Most people have three things in common when they buy a car.

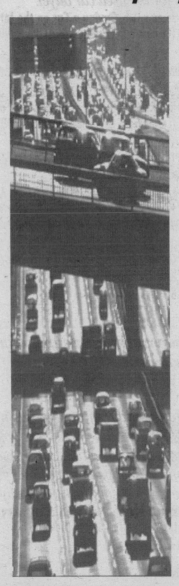

They pay too much.

They waste time.

They hate the experience.

Which is exactly why you should call the Consumers Car Club, a nationwide auto buying service. We offer the quickest and most convenient way to save time and money when you buy a new car or truck. Simple as that. Just tell us the vehicle and options you want (any make or model-foreign or domestic) and we'll get you a lower price than you can get on your own. Guaranteed in writing. We can factory order any domestic vehicle and usually save you even more. No haggling. No hassles. No games.

Don't forget to ask about our loans, leases and extended service contracts. It's a terrific way to save even more money on the purchase of your new car. For more information, call the Consumers Car Club at 1-800-CAR-CLUB (1-800-227-2582).

The Smart New Way to Buy Your Car™

All new cars arranged for sale are subject to price & availability from the selling franchised new car dealer.

2000

edmunds.com
where smart car buyers start

USED CARS & TRUCKS

PRICES & RATINGS

"THE ORIGINAL CONSUMER PRICE AUTHORITY"

You Drive, You Decide...

Announcing an innovative type of "auto show" where you can test drive cars and experience all things automotive in one comfortable, convenient and entertaining location!

EdmundsLIVE is the industry's first automotive event of its kind. With over 50 of the industry's top vehicles on site, EdmundsLIVE enables you to research and compare vehicles in a no-pressure, sales-free environment. Come to this exciting event where you can attend informational workshops on car-related issues, receive information on specific models and test drive any number of the vehicles we have to offer on our eight specially designed tracks.

Sound good? Thousands of others agree, which is why a reservation for the EdmundsLIVE event is required. Reservations are made on a first-come, first-served basis, so don't delay. Click on the Edmunds-LIVE link on our homepage at www.edmunds.com to make your reservation NOW!

Cover photo:
1997 Nissan 200SX SE-R

ISBN: 0-87759-659-X
ISSN: 1523-8024

USED CARS & TRUCKS

T A B L E   O F   C O N T E N T S

FALL 2000

VOL. U3403-0010

Publisher:
Peter Steinlauf

Editor-in-Chief:
Christian Wardlaw

Director, Data Content:
Alison Cooper

Production Manager:
Lynette Archbold

Managing Editor:
Karl Brauer

Detroit Editor:
John Clor

Senior Features Editor:
Brent Romans

Features Editor:
Scott Mead

Technical Editor:
Scott Memmer

News Editor:
Gonzo Schexnayder

Road Test Editor:
Dan Gardner

Copy Editors:
Erin Mahoney
Deborah Greenbaum

Photography Editor:
Scott Jacobs

Associate Editor:
Liz Kim

Sr. Layout and Design Artist:
Robert Archbold

Editorial Assistant:
Erin Riches

Used Vehicle Data Editors:
John DiPietro
Wandile Kunene

Maintenance Data Editor:
Jose Luis Munoz

Photo Archivist:
Letitia Poteet

Printed in U.S.A.

Edmund's® books are available at special quantity discounts when purchased in bulk by credit unions, corporations, organizations, and other special interest groups. Custom covers and/or customized copy on available pages may also be prepared to fit particular needs.

INTRODUCTION

Thanks for consulting *Edmund's® Used Cars & Trucks Prices & Ratings*! You've made a wise purchase, because the values contained within this publication represent a current snapshot of the U.S. used car market as it exists for the consumer. Unlike other guides, we aren't publishing data sourced strictly from dealer-only auction houses or dealership sales records. Our values are based on advertised and actual transaction prices between private owners, between private owners and dealers, and between dealers. You won't find a dealer slant to our data, because one doesn't exist.

The Edmund's® Philosophy

For years Edmund's® followed tradition and published wholesale and retail values for vehicles. But we found that the commonly accepted method of providing a wholesale value and a retail value was based on a dealer's market, making such a system unreliable for and misleading to the average consumer. Dealers and private owners almost never sell a car for retail, and dealers almost never give wholesale value when assessing a trade-in. In years past we based our pricing on actual dealer advertised prices and auction data to generate retail and wholesale price. Our current pricing is gathered using a similar methodology, but we've modified the process to arrive at what we call Market Value and Trade-in Value.

Market Value

Market Value is a national average of prices asked by private sellers and dealers. Our source compiles hundreds of thousands of advertised prices nationwide, and interviews thousands of sellers by phone each week to find out their bottom-line price (the take price, as it is referred to in the industry), or the actual transaction price if the car has been sold. Data gleaned from telephone interviews, combined with national averages from the advertised price database, is used to create the Market Value. By including private sellers in the tabulation, we've effectively generated a more accurate, more reliable average value for any given make and model.

Trade-in Value

Trade-in Value is the amount that a consumer might expect to get from a dealer for a trade-in. Most dealers won't give a customer wholesale value (the average value a dealer could expect to receive at an auction) on a trade-in unless there is profit to be made from some other aspect of the deal. Why won't they? Because the dealer is assuming the customer's risk. If the car has a problem, the dealer must fix it. If the car is only in fair condition, the dealer must recondition it. If the car won't pass emissions inspection, the dealer must repair it. Then there is no guarantee that the car will sell on the dealer's used car lot, so the dealer must anticipate taking the car to the auction house, where a profit, no matter how meager, will be expected. So, when assessing a customer's trade-in, the dealer will value it lower than wholesale price.

Our Trade-in Value, calculated as a percentage of Market Value, is designed to provide consumers with a more realistic guide to valuing a trade-in.

When buying or selling a car, a price close to Market Value is a fair price. When trading a car, a price close to Trade-in Value is a fair price. Keep in mind that dealers will use whatever regional price guide favors them the most to value your trade-in and price the used cars on their lot. Sometimes, they will consult two different guides; one that undervalues trades, and one that overvalues retail prices for used cars. Since Edmund's® does not cater to the dealer or sell dealer-specific value guides like many of our competitors, expect initial resistance by the dealer to the prices we publish, but don't give in to dealer claims that our numbers are wrong. Also, keep the following guideline in mind: *A car is only worth as much as someone is willing to pay for it.*

Where's the Recall Data?

We've stopped publishing recall data, and here's the reason why. If you have Internet access, go to http://www.nhtsa.dot.gov, which is the address for the National Highway and Traffic Safety Administration's website. There you can search archives of recalls, technical service bulletins, and crash tests. The data found at this website is much more comprehensive and detailed than we could ever hope to provide, and you'll be better off arming yourself with this information before heading down to the local dealership for a chat with the service advisor.

How Do I Use Edmund's® Data?

Among Edmunds.com's long-term test cars is a 1999 Mazda Miata. As of this writing, the car has 19,987 miles on it. Options include air conditioning and the leather package. We would value the car like this:

	Trade-in Value	Market Value
1999 Mazda Miata	**$13,030**	**$15,330**
Air Conditioning	$620	$620
Leather Package	$2700	$2700
Mileage Adjustment	-$134	-$134
TOTAL:	**$16,216**	**$18,516**

Since these figures are for a car in average shape, we could adjust the numbers slightly upward since this car is in showroom condition. Also keep in mind that the value of this type of car increases during "top-down" season (when demand is higher) and decreases as the colder months approach (when demand is lower).

Remember that vehicle condition affects the car's value, as does having receipts for all the maintenance done on the car. Obviously, a car in excellent condition with receipts proving strict maintenance will be worth more than an average car without records. Other variables can affect the price as well, such as demand for this particular model and the time of year that the car is sold.

However, just because our book claims a fair value for this car of about $18,516, that doesn't mean we can automatically sell it for that amount of money. *A used car is only worth as much as someone is willing to pay for it.*

Contact Us

We believe that this guide is much more accurate and easy-to-understand than ever before. If you have questions, comments, suggestions, or complaints, you can write to us at the following address:

Automotive Editors
Edmunds.com
P.O. Box 25906
Los Angeles, CA 90025-9998

Or, you can send us e-mail to editors@edmunds.com. We look forward to your feedback!

HOW TO USE THIS GUIDE

Understanding the Layout

Finding the Right Model

We've listed all makes and models in alphabetical order, from Acura to Volvo. To find the make and model you want to value, look at the title bar at the top of each page. The title bar defines each section of the book by listing the *Automobile Make* and *Model Year* covered on each page. When the proper section has been found, you can find the right model by looking at the gray shaded title bars that begin each model listing. In this gray bar, you will find the *Model Name* and *Model Year*. To distinguish cars from trucks, we've printed truck data over a gray background.

What's New and Ratings

Beneath the model title bar is a section of text, called a *Yearly Feature Update*, which explains what changed on the model for that particular model year. Next is a *Ratings Chart*, containing a synopsis of heavily researched data about the model you're valuing. Most of the vehicles covered in this book have a ratings chart, but some vehicles cannot be rated because there is not enough data to calculate accurate ratings. Below the ratings chart is a *Mileage Category Designation*.

Mileage Categories

Each vehicle in this guide has been assigned to a specific mileage category, which contains other vehicles with similar characteristics. For example, Category C contains mid-sized American cars like the Ford Contour. Category E contains economy cars like the Toyota Tercel. And, Category G contains compact pickups, compact SUVs, and minivans like the Chevrolet S-10, the Nissan Pathfinder, and the Dodge Caravan. The mileage adjustment table is keyed to each vehicle by category. Sometimes, different versions of the same model may fall into different categories. In this event, versions belonging to different categories will be listed separately within the individual model listing section.

Data Presentations

The first column of data contains a *Model Description* for each individual model that has pricing data. The number of doors, trim level, drive system (if something other than two-wheel drive), and body style are described here. The middle column is the baseline *Trade-in Value*, which is used to calculate the amount of money you might expect a dealership to offer you if you traded the car in. The third column is the baseline *Market Value*, which is used to calculate the amount of money you might expect to receive for your car on the open market, or the amount of money you might pay a dealership for a used car. Beneath the pricing data for each individual model you might find values for *Optional Equipment*. Conveniently located on the last page of this book is a *Mileage Adjustment Table*.

Pricing a Vehicle

Market or Trade-in Value?

To find an accurate value for a vehicle, you must make adjustments to the baseline values for equipment and mileage. Realistically, you should use Market Value if selling to a private party or buying from a private party or dealer, and use Trade-in Value if selling to a dealer.

Options and Packages

Below the baseline pricing data for most vehicles are lists of optional equipment that require price adjustments. If the vehicle you're valuing is equipped with any of these items, you must add the appropriate value to the baseline values. Also listed with the options are expensive option packages. For example, a BMW might be equipped with a Luxury Package that includes power leather seats, cruise control, an onboard computer, wood trim, special aluminum wheels, and special trim. Some of these items might be found separately in the equipment list, and some might not. The published package price includes the intrinsic value for those items that are not otherwise listed as options. Most private sellers will be able to tell you if a vehicle is equipped with a certain package, but don't expect a dealer to know much about a used car except the price. Do your homework!

Transmissions

Our Market Value and Trade-in Value includes the standard transmission on that model, whether manual shift or automatic. Keep in mind that sometimes manufacturers would install a 3-speed automatic transmission as standard equipment, but would offer an upgraded 4-speed automatic transmission as an option. Newer Chevrolet Cavalier LS sedans provide an excellent example of this practice; the 3-speed automatic is standard, and the 4-speed automatic is optional. Don't assume that a listing for an optional automatic transmission means that the basic vehicle came with a stick shift.

Engines

There are five basic engine types: gasoline; diesel; supercharged gasoline; turbocharged gasoline and turbocharged diesel. Some engines appear in the optional equipment listings. Each vehicle record is listed including the standard gasoline engine. Similarly, models with standard turbocharged or supercharged engines are listed individually. The only engines contained in the optional equipment lists are optional gasoline- or diesel-powered powerplants. Make sure you find out what engine is under the hood of the vehicle you're valuing. If the vehicle you're buying or selling has an optional engine, look for the value in the optional equipment list.

The Mileage Table

Once the proper adjusted value has been determined, you must further modify the price of the vehicle using the Mileage Table on the last page of this book. Edmund's links mileage adjustments directly to each vehicle category and presents the data in a single table. The table features an average mileage range for each category and model year, and provides an exact value to be added or subtracted **per mile** over or under the average mileage range. No other value guide provides such detailed, or realistic, mileage adjustments. Because the acceptable mileage range is based on an actual average mileage of all vehicles within a given category, an exotic car like the Acura NSX will be valued according to a substantially lower and tighter average mileage range than a mid-sized import like the Honda Accord. If the vehicle you're valuing has excessively high or low mileage, you should not add or subtract value in excess of half of the vehicle's adjusted trade-in value.

The Disclaimer

That's all there is to valuing a used car with Edmund's. Now you've got accurate ballpark values for trade-in value and market value. *Keep the following in mind, however. Regional price differences, seasonal price differences, seasonal demand, vehicle condition, and the economic laws of supply and demand all help determine the actual worth of a used car. The values calculated using this guide are designed to represent average values nationwide for a used car in average condition, and should be used only as a guide to set an acceptable price range for selling or purchasing. None of the values published herein are intended to represent absolute values.*

Pricing Examples

	Trade-in Value	Market Value
1. 1996 Ford Explorer XLT 4WD	**$11,550**	**$14,260**
Automatic Transmission	380	380
Aluminum Alloy Wheels	135	135
AM/FM Stereo Tape	90	90
Dual Power Seats	155	155
JBL Sound System	310	310
Keyless Entry System	80	80
Leather Seats	315	315
Luggage Rack	65	65
Value before Mileage Adjustment	$13,080	$ 15,790
60,850 miles (Category G)	0	0
	---------	---------
TOTAL ADJUSTED VALUE:	**$13,080**	**$15,790**
2. 1993 Nissan Altima GXE	**$3,810**	**$5,010**
Automatic Transmission	185	185
Air Conditioning	190	190
Cruise Control	55	55
Value before Mileage Adjustment	$4,240	$5,440
117,200 miles (Category D)	-654	-654
	---------	---------
TOTAL ADJUSTED VALUE:	**$3,586**	**$4,786**
3. 1991 BMW 325i Sedan	**$5,365**	**$7,350**
Leather Seats	95	95
Power Sunroof	100	100
Value before Mileage Adjustment	$5,560	$7,545
87,250 miles (Category F)	+1,233	+1,233
	---------	---------
TOTAL ADJUSTED VALUE:	**$6,793**	**$8,778**

HOW WE RATE THE CARS

Each spring, we update our ratings for used cars. Currently, we offer ratings for many vehicles built between 1990 and 1999. Edmund's ratings are presented in chart form, on a 1 to 10 numerical scale where 10 is best. Some ratings data is supplied by IntelliChoice, Inc., 471 Division Street, Campbell, CA 95008. IntelliChoice, a respected automotive data provider, has contributed information to our Safety and Reliability ratings for used cars and trucks.

Safety Rating

We examine nine factors that determine vehicle safety. First, we check frontal impact crash test data from the National Highway and Traffic Safety Administration (NHTSA). The NHTSA selects several models each year for crash testing, which is conducted at 35 mph into a fixed barrier. Federal standards require that all cars pass a 30 mph test to be sold in the United States. The higher speed used by the NHTSA allows for comparison outside of federal regulations. By crashing into a fixed barrier, the NHTSA simulates a head-on collision with another vehicle of similar size and weight traveling at the same rate of speed. The NHTSA assigns specific scores to the driver and front passenger. The higher the score, the more likely a person is to escape such a crash with minimal injuries. *If a vehicle has not been crash tested, we do not rate the vehicle in this category.* Crash test data is the most important ingredient of our safety score. Without it, a safety rating means little.

Other factors that are used to determine a safety rating include the number of times the model has been recalled for non-emissions-related issues and the presence of safety equipment like airbags and anti-lock brakes (ABS). On later model vehicles, offset crash test scores, which the Insurance Institute for Highway Safety (IIHS) began conducting in 1994, are rolled into the tabulation if available. In 1996, Volvo equipped their entire model lineup with side-impact airbags. Therefore, all 1996 through 1999 Volvos include side-impact airbags in the safety calculation. If a 1995 model that is identical to a 1996 model but is not equipped with side-impact airbags has a slightly lower safety rating than the newer vehicle, now you know why.

Important Note About Airbags and ABS: These days, it seems like everybody is talking about how unsafe these systems are. Edmund's® does not consider airbags or ABS to be unsafe. In defense of airbags, they have saved approximately 25 people for every one person they have killed. True, they shouldn't be killing anyone. Unfortunately, airbags were designed to protect a 165-lb. person not wearing a seatbelt. To accomplish this mandate, airbags must inflate rapidly, expanding at a rate of approximately 200 mph. Children and adults are getting hurt or killed because of these rapid inflation rates, but it is important to note that in almost all cases involving death, the person killed was not properly restrained by a seatbelt.

Problems with airbags seem particularly acute in low-speed collisions, such as tapping a car in a parking lot, which do not require the protection the airbag provides. The sensors that control the airbag may not be without fault or flaw, but neither are most other sophisticated systems in today's cars. The best way to avoid injury or loss with airbag-equipped cars is to sit as far away from the airbag as possible, wear your seat belt and strap youngsters into the back seat.

The lawmakers who forced automobile manufacturers to install airbags may have gone about doing so in a misguided and uneducated fashion, but the fact of the matter is that these supplemental restraints do save lives and are improved with each passing model year. In fact, many 1998 model year cars and trucks came equipped with airbags that deploy at lower speeds. This recently accepted lower deployment speed will save more properly belted vehicle occupants, but those who do not wear a seatbelt will be more at risk than if they rode in a vehicle with airbags that deployed at higher speeds.

Recent reports claim that vehicles equipped with anti-lock brakes are more likely to be involved in single vehicle crashes than cars that are not equipped with anti-lock brakes. Why is this? ABS is misunderstood, and is misused in general by the driving public.

Here are the facts. ABS will not shorten stopping distances. ABS will not prevent all skids. What ABS is designed to do, and it does this very well, is allow the driver to steer around danger while simultaneously using maximum braking ability. A car without ABS will skid when the wheels lock up, and when the car is skidding all steering ability is lost. So, in such a car, it is highly likely that the driver will lock up the brakes, and slide into whatever situation or object caused him to apply the brakes in the first place.

With ABS, the driver can hit the brakes hard and steer around the situation or object in the road because the front wheels are not locked up. However, it is important that the driver steer carefully and not wildly. Once the car begins to change direction, it may begin to skid sideways, or laterally, if direction is changed too quickly. ABS cannot help control a lateral skid. One theory says that drivers of ABS-equipped cars are steering around immediate danger successfully, but then skidding laterally off the road and hitting a tree, a road sign, or a building. Also, some drivers of ABS-equipped cars may be pumping the brakes in moments of panic, because that's what has been taught for decades to stop a car without ABS.

Owners of ABS-equipped cars should practice using the system in a vacant parking lot before the need to use ABS in a panic situation arises. For the record, Edmund's staff members prefer ABS on all surfaces except narrow dirt or gravel roads, where there is little room to steer and a locked tire can dig into the earth and drop speed more rapidly.

Finally, consider this. Bob Bondurant (famed racing legend and operator of the acclaimed Bob Bondurant School of High Performance Driving in Phoenix, AZ) told us that when ABS-equipped Mustangs were introduced to his fleet of student cars, the accident rate on his track dropped a whopping 40 percent. Bondurant believes in ABS, but concedes that most drivers have no idea how to use them. Do all of us a favor – learn.

Reliability Rating

Our reliability rating is based on three factors that determine how trouble-free a vehicle is likely to be. Intellichoice, Inc. tracks complaints from vehicle owners. For any given make and model, we combine data regarding specific reported problem areas with the number of mechanically-related recalls issued by NHTSA. Finally, we consult our records regarding build quality inside and out when the car was new.

Performance Rating

We take into consideration a vehicle's ability to accelerate, stop, and turn, then compare it to other models in the same vehicle class. So, the performance rating for the Dodge Neon is to be compared to the Chevrolet Cavalier or Ford Escort rather than the Chevrolet Camaro or Ford Mustang. Additionally, we toss transmission performance and steering ability into the recipe. Since performance often means different things to different people, we'll define it this way. A fast car with good brakes, communicative steering, a smooth-shifting transmission, and the ability to get around a turn without keeling over and begging for mercy gets a higher rating than a car that, uh, doesn't.

Comfort Rating

Another subjective category, rated by our staffers, is overall comfort. We look for a comfortable position behind the steering wheel on a supportive seat with a clear view of gauges and an easy stretch to controls that operate with minimum amounts of concentration. A car or truck with a quiet ride that doesn't jar occupants, clear sightlines front and rear, and easy ingress and egress will get a better score than one that rattles teeth and requires a stepladder to enter. So, if your idea of comfort is a rolling Barcalounger surrounded by look-alike chrome buttons and switches, you can ignore our rating.

Value Rating

To determine value, we examine nationally averaged theft rates, parts costs if purchased at the dealership, the likelihood that a vehicle will break down or run reliably and average insurance rates based on claims losses from a nationally-known insurance company. The icing on the value cupcake is the vehicle's degree of versatility. A full-size 4WD Suburban is infinitely more useable than a Mazda Miata, and therefore, offers better overall versatility.

Overall Rating

Add 'em all together, and you come up with an overall rating. We do not weight the overall rating, allowing each factor to count equally toward the final tally. If any of the five factors is missing from the equation due to insufficient data, we do not provide an overall rating.

Important Note: If data was unavailable for more than two of the five factors, we did not rate the vehicle at all. For those cars without ratings, the reason a rating is not given in any category is because of scarce data for at least three of the rating factors listed above.

Car Buying and Selling Tips

Buying a Used Car

- Visually inspect the car in daylight. If buying from a dealer, request that any items that are broken or damaged be repaired. If buying from a private seller, devalue the vehicle for broken or damaged items. Signs of paint overspray may indicate a history of bodywork.

- Have the car thoroughly inspected by a mechanic. If mechanical repair is necessary, devalue the vehicle accordingly.

- Have the car looked at by a body shop technician for signs of accident repair. Inspect the title, too. If the car has been wrecked and repaired, but has a clear title, chances are good that the vehicle is still in sound condition. If the vehicle is saddled with a salvage title, you should steer clear of it. This means it has been damaged so badly that the insurance company totaled it, and an enterprising person has repaired the vehicle for sale.

- Do a VIN search to help determine if the car has a clear title. Visit our website at http://www.edmunds.com to run a CarFax VIN report on any used car you're considering.

- Pay for the car with a cashier's check.

- Prepare a bill of sale. The bill of sale can be written in crayon on the back of a paper towel as long as a notary public witnesses the signatures of both parties. If the owner of the car has a lien against it, the bill of sale, when properly notarized, will serve as proof of purchase until the owner's loan is paid and you receive the title.

Selling a Used Car

- Clean the vehicle thoroughly, and make sure it is in good operating condition.

- Make sure all paperwork related to the vehicle is in order, particularly the title and registration.

- Advertise, advertise, advertise in major newspapers and used car magazine classifieds. If possible, park the car in high-traffic areas with For Sale signs in the windows and flyers tucked under the wiper blade that explain why someone would want your car. However, beware of local ordinances prohibiting the display of vehicles for sale.

- Realize that Japanese cars are generally in more demand than most American and European cars on the used car market.

Trading a Used Car

- Clean the vehicle thoroughly, and make sure it is in good operating condition.

- Make sure all paperwork related to the vehicle is in order, particularly the title and registration.

- Expect the dealer to offer far less than the car is worth. Negotiate as close to Trade-in Value as possible.

- Make sure the trade-in value doesn't get lost in the purchase or lease contract. Keep your eye on the ball.

1997 Nissan 200 SX

S E - R

By Christian J. Wardlaw

Photography courtesy of Nissan Motors Corporation, USA

Two punks driving erratically bore down on the family sedan. The first was driving a beat-to-hell Honda CRX, and he rode the Camry's tail uncomfortably closely. The second piloted a brand-spanking-new Nissan 200SX, replete with dealer advertising tags front and rear. When the road widened to four lanes, the weaving CRX wheezed alongside my family on the right, windows down, Tupac blasting from within. Next came the new 200SX, freshly minted engine running near redline, skinny driver slouched in a gangsta's protective position behind the B-pillar, baseball hat turned backward. He and his pal were playing a dangerous game of vehicular tag, and I quickly tired of it. With a push of the accelerator, the Camry's V-6 engine revved up and we blew past both of them, leaving them choking on bland, non-descript sedan dust. "Ha!" I thought as the Camry slowed, "That's what you guys get for buying girlie-mobiles with no *cojones.*"

A week later, a girlie-mobile showed up at the office. Painted a Halloweenish shade of orange called Autumn Sunburst, our Nissan 200SX test car was nearly identical to what our gangsta' wannabe friend was driving, with some important differences under the sheetmetal. See, Mr. GW bought himself the SE model,

IOUS

which amounts to little more than a two-door Sentra. Nissan sent us the SE-R, which makes more power, handles better, and looks sharper than other 200SX models.

At first we were skeptical. Several staffers were immediately turned off by the paint color, while others liked the way the sunlight glinted off the Nissan's flanks just before dipping below the horizon. Styling was not cited as exciting by anyone who saw the car. Some of us found certain interior elements to be less than perfect, like the low seating position and busy climate control markings. But by the end of the week, an editor and a graphic artist were serious about buying the 200SX when its tour of duty in the press fleet was over.

Everybody liked the 200SX SE-R. In fact, no other car we've tested in the past two years has met with such universal approval. My wife thought it would be a perfect car for her mom, who needs to replace her 1987 Chevrolet Nova

FUN

sometime very soon. Greg Anderson, our online editor and resident photographer, had his wife drive the 200SX for a day, and she deemed the car perfect except for the paint color. Down to Colorado Springs the 200SX went where it appealed to graphic artist John Davis and his longtime companion, Dolores. Autumn Sunburst reminded her of the color that her first Volvo was painted. When Anderson and Davis found out Nissan was ready to reclaim the 200SX and send it to auction, a war started over whom would be able to purchase the car. Rock, paper, scissors solved that issue. Davis got first dibs.

Personally, I felt the Nissan 200SX SE-R proved a theorem I've held since the days when my father drove a Saab 900 Turbo. Looks aren't everything when it comes to cars. They matter quite a bit, but often the driving experience is so exceptional, so outstanding, that styling matters little. The 200SX SE-R is serious fun. Under the hood is a 2.0-liter twin-cam four cylinder engine that makes 140 horsepower. Fat Goodyear tires are mounted on attractive alloy wheels at each corner, and do an excellent job of keeping the little Nissan planted to the ground on smooth winding roads and in pockmarked urban corners. The suspension provides a firm ride, and the nicely weighted steering

gives the driver all the information he needs to know about what's happening at street-level.

Applied to spirited driving, the 200SX SE-R is a hoot, albeit a refined one. The main source of refinement is the engine, which revs happily, not raucously, to redline. Zooming along I-25 at 85 mph one afternoon, I realized after several miles that I'd been traveling in fourth gear, tach needle pegged up near the 5,000 rpm mark. There was no excessive noise or vibration coming from beyond the firewall, just instantaneous bursts of power as demanded. At rest, this sophisticated four banger transmitted no vibration through the steering column, and the hood provided mirror-like images at idle. Furthermore, the 200SX we drove was equipped with Goodyear Eagle RS-A tires. On other cars we've found these Eagles to be substandard in terms of handling, but on the SE-R, they gripped the pavement tenaciously, and emitted little protest when pushed hard. This is a car that could threaten your driver's license.

The in-dash disc changer had eaten my new Janet Jackson CD (thanks to my idiocy, not an ergonomic flaw with the car), and I'd been attempting to extract it from the dashboard slot. As I looked up at the road, a Crown Vic with a light bar passed on the left,

Looks aren't everything when it comes to cars. Often the driving experience is so exceptional, so outstanding, that styling matters little.

while I passed a Dodge Caravan on the right. A glance at the speedometer confirmed the bad news. I pulled over before the Douglas Country sheriff could get the Crown Vic turned around. "Can I see your license and registration, please?"

I handed the officer my license and the form Nissan had me sign when I took possession of the car. From the glovebox I fished out a California proof of insurance. "I clocked you at 54 mph in a 40 mph zone, while passing on the right."

Ayuh. But see, I was trying to get my CD out of the disc changer and I wasn't paying attention to my speed. I live right here in the neighborhood, and know the speed limit is 40 mph. "Well, I'll let you off with a warning this time, but if I catch you speeding again, I'll give you a ticket." So, if you admit you know what the speed limit is, and you confess that you weren't paying attention to your driving, you actually get out of it? Wow, that's almost scary. Hopefully, the gangsta' wannabe in the nearly identical girlie-mobile

200SX SE got nailed later in the week, because he actually deserved a ticket.

In short, we all loved to drive the 200SX SE-R. Otherwise, the car was rather dull and unexceptional. Exterior styling is contemporary, but devoid of character. Inside, muted black and gray tones were the rule, and all the gauges and controls were logically placed for easy use. Unfortunately, the markings on the climate controls and the stereo were fussy and sized too small. The seats, while comfortable, did not offer a height adjuster to raise them from their position at floor level. The gearshift was unusually tall for a sporting car, and throws between ratios were precise but long. The sunroof on our test car was quite noisy when open, and the stereo's sound quality was mediocre at best.

At least the 200SX is equipped with useable interior space and a sizable trunk. My wife and I had no trouble toting baby Sarah around in her rear-facing car seat, thanks to the easy-entry feature on the front passenger seat and an unobtru-

Exterior styling is contemporary, but devoid of character. Inside, muted black and gray tones were the rule, and all the gauges and controls were logically placed for easy use.

sive dashboard forward of the front passenger. There was also plenty of room in the trunk for the assorted detritus that accompanies all travel with infants. We found the split-folding rear seat to be quite handy, though we would have preferred a true hatchback to the current coupe configuration. But then we'd have to give up some structural rigidity, and the car we drove was tight and rattle-free at 20,000 miles. As the end of our week with the 200SX SE-R approached, we had decided we didn't want to give it back.

"So, are you guys coming to pick up the Nissan today?" No, we aren't. We wanted to get you the 1998 Blazer, but Billy Bob (name changed to protect the innocent) has decided he doesn't want to give it back just yet. The Volvo wagon isn't in from Utah until tomorrow, and then it goes to service. Can you guys sit tight with the Nissan a few more days?

"No problem. We love this car. In fact, we've got a couple of guys on staff who want to buy it." In the end, we drove the SE-R for nearly another week, but nobody on staff bought it. Davis decided to get something less expensive, and Anderson's wife couldn't live with the Autumn Sunburst paint job. To date, this is one of the few test cars we've all universally enjoyed, and it's only the second one any of us has considered buying from a

press fleet (I considered the 1997 Miata M-Edition for awhile a few months back). That says something about the fun-to-drive nature of the 200SX SE-R and our confidence in its ability to withstand many miles of hard use. If you're shopping any sporty coupe in this class, you owe it to yourself to drive the SE-R. ■

1997 Nissan 200SX SE-R

Base Price of Test Vehicle $17,219
Options on Test Vehicle .... Anti-lock Brakes, Power Sunroof, In-Dash CD Changer
Price of Vehicle as Tested .... $18,836 (includes destination charge)

Engine
Number of Cylinders 4
Displacement (liters) 2
Compression Ratio 9.5:1
Horsepower @ RPM .... 140 @ 6400
Torque @ RPM .... 132 @ 4800

Fuel
Fuel Capacity 13.2
EPA City (mpg) - Manual 23
EPA Hwy (mpg) - Manual 31
EPA City (mpg) - Auto 24
EPA Hwy (mpg) - Auto 31

Performance

Acceleration (0-60/sec) .... 8.1 (5M), NA (AT)
Braking Distance (60-0/ft) ... 144
Cornering Index (g's) 0.85

Measurements

Length (in.) 170.1
Width (in.) 66.6
Height (in.) 54.2
Curb Weight (lbs.) 2491 (5M),
                                     2564 (AT)

Wheelbase (in.) 99.8
Front Head Room (in.) 39.1
Rear Head Room (in.) 35.4
Front Shoulder Room (in.) 52.1
Rear Shoulder Room (in.) 52.9
Front Hip Room (in.) 50.3
Rear Hip Room (in.) 52.5
Front Leg Room (in.) 42.3
Rear Leg Room (in.) 31.4
Luggage Capacity (cu ft.) 10.4

ACURA 99-98

Model Description	Trade-in Value	Market Value	Model Description	Trade-in Value	Market Value

ACURA   Japan

1997 Acura TL

1999 ACURA

CL-SERIES   1999

The previously optional Premium package, consisting of leather seats, is now standard.

RATINGS (SCALE OF 1-10)

Overall	Safety	Reliability	Performance	Comfort	Value
N/A	N/A	N/A	7.8	7.5	N/A

Category J
2 Dr 2.3 Cpe	15415	18350
2 Dr 3.0 Cpe	16625	19790

OPTIONS FOR CL-SERIES
Auto 4-Speed Transmission[Std on 3.0] +590

INTEGRA   1999

In a small step up-market, Acura has decided to kill the Integra's entry-level RS trim. The LS gets leather accents and 15-inch wheels, and the sporty GS-R now comes with leather seats. Type R will return in limited numbers later in the year.

RATINGS (SCALE OF 1-10)

Overall	Safety	Reliability	Performance	Comfort	Value
N/A	6.9	N/A	8.6	7.8	N/A

Category E
2 Dr GS Hbk	13605	16390
4 Dr GS Sdn	13475	16235
2 Dr GS-R Hbk	14615	17610
4 Dr GS-R Sdn	14465	17430
2 Dr LS Hbk	12610	15195
4 Dr LS Sdn	12460	15010

OPTIONS FOR INTEGRA
Auto 4-Speed Transmission +590
Fog Lights +110
Keyless Entry System +115

RL-SERIES   1999

There are more than 300 changes to the RL this year, so we'll just touch on the important ones: the suspension has been revised for better handling and a firmer ride, brake rotors have added mass, side air bags are standard, styling is more aggressive, the Premium features have been incorporated into one trim level, and, best of all, the price has been slashed.

RATINGS (SCALE OF 1-10)

Overall	Safety	Reliability	Performance	Comfort	Value
N/A	N/A	N/A	7.8	8.9	N/A

Category A
4 Dr STD Sdn	28760	33835

OPTIONS FOR RL-SERIES
Navigation System +1480

SLX   1999

The SLX is carried over unchanged from a year ago.

RATINGS (SCALE OF 1-10)

Overall	Safety	Reliability	Performance	Comfort	Value
N/A	7.3	N/A	N/A	7.6	N/A

Category G
4 Dr STD 4WD Wgn	22010	26200

TL-SERIES   1999

The TL has been redesigned for 1999, with everything just getting better. The 2.5-liter engine is gone, making way for an all-new 3.2-liter V6. The transmission has been refined, the interior design makes better use of space, and the exterior is updated with a less stodgy appearance.

RATINGS (SCALE OF 1-10)

Overall	Safety	Reliability	Performance	Comfort	Value
N/A	7.6	9.6	7.8	N/A	N/A

Category A
4 Dr 3.2 Sdn	20660	24305

OPTIONS FOR TL-SERIES
Navigation System +1480

1998 ACURA

CL-SERIES   1998

A new 2.3L engine replaces last year's 2.2L unit. All CL models get a revised grille and new alloy wheels.

Don't forget to refer to the Mileage Adjustment Table at the back of this book!

ACURA 98-97

Model Description	Trade-in Value	Market Value	Model Description	Trade-in Value	Market Value

RATINGS (SCALE OF 1-10)

Overall	Safety	Reliability	Performance	Comfort	Value
N/A	N/A	9.1	7.8	7.5	N/A

Category J

	Trade-in	Market
2 Dr 2.3 Cpe	13215	15730
2 Dr 2.3 Premium Cpe	13820	16455
2 Dr 3.0 Cpe	14720	17525
2 Dr 3.0 Premium Cpe	15295	18210

OPTIONS FOR CL-SERIES

Auto 4-Speed Transmission[Opt on 2.3, 2.3 Premium] +490
Rear Spoiler +245

INTEGRA 1998

A slight nose job, designed for a more aerodynamic approach, is added this year. LS, GS and GS-R models get a little more comfortable with a tilt- and height-adjustable driver's seat and new alloy wheels appear on the LS and GS-R. The performance edition Type R is available again this year.

RATINGS (SCALE OF 1-10)

Overall	Safety	Reliability	Performance	Comfort	Value
7.4	6.9	9.1	9.2	7.8	4

Category E

	Trade-in	Market
2 Dr GS Hbk	12785	15405
4 Dr GS Sdn	12660	15250
2 Dr GS-R Hbk	13630	16420
4 Dr GS-R Sdn	13485	16245
2 Dr LS Hbk	11830	14250
4 Dr LS Sdn	11640	14025
2 Dr RS Hbk	9950	11990
2 Dr Type R Hbk	13940	16795

OPTIONS FOR INTEGRA

Auto 4-Speed Transmission +490
Air Conditioning[Opt on RS, Type R] +495
Aluminum/Alloy Wheels[Opt on RS] +200
Fog Lights +90
Keyless Entry System +95
Leather Seats[Std on GS] +530

RL-SERIES 1998

Slight suspension enhancements provide more sporty handling without sacrificing the ride.

RATINGS (SCALE OF 1-10)

Overall	Safety	Reliability	Performance	Comfort	Value
N/A	N/A	9.6	8.2	8.9	4.2

Category A

	Trade-in	Market
4 Dr Premium Sdn	24725	29435
4 Dr STD Sdn	23065	27460
4 Dr Special Edition Sdn	23795	28325

OPTIONS FOR RL-SERIES

Navigation System +1265
Compact Disc Changer[Opt on STD] +480

SLX 1998

Acura's rebadged Isuzu Trooper gets more power and torque, a trick new 4WD system and revised styling for 1998.

RATINGS (SCALE OF 1-10)

Overall	Safety	Reliability	Performance	Comfort	Value
6.9	6.5	9.2	6.8	7.6	4.6

Category G

	Trade-in	Market
4 Dr STD 4WD Wgn	18445	21960

TL-SERIES 1998

The premium level is gone, but the TL-Series gets more standard equipment.

RATINGS (SCALE OF 1-10)

Overall	Safety	Reliability	Performance	Comfort	Value
7.6	7.6	9.6	7.4	8	5.3

Category A

	Trade-in	Market
4 Dr 2.5 Sdn	16290	19395
4 Dr 3.2 Sdn	18055	21495

1997 ACURA

CL-SERIES 1997

Introduced as a 1997 model, the CL is supposed to compete in the growing personal coupe segment. Like many Acura products, the CL is based on a Honda platform, in this case the Honda Accord. The CL's sights are aimed squarely at BMW's 3-Series coupes.

RATINGS (SCALE OF 1-10)

Overall	Safety	Reliability	Performance	Comfort	Value
N/A	N/A	8.8	7.8	7.5	N/A

Category J

	Trade-in	Market
2 Dr 2.2 Cpe	11865	14295
2 Dr 2.2 Premium Cpe	12355	14885
2 Dr 3.0 Cpe	12910	15555
2 Dr 3.0 Premium Cpe	13370	16110

OPTIONS FOR CL-SERIES

Auto 4-Speed Transmission[Opt on 2.2CL] +400

INTEGRA 1997

No major changes to what may be the last Acura Integra. The good news is that prices for Special Edition (now called GS), LS and RS models remain the same as last year.

Model Description	Trade-in Value	Market Value

Model Description	Trade-in Value	Market Value

RATINGS (SCALE OF 1-10)

Overall	Safety	Reliability	Performance	Comfort	Value
7.2	6.9	9.1	9.2	7.8	3

Category E

2 Dr GS Hbk	11585	14130
4 Dr GS Sdn	11425	13930
2 Dr GS-R Hbk	12365	15080
4 Dr GS-R Sdn	12165	14835
2 Dr LS Hbk	10605	12935
4 Dr LS Sdn	10445	12735
2 Dr RS Hbk	9065	11055
2 Dr Type R Hbk	12675	15460

OPTIONS FOR INTEGRA

Auto 4-Speed Transmission +400
AM/FM Stereo Tape[Std on LS] +150
Air Conditioning[Opt on RS, Type R] +405
Aluminum/Alloy Wheels[Opt on LS] +165
Leather Seats[Std on GS] +430

RL-SERIES 1997

No changes for the 1997 3.5RL.

RATINGS (SCALE OF 1-10)

Overall	Safety	Reliability	Performance	Comfort	Value
N/A	N/A	9.5	8.2	8.9	4.2

Category A

4 Dr Premium Sdn	22695	27020
4 Dr STD Sdn	21005	25005

OPTIONS FOR RL-SERIES

Elect. Navigation System +1005
Alarm System +140
Compact Disc Changer[Opt on STD] +395
Compact Disc W/fm/tape +320

SLX 1997

No changes to Acura's upscale Isuzu Trooper twin.

RATINGS (SCALE OF 1-10)

Overall	Safety	Reliability	Performance	Comfort	Value
6.7	6.5	8	6.8	7.6	4.6

Category G

4 Dr Premium 4WD Wgn	16700	20120
4 Dr STD 4WD Wgn	15750	18975

TL-SERIES 1997

The TL is unchanged for 1997.

RATINGS (SCALE OF 1-10)

Overall	Safety	Reliability	Performance	Comfort	Value
7.5	7.6	9.5	7.4	8	5

Category A

4 Dr 2.5 Sdn	14875	17710
4 Dr 2.5 Premium Sdn	15540	18500

4 Dr 3.2 Sdn	16010	19060
4 Dr 3.2 Premium Sdn	16700	19880

1996 ACURA

INTEGRA 1996

All Integras get new wheel cover and alloy wheel designs this year, as well as green tinted glass. LS models receive body-colored moldings. Three new colors can be applied to the 1996 Integra: pearls in red, green or black.

RATINGS (SCALE OF 1-10)

Overall	Safety	Reliability	Performance	Comfort	Value
7.3	6.9	9	9.2	7.8	3.4

Category E

2 Dr GS-R Hbk	10750	13435
4 Dr GS-R Sdn	10590	13235
2 Dr LS Hbk	9650	12065
4 Dr LS Sdn	9535	11920
2 Dr RS Hbk	8370	10460
4 Dr RS Sdn	8210	10260
2 Dr Special Edition Hbk	10030	12540
4 Dr Special Edition Sdn	9850	12310

OPTIONS FOR INTEGRA

Auto 4-Speed Transmission +325
Air Conditioning[Opt on RS] +330
Aluminum/Alloy Wheels[Opt on LS] +135
Leather Seats[Opt on GS-R] +355

NSX 1996

The hardtop NSX is reintroduced to the Acura lineup.
Category K

2 Dr NSX-T Cpe	43355	50410
2 Dr STD Cpe	38715	45020

OPTIONS FOR NSX

Auto 4-Speed Transmission +1410

RL-SERIES 1996

The replacement for the Legend arrives wearing Acura's new alphanumeric naming system: the 3.5 RL. The 3.5 refers to the Acura's engine size. Detractors claim that the RL stands for little more than "Revised Legend." While the 3.5 RL is definitely luxurious, we think that many will miss the Legend's sporty feel. The front wheels of the 3.5 RL are powered by a torquey V6 engine mated to an electronic four-speed automatic transmission. Other changes include 101 ways to isolate bumps, vibrations and road noise. Acura's new flagship promises to be about as noisy as a sensory-deprivation chamber.

Don't forget to refer to the Mileage Adjustment Table at the back of this book!

Model Description	Trade-in Value	Market Value
Model Description	Trade-in Value	Market Value

RATINGS (SCALE OF 1-10)

Overall	Safety	Reliability	Performance	Comfort	Value
N/A	N/A	9.5	8.2	8.9	3.1

Category A

	Trade-in	Market
4 Dr 3.5 Sdn	17855	21515
4 Dr 3.5 Premium Sdn	19180	23105

OPTIONS FOR RL-SERIES
Navigation System +805
AM/FM Compact Disc Player +200
Compact Disc Changer[Opt on 3.5] +320

SLX   1996

In typical Acura form, the SLX is one of the first luxury-badged sport-utes to be released in this country. Based on the successful Isuzu Trooper, the SLX is very similar to its twin.

RATINGS (SCALE OF 1-10)

Overall	Safety	Reliability	Performance	Comfort	Value
N/A	N/A	7	6.8	7.6	5.5

Category G

	Trade-in	Market
4 Dr STD 4WD Wgn	13815	16845

OPTIONS FOR SLX
Premium Pkg +1180
Dual Power Seats +155
Leather Seats +315
Limited Slip Diff +110
Power Moonroof +350

TL-SERIES   1996

Vigor replacement designed to do battle with new Infiniti I30 and the Lexus ES300 in the near-luxury segment. Cleanly styled with room for four, the new TL-Series comes with either a 2.5-liter, inline five- cylinder, or a smooth, 3.2-liter V6.

RATINGS (SCALE OF 1-10)

Overall	Safety	Reliability	Performance	Comfort	Value
N/A	N/A	9.4	7.4	8	5

Category A

	Trade-in	Market
4 Dr 2.5 Sdn	12740	15350
4 Dr 2.5 Premium Sdn	13321	16050
4 Dr 3.2 Sdn	14525	17500
4 Dr 3.2 Premium Sdn	15135	18235

OPTIONS FOR TL-SERIES
Compact Disc Changer +320

1995 ACURA

INTEGRA   1995

A Special Edition model debuts, sporting leather interior, spoiler and larger tires. All LS models receive a sunroof.

RATINGS (SCALE OF 1-10)

Overall	Safety	Reliability	Performance	Comfort	Value
7.3	7.1	8.9	9.2	7.8	3.4

Category E

	Trade-in	Market
2 Dr GS-R Hbk	9115	11835
4 Dr GS-R Sdn	8945	11620
2 Dr LS Hbk	7790	10120
4 Dr LS Sdn	7625	9905
2 Dr RS Hbk	6970	9050
4 Dr RS Sdn	6835	8875
2 Dr Special Edition Hbk	8160	10600
4 Dr Special Edition Sdn	8025	10420

OPTIONS FOR INTEGRA
Auto 4-Speed Transmission +245
AM/FM Compact Disc Player +150
Air Conditioning[Opt on RS] +270
Alarm System +135
Aluminum/Alloy Wheels[Std on GS-R] +110
Compact Disc W/fm/tape +190
Leather Seats[Opt on GS-R] +290

LEGEND   1995

Last year for the Acura flagship, the 1996 model will bear Acura's new alphanumeric nomenclature. No changes for this year's model.

RATINGS (SCALE OF 1-10)

Overall	Safety	Reliability	Performance	Comfort	Value
7.9	8	9.6	8.6	8	5.4

Category A

	Trade-in	Market
4 Dr GS Sdn	14510	17695
2 Dr L Cpe	14340	17490
4 Dr L Sdn	12595	15360
2 Dr LS Cpe	15265	18615
4 Dr LS Sdn	13820	16855
4 Dr SE Sdn	14150	17255

OPTIONS FOR LEGEND
Auto 4-Speed Transmission[Opt on GS,L,Cpe] +265
Compact Disc Changer[Opt on L] +265
Leather Seats[Opt on L Sdn] +220

NSX   1995

The NSX coupe is dropped in favor of the NSX-T. The "T" stands for targa (removeable) top; all 1995 models are so equipped. Designed to boost sales of this slow-

ACURA 95-93

Model Description	Trade-in Value	Market Value	Model Description	Trade-in Value	Market Value

selling sports car, the NSX-T is otherwise identical to last year's fixed-roof coupe.

Category K

	Trade-in	Market
2 Dr STD Cpe	35410	41660

OPTIONS FOR NSX
Auto 4-Speed Transmission +1155

1994 ACURA

INTEGRA   1994

Redesigned for 1994, the Integra sports a distinctive four-headlight front end. All models receive four-wheel disc brakes to aid stopping; LS and GS-R models get antilock brakes. GS-Rs get a 10-horsepower boost over last year to improve performance. Dual airbags finally replace the annoying motorized seat belts as the passive restraint system on the Integra.

RATINGS (SCALE OF 1-10)

Overall	Safety	Reliability	Performance	Comfort	Value
7.2	7.1	8.1	9.2	7.8	3.8

Category E

	Trade-in	Market
2 Dr GS-R Hbk	7470	9960
4 Dr GS-R Sdn	7320	9760
2 Dr LS Hbk	6295	8395
4 Dr LS Sdn	6170	8225
2 Dr RS Hbk	5905	7870
4 Dr RS Sdn	5725	7630

OPTIONS FOR INTEGRA
Auto 4-Speed Transmission +205
Air Conditioning[Opt on RS] +220
Alarm System +110
Aluminum/Alloy Wheels[Opt on LS] +90

LEGEND   1994

The base Legend is dropped from the lineup and a GS sedan is added. The new sedan offers the same 230-horsepower engine found in the coupe as well as traction control and a sport-tuned suspension. A new grille and bumpers find their way to all Legends and the LS coupe gets a new chin-spoiler. An automatically tilting steering wheel raises as soon as the key is removed from the ignition. Further improvements include a steering wheel position memory that is incorporated into the seat memory feature.

RATINGS (SCALE OF 1-10)

Overall	Safety	Reliability	Performance	Comfort	Value
7.9	8	9.6	8.6	8	5.4

Category A

	Trade-in	Market
4 Dr GS Sdn	12670	15640
2 Dr L Cpe	12430	15345

	Trade-in Value	Market Value
4 Dr L Sdn	10940	13505
2 Dr LS Cpe	13185	16280
4 Dr LS Sdn	12045	14870

OPTIONS FOR LEGEND
Auto 4-Speed Transmission[Opt on GS,L,Cpe] +220
Leather Seats[Opt. on L Sdn] +180

NSX   1994

Still no changes for the four-year-old NSX.

Category K

	Trade-in	Market
2 Dr STD Cpe	31065	36980

OPTIONS FOR NSX
Auto 4-Speed Transmission +1095

VIGOR   1994

Dual airbags are now standard on all Vigors. Burled walnut trim replaces the Zebrano wood trim and GS models get a standard CD player. This is the final year for the Vigor.

Category D

	Trade-in	Market
4 Dr GS Sdn	8325	10670
4 Dr LS Sdn	7455	9560

OPTIONS FOR VIGOR
Auto 4-Speed Transmission +205

1993 ACURA

INTEGRA   1993

An LS Special model is introduced to the Integra line-up. Standard leather upholstery, rear spoiler and bigger tires make this midlevel Integra attractive to luxury-oriented buyers. An improved warranty boosts coverage to four years/45,000 miles.

RATINGS (SCALE OF 1-10)

Overall	Safety	Reliability	Performance	Comfort	Value
N/A	N/A	8.8	8.8	7.9	3.7

Category E

	Trade-in	Market
2 Dr GS Hbk	5495	7530
4 Dr GS Sdn	5400	7395
2 Dr GS-R Hbk	5720	7835
2 Dr LS Hbk	4875	6675
4 Dr LS Sdn	4805	6580
2 Dr LS Special Hbk	4875	6675
2 Dr RS Hbk	4495	6155
4 Dr RS Sdn	4320	5920

OPTIONS FOR INTEGRA
Auto 4-Speed Transmission +170
Air Conditioning +180
Leather Seats[Opt on GS] +195

Don't forget to refer to the Mileage Adjustment Table at the back of this book!

ACURA 93-92

Model Description	Trade-in Value	Market Value	Model Description	Trade-in Value	Market Value

LEGEND 1993

Thirty more horsepower and a six-speed manual transmission make the Legend coupe a viable luxury-performance contender. A passenger airbag is now standard on the base Legend. Upgraded stereos are standard on the L and LS models. Warranty coverage is extended to four years/45,000 miles.

RATINGS (SCALE OF 1-10)

Overall	Safety	Reliability	Performance	Comfort	Value
7.8	8	9.1	8.6	8	5.3

Category A

2 Dr L Cpe	9860	12480
4 Dr L Sdn	8805	11145
2 Dr LS Cpe	10620	13440
4 Dr LS Sdn	9515	12045
4 Dr STD Sdn	8055	10195

OPTIONS FOR LEGEND
· Auto 4-Speed Transmission +180
· AM/FM Compact Disc Player +110
· Compact Disc W/fm/tape +145
· Leather Seats[Opt on L] +150

NSX 1993

A passenger airbag is introduced this year, as is a cupholder for the center console. Warranty coverage is improved from three years/36,000 miles to four years/45,000 miles.

Category K

2 Dr STD Cpe	26290	32060

OPTIONS FOR NSX
Auto 4-Speed Transmission +895

VIGOR 1993

A passenger airbag debuts on the up-level GS Vigor. Restyled front grille and sound insulation mark the other changes to this car. Warranty coverage increases to four years/45,000 miles.

Category D

4 Dr GS Sdn	6695	8810
4 Dr LS Sdn	5915	7785

OPTIONS FOR VIGOR
Auto 4-Speed Transmission +170

1992 ACURA

INTEGRA 1992

A minor facelift and more horsepower are the only changes for the '92 Integra. A GS-R performance model is introduced with a 160 horsepower VTEC engine.

RATINGS (SCALE OF 1-10)

Overall	Safety	Reliability	Performance	Comfort	Value
N/A	N/A	8.6	8.8	7.9	5.1

Category E

2 Dr GS Hbk	4600	6570
4 Dr GS Sdn	4480	6400
2 Dr GS-R Hbk	4815	6875
2 Dr LS Hbk	4095	5850
4 Dr LS Sdn	3990	5700
2 Dr RS Hbk	3700	5285
4 Dr RS Sdn	3590	5130

OPTIONS FOR INTEGRA
Auto 4-Speed Transmission +135
Air Conditioning +145

LEGEND 1992

A passenger airbag joins the standard equipment list on LS models. Cupholders are finally available to front-seat passengers. LS models are now available with heated front seats.

RATINGS (SCALE OF 1-10)

Overall	Safety	Reliability	Performance	Comfort	Value
7.7	7.5	8.2	8.6	8	6.1

Category A

2 Dr L Cpe	8135	10565
4 Dr L Sdn	7335	9525
2 Dr LS Cpe	8715	11315
4 Dr LS Sdn	8010	10400
4 Dr STD Sdn	6705	8710

OPTIONS FOR LEGEND
Auto 4-Speed Transmission +145

NSX 1992

No changes for the sweetest looking car since the Ferrari 308.

Category K

2 Dr STD Cpe	22160	27025

OPTIONS FOR NSX
Auto 4-Speed Transmission +720

VIGOR 1992

The Vigor is introduced to broaden Acura's market. It is a midsized near-luxury sedan based on the Honda Accord. Offered in two trim levels, the Vigor can be had with an automatic or manual transmission. Power comes via an inline five-cylinder engine. Antilock brakes, power everything and a security system are standard on the Vigor.

Don't forget to refer to the Mileage Adjustment Table at the back of this book!

Model Description	Trade-in Value	Market Value

Category D

Model Description	Trade-in Value	Market Value
4 Dr GS Sdn	5790	7720
4 Dr LS Sdn	5235	6980

OPTIONS FOR VIGOR
Auto 4-Speed Transmission +135

1991 ACURA

INTEGRA 1991

No significant changes are made to the 1991 Integra.

RATINGS (SCALE OF 1-10)

Overall	Safety	Reliability	Performance	Comfort	Value
N/A	N/A	7.5	8.8	7.9	4.1

Category E

2 Dr GS Hbk	3785	5565
4 Dr GS Sdn	3690	5430
2 Dr LS Hbk	3510	5160
4 Dr LS Sdn	3395	4990
2 Dr LS Special Hbk	3510	5165
2 Dr RS Hbk	3060	4500
4 Dr RS Sdn	2950	4335

OPTIONS FOR INTEGRA
Auto 4-Speed Transmission +105
Air Conditioning +120

LEGEND 1991

Redesigned for 1991, the Legend gets longer and larger. A more powerful (200 horsepower) engine keeps this car competitive with domestic and import rivals.

RATINGS (SCALE OF 1-10)

Overall	Safety	Reliability	Performance	Comfort	Value
7.6	7.4	7.5	8.6	8	6.6

Category A

2 Dr L Cpe	6725	8365
4 Dr L Sdn	6275	8965
2 Dr LS Cpe	7220	9625
4 Dr LS Sdn	6640	8855
2 Dr STD Cpe	6175	7775
4 Dr STD Sdn	5830	8235

OPTIONS FOR LEGEND
Auto 4-Speed Transmission +120
Compact Disc W/fm/tape +95
Leather Seats[Opt on L] +100

1990 ACURA

INTEGRA 1990

The Integra is redesigned. The five-door hatchback is replaced by a sedan and a two-door hatchback continues. Horsepower and torque figures are up for this entry-level Acura, but so is weight. Suspension upgrades improve handling.

RATINGS (SCALE OF 1-10)

Overall	Safety	Reliability	Performance	Comfort	Value
N/A	N/A	7.3	8.8	7.9	4.6

Category E

2 Dr GS Hbk	3140	4760
4 Dr GS Sdn	3050	4620
2 Dr LS Hbk	2890	4380
4 Dr LS Sdn	2795	4235
2 Dr RS Hbk	2515	3810
4 Dr RS Sdn	2410	3650

OPTIONS FOR INTEGRA
Auto 4-Speed Transmission +90
Air Conditioning +100

LEGEND 1990

LS models get a spoiler. A new grille appears on all Legends. Interior changes include an authentic burled walnut center console and improved seats.

Category A

2 Dr L Cpe	4320	5835
4 Dr L Sdn	4005	5410
2 Dr LS Cpe	4660	6300
4 Dr LS Sdn	4330	5850
2 Dr STD Cpe	4005	5415
4 Dr STD Sdn	3680	4970

OPTIONS FOR LEGEND
Auto 4-Speed Transmission +100
Leather Seats[Opt on L] +80
Power Sunroof[Std on L,LS,Cpe] +170

Don't forget to refer to the Mileage Adjustment Table at the back of this book!

AUDI 99-98

Model Description	Trade-in Value	Market Value	Model Description	Trade-in Value	Market Value

AUDI Germany

1997 Audi A8

1999 AUDI

A4 1999

Audi introduces the 1.8T Avant wagon to its lineup, while other A4 models gain standard equipment and new options.

RATINGS (SCALE OF 1-10)

Overall	Safety	Reliability	Performance	Comfort	Value
N/A	8.7	9.6	8.8	8.1	N/A

Category D
4 Dr Quattro 1.8T 4WD Sdn	19220	22350
4 Dr Quattro 2.8 4WD Sdn	20485	23820
4 Dr STD 2.8 Sdn	19460	22630
4 Dr STD 1.8T Sdn	17920	20840

OPTIONS FOR A4
Auto Manual Transmission +795
Compact Disc Changer +500
Heated Front Seats +300
Leather Seats +820
Power Moonroof +620

A6 1999

The A6 continues basically unchanged after last year's redesign.

RATINGS (SCALE OF 1-10)

Overall	Safety	Reliability	Performance	Comfort	Value
N/A	9.3	N/A	8.2	8.1	N/A

Category D
4 Dr Avant 4WD Wgn	27135	31550
4 Dr Quattro 4WD Sdn	25475	29620
4 Dr STD Sdn	24435	28410

OPTIONS FOR A6
Enhanced Security Pkg +700
Warm Weather Pkg +935
Automatic Dimming Mirror +180
Compact Disc Changer +500
Leather Seats +820
Power Moonroof +620
Ski Sack[Std on Avant] +145

A8 1999

The A8's warm weather package is modified to improve electronic accessory performance, while dual pane laminated glass replaces insulated glass. Standard on the A8 is a larger right outside mirror, a first aid kit and a CD changer. A premium leather/alcantra trim package and a new volcano black exterior paint color are optional. A8 prices will remain unchanged from 1998.

RATINGS (SCALE OF 1-10)

Overall	Safety	Reliability	Performance	Comfort	Value
N/A	N/A	N/A	7.6	8	N/A

Category D
4 Dr Quattro 4WD Sdn	40075	46600

OPTIONS FOR A8
Alcantara & Leather Pkg +2585
Electronics Pkg +1035
Polished Alloy Wheels +740
Warm Weather Pkg +885

1998 AUDI

A4 1998

The 2.8 sedan gets a valve job resulting in 18 more horsepower and additional torque. Side-impact airbags are standard, as is traction control. Opt for the automatic and you'll get the same Tiptronic technology that allows Biff to manually shift Buffy's 911 Cabriolet. A new station wagon called Avant debuts, while the A4 1.8T gets new wheels, a sport package and an ambient temperature gauge. New colors and stereo improvements round out the changes for 1998.

RATINGS (SCALE OF 1-10)

Overall	Safety	Reliability	Performance	Comfort	Value
7.9	8.6	9.3	8.8	8.1	4.9

Category J
4 Dr Avant 2.8 Wgn	20135	23410
4 Dr Avant 2.8 4WD Wgn	21200	24650
4 Dr Quattro 1.8T 4WD Sdn	17370	20200
4 Dr Quattro 2.8 4WD Sdn	18595	21620
4 Dr STD 1.8T Sdn	16365	19030
4 Dr STD 2.8 Sdn	17505	20355

Don't forget to refer to the Mileage Adjustment Table at the back of this book!

Model Description	Trade-in Value	Market Value

Model Description	Trade-in Value	Market Value

OPTIONS FOR A4
Bose Sound System +495
Compact Disc Changer +560
Heated Front Seats +255
Leather Seats +705
Power Moonroof +570
Special Factory Paint +1020

A6 1998

Stretch an A4 platform, add rounded styling with plenty of edges for character, toss in a sumptuously comfortable interior available in several "atmosphere" styles, blend it all with traditional Germanic handling, and what do you get? The excellent new Audi A6 sedan. Our only quibble is the with the dorky taillights, which appear to have been inspired by the Chevrolet S-10 pickup. The wagon is carried over from 1997.

RATINGS (SCALE OF 1-10)

Overall	Safety	Reliability	Performance	Comfort	Value
N/A	9.1	N/A	8.6	8.1	N/A

Category J

4 Dr Quattro 4WD Sdn	21805	25355
4 Dr Quattro 4WD Wgn	23300	27095
4 Dr STD Sdn	20475	23810
4 Dr STD Wgn	22110	25710

OPTIONS FOR A6
Enhanced Security Pkg +585
Warm Weather Pkg +920
Bose Sound System +495
Compact Disc Changer +560
Dual Power Seats +450
Heated Front Seats +255
Leather Seats +705
Metallic Paint +405
Power Moonroof +570

A8 1998

Tiptronic automanual gear shifting is standard, as is a glass sunroof, dual-pane laminated window glass, an improved stereo and an upgraded antilock braking system.

Category L

4 Dr Quattro 4WD Sdn	37195	43760

OPTIONS FOR A8
Polished Alloy Wheels +615
Warm Weather Pkg +1230
Bose Sound System[Opt on STD] +335

CABRIOLET 1998

Here's an argument for euthanasia. Based on the ancient 80/90 platform from the late 80s, the Cabriolet soldiers on with minimal change. A new steering wheel design is standard, and the Audi logo disappears from the side moldings.

Category F

2 Dr STD Conv	17425	20500

OPTIONS FOR CABRIOLET
Premium Equipment Pkg +1670

1997 AUDI

A4 1997

A cheaper Audi A4 1.8T debuts, featuring a 150-horsepower, 20-valve, turbocharged inline four-cylinder engine and a base price in the low 20s. The 2.8 gains a revised decklid and expanded central locking features. All models have new cloth upholstery, and the console and armrests are trimmed with the same fabric as the seats. Three new colors debut for 1997.

RATINGS (SCALE OF 1-10)

Overall	Safety	Reliability	Performance	Comfort	Value
7.7	7.6	9	8.8	8.1	4.9

Category J

4 Dr Quattro 2.8 4WD Sdn	16475	19380
4 Dr Quattro 1.8T 4WD Sdn	15980	18800
4 Dr STD 2.8 Sdn	15515	18255
4 Dr STD 1.8T Sdn	15010	17660

OPTIONS FOR A4
Auto 5-Speed Transmission +490
Bose Sound System +405
Heated Front Seats +210
Leather Seats +580
Power Moonroof +465
Special Factory Paint +835
Sport Seats +370

A6 1997

A new Quattro Value Package is available with a power glass sunroof, larger alloy wheels, bigger tires, and, of course, the quattro all-wheel drive system. Selective unlocking capability expands to the remote keyless entry fob, and the alarm system now features interior monitoring. Jacquard cloth upholstery is new, and three new colors debut: Tornado Red, Volcano Black metallic and Byzantine metallic.

RATINGS (SCALE OF 1-10)

Overall	Safety	Reliability	Performance	Comfort	Value
N/A	8.2	N/A	8	8	5.8

Category J

4 Dr Quattro 4WD Sdn	18045	21230
4 Dr Quattro 4WD Wgn	19820	23320
4 Dr STD Sdn	17050	20060
4 Dr STD Wgn	18715	22020

Don't forget to refer to the Mileage Adjustment Table at the back of this book!

Model Description	Trade-in Value	Market Value	Model Description	Trade-in Value	Market Value

OPTIONS FOR A6
Bose Sound System +405
Dual Power Seats +365
Headlight Washers +120
Heated Front Seats +210
Leather Seats +580
Metallic Paint +330
Power Moonroof +465

A8 · 1997

Audi revolutionizes luxury sedan construction with the Audi Space Frame, which employs seven new aircraft-grade aluminum alloys to lighten weight and provide a tighter, more crashworthy structure. The new A8 is also the first passenger car equipped with six airbags. The usual accouterments associated with a premium German sedan are all in place.

Category L

4 Dr Quattro 4WD Sdn	32505	38240
4 Dr STD Sdn	30620	36025

OPTIONS FOR A8
Cold Weather Pkg +380
Polished Alloy Wheels +500
Warm Weather Pkg +1005
Bose Sound System [Opt on STD] +275
Heated Seats +190
Metallic Paint +300

CABRIOLET · 1997

Base price drops a couple grand, but at the expense of the power top, burled walnut wood trim, and leather seats. Opt for the Premium Equipment Package, and these items magically reappear. Casablanca White and Cactus Green join the list of paint colors, and three new top colors debut. Leather seats can be had in two new shades, too.

Category F

2 Dr STD Conv	16170	19250

OPTIONS FOR CABRIOLET
Premium Equipment Pkg +1490

1996 AUDI

A4 · 1996

All-new, the A4 replaces the compact 90. This car performs better than the lackluster 90, and features a full load of standard features. Plus, it's drop-dead gorgeous. For the first time, a five-speed automatic transmission is available with the optional Quattro all-wheel-drive system.

RATINGS (SCALE OF 1-10)

Overall	Safety	Reliability	Performance	Comfort	Value
N/A	N/A	8.4	8.8	8.1	6.1

Category J

4 Dr Quattro 2.8 4WD Sdn	14850	17680
4 Dr STD 2.8 Sdn	14075	16755

OPTIONS FOR A4
Auto 5-Speed Transmission +375
Bose Sound System +330
Heated Front Seats +170
Leather Seats +470
Metallic Paint +270
Power Moonroof +380

A6 · 1996

Traction control systems have been improved this year. Fans of the manual transmission will mourn the loss of it; all 1996 A6 models are saddled with an automatic shifter.

RATINGS (SCALE OF 1-10)

Overall	Safety	Reliability	Performance	Comfort	Value
N/A	8.2	N/A	8	8	5.7

Category J

4 Dr Quattro 4WD Sdn	14970	17820
4 Dr Quattro 4WD Wgn	16715	19900
4 Dr STD Sdn	13955	16615
4 Dr STD Wgn	15685	18675

OPTIONS FOR A6
Bose Sound System +330
Dual Power Seats +300
Headlight Washers +100
Heated Front Seats +170
Leather Seats +470
Metallic Paint +270
Power Moonroof +380

CABRIOLET · 1996

Better acceleration, a new radio, a new color and revised alloy wheels are the only changes.

Category F

2 Dr STD Conv	14905	17745

1995 AUDI

90 · 1995

Sport 90 model introduced, featuring lowered suspension.

Category D

4 Dr Quattro 4WD Sdn	10310	13050
4 Dr STD Sdn	8785	11120
4 Dr Sport Sdn	8945	11325

OPTIONS FOR 90
Auto 4-Speed Transmission +295
Heated Front Seats +135
Keyless Entry System +105

Don't forget to refer to the Mileage Adjustment Table at the back of this book!

Leather Seats +365
Power Sunroof +245

A6 — 1995

Subtle restyle of last year's 100 brings new name. Sedan or wagon available in either front- or all-wheel drive. Wagon comes only with an automatic transmission.

RATINGS (SCALE OF 1-10)

Overall	Safety	Reliability	Performance	Comfort	Value
N/A	9	N/A	8	8	7

Category J

	Trade-in	Market
4 Dr Quattro 4WD Sdn	13095	15780
4 Dr Quattro 4WD Wgn	14365	17310
4 Dr STD Sdn	12175	14670
4 Dr STD Wgn	13345	16080

OPTIONS FOR A6

Auto 4-Speed Transmission[Std on Wgn] +295
Bose Sound System +270
Dual Power Seats +245
Heated Front Seats +140
Leather Seats +385
Power Moonroof +310

CABRIOLET — 1995

No changes.
Category F

	Trade-in	Market
2 Dr STD Conv	12955	15800

S6 — 1995

Category F

	Trade-in	Market
4 Dr STD Turbo 4WD Sdn	19690	24015

OPTIONS FOR S6

Compact Disc Changer +215

1994 AUDI

100 — 1994

Base sedan dropped. CS sedan gets standard automatic transmission. Rear ashtrays and cigarette lighters disappear from all models.

RATINGS (SCALE OF 1-10)

Overall	Safety	Reliability	Performance	Comfort	Value
N/A	N/A	N/A	8	8.1	7

Category D

	Trade-in	Market
4 Dr CS Sdn	9750	12665
4 Dr CS Quattro 4WD Sdn	10565	13720
4 Dr S Sdn	8160	10600
4 Dr S Wgn	9515	12355

OPTIONS FOR 100

Auto 4-Speed Transmission[Std on CS,Wgn] +220
Bose Sound System[Opt on S Sdn] +205
Heated Front Seats[Opt on S,Sdn] +110
Leather Seats[Opt on S Sdn] +300

90 — 1994

Passenger airbag newly standard. S model can be equipped with leather and a power sunroof.
Category D

	Trade-in	Market
4 Dr CS Sdn	8445	10970
4 Dr CS Quattro 4WD Sdn	9080	11795
4 Dr S Sdn	7405	9620

OPTIONS FOR 90

Auto 4-Speed Transmission +220
Heated Front Seats +110
Power Sunroof[Opt on S] +200

CABRIOLET — 1994

Based on 90 platform. Features dual airbags, ABS and 2.8-liter V6 engine. No manual transmission available. Rear window is plastic.
Category F

	Trade-in	Market
2 Dr STD Conv	11030	13785

OPTIONS FOR CABRIOLET

Heated Front Seats +105

S4 — 1994

Category F

	Trade-in	Market
4 Dr STD Turbo 4WD Sdn	15720	19650

V8 — 1994

Category F

	Trade-in	Market
4 Dr Quattro 4WD Sdn	8995	11245

1993 AUDI

100 — 1993

Passenger airbag standard.

RATINGS (SCALE OF 1-10)

Overall	Safety	Reliability	Performance	Comfort	Value
N/A	N/A	N/A	8	8.1	6.9

Category D

	Trade-in	Market
4 Dr CS Sdn	7900	10530
4 Dr CS Quattro 4WD Sdn	8710	11610
4 Dr CS Quattro 4WD Wgn	9425	12565
4 Dr S Sdn	6790	9055
4 Dr STD Sdn	6150	8200

OPTIONS FOR 100

Auto 4-Speed Transmission[Std on CS,Wgn] +180
Heated Front Seats +90
Leather Seats[Opt on S] +245

Don't forget to refer to the Mileage Adjustment Table at the back of this book!

Model Description	Trade-in Value	Market Value

90 — 1993

All-new 90 model debuts, with 2.8-liter V6 under the hood. ABS and driver airbag standard. Quattro AWD system still available.

Category D

4 Dr CS Sdn	6745	8990
4 Dr S Sdn	5760	7680

OPTIONS FOR 90
Auto 4-Speed Transmission +180
Heated Front Seats +90
Power Sunroof[Opt on S] +165

S4 — 1993

Passenger airbag standard.

Category F

4 Dr STD Turbo 4WD Sdn	13630	17700

V8 — 1993

Category F

4 Dr Quattro 4WD Sdn	7875	10225

1992 AUDI

100 — 1992

Sheetmetal redesigned, and 2.8-liter V6 replaces five-cylinder motor. Quattro models available with automatic transmission. Driver airbag and ABS standard. All wagons are Quattro-equipped.

RATINGS (SCALE OF 1-10)

Overall	Safety	Reliability	Performance	Comfort	Value
N/A	N/A	N/A	8	8.1	6.9

Category D

4 Dr CS Sdn	6335	8560
4 Dr CS Quattro 4WD Sdn	6965	9410
4 Dr CS Quattro 4WD Wgn	8105	10950
4 Dr S Sdn	5570	7525
4 Dr STD Sdn	5010	6770

OPTIONS FOR 100
Auto 4-Speed Transmission[Std on Wgn] +145
Pearlescent Met. Paint +170
Heated Front Seats[Std on Wgn] +75
Leather Seats[Std on Wgn] +200

80 — 1992

90 model discontinued. Coupe Quattro disappears. Antilock brakes made standard on 80, and optional power sunroof replaces last year's manual one.

Category D

4 Dr STD Sdn	3870	5230

OPTIONS FOR 80
Auto 4-Speed Transmission +160
Power Sunroof +135

V8 — 1992

Category F

4 Dr Quattro 4WD Sdn	6095	8125

1991 AUDI

100 — 1991

100E dropped. New programmable four-speed automatic transmission for 100 models.

Category D

4 Dr Quattro 4WD Sdn	4610	6315
4 Dr STD Sdn	3695	5060

OPTIONS FOR 100
Bose Sound System +110
Heated Front Seats +60
Leather Seats +165

200 — 1991

New 20-valve turbo engine installed in 200 Quattro models.

Category F

4 Dr Quattro Turbo 4WD Sdn	5625	7500
4 Dr STD Turbo Sdn	5035	6715

OPTIONS FOR 200
Heated Front Seats +55

80 — 1991

Programmable four-speed automatic transmission introduced. 80 dumps weak, 2.0-liter, four-cylinder engine in favor of more powerful, 2.3-liter, five-cylinder engine.

Category D

4 Dr STD Sdn	3170	4345

OPTIONS FOR 80
Auto 4-Speed Transmission +125
Sunroof +65

90 — 1991

Programmable four-speed automatic transmission introduced.

Category D

4 Dr Quattro 4WD Sdn	5260	7205
4 Dr STD Sdn	3975	5445

OPTIONS FOR 90
Heated Front Seats +60
Leather Seats +165

Don't forget to refer to the Mileage Adjustment Table at the back of this book!

AUDI 91-90

Model Description	Trade-in Value	Market Value
COUPE		**1991**
Category F		
2 Dr Quattro 4WD Cpe	6070	8090
V8		**1991**
Category F		
4 Dr Quattro 4WD Sdn	5395	7190

1990 AUDI

Model Description	Trade-in Value	Market Value
100		**1990**
No changes.		
Category D		
4 Dr STD Sdn	3045	4230
OPTIONS FOR 100		
Bose Sound System +90		
Leather Seats +135		
200		**1990**
No changes.		
Category F		
4 Dr Quattro Turbo 4WD Sdn	4535	6210
4 Dr STD Turbo Sdn	3970	5435

Model Description	Trade-in Value	Market Value
80		**1990**
No changes.		
Category D		
4 Dr Quattro 4WD Sdn	2960	4110
4 Dr STD Sdn	2515	3490
OPTIONS FOR 80		
Power Sunroof +90		
90		**1990**
No changes.		
Category D		
4 Dr Quattro 4WD Sdn	4180	5810
4 Dr STD Sdn	3475	4825
OPTIONS FOR 90		
Leather Seats +135		
COUPE		**1990**
New Coupe Quattro debuts, with 164-horsepower 20-valve engine.		
Category F		
2 Dr Quattro 4WD Cpe	4705	6445

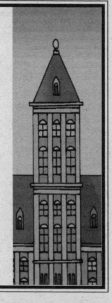
Don't forget to refer to the Mileage Adjustment Table at the back of this book!

BMW 99

Model Description	Trade-in Value	Market Value	Model Description	Trade-in Value	Market Value

BMW   Germany

1990 BMW M3 Coupe

1999 BMW

3-SERIES   1999

3-Series sedans redesigned for 1999, offering 5-Series style along with more room for rear seat passengers.

RATINGS (SCALE OF 1-10)

Overall	Safety	Reliability	Performance	Comfort	Value
N/A	8.5	9.4	8.8	8.4	N/A

Category D

2 Dr 323i Conv	23835	27715
4 Dr 323i Sdn	19500	22675
2 Dr 323is Cpe	20905	24310
2 Dr 328i Conv	29085	33820
4 Dr 328i Sdn	23890	27780
2 Dr 328i Cpe	25240	29350

OPTIONS FOR 3-SERIES

Auto 4-Speed Transmission +720
Auto 5-Speed Transmission[Opt on Sedans, M3] +830
California Roof +1180
Navigation System +1400
Premium Pkg +720
Sport Handling Pkg +670
Alarm System[Std on 328i,Sdn] +390
Aluminum/Alloy Wheels[Opt on 323i Sedan] +345
Automatic Dimming Mirror +180
Compact Disc Changer +500
Cruise Control[Opt on 318ti,323i Sedan] +180
Dual Power Seats[Opt on 323i] +625
Fog Lights[Opt on 323i,323is] +175
Heated Front Seats +300
Leather Seats[Std on 318ti] +820
Onboard Computer[Std on 328i Sedan] +320

Power Sunroof +550
Sport Suspension[Std on 318ti] +235
Xenon Headlamps[Opt on Sedans] +370

5-SERIES   1999

This fall, new 528i and 540i sport wagons debut, all 5-Series models achieve Low Emission Vehicle (LEV) status, and consumers will find extensive new standard and optional equipment on the cars.

RATINGS (SCALE OF 1-10)

Overall	Safety	Reliability	Performance	Comfort	Value
N/A	N/A	N/A	9.4	8.8	N/A

Category J

4 Dr 528i Sdn	30235	34750
4 Dr 540i Sdn	37760	43405
4 Dr 528iT Wgn	31510	36220

OPTIONS FOR 5-SERIES

6-Speed Transmission +2070
Auto 4-Speed Transmission +720
Comfort Seats +885
Navigation System +1310
Premium Hi-fi +885
Premium Hi-fi Sound +885
Premium Pkg +1155
Sport Handling Pkg +1640
Sport Premium Pkg +2100
Automatic Dimming Mirror[Std on 540i Sedan,540iT Sport Wagon] +330
Leather Seats[Std on 540i Sedan,540iT Sport Wagon] +865
Metallic Paint +495
Power Moonroof[Std on 540i Sedan,540iT Sport Wagon] +695
Premium Sound System[Std on 540iT Sport Wagon] +970

7-SERIES   1999

All 7-Series engines achieve LEV (Low Emission Vehicle) status. Revised standard and optional equipment add to the cars' appeal.

Category L

4 Dr 740i Sdn	41390	48130
4 Dr 740iL Sdn	43055	50065

OPTIONS FOR 7-SERIES

Comfort Seats +885
Elect. Damping Control Susp. +1110
Navigation System +1330
Park Distance Control +665
Security Glass +1920
Security Sun Roof +1920
Sport Handling Pkg +1790
Compact Disc Changer[Std on 750iL] +825
Headlight Washers[Std on 750iL] +240
Heated Front Seats[Std on 750iL] +355
Power Sunroof +685

Model Description	Trade-in Value	Market Value

M3 1999

Production of M3 four-door sedans ends this year as BMW concentrates on selling the M3 coupe and recently introduced M3 convertible. These models go unchanged for 1999.

Category J

2 Dr STD Conv	32725	37615
2 Dr STD Cpe	29320	33700

OPTIONS FOR M3

Auto 5-Speed Transmission +885
Forged Alloy Wheels +1070
Cruise Control +355
Dual Power Seats +550
Harman Kardon Sound Sys +1055
Heated Front Seats +310
Power Moonroof +695

Z3 COUPE/CONVERTIBLE 1999

RATINGS (SCALE OF 1-10)

Overall	Safety	Reliability	Performance	Comfort	Value
N/A	N/A	N/A	8.8	7.6	N/A

M

Category F

2 Dr M Conv	31620	36770
2 Dr M Cpe	28975	33690

Z3

Category F

2 Dr 2.3 Conv	22800	26510
2 Dr 2.8 Conv	25795	29995
2 Dr 2.8 Cpe	24010	27920

OPTIONS FOR Z3 COUPE/CONVERTIBLE

Auto 4-Speed Transmission +720
Extended Leather Trim +885
Round Spoke Alloy Wheels +830
AM/FM Compact Disc Player +355
Cruise Control[Opt on 2.3] +155
Leather Seats[Opt on 2.3] +485
Power Convertible Top[Std on M] +555

1998 BMW

3-SERIES 1998

BMW adds a 2.5-liter inline-six engine to their entry-level coupe and convertible, making them the cheapest six-cylinder BMWs in years. Also new are standard side-impact airbags for front seat passengers in all models except the 318ti, in which they're optional.

RATINGS (SCALE OF 1-10)

Overall	Safety	Reliability	Performance	Comfort	Value
7.7	8.4	9.4	9.4	8	3.5

Category D

4 Dr 318i Sdn	16480	19390
2 Dr 318ti Hbk	13625	16030
2 Dr 323i Conv	22480	26445
2 Dr 323is Cpe	19565	23020
2 Dr 328i Conv	26755	31475
4 Dr 328i Sdn	21530	25330

Category F

2 Dr 328is Cpe	22375	26325

Category J

2 Dr M3 Conv	31930	37125
2 Dr M3 Cpe	26620	30955
4 Dr M3 Sdn	26030	30265

OPTIONS FOR 3-SERIES

Auto 4-Speed Transmission +600
Auto 5-Speed Transmission[Opt on M3] +770
California Roof +985
Forged Alloy Wheels +915
Rollover Protection System(Opt on Conv) +890
Sport Handling Pkg +1305
Aluminum/Alloy Wheels[Opt on 318i, 318ti] +280
Compact Disc Changer +390
Cruise Control[Opt on 318ti, M3] +145
Dual Power Seats[Opt on M3] +450
Heated Front Seats +235
Keyless Entry System +110
Leather Seats[Std on M3] +395
Metallic Paint +175
Onboard Computer +225
Power Sunroof +410
Side Air Bag Restraint[Opt on 318ti] +180
Sport Suspension[Std on M3] +110

5-SERIES 1998

Side-impact airbags are now available for rear-seat passengers, as is break-resistant glass for the windows and moonroof.

RATINGS (SCALE OF 1-10)

Overall	Safety	Reliability	Performance	Comfort	Value
N/A	N/A	9.1	9.4	8.8	N/A

Category F

4 Dr 528i Sdn	27620	32495

Category J

4 Dr 540i Sdn	33585	39050

OPTIONS FOR 5-SERIES

6-Speed Transmission[Opt on 540i] +1720
Auto 4-Speed Transmission +600
Comfort Seats +735
Navigation System +1595
Premium Pkg +1525
Sport Handling Pkg +1420
Heated Front Seats +235
Leather Seats[Opt on 528i] +395
Metallic Paint +240

Don't forget to refer to the Mileage Adjustment Table at the back of this book!

Power Moonroof[Opt on 528i] +395
Premium Sound System +225
Sport Suspension +110

7-SERIES 1998

BMW introduces Dynamic Stability Control (DSC) to the big Bimmer. DSC is designed to automatically correct the yaw on all 7-Series cars, preventing plowing and fishtailing. Guess this means no more smoky burnouts in the Beverly Hilton's parking lot.

Category L

4 Dr 740i Sdn	35100	41295
4 Dr 740iL Sdn	36670	43140
4 Dr 750iL Sdn	44250	52060

OPTIONS FOR 7-SERIES
Comfort Seats +735
Elect. Damping Control Susp. +1230
Navigation System +1535
Park Distance Control +555
Security Sun Roof +1595
Auto Load Leveling[Opt on 740iL] +680
Compact Disc W/fm/tape[Std on 750iL] +390
Heated Front Seats[Std on 750iL] +290
Metallic Paint +365
Power Sunroof +560

Z3 1998

The M Roadster, a 240-horsepower version of the Z3 convertible, arrives for 1998. An electric top also becomes available this year.

RATINGS (SCALE OF 1-10)

Overall	Safety	Reliability	Performance	Comfort	Value
N/A	N/A	8.9	9	7.5	N/A

Category F

2 Dr 1.9 Conv	20035	23570
2 Dr 2.8 Conv	23030	27095
2 Dr M Conv	28470	33495

OPTIONS FOR Z3
Auto 4-Speed Transmission +600
Alloy Wheels W/17in. Tires +690
Extended Leather Trim +735
Heated Front Seats[Std on M] +235
Heated Power Mirrors[Std on M] +135
Leather Seats[Opt on 1.9] +395
Metallic Paint[Std on M] +240
Onboard Computer +225
Power Convertible Top[Std on M] +455
Premium Sound System[Opt on 1.9] +225
Side Air Bag Restraint +240

1997 BMW

3-SERIES 1997

An M3 sedan has arrived at a store near you. Those of you claiming to want power and practicality no longer have an excuse for driving that old jalopy currently parked in your driveway. Buy one now. Also, All-Season Traction is now standard on all models.

RATINGS (SCALE OF 1-10)

Overall	Safety	Reliability	Performance	Comfort	Value
7.3	7.4	9	9.4	8	2.9

Category D

2 Dr 318i Conv	18110	21820
4 Dr 318i Sdn	14360	17300
2 Dr 318ti Hbk	12070	14545
2 Dr 328i Conv	23495	28310
4 Dr 328i Sdn	18645	22465
2 Dr 328i Luxury Conv	25355	30550

Category F

2 Dr 318is Cpe	16165	19245
2 Dr 328is Cpe	19885	23670

Category J

2 Dr M3 Cpe	23695	27875
4 Dr M3 Sdn	22940	26990

OPTIONS FOR 3-SERIES
Auto 4-Speed Transmission +490
Forged Alloy Wheels +730
Luxury Pkg +1095
Rollover Protection System(Opt on Conv) +730
Sports Pkg +670
AM/FM Compact Disc Player +260
Aluminum/Alloy Wheels[Opt on 318ti,318i] +230
Compact Disc W/fm/tape +400
Heated Front Seats +190
Leather Seats[Std on M3,Luxury,328i STD Conv] +325
Onboard Computer +185
Power Sunroof +335
Premium Sound System +185
Sport Seats +245

5-SERIES 1997

The 5-Series is redesigned and introduced midway through 1996 as a 1997 model. Bearing a strong resemblance to its 3- and 7-Series siblings, the 5-Series offers a lot of car for a lot of money. The Touring wagons are no longer available, and the 3.0-liter V8 is history. New 5-Series models can be had as a six-cylinder 528i or a V8 540i. Both models feature new engines, all-aluminum suspensions, improved brakes and available side impact airbag protection.

Model Description	Trade-in Value	Market Value

RATINGS (SCALE OF 1-10)

Overall	Safety	Reliability	Performance	Comfort	Value
N/A	N/A	8.9	9.4	8.8	N/A

Category F

Model Description	Trade-in Value	Market Value
4 Dr 528i Sdn	23750	28275

Category J

4 Dr 540i Sdn	29720	34965

OPTIONS FOR 5-SERIES

6-Speed Transmission[Opt on 540i] +1075
Auto 4-Speed Transmission +430
Comfort Seats +525
Navigation System +1230
Premium Pkg +750
Heated Front Seats +190
Leather Seats[Opt on 528i] +325
Power Moonroof[Opt on 528i] +320
Premium Sound System +185
Sport Suspension +210

7-SERIES 1997

BMW reintroduces the regular length 740i after the uproar caused over its cancellation for the 1996 model year. Like the rest of the 7-Series, the 740i has a standard equipment list that will leave the Sultan of Brunei drooling with desire.

Category L

4 Dr 740i Sdn	31010	36480
4 Dr 740iL Sdn	32285	37980
4 Dr 750iL Sdn	38855	45710

OPTIONS FOR 7-SERIES

Cold Weather Pkg +400
Comfort Seats +585
Elect. Damping Control Susp. +970
Navigation System +1360
Park Distance Control +435
Auto Load Leveling[Opt on 740iL] +555
Headlight Washers[Std on 750iL] +160
Heated Front Seats[Std on 750iL] +235

8-SERIES 1997

Engine displacement is bumped, making the 1997 840Ci and 850Ci a bit stronger than last year's models. BMW's five-speed Steptronic is now standard on both models.

Category L

2 Dr 840Ci Cpe	37775	44440

OPTIONS FOR 8-SERIES

Forged Alloy Wheels +605

Z3 1997

Hooray, the market for sports cars is alive and kicking. Despite the ever-increasing number of minivans and sport-utes on our clogged highways, there are still enough of us that like to drive to support this wonderful little car. As a reward for keeping the segment alive, BMW makes its 190-horsepower six-cylinder engine available in the Z3 2.8.

RATINGS (SCALE OF 1-10)

Overall	Safety	Reliability	Performance	Comfort	Value
N/A	N/A	8.3	9	7.5	N/A

Category F

2 Dr 1.9 Conv	18320	21810
2 Dr 2.8 Conv	21645	25770

OPTIONS FOR Z3

Auto 4-Speed Transmission +490
Extended Leather Trim +600
Compact Disc Changer +320
Heated Front Seats +190
Leather Seats[Opt on 1.9] +325
Onboard Computer +185
Traction Control System[Opt on 1.9] +215

1996 BMW

3-SERIES 1996

BMW's highly acclaimed 3-series receives new engines across the board. The 318 remains a 318 despite an increase in displacement to 1.9 liters. The six-cylinder model becomes the 328 with an improved engine that increases torque by a whopping 14 percent. Vented rear disc brakes aid the 328's stopping power by reducing brake fade. Automatic climate control is standard, except in the 318ti, and improved sound systems are optional on all models.

RATINGS (SCALE OF 1-10)

Overall	Safety	Reliability	Performance	Comfort	Value
7.4	7.4	8.7	9.4	8	3.3

Category D

2 Dr 318i Conv	16765	20955
4 Dr 318i Sdn	12315	15395
2 Dr 318ti Hbk	10085	12605
2 Dr 328i Conv	21255	26570
4 Dr 328i Sdn	16390	20490

Category F

2 Dr 318is Cpe	14230	16940
2 Dr 328is Cpe	18095	21540

Category J

2 Dr M3 Cpe	20990	24990

OPTIONS FOR 3-SERIES

Auto 4-Speed Transmission +395
Rollover Protection System(Opt on Conv) +585
Sports Pkg +380
AM/FM Compact Disc Player +210
Air Conditioning[Opt on 318ti] +345
Aluminum/Alloy Wheels[Opt on 318ti,318i Sdn] +190
Cruise Control[Opt on 318ti,M3] +100

Don't forget to refer to the Mileage Adjustment Table at the back of this book!

BMW 96-95

Model Description	Trade-in Value	Market Value	Model Description	Trade-in Value	Market Value

Heated Front Seats +155
Keyless Entry System +125
Leather Seats[Std on M3,328i Conv] +265
Onboard Computer +150
Power Sunroof[Opt on 318ti,M3] +300
Premium Sound System +150
Sport Seats +200
Traction Control System +175

7-SERIES   1996

BMW's flagship gets stretched; the only 7-Series models available for 1996 are long wheelbase models. The 740iL receives a larger V8 that substantially increases torque. BMW's killer 440-watt sound system is now standard on the 750iL and optional on the 740iL. A sophisticated interior-motion theft-deterrent system is now available.

Category L

	Trade-in	Market
4 Dr 740i Sdn	27785	33075
4 Dr 740iL Sdn	28775	34255
4 Dr 750iL Sdn	35025	41695

OPTIONS FOR 7-SERIES
Comfort Seats +445
Park Distance Control +365
Compact Disc Changer[Opt on 740i] +450
Headlight Washers[Std on 750iL] +130
Heated Front Seats[Opt on 740i] +195
Traction Control System[Opt on 740i] +575

8-SERIES   1996

Category L

	Trade-in	Market
2 Dr 840Ci Cpe	31515	37520

OPTIONS FOR 8-SERIES
Forged Alloy Wheels +505
Aluminum/Alloy Wheels[Std on 850Ci] +175

Z3   1996

BMW follows Mazda's lead and introduces a roadster. This dreamy two-seater made its debut in the James Bond movie, Golden Eye, and has had enthusiasts across the country drooling over its smart styling and impressive refinement. Featured as the perfect Christmas gift in the 1995 Neiman Marcus Christmas catalog, BMW sold out of Z3s before the first one was released to the public.

RATINGS (SCALE OF 1-10)

Overall	Safety	Reliability	Performance	Comfort	Value
N/A	N/A	8.3	8.6	7.5	N/A

Category F

	Trade-in	Market
2 Dr 007 Conv	17305	20600
2 Dr STD Conv	17020	20260

OPTIONS FOR Z3
Auto 4-Speed Transmission +395
Heated Front Seats +155
Leather Seats +265
Onboard Computer +150
Traction Control System +175

1995 BMW

3-SERIES   1995

A new M3 coupe debuts with blistering performance and exceptional grace. Available only as a five-speed manual, the M3 has Z-rated tires, a limited-slip differential and 17-inch wheels. The 318 series gains a convertible. Two new packages debut that allow a driver to choose between a sports or luxury orientation.

RATINGS (SCALE OF 1-10)

Overall	Safety	Reliability	Performance	Comfort	Value
7.1	7.9	7.4	9.2	8	3.1

Category D

	Trade-in	Market
2 Dr 318i Conv	13760	17420
4 Dr 318i Sdn	10655	13490
2 Dr 318ti Hbk	8305	10515
2 Dr 325i Conv	17905	22665
4 Dr 325i Sdn	13835	17510

Category F

	Trade-in	Market
2 Dr 318is Cpe	12100	14755
2 Dr 325is Cpe	14975	18260

Category J

	Trade-in	Market
2 Dr M3 Cpe	18665	22490

OPTIONS FOR 3-SERIES
Auto 4-Speed Transmission +300
Luxury Pkg +410
Rollover Protection Sys. +470
Sports Pkg +640
AM/FM Compact Disc Player +160
Heated Front Seats +130
Keyless Entry System +105
Leather Seats[Opt on 318i,318is,318ti] +215
Onboard Computer +125
Power Sunroof[Opt on 318ti,M3] +245
Sport Seats +155
Traction Control System +145

5-SERIES   1995

BMW sports up its 540i by making a six-speed manual transmission available. That option includes 12-way power sport seats, a sport suspension and beefy anti-roll bars. Unfortunately, all models lose their V-rated tires in favor of wimpy H-rated tires in an attempt to improve fuel economy.

Model Description	Trade-in Value	Market Value

Model Description	Trade-in Value	Market Value

RATINGS (SCALE OF 1-10)

Overall	Safety	Reliability	Performance	Comfort	Value
N/A	N/A	8.6	8.8	8	N/A

Category J

Model	Trade-in	Market
4 Dr 525i Sdn	15835	19080
4 Dr 525i Touring Wgn	16650	20060
4 Dr 530i Sdn	17725	21355
4 Dr 540i Sdn	19275	23225

OPTIONS FOR 5-SERIES

6-Speed Transmission[Opt on 540i] +295
Auto 4-Speed Transmission[Std on Touring] +345
Premium Pkg +725
AM/FM Compact Disc Player +145
Heated Front Seats +140
Leather Seats[Opt on 525i] +385
Onboard Computer[Opt on 525i] +145
Power Sunroof[Std on 530i,540i] +375
Traction Control System +390

7-SERIES   1995

The big Bimmer is totally redesigned for 1995. The flagship sedan now features sleek styling and a lengthened wheelbase. Three models are available for 1995, including a new 740i regular-wheelbase model. The V12 engine found in the 750iL gains 27 horsepower and 30 foot-pounds of torque. New interior refinements include a residual heat system which will continue to heat the car after the power has been turned off, and 14-way power seats.

Category L

Model	Trade-in	Market
4 Dr 740i Sdn	22465	27395
4 Dr 740iL Sdn	23655	28850
4 Dr 750iL Sdn	30745	37495

OPTIONS FOR 7-SERIES

Comfort Seats +330
Park Distance Control +270
Compact Disc Changer[Std on 750iL] +370
Heated Front Seats[Std on 750iL] +160
Traction Control System[Std on 750iL] +470

8-SERIES   1995

No changes for the 8-Series.
Category L

Model	Trade-in	Market
2 Dr 840Ci Cpe	26265	32030

OPTIONS FOR 8-SERIES

Electronic Damp Control +625
Forged Alloy Wheels +365

1994 BMW

3-SERIES   1994

Dual airbags appear on all 3-series models. A new six-cylinder convertible joins the stable and traction control becomes optional for all cars.

RATINGS (SCALE OF 1-10)

Overall	Safety	Reliability	Performance	Comfort	Value
7	7.9	7.5	9.2	8	2.6

Category D

Model	Trade-in	Market
4 Dr 318i Sdn	8665	11250
4 Dr 325i Sdn	11090	14405

Category F

Model	Trade-in	Market
2 Dr 318i Conv	12360	15450
2 Dr 318is Cpe	9950	12440
2 Dr 325i Conv	15460	19325
2 Dr 325is Cpe	12330	15415

OPTIONS FOR 3-SERIES

Auto 4-Speed Transmission +245
Rollover Protection System(Opt on Conv) +380
AM/FM Compact Disc Player +130
Heated Front Seats +105
Leather Seats[Opt on 318is,Sdn] +175
Onboard Computer +100
Sport Seats +130
Traction Control System +115

5-SERIES   1994

A passenger airbag debuts on all models and two new V8s join the lineup. The 535i and M5 are dropped. BMW's traction control system becomes standard on the 530i Touring and optional on other models. Both 525i models gain a premium sound system.

RATINGS (SCALE OF 1-10)

Overall	Safety	Reliability	Performance	Comfort	Value
N/A	N/A	8.7	8.8	8	N/A

Category J

Model	Trade-in	Market
4 Dr 525i Sdn	13765	16585
4 Dr 525i Touring Wgn	14690	17700
4 Dr 530i Sdn	15315	18450
4 Dr 540i Sdn	16990	20470

OPTIONS FOR 5-SERIES

Auto 4-Speed Transmission[Std on Touring] +245
AM/FM Compact Disc Player +120
Heated Front Seats +115
Onboard Computer[Std on 540i] +120
Traction Control System[Opt on 525i,540i] +320

Model Description	Trade-in Value	Market Value

7-SERIES 1994

No changes for the 7-Series.

Category L

4 Dr 740i Sdn	14990	18735
4 Dr 740iL Sdn	15935	19920

OPTIONS FOR 7-SERIES

Elec. Damping Cntrl. Susp +410
Heated Front Seats[Std on 750iL] +130
Traction Control System[Std on 750iL] +385

8-SERIES 1994

Two new models are introduced to the 8-Series: the 840Ci and the 850CSi. The 840Ci has the same V8 power found in the 740 and 540. The 850CSi gets an increased displacement V12 that offers a whopping 372-horsepower. The CSi comes standard with a sports suspension and a six-speed manual transmission. Unfortunately, the introduction of the CSi takes away from the sportiness of the 850Ci, which is now saddled with a four-speed automatic as the only transmission choice.

Category L

2 Dr 840Ci Cpe	23280	29100

OPTIONS FOR 8-SERIES

Elec. Damping Cntrl. Susp +410
Forged Alloy Wheels +300

1993 BMW

3-SERIES 1993

Four-bangers can now be equipped with an automatic transmission. Six-cylinder models get a variable valve timing system that improves low-end torque.

RATINGS (SCALE OF 1-10)

Overall	Safety	Reliability	Performance	Comfort	Value
6.7	6.5	7.4	9.2	8	2.4

Category D

4 Dr 318i Sdn	7440	9920
4 Dr 325i Sdn	9315	12420

Category F

2 Dr 318is Cpe	8305	10785
2 Dr 325i Conv	11425	14840
2 Dr 325is Cpe	10060	13065

OPTIONS FOR 3-SERIES

Auto 4-Speed Transmission +190
Sports Pkg +190
Heated Front Seats +85
Leather Seats[Opt on Sdn] +245
Onboard Computer[Std on Conv] +85
Sport Seats +105

5-SERIES 1993

Bad news for trees and cows: wood trim and leather upholstery are now standard on the 525i. The 525i gets a variable valve timing system that improves low-end torque. The M5 gets new wheels for 1993.

RATINGS (SCALE OF 1-10)

Overall	Safety	Reliability	Performance	Comfort	Value
N/A	N/A	8.5	8.6	8	N/A

Category J

4 Dr 525i Sdn	11680	14420
4 Dr 525i Touring Wgn	12565	15510
4 Dr 535i Sdn	12920	15950

OPTIONS FOR 5-SERIES

Auto 4-Speed Transmission[Std on Touring] +190
Auto Stab Cntrl Susp. +290
Heated Front Seats[Opt on 525i] +95
Leather Seats[Opt on Touring] +260
Onboard Computer[Opt on 525i] +95

7-SERIES 1993

The 7-Series' cheapest model swaps I-6 for V8 power. The entry-level 7-Series is now called the 740 to denote this change. The new engine has 282-horsepower that is mated to a five-speed automatic transmission. More wood for the interior, Z-rated tires, and an upgraded stereo round out the changes for the 1993 7-Series.

Category L

4 Dr 740i Sdn	13070	16545
4 Dr 740iL Sdn	13880	17570
4 Dr 750iL Sdn	17425	22060

OPTIONS FOR 7-SERIES

Elect Damp Cntrl Susp. +330
Heated Seats[Opt on 740i] +85
Traction Control System[Std on 750iL] +315

8-SERIES 1993

The 850i is now called the 850Ci. A passenger airbag is added to the standard equipment list, as is a split-fold rear seat. All interior materials have been upgraded over previous models.

Category J

2 Dr 850Ci Cpe	21655	26735

OPTIONS FOR 8-SERIES

Forged Alloy Wheels +225

1992 BMW

3-SERIES 1992

New sheetmetal for the 3-series; all the corners are rounded and the wheelbase is stretched. Interior space is marginally greater than previous models. A driver airbag is added to the equipment list. Buyers can choose between a-sports or luxury package, depending on their predilections.

RATINGS (SCALE OF 1-10)

Overall	Safety	Reliability	Performance	Comfort	Value
6.7	6.4	6.7	9.2	8	3.3

Category D

2 Dr 318i Conv	7525	10170
4 Dr 318i Sdn	6175	8345
2 Dr 325i Conv	9160	12380
4 Dr 325i Sdn	7720	10430

Category F

2 Dr 318is Cpe	6895	9190
2 Dr 325is Cpe	8280	11040

OPTIONS FOR 3-SERIES

Auto 4-Speed Transmission +145
Appearance Pkg +335
Compact Disc W/fm/tape +145
Heated Front Seats[Std on 318i STD Conv] +70
Leather Seats[Opt on Sdn] +120
Onboard Computer[Std on Conv] +70

5-SERIES   1992

The 525 loses some luxury items from its standard equipment list; the steering wheel is now wrapped in leatherette instead of leather and the spare tire is shod with a steel wheel instead of an alloy. The 535 gains options like a nifty on-board computer and a power-adjustable steering wheel with a position memory. A security system is now standard. The M5 gets better power steering and a higher final-drive ratio. A Touring model is introduced as a wagon body style.

RATINGS (SCALE OF 1-10)

Overall	Safety	Reliability	Performance	Comfort	Value
N/A	N/A	8.1	8.6	8	N/A

Category J

4 Dr 525i Sdn	9380	12025
4 Dr 525i Touring Wgn	10190	13065
4 Dr 535i Sdn	10555	13535

OPTIONS FOR 5-SERIES

Auto 4-Speed Transmission[Std on 535i,Touring] +145
Auto Stability Control +230
Wood & Leather Pkg +205
Heated Front Seats +75
Leather Seats[Opt on 525i] +210
Onboard Computer[Opt on Touring] +80

7-SERIES   1992

7-Series cars equipped with an automatic transmission now have a shift interlock that prevents the car from being shifted out of park without simultaneously

applying the brake. The one-touch-down power window feature now applies to all windows, not just the driver's. The 750iL model receives double-paned windows to improve noise reduction. All 1992 7-Series cars get a new Infinity stereo.

Category L

4 Dr 735i Sdn	9835	12775
4 Dr 735iL Sdn	10355	13450
4 Dr 750iL Sdn	12370	16065

OPTIONS FOR 7-SERIES

Auto Stability Control +230
Elect Damping Control +265
Elect. Damping Control Susp. +265
Heated Front Seats[Std on 750iL] +85

8-SERIES   1992

BMW's most expensive coupe gets a few tweaks for 1992. Models equipped with an automatic transmission now have a shift interlock to prevent the car from unintentionally being shifted out of "park". BMW's Electronic Damping System is improved for 1992 as well, offering greater diversity between the sports and comfort settings.

Category J

2 Dr 850i Cpe	19420	24895

OPTIONS FOR 8-SERIES

Auto Stability Control +270
Elect Damping Control +265
Forged Alloy Wheels +180

1991 BMW

3-SERIES   1991

No changes for the 3-Series.

Category D

2 Dr 318i Conv	5775	7910
4 Dr 318i Sdn	4315	5910
2 Dr 325i Conv	7525	10310
2 Dr 325i Sdn	5365	7350
4 Dr 325i Sdn	5480	7505

Category F

2 Dr 318is Sdn	4745	6325
2 Dr 325iX 4WD Sdn	6520	8695
4 Dr 325iX 4WD Sdn	6565	8755

OPTIONS FOR 3-SERIES

Auto 3-Speed Transmission +95
Sport Handling Pkg +285
Leather Seats[Std on M3,Conv] +95
Power Sunroof[Std on M3] +100

Don't forget to refer to the Mileage Adjustment Table at the back of this book!

Model Description	Trade-in Value	Market Value

5-SERIES 1991

No changes for the 1991 5-Series.

RATINGS (SCALE OF 1-10)

Overall	Safety	Reliability	Performance	Comfort	Value
N/A	N/A	7.8	8.6	8	N/A

Category J

4 Dr 525i Sdn	7725	10030
4 Dr 535i Sdn	8800	11430
4 Dr M5 Sdn	14750	19155

OPTIONS FOR 5-SERIES

Auto 4-Speed Transmission +105
Stability Control +190
Heated Front Seats +60
Leather Seats[Opt on 525i] +170

7-SERIES 1991

No changes for the 7-Series.
Category L

4 Dr 735i Sdn	8390	11040
4 Dr 735iL Sdn	8810	11590
4 Dr 750iL Sdn	10065	13245

OPTIONS FOR 7-SERIES

Electronic Susp. +215
Stability Control +190
Heated Front Seats[Std on 750iL] +70

8-SERIES 1991

BMW's replacement for the 635CSi, the 850i offers V12 power, a six-speed manual transmission and rear-wheel drive. Standard traction control, a driver airbag, antilock brakes and power head restraints are a few of the safety features found on this expensive BMW coupe. A four-speed automatic transmission is optional.
Category J

2 Dr 850i Cpe	17685	22970

OPTIONS FOR 8-SERIES

Electronic Susp. +215
Forged Alloy Wheels +145
Stability Control +220

1990 BMW

3-SERIES 1990

No changes for the 1990 3-Series.
Category D

2 Dr 325i Conv	6275	8715
2 Dr 325i Sdn	4740	6585
4 Dr 325i Sdn	4830	6705

Category F

2 Dr 325iX 4WD Sdn	6055	8295
4 Dr 325iX 4WD Sdn	6155	8430
2 Dr 325is Sdn	4995	6840

Category J

2 Dr M3 Sdn	7335	9780

OPTIONS FOR 3-SERIES

Auto 4-Speed Transmission +85
Leather Seats[Opt on 325i STD Sdn] +135
Power Sunroof[Std on 325is,M3] +80

5-SERIES 1990

BMW Motorsports unleashes 5-Series M-car. Serious inquiries only; this car has a bone-jarring suspension and more performance than most drivers can handle.

RATINGS (SCALE OF 1-10)

Overall	Safety	Reliability	Performance	Comfort	Value
N/A	N/A	7.4	8.4	8	N/A

Category J

4 Dr 525i Sdn	6205	8270
4 Dr 535i Sdn	7200	9600

OPTIONS FOR 5-SERIES

Auto 4-Speed Transmission[Opt on 525i] +85
Leather Seats[Opt on 525i] +140

7-SERIES 1990

No changes for the 7-Series.
Category L

4 Dr 735i Sdn	7600	10135
4 Dr 735iL Sdn	7785	10380
4 Dr 750iL Sdn	8995	11995

Don't forget to refer to the Mileage Adjustment Table at the back of this book!

BUICK 99

Model Description	Trade-in Value	Market Value	Model Description	Trade-in Value	Market Value

BUICK   USA

1995 Buick Riviera

1999 BUICK

CENTURY   1999

After a complete redesign in 1997 put the Century into carryover status last year, 1999 brings a host of safety feature improvements, many of them standard. Additionally, the suspension has been retuned for less body roll, the sound systems have been upgraded and one new paint color, called Auburn Nightmist, has been added.

RATINGS (SCALE OF 1-10)

Overall	Safety	Reliability	Performance	Comfort	Value
N/A	7.3	8.7	8	7.9	N/A

Category C

4 Dr Custom Sdn	11295	13610
4 Dr Limited Sdn	12000	14460

OPTIONS FOR CENTURY

AM/FM Stereo Tape +120
Aluminum/Alloy Wheels +225
Automatic Dimming Mirror +90
Climate Control for AC +125
Cruise Control +155
Dual Power Seats +440
Leather Seats +450

LESABRE   1999

Buick's LeSabre celebrates its 40th year in the marketplace as a carryover model for 1999. Perhaps deciding there's no need to mess with success (more than 6 million LeSabres have been sold since the nameplate's 1959 introduction), Buick has merely made some emissions system improvements for '99, and added two exterior metallic paint choices, Sterling Silver and Dark Bronzemist.

RATINGS (SCALE OF 1-10)

Overall	Safety	Reliability	Performance	Comfort	Value
N/A	7.6	8.9	8.6	8.1	N/A

Category B

4 Dr Custom Sdn	13330	16060
4 Dr Limited Sdn	15320	18455

OPTIONS FOR LESABRE

AM/FM Stereo Tape[Opt on Custom] +130
Aluminum/Alloy Wheels[Opt on Custom] +245
Compact Disc W/fm/tape +285
Leather Seats +505
Power Drivers Seat +230
Power Mirrors +75

PARK AVENUE   1999

Riding a wave of sales success since its 1997 redesign, Buick didn't feel like fiddling much with its Park Avenue recipe for 1999. One noticeable change is a revision of the Park Avenue's taillamps, which are now similar to those found on the upscale Ultra model. Also new this year is an enhanced eight-speaker audio system dubbed Concert Sound III, a new hood-to-fender seal for improved appearance, an adjustable rubber bumper for the decklid, and four new exterior colors.

RATINGS (SCALE OF 1-10)

Overall	Safety	Reliability	Performance	Comfort	Value
N/A	N/A	9	8.4	8.4	N/A

Category A

4 Dr STD Sdn	18735	22040
4 Dr Ultra Sprchgd Sdn	21040	24750

OPTIONS FOR PARK AVENUE

Compact Disc W/fm/tape +480
Leather Seats[Opt on STD] +495

REGAL   1999

Performance-oriented changes, such as more power, sporty tweaks to the steering and suspension, firmer motor mounts and the addition of a strut tower brace underhood, lead the news for the '99 Regal. Other changes include enhancements to the ABS and traction control systems, as well as the addition of a tire inflation monitor, perimeter lighting and the Concert Sound II audio system to Regal's already long list of standard equipment. New options include a self-dimming electrochromic outside rearview mirror, redesigned 15-inch alloy wheels and the eight-speaker, 220-watt Monsoon audio system. And that's all in addition to a new exterior paint color, Auburn Nightmist.

Model Description	Trade-in Value	Market Value

RATINGS (SCALE OF 1-10)

Overall	Safety	Reliability	Performance	Comfort	Value
N/A	N/A	8.8	8.4	7.8	N/A

Category C

	Trade-in	Market
4 Dr GS Sprchgd Sdn	15980	19250
4 Dr LS Sdn	13880	16720

OPTIONS FOR REGAL

LSE Pkg +955
Aluminum/Alloy Wheels[Std on GS] +225
Bucket Seats +140
Compact Disc W/fm/tape +250
Leather Seats[Std on GS] +450
Power Drivers Seat[Std on GS] +220

RIVIERA   1999

We were going to mention that traction control is now standard on the Riviera and that this year brings the choice of four new paint colors (Sterling Silver, Titanium Blue, Gold Firemist and Dark Bronzemist), but that was before Buick decided to pull the plug on the big coupe soon after production began. Now you also need to know that only approximately 2,000 Riveras will be built for the 1999 model year, along with a special run of 200 special edition models dubbed "Silver Arrow."

RATINGS (SCALE OF 1-10)

Overall	Safety	Reliability	Performance	Comfort	Value
N/A	N/A	N/A	8.6	8	N/A

Category B

	Trade-in	Market
2 Dr STD Sprchgd Cpe	18940	22820

1998 BUICK

CENTURY   1998

The addition of second-generation airbags, three new exterior colors, one new interior color and the availability of OnStar mobile communications are this year's changes.

RATINGS (SCALE OF 1-10)

Overall	Safety	Reliability	Performance	Comfort	Value
8.1	7.2	8.4	8	7.9	8.8

Category C

	Trade-in	Market
4 Dr Custom Sdn	10420	12705
4 Dr Limited Sdn	11080	13510

OPTIONS FOR CENTURY

AM/FM Compact Disc Player +220
Aluminum/Alloy Wheels +180
Climate Control for AC +100
Cruise Control +130
Heated Power Mirrors[Opt on Custom] +65
Leather Seats +365
Power Drivers Seat +180
Power Moonroof +415

LESABRE   1998

Cruise control is standard on base models, OnStar Mobile Communications is a dealer-installed option, Limited models get a couple of electrochromic mirrors, and new colors are on tap inside and out. Second-generation airbags are made standard.

RATINGS (SCALE OF 1-10)

Overall	Safety	Reliability	Performance	Comfort	Value
8.5	7.6	9.1	8.6	8.1	8.9

Category B

	Trade-in	Market
4 Dr Custom Sdn	11790	14205
4 Dr Limited Sdn	13505	16270

OPTIONS FOR LESABRE

AM/FM Compact Disc Player +200
Aluminum/Alloy Wheels[Opt on Custom] +200
Auto Load Leveling +110
Dual Power Seats[Opt on Custom] +230
Keyless Entry System[Opt on Custom] +105
Leather Seats +410
Power Mirrors +60
Traction Control System +105

PARK AVENUE   1998

Exterior mirrors can be folded away, a new optional feature tilts the exterior mirrors down for curb viewing during reversing, dealers can install an OnStar Communications system and new colors are available inside and out. Second-generation airbags are made standard.

RATINGS (SCALE OF 1-10)

Overall	Safety	Reliability	Performance	Comfort	Value
N/A	N/A	9	8.4	8.4	8.9

Category A

	Trade-in	Market
4 Dr STD Sdn	15560	18525
4 Dr Ultra Sprchgd Sdn	17600	20950

OPTIONS FOR PARK AVENUE

AM/FM Compact Disc Player[Opt on STD] +300
Heads-up Display +165
Heated Front Seats[Opt on STD] +120
Heated Power Mirrors[Opt on STD] +60
Leather Seats[Opt on STD] +405
Power Moonroof +825
Traction Control System[Opt on STD] +130

REGAL   1998

Regal LS gets a new standard four-speed automatic transmission, and three new exterior colors are available. Dealers will install an OnStar Mobile Communications system if the buyer desires, and second-generation airbags are added.

Don't forget to refer to the Mileage Adjustment Table at the back of this book!

Model Description	Trade-in Value	Market Value

RATINGS (SCALE OF 1-10)

Overall	Safety	Reliability	Performance	Comfort	Value
N/A	N/A	8.2	8.4	7.8	8.2

Category C

	Trade-in	Market
4 Dr 25TH Anniversary Sdn	12010	14645
4 Dr GS Sprchgd Sdn	13490	16450
4 Dr LS Sdn	11695	14260

OPTIONS FOR REGAL

Aluminum/Alloy Wheels[Opt on LS] +180
Chrome Wheels[Opt on GS,LS] +370
Climate Control for AC +100
Compact Disc W/fm/tape[Opt on GS,LS] +200
Dual Power Seats +360
Heated Front Seats +135
Leather Seats[Opt on LS] +365
Power Drivers Seat[Opt on LS] +180
Power Moonroof +415

RIVIERA   1998

Supercharged power is standard, OnStar satellite communications system is a new option and de-powered airbags debut. Four exterior colors are new, suspension and steering have been massaged and a heated passenger seat with lumbar support has been added to the options list.

RATINGS (SCALE OF 1-10)

Overall	Safety	Reliability	Performance	Comfort	Value
N/A	N/A	8.4	8.6	8	8.1

Category B

	Trade-in	Market
2 Dr STD Sprchgd Cpe	16310	19650

OPTIONS FOR RIVIERA

Chrome Wheels +415
Heated Front Seats +185
Power Moonroof +590
Special Factory Paint +120
Traction Control System +105

SKYLARK   1998

Skylark was sold strictly to fleets for 1998. If you're buying one used, chances are good that it was once a rental car.

Category C

	Trade-in	Market
4 Dr Custom Sdn	7780	9490

OPTIONS FOR SKYLARK

6 cyl 3.1 L Engine +275
Cruise Control +130
Power Windows +190

CENTURY   1997

After a decade and a half, Buick finally redesigns its bread-and-butter mid-size sedan, dropping the wagon variant in the process. A spunky 3.1-liter V6 engine, roomier interior, larger trunk and traditional Buick styling cues should convince Grandpa to trade the old warhorse in on a new one.

RATINGS (SCALE OF 1-10)

Overall	Safety	Reliability	Performance	Comfort	Value
7.4	7.2	8	8	7.9	5.9

Category C

	Trade-in	Market
4 Dr Custom Sdn	9410	11620
4 Dr Limited Sdn	10050	12410

OPTIONS FOR CENTURY

Prestige Pkg +430
AM/FM Compact Disc Player +180
Aluminum/Alloy Wheels +150
Automatic Dimming Mirror +60
Climate Control for AC +85
Compact Disc W/fm/tape +165
Cruise Control +105
Dual Power Seats +295
Leather Seats +300
Power Drivers Seat +145
Power Moonroof +340

LESABRE   1997

Buick freshens the somewhat stale LeSabre with new front and rear styling. Redesigned wheel selections, new seats on Custom models, and walnut instrument panel appliques round out the visual changes. Structurally, the LeSabre now meets side-impact standards.

RATINGS (SCALE OF 1-10)

Overall	Safety	Reliability	Performance	Comfort	Value
8.2	7.5	8.3	8.6	8.1	8.3

Category B

	Trade-in	Market
4 Dr Custom Sdn	9860	12025
4 Dr Limited Sdn	11160	13610

OPTIONS FOR LESABRE

Prestige Pkg +370
AM/FM Compact Disc Player +160
Aluminum/Alloy Wheels[Opt on Custom] +165
Automatic Dimming Mirror +40
Cruise Control[Opt on Custom] +110
Dual Power Seats[Opt on Custom] +190
Keyless Entry System[Opt on Custom] +85
Leather Seats +335
Power Drivers Seat +155

Don't forget to refer to the Mileage Adjustment Table at the back of this book!

Model Description	Trade-in Value	Market Value

Power Mirrors[Opt on Custom] +50
Traction Control System +85

PARK AVENUE 1997

Buick engineers substantially improve the Park Avenue for 1997 by strengthening the body structure, improving interior ergonomics, and introducing a sleek new look. Powertrains are carried over, and two models are available: base and Ultra. Prices have risen, but the Park Avenue represents real value in comparison to other traditional luxury sedans.

RATINGS (SCALE OF 1-10)

Overall	Safety	Reliability	Performance	Comfort	Value
N/A	N/A	8.2	8.4	8.4	8.3

Category A
4 Dr STD Sdn	13340	16075
4 Dr Ultra Sprchgd Sdn	15100	18195

OPTIONS FOR PARK AVENUE
AM/FM Compact Disc Player[Opt on STD] +245
Automatic Dimming Mirror +80
Chrome Wheels +500
Compact Disc Changer +395
Heated Front Seats[Opt on STD] +100
Heated Power Mirrors[Opt on STD] +50
Leather Seats[Opt on STD] +330
Power Moonroof +675
Traction Control System[Opt on STD] +105

REGAL 1997

Long overdue, the complete redesign of the Regal means Buick finally has a viable entry in the midsized sedan marketplace. The standard equipment list is a mile long, including ABS, traction control, dual-zone climate controls, heated exterior mirrors, retained accessory power and battery rundown protection.

RATINGS (SCALE OF 1-10)

Overall	Safety	Reliability	Performance	Comfort	Value
N/A	N/A	7.7	8.4	7.8	8.1

Category C
4 Dr GS Sprchgd Sdn	12035	14855
4 Dr LS Sdn	10855	13400

OPTIONS FOR REGAL
Aluminum/Alloy Wheels[Opt on LS] +150
Automatic Dimming Mirror +60
Chrome Wheels +300
Climate Control for AC +85
Compact Disc W/fm/tape +165
Heated Front Seats +110
Leather Seats[Opt on LS] +300
Power Drivers Seat +145
Power Moonroof +340

RIVIERA 1997

Upgraded transmissions, several new colors inside and out, additional standard equipment and new options summarize minimal changes to the Riviera.

RATINGS (SCALE OF 1-10)

Overall	Safety	Reliability	Performance	Comfort	Value
N/A	N/A	8.1	8.6	8	7.5

Category B
2 Dr STD Cpe	12995	15850
2 Dr STD Sprchgd Cpe	13610	16600

OPTIONS FOR RIVIERA
Automatic Dimming Mirror +40
Chrome Wheels +340
Heated Front Seats +155
Leather Seats +335
Power Moonroof +485
Traction Control System +85

SKYLARK 1997

Skylark gets minimal revisions this year. The standard equipment list is expanded.

RATINGS (SCALE OF 1-10)

Overall	Safety	Reliability	Performance	Comfort	Value
7.8	7.7	8.5	7.2	7.3	8.2

Category C
2 Dr Custom Cpe	6455	7970
4 Dr Custom Sdn	6845	8450
2 Dr Gran Sport Cpe	7500	9260
4 Dr Gran Sport Sdn	7695	9500

OPTIONS FOR SKYLARK
6 cyl 3.1 L Engine[Opt on Custom] +215
AM/FM Stereo Tape[Opt on Custom] +80
Aluminum/Alloy Wheels[Opt on Custom] +150
Cruise Control[Opt on Custom] +105
Keyless Entry System +95
Leather Seats +300
Power Drivers Seat +145
Power Mirrors[Opt on Custom] +55
Power Moonroof +340
Power Windows[Opt on Custom] +155

1996 BUICK

CENTURY 1996

In many states, this design is just a decade away from antique car status. Wagons get the V6 as standard equipment. Power windows, cassette player, rear window defogger and a remote trunk release make the standard equipment list as this ancient A-body rolls into its final year of production.

Model Description	Trade-in Value	Market Value
RATINGS (SCALE OF 1-10)		

Overall	Safety	Reliability	Performance	Comfort	Value
7.5	6.5	7.7	7.4	7.3	8.4

Category C

Model Description	Trade-in Value	Market Value
4 Dr STD Sdn	6180	7925
4 Dr STD Wgn	6375	8170

OPTIONS FOR CENTURY
6 cyl 3.1 L Engine[Opt on Sdn] +185
Auto 4-Speed Transmission[Opt on Sdn] +75
AM/FM Stereo Tape +65
Cruise Control +85
Keyless Entry System +75
Leather Seats +245
Luggage Rack +45
Power Drivers Seat +120
Wire Wheel Covers +90

LESABRE 1996

Finally, the Series II engine is standard on LeSabre. Order the Gran Touring suspension, and get the same magnetic variable effort steering found on the Park Avenue Ultra. Now standard on the Custom is an electric rear window defogger and storage armrest. Limited trim levels get Twilight Sentinel, dual automatic ComforTemp climate controls, and a rear seat center armrest.

RATINGS (SCALE OF 1-10)

Overall	Safety	Reliability	Performance	Comfort	Value
8.1	7.5	8.1	8.6	8.1	8.3

Category B

	Trade-in	Market
4 Dr Custom Sdn	7960	9950
4 Dr Limited Sdn	9085	11355

OPTIONS FOR LESABRE
Prestige Pkg +460
AM/FM Compact Disc Player +135
Cruise Control[Opt on Custom] +90
Keyless Entry System[Opt on Custom] +70
Leather Seats +275
Power Drivers Seat +125
Power Passenger Seat +135

PARK AVENUE 1996

Ultra gets new Series II supercharged engine as standard equipment, as well as magnetic variable effort steering gear. Colors and trim are revised, battery rundown protection is added, and long-life engine components keep the Park going longer between maintenance stops.

RATINGS (SCALE OF 1-10)

Overall	Safety	Reliability	Performance	Comfort	Value
8.1	7.4	7.9	8.6	8.1	8.3

Category A

	Trade-in	Market
4 Dr STD Sdn	10650	12985
4 Dr Ultra Sprchgd Sdn	11940	14560

OPTIONS FOR PARK AVENUE
Luxury Pkg +645
Prestige Pkg +760
AM/FM Compact Disc Player +200
Automatic Dimming Mirror +65
Heated Front Seats +80
Keyless Entry System[Opt on STD] +100
Leather Seats[Opt on STD] +270
Power Moonroof +550
Traction Control System +85

REGAL 1996

The Series II 3.8-liter V6 is standard on Limited and Gran Sport, optional on base Custom models. Standard equipment now includes dual ComforTemp climate controls and a cassette player. Revised wheels, available in chrome, are standard on the Gran Sport. Base V6 is upgraded, and both engines feature long-life engine components.

RATINGS (SCALE OF 1-10)

Overall	Safety	Reliability	Performance	Comfort	Value
N/A	N/A	8	7.4	7.6	8.1

Category C

	Trade-in	Market
2 Dr Custom Cpe	7290	9345
4 Dr Custom Sdn	7420	9510
2 Dr Gran Sport Cpe	8185	10495
4 Dr Gran Sport Sdn	8380	10745
4 Dr Limited Sdn	8145	10445
4 Dr Olympic Gold Sdn	7675	9840

OPTIONS FOR REGAL
6 cyl 3.8 L Engine[Opt on Custom] +150
AM/FM Compact Disc Player +145
Keyless Entry System +75
Leather Seats +245
Power Drivers Seat[Std on Gran Sport] +120
Power Moonroof +280
Premium Sound System +160

RIVIERA 1996

Series II supercharged engine gives top-of-the-line Riv 240 horsepower. There are new colors inside and out, real wood on the dash, and revised climate and radio controls. Chrome wheels are optional.

RATINGS (SCALE OF 1-10)

Overall	Safety	Reliability	Performance	Comfort	Value
N/A	N/A	7.5	8.6	8	8

Category B

	Trade-in	Market
2 Dr STD Cpe	10710	13385
2 Dr STD Sprchgd Cpe	11105	13880

Don't forget to refer to the Mileage Adjustment Table at the back of this book!

OPTIONS FOR RIVIERA
Prestige Pkg +295
Chrome Wheels +280
Heated Front Seats +125
Leather Seats +275
Power Moonroof +395
Traction Control System +70

ROADMASTER 1996
Last year for 260 hp land yacht. All models are designated Collector's Editions.

RATINGS (SCALE OF 1-10)
Overall	Safety	Reliability	Performance	Comfort	Value
7.6	7.2	6.5	7.8	8.4	8.3

Category B
4 Dr Estate Wgn	12340	15425
4 Dr Limited Sdn	11240	14050
4 Dr STD Sdn	10095	12620

OPTIONS FOR ROADMASTER
Limited Pkg +450
Prestige Pkg +310
Auto Load Leveling +75
Camper/Towing Package +150
Compact Disc W/fm/tape +155
Heated Front Seats +125
Keyless Entry System[Std on Limited] +70
Leather Seats +275
Power Drivers Seat +125
Power Passenger Seat +135

SKYLARK 1996
Styling changes inside and out make the Skylark far more marketable, and credible. Dual airbags are new, as are three-point seatbelts mounted to the B-pillar where they should be. A new twin-cam engine replaces the 2.3-liter Quad 4, and automatic transmissions include traction control. Air conditioning, a rear window defroster, and a tilt wheel are now standard. Long-life engine components round out the long list of improvements to Buick's lame duck.

RATINGS (SCALE OF 1-10)
Overall	Safety	Reliability	Performance	Comfort	Value
7.8	7.8	8.2	7.2	7.3	8.5

Category C
2 Dr Custom Cpe	5645	7240
4 Dr Custom Sdn	5830	7475
4 Dr Olympic Gold Sdn	5975	7660

OPTIONS FOR SKYLARK
6 cyl 3.1 L Engine +185
Gran Sport Pkg +540
AM/FM Stereo Tape +65
Cruise Control[Opt on Custom] +85
Keyless Entry System +75

Leather Seats +245
Power Drivers Seat +120
Power Moonroof +280
Power Windows +125 .

1995 BUICK

CENTURY 1995
Instruments newly backlit, and seats are revised.

RATINGS (SCALE OF 1-10)
Overall	Safety	Reliability	Performance	Comfort	Value
7.3	7	7.3	7.4	7.3	7.4

Category C
4 Dr Custom Sdn	5225	6965
4 Dr Limited Sdn	5470	7295
4 Dr Special Sdn	4930	6570
4 Dr Special Wgn	5105	6805

OPTIONS FOR CENTURY
6 cyl 3.1 L Engine[Opt on Special] +160
Auto 4-Speed Transmission[Opt on Special] +65
AM/FM Stereo Tape[Std on Limited] +55
Cruise Control[Std on Limited] +70
Keyless Entry System[Std on Limited] +60
Power Drivers Seat[Std on Limited] +100
Power Windows[Opt on Special] +105

LESABRE 1995
New climate controls and radios are major changes.

RATINGS (SCALE OF 1-10)
Overall	Safety	Reliability	Performance	Comfort	Value
8.2	8.3	7.9	8.6	8.1	8.2

Category B
4 Dr Custom Sdn	6930	8885
4 Dr Limited Sdn	7810	10010

OPTIONS FOR LESABRE
AM/FM Compact Disc Player +110
Cruise Control[Opt on Custom] +75
Keyless Entry System[Opt on Custom] +55
Leather Seats +225
Power Drivers Seat[Opt on Custom] +105

PARK AVENUE 1995
Base engine upgraded to 3800 Series II status; makes 35 more horsepower than previous year. Base models get styling tweaks front and rear. New climate controls and radios are added.

RATINGS (SCALE OF 1-10)
Overall	Safety	Reliability	Performance	Comfort	Value
8.2	8.3	7.9	8.6	8.1	8.2

Model Description	Trade-in Value	Market Value

Category A

Model Description	Trade-in Value	Market Value
4 Dr STD Sdn	8680	10850
4 Dr Ultra Sprchgd Sdn	9630	12040

OPTIONS FOR PARK AVENUE
Luxury Pkg +410
Prestige Pkg +735
AM/FM Compact Disc Player +165
Heated Front Seats +65
Keyless Entry System[Opt on STD] +80
Leather Seats[Opt on STD] +220
Power Moonroof +450

REGAL   1995

New interior has dual airbags housed in revised instrument panel. Gauges are actually legible. Seats are new, too. Fake wood has been chopped from door panels. Exterior styling is updated.

RATINGS (SCALE OF 1-10)

Overall	Safety	Reliability	Performance	Comfort	Value
N/A	N/A	5.6	7.4	7.6	8.1

Category C

Model	Trade-in	Market
2 Dr Custom Cpe	5680	7575
4 Dr Custom Sdn	5820	7760
4 Dr Custom Select Sdn	5925	7900
2 Dr Gran Sport Cpe	6540	8720
4 Dr Gran Sport Sdn	6645	8860
4 Dr Limited Sdn	6475	8635

OPTIONS FOR REGAL
6 cyl 3.8 L Engine[Opt on Custom] +120
AM/FM Compact Disc Player +120
Keyless Entry System[Std on Custom Select] +60
Leather Seats +200
Power Drivers Seat[Std on Custom Select] +100
Power Moonroof +225

RIVIERA   1995

All-new Riv debuts with controversial styling. Dual airbags and ABS are standard. Base engine is 3800 Series II V6; optional is a supercharged 3.8-liter. Traction control is optional.

RATINGS (SCALE OF 1-10)

Overall	Safety	Reliability	Performance	Comfort	Value
N/A	N/A	7.3	8.6	8	7

Category B

Model	Trade-in	Market
2 Dr STD Cpe	8765	11240
2 Dr STD Sprchgd Cpe	9095	11660

OPTIONS FOR RIVIERA
AM/FM Compact Disc Player +110
Heated Front Seats +100
Leather Seats +225
Power Moonroof +325

ROADMASTER   1995

New radios and larger rearview mirrors are added. Cassette player is made standard. Wagon gets standard alloy wheels. New options are heated front seats and memory feature for power driver's seat.

RATINGS (SCALE OF 1-10)

Overall	Safety	Reliability	Performance	Comfort	Value
7.5	7.9	5.2	7.8	8.4	8.3

Category B

Model	Trade-in	Market
4 Dr Estate Wgn	10500	13460
4 Dr Limited Sdn	9505	12185
4 Dr STD Sdn	8445	10825

OPTIONS FOR ROADMASTER
Limited Wagon Pkg +290
Camper/Towing Package +125
Compact Disc W/fm/tape +125
Keyless Entry System[Std on Limited] +55
Leather Seats +225
Power Drivers Seat[Std on Limited] +105

SKYLARK   1995

Rear suspension is revised. New base engine is 150-horsepower Quad 4, packing 35 more ponies than previous base engine. GS gets 3.1-liter V6 standard. Power sunroof is a new option.

RATINGS (SCALE OF 1-10)

Overall	Safety	Reliability	Performance	Comfort	Value
7.3	7.2	7.7	7.2	7	7.2

Category C

Model	Trade-in	Market
2 Dr Custom Cpe	4160	5545
4 Dr Custom Sdn	4320	5760
2 Dr Gran Sport Cpe	5495	7325
4 Dr Gran Sport Sdn	5605	7475

OPTIONS FOR SKYLARK
6 cyl 3.1 L Engine[Opt on Custom] +160
Auto 4-Speed Transmission[Opt on Custom] +65
AM/FM Stereo Tape[Opt on Custom] +55
Air Conditioning[Opt on Custom] +265
Cruise Control[Opt on Custom] +70
Keyless Entry System +60
Power Drivers Seat +100
Power Moonroof +225
Power Windows[Opt on Custom] +105

1994 BUICK

CENTURY   1994

A driver airbag and ABS are standard on all models. This marks the first time ABS is offered on the Century. Coupe trimmed from lineup. The 2.2-liter engine gains 10 horsepower, and the optional 3.3-liter V6 is replaced by a 3.1-liter unit. When transmission is shifted into "Park," automatic door locks unlock themselves. Defeat this feature by removing a fuse. Tilt steering is standard on Special. New gauges debut.

RATINGS (SCALE OF 1-10)

Overall	Safety	Reliability	Performance	Comfort	Value
7	6.5	5.8	7.4	7.3	7.8

Category C

4 Dr Custom Sdn	4235	5720
4 Dr Special Sdn	4095	5535
4 Dr Special Wgn	4230	5715

OPTIONS FOR CENTURY

6 cyl 3.1 L Engine +140
Auto 4-Speed Transmission +55
AM/FM Stereo Tape +45
Cruise Control +55
Keyless Entry System +50
Power Drivers Seat +80
Power Windows +85

LESABRE   1994

Passenger airbag installed. Traction control system now cuts engine power to slipping wheels in addition to applying brake. Front seat travel increased one inch.

RATINGS (SCALE OF 1-10)

Overall	Safety	Reliability	Performance	Comfort	Value
8.3	8.4	7.9	8.6	8.1	8.5

Category B

4 Dr Custom Sdn	5740	7550
4 Dr Limited Sdn	6395	8415

OPTIONS FOR LESABRE

AM/FM Stereo Tape[Opt on Custom] +50
Keyless Entry System[Opt on Custom] +45
Leather Seats +185
Power Drivers Seat[Opt on Custom] +85

PARK AVENUE   1994

Passenger airbag debuts, and Ultra model gets 20 more horsepower. Traction control system now cuts engine power to slipping wheels in addition to applying brake, and can be turned off if desired. Remote keyless entry, power trunk pull-down and auto dimming rearview mirror added to Ultra standard equipment list. Front seat travel increased one inch. Heated front seats are newly optional.

RATINGS (SCALE OF 1-10)

Overall	Safety	Reliability	Performance	Comfort	Value
8.4	8.4	8.4	8.6	8.1	8.6

Category A

4 Dr STD Sdn	6840	8770
4 Dr Ultra Sprchgd Sdn	7610	9755

OPTIONS FOR PARK AVENUE

Prestige Pkg +320
AM/FM Compact Disc Player +135
Astro Roof +380
Keyless Entry System[Opt on STD] +65
Leather Seats[Opt on STD] +180

REGAL   1994

Driver airbag and ABS standard on all Regals. 3.1-liter V6 gets 20 more horsepower. Power windows standard across the board, and automatic door locks automatically unlock when car is shifted into "Park." Defeat this feature by removing a fuse.

RATINGS (SCALE OF 1-10)

Overall	Safety	Reliability	Performance	Comfort	Value
7.4	6.5	6.3	8.2	7.3	8.5

Category C

2 Dr Custom Cpe	4895	6615
4 Dr Custom Sdn	5030	6800
2 Dr Gran Sport Cpe	5555	7510
4 Dr Gran Sport Sdn	5670	7665
4 Dr Limited Sdn	5430	7340

OPTIONS FOR REGAL

6 cyl 3.8 L Engine[Opt on Custom] +110
AM/FM Stereo Tape +45
Cruise Control +55
Leather Seats +165
Power Drivers Seat +80
Power Moonroof +185

ROADMASTER   1994

Detuned Corvette engine transplanted into big Buick, giving Roadmaster 80 additional horsepower. Dual airbags housed in redesigned dashboard with new gauges.

RATINGS (SCALE OF 1-10)

Overall	Safety	Reliability	Performance	Comfort	Value
7.9	8	5.7	7.8	8.4	9.4

Category B

4 Dr Estate Wgn	8320	10950
4 Dr Limited Sdn	7550	9935
4 Dr STD Sdn	6770	8905

OPTIONS FOR ROADMASTER

AM/FM Compact Disc Player +90
Camper/Towing Package +100
Keyless Entry System[Std on Limited] +45
Leather Seats +185
Power Drivers Seat[Opt on STD] +85

Don't forget to refer to the Mileage Adjustment Table at the back of this book!

SKYLARK 1994

Driver airbag added to all models. New 3.1-liter V6 replaces 3.3-liter V6 from 1993. Automatic transmission gets overdrive gear. Gran Sport and Limited gain standard equipment including air conditioning, power windows, cruise control and tilt steering wheel. Automatic door locks automatically unlock when car is put in "Park." Defeat this feature by removing a fuse.

RATINGS (SCALE OF 1-10)

Overall	Safety	Reliability	Performance	Comfort	Value
7.1	7.2	7.3	7.2	7	7

Category C

	Trade-in	Market
2 Dr Custom Cpe	3635	4910
4 Dr Custom Sdn	3775	5100
2 Dr Gran Sport Cpe	4575	6185
4 Dr Gran Sport Sdn	4700	6350
4 Dr Limited Sdn	4190	5665

OPTIONS FOR SKYLARK

6 cyl 3.1 L Engine[Std on Gran Sport] +140
Auto 4-Speed Transmission[Std on Gran Sport] +55
AM/FM Stereo Tape +45
Air Conditioning[Opt on Custom] +220
Cruise Control[Opt on Custom] +55
Power Drivers Seat +80
Power Windows[Opt on Custom] +85

1993 BUICK

CENTURY 1993

Driver airbag standard on Custom and Limited; optional on Special. New 2.2-liter four-cylinder replaces old 2.5-liter unit with no loss of power. Fuel tank capacity increased.

RATINGS (SCALE OF 1-10)

Overall	Safety	Reliability	Performance	Comfort	Value
7	4.6	7.4	7.4	7.3	8.3

Category C

	Trade-in	Market
2 Dr Custom Cpe	3165	4395
4 Dr Custom Sdn	3320	4610
4 Dr Custom Wgn	3515	4885
4 Dr Limited Sdn	3660	5080
4 Dr Special Sdn	3280	4555
4 Dr Special Wgn	3400	4720

OPTIONS FOR CENTURY

6 cyl 3.3 L Engine +120
Auto 4-Speed Transmission +45
Premium Pkg +170
Prestige Pkg +220
Cruise Control +45
Keyless Entry System +40

Power Drivers Seat +65
Power Windows +70

LESABRE 1993

Engine gets more torque, and both ABS and power door locks standard on all models. Limited offers variable-assist steering.

RATINGS (SCALE OF 1-10)

Overall	Safety	Reliability	Performance	Comfort	Value
7.8	7.2	7.2	8.6	8.1	8

Category B

	Trade-in	Market
4 Dr 90th Anniversary Sdn	4825	6610
4 Dr Custom Sdn	4685	6420
4 Dr Limited Sdn	5115	7005

OPTIONS FOR LESABRE

Luxury Pkg +290
Premium Pkg +210
Prestige Pkg +225
Aluminum/Alloy Wheels +75
Cruise Control[Opt on Custom,Limited] +50
Leather Seats +150
Power Drivers Seat[Opt on Custom,Limited] +70

PARK AVENUE 1993

Base V6 gains power. Revisions made to grilles and taillights. An automatic ride control system adjusts the suspension between three different modes ranging from soft to firm.

RATINGS (SCALE OF 1-10)

Overall	Safety	Reliability	Performance	Comfort	Value
N/A	N/A	7.5	8.6	8.1	8.5

Category A

	Trade-in	Market
4 Dr STD Sdn	5630	7605
4 Dr Ultra Sprchgd Sdn	6125	8275

OPTIONS FOR PARK AVENUE

AM/FM Compact Disc Player +110
Leather Seats[Opt on STD] +150
Power Sunroof +310

REGAL 1993

A new transmission, grille and taillights debut. The 3.8-liter V6 gains torque. 15-inch wheels replace 14-inch wheels. Optional on Limited and Gran Sport is a steering wheel with radio controls.

RATINGS (SCALE OF 1-10)

Overall	Safety	Reliability	Performance	Comfort	Value
7.1	4.8	6.6	8.2	7.3	8.4

Category C

	Trade-in	Market
2 Dr Custom Cpe	3895	5410
4 Dr Custom Sdn	4070	5650
2 Dr Gran Sport Cpe	4400	6110

Don't forget to refer to the Mileage Adjustment Table at the back of this book!

Model Description	Trade-in Value	Market Value
4 Dr Gran Sport Sdn	4510	6265
2 Dr Limited Cpe	4145	5755
4 Dr Limited Sdn	4260	5920

OPTIONS FOR REGAL

6 cyl 3.8 L Engine[Std on Gran Sport] +80
AM/FM Stereo Tape +35
Aluminum/Alloy Wheels[Std on Gran Sport] +65
Anti-Lock Brakes[Opt on Custom] +135
Cruise Control +45
Leather Seats +135
Power Drivers Seat +65
Power Sunroof +150
Power Windows +70

RIVIERA   1993

Gran Touring model gets larger wheels and tires from defunct Reatta.

Category B

	Trade-in Value	Market Value
2 Dr STD Cpe	6255	8570

OPTIONS FOR RIVIERA

AM/FM Compact Disc Player +70
Aluminum/Alloy Wheels +75
Leather Seats +150
Power Sunroof +250

ROADMASTER   1993

Wagons get Solar-Ray tinted windshield. Both models receive power window lockout switch and more sound deadening.

RATINGS (SCALE OF 1-10)

Overall	Safety	Reliability	Performance	Comfort	Value
N/A	N/A	7.3	7.4	8.4	9.3

Category B

	Trade-in Value	Market Value
4 Dr Estate Wgn	5930	8120
4 Dr Limited Sdn	5415	7420
4 Dr STD Sdn	4900	6715

OPTIONS FOR ROADMASTER

Prestige Pkg +200
AM/FM Compact Disc Player +70
Aluminum/Alloy Wheels[Std on Estate] +75
Camper/Towing Package +80
Leather Seats +150
Power Drivers Seat[Std on Limited] +70

SKYLARK   1993

New entry-level Custom model debuts. Base engine loses five horsepower. Split-folding rear seat optional on Limited; not available on Custom. Adjustable Ride Control moves to GS options list from standard equipment roster.

RATINGS (SCALE OF 1-10)

Overall	Safety	Reliability	Performance	Comfort	Value
6.5	4.1	7	7.2	7	7

Category C

	Trade-in Value	Market Value
2 Dr Custom Cpe	2770	3850
4 Dr Custom Sdn	2885	4010
2 Dr Gran Sport Cpe	3405	4730
4 Dr Gran Sport Sdn	3540	4920
2 Dr Limited Cpe	2970	4125
4 Dr Limited Sdn	3090	4295

OPTIONS FOR SKYLARK

6 cyl 3.3 L Engine[Std on Gran Sport] +120
AM/FM Stereo Tape +35
Air Conditioning +180
Cruise Control +45
Power Drivers Seat +65
Power Windows +70

1992 BUICK

CENTURY   1992

Power door locks made standard.

RATINGS (SCALE OF 1-10)

Overall	Safety	Reliability	Performance	Comfort	Value
6.8	4.1	7	7.4	7.3	8.2

Category C

	Trade-in Value	Market Value
2 Dr Custom Cpe	2555	3705
4 Dr Custom Sdn	2660	3855
4 Dr Custom Wgn	2815	4080
4 Dr Limited Sdn	2875	4170
4 Dr Limited Wgn	3010	4360
4 Dr Special Sdn	2570	3725

OPTIONS FOR CENTURY

6 cyl 3.3 L Engine +100
Auto 4-Speed Transmission +35
Cruise Control +40
Power Drivers Seat +55
Power Windows +55

LESABRE   1992

All-new car debuts based on 1991 Park Avenue redesign. ABS is standard on Limited, optional on Custom. Driver airbag is standard. Coupe dropped; all LeSabres are sedans. 3.8-liter V6 gets more power. Theft-deterrent system, power windows, and child-proof rear door locks are standard.

RATINGS (SCALE OF 1-10)

Overall	Safety	Reliability	Performance	Comfort	Value
7.6	6.6	6.7	8.6	8.1	7.9

Don't forget to refer to the Mileage Adjustment Table at the back of this book!

BUICK 92

Model Description	Trade-in Value	Market Value	Model Description	Trade-in Value	Market Value

Category B

Model	Trade-in Value	Market Value
4 Dr Custom Sdn	3615	5165
4 Dr Limited Sdn	3995	5710

OPTIONS FOR LESABRE

Anti-Lock Brakes[Opt on Custom] +125
Leather Seats +125
Power Drivers Seat +55

PARK AVENUE 1992

Ultra gets 205-horsepower supercharged V6. Traction control is a new option. Variable-effort power steering and dual cupholders are new for all Park Avenues.

RATINGS (SCALE OF 1-10)

Overall	Safety	Reliability	Performance	Comfort	Value
N/A	N/A	7	8.6	8.1	7.9

Category A

Model	Trade-in Value	Market Value
4 Dr STD Sdn	4540	6395
4 Dr Ultra Sprchgd Sdn	5005	7050

OPTIONS FOR PARK AVENUE

Premium Pkg +140
Prestige Pkg +270
AM/FM Compact Disc Player +90
Astro Roof +255
Leather Seats[Opt on STD] +120

REGAL 1992

Gran Sport no longer an option package; becomes a full-fledged model designation. ABS newly standard on Gran Sport and Limited. Power door locks made standard on all Regals. Power front passenger seat is new option.

RATINGS (SCALE OF 1-10)

Overall	Safety	Reliability	Performance	Comfort	Value
7	4.9	6.2	8.2	7.3	8.3

Category C

Model	Trade-in Value	Market Value
2 Dr Custom Cpe	3205	4645
4 Dr Custom Sdn	3345	4845
2 Dr Gran Sport Cpe	3725	5400
4 Dr Gran Sport Sdn	3820	5535
2 Dr Limited Cpe	3395	4920
4 Dr Limited Sdn	3505	5080

OPTIONS FOR REGAL

6 cyl 3.8 L Engine[Std on Gran Sport] +90
Anti-Lock Brakes[Opt on Custom] +110
Leather Seats +110
Power Drivers Seat +55
Power Sunroof +125
Power Windows +55

RIVIERA 1992

Solar-control glass is standard. Brake system gets larger rotors and calipers.

Category B

Model	Trade-in Value	Market Value
2 Dr STD Cpe	4775	6820

OPTIONS FOR RIVIERA

Astro Roof +230
Leather Seats +125
Power Passenger Seat +60

ROADMASTER 1992

Wagon gets 5.7-liter engine. Sedan debuts.

RATINGS (SCALE OF 1-10)

Overall	Safety	Reliability	Performance	Comfort	Value
N/A	N/A	5.7	7.4	8.4	8.6

Category B

Model	Trade-in Value	Market Value
4 Dr Estate Wgn	4665	6665
4 Dr Limited Sdn	4400	6285
4 Dr STD Sdn	4090	5845

OPTIONS FOR ROADMASTER

Cruise Control[Opt on Estate] +40
Leather Seats +125
Power Drivers Seat[Std on Limited] +55

SKYLARK 1992

Redesign meant to bring younger buyers into showrooms backfires. Choice of four- or six-cylinder engines available. Automatic transmission, ABS, power door locks and split-folding rear seat are standard. Still has door-mounted seatbelts. Adjustable Ride Control, standard on GS and optional on other Skylarks, allows driver to select one of three suspension settings.

RATINGS (SCALE OF 1-10)

Overall	Safety	Reliability	Performance	Comfort	Value
6.4	4.1	6.7	7.2	7	6.9

Category C

Model	Trade-in Value	Market Value
2 Dr Gran Sport Cpe	2720	3940
4 Dr Gran Sport Sdn	2830	4100
2 Dr STD Cpe	2320	3360
4 Dr STD Sdn	2420	3505

OPTIONS FOR SKYLARK

6 cyl 3.3 L Engine[Opt on STD] +100
Air Conditioning +145
Power Drivers Seat +55
Power Windows +55

Don't forget to refer to the Mileage Adjustment Table at the back of this book!

1991 BUICK

CENTURY 1991

Remote keyless entry and steering wheel radio controls are newly available.

RATINGS (SCALE OF 1-10)

Overall	Safety	Reliability	Performance	Comfort	Value
6.7	3.7	7	7.4	7.3	8.1

Category C

	Trade-in	Market
2 Dr Custom Cpe	1990	3060
4 Dr Custom Sdn	2030	3125
4 Dr Limited Sdn	2095	3220
4 Dr Limited Wgn	2255	3470

OPTIONS FOR CENTURY

6 cyl 3.3 L Engine +95
Auto 4-Speed Transmission +30
Prestige Pkg +125
Power Door Locks +35
Power Drivers Seat +45
Power Windows +45

LESABRE 1991

New 3.8-liter V6 engine replaces old one.

Category B

	Trade-in	Market
4 Dr Custom Sdn	2715	3990
2 Dr Limited Cpe	2545	3740
4 Dr Limited Sdn	2860	4205
2 Dr STD Cpe	2405	3535

OPTIONS FOR LESABRE

Anti-Lock Brakes +100
Leather Seats +100
Power Door Locks +40
Power Drivers Seat +45
Power Windows +45

PARK AVENUE 1991

All-new design debuts. New 3.8-liter V6 engine installed under the hood. Driver airbag and ABS are standard. Ultra gets standard dual-zone climate controls; this feature is optional on base car.

RATINGS (SCALE OF 1-10)

Overall	Safety	Reliability	Performance	Comfort	Value
N/A	N/A	7	8.6	8.1	7.9

Category A

	Trade-in	Market
4 Dr STD Sdn	3665	5315
4 Dr Ultra Sdn	4050	5870

OPTIONS FOR PARK AVENUE

Astro Roof +210
Leather Seats[Opt on STD] +100

REATTA 1991

New transmission and alloy wheels debut. New 3.8-liter V6 installed under the hood. Final year for slow-selling sportster.

Category C

	Trade-in	Market
2 Dr STD Conv	7965	12250
2 Dr STD Cpe	5235	8050

OPTIONS FOR REATTA

Power Sunroof +100

REGAL 1991

Teensy analog gauges replace yucky digital readouts, except on Custom coupe. New 3.8-liter V6 is optional on Regal except Gran Sport, on which it is standard. ABS optional on all Regals.

RATINGS (SCALE OF 1-10)

Overall	Safety	Reliability	Performance	Comfort	Value
6.7	4.6	5.3	8.2	7.3	8.3

Category C

	Trade-in	Market
2 Dr Custom Cpe	2455	3780
4 Dr Custom Sdn	2555	3930
2 Dr Limited Cpe	2570	3950
4 Dr Limited Sdn	2695	4145

OPTIONS FOR REGAL

6 cyl 3.8 L Engine +65
Anti-Lock Brakes +90
Leather Seats +90
Power Door Locks +35
Power Drivers Seat +45
Power Sunroof +100
Power Windows +45

RIVIERA 1991

Improved 3.8-liter V6 powers Riviera. Concert Sound II speaker system made standard. Retained accessory power means windows and sunroof can be shut after car is turned off.

Category B

	Trade-in	Market
2 Dr STD Cpe	3780	5560

OPTIONS FOR RIVIERA

Astro Roof +185
Leather Seats +100

ROADMASTER 1991

Buick revives legendary moniker for huge new rear-drive wagon with glass Vista Roof over rear seat. ABS and driver airbag are standard. Powered by 5.0-liter V8.

RATINGS (SCALE OF 1-10)

Overall	Safety	Reliability	Performance	Comfort	Value
N/A	N/A	5.9	7.4	8.4	7.6

Don't forget to refer to the Mileage Adjustment Table at the back of this book!

Model Description	Trade-in Value	Market Value
Category B		
4 Dr Estate Wgn	3690	5425

OPTIONS FOR ROADMASTER
Leather Seats +100
Power Door Locks +40
Power Drivers Seat +45

SKYLARK 1991

No changes.

Model	Trade-in Value	Market Value
Category C		
2 Dr Custom Cpe	1855	2855
4 Dr Custom Sdn	1955	3010
2 Dr Gran Sport Cpe	2080	3200
4 Dr Luxury Sdn	2095	3220
2 Dr STD Cpe	1845	2840
4 Dr STD Sdn	1935	2980

OPTIONS FOR SKYLARK
4 cyl 2.3 L Quad 4 Engine +95
6 cyl 3.3 L Engine +95
Air Conditioning +120
Power Door Locks +35
Power Drivers Seat +45
Power Windows +45

1990 BUICK

CENTURY 1990

New door trim, passive restraints and an improved suspension debut. Air conditioning now standard. 2.5-liter engine gets more power. Power seat switches relocated.

RATINGS (SCALE OF 1-10)

Overall	Safety	Reliability	Performance	Comfort	Value
6.6	3.8	6.9	7.4	7.3	7.6

Model	Trade-in Value	Market Value
Category C		
2 Dr Custom Cpe	1600	2620
4 Dr Custom Sdn	1665	2730
4 Dr Custom Wgn	1570	2570
4 Dr Limited Sdn	1695	2780
4 Dr Limited Wgn	1420	2325

OPTIONS FOR CENTURY
6 cyl 3.3 L Engine +75
Leather Seats +75
Power Door Locks +30
Power Drivers Seat +35
Power Windows +35

ELECTRA 1990

Cassette player and rear defogger made standard. Limited and Park Avenue get wire wheel covers; Limited and T-Type get cruise control. Steering feel is improved.

Model Description	Trade-in Value	Market Value
Category A		
4 Dr Limited Sdn	2435	3690
4 Dr Park Ave Ultra Sdn	2880	4365
4 Dr Park Avenue Sdn	2675	4055
4 Dr T Type Sdn	2495	3780

OPTIONS FOR ELECTRA
Luxury Pkg +115
Prestige Pkg +125
Anti-Lock Brakes[Opt on Limited,Park Avenue] +110
Astro Roof +170
Leather Seats[Std on Park Ave Ultra] +80

ESTATE WAGON 1990

LeSabre model dropped. Third seat can be deleted, and hood is garnished by new ornament.

Model	Trade-in Value	Market Value
Category B		
4 Dr STD Wgn	1770	2725

OPTIONS FOR ESTATE WAGON
Leather Seats +80
Power Door Locks +30
Power Drivers Seat +40
Power Windows +35

LESABRE 1990

New front and rear styling debuts, including composite headlamps, new grille and body-color fascia. T-Type model dropped. Steering feel is improved.

Model	Trade-in Value	Market Value
Category B		
4 Dr Custom Sdn	2150	3305
2 Dr Limited Cpe	2075	3190
4 Dr Limited Sdn	2315	3565
2 Dr STD Cpe	2000	3075

OPTIONS FOR LESABRE
Luxury Pkg +195
Leather Seats +80
Power Door Locks +30
Power Drivers Seat +40
Power Windows +35

REATTA 1990

Convertible introduced. Coupe gets analog gauges. New stereo with cassette and CD player is available. Distracting Video Touch Screen replaced by conventional controls.

Model	Trade-in Value	Market Value
Category C		
2 Dr STD Conv	6740	11050
2 Dr STD Cpe	4060	6655

OPTIONS FOR REATTA
Power Sunroof +80

Don't forget to refer to the Mileage Adjustment Table at the back of this book!

Model Description	Trade-in Value	Market Value

REGAL   1990

Sedan debuted midyear. New 3.8-liter engine is optional. ABS is part of SE package on Limited sedan. Leather is optional on Gran Sport coupe and Limited sedan.

RATINGS (SCALE OF 1-10)

Overall	Safety	Reliability	Performance	Comfort	Value
6.4	4.2	4.1	8.2	7.3	8.3

Category C

	Trade-in	Market
2 Dr Custom Cpe	1855	3040
2 Dr Limited Cpe	1925	3155

OPTIONS FOR REGAL
6 cyl 3.8 L Engine +50
Gran Sport Pkg +120
Leather Seats +75
Power Door Locks +30
Power Drivers Seat +35
Power Windows +35

RIVIERA   1990

Video Touch Screen killed in favor of conventional radio and climate controls. Driver airbag added this year. Anti-theft ignition system made standard. Seats redesigned, and 14-way power adjustment is available. Taillights are revised. Ergonomics improved with relocated switches for various accessories.

Category B

	Trade-in	Market
2 Dr STD Cpe	2950	4540

OPTIONS FOR RIVIERA
Anti-Lock Brakes +85
Astro Roof +155
Leather Seats +80

SKYLARK   1990

Base 2.5-liter engine gets more horsepower. Turn signal chime reminds driver when signal has been on for more than half-a-mile.

Category C

	Trade-in	Market
2 Dr Custom Cpe	1560	2560
4 Dr Custom Sdn	1660	2720
2 Dr Gran Sport Cpe	1865	3060
4 Dr Luxury Sdn	1805	2955
2 Dr STD Cpe	1495	2450
4 Dr STD Sdn	1555	2550

OPTIONS FOR SKYLARK
4 cyl 2.3 L Quad 4 Engine +75
6 cyl 3.3 L Engine +75
Air Conditioning +95
Power Door Locks +30
Power Drivers Seat +35
Power Windows +35

CADILLAC 99

Model Description	Trade-in Value	Market Value	Model Description	Trade-in Value	Market Value

CADILLAC · USA

1997 Cadillac DeVille

1999 CADILLAC

CATERA · 1999

Catera's "black chrome" grille will be darkened this year, while new electronics and emissions systems make the '99 Catera the first Cadillac to meet the federal Low Emissions Vehicle (LEV) standards. There's also a redesigned fuel cap and tether with an instrument cluster telltale to indicate a loose fuel cap. Up to four remote entry key fobs can now be programmed for separate memory settings, all with enhanced automatic door lock/unlock functions. Cadillac is rumored to be working on a special Sport Edition planned for later in the model year.

RATINGS (SCALE OF 1-10)

Overall	Safety	Reliability	Performance	Comfort	Value
N/A	N/A	N/A	8.6	8.6	N/A

Category A

4 Dr STD Sdn	20075	23620

OPTIONS FOR CATERA
Sport Handling Pkg +585

DEVILLE · 1999

Comfort is big with Cadillac, so who else would offer massaging lumbar seats? Sure enough, this industry-first option is available on '99 d'Elegance and Concours models. All DeVilles get an electrochromic inside rearview mirror with compass added to the standard equipment list, in addition to an audible theft deterrent system. There are three new exterior colors this year, and one different shade of leather inside. As if that weren't enough, side airbag deployment now communicates with the optional OnStar

communications system, so the outside world will know when you've taken a broadside hit. Comforting, indeed. Look for a limited run of about 2000 specially badged and optioned Golden Anniversary Edition DeVilles, painted White Diamond with gold trim, to celebrate the nameplate's 50th anniversary.

RATINGS (SCALE OF 1-10)

Overall	Safety	Reliability	Performance	Comfort	Value
N/A	8.9	9.1	N/A	8.3	N/A

Category A

4 Dr Concours Sdn	27455	32300
4 Dr D'elegance Sdn	26770	31495
4 Dr STD Sdn	23560	27720

OPTIONS FOR DEVILLE
Leather Seats[Opt on STD] +495

ELDORADO · 1999

Colors are big each year with Cadillac, and 1999 is no different. Cashmere, Parisian Blue and Sterling Silver replace Frost Beige, Baltic Blue Silver Mist and Shale on Eldorado's exterior color chart. Oatmeal leather replaces Cappuccino Cream as an interior color, while Pewter cloth has been deleted, leaving only Shale and Blue cloth available. In the hardware department, an electrochromic inside rearview mirror with compass and an audible theft deterrent system are now standard equipment. The Eldorado Touring Coupe (ETC) also gets the Bose four-speaker AM/FM cassette/single-slot CD & Weather Band audio system standard, with the option of adding massaging lumbar seats that provide a gentle back rub as you drive.

RATINGS (SCALE OF 1-10)

Overall	Safety	Reliability	Performance	Comfort	Value
N/A	8	N/A	8.6	7.6	N/A

Category A

2 Dr STD Cpe	28095	33055
2 Dr Touring Cpe	29070	34200

OPTIONS FOR ELDORADO
Leather Seats[Opt on STD] +495
Power Moonroof +1010

ESCALADE · 1999

The new Cadillac Escalade is really more a 1999 GMC Yukon Denali than it is a Cadillac. (And GMC's Yukon Denali is really more Yukon than anything else-except, perhaps, a Chevrolet Tahoe, but that's another story) Regardless of its origins, think of the Escalade as a big, four-wheel-drive Cadillac limo for well-heeled, outdoorsy types. Loaded with luxury touches and every possible convenience (even GM's OnStar mobile communications system), Escalade comes in four

Don't forget to refer to the Mileage Adjustment Table at the back of this book!

Model Description	Trade-in Value	Market Value	Model Description	Trade-in Value	Market Value

CADILLAC 99-98

special colors and lacks only one thing: an options list. Why? It's got it all.

RATINGS (SCALE OF 1-10)

Overall	Safety	Reliability	Performance	Comfort	Value
N/A	N/A	N/A	6	8	N/A

Category G

	Trade-in	Market
4 Dr STD 4WD Wgn	30295	36065

SEVILLE 1999

The Seville sees only minor changes after its successful redesign in 1998. Cadillac's new massaging lumbar seats are offered as an option on the STS. Heated seats become part of the adaptive seat package, which is now available on both SLS and STS trim levels. And the optional OnStar mobile communications system will automatically notify the OnStar customer assistance center in the case of any airbag deployment, front or side, so that the center can dispatch emergency services to the scene. Previously, notification occurred only with a front airbag deployment. There are also three new exterior colors, Cashmere, Parisian Blue and Sterling Silver, and one new interior shade called Oatmeal.

RATINGS (SCALE OF 1-10)

Overall	Safety	Reliability	Performance	Comfort	Value
N/A	N/A	9.2	8.8	8.6	N/A

Category A

	Trade-in	Market
4 Dr SLS Sdn	29750	35000
4 Dr STS Sdn	31210	36720

OPTIONS FOR SEVILLE

Adaptive Seat Pkg +1250
Personalization Pkg +870
Garage Door Opener +85
Power Moonroof +1010

1998 CADILLAC

CATERA 1998

New radios are available across the board, and a new option is a power rear sunshade. Second-generation airbags arrived during the middle of the model year.

RATINGS (SCALE OF 1-10)

Overall	Safety	Reliability	Performance	Comfort	Value
N/A	N/A	9.3	8.6	8.6	N/A

Category A

	Trade-in	Market
4 Dr STD Sdn	16365	19480

OPTIONS FOR CATERA

Leather Pkg +1565
Bose Sound System +355
Chrome Wheels +610
Dual Power Seats +230

Heated Seats +225
Leather Seats +405
Power Moonroof +825

DEVILLE 1998

StabiliTrak, an integrated chassis control system that corrects four-wheel lateral skids, is available on base and d'Elegance. New radio systems debut, and door lock programmability is enhanced. An idiot light is added to warn about loose fuel caps, and new colors are available inside and out. Heated seats are added to the d'Elegance and Concours while the Concours also gets a much-needed alloy wheel redesign. Second-generation airbags debut as standard equipment.

RATINGS (SCALE OF 1-10)

Overall	Safety	Reliability	Performance	Comfort	Value
8.2	8.7	8.5	8.2	8.3	7.4

Category A

	Trade-in	Market
4 Dr Concours Sdn	21435	25520
4 Dr D'elegance Sdn	21005	25005
4 Dr STD Sdn	18735	22305

OPTIONS FOR DEVILLE

Alarm System +175
Chrome Wheels[Std on D'elegance] +610
Compact Disc W/fm/tape[Opt on STD] +390
Heated Front Seats[Opt on STD] +120
Leather Seats[Opt on STD] +405

ELDORADO 1998

New radios, a revised interior electrochromic mirror, enhanced programmable features, second-generation airbags and the addition of StabiliTrak to the base model's option list are the major improvements for 1998.

RATINGS (SCALE OF 1-10)

Overall	Safety	Reliability	Performance	Comfort	Value
7.5	7.9	8.4	8.6	7.6	4.9

Category A

	Trade-in	Market
2 Dr STD Cpe	22155	26375
2 Dr Touring Cpe	23225	27650

OPTIONS FOR ELDORADO

Bose Sound System[Opt on STD] +355
Chrome Wheels +610
Compact Disc Changer +480
Heated Front Seats[Opt on STD] +120
Leather Seats[Opt on STD] +405
Power Moonroof +825

SEVILLE 1998

Cadillac redefines the American luxury car by debuting an athletic sedan that boasts the performance, style,

CADILLAC 98-97

Model Description	Trade-in Value	Market Value	Model Description	Trade-in Value	Market Value

refinement and technological innovation necessary to play ball on a global level.

RATINGS (SCALE OF 1-10)

Overall	Safety	Reliability	Performance	Comfort	Value
N/A	N/A	8.6	8.8	8.8	6.2

Category A

4 Dr SLS Sdn	24825	29555
4 Dr STS Sdn	26215	31210

OPTIONS FOR SEVILLE
Adaptive Seat Pkg +675
Personalization Pkg +730
Bose Sound System[Opt on SLS] +355
Chrome Wheels +610
Compact Disc Changer +480
Heated Seats +225
Power Moonroof +825

1997 CADILLAC

CATERA   1997

Cadillac leaps into the near luxury segment of the market with a stylish, German-engineered sedan that features a 200-horsepower V6, an impressive load of standard equipment, and proper rear-wheel drive.

RATINGS (SCALE OF 1-10)

Overall	Safety	Reliability	Performance	Comfort	Value
N/A	N/A	8.8	8.6	8.6	N/A

Category A

4 Dr STD Sdn	13975	16840

OPTIONS FOR CATERA
Leather Pkg +830
Bose Sound System +290
Chrome Wheels +500
Dual Power Seats +185
Heated Seats +185
Leather Seats +330
Power Moonroof +675

DEVILLE   1997

DeVille undergoes a substantial revamp for 1997, including revised styling, the addition of standard side-impact airbags, and a fresh interior that is actually functional. Concours receives stability enhancement and road texture detection as part of its Integrated Chassis Control System (ICCS), while a new D'elegance model picks up where the defunct Fleetwood left off. Finally, the OnStar Services package provides DeVille owners with security and convenience features that will pinpoint the car's location at any given time or allow you to book a flight to Paris from the comfort of your driver's seat.

RATINGS (SCALE OF 1-10)

Overall	Safety	Reliability	Performance	Comfort	Value
8.3	8.9	8.6	8.2	8.3	7.3

Category A

4 Dr Concours Sdn	18730	22565
4 Dr D'elegance Sdn	17675	21295
4 Dr STD Sdn	16620	20025

OPTIONS FOR DEVILLE
Alarm System +140
Chrome Wheels[Std on D'elegance] +500
Compact Disc W/fm/tape +320
Leather Seats[Opt on STD] +330

ELDORADO   1997

Structural, suspension, and brake system enhancements are made across the board. Base models get MagnaSteer variable effort steering, while the Eldorado Touring Coupe (ETC) receives a new Integrated Chassis Control System (ICCS) that includes stability enhancement and road texture detection. All Eldos have slightly revised stereo and climate controls, and the OnStar services package is a slick new option that can notify emergency personnel where your disabled car is located or can allow you to book dinner reservations from the driver's seat.

RATINGS (SCALE OF 1-10)

Overall	Safety	Reliability	Performance	Comfort	Value
7.3	7.9	7.9	8.6	7.6	4.6

Category A

2 Dr STD Cpe	19655	23680
2 Dr Touring Cpe	20680	24915

OPTIONS FOR ELDORADO
Automatic Dimming Mirror +80
Bose Sound System +290
Chrome Wheels +500
Compact Disc Changer +395
Heated Front Seats +100
Leather Seats[Opt on STD] +330
Power Moonroof +675

SEVILLE   1997

All Sevilles receive body structure, suspension, brake system, and interior enhancements. STS models get a new stability enhancement feature designed to correct lateral skids, and road texture detection, which helps modulate the ABS more effectively on rough roads. Enhanced, programmable memory systems are new to both models, as is a revised rear seatback and the availability of OnStar, a vehicle information and communications service. SLS models get MagnaSteer variable-effort steering.

Don't forget to refer to the Mileage Adjustment Table at the back of this book!

RATINGS (SCALE OF 1-10)

Overall	Safety	Reliability	Performance	Comfort	Value
7.7	7.6	8.4	8.2	8.1	6.1

Category A

	Trade-in	Market
4 Dr SLS Sdn	19140	23060
4 Dr STS Sdn	20335	24500

OPTIONS FOR SEVILLE
Automatic Dimming Mirror +80
Bose Sound System +290
Chrome Wheels +500
Compact Disc Changer +395
Heated Front Seats +100
Leather Seats[Opt on SLS] +330
Power Moonroof +675

1996 CADILLAC

DEVILLE   1996

Northstar V8 is installed in base DeVille, along with a new transmission, Integrated Chassis Control System, and Road-Sensing Suspension. Concours gets 25 horsepower boost to 300, along with a higher final-drive ratio for quicker pickup and an improved continuously-variable Road-Sensing Suspension. Automatic windshield wipers and new variable-effort steering are standard on the Concours. Daytime running lights debut on both of these monsters.

RATINGS (SCALE OF 1-10)

Overall	Safety	Reliability	Performance	Comfort	Value
8	8	8.4	8.2	8.3	7.2

Category A

	Trade-in	Market
4 Dr Concours Sdn	15225	18570
4 Dr STD Sdn	13660	16660

OPTIONS FOR DEVILLE
Alarm System +115
Leather Seats[Opt on STD] +270

ELDORADO   1996

Sea Mist Green is a new interior and exterior color, and daytime running lights are standard. Eldorado gets new seats and revised audio systems. Touring Coupe interior is revised, with a center-stack console, bigger gauges, and seamless passenger airbag. Rainsense, an automatic windshield wiper system, is standard on the ETC, as is an updated continuously-variable Road-Sensing Suspension.

RATINGS (SCALE OF 1-10)

Overall	Safety	Reliability	Performance	Comfort	Value
7.2	7.7	7.3	8.6	7.6	4.6

Category A

	Trade-in	Market
2 Dr STD Cpe	16250	19815
2 Dr Touring Cpe	17065	20810

OPTIONS FOR ELDORADO
Bose Sound System +240
Chrome Wheels +410
Compact Disc Changer +320
Heated Front Seats +80
Leather Seats[Opt on STD] +270
Power Moonroof +550

FLEETWOOD   1996

Final year for the longest production car sold in the U.S. Updates are limited to a new audio system, revised center storage armrest, and pre-wiring for Cadillac's Dual Mode cellular phone.

RATINGS (SCALE OF 1-10)

Overall	Safety	Reliability	Performance	Comfort	Value
N/A	N/A	7.3	7.6	8.1	6.7

Category A

	Trade-in	Market
4 Dr STD Sdn	14705	17930

OPTIONS FOR FLEETWOOD
Camper/Towing Package +135
Chrome Wheels +410
Compact Disc W/fm/tape +260
Heated Seats +150
Leather Seats +270
Power Moonroof +550

SEVILLE   1996

All Sevilles get new seats and seat trim, redesigned sound systems, an (optional) integrated voice-activated cellular phone, daytime running lights, and programmable door lock functions and seating positions. The STS also receives an updated instrument panel with big gauges and a new center console, the Cadillac-exclusive Rainsense Wiper System (which detects rainfall and turns the wipers on automatically) and a newly improved continuously-variable Road-Sensing Suspension. Magnasteer variable-assist steering replaces the old speed-sensitive gear on last year's STS.

RATINGS (SCALE OF 1-10)

Overall	Safety	Reliability	Performance	Comfort	Value
7.6	7.4	8.1	8.2	8.1	6

Category A

	Trade-in	Market
4 Dr SLS Sdn	15975	19480
4 Dr STS Sdn	17070	20815

OPTIONS FOR SEVILLE
Bose Sound System +240
Chrome Wheels +410
Compact Disc Changer +320

Don't forget to refer to the Mileage Adjustment Table at the back of this book!

EDMUND'S® USED CARS & TRUCKS   www.edmunds.com   65

Model Description	Trade-in Value	Market Value	Model Description	Trade-in Value	Market Value

Heated Front Seats +80
Leather Seats[Opt on SLS] +270
Power Moonroof +550

1995 CADILLAC

DEVILLE   1995

Traction control (which can be shut off) is standard on base DeVille. Headlights come on automatically when windshield wipers are activated. Chrome wheels can be ordered on Concours. Garage door opener is optional on DeVille; standard on Concours.

RATINGS (SCALE OF 1-10)

Overall	Safety	Reliability	Performance	Comfort	Value
8.1	8.6	8.4	8.2	8.3	7.1

Category A

4 Dr Concours Sdn	12325	15405
4 Dr STD Sdn	11070	13840

OPTIONS FOR DEVILLE
Compact Disc W/fm/tape +215
Leather Seats[Opt on STD] +220

ELDORADO   1995

Northstar V8 power is increased. Electronic chassis controls now evaluate steering angle when deciding what to do with the Road Sensing Suspension, traction control, and ABS. Styling is slightly revised front and rear. Headlights come on automatically when windshield wipers are activated.

RATINGS (SCALE OF 1-10)

Overall	Safety	Reliability	Performance	Comfort	Value
7.9	8.5	8	8.6	7.6	6.6

Category A

2 Dr STD Cpe	12860	16075
2 Dr Touring Cpe	13510	16885

OPTIONS FOR ELDORADO
Chrome Wheels +335
Compact Disc W/fm/tape +215
Heated Front Seats +65
Leather Seats[Opt on STD] +220
Power Moonroof +450

FLEETWOOD   1995

Traction control gets on/off switch. Platinum-tipped spark plugs are added, allowing tune-ups to occur every 100,000 miles. Anti-lockout feature added. Remote keyless entry, central unlocking, and fold-away outside mirrors are added. Garage door opener is new option.

RATINGS (SCALE OF 1-10)

Overall	Safety	Reliability	Performance	Comfort	Value
N/A	N/A	7.2	7.6	8.1	6.6

Category A

4 Dr STD Sdn	12045	15055

OPTIONS FOR FLEETWOOD
Camper/Towing Package +110
Chrome Wheels +335
Compact Disc W/fm/tape +215
Heated Front Seats +65
Leather Seats +220
Power Moonroof +450

SEVILLE   1995

Northstar V8 power is increased. Electronic chassis controls now evaluate steering angle when deciding what to do with the Road Sensing Suspension, traction control, and ABS. Headlights come on automatically when windshield wipers are activated. Chrome wheels are new option.

RATINGS (SCALE OF 1-10)

Overall	Safety	Reliability	Performance	Comfort	Value
7.6	8.5	7.9	8.2	8.1	5.5

Category A

4 Dr SLS Sdn	12610	15765
4 Dr STS Sdn	13435	16795

OPTIONS FOR SEVILLE
Chrome Wheels +335
Compact Disc W/fm/tape +215
Heated Front Seats +65
Leather Seats[Opt on SLS] +220
Power Moonroof +450

1994 CADILLAC

DEVILLE   1994

Redesigned with dual airbags, height-adjustable seat belts, and side-impact protection meeting 1997 standards. Base and Concours models available, with Concours replacing Touring Sedan. Concours comes with Northstar V8 and Road Sensing Suspension. Coupe DeVille and Sixty Special are retired. Base DeVille powered by 1993's 4.9-liter V8. Remote keyless entry is standard.

RATINGS (SCALE OF 1-10)

Overall	Safety	Reliability	Performance	Comfort	Value
N/A	N/A	7.7	8.2	8.3	8

Category A

4 Dr Concours Sdn	10035	12865
4 Dr STD Sdn	8960	11485

OPTIONS FOR DEVILLE
Compact Disc W/fm/tape +175
Leather Seats[Opt on STD] +180

Don't forget to refer to the Mileage Adjustment Table at the back of this book!

CADILLAC 94-93

Model Description	Trade-in Value	Market Value	Model Description	Trade-in Value	Market Value

ELDORADO 1994

Base model gets Northstar V8, Road Sensing Suspension, and traction control. Remote keyless entry and automatic door locks are made standard.

RATINGS (SCALE OF 1-10)

Overall	Safety	Reliability	Performance	Comfort	Value
7.5	8.4	7.3	8.6	7.6	5.5

Category A

2 Dr STD Cpe	10450	13395
2 Dr Touring Cpe	11015	14120

OPTIONS FOR ELDORADO
Astro Roof +380
Chrome Wheels +275
Compact Disc W/fm/tape +175
Leather Seats[Opt on STD] +180

FLEETWOOD 1994

Detuned Corvette 5.7-liter engine makes its way under Fleetwood's gargantuan hood. Performance is much improved. New transmission comes with new engine. Brougham package includes padded vinyl roof and alloy wheels. Flash-to-pass is a new feature, and a battery saver is installed.

RATINGS (SCALE OF 1-10)

Overall	Safety	Reliability	Performance	Comfort	Value
N/A	N/A	7.4	7.6	8.1	7.1

Category A

4 Dr STD Sdn	9280	11900

OPTIONS FOR FLEETWOOD
Cloth Brougham Pkg +385
Leather Brougham Pkg +350
Astro Roof +380
Camper/Towing Package +90
Chrome Wheels +275
Compact Disc W/fm/tape +175
Leather Seats +180

SEVILLE 1994

Base model now called SLS. SLS gets Northstar V8, traction control, and Road Sensing Suspension. Remote keyless entry is standard this year.

RATINGS (SCALE OF 1-10)

Overall	Safety	Reliability	Performance	Comfort	Value
7.5	8.4	6.9	8.2	8.1	5.8

Category A

4 Dr STD Sdn	10410	13345
4 Dr STS Sdn	11075	14200

OPTIONS FOR SEVILLE
Astro Roof +380
Chrome Wheels +275
Compact Disc W/fm/tape +175
Leather Seats[Opt on STD] +180

1993 CADILLAC

60 SPECIAL 1993

Speed-sensitive steering debuts. Speed Sensitive Suspension is standard on all models. Grille is revised.

Category A

4 Dr STD Sdn	6795	9180

OPTIONS FOR 60 SPECIAL
Ultra Seating Pkg +525
AM/FM Compact Disc Player +110
Astro Roof +310
Chrome Wheels +225
Keyless Entry System +55
Leather Seats +150
Power Passenger Seat +65

ALLANTE 1993

Final year for ill-fated convertible, and this is the year to buy. Why? This is the only Allante with Northstar V8 engine. Along with the superb engine, Allante gets a new transmission, new traction control system, and a Road Sensing Suspension. Rear suspension is redesigned, and tires are rated to 155 mph. Audio system is revised, dual cupholders are added, alloy wheels are restyled, and seats are all-new. Buy one. Store it.

Category J

2 Dr STD Conv	18740	23720

DEVILLE 1993

Fleetwood tag moved to big new rear-drive sedan. Speed-sensitive steering debuts. Speed Sensitive Suspension is standard on all models. Grille is revised. Special Edition option packages include really cool stuff like gold trim and Phaeton roof.

RATINGS (SCALE OF 1-10)

Overall	Safety	Reliability	Performance	Comfort	Value
N/A	N/A	7.6	8	8	7.4

Category A

2 Dr STD Cpe	6580	8895
4 Dr STD Sdn	6845	9250
4 Dr Touring Sdn	7465	10085

OPTIONS FOR DEVILLE
Leather Seats[Opt on STD] +150

ELDORADO 1993

Touring Coupe gets stellar Northstar V8, Road Sensing Suspension, and traction control. Passenger airbag debuts. Rear suspension redesigned. Speed-

CADILLAC 93-92

Model Description	Trade-in Value	Market Value	Model Description	Trade-in Value	Market Value

sensitive steering made standard. Base Eldo gets Speed Sensitive Suspension standard. Sport Performance package is a blend of base model and TC with detuned Northstar. Sport Appearance package gives look of Sport Performance package with 4.9-liter V8 from base coupe. Got that?

RATINGS (SCALE OF 1-10)

Overall	Safety	Reliability	Performance	Comfort	Value
7.3	8.4	6.7	8.6	7.6	5.4

Category A
2 Dr STD Cpe	8175	11050
2 Dr Touring Cpe	8660	11700

OPTIONS FOR ELDORADO
Sport Appearance Pkg +195
Astro Roof +310
Chrome Wheels +225
Compact Disc W/fm/tape +145
Leather Seats +150
Traction Control System +45

FLEETWOOD   1993

Dual airbags and rounded styling characterize this Brougham replacement, which is based on stretched Chevy Caprice chassis. Length is up 4.1 inches. Yowza! Traction control and ABS are standard. Optional trailer tow group gives car a 7,000-lb. towing capacity. Goofy digital dashboard standard.

RATINGS (SCALE OF 1-10)

Overall	Safety	Reliability	Performance	Comfort	Value
N/A	N/A	6.8	7.2	8.1	7.9

Category A
4 Dr STD Sdn	7125	9630

OPTIONS FOR FLEETWOOD
AM/FM Compact Disc Player +110
Astro Roof +310
Leather Seats +150

SEVILLE   1993

STS gets Northstar V8, Road Sensing Suspension, and traction control. Passenger airbag added to all Sevilles. Base Seville gets Speed Sensitive Suspension. Bigger fuel tank is added, rear suspension is redesigned, and a cupholder is added to center console. ABS and speed-sensitive steering standard on all Sevilles.

RATINGS (SCALE OF 1-10)

Overall	Safety	Reliability	Performance	Comfort	Value
7.5	8.4	7	8.2	8.1	5.9

Category A
4 Dr STD Sdn	7675	10370
4 Dr STS Sdn	8320	11245

OPTIONS FOR SEVILLE
AM/FM Compact Disc Player +110
Astro Roof +310
Bose Sound System +130
Chrome Wheels +225
Keyless Entry System[Opt on STD] +55
Leather Seats[Opt on STD] +150

1992 CADILLAC

ALLANTE   1992

No changes.
Category J
2 Dr STD Conv	13155	16865

OPTIONS FOR ALLANTE
Hardtop Roof +530

BROUGHAM   1992

5.7-liter V8 escapes gas-guzzler tax. Towing capacity increased 2,000 lbs. Final edition.
Category A
4 Dr STD Sdn	5710	8040

OPTIONS FOR BROUGHAM
8 cyl 5.7 L Engine +45
D'Elegance Pkg +340
Astro Roof +255
Leather Seats +120

DEVILLE   1992

Traction control optional on base DeVille; standard on all others. Platinum-tipped spark plugs mean tune-ups happen every 100,000 miles. Power passenger seat made standard on DeVille. Electrochromic rearview mirror made standard on all models.

RATINGS (SCALE OF 1-10)

Overall	Safety	Reliability	Performance	Comfort	Value
N/A	N/A	7.5	8	8	7.3

Category A
2 Dr STD Cpe	5280	7440
4 Dr STD Sdn	5465	7700
4 Dr Touring Sdn	6060	8535

OPTIONS FOR DEVILLE
Phaeton Roof +195
Astro Roof +255
Bose Sound System +105
Leather Seats[Opt on STD] +120

ELDORADO   1992

Complete makeover results in distinctly European-flavored coupe. Powertrains are carried over from 1991. ABS and driver airbag are standard. Sport interior option includes analog gauges rather than digital gauges.

Don't forget to refer to the Mileage Adjustment Table at the back of this book!

Model Description	Trade-in Value	Market Value

Model Description	Trade-in Value	Market Value

RATINGS (SCALE OF 1-10)

Overall	Safety	Reliability	Performance	Comfort	Value
7.2	7.5	6.9	8.2	7.6	5.8

Category A

2 Dr STD Cpe	6410	9030

OPTIONS FOR ELDORADO
Stars & Stripes Pkg +160
Touring Pkg +510
Astro Roof +255
Compact Disc W/fm/tape +115
Leather Seats +120

FLEETWOOD   1992

Traction control standard. Platinum-tipped spark plugs mean tune-ups happen every 100,000 miles. Electrochromatic rearview mirror made standard on all models.
Category A

2 Dr STD Cpe	5235	7375
4 Dr STD Sdn	5340	7520
4 Dr Sixty Special Sdn	5845	8235

OPTIONS FOR FLEETWOOD
Astro Roof +255
Bose Sound System +105
Leather Seats[Opt on STD] +120

SEVILLE   1992

Complete makeover results in distinctly European-flavored sedan. Powertrains are carried over from 1991. ABS and driver airbag are standard. Sport interior option includes analog gauges rather than digital gauges. Leather upholstery and analog gauges are standard on STS.

RATINGS (SCALE OF 1-10)

Overall	Safety	Reliability	Performance	Comfort	Value
7.6	7.5	7.6	8	8.1	6.8

Category A

4 Dr STD Sdn	5980	8420
4 Dr STS Sdn	6645	9360

OPTIONS FOR SEVILLE
Phaeton Roof +195
Astro Roof +255
Leather Seats[Opt on STD] +120

1991 CADILLAC

ALLANTE   1991

Traction control debuts. Power latching mechanism added to manual top.
Category J

2 Dr STD Conv	10605	13770

OPTIONS FOR ALLANTE
Hardtop Roof +435

BROUGHAM   1991

Standard and optional engines gain more power. Optional 5.7-liter motor slapped with gas-guzzler tax for city rating of 15 mpg.
Category A

4 Dr STD Sdn	4760	6895

OPTIONS FOR BROUGHAM
8 cyl 5.7 L Engine +35
D'elegance Pkg +265
Astro Roof +210
Leather Seats +100
Wire Wheels +145

DEVILLE   1991

Engine upgraded to 200-horsepower, 4.9-liter V8 from 180-horsepower, 4.5-liter V8. DeVille Touring Sedan debuted late in model year, with monotone exterior paint, performance tires, quicker-ratio steering, and thicker stabilizer bars.

RATINGS (SCALE OF 1-10)

Overall	Safety	Reliability	Performance	Comfort	Value
N/A	N/A	7	8	8	7.8

Category A

2 Dr STD Cpe	3980	5765
4 Dr STD Sdn	4145	6010
4 Dr Touring Sdn	4870	7055

OPTIONS FOR DEVILLE
Phaeton Roof +160
Astro Roof +210
Bose Sound System +85
Leather Seats[Opt on STD] +100

ELDORADO   1991

Engine upgraded to 200-horsepower, 4.9-liter V8 from 180-horsepower, 4.5-liter V8. Transmission modified to generate better acceleration. Touring Coupe debuts, featuring Seville STS styling and suspension modifications.
Category A

2 Dr Biarritz Cpe	5005	7250
2 Dr STD Cpe	4830	7000

OPTIONS FOR ELDORADO
Touring Coupe Pkg +230
Astro Roof +210
Bose Sound System +85
Leather Seats[Opt on STD] +100

FLEETWOOD   1991

Engine upgraded to 200-horsepower, 4.9-liter V8 from 180-horsepower, 4.5-liter V8.

Don't forget to refer to the Mileage Adjustment Table at the back of this book!

Model Description	Trade-in Value	Market Value
Category A		
4 Dr STD Sdn	4680	6785
4 Dr Sixty Special Sdn	4835	7005

OPTIONS FOR FLEETWOOD
Astro Roof +210
Bose Sound System +85
Leather Seats[Opt on STD] +100

SEVILLE   1991

Engine upgraded to 200-horsepower, 4.9-liter V8 from 180-horsepower, 4.5-liter V8. Transmission modified to generate better acceleration.

Category A		
4 Dr STD Sdn	4495	6515
4 Dr STS Sdn	5025	7285

OPTIONS FOR SEVILLE
Phaeton Roof +175
Astro Roof +210
Bose Sound System +85
Leather Seats[Opt on STD] +100

1990 CADILLAC

ALLANTE   1990

CD player is standard, as is Natural Beige interior color.

Category J		
2 Dr STD Conv	9365	12320

OPTIONS FOR ALLANTE
Hardtop Roof +355

BROUGHAM   1990

5.7-liter engine is optional, but when only ordered with trailer towing or Coachbuilder packages. ABS is standard. Composite headlights and new front bumper update Brougham's dated styling. Can't forget to mention the new standard padded vinyl roof, can we? Rear styling is updated as well.

Category A		
4 Dr D'elegance Sdn	3625	5490
4 Dr STD Sdn	3495	5295

OPTIONS FOR BROUGHAM
8 cyl 5.7L Engine +30
Astro Roof +170
Leather Seats +80
Wire Wheels +120

DEVILLE   1990

More powerful 4.5-liter V8 debuts. Driver airbag is made standard. Anti-theft ignition lock is standard.

RATINGS (SCALE OF 1-10)

Overall	Safety	Reliability	Performance	Comfort	Value
N/A	N/A	6.6	8	8	6.2

Model Description	Trade-in Value	Market Value
Category A		
2 Dr STD Cpe	3105	4705
4 Dr STD Sdn	3205	4855

OPTIONS FOR DEVILLE
DeVille Spring Edition +250
Leather Seats +80

ELDORADO   1990

Stronger 4.5-liter V8 installed under the hood. Suspension is upgraded. Onboard computer added. Driver airbag is standard. Rear defogger, heated outside mirrors, and illuminated entry system made standard. Styling is tweaked.

Category A		
2 Dr Biarritz Cpe	3775	5720
2 Dr STD Cpe	3635	5510
2 Dr Touring Cpe	3830	5805

OPTIONS FOR ELDORADO
Anti-Lock Brakes +110
Astro Roof +170
Leather Seats[Opt on STD] +80

FLEETWOOD   1990

More powerful 4.5-liter V8 debuts. Driver airbag is made standard. Anti-theft ignition lock is standard.

Category A		
2 Dr STD Cpe	3810	5770
4 Dr STD Sdn	3895	5905
4 Dr Sixty Special Sdn	3990	6045

OPTIONS FOR FLEETWOOD
AM/FM Compact Disc Player +60
Astro Roof +170
Leather Seats[Opt on STD] +80

SEVILLE   1990

Stronger 4.5-liter V8 installed under the hood. Suspension is upgraded. Onboard computer added. Driver airbag is standard. Rear defogger, heated outside mirrors, and illuminated entry system made standard. Styling is tweaked. STS gets dual exhaust system and firmer suspension.

Category A		
4 Dr STD Sdn	3750	5685
4 Dr STS Sdn	4105	6220

OPTIONS FOR SEVILLE
Phaeton Roof +145
Anti-Lock Brakes[Opt on STD] +110
Astro Roof +170
Leather Seats[Opt on STD] +80

CHEVROLET 99

Model Description	Trade-in Value	Market Value	Model Description	Trade-in Value	Market Value

CHEVROLET   USA

1995 Chevrolet Suburban

1999 CHEVROLET

ASTRO   1999

A new, all-wheel-drive active transfer case replaces the previous AWD system, and includes a new control module and service light. There are two new interior roof consoles: one with storage is optional on base model, another with trip computer is standard on LS and LT trim. A new LT stripe design comes in three new colors. Dealer-installed running boards are available, as are new optional aluminum wheels. Three exterior paint colors are added for '99, while depowered airbags finally arrive this year. Finally, the outside mirrors are redesigned, available heated and with or without electrochromatic glare reduction.

RATINGS (SCALE OF 1-10)

Overall	Safety	Reliability	Performance	Comfort	Value
N/A	7	8.5	5.8	6.1	N/A

Category G

	Trade-in	Market
2 Dr LS Pass. Van Ext	13480	16045
2 Dr LS 4WD Pass. Van Ext	15225	18125
2 Dr LT Pass. Van Ext	14110	16795
2 Dr LT 4WD Pass. Van Ext	15920	18950
2 Dr STD Cargo Van Ext	11195	13325
2 Dr STD 4WD Cargo Van Ext	12990	15465
2 Dr STD Pass. Van Ext	12035	14330
2 Dr STD 4WD Pass. Van Ext	13910	16560

OPTIONS FOR ASTRO

AM/FM Stereo Tape[Opt on STD] +170
Compact Disc W/fm/tape +355
Cruise Control[Opt on STD] +155
Luggage Rack[Opt on STD] +115

Power Door Locks[Opt on STD] +170
Power Mirrors[Opt on STD] +100
Power Windows[Opt on STD] +175
Privacy Glass[Opt on STD] +195
Rear Heater +150
Rear Window Defroster[Opt on LS,STD,4WD] +125
Rear Window Wiper +115
Tilt Steering Wheel[Opt on STD] +130
Tutone Paint +195

BLAZER   1999

Blazer gets automatic transmission improvements, new exterior colors and larger outside mirrors, while four-wheel-drive versions can be equipped with GM's AutoTrac active transfer case. Inside, there're new power-seating features, upgraded sound system options and available redundant radio controls in the steering wheel. On the safety side, the '99 Blazer now offers a vehicle content theft alarm, flash-to-pass headlamp feature, and a liftgate ajar warning lamp. What's more, a new TrailBlazer trim package is available on four-door versions, featuring monochrome paint with gold accents, unique aluminum wheels, touring suspension and leather-lined interior.

RATINGS (SCALE OF 1-10)

Overall	Safety	Reliability	Performance	Comfort	Value
N/A	7.3	8.7	8	7.9	N/A

Category G

	Trade-in	Market
2 Dr LS Utility	14750	17560
2 Dr LS 4WD Utility	15415	18350
4 Dr LS Wgn	16315	19425
4 Dr LS 4WD Wgn	17070	20320
4 Dr LT Wgn	17235	20520
4 Dr LT 4WD Wgn	17925	21340
2 Dr STD Utility	13060	15550
2 Dr STD 4WD Utility	13685	16290
4 Dr STD Wgn	14475	17230
4 Dr STD 4WD Wgn	15185	18080
4 Dr Trailblazer Wgn	18255	21735
4 Dr Trailblazer 4WD Wgn	18985	22600

OPTIONS FOR BLAZER

Auto 4-Speed Transmission[Opt on Utility] +740
ZR2 Suspension Pkg +1255
AM/FM Compact Disc Player[Std on Utility] +245
AM/FM Stereo Tape[Std on LS,LT,Trailblazer,Utility] +170
Aluminum/Alloy Wheels[Std on LS,LT,Trailblazer,Utility] +245
Compact Disc W/fm/tape +355
Cruise Control[Opt on STD] +155
Heated Front Seats +195
Luggage Rack[Std on LS,LT,Trailblazer,Utility] +115
Overhead Console[Opt on LS,STD] +120
Power Door Locks[Opt on STD] +170
Power Drivers Seat[Opt on Wgn] +210
Power Sunroof[Opt on LS] +580

Don't forget to refer to the Mileage Adjustment Table at the back of this book!

Model Description	Trade-in Value	Market Value	Model Description	Trade-in Value	Market Value

Power Windows[Opt on STD] +175
Rear Window Defroster[Opt on STD] +125
Rear Window Wiper[Opt on STD] +115
Swing Out Tire Carrier +145
Tilt Steering Wheel[Opt on STD] +130

C/K PICKUP — 1999

C/K 1500 SERIES
Category H

2 Dr LS Ext Cab SB	15910	18715
2 Dr LS 4WD Ext Cab SB	17695	20815

C/K 2500 SERIES
Category H

4 Dr LS 4WD Crew Cab SB	21505	25300
4 Dr LS 4WD Ext Cab LB	20190	23755
2 Dr LS 4WD Ext Cab SB	19975	23500
2 Dr LS Std Cab LB	17100	20115
2 Dr LS 4WD Std Cab LB	18190	21400
4 Dr STD Crew Cab SB	18350	21590
4 Dr STD 4WD Crew Cab SB	20040	23575
2 Dr STD 4WD Ext Cab LB	18905	22240
2 Dr STD 4WD Ext Cab SB	18715	22015
2 Dr STD Std Cab LB	16025	18850
2 Dr STD 4WD Std Cab LB	16985	19985

C/K 3500 SERIES
Category H

4 Dr LS Crew Cab LB	20740	24400
4 Dr LS 4WD Crew Cab LB	22960	27010
4 Dr LS Crew Cab SB	20555	24180
4 Dr LS 4WD Crew Cab SB	22780	26800
2 Dr LS Ext Cab LB	19720	23200
2 Dr LS 4WD Ext Cab LB	21940	25810
2 Dr LS Std Cab LB	18790	22105
2 Dr LS 4WD Std Cab LB	20825	24500
4 Dr STD Crew Cab LB	19805	23300
4 Dr STD 4WD Crew Cab LB	21940	25810
4 Dr STD Crew Cab SB	19645	23110
4 Dr STD 4WD Crew Cab SB	21770	25610
2 Dr STD Ext Cab LB	18615	21900
2 Dr STD 4WD Ext Cab LB	21010	24720
2 Dr STD Std Cab LB	17625	20735
2 Dr STD 4WD Std Cab LB	19915	23430

OPTIONS FOR C/K PICKUP
8 cyl 5.7 L Engine[Opt on C/K 1500] +750
8 cyl 6.5 L Turbodsl Engine +2115
Auto 4-Speed Transmission[Std on C/K 1500] +735
AM/FM Compact Disc Player +230
Air Conditioning[Opt on STD] +600
Aluminum/Alloy Wheels +235
Bed Liner +165
Camper/Towing Package +255
Cruise Control[Opt on STD] +140

Keyless Entry System +130
Leather Seats +730
Power Door Locks[Opt on STD] +140
Power Drivers Seat +210
Privacy Glass +125
Skid Plates +80
Sliding Rear Window +85
Tilt Steering Wheel[Opt on STD] +135

CAMARO — 1999

Traction control (Acceleration Slip Regulation in Chevrolet parlance) is available on all models in 1999, and on the Z28 ASR allows for some tire slip before killing the power to the rear wheels. Electronic throttle control is newly standard on V6 models, a new engine oil-life monitor tracks specific driving conditions to determine when the next change should occur and a Zexel Torsen differential is employed in the limited-slip rear axle.

RATINGS (SCALE OF 1-10)

Overall	Safety	Reliability	Performance	Comfort	Value
N/A	8	N/A	9	6.8	N/A

Category F

2 Dr STD Conv	14170	17070
2 Dr STD Cpe	11855	14285
2 Dr Z28 Conv	17620	21230
2 Dr Z28 Cpe	15065	18150
2 Dr Z28 SS Conv	20420	24600
2 Dr Z28 SS Cpe	16650	20060

OPTIONS FOR CAMARO
Auto 4-Speed Transmission[Opt on STD] +600
Performance Pkg +1010
*Sport Appearance Pkg +1085 ***
AM/FM Compact Disc Player +355
Alarm System[Opt on STD,Cpe] +140
Aluminum/Alloy Wheels[Opt on STD] +230
Cruise Control[Opt on STD,Cpe] +155
Fog Lights[Opt on STD,Cpe] +135
Glass Panel T-tops +730
Keyless Entry System[Opt on STD,Cpe] +130
Leather Seats +485
Power Door Locks[Opt on STD,Cpe] +150
Power Drivers Seat[Opt on STD,Cpe] +180
Power Mirrors[Opt on STD,Cpe] +95
Power Windows[Opt on STD,Cpe] +165
Rear Window Defroster[Opt on Cpe] +125

CAVALIER — 1999

Chevrolet changes little on this slow-selling compact for 1999. The 2.4 twin cam engine benefits from reliability, emissions and fuel economy enhancements, and new front brake linings increase pad life. Minor interior and exterior revisions have been made, and

Fern Green Metallic and Sandrift Metallic replace Bright Aqua and Deep Purple on the paint chart.

RATINGS (SCALE OF 1-10)

Overall	Safety	Reliability	Performance	Comfort	Value
N/A	6.8	8.8	6.6	7.5	N/A

Category E

	Trade-in	Market
4 Dr LS Sdn	8980	10950
2 Dr RS Cpe	7720	9415
2 Dr STD Cpe	7390	9015
4 Dr STD Sdn	7545	9200
2 Dr Z24 Conv	10535	12845
2 Dr Z24 Cpe	9215	11235

OPTIONS FOR CAVALIER

4 cyl 2.4 L Engine[Opt on LS] +335
Auto 3-Speed Transmission +445
Auto 4-Speed Transmission[Std on LS] +575
AM/FM Compact Disc Player +340
AM/FM Stereo Tape[Std on LS,Z24] +225
Air Conditioning[Std on LS,Z24] +605
Bucket Seats +85
Power Door Locks[Std on Z24] +180
Power Mirrors[Std on Z24] +80
Power Sunroof +455
Power Windows[Std on Z24] +195
Rear Window Defroster[Std on Conv] +120

CORVETTE   1999

A hardtop model aimed at enthusiasts is introduced, and it's options list is short. Other Corvettes can be equipped with numerous options including a new heads-up display and a power tilt/telescope steering wheel.

RATINGS (SCALE OF 1-10)

Overall	Safety	Reliability	Performance	Comfort	Value
N/A	N/A	N/A	8.8	7.1	N/A

Category J

	Trade-in	Market
2 Dr STD Conv	34950	41115
2 Dr STD Cpe	30360	35715
2 Dr STD Hardtop	29615	34840

OPTIONS FOR CORVETTE

6-Speed Transmission[Std on Hardtop] +600
Damping Suspension +1255
Sport Magnesium Wheels +2215
AM/FM Compact Disc Player +325
Bose Sound System +610
Climate Control for AC +200
Dual Power Seats +550
Fog Lights +50
Power Drivers Seat[Opt on Hardtop] +255

EXPRESS   1999

The Chevy Express line of full-size vans now include both the Passenger Van version and the newly renamed Cargo Van, in a variety of configurations, including the G1500 (1/2-ton), G2500 (3/4-ton) and G3500 (1-ton) series. Two wheelbases (135-inches and 155-inches) are available on 2500 and 3500 models. For '99, all Express vans get automatic transmission enhancements to increase durability and improve sealing, plus de-powered dual front airbags. There are also two new exterior paint colors and one new interior shade for the 1999 model year.

RATINGS (SCALE OF 1-10)

Overall	Safety	Reliability	Performance	Comfort	Value
N/A	N/A	N/A	4.8	6.5	N/A

Category H

	Trade-in	Market
2 Dr G15 Cargo Van	13440	15810
2 Dr G15 Pass. Van	16050	18880
2 Dr G15 LS Pass. Van	17795	20935
2 Dr G25 Cargo Van	14205	16710
2 Dr G25 Cargo Van Ext	14640	17225
2 Dr G25 Pass. Van	16610	19540
2 Dr G25 Pass. Van Ext	17110	20130
2 Dr G25 LS Pass. Van	18345	21585
2 Dr G25 LS Pass. Van Ext	18630	21920
2 Dr G35 Cargo Van	14535	17100
2 Dr G35 Cargo Van Ext	14975	17620
2 Dr G35 Pass. Van	17010	20010
2 Dr G35 Pass. Van Ext	17450	20530
2 Dr G35 LS Pass. Van	18750	22060
2 Dr G35 LS Pass. Van Ext	19125	22500

OPTIONS FOR EXPRESS

8 cyl 5.0 L Engine +365
8 cyl 5.7 L Engine[Opt on G15,G25] +750
8 cyl 6.5 L Turbodsl Engine +2115
8 cyl 7.4 L Engine +445
15 Passenger Seating +615
AM/FM Compact Disc Player +230
Air Conditioning[Opt on Cargo Van,Cargo Van Ext] +600
Aluminum/Alloy Wheels +235
Cruise Control[Std on LS] +140
Dual Air Conditioning +990
Keyless Entry System +130
Power Door Locks[Std on LS] +140
Power Drivers Seat +210
Power Windows[Std on LS] +140
Rear Heater +160
Tilt Steering Wheel[Std on LS] +135

LUMINA   1999

Chevrolet adds standard equipment to the LTZ and introduces Auburn Nightmist Medium Metallic to the base and LS models.

Model Description	Trade-in Value	Market Value

RATINGS (SCALE OF 1-10)

Overall	Safety	Reliability	Performance	Comfort	Value
N/A	7.8	7.9	7.4	7.3	N/A

Category C

	Trade-in	Market
4 Dr LS Sdn	11645	14030
4 Dr LTZ Sdn	12035	14500
4 Dr STD Sdn	10350	12470

OPTIONS FOR LUMINA

AM/FM Compact Disc Player +270
Aluminum/Alloy Wheels[Opt on STD] +225
Anti-Lock Brakes[Opt on STD] +450
Keyless Entry System +140
Leather Seats +450
Power Drivers Seat +220
Power Mirrors[Opt on STD] +85

MALIBU 1999

The 1999 Malibu is identical to the 1998 model, unless you consider the addition of Medium Bronzemist Metallic to the paint chart big news.

RATINGS (SCALE OF 1-10)

Overall	Safety	Reliability	Performance	Comfort	Value
N/A	N/A	N/A	8	8.3	N/A

Category C

	Trade-in	Market
4 Dr LS Sdn	11565	13935
4 Dr STD Sdn	9860	11880

OPTIONS FOR MALIBU

6 cyl 3.1 L Engine[Std on LS] +440
AM/FM Stereo Tape[Std on LS] +120
Cruise Control[Std on LS] +155
Power Door Locks[Std on LS] +185
Power Mirrors[Std on LS] +85
Power Windows[Std on LS] +230
Rear Window Defroster[Std on LS] +125

METRO 1999

After getting a makeover last year to mark its move from the old Geo nameplate to the Chevrolet model family, the Metro is a carryover product for 1999, save for the addition of two new exterior colors: Dark Green Metallic and Silver Metallic.

RATINGS (SCALE OF 1-10)

Overall	Safety	Reliability	Performance	Comfort	Value
N/A	6.3	N/A	5.2	6.4	N/A

Category E

	Trade-in	Market
2 Dr LSi Hbk	5470	6670
4 Dr LSi Sdn	6145	7495
2 Dr STD Hbk	5150	6280

OPTIONS FOR METRO

Auto 3-Speed Transmission +440
AM/FM Stereo Tape +225

Air Conditioning +605
Power Steering +190
Rear Window Defroster +120

MONTE CARLO 1999

Deep Purple is gone. No, we're not talking about '70s rock bands here, just metallic paint. Meaning that, except for Medium Auburn Nightmist replacing Deep Purple on Chevy's color availability chart (we could guess what Deep Purple looked like, but Medium Auburn Nightmist?), the Monte Carlo is a carryover model. Unless, of course, you count the availability of the optional OnStar communications system, a 24-hour roadside assistance network that is accessed through a dealer-installed cellular phone.

RATINGS (SCALE OF 1-10)

Overall	Safety	Reliability	Performance	Comfort	Value
N/A	7.6	N/A	7.4	7.5	N/A

Category C

	Trade-in	Market
2 Dr LS Cpe	11365	13695
2 Dr Z34 Cpe	12390	14930

OPTIONS FOR MONTE CARLO

AM/FM Compact Disc Player +270
Aluminum/Alloy Wheels[Opt on LS] +225
Bucket Seats[Opt on LS] +140
Leather Seats +450
Power Drivers Seat +220
Power Moonroof +510
Rear Spoiler +130

PRIZM 1999

After a thorough revision last year, the only changes for 1999 are four new paint colors.

RATINGS (SCALE OF 1-10)

Overall	Safety	Reliability	Performance	Comfort	Value
N/A	7.2	9.2	7.2	7.8	N/A

Category E

	Trade-in	Market
4 Dr LSi Sdn	8470	10330
4 Dr STD Sdn	7215	8800

OPTIONS FOR PRIZM

Auto 3-Speed Transmission +365
Auto 4-Speed Transmission +590
AM/FM Compact Disc Player +340
Air Conditioning[Std on LSi] +605
Power Windows +195
Rear Window Defroster +120
Tilt Steering Wheel +110

S-10 1999

An all-new sport package called the Xtreme replaces the old SS model. All S-10s get automatic transmission enhancements to improve sealing and durability and larger outside mirrors with an optional power heated mirror. Other changes for '99 include a content theft alarm, headlamp flash-to-pass feature, three new exterior paint choices and the availability of GM's AutoTrac electronic push-button transfer case on select four-wheel-drive models.

RATINGS (SCALE OF 1-10)

Overall	Safety	Reliability	Performance	Comfort	Value
N/A	6.5	N/A	6.6	8.1	N/A

Category G

	Trade-in	Market
2 Dr LS Ext Cab SB	9930	11820
2 Dr LS 4WD Ext Cab SB	12800	15240
2 Dr LS Ext Cab Stepside SB	10250	12200
2 Dr LS 4WD Ext Cab Stepside SB		
	13020	15500
2 Dr LS Std Cab LB	8845	10530
2 Dr LS 4WD Std Cab LB	11775	14020
2 Dr LS Std Cab SB	8660	10310
2 Dr LS 4WD Std Cab SB	11540	13740
2 Dr LS Std Cab Stepside SB	9015	10730
2 Dr LS 4WD Std Cab Stepside SB		
	11970	14250
2 Dr LS Wide Stance 4WD Ext Cab SB		
	13660	16260
2 Dr LS Wide Stance 4WD Std Cab SB		
	12395	14755
2 Dr STD Std Cab LB	8190	9750
2 Dr STD 4WD Std Cab LB	12035	14325
2 Dr STD Std Cab SB	8040	9570
2 Dr STD 4WD Std Cab SB	11045	13150

OPTIONS FOR S-10

6 cyl 4.3 L Engine[Std on 4WD] +805
6 cyl 4.3 L Vortec Engine[Std on LS Wide Stance] +680
Auto 4-Speed Transmission +790
AM/FM Compact Disc Player +245
Air Conditioning[Std on ZR2] +605
Aluminum/Alloy Wheels[Std on ZR2] +245
Cruise Control[Std on LS Wide Stance,2 Dr LS 4WD
    Extended Cab Stepside SB] +155
Hinged Third Door (PU)[Opt on LS Xtreme,2,
    LS 4WD Extended Cab SB] +255
Power Door Locks[Opt on LS,LS Xtreme] +170
Power Windows[Opt on LS,LS Xtreme] +175
Privacy Glass[Std on LS Wide Stance,2 Dr LS 4WD
    Extended Cab Stepside SB] +195
Tilt Steering Wheel[Std on LS Wide Stance,2 Dr LS
    4WD Extended Cab Stepside SB] +130

SILVERADO   1999

RATINGS (SCALE OF 1-10)

Overall	Safety	Reliability	Performance	Comfort	Value
N/A	N/A	N/A	7.6	8.5	N/A

SILVERADO 1500

Category H

	Trade-in	Market
2 Dr LS Ext Cab LB	16175	19030
2 Dr LS 4WD Ext Cab LB	18190	21400
2 Dr LS Ext Cab SB	15965	18785
2 Dr LS 4WD Ext Cab SB	18005	21180
2 Dr LS Ext Cab Stepside SB	16425	19325
2 Dr LS 4WD Ext Cab Stepside SB		
	18370	21610
2 Dr LS Std Cab LB	13945	16405
2 Dr LS 4WD Std Cab LB	16365	19250
2 Dr LS Std Cab SB	13785	16220
2 Dr LS 4WD Std Cab SB	16210	19070
2 Dr LS Std Cab Stepside SB	14225	16735
2 Dr LS 4WD Std Cab Stepside SB		
	16575	19500
2 Dr LT Ext Cab LB	18090	21280
2 Dr LT 4WD Ext Cab LB	20495	24110
2 Dr LT Ext Cab SB	17915	21075
2 Dr LT 4WD Ext Cab SB	20315	23900
2 Dr STD Ext Cab LB	13450	15825
2 Dr STD 4WD Ext Cab LB	15515	18250
2 Dr STD Ext Cab SB	13245	15580
2 Dr STD 4WD Ext Cab SB	15295	17995
2 Dr STD Ext Cab Stepside SB	13670	16080
2 Dr STD 4WD Ext Cab Stepside SB		
	15715	18490
2 Dr STD Std Cab LB	11220	13200
2 Dr STD 4WD Std Cab LB	13415	15780
2 Dr STD Std Cab SB	11005	12945
2 Dr STD 4WD Std Cab SB	13245	15580
2 Dr STD Std Cab Stepside SB	11435	13455
2 Dr STD 4WD Std Cab Stepside SB		
	13635	16040

SILVERADO 2500

Category H

	Trade-in	Market
2 Dr LS Ext Cab SB	19635	23100
2 Dr LT Ext Cab SB	21125	24855
2 Dr STD Ext Cab SB	17875	21030

OPTIONS FOR SILVERADO

8 cyl 4.8 L Engine[Opt on Std Cab, 2WD Ext. Cab SB] +440
8 cyl 5.3 L Engine[Std on Silverado 2500,LT] +755
8 cyl 6.0 L Engine +370
Auto 4-Speed Transmission[Std on Silverado 2500,LT] +735
AM/FM Stereo Tape +160
Air Conditioning[Opt on STD] +600
Aluminum/Alloy Wheels[Std on LT] +235
Bucket Seats +280
Camper/Towing Package +255
Chrome Wheels[Std on LS] +220
Cruise Control[Opt on STD] +140

Locking Differential +185
Power Door Locks[Opt on STD] +140
Privacy Glass[Std on LT] +125
Skid Plates +80

SUBURBAN   1999

A couple of new colors are the only modifications to the Suburban as Chevrolet prepares a redesigned model for 2000.

RATINGS (SCALE OF 1-10)

Overall	Safety	Reliability	Performance	Comfort	Value
N/A	8.2	8.1	7	7.9	N/A

Category H

4 Dr C1500 Wgn	20245	23820
4 Dr C2500 Wgn	21465	25250
4 Dr K1500 4WD Wgn	22125	26030
4 Dr K2500 4WD Wgn	23325	27440

OPTIONS FOR SUBURBAN

8 cyl 6.5 L Turbodsl Engine +2115
8 cyl 7.4 L Engine +445
LS Pkg +1640
LT Pkg +2175
AM/FM Compact Disc Player +230
Air Conditioning +600
Aluminum/Alloy Wheels +235
Camper/Towing Package +255
Center & Rear Bench Seat +810
Center Console +105
Cruise Control +140
Dual Air Conditioning +990
Keyless Entry System +130
Leather Seats +730
Luggage Rack +115
Overhead Console +95
Power Drivers Seat +210
Power Mirrors +75
Power Windows +140
Privacy Glass +125
Rear Heater +160
Rear Window Defroster +115
Rear Window Wiper +90
Tilt Steering Wheel +135

TAHOE   1999

The standard cargo net is deleted, and new colors are added as Tahoe cruises into final model year in current guise.

RATINGS (SCALE OF 1-10)

Overall	Safety	Reliability	Performance	Comfort	Value
N/A	N/A	N/A	7.4	8	N/A

Category H

2 Dr LS Utility	19220	22610
2 Dr LS 4WD Utility	20825	24500
4 Dr LS Wgn	20955	24650
4 Dr LS 4WD Wgn	22975	27030
2 Dr LT Utility	20570	24200
2 Dr LT 4WD Utility	21805	25650
4 Dr LT Wgn	22245	26170
4 Dr LT 4WD Wgn	23645	27820
2 Dr STD Utility	17200	20235
2 Dr STD 4WD Utility	18165	21370

OPTIONS FOR TAHOE

8 cyl 6.5 L Turbodsl Engine +2115
Special Z-71 Pkg +1690
Air Conditioning[Opt on STD] +600
Aluminum/Alloy Wheels[Opt on STD] +235
Bucket Seats +280
Camper/Towing Package +255
Compact Disc W/fm/tape[Std on LT] +230
Cruise Control[Opt on STD] +140
Dual Air Conditioning +990
Dual Power Seats +345
Rear Window Defroster[Opt on STD] +115
Running Boards +255
Tilt Steering Wheel[Opt on STD] +135

TRACKER   1999

The redesigned-for-1999 Tracker, available in either two-door convertible or four-door hardtop versions and in two- or four-wheel drive, features sporty new looks, more power, improved ride and handling and a roomier, more comfortable interior.

RATINGS (SCALE OF 1-10)

Overall	Safety	Reliability	Performance	Comfort	Value
N/A	N/A	N/A	6.6	7.4	N/A

Category G

2 Dr STD Conv	7730	9200
2 Dr STD 4WD Conv	8580	10215
4 Dr STD Wgn	8510	10130
4 Dr STD 4WD Wgn	9305	11080

OPTIONS FOR TRACKER

4 cyl 2.0 L Engine[Std on Wgn] +295
Auto 4-Speed Transmission +740
AM/FM Compact Disc Player +245
AM/FM Stereo Tape +170
Air Conditioning +605
Aluminum/Alloy Wheels +245
Cruise Control +155
Luggage Rack +115
Power Door Locks +170
Power Mirrors +100
Power Windows +175
Rear Window Wiper +115
Tilt Steering Wheel +130

Don't forget to refer to the Mileage Adjustment Table at the back of this book!

VENTURE 1999

Venture gets some performance and safety enhancements. Other changes include additional seating choices, four new exterior and two new interior colors, as well as fatter standard tires. What's more, there's a newly badged LT model that packages an upgraded audio system with a touring suspension, traction control and captain's seats with available leather.

RATINGS (SCALE OF 1-10)

Overall	Safety	Reliability	Performance	Comfort	Value
N/A	8	8.5	7.4	7.9	N/A

Category G
4 Dr LS Pass. Van	14825	17650
4 Dr LS Pass. Van Ext	15800	18810
4 Dr LT Pass. Van Ext	17960	21380
4 Dr STD Pass. Van	13735	16350
4 Dr STD Pass. Van Ext	14515	17280

OPTIONS FOR VENTURE
AM/FM Stereo Tape[Std on LS] +170
Compact Disc W/fm/tape[Std on LT] +355
Cruise Control[Opt on STD] +155
Keyless Entry System[Opt on STD] +150
Luggage Rack[Opt on STD] +115
Power Windows[Opt on STD] +175
Privacy Glass[Opt on STD] +195

1998 CHEVROLET

ASTRO 1998

New colors, improved clearcoating, a standard theft deterrent system (like anybody wants to steal one of these) and the addition of composite headlights and an uplevel grille to base models are all that's different on this year's Astro. Full-power airbags continue for 1998.

RATINGS (SCALE OF 1-10)

Overall	Safety	Reliability	Performance	Comfort	Value
7.4	6.9	8.1	6.8	6.5	8.5

Category G
2 Dr LS Pass. Van Ext	12115	14420
2 Dr LS 4WD Pass. Van Ext	14020	16690
2 Dr LT Pass. Van Ext	12725	15150
2 Dr LT 4WD Pass. Van Ext	14450	17200
2 Dr STD Cargo Van Ext	10305	12265
2 Dr STD 4WD Cargo Van Ext	12160	14475
2 Dr STD Pass. Van Ext	11135	13255
2 Dr STD 4WD Pass. Van Ext	12930	15390

OPTIONS FOR ASTRO
AM/FM Compact Disc Player +200
Aluminum/Alloy Wheels[Std on LT] +200
Cruise Control[Opt on STD] +125
Dual Air Conditioning +575
Dual Power Seats +235
Keyless Entry System[Std on LT] +120
Leather Seats +470
Power Door Locks[Opt on STD] +140
Power Drivers Seat[Std on LT] +170
Power Mirrors[Opt on STD] +80
Power Windows[Opt on STD] +145
Rear Heater +125
Rear Window Defroster[Std on LT] +105
Tilt Steering Wheel[Opt on STD] +105

BLAZER 1998

Blazer gets a nose job and an interior redesign. New standard equipment includes a theft deterrent system, automatic headlight control, four-wheel disc brakes and dual airbags incorporating second-generation technology to reduce the bags' inflation force. New radios, colors, and a column-mounted automatic shift selector round out the major changes.

RATINGS (SCALE OF 1-10)

Overall	Safety	Reliability	Performance	Comfort	Value
7.6	7.4	7.7	8	7.9	7

Category G
2 Dr LS Utility	12990	15465
2 Dr LS 4WD Utility	13740	16355
4 Dr LS Wgn	14175	16875
4 Dr LS 4WD Wgn	14725	17530
4 Dr LT Wgn	15035	17900
4 Dr LT 4WD Wgn	15605	18580
2 Dr STD Utility	11810	14060
2 Dr STD 4WD Utility	12070	14370
4 Dr STD Wgn	12700	15120
4 Dr STD 4WD Wgn	13350	15895

OPTIONS FOR BLAZER
Auto 4-Speed Transmission[Opt on Utility] +545
Wide Stance Suspension +1050
AM/FM Compact Disc Player +200
Aluminum/Alloy Wheels[Opt on STD] +200
Cruise Control[Opt on STD] +125
Fog Lights[Opt on LS] +90
Heated Front Seats +160
Keyless Entry System[Opt on LS] +120
Power Door Locks[Opt on STD] +140
Power Drivers Seat[Opt on LS] +170
Power Mirrors +80
Power Sunroof +470
Power Windows[Opt on STD] +145
Rear Window Defroster[Opt on STD] +105
Rear Window Wiper[Opt on STD] +95

Don't forget to refer to the Mileage Adjustment Table at the back of this book!

Model Description	Trade-in Value	Market Value

Model Description	Trade-in Value	Market Value

Sport Suspension +285
Tilt Steering Wheel[Opt on STD] +105

C/K PICKUP 1998

This year's big news is a standard theft deterrent system, revised color choices, and fresh tailgate lettering. The Sport package has been dropped from the option list. Second generation airbags are standard on models under 8,600 GVWR.

RATINGS (SCALE OF 1-10)

Overall	Safety	Reliability	Performance	Comfort	Value
N/A	8	6.9	7.8	8.4	N/A

C/K 1500 SERIES

Category H

	Trade-in	Market
2 Dr C1500 Cheyenne Ext Cab LB	12535	14920
2 Dr C1500 Cheyenne Ext Cab SB	12360	14715
2 Dr C1500 Cheyenne Std Cab LB	10875	12945
2 Dr C1500 Cheyenne Std Cab SB	10720	12760
2 Dr C1500 Cheyenne Std Cab Stepside SB	11140	13260
2 Dr C1500 Silverado Ext Cab LB	13850	16490
2 Dr C1500 Silverado Ext Cab SB	13680	16285
2 Dr C1500 Silverado Ext Cab Stepside SB	14110	16800
2 Dr C1500 Silverado Std Cab LB	12870	15320
2 Dr C1500 Silverado Std Cab SB	12720	15140
2 Dr C1500 Silverado Std Cab Stepside SB	13200	15715
2 Dr C1500 WT Std Cab LB	8820	10500
2 Dr C1500 WT Std Cab SB	8660	10310
2 Dr K1500 Cheyenne 4WD Ext Cab LB	14455	17210
2 Dr K1500 Cheyenne 4WD Ext Cab SB	14320	17050
2 Dr K1500 Cheyenne 4WD Std Cab LB	13690	16300
2 Dr K1500 Cheyenne 4WD Std Cab SB	13530	16105
2 Dr K1500 Cheyenne 4WD Std Cab Stepside SB	13980	16645
2 Dr K1500 Silverado 4WD Ext Cab LB	15815	18830
2 Dr K1500 Silverado 4WD Ext Cab SB	15650	18630
2 Dr K1500 Silverado 4WD Ext Cab Stepside SB	16190	19275
2 Dr K1500 Silverado 4WD Std Cab LB	15295	18210
2 Dr K1500 Silverado 4WD Std Cab SB	15135	18015
2 Dr K1500 Silverado 4WD Std Cab Stepside SB	15420	18355
2 Dr K1500 WT 4WD Std Cab LB	12765	15195
2 Dr K1500 WT 4WD Std Cab SB	12615	15020

C/K 2500 SERIES

Category H

	Trade-in	Market
2 Dr C2500 Cheyenne Ext Cab SB	13265	15790
2 Dr C2500 Cheyenne Std Cab LB	12435	14805
2 Dr C2500 HD Cheyenne Ext Cab LB	13815	16445
2 Dr C2500 HD Silverado Ext Cab LB	15130	18010
2 Dr C2500 Silverado Ext Cab SB	14055	16730
2 Dr C2500 Silverado Std Cab LB	13110	15605
2 Dr K2500 HD Cheyenne 4WD Ext Cab LB	15705	18695
2 Dr K2500 HD Cheyenne 4WD Ext Cab SB	15515	18470
2 Dr K2500 HD Cheyenne 4WD Std Cab LB	14330	17060
2 Dr K2500 HD Silverado 4WD Ext Cab LB	16420	19545
2 Dr K2500 HD Silverado 4WD Ext Cab SB	16220	19310
2 Dr K2500 HD Silverado 4WD Std Cab LB	15280	18190

C/K 3500 SERIES

Category H

	Trade-in	Market
4 Dr C3500 Cheyenne Crew Cab LB	15605	18575
2 Dr C3500 Cheyenne Ext Cab LB	14770	17585
2 Dr C3500 Cheyenne Std Cab LB	13770	16395
4 Dr C3500 Silverado Crew Cab LB	16330	19440
2 Dr C3500 Silverado Ext Cab LB	15580	18545

Don't forget to refer to the Mileage Adjustment Table at the back of this book!

Model Description	Trade-in Value	Market Value
2 Dr C3500 Silverado Std Cab LB	14660	17455
4 Dr K3500 Cheyenne 4WD Crew Cab LB	17205	20480
2 Dr K3500 Cheyenne 4WD Ext Cab LB	16325	19435
2 Dr K3500 Cheyenne 4WD Std Cab LB	15055	17925
4 Dr K3500 Silverado 4WD Crew Cab LB	18075	21520
2 Dr K3500 Silverado 4WD Ext Cab LB	17150	20415
2 Dr K3500 Silverado 4WD Std Cab LB	15885	18910

OPTIONS FOR C/K PICKUP

8 cyl 5.0 L Engine[Std on C1500 Silverado Ext. Cab, C2500, K1500] +305
8 cyl 5.7 L Engine[Opt on C1500, C2500, K1500, K2500 LD] +615
8 cyl 6.5 L Turbodsl Engine +1845
8 cyl 7.4 L Engine +370
Auto 4-Speed Transmission +595
AM/FM Compact Disc Player +190
Air Conditioning[Std on Silverado] +490
Aluminum/Alloy Wheels +190
Bed Liner +135
Camper/Towing Package +205
Cruise Control[Std on Silverado] +115
Hinged Third Door (PU) +255
Keyless Entry System +105
Leather Seats +595
Power Door Locks[Opt on Cheyenne] +115
Power Drivers Seat +170
Rear Window Defroster +95
Skid Plates +65
Sliding Rear Window +70
Tilt Steering Wheel[Std on Silverado] +110

CAMARO 1998

Chevrolet dumps a 305-horsepower version of the Corvette's V8 engine under a new front end, adds standard four-wheel disc brakes on all models, adds a couple of new colors, makes second generation airbags standard, and revises trim levels. The midyear SS package makes 320 horsepower. Uh, why were you considering that Mustang again?

RATINGS (SCALE OF 1-10)

Overall	Safety	Reliability	Performance	Comfort	Value
7.2	8	7.8	9.2	6.8	4.1

Category F

	Trade-in	Market
2 Dr STD Conv	12385	15105
2 Dr STD Cpe	10315	12580
2 Dr Z28 Conv	14950	18230
2 Dr Z28 Cpe	13085	15960
2 Dr Z28 SS Cpe	14695	17920

OPTIONS FOR CAMARO

Auto 4-Speed Transmission[Opt on STD] +500
Performance Pkg +720
Sport Appearance Pkg +910
AM/FM Compact Disc Player +290
Aluminum/Alloy Wheels[Opt on STD] +185
Chrome Wheels +355
Cruise Control[Opt on STD, Cpe] +125
Fog Lights[Opt on STD, Cpe] +110
Glass Panel T-tops +595
Keyless Entry System[Opt on STD, Cpe] +110
Leather Seats +395
Limited Slip Diff[Opt on STD] +205
Power Door Locks[Opt on STD, Cpe] +120
Power Drivers Seat[Opt on STD, Cpe] +150
Power Mirrors[Opt on STD, Cpe] +75
Power Windows[Opt on STD, Z28, Cpe] +135
Rear Window Defroster[Opt on Cpe] +100

CAVALIER 1998

A Z24 convertible is introduced, cruise control is standard on all but base models, power windows and remote keyless entry are no longer available on base cars, and...hold on to your seats, buyers can no longer delete the AM/FM radio. Second-generation airbags debut on all models.

RATINGS (SCALE OF 1-10)

Overall	Safety	Reliability	Performance	Comfort	Value
7.1	6.8	8.3	7	7.6	5.8

Category E

	Trade-in	Market
4 Dr LS Sdn	7970	9840
2 Dr RS Cpe	6895	8515
2 Dr STD Cpe	6540	8075
4 Dr STD Sdn	6720	8295
2 Dr Z24 Conv	9415	11625
2 Dr Z24 Cpe	8105	10005

OPTIONS FOR CAVALIER

4 cyl 2.4 L Engine[Opt on LS] +275
Auto 3-Speed Transmission +370
Auto 4-Speed Transmission[Std on LS] +480
AM/FM Compact Disc Player +275
Air Conditioning[Opt on RS, STD] +495
Aluminum/Alloy Wheels[Std on Z24] +200
Cruise Control[Opt on STD] +135
Keyless Entry System[Std on Z24] +95
Power Door Locks[Std on Z24] +145
Power Mirrors[Std on Z24] +65
Power Sunroof +375
Power Windows[Std on Z24] +160
Rear Window Defroster[Std on Conv] +100
Tilt Steering Wheel[Opt on STD] +90
Traction Control System[Std on LS] +30

CHEVROLET 98

Model Description	Trade-in Value	Market Value	Model Description	Trade-in Value	Market Value

CHEVY VAN/EXPRESS 1998

All vans equipped with airbags switch to mini-module bag designs for the driver, but they still deploy with more force than second-generation types. A theft-deterrent system is standard, and three new colors debut.

CHEVY VAN

Category H

	Trade-in	Market
2 Dr G1500 Chevy Van	12635	15040
2 Dr G2500 Chevy Van	12850	15300
2 Dr G2500 Chevy Van Ext	13195	15710
2 Dr G3500 Chevy Van	12980	15450
2 Dr G3500 Chevy Van Ext	13355	15900

EXPRESS

Category H

	Trade-in	Market
2 Dr G15 Express Van	14150	16845
2 Dr G15 LS Express Van	14820	17640
2 Dr G35 Express Van Ext	15300	18215
2 Dr G35 LS Express Van Ext	16445	19575

OPTIONS FOR CHEVY VAN/EXPRESS
8 cyl 5.0 L Engine +305
8 cyl 5.7 L Engine[Opt on G15, G25 Chevy Van] +615
8 cyl 6.5 L Turbodsl Engine +1845
8 cyl 7.4 L Engine +370
15 Passenger Seating +505
8 Passenger Seating[Std on G15] +225
AM/FM Compact Disc Player +190
Air Conditioning[Opt on Chevy Van, Chevy Van Ext] +490
Aluminum/Alloy Wheels +190
Cruise Control[Std on LS] +115
Dual Air Conditioning +810
Heated Power Mirrors +60
Keyless Entry System +105
Power Door Locks[Std on LS] +115
Power Drivers Seat +170
Power Windows[Std on LS] +115
Rear Heater +130
Tilt Steering Wheel[Std on LS] +110

CORVETTE 1998

Two fresh colors are available, but the new convertible model steals the show. Equipped with a manual folding top, a hard tonneau that extends along the rear wall of the passenger compartment and a real live trunk that holds golf bags, this new drop top should prove quite popular. Lower-powered airbags are not available on the Corvette.

Category J

	Trade-in	Market
2 Dr STD Conv	31835	37900
2 Dr STD Cpe	27890	33205

OPTIONS FOR CORVETTE
6-Speed Transmission +500
Selective Damping System +1040

Sport Magnesium Wheels +1845
AM/FM Compact Disc Player +265
Climate Control for AC +165
Dual Power Seats +450
Fog Lights +40
Glass Targa Top +390

LUMINA 1998

Last year's aborted LTZ sport sedan comes on strong for 1998, with a 200-horsepower 3800 V6 engine and machine-faced aluminum wheels. Four new exterior colors and one new interior color are also available on all Lumina models. To help give Lumina a more upscale image than Malibu, an OnStar Mobile Communications system is a dealer-installed option. Second-generation airbags are standard equipment.

RATINGS (SCALE OF 1-10)

Overall*	Safety	Reliability	Performance	Comfort	Value
7.9	7.8	8	7.6	7.3	8.8

Category C

	Trade-in	Market
4 Dr LS Sdn	9795	11945
4 Dr LTZ Sdn	10170	12400
4 Dr STD Sdn	8585	10470

OPTIONS FOR LUMINA
6 cyl 3.8 L Engine[Opt on LTZ] +265
AM/FM Compact Disc Player +220
Aluminum/Alloy Wheels[Opt on STD] +180
Anti-Lock Brakes[Opt on STD] +370
Cruise Control +130
Keyless Entry System +115
Leather Seats +365
Power Drivers Seat +180
Power Mirrors[Opt on STD] +70
Power Moonroof +415
Power Windows[Opt on STD] +190
Rear Window Defroster +100

MALIBU 1998

Leather trim is newly optional on LS models, aluminum wheels are revised, a sunroof can be ordered and Base models can be equipped with Medium Oak colored interior. Second-generation airbags debut.

RATINGS (SCALE OF 1-10)

Overall	Safety	Reliability	Performance	Comfort	Value
N/A	N/A	8.3	8	8.3	7.5

Category C

	Trade-in	Market
4 Dr LS Sdn	10120	12340
4 Dr STD Sdn	8445	10300

OPTIONS FOR MALIBU
6 cyl 3.1 L Engine[Std on LS] +275
AM/FM Compact Disc Player +220
Aluminum/Alloy Wheels[Std on LS] +180
Cruise Control[Std on LS] +130

Don't forget to refer to the Mileage Adjustment Table at the back of this book!

CHEVROLET 98

Model Description	Trade-in Value	Market Value	Model Description	Trade-in Value	Market Value

Keyless Entry System[Std on LS] +115
Leather Seats +365
Power Door Locks[Std on LS] +150
Power Drivers Seat[Std on LS] +180
Power Mirrors[Std on LS] +70
Power Sunroof +410
Power Windows[Std on LS] +190
Rear Window Defroster[Std on LS] +100

METRO 1998

The Geo badge is replaced with a Chevy bowtie. Styling is updated front and rear. The LSi's four-cylinder engine gets four valves per cylinder for more power and better acceleration. Second-generation airbags are standard equipment. Wheel covers are revised, new radios, new interior fabrics, and the addition of California Gold Metallic to the paint palette round out the changes.

RATINGS (SCALE OF 1-10)

Overall	Safety	Reliability	Performance	Comfort	Value
6.1	6.3	8	5.2	6.4	4.8

Category E
2 Dr LSi Hbk	4900	6050
4 Dr LSi Sdn	5445	6720
2 Dr STD Hbk	4600	5680

OPTIONS FOR METRO

Auto 3-Speed Transmission +355
AM/FM Compact Disc Player +275
Air Conditioning +495
Anti-Lock Brakes +410
Power Door Locks +145
Power Steering +155
Rear Window Defroster +100
Rear Window Wiper +75

MONTE CARLO 1998

The Z34 model gets a different engine and fresh wheels. Second-generation airbags are added. New paint colors and one new interior hue round out the changes.

RATINGS (SCALE OF 1-10)

Overall	Safety	Reliability	Performance	Comfort	Value
7.5	7.6	7.7	7.4	7.5	7.1

Category C
2 Dr LS Cpe	9640	11755
2 Dr Z34 Cpe	10605	12935

OPTIONS FOR MONTE CARLO

AM/FM Compact Disc Player +220
Aluminum/Alloy Wheels[Opt on LS] +180
Cruise Control[Opt on LS] +130
Keyless Entry System[Opt on LS] +115
Leather Seats +365
Power Drivers Seat +180

Power Moonroof +415
Rear Window Defroster +100

PRIZM 1998

The Prizm is completely redesigned, though it might not look like it at first glance. Among the improvements are a larger standard engine, optional side airbags, an optional handling package for LSi models and new colors inside and out. Front airbags are of the de-powered variety.

RATINGS (SCALE OF 1-10)

Overall	Safety	Reliability	Performance	Comfort	Value
7.5	7.2	9.2	7.2	7.8	6

Category E
4 Dr LSi Sdn	7695	9500
4 Dr STD Sdn	6525	8055

OPTIONS FOR PRIZM

Auto 3-Speed Transmission +305
Auto 4-Speed Transmission +490
AM/FM Compact Disc Player +275
Air Conditioning +495
Aluminum/Alloy Wheels +200
Anti-Lock Brakes +410
Cruise Control +135
Power Door Locks[Opt on STD] +145
Power Sunroof +375
Power Windows +160
Rear Window Defroster +100
Side Air Bag Restraint +155
Tilt Steering Wheel +90

S-10 1998

The S-10 gets a sheetmetal makeover and a new interior with dual airbags that incorporate second-generation technology for reduced force deployments. The basic four-cylinder engine benefits from Vortec technology this year, while 4WD models now have four-wheel disc brakes and a more refined transfer case on trucks with an automatic transmission. New radios, automatic headlight control, and a standard theft-deterrent system sum up the changes.

RATINGS (SCALE OF 1-10)

Overall	Safety	Reliability	Performance	Comfort	Value
N/A	6.6	7.3	6.6	8.1	N/A

Category G
2 Dr LS Ext Cab SB	8905	10600
2 Dr LS 4WD Ext Cab SB	11625	13840
2 Dr LS Ext Cab Stepside SB	9180	10930
2 Dr LS 4WD Ext Cab Stepside SB		
	11900	14165
2 Dr LS Std Cab LB	8010	9535
2 Dr LS 4WD Std Cab LB	10710	12750

CHEVROLET 98

Model Description	Trade-in Value	Market Value
2 Dr LS Std Cab SB	7845	9340
2 Dr LS 4WD Std Cab SB	10530	12535
2 Dr LS Std Cab Stepside SB	8175	9730
2 Dr LS 4WD Std Cab Stepside SB	10900	12975
2 Dr STD Std Cab LB	7475	8900
2 Dr STD 4WD Std Cab LB	10440	12430
2 Dr STD Std Cab SB	7325	8720
2 Dr STD 4WD Std Cab SB	10115	12040
2 Dr ZR2 4WD Ext Cab SB	13430	15990
2 Dr ZR2 4WD Std Cab SB	12035	14330

OPTIONS FOR S-10

6 cyl 4.3 L Engine[Opt on 2WD] +670
6 cyl 4.3 L Vortec Engine[Std on ZR2] +495
Auto 4-Speed Transmission[Std on ZR2] +655
AM/FM Compact Disc Player +200
Air Conditioning[Std on ZR2] +495
Aluminum/Alloy Wheels[Opt on LS] +200
Cruise Control[Std on ZR2] +125
Fog Lights +90
Heavy Duty Suspension +85
Hinged Third Door (PU) +205
Keyless Entry System[Opt on LS] +120
Power Door Locks[Opt on LS] +140
Power Mirrors[Opt on LS] +80
Power Windows[Opt on LS] +145
Premium Sound System +210
Skid Plates[Std on ZR2] +80
Sliding Rear Window +70
Sport Suspension +285
Tilt Steering Wheel[Std on ZR2] +105

SUBURBAN   1998

New colors, a standard theft deterrent system, optional heated seats, second generation airbags, and an automatic 4WD system improve the 1998 Suburban.

RATINGS (SCALE OF 1-10)

Overall	Safety	Reliability	Performance	Comfort	Value
7.6	8.1	7.8	7	7.9	7.4

Category H

	Trade-in	Market
4 Dr C1500 Wgn	17975	21400
4 Dr C2500 Wgn	19100	22740
4 Dr K1500 4WD Wgn	19655	23400
4 Dr K2500 4WD Wgn	20800	24760

OPTIONS FOR SUBURBAN

8 cyl 6.5 L Turbodsl Engine[Opt on 2500] +1845
8 cyl 7.4 L Engine[Opt on 2500] +370
LS Pkg +2075
LT Pkg +2470
AM/FM Compact Disc Player +190
Air Conditioning +490
Aluminum/Alloy Wheels +190
Camper/Towing Package +205
Cruise Control +115

Dual Air Conditioning +810
Heated Front Seats +205
Keyless Entry System +105
Leather Seats +595
Power Drivers Seat +170
Power Mirrors +60
Power Windows +115
Privacy Glass +100
Rear Heater +130
Rear Window Defroster +95
Rear Window Wiper +75
Tilt Steering Wheel +110

TAHOE   1998

Autotrac is a new optional automatic four-wheel drive system that switches from 2WD to 4WD automatically as conditions warrant. A new option package includes heated seats and heated exterior mirrors. Second generation airbags deploy with less force than last year. A theft deterrent system is standard, and color selections are modified.

RATINGS (SCALE OF 1-10)

Overall	Safety	Reliability	Performance	Comfort	Value
7.7	8.2	7.7	7.4	8	7.4

Category H

	Trade-in	Market
2 Dr LS Utility	17735	21115
2 Dr LS 4WD Utility	19380	23070
4 Dr LS Wgn	19440	23140
4 Dr LS 4WD Wgn	20850	24820
2 Dr LT Utility	18850	22440
2 Dr LT 4WD Utility	20210	24060
4 Dr LT Wgn	20480	24380
4 Dr LT 4WD Wgn	21690	25820
2 Dr STD Utility	15615	18590
2 Dr STD 4WD Utility	16600	19760

OPTIONS FOR TAHOE

8 cyl 6.5 L Turbodsl Engine[Opt on 2 Dr] +1845
AM/FM Compact Disc Player +190
Air Conditioning[Opt on STD] +490
Aluminum/Alloy Wheels[Opt on STD] +190
Camper/Towing Package +205
Cruise Control[Opt on STD] +115
Heated Front Seats +205
Rear Window Defroster[Opt on STD] +95
Rear Window Wiper[Opt on STD] +75
Running Boards +210
Tilt Steering Wheel[Opt on STD] +110

TRACKER   1998

Geo is gone, so all Trackers are now badged as Chevrolets. The LSi models are dropped, though an LSi equipment package is available on Base models. Two new colors are available. Second-generation airbags are standard.

Don't forget to refer to the Mileage Adjustment Table at the back of this book!

CHEVROLET 98-97

Model Description	Trade-in Value	Market Value	Model Description	Trade-in Value	Market Value

RATINGS (SCALE OF 1-10)

Overall	Safety	Reliability	Performance	Comfort	Value
6.2	5.8	8.6	5.8	6.8	4.2

Category G
2 Dr STD Conv	6780	8070
2 Dr STD 4WD Conv	7595	9040
4 Dr STD 4WD Wgn	8150	9700

OPTIONS FOR TRACKER

Auto 3-Speed Transmission +385
Auto 4-Speed Transmission +615
AM/FM Compact Disc Player +200
Air Conditioning +495
Aluminum/Alloy Wheels +200
Anti-Lock Brakes +365
Auto Locking Hubs (4WD) +155
Cruise Control +125
Power Door Locks +140
Power Mirrors +80
Power Steering[Std on Wgn,4WD] +170
Power Windows +145
Rear Window Wiper +95

VENTURE   1998

Venture is the first minivan to get side-impact airbags. Other changes include the availability of a cargo van edition, a wider variety of dual door models, and an optional power sliding door on regular wheelbase vans. Power rear window vents are also added for 1998. Front airbags deploy with less force thanks to second-generation technology.

RATINGS (SCALE OF 1-10)

Overall	Safety	Reliability	Performance	Comfort	Value
7.6	7.8	7.7	7.8	7.9	7

Category G
2 Dr LS Pass. Van	12265	14600
2 Dr LS Pass. Van Ext	13130	15630
2 Dr STD Pass. Van	11650	13870
2 Dr STD Pass. Van Ext	12450	14820

OPTIONS FOR VENTURE

AM/FM Compact Disc Player +200
Aluminum/Alloy Wheels +200
Cruise Control[Std on LS] +125
Keyless Entry System[Std on LS] +120
Power Drivers Seat +170
Power Windows[Std on LS] +145
Privacy Glass +160
Rear Window Defroster +105
Sliding Driver Side Door +320
Traction Control System +165

1997 CHEVROLET

ASTRO   1997

Daytime running lights debut, and LT models can be equipped with leather upholstery. Also optional this year is a HomeLink three-channel transmitter. Delayed entry/exit lighting is now standard on all Astro passenger vans. Transmission refinements mean smoother shifts, and electronic variable orifice steering eases steering effort at low speeds.

RATINGS (SCALE OF 1-10)

Overall	Safety	Reliability	Performance	Comfort	Value
7.2	6.8	7.4	6.8	6.5	8.4

Category G
2 Dr LS Pass. Van Ext	10510	12665
2 Dr LS 4WD Pass. Van Ext	12005	14465
2 Dr LT Pass. Van Ext	11010	13265
2 Dr LT 4WD Pass. Van Ext	12440	14990
2 Dr STD Cargo Van Ext	8630	10395
2 Dr STD 4WD Cargo Van Ext	10085	12150
2 Dr STD Pass. Van Ext	9580	11545
2 Dr STD 4WD Pass. Van Ext	11045	13310

OPTIONS FOR ASTRO

8 Passenger Seating[Opt on STD] +195
AM/FM Compact Disc Player +160
Aluminum/Alloy Wheels[Std on LT] +165
Child Seats (2) +125
Cruise Control[Opt on STD] +105
Dual Air Conditioning +470
Keyless Entry System[Std on LT] +100
Leather Seats +385
Power Door Locks[Opt on STD] +115
Power Drivers Seat[Std on LT] +140
Power Mirrors[Std on LT] +65
Power Windows[Opt on STD] +120
Privacy Glass[Opt on STD] +130
Rear Heater +100
Tilt Steering Wheel[Opt on STD] +85

BLAZER   1997

Those who prefer a liftgate over a tailgate have that option on 1997 four-door Blazers. A power sunroof is a new option for all Blazers, and models equipped with LT decor are equipped with a HomeLink transmitter that will open your garage, among other things. All-wheel drive Blazers get four-wheel disc brakes, and automatic transmissions are revised for smoother shifting. Early production 4WD two-door Blazers could be ordered with a ZR2 suspension package, but by the time we got pricing, Chevrolet had cancelled the option. Base Blazers get a chrome grille, while LT four-

Model Description	Trade-in Value	Market Value

door models have body-color grilles in six exterior colors. Two new paint colors round out the changes.

RATINGS (SCALE OF 1-10)

Overall	Safety	Reliability	Performance	Comfort	Value
7.1	5.3	7.4	8	7.9	6.9

Category G

	Trade-in	Market
2 Dr LS Utility	11600	13975
2 Dr LS 4WD Utility	12250	14760
4 Dr LS Wgn	12545	15115
4 Dr LS 4WD Wgn	13220	15925
4 Dr LT Wgn	13450	16205
4 Dr LT 4WD Wgn	14065	16945
2 Dr STD Utility	10345	12465
2 Dr STD 4WD Utility	11010	13265
4 Dr STD Wgn	11340	13660
4 Dr STD 4WD Wgn	11885	14320

OPTIONS FOR BLAZER

Auto 4-Speed Transmission[Std on Wgn] +445
Wide Stance Suspension +930
AM/FM Compact Disc Player +160
Aluminum/Alloy Wheels[Opt on STD] +165
Cruise Control[Opt on STD] +105
Keyless Entry System[Opt on LS] +100
Power Door Locks[Opt on STD] +115
Power Drivers Seat[Opt on LS] +140
Power Mirrors[Opt on STD] +65
Power Sunroof +385
Power Windows[Opt on STD] +120
Running Boards +190
Skid Plates +65
Swing Out Tire Carrier[Opt on 4WD,Utility] +95
Tilt Steering Wheel[Opt on STD] +85

C/K PICKUP   1997

Order a truck under 8,600 lbs. GVWR, and you'll get a passenger airbag. The airbag can be deactivated when a rear-facing child safety seat is installed. Low-speed steering effort is reduced this year, and a refined transmission fluid pump results in smoother shifts. An alternative fuel version of the Vortec 5700 is available, but only on a specific model. K1500's get a tighter turning radius, and three new colors debut. The third door option will be more widely available, because it is now a required option on all C/K 1500 shortbed extended cab trucks.

RATINGS (SCALE OF 1-10)

Overall	Safety	Reliability	Performance	Comfort	Value
N/A	8	6.7	7.8	8.4	N/A

C/K 1500 SERIES

Category H

	Trade-in	Market
2 Dr C1500 Cheyenne Ext Cab LB	11250	13390
2 Dr C1500 Cheyenne Ext Cab SB	11095	13210
2 Dr C1500 Cheyenne Ext Cab Stepside SB	11460	13645
2 Dr C1500 Cheyenne Std Cab LB	10105	12030
2 Dr C1500 Cheyenne Std Cab SB	9960	11860
2 Dr C1500 Cheyenne Std Cab Stepside SB	10230	12180
2 Dr C1500 Silverado Ext Cab LB	12490	14870
2 Dr C1500 Silverado Ext Cab SB	12340	14690
2 Dr C1500 Silverado Ext Cab Stepside SB	12710	15130
2 Dr C1500 Silverado Std Cab LB	11995	14280
2 Dr C1500 Silverado Std Cab SB	11850	14105
2 Dr C1500 Silverado Std Cab Stepside SB	12210	14535
2 Dr C1500 WT Std Cab LB	8300	9880
2 Dr C1500 WT Std Cab SB	8130	9680
2 Dr K1500 Cheyenne 4WD Ext Cab LB	13075	15565
2 Dr K1500 Cheyenne 4WD Ext Cab SB	12910	15370
2 Dr K1500 Cheyenne 4WD Ext Cab Stepside SB	13285	15815
2 Dr K1500 Cheyenne 4WD Std Cab LB	12260	14595
2 Dr K1500 Cheyenne 4WD Std Cab SB	12110	14415
2 Dr K1500 Cheyenne 4WD Std Cab Stepside SB	12520	14905
2 Dr K1500 Silverado 4WD Ext Cab LB	14315	17040
2 Dr K1500 Silverado 4WD Ext Cab SB	14095	16780
2 Dr K1500 Silverado 4WD Ext Cab Stepside SB	14530	17300
2 Dr K1500 Silverado 4WD Std Cab LB	13665	16270
2 Dr K1500 Silverado 4WD Std Cab SB	13470	16035
2 Dr K1500 Silverado 4WD Std Cab Stepside SB	13830	16465
2 Dr K1500 WT 4WD Std Cab LB	10460	12455
2 Dr K1500 WT 4WD Std Cab SB	10285	12245

Model Description	Trade-in Value	Market Value

C/K 2500 SERIES
Category H

Model Description	Trade-in Value	Market Value
2 Dr C2500 Cheyenne Ext Cab SB	11460	13640
2 Dr C2500 Cheyenne Std Cab LB	10435	12420
2 Dr C2500 HD Cheyenne Ext Cab LB	12070	14370
2 Dr C2500 HD Silverado Ext Cab LB	13610	16200
2 Dr C2500 Silverado Ext Cab SB	12750	15180
2 Dr C2500 Silverado Std Cab LB	11705	13935
2 Dr K2500 HD Cheyenne 4WD Ext Cab LB	14065	16745
2 Dr K2500 HD Cheyenne 4WD Ext Cab SB	13930	16585
2 Dr K2500 HD Cheyenne 4WD Std Cab LB	12960	15430
2 Dr K2500 HD Silverado 4WD Ext Cab LB	14620	17405
2 Dr K2500 HD Silverado 4WD Ext Cab SB	14505	17265
2 Dr K2500 HD Silverado 4WD Std Cab LB	13585	16170

C/K 3500 SERIES
Category H

Model Description	Trade-in Value	Market Value
4 Dr C3500 Cheyenne Crew Cab LB	14195	16900
2 Dr C3500 Cheyenne Ext Cab LB	13345	15885
2 Dr C3500 Cheyenne Std Cab LB	12665	15075
4 Dr C3500 Silverado Crew Cab LB	15475	18420
2 Dr C3500 Silverado Ext Cab LB	14675	17470
2 Dr C3500 Silverado Std Cab LB	13865	16505
4 Dr K3500 Cheyenne 4WD Crew Cab LB	16405	19530
2 Dr K3500 Cheyenne 4WD Ext Cab LB	15515	18470
2 Dr K3500 Cheyenne 4WD Std Cab LB	14240	16950
4 Dr K3500 Silverado 4WD Crew Cab LB	17305	20600
2 Dr K3500 Silverado 4WD Ext Cab LB	16420	19550
2 Dr K3500 Silverado 4WD Std Cab LB	15055	17920

OPTIONS FOR C/K PICKUP
8 cyl 5.0 L Engine +250
8 cyl 5.7 L Engine +520
8 cyl 6.5 L Turbodsl Engine +1535
8 cyl 7.4 L Engine +300
Auto 4-Speed Transmission +485
AM/FM Compact Disc Player +155
Air Conditioning[Std on Silverado] +400
Aluminum/Alloy Wheels +155
Automatic Dimming Mirror[Std on Crew Cab] +70
Bed Liner +110
Camper/Towing Package +170
Cruise Control[Std on Silverado] +95
Hinged Third Door (PU) +205
Keyless Entry System +85
Leather Seats +485
Power Door Locks[Opt on Cheyenne] +95
Power Drivers Seat +140
Tilt Steering Wheel[Std on Silverado] +90

CAMARO 1997

Chevrolet celebrates the Camaro's 30th Anniversary with a special-edition Z28 that emulates the appearance of the 1969 SS Indy Pace Car with white paint, Hugger Orange stripes, and black-and-white houndstooth seat inserts. Interior revisions to seats, center console and dashboard freshen the look inside for 1997. Two new shades of gray are available for interiors, while exteriors get new green and purple hues. Tri-color taillamps debut, and new five-spoke alloy wheels are optional. On the safety front, daytime running lights are standard and side-impact regulations are met.

RATINGS (SCALE OF 1-10)

Overall	Safety	Reliability	Performance	Comfort	Value
7.2	7.9	7.4	9.2	6.8	4.5

Category F

Model	Trade-in	Market
2 Dr RS Conv	11160	13610
2 Dr RS Cpe	9955	12140
2 Dr STD Conv	10335	12605
2 Dr STD Cpe	8760	10680
2 Dr Z28 Conv	12650	15425
2 Dr Z28 Cpe	11235	13700
2 Dr Z28 SS Cpe	12840	15660

OPTIONS FOR CAMARO
Auto 4-Speed Transmission[Std on Z28,SS] +395
Performance Pkg +570
Sport Suspension Pkg +590
Torsen Torque Sensing Axle +500

Don't forget to refer to the Mileage Adjustment Table at the back of this book!

CHEVROLET 97

Model Description	Trade-in Value	Market Value	Model Description	Trade-in Value	Market Value

AM/FM Compact Disc Player +235
Aluminum/Alloy Wheels[Opt on STD] +150
Cruise Control +105
Fog Lights +90
Glass Panel T-tops +490
Keyless Entry System +90
Leather Seats +325
Limited Slip Diff[Opt on RS,STD] +170
Power Door Locks +100
Power Drivers Seat +120
Power Mirrors +60
Power Windows +110

CAVALIER   1997

The historically on-again off-again Rally Sport (RS) trim level is evidently on-again, attached for 1997 to the coupe and slotted between base and Z24 editions of the Cavalier. RS trim nets buyers the rear spoiler from the Z24, 15-inch tires, AM/FM stereo, tachometer, interior and exterior trim goodies, and a really cool (yeah, right) 3D rear quarter panel decal. Base coupes have new wheel covers and safety belt guide loops. All 1997 Cavaliers meet federal side-impact standards for the first time. One new interior color and three new exterior colors freshen the lineup.

RATINGS (SCALE OF 1-10)

Overall	Safety	Reliability	Performance	Comfort	Value
6.7	6.5	7.3	7	7.6	5.3

Category E

2 Dr LS Conv	7690	9735
4 Dr LS Sdn	6650	8415
2 Dr RS Cpe	5920	7495
2 Dr STD Cpe	5590	7075
4 Dr STD Sdn	5750	7280
2 Dr Z24 Cpe	6960	8810

OPTIONS FOR CAVALIER

4 cyl 2.4 L Engine[Opt on LS, Z24] +215
Auto 3-Speed Transmission[Std on LS] +265
Auto 4-Speed Transmission[Std on LS] +385
AM/FM Compact Disc Player +225
Air Conditioning[Opt on RS,STD] +405
Aluminum/Alloy Wheels[Std on Z24] +165
Cruise Control +110
Keyless Entry System +80
Power Door Locks +120
Power Mirrors +55
Power Sunroof +305
Power Windows +130
Tilt Steering Wheel[Std on Z24] +75

CHEVY VAN/EXPRESS   1997

Dual airbags appear on the G3500 model, while daytime running lights and three fresh exterior colors make this van easier to see. (Editor's Note: If you can't

see this monster van without DRL's, perhaps you should consider surrendering your driver's license.) Electronic variable orifice steering reduces effort at low speeds for easier parking, and automatic transmissions shift more smoothly.

CHEVY VAN

Category H

2 Dr G1500 Chevy Van	11065	13170
2 Dr G2500 Chevy Van	11180	13310
2 Dr G2500 Chevy Van Ext	11440	13620
2 Dr G3500 Chevy Van	11280	13430
2 Dr G3500 Chevy Van Ext	11590	13800

EXPRESS

Category H

2 Dr G1500 Express Van	12365	14720
2 Dr G1500 LS Express Van	13505	16075

OPTIONS FOR CHEVY VAN/EXPRESS

8 cyl 5.0 L Engine +250
8 cyl 5.7 L Engine[Opt on G15] +520
8 cyl 6.5 L Turbodsl Engine +1535
8 cyl 7.4 L Engine +300
15 Passenger Seating +410
8 Passenger Seating[Std on G15] +180
AM/FM Compact Disc Player +155
Aluminum/Alloy Wheels +155
Cruise Control[Std on LS] +95
Dual Air Conditioning +660
Keyless Entry System +85
Power Door Locks[Std on LS] +95
Power Drivers Seat +140
Power Windows[Std on LS] +95
Privacy Glass +85
Rear Heater +105
Tilt Steering Wheel[Std on LS] +90

CORVETTE   1997

Fifth-generation Corvette debuts 44 years after the original, and is better than ever with world-class build quality and performance at a bargain price.

Category J

2 Dr STD Cpe	26290	31295

OPTIONS FOR CORVETTE

6-Speed Transmission +445
Selective Damping System +925
AM/FM Compact Disc Player +215
Climate Control for AC +135
Dual Power Seats +365
Fog Lights +35
Glass Targa Top +320
Solid & Glass Targa Tops +465
Sport Seats +370

Don't forget to refer to the Mileage Adjustment Table at the back of this book!

Model Description	Trade-in Value	Market Value	Model Description	Trade-in Value	Market Value

LUMINA 1997

Performance-oriented Lumina LTZ debuts, though a spoiler, special front and rear styling, graphics, and alloy wheels don't amount to performance in our book. Daytime running lamps are standard on all Luminas, and the power sunroof expected last year finally arrives. New colors and an oil life monitor round out changes to Lumina for 1997.

RATINGS (SCALE OF 1-10)

Overall	Safety	Reliability	Performance	Comfort	Value
7.7	7.8	7.8	7.6	7.3	8.2

Category C

4 Dr LS Sdn	7985	9855
4 Dr LTZ Sdn	8350	10310
4 Dr STD Sdn	7210	8900

OPTIONS FOR LUMINA

6 cyl 3.4 L Engine +550
AM/FM Compact Disc Player +180
Aluminum/Alloy Wheels[Opt on STD] +150
Anti-Lock Brakes[Opt on STD] +300
Child Seat (1) +60
Cruise Control[Std on LS] +105
Keyless Entry System +95
Leather Seats +300
Power Drivers Seat +145
Power Moonroof +340
Power Windows[Opt on STD] +155

MALIBU 1997

Malibu returns after consumer clinics tell Chevrolet they want a tight, solid, roomy, fun-to-drive midsize sedan. Guess what? Chevrolet delivers.

RATINGS (SCALE OF 1-10)

Overall	Safety	Reliability	Performance	Comfort	Value
N/A	N/A	7.3	8	8.3	N/A

Category C

4 Dr LS Sdn	8815	10880
4 Dr STD Sdn	7065	8720

OPTIONS FOR MALIBU

6 cyl 3.1 L Engine[Std on LS] +215
AM/FM Compact Disc Player +180
Aluminum/Alloy Wheels[Std on LS] +150
Cruise Control[Std on LS] +105
Keyless Entry System[Std on LS] +95
Power Door Locks[Std on LS] +125
Power Drivers Seat[Std on LS] +145
Power Mirrors[Std on LS] +55
Power Windows[Std on LS] +155
Rear Window Defroster[Std on LS] +80

MONTE CARLO 1997

Hot-rod Z34 gets a new transmission, while all models have daytime running lights. Newly optional is a power sunroof. Two new colors freshen the rather dull sheetmetal.

RATINGS (SCALE OF 1-10)

Overall	Safety	Reliability	Performance	Comfort	Value
7.3	7.6	7.5	7.4	7.5	6.5

Category C

2 Dr LS Cpe	8330	10285
2 Dr Z34 Cpe	9265	11440

OPTIONS FOR MONTE CARLO

AM/FM Compact Disc Player +180
Aluminum/Alloy Wheels[Opt on LS] +150
Cruise Control[Opt on LS] +105
Keyless Entry System[Opt on LS] +95
Leather Seats +300
Power Drivers Seat +145
Power Sunroof +335

S-10 1997

Chevy strengthens the 2WD S-10 frame by using tougher components. Refinements to the automatic transmission result in improved efficiency and smoother shifts. 4WD models have lighter-weight plug-in half shafts. Two new colors are available.

RATINGS (SCALE OF 1-10)

Overall	Safety	Reliability	Performance	Comfort	Value
N/A	5	7.1	6.6	8.1	N/A

Category G

2 Dr LS Ext Cab SB	7660	9230
2 Dr LS 4WD Ext Cab SB	10190	12280
2 Dr LS Ext Cab Stepside SB	7925	9550
2 Dr LS 4WD Ext Cab Stepside SB	10290	12400
2 Dr LS Std Cab LB	7010	8445
2 Dr LS 4WD Std Cab LB	9215	11100
2 Dr LS Std Cab SB	6855	8260
2 Dr LS 4WD Std Cab SB	9040	10890
2 Dr LS Std Cab Stepside SB	7175	8645
2 Dr LS 4WD Std Cab Stepside SB	9365	11285
2 Dr STD Std Cab LB	6890	8300
2 Dr STD 4WD Std Cab LB	8760	10555
2 Dr STD Std Cab SB	6740	8120
2 Dr STD 4WD Std Cab SB	8670	10445

OPTIONS FOR S-10

6 cyl 4.3 L Engine[Opt on 2WD] +495
6 cyl 4.3 L Vortec Engine +380
Auto 4-Speed Transmission +535

Don't forget to refer to the Mileage Adjustment Table at the back of this book!

CHEVROLET 97

Model Description	Trade-in Value	Market Value	Model Description	Trade-in Value	Market Value

Wide Stance Suspension +845
AM/FM Compact Disc Player +160
Air Conditioning +405
Aluminum/Alloy Wheels +165
Cruise Control +105
Heavy Duty Suspension +70
Hinged Third Door (PU) +170
Keyless Entry System +100
Power Door Locks +115
Power Mirrors +65
Power Windows +120
Skid Plates +65
Tilt Steering Wheel +85

SUBURBAN 1997

Dual airbags debut, and a cargo area power lock switch makes locking up the vehicle after unloading cargo more convenient. Electronic Variable Orifice power steering lightens low-speed steering effort, and automatic transmissions are improved. Two new exterior colors are added to the paint roster.

RATINGS (SCALE OF 1-10)

Overall	Safety	Reliability	Performance	Comfort	Value
7.5	8.1	7.3	7	7.9	7.2

Category H

	Trade-in	Market
4 Dr C1500 Wgn	16125	19195
4 Dr C2500 Wgn	17135	20400
4 Dr K1500 4WD Wgn	17655	21020
4 Dr K2500 4WD Wgn	18715	22280

OPTIONS FOR SUBURBAN

8 cyl 6.5 L Turbodsl Engine +1535
8 cyl 7.4 L Engine +300
LS Pkg +1765
LT Pkg +1570
AM/FM Compact Disc Player +155
Air Conditioning +400
Aluminum/Alloy Wheels +155
Automatic Dimming Mirror[Std on K2500] +70
Camper/Towing Package +170
Cruise Control +95
Dual Air Conditioning +660
Keyless Entry System +85
Leather Seats +485
Power Drivers Seat +140
Power Mirrors +50
Power Windows +95
Privacy Glass +85
Rear Heater +105
Tilt Steering Wheel +90

TAHOE 1997

A passenger-side airbag is added, and the automatic transmission is improved. Electronic Variable Orifice steering debuts, and cargo areas have a power door lock switch. A new center console comes with high-back bucket seats, and two new paint colors are available.

RATINGS (SCALE OF 1-10)

Overall	Safety	Reliability	Performance	Comfort	Value
7.7	8.2	7.4	7.4	8	7.3

Category H

	Trade-in	Market
2 Dr LS Utility	16155	19230
2 Dr LS 4WD Utility	17655	21020
4 Dr LS Wgn	17885	21290
4 Dr LS 4WD Wgn	19255	22925
2 Dr LT Utility	17095	20350
2 Dr LT 4WD Utility	18400	21905
4 Dr LT Wgn	18740	22310
4 Dr LT 4WD Wgn	20095	23920
2 Dr STD 4WD Utility	15370	18300

OPTIONS FOR TAHOE

8 cyl 6.5 L Turbodsl Engine +1535
AM/FM Compact Disc Player +155
Air Conditioning[Opt on STD] +400
Aluminum/Alloy Wheels[Opt on STD] +155
Camper/Towing Package +170
Cruise Control[Opt on STD] +95
Keyless Entry System[Std on LT,LS Utility] +85
Power Drivers Seat[Opt on LS] +140
Privacy Glass[Opt on STD] +85
Tilt Steering Wheel[Opt on STD] +90
Velour/Cloth Seats[Std on LS] +65

VENTURE 1997

Complete redesign of Chevy's minivan results in a new name, a left-side sliding door, optional traction control, a powerful standard engine, and a fun-to-drive demeanor. Nice van, except for the big chrome grille.

RATINGS (SCALE OF 1-10)

Overall	Safety	Reliability	Performance	Comfort	Value
7.4	7	7.6	7.8	7.9	6.8

Category G

	Trade-in	Market
2 Dr LS Pass. Van	10705	12900
2 Dr LS Pass. Van Ext	11295	13610
2 Dr STD Pass. Van	10195	12285
2 Dr STD Pass. Van Ext	10980	13230

OPTIONS FOR VENTURE

AM/FM Compact Disc Player +160
Aluminum/Alloy Wheels +165
Child Seat (1) +85
Cruise Control +105
Dual Air Conditioning +470
Keyless Entry System +100
Power Drivers Seat +140
Power Windows +120
Privacy Glass +130

Don't forget to refer to the Mileage Adjustment Table at the back of this book!

Sliding Driver Side Door +260
Traction Control System +135

1996 CHEVROLET

ASTRO   1996

A new interior with dual airbags, new radio systems, an improved V6, and three new paint colors are the changes for this year.

RATINGS (SCALE OF 1-10)

Overall	Safety	Reliability	Performance	Comfort	Value
7.2	6.9	7.5	6.8	6.5	8.3

Category G

2 Dr LS Pass. Van Ext	9090	11220
2 Dr LS 4WD Pass. Van Ext	10005	12350
2 Dr LT Pass. Van Ext	9520	11755
2 Dr LT 4WD Pass. Van Ext	10465	12920
2 Dr STD Cargo Van Ext	6845	8450
2 Dr STD 4WD Cargo Van Ext	8490	10480
2 Dr STD Pass. Van Ext	8085	9980
2 Dr STD 4WD Pass. Van Ext	9220	11385

OPTIONS FOR ASTRO

8 Passenger Seating[Opt on STD] +160
AM/FM Compact Disc Player +135
Aluminum/Alloy Wheels[Std on LT] +135
Child Seats (2) +105
Cruise Control[Opt on STD] +85
Dual Air Conditioning +385
Keyless Entry System[Std on LT] +80
Power Door Locks[Opt on STD] +95
Power Drivers Seat[Std on LT] +115
Power Mirrors[Std on LT] +55
Power Windows[Opt on STD] +95
Privacy Glass[Opt on STD] +110
Rear Heater +80
Tilt Steering Wheel[Opt on STD] +70

BERETTA   1996

Final year for Beretta. Only change is the addition of long-life coolant to the engine.

RATINGS (SCALE OF 1-10)

Overall	Safety	Reliability	Performance	Comfort	Value
6.8	6.4	7.7	7.8	7	5

Category E

2 Dr STD Cpe	4930	6485
2 Dr Z26 Cpe	6075	7995

OPTIONS FOR BERETTA

6 cyl 3.1 L Engine[Opt on STD] +190
Auto 3-Speed Transmission +215
Auto 4-Speed Transmission[Opt on STD] +295
AM/FM Compact Disc Player +185
Aluminum/Alloy Wheels +135

Cruise Control +90
Power Windows +105
Sunroof +140
Tilt Steering Wheel +60

BLAZER   1996

More power, available all-wheel drive, and five new colors improve the 1996 Blazer. A five-speed manual transmission is optional on two-door models.

RATINGS (SCALE OF 1-10)

Overall	Safety	Reliability	Performance	Comfort	Value
6.4	4.9	6.6	8	7.9	4.8

Category G

2 Dr LS Utility	10135	12510
2 Dr LS 4WD Utility	10990	13570
4 Dr LS Wgn	10940	13505
4 Dr LS 4WD Wgn	11765	14525
4 Dr LT Wgn	11775	14535
4 Dr LT 4WD Wgn	12510	15445
2 Dr STD Utility	8865	10945
2 Dr STD 4WD Utility	9645	11905
4 Dr STD Wgn	9770	12060
4 Dr STD 4WD Wgn	10455	12910

OPTIONS FOR BLAZER

Auto 4-Speed Transmission[Std on Wgn] +350
AM/FM Compact Disc Player +135
Cruise Control[Opt on STD] +85
Keyless Entry System[Std on LT] +80
Power Door Locks[Opt on STD] +95
Power Drivers Seat[Std on LT] +115
Power Mirrors[Opt on STD] +55
Power Windows[Opt on STD] +95
Running Boards +155
Skid Plates +55
Tilt Steering Wheel[Opt on STD] +70

C/K PICKUP   1996

Major engine improvements result in more horsepower and torque. Extended-cab models can be equipped with an access panel that opens to the rear of the cab from the passenger side of the truck. Daytime running lights are added, and K1500 models offer an optional electronic shift transfer case.

RATINGS (SCALE OF 1-10)

Overall	Safety	Reliability	Performance	Comfort	Value
N/A	7.4	6	7.8	8.4	N/A

C/K 1500 SERIES

Category H

2 Dr C1500 Cheyenne Ext Cab LB	10290	12400
2 Dr C1500 Cheyenne Ext Cab SB	10145	12220

Don't forget to refer to the Mileage Adjustment Table at the back of this book!

Model Description	Trade-in Value	Market Value
2 Dr C1500 Cheyenne Ext Cab Stepside SB	10415	12550
2 Dr C1500 Cheyenne Std Cab LB	9205	11090
2 Dr C1500 Cheyenne Std Cab SB	9005	10850
2 Dr C1500 Cheyenne Std Cab Stepside SB	9280	11180
2 Dr C1500 Silverado Ext Cab LB	11170	13460
2 Dr C1500 Silverado Ext Cab SB	11000	13250
2 Dr C1500 Silverado Ext Cab Stepside SB	11420	13760
2 Dr C1500 Silverado Std Cab LB	10400	12530
2 Dr C1500 Silverado Std Cab SB	10215	12310
2 Dr C1500 Silverado Std Cab Stepside SB	10670	12855
2 Dr C1500 WT Std Cab LB	7675	9245
2 Dr C1500 WT Std Cab SB	7475	9005
2 Dr K1500 Cheyenne 4WD Ext Cab LB	11830	14250
2 Dr K1500 Cheyenne 4WD Ext Cab SB	11705	14105
2 Dr K1500 Cheyenne 4WD Ext Cab Stepside SB	11965	14415
2 Dr K1500 Cheyenne 4WD Std Cab LB	11115	13390
2 Dr K1500 Cheyenne 4WD Std Cab SB	10955	13200
2 Dr K1500 Cheyenne 4WD Std Cab Stepside SB	11265	13575
2 Dr K1500 Silverado 4WD Ext Cab LB	12805	15425
2 Dr K1500 Silverado 4WD Ext Cab SB	12625	15210
2 Dr K1500 Silverado 4WD Ext Cab Stepside SB	12950	15600
2 Dr K1500 Silverado 4WD Std Cab LB	12190	14685
2 Dr K1500 Silverado 4WD Std Cab SB	12045	14510
2 Dr K1500 Silverado 4WD Std Cab Stepside SB	12325	14850
2 Dr K1500 WT 4WD Std Cab LB	9405	11330
2 Dr K1500 WT 4WD Std Cab SB	9305	11210

C/K 2500 SERIES
Category H

Model Description	Trade-in Value	Market Value
2 Dr C2500 Cheyenne Ext Cab SB	10055	12115
2 Dr C2500 Cheyenne Std Cab LB	9375	11295
2 Dr C2500 HD Cheyenne Ext Cab LB	10230	12325
2 Dr C2500 HD Silverado Ext Cab LB	11660	14050
2 Dr C2500 Silverado Std Cab LB	10315	12430
2 Dr K2500 Cheyenne 4WD Ext Cab LB	11705	14100
2 Dr K2500 Cheyenne 4WD Ext Cab SB	11555	13920
2 Dr K2500 Cheyenne 4WD Std Cab LB	10880	13110
2 Dr K2500 Silverado 4WD Ext Cab LB	12730	15335
2 Dr K2500 Silverado 4WD Ext Cab SB	12610	15195
2 Dr K2500 Silverado 4WD Std Cab LB	11950	14400

C/K 3500 SERIES
Category H

Model Description	Trade-in Value	Market Value
4 Dr C3500 Cheyenne Crew Cab LB	12510	15070
2 Dr C3500 Cheyenne Ext Cab LB	11785	14200
2 Dr C3500 Cheyenne Std Cab LB	11165	13450
4 Dr C3500 Silverado Crew Cab LB	13860	16700
2 Dr C3500 Silverado Ext Cab LB	13120	15805
2 Dr C3500 Silverado Std Cab LB	12170	14665
4 Dr K3500 Cheyenne 4WD Crew Cab LB	13755	16570
2 Dr K3500 Cheyenne 4WD Ext Cab LB	13265	15980
2 Dr K3500 Cheyenne 4WD Std Cab LB	12705	15310
4 Dr K3500 Silverado 4WD Crew Cab LB	15050	18130
2 Dr K3500 Silverado 4WD Ext Cab LB	14170	17070
2 Dr K3500 Silverado 4WD Std Cab LB	13280	16000

Don't forget to refer to the Mileage Adjustment Table at the back of this book!

Model Description	Trade-in Value	Market Value

OPTIONS FOR C/K PICKUP

8 cyl 5.0 L Engine +230
8 cyl 5.7 L Engine +410
8 cyl 6.5 L Turbodsl Engine +1340
8 cyl 7.4 L Engine +245
Auto 4-Speed Transmission +390
Silverado Pkg 2 +615
AM/FM Compact Disc Player +125
Air Conditioning[Std on Silverado] +330
Automatic Dimming Mirror +60
Bed Liner +90
Camper/Towing Package +140
Cruise Control[Std on Silverado] +75
Hinged Third Door (PU) +170
Keyless Entry System +70
Leather Seats +400
Power Door Locks[Std on Silverado] +75
Power Drivers Seat +115
Tilt Steering Wheel[Std on Silverado] +75

CAMARO 1996

Hot, new, 200 hp base V6 whumps the Mustang. Z28's 285 hp, LT1 V8 (with 10 more horsepower this year), whumps the Mustang GT. SLP Engineering provides a 305-horse Z28 SS, which ties the new Mustang Cobra for horsepower. The RS trim level returns, and chrome aluminum wheels are optional.

RATINGS (SCALE OF 1-10)

Overall	Safety	Reliability	Performance	Comfort	Value
7.2	8	7.4	9.2	6.8	4.4

Category F

2 Dr RS Conv	9570	12115
2 Dr RS Cpe	8250	10440
2 Dr STD Conv	8610	10900
2 Dr STD Cpe	6965	8815
2 Dr Z28 Conv	10605	13425
2 Dr Z28 Cpe	9190	11635
2 Dr Z28 SS Cpe	10730	13580

OPTIONS FOR CAMARO

Auto 4-Speed Transmission +310
Performance Pkg +475
R1 Wheels/tires Pkg +765
Suspension Pkg +405
Torque-sensing Axle +405
AM/FM Compact Disc Player +195
Air Conditioning[Opt on STD Cpe] +340
Aluminum/Alloy Wheels[Opt on STD] +125
Bose Sound System +220
Cruise Control +85
Fog Lights +75
Glass Panel T-tops +400
Keyless Entry System +70
Leather Seats +265
Limited Slip Diff[Opt on RS,STD] +140
Power Door Locks +80

Power Drivers Seat +100
Power Mirrors +50
Power Windows +90

CAPRICE 1996

Zero changes as Caprice enters final year of production.

RATINGS (SCALE OF 1-10)

Overall	Safety	Reliability	Performance	Comfort	Value
7.7	7.2	6.3	8.2	8.3	8.4

Category B

4 Dr STD Sdn	7720	9650

OPTIONS FOR CAPRICE

8 cyl 5.7 L Engine[Opt on Sdn] +210
Special Value Pkg 3 +330
Auto Load Leveling +75
Cruise Control +90
Dual Power Seats +155
Keyless Entry System +70
Leather Seats +275
Power Windows +120

CAVALIER 1996

The 2.3-liter Quad 4 is replaced after just one year by a 2.4-liter twin-cam engine. Four-speed automatic transmission includes traction control. Daytime running lights debut, remote keyless entry is optional on LS and Z24, and base models get new interior fabrics and an Appearance Package.

RATINGS (SCALE OF 1-10)

Overall	Safety	Reliability	Performance	Comfort	Value
6.8	6.4	6.7	7	7.6	6.1

Category E

2 Dr LS Conv	6355	8360
4 Dr LS Sdn	5485	7215
2 Dr STD Cpe	4745	6245
4 Dr STD Sdn	4885	6425
2 Dr Z24 Cpe	6000	7895

OPTIONS FOR CAVALIER

4 cyl 2.4 L Engine[Opt on LS] +140
Auto 3-Speed Transmission[Std on LS] +210
Auto 4-Speed Transmission +305
Preferred Equipment Grp-3 +305
AM/FM Compact Disc Player +185
Air Conditioning[Opt on STD] +330
Cruise Control +90
Keyless Entry System +65
Power Door Locks +100
Power Mirrors +45
Power Sunroof +250
Power Windows +105
Tilt Steering Wheel[Std on Z24] +60

CHEVROLET 96

Model Description	Trade-in Value	Market Value	Model Description	Trade-in Value	Market Value

CHEVY VAN/EXPRESS 1996

First all-new full-size cargo van for Chevrolet in 25 years sports dual airbags, standard four-wheel antilock brakes, up to 317 cubic feet of cargo room and 10,000 pounds of towing capacity. Full-frame construction replaces the less rugged unibody configuration of the previous model. Sportvan replacement, the Express, carries up to 15 passengers and offers full-frame rather than unibody construction. Dual airbags and four-wheel antilock brakes are standard. Long-wheelbase models can carry 317 cubic feet of cargo with the rear seats removed. 3500 models can tow up to 10,000 pounds.

CHEVY VAN

Category H

2 Dr G1500 Chevy Van	9045	10895
2 Dr G2500 Chevy Van	9155	11030
2 Dr G2500 Chevy Van Ext	9455	11390
2 Dr G3500 Chevy Van	9295	11200
2 Dr G3500 Chevy Van Ext	9560	11520

OPTIONS FOR CHEVY VAN/EXPRESS
8 cyl 5.0 L Engine +230
8 cyl 5.7 L Engine[Opt on G15] +410
8 cyl 6.5 L Turbodsl Engine +1340
8 cyl 7.4 L Engine +245
15 Passenger Seating +335
AM/FM Compact Disc Player +125
Aluminum/Alloy Wheels +125
Cruise Control +75
Dual Air Conditioning +540
Power Door Locks +75
Power Drivers Seat +115
Power Windows +75
Privacy Glass +70
Rear Heater +90
Tilt Steering Wheel +75

CHEVY VAN/SPORTVAN CLASSIC 1996

Final year for ancient GM vans dating to 1971.

CHEVY VAN CLASSIC

Category H

2 Dr G30 Chevy Van	9555	11515
2 Dr G30 Chevy Van Ext	9735	11730

SPORTVAN

Category H

2 Dr G30 Sportvan	10415	12550
2 Dr G30 Sportvan Ext	10895	13125

OPTIONS FOR CHEVY VAN/SPORTVAN CLASSIC
8 cyl 6.5 L Dsl Engine +670
8 cyl 7.4 L Engine +245
15 Passenger Seating +335
AM/FM Stereo Tape[Opt on STD] +85

Air Conditioning[Opt on STD] +330
Cruise Control[Opt on STD] +75
Dual Air Conditioning +540
Power Door Locks[Opt on STD] +75
Power Windows[Opt on STD] +75
Privacy Glass +70
Rear Heater +90
Tilt Steering Wheel[Opt on STD] +75

CORSICA 1996

Chevy's fleet favorite rolls into the sunset with long-life coolant.

RATINGS (SCALE OF 1-10)

Overall	Safety	Reliability	Performance	Comfort	Value
6.7	5.3	7.4	8	7.5	5.1

Category C

4 Dr STD Sdn	4670	5990

OPTIONS FOR CORSICA
6 cyl 3.1 L Engine +185
AM/FM Stereo Tape +65
Cruise Control +85
Power Windows +125
Tilt Steering Wheel +60

CORVETTE 1996

New 330-horsepower LT4 engine debuts on all manually shifted Corvettes. Two special editions are available, the Collector Edition and the Grand Sport, to send the fourth-generation Vette off in style. Next year, an all-new Corvette debuts. Other additions for 1996 include a Selective Real Time Damping system for the shock absorbers, and a tooth-jarring Z51 suspension setup.

Category J

2 Dr Grand Sport Cpe	20520	24725
2 Dr STD Conv	19630	23650
2 Dr STD Cpe	17830	21480

OPTIONS FOR CORVETTE
8 cyl 5.7 L LT4 Engine[Opt on STD,Conv] +555
Electronic Suspension +650
Bose Sound System +330
Climate Control for AC +110
Compact Disc W/fm/tape +325
Dual Power Seats +300
Power Drivers Seat +140
Solid & Glass Targa Tops +380
Sport Seats[Opt on STD] +305
Sport Suspension +170

IMPALA 1996

Big surprise. The car is finally correct with the addition of a tachometer and floor shifter, and General Motors kills it. Take note collectors: the 1996 Impala SS should be on your list.

Don't forget to refer to the Mileage Adjustment Table at the back of this book!

Model Description	Trade-in Value	Market Value

Model Description	Trade-in Value	Market Value

RATINGS (SCALE OF 1-10)

Overall	Safety	Reliability	Performance	Comfort	Value
7.8	7.2	6.3	9	8.3	8.1

Category B
4 Dr SS Sdn — 15150 18935

OPTIONS FOR IMPALA
AM/FM Compact Disc Player +135
Keyless Entry System +70
Power Passenger Seat +135

LUMINA   1996

The ultimate family sedan is now available with an integrated child safety seat. Driver and passenger get their own climate controls. LS models offer available leather, and four-wheel disc brakes when equipped with the 3.4-liter V6.

RATINGS (SCALE OF 1-10)

Overall	Safety	Reliability	Performance	Comfort	Value
7.8	7.7	7.2	7.6	7.3	9.1

Category C
4 Dr LS Sdn — 6905 8850
4 Dr STD Sdn — 6255 8020

OPTIONS FOR LUMINA
6 cyl 3.4 L Engine +420
AM/FM Compact Disc Player +145
Anti-Lock Brakes[Std on LS] +245
Child Seat (1) +50
Cruise Control +85
Keyless Entry System +75
Leather Seats +245
Power Drivers Seat +120
Power Windows[Std on LS] +125

LUMINA MINIVAN   1996

Last year for sloped-nose, plastic-bodied van. A 3.4-liter V6 good for 180 horsepower replaces standard and optional V6 engines from last year. Air conditioning, seven-passenger seating, and an electronically controlled four-speed automatic transmission are standard.

RATINGS (SCALE OF 1-10)

Overall	Safety	Reliability	Performance	Comfort	Value
7.6	6.3	8.1	7.6	7.3	8.5

Category G
2 Dr STD Cargo Van — 6275 7745
2 Dr STD Pass. Van — 7210 8900

OPTIONS FOR LUMINA MINIVAN
AM/FM Stereo Tape +90
Aluminum/Alloy Wheels +135
Child Seat (1) +70
Cruise Control +85

Keyless Entry System +80
Power Door Locks +95
Power Drivers Seat +115
Power Mirrors +55
Power Sliding Door +160
Power Windows +95
Privacy Glass +110
Tilt Steering Wheel +70

MONTE CARLO   1996

Dual-zone climate controls reduce marital spats. The 3.4-liter V6 makes more power this year, and four-wheel disc brakes, standard on the Z34, are optional on the LS.

RATINGS (SCALE OF 1-10)

Overall	Safety	Reliability	Performance	Comfort	Value
7.4	7.5	6.3	7.4	7.5	8.5

Category C
2 Dr LS Cpe — 7055 9045
2 Dr Z34 Cpe — 7840 10050

OPTIONS FOR MONTE CARLO
AM/FM Compact Disc Player +145
Cruise Control[Opt on LS] +85
Keyless Entry System[Opt on LS] +75
Leather Seats +245
Power Drivers Seat +120
Power Sunroof +275

S10 PICKUP   1996

Improved V6 engines make more power and torque this year. A new five-speed manual gives four-cylinder models better acceleration, and four-bangers also get four-wheel antilock brakes. Extended-cab models get third-door access panel on the driver's side to make loading cargo and passengers easier. A new sport suspension turns the S-10 into a competent sports truck, and the new Sportside cargo box allows the S-Series to go head-to-head with the Ford Ranger Splash.

RATINGS (SCALE OF 1-10)

Overall	Safety	Reliability	Performance	Comfort	Value
N/A	5.1	6.3	6.6	8.1	N/A

Category G
2 Dr LS Ext Cab SB — 6805 8400
2 Dr LS 4WD Ext Cab SB — 8950 11050
2 Dr LS Ext Cab Stepside SB — 7055 8710
2 Dr LS 4WD Ext Cab Stepside SB
— 9190 11345
2 Dr LS Std Cab LB — 6360 7850
2 Dr LS 4WD Std Cab LB — 8360 10320
2 Dr LS Std Cab SB — 6170 7620
2 Dr LS 4WD Std Cab SB — 8180 10100
2 Dr LS Std Cab Stepside SB — 6515 8045

Don't forget to refer to the Mileage Adjustment Table at the back of this book!

Model Description	Trade-in Value	Market Value
2 Dr LS 4WD Std Cab Stepside SB		
	8535	10540
2 Dr STD Std Cab LB	6035	7450
2 Dr STD 4WD Std Cab LB	7710	9520
2 Dr STD Std Cab SB	5870	7245
2 Dr STD 4WD Std Cab SB	7580	9355

OPTIONS FOR S10 PICKUP

6 cyl 4.3 L Engine[Opt on 2WD] +400
6 cyl 4.3 L Vortec Engine +305
Auto 4-Speed Transmission +400
Wide Stance Suspension +640
AM/FM Compact Disc Player +135
Air Conditioning +330
Aluminum/Alloy Wheels +135
Anti-Lock Brakes[Opt on 2WD] +245
Cruise Control +85
Heavy Duty Suspension +60
Hinged Third Door (PU) +140
Keyless Entry System +80
Power Door Locks +95
Power Mirrors +55
Power Windows +95
Tilt Steering Wheel +70

SUBURBAN   1996

Improved engines generate lots of horsepower and torque. Four-wheel-drive models get an optional electronic shift transfer case. Daytime running lights, rear seat heating ducts, and two new paint colors summarize the changes to Chevy's Texas Cadillac.

RATINGS (SCALE OF 1-10)

Overall	Safety	Reliability	Performance	Comfort	Value
7.2	6.6	6.9	7	7.9	7.6

Category H

	Trade-in	Market
4 Dr C1500 Wgn	14755	17780
4 Dr C2500 Wgn	15810	19050
4 Dr K1500 4WD Wgn	16060	19350
4 Dr K2500 4WD Wgn	16960	20435

OPTIONS FOR SUBURBAN

8 cyl 6.5 L Turbodsl Engine +1340
8 cyl 7.4 L Engine +245
LS Pkg +915
LS Preferred Equip. Pkg +1515
LT Pkg +1085
LT Preferred Equip. Pkg +1595
AM/FM Compact Disc Player +125
Air Conditioning +330
Automatic Dimming Mirror +60
Camper/Towing Package +140
Cruise Control +75
Dual Air Conditioning +540
Keyless Entry System +70
Leather Seats +400
Power Door Locks +75

Power Drivers Seat +115
Power Mirrors +40
Power Windows +75
Privacy Glass +70
Rear Heater +90
Tilt Steering Wheel +75

TAHOE   1996

For 1996, Tahoe gets 50 additional horsepower and more torque out of a new 5700 V8. Other improvements include rear seat heating ducts, quieter-riding P-metric tires, improved automatic transmissions, and extended interval service schedules. Daytime running lights are new for 1996.

RATINGS (SCALE OF 1-10)

Overall	Safety	Reliability	Performance	Comfort	Value
7.4	6.9	6.9	7.4	8	7.6

Category H

	Trade-in	Market
2 Dr LS Utility	15035	18115
2 Dr LS 4WD Utility	16185	19500
4 Dr LS Wgn	16475	19850
4 Dr LS 4WD Wgn	17615	21225
2 Dr LT Utility	14590	17580
2 Dr LT 4WD Utility	16715	20140
4 Dr LT Wgn	17115	20620
4 Dr LT 4WD Wgn	18220	21950
2 Dr STD Utility	13245	15955
2 Dr STD 4WD Utility	14210	17120

OPTIONS FOR TAHOE

8 cyl 6.5 L Turbodsl Engine +1340
Auto 4-Speed Transmission[Std on STD Utility, Wgn] +375
AM/FM Compact Disc Player +125
Air Conditioning[Opt on STD] +330
Aluminum/Alloy Wheels[Opt on STD] +125
Camper/Towing Package +140
Cruise Control[Opt on STD] +75
Keyless Entry System[Opt on LS] +70
Power Drivers Seat[Opt on LS] +115
Privacy Glass[Opt on STD] +70
Tilt Steering Wheel[Opt on STD,LS Utility] +75

1995 CHEVROLET

ASTRO   1995

Front sheetmetal is restyled. Regular-length versions are dropped from the lineup, leaving only the extended-length model. Multi-leaf steel springs replace single-leaf plastic springs. One engine is available, the 190-horsepower, 4.3-liter V6. Air conditioning is newly standard, and remote keyless entry is a new option.

CHEVROLET 95

Model Description	Trade-in Value	Market Value	Model Description	Trade-in Value	Market Value

RATINGS (SCALE OF 1-10)

Overall	Safety	Reliability	Performance	Comfort	Value
7	6	6.3	7.2	6.6	8.7

Category G

	Trade-in	Market
2 Dr CL Pass. Van Ext	7615	9640
2 Dr CL 4WD Pass. Van Ext	8340	10555
2 Dr CS Pass. Van Ext	7230	9155
2 Dr CS 4WD Pass. Van Ext	7910	10010
2 Dr LT Pass. Van Ext	7840	9925
2 Dr LT 4WD Pass. Van Ext	8875	11235
2 Dr STD 4WD Cargo Van	7190	9100
2 Dr STD Pass. Van Ext	6800	8610
2 Dr STD 4WD Pass. Van Ext	7875	9970

OPTIONS FOR ASTRO

8 Passenger Seating[Std on CL,LT] +130
AM/FM Compact Disc Player +110
Cruise Control[Opt on STD] +70
Dual Air Conditioning +315
Keyless Entry System[Std on LT] +65
Power Door Locks[Std on CL,LT] +75
Power Drivers Seat +95
Power Mirrors[Std on LT] +45
Power Windows[Opt on CS,STD,CL Pass. Van Ext] +80
Privacy Glass[Opt on CS,STD,CL Pass. Van Ext] +90
Rear Heater +65
Tilt Steering Wheel[Opt on STD] +60

BERETTA   1995

Daytime running lights are newly standard. 170-horse Quad 4 engine is dropped, and 3.1-liter V6 loses five horsepower. Platinum-tipped spark plugs are standard on both engines.

RATINGS (SCALE OF 1-10)

Overall	Safety	Reliability	Performance	Comfort	Value
6.9	7	7.8	7.8	7	4.9

Category E

	Trade-in	Market
2 Dr STD Cpe	4205	5760
2 Dr Z26 Cpe	4930	6750

OPTIONS FOR BERETTA

6 cyl 3.1 L Engine[Opt on STD] +420
Auto 3-Speed Transmission +180
Auto 4-Speed Transmission[Opt on STD] +330
AM/FM Compact Disc Player +150
Cruise Control +75
Power Windows +85
Sunroof +115
Tilt Steering Wheel +50

BLAZER   1995

All-new SUV appears based on revamped S10. S10 nomenclature is dropped, and full-size Blazer becomes Tahoe. Four-wheel-drive models have electronic transfer case as standard equipment. Spare tire on four-door model is mounted beneath cargo bay instead of in it. Five different suspension packages are available. One engine, a 195-horsepower 4.3-liter V6, is available. All-wheel drive is optional. Driver airbag and air conditioning are standard equipment.

RATINGS (SCALE OF 1-10)

Overall	Safety	Reliability	Performance	Comfort	Value
6.5	5.3	5.3	8	7.9	6.1

Category G

	Trade-in	Market
2 Dr LS Utility	8265	10460
2 Dr LS 4WD Utility	9300	11775
4 Dr LS Wgn	8980	11370
4 Dr LS 4WD Wgn	9985	12640
4 Dr LT Wgn	9635	12195
4 Dr LT 4WD Wgn	10570	13380
2 Dr STD Utility	7750	9810
2 Dr STD 4WD Utility	8360	10585
4 Dr STD Wgn	8755	11080
4 Dr STD 4WD Wgn	9225	11680

OPTIONS FOR BLAZER

AM/FM Compact Disc Player +110
Cruise Control[Opt on STD] +70
Keyless Entry System[Std on LT] +65
Power Door Locks[Opt on STD] +75
Power Drivers Seat[Std on LT] +95
Power Mirrors[Opt on STD] +45
Power Windows[Opt on STD] +80
Skid Plates +45
Swing Out Tire Carrier +65
Tilt Steering Wheel[Opt on STD] +60

C/K PICKUP   1995

New interior with driver airbag (models under 8,500-lb. GVWR) and standard four-wheel ABS debut. New dashboard features modular design with controls that are much easier to read and use. Power mirrors and remote keyless entry are new options. Uplevel radios come with automatic volume control that raises or lowers the volume depending on vehicle speed.

RATINGS (SCALE OF 1-10)

Overall	Safety	Reliability	Performance	Comfort	Value
N/A	8.1	6	7.6	8.4	N/A

C/K 1500 SERIES

Category H

	Trade-in	Market
2 Dr C1500 Cheyenne Ext Cab LB		
	8885	10970
2 Dr C1500 Cheyenne Ext Cab SB		
	8735	10785
2 Dr C1500 Cheyenne Ext Cab Stepside SB		
	9115	11250

Model Description	Trade-in Value	Market Value
2 Dr C1500 Cheyenne Std Cab LB	8150	10060
2 Dr C1500 Cheyenne Std Cab SB	7940	9800
2 Dr C1500 Cheyenne Std Cab Stepside SB	8280	10225
2 Dr C1500 Silverado Ext Cab LB	9540	11775
2 Dr C1500 Silverado Ext Cab SB	9465	11685
2 Dr C1500 Silverado Ext Cab Stepside SB	9750	12035
2 Dr C1500 Silverado Std Cab LB	9205	11365
2 Dr C1500 Silverado Std Cab SB	9060	11185
2 Dr C1500 Silverado Std Cab Stepside SB	9380	11580
2 Dr C1500 WT Std Cab LB	6765	8350
2 Dr C1500 WT Std Cab SB	6600	8150
2 Dr K1500 Cheyenne 4WD Ext Cab LB	10115	12490
2 Dr K1500 Cheyenne 4WD Ext Cab SB	9965	12305
2 Dr K1500 Cheyenne 4WD Ext Cab Stepside SB	10270	12680
2 Dr K1500 Cheyenne 4WD Std Cab LB	9410	11620
2 Dr K1500 Cheyenne 4WD Std Cab SB	9265	11440
2 Dr K1500 Cheyenne 4WD Std Cab Stepside SB	9580	11825
2 Dr K1500 Silverado 4WD Ext Cab LB	11160	13775
2 Dr K1500 Silverado 4WD Ext Cab SB	11000	13580
2 Dr K1500 Silverado 4WD Ext Cab Stepside SB	11290	13940
2 Dr K1500 Silverado 4WD Std Cab LB	10380	12815
2 Dr K1500 Silverado 4WD Std Cab SB	10205	12600
2 Dr K1500 Silverado 4WD Std Cab Stepside SB	10650	13150
2 Dr K1500 WT 4WD Std Cab LB	7685	9485
2 Dr K1500 WT 4WD Std Cab SB	7570	9345

C/K 2500 SERIES
Category H

Model Description	Trade-in Value	Market Value
2 Dr C2500 Cheyenne Ext Cab LB	9265	11440
2 Dr C2500 Cheyenne Ext Cab SB	9155	11305
2 Dr C2500 Cheyenne Std Cab LB	8510	10505
2 Dr C2500 Silverado Ext Cab LB	9880	12200
2 Dr C2500 Silverado Ext Cab SB	9760	12050
2 Dr C2500 Silverado Std Cab LB	9115	11255
2 Dr K2500 Cheyenne 4WD Ext Cab LB	10255	12660
2 Dr K2500 Cheyenne 4WD Ext Cab SB	10140	12520
2 Dr K2500 Cheyenne 4WD Std Cab LB	9475	11700
2 Dr K2500 Silverado 4WD Ext Cab LB	10935	13500
2 Dr K2500 Silverado 4WD Ext Cab SB	10840	13380
2 Dr K2500 Silverado 4WD Std Cab LB	10245	12650

C/K 3500 SERIES
Category H

Model Description	Trade-in Value	Market Value
4 Dr C3500 Cheyenne Crew Cab LB	10930	13495
2 Dr C3500 Cheyenne Ext Cab LB	10510	12975
2 Dr C3500 Cheyenne Std Cab LB	9850	12160
4 Dr C3500 Silverado Crew Cab LB	11815	14585
2 Dr C3500 Silverado Ext Cab LB	10905	13460
2 Dr C3500 Silverado Std Cab LB	10305	12725
4 Dr K3500 Cheyenne 4WD Crew Cab LB	12715	15700
2 Dr K3500 Cheyenne 4WD Ext Cab LB	11950	14750
2 Dr K3500 Cheyenne 4WD Std Cab LB	11260	13900
4 Dr K3500 Silverado 4WD Crew Cab LB	13460	16615
2 Dr K3500 Silverado 4WD Ext Cab LB	12840	15850
2 Dr K3500 Silverado 4WD Std Cab LB	12205	15070

OPTIONS FOR C/K PICKUP
8 cyl 5.0 L Engine +200
8 cyl 5.7 L Engine +250

Don't forget to refer to the Mileage Adjustment Table at the back of this book!

Model Description	Trade-in Value	Market Value
8 cyl 6.5 L Dsl Engine +740		
8 cyl 6.5 L Turbodsl Engine +1055		
8 cyl 7.4 L Engine +185		
Auto 4-Speed Transmission +310		
AM/FM Compact Disc Player +105		
Air Conditioning +270		
Bed Liner +75		
Cruise Control[Opt on STD,WT] +60		
Keyless Entry System +55		
Leather Seats +325		
Power Door Locks[Opt on STD] +60		
Power Drivers Seat +95		
Power Mirrors +35		
Tilt Steering Wheel[Opt on STD,WT] +60		

CAMARO 1995

Z28 gets optional traction control. Z28 can now be ordered with body-color roof and side mirrors (standard color is gloss black). Chrome-plated alloys are newly optional.

RATINGS (SCALE OF 1-10)

Overall	Safety	Reliability	Performance	Comfort	Value
7.3	8.7	6.9	9.2	6.8	4.9

Category F

	Trade-in	Market
2 Dr STD Conv	7545	9675
2 Dr STD Cpe	6050	7755
2 Dr Z28 Conv	9310	11935
2 Dr Z28 Cpe	7950	10190

OPTIONS FOR CAMARO

6 cyl 3.8 L Engine +140
Auto 4-Speed Transmission +250
AM/FM Compact Disc Player +160
Air Conditioning +275
Bose Sound System +180
Cruise Control +70
Fog Lights +60
Glass Panel T-tops +325
Keyless Entry System +60
Leather Seats +215
Power Door Locks +65
Power Drivers Seat +80
Power Mirrors[Std on Cpe] +40
Power Windows +75

CAPRICE 1995

Impala SS styling treatment for C-pillar is carried over to more mainstream sedan. New seats and radios debut. Outside mirrors can be folded in, and a new option is a radio with speed-compensated volume control.

RATINGS (SCALE OF 1-10)

Overall	Safety	Reliability	Performance	Comfort	Value
7.7	7.9	5.7	8.2	8.3	8.3

Category B

	Trade-in	Market
4 Dr STD Sdn	6300	8075
4 Dr STD Wgn	7930	10165

OPTIONS FOR CAPRICE

8 cyl 5.7 L Engine[Std on Wgn] +180
AM/FM Stereo Tape[Std on Wgn] +60
Auto Load Leveling +60
Cruise Control +75
Keyless Entry System +55
Leather Seats +225
Power Drivers Seat +105
Power Mirrors +35
Power Windows +100

CAVALIER 1995

First redesign since 1982 debut. Sedan, coupe and convertible are available. Wagon is dropped. Sedan comes in base and LS trim. Coupe comes in base and Z24 trim. Convertible is available as LS only. Dual airbags and ABS are standard. Base engine is a 2.2-liter, 120-horsepower four-cylinder engine. Optional on LS sedan and convertible is the Z24's standard powerplant; a 2.3-liter, DOHC four-cylinder making 150 horsepower.

RATINGS (SCALE OF 1-10)

Overall	Safety	Reliability	Performance	Comfort	Value
7.3	7.2	7	7	7.6	7.9

Category E

	Trade-in	Market
2 Dr LS Conv	5285	7240
4 Dr LS Sdn	4445	6090
2 Dr STD Cpe	4035	5530
4 Dr STD Sdn	4170	5715
2 Dr Z24 Cpe	5090	6970

OPTIONS FOR CAVALIER

4 cyl 2.3 L Quad 4 Engine[Opt on LS] +130
Auto 3-Speed Transmission[Std on LS] +165
Auto 4-Speed Transmission +120
AM/FM Compact Disc Player +150
Air Conditioning[Opt on STD] +270
Cruise Control +75
Power Door Locks +80
Power Mirrors +35
Power Sunroof +205
Power Windows +85
Tilt Steering Wheel[Std on Z24] +50

CHEVY VAN/SPORTVAN 1995

No changes.

CHEVY VAN

Category H

	Trade-in	Market
2 Dr G10 Chevy Van	6685	8255
2 Dr G10 Chevy Van Ext	7065	8720
2 Dr G20 Chevy Van	7000	8645

Don't forget to refer to the Mileage Adjustment Table at the back of this book!

Model Description	Trade-in Value	Market Value
2 Dr G20 Chevy Van Ext	7230	8925
2 Dr G30 Chevy Van	7255	8955
2 Dr G30 Chevy Van Ext	7515	9280

SPORTVAN

Category H

Model Description	Trade-in Value	Market Value
2 Dr G20 Sportvan	7225	8920
2 Dr G20 Beauville Sportvan	7905	9760
2 Dr G30 Sportvan	7905	9760
2 Dr G30 Sportvan Ext	8260	10200
2 Dr G30 Beauville Sportvan	8390	10355
2 Dr G30 Beauville Sportvan Ext	8715	10760

OPTIONS FOR CHEVY VAN/SPORTVAN

8 cyl 5.0 L Engine +200
8 cyl 5.7 L Engine[Opt on G20,Chevy Van] +250
8 cyl 6.5 L Dsl Engine +740
8 cyl 7.4 L Engine +185
16 Passenger Seating +120
AM/FM Stereo Tape[Opt on G10,STD] +70
Air Conditioning[Opt on G10,STD] +270
Cruise Control[Opt on G10,STD] +60
Dual Air Conditioning +440
Power Door Locks[Opt on G10,STD] +60
Power Windows[Opt on G10,STD] +65
Privacy Glass +55
Rear Heater +70
Tilt Steering Wheel[Opt on G10,STD] +60

CORSICA   1995

Daytime running lights debut. Rear suspension is revised, and larger tires are standard.

RATINGS (SCALE OF 1-10)

Overall	Safety	Reliability	Performance	Comfort	Value
6.8	5.8	7.5	8	7.5	5

Category C

	Trade-in	Market
4 Dr STD Sdn	3675	4900

OPTIONS FOR CORSICA

6 cyl 3.1 L Engine +160
AM/FM Stereo Tape +55
Cruise Control +70
Power Windows +105
Tilt Steering Wheel +50

CORVETTE   1995

ZR-1's brakes trickle down to base models. Front fenders get revised gills. Only 448 ZR-1s were produced in 1995.

Category J

	Trade-in	Market
2 Dr STD Conv	17665	21540
2 Dr STD Cpe	15790	19255
2 Dr ZR1 Cpe	23015	28065

OPTIONS FOR CORVETTE

Handling Pkg +675
Selective Ride Suspension +560
Bose Sound System +270
Climate Control for AC[Opt on STD] +90
Compact Disc W/fm/tape[Opt on STD] +265
Power Drivers Seat[Opt on STD] +115
Solid & Glass Targa Tops +310

IMPALA   1995

Dark Cherry and Green Gray paint colors join basic black. New seats and radios debut. Outside mirrors can be folded in, and a new option is a radio with speed-compensated volume control.

RATINGS (SCALE OF 1-10)

Overall	Safety	Reliability	Performance	Comfort	Value
7.8	7.9	5.7	9	8.3	8

Category B

	Trade-in	Market
4 Dr SS Sdn	12665	16235

OPTIONS FOR IMPALA

AM/FM Compact Disc Player +110
Keyless Entry System +55
Power Passenger Seat +110

LUMINA   1995

Midsize sedan is redesigned; features dual airbags. Base and LS trim levels are available. ABS is optional on base model; standard on LS. Standard powerplant is a 160-horsepower, 3.1-liter V6. Optional on LS is a 210-horsepower, 3.4-liter V6. Air conditioning is standard.

RATINGS (SCALE OF 1-10)

Overall	Safety	Reliability	Performance	Comfort	Value
7.2	7.9	5.6	7.6	7.3	7.5

Category C

	Trade-in	Market
4 Dr LS Sdn	5645	7525
4 Dr STD Sdn	5205	6940

OPTIONS FOR LUMINA

6 cyl 3.4 L Engine +315
AM/FM Compact Disc Player +120
Anti-Lock Brakes[Std on LS] +200
Cruise Control +70
Keyless Entry System +60
Power Drivers Seat +100
Power Windows[Std on LS] +105

LUMINA MINIVAN   1995

Transmission gets brake/shift interlock.

RATINGS (SCALE OF 1-10)

Overall	Safety	Reliability	Performance	Comfort	Value
6.9	6.9	6	7.6	7.3	6.6

Don't forget to refer to the Mileage Adjustment Table at the back of this book!

Model Description	Trade-in Value	Market Value
Category G		
2 Dr STD Cargo Van	4770	6040
2 Dr STD Pass. Van	5860	7420

OPTIONS FOR LUMINA MINIVAN

6 cyl 3.8 L Engine +140
Auto 4-Speed Transmission +65
AM/FM Stereo Tape +75
Air Conditioning +270
Child Seat (1) +55
Cruise Control +70
Keyless Entry System +65
Power Door Locks +75
Power Drivers Seat +95
Power Mirrors +45
Power Windows +80
Privacy Glass +90
Tilt Steering Wheel +60

MONTE CARLO 1995

Chevy slaps revered moniker on coupe version of Lumina. Available in LS or Z34 trim levels. Dual airbags and ABS are standard. LS comes with 160-horsepower, 3.1-liter V6, while Z34 is powered by 3.4-liter, twin-cam V6 good for 210 horsepower. All Monte Carlos have automatic transmissions. Air conditioning is standard.

RATINGS (SCALE OF 1-10)

Overall	Safety	Reliability	Performance	Comfort	Value
7	7.8	5.4	7.4	7.5	7.1

	Trade-in	Market
Category C		
2 Dr LS Cpe	6095	8125
2 Dr Z34 Cpe	6835	9115

OPTIONS FOR MONTE CARLO

Cruise Control[Opt on LS] +70
Keyless Entry System[Opt on LS] +60
Leather Seats +200
Power Drivers Seat +100
Power Mirrors[Opt on LS] +35

S10 PICKUP 1995

Driver airbag is added, and daytime running lights are standard. ZR2 off-road package can be ordered on the extended-cab. Power window and lock buttons are illuminated at night. Remote keyless entry is a new option. A single key operates both the door locks and the ignition. A manual transmission can now be ordered with the 191-horsepower, 4.3-liter V6.

RATINGS (SCALE OF 1-10)

Overall	Safety	Reliability	Performance	Comfort	Value
N/A	5.1	5.7	6.6	8.1	N/A

	Trade-in	Market
Category G		
2 Dr LS Ext Cab SB	5785	7320
2 Dr LS 4WD Ext Cab SB	7585	9600
2 Dr LS Std Cab LB	5350	6770

Model Description	Trade-in Value	Market Value
2 Dr LS 4WD Std Cab LB	7120	9010
2 Dr LS Std Cab SB	5215	6600
2 Dr LS 4WD Std Cab SB	6970	8820
2 Dr STD Std Cab LB	5055	6400
2 Dr STD 4WD Std Cab LB	6745	8540
2 Dr STD Std Cab SB	4910	6215
2 Dr STD 4WD Std Cab SB	6635	8400

OPTIONS FOR S10 PICKUP

6 cyl 4.3 L Engine[Opt on 2WD] +265
6 cyl 4.3 L CPI Engine +275
Auto 4-Speed Transmission +330
Wide Stance Suspension +570
AM/FM Compact Disc Player +110
AM/FM Stereo Tape +75
Air Conditioning +270
Anti-Lock Brakes[Opt on 2WD] +200
Cruise Control +70
Heavy Duty Suspension +45
Keyless Entry System +65
Power Door Locks +75
Power Windows +80
Tilt Steering Wheel +60

SUBURBAN 1995

New interior with driver airbag debuts. New dashboard features modular design with controls that are much easier to read and use. 1500 models can now be ordered with turbodiesel engine. Brake/transmission shift interlock is added to automatic transmission. Seats and door panels are revised. New console on models with bucket seats features pivoting writing surface, along with rear cupholders and storage drawer. Uplevel radios come with automatic volume controls that raise or lower the volume depending on vehicle speed.

RATINGS (SCALE OF 1-10)

Overall	Safety	Reliability	Performance	Comfort	Value
6.9	6.9	5.2	6.8	7.9	7.5

	Trade-in	Market
Category H		
4 Dr C1500 Wgn	12570	15520
4 Dr C2500 Wgn	13525	16700
4 Dr K1500 4WD Wgn	13770	17000
4 Dr K2500 4WD Wgn	14750	18210

OPTIONS FOR SUBURBAN

8 cyl 6.5 L Turbodsl Engine +1055
8 cyl 7.4 L Engine +185
LS Pkg +1085
LS Preferred Equip. Pkg +1195
LT Pkg +1580
LT Preferred Equip. Pkg +1240
AM/FM Compact Disc Player +105
Air Conditioning +270
Automatic Dimming Mirror +50
Camper/Towing Package +115
Cruise Control +60

Don't forget to refer to the Mileage Adjustment Table at the back of this book!

CHEVROLET 95-94

Model Description	Trade-in Value	Market Value	Model Description	Trade-in Value	Market Value

Dual Air Conditioning +440
Keyless Entry System +55
Leather Seats +325
Power Door Locks +60
Power Drivers Seat +95
Power Mirrors +35
Power Windows +65
Privacy Glass +55
Rear Heater +70
Tilt Steering Wheel +60

TAHOE 1995

Full-size SUV gets a new name as S10-based model takes Blazer moniker. New interior with driver airbag debuts. New dashboard features modular design with controls that are much easier to read and use. New five-door model is added midyear, nicely sized between Blazer and Suburban. New model is offered only in LS or LT trim with a 5.7-liter V8 and an automatic transmission in either 2WD or 4WD. Brake/transmission shift interlock is added to automatic transmission. New console on models with bucket seats features pivoting writing surface, along with rear cupholders and storage drawer.

RATINGS (SCALE OF 1-10)

Overall	Safety	Reliability	Performance	Comfort	Value
7.2	7.6	5.6	7.2	8	7.6

Category H
2 Dr LS 4WD Utility	12890	15915
4 Dr LS Wgn	12650	15615
4 Dr LS 4WD Wgn	13795	17030
2 Dr LT 4WD Utility	13425	16575
4 Dr LT Wgn	13275	16390
4 Dr LT 4WD Wgn	14400	17780
2 Dr STD 4WD Utility	11670	14410

OPTIONS FOR TAHOE

8 cyl 6.5 L Turbodsl Engine +1055
Auto 4-Speed Transmission[Std on Wgn] +305
AM/FM Compact Disc Player +105
AM/FM Stereo Tape[Opt on STD] +70
Air Conditioning[Opt on STD] +270
Cruise Control[Opt on STD] +60
Keyless Entry System[Std on LT] +55
Power Door Locks[Opt on STD] +60
Power Drivers Seat[Opt on LS] +95
Privacy Glass[Opt on STD] +55
Tilt Steering Wheel[Opt on STD] +60

1994 CHEVROLET

ASTRO 1994

Driver airbag is made standard. Side-door guard beams are stronger, and air conditioners use CFC-free refrigerant. A high-mount center brake light is added. Analog gauges get new graphics, and carpet is treated with Scotchgard.

RATINGS (SCALE OF 1-10)

Overall	Safety	Reliability	Performance	Comfort	Value
7.1	5.8	6.5	7.2	6.6	9.2

Category G
2 Dr CL Pass. Van	5120	6650
2 Dr CL 4WD Pass. Van	6055	7865
2 Dr CL Pass. Van Ext	5605	7280
2 Dr CL 4WD Pass. Van Ext	6560	8520
2 Dr LT Pass. Van	5405	7020
2 Dr LT 4WD Pass. Van	6515	8460
2 Dr LT Pass. Van Ext	5905	7670
2 Dr LT 4WD Pass. Van Ext	6905	8965
2 Dr STD Cargo Van	3775	4900
2 Dr STD 4WD Cargo Van	5050	6560
2 Dr STD Cargo Van Ext	4180	5430
2 Dr STD 4WD Cargo Van Ext	5465	7095
2 Dr STD Pass. Van	5060	6570
2 Dr STD 4WD Pass. Van	5720	7430
2 Dr STD Pass. Van Ext	5450	7080
2 Dr STD 4WD Pass. Van Ext	6100	7925

OPTIONS FOR ASTRO

6 cyl 4.3 L CPI Engine[Opt on 2WD] +155
8 Passenger Seating +105
AM/FM Stereo Tape +60
Air Conditioning +220
Cruise Control +55
Dual Air Conditioning +255
Power Door Locks +65
Power Drivers Seat +75
Power Windows +65
Privacy Glass[Std on LT] +70
Tilt Steering Wheel +50

BERETTA 1994

GT and GTZ are dropped in favor of Z26 model, which offers a standard 170-horsepower Quad 4 engine. Base models get 10 more horsepower, and the 3.1-liter V6 makes an additional 20 horsepower, up to 160. Automatic transmission is unavailable with Quad 4; manual transmission is unavailable with V6. Door-mounted seat belts are added. Automatic door locks lock doors once Beretta is underway, and unlock when car is stopped. Disable this feature by yanking a fuse. Interior lights shut off after 10 minutes to save battery. Warning chime reminds driver that turn signal has been left on.

RATINGS (SCALE OF 1-10)

Overall	Safety	Reliability	Performance	Comfort	Value
6.8	6.6	7.5	7.8	7	4.9

Don't forget to refer to the Mileage Adjustment Table at the back of this book!

Model Description	Trade-in Value	Market Value
Category E		
2 Dr STD Cpe	3540	5055
2 Dr Z26 Cpe	3940	5630

OPTIONS FOR BERETTA

6 cyl 3.1 L Engine +200
Auto 3-Speed Transmission +150
Auto 4-Speed Transmission +185
AM/FM Stereo Tape[Opt on STD] +80
Cruise Control +60
Power Windows +70
Sunroof +95
Tilt Steering Wheel +40

BLAZER   1994

Air conditioning receives CFC-free coolant. Side-door guard beams are added. A new grille appears, and models equipped with a decor package get composite headlamps. A turbocharged diesel is newly optional. Third brake light is added.

Category H		
2 Dr STD 4WD Utility	8400	10635
2 Dr Silverado 4WD Utility	9180	11620
2 Dr Sport 4WD Utility	8765	11095

OPTIONS FOR BLAZER

8 cyl 6.5 L Turbodsl Engine +845
Auto 4-Speed Transmission +245
AM/FM Stereo Tape +60
Air Conditioning[Opt on STD] +220
Cruise Control[Opt on STD] +50
Power Door Locks[Std on Sport] +50
Power Drivers Seat +75
Power Windows[Std on Sport] +50
Tilt Steering Wheel[Opt on STD] +50

C/K PICKUP   1994

454 SS dropped. Grilles are restyled, side-door guard beams are added, and a third brake light is installed. Leather seats are available. Front seatback on extended-cab models gets memory feature to improve entry and exit to rear seat. A 6.5-liter diesel replaces last year's 6.2-liter unit, and a turbocharged version is also available for 1500 and 2500 models.

RATINGS (SCALE OF 1-10)

Overall	Safety	Reliability	Performance	Comfort	Value
N/A	6	6.4	7.4	8.4	N/A

C/K 1500 SERIES

Category H		
2 Dr C1500 Cheyenne Ext Cab LB	7835	9920
2 Dr C1500 Cheyenne Ext Cab SB	7710	9760
2 Dr C1500 Cheyenne Ext Cab Stepside SB	8005	10130
2 Dr C1500 Cheyenne Std Cab LB	7080	8965
2 Dr C1500 Cheyenne Std Cab SB	6975	8830
2 Dr C1500 Cheyenne Std Cab Stepside SB	7285	9220
2 Dr C1500 Silverado Ext Cab LB	8105	10260
2 Dr C1500 Silverado Ext Cab SB	7970	10090
2 Dr C1500 Silverado Ext Cab Stepside SB	8210	10390
2 Dr C1500 Silverado Std Cab LB	7385	9350
2 Dr C1500 Silverado Std Cab SB	7235	9160
2 Dr C1500 Silverado Std Cab Stepside SB	7560	9570
2 Dr C1500 Work Truck Std Cab LB	5750	7280
2 Dr C1500 Work Truck Std Cab SB	5575	7060
2 Dr K1500 Cheyenne 4WD Ext Cab LB	8455	10700
2 Dr K1500 Cheyenne 4WD Ext Cab SB	8325	10535
2 Dr K1500 Cheyenne 4WD Ext Cab Stepside SB	8625	10920
2 Dr K1500 Cheyenne 4WD Std Cab LB	7975	10095
2 Dr K1500 Cheyenne 4WD Std Cab SB	7820	9900
2 Dr K1500 Cheyenne 4WD Std Cab Stepside SB	8140	10305
2 Dr K1500 Silverado 4WD Ext Cab LB	9355	11840
2 Dr K1500 Silverado 4WD Ext Cab SB	9205	11650
2 Dr K1500 Silverado 4WD Ext Cab Stepside SB	9560	12100
2 Dr K1500 Silverado 4WD Std Cab LB	8995	11385
2 Dr K1500 Silverado 4WD Std Cab SB	8865	11220
2 Dr K1500 Silverado 4WD Std Cab Stepside SB	9100	11520
2 Dr K1500 Sport 4WD Std Cab Stepside SB	9115	11540
2 Dr K1500 Work Truck 4WD Std Cab LB	6745	8540

Don't forget to refer to the Mileage Adjustment Table at the back of this book!

Model Description	Trade-in Value	Market Value
2 Dr K1500 Work Truck 4WD Std Cab SB	6615	8375

C/K 2500 SERIES

Category H

Model Description	Trade-in Value	Market Value
2 Dr C2500 Cheyenne Ext Cab LB	8020	10155
2 Dr C2500 Cheyenne Ext Cab SB	7925	10030
2 Dr C2500 Cheyenne Std Cab LB	7275	9210
2 Dr C2500 Silverado Ext Cab LB	8485	10740
2 Dr C2500 Silverado Ext Cab SB	8380	10610
2 Dr C2500 Silverado Std Cab LB	7725	9780
2 Dr K2500 Cheyenne 4WD Ext Cab LB	8895	11260
2 Dr K2500 Cheyenne 4WD Ext Cab SB	8790	11125
2 Dr K2500 Cheyenne 4WD Std Cab LB	8250	10440
2 Dr K2500 Silverado 4WD Ext Cab LB	9560	12100
2 Dr K2500 Silverado 4WD Ext Cab SB	9395	11895
2 Dr K2500 Silverado 4WD Std Cab LB	8925	11300

C/K 3500 SERIES

Category H

Model Description	Trade-in Value	Market Value
4 Dr C3500 Cheyenne Crew Cab LB	10100	12785
2 Dr C3500 Cheyenne Ext Cab LB	9615	12170
2 Dr C3500 Cheyenne Std Cab LB	9150	11585
4 Dr C3500 Silverado Crew Cab LB	10310	13050
2 Dr C3500 Silverado Ext Cab LB	9935	12575
2 Dr C3500 Silverado Std Cab LB	9455	11970
4 Dr K3500 4WD Crew Cab LB	10760	13620
2 Dr K3500 Cheyenne 4WD Ext Cab LB	10470	13250
2 Dr K3500 Cheyenne 4WD Std Cab LB	9755	12350
4 Dr K3500 Silverado 4WD Crew Cab LB	11365	14385
2 Dr K3500 Silverado 4WD Ext Cab LB	11020	13950
2 Dr K3500 Silverado 4WD Std Cab LB	10610	13430

OPTIONS FOR C/K PICKUP

8 cyl 5.0 L Engine +165
8 cyl 5.7 L Engine +195
8 cyl 6.5 L Dsl Engine +735
8 cyl 6.5 L Turbodsl Engine +845
8 cyl 7.4 L Engine +160
Auto 4-Speed Transmission +245
LT Pkg +220
AM/FM Stereo Tape[Std on Sport] +60
Air Conditioning[Opt on STD,Work Truck] +220
Bed Liner +60
Camper/Towing Package +90
Cruise Control[Std on Sport] +50
Power Door Locks[Std on Sport] +50
Power Drivers Seat +75
Power Windows[Std on Sport] +50
Tilt Steering Wheel[Std on Sport] +50

CAMARO   1994

Convertible returns in base and Z28 trim. First-to-fourth shift pattern added to six-speed manual transmission to meet fuel economy regulations. Z28 with manual transmission gets revised gearing for better acceleration.

RATINGS (SCALE OF 1-10)

Overall	Safety	Reliability	Performance	Comfort	Value
7.2	8.7	7	9.2	6.8	4.4

Category F

Model	Trade-in	Market
2 Dr STD Conv	6420	8445
2 Dr STD Cpe	5110	6725
2 Dr Z28 Conv	7720	10160
2 Dr Z28 Cpe	6505	8560

OPTIONS FOR CAMARO

Auto 4-Speed Transmission +185
Air Conditioning +225
Bose Sound System +145
Fog Lights +50
Glass Panel T-tops +265
Keyless Entry System +50
Leather Seats +175
Power Door Locks +55
Power Drivers Seat +65
Power Windows +60

CAPRICE   1994

Passenger airbag added. New base engine for sedan is a 200-horsepower, 4.3-liter V8. Optional on sedan and standard on wagon is a more powerful 260-horsepower, 5.7-liter V8. Automatic transmissions get electronic controls. Pass-Key II is a standard theft-deterrent system, and CFC-free refrigerant is added to air conditioning systems.

Don't forget to refer to the Mileage Adjustment Table at the back of this book!

Model Description	Trade-in Value	Market Value
RATINGS (SCALE OF 1-10)		

Overall	Safety	Reliability	Performance	Comfort	Value
7.9	8	6	8.2	8.3	8.8

Category B

	Trade-in	Market
4 Dr LS Sdn	6350	8355
4 Dr STD Sdn	5165	6795
4 Dr STD Wgn	6815	8965

OPTIONS FOR CAPRICE
8 cyl 5.7 L Engine[Std on Wgn] +90
AM/FM Stereo Tape[Std on LS,Wgn] +50
Cruise Control[Std on LS] +60
Leather Seats +185
Power Door Locks[Std on LS] +70
Power Drivers Seat[Std on LS] +85
Power Windows[Std on LS] +80

CAVALIER   1994

Wagon is sold without trim designation. Base engine is up 10 horsepower to 120. Automatic door locks unlock when ignition is turned off. Feature is defeated by yanking a fuse.

RATINGS (SCALE OF 1-10)

Overall	Safety	Reliability	Performance	Comfort	Value
N/A	N/A	6.7	6.4	6.8	8.5

Category E

	Trade-in	Market
2 Dr RS Conv	3935	5620
2 Dr RS Cpe	2835	4050
4 Dr RS Sdn	2910	4160
4 Dr STD Wgn	2845	4065
2 Dr VL Cpe	2380	3400
4 Dr VL Sdn	2450	3500
2 Dr Z24 Conv	5100	7285
2 Dr Z24 Cpe	4035	5765

OPTIONS FOR CAVALIER
6 cyl 3.1 L Engine[Std on Z24] +200
Auto 3-Speed Transmission[Opt on Coupes] +135
AM/FM Stereo Tape[Std on Z24] +80
Air Conditioning[Opt on VL] +220
Cruise Control +60
Power Windows[Std on Conv] +70
Sunroof +95
Tilt Steering Wheel[Std on Z24] +40

CHEVY VAN / SPORTVAN   1994

Driver airbag is added to all models under 8,500-lb. GVWR. Side-door guard beams are installed in front doors and a high-mount center brake light is added.

CHEVY VAN

Category H

	Trade-in	Market
2 Dr G10 Chevy Van	5310	6720
2 Dr G10 Chevy Van Ext	5650	7155
2 Dr G20 Chevy Van	5595	7080
2 Dr G20 Chevy Van Ext	5855	7410
2 Dr G30 Chevy Van	5785	7320
2 Dr G30 Chevy Van Ext	6060	7670

SPORTVAN

Category H

	Trade-in	Market
2 Dr G20 Sportvan	5520	6990
2 Dr G20 Beauville Sportvan	6085	7700
2 Dr G30 Sportvan	6160	7800
2 Dr G30 Sportvan Ext	6500	8230
2 Dr G30 Beauville Sportvan	6560	8305
2 Dr G30 Beauville Sportvan Ext	6880	8710

OPTIONS FOR CHEVY VAN/SPORTVAN
8 cyl 5.0 L Engine +165
8 cyl 5.7 L Engine[Opt on G20] +195
8 cyl 6.5 L Dsl Engine +735
8 cyl 7.4 L Engine +160
15 Passenger Seating +225
AM/FM Stereo Tape +60
Air Conditioning[Opt on G10,STD] +220
Cruise Control[Opt on G10,STD] +50
Dual Air Conditioning +360
Power Door Locks[Opt on G10,STD] +50
Power Windows[Opt on G10,STD] +50
Privacy Glass +45
Tilt Steering Wheel[Opt on G10,STD] +50

CORSICA   1994

Door mounted seatbelts are added. Engines gain power; the 2.2-liter unit is up to 120 horsepower, and the optional, 3.1-liter V6 now makes 160 horsepower. Sport Handling Package dropped from options list. Manual transmission dropped. Automatic door locks now unlock when car is shut off. This feature can be disabled by pulling a fuse. Interior lights will shut off automatically after 10 minutes to save the battery. Warning chime sounds if turn signal is left on.

RATINGS (SCALE OF 1-10)

Overall	Safety	Reliability	Performance	Comfort	Value
6.9	5.8	7.3	8	7.5	6.1

Category C

	Trade-in	Market
4 Dr STD Sdn	2710	3665

OPTIONS FOR CORSICA
6 cyl 3.1 L Engine +140
AM/FM Stereo Tape +45
Cruise Control +55
Power Windows +85
Tilt Steering Wheel +40

CORVETTE   1994

Passenger airbag is added. Traction control is standard. A new steering wheel and redesigned seats are added inside. Leather upholstery is standard.

CHEVROLET 94

Model Description	Trade-in Value	Market Value	Model Description	Trade-in Value	Market Value

Automatic transmission gets electronic shift controls and brake/transmission shift interlock. Convertible gets glass rear window with defogger. ZR-1 has new five-spoke alloys. Power windows gain express-down feature for driver's side. Selective Ride Control system has softer springs.

Category J

2 Dr STD Conv	14540	18175
2 Dr STD Cpe	12880	16100
2 Dr ZR1 Cpe	20755	25945

OPTIONS FOR CORVETTE

Adjustable Handling Pkg +560
Selective Ride & Handling +465
Bose Sound System[Opt on STD] +220
Power Drivers Seat[Opt on STD] +90
Power Passenger Seat[Opt on STD] +90
Solid & Glass Targa Tops +255

IMPALA   1994

Caprice-based sedan powered by 260-horsepower, 5.7-liter V8 and sporting monochromatic black paint debuts to critical acclaim. Has four-wheel disc brakes, dual airbags, ABS, five-spoke alloys, and restyled C-pillars.

RATINGS (SCALE OF 1-10)

Overall	Safety	Reliability	Performance	Comfort	Value
8	8	6	9	8.3	8.5

Category B

4 Dr SS Sdn	9400	12370

OPTIONS FOR IMPALA

AM/FM Compact Disc Player +90
Keyless Entry System +45

LUMINA   1994

Base coupe is dropped from lineup. Manual transmission disappears.

RATINGS (SCALE OF 1-10)

Overall	Safety	Reliability	Performance	Comfort	Value
N/A	N/A	7.8	8.2	7.6	7.9

Category C

2 Dr Euro Cpe	4510	6095
4 Dr Euro Sdn	4590	6200
4 Dr STD Sdn	3945	5330
2 Dr Z34 Cpe	5075	6855

OPTIONS FOR LUMINA

6 cyl 3.4 L Engine[Std on Z34] +310
AM/FM Stereo Tape[Opt on STD] +45
Anti-Lock Brakes[Opt on STD] +165
Cruise Control[Std on Z34] +55
Power Drivers Seat +80
Power Windows[Opt on STD] +85

LUMINA MINIVAN   1994

APV designation dropped in favor of more descriptive "Minivan" nomenclature. Front styling is revised; overall length drops three inches. Driver airbag is standard. Integrated child seats and remote keyless entry are newly optional. Midyear, traction control becomes available on LS model.

RATINGS (SCALE OF 1-10)

Overall	Safety	Reliability	Performance	Comfort	Value
7.3	6.9	6.3	7.6	7.5	8.4

Category G

2 Dr STD Cargo Van	3435	4460
2 Dr STD Pass. Van	4695	6100

OPTIONS FOR LUMINA MINIVAN

6 cyl 3.8 L Engine +170
Auto 4-Speed Transmission +55
AM/FM Stereo Tape +60
Air Conditioning +220
Cruise Control +55
Power Door Locks +65
Power Drivers Seat +75
Power Windows +65
Privacy Glass +70
Tilt Steering Wheel +50

S10 BLAZER   1994

Side-door guard beams and a high-mount center brake light are added. Front bench seat is now standard on four-door models.

RATINGS (SCALE OF 1-10)

Overall	Safety	Reliability	Performance	Comfort	Value
6	5.1	6.6	6.8	7.1	4.6

Category G

2 Dr STD Utility	5220	6780
2 Dr STD 4WD Utility	5700	7405
4 Dr STD Wgn	5750	7465
4 Dr STD 4WD Wgn	6235	8100
2 Dr Tahoe Utility	5400	7015
2 Dr Tahoe 4WD Utility	6170	8015
4 Dr Tahoe Wgn	5950	7730
4 Dr Tahoe 4WD Wgn	6605	8575
2 Dr Tahoe LT Utility	6100	7920
2 Dr Tahoe LT 4WD Utility	6785	8810
4 Dr Tahoe LT Wgn	6585	8550
4 Dr Tahoe LT 4WD Wgn	7255	9420

OPTIONS FOR S10 BLAZER

6 cyl 4.3 L CPI Engine +155
Auto 4-Speed Transmission +245
AM/FM Stereo Tape[Std on Tahoe LT] +60
Air Conditioning[Std on Tahoe LT] +220

Don't forget to refer to the Mileage Adjustment Table at the back of this book!

Model Description	Trade-in Value	Market Value	Model Description	Trade-in Value	Market Value

CHEVROLET 94-93

Cruise Control[Opt on STD] +55
Keyless Entry System[Std on Tahoe LT] +55
Power Door Locks[Std on Tahoe LT] +65
Power Drivers Seat[Std on Tahoe LT] +75
Power Windows[Std on Tahoe LT] +65
Tilt Steering Wheel[Opt on STD] +50

S10 PICKUP   1994

All-new truck debuts with more powerful engines and available four-wheel ABS. Side-door guard beams are standard. Rear ABS is standard on four cylinder models; V6 trucks get the new, four-wheel ABS system that works in both two- and four-wheel drive. ZR2 package is for serious off-roaders. Available only on regular-cab shortbed models, the ZR2 package includes four-inch wider track, three-inch height increase, off-road suspension and tires, wheel flares and thick skid plates. Base engine is 118-horse, 2.2-liter four cylinder. Standard on 4WD models is a 165-horsepower 4.3-liter V6. Optional on all models is a 195-horsepower, high-output 4.3-liter V6. SS package available with high-output engine, sport suspension and alloy wheels.

RATINGS (SCALE OF 1-10)

Overall	Safety	Reliability	Performance	Comfort	Value
N/A	5.2	6.5	6.6	8.1	N/A

Category G

	Trade-in	Market
2 Dr LS Ext Cab SB	4780	6210
2 Dr LS 4WD Ext Cab SB	6305	8190
2 Dr LS Std Cab LB	4375	5680
2 Dr LS 4WD Std Cab LB	5875	7630
2 Dr LS Std Cab SB	4235	5500
2 Dr LS 4WD Std Cab SB	5745	7460
2 Dr STD Std Cab LB	4110	5340
2 Dr STD 4WD Std Cab LB	5790	7520
2 Dr STD Std Cab SB	3985	5175
2 Dr STD 4WD Std Cab SB	5675	7370

OPTIONS FOR S10 PICKUP

6 cyl 4.3 L Engine[Opt on 2WD] +235
Auto 4-Speed Transmission +255
Wide Stance Pkg +460
AM/FM Stereo Tape +60
Air Conditioning +220
Anti-Lock Brakes[Opt on 2WD] +160
Cruise Control +55
Power Door Locks +65
Power Windows +65
Tilt Steering Wheel +50

SUBURBAN   1994

Side-door guard beams are added, as well as a high-mounted center brake light. A turbocharged diesel is newly optional on 2500 models. A new grille appears.

RATINGS (SCALE OF 1-10)

Overall	Safety	Reliability	Performance	Comfort	Value
6.7	6.4	6.7	6.8	7.5	6.3

Category H

	Trade-in	Market
4 Dr C1500 Wgn	10175	12880
4 Dr C2500 Wgn	10995	13920
4 Dr K1500 4WD Wgn	11220	14200
4 Dr K2500 4WD Wgn	12135	15360

OPTIONS FOR SUBURBAN

8 cyl 6.5 L Turbodsl Engine +845
8 cyl 7.4 L Engine +160
Silverado Pkg +560
AM/FM Stereo Tape +60
Air Conditioning +220
Camper/Towing Package +90
Cruise Control +50
Dual Air Conditioning +360
Leather Seats +265
Power Door Locks +50
Power Drivers Seat +75
Power Windows +50
Tilt Steering Wheel +50

1993 CHEVROLET

ASTRO   1993

Base 4.3-liter V6 gets 15 additional horsepower. Automatic transmission gets electronic shift controls and second-gear start feature. New speedometer reads to 100 mph. Driver airbag is offered as an option midyear.

RATINGS (SCALE OF 1-10)

Overall	Safety	Reliability	Performance	Comfort	Value
6.6	4	6.3	7.2	6.6	9

Category G

	Trade-in	Market
2 Dr CL Pass. Van	3810	5080
2 Dr CL 4WD Pass. Van	4615	6150
2 Dr CL Pass. Van Ext	4290	5720
2 Dr CL 4WD Pass. Van Ext	4965	6620
2 Dr LT Pass. Van	4025	5365
2 Dr LT 4WD Pass. Van	5210	6945
2 Dr LT Pass. Van Ext	4540	6050
2 Dr LT 4WD Pass. Van Ext	5500	7330
2 Dr STD Cargo Van	2845	3790
2 Dr STD 4WD Cargo Van	4075	5435
2 Dr STD Cargo Van Ext	3080	4105
2 Dr STD 4WD Cargo Van Ext	4415	5885
2 Dr STD Pass. Van	3670	4890
2 Dr STD 4WD Pass. Van	4575	6100
2 Dr STD Pass. Van Ext	3920	5225

Don't forget to refer to the Mileage Adjustment Table at the back of this book!

Model Description	Trade-in Value	Market Value

Model Description	Trade-in Value	Market Value

OPTIONS FOR ASTRO
6 cyl 4.3 L CPI Engine[Opt on CL,Pass. Van Ext,2WD] +110
8 Passenger Seating +90
AM/FM Stereo Tape +50
Air Conditioning +180
Cruise Control +45
Dual Air Conditioning +210
Power Door Locks +50
Power Drivers Seat +60
Power Windows +55
Privacy Glass[Std on LT] +60

BERETTA   1993

Standard engine on the GT is now a ridiculous 110-horsepower four-cylinder from the base car. The V6 is optional. GTZ's Quad 4 engine loses five horsepower to emissions regulations. A brake/shift interlock has been added to automatic transmissions. Manuals get an improved clutch.

RATINGS (SCALE OF 1-10)

Overall	Safety	Reliability	Performance	Comfort	Value
6.9	6.6	7.7	7.8	7	5.3

Category E

		Trade-in	Market
2 Dr GT Cpe		2785	4155
2 Dr GTZ Cpe		3185	4750
2 Dr STD Cpe		2490	3720

OPTIONS FOR BERETTA
6 cyl 3.1 L Engine +135
Auto 3-Speed Transmission +125
AM/FM Stereo Tape +65
Air Conditioning[Std on GTZ] +180
Cruise Control +50
Power Door Locks +55
Power Windows +60
Tilt Steering Wheel +35

BLAZER   1993

No changes.
Category H

		Trade-in	Market
2 Dr STD 4WD Utility		7760	9825
2 Dr Silverado 4WD Utility		8435	10675
2 Dr Sport 4WD Utility		8155	10325

OPTIONS FOR BLAZER
Auto 4-Speed Transmission +200
AM/FM Stereo Tape +45
Air Conditioning[Opt on Sport,STD] +180
Cruise Control[Opt on Sport,STD] +40
Power Door Locks +40
Power Drivers Seat +60
Power Windows +40
Tilt Steering Wheel[Opt on Sport,STD] +40

C/K PICKUP   1993

Solar-Ray tinted glass is made standard. Cloth interior surfaces are now protected by Scotchgard fabric protection. Automatic transmissions get electronic shift controls. Base V6 gets five additional horsepower.

RATINGS (SCALE OF 1-10)

Overall	Safety	Reliability	Performance	Comfort	Value
N/A	5.6	7.1	7.4	8	N/A

C/K 1500 SERIES

Category H

	Trade-in	Market
2 Dr C1500 Cheyenne Ext Cab LB	6665	8435
2 Dr C1500 Cheyenne Ext Cab SB	6600	8355
2 Dr C1500 Cheyenne Ext Cab Stepside SB	6815	8625
2 Dr C1500 Cheyenne Std Cab LB	5975	7565
2 Dr C1500 Cheyenne Std Cab SB	5895	7465
2 Dr C1500 Cheyenne Std Cab Stepside SB	6150	7785
2 Dr C1500 Silverado Ext Cab LB	7015	8880
2 Dr C1500 Silverado Ext Cab SB	6910	8745
2 Dr C1500 Silverado Ext Cab Stepside SB	7120	9015
2 Dr C1500 Silverado Std Cab LB	6160	7800
2 Dr C1500 Silverado Std Cab SB	6035	7640
2 Dr C1500 Silverado Std Cab Stepside SB	6330	8010
2 Dr C1500 Sport Std Cab Stepside SB	6350	8040
2 Dr C1500 Work Truck Std Cab LB	4855	6145
2 Dr K1500 Cheyenne 4WD Ext Cab LB	7245	9170
2 Dr K1500 Cheyenne 4WD Ext Cab SB	7135	9030
2 Dr K1500 Cheyenne 4WD Ext Cab Stepside SB	7315	9260
2 Dr K1500 Cheyenne 4WD Std Cab LB	6615	8375
2 Dr K1500 Cheyenne 4WD Std Cab SB	6530	8265

Don't forget to refer to the Mileage Adjustment Table at the back of this book!

Model Description	Trade-in Value	Market Value
2 Dr K1500 Cheyenne 4WD Std Cab Stepside SB	6715	8500
2 Dr K1500 Silverado 4WD Ext Cab LB	8155	10320
2 Dr K1500 Silverado 4WD Ext Cab SB	8095	10245
2 Dr K1500 Silverado 4WD Ext Cab Stepside SB	8305	10510
2 Dr K1500 Silverado 4WD Std Cab LB	7195	9105
2 Dr K1500 Silverado 4WD Std Cab SB	7110	9000
2 Dr K1500 Silverado 4WD Std Cab Stepside SB	7720	9770
2 Dr K1500 Work Truck 4WD Std Cab LB	5680	7190

C/K 2500 SERIES

Category H

Model Description	Trade-in Value	Market Value
2 Dr C2500 Cheyenne Ext Cab LB	6990	8850
2 Dr C2500 Cheyenne Ext Cab SB	6930	8775
2 Dr C2500 Cheyenne Std Cab LB	6285	7955
2 Dr C2500 Silverado Ext Cab LB	6975	8830
2 Dr C2500 Silverado Ext Cab SB	6915	8755
2 Dr C2500 Silverado Std Cab LB	6385	8080
2 Dr K2500 Cheyenne 4WD Ext Cab LB	8355	10575
2 Dr K2500 Cheyenne 4WD Ext Cab SB	8260	10455
2 Dr K2500 Cheyenne 4WD Std Cab LB	7610	9635
2 Dr K2500 Silverado 4WD Ext Cab LB	8465	10715
2 Dr K2500 Silverado 4WD Ext Cab SB	8655	10955
2 Dr K2500 Silverado 4WD Std Cab LB	7760	9820

C/K 3500 SERIES

Category H

Model Description	Trade-in Value	Market Value
4 Dr C3500 Crew Cab LB	9075	11490
2 Dr C3500 Ext Cab LB	8425	10665
2 Dr C3500 Cheyenne Std Cab LB	7690	9735
4 Dr C3500 Silverado Crew Cab LB	9045	11450

Model Description	Trade-in Value	Market Value
4 Dr C3500 Silverado Turbodsl Crew Cab SB	9305	11780
2 Dr C3500 Silverado Ext Cab LB	8630	10925
2 Dr C3500 Silverado Std Cab LB	8050	10190
4 Dr K3500 4WD Crew Cab LB	9775	12375
2 Dr K3500 Cheyenne 4WD Ext Cab LB	9335	11815
2 Dr K3500 Cheyenne 4WD Std Cab LB	8775	11110
4 Dr K3500 Silverado 4WD Crew Cab LB	10075	12750
2 Dr K3500 Silverado 4WD Ext Cab LB	9920	12560
2 Dr K3500 Silverado 4WD Std Cab LB	9000	11390

OPTIONS FOR C/K PICKUP

8 cyl 5.0 L Engine +135
8 cyl 5.7 L Engine +190
8 cyl 6.2 L Dsl Engine +475
8 cyl 6.5 L Turbodsl Engine +625
8 cyl 7.4 L Engine +175
Auto 4-Speed Transmission[Std on 454SS] +200
AM/FM Stereo Tape[Std on Sport] +45
Air Conditioning[Opt on Cheyenne,STD,Work Truck] +180
Bed Liner +50
Camper/Towing Package +75
Cruise Control[Std on 454SS,Sport,Silverado] +40
Power Door Locks[Std on 454SS,Sport] +40
Power Drivers Seat +60
Power Windows[Std on 454SS,Sport] +40

CAMARO   1993

All-new sports coupe is redesigned for the first time in 12 years. Dual airbags and ABS are standard. Convertible disappears for one year. Available in base and Z28 trim. Base model powered by 3.4-liter V6; Z28 gets 5.7-liter V8 rated at 275 horsepower (115 more than base Camaro). Z28 has a six-speed manual transmission standard.

RATINGS (SCALE OF 1-10)

Overall	Safety	Reliability	Performance	Comfort	Value
7.4	8.7	6.9	9.2	6.8	5.3

Category F

Model Description	Trade-in Value	Market Value
2 Dr STD Cpe	4405	5875
2 Dr Z28 Cpe	5840	7785

OPTIONS FOR CAMARO

Auto 4-Speed Transmission +135
Air Conditioning +185
Aluminum/Alloy Wheels[Opt on STD] +70
Bose Sound System +120
Glass Panel T-tops +220

Don't forget to refer to the Mileage Adjustment Table at the back of this book!

CHEVROLET 93

Model Description	Trade-in Value	Market Value	Model Description	Trade-in Value	Market Value

Power Door Locks +45
Power Drivers Seat +55
Power Windows +50

CAPRICE 1993

Rear styling is revised, and rear wheel wells are opened up. Rear track is increased 1.6 inches. LTZ gets a 180-horsepower 5.7-liter V8 standard. Acoustical package added to reduce noise. LS trim level gets gold accents on wheels and trim.

RATINGS (SCALE OF 1-10)

Overall	Safety	Reliability	Performance	Comfort	Value
7.9	7	7.3	7.6	8.3	9.3

Category B
4 Dr LS Sdn	4805	6580
4 Dr LTZ Sdn	4695	6430
4 Dr STD Sdn	3960	5425
4 Dr STD Wgn	5225	7155

OPTIONS FOR CAPRICE
8 cyl 5.7 L Engine +55
AM/FM Stereo Tape +40
Cruise Control +50
Leather Seats +150
Power Door Locks[Std on LS,LTZ] +55
Power Drivers Seat +70
Power Windows[Std on LTZ] +65

CAVALIER 1993

Convertible gets glass rear window, and RS coupes and sedans can be equipped with the Z24's 3.1-liter V6. A CD player is a new option on VL models. RS gets Z24 interior trimmings.

RATINGS (SCALE OF 1-10)

Overall	Safety	Reliability	Performance	Comfort	Value
N/A	N/A	7.1	6.4	6.8	7.2

Category E
2 Dr RS Conv	3010	4490
2 Dr RS Cpe	2030	3030
4 Dr RS Sdn	2110	3150
4 Dr RS Wgn	2190	3265
2 Dr VL Cpe	1835	2740
4 Dr VL Sdn	1930	2880
4 Dr VL Wgn	2045	3050
2 Dr Z24 Conv	4055	6050
2 Dr Z24 Cpe	3025	4515

OPTIONS FOR CAVALIER
6 cyl 3.1 L Engine[Opt on RS] +135
Auto 3-Speed Transmission[Std on Wgn] +110
AM/FM Stereo Tape +65
Air Conditioning +180
Cruise Control +50
Power Windows[Std on Conv] +60

CHEVY VAN/SPORTVAN 1993

Solar-Ray tinted glass and Scotchgard fabric protectant are both standard. Four-wheel ABS is a new standard feature. Remote keyless entry joins the options list.

CHEVY VAN

Category H
2 Dr G10 Chevy Van	4455	5640
2 Dr G10 Chevy Van Ext	4645	5880
2 Dr G20 Chevy Van	4715	5970
2 Dr G20 Chevy Van Ext	4910	6215
2 Dr G30 Chevy Van	4835	6120
2 Dr G30 Chevy Van Ext	5070	6420

SPORTVAN

Category H
2 Dr G10 Sportvan	4725	5980
2 Dr G10 Sportvan Ext	4845	6135
2 Dr G10 Beauville Sportvan	4955	6270
2 Dr G10 Beauville Sportvan Ext	5130	6495
2 Dr G20 Sportvan Ext	4995	6320
2 Dr G20 Beauville Sportvan Ext	5195	6575
2 Dr G30 Sportvan	5035	6375
2 Dr G30 Sportvan Ext	5245	6640
2 Dr G30 Beauville Sportvan	5365	6790
2 Dr G30 Beauville Sportvan Ext	5600	7090

OPTIONS FOR CHEVY VAN/SPORTVAN
8 cyl 5.0 L Engine +135
8 cyl 5.7 L Engine[Opt on G10,G20,Chevy Van] +190
8 cyl 6.2 L Dsl Engine +475
8 cyl 7.4 L Engine +175
12 Passenger Seating +135
AM/FM Stereo Tape +45
Air Conditioning +180
Cruise Control +40
Dual Air Conditioning +295
Power Door Locks +40
Power Windows +40
Tilt Steering Wheel +40

CORSICA 1993

Wow. A brake/transmission shift interlock is added. Larger muffler is supposed to make Corsica quieter.

RATINGS (SCALE OF 1-10)

Overall	Safety	Reliability	Performance	Comfort	Value
6.8	5.8	7.6	6.8	7.3	6.4

Category C
4 Dr LT Sdn	2085	2895

Model Description	Trade-in Value	Market Value	Model Description	Trade-in Value	Market Value

OPTIONS FOR CORSICA

6 cyl 3.1 L Engine +135
Auto 3-Speed Transmission +125
AM/FM Stereo Tape +35
Air Conditioning +180
Cruise Control +45
Power Door Locks +55
Power Drivers Seat +65
Power Windows +70
Tilt Steering Wheel +35

CORVETTE   1993

Base model gets narrower front tires and wider rear tires. LT1 V8 gets additional torque. ZR-1 horsepower is up to 405 this year. All models can be ordered in 40th Anniversary trim, consisting of Ruby Red paint and badging. Passive Keyless Entry is newly optional, and locks or unlocks the doors simply by having the key fob close to the car.

Category J

	Trade-in	Market
2 Dr STD Conv	13255	16780
2 Dr STD Cpe	11800	14935
2 Dr ZR1 Cpe	19450	24620

OPTIONS FOR CORVETTE

Adjustable Handling Pkg +305
Selective Ride Suspension +380
Bose Sound System +180
Leather Seats[Opt on STD] +260
Power Drivers Seat[Opt on STD] +75
Solid & Glass Targa Tops +210

LUMINA   1993

Base sedans get five more horsepower this year, and base coupes now have standard V6 power. Doors lock automatically when vehicle reaches eight mph.

RATINGS (SCALE OF 1-10)

Overall	Safety	Reliability	Performance	Comfort	Value
N/A	N/A	7.5	8.2	7.6	8.4

Category C

	Trade-in	Market
2 Dr Euro Cpe	3395	4715
4 Dr Euro Sdn	3465	4810
2 Dr STD Cpe	2770	3845
4 Dr STD Sdn	2840	3945
2 Dr Z34 Cpe	4095	5685

OPTIONS FOR LUMINA

6 cyl 3.1 L Engine[Std on Euro,Cpe] +135
6 cyl 3.4 L Engine[Std on Z34] +225
Auto 4-Speed Transmission +45
AM/FM Stereo Tape[Std on Z34] +35
Air Conditioning[Opt on STD Sdn] +180
Anti-Lock Brakes[Opt on STD] +135
Cruise Control[Std on Z34] +45
Power Drivers Seat +65
Power Windows +70
Tilt Steering Wheel[Std on Z34] +35

LUMINA MINIVAN   1993

Uplevel trim switches from CL to LS designation. Sunroof joins options list this year. Center console is redesigned to include dual cupholders.

RATINGS (SCALE OF 1-10)

Overall	Safety	Reliability	Performance	Comfort	Value
7.1	5.8	6.5	7.6	7.5	8.3

Category G

	Trade-in	Market
2 Dr LS Pass. Van	3760	5015
2 Dr STD Pass. Van	3530	4705

OPTIONS FOR LUMINA MINIVAN

6 cyl 3.8 L Engine +140
Auto 4-Speed Transmission +45
AM/FM Stereo Tape +50
Air Conditioning[Std on LS] +180
Cruise Control +45
Power Door Locks +50
Power Drivers Seat +60
Power Windows +55
Privacy Glass +60
Tilt Steering Wheel[Std on LS] +40

S10 BLAZER   1993

Two-door model available in LT trim. All models get two-tone paint scheme in LT trim. V6 engines get internal balance shaft designed to reduce vibration. Automatic transmission receives electronic shift controls and second-gear start feature. Manual lumbar adjusters are newly standard on front seats.

RATINGS (SCALE OF 1-10)

Overall	Safety	Reliability	Performance	Comfort	Value
5.9	5.1	6.1	6.8	7.1	4.3

Category G

	Trade-in	Market
2 Dr STD Utility	4245	5660
2 Dr STD 4WD Utility	4730	6305
4 Dr STD Wgn	4615	6150
4 Dr STD 4WD Wgn	5235	6980
2 Dr Tahoe Utility	4410	5880
2 Dr Tahoe 4WD Utility	5050	6735
4 Dr Tahoe Wgn	4810	6410
4 Dr Tahoe 4WD Wgn	5490	7320
2 Dr Tahoe LT Utility	4990	6655
2 Dr Tahoe LT 4WD Utility	5580	7440
4 Dr Tahoe LT Wgn	5350	7130
4 Dr Tahoe LT 4WD Wgn	6060	8080

OPTIONS FOR S10 BLAZER

6 cyl 4.3 L CPI Engine +110
Auto 4-Speed Transmission +200
AM/FM Stereo Tape[Std on Tahoe LT] +50
Air Conditioning[Std on Tahoe LT] +180
Cruise Control[Std on Tahoe LT] +45

Don't forget to refer to the Mileage Adjustment Table at the back of this book!

CHEVROLET 93-92

Model Description	Trade-in Value	Market Value	Model Description	Trade-in Value	Market Value

Leather Seats[Std on Tahoe LT] +170
Power Door Locks[Std on Tahoe LT] +50
Power Drivers Seat[Std on Tahoe LT] +60
Power Windows[Std on Tahoe LT] +55
Tilt Steering Wheel[Opt on STD] +40

S10 PICKUP   1993

V6 engines get internal balance shaft designed to reduce vibration. Automatic transmission gets electronic shift controls.

RATINGS (SCALE OF 1-10)

Overall	Safety	Reliability	Performance	Comfort	Value
N/A	3.4	6.6	7.2	7	N/A

Category G

2 Dr EL Std Cab SB	2880	3840
2 Dr EL 4WD Std Cab SB	4320	5760
2 Dr STD Ext Cab SB	3860	5145
2 Dr STD 4WD Ext Cab SB	5095	6790
2 Dr STD Std Cab LB	3225	4300
2 Dr STD 4WD Std Cab LB	4720	6290
2 Dr STD Std Cab SB	3160	4210
2 Dr STD 4WD Std Cab SB	4645	6195
2 Dr Tahoe Ext Cab SB	3985	5315
2 Dr Tahoe 4WD Ext Cab SB	5185	6910
2 Dr Tahoe Std Cab LB	3495	4660
2 Dr Tahoe 4WD Std Cab LB	4870	6490
2 Dr Tahoe Std Cab SB	3395	4525
2 Dr Tahoe 4WD Std Cab SB	4755	6340

OPTIONS FOR S10 PICKUP

6 cyl 2.8 L Engine +85
6 cyl 4.3 L Engine[Opt on 2WD] +140
Auto 4-Speed Transmission +200
AM/FM Stereo Tape[Opt on EL,STD] +50
Air Conditioning +180
Cruise Control +45
Power Windows +55
Tilt Steering Wheel +40

SUBURBAN   1993

No changes.

RATINGS (SCALE OF 1-10)

Overall	Safety	Reliability	Performance	Comfort	Value
6.9	6.6	6.9	6.8	7.5	6.7

Category H

4 Dr C1500 Wgn	8860	11215
4 Dr C2500 Wgn	9500	12025
4 Dr K1500 4WD Wgn	9770	12365
4 Dr K2500 4WD Wgn	10435	13210

OPTIONS FOR SUBURBAN

8 cyl 7.4 L Engine +175
Silverado Pkg +475
AM/FM Stereo Tape +45

Air Conditioning +180
Camper/Towing Package +75
Cruise Control +40
Dual Air Conditioning +295
Leather Seats +215
Power Door Locks +40
Power Drivers Seat +60
Power Windows +40
Tilt Steering Wheel +40

1992 CHEVROLET

ASTRO   1992

Dutch rear door treatment is available. With Dutch doors, a rear washer/wiper and rear defogger can be ordered. All-wheel-drive models get high-output, 200-horsepower, V6 standard. Engine is optional on 2WD models.

RATINGS (SCALE OF 1-10)

Overall	Safety	Reliability	Performance	Comfort	Value
6.5	3.6	6.9	7.2	6.6	8

Category G

2 Dr CL Pass. Van	3130	4290
2 Dr CL 4WD Pass. Van	3795	5200
2 Dr CL Pass. Van Ext	3575	4895
2 Dr CL 4WD Pass. Van Ext	4155	5695
2 Dr LT Pass. Van	3310	4535
2 Dr LT 4WD Pass. Van	4245	5815
2 Dr LT Pass. Van Ext	3745	5130
2 Dr LT 4WD Pass. Van Ext	4470	6125
2 Dr STD Cargo Van	2395	3280
2 Dr STD 4WD Cargo Van	3135	4295
2 Dr STD Cargo Van Ext	2630	3600
2 Dr STD 4WD Cargo Van Ext	3490	4780
2 Dr STD Pass. Van	3210	4400
2 Dr STD 4WD Pass. Van	3805	5210
2 Dr STD Pass. Van Ext	3455	4730
2 Dr STD 4WD Pass. Van Ext	4130	5655

OPTIONS FOR ASTRO

6 cyl 4.3 L CPI Engine +95
8 Passenger Seating +70
Air Conditioning +145
Power Door Locks +40
Power Drivers Seat +50
Power Windows +45

BERETTA   1992

ABS is standard. Base engine gains 15 horsepower. GTZ gets revised gearing for better off-the-line acceleration. Base V6 models get gearing change designed to save fuel. Order a GTZ with the V6, and you'll get touring tires instead of high-performance rubber. Front brakes are slightly larger on all models.

Model Description	Trade-in Value	Market Value

RATINGS (SCALE OF 1-10)

Overall	Safety	Reliability	Performance	Comfort	Value
6.8	6.6	6.7	7.8	7	5.7

Category E

2 Dr GT Cpe	2255	3520
2 Dr GTZ Cpe	2505	3915
2 Dr STD Cpe	1940	3030

OPTIONS FOR BERETTA

6 cyl 3.1 L Engine +110
Auto 3-Speed Transmission +100
Air Conditioning[Std on GT] +145
Cruise Control +40
Power Door Locks +45
Power Windows +50

BLAZER   1992

Totally redesigned and based on same platform and sheetmetal as C/K pickup. Six-passenger seating is standard. Cargo area gets fixed metal roof rather than fiberglass shell. Four-wheel ABS is standard and works in 4WD. New Sport appearance package includes two-tone paint and wheelwell flares. Diesel option is dropped. Five-speed manual is standard transmission. An automatic is optional. Shift-on-the-fly 4WD is standard.

Category H

2 Dr STD 4WD Utility	6755	8775
2 Dr Silverado 4WD Utility	7255	9425
2 Dr Sport 4WD Utility	7085	9200

OPTIONS FOR BLAZER

Auto 4-Speed Transmission +160
Air Conditioning +145
Cruise Control +35
Power Door Locks +35
Power Drivers Seat +50
Power Windows +35

C/K PICKUP   1992

Extended-cab models get Sportside box option. Crew Cab model is all-new, sporting same engineering and styling as rest of C/K line. Front buckets have been redesigned. Standard gauge cluster is restyled. Integral head restraints are added for outboard passengers. A new turbocharged, 6.5-liter diesel V8 is optional in C/K 2500 and regular cab C/K 3500 models. Four-speed manual transmission is dropped.

RATINGS (SCALE OF 1-10)

Overall	Safety	Reliability	Performance	Comfort	Value
N/A	5.6	6.8	7.4	8	N/A

C/K 1500 SERIES

Category H

2 Dr C1500 Ext Cab LB	5485	7125
2 Dr C1500 Ext Cab SB	5420	7040
2 Dr C1500 Ext Cab Stepside SB	5565	7230
2 Dr C1500 Std Cab LB	5040	6545
2 Dr C1500 Std Cab SB	4945	6425
2 Dr C1500 Std Cab Stepside SB	5150	6690
2 Dr C1500 454SS Std Cab SB	8625	11200
2 Dr C1500 Scottsdale Ext Cab LB	5645	7330
2 Dr C1500 Scottsdale Ext Cab SB	5565	7225
2 Dr C1500 Scottsdale Ext Cab Stepside SB	5780	7505
2 Dr C1500 Scottsdale Std Cab LB	5145	6680
2 Dr C1500 Scottsdale Std Cab SB	5030	6535
2 Dr C1500 Scottsdale Std Cab Stepside SB	5220	6780
2 Dr C1500 Silverado Ext Cab LB	5985	7775
2 Dr C1500 Silverado Ext Cab SB	5915	7685
2 Dr C1500 Silverado Ext Cab Stepside SB	6085	7905
2 Dr C1500 Silverado Std Cab LB	5360	6960
2 Dr C1500 Silverado Std Cab SB	5260	6830
2 Dr C1500 Silverado Std Cab Stepside SB	5465	7100
2 Dr C1500 Work Truck Std Cab LB	4250	5520
2 Dr K1500 4WD Ext Cab LB	6855	8900
2 Dr K1500 4WD Ext Cab SB	6745	8760
2 Dr K1500 4WD Ext Cab Stepside SB	6970	9050
2 Dr K1500 4WD Std Cab LB	6050	7855
2 Dr K1500 4WD Std Cab SB	5930	7700
2 Dr K1500 4WD Std Cab Stepside SB	6205	8060
2 Dr K1500 Scottsdale 4WD Ext Cab LB	6730	8740
2 Dr K1500 Scottsdale 4WD Ext Cab SB	6635	8620
2 Dr K1500 Scottsdale 4WD Ext Cab Stepside SB	6845	8890

Model Description	Trade-in Value	Market Value
2 Dr K1500 Scottsdale 4WD Std Cab LB		
	6065	7875
2 Dr K1500 Scottsdale 4WD Std Cab SB		
	5985	7775
2 Dr K1500 Scottsdale 4WD Std Cab Stepside SB		
	6190	8040
2 Dr K1500 Silverado 4WD Ext Cab LB		
	6975	9060
2 Dr K1500 Silverado 4WD Ext Cab SB		
	6905	8970
2 Dr K1500 Silverado 4WD Ext Cab Stepside SB		
	7075	9190
2 Dr K1500 Silverado 4WD Std Cab LB		
	6370	8275
2 Dr K1500 Silverado 4WD Std Cab SB		
	6285	8165
2 Dr K1500 Silverado 4WD Std Cab Stepside SB		
	6440	8365
2 Dr K1500 Work Truck 4WD Std Cab LB		
	5150	6690

C/K 2500 SERIES
Category H

Model Description	Trade-in Value	Market Value
2 Dr C2500 Ext Cab LB	6005	7800
2 Dr C2500 Ext Cab SB	5915	7685
2 Dr C2500 Std Cab LB	5275	6850
2 Dr C2500 Scottsdale Ext Cab LB		
	6175	8020
2 Dr C2500 Scottsdale Ext Cab SB		
	6050	7860
2 Dr C2500 Scottsdale Std Cab LB		
	5565	7225
2 Dr C2500 Silverado Ext Cab LB		
	6255	8125
2 Dr C2500 Silverado Ext Cab SB		
	6175	8020
2 Dr C2500 Silverado Std Cab LB		
	5475	7110
2 Dr K2500 4WD Ext Cab LB	6685	8680
2 Dr K2500 4WD Ext Cab SB	6585	8550
2 Dr K2500 4WD Std Cab LB	6060	7870
2 Dr K2500 Scottsdale 4WD Ext Cab LB		
	6720	8725
2 Dr K2500 Scottsdale 4WD Ext Cab SB		
	6615	8590
2 Dr K2500 Scottsdale 4WD Std Cab LB		
	6195	8045
2 Dr K2500 Silverado 4WD Ext Cab LB		
	7130	9260
2 Dr K2500 Silverado 4WD Ext Cab SB		
	7035	9135

Model Description	Trade-in Value	Market Value
2 Dr K2500 Silverado 4WD Std Cab LB		
	6495	8435

C/K 3500 SERIES
Category H

Model Description	Trade-in Value	Market Value
2 Dr C3500 Ext Cab LB	7260	9430
2 Dr C3500 Std Cab LB	6705	8710
2 Dr C3500 Scottsdale Ext Cab LB		
	7510	9750
2 Dr C3500 Scottsdale Std Cab LB		
	7045	9150
2 Dr C3500 Silverado Ext Cab LB		
	7710	10010
2 Dr C3500 Silverado Std Cab LB		
	7205	9355
4 Dr K3500 4WD Crew Cab LB	8315	10800
2 Dr K3500 4WD Ext Cab LB	7875	10230
2 Dr K3500 4WD Std Cab LB	7065	9175
2 Dr K3500 Scottsdale 4WD Ext Cab LB		
	8185	10630
2 Dr K3500 Scottsdale 4WD Std Cab LB		
	7750	10065
2 Dr K3500 Silverado 4WD Ext Cab LB		
	8400	10910
2 Dr K3500 Silverado 4WD Std Cab LB		
	7825	10160
4 Dr Silverado Crew Cab LB	8595	11165

OPTIONS FOR C/K PICKUP
8 cyl 5.0 L Engine +105
8 cyl 5.7 L Engine +150
8 cyl 6.2 L Dsl Engine +375
8 cyl 6.5 L Turbodsl Engine +480
8 cyl 7.4 L Engine +135
Auto 4-Speed Transmission[Std on 454SS] +160
Silverado Pkg +190
Sport Handling Pkg +160
Air Conditioning +145
Camper/Towing Package +60
Cruise Control[Std on 454SS,Silverado] +35
Power Door Locks[Std on 454SS] +35
Power Drivers Seat +50
Power Windows[Std on 454SS] +35

CAMARO   1992

Heritage Appearance option, essentially a couple of sport stripes and a dashboard plaque, commemorates Camaro's 25th anniversary. Z28 models get quicker steering and an improved suspension.

Category F

Model Description	Trade-in Value	Market Value
2 Dr RS Conv	4850	6645
2 Dr RS Cpe	3600	4930
2 Dr Z28 Conv	5615	7690
2 Dr Z28 Cpe	4595	6295

Don't forget to refer to the Mileage Adjustment Table at the back of this book!

OPTIONS FOR CAMARO
8 cyl 5.0 L Engine[Opt on RS] +65
8 cyl 5.7 L Engine +80
Auto 4-Speed Transmission +95
Air Conditioning +150
Bose Sound System +95
Glass Panel T-tops +180
Leather Seats +120
Power Door Locks +35
Power Drivers Seat +45
Power Windows +40

CAPRICE 1992

Station wagon gets more powerful V8 option. Speedometer now reads to 100 mph, tilt steering is standard, and wagon's quarter vent windows are power operated.

RATINGS (SCALE OF 1-10)

Overall	Safety	Reliability	Performance	Comfort	Value
7.2	6.6	5.5	7.6	8.3	8.1

Category B
4 Dr Classic Sdn	3610	5160
4 Dr STD Sdn	2895	4135
4 Dr STD Wgn	4060	5800

OPTIONS FOR CAPRICE
8 cyl 5.7 L Engine +45
Cruise Control +40
Leather Seats +125
Power Door Locks[Std on Classic] +45
Power Drivers Seat +55
Power Windows +55

CAVALIER 1992

ABS is standard, and base engines are bumped 15 horsepower to 110. RS and Z24 convertibles are back after two-year hiatus. Automatic door locks are added. VL and RS models get new wheelcovers. Z24 trades performance tires for touring.

RATINGS (SCALE OF 1-10)

Overall	Safety	Reliability	Performance	Comfort	Value
N/A	N/A	6.8	6.4	6.8	5.6

Category E
2 Dr RS Conv	2335	3650
2 Dr RS Cpe	1715	2680
4 Dr RS Sdn	1795	2805
4 Dr RS Wgn	1860	2905
2 Dr VL Cpe	1465	2290
4 Dr VL Sdn	1535	2400
4 Dr VL Wgn	1605	2510
2 Dr Z24 Conv	3305	5165
2 Dr Z24 Cpe	2495	3900

OPTIONS FOR CAVALIER
6 cyl 3.1 L Engine[Opt on RS] +110
Auto 3-Speed Transmission[Std on Wgn] +90
Air Conditioning +145
Cruise Control +40
Power Windows[Std on Conv] +50

CHEVY VAN / SPORTVAN 1992

Minor suspension modifications improve the ride.

CHEVY VAN
Category H
2 Dr G10 Chevy Van	3165	4110
2 Dr G10 Chevy Van Ext	3325	4320
2 Dr G20 Chevy Van	3390	4405
2 Dr G20 Chevy Van Ext	3600	4675
2 Dr G30 Chevy Van	3595	4670
2 Dr G30 Chevy Van Ext	3925	5100

SPORTVAN
Category H
2 Dr G10 Sportvan	3665	4760
2 Dr G10 Sportvan Ext	3780	4910
2 Dr G10 Beauville Sportvan	3795	4930
2 Dr G10 Beauville Sportvan Ext	3950	5130
2 Dr G20 Sportvan Ext	3995	5190
2 Dr G20 Beauville Sportvan Ext	4120	5350
2 Dr G30 Sportvan	4380	5690
2 Dr G30 Sportvan Ext	4545	5900
2 Dr G30 Beauville Sportvan Ext	4655	6045

OPTIONS FOR CHEVY VAN/SPORTVAN
8 cyl 5.0 L Engine +105
8 cyl 5.7 L Engine[Opt on G10,G20,Chevy Van Ext] +150
8 cyl 6.2 L Dsl Engine +375
8 cyl 7.4 L Engine +135
12 Passenger Seating +110
Air Conditioning +145
Cruise Control +35
Dual Air Conditioning +240
Power Door Locks +35
Power Windows +35

CORSICA 1992

Five-door hatchback is dropped. ABS is standard, and base engine makes more power. Manual transmission cannot be ordered with V6 this year. V6 models get more fuel-efficient gearing. Front brakes are larger, and optional CD player gets theft-deterrent system. Outside mirrors are body-color.

RATINGS (SCALE OF 1-10)

Overall	Safety	Reliability	Performance	Comfort	Value
6.6	5.8	6.5	6.8	7.3	6.8

Don't forget to refer to the Mileage Adjustment Table at the back of this book!

Model Description	Trade-in Value	Market Value

Category C

| 4 Dr LT Sdn | 1720 | 2495 |

OPTIONS FOR CORSICA
6 cyl 3.1 L Engine +115
Auto 3-Speed Transmission +100
Air Conditioning +145
Cruise Control +40
Power Door Locks +45
Power Windows +55

CORVETTE   1992

New base V8 is the LT1 engine, making 300 horsepower. ZR-1 gets fender badging to distinguish itself from lesser Corvettes. All Corvettes get traction control standard. Speedometer swaps spots with the fuel gauge for better readability. A Quiet Car option adds weather-stripping and sound insulation.

Category J

2 Dr STD Conv	12080	15490
2 Dr STD Cpe	10835	13890
2 Dr ZR1 Cpe	18055	23150

OPTIONS FOR CORVETTE
Handling Pkg +370
Selective Suspension +305
Bose Sound System +150
Compact Disc W/fm/tape[Opt on STD] +145
Leather Seats[Opt on STD] +210
Power Drivers Seat[Opt on STD] +60
Solid & Glass Targa Tops +170

LUMINA   1992

Euro sedan can be equipped with 3.4-liter twin-cam engine. Base engine loses five horsepower. ABS is standard on Z34 and Euro; optional on base models. A CD player joins the options sheet.

RATINGS (SCALE OF 1-10)

Overall	Safety	Reliability	Performance	Comfort	Value
N/A	N/A	6.6	8.2	7.6	8.3

Category C

2 Dr Euro Cpe	2805	4065
4 Dr Euro Sdn	2890	4185
2 Dr STD Cpe	2150	3115
4 Dr STD Sdn	2220	3220
2 Dr Z34 Cpe	3335	4835

OPTIONS FOR LUMINA
6 cyl 3.1 L Engine[Opt on STD] +115
6 cyl 3.4 L Engine[Std on Z34] +180
Auto 4-Speed Transmission +35
Euro 3.4 Pkg +305
Air Conditioning[Opt on STD] +145
Anti-Lock Brakes[Opt on STD] +110
Cruise Control[Std on Z34] +40
Power Door Locks +45

Power Drivers Seat +55
Power Windows +55

LUMINA MINIVAN   1992

An optional 165-horsepower, 3.8-liter V6 with a four-speed automatic is newly available. Wheels and tires are larger this year. Power mirrors and a four-way manual seat adjuster for the driver are new options.

RATINGS (SCALE OF 1-10)

Overall	Safety	Reliability	Performance	Comfort	Value
7.1	5.9	6.3	7.6	7.5	8.3

Category G

2 Dr CL Pass. Van	3245	4445
2 Dr STD Cargo Van	1980	2710
2 Dr STD Pass. Van	3050	4175

OPTIONS FOR LUMINA MINIVAN
6 cyl 3.8 L Engine +120
Auto 4-Speed Transmission +35
Air Conditioning[Std on CL] +145
Cruise Control +40
Power Door Locks +40
Power Drivers Seat +50
Power Windows +45

S10 BLAZER   1992

Four-wheel ABS is standard on all models. Electronic-shift transfer case is added to options list of 4WD models. A high-performance 4.3-liter V6 debuts with 40 additional horsepower, bringing total output to 200 ponies. Bucket seats are redesigned, a new speedometer is installed, and a four-spoke steering wheel is added.

RATINGS (SCALE OF 1-10)

Overall	Safety	Reliability	Performance	Comfort	Value
5.8	3.9	6.2	6.8	7.1	4.9

Category G

2 Dr STD Utility	3550	4865
2 Dr STD 4WD Utility	4010	5495
4 Dr STD Wgn	3780	5180
2 Dr Tahoe Utility	3775	5170
2 Dr Tahoe 4WD Utility	4275	5855
4 Dr Tahoe Wgn	4085	5595
4 Dr Tahoe 4WD Wgn	4715	6460

OPTIONS FOR S10 BLAZER
6 cyl 4.3 L CPI Engine +95
Auto 4-Speed Transmission +160
LT Pkg +150
Air Conditioning +145
Cruise Control +40
Power Door Locks +40
Power Windows +45

Don't forget to refer to the Mileage Adjustment Table at the back of this book!

Model Description	Trade-in Value	Market Value

Model Description	Trade-in Value	Market Value

S10 PICKUP 1992

Base EL model can be equipped with four-wheel drive. Baja package dropped. Front bucket seats are redesigned, integral head restraints are added, and Extended Cabs can be equipped with leather seats. New speedometer and four-spoke steering wheel are installed. Premium sound system with CD player is added to options list. Four-wheel-drive models can be equipped with an electronic-shift transfer case.

RATINGS (SCALE OF 1-10)

Overall	Safety	Reliability	Performance	Comfort	Value
N/A	3.5	6.6	7.2	7	N/A

Category G

	Trade-in	Market
2 Dr EL Std Cab SB	2455	3365
2 Dr EL 4WD Std Cab SB	3750	5135
2 Dr STD Ext Cab SB	3155	4325
2 Dr STD 4WD Ext Cab SB	4150	5685
2 Dr STD Std Cab LB	2710	3715
2 Dr STD 4WD Std Cab LB	3860	5285
2 Dr STD Std Cab SB	2630	3605
2 Dr STD 4WD Std Cab SB	3740	5120
2 Dr Tahoe Ext Cab SB	3275	4485
2 Dr Tahoe 4WD Ext Cab SB	4175	5720
2 Dr Tahoe Std Cab LB	2815	3855
2 Dr Tahoe 4WD Std Cab LB	3870	5300
2 Dr Tahoe Std Cab SB	2750	3765
2 Dr Tahoe 4WD Std Cab SB	3790	5195

OPTIONS FOR S10 PICKUP

6 cyl 2.8 L Engine +70
6 cyl 4.3 L Engine [Opt on 2WD] +110
Auto 4-Speed Transmission +160
Air Conditioning +145
Cruise Control +40
Power Door Locks +40
Power Windows +45

SUBURBAN 1992

All-new design debuts based on platform and styling of C/K pickup. Cargo space and towing capacity are up. ABS works on all four wheels even in 4WD. Tailgate glass is lifted up instead of powered down. No diesel is offered. GM's Instatrac 4WD system is standard on K models.

RATINGS (SCALE OF 1-10)

Overall	Safety	Reliability	Performance	Comfort	Value
6.7	6.4	6.3	6.8	7.5	6.6

Category H

	Trade-in	Market
4 Dr C1500 Wgn	7355	9550
4 Dr C2500 Wgn	7895	10250
4 Dr K1500 4WD Wgn	8175	10615
4 Dr K2500 4WD Wgn	8770	11390

OPTIONS FOR SUBURBAN

8 cyl 7.4 L Engine +135
Silverado Pkg +330
Air Conditioning +145
Cruise Control +35
Dual Air Conditioning +240
Power Door Locks +35
Power Drivers Seat +50
Power Windows +35

1991 CHEVROLET

ASTRO 1991

Cargo models gain the 4.3-liter V6 as standard equipment. A revised Sport Package is available with sport suspension, rally wheels, front air dam with fog lights, and a sport steering wheel. Side and rear windows now have swing-out glass. Extended-length models can be ordered with the Sport Package.

RATINGS (SCALE OF 1-10)

Overall	Safety	Reliability	Performance	Comfort	Value
6.2	3.4	*6.2	7.2	6.6	7.6

Category G

	Trade-in	Market
2 Dr CL Pass. Van	2485	3550
2 Dr CL 4WD Pass. Van	3170	4530
2 Dr CL Pass. Van Ext	2870	4100
2 Dr CL 4WD Pass. Van Ext	3555	5080
2 Dr LT Pass. Van	2680	3825
2 Dr LT 4WD Pass. Van	3615	5165
2 Dr LT Pass. Van Ext	3140	4485
2 Dr LT 4WD Pass. Van Ext	3845	5490
2 Dr STD Cargo Van	2025	2895
2 Dr STD 4WD Cargo Van	2660	3800
2 Dr STD Cargo Van Ext	2260	3230
2 Dr STD 4WD Cargo Van Ext	2940	4200
2 Dr STD Pass. Van	2655	3790
2 Dr STD 4WD Pass. Van	3285	4695
2 Dr STD Pass. Van Ext	2820	4030
2 Dr STD 4WD Pass. Van Ext	3515	5020

OPTIONS FOR ASTRO

6 cyl 4.3 L HO Engine +60
Sport Handling Pkg +135
8 Passenger Seating +60
Air Conditioning +120
Power Door Locks +35
Power Drivers Seat +40
Power Windows +35

Don't forget to refer to the Mileage Adjustment Table at the back of this book!

BERETTA 1991

New dashboard debuts, and a driver airbag is added. Color-keyed lace-spoke alloys are available on GT, along with revised graphics. A CD player is newly optional. GTZ can be ordered with the more tame 3.1-liter V6 found in other Berettas so that folks who hate to shift their own gears can get a GTZ with an automatic transmission. All Quad 4 GTZs come with a five-speed only.

RATINGS (SCALE OF 1-10)

Overall	Safety	Reliability	Performance	Comfort	Value
6.5	5.5	6.9	7.8	7	5.1

Category E
2 Dr GT Cpe	1815	3075
2 Dr GTZ Cpe	2025	3435
2 Dr STD Cpe	1505	2555

OPTIONS FOR BERETTA
6 cyl 3.1 L Engine[Opt on STD] +100
Auto 3-Speed Transmission +80
Air Conditioning[Opt on STD] +120
Cruise Control +35
Power Door Locks +35
Power Windows +40

BLAZER 1991

Throttle-body fuel injection is improved, and more powerful alternator is standard.
Category H
2 Dr STD 4WD Utility	5200	7120
2 Dr Silverado 4WD Utility	5540	7590

OPTIONS FOR BLAZER
8 cyl 6.2 L Dsl Engine +345
Auto 4-Speed Transmission +130
Air Conditioning +120
Cruise Control +30
Power Door Locks +30
Power Windows +30

C/K PICKUP 1991

7.4-liter V8 is reworked, and can be mated to four-speed automatic transmission. 454 SS gets 25 more horsepower. New gauge cluster includes a tachometer. Bucket seats are a new option. Air conditioners get a new recirculation mode. Two-wheel-drive models add tow hooks to the options list. W/T gets new steering wheel and revised outside mirrors.

RATINGS (SCALE OF 1-10)

Overall	Safety	Reliability	Performance	Comfort	Value
N/A	5.7	6.8	7.4	8	N/A

C/K 1500 SERIES

Category H
2 Dr C1500 Ext Cab LB	4695	6430
2 Dr C1500 Ext Cab SB	4610	6315
2 Dr C1500 Std Cab LB	4270	5850
2 Dr C1500 Std Cab SB	4150	5685
2 Dr C1500 Std Cab Stepside SB	4370	5985
2 Dr C1500 454SS Std Cab SB	7120	9750
2 Dr C1500 Scottsdale Ext Cab LB	4900	6710
2 Dr C1500 Scottsdale Ext Cab SB	4835	6625
2 Dr C1500 Scottsdale Std Cab LB	4345	5950
2 Dr C1500 Scottsdale Std Cab SB	4255	5830
2 Dr C1500 Scottsdale Std Cab Stepside SB	4440	6085
2 Dr C1500 Silverado Ext Cab LB	5225	7160
2 Dr C1500 Silverado Ext Cab SB	5160	7070
2 Dr C1500 Silverado Ext Cab Stepside SB	5160	7070
2 Dr C1500 Silverado Std Cab LB	4605	6310
2 Dr C1500 Silverado Std Cab SB	4525	6200
2 Dr C1500 Silverado Std Cab Stepside SB	4725	6470
2 Dr C1500 WT Std Cab LB	3685	5045
2 Dr K1500 4WD Ext Cab LB	5725	7845
2 Dr K1500 4WD Ext Cab SB	5620	7700
2 Dr K1500 4WD Std Cab LB	5230	7165
2 Dr K1500 4WD Std Cab SB	5170	7085
2 Dr K1500 4WD Std Cab Stepside SB	5330	7300
2 Dr K1500 Scottsdale 4WD Ext Cab LB	5790	7930
2 Dr K1500 Scottsdale 4WD Ext Cab SB	5695	7800
2 Dr K1500 Scottsdale 4WD Std Cab LB	5315	7280
2 Dr K1500 Scottsdale 4WD Std Cab SB	5225	7160
2 Dr K1500 Scottsdale 4WD Std Cab Stepside SB	5415	7420
2 Dr K1500 Silverado 4WD Ext Cab LB	6060	8300

Don't forget to refer to the Mileage Adjustment Table at the back of this book!

Model Description	Trade-in Value	Market Value
2 Dr K1500 Silverado 4WD Ext Cab SB		
	5960	8165
2 Dr K1500 Silverado 4WD Ext Cab Stepside SB		
	6130	8400
2 Dr K1500 Silverado 4WD Std Cab LB		
	5470	7490
2 Dr K1500 Silverado 4WD Std Cab SB		
	5385	7380
2 Dr K1500 Silverado 4WD Std Cab Stepside SB		
	5575	7635
2 Dr K1500 WT 4WD Std Cab LB	4425	6065

C/K 2500 SERIES
Category H

Model Description	Trade-in Value	Market Value
2 Dr C2500 Ext Cab LB	4970	6805
2 Dr C2500 Ext Cab SB	4860	6655
2 Dr C2500 Std Cab LB	4355	5965
2 Dr C2500 Scottsdale Ext Cab LB		
	5090	6975
2 Dr C2500 Scottsdale Ext Cab SB		
	4995	6845
2 Dr C2500 Scottsdale Std Cab LB		
	4530	6205
2 Dr C2500 Silverado Ext Cab LB		
	5110	7000
2 Dr C2500 Silverado Ext Cab SB		
	5010	6860
2 Dr C2500 Silverado Std Cab LB		
	4520	6190
2 Dr K2500 4WD Ext Cab LB	5780	7920
2 Dr K2500 4WD Ext Cab SB	5750	7875
2 Dr K2500 4WD Std Cab LB	5265	7210
2 Dr K2500 Scottsdale 4WD Ext Cab LB		
	5930	8120
2 Dr K2500 Scottsdale 4WD Ext Cab SB		
	5815	7965
2 Dr K2500 Scottsdale 4WD Std Cab LB		
	5325	7295
2 Dr K2500 Silverado 4WD Ext Cab LB		
	5995	8210
2 Dr K2500 Silverado 4WD Ext Cab SB		
	5910	8095
2 Dr K2500 Silverado 4WD Std Cab LB		
	5395	7390

C/K 3500 SERIES
Category H

Model Description	Trade-in Value	Market Value
2 Dr C3500 Ext Cab LB	6140	8410
2 Dr C3500 Std Cab LB	5815	7965
2 Dr C3500 Scottsdale Ext Cab LB		
	6280	8600
2 Dr C3500 Scottsdale Std Cab LB		
	5930	8120

Model Description	Trade-in Value	Market Value
2 Dr C3500 Silverado Ext Cab LB		
	6530	8945
2 Dr C3500 Silverado Std Cab LB		
	6065	8310
2 Dr K3500 Silverado 4WD Ext Cab LB		
	7200	9860

OPTIONS FOR C/K PICKUP
8 cyl 5.0 L Engine +85
8 cyl 5.7 L Engine +120
8 cyl 6.2 L Dsl Engine +345
8 cyl 7.4 L Engine +115
Auto 4-Speed Transmission[Std on 454SS] +130
Sport Handling Pkg +135
Air Conditioning[Std on 454SS] +120
Cruise Control[Std on 454SS] +30
Power Door Locks[Std on 454SS] +30
Power Windows[Std on 454SS] +30

CAMARO   1991

Chevy loses IROC sponsorship to Dodge, and right to use IROC name. Z28 nomenclature returns on top-level Camaro. Order your RS with the 5.0-liter V8 engine, and you can opt for a 16-inch wheel and tire combination. Z28 models have a revised hood, scooped rocker panels, and a more aggressive rear spoiler. Color-keyed alloys are available.

Category F

Model Description	Trade-in Value	Market Value
2 Dr RS Conv	4525	6375
2 Dr RS Cpe	2915	4105
2 Dr Z28 Conv	5000	7045
2 Dr Z28 Cpe	3795	5345

OPTIONS FOR CAMARO
8 cyl 5.0 L Engine[Opt on RS] +50
8 cyl 5.7 L Engine +70
Auto 4-Speed Transmission +75
Air Conditioning +125
Power Door Locks +30
Power Drivers Seat +35
Power Windows +35
T-Tops (solid/Colored) +140

CAPRICE   1991

Shamu arrives! Sedan and wagon are totally re ...ahem, designed. Retain rear-wheel drive. Standard engine is a 5.0-liter V8. Driver airbag and ABS are standard. Wagon provides over 92 cubic feet of cargo volume. LTZ model added midyear sporting wider tires, sport suspension, and heavy-duty cooling and braking systems.

RATINGS (SCALE OF 1-10)

Overall	Safety	Reliability	Performance	Comfort	Value
7	6.7	4.7	7.6	8.3	7.5

Model Description	Trade-in Value	Market Value
Category B		
4 Dr Classic Sdn	2885	4240
4 Dr STD Sdn	2225	3270
4 Dr STD Wgn	3300	4855

OPTIONS FOR CAPRICE

Cruise Control +30
Power Door Locks[Std on Classic] +40
Power Drivers Seat +45
Power Windows[Std on Classic] +45

CAVALIER   1991

Styling is revised front and rear for a more aerodynamic look. Cupholders and storage cubbies are added to a restyled dashboard. RS trim level reappears for coupe and sedan after two-year hiatus. Z51 Performance Handling Package is available on Cavalier RS coupe, and includes sport suspension, performance tires and gauge package. Scotchgard protectant covers cloth seats and door trim. Z24 gets new alloy wheels.

RATINGS (SCALE OF 1-10)

Overall	Safety	Reliability	Performance	Comfort	Value
N/A	N/A	6.6	6.4	6.8	5.4

	Trade-in	Market
Category E		
2 Dr RS Conv	1925	3260
2 Dr RS Cpe	1355	2295
4 Dr RS Sdn	1430	2425
4 Dr RS Wgn	1485	2515
2 Dr VL Cpe	1130	1915
4 Dr VL Sdn	1205	2040
4 Dr VL Wgn	1275	2165
2 Dr Z24 Cpe	1965	3330

OPTIONS FOR CAVALIER

6 cyl 3.1 L Engine[Opt on Wgn] +100
Auto 3-Speed Transmission[Std on Wgn] +70
Air Conditioning +120
Cruise Control +35
Power Door Locks[Std on Conv] +35
Power Windows[Std on Conv] +40

CHEVY VAN/SPORTVAN   1991

7.4-liter engine can be equipped with a four-speed automatic transmission.

CHEVY VAN

	Trade-in	Market
Category H		
2 Dr G10 Chevy Van	2700	3700
2 Dr G10 Chevy Van Ext	2885	3950
2 Dr G20 Chevy Van	2965	4065
2 Dr G30 Chevy Van	3070	4205
2 Dr G30 Chevy Van Ext	3240	4440

SPORTVAN

Model Description	Trade-in Value	Market Value
Category H		
2 Dr G10 Sportvan	3200	4385
2 Dr G20 Sportvan	3495	4790
2 Dr G20 Beauville Sportvan	3620	4960
2 Dr G30 Sportvan	3665	5020
2 Dr G30 Sportvan Ext	3795	5200
2 Dr G30 Beauville Sportvan	3805	5210
2 Dr G30 Beauville Sportvan Ext	3955	5415

OPTIONS FOR CHEVY VAN/SPORTVAN

8 cyl 5.0 L Engine +85
8 cyl 5.7 L Engine[Std on G30, Chevy Van Ext] +120
12 Passenger Seating +90
Air Conditioning +120
Cruise Control +30
Power Door Locks +30
Power Windows +30

CORSICA   1991

New dashboard debuts, and a driver airbag is added. LTZ model is dropped, leaving one trim level available. Sport Handling Package includes LTZ suspension, trim, and wheels. A CD player joins the options sheet.

RATINGS (SCALE OF 1-10)

Overall	Safety	Reliability	Performance	Comfort	Value
6.4	4.7	6.7	6.8	7.3	6.3

	Trade-in	Market
Category C		
4 Dr LT Hbk	1465	2250
4 Dr LT Sdn	1400	2150

OPTIONS FOR CORSICA

6 cyl 3.1 L Engine +80
Auto 3-Speed Transmission +80
Air Conditioning +120
Cruise Control +30
Power Door Locks +35
Power Windows +45

CORVETTE   1991

Styling is tweaked front and rear for a more aerodynamic appearance. All Corvettes get the ZR-1's rear styling treatment. New alloy wheels are standard across the line.

	Trade-in	Market
Category J		
2 Dr STD Conv	10840	14080
2 Dr STD Cpe	9750	12660
2 Dr ZR1 Cpe	16785	21800

OPTIONS FOR CORVETTE

Adj. Leather Seats +160
Electronic Ride Select. +250
Bose Sound System +120
Leather Seats[Opt on STD] +170

Power Drivers Seat[Opt on STD] +50
Solid & Glass Targa Tops +140

LUMINA 1991

Euro models get standard alloy wheels. Newly optional is a Delco/Bose sound system. Coupes can be ordered in new Z34 trim, which comes standard with a 3.4-liter twin-cam V6, sport suspension and louvered hood.

RATINGS (SCALE OF 1-10)

Overall	Safety	Reliability	Performance	Comfort	Value
N/A	N/A	6.1	8.2	7.6	8.2

Category C
2 Dr Euro Cpe	2250	3460
4 Dr Euro Sdn	2300	3540
2 Dr STD Cpe	1770	2720
4 Dr STD Sdn	1820	2800
2 Dr Z34 Cpe	2695	4145

OPTIONS FOR LUMINA

6 cyl 3.1 L Engine[Opt on STD] +80
Auto 4-Speed Transmission +30
Air Conditioning[Opt on STD] +120
Cruise Control[Std on Z34] +30
Power Door Locks +35
Power Drivers Seat +45
Power Windows +45

LUMINA MINIVAN 1991

A CD player is newly optional. Non-reflective carpet is added to the top of the dashboard.

RATINGS (SCALE OF 1-10)

Overall	Safety	Reliability	Performance	Comfort	Value
6.7	4.9	6.5	7	7.5	7.7

Category G
2 Dr CL Pass. Van	2590	3700
2 Dr STD Pass. Van	2315	3310

OPTIONS FOR LUMINA MINIVAN

Air Conditioning +120
Cruise Control +30
Power Door Locks +35
Power Drivers Seat +40
Power Windows +35

R3500 PICKUP 1991

Category H
4 Dr STD Crew Cab LB	5020	6880
4 Dr Silverado Crew Cab LB	5215	7145

OPTIONS FOR R3500 PICKUP

8 cyl 6.2 L Dsl Engine +345
8 cyl 7.4 L Engine +115
Auto 4-Speed Transmission +145
Air Conditioning +120
Cruise Control +30

Dual Rear Wheels +120
Power Door Locks +30
Power Windows +30

S10 BLAZER 1991

Four-door models get new Sport Package on the options list. It includes two-tone paint, alloy wheels and chrome trim. A heavy-duty battery is standard on all models, and 2WD Blazers can be equipped with 15-inch alloy wheels. Front bench seat option will give four-door models six-passenger capacity. Softer suspension available midyear with Tahoe LT trim.

RATINGS (SCALE OF 1-10)

Overall	Safety	Reliability	Performance	Comfort	Value
5.5	3.7	5.4	6.8	7.1	4.3

Category G
2 Dr STD Utility	2760	3940
2 Dr STD 4WD Utility	3205	4580
4 Dr STD Wgn	3005	4295
4 Dr STD 4WD Wgn	3540	5060
2 Dr Sport Utility	2950	4215
2 Dr Sport 4WD Utility	3310	4730
4 Dr Sport 4WD Wgn	3740	5345
2 Dr Tahoe Utility	2895	4135
2 Dr Tahoe 4WD Utility	3410	4870
4 Dr Tahoe Wgn	3180	4545
4 Dr Tahoe 4WD Wgn	3665	5235

OPTIONS FOR S10 BLAZER

Auto 4-Speed Transmission +130
LT Pkg +145
Air Conditioning +120
Cruise Control +30
Power Door Locks +35
Power Windows +35

S10 PICKUP 1991

Exterior facelift that includes a new grille, fresh trim and restyled wheels debuted early in 1990. Four-wheel-drive models get the 4.3-liter V6 as standard equipment. Durango trim is dropped. Midyear, the base four-cylinder powerplant gets more horsepower.

RATINGS (SCALE OF 1-10)

Overall	Safety	Reliability	Performance	Comfort	Value
N/A	3.4	6	7.2	7	N/A

Category G
2 Dr Baja 4WD Ext Cab SB	3240	4630
2 Dr Baja 4WD Std Cab LB	3040	4345
2 Dr Baja 4WD Std Cab SB	2985	4265
2 Dr EL Std Cab SB	1950	2785
2 Dr STD Ext Cab SB	2550	3645
2 Dr STD 4WD Ext Cab SB	3520	5025

Don't forget to refer to the Mileage Adjustment Table at the back of this book!

Model Description	Trade-in Value	Market Value
2 Dr STD Std Cab LB	2185	3120
2 Dr STD 4WD Std Cab LB	3325	4750
2 Dr STD Std Cab SB	2140	3055
2 Dr STD 4WD Std Cab SB	3225	4605
2 Dr Tahoe Ext Cab SB	2685	3835
2 Dr Tahoe 4WD Ext Cab SB	3665	5235
2 Dr Tahoe Std Cab LB	2420	3460
2 Dr Tahoe 4WD Std Cab LB	3240	4630
2 Dr Tahoe Std Cab SB	2410	3440
2 Dr Tahoe 4WD Std Cab SB	3165	4520

OPTIONS FOR S10 PICKUP
6 cyl 2.8 L Engine +60
6 cyl 4.3 L Engine [Opt on 2WD] +90
Auto 4-Speed Transmission +130
Air Conditioning +120
Cruise Control +30
Power Door Locks +35
Power Windows +35

SUBURBAN 1991

Manual transmission is dropped.
Category H

Model	Trade-in	Market
4 Dr R1500 Wgn	4780	6545
4 Dr R2500 Wgn	5035	6900
4 Dr V1500 4WD Wgn	5660	7750
4 Dr V2500 4WD Wgn	5960	8165

OPTIONS FOR SUBURBAN
8 cyl 6.2 L Dsl Engine +345
8 cyl 7.4 L Engine +115
Silverado Pkg +220
Air Conditioning +120
Cruise Control +30
Dual Air Conditioning +195
Power Door Locks +30
Power Windows +30

V3500 PICKUP 1991

Category H

Model	Trade-in	Market
4 Dr STD 4WD Crew Cab LB	5615	7690
4 Dr Silverado 4WD Crew Cab LB	6115	8375

OPTIONS FOR V3500 PICKUP
8 cyl 6.2 L Dsl Engine +345
8 cyl 7.4 L Engine +115
Auto 4-Speed Transmission +130
Air Conditioning +120
Cruise Control +30
Dual Rear Wheels +120
Power Door Locks +30
Power Windows +30

1990 CHEVROLET

ASTRO 1990

All-wheel drive is newly optional, and an extended body style is introduced. Standard engine on passenger models is a 150-horsepower, 4.3-liter V6. The optional sport suspension will not be available on AWD vans. Four-wheel ABS is standard on all but commercially purchased cargo vans.

RATINGS (SCALE OF 1-10)

Overall	Safety	Reliability	Performance	Comfort	Value
6.1	2.8	5.7	7.2	6.6	8

Category G

Model	Trade-in	Market
2 Dr CL Pass. Van	2005	3035
2 Dr CL 4WD Pass. Van	2695	4080
2 Dr CL Pass. Van Ext	2350	3560
2 Dr CL 4WD Pass. Van Ext	2960	4485
2 Dr LT Pass. Van	2200	3330
2 Dr LT 4WD Pass. Van	2925	4435
2 Dr LT Pass. Van Ext	2605	3945
2 Dr LT 4WD Pass. Van Ext	3130	4740
2 Dr STD Cargo Van	1660	2515
2 Dr STD 4WD Cargo Van	2205	3340
2 Dr STD Cargo Van Ext	1890	2865
2 Dr STD 4WD Cargo Van Ext	2460	3725
2 Dr STD Pass. Van	2195	3325
2 Dr STD 4WD Pass. Van	2705	4100
2 Dr STD Pass. Van Ext	2410	3650
2 Dr STD 4WD Pass. Van Ext	2960	4485

OPTIONS FOR ASTRO
6 cyl 4.3 L Engine +75
Sport Handling Pkg +160
8 Passenger Seating +50
Air Conditioning +100
Power Door Locks +30
Power Drivers Seat +35
Power Windows +30

BERETTA 1990

GTZ model debuts, with high-output version of Quad 4 engine. GTZ has 180-horsepower, and is available only with five-speed transmission. Short-lived GTU is dropped. An aggressively hyped convertible model never made it to production. Base 2.0-liter engine is swapped for peppier 2.2-liter unit. Optional V6 goes from 2.8 liters to 3.1, and now makes 140 horsepower. Air conditioning is made standard on all but the base model. All Berettas get new cloth seat covers and cushions.

CHEVROLET 90

Model Description	Trade-in Value	Market Value

RATINGS (SCALE OF 1-10)

Overall	Safety	Reliability	Performance	Comfort	Value
6.3	5.2	6.7	7.8	6.8	5.1

Category E

Model	Trade-in	Market
2 Dr GT Cpe	1340	2580
2 Dr GTZ Cpe	1475	2835
2 Dr Indy GT Cpe	1520	2920
2 Dr STD Cpe	995	1915

OPTIONS FOR BERETTA

6 cyl 3.1 L Engine[Opt on STD] +85
Auto 3-Speed Transmission +65
Air Conditioning[Opt on STD] +100
Power Door Locks +30
Power Windows +30

BLAZER 1990

Rear-wheel ABS that works only in 2WD is added.

Category H

Model	Trade-in	Market
2 Dr STD 4WD Utility	4480	6220
2 Dr Silverado 4WD Utility	4685	6510

OPTIONS FOR BLAZER

8 cyl 6.2 L Dsl Engine +290
Auto 4-Speed Transmission +105
Air Conditioning +100

C/K PICKUP 1990

Stripped W/T (Work Truck) model is added to serve as a serious, and affordable, work truck. C/K 2500 Crew Cab model dropped. 454 SS model introduced, with powerful 7.4-liter V8 and sport suspension installed in regular-cab shortbox.

RATINGS (SCALE OF 1-10)

Overall	Safety	Reliability	Performance	Comfort	Value
N/A	5.5	6.4	7.4	8	N/A

C/K 1500 SERIES

Category H

Model	Trade-in	Market
2 Dr C1500 Ext Cab LB	4290	5955
2 Dr C1500 Ext Cab SB	4175	5800
2 Dr C1500 Ext Cab Stepside SB	4455	6185
2 Dr C1500 Std Cab LB	3780	5250
2 Dr C1500 Std Cab SB	3720	5170
2 Dr C1500 Std Cab Stepside SB	3850	5345
2 Dr C1500 454SS Std Cab SB	5945	8260
2 Dr C1500 Scottsdale Ext Cab LB	4325	6005
2 Dr C1500 Scottsdale Ext Cab SB	4290	5955
2 Dr C1500 Scottsdale Std Cab LB	3965	5505
2 Dr C1500 Scottsdale Std Cab SB	3915	5440
2 Dr C1500 Scottsdale Std Cab Stepside SB	4040	5610
2 Dr C1500 Silverado Ext Cab LB	4695	6520
2 Dr C1500 Silverado Ext Cab SB	4610	6405
2 Dr C1500 Silverado Std Cab LB	4290	5955
2 Dr C1500 Silverado Std Cab SB	4175	5800
2 Dr C1500 Silverado Std Cab Stepside SB	4405	6120
2 Dr C1500 Work Truck Std Cab LB	3395	4715
2 Dr K1500 4WD Ext Cab LB	5200	7220
2 Dr K1500 4WD Ext Cab SB	5095	7075
2 Dr K1500 4WD Std Cab LB	4905	6815
2 Dr K1500 4WD Std Cab SB	4840	6720
2 Dr K1500 4WD Std Cab Stepside SB	4970	6900
2 Dr K1500 Scottsdale 4WD Ext Cab LB	5105	7090
2 Dr K1500 Scottsdale 4WD Ext Cab SB	5030	6985
2 Dr K1500 Scottsdale 4WD Std Cab LB	4995	6940
2 Dr K1500 Scottsdale 4WD Std Cab SB	4890	6790
2 Dr K1500 Scottsdale 4WD Std Cab Stepside SB	5140	7140
2 Dr K1500 Silverado 4WD Ext Cab LB	5355	7435
2 Dr K1500 Silverado 4WD Ext Cab SB	5265	7315
2 Dr K1500 Silverado 4WD Std Cab LB	5055	7020
2 Dr K1500 Silverado 4WD Std Cab SB	4965	6895
2 Dr K1500 Silverado 4WD Std Cab Stepside SB	5165	7175
2 Dr K1500 WT 4WD Std Cab LB	3940	5470

C/K 2500 SERIES

Category H

Model	Trade-in	Market
2 Dr C2500 Ext Cab LB	4315	5995
2 Dr C2500 Ext Cab SB	4235	5880
2 Dr C2500 Std Cab LB	3930	5455
2 Dr C2500 Scottsdale Ext Cab LB	4520	6280

Don't forget to refer to the Mileage Adjustment Table at the back of this book!

Model Description	Trade-in Value	Market Value
2 Dr C2500 Scottsdale Ext Cab SB	4470	6210
2 Dr C2500 Scottsdale Std Cab LB	3935	5465
2 Dr C2500 Silverado Ext Cab LB	4610	6400
2 Dr C2500 Silverado Ext Cab SB	4545	6310
2 Dr C2500 Silverado Std Cab LB	4025	5590
2 Dr K2500 4WD Ext Cab LB	5305	7365
2 Dr K2500 4WD Ext Cab SB	5235	7270
2 Dr K2500 4WD Std Cab LB	4750	6595
2 Dr K2500 Scottsdale 4WD Ext Cab LB	5485	7620
2 Dr K2500 Scottsdale 4WD Ext Cab SB	5370	7460
2 Dr K2500 Scottsdale 4WD Std Cab LB	4815	6685
2 Dr K2500 Silverado 4WD Ext Cab LB	5510	7655
2 Dr K2500 Silverado 4WD Ext Cab SB	5385	7480
2 Dr K2500 Silverado 4WD Std Cab LB	4950	6875

C/K 3500 SERIES

Category H

	Trade-in Value	Market Value
2 Dr C3500 Ext Cab LB	5560	7720
2 Dr C3500 Std Cab LB	5230	7265
2 Dr C3500 Scottsdale Ext Cab LB	5670	7875
2 Dr C3500 Scottsdale Std Cab LB	5375	7465
2 Dr C3500 Silverado Ext Cab LB	5900	8195
2 Dr C3500 Silverado Std Cab LB	5610	7795
2 Dr K3500 4WD Ext Cab LB	5730	7960
2 Dr K3500 4WD Std Cab LB	5295	7355
2 Dr K3500 Scottsdale 4WD Ext Cab LB	5765	8005
2 Dr K3500 Scottsdale 4WD Std Cab LB	5370	7460
2 Dr K3500 Silverado 4WD Ext Cab LB	6155	8550
2 Dr K3500 Silverado 4WD Std Cab LB	5610	7795

OPTIONS FOR C/K PICKUP
8 cyl 5.0 L Engine +70
8 cyl 5.7 L Engine +95
8 cyl 6.2 L Dsl Engine +290

Auto 3-Speed Transmission[Std on 454SS] +75
Auto 4-Speed Transmission +105
Sport Handling Pkg +120
Air Conditioning[Std on 454SS] +100
Dual Rear Wheels +100

CAMARO 1990

Driver airbag is standard. The 2.8-liter V6 is replaced by a 3.1-liter motor making 140 horsepower. The 5.7-liter V8 is redesigned with lighter-weight pistons. IROC models get a limited-slip differential, and IROC convertibles have new 16-inch alloy wheels. Delco/Bose sound system is upgraded. Buyers can order a Flame Red interior, though we don't know why they would.

Category F

	Trade-in Value	Market Value
2 Dr IROC Z Conv	4295	6225
2 Dr IROC Z Cpe	3420	4955
2 Dr RS Conv	3750	5435
2 Dr RS Cpe	2305	3340

OPTIONS FOR CAMARO
8 cyl 5.0 L Engine[Opt on RS Cpe] +60
8 cyl 5.7 L Engine +65
Auto 4-Speed Transmission +65
Air Conditioning +100
Power Drivers Seat +30
Power Windows +25
T-Tops (solid/Colored) +115

CAPRICE 1990

No changes.

Category B

	Trade-in Value	Market Value
4 Dr Classic Sdn	2085	3205
4 Dr Classic Wgn	1830	2815
4 Dr Classic Brougham Sdn	2345	3605
4 Dr LS Brougham Sdn	2780	4275
4 Dr STD Sdn	1650	2535

OPTIONS FOR CAPRICE
Preferred Equipment Pkg +100
Power Door Locks +30
Power Drivers Seat +40
Power Windows +35

CAVALIER 1990

Convertible model disappears. New engines have more power; base 2.2-liter motor pumps out 95 horsepower, while the 3.1-liter V6 makes 140 horsepower. Door-mounted passive seatbelts have been added. Seats and fabrics are new this year. RS trim level reappears on wagon models.

RATINGS (SCALE OF 1-10)

Overall	Safety	Reliability	Performance	Comfort	Value
N/A	N/A	7.2	6.4	6.8	5.4

Don't forget to refer to the Mileage Adjustment Table at the back of this book!

Model Description	Trade-in Value	Market Value
Category E		
2 Dr RS Cpe	960	1845
2 Dr STD Cpe	830	1600
4 Dr STD Wgn	900	1730
2 Dr VL Cpe	785	1510
4 Dr VL Sdn	870	1670
4 Dr VL Wgn	860	1650
2 Dr Z24 Cpe	1440	2770

OPTIONS FOR CAVALIER
6 cyl 3.1 L Engine[Opt on STD] +85
Auto 3-Speed Transmission +55
Air Conditioning +100
Power Door Locks +30
Power Windows +30

CELEBRITY 1990

Sedan model dropped, leaving a wagon only. Base engine makes more power, and optional, 2.8-liter V6 is replaced by a 3.1-liter motor that makes 135 horsepower. All models get a heavy-duty suspension. The rear seat is now of the split-folding variety. Door-mounted passive restraints have been added.

	Trade-in	Market
Category C		
4 Dr Eurosport Wgn	1630	2670
4 Dr STD Wgn	1395	2290

OPTIONS FOR CELEBRITY
6 cyl 3.1 L Engine +75
Air Conditioning[Opt on STD] +95
Power Door Locks +30
Power Drivers Seat +35
Power Windows +35

CHEVY VAN/SPORTVAN 1990

No changes.
CHEVY VAN

	Trade-in	Market
Category H		
2 Dr G10 Chevy Van	2180	3025
2 Dr G10 Chevy Van Ext	2335	3240
2 Dr G20 Chevy Van	2310	3205
2 Dr G20 Chevy Van Ext	2435	3380
2 Dr G30 Chevy Van	2455	3410
2 Dr G30 Chevy Van Ext	2565	3565

SPORTVAN

	Trade-in	Market
Category H		
2 Dr G10 Sportvan	2690	3735
2 Dr G10 Sportvan Ext	2820	3920
2 Dr G10 Beauville Sportvan	2945	4090
2 Dr G10 Beauville Sportvan Ext	3050	4235
2 Dr G20 Sportvan	2810	3900
2 Dr G20 Beauville Sportvan	3080	4280
2 Dr G30 Sportvan	3105	4310
2 Dr G30 Beauville Sportvan	3325	4620

OPTIONS FOR CHEVY VAN/SPORTVAN
8 cyl 5.0 L Engine +70
8 cyl 5.7 L Engine[Opt on G10,G20,Chevy Van Ext] +95
Auto 4-Speed Transmission[Std on G30,Beauville, Sportvan] +30
12 Passenger Seating +75
Air Conditioning +100

CORSICA 1990

Base model replaced by LT trim level. A 2.2-liter engine replaces the base 2.0-liter motor. A 3.1-liter V6 replaces the 2.8-liter V6. Seats get new cloth covers and cushions. All models except the LT comes with air conditioning standard.

RATINGS (SCALE OF 1-10)

Overall	Safety	Reliability	Performance	Comfort	Value
6.3	4	6.5	6.8	6.9	7.4

	Trade-in	Market
Category C		
4 Dr LT Hbk	1270	2085
4 Dr LT Sdn	1160	1900
4 Dr LTZ Sdn	1420	2330

OPTIONS FOR CORSICA
6 cyl 3.1 L Engine[Opt on LT] +75
Auto 3-Speed Transmission +65
Air Conditioning[Opt on LT] +95
Power Door Locks +30
Power Windows +35

CORVETTE 1990

King-of-the-hill ZR-1 appears with aluminum DOHC 32-valve, 5.7-liter V8 built by Mercury Marine. ZF six-speed transmission is standard on ZR-1, as is blistering performance and ultra-wide rear wheels. ZR-1 is distinguished by unique rear-body work. All Corvettes get a driver airbag and ABS. New dashboard debuts with several analog gauges and a real glovebox. Base Corvettes get five additional horsepower. The radiator is sloped for better cooling. Seventeen-inch alloys are lighter-weight. A 200-watt sound system with cassette or CD player is available.

	Trade-in	Market
Category J		
2 Dr STD Conv	9630	12670
2 Dr STD Cpe	8800	11580

OPTIONS FOR CORVETTE
Electronic Ride Selection +205
Handling Suspension (FX3) +205
Roof Option +110
Bose Sound System +100
Leather Seats[Opt on STD] +140
Power Drivers Seat[Opt on STD] +40
Solid & Glass Targa Tops +115

Don't forget to refer to the Mileage Adjustment Table at the back of this book!

Model Description	Trade-in Value	Market Value	Model Description	Trade-in Value	Market Value

LUMINA　　　　1990

Sedan bowed in March, 1989. Coupe is added this year. Base engine is a 110-horsepower 2.5-liter four cylinder. Optional is a 135-horsepower 3.1-liter V6. Euro models include V6 engine, sport suspension, air conditioning, bigger wheels, and decklid spoiler.

RATINGS (SCALE OF 1-10)

Overall	Safety	Reliability	Performance	Comfort	Value
N/A	N/A	5.6	8.2	7.6	8.1

Category C

2 Dr Euro Cpe	1770	2900
4 Dr Euro Sdn	1860	3050
2 Dr STD Cpe	1360	2230
4 Dr STD Sdn	1415	2320

OPTIONS FOR LUMINA

6 cyl 3.1 L Engine[Opt on STD] +75
Air Conditioning[Opt on STD] +95
Power Door Locks +30
Power Drivers Seat +35
Power Windows +35

LUMINA MINIVAN　　　　1990

New minivan suffering from inadequate powerplant debuts. Body panels are composite plastic mounted to a steel-space frame. Modular seating accommodates up to seven passengers. Standard and only engine is a 3.1-liter V6 offering 120 measly horsepower.

RATINGS (SCALE OF 1-10)

Overall	Safety	Reliability	Performance	Comfort	Value
6.5	4.9	5.8	7	7.5	7.2

Category G

2 Dr CL Pass. Van	2045	3100
2 Dr STD Pass. Van	1860	2815

OPTIONS FOR LUMINA MINIVAN

Air Conditioning[Std on CL] +100
Power Door Locks +30
Power Drivers Seat +35
Power Windows +30

R3500 PICKUP　　　　1990

Category H

4 Dr STD Crew Cab LB	4470	6210
4 Dr Silverado Crew Cab LB	4715	6550

OPTIONS FOR R3500 PICKUP

8 cyl 6.2 L Dsl Engine +290
Auto 3-Speed Transmission +80
Air Conditioning +100
Dual Rear Wheels +100

S10 BLAZER　　　　1990

A four-door model with standard four-wheel ABS is added to the lineup, and the 2.8-liter engine is dropped in favor of a more powerful 160-horsepower, 4.3-liter V6.

RATINGS (SCALE OF 1-10)

Overall	Safety	Reliability	Performance	Comfort	Value
5.9	3.7	5.7	6.8	7.1	6.2

Category G

2 Dr STD Utility	2040	3090
2 Dr STD 4WD Utility	2540	3850
2 Dr Sport Utility	2200	3335
2 Dr Sport 4WD Utility	2615	3965
2 Dr Tahoe Utility	2275	3450
2 Dr Tahoe 4WD Utility	2750	4165

OPTIONS FOR S10 BLAZER

Auto 4-Speed Transmission +105
Air Conditioning +100
Power Door Locks +30
Power Windows +30

S10 PICKUP　　　　1990

No changes.

RATINGS (SCALE OF 1-10)

Overall	Safety	Reliability	Performance	Comfort	Value
N/A	3.4	6.4	7.2	7	N/A

Category G

2 Dr Baja 4WD Std Cab SB	2540	3845
2 Dr Durango 4WD Ext Cab SB	2815	4265
2 Dr Durango Std Cab LB	1935	2935
2 Dr Durango 4WD Std Cab LB	2510	3800
2 Dr Durango Std Cab SB	1905	2885
2 Dr Durango 4WD Std Cab SB	2410	3655
2 Dr EL Std Cab SB	1725	2615
2 Dr STD Ext Cab SB	2005	3040
2 Dr STD 4WD Ext Cab SB	2680	4060
2 Dr STD Std Cab LB	1810	2745
2 Dr STD 4WD Std Cab LB	2430	3680
2 Dr STD Std Cab SB	1770	2685
2 Dr STD 4WD Std Cab SB	2355	3565
2 Dr Tahoe Ext Cab SB	2295	3480
2 Dr Tahoe 4WD Ext Cab SB	2920	4425
2 Dr Tahoe Std Cab LB	2015	3050
2 Dr Tahoe 4WD Std Cab LB	2615	3960
2 Dr Tahoe Std Cab SB	1915	2900
2 Dr Tahoe 4WD Std Cab SB	2515	3810

OPTIONS FOR S10 PICKUP

6 cyl 2.8 L Engine +45
6 cyl 4.3 L Engine[Opt on 2WD] +75

Don't forget to refer to the Mileage Adjustment Table at the back of this book!

Model Description	Trade-in Value	Market Value	Model Description	Trade-in Value	Market Value
Auto 4-Speed Transmission +105			4 Dr V1500 4WD Wgn	5095	7075
Baja Preferred Pkg 1 +230			4 Dr V2500 4WD Wgn	5425	7535
Baja Preferred Pkg 2 +190					
Air Conditioning +100			OPTIONS FOR SUBURBAN		
Power Door Locks +30			8 cyl 6.2 L Dsl Engine +290		
Power Windows +30			8 cyl 7.4 L Engine +55		
			Auto 3-Speed Transmission +75		
SUBURBAN		**1990**	Auto 4-Speed Transmission[Opt on V15] +105		
Rear-wheel ABS that works in 2WD only is added.			Silverado Pkg +165		
Category H			Air Conditioning +100		
4 Dr R1500 Wgn	4150	5765	Dual Air Conditioning +160		
4 Dr R2500 Wgn	4445	6175			

Don't forget to refer to the Mileage Adjustment Table at the back of this book!

CHRYSLER 99

Model Description	Trade-in Value	Market Value	Model Description	Trade-in Value	Market Value

CHRYSLER USA

1995 Chrysler Sebring

1999 CHRYSLER

300M — 1999

This all-new car from Chrysler will try to win some international recognition for the marque.

RATINGS (SCALE OF 1-10)

Overall	Safety	Reliability	Performance	Comfort	Value
N/A	N/A	N/A	8.4	8.3	N/A

Category A
4 Dr STD Sdn	18915	22250

OPTIONS FOR 300M
Chrome Wheels +750
Power Moonroof +1010

CIRRUS — 1999

A slightly revised suspension gives the Cirrus a softer ride, and the interior improvements include a new instrument cluster and lower NVH levels. Outside, 15-inch chrome wheel covers are standard, and a winged Chrysler badge now decorates the front grille.

RATINGS (SCALE OF 1-10)

Overall	Safety	Reliability	Performance	Comfort	Value
N/A	6.8	8.2	7.6	7.8	N/A

Category C
4 Dr LXi Sdn	10915	13150

OPTIONS FOR CIRRUS
Aluminum/Alloy Wheels +225

CONCORDE — 1999

Bigger sway bar links and tubular rear trailing arms will be phased in during the model year, two changes that Chrysler promises will provide more road isolation for a more luxurious ride. Premium carpeting is added to the interior, and the LXi leather is improved.

RATINGS (SCALE OF 1-10)

Overall	Safety	Reliability	Performance	Comfort	Value
N/A	7.2	8.1	N/A	8.5	N/A

Category B
4 Dr LX Sdn	14235	17150
4 Dr LXi Sdn	15535	18715

OPTIONS FOR CONCORDE
Aluminum/Alloy Wheels[Opt on LX] +245
Compact Disc W/fm/tape +285
Dual Power Seats[Opt on LX] +280

LHS — 1999

What a difference two years can make. The luxury-tuned LHS has been completely redesigned for 1999. In fact, it's such a new car, we're kinda' disappointed that they kept the name.

RATINGS (SCALE OF 1-10)

Overall	Safety	Reliability	Performance	Comfort	Value
N/A	7.8	8.3	7.8	8.3	N/A

Category A
4 Dr STD Sdn	18345	21585

SEBRING COUPE/CONVERTIBLE — 1999

RATINGS (SCALE OF 1-10)

Overall	Safety	Reliability	Performance	Comfort	Value
N/A	7.5	N/A	6.8	7.5	N/A

Sebring
Category C
2 Dr LX Cpe	10415	12550
2 Dr LXi Cpe	12620	15205

Sebring Convertible
Category C
2 Dr JX Conv	12745	15355
2 Dr JXi Conv	14880	17930

OPTIONS FOR SEBRING COUPE/CONVERTIBLE
6 cyl 2.5 L Engine[Opt on LX] +500
Auto 4-Speed Transmission[Opt on LX] +515
Aluminum/Alloy Wheels[Opt on JX,LX] +225
Anti-Lock Brakes[Opt on Sebring] +450
Cruise Control[Opt on LX] +155
Power Door Locks[Opt on LX] +185
Power Drivers Seat[Opt on Sebring] +220
Power Mirrors +85
Power Sunroof +505
Power Windows[Opt on LX] +230

Don't forget to refer to the Mileage Adjustment Table at the back of this book!

CHRYSLER 99-98

Model Description	Trade-in Value	Market Value	Model Description	Trade-in Value	Market Value

TOWN & COUNTRY 1999

The top-of-the-line trim level is now called "Limited," and it offers more standard equipment (hence less options) than any other Chrysler minivan. Leather upgrades, steering wheel mounted stereo controls, and a center armrest in the rear bench are new this year, and the exterior features such details as 16-inch 15-spoke chrome wheels and chrome door handles.

RATINGS (SCALE OF 1-10)

Overall	Safety	Reliability	Performance	Comfort	Value
N/A	7	8.8	6.8	7.9	N/A

Category G

	Trade-in	Market
2 Dr LX Pass. Van Ext	16400	19525
2 Dr LX 4WD Pass. Van Ext	17325	20625
2 Dr LXi Pass. Van Ext	19735	23495
2 Dr LXi 4WD Pass. Van Ext	20550	24465
2 Dr Limited Pass. Van Ext	20065	23885
2 Dr Limited 4WD Pass. Van Ext	20915	24900
2 Dr SX Pass. Van	15580	18545

OPTIONS FOR TOWN & COUNTRY

6 cyl 3.8 L Engine[Opt on SX,LX FWD] +275
Aluminum/Alloy Wheels[Opt on LX] +245
Compact Disc W/fm/tape[Opt on LX,SX] +355
Dual Air Conditioning[Opt on LX] +700
Heated Front Seats[Opt on LX] +195
Luggage Rack[Opt on LX] +115
Sunscreen Glass[Opt on LX,SX] +275
Traction Control System[Opt on SX,LX FWD] +200

1998 CHRYSLER

CIRRUS 1998

There's just one model to choose from this year, as Chrysler says "goodbye" to the base LX, and "hello" to a higher price. That means that leather seats, a powered driver's seat, a 2.5-liter V6 engine, a tilt wheel, and power windows, locks, and mirrors are now standard equipment. The LXi also comes in five new colors and as with all other Chrysler products, depowered airbags are standard.

RATINGS (SCALE OF 1-10)

Overall	Safety	Reliability	Performance	Comfort	Value
7.6	6.8	8	7.6	7.6	8.1

Category C

	Trade-in	Market
4 Dr LXi Sdn	10025	12225

OPTIONS FOR CIRRUS

Chrome Wheels +370
Power Moonroof +415

CONCORDE 1998

The Concorde is all-new for 1998. The only thing they didn't change is the name.

RATINGS (SCALE OF 1-10)

Overall	Safety	Reliability	Performance	Comfort	Value
8.1	7.1	8.1	7.8	8.5	9

Category B

	Trade-in	Market
4 Dr LX Sdn	12555	15125
4 Dr LXi Sdn	13845	16680

OPTIONS FOR CONCORDE

Aluminum/Alloy Wheels[Opt on LX] +200
Anti-Lock Brakes[Opt on LX] +420
Compact Disc W/fm/tape +235
Dual Power Seats[Opt on LX] +230
Power Moonroof +590
Traction Control System[Opt on LX] +105

SEBRING 1998

Evolutionary, mostly aesthetic changes enhance the Sebrings this year. The Sebring Coupe LX and LXi now offer a black and gray interior, and the exterior color of the day is "Caffe Latte" (not to be confused with Macchiato or Cappuccino).

RATINGS (SCALE OF 1-10)

Overall	Safety	Reliability	Performance	Comfort	Value
7.2	7.5	7.7	7.6	7.5	5.5

Category C

	Trade-in	Market
2 Dr JX Conv	11815	14410
2 Dr JXi Conv	13730	16745
2 Dr LX Cpe	9505	11590
2 Dr LXi Cpe	11585	14125

OPTIONS FOR SEBRING

6 cyl 2.5 L Engine[Std on LXi] +415
Auto 4-Speed Transmission[Opt on LX] +425
Aluminum/Alloy Wheels[Opt on JX, LX] +180
Anti-Lock Brakes[Opt on JX, LX] +370
Chrome Wheels +370
Compact Disc W/fm/tape[Std on LXi] +200
Cruise Control[Opt on JX, LX] +130
Heated Power Mirrors[Opt on JX] +65
Keyless Entry System[Opt on JX, LX] +115
Power Door Locks[Opt on JX, LX] +150
Power Drivers Seat[Std on JXi] +180
Power Mirrors +70
Power Sunroof +410
Power Windows[Opt on LX] +190
Remote Trunk Release[Opt on JX] +50
Traction Control System +150

TOWN & COUNTRY 1998

Chrysler's luxury minivans get a few improvements this year, with the addition of a new Chrysler-signature

CHRYSLER 98-97

Model Description	Trade-in Value	Market Value	Model Description	Trade-in Value	Market Value

grille, more powerful 3.8-liter V6, high-performance headlights, and three fancy new colors.

RATINGS (SCALE OF 1-10)

Overall	Safety	Reliability	Performance	Comfort	Value
7.9	6.9	8.5	7.4	7.9	8.8

Category G

	Trade-in	Market
2 Dr LX Pass. Van Ext	14070	16750
2 Dr LX 4WD Pass. Van Ext	14740	17550
2 Dr LXi Pass. Van Ext	16955	20185
2 Dr LXi 4WD Pass. Van Ext	17940	21355
2 Dr SX Pass. Van	13460	16025

OPTIONS FOR TOWN & COUNTRY

6 cyl 3.8 L Engine[Std on LXi, 4WD] +255
Auto Load Leveling[Std on LXi, 4WD] +135
Camper/Towing Package +180
Compact Disc W/fm/tape[Std on LXi] +290
Dual Air Conditioning[Opt on LX] +575
Garage Door Opener[Std on LXi] +85
Heated Front Seats +160
Leather Seats[Std on LXi] +470
Power Drivers Seat +170
Rear Heater[Opt on LX] +125
Special Factory Paint +90

1997 CHRYSLER

CIRRUS   1997

New wheels for everyone; the LXi trim level gets chrome wheels and the LX gets optional aluminum wheels. The Gold Package is also available on the LX, for any driver who wants to be mistaken for Slick Jimmy, your friendly, neighborhood pimp. On a more positive note, an in-dash CD changer is now available on LX and LXi models, as is a trip computer.

RATINGS (SCALE OF 1-10)

Overall	Safety	Reliability	Performance	Comfort	Value
7.2	6.6	7	7.6	7.6	7.4

Category C

	Trade-in	Market
4 Dr LX Sdn	7860	9705
4 Dr LXi Sdn	8695	10735

OPTIONS FOR CIRRUS

6 cyl 2.5 L Engine +455
AM/FM Compact Disc Player +180
Aluminum/Alloy Wheels +150
Child Seat (1) +60
Gold Package +190
Keyless Entry System[Opt on LX] +95
Power Drivers Seat[Opt on LX] +145
Trip Computer +95

CONCORDE   1997

The 3.5-liter engine is now standard on the LX trim level. An upgraded stereo debuts along with hood-mounted windshield-washer nozzles. The automatic transmission receives refinements.

RATINGS (SCALE OF 1-10)

Overall	Safety	Reliability	Performance	Comfort	Value
8.1	7.1	7.5	8.2	8.5	9.3

Category B

	Trade-in	Market
4 Dr LX Sdn	9760	11905
4 Dr LXi Sdn	10770	13135

OPTIONS FOR CONCORDE

Aluminum/Alloy Wheels[Std on LXi] +165
Anti-Lock Brakes[Std on LXi] +340
Compact Disc W/fm/tape +190
Dual Power Seats +190
Leather Seats[Opt on LX] +335
Power Moonroof +485
Premium Sound System[Opt on LX] +195
Traction Control System[Opt on LX] +85

LHS   1997

What's new for 1997? Deep Amethyst Pearl Paint. Oh yeah, the automatic transmission receives some fine-tuning.

RATINGS (SCALE OF 1-10)

Overall	Safety	Reliability	Performance	Comfort	Value
8	7.5	7.7	8.4	8.1	8.2

Category A

	Trade-in	Market
4 Dr STD Sdn	12000	14455

OPTIONS FOR LHS

Compact Disc W/fm/tape +320
Power Moonroof +675

SEBRING   1997

After just one year in production, the Sebring Convertible receives a rash of changes. The most significant are a quieter intake manifold for the 2.4-liter engine and the availability of Chrysler's AutoStick transmission. Other changes include the addition of new colors, auto-dimming mirror, trip computer, enhanced vehicle theft system, and damage resistant power antenna to the options list.

RATINGS (SCALE OF 1-10)

Overall	Safety	Reliability	Performance	Comfort	Value
6.9	7.4	6.7	7.6	7.5	5.4

Category C

	Trade-in	Market
2 Dr JX Conv	10230	12630
2 Dr JXi Conv	12005	14820

Don't forget to refer to the Mileage Adjustment Table at the back of this book!

Model Description	Trade-in Value	Market Value
2 Dr LX Cpe	8470	10455
2 Dr LXi Cpe	10550	13025

OPTIONS FOR SEBRING

6 cyl 2.5 L Engine[Std on LXi] +455
Auto 4-Speed Transmission[Opt on LX] +350
Aluminum/Alloy Wheels[Opt on JX,LX] +150
Anti-Lock Brakes[Opt on JX,LX] +300
Compact Disc W/fm/tape[Std on LXi] +165
Cruise Control[Opt on JX,LX] +105
Keyless Entry System[Opt on JX,LX] +95
Leather Seats[Opt on LXi] +300
Power Door Locks[Opt on JX,LX] +125
Power Drivers Seat[Std on JXi] +145
Power Sunroof +335
Power Windows[Opt on LX] +155

TOWN & COUNTRY 1997

Chrysler's luxury minivans get a few improvements this year, as AWD extended length models are added to the lineup. Also new this year is a sporty SX model, which replaces last year's LX as the regular length Town & Country. Families with kids will love the standard left side sliding door on this vehicle.

RATINGS (SCALE OF 1-10)

Overall	Safety	Reliability	Performance	Comfort	Value
7.4	6.8	7.6	7.4	7.9	7.1

Category G
2 Dr LX Pass. Van Ext	12220	14720
2 Dr LX 4WD Pass. Van Ext	12745	15355
2 Dr LXi Pass. Van Ext	14585	17570
2 Dr LXi 4WD Pass. Van Ext	15480	18650
2 Dr SX Pass. Van	11725	14125

OPTIONS FOR TOWN & COUNTRY

6 cyl 3.8 L Engine[Std on LXi,LX 4WD] +205
Auto Load Leveling[Std on LXi,LX 4WD] +110
Child Seats (2) +125
Compact Disc W/fm/tape[Std on LXi] +240
Dual Air Conditioning[Std on LXi] +470
Leather Seats[Std on LXi] +385
Luggage Rack[Std on LXi] +80
Power Drivers Seat +140

1996 CHRYSLER

CIRRUS 1996

Base LX model gets a four-cylinder engine in a cost-cutting move. Uplevel LXi gets revised torque converter for better V6 response. A power sunroof, chrome-plated aluminum wheels, and new colors are available for 1996.

RATINGS (SCALE OF 1-10)

Overall	Safety	Reliability	Performance	Comfort	Value
6.6	6.3	5.4	7.6	7.6	6.1

Model Description	Trade-in Value	Market Value
Category C		
4 Dr LX Sdn	6900	8845
4 Dr LXi Sdn	7600	9745

OPTIONS FOR CIRRUS

6 cyl 2.5 L Engine[Opt on LX] +405
AM/FM Compact Disc Player +145
Aluminum/Alloy Wheels +120
Child Seat (1) +50
Chrome Wheels +245
Power Drivers Seat[Opt on LX] +120
Power Sunroof +275

CONCORDE 1996

Improved headlight illumination, a revised exterior appearance, a quieter interior and new colors bow on all Concorde models. Base cars get standard 16-inch wheels. LXi models get gold accented wheels and trim.

RATINGS (SCALE OF 1-10)

Overall	Safety	Reliability	Performance	Comfort	Value
8	7.1	7.1	8.2	8.5	9.1

Category B
4 Dr LX Sdn	8125	10155
4 Dr LXi Sdn	8890	11115

OPTIONS FOR CONCORDE

6 cyl 3.5 L Engine +260
Child Seat (1) +40
Climate Control for AC[Opt on LX] +70
Compact Disc W/fm/tape +155
Dual Power Seats +155
Keyless Entry System +70
Power Moonroof +395
Premium Sound System[Opt on LX] +160
Traction Control System[Opt on LX] +70
Trip Computer[Opt on LX] +160

LHS 1996

A quieter interior and new colors entice buyers for 1996. Revised sound systems and a HomeLink Universal transmitter that opens your garage door for you when you pull in the driveway debut.

RATINGS (SCALE OF 1-10)

Overall	Safety	Reliability	Performance	Comfort	Value
7.8	7.5	7.6	8.4	8.1	7.6

Category A
4 Dr STD Sdn	9740	11880

OPTIONS FOR LHS

AM/FM Compact Disc Player +200
Infinity Sound System +120
Power Moonroof +550

NEW YORKER 1996

Gets same changes as LHS, plus added standard equipment over last year's New Yorker. After a short

Model Description	Trade-in Value	Market Value

Model Description	Trade-in Value	Market Value

1996 production run, the New Yorker is axed from the lineup in favor of the more popular LHS.

RATINGS (SCALE OF 1-10)

Overall	Safety	Reliability	Performance	Comfort	Value
7.9	7.6	7.9	8.4	8.1	7.6

Category B

4 Dr STD Sdn	8535	10670

OPTIONS FOR NEW YORKER

Compact Disc Changer +180
Leather Seats +275
Power Moonroof +395
Power Passenger Seat +135
Traction Control System +70

SEBRING   1996

Remote keyless entry system gets a panic feature, and a HomeLink Universal Transmitter debuts on this suave sport coupe. Three new paint colors are also available. Chrysler dumps its final K-Car variant this year in favor of the fine looking Sebring Convertible. Based on the Cirrus platform and drivetrains, this drop top shares only the name of the Sebring coupe.

RATINGS (SCALE OF 1-10)

Overall	Safety	Reliability	Performance	Comfort	Value
6.4	6.7	6.4	7.6	7.5	3.8

Category C

2 Dr JX Conv	8635	11070
2 Dr JXi Conv	10280	13180
2 Dr LX Cpe	6945	8905
2 Dr LXi Cpe	8625	11060

OPTIONS FOR SEBRING

6 cyl 2.5 L Engine[Opt on JX,LX] +405
Auto 4-Speed Transmission[Opt on LX] +260
Anti-Lock Brakes[Opt on JX] +245
Compact Disc Changer +195
Compact Disc W/fm/tape +135
Cruise Control[Opt on JX,LX] +85
Keyless Entry System[Opt on JX,LX] +75
Leather Seats[Opt on LXi] +245
Power Door Locks[Opt on JX,LX] +100
Power Drivers Seat[Std on JXi] +120
Power Sunroof +275
Power Windows[Opt on LX] +125
Premium Sound System[Opt on LX] +160

TOWN & COUNTRY   1996

Totally redesigned for 1996, the T&C raises the bar for luxury minivans. In a departure from last year, the T&C is offered in a short wheelbase version, and is available in two trim levels: LX and LXi. New innovations include a driver's side passenger door, dual-zone temperature controls, and a one-hand latch system on the integrated child safety seats.

RATINGS (SCALE OF 1-10)

Overall	Safety	Reliability	Performance	Comfort	Value
7	6.5	6.1	7.4	7.9	6.9

Category G

2 Dr LX Pass. Van	11135	13745
2 Dr LXi Pass. Van Ext	12655	15625
2 Dr STD Pass. Van Ext	10565	13045

OPTIONS FOR TOWN & COUNTRY

6 cyl 3.8 L Engine[Std on LXi] +175
Captain Chairs (4)[Std on LXi] +255
Child Seats (2) +105
Compact Disc W/fm/tape[Std on LXi] +195
Dual Air Conditioning[Opt on STD] +385
Infinity Sound System +175
Keyless Entry System[Std on LXi] +80
Leather Seats[Std on LXi] +315
Luggage Rack[Std on LXi] +65
Power Drivers Seat +115
Sliding Driver Side Door[Std on LXi] +215
Sunscreen Glass[Std on LXi] +150

1995 CHRYSLER

CIRRUS   1995

The Cirrus is replacing the LeBaron sedan. A cab-forward design, a 164-horsepower V6 coupled with an automatic transmission, dual airbags, antilock brakes, air conditioning, power door locks, and power windows are just a few of the improvements this car has over the LeBaron.

RATINGS (SCALE OF 1-10)

Overall	Safety	Reliability	Performance	Comfort	Value
7	6.9	5.2	7.6	7.6	7.5

Category C

4 Dr LX Sdn	5890	7850
4 Dr LXi Sdn	6405	8540

OPTIONS FOR CIRRUS

4 cyl 2.4 L Engine +145
AM/FM Compact Disc Player +120
Child Seat (1) +40
Power Drivers Seat[Opt on LX] +100
Premium Sound System[Opt on LX] +130

CONCORDE   1995

No significant changes for the 1995 Concorde.

RATINGS (SCALE OF 1-10)

Overall	Safety	Reliability	Performance	Comfort	Value
7.9	7.8	6.7	8.2	8.5	8.5

Category B

4 Dr STD Sdn	6505	8340

Don't forget to refer to the Mileage Adjustment Table at the back of this book!

OPTIONS FOR CONCORDE

6 cyl 3.5 L Engine +240
Aluminum/Alloy Wheels +110
Child Seat (1) +35
Infinity Sound System +210
Keyless Entry System +55
Leather Seats +225
Power Drivers Seat +105
Power Moonroof +325
Power Passenger Seat +110
Traction Control System +60

LE BARON 1995

The last of the K-cars, the LeBaron convertible rides into the sunset in GTC trim.

RATINGS (SCALE OF 1-10)

Overall	Safety	Reliability	Performance	Comfort	Value
7.8	8.5	7.8	7.8	6.6	8.4

Category C
2 Dr GTC Conv   5545   7395

OPTIONS FOR LE BARON

AM/FM Compact Disc Player +120
Anti-Lock Brakes +200
Cruise Control +70
Keyless Entry System +60
Leather Seats +200
Power Door Locks +80
Power Drivers Seat +100
Premium Sound System +130
Trip Computer +60

LHS 1995

No changes to the highly acclaimed LHS.

RATINGS (SCALE OF 1-10)

Overall	Safety	Reliability	Performance	Comfort	Value
8	8.4	7.7	8.4	8.1	7.4

Category A
4 Dr STD Sdn   7665   9580

OPTIONS FOR LHS

AM/FM Compact Disc Player +165
Power Moonroof +450

NEW YORKER 1995

No changes to the highly acclaimed New Yorker.

RATINGS (SCALE OF 1-10)

Overall	Safety	Reliability	Performance	Comfort	Value
7.9	8.4	7.4	8.4	8.1	7.4

Category B
4 Dr STD Sdn   7010   8985

OPTIONS FOR NEW YORKER

Climate Control for AC +55
Infinity Sound System +210

Keyless Entry System +55
Leather Seats +225
Power Moonroof +325
Power Passenger Seat +110
Traction Control System +60

SEBRING 1995

Chrysler's sporty replacement for the LeBaron coupe is the Sebring. Based on the Dodge Avenger, the Sebring offers more luxury than its corporate cousin. The Sebring is available as a four-cylinder LX or an upscale 2.5-liter V6 LXi; both come standard with an automatic transmission.

RATINGS (SCALE OF 1-10)

Overall	Safety	Reliability	Performance	Comfort	Value
7.2	7.8	6.9	7.6	7.5	6.3

Category C
2 Dr LX Cpe   5850   7800
2 Dr LXi Cpe   7090   9450

OPTIONS FOR SEBRING

6 cyl 2.5 L Engine[Opt on LX] +320
Auto 4-Speed Transmission[Opt on LX] +225
AM/FM Compact Disc Player +120
Cruise Control[Opt on LX] +70
Keyless Entry System[Opt on LX] +60
Leather Seats +200
Power Door Locks[Opt on LX] +80
Power Drivers Seat +100
Power Sunroof +225
Power Windows[Opt on LX] +105
Premium Sound System +130

TOWN & COUNTRY 1995

There are no changes for the 1995 Town & Country.

RATINGS (SCALE OF 1-10)

Overall	Safety	Reliability	Performance	Comfort	Value
7.9	8.4	7.5	7.8	8	7.9

Category G
2 Dr STD Pass. Van   8485   10740
2 Dr STD 4WD Pass. Van   9060   11470

OPTIONS FOR TOWN & COUNTRY

AM/FM Compact Disc Player +110
Child Seats (2) +85

1994 CHRYSLER

CONCORDE 1994

The base 3.3-liter engine is upped to 161 horsepower. A flexible-fuel version of the Concorde is available that will allow the car to run on alternative fuels such as methanol. Variable-assist power steering and a touring suspension are also added to the standard equipment list.

Don't forget to refer to the Mileage Adjustment Table at the back of this book!

Model Description	Trade-in Value	Market Value

RATINGS (SCALE OF 1-10)

Overall	Safety	Reliability	Performance	Comfort	Value
7.8	7.7	6.4	8.2	8.5	8.4

Category B

	Trade-in	Market
4 Dr STD Sdn	5230	6880

OPTIONS FOR CONCORDE

6 cyl 3.5 L Engine +200
AM/FM Compact Disc Player +90
Aluminum/Alloy Wheels +90
Child Seat (1) +25
Infinity Sound System +170
Keyless Entry System +45
Leather Seats +185
Power Door Locks +70
Power Drivers Seat +85
Power Moonroof +265
Power Windows +80
Traction Control System +50

LE BARON 1994

The two-door coupe is cancelled, leaving the convertible and sedan in place. The 100-horsepower four-cylinder engine is dropped, leaving the 141-horsepower V6 as the sole powerplant.

RATINGS (SCALE OF 1-10)

Overall	Safety	Reliability	Performance	Comfort	Value
7.7	8.5	7.8	7.8	6.6	7.7

Category C

	Trade-in	Market
2 Dr GTC Conv	4630	6260
4 Dr LE Sdn	4190	5665
4 Dr Landau Sdn	4570	6175

OPTIONS FOR LE BARON

6 cyl 3.0 L Engine[Opt on LE] +185
Auto 4-Speed Transmission[Opt on LE] +45
AM/FM Compact Disc Player +100
Air Conditioning[Opt on LE] +220
Aluminum/Alloy Wheels +80
Anti-Lock Brakes +165
Cruise Control[Opt on GTC] +55
Infinity Sound System +175
Leather Seats +165
Power Door Locks[Opt on GTC,LE] +65
Power Drivers Seat +80
Premium Sound System +105
Trip Computer +50

LHS 1994

The de-chromed LHS model is the sporty edition of the New Yorker.

RATINGS (SCALE OF 1-10)

Overall	Safety	Reliability	Performance	Comfort	Value
7.7	8.2	6.5	8.4	8.1	7.4

Category A

	Trade-in	Market
4 Dr STD Sdn	6535	8375

OPTIONS FOR LHS

AM/FM Compact Disc Player +135

NEW YORKER 1994

An all-new New Yorker replaces the stodgy car of yesteryear. Improved handling, styling and luxury mark a significant change in direction for the once-ailing Chrysler corporation.

RATINGS (SCALE OF 1-10)

Overall	Safety	Reliability	Performance	Comfort	Value
8	8.4	7.7	8.4	8.1	7.4

Category B

	Trade-in	Market
4 Dr STD Sdn	5280	6945

OPTIONS FOR NEW YORKER

AM/FM Compact Disc Player +90
Aluminum/Alloy Wheels +90
Climate Control for AC +45
Keyless Entry System +45
Leather Seats +185
Power Moonroof +265
Power Passenger Seat +90
Premium Sound System +105
Traction Control System +50

TOWN & COUNTRY 1994

A passenger airbag joins the standard equipment list of the Chrysler Town & Country, once again pushing the envelope of the growing minivan segment. A larger engine is also available in the 1994 Town & Country.

RATINGS (SCALE OF 1-10)

Overall	Safety	Reliability	Performance	Comfort	Value
7.4	8.3	5.9	7.8	8	6.8

Category G

	Trade-in	Market
2 Dr STD Pass. Van	6785	8810
2 Dr STD 4WD Pass. Van	7200	9350

OPTIONS FOR TOWN & COUNTRY

AM/FM Compact Disc Player +90
Child Seats (2) +70

1993 CHRYSLER

CONCORDE 1993

Chrysler's new near-luxury sedan is designed to compete with cars like the Acura Vigor and the Lexus ES 300. Standard antilock brakes, dual airbags, an optional integrated child-seat, and optional traction control are some of the Concorde's available safety features. Cab-forward design and a long wheelbase insure good passenger space and a comfortable ride

---

Don't forget to refer to the Mileage Adjustment Table at the back of this book!

for all occupants. A 3.5-liter V6 engine that produces 214 horsepower is available instead of the standard 3.3-liter V6 that produces 153 horsepower.

RATINGS (SCALE OF 1-10)

Overall	Safety	Reliability	Performance	Comfort	Value
7.6	7.6	5.8	8.2	8.5	7.8

Category B

	Trade-in	Market
4 Dr STD Sdn	4190	5740

OPTIONS FOR CONCORDE
6 cyl 3.5 L Engine +140
AM/FM Compact Disc Player +70
Aluminum/Alloy Wheels +75
Cruise Control +50
Keyless Entry System +40
Leather Seats +150
Power Door Locks +55
Power Drivers Seat +70
Power Passenger Seat +75
Power Windows +65
Premium Sound System +90
Traction Control System +40

FIFTH AVENUE 1993

A new stereo is available on the Fifth Avenue; buyers can now choose between a CD player or a cassette player for their listening pleasure. A tamper-resistant odometer is also added.

Category C

	Trade-in	Market
4 Dr STD Sdn	4325	6005

OPTIONS FOR FIFTH AVENUE
6 cyl 3.8 L Engine +80
AM/FM Compact Disc Player +80
AM/FM Stereo Tape +35
Aluminum/Alloy Wheels +65
Anti-Lock Brakes +135
Infinity Sound System +145
Keyless Entry System +40
Leather Seats +135
Power Passenger Seat +60
Premium Sound System +85

IMPERIAL 1993

A new stereo is available on the Imperial. Buyers can choose between a CD player or a cassette player. A tamper-resistant odometer is also added; this means that the miles displayed should be true.

Category A

	Trade-in	Market
4 Dr STD Sdn	4520	6105

OPTIONS FOR IMPERIAL
AM/FM Compact Disc Player +110
Aluminum/Alloy Wheels +100
Dual Power Seats +85
Keyless Entry System +55
Leather Seats +150

LE BARON 1993

The turbocharged engine is dropped and a new grille is added.

RATINGS (SCALE OF 1-10)

Overall	Safety	Reliability	Performance	Comfort	Value
6.9	5.9	7.6	7.8	6.6	6.8

Category C

	Trade-in	Market
2 Dr GTC Conv	3685	5115
2 Dr GTC Cpe	3115	4325
4 Dr LE Sdn	2975	4135
2 Dr LX Conv	4210	5845
2 Dr LX Cpe	3505	4870
4 Dr Landau Sdn	3415	4745
2 Dr STD Conv	3465	4815
2 Dr STD Cpe	2810	3905

OPTIONS FOR LE BARON
6 cyl 3.0 L Engine[Opt on LE,STD] +155
Auto 4-Speed Transmission[Std on Landau,LX] +90
AM/FM Compact Disc Player +80
Air Conditioning[Opt on LE,STD] +180
Aluminum/Alloy Wheels[Std on GTC Conv] +65
Anti-Lock Brakes +135
Cruise Control[Opt on STD] +45
Leather Seats[Std on LX Conv] +135
Power Door Locks[Std on GTC,LX] +55
Power Drivers Seat[Std on LX Conv] +65
Power Windows[Opt on Landau,LE] +70
Premium Sound System +85
Sport Suspension[Opt on LX] +45
Trip Computer +40

NEW YORKER 1993

This is the last model year for the New Yorker in its current form. Interior changes include a six-way power seat and an upgraded stereo.

Category B

	Trade-in	Market
4 Dr Salon Sdn	3980	5455

OPTIONS FOR NEW YORKER
AM/FM Stereo Tape +40
Aluminum/Alloy Wheels +75
Anti-Lock Brakes +155
Cruise Control +50
Infinity Sound System +140
Keyless Entry System +40
Leather Seats +150
Power Door Locks +55
Power Passenger Seat +75

TOWN & COUNTRY 1993

A stainless-steel exhaust system, new wheels and adjustable front shoulder belts are the main changes for the 1993 Town & Country.

Model Description	Trade-in Value	Market Value

Model Description	Trade-in Value	Market Value

RATINGS (SCALE OF 1-10)

Overall	Safety	Reliability	Performance	Comfort	Value
6.7	6.2	4.8	7.8	8	6.7

Category G

2 Dr STD Pass. Van	5490	7320
2 Dr STD 4WD Pass. Van	5815	7755

OPTIONS FOR TOWN & COUNTRY
AM/FM Compact Disc Player +70
Air Conditioning +180
Leather Seats +170

1992 CHRYSLER

FIFTH AVENUE   1992

The Fifth Avenue gets revised front-end styling that includes a new hood, grille and headlights.
Category C

4 Dr STD Sdn	3475	5035

OPTIONS FOR FIFTH AVENUE
Electronic Features Pkg +180
Anti-Lock Brakes +110
Infinity Sound System +120
Leather Seats +110

IMPERIAL   1992

No changes for 1992.
Category A

4 Dr STD Sdn	3700	5210

OPTIONS FOR IMPERIAL
Electronic Features Pkg +325
Infinity Sound System +55
Leather Seats +120

LE BARON   1992

Antilock brakes become an available option on the 1992 LeBaron. A transmission interlock also joins the list of safety equipment. Designed to keep the car from being started while in gear, the interlock requires that the clutch be fully depressed before the car will start. This year there are three trim levels available for the LeBaron, including a Landau and base model that have a 100-horsepower four-cylinder engine.

RATINGS (SCALE OF 1-10)

Overall	Safety	Reliability	Performance	Comfort	Value
6.7	5.8	6.7	7.8	6.6	6.7

Category C

2 Dr GTC Conv	3090	4480
2 Dr GTC Cpe	2355	3410
2 Dr LX Conv	3315	4805
2 Dr LX Cpe	2775	4020
4 Dr LX Sdn	2530	3665

4 Dr Landau Sdn	2700	3910
2 Dr STD Conv	2770	4015
2 Dr STD Cpe	2310	3345
4 Dr STD Sdn	2420	3505

OPTIONS FOR LE BARON
6 cyl 3.0 L Engine[Std on GTC,LX] +125
Auto 4-Speed Transmission[Std on LX] +75
Air Conditioning[Opt on STD,LX Sdn] +145
Anti-Lock Brakes +110
Cruise Control[Std on GTC,Landau,LX,Sdn] +40
Leather Seats[Std on LX Conv] +110
Power Door Locks[Opt on Landau,STD,Sdn] +45
Power Drivers Seat[Std on LX Conv] +55
Power Windows[Opt on Landau,Sdn] +55

NEW YORKER   1992

Revised styling results in rounded front and rear corners on Chrysler's midsized luxury cars. The landau top is reintroduced and an electromagnetic mirror is added to the options list.
Category B

4 Dr Salon Sdn	3260	4655

OPTIONS FOR NEW YORKER
Anti-Lock Brakes +125
Cruise Control +40
Infinity Sound System +115
Leather Seats +125
Power Door Locks +45

TOWN & COUNTRY   1992

The Town & Country can finally be ordered without the awful wood paneling that has "graced" previous year's models.

RATINGS (SCALE OF 1-10)

Overall	Safety	Reliability	Performance	Comfort	Value
6.6	5.5	4	7.8	8	7.6

Category G

2 Dr STD Pass. Van	4710	6450
2 Dr STD 4WD Pass. Van	4985	6830

OPTIONS FOR TOWN & COUNTRY
Dual Air Conditioning +170
Leather Seats +140

1991 CHRYSLER

IMPERIAL   1991

No changes for 1991.
Category A

4 Dr STD Sdn	3085	4470

OPTIONS FOR IMPERIAL
Electronic Features Pkg +205
Infinity Sound System +45
Leather Seats +100

Don't forget to refer to the Mileage Adjustment Table at the back of this book!

Model Description	Trade-in Value	Market Value

LE BARON 1991

No major changes for the 1991 Chrysler LeBaron.

RATINGS (SCALE OF 1-10)

Overall	Safety	Reliability	Performance	Comfort	Value
6.5	5.8	5.7	7.8	6.6	6.6

Category C

2 Dr GTC Conv	2470	3800
2 Dr GTC Turbo Conv	2560	3935
2 Dr Highline Conv	2345	3610
2 Dr Highline Turbo Conv	2400	3695
2 Dr Highline Cpe	1760	2705
2 Dr Highline Turbo Cpe	1805	2780
2 Dr Premium LX Conv	2665	4100
2 Dr Premium LX Cpe	2150	3305
4 Dr STD Sdn	2030	3120

OPTIONS FOR LE BARON

6 cyl 3.0 L Engine[Opt on Highline,STD] +100
Auto 4-Speed Transmission[Opt on GTC,Highline] +60
Air Conditioning[Opt on Highline] +120
Anti-Lock Brakes +90
Cruise Control[Opt on Highline] +30
Infinity Sound System +95
Leather Seats[Opt on GTC,STD] +90
Power Door Locks[Opt on Highline,STD] +35
Power Drivers Seat +45
Power Windows[Opt on STD] +45

NEW YORKER 1991

No changes for the 1991 New Yorker.

Category B

4 Dr Fifth Avenue Sdn	2820	4145
4 Dr Salon Sdn	2560	3765

OPTIONS FOR NEW YORKER

Electronic Features Pkg +185
Luxury Pkg +185
Anti-Lock Brakes +100
Cruise Control[Opt on Salon] +30
Infinity Sound System +95
Leather Seats +100
Power Door Locks[Opt on Salon] +40
Power Drivers Seat[Opt on Salon] +45

TOWN & COUNTRY 1991

Antilock brakes and a driver airbag are added to the all-new Town & Country option lists.

RATINGS (SCALE OF 1-10)

Overall	Safety	Reliability	Performance	Comfort	Value
6.6	5	3.8	7.8	8	8.6

Category G

2 Dr STD Pass. Van	4045	5775

OPTIONS FOR TOWN & COUNTRY

Captain Chairs (4) +90
Dual Air Conditioning +140

1990 CHRYSLER

FIFTH AVENUE 1990

Wow, this car gets big changes in 1990. The car goes from being a V8/rear-wheel-drive platform to a smaller V6 powered chassis with front-wheel drive. Performance actually improves. This totally redesigned sedan actually uses the Dodge Dynasty's platform. Luxury content is up and rear seat passengers will appreciate the commodious legroom.

Category C

4 Dr Mark Cross Sdn	2240	3670
4 Dr STD Sdn	2055	3370

OPTIONS FOR FIFTH AVENUE

Electronic Features Pkg +110

IMPERIAL 1990

Yet another Chrysler Imperial is unleashed on the unsuspecting public. This one has front-wheel drive and is larger than the New Yorker Fifth Avenue. It is loaded with standard equipment and is equipped with Chrysler's new 3.3 V6 engine and a four-speed transmission.

Category A

4 Dr STD Sdn	2605	3950

LE BARON 1990

The LeBaron hatchback is dropped, moving the Chrysler coupe and convertible closer to enthusiast respectability. A new V6 engine is introduced offering smoother operation than the raspy turbo. Speaking of turbos, the next generation turbo is released for the LeBaron; horsepower figures are the same but turbo lag is reduced. A LeBaron Sedan is reintroduced this year with a 3.0-liter engine and room for six.

RATINGS (SCALE OF 1-10)

Overall	Safety	Reliability	Performance	Comfort	Value
6.5	5.2	6.1	7.8	6.6	6.6

Category C

2 Dr GT Conv	2120	3475
2 Dr GT Turbo Conv	2135	3500
2 Dr GT Cpe	1805	2955
2 Dr GT Turbo Cpe	1860	3050
2 Dr GTC Turbo Conv	2220	3640
2 Dr GTC Turbo Cpe	1910	3130
2 Dr Highline Conv	1950	3200
2 Dr Highline Turbo Conv	2040	3345

Model Description	Trade-in Value	Market Value
2 Dr Highline Cpe	1335	2190
2 Dr Highline Turbo Cpe	1395	2290
2 Dr Premium Conv	2135	3500
2 Dr Premium Cpe	1840	3015
4 Dr STD Sdn	1640	2685

OPTIONS FOR LE BARON
6 cyl 3.0 L Engine[Opt on Highline] +85
Auto 4-Speed Transmission[Opt on GT,Highline] +45
Air Conditioning[Opt on Highline] +95
Cruise Control[Opt on Highline,Premium Cpe] +25
Leather Seats[Std on GTC Turbo Conv] +75
Power Door Locks[Opt on Highline,STD] +30
Power Drivers Seat[Std on GTC] +35
Power Windows[Opt on STD] +35

NEW YORKER   1990

The New Yorker Landau and Salon models are introduced to the New Yorker lineup, as is a Chrysler-built 3.3-liter V6 engine. A new four-speed automatic is mated to the new powerplant.

Category B

Model Description	Trade-in Value	Market Value
4 Dr Mark Cross Sdn	2345	3610
4 Dr Salon Sdn	2100	3230

Category C

4 Dr Landau Sdn	2045	3350

OPTIONS FOR NEW YORKER
Air Conditioning[Opt on Salon] +100
Anti-Lock Brakes +75
Leather Seats[Opt on Landau] +75
Power Door Locks[Std on Mark Cross] +30
Power Drivers Seat[Std on Mark Cross] +35
Power Windows[Opt on Salon] +35

TOWN & COUNTRY   1990

Chrysler releases an upscale version of its popular minivan. Luxury appointments and fake wood-grain body-side paneling hearken back to the days of the full-size luxury station wagon. Power comes via 3.3-liter V6 engine that is good for 150 horsepower.

Category G

Model Description	Trade-in Value	Market Value
2 Dr STD Pass. Van	3135	4750

OPTIONS FOR TOWN & COUNTRY
Dual Air Conditioning +115

Don't forget to refer to the Mileage Adjustment Table at the back of this book!

Model Description	Trade-in Value	Market Value
DAEWOO S. Korea		

1999 Daewoo Leganza

1999 DAEWOO

LANOS 1999

This entry into the subcompact class is Daewoo's attack on the Honda Civic.
Category E

Model Description	Trade-in Value	Market Value
2 Dr S Hbk	5480	6685
4 Dr S Sdn	6230	7600
2 Dr SE Hbk	6490	7915
4 Dr SE Sdn	7955	9700
2 Dr SX Hbk	7020	8560
4 Dr SX Sdn	9125	11130

OPTIONS FOR LANOS
Auto 4-Speed Transmission +590
Air Conditioning[Std on SX] +605

LEGANZA 1999

The whole car is new to the United States, as is the motor company that makes it.
Category E

Model Description	Trade-in Value	Market Value
4 Dr CDX Sdn	11585	14125
4 Dr SE Sdn	8870	10820
4 Dr SX Sdn	10445	12735

OPTIONS FOR LEGANZA
Auto 4-Speed Transmission[Opt on SE] +590
Power Drivers Seat +230
Power Moonroof[Opt on SX] +425

NUBIRA 1999

Want a car that looks just like a Nissan Maxima, yet costs thousands less? Dae Woo's Nubira is it.
Category E

Model Description	Trade-in Value	Market Value
4 Dr CDX Hbk	8890	10840
4 Dr SX Hbk	8030	9790

OPTIONS FOR NUBIRA
Auto 4-Speed Transmission +590

Don't forget to refer to the Mileage Adjustment Table at the back of this book!

DODGE USA

1994 Dodge Ram 1500 2WD

1999 DODGE

AVENGER 1999

One new color for the exterior: Shark Blue (replaces Silver Mist).

RATINGS (SCALE OF 1-10)

Overall	Safety	Reliability	Performance	Comfort	Value
N/A	7.7	N/A	7.6	7.4	N/A

Category F
2 Dr ES Cpe	10300	12410
2 Dr STD Cpe	9160	11035

OPTIONS FOR AVENGER
6 cyl 2.5 L Engine +475
Auto 4-Speed Transmission +515
Air Conditioning[Std on ES] +620
Aluminum/Alloy Wheels[Std on ES] +230
Anti-Lock Brakes +505
Compact Disc W/fm/tape +375
Cruise Control[Std on ES] +155
Keyless Entry System +130
Leather Seats +485
Power Door Locks +150
Power Drivers Seat +180
Power Mirrors +95
Power Moonroof +480
Power Windows +165
Rear Spoiler[Std on ES] +185

CARAVAN/GRAND CARAVAN 1999

RATINGS (SCALE OF 1-10)

Overall	Safety	Reliability	Performance	Comfort	Value
N/A	6.6	8.4	6.6	7.4	N/A

CARAVAN
Category G
2 Dr LE Pass. Van	15315	18230
2 Dr SE Pass. Van	13590	16180
2 Dr STD Pass. Van	11255	13400

GRAND CARAVAN
Category G
2 Dr Grand Pass. Van	12665	15080
2 Dr Grand ES Pass. Van	17325	20625
2 Dr Grand ES 4WD Pass. Van	18325	21815
2 Dr Grand LE Pass. Van	16405	19530
2 Dr Grand LE 4WD Pass. Van	17400	20715
2 Dr Grand SE Pass. Van	14870	17700
2 Dr Grand SE 4WD Pass. Van	15895	18920

OPTIONS FOR CARAVAN/GRAND CARAVAN
6 cyl 3.0 L Engine +415
6 cyl 3.3 L Engine[Std on Grand] +715
6 cyl 3.8 L Engine[Std on Grand ES,4WD] +275
Auto 4-Speed Transmission[Opt on STD] +150
7 Passenger Seating[Opt on STD] +385
AM/FM Stereo Tape[Opt on Grand,STD] +170
Air Conditioning[Opt on Grand,STD] +605
Captain Chairs (4) +465
Compact Disc W/fm/tape[Std on Grand ES] +355
Cruise Control[Opt on Grand,STD] +155
Dual Air Conditioning +700
Dual Power Seats +285
Leather Seats +575
Luggage Rack +115
Power Door Locks[Std on Grand ES,Grand LE,LE] +170
Power Windows[Std on Grand ES,Grand LE,LE] +175
Rear Window Defroster[Opt on Grand,STD] +125
Tilt Steering Wheel[Opt on Grand,STD] +130

DAKOTA 1999

Solar Yellow paint is now available for those who want their pickups to get noticed. Other un-pickup-like refinements include an express down feature for the driver's window, extra storage space for cassettes or CDs, and remote radio controls on the steering wheel.

RATINGS (SCALE OF 1-10)

Overall	Safety	Reliability	Performance	Comfort	Value
N/A	N/A	N/A	6.6	7.1	N/A

Category G
2 Dr R/T Sport Ext Cab SB	12305	14650
2 Dr R/T Sport Std Cab SB	11300	13455
2 Dr SLT Ext Cab SB	12145	14460
2 Dr SLT 4WD Ext Cab SB	13770	16390
2 Dr SLT Std Cab LB	11380	13545
2 Dr SLT Std Cab SB	11200	13335
2 Dr SLT 4WD Std Cab SB	12905	15365
2 Dr STD Ext Cab SB	10750	12800

Don't forget to refer to the Mileage Adjustment Table at the back of this book!

Model Description	Trade-in Value	Market Value
2 Dr STD 4WD Ext Cab SB	12615	15020
2 Dr STD Std Cab LB	9720	11570
2 Dr STD Std Cab SB	9560	11380
2 Dr STD 4WD Std Cab SB	11515	13710
2 Dr Sport Ext Cab SB	11555	13755
2 Dr Sport 4WD Ext Cab SB	13295	15825
2 Dr Sport Std Cab LB	10485	12485
2 Dr Sport Std Cab SB	10355	12325
2 Dr Sport 4WD Std Cab SB	12195	14515

OPTIONS FOR DAKOTA

6 cyl 3.9 L Engine[Std on 4WD and Ext. Cab] +415
8 cyl 5.2 L Engine +660
8 cyl 5.9 L Engine[Std on R/T Sport] +1245
Auto 4-Speed Transmission[Std on R/T Sport] +720
AM/FM Compact Disc Player +245
Air Conditioning[Std on SLT] +605
Anti-Lock Brakes +445
Bed Liner +210
Cruise Control[Std on R/T Sport] +155
Fog Lights +105
Overhead Console +120
Power Door Locks +170
Power Mirrors +100
Power Windows +175
Sliding Rear Window +90
Tilt Steering Wheel[Std on R/T Sport] +130

DURANGO 1999

Two-wheel drive models finally show up for true flatlander use, and all Durangos gain a rear power outlet. Also available are steering wheel-mounted radio controls, heated mirrors, and two new colors: Bright Platinum Metallic and Patriot Blue.

RATINGS (SCALE OF 1-10)

Overall	Safety	Reliability	Performance	Comfort	Value
N/A	N/A	N/A	6.6	7.6	N/A

Category H

	Trade-in Value	Market Value
4 Dr SLT Wgn	18175	21380
4 Dr SLT 4WD Wgn	19935	23450

OPTIONS FOR DURANGO

8 cyl 5.2 L Engine +435
8 cyl 5.9 L Engine +540
Compact Disc W/fm/tape +230
Dual Air Conditioning +990
Fog Lights +90
Leather Seats +730
Overhead Console +95
Power Drivers Seat +210
Third Seat +470

INTREPID 1999

Minor appearance tweaks such as chrome badging and improved floor carpeting debut for 1999. A new engine immobilizer is now available on the ES.

RATINGS (SCALE OF 1-10)

Overall	Safety	Reliability	Performance	Comfort	Value
N/A	7.2	8	8.2	8.5	N/A

Category B

	Trade-in Value	Market Value
4 Dr ES Sdn	13985	16850
4 Dr STD Sdn	12600	15180

OPTIONS FOR INTREPID

AM/FM Compact Disc Player +245
Anti-Lock Brakes[Std on ES] +510
Keyless Entry System[Std on ES] +130
Leather Seats +505
Power Drivers Seat[Std on ES] +230
Power Sunroof +845
Traction Control System +130

NEON 1999

One new color is available for the Neon Style Package: Inferno Red. Disco, anyone?

RATINGS (SCALE OF 1-10)

Overall	Safety	Reliability	Performance	Comfort	Value
N/A	6	7.6	7.4	7.6	N/A

Category E

	Trade-in Value	Market Value
2 Dr Competition Cpe	7595	9260
4 Dr Competition Sdn	7750	9450
2 Dr Highline Cpe	6730	8210
4 Dr Highline Sdn	6890	8400
2 Dr R/T Cpe	9200	11220
4 Dr R/T Sdn	9350	11400
2 Dr Sport Cpe	7040	8585
4 Dr Sport Sdn	7210	8790

OPTIONS FOR NEON

4 cyl 2.0 L DOHC Engine[Std on R/T,Sport] +110
Auto 3-Speed Transmission +445
Competition Pkg +1115
AM/FM Compact Disc Player +340
AM/FM Stereo Tape[Std on R/T] +225
Air Conditioning[Std on R/T,Sport] +605
Aluminum/Alloy Wheels[Std on R/T] +245
Cruise Control +165
Power Door Locks +180
Power Mirrors +80
Power Windows +195
Rear Window Defroster[Opt on Competition] +120
Tilt Steering Wheel +110

RAM PICKUP 1999

RATINGS (SCALE OF 1-10)

Overall	Safety	Reliability	Performance	Comfort	Value
N/A	N/A	N/A	7	8	N/A

Model Description	Trade-in Value	Market Value
RAM 1500		
Category H		
2 Dr Laramie SLT Ext Cab LB	15745	18525
2 Dr Laramie SLT 4WD Ext Cab LB	18230	21445
4 Dr Laramie SLT Ext Cab LB	16115	18960
4 Dr Laramie SLT 4WD Ext Cab LB	18540	21810
2 Dr Laramie SLT Ext Cab SB	15565	18310
2 Dr Laramie SLT 4WD Ext Cab SB	18035	21220
4 Dr Laramie SLT Ext Cab SB	15940	18750
4 Dr Laramie SLT 4WD Ext Cab SB	18430	21685
2 Dr Laramie SLT Std Cab LB	13615	16015
2 Dr Laramie SLT 4WD Std Cab LB	16710	19660
2 Dr Laramie SLT Std Cab SB	13455	15830
2 Dr Laramie SLT 4WD Std Cab SB	16555	19475
2 Dr ST Ext Cab LB	13445	15820
2 Dr ST 4WD Ext Cab LB	15965	18785
4 Dr ST Ext Cab LB	13830	16270
4 Dr ST 4WD Ext Cab LB	16330	19210
2 Dr ST Ext Cab SB	13270	15610
4 Dr ST Ext Cab SB	13675	16090
2 Dr ST 4WD Ext Cab SB	15765	18545
4 Dr ST 4WD Ext Cab SB	16165	19020
2 Dr ST Std Cab LB	10965	12900
2 Dr ST 4WD Std Cab LB	14120	16610
2 Dr ST Std Cab SB	10810	12715
2 Dr ST 4WD Std Cab SB	13935	16395
2 Dr WS Std Cab LB	9425	11090
2 Dr WS Std Cab SB	9250	10880
RAM 2500		
Category H		
2 Dr Laramie SLT Ext Cab LB	19050	22410
2 Dr Laramie SLT 4WD Ext Cab LB	20410	24010
4 Dr Laramie SLT Ext Cab LB	19440	22870
4 Dr Laramie SLT 4WD Ext Cab LB	20780	24445
2 Dr Laramie SLT Ext Cab SB	18905	22240
2 Dr Laramie SLT 4WD Ext Cab SB	20230	23800
4 Dr Laramie SLT Ext Cab SB	19280	22680
4 Dr Laramie SLT 4WD Ext Cab SB	20560	24190
2 Dr Laramie SLT Std Cab LB	17270	20320
2 Dr Laramie SLT 4WD Std Cab LB	18990	22340

Model Description	Trade-in Value	Market Value
2 Dr ST Ext Cab LB	17160	20190
2 Dr ST 4WD Ext Cab LB	19380	22800
4 Dr ST Ext Cab LB	17575	20675
4 Dr ST 4WD Ext Cab LB	19720	23200
2 Dr ST Ext Cab SB	16980	19975
2 Dr ST 4WD Ext Cab SB	19235	22630
4 Dr ST Ext Cab SB	17350	20410
4 Dr ST 4WD Ext Cab SB	19560	23010
2 Dr ST Std Cab LB	15805	18595
2 Dr ST 4WD Std Cab LB	17520	20610
RAM 3500		
Category H		
4 Dr Laramie SLT Ext Cab LB	19885	23395
4 Dr Laramie SLT 4WD Ext Cab LB	22675	26675
2 Dr Laramie SLT Std Cab LB	18540	21810
4 Dr ST Ext Cab LB	18565	21840
4 Dr ST 4WD Ext Cab LB	21575	25380
2 Dr ST Std Cab LB	16985	19985

OPTIONS FOR RAM PICKUP

10 cyl 8.0 L Engine +345
6 cyl 5.9 L Turbodsl Engine +3385
8 cyl 5.2 L Engine[Std on Ext Cab,4WD] +435
8 cyl 5.9 L Engine[Opt on Ram 1500] +540
Auto 4-Speed Transmission +720
AM/FM Compact Disc Player +230
Air Conditioning[Opt on ST,WS] +600
Anti-Lock Brakes[Std on Ram 3500] +370
Bed Liner +165
Camper/Towing Package +255
Cruise Control[Opt on ST,WS] +140
Fog Lights +90
Keyless Entry System +130
Leather Seats +730
Limited Slip Diff +190
Power Drivers Seat +210
Sliding Rear Window +85
Tilt Steering Wheel[Opt on ST,WS] +135
Tutone Paint +190

RAM VAN/WAGON   1999

RATINGS (SCALE OF 1-10)

Overall	Safety	Reliability	Performance	Comfort	Value
N/A	N/A	N/A	6.2	6.9	N/A

VAN

Model Description	Trade-in Value	Market Value
Category H		
2 Dr 2500 Maxi Cargo Van Ext	13275	15620
2 Dr 3500 Maxi Cargo Van Ext	13940	16400
2 Dr 1500 STD Cargo Van	12490	14695
2 Dr 1500 STD Cargo Van Ext	12955	15240
2 Dr 3500 STD Cargo Van Ext	13625	16030

Don't forget to refer to the Mileage Adjustment Table at the back of this book!

Model Description	Trade-in Value	Market Value

WAGON
Category H

Model Description	Trade-in Value	Market Value
2 Dr 3500 Maxi Pass. Van Ext	14690	17280
2 Dr 1500 STD Pass. Van	12845	15110
2 Dr 2500 STD Pass. Van Ext	13670	16080

OPTIONS FOR RAM VAN/WAGON
8 cyl 5.2 L Engine[Opt on B150] +435
8 cyl 5.9 L Engine +540
Auto 4-Speed Transmission[Opt on B150] +220
Tradesman Upfitter Pkg +735
AM/FM Stereo Tape[Opt on Van] +160
Air Conditioning[Opt on Van] +600
Aluminum/Alloy Wheels +235
Cruise Control +140
Keyless Entry System +130
Power Door Locks +140
Power Mirrors +75
Power Windows +140
Rear Heater +160
Rear Window Defroster +115
Sunscreen Glass +175

STRATUS   1999
The instrument panel gauges are now white-faced, wheels are better looking, and some work has been done to reduce the interior noise levels.

RATINGS (SCALE OF 1-10)

Overall	Safety	Reliability	Performance	Comfort	Value
N/A	6.4	N/A	6.4	7.9	N/A

Category C

	Trade-in	Market
4 Dr ES Sdn	11080	13350
4 Dr STD Sdn	8655	10430

OPTIONS FOR STRATUS
4 cyl 2.4 L Engine +335
Auto 4-Speed Transmission[Std on ES] +775
AM/FM Compact Disc Player +270
Cruise Control[Std on ES] +155
Keyless Entry System +140
Power Door Locks[Std on ES] +185
Power Drivers Seat +220
Power Windows[Std on ES] +230

VIPER   1999
Goodies for the '99 Viper include power mirrors, Connolly leather for various interior surfaces, a new shift knob, aluminum interior accents, and a remote release for the glass hatch on the GTS. Black is again an exterior color choice, available with or without silver stripes. New 18-inch aluminum wheels with the Viper logo on the caps round out the changes.
Category K

	Trade-in	Market
2 Dr GTS Cpe	53215	62605

OPTIONS FOR VIPER
Dual Stripes +1480

1998 DODGE

AVENGER   1998
Interior fabrics are new, as is a black and gray color scheme. The ES model gets a new Sport package that affects appearance, not performance. Also available for the ES are new 16-inch aluminum wheels and a rear sway bar that improves handling.

RATINGS (SCALE OF 1-10)

Overall	Safety	Reliability	Performance	Comfort	Value
7.2	7.5	7.1	7.6	7.6	6

Category F

	Trade-in	Market
2 Dr ES Cpe	9485	11565
2 Dr STD Cpe	8445	10300

OPTIONS FOR AVENGER
6 cyl 2.5 L Engine +395
Auto 4-Speed Transmission +425
Air Conditioning[Std on ES] +505
Aluminum/Alloy Wheels[Std on ES] +185
Anti-Lock Brakes +415
Compact Disc W/fm/tape +305
Cruise Control[Std on ES] +125
Keyless Entry System +110
Leather Seats +395
Leather Steering Wheel[Std on ES] +90
Power Door Locks +120
Power Drivers Seat +150
Power Mirrors +75
Power Sunroof +410
Power Windows +135

CARAVAN   1998
Available this year is a 3.8-liter V6 that puts out 180 horsepower and 240 foot-pounds of torque. And for convenience, Caravans come with rear-seat mounted grocery bag hooks, and driver's-side easy-entry Quad seating. All Chrysler products are equipped with "Next Generation" depowered airbags.

RATINGS (SCALE OF 1-10)

Overall	Safety	Reliability	Performance	Comfort	Value
7.6	6.8	8.1	6.6	7.4	9.3

Category G

	Trade-in	Market
2 Dr Grand Pass. Van	11320	13475
2 Dr Grand ES Pass. Van	15500	18450
2 Dr Grand ES 4WD Pass. Van	16130	19200
2 Dr Grand LE Pass. Van	14885	17720
2 Dr Grand LE 4WD Pass. Van	15565	18530
2 Dr Grand SE Pass. Van	12620	15025
2 Dr Grand SE 4WD Pass. Van	13280	15810

Don't forget to refer to the Mileage Adjustment Table at the back of this book!

Model Description	Trade-in Value	Market Value
2 Dr LE Pass. Van	13635	16235
2 Dr SE Pass. Van	11420	13595
2 Dr STD Pass. Van	9825	11695

OPTIONS FOR CARAVAN
6 cyl 3.0 L Engine[Std on Grand, SE] +305
6 cyl 3.3 L Engine[Std on Grand ES, Grand LE, LE] +210
6 cyl 3.8 L Engine[Std on 4WD] +255
Auto 4-Speed Transmission[Opt on Grand, STD] +155
AM/FM Compact Disc Player +200
Air Conditioning[Std on Grand ES,Grand LE,LE,4WD] +495
Aluminum/Alloy Wheels[Std on Grand ES] +200
Anti-Lock Brakes[Opt on Grand, STD] +365
Auto Load Leveling[Std on 4WD] +135
Captain Chairs (4) +380
Cruise Control[Opt on Grand, STD] +125
Dual Air Conditioning +575
Keyless Entry System[Opt on Grand SE, SE] +120
Leather Seats +470
Power Door Locks[Std on Grand ES, Grand LE, LE] +140
Power Drivers Seat +170
Power Mirrors[Opt on Grand, STD] +80
Power Windows[Opt on Grand SE, SE] +145
Rear Window Defroster[Std on Grand ES, Grand LE, LE] +105
Sliding Driver Side Door[Opt on STD] +320
Sunscreen Glass[Std on Grand ES,Grand LE,LE] +225
Tilt Steering Wheel[Opt on Grand, STD] +105
Traction Control System +165
Trip Computer[Opt on Grand SE, SE] +90

DAKOTA   1998
The Dakota R/T, featuring a 250-horsepower V8, is available for those seeking a performance pickup. The passenger airbag can now be deactivated in all Dakotas, so a rear-facing child seat is perfectly safe. The Dakota is also available in three new colors.

RATINGS (SCALE OF 1-10)

Overall	Safety	Reliability	Performance	Comfort	Value
N/A	N/A	N/A	7	7.1	N/A

Category G

Model Description	Trade-in Value	Market Value
2 Dr R/T Sport Ext Cab SB	11460	13640
2 Dr R/T Sport Std Cab SB	10230	12180
2 Dr SLT Ext Cab SB	11300	13450
2 Dr SLT 4WD Ext Cab SB	12775	15210
2 Dr SLT Std Cab LB	10410	12390
2 Dr SLT Std Cab SB	10250	12200
2 Dr SLT 4WD Std Cab SB	11935	14210
2 Dr STD Ext Cab SB	10030	11940
2 Dr STD 4WD Ext Cab SB	11800	14050
2 Dr STD Std Cab LB	8895	10590
2 Dr STD Std Cab SB	8720	10380
2 Dr STD 4WD Std Cab SB	10655	12685
2 Dr Sport Ext Cab SB	10505	12505
2 Dr Sport 4WD Ext Cab SB	12305	14650

Model Description	Trade-in Value	Market Value
2 Dr Sport Std Cab LB	9655	11495
2 Dr Sport Std Cab SB	9510	11320
2 Dr Sport 4WD Std Cab SB	11255	13400

OPTIONS FOR DAKOTA
6 cyl 3.9 L Engine[Std on 4WD, SLT 2WD Ext Cab SB] +305
8 cyl 5.2 L Engine +535
8 cyl 5.9 L Engine[Std on R/T Sport] +975
Auto 4-Speed Transmission[Std on R/T Sport] +585
AM/FM Compact Disc Player +200
Air Conditioning[Std on SLT] +495
Anti-Lock Brakes +365
Bed Liner +170
Cruise Control[Std on R/T Sport] +125
Fog Lights +90
Keyless Entry System +120
Limited Slip Diff[Std on R/T Sport] +165
Power Door Locks +140
Power Drivers Seat +170
Power Mirrors +80
Power Windows +145
Sliding Rear Window +70
Tilt Steering Wheel[Std on R/T Sport] +105

DURANGO   1998
As the most recent addition to the Dodge truck lineup, the Durango makes quite an entry. Offering the most cargo space in its class, along with eight-passenger seating and three-and-a-half tons of towing capacity, the Durango is the most versatile sport-utility on the market.

RATINGS (SCALE OF 1-10)

Overall	Safety	Reliability	Performance	Comfort	Value
N/A	N/A	8.8	6.8	7.6	N/A

Category H

Model Description	Trade-in Value	Market Value
4 Dr SLT 4WD Wgn	18700	22260
4 Dr STD 4WD Wgn	17260	20550

OPTIONS FOR DURANGO
8 cyl 5.2 L Engine +360
8 cyl 5.9 L Engine +365
Anti-Lock Brakes +300
Camper/Towing Package +205
Compact Disc W/fm/tape +190
Fog Lights +75
Leather Seats +595
Limited Slip Diff +155
Power Drivers Seat +170
Third Seat +385

INTREPID   1998
Completely redesigned for 1998, the Intrepid is a sedan that has the graceful styling of a coupe, thanks to a continuation of Chrysler's cab-forward design. Dodge's trademark cross hair grille dominates the front end along with two large, sparkling headlights. And the

DODGE 98

Model Description	Trade-in Value	Market Value	Model Description	Trade-in Value	Market Value

new Intrepid is powered by your choice of two new V6 engines.

RATINGS (SCALE OF 1-10)

Overall	Safety	Reliability	Performance	Comfort	Value
8.1	7.1	7.8	8.2	8.5	9

Category B

	Trade-in	Market
4 Dr ES Sdn	12450	15000
4 Dr STD Sdn	11090	13360

OPTIONS FOR INTREPID

AM/FM Compact Disc Player +200
Anti-Lock Brakes[Std on ES] +420
Climate Control for AC +105
Dual Power Seats +230
Keyless Entry System[Std on ES] +105
Leather Seats +410
Power Drivers Seat[Std on ES] +190
Power Moonroof +590
Traction Control System +105

NEON   1998

An R/T appearance package makes people think you're driving a Viper! Improved option packages, LEV emissions and next-generation airbags round out the changes.

RATINGS (SCALE OF 1-10)

Overall	Safety	Reliability	Performance	Comfort	Value
7.1	6.1	7.7	7.4	7.6	6.8

Category E

	Trade-in	Market
2 Dr Competition Cpe	6965	8600
4 Dr Competition Sdn	7135	8810
2 Dr Highline Cpe	5975	7375
4 Dr Highline Sdn	6130	7570
2 Dr R/T Cpe	8245	10180
4 Dr R/T Sdn	8390	10360
2 Dr Sport Cpe	6450	7960
4 Dr Sport Sdn	6620	8170

OPTIONS FOR NEON

Auto 3-Speed Transmission +370
Competition Pkg +930
AM/FM Compact Disc Player +275
Air Conditioning[Std on R/T, Sport] +495
Aluminum/Alloy Wheels[Std on R/T] +200
Anti-Lock Brakes +410
Cruise Control +135
Keyless Entry System +95
Power Door Locks +145
Power Mirrors +65
Power Windows +160
Rear Window Defroster[Opt on Competition] +100
Tilt Steering Wheel +90

RAM PICKUP   1998

All Rams get a totally redesigned interior, standard passenger-side airbag with cutoff switch, and all airbags are "depowered" for safety.

RATINGS (SCALE OF 1-10)

Overall	Safety	Reliability	Performance	Comfort	Value
N/A	N/A	8.9	7	8	N/A

RAM 1500

Category H

	Trade-in	Market
2 Dr Laramie SLT Ext Cab LB	14270	16990
2 Dr Laramie SLT 4WD Ext Cab LB	16295	19400
4 Dr Laramie SLT Ext Cab LB	14635	17420
4 Dr Laramie SLT 4WD Ext Cab LB	16630	19800
2 Dr Laramie SLT Ext Cab SB	14065	16745
2 Dr Laramie SLT 4WD Ext Cab SB	16155	19230
4 Dr Laramie SLT Ext Cab SB	14450	17200
4 Dr Laramie SLT 4WD Ext Cab SB	17120	20380
2 Dr Laramie SLT Std Cab LB	12670	15085
2 Dr Laramie SLT 4WD Std Cab LB	14975	17830
2 Dr Laramie SLT Std Cab SB	12505	14885
2 Dr Laramie SLT 4WD Std Cab SB	14800	17620
2 Dr SS/T Std Cab SB	12195	14520
2 Dr ST Ext Cab LB	12255	14590
2 Dr ST 4WD Ext Cab LB	14450	17205
4 Dr ST Ext Cab LB	12625	15030
4 Dr ST 4WD Ext Cab LB	14820	17640
2 Dr ST Ext Cab SB	12105	14410
2 Dr ST 4WD Ext Cab SB	14320	17050
4 Dr ST Ext Cab SB	12475	14850
4 Dr ST 4WD Ext Cab SB	14640	17430
2 Dr ST Std Cab LB	10130	12060
2 Dr ST 4WD Std Cab LB	12720	15140
2 Dr ST Std Cab SB	9975	11875
2 Dr ST 4WD Std Cab SB	12565	14960
2 Dr WS Std Cab LB	8860	10550
2 Dr WS Std Cab SB	8700	10360

RAM 2500

Category H

	Trade-in	Market
2 Dr Laramie SLT Ext Cab LB	17105	20365
2 Dr Laramie SLT 4WD Ext Cab LB	18580	22120
4 Dr Laramie SLT Ext Cab LB	17470	20795

Don't forget to refer to the Mileage Adjustment Table at the back of this book!

Model Description	Trade-in Value	Market Value
4 Dr Laramie SLT 4WD Ext Cab LB		
	18910	22510
2 Dr Laramie SLT Ext Cab SB	16940	20165
2 Dr Laramie SLT 4WD Ext Cab SB		
	18405	21910
4 Dr Laramie SLT Ext Cab SB	17300	20595
4 Dr Laramie SLT 4WD Ext Cab SB		
	18745	22315
2 Dr Laramie SLT Std Cab LB	15410	18345
2 Dr Laramie SLT 4WD Std Cab LB		
	16780	19975
2 Dr ST Ext Cab LB	15600	18570
2 Dr ST 4WD Ext Cab LB	17235	20520
4 Dr ST Ext Cab LB	16305	19410
4 Dr ST 4WD Ext Cab LB	17555	20900
2 Dr ST Ext Cab SB	15435	18375
2 Dr ST 4WD Ext Cab SB	17050	20300
4 Dr ST Ext Cab SB	15790	18800
4 Dr ST 4WD Ext Cab SB	17395	20710
2 Dr ST Std Cab LB	14475	17235
2 Dr ST 4WD Std Cab LB	16210	19300

RAM 3500

Category H

Model Description	Trade-in Value	Market Value
4 Dr Laramie SLT Ext Cab LB	17860	21260
4 Dr Laramie SLT 4WD Ext Cab LB		
	20830	24800
2 Dr Laramie SLT Std Cab LB	16670	19845
2 Dr Laramie SLT 4WD Std Cab LB		
	19440	23145
4 Dr ST Ext Cab LB	16785	19980
4 Dr ST 4WD Ext Cab LB	19595	23330
2 Dr ST Std Cab LB	15650	18630
2 Dr ST 4WD Std Cab LB	18245	21720

OPTIONS FOR RAM PICKUP

10 cyl 8.0 L Engine +600
6 cyl 5.9 L Turbodsl Engine +2730
8 cyl 5.2 L Engine[Std on Ext Cab, 4WD] +360
8 cyl 5.9 L Engine[Std on Ram 2500, Ram 3500, SS/T] +365
Auto 4-Speed Transmission +585
AM/FM Compact Disc Player +190
Air Conditioning[Opt on ST, WS] +490
Aluminum/Alloy Wheels[Opt on Ram 2500, ST] +190
Anti-Lock Brakes +300
Bed Liner +135
Camper/Towing Package +205
Cruise Control[Opt on ST, WS] +115
Fog Lights[Std on SS/T] +75
Heated Power Mirrors[Std on Ram 3500, Laramie SLT, SS/T] +60
Keyless Entry System +105
Leather Seats +595
Limited Slip Diff +155
Power Drivers Seat +170

Skid Plates[Std on Ram 3500] +65
Sliding Rear Window +70
Tilt Steering Wheel[Opt on ST, WS] +110
Tutone Paint +155

RAM VAN/WAGON   1998

A minor redesign this year includes better build quality, so we're told. Of note are the appearance of dual airbags in the revised dash and upgrades to the brakes and sound systems. The V8 engines have also been relocated forward to reduce the size of that annoying "doghouse."

RATINGS (SCALE OF 1-10)

Overall	Safety	Reliability	Performance	Comfort	Value
N/A	N/A	8.3	6.2	6.9	N/A

VAN

Category H

Model Description	Trade-in Value	Market Value
2 Dr 1500 Ram Van	10925	13005
2 Dr 1500 Ram Van Ext	11460	13645
2 Dr 2500 Ram Van Ext	11960	14240
2 Dr 2500 Maxi Ram Van Ext	12430	14800
2 Dr 3500 Ram Van Ext	12430	14800
2 Dr 3500 Maxi Ram Van Ext	12960	15430

WAGON

Category H

Model Description	Trade-in Value	Market Value
2 Dr 1500 Ram Wagon	10920	13000
2 Dr 1500 SLT Ram Wagon	11705	13935
2 Dr 2500 Ram Wagon Ext	12070	14370
2 Dr 2500 SLT Ram Wagon Ext	12885	15340
2 Dr 3500 Maxi Ram Wagon Ext	13185	15695
2 Dr 3500 SLT Maxi Ram Wagon Ext		
	13885	16530

OPTIONS FOR RAM VAN/WAGON

8 cyl 5.2 L Engine[Opt on B150] +360
8 cyl 5.9 L Engine +365
Auto 4-Speed Transmission[Opt on B150] +185
AM/FM Compact Disc Player +190
Air Conditioning[Opt on Ram Van, Ram Van Ext] +490
Aluminum/Alloy Wheels +190
Anti-Lock Brakes +300
Cruise Control +115
Keyless Entry System +105
Power Door Locks +115
Power Drivers Seat +170
Power Mirrors +60
Power Windows +115
Premium Sound System +235
Rear Heater +130
Rear Window Defroster +95
Sunscreen Glass +140

Don't forget to refer to the Mileage Adjustment Table at the back of this book!

Model Description	Trade-in Value	Market Value

STRATUS 1998

The 2.4-liter engine with automatic transmission is now standard on the ES. New colors are available this year and numerous refinements were made to reduce noise and vibration.

RATINGS (SCALE OF 1-10)

Overall	Safety	Reliability	Performance	Comfort	Value
7.3	6.3	7.9	6.4	7.8	8.1

Category C
4 Dr ES Sdn	9170	11185
4 Dr STD Sdn	7420	9050

OPTIONS FOR STRATUS

4 cyl 2.4 L Engine[Std on ES] +275
6 cyl 2.5 L Engine +415
Auto 4-Speed Transmission[Std on ES] +645
AM/FM Compact Disc Player +220
Anti-Lock Brakes +370
Cruise Control[Std on ES] +130
Heated Power Mirrors[Std on ES] +65
Keyless Entry System +115
Leather Seats +365
Power Door Locks[Std on ES] +150
Power Drivers Seat +180
Power Sunroof +410
Power Windows[Std on ES] +190

VIPER 1998

Tubular, stainless steel exhaust manifolds help reduce emissions and weight. Silver Metallic paint is a new option and the powerful Dodge gets a passenger airbag cutoff switch and second-generation depowered airbags.

Category K
2 Dr GTS Cpe	48625	57205

OPTIONS FOR VIPER

Dual Painted Stripes +920

1997 DODGE

AVENGER 1997

Front and rear styling is updated, while ES models lose the standard V6 engine. The V6 is available on base and ES models, and includes 17-inch wheels and tires on the ES. New colors inside and out and two additional speakers with cassette stereos further broaden the appeal of this roomy coupe.

RATINGS (SCALE OF 1-10)

Overall	Safety	Reliability	Performance	Comfort	Value
6.8	7.4	6.7	7.6	7.6	4.9

Category F
2 Dr ES Cpe	8545	10420
2 Dr STD Cpe	7560	9220

OPTIONS FOR AVENGER

6 cyl 2.5 L Engine +390
Auto 4-Speed Transmission +345
Air Conditioning[Std on ES] +415
Aluminum/Alloy Wheels[Std on ES] +150
Anti-Lock Brakes[Std on ES] +335
Compact Disc W/fm/tape +240
Cruise Control[Std on ES] +105
Keyless Entry System +90
Leather Seats +325
Power Door Locks +100
Power Drivers Seat +120
Power Sunroof +335
Power Windows +110

CARAVAN 1997

Traction control is a new option, so long as you get LE or ES trim, and an enhanced accident response system will automatically unlock the doors and illuminate the interior when an airbag deploys. Appearance and equipment refinements complete the modest changes to this best-in-class minivan.

RATINGS (SCALE OF 1-10)

Overall	Safety	Reliability	Performance	Comfort	Value
7	6.4	6.6	6.6	7.4	8.1

Category G
2 Dr ES Pass. Van	12270	14785
2 Dr Grand Pass. Van	9665	11645
2 Dr Grand ES Pass. Van	13210	15915
2 Dr Grand ES 4WD Pass. Van	13885	16730
2 Dr Grand LE Pass. Van	12735	15345
2 Dr Grand LE 4WD Pass. Van	13430	16180
2 Dr Grand SE Pass. Van	10690	12880
2 Dr Grand SE 4WD Pass. Van	11370	13700
2 Dr LE Pass. Van	11455	13800
2 Dr SE Pass. Van	9395	11320
2 Dr STD Pass. Van	8155	9825

OPTIONS FOR CARAVAN

6 cyl 3.0 L Engine +345
6 cyl 3.3 L Engine[Opt on Grand,Grand SE,SE,STD] +460
6 cyl 3.8 L Engine[Opt on ES,LE] +205
Auto 4-Speed Transmission[Opt on Grand,STD] +125
Sport Handling Pkg +480
7 Passenger Seating[Opt on STD] +260
Air Conditioning[Opt on Grand,Grand SE,SE,STD] +405
Aluminum/Alloy Wheels[Std on ES,Grand ES] +165
Anti-Lock Brakes[Opt on Grand,STD] +295
Auto Load Leveling +110
Captain Chairs (4) +310
Child Seats (2) +125
Compact Disc W/fm/tape +240

DODGE 97

Model Description	Trade-in Value	Market Value	Model Description	Trade-in Value	Market Value

Cruise Control[Opt on Grand,STD] +105
Dual Air Conditioning +470
Keyless Entry System[Opt on Grand SE,SE] +100
Leather Seats +385
Luggage Rack +80
Power Door Locks[Opt on Grand,Grand SE,SE,STD] +115
Power Drivers Seat +140
Power Windows[Opt on Grand SE,SE] +120
Premium Sound System +170
Sliding Driver Side Door[Opt on Grand,Grand SE, SE,STD] +260
Traction Control System +135

DAKOTA 1997

What's new? Almost the entire truck, that's what. Powertrains are carried over, but everything else is new. Distinctions? Tightest turning circle in class, roomiest cabs and dual airbags are standard. Faux pas? No third door option, and the passenger airbag cannot be deactivated, so a rear-facing child seat is out of the question unless you cram it into the rear of the Club Cab.

RATINGS (SCALE OF 1-10)

Overall	Safety	Reliability	Performance	Comfort	Value
N/A	7.1	8.3	7	7.1	N/A

Category G
2 Dr SLT Ext Cab SB	9975	12020
2 Dr SLT 4WD Ext Cab SB	11575	13945
2 Dr SLT Std Cab LB	9170	11050
2 Dr SLT Std Cab SB	8940	10770
2 Dr SLT 4WD Std Cab SB	10799	13010
2 Dr STD Ext Cab SB	8865	10680
2 Dr STD 4WD Ext Cab SB	10605	12780
2 Dr STD Std Cab LB	7900	9520
2 Dr STD Std Cab SB	7730	9315
2 Dr STD 4WD Std Cab SB	9655	11630
2 Dr Sport Ext Cab SB	9380	11300
2 Dr Sport 4WD Ext Cab SB	11080	13350
2 Dr Sport Std Cab LB	8530	10275
2 Dr Sport Std Cab SB	8365	10080
2 Dr Sport 4WD Std Cab SB	10190	12280

OPTIONS FOR DAKOTA

6 cyl 3.9 L Engine +250
8 cyl 5.2 L Engine +420
Auto 4-Speed Transmission +475
Air Conditioning[Std on SLT] +405
Anti-Lock Brakes +295
Camper/Towing Package +150
Compact Disc W/fm/tape +240
Cruise Control +105
Keyless Entry System +100
Limited Slip Diff +135
Power Door Locks +115
Power Windows +120

Skid Plates +65
Velour/Cloth Seats[Opt on STD,Std Cab LB] +105

INTREPID 1997

Few changes as first-generation Intrepid enters final year of production. A Sport Group including the 3.5-liter V6 engine is optional on base models, which also get an upgraded cassette stereo standard. Bolt-on wheel covers debut, and a new exterior color is introduced. Automatic transmissions get new software.

RATINGS (SCALE OF 1-10)

Overall	Safety	Reliability	Performance	Comfort	Value
8.2	7.1	7.5	8.4	8.6	9.3

Category B
4 Dr ES Sdn	9555	11650
4 Dr STD Sdn	8385	10225

OPTIONS FOR INTREPID

6 cyl 3.5 L Engine[Std on ES] +95
Anti-Lock Brakes[Std on ES] +340
Climate Control for AC +85
Compact Disc W/fm/tape +190
Dual Power Seats +190
Keyless Entry System[Std on ES] +85
Power Moonroof +485
Premium Sound System +195
Traction Control System +85

NEON 1997

Sport trim level disappears in favor of Sport Package for Highline models. Twin-cam engine is now optional on Highline models. Federal side-impact standards are met for the first time. More work has been done to quiet the Neon's boisterous demeanor.

RATINGS (SCALE OF 1-10)

Overall	Safety	Reliability	Performance	Comfort	Value
7.1	6	7.6	7.4	7.6	6.8

Category E
2 Dr Highline Cpe	4975	6300
4 Dr Highline Sdn	5145	6510
2 Dr STD Cpe	4595	5815
4 Dr STD Sdn	4775	6045
2 Dr Sport Cpe	5750	7280
4 Dr Sport Sdn	5915	7485

OPTIONS FOR NEON

4 cyl 2.0 L DOHC Engine +75
Auto 3-Speed Transmission +295
Competition Pkg +680
AM/FM Compact Disc Player +225
Air Conditioning[Opt on STD] +405
Aluminum/Alloy Wheels +165
Anti-Lock Brakes +335
Child Seat (1) +55
Cruise Control +110

Don't forget to refer to the Mileage Adjustment Table at the back of this book!

Model Description	Trade-in Value	Market Value

Keyless Entry System +80
Power Door Locks +120
Power Moonroof +285
Power Windows +130
Tilt Steering Wheel +75

RAM PICKUP 1997

No major changes to this popular truck for 1997. Refinements include available leather seating and wood-grain trim on SLT models, optional remote keyless entry, and standard deep-tinted quarter glass on Club Cab models. Newly available is a combination CD/cassette stereo. Items from the 1996 Indy 500 Special Edition are available in a new Sport Package upgrade. Fresh interior and exterior colors sum up the changes this year.

RATINGS (SCALE OF 1-10)

Overall	Safety	Reliability	Performance	Comfort	Value
N/A	5.9	8.2	7	8	N/A

RAM 1500

Category H

Model Description	Trade-in Value	Market Value
2 Dr LT Std Cab LB	10500	12500
2 Dr LT 4WD Std Cab LB	12430	14800
2 Dr LT Std Cab SB	10350	12320
2 Dr LT 4WD Std Cab SB	12280	14620
2 Dr Laramie SLT Ext Cab LB	13055	15540
2 Dr Laramie SLT 4WD Ext Cab LB	14675	17470
2 Dr Laramie SLT Ext Cab SB	12850	15300
2 Dr Laramie SLT 4WD Ext Cab SB	14530	17300
2 Dr Laramie SLT Std Cab LB	12035	14330
2 Dr Laramie SLT 4WD Std Cab LB	13695	16305
2 Dr Laramie SLT Std Cab SB	11880	14145
2 Dr Laramie SLT 4WD Std Cab SB	13575	16160
2 Dr SS/T Std Cab SB	11455	13635
2 Dr ST Ext Cab LB	11550	13750
2 Dr ST 4WD Ext Cab LB	13220	15740
2 Dr ST Ext Cab SB	11380	13550
2 Dr ST 4WD Ext Cab SB	13080	15570
2 Dr WS Std Cab LB	8405	10005
2 Dr WS Std Cab SB	8230	9800

RAM 2500

Category H

Model Description	Trade-in Value	Market Value
2 Dr LT Std Cab LB	10990	13085
2 Dr LT 4WD Std Cab LB	12760	15190
2 Dr Laramie SLT Ext Cab LB	14715	17515
2 Dr Laramie SLT 4WD Ext Cab LB	16135	19210
2 Dr Laramie SLT Ext Cab SB	14550	17320
2 Dr Laramie SLT 4WD Ext Cab SB	15995	19040
2 Dr Laramie SLT Std Cab LB	13340	15880
2 Dr Laramie SLT 4WD Std Cab LB	14710	17510
2 Dr ST Ext Cab LB	13615	16210
2 Dr ST 4WD Ext Cab LB	15715	18710
2 Dr ST Ext Cab SB	13455	16020
2 Dr ST 4WD Ext Cab SB	15540	18500
2 Dr ST Std Cab LB	12685	15100
2 Dr ST 4WD Std Cab LB	14345	17080

RAM 3500

Category H

Model Description	Trade-in Value	Market Value
2 Dr LT Std Cab LB	13850	16490
2 Dr LT 4WD Std Cab LB	16210	19295
2 Dr Laramie SLT Ext Cab LB	16170	19250
2 Dr Laramie SLT 4WD Ext Cab LB	18680	22240
2 Dr Laramie SLT Std Cab LB	15215	18115
2 Dr Laramie SLT 4WD Std Cab LB	17630	20990
2 Dr ST Ext Cab LB	15290	18200
2 Dr ST 4WD Ext Cab LB	16785	19985
2 Dr ST Std Cab LB	14240	16950
2 Dr ST 4WD Std Cab LB	15710	18700

OPTIONS FOR RAM PICKUP

10 cyl 8.0 L Engine +490
6 cyl 5.9 L Turbodsl Engine +2185
8 cyl 5.2 L Engine +285
8 cyl 5.9 L Engine +220
Auto 4-Speed Transmission +480
Sport Appearance Group +395
Air Conditioning[Opt on LT,ST,WS] +400
Aluminum/Alloy Wheels[Std on SS/T] +155
Anti-Lock Brakes +245
Camper/Towing Package +170
Chrome Wheels[Std on Laramie SLT] +145
Compact Disc W/fm/tape +155
Cruise Control[Opt on LT,ST,WS] +95
Keyless Entry System +85
Leather Seats +485
Limited Slip Diff +130
Power Drivers Seat +140
Premium Sound System +190
Rear Step Bumper[Std on Laramie SLT,SS/T] +75
Skid Plates[Std on Ram 3500 ST 4WD Ext Cab LB] +55

RAM VAN/WAGON 1997

New this year are wider cargo doors, upgraded stereo systems, and an improved ignition switch with anti-theft protection. Front quarter vent windows disappear for 1997, and underhood service points feature colored identification.

Don't forget to refer to the Mileage Adjustment Table at the back of this book!

DODGE 97-96

Model Description	Trade-in Value	Market Value	Model Description	Trade-in Value	Market Value

RATINGS (SCALE OF 1-10)

Overall	Safety	Reliability	Performance	Comfort	Value
N/A	6.5	7.8	6.2	6.9	N/A

VAN

Category H

Model	Trade-in	Market
2 Dr 1500 Ram Van	7800	9285
2 Dr 1500 Ram Van Ext	8245	9815
2 Dr 2500 Ram Van	9280	11050
2 Dr 2500 Ram Van Ext	9810	11680
2 Dr 2500 Maxi Ram Van Ext	10275	12235
2 Dr 3500 Ram Van Ext	10350	12320
2 Dr 3500 Maxi Ram Van Ext	10835	12900

WAGON

Category H

Model	Trade-in	Market
2 Dr 1500 Ram Wagon	9515	11330
2 Dr 1500 SLT Ram Wagon	10255	12210
2 Dr 2500 Ram Wagon Ext	10580	12595
2 Dr 2500 SLT Ram Wagon Ext	11265	13410
2 Dr 3500 Ram Wagon Ext	11095	13210
2 Dr 3500 Maxi Ram Wagon Ext	11525	13720
2 Dr 3500 SLT Ram Wagon Ext	11820	14070
2 Dr 3500 SLT Maxi Ram Wagon Ext	12265	14600

OPTIONS FOR RAM VAN/WAGON

8 cyl 5.2 L Engine[Std on B350,B250 Ram Wagon Ext] +285
8 cyl 5.9 L Engine +220
Auto 4-Speed Transmission[Std on B350,Ram Wagon Ext] +150
Tradesman Upfitter Pkg +500
AM/FM Compact Disc Player +155
Air Conditioning[Opt on Ram Van,Ram Van Ext] +400
Aluminum/Alloy Wheels +155
Anti-Lock Brakes +245
Camper/Towing Package +170
Chrome Bumpers[Std on SLT] +85
Chrome Wheels[Opt on STD] +145
Cruise Control[Opt on Maxi,STD] +95
Dual Air Conditioning[Opt on B150,B250,Maxi,STD] +660
Keyless Entry System[Opt on Maxi,STD] +85
Limited Slip Diff +130
Power Door Locks[Opt on Maxi,STD] +95
Power Drivers Seat +140
Power Windows[Opt on Maxi,STD] +95
Premium Sound System +190

STRATUS   1997

Subtle styling revisions are the most obvious change to the Stratus for 1997. Sound systems have been improved, rear seat heat ducts benefit from improved flow, and the optional 2.4-liter engine runs quieter. New colors and a revised console round out changes.

RATINGS (SCALE OF 1-10)

Overall	Safety	Reliability	Performance	Comfort	Value
N/A	6.2	6.9	N/A	7.8	7.4

Category C

Model	Trade-in	Market
4 Dr ES Sdn	7775	9600
4 Dr STD Sdn	6505	8030

OPTIONS FOR STRATUS

4 cyl 2.4 L Engine +220
6 cyl 2.5 L Engine +455
Auto 4-Speed Transmission +455
Anti-Lock Brakes[Std on ES] +300
Child Seat (1) +60
Compact Disc W/fm/tape +165
Cruise Control[Std on ES] +105
Keyless Entry System +95
Leather Seats +300
Lighted Entry System +75
Power Door Locks[Std on ES] +125
Power Windows[Std on ES] +155

VIPER   1997

One new color, flame red, with or without white stripes, is available for 1997. Silver, sparkle gold or yellow gold wheels come with red Vipers. The original blue with white stripes paint scheme is available as an option, as are last year's standard polished aluminum wheels. The RT/10 roadster is set to return later this year, with dual airbags, power windows and door locks, and the 450-horsepower V10 from the GTS. Also set to debut on the revamped drop top are the four-wheel independent suspension and adjustable pedals from the GTS.

Category K

Model	Trade-in	Market
2 Dr GTS Cpe	43050	51250

OPTIONS FOR VIPER

Blue Pearlcoat Paint +600
Air Conditioning[Std on GTS] +565
Hardtop Roof +1235

1996 DODGE

AVENGER   1996

Dodge's sporty coupe gets a panic mode for the remote keyless entry system and a HomeLink transmitter that will open your garage door. ES models get new seat fabric, and three new colors are on the roster.

RATINGS (SCALE OF 1-10)

Overall	Safety	Reliability	Performance	Comfort	Value
6.5	7.4	6.3	7.6	7.6	3.7

Category F

Model	Trade-in	Market
2 Dr ES Cpe	7515	9515
2 Dr STD Cpe	6480	8200

Don't forget to refer to the Mileage Adjustment Table at the back of this book!

Model Description	Trade-in Value	Market Value

OPTIONS FOR AVENGER

Auto 4-Speed Transmission[Std on ES] +260
Air Conditioning[Std on ES] +340
Anti-Lock Brakes[Std on ES] +275
Compact Disc W/fm/tape +205
Cruise Control[Std on ES] +85
Keyless Entry System +70
Leather Seats +265
Power Door Locks +80
Power Drivers Seat +100
Power Sunroof +275
Power Windows +90
Premium Sound System +150

CARAVAN 1996

Completely redesigned with cavernous interiors, best-in-class driveability, and new innovations such as the optional driver's side passenger door. Caravan, and the extended-length Grand Caravan, have dethroned the Ford Windstar, once again reigning as king of the minivans.

RATINGS (SCALE OF 1-10)

Overall	Safety	Reliability	Performance	Comfort	Value
6.9	6.2	5.2	6.6	7.4	8.9

Category G

	Trade-in	Market
2 Dr ES Pass. Van	10330	12755
2 Dr Grand Pass. Van	8450	10435
2 Dr Grand ES Pass. Van	11370	14040
2 Dr Grand LE Pass. Van	10740	13260
2 Dr Grand SE Pass. Van	9230	11395
2 Dr LE Pass. Van	9640	11900
2 Dr SE Pass. Van	8000	9875
2 Dr STD Pass. Van	7255	8955

OPTIONS FOR CARAVAN

6 cyl 3.0 L Engine +290
6 cyl 3.3 L Engine[Opt on Grand SE,SE] +350
6 cyl 3.3 L CNG Engine +355
6 cyl 3.8 L Engine[Opt on LE, ES] +175
Auto 4-Speed Transmission[Opt on SE,STD] +80
7 Passenger Seating[Opt on STD] +210
Air Conditioning[Opt on Grand,Grand SE,SE,STD] +330
Anti-Lock Brakes[Opt on SE,STD] +245
Captain Chairs (4) +255
Child Seats (2) +105
Compact Disc W/fm/tape +195
Cruise Control[Opt on Grand,STD] +85
Dual Air Conditioning +385
Infinity Sound System +175
Keyless Entry System[Std on LE] +80
Leather Seats +315
Luggage Rack +65
Power Door Locks[Opt on Grand,Grand SE,SE,STD] +95
Power Drivers Seat +115
Power Windows[Opt on Grand SE,SE] +95
Sliding Driver Side Door +215

DAKOTA 1996

America's first midsized pickup gets a more powerful standard four-cylinder engine, revised sound system, and three new colors.

RATINGS (SCALE OF 1-10)

Overall	Safety	Reliability	Performance	Comfort	Value
N/A	6.5	7.7	7	7.1	N/A

Category G

	Trade-in	Market
2 Dr SLT Ext Cab SB	8510	10505
2 Dr SLT 4WD Ext Cab SB	10435	12880
2 Dr SLT Std Cab LB	7555	9325
2 Dr SLT 4WD Std Cab LB	9665	11935
2 Dr SLT Std Cab SB	7385	9120
2 Dr SLT 4WD Std Cab SB	9515	11745
2 Dr STD Ext Cab SB	7585	9365
2 Dr STD 4WD Ext Cab SB	9460	11680
2 Dr STD Std Cab LB	6640	8200
2 Dr STD 4WD Std Cab LB	8650	10680
2 Dr STD Std Cab SB	6520	8050
2 Dr STD 4WD Std Cab SB	8495	10490
2 Dr Sport Ext Cab SB	7875	9720
2 Dr Sport 4WD Ext Cab SB	9610	11865
2 Dr Sport Std Cab SB	6815	8415
2 Dr Sport 4WD Std Cab SB	8830	10900
2 Dr WS Std Cab LB	5830	7200
2 Dr WS 4WD Std Cab LB	8035	9920
2 Dr WS Std Cab SB	5680	7010
2 Dr WS 4WD Std Cab SB	7865	9710

OPTIONS FOR DAKOTA

6 cyl 3.9 L Engine +280
8 cyl 5.2 L Engine +300
Auto 4-Speed Transmission +370
AM/FM Compact Disc Player +135
Air Conditioning[Std on SLT] +330
Aluminum/Alloy Wheels[Opt on SLT] +135
Anti-Lock Brakes +245
Camper/Towing Package +120
Chrome Bumpers[Std on SLT] +65
Chrome Wheels[Std on SLT] +70
Cruise Control[Opt on Sport,STD] +85
Limited Slip Diff +110
Power Door Locks +95
Power Windows +95
Premium Sound System +140
Velour/Cloth Seats[Std on SLT,Sport,Ext Cab] +85

INTREPID 1996

ES carries over, but the base model gets several improvements to remain competitive with the new Ford Taurus. ES styling cues and 16-inch wheels come standard on the base Intrepid. New colors and seat

Don't forget to refer to the Mileage Adjustment Table at the back of this book!

EDMUND'S® USED CARS & TRUCKS   www.edmunds.com   149

fabrics update this full-size sedan, and all Intrepids get noise, vibration and harshness improvements.

RATINGS (SCALE OF 1-10)

Overall	Safety	Reliability	Performance	Comfort	Value
8.1	7.1	7.1	8.4	8.6	9.1

Category B

	Trade-in	Market
4 Dr ES Sdn	7750	9690
4 Dr STD Sdn	6750	8440

OPTIONS FOR INTREPID

6 cyl 3.5 L Engine +260
AM/FM Compact Disc Player +135
Aluminum/Alloy Wheels +135
Anti-Lock Brakes[Std on ES] +280
Child Seat (1) +40
Climate Control for AC +70
Keyless Entry System +70
Leather Seats +275
Power Drivers Seat +125
Power Moonroof +395
Power Passenger Seat +135
Traction Control System +70

NEON   1996

A raft of improvements make the sprightly Neon even more attractive to compact buyers. Base models get more equipment, and the ugly gray bumpers are history. A base coupe is newly available. Interior noise levels are supposedly subdued this year. ABS is available across the board this year.

RATINGS (SCALE OF 1-10)

Overall	Safety	Reliability	Performance	Comfort	Value
6.7	5.9	6.7	7.4	7.6	6.1

Category E

	Trade-in	Market
2 Dr Highline Cpe	4260	5605
4 Dr Highline Sdn	4410	5800
2 Dr STD Cpe	3875	5100
4 Dr STD Sdn	4020	5290
2 Dr Sport Cpe	4725	6215
4 Dr Sport Sdn	4885	6430

OPTIONS FOR NEON

4 cyl 2.0 L DOHC Engine[Std on Sport] +60
Auto 3-Speed Transmission +215
AM/FM Compact Disc Player +185
Air Conditioning +330
Anti-Lock Brakes[Std on Sport] +275
Child Seat (1) +45
Cruise Control +90
Power Door Locks[Std on Sport] +100
Power Steering[Opt on STD] +105
Power Windows +105
Rear Spoiler[Std on Sport] +85
Tilt Steering Wheel[Std on Sport] +60

RAM PICKUP   1996

Best-selling Ram has a more powerful diesel engine option for 1996, an available "Camper Special" suspension package, and new wheels on the 1500 SLT and Sport. Two new colors, a revised sound system, and easy-to-see yellow under-hood service point identification all debut for 1996.

RATINGS (SCALE OF 1-10)

Overall	Safety	Reliability	Performance	Comfort	Value
N/A	N/A	7.8	7	8	N/A

RAM 1500

Category H

	Trade-in	Market
2 Dr LT Std Cab LB	9120	10985
2 Dr LT 4WD Std Cab LB	11300	13615
2 Dr LT Std Cab SB	8935	10765
2 Dr LT 4WD Std Cab SB	11135	13415
2 Dr Laramie SLT Ext Cab LB	11280	13590
2 Dr Laramie SLT 4WD Ext Cab LB	12810	15435
2 Dr Laramie SLT Ext Cab SB	11195	13490
2 Dr Laramie SLT 4WD Ext Cab SB	12670	15265
2 Dr Laramie SLT Std Cab LB	10385	12510
2 Dr Laramie SLT 4WD Std Cab LB	11925	14365
2 Dr Laramie SLT Std Cab SB	10220	12315
2 Dr Laramie SLT 4WD Std Cab SB	11720	14120
2 Dr ST Ext Cab LB	9970	12015
2 Dr ST 4WD Ext Cab LB	11680	14075
2 Dr ST Ext Cab SB	9860	11880
2 Dr ST 4WD Ext Cab SB	11500	13855
2 Dr WS Std Cab LB	7230	8710
2 Dr WS Std Cab SB	7070	8520

RAM 2500

Category H

	Trade-in	Market
2 Dr LT Std Cab LB	10145	12220
2 Dr LT 4WD Std Cab LB	11025	13285
2 Dr Laramie SLT Ext Cab LB	13090	15770
2 Dr Laramie SLT 4WD Ext Cab LB	13565	16345
2 Dr Laramie SLT Ext Cab SB	12910	15555
2 Dr Laramie SLT 4WD Ext Cab SB	13420	16170
2 Dr Laramie SLT Std Cab LB	11800	14215
2 Dr Laramie SLT 4WD Std Cab LB	12595	15175
2 Dr ST Ext Cab LB	11625	14005
2 Dr ST 4WD Ext Cab LB	12710	15315

Don't forget to refer to the Mileage Adjustment Table at the back of this book!

Model Description	Trade-in Value	Market Value
2 Dr ST Ext Cab SB	11445	13790
2 Dr ST 4WD Ext Cab SB	12535	15100
2 Dr ST Std Cab LB	10750	12950
2 Dr ST 4WD Std Cab LB	11545	13910
RAM 3500		
Category H		
2 Dr LT Std Cab LB	12160	14650
2 Dr LT 4WD Std Cab LB	13780	16600
2 Dr Laramie SLT Ext Cab LB	14275	17200
2 Dr Laramie SLT 4WD Ext Cab LB		
	15585	18780
2 Dr Laramie SLT Std Cab LB	13405	16150
2 Dr Laramie SLT 4WD Std Cab LB		
	14625	17620
2 Dr ST Ext Cab LB	13455	16210
2 Dr ST 4WD Ext Cab LB	14255	17175
2 Dr ST Std Cab LB	12510	15075
2 Dr ST 4WD Std Cab LB	13395	16140

OPTIONS FOR RAM PICKUP

10 cyl 8.0 L Engine +190
6 cyl 5.9 L Turbodsl Engine +1660
8 cyl 5.2 L Engine +245
8 cyl 5.9 L Engine +170
Auto 4-Speed Transmission +375
Heavy Duty Pkg +465
AM/FM Compact Disc Player +125
Air Conditioning[Opt on LT,ST,WS] +330
Aluminum/Alloy Wheels[Std on Laramie SLT] +125
Anti-Lock Brakes +200
Bed Liner +90
Camper/Towing Package +140
Chrome Bumpers[Opt on ST] +70
Chrome Wheels[Opt on LT,ST] +120
Cruise Control[Opt on LT,ST,WS] +75
Limited Slip Diff +105
Power Door Locks[Opt on LT,ST] +75
Power Drivers Seat +115
Premium Sound System +155
Rear Step Bumper[Std on Laramie SLT] +60
Skid Plates +45
Split Front Bench Seat +140

RAM VAN/WAGON 1996

New interior and exterior colors, a revised stereo system, and improved ventilation freshen this ancient design. Also new: a higher GVWR and new cruise control switches.

RATINGS (SCALE OF 1-10)

Overall	Safety	Reliability	Performance	Comfort	Value
N/A	6.5	7.6	6.2	6.9	N/A

RAM VAN

Category H

	Trade-in	Market
2 Dr 1500 Ram Van	7170	8640

Model Description	Trade-in Value	Market Value
2 Dr 1500 Ram Van Ext	7429	8950
2 Dr 2500 Ram Van	7725	9305
2 Dr 2500 Ram Van Ext	7990	9625
2 Dr 2500 Maxi Ram Van Ext	8180	9855
2 Dr 3500 Ram Van Ext	7895	9510
2 Dr 3500 Maxi Ram Van Ext	8220	9905
RAM WAGON		
Category H		
2 Dr 1500 Ram Wagon	8150	9820
2 Dr 1500 SLT Ram Wagon	9030	10880
2 Dr 2500 Ram Wagon Ext	9140	11015
2 Dr 2500 SLT Ram Wagon Ext	9870	11890
2 Dr 3500 Ram Wagon Ext	9155	11030
2 Dr 3500 Maxi Ram Wagon Ext	9435	11365
2 Dr 3500 SLT Ram Wagon Ext	10240	12340
2 Dr 3500 SLT Maxi Ram Wagon Ext		
	10520	12675

OPTIONS FOR RAM VAN/WAGON

8 cyl 5.2 L Engine[Std on B350] +245
8 cyl 5.9 L Engine +170
Auto 4-Speed Transmission[Std on B350] +100
AM/FM Compact Disc Player +125
Air Conditioning[Std on B350 Ram Wagon] +330
Anti-Lock Brakes[Opt on B350,Maxi,Ram Van,
    Ram Van Ext] +200
Camper/Towing Package +140
Chrome Bumpers[Std on SLT] +70
Chrome Wheels[Opt on STD] +120
Cruise Control[Opt on Maxi,STD] +75
Dual Air Conditioning[Opt on B150,B250,Maxi,STD] +540
Keyless Entry System[Std on SLT,SLT Maxi] +70
Limited Slip Diff +105
Power Door Locks[Opt on Maxi,STD] +75
Power Drivers Seat +115
Power Windows[Opt on Maxi,STD] +75
Premium Sound System +155
Velour/Cloth Seats[Opt on B150,STD] +55

STEALTH 1996

Final year for slow-selling Japanese-built sports car. A new rear spoiler and body-color roof mark the 1996 model. A chrome 18-inch wheel package is available with Pirelli P-Zero tires and base models get an optional Infinity sound system.

RATINGS (SCALE OF 1-10)

Overall	Safety	Reliability	Performance	Comfort	Value
N/A	N/A	7.8	N/A	N/A	N/A

Category F

	Trade-in	Market
2 Dr R/T Hbk	10810	13685
2 Dr STD Hbk	9545	12085

OPTIONS FOR STEALTH

Auto 4-Speed Transmission +355
AM/FM Compact Disc Player +195

Don't forget to refer to the Mileage Adjustment Table at the back of this book!

DODGE 96-95

Model Description	Trade-in Value	Market Value	Model Description	Trade-in Value	Market Value

Anti-Lock Brakes +275
Chrome Wheels +235
Cruise Control[Std on 4WD] +85
Keyless Entry System[Std on 4WD] +70
Leather Seats +265
Power Door Locks[Std on 4WD] +80
Power Drivers Seat +100
Power Sunroof +275
Power Windows[Std on 4WD] +90

STRATUS   1996

Excellent midsized sedan gets a more responsive torque converter when equipped with the 2.5-liter V6. New colors and a power sunroof are also new for 1996.

RATINGS (SCALE OF 1-10)

Overall	Safety	Reliability	Performance	Comfort	Value
N/A	5.9	5.6	N/A	7.8	7.4

Category C

4 Dr ES Sdn	6635	8505
4 Dr STD Sdn	5725	7340

OPTIONS FOR STRATUS

4 cyl 2.4 L Engine +180
6 cyl 2.5 L Engine +405
Auto 4-Speed Transmission +335
AM/FM Compact Disc Player +145
Anti-Lock Brakes[Std on ES] +245
Child Seat (1) +50
Keyless Entry System +75
Leather Seats +245
Lighted Entry System +65
Power Door Locks[Std on ES] +100
Power Drivers Seat +120
Power Sunroof +275
Power Windows[Std on ES] +125
Premium Sound System +160

VIPER   1996

Final year for Viper in current form. More power is eked from the V10 engine via a low-restriction rear outlet exhaust system, and an optional hardtop with sliding side curtains is available. Five-spoke aluminum wheels and three exterior styling themes replace the trim on the 1995 Viper. GTS coupe begins production when convertibles have completed their run. Scheduled to pace the 1996 Indianapolis 500, the GTS will arrive in showrooms with dual airbags and air conditioning.

Category K

2 Dr GTS Cpe	37320	44430
2 Dr RT/10 Conv	32905	39170

OPTIONS FOR VIPER

Air Conditioning[Std on GTS] +460
Hardtop Roof +1010

1995 DODGE

AVENGER   1995

New coupe is late replacement for Daytona. Based on a Mitsubishi Galant platform, the Avenger is about the size of a Camry coupe. Base and ES models are available. Base cars have a 2.0-liter, 140-horsepower four-cylinder engine underhood. ES gets a Mitsubishi-built 2.5-liter V6 making 155 horsepower. An automatic is the only transmission available on the ES. ABS is optional on base models; standard on ES. All Avengers have dual airbags, height-adjustable driver's seat, split-folding rear seat, rear defroster, and tilt steering wheel.

RATINGS (SCALE OF 1-10)

Overall	Safety	Reliability	Performance	Comfort	Value
7.4	8.4	7.2	7.6	7.6	6.3

Category C

2 Dr ES Cpe	6800	8720
2 Dr Highline Cpe	5795	7430

OPTIONS FOR AVENGER

Auto 4-Speed Transmission[Std on ES] +225
AM/FM Compact Disc Player +160
Air Conditioning[Std on ES] +275
Anti-Lock Brakes[Std on ES] +225
Cruise Control[Std on ES] +70
Infinity Sound System +215
Keyless Entry System +60
Leather Seats +215
Power Door Locks +65
Power Drivers Seat +80
Power Sunroof +225
Power Windows +75
Premium Sound System +125

CARAVAN   1995

Newly optional is a 3.3-liter V6 engine designed to operate on compressed natural gas. Sport and SE decor packages are available this year. The five-speed manual transmission, available only with the four-cylinder engine, has been canceled.

RATINGS (SCALE OF 1-10)

Overall	Safety	Reliability	Performance	Comfort	Value
7.8	8.2	6.6	7.4	8.3	8.5

Category G

2 Dr ES Pass. Van	7270	9200
2 Dr Grand Pass. Van	5920	7495
2 Dr Grand ES Pass. Van	7930	10040
2 Dr Grand ES 4WD Pass. Van	8140	10305
2 Dr Grand LE Pass. Van	7440	9420
2 Dr Grand LE 4WD Pass. Van	7720	9770

Model Description	Trade-in Value	Market Value	Model Description	Trade-in Value	Market Value
2 Dr Grand SE Pass. Van	6595	8350	2 Dr WS Std Cab SB	4820	6100
2 Dr Grand SE 4WD Pass. Van	6915	8755	2 Dr WS 4WD Std Cab SB	6405	8105
2 Dr LE Pass. Van	6680	8455			
2 Dr SE Pass. Van	5540	7010			
2 Dr STD Cargo Van	2935	3715			
2 Dr STD Cargo Van Ext	3395	4300			
2 Dr STD Pass. Van	4665	5905			

OPTIONS FOR CARAVAN

6 cyl 3.0 L Engine[Opt on STD] +235
6 cyl 3.3 L Engine[Opt on ES,LE,SE] +75
6 cyl 3.3 L CNG Engine +290
6 cyl 3.8 L Engine +140
Auto 4-Speed Transmission[Opt on SE,Cargo Van, STD] +65
7 Passenger Seating[Opt on STD] +170
Air Conditioning[Opt on Grand,Grand SE,SE,STD] +270
Anti-Lock Brakes[Std on ES,Grand ES,Grand LE,
    LE,4WD] +200
Captain Chairs (4) +205
Child Seats (2) +85
Cruise Control[Opt on Grand,STD] +70
Dual Air Conditioning +315
Keyless Entry System[Opt on Grand SE,SE] +65
Leather Seats +255
Luggage Rack +50
Power Door Locks[Opt on Grand,Grand SE,SE,STD] +75
Power Drivers Seat +95
Power Windows +80
Premium Sound System +115

OPTIONS FOR DAKOTA

6 cyl 3.9 L Engine +225
8 cyl 5.2 L Engine +245
Auto 4-Speed Transmission +300
AM/FM Compact Disc Player +110
Air Conditioning[Std on SLT] +270
Anti-Lock Brakes +200
Camper/Towing Package +100
Chrome Wheels[Std on SLT] +55
Cruise Control[Std on SLT Ext Cab SB] +70
Limited Slip Diff +90
Power Door Locks +75
Power Windows +80
Premium Sound System +115
Rear Step Bumper[Opt on WS] +50
Sliding Rear Window[Std on SLT] +40
Velour/Cloth Seats[Std on SLT,Sport,Ext Cab] +70

DAKOTA 1995

A 2WD Club Cab Sport is added to the model mix.

RATINGS (SCALE OF 1-10)

Overall	Safety	Reliability	Performance	Comfort	Value
N/A	7.1	7.7	7	7.1	N/A

Category G

	Trade-in	Market
2 Dr SLT Ext Cab SB	7025	8895
2 Dr SLT 4WD Ext Cab SB	8815	11160
2 Dr SLT Std Cab LB	6300	7975
2 Dr SLT 4WD Std Cab LB	8210	10395
2 Dr SLT Std Cab SB	6170	7810
2 Dr SLT 4WD Std Cab SB	8100	10250
2 Dr STD Ext Cab SB	6320	8000
2 Dr STD 4WD Ext Cab SB	7925	10030
2 Dr STD Std Cab LB	5475	6930
2 Dr STD 4WD Std Cab LB	7265	9195
2 Dr STD Std Cab SB	5310	6720
2 Dr STD 4WD Std Cab SB	7150	9050
2 Dr Sport Ext Cab SB	6495	8220
2 Dr Sport 4WD Ext Cab SB	8200	10380
2 Dr Sport Std Cab SB	5480	6935
2 Dr Sport 4WD Std Cab SB	7330	9280
2 Dr WS Std Cab LB	4955	6270
2 Dr WS 4WD Std Cab LB	6565	8310

INTREPID 1995

ABS is now standard on ES. Traction control is a new ES option.

RATINGS (SCALE OF 1-10)

Overall	Safety	Reliability	Performance	Comfort	Value
8	7.8	6.7	8.4	8.6	8.5

Category B

	Trade-in	Market
4 Dr ES Sdn	6480	8305
4 Dr STD Sdn	5535	7095

OPTIONS FOR INTREPID

6 cyl 3.3 L FLEX Engine +50
6 cyl 3.5 L Engine +240
AM/FM Compact Disc Player +110
Anti-Lock Brakes[Std on ES] +230
Child Seat (1) +35
Climate Control for AC +55
Cruise Control[Std on ES] +75
Dual Power Seats +125
Keyless Entry System +55
Power Door Locks[Std on ES] +85
Power Drivers Seat +105
Power Moonroof +325
Power Windows[Std on ES] +100
Traction Control System +60

NEON 1995

This spunky Shadow replacement is cleverly designed, adequately powered, and cute to boot. Base, Highline and Sport models are available. Coupe and sedan body styles are offered. All except Sport Coupe have a 132-horsepower, 2.0-liter four-cylinder engine. Sport Coupe gets a 150-horsepower twin-cam edition of the base motor. Dual airbags are standard on all models; ABS is standard on Sport and optional on others. Integrated child seats are optional.

Don't forget to refer to the Mileage Adjustment Table at the back of this book!

Model Description	Trade-in Value	Market Value

RATINGS (SCALE OF 1-10)

Overall	Safety	Reliability	Performance	Comfort	Value
6.5	5.6	5	7.4	7.6	6.9

Category E

Model Description	Trade-in Value	Market Value
2 Dr Highline Cpe	3285	4500
4 Dr Highline Sdn	3420	4685
4 Dr STD Sdn	3035	4155
2 Dr Sport Cpe	3665	5020
4 Dr Sport Sdn	3805	5210

OPTIONS FOR NEON

4 cyl 2.0 L DOHC Engine[Std on Sport] +55
Auto 3-Speed Transmission +200
AM/FM Compact Disc Player +150
Air Conditioning +270
Anti-Lock Brakes[Std on Sport] +225
Child Seat (1) +35
Cruise Control +75
Power Door Locks[Std on Sport] +80
Power Steering[Opt on STD] +85
Power Windows +85
Premium Sound System +110
Rear Spoiler[Opt on Sdn] +70
Tilt Steering Wheel[Std on Sport] +50
Tinted Glass[Opt on STD] +35

RAM PICKUP   1995

A Club Cab model is added in 1500-, 2500-, and 3500-series levels with either two- or four-wheel drive. The Club Cab is available only in ST or Laramie SLT trim. Regular-cab models can be equipped with Sport trim midyear. Sport models have a sport suspension, chrome wheels, and a body-color grille with fog lights. Four-wheel ABS moves to the 3500 options list midyear.

RATINGS (SCALE OF 1-10)

Overall	Safety	Reliability	Performance	Comfort	Value
N/A	N/A	7.5	7	8	N/A

RAM 1500

Category H

Model Description	Trade-in Value	Market Value
2 Dr LT Std Cab LB	7460	9210
2 Dr LT 4WD Std Cab LB	9345	11535
2 Dr LT Std Cab SB	7340	9060
2 Dr LT 4WD Std Cab SB	9165	11315
2 Dr Laramie SLT Ext Cab LB	9580	11825
2 Dr Laramie SLT 4WD Ext Cab LB	10790	13320
2 Dr Laramie SLT Ext Cab SB	9420	11630
2 Dr Laramie SLT 4WD Ext Cab SB	10645	13140
2 Dr Laramie SLT Std Cab LB	8550	10555
2 Dr Laramie SLT 4WD Std Cab LB	10100	12470
2 Dr Laramie SLT Std Cab SB	8380	10345

Model Description	Trade-in Value	Market Value
2 Dr Laramie SLT 4WD Std Cab SB	9945	12280
2 Dr ST Ext Cab LB	8625	10650
2 Dr ST 4WD Ext Cab LB	9870	12185
2 Dr ST Ext Cab SB	8495	10490
2 Dr ST 4WD Ext Cab SB	9730	12015
2 Dr WS Std Cab LB	6025	7440
2 Dr WS Std Cab SB	5870	7245

RAM 2500

Category H

Model Description	Trade-in Value	Market Value
2 Dr LT Std Cab LB	9305	11485
2 Dr LT 4WD Std Cab LB	9680	11950
2 Dr Laramie SLT Ext Cab LB	11010	13595
2 Dr Laramie SLT 4WD Ext Cab LB	11600	14320
2 Dr Laramie SLT 4WD Ext Cab SB	11465	14155
2 Dr Laramie SLT Std Cab LB	10190	12580
2 Dr Laramie SLT 4WD Std Cab LB	10690	13200
2 Dr ST Ext Cab LB	10120	12495
2 Dr ST 4WD Ext Cab LB	9995	12340
2 Dr ST Ext Cab SB	9980	12320
2 Dr ST 4WD Ext Cab SB	10675	13180
2 Dr ST Std Cab LB	9230	11395
2 Dr ST 4WD Std Cab LB	9830	12135
2 Dr Sport Ext Cab SB	10135	12510
2 Dr Sport 4WD Ext Cab SB	10000	12345

RAM 3500

Category H

Model Description	Trade-in Value	Market Value
2 Dr LT Std Cab LB	9640	11900
2 Dr LT 4WD Std Cab LB	11435	14115
2 Dr Laramie SLT Ext Cab LB	11470	14160
2 Dr Laramie SLT 4WD Ext Cab LB	13525	16700
2 Dr Laramie SLT Std Cab LB	10670	13175
2 Dr Laramie SLT 4WD Std Cab LB	12785	15785
2 Dr ST Ext Cab LB	10610	13100
2 Dr ST 4WD Ext Cab LB	12025	14845
2 Dr ST Std Cab LB	9950	12285

OPTIONS FOR RAM PICKUP

10 cyl 8.0 L Engine +155
6 cyl 5.9 L Turbodsl Engine +1345
8 cyl 5.2 L Engine +200
8 cyl 5.9 L Engine +150
Auto 4-Speed Transmission +305
Sport Appearance Grp +280
AM/FM Compact Disc Player +105
Air Conditioning[Std on Laramie SLT] +270
Aluminum/Alloy Wheels +105
Anti-Lock Brakes +165

Model Description	Trade-in Value	Market Value	Model Description	Trade-in Value	Market Value

Camper/Towing Package +115
Chrome Wheels[Opt on LT,ST] +100
Cruise Control[Std on Laramie SLT] +60
Limited Slip Diff +85
Power Door Locks[Opt on LT,ST] +60
Power Drivers Seat +95
Power Windows[Opt on ST] +65
Premium Sound System +130
Rear Step Bumper[Opt on Ram 3500,WS] +50
Skid Plates +35

RAM VAN/WAGON   1995

A driver airbag is added, and four-wheel ABS is now standard on Wagons and Vans sent to conversion outfitters. LE trim changes to SLT. Chrome wheels and a CD player are new options.

RATINGS (SCALE OF 1-10)

Overall	Safety	Reliability	Performance	Comfort	Value
N/A	7.2	7.4	6.2	6.9	N/A

RAM VAN

Category H

2 Dr 1500 Ram Van	5960	7355
2 Dr 1500 Ram Van Ext	6130	7570
2 Dr 2500 Ram Van	6500	8025
2 Dr 2500 Ram Van Ext	6665	8230
2 Dr 2500 Maxi Ram Van Ext	6855	8460
2 Dr 3500 Ram Van	6985	8625
2 Dr 3500 Ram Van Ext	7225	8920

RAM WAGON

Category H

2 Dr 1500 Ram Wagon	6810	8405
2 Dr 1500 SLT Ram Wagon	7555	9325
2 Dr 2500 Ram Wagon	7085	8745
2 Dr 2500 Maxi Ram Wagon Ext	7405	9140
2 Dr 2500 SLT Ram Wagon	7655	9450
2 Dr 2500 SLT Ram Wagon Ext	7835	9670
2 Dr 3500 Ram Wagon	7305	9020
2 Dr 3500 Ram Wagon Ext	7555	9330
2 Dr 3500 SLT Ram Wagon	7940	9800
2 Dr 3500 SLT Ram Wagon Ext	8195	10120

OPTIONS FOR RAM VAN/WAGON

8 cyl 5.2 L Engine[Std on B350,Ram Wagon Ext] +200
8 cyl 5.9 L Engine +150
Auto 4-Speed Transmission[Std on B350] +80
Rear A/C W/Rear Heater +270
AM/FM Compact Disc Player +105
Air Conditioning[Std on B250 SLT] +270
Anti-Lock Brakes[Opt on Ram Van,Ram Van Ext] +165
Chrome Bumpers[Std on SLT] +60
Chrome Wheels[Std on SLT] +100
Cruise Control[Std on SLT] +60
Dual Air Conditioning[Opt on B250,STD] +440
Keyless Entry System[Std on SLT] +55

Limited Slip Diff[Opt on B250,B350] +85
Power Door Locks[Opt on Maxi,STD] +60
Power Drivers Seat +95
Power Windows[Opt on Maxi,STD] +65
Premium Sound System +130
Velour/Cloth Seats[Opt on B150,Maxi,STD] +45

SPIRIT   1995

Flexible fuel model and optional four-speed automatic transmission are dropped. A three-speed automatic continues as standard equipment.

RATINGS (SCALE OF 1-10)

Overall	Safety	Reliability	Performance	Comfort	Value
7	6.7	7.5	6.8	7.4	6.8

Category C

4 Dr STD Sdn	3980	5310

OPTIONS FOR SPIRIT

6 cyl 3.0 L Engine +265
Power Door Locks +80
Power Drivers Seat +100
Power Windows +105

STEALTH   1995

Chromed 18-inch aluminum wheels are available on R/T Turbo.

RATINGS (SCALE OF 1-10)

Overall	Safety	Reliability	Performance	Comfort	Value
N/A	N/A	7.7	9.4	6.8	N/A

Category F

2 Dr R/T Hbk	9480	12155
2 Dr R/T Turbo 4WD Hbk	12665	16240
2 Dr STD Hbk	8295	10635

OPTIONS FOR STEALTH

Auto 4-Speed Transmission +290
Anti-Lock Brakes[Std on 4WD] +225
Chrome Wheels +195
Compact Disc Changer +215
Cruise Control[Opt on STD] +70
Keyless Entry System +60
Leather Seats +215
Power Door Locks[Std on 4WD] +65
Power Sunroof +225
Power Windows[Std on 4WD] +75

STRATUS   1995

Spirit replacement features cutting-edge styling and class-leading accommodations. Dual airbags and ABS are standard. Base and ES models are available. Base model has 2.0-liter, four-cylinder engine making 132 horsepower and a five-speed manual transmission. ES is powered by 155-horsepower, Mitsubishi 2.5-liter V6. A credit option on the ES is the Neon's 2.0-liter four hooked to a five-speed manual transmission.

Don't forget to refer to the Mileage Adjustment Table at the back of this book!

Model Description	Trade-in Value	Market Value

RATINGS (SCALE OF 1-10)

Overall	Safety	Reliability	Performance	Comfort	Value
N/A	6.5	5.2	N/A	7.8	7.5

Category C

4 Dr ES Sdn	5530	7370
4 Dr STD Sdn	4795	6390

OPTIONS FOR STRATUS

4 cyl 2.4 L Engine +145
Auto 4-Speed Transmission[Std on ES] +240
AM/FM Compact Disc Player +120
Anti-Lock Brakes[Std on ES] +200
Child Seat (1) +40
Keyless Entry System +60
Leather Seats +200
Lighted Entry System +50
Power Door Locks[Std on ES] +80
Power Drivers Seat +100
Power Windows[Std on ES] +105
Premium Sound System +130

VIPER   1995

No changes.
Category K

2 Dr RT/10 Conv	28170	34355

OPTIONS FOR VIPER

Air Conditioning +375

1994 DODGE

CARAVAN   1994

A passenger airbag is added to a redesigned dashboard, and new side-door guard beams meet 1997 passenger car safety standards. All-wheel drive is no longer available on regular-length models. Bumpers are restyled, and seats with integrated child seats can be reclined for the first time.

RATINGS (SCALE OF 1-10)

Overall	Safety	Reliability	Performance	Comfort	Value
7.6	8.2	6.2	7.4	8.3	7.9

Category G

2 Dr ES Pass. Van	5815	7550
2 Dr Grand Pass. Van	4535	5890
2 Dr Grand ES Pass. Van	6290	8170
2 Dr Grand ES 4WD Pass. Van	6510	8455
2 Dr Grand LE Pass. Van	5840	7585
2 Dr Grand LE 4WD Pass. Van	6235	8095
2 Dr Grand SE Pass. Van	5350	6950
2 Dr Grand SE 4WD Pass. Van	5765	7485
2 Dr LE Pass. Van	5405	7020
2 Dr SE Pass. Van	4480	5815
2 Dr STD Cargo Van	2235	2905
2 Dr STD Cargo Van Ext	2770	3500
2 Dr STD Pass. Van	3605	4685

OPTIONS FOR CARAVAN

6 cyl 3.0 L Engine[Opt on STD] +165
6 cyl 3.3 L Engine[Opt on Grand,SE] +30
6 cyl 3.8 L Engine +110
Auto 3-Speed Transmission[Opt on STD] +165
Auto 4-Speed Transmission[Opt on Grand,SE, STD] +110
7 Passenger Seating[Opt on SE,STD] +140
AM/FM Compact Disc Player +90
Air Conditioning[Std on Grand LE,LE] +220
Anti-Lock Brakes +160
Captain Chairs (4) +170
Child Seats (2) +70
Cruise Control[Opt on Grand,STD] +55
Dual Air Conditioning +255
Heavy Duty Suspension[Opt on LE] +40
Infinity Sound System +115
Keyless Entry System[Std on Grand LE,LE] +55
Leather Seats +210
Lighted Entry System[Opt on Grand SE] +40
Power Door Locks[Std on Grand LE,LE] +65
Power Drivers Seat +75
Power Windows[Std on LE] +65
Sport Suspension +125

COLT   1994

A driver airbag debuts. ES trim replaces GL nomenclature. Order ABS on an ES sedan and you'll get rear discs instead of drums. The optional 1.8-liter engine is available on the coupe this year, but only with ES trim. Sedans gain standard power steering. Air conditioners use CFC-free refrigerant.

RATINGS (SCALE OF 1-10)

Overall	Safety	Reliability	Performance	Comfort	Value
6.6	5.5	7.4	8	7.4	4.7

Category E

2 Dr ES Sdn	2420	3460
4 Dr ES Sdn	2550	3650
2 Dr STD Sdn	2205	3150
4 Dr STD Sdn	2331	3330

OPTIONS FOR COLT

4 cyl 1.8 L Engine[Opt on ES Sdn] +125
Auto 3-Speed Transmission +140
Auto 4-Speed Transmission +185
AM/FM Stereo Tape +80
Air Conditioning +220
Aluminum/Alloy Wheels +90
Anti-Lock Brakes +180
Cruise Control +60
Power Door Locks +65
Power Windows +70

DODGE 94

Model Description	Trade-in Value	Market Value	Model Description	Trade-in Value	Market Value

DAKOTA 1994

Driver airbag is added, along with side-door guard beams. LE trim level now called SLT. A strengthened roof now meets passenger car crush standards. The 5.2-liter V8 loses horsepower but gains torque.

RATINGS (SCALE OF 1-10)

Overall	Safety	Reliability	Performance	Comfort	Value
N/A	7	7.3	7	7.1	N/A

Category G

	Trade-in	Market
2 Dr SLT Ext Cab SB	5850	7600
2 Dr SLT 4WD Ext Cab SB	7095	9215
2 Dr SLT Std Cab LB	5300	6880
2 Dr SLT 4WD Std Cab LB	6520	8470
2 Dr SLT Std Cab SB	5195	6745
2 Dr SLT 4WD Std Cab SB	6415	8330
2 Dr STD Ext Cab SB	5245	6810
2 Dr STD 4WD Ext Cab SB	7005	9100
2 Dr STD Std Cab LB	4520	5870
2 Dr STD 4WD Std Cab LB	6420	8335
2 Dr STD Std Cab SB	4380	5690
2 Dr STD 4WD Std Cab SB	6300	8185
2 Dr Sport Ext Cab SB	5530	7185
2 Dr Sport 4WD Ext Cab SB	7205	9355
2 Dr Sport Std Cab SB	4535	5890
2 Dr Sport 4WD Std Cab SB	6505	8445
2 Dr WS Std Cab LB	3875	5030
2 Dr WS 4WD Std Cab LB	6235	8100
2 Dr WS Std Cab SB	3740	4855
2 Dr WS 4WD Std Cab SB	6100	7920

OPTIONS FOR DAKOTA

6 cyl 3.9 L Engine +145
8 cyl 5.2 L Engine +190
Auto 4-Speed Transmission +245
AM/FM Stereo Tape[Opt on STD,WS] +60
Air Conditioning[Opt on Sport,STD,WS] +220
Anti-Lock Brakes +160
Camper/Towing Package +80
Chrome Bumpers[Std on SLT] +45
Chrome Wheels[Std on SLT] +45
Cruise Control[Opt on Sport,STD] +55
Limited Slip Diff +75
Power Door Locks +65
Power Windows +65
Premium Sound System +95
Rear Step Bumper[Opt on STD,WS] +40

INTREPID 1994

Base engine is upgraded with eight more horsepower. A flexible-fuel model is introduced to all states except California. Standard equipment now includes air conditioning and a touring suspension. ES models gain variable-assist power steering, which is optional on base models with the Wheel and Handling Group. New options include a power sunroof, security alarm and power passenger seat.

RATINGS (SCALE OF 1-10)

Overall	Safety	Reliability	Performance	Comfort	Value
7.9	7.7	6.4	8.4	8.6	8.4

Category B

	Trade-in	Market
4 Dr ES Sdn	5170	6805
4 Dr STD Sdn	4490	5910

OPTIONS FOR INTREPID

6 cyl 3.5 L Engine +200
Anti-Lock Brakes +185
Child Seat (1) +25
Climate Control for AC +45
Compact Disc W/fm/tape +105
Cruise Control[Std on ES] +60
Dual Power Seats +105
Keyless Entry System +45
Leather Seats +185
Power Door Locks +70
Power Moonroof +265
Power Windows +80
Traction Control System +50

RAM PICKUP 1994

Brand-new truck replaces 22-year-old D-Series model. New truck sports big-rig styling, driver airbag, available V10 engine, and a commodious cabin. All 1994 Rams are regular-cab models in shortbed or longbed configuration with 2WD or 4WD. Optional on 1500 and 2500 models is four-wheel ABS that works in both 2WD and 4WD.

RATINGS (SCALE OF 1-10)

Overall	Safety	Reliability	Performance	Comfort	Value
N/A	N/A	7.4	7	8	N/A

RAM 1500

Category H

	Trade-in	Market
2 Dr LT Std Cab LB	6405	8105
2 Dr LT 4WD Std Cab LB	7880	9975
2 Dr LT Std Cab SB	6320	8000
2 Dr LT 4WD Std Cab SB	7825	9905
2 Dr Laramie SLT Std Cab LB	7245	9170
2 Dr Laramie SLT 4WD Std Cab LB	8560	10835
2 Dr Laramie SLT Std Cab SB	7155	9055
2 Dr Laramie SLT 4WD Std Cab SB	8475	10725
2 Dr ST Std Cab LB	6060	7670
2 Dr ST 4WD Std Cab LB	7905	10005
2 Dr ST Std Cab SB	5950	7530
2 Dr ST 4WD Std Cab SB	7835	9920

Model Description	Trade-in Value	Market Value	Model Description	Trade-in Value	Market Value
2 Dr WS Std Cab LB	5200	6585	2 Dr 3500 Ram Van Ext	5650	7150
2 Dr WS Std Cab SB	5130	6495	2 Dr 3500 Maxi Ram Van Ext	5815	7360

RAM 2500
Category H

Model	Trade-in	Market
2 Dr LT Std Cab LB	7105	8995
2 Dr LT 4WD Std Cab LB	8605	10890
2 Dr Laramie SLT Std Cab LB	8010	10140
2 Dr Laramie SLT 4WD Std Cab LB	9260	11720
2 Dr ST Std Cab LB	7230	9155
2 Dr ST 4WD Std Cab LB	8610	10900

RAM 3500
Category H

Model	Trade-in	Market
2 Dr LT Std Cab LB	8400	10630
2 Dr Laramie SLT Std Cab LB	9565	12105
2 Dr ST Std Cab LB	8720	11040

OPTIONS FOR RAM PICKUP
10 cyl 8.0 L Engine +130
6 cyl 5.9 L Turbodsl Engine +1205
8 cyl 5.2 L Engine +140
8 cyl 5.9 L Engine +135
Auto 4-Speed Transmission +245
Air Conditioning[Opt on LT,ST,WS] +220
Anti-Lock Brakes +135
Bed Liner +60
Camper/Towing Package +90
Chrome Bumpers[Opt on LT] +45
Chrome Wheels[Opt on LT,ST] +80
Compact Disc W/fm/tape +85
Cruise Control[Opt on LT,ST,WS] +50
Limited Slip Diff +70
Power Drivers Seat +75
Premium Sound System +105
Rear Step Bumper +40

RAM VAN / WAGON   1994

A reskinned full-size van debuted in mid-1993, featuring new front and rear styling. Early-build vans did not include side-door guard beams for the front doors or improved roof crush protection. Air conditioning now uses CFC-free refrigerant.

RATINGS (SCALE OF 1-10)

Overall	Safety	Reliability	Performance	Comfort	Value
N/A	6.3	7.7	6.2	6.9	N/A

RAM VAN
Category H

Model	Trade-in	Market
2 Dr 1500 Ram Van	4365	5525
2 Dr 1500 Ram Van Ext	4505	5700
2 Dr 2500 Ram Van	4935	6245
2 Dr 2500 Ram Van Ext	5075	6425
2 Dr 2500 Maxi Ram Van Ext	5300	6710

RAM WAGON
Category H

Model	Trade-in	Market
2 Dr 1500 Ram Wagon	5485	6940
2 Dr 1500 LE Ram Wagon	5880	7440
2 Dr 2500 Ram Wagon	6010	7605
2 Dr 2500 LE Ram Wagon	6340	8025
2 Dr 2500 Maxi Ram Wagon	6425	8135
2 Dr 3500 Ram Wagon	6330	8010
2 Dr 3500 Ram Wagon Ext	6525	8260
2 Dr 3500 LE Ram Wagon	6740	8530
2 Dr 3500 LE Ram Wagon Ext	6950	8800

OPTIONS FOR RAM VAN/WAGON
8 cyl 5.2 L Engine[Std on B350] +140
8 cyl 5.9 L Engine +135
Auto 4-Speed Transmission[Std on B350] +70
AM/FM Stereo Tape +60
Air Conditioning[Std on LE] +220
Aluminum/Alloy Wheels +85
Anti-Lock Brakes +135
Auxiliary Fuel Tank +40
Cruise Control[Opt on Maxi,STD] +50
Dual Air Conditioning[Opt on B250] +360
Infinity Sound System +60
Keyless Entry System[Opt on Maxi,STD] +45
Limited Slip Diff +70
Power Door Locks[Opt on Maxi,STD] +50
Power Windows[Opt on Maxi,STD] +50
Premium Sound System +105
Velour/Cloth Seats[Std on LE,Maxi LE] +35

SHADOW   1994

Four-door hatchback production stops midyear. Front passengers are now restrained by the dreaded motorized seatbelt to comply with federal regulations. Air conditioning runs on CFC-free coolant this year.

RATINGS (SCALE OF 1-10)

Overall	Safety	Reliability	Performance	Comfort	Value
6.5	6.5	6.9	7.2	6.8	5.1

Category E

Model	Trade-in	Market
2 Dr ES Hbk	2765	3950
4 Dr ES Hbk	2830	4040
2 Dr STD Hbk	2400	3430
4 Dr STD Hbk	2470	3525

OPTIONS FOR SHADOW
4 cyl 2.5 L Engine[Std on ES] +80
6 cyl 3.0 L Engine +220
Auto 3-Speed Transmission +155
Auto 4-Speed Transmission +200
AM/FM Compact Disc Player +125
Air Conditioning +220
Aluminum/Alloy Wheels +90

DODGE 94-93

Model Description	Trade-in Value	Market Value	Model Description	Trade-in Value	Market Value

Anti-Lock Brakes +180
Cruise Control +60
Power Door Locks +65
Power Drivers Seat +85
Power Windows +70
Premium Sound System +90
Sunroof +95

SPIRIT 1994

Motorized seatbelt is introduced for front passengers. Highline and ES trim designations are retired in favor of ... well, nothing. All 1994 Spirits come equipped one way, with various option packages available.

RATINGS (SCALE OF 1-10)

Overall	Safety	Reliability	Performance	Comfort	Value
7.1	6.6	7.5	6.8	7.4	7.4

Category C
4 Dr STD Sdn   3090   4175

OPTIONS FOR SPIRIT

6 cyl 3.0 L Engine +185
Auto 4-Speed Transmission +45
AM/FM Stereo Tape +45
Anti-Lock Brakes +165
Power Door Locks +65
Power Drivers Seat +80
Power Windows +85

STEALTH 1994

Passenger airbag is added. R/T Turbo gains 20 horsepower and a six-speed transmission. ES trim level is dropped. Styling is slightly revised front and rear, revealing the addition of projector-beam headlamps in place of the hidden lights used previously. CFC-free refrigerant is used in the air conditioning system, and R/T models can be painted a really bright shade of yellow.

RATINGS (SCALE OF 1-10)

Overall	Safety	Reliability	Performance	Comfort	Value
N/A	N/A	7.6	9.4	6.8	N/A

Category F
2 Dr R/T Hbk   7345   9665
2 Dr R/T Turbo 4WD Hbk   10745   14140
2 Dr R/T Luxury Hbk   8115   10680
2 Dr STD Hbk   6280   8260

OPTIONS FOR STEALTH

Auto 4-Speed Transmission +265
AM/FM Stereo Tape +60
Air Conditioning[Std on R/T Luxury,4WD] +225
Anti-Lock Brakes[Std on 4WD] +185
Chrome Wheels +160
Compact Disc Changer[Opt on R/T,STD] +175
Cruise Control[Std on R/T Luxury,4WD] +55
Keyless Entry System[Opt on R/T,STD] +50

Leather Seats +175
Power Door Locks[Std on R/T Luxury,4WD] +55
Power Sunroof +185
Power Windows[Std on R/T Luxury,4WD] +60
Premium Sound System[Std on R/T Luxury,4WD] +100
Rear Spoiler[Std on R/T Luxury,4WD] +65

1993 DODGE

CARAVAN 1993

No changes.

RATINGS (SCALE OF 1-10)

Overall	Safety	Reliability	Performance	Comfort	Value
6.9	6	4.7	7.4	8.3	8.3

Category G
2 Dr ES Pass. Van   4575   6100
2 Dr ES 4WD Pass. Van   5020   6695
2 Dr Grand Pass. Van   3655   4870
2 Dr Grand ES Pass. Van   5225   6965
2 Dr Grand LE Pass. Van   4945   6590
2 Dr Grand LE 4WD Pass. Van   5310   7080
2 Dr Grand SE Pass. Van   4155   5540
2 Dr Grand SE 4WD Pass. Van   4575   6100
2 Dr LE Pass. Van   4395   5860
2 Dr LE 4WD Pass. Van   4725   6300
2 Dr SE Pass. Van   3750   5000
2 Dr SE 4WD Pass. Van   4290   5720
2 Dr STD Cargo Van   1960   2615
2 Dr STD Cargo Van Ext   2490   3320
2 Dr STD Pass. Van   2860   3815

OPTIONS FOR CARAVAN

6 cyl 3.0 L Engine[Opt on SE,STD] +145
6 cyl 3.3 L Engine[Std on Grand ES,Grand LE,
*   Grand SE,4WD] +95*
Auto 3-Speed Transmission[Opt on STD] +135
Auto 4-Speed Transmission[Opt on SE Pass. Van,
*   LE Pass. Van] +55*
7 Passenger Seating[Std on Grand ES] +115
AM/FM Compact Disc Player +70
Air Conditioning[Std on ES,Grand ES,Grand LE, LE] +180
Aluminum/Alloy Wheels +75
Anti-Lock Brakes +135
Captain Chairs (4) +140
Child Seats (2) +55
Cruise Control[Opt on Grand,Grand SE,SE,STD] +45
Dual Air Conditioning +210
Leather Seats +170
Luggage Rack +35
Power Door Locks[Opt on Grand,Grand SE,SE,STD] +50
Power Drivers Seat +60
Power Windows +55
Premium Sound System +75

DODGE 93

Model Description	Trade-in Value	Market Value	Model Description	Trade-in Value	Market Value

COLT 1993

Complete redesign results in two- and four-door notchback models; the hatchback is dropped. Coupes and sedans come in base or GL trim. Coupe and base sedan are powered by same 1.5-liter engine from last year. GL has a stronger 113-horsepower, 1.8-liter engine; this powerplant is optional on base sedan. GL sedan is only Colt that can be equipped with optional ABS.

RATINGS (SCALE OF 1-10)

Overall	Safety	Reliability	Performance	Comfort	Value
N/A	N/A	6	8	7.4	6.6

Category E

2 Dr GL Sdn	1725	2575
4 Dr GL Sdn	1842	2750
2 Dr STD Sdn	1590	2370
4 Dr STD Sdn	1711	2550

OPTIONS FOR COLT

4 cyl 1.8 L Engine[Std on GL] +85
Auto 3-Speed Transmission +115
Auto 4-Speed Transmission +150
AM/FM Stereo Tape +65
Air Conditioning +180
Aluminum/Alloy Wheels +75
Anti-Lock Brakes +150
Cruise Control +50
Power Door Locks +55
Power Steering +55
Power Windows +60

DAKOTA 1993

Sport model gets new graphics.

RATINGS (SCALE OF 1-10)

Overall	Safety	Reliability	Performance	Comfort	Value
N/A	4.8	7.1	7	7.1	N/A

Category G

2 Dr LE Ext Cab SB	4775	6365
2 Dr LE 4WD Ext Cab SB	5930	7905
2 Dr LE Std Cab LB	4100	5465
2 Dr LE 4WD Std Cab LB	5460	7280
2 Dr LE Std Cab SB	4015	5355
2 Dr LE 4WD Std Cab SB	5400	7200
2 Dr S Std Cab SB	3555	4740
2 Dr STD Ext Cab SB	4270	5695
2 Dr STD 4WD Ext Cab SB	5635	7510
2 Dr STD Std Cab LB	3710	4945
2 Dr STD 4WD Std Cab LB	5275	7030
2 Dr STD Std Cab SB	3630	4840
2 Dr STD 4WD Std Cab SB	5195	6925
2 Dr Sport Std Cab SB	3780	5040
2 Dr Sport 4WD Std Cab SB	5340	7120

OPTIONS FOR DAKOTA

6 cyl 3.9 L Engine +120
8 cyl 5.2 L Engine +195
Auto 4-Speed Transmission +200
Dakota Snowplow Prep Grp. +170
AM/FM Stereo Tape[Opt on S,STD] +50
Air Conditioning[Std on LE] +180
Aluminum/Alloy Wheels[Opt on STD] +75
Anti-Lock Brakes +135
Camper/Towing Package +65
Chrome Bumpers +35
Chrome Wheels +40
Cruise Control[Std on LE] +45
Limited Slip Diff +60
Power Door Locks +50
Power Steering[Std on LE,Sport,4WD] +60
Power Windows +55
Premium Sound System +75
Rear Step Bumper[Opt on S,STD] +30

DAYTONA 1993

ABS is now available on base model. IROC loses turbocharged engine, though the limited-edition IROC R/T continues with turbo power.

Category C

2 Dr ES Hbk	2815	3910
2 Dr STD Hbk	2490	3460

Category F

2 Dr IROC Hbk	3750	5000

OPTIONS FOR DAYTONA

6 cyl 3.0 L Engine[Std on IROC] +155
Auto 3-Speed Transmission +125
Auto 4-Speed Transmission +160
AM/FM Compact Disc Player +80
Air Conditioning[Std on IROC R/T] +180
Aluminum/Alloy Wheels[Opt on STD] +65
Anti-Lock Brakes[Opt on ES] +135
Cruise Control +45
Leather Seats +135
Power Door Locks +45
Power Drivers Seat +55
Power Windows +50
Premium Sound System +80
Tilt Steering Wheel +35

DYNASTY 1993

Audio system is upgraded, a tamper-resistant odometer is added, and a stainless steel exhaust system is installed.

Category C

4 Dr LE Sdn	3025	4200
4 Dr STD Sdn	2660	3695

OPTIONS FOR DYNASTY

6 cyl 3.0 L Engine[Std on LE] +155
6 cyl 3.3 L Engine +120
Auto 4-Speed Transmission[Std on LE] +30

Don't forget to refer to the Mileage Adjustment Table at the back of this book!

Model Description	Trade-in Value	Market Value	Model Description	Trade-in Value	Market Value
AM/FM Stereo Tape +35			2 Dr LE Std Cab SB	4865	6160
Air Conditioning +180			2 Dr LE 4WD Std Cab SB	5845	7400
Anti-Lock Brakes +135			2 Dr STD Ext Cab LB	5060	6405
Cruise Control +45			2 Dr STD 4WD Ext Cab LB	6085	7700
Keyless Entry System +40			2 Dr STD Ext Cab SB	4990	6315
Leather Seats +135			2 Dr STD Std Cab LB	4580	5800
Power Door Locks +55			2 Dr STD 4WD Std Cab LB	5590	7075
Power Drivers Seat +65			2 Dr STD Std Cab SB	4485	5680
Power Passenger Seat +60			2 Dr STD 4WD Std Cab SB	5488	6950
Power Windows +70					
Premium Sound System +85					
Wire Wheel Covers +50					

INTREPID 1993

This midsized car represents the beginning of a revolution at Chrysler. Introducing cab-forward styling, Intrepid is powered by one of two V6 engines and comes in base or ES trim. ES model has four-wheel disc brakes. ABS is optional on base and ES. All Intrepids are equipped with dual airbags and height-adjustable seatbelts, while an integrated child seat is optional.

RATINGS (SCALE OF 1-10)

Overall	Safety	Reliability	Performance	Comfort	Value
7.6	7.6	5.8	8.4	8.6	7.8

Category B

4 Dr ES Sdn	3770	5165
4 Dr STD Sdn	3325	4555

OPTIONS FOR INTREPID

6 cyl 3.5 L Engine +140
Air Conditioning +180
Aluminum/Alloy Wheels +75
Anti-Lock Brakes +155
Climate Control for AC +40
Compact Disc W/fm/tape +85
Cruise Control +50
Leather Seats +150
Power Door Locks +55
Power Drivers Seat +70
Power Passenger Seat +75
Power Windows +65
Premium Sound System +90
Traction Control System +40

RAM PICKUP 1993

The optional 5.9-liter V8 is upgraded. New steel and alloy wheel designs debut.

RAM 150

Category H

2 Dr LE Ext Cab LB	5390	6825
2 Dr LE 4WD Ext Cab LB	6910	8300
2 Dr LE Ext Cab SB	5330	6745
2 Dr LE Std Cab LB	4960	6280
2 Dr LE 4WD Std Cab LB	5955	7540

RAM 250

Category H

2 Dr LE Turbodsl Ext Cab LB	8215	10400
2 Dr LE Std Cab LB	5370	6800
2 Dr STD Std Cab LB	5065	6410

RAM 350

Category H

2 Dr LE Turbodsl Ext Cab LB	7750	9810
2 Dr LE Turbodsl 4WD Ext Cab LB	9240	11695
2 Dr STD Turbodsl Ext Cab LB	7405	9375
2 Dr STD Turbodsl 4WD Ext Cab LB	8700	11010

OPTIONS FOR RAM PICKUP

6 cyl 5.9 L Turbodsl Engine +875
8 cyl 5.2 L Engine +130
8 cyl 5.9 L Engine +120
Auto 3-Speed Transmission +145
Auto 4-Speed Transmission +200
Snow Plow Prep Pkg +185
AM/FM Stereo Tape[Opt on STD] +45
Air Conditioning[Opt on STD] +180
Aluminum/Alloy Wheels +70
Camper/Towing Package +75
Chrome Step Bumper +45
Cruise Control[Opt on STD,] +40
Dual Rear Wheels +185
Limited Slip Diff +55
Power Door Locks[Opt on STD] +40
Power Windows[Opt on STD] +40
Premium Sound System +85
Rear Step Bumper[Opt on STD] +35

RAM VAN/WAGON 1993

The optional 5.9-liter V8 is upgraded.

RAM VAN

Category H

2 Dr 1500 Ram Van	3150	3985
2 Dr 1500 Ram Van Ext	3300	4180
2 Dr 2500 Ram Van	3565	4515
2 Dr 2500 Ram Van Ext	3790	4800
2 Dr 2500 Maxi Ram Van Ext	4035	5110
2 Dr 3500 Ram Van Ext	4045	5120
2 Dr 3500 Maxi Ram Van Ext	4290	5430

Don't forget to refer to the Mileage Adjustment Table at the back of this book!

DODGE 93

RAM WAGON

Category H

Model Description	Trade-in Value	Market Value
2 Dr 1500 Ram Wagon	3885	4915
2 Dr 1500 Ram Wagon Ext	4035	5105
2 Dr 1500 LE Ram Wagon	4110	5205
2 Dr 1500 LE Ram Wagon Ext	4185	5300
2 Dr 1500 Value Ram Wagon	3995	5060
2 Dr 1500 Value Ram Wagon Ext	4155	5260
2 Dr 2500 Ram Wagon Ext	5160	6530
2 Dr 2500 LE Ram Wagon Ext	5290	6695
2 Dr 2500 LE Maxi Ram Wagon Ext	5635	7130
2 Dr 2500 Maxi Ram Wagon Ext	5540	7010
2 Dr 2500 Value Ram Wagon Ext	5270	6670
2 Dr 2500 Value Maxi Ram Wagon Ext	5675	7185
2 Dr 3500 Ram Wagon Ext	5310	6720
2 Dr 3500 LE Ram Wagon Ext	5490	6950

OPTIONS FOR RAM VAN/WAGON

8 cyl 5.2 L Engine[Std on B350,LE Maxi,Value Maxi, B250 Maxi Ram Wagon Ext] +130
8 cyl 5.9 L Engine +120
Auto 3-Speed Transmission[Opt on B150,Ram Van, Ram Van Ext] +75
Auto 4-Speed Transmission[Std on B350] +95
8 Pass W/Travel Seat Pkg +205
AM/FM Stereo Tape +45
Air Conditioning[Opt on Maxi,STD,B150, LE Ram Wagon Ext] +180
Aluminum/Alloy Wheels +70
Cruise Control[Std on LE,LE Maxi] +40
Dual Air Conditioning +295
Limited Slip Diff +55
Power Door Locks[Opt on Value] +40
Power Windows[Opt on Value] +40
Premium Sound System[Opt on Value] +85

RAMCHARGER 1993

The optional 5.9-liter V8 is upgraded.

Category H

Model Description	Trade-in Value	Market Value
2 Dr Canyon Sport 4WD Utility	6085	7705
2 Dr LE 4WD Utility	5955	7540
2 Dr S 4WD Utility	5255	6650
2 Dr STD 4WD Utility	5595	7080

OPTIONS FOR RAMCHARGER

8 cyl 5.9 L Engine +120
Ramcharger Snow Plow Pkg +235
AM/FM Stereo Tape +45
Air Conditioning[Std on LE] +180
Aluminum/Alloy Wheels +70
Camper/Towing Package +75
Cruise Control[Std on LE] +40
Limited Slip Diff +55
Locking Differential +55

Power Door Locks[Std on LE] +40
Power Windows[Std on LE] +40
Premium Sound System +85
Velour/Cloth Seats[Opt on Canyon Sport,S,4WD] +30

SHADOW 1993

America model is dropped. Convertible disappears midyear. ABS is newly optional.

RATINGS (SCALE OF 1-10)

Overall	Safety	Reliability	Performance	Comfort	Value
6.6	6.5	7.7	7.2	6.8	5

Category E

Model Description	Trade-in Value	Market Value
2 Dr ES Conv	2780	4150
2 Dr ES Hbk	2190	3270
4 Dr ES Hbk	2260	3370
2 Dr Highline Conv	2515	3755
2 Dr STD Hbk	1910	2850
4 Dr STD Hbk	2010	3000

OPTIONS FOR SHADOW

4 cyl 2.5 L Engine[Opt on STD] +65
6 cyl 3.0 L Engine +155
Auto 3-Speed Transmission +125
Auto 4-Speed Transmission +155
AM/FM Compact Disc Player +100
Air Conditioning +180
Aluminum/Alloy Wheels +75
Anti-Lock Brakes +150
Cruise Control +50
Power Door Locks +55
Power Drivers Seat +70
Power Windows[Opt on STD] +60
Premium Sound System +70
Sunroof +75

SPIRIT 1993

LE and R/T models are dropped from lineup. Turbocharged engines are banished. Four thousand flexible-fuel models are produced. Grille is now color keyed. CD player is added to options list. Rear styling is revised.

RATINGS (SCALE OF 1-10)

Overall	Safety	Reliability	Performance	Comfort	Value
7.1	6.1	8	6.8	7.4	7.4

Category C

Model Description	Trade-in Value	Market Value
4 Dr ES Sdn	3115	4325
4 Dr Highline Sdn	2770	3845

OPTIONS FOR SPIRIT

6 cyl 3.0 L Engine +155
Auto 3-Speed Transmission[Std on ES] +125
Auto 4-Speed Transmission +95
AM/FM Stereo Tape +35
Air Conditioning +180
Aluminum/Alloy Wheels[Std on ES] +65

Don't forget to refer to the Mileage Adjustment Table at the back of this book!

EDMUND'S® USED CARS & TRUCKS

Model Description	Trade-in Value	Market Value
Anti-Lock Brakes +135		
Cruise Control[Std on ES] +45		
Power Door Locks +55		
Power Drivers Seat +65		
Power Windows +70		
Premium Sound System +85		

STEALTH 1993

Base model gets ES sill moldings, while R/T's spoiler is optional across the line. R/T Turbo can be ordered with chrome wheels. Remote keyless entry and a CD changer are new options.

RATINGS (SCALE OF 1-10)

Overall	Safety	Reliability	Performance	Comfort	Value
N/A	6.3	7.5	9.4	6.8	N/A

Category F

	Trade-in	Market
2 Dr ES Hbk	5705	7605
2 Dr R/T Hbk	6525	8700
2 Dr R/T Turbo 4WD Hbk	8700	11600
2 Dr STD Hbk	4925	6565

OPTIONS FOR STEALTH

Auto 4-Speed Transmission +195
AM/FM Stereo Tape +45
Air Conditioning[Std on R/T] +185
Anti-Lock Brakes[Std on R/T] +150
Chrome Wheels +130
Compact Disc Changer +140
Cruise Control[Std on R/T] +45
Keyless Entry System +40
Leather Seats +145
Power Door Locks[Std on R/T] +45
Power Sunroof +150
Power Windows[Std on R/T] +50
Premium Sound System[Std on R/T] +80
Rear Spoiler[Std on R/T] +55

1992 DODGE

CARAVAN 1992

Integrated child seats are a new option. Exterior door handles are flush-mounted, and new wheels debut.

RATINGS (SCALE OF 1-10)

Overall	Safety	Reliability	Performance	Comfort	Value
6.6	5.3	3.9	7.4	8.3	8.1

Category G

	Trade-in	Market
2 Dr ES Pass. Van	3690	5055
2 Dr ES 4WD Pass. Van	4090	5600
2 Dr Grand Pass. Van	3020	4140
2 Dr Grand ES Pass. Van	4265	5845
2 Dr Grand ES 4WD Pass. Van	4380	6000
2 Dr Grand LE Pass. Van	4055	5555
2 Dr Grand LE 4WD Pass. Van	4265	5840
2 Dr Grand SE Pass. Van	3390	4645
2 Dr Grand SE 4WD Pass. Van	3905	5350
2 Dr LE Pass. Van	3615	4955
2 Dr LE 4WD Pass. Van	3940	5395
2 Dr SE Pass. Van	2885	3950
2 Dr SE 4WD Pass. Van	3550	4860
2 Dr STD Cargo Van	1680	2300
2 Dr STD 4WD Cargo Van	2245	3075
2 Dr STD Cargo Van Ext	2195	3010
2 Dr STD 4WD Cargo Van Ext	2590	3550
2 Dr STD Pass. Van	2510	3440

OPTIONS FOR CARAVAN

6 cyl 3.0 L Engine[Opt on SE,STD] +140
6 cyl 3.3 L Engine[Std on Grand ES,Grand LE, Grand SE,Cargo Van,4WD] +70
Auto 3-Speed Transmission[Opt on STD] +105
Auto 4-Speed Transmission[Std on ES,Grand ES, Grand LE,Grand SE,LE,4WD] +105
7 Passenger Seating[Opt on STD] +95
Air Conditioning[Opt on Grand,Grand SE,SE,STD] +145
Captain Chairs (4) +115
Cruise Control[Opt on Grand,Grand SE,SE,STD] +40
Infinity Sound System +75
Power Door Locks[Opt on Grand,Grand SE,SE,STD] +40
Power Drivers Seat +50
Power Windows[Opt on Grand SE,SE] +45

COLT 1992

GL models can be equipped with a digital clock, but all Colts lose options such as factory floor mats, intermittent wipers, wheel trim rings, and alloy wheels.

Category E

	Trade-in	Market
2 Dr GL Hbk	1475	2305
2 Dr STD Hbk	1390	2170

OPTIONS FOR COLT

Auto 3-Speed Transmission +100
Air Conditioning +145
Power Steering +45

DAKOTA 1992

V6 and V8 engines get more power. The V6 is up considerably, from 125 to 180 horsepower. V8 models add a whopping 65 horsepower and 30 foot-pounds of torque. Four-wheel drive models can be equipped with an optional Off-Road Appearance package.

RATINGS (SCALE OF 1-10)

Overall	Safety	Reliability	Performance	Comfort	Value
N/A	4.7	7.1	7	7.1	N/A

Category G

	Trade-in	Market
2 Dr LE Ext Cab SB	3760	5150
2 Dr LE 4WD Ext Cab SB	5010	6860
2 Dr LE Std Cab LB	3355	4595
2 Dr LE 4WD Std Cab LB	4700	6440

Don't forget to refer to the Mileage Adjustment Table at the back of this book!

Model Description	Trade-in Value	Market Value
2 Dr LE Std Cab SB	3280	4490
2 Dr LE 4WD Std Cab SB	4640	6355
2 Dr S Std Cab SB	2825	3870
2 Dr STD Ext Cab SB	3480	4765
2 Dr STD 4WD Ext Cab SB	4710	6450
2 Dr STD Std Cab LB	3195	4375
2 Dr STD 4WD Std Cab LB	4385	6010
2 Dr STD Std Cab SB	3135	4295
2 Dr STD 4WD Std Cab SB	4320	5920
2 Dr Sport Ext Cab SB	3520	4820
2 Dr Sport 4WD Ext Cab SB	4831	6620
2 Dr Sport Std Cab SB	3105	4255
2 Dr Sport 4WD Std Cab SB	4480	6140

OPTIONS FOR DAKOTA
6 cyl 3.9 L Engine +95
8 cyl 5.2 L Engine +150
Auto 4-Speed Transmission +160
Snow Plow Prep Pkg +135
Air Conditioning +145
Cruise Control +40
Limited Slip Diff +50
Power Door Locks +40
Power Steering[Std on Sport,4WD] +50
Power Windows +45

DAYTONA   1992

Front and rear styling is revised, unsuccessfully. ABS is a new option. Shelby model is replaced midyear by IROC R/T model, powered by a 224-horsepower, 2.2-liter turbocharged engine and limited to a production run of 800 units.

Category C

Model Description	Trade-in Value	Market Value
2 Dr ES Hbk	2255	3270
2 Dr STD Hbk	2000	2895

Category F

Model Description	Trade-in Value	Market Value
2 Dr IROC Hbk	2925	4005

OPTIONS FOR DAYTONA
6 cyl 3.0 L Engine[Std on IROC] +125
Auto 3-Speed Transmission +100
Auto 4-Speed Transmission +115
Air Conditioning +145
Anti-Lock Brakes +110
Cruise Control +40
Power Door Locks +35
Power Drivers Seat[Std on IROC R/T] +45
Power Windows +40

DYNASTY   1992

Child-proof door locks are added, and options include an overhead console with storage bin and console with cassette storage.

Category C

Model Description	Trade-in Value	Market Value
4 Dr LE Sdn	2485	3600
4 Dr STD Sdn	2145	3110

OPTIONS FOR DYNASTY
6 cyl 3.0 L Engine[Std on LE] +125
Air Conditioning +145
Cruise Control +40
Power Door Locks +45
Power Drivers Seat +55
Power Windows +55

MONACO   1992

No changes.
Category C

Model Description	Trade-in Value	Market Value
4 Dr ES Sdn	1545	2240
4 Dr LE Sdn	1485	2155

OPTIONS FOR MONACO
Air Conditioning[Opt on LE] +145
Cruise Control +40
Power Door Locks +45
Power Drivers Seat +55
Power Windows +55

RAM 50 PICKUP   1992

The V6 engine, rear ABS, and extended-cab models are dropped from the lineup. Left are regular-cab trucks in 2WD or 4WD in base or SE trim.

Category G

Model Description	Trade-in Value	Market Value
2 Dr SE Std Cab LB	2315	3170
2 Dr SE Std Cab SB	2235	3065
2 Dr STD Std Cab LB	2110	2890
2 Dr STD Std Cab SB	1989	2725

OPTIONS FOR RAM 50 PICKUP
Auto 4-Speed Transmission +125
Air Conditioning +145
Power Steering[Std on SE,4WD] +50

RAM PICKUP   1992

Gasoline engines make more horsepower, and the Cummins Turbo Diesel engine is newly optional on Club Cab models. A one-ton duallie is introduced. Club Cabs have larger fuel tanks.

RAM 150

Category H

Model Description	Trade-in Value	Market Value
2 Dr LE Ext Cab LB	4685	6085
2 Dr LE 4WD Ext Cab LB	5955	7735
2 Dr LE Ext Cab SB	4580	5950
2 Dr LE Std Cab LB	3860	5010
2 Dr LE 4WD Std Cab LB	5165	6705
2 Dr LE Std Cab SB	3825	4970
2 Dr LE 4WD Std Cab SB	5080	6600
2 Dr STD Ext Cab LB	4230	5495
2 Dr STD 4WD Ext Cab LB	5700	7405
2 Dr STD Ext Cab SB	4125	5355
2 Dr STD Std Cab LB	3675	4775
2 Dr STD 4WD Std Cab LB	4840	6285

Model Description	Trade-in Value	Market Value
2 Dr STD Std Cab SB	3585	4655
2 Dr STD 4WD Std Cab SB	4750	6170

RAM 250

Category H

2 Dr LE Std Cab LB	4685	6085
2 Dr LE 4WD Std Cab LB	5415	7035
2 Dr STD Std Cab LB	4360	5665
2 Dr STD 4WD Std Cab LB	5660	7350

RAM 350

Category H

2 Dr LE Turbodsl Ext Cab LB	6685	8680
2 Dr LE Turbodsl 4WD Ext Cab LB	8285	10760
2 Dr STD Turbodsl Ext Cab LB	6275	8150
2 Dr STD Turbodsl 4WD Ext Cab LB	7775	10095

OPTIONS FOR RAM PICKUP

6 cyl 5.9 L Turbodsl Engine +700
8 cyl 5.2 L Engine +105
8 cyl 5.9 L Engine +80
Auto 3-Speed Transmission +115
Auto 4-Speed Transmission +160
Snow Plow Prep Pkg +150
Air Conditioning +145
Camper/Towing Package +60
Cruise Control +35
Dual Rear Wheels[Opt on 4WD] +150
Limited Slip Diff +45
Power Door Locks +35
Power Windows +35

RAM VAN/WAGON   1992

Alloy wheels and moldings are revised, and two engines get an infusion of horsepower.

RAM VAN

Category H

2 Dr 1500 Ram Van	2635	3425
2 Dr 1500 Ram Van Ext	2740	3560
2 Dr 2500 Ram Van	3055	3970
2 Dr 2500 Ram Van Ext	3325	4320
2 Dr 2500 Maxi Ram Van Ext	3580	4650
2 Dr 3500 Ram Van Ext	3575	4640
2 Dr 3500 Maxi Ram Van Ext	3790	4920

RAM WAGON

Category H

2 Dr 1500 Ram Wagon	3415	4435
2 Dr 1500 LE Ram Wagon	3690	4795
2 Dr 2500 Ram Wagon Ext	4180	5430
2 Dr 2500 LE Ram Wagon Ext	4445	5775
2 Dr 2500 LE Maxi Ram Wagon Ext	4825	6265
2 Dr 2500 Maxi Ram Wagon Ext	4560	5925

2 Dr 3500 Ram Wagon Ext	4445	5770
2 Dr 3500 LE Ram Wagon Ext	4560	5920
2 Dr 3500 Maxi Ram Wagon Ext	4425	5745

OPTIONS FOR RAM VAN/WAGON

8 cyl 5.2 L Engine[Std on B350] +105
8 cyl 5.9 L Engine[Opt on B150,B250,B350] +80
Auto 3-Speed Transmission[Opt on B150,Ram Van, Ram Van Ext] +60
Auto 4-Speed Transmission +80
Travel Seating Pkg +165
Air Conditioning[Opt on B150,B250,Maxi,STD] +145
Cruise Control[Opt on B150,B250,Maxi,STD] +35
Dual Air Conditioning +240
Limited Slip Diff +45
Power Door Locks[Opt on B150,B250,Maxi,STD] +35
Power Windows[Opt on B150,B250,Maxi,STD] +35

RAMCHARGER   1992

The 5.2-liter engine gains 50 horsepower, and manual transmissions have five speeds rather than four. A Canyon Sport trim level is available this year.

Category H

2 Dr Canyon Sport 4WD Utility	5000	6495
2 Dr LE 4WD Utility	4880	6340
2 Dr S 4WD Utility	4195	5450
2 Dr STD 4WD Utility	4545	5900

OPTIONS FOR RAMCHARGER

8 cyl 5.9 L Engine +80
Auto 4-Speed Transmission[Opt on 4WD] +160
Air Conditioning +145
Cruise Control +35
Limited Slip Diff +45
Power Door Locks +35
Power Windows +35

SHADOW   1992

ES model gets body-color bumpers. Midyear, the turbo engine found in the ES is swapped for a 3.0-liter V6.

RATINGS (SCALE OF 1-10)

Overall	Safety	Reliability	Performance	Comfort	Value
6.3	5.9	6.1	7.2	6.8	5.4

Category E

2 Dr America Hbk	1425	2230
4 Dr America Hbk	1500	2345
2 Dr ES Conv	2305	3605
2 Dr ES Hbk	1855	2900
4 Dr ES Hbk	1925	3010
2 Dr Highline Conv	2030	3170
2 Dr Highline Hbk	1755	2740
4 Dr Highline Hbk	1805	2820

OPTIONS FOR SHADOW

4 cyl 2.5 L Engine[Std on ES,Conv] +50
6 cyl 3.0 L Engine +135

Don't forget to refer to the Mileage Adjustment Table at the back of this book!

DODGE 92-91

Model Description	Trade-in Value	Market Value	Model Description	Trade-in Value	Market Value

Auto 3-Speed Transmission +100
Auto 4-Speed Transmission +125
Air Conditioning +145
Cruise Control +40
Power Door Locks +45
Power Windows +50

SPIRIT   1992

R/T gets revised gear ratios to make it accelerate faster, and revised suspension tuning to make it handle better. V6 models can be equipped with either a three-speed automatic or a four-speed unit. Alloy wheels are restyled.

RATINGS (SCALE OF 1-10)

Overall	Safety	Reliability	Performance	Comfort	Value
7	6.1	7.1	6.8	7.4	7.7

Category C

4 Dr ES Sdn	2445	3540
4 Dr LE Sdn	2230	3230
4 Dr STD Sdn	2025	2935

OPTIONS FOR SPIRIT

6 cyl 3.0 L Engine[Std on ES] +125
Auto 3-Speed Transmission[Std on LE] +100
Auto 4-Speed Transmission +80
Air Conditioning +145
Anti-Lock Brakes +110
Cruise Control[Opt on STD] +40
Power Door Locks +45
Power Drivers Seat +55
Power Windows +55

STEALTH   1992

A tilt/removable glass sunroof becomes available midyear.

RATINGS (SCALE OF 1-10)

Overall	Safety	Reliability	Performance	Comfort	Value
N/A	6.3	7.5	9.4	6.8	N/A

Category F

2 Dr ES Hbk	5050	6915
2 Dr R/T Hbk	5850	8015
2 Dr R/T Turbo 4WD Hbk	7180	9835
2 Dr STD Hbk	4315	5910

OPTIONS FOR STEALTH

Auto 4-Speed Transmission +150
Air Conditioning[Std on R/T] +150
Anti-Lock Brakes[Std on R/T] +125
Cruise Control[Std on R/T] +40
Leather Seats +120
Power Door Locks[Std on R/T] +35
Power Windows[Std on R/T] +40
Sunroof +70

1991 DODGE

CARAVAN   1991

Van is substantially reworked, with new styling, new interior, available all-wheel drive, and optional ABS. A driver airbag is standard on models built after February 1, 1991. All models have an automatic transmission, and the turbocharged model has been dropped.

RATINGS (SCALE OF 1-10)

Overall	Safety	Reliability	Performance	Comfort	Value
6.6	4.8	3.7	7.4	8.3	8.6

Category G

2 Dr ES Pass. Van	2795	3995
2 Dr ES 4WD Pass. Van	3235	4620
2 Dr Grand LE Pass. Van	2868	4100
2 Dr Grand LE 4WD Pass. Van	3335	4765
2 Dr Grand SE Pass. Van	2575	3680
2 Dr Grand SE 4WD Pass. Van	2980	4255
2 Dr LE Pass. Van	2815	4020
2 Dr LE 4WD Pass. Van	3040	4345
2 Dr SE Pass. Van	2305	3295
2 Dr SE 4WD Pass. Van	2710	3870
2 Dr STD Cargo Van	1450	2070
2 Dr STD 4WD Cargo Van	1945	2775
2 Dr STD Cargo Van Ext	1710	2445
2 Dr STD Pass. Van	2050	2930

OPTIONS FOR CARAVAN

6 cyl 3.0 L Engine[Std on ES,Cargo Van Ext] +105
6 cyl 3.3 L Engine[Opt on ES,SE,LE,STD,Cargo Van Ext] +85
Auto 4-Speed Transmission[Std on ES,Grand LE,
    Grand SE,Cargo Van,Cargo Van Ext,4WD] +25
Luxury Pkg +145
Premium Decor Pkg +120
7 Passenger Seating[Std on ES,Grand LE,Grand SE,
    LE,SE] +75
Air Conditioning[Std on ES,Grand LE,LE] +120
Anti-Lock Brakes +90
Captain Chairs (4) +90
Cruise Control[Std on ES,Grand LE,LE] +30
Power Door Locks[Std on ES,Grand LE,LE] +35
Power Drivers Seat +40
Power Windows +35

COLT   1991

GT model dropped from lineup due to lack of interest.

Category E

2 Dr GL Hbk	1105	1870
2 Dr STD Hbk	950	1610
4 Dr STD Wgn	1300	2205
4 Dr STD 4WD Wgn	1480	2510

DODGE 91

Model Description	Trade-in Value	Market Value	Model Description	Trade-in Value	Market Value

OPTIONS FOR COLT

Auto 3-Speed Transmission +80
Air Conditioning +120
Power Door Locks +35
Power Steering[Std on 4WD] +40
Power Windows +40

DAKOTA 1991

Base four-cylinder engine gets more horsepower. Club Cab can be ordered with four-wheel drive. Slow-selling convertible model is dropped from lineup. Front styling is freshened with composite headlamps (LE and Sport), new bumper, new grille, and extended sheetmetal to better accommodate the optional V8 engine. Exterior door handles are now metal instead of plastic. Front disc brake calipers are larger. Ignition and lock keys are double-sided.

RATINGS (SCALE OF 1-10)

Overall	Safety	Reliability	Performance	Comfort	Value
N/A	4.6	6.6	6.6	7.1	N/A

Category G		
2 Dr LE Ext Cab SB	3110	4445
2 Dr LE 4WD Ext Cab SB	4325	6175
2 Dr LE Std Cab LB	2830	4040
2 Dr LE 4WD Std Cab LB	3920	5600
2 Dr LE Std Cab SB	2715	3880
2 Dr LE 4WD Std Cab SB	3870	5525
2 Dr S Std Cab SB	2325	3320
2 Dr SE Ext Cab SB	3205	4575
2 Dr SE 4WD Ext Cab SB	4095	5850
2 Dr SE Std Cab LB	2770	3960
2 Dr SE 4WD Std Cab LB	3765	5380
2 Dr SE Std Cab SB	2710	3870
2 Dr SE 4WD Std Cab SB	3690	5270
2 Dr STD Ext Cab SB	2870	4100
2 Dr STD 4WD Ext Cab SB	4095	5850
2 Dr STD Std Cab LB	2700	3860
2 Dr STD 4WD Std Cab LB	3710	5300
2 Dr STD Std Cab SB	2610	3725
2 Dr STD 4WD Std Cab SB	3630	5185
2 Dr Sport Ext Cab SB	2930	4185
2 Dr Sport 4WD Ext Cab SB	4215	6020
2 Dr Sport Std Cab LB	2980	4255
2 Dr Sport 4WD Std Cab LB	3815	5450
2 Dr Sport Std Cab SB	2590	3700
2 Dr Sport 4WD Std Cab SB	3730	5330

OPTIONS FOR DAKOTA

6 cyl 3.9 L Engine +80
8 cyl 5.2 L Engine +145
Auto 4-Speed Transmission +130
Snow Plow Prep Pkg +110
Air Conditioning +120

Camper/Towing Package +45
Cruise Control +30
Limited Slip Diff +40
Power Door Locks +35
Power Steering[Std on 4WD] +40
Power Windows +35

DAYTONA 1991

No changes.

Category C		
2 Dr ES Hbk	1815	2795
2 Dr STD Hbk	1480	2275
Category F		
2 Dr IROC Hbk	2450	3450
2 Dr IROC Turbo Hbk	2555	3600
2 Dr Shelby Turbo Hbk	2090	2945

OPTIONS FOR DAYTONA

6 cyl 3.0 L Engine[Std on IROC] +100
Auto 3-Speed Transmission +90
Auto 4-Speed Transmission +100
CS Competition Pkg +320
Leather Enthusiast Seats +195
Air Conditioning +120
Anti-Lock Brakes +100
Cruise Control +30
Power Door Locks +30
Power Drivers Seat +35
Power Windows +35

DYNASTY 1991

Remote keyless entry is a new option, available with a security system and illuminated entry in an option package. Door glass is thicker, and front suspensions are improved.

Category C		
4 Dr LE Sdn	2040	3135
4 Dr STD Sdn	1775	2730

OPTIONS FOR DYNASTY

6 cyl 3.0 L Engine[Std on LE] +100
Luxury Pkg +130
Air Conditioning +120
Anti-Lock Brakes +90
Cruise Control +30
Power Door Locks +35
Power Windows +45

MONACO 1991

No changes.

Category C		
4 Dr ES Sdn	1315	2025
4 Dr LE Sdn	1250	1925

OPTIONS FOR MONACO

Air Conditioning[Opt on LE] +120
Cruise Control +30
Power Door Locks +35

Don't forget to refer to the Mileage Adjustment Table at the back of this book!

Model Description	Trade-in Value	Market Value	Model Description	Trade-in Value	Market Value

Power Drivers Seat +45
Power Windows +45

RAM 50 PICKUP 1991

Rear-wheel ABS is standard on top models. V6 engine is infused with additional power. Upholstery is revised.

Category G

Model Description	Trade-in Value	Market Value
2 Dr SE Std Cab SB	1935	2765
2 Dr SE 4WD Std Cab SB	3365	4810
2 Dr STD Std Cab LB	1780	2540
2 Dr STD Std Cab SB	1700	2425
2 Dr STD 4WD Std Cab SB	3165	4520

OPTIONS FOR RAM 50 PICKUP
6 cyl 3.0 L Engine +105
Auto 4-Speed Transmission +100
Air Conditioning +120
Power Steering[Std on LE,4WD] +40
Power Windows +35

RAM PICKUP 1991

New rear step bumper increases towing capacity from 3,000 to 5,000 pounds. An intercooler for turbodiesel models debuts midyear. Grille is revised, and Ram's-head hood ornament has been axed.

RAM 150

Category H

Model Description	Trade-in Value	Market Value
2 Dr LE Ext Cab SB	3975	5445
2 Dr LE Std Cab LB	3210	4400
2 Dr LE 4WD Std Cab LB	4320	5920
2 Dr LE Std Cab SB	3150	4315
2 Dr LE 4WD Std Cab SB	4255	5830
2 Dr S Std Cab LB	2860	3915
2 Dr S 4WD Std Cab LB	3665	5020
2 Dr S Std Cab SB	2780	3810
2 Dr S 4WD Std Cab SB	3565	4885
2 Dr SE Std Cab LB	3075	4210
2 Dr SE 4WD Std Cab LB	4155	5690
2 Dr SE Std Cab SB	3010	4120
2 Dr SE 4WD Std Cab SB	4060	5560
2 Dr STD Std Cab LB	3020	4140
2 Dr STD 4WD Std Cab LB	4015	5500
2 Dr STD Std Cab SB	2930	4015
2 Dr STD 4WD Std Cab SB	3950	5410

RAM 250

Category H

Model Description	Trade-in Value	Market Value
2 Dr LE Std Cab LB	3780	5180
2 Dr SE Std Cab LB	3590	4920
2 Dr STD Std Cab LB	3515	4815

RAM 350

Category H

Model Description	Trade-in Value	Market Value
2 Dr LE Std Cab LB	4165	5705
2 Dr SE Std Cab LB	4010	5495
2 Dr STD Std Cab LB	3905	5350

OPTIONS FOR RAM PICKUP
6 cyl 5.9 L Turbodsl Engine +500
8 cyl 5.2 L Engine +85
8 cyl 5.9 L Engine +70
Auto 3-Speed Transmission +95
Auto 4-Speed Transmission +130
Snow Plow Pkg +155
Air Conditioning +120
Cruise Control +30
Dual Rear Wheels +120
Limited Slip Diff +40
Power Door Locks +30
Power Windows +30

RAM VAN / WAGON 1991

Cruise control buttons now located on steering wheel. A new air conditioning outlet next to the second rear seat of Wagons improves cooling.

RAM VAN

Category H

Model Description	Trade-in Value	Market Value
2 Dr 1500 Ram Van	2090	2865
2 Dr 1500 Ram Van Ext	2220	3040
2 Dr 2500 Ram Van	2420	3315
2 Dr 2500 Ram Van Ext	2655	3635
2 Dr 3500 Ram Van	2630	3605
2 Dr 3500 Ram Van Ext	2855	3910

RAM WAGON

Category H

Model Description	Trade-in Value	Market Value
2 Dr 1500 Ram Wagon	2495	3415
2 Dr 1500 LE Ram Wagon	2755	3775
2 Dr 1500 LE Ram Wagon Ext	2835	3885
2 Dr 2500 Ram Wagon	2915	3990
2 Dr 2500 Ram Wagon Ext	3090	4235
2 Dr 2500 LE Ram Wagon	3200	4385
2 Dr 2500 LE Ram Wagon Ext	3350	4590
2 Dr 3500 Ram Wagon	3140	4300
2 Dr 3500 Ram Wagon Ext	3300	4520
2 Dr 3500 LE Ram Wagon	3365	4610
2 Dr 3500 LE Ram Wagon Ext	3495	4790

OPTIONS FOR RAM VAN/WAGON
8 cyl 5.2 L Engine[Std on B350] +85
8 cyl 5.9 L Engine[Std on Maxi] +70
Auto 3-Speed Transmission[Opt on B150,Ram Van, Ram Van Ext] +50
Auto 4-Speed Transmission[Std on B350,B150 STD Ram Van Ext] +70
Travel Seating Pkg +185
Air Conditioning +120
Captain Chairs (2) +80
Cruise Control +30
Dual Air Conditioning +195
Power Door Locks +30
Power Windows +30

Don't forget to refer to the Mileage Adjustment Table at the back of this book!

Model Description	Trade-in Value	Market Value

RAMCHARGER   1991

Front styling is revised with a new grille and the exclusion of the Ram's head hood ornament. A stronger rear bumper provides more towing capacity. Models equipped with a manual transmission can be ordered with tilt steering.

Category H

	Trade-in	Market
2 Dr LE 4WD Utility	4045	5540
2 Dr S 4WD Utility	3595	4925
2 Dr STD 4WD Utility	3860	5290

OPTIONS FOR RAMCHARGER
8 cyl 5.9 L Engine +70
Auto 4-Speed Transmission[Opt on 4WD] +130
Snow Plow Pkg +145
Air Conditioning +120
Camper/Towing Package +50
Cruise Control +30
Limited Slip Diff +40
Power Door Locks +30
Power Windows +30

SHADOW   1991

A bargain-basement America model is introduced, and convertible body style is added to the lineup.

RATINGS (SCALE OF 1-10)

Overall	Safety	Reliability	Performance	Comfort	Value
6.2	5.8	5.4	7.4	6.8	5.8

Category E

	Trade-in	Market
2 Dr America Hbk	1125	1910
4 Dr America Hbk	1225	2080
2 Dr ES Conv	1935	3280
2 Dr ES Turbo Conv	1990	3375
2 Dr ES Hbk	1340	2270
2 Dr ES Turbo Hbk	1395	2365
4 Dr ES Hbk	1410	2390
2 Dr Highline Conv	1580	2680
2 Dr Highline Turbo Conv	1690	2865
2 Dr Highline Hbk	1290	2185
4 Dr Highline Hbk	1315	2230

OPTIONS FOR SHADOW
4 cyl 2.5 L Engine[Std on ES,Conv] +40
Auto 3-Speed Transmission +80
Air Conditioning +120
Cruise Control +35
Power Door Locks +35
Power Windows[Std on Conv] +40

SPIRIT   1991

R/T trim level debuts with monochromatic paint scheme, sport-tuned suspension, 2.2-liter twin-cam turbocharged engine good for 224 horsepower, and 6.5 second zero-to-60 times. Four-wheel ABS is newly optional on all Spirit models.

RATINGS (SCALE OF 1-10)

Overall	Safety	Reliability	Performance	Comfort	Value
6.9	6	6.2	6.8	7.4	8.2

Category C

	Trade-in	Market
4 Dr ES Sdn	1895	2915
4 Dr ES Turbo Sdn	1955	3005
4 Dr LE Sdn	1770	2725
4 Dr LE Turbo Sdn	1840	2830
4 Dr R/T Turbo Sdn	2450	3770
4 Dr STD Sdn	1565	2405

OPTIONS FOR SPIRIT
6 cyl 3.0 L Engine[Std on ES] +100
Auto 3-Speed Transmission[Std on LE] +80
Auto 4-Speed Transmission +60
Air Conditioning[Std on R/T] +120
Cruise Control[Opt on STD] +30
Power Door Locks +35
Power Drivers Seat +45
Power Windows +45

STEALTH   1991

Brand-new sports car based on Mitsubishi 3000GT is available with front- or all-wheel drive. Four-wheel steering is standard with the all-wheel drive R/T Turbo model, powered by a twin-turbocharged 300-horsepower V6. Base models have a 164-horse SOHC V6 engine, ES and R/T a DOHC V6 making 222 horsepower.

RATINGS (SCALE OF 1-10)

Overall	Safety	Reliability	Performance	Comfort	Value
N/A	6.2	7.1	9.4	6.8	N/A

Category F

	Trade-in	Market
2 Dr ES Hbk	4435	6245
2 Dr R/T Hbk	5180	7295
2 Dr R/T Turbo 4WD Hbk	6365	8965
2 Dr STD Hbk	3815	5370

OPTIONS FOR STEALTH
Auto 4-Speed Transmission +120
Air Conditioning[Std on R/T] +125
Anti-Lock Brakes[Std on R/T] +100
Cruise Control[Std on R/T] +30
Leather Seats +95
Power Door Locks[Std on R/T] +30
Power Windows[Std on R/T] +35

1990 DODGE

CARAVAN   1990

All models get a 20-gallon fuel tank. New 3.3-liter V6 option is added to Grand Caravan engine lineup.

Don't forget to refer to the Mileage Adjustment Table at the back of this book!

Model Description	Trade-in Value	Market Value
Category G		
2 Dr ES Pass. Van	2075	3145
2 Dr ES Turbo Pass. Van	2125	3220
2 Dr Grand LE Pass. Van	2335	3535
2 Dr Grand SE Pass. Van	1935	2935
2 Dr LE Pass. Van	1645	2495
2 Dr LE Turbo Pass. Van	1695	2570
2 Dr SE Pass. Van	1695	2570
2 Dr SE Turbo Pass. Van	1645	2495
2 Dr STD Cargo Van	1065	1610
2 Dr STD Cargo Van Ext	1345	2035
2 Dr STD Pass. Van	1470	2225
2 Dr STD Turbo Pass. Van	1550	2350

OPTIONS FOR CARAVAN

6 cyl 3.0 L Engine[Std on ES] +110
6 cyl 3.3 L Engine[Opt on STD] +140
Auto 3-Speed Transmission +70
Auto 4-Speed Transmission[Opt on ES,LE,SE,STD] +90
Royal Pkg +145
Air Conditioning[Std on ES,Grand LE,LE] +100
Power Door Locks[Std on ES,Grand LE,LE] +30
Power Windows[Std on ES,Grand LE,LE] +30

COLT   1990

Outstanding GT model loses turbocharged engine. To compensate, a 1.6-liter twin-cam has been installed in the GT, making 113 horsepower. That's 22 fewer ponies than in 1989. Other changes include a switch from E to GL trim for the midrange hatchback. Vista 4WD system is now full-time rather than part-time. Vista body-side moldings and the grille have fresh appearance.

Model Description	Trade-in Value	Market Value
Category E		
4 Dr DL Wgn	1160	2235
4 Dr DL 4WD Wgn	1280	2465
2 Dr GL Hbk	765	1475
2 Dr GT Hbk	965	1855
2 Dr STD Hbk	695	1340
4 Dr STD Wgn	970	1865
4 Dr STD 4WD Wgn	1105	2125

OPTIONS FOR COLT

Auto 3-Speed Transmission +60
Auto 4-Speed Transmission +80
Performance Pkg +185
Sport Appearance Pkg +100
Air Conditioning +100
Power Door Locks +30
Power Windows +30

DAKOTA   1990

Big news is the addition of an extended-cab model. Base, SE, LE, and Sport versions of new Club Cab are available. Shelby model dropped from lineup, while convertible availability expands to base trim.

RATINGS (SCALE OF 1-10)

Overall	Safety	Reliability	Performance	Comfort	Value
N/A	4.7	6.6	6.6	7.1	N/A

Model Description	Trade-in Value	Market Value
Category G		
2 Dr Convertible Std Cab SB	2520	3820
2 Dr LE Ext Cab SB	2435	3690
2 Dr LE Std Cab LB	2220	3360
2 Dr LE 4WD Std Cab LB	2770	4200
2 Dr LE Std Cab SB	2135	3235
2 Dr LE 4WD Std Cab SB	2725	4125
2 Dr S Std Cab SB	1780	2700
2 Dr SE Ext Cab SB	2425	3675
2 Dr SE Std Cab LB	2160	3275
2 Dr SE 4WD Std Cab LB	2510	3800
2 Dr SE Std Cab SB	2090	3165
2 Dr SE 4WD Std Cab SB	2420	3670
2 Dr STD Ext Cab SB	2185	3310
2 Dr STD Std Cab LB	2025	3070
2 Dr STD 4WD Std Cab LB	2515	3810
2 Dr STD Std Cab SB	1935	2930
2 Dr STD 4WD Std Cab SB	2445	3705
2 Dr Sport Ext Cab SB	2310	3500
2 Dr Sport Std Cab SB	2000	3030
2 Dr Sport 4WD Std Cab SB	2540	3850
2 Dr Sport Convertible Std Cab SB	2890	4375
2 Dr Sport Convertible 4WD Std Cab SB	3355	5080

OPTIONS FOR DAKOTA

6 cyl 3.9 L Engine +65
Auto 4-Speed Transmission +105
Air Conditioning +100
Power Door Locks +30
Power Windows +30

DAYTONA   1990

Top-shelf Turbo II engine replaced by Turbo IV, which utilizes a variable-nozzle turbine to reduce turbo lag. Manual transmission has been reworked to provide less shift lever travel and easier use. Optional on base and ES models is a Mitsubishi-built V6 engine. Instrument panel is completely revised.

Model Description	Trade-in Value	Market Value
Category C		
2 Dr ES Hbk	1460	2395
2 Dr ES Turbo Hbk	1505	2465
2 Dr STD Hbk	1125	1845
Category F		
2 Dr Shelby Turbo Hbk	1780	2580

OPTIONS FOR DAYTONA

6 cyl 3.0 L Engine +85
Auto 3-Speed Transmission +65
Auto 4-Speed Transmission +75

Don't forget to refer to the Mileage Adjustment Table at the back of this book!

Model Description	Trade-in Value	Market Value	Model Description	Trade-in Value	Market Value

CS Performance Pkg +145
Air Conditioning +95
Power Windows +25

DYNASTY 1990

Driver airbag debuts. A new 3.3-liter V6 engine is available. New options include an automatic day/night mirror, and leather seating for LE models. Power windows can have a one-touch down feature for the driver's side, and bumpers are upgraded to withstand five-mph impacts. Outboard rear seat passengers are treated to three-point seatbelts.

Category C

4 Dr LE Sdn	1625	2665
4 Dr STD Sdn	1450	2380

OPTIONS FOR DYNASTY

6 cyl 3.0 L Engine[Std on LE] +85
Air Conditioning +95
Anti-Lock Brakes +75
Cruise Control +25
Power Door Locks +30
Power Windows +35

MONACO 1990

New model is virtually identical to Eagle Premier. LS and ES trim levels are available, with ES including four-wheel disc brakes, touring suspension and alloy wheels. An automatic is the only transmission choice.

Category C

4 Dr ES Sdn	1115	1830
4 Dr LE Sdn	1040	1705

OPTIONS FOR MONACO

Air Conditioning[Opt on LE] +95
Cruise Control +25
Power Door Locks +30
Power Drivers Seat +35
Power Windows +35

OMNI 1990

A driver airbag is added to this ancient econocar. Production finally ceased midyear.

Category E

4 Dr America Hbk	660	1270

OPTIONS FOR OMNI

Air Conditioning +100

RAM 50 PICKUP 1990

Sport trim becomes SE, while extended-cabs are now known as Sport Cabs. A V6 engine is newly standard on 4WD models.

Category G

2 Dr SE Std Cab SB	1595	2420
2 Dr STD Std Cab LB	1500	2275
2 Dr STD Std Cab SB	1415	2145

OPTIONS FOR RAM 50 PICKUP

6 cyl 3.0 L Engine +110
Auto 4-Speed Transmission +85
Air Conditioning +100
Power Steering[Std on LE, 4WD] +35
Power Windows +30

RAM PICKUP 1990

Finally, an extended-cab model is available in D150 and D250 series. D100 trucks dropped from the lineup.

RAM 150

Category H

2 Dr LE Ext Cab LB	3095	4300
2 Dr LE Ext Cab SB	3025	4200
2 Dr LE Std Cab LB	2695	3745
2 Dr LE 4WD Std Cab LB	3630	5040
2 Dr LE Std Cab SB	2610	3625
2 Dr LE 4WD Std Cab SB	3535	4910
2 Dr S Std Cab LB	2190	3040
2 Dr S 4WD Std Cab LB	3040	4225
2 Dr S Std Cab SB	2150	2985
2 Dr S 4WD Std Cab SB	2990	4150
2 Dr SE Std Cab LB	2560	3555
2 Dr SE 4WD Std Cab LB	3505	4870
2 Dr SE Std Cab SB	2475	3440
2 Dr SE 4WD Std Cab SB	3430	4765
2 Dr STD 4WD Ext Cab LB	3785	5255
2 Dr STD Std Cab LB	2405	3340
2 Dr STD 4WD Std Cab LB	3345	4645
2 Dr STD Std Cab SB	2360	3280
2 Dr STD 4WD Std Cab SB	3275	4550

RAM 250

Category H

2 Dr LE Std Cab LB	3055	4240
2 Dr LE 4WD Std Cab LB	3760	5220
2 Dr SE Std Cab LB	2870	3985
2 Dr SE 4WD Std Cab LB	3565	4950
2 Dr STD 4WD Ext Cab LB	3890	5400
2 Dr STD Std Cab LB	2745	3810
2 Dr STD 4WD Std Cab LB	3415	4740

RAM 350

Category H

2 Dr LE Std Cab LB	3750	5205
2 Dr SE Std Cab LB	3615	5020
2 Dr STD Std Cab LB	3440	4780

OPTIONS FOR RAM PICKUP

6 cyl 5.9 L Turbodsl Engine +395
8 cyl 5.2 L Engine +70
8 cyl 5.9 L Engine +65
Auto 3-Speed Transmission +75
Auto 4-Speed Transmission +105
Snow Plow Prep Pkg +140

Don't forget to refer to the Mileage Adjustment Table at the back of this book!

DODGE 90

Model Description	Trade-in Value	Market Value	Model Description	Trade-in Value	Market Value

Air Conditioning +100
Dual Rear Wheels +100
Limited Slip Diff +30

RAM VAN/WAGON 1990

Prospector trim dropped, as well as Value Wagon and Long Range Ram Van models.

RAM VAN

Category H

2 Dr 1500 Ram Van	1705	2370
2 Dr 1500 Ram Van Ext	1765	2450
2 Dr 2500 Ram Van	1985	2760
2 Dr 2500 Ram Van Ext	2165	3010
2 Dr 3500 Ram Van	2220	3080
2 Dr 3500 Ram Van Ext	2450	3400

RAM WAGON

Category H

2 Dr 1500 Ram Wagon	2020	2805
2 Dr 1500 LE Ram Wagon	2280	3165
2 Dr 2500 Ram Wagon	2310	3210
2 Dr 2500 Ram Wagon Ext	2490	3460
2 Dr 2500 LE Ram Wagon	2585	3590
2 Dr 2500 LE Ram Wagon Ext	2760	3835
2 Dr 3500 Ram Wagon	2500	3470
2 Dr 3500 Ram Wagon Ext	2680	3720
2 Dr 3500 LE Ram Wagon Ext	2910	4040

OPTIONS FOR RAM VAN/WAGON
8 cyl 5.2 L Engine[Std on B350] +70
8 cyl 5.9 L Engine +65
Auto 3-Speed Transmission[Opt on B150 ,B250] +40
Auto 4-Speed Transmission[Std on B350] +50
Travel Seating Pkg +150
Air Conditioning +100
Dual Air Conditioning +160

RAMCHARGER 1990

Base 100-series model is replaced by a 150-series S trim level. Prospector trim package dropped.

Category H

2 Dr LE 4WD Utility	3335	4630
2 Dr S 4WD Utility	2605	3615
2 Dr STD 4WD Utility	2940	4085

OPTIONS FOR RAMCHARGER
8 cyl 5.9 L Engine +65
Auto 4-Speed Transmission[Opt on 4WD] +105
Snow Plow Pkg Ramcharger +120
Air Conditioning +100
Camper/Towing Package +40

SHADOW 1990

A driver airbag is installed. An optional Turbo IV engine with variable-nozzle turbine pumps 174 horsepower to Shadow ES's front axle. Manual transmissions have been redesigned.

RATINGS (SCALE OF 1-10)

Overall	Safety	Reliability	Performance	Comfort	Value
6.4	5.5	5.8	7.4	6.8	6.7

Category E

2 Dr ES Hbk	985	1890
2 Dr ES Turbo Hbk	1005	1930
4 Dr ES Hbk	1015	1950
4 Dr ES Turbo Hbk	1070	2055
2 Dr STD Hbk	840	1620
2 Dr STD Turbo Hbk	885	1700
4 Dr STD Hbk	910	1750
4 Dr STD Turbo Hbk	960	1845

OPTIONS FOR SHADOW
Auto 3-Speed Transmission +65
Competition Pkg +120
Air Conditioning +100
Cruise Control +25
Power Door Locks +30
Power Windows +30

SPIRIT 1990

Base models can be equipped with V6 power. A driver airbag is newly standard.* ES model gets four-wheel disc brakes and more sound insulation.

RATINGS (SCALE OF 1-10)

Overall	Safety	Reliability	Performance	Comfort	Value
6.9	5.5	6.6	6.8	7.4	8.1

Category C

4 Dr ES Sdn	1445	2370
4 Dr ES Turbo Sdn	1490	2440
4 Dr LE Sdn	1325	2170
4 Dr LE Turbo Sdn	1375	2250
4 Dr STD Sdn	1215	1990
4 Dr STD Turbo Sdn	1280	2100

OPTIONS FOR SPIRIT
6 cyl 3.0 L Engine[Std on ES] +85
Auto 3-Speed Transmission +70
Auto 4-Speed Transmission +75
Air Conditioning +95
Cruise Control[Opt on STD] +25
Power Door Locks +30
Power Drivers Seat +35
Power Windows +35

EAGLE 98-97

Model Description	Trade-in Value	Market Value	Model Description	Trade-in Value	Market Value

EAGLE · USA

1993 Eagle Talon

1998 EAGLE

TALON 1998

New silver exterior badging and a new black and gray interior mark the Eagle in its final year of production. A new four-speaker CD/cassette player is now optional on the ESi, and all Talons benefit from Chrysler's next generation depowered airbags.

RATINGS (SCALE OF 1-10)

Overall	Safety	Reliability	Performance	Comfort	Value
6.7	6.8	7.6	8.4	6.6	4.2

Category F

	Trade-in	Market
2 Dr ESi Hbk	8700	10610
2 Dr STD Hbk	8300	10120
2 Dr TSi Turbo Hbk	11345	13835
2 Dr TSi Turbo 4WD Hbk	12340	15050

OPTIONS FOR TALON
Auto 4-Speed Transmission +505
AM/FM Compact Disc Player +290
Air Conditioning +505
Aluminum/Alloy Wheels[Opt on ESi] +185
Anti-Lock Brakes +415
Cruise Control[Std on 4WD] +125
Infinity Sound System +390
Keyless Entry System +110
Leather Seats +395
Power Door Locks[Std on 4WD] +120
Power Drivers Seat +150
Power Mirrors[Opt on ESi] +75
Power Sunroof +410
Power Windows[Std on 4WD] +135
Rear Window Defroster[Std on TSi] +100

1997 EAGLE

TALON 1997

Eagle's sporty Talon sees a host of changes as Chrysler Corp. seeks to rescue this endangered species. New front and rear fascias, bodyside cladding, bright new paint colors and "sparkle" wheels and wheel covers are guaranteed to attract attention to this overshadowed model. A bargain-basement Talon is introduced with minimal standard equipment to serve as a value leader for the model.

RATINGS (SCALE OF 1-10)

Overall	Safety	Reliability	Performance	Comfort	Value
6.8	6.8	6.9	8.4	6.6	5.1

Category F

	Trade-in	Market
2 Dr ESi Hbk	7965	9715
2 Dr STD Hbk	7590	9255
2 Dr TSi Turbo Hbk	9530	11620
2 Dr TSi Turbo 4WD Hbk	10415	12700

OPTIONS FOR TALON
Auto 4-Speed Transmission +400
Air Conditioning +415
Aluminum/Alloy Wheels[Opt on ESi] +150
Anti-Lock Brakes +335
Compact Disc W/fm/tape +250
Cruise Control[Std on 4WD] +105
Keyless Entry System +90
Leather Seats +325
Limited Slip Diff +170
Power Door Locks[Std on 4WD] +100
Power Drivers Seat +120
Power Sunroof +335
Power Windows[Std on 4WD] +110
Premium Sound System +185

VISION 1997

The 3.5-liter engine formerly exclusive to the TSi is now available on the ESi. Automatic transmission refinements are intended to improve shifting. Eagle Vision ESis gets an improved stereo. A new color, Deep Amethyst Pearl, is now available.

RATINGS (SCALE OF 1-10)

Overall	Safety	Reliability	Performance	Comfort	Value
8.1	7.2	7.8	8.4	8.5	8.8

Category B

	Trade-in	Market
4 Dr ESi Sdn	8060	9830
4 Dr TSi Sdn	9535	11625

OPTIONS FOR VISION
Anti-Lock Brakes[Opt on ESi] +340
Compact Disc W/fm/tape +190
Keyless Entry System[Opt on ESi] +85
Leather Seats +335

EAGLE 97-95

Model Description	Trade-in Value	Market Value	Model Description	Trade-in Value	Market Value

Lighted Entry System[Opt on ESi] +50
Power Drivers Seat +155
Power Moonroof +485
Trip Computer[Opt on ESi] +195

Keyless Entry System[Opt on ESi] +70
Leather Seats +275
Power Drivers Seat[Opt on ESi] +125
Power Moonroof +395
Premium Sound System +160

1996 EAGLE

TALON   1996

Based on Mitsubishi mechanicals, Talon receives minor upgrades for 1996, including revised sound systems, a panic alarm, a HomeLink transmitter, and two new colors. ESi trim level gets standard 16-inch wheels.

RATINGS (SCALE OF 1-10)

Overall	Safety	Reliability	Performance	Comfort	Value
6.7	6.8	6.8	8.4	6.6	5

Category F
2 Dr ESi Hbk	6745	8535
2 Dr STD Hbk	6375	8070
2 Dr TSi Turbo Hbk	7545	9550
2 Dr TSi Turbo 4WD Hbk	8380	10610

OPTIONS FOR TALON
Auto 4-Speed Transmission +315
Air Conditioning +340
Aluminum/Alloy Wheels +125
Anti-Lock Brakes +275
Compact Disc W/fm/tape +205
Cruise Control[Std on 4WD] +85
Leather Seats +265
Power Door Locks[Std on 4WD] +80
Power Drivers Seat +100
Power Sunroof +275
Power Windows[Std on 4WD] +90

VISION   1996

An automanual transmission called AutoStick gives the 1996 Vision a feature to distinguish it as Chrysler's premier sport sedan. Interiors have been quieted down, and the ESi gets standard 16-inch wheels. Headlight illumination has been improved, new colors and seat fabrics are on board, and improved sound systems debut; all in the hope that some interest can be sparked in this slow-selling Eagle.

RATINGS (SCALE OF 1-10)

Overall	Safety	Reliability	Performance	Comfort	Value
8	7.2	7.4	8.4	8.5	8.6

Category B
4 Dr ESi Sdn	7280	9100
4 Dr TSi Sdn	7900	9870

OPTIONS FOR VISION
Anti-Lock Brakes[Opt on ESi] +280
Child Seat (1) +40
Compact Disc W/fm/tape +155

1995 EAGLE

SUMMIT   1995

Dual airbags for the slow-selling Eagle Summit are the only change for 1995.

RATINGS (SCALE OF 1-10)

Overall	Safety	Reliability	Performance	Comfort	Value
6.7	6.5	7.5	8.2	7	4.3

Category E
2 Dr DL Cpe	3385	4635
4 Dr DL Wgn	4640	6355
2 Dr ESi Cpe	3795	5200
4 Dr ESi Sdn	4035	5530
4 Dr LX Sdn	3925	5380
4 Dr LX Wgn	5015	6870

OPTIONS FOR SUMMIT
4 cyl 1.8 L Engine[Opt on Wgn] +215
4 cyl 2.4 L Engine[Opt on DL] +60
Auto 3-Speed Transmission +175
Auto 4-Speed Transmission +235
AM/FM Stereo Tape +100
Air Conditioning +270
Anti-Lock Brakes +225
Cruise Control +75
Keyless Entry System +50
Luggage Rack +45
Power Door Locks[Std on LX] +80
Power Steering[Opt on Cpe] +85
Power Windows +85
Tilt Steering Wheel[Opt on ESi] +50
Two-Tone Paint[Std on LX] +50

TALON   1995

The Talon is redesigned for 1995. The new model features gorgeous curves and more power. Base engine creeps up to 140 horsepower, the turbo to 210 horsepower. Dual airbags replace the antiquated motorized seatbelts on the previous edition, and the Talon now meets 1997 federal side-impact standards.

RATINGS (SCALE OF 1-10)

Overall	Safety	Reliability	Performance	Comfort	Value
6.4	7.5	5.7	8.4	6.6	3.8

Category F
2 Dr ESi Hbk	5445	6980
2 Dr TSi Turbo Hbk	6525	8365
2 Dr TSi Turbo 4WD Hbk	6900	8845

Don't forget to refer to the Mileage Adjustment Table at the back of this book!

Model Description	Trade-in Value	Market Value	Model Description	Trade-in Value	Market Value

OPTIONS FOR TALON

Auto 4-Speed Transmission +270
Air Conditioning +275
Anti-Lock Brakes +225
Compact Disc W/fm/tape +165
Cruise Control[Std on 4WD] +70
Keyless Entry System +60
Leather Seats +215
Power Door Locks[Std on 4WD] +65
Power Drivers Seat +80
Power Sunroof +225
Power Windows[Std on 4WD] +75

VISION   1995

No changes to the Vision.

RATINGS (SCALE OF 1-10)

Overall	Safety	Reliability	Performance	Comfort	Value
8.1	7.9	7	8.4	8.5	8.5

Category B

4 Dr ESi Sdn	5680	7280
4 Dr TSi Sdn	6530	8370

OPTIONS FOR VISION

6 cyl 3.5 L Engine[Opt on ESi] +240
AM/FM Compact Disc Player +110
Anti-Lock Brakes[Opt on ESi] +230
Child Seat (1)[Opt on TSi] +35
Climate Control for AC[Opt on ESi] +55
Keyless Entry System[Opt on ESi] +55
Leather Seats +225
Power Drivers Seat[Opt on ESi] +105
Power Moonroof +325
Power Passenger Seat +110
Traction Control System +60

1994 EAGLE

SUMMIT   1994

A driver airbag is added to the standard equipment list of the Eagle Summit. CFC-free air conditioning is now standard on all models equipped with air conditioning. Power steering is standard on all sedan models.

RATINGS (SCALE OF 1-10)

Overall	Safety	Reliability	Performance	Comfort	Value
N/A	N/A	7.2	8.2	7	4.7

Category E

2 Dr DL Cpe	2505	3580
4 Dr DL Wgn	3770	5385
2 Dr ES Cpe	2785	3975
4 Dr ES Sdn	2975	4250
2 Dr ESi Cpe	2955	4220
4 Dr ESi Sdn	3150	4500
4 Dr LX Sdn	3045	4350
4 Dr LX Wgn	4110	5870

OPTIONS FOR SUMMIT

4 cyl 2.4 L Engine[Opt on DL] +50
Auto 3-Speed Transmission +140
Auto 4-Speed Transmission +190
AM/FM Stereo Tape +80
Air Conditioning +220
Anti-Lock Brakes +180
Cruise Control +60
Keyless Entry System +45
Luggage Rack +35
Power Door Locks[Std on LX] +65
Power Steering[Opt on ES Cpe] +70
Power Windows +70
Tilt Steering Wheel[Opt on ES, ESi] +40

TALON   1994

No changes for the Talon.

RATINGS (SCALE OF 1-10)

Overall	Safety	Reliability	Performance	Comfort	Value
N/A	N/A	8	8.4	6.8	3.9

Category F

2 Dr DL Hbk	3565	4690
2 Dr ES Hbk	4095	5385
2 Dr TSi Turbo Hbk	4900	6450
2 Dr TSi Turbo 4WD Hbk	5250	6910

OPTIONS FOR TALON

Auto 4-Speed Transmission +215
Air Conditioning +225
Aluminum/Alloy Wheels[Std on 4WD] +85
Anti-Lock Brakes +185
Compact Disc W/fm/tape +135
Cruise Control +55
Leather Seats +175
Power Door Locks +55
Power Steering[Opt on DL] +95
Power Windows +60
Premium Sound System +100
Sunroof +105

VISION   1994

ESi models restyled to resemble their TSi stablemates by adding body cladding and a similar front fascia. The ESi's engine gains an increase in horsepower for 1994 as well. A flexible fuel version of the Vision is released in all states but California.

RATINGS (SCALE OF 1-10)

Overall	Safety	Reliability	Performance	Comfort	Value
8	7.9	6.7	8.4	8.5	8.4

Category B

4 Dr ESi Sdn	4695	6175
4 Dr TSi Sdn	5365	7060

EAGLE 94-93

Model Description	Trade-in Value	Market Value	Model Description	Trade-in Value	Market Value

OPTIONS FOR VISION

AM/FM Compact Disc Player +90
Child Seat (1) +25
Climate Control for AC[Opt on ESi] +45
Infinity Sound System +170
Leather Seats +185
Lighted Entry System +25
Overhead Console[Opt on ESi] +100
Power Drivers Seat[Opt on ESi] +85
Power Passenger Seat +90
Traction Control System +50

1993 EAGLE

SUMMIT   1993

The Eagle Summit is redesigned and in the process loses its hatchback. Offered as a coupe or sedan, the new Summit is longer than the one it replaces, which translates into more interior room for passengers. The Summit is now available as a base DL or upscale ES. Fortunately, the 113-horsepower engine can be had on both models. Antilock brakes are a thoughtful option on the ES models and wagons. The minivan/station wagon hybrid is positioned to take advantage of those consumers who want the convenience of a minivan and the driveability of a car. There is seating for five in the Summit Wagon, which is available as a DL, LX or all-wheel-drive model.

RATINGS (SCALE OF 1-10)

Overall	Safety	Reliability	Performance	Comfort	Value
N/A	N/A	5.9	8.2	7	6.6

Category E
2 Dr DL Cpe	1925	2875
4 Dr DL Sdn	2030	3030
4 Dr DL Wgn	2850	4250
2 Dr ES Cpe	2130	3180
4 Dr ES Sdn	2220	3315
4 Dr LX Wgn	3245	4840

OPTIONS FOR SUMMIT

4 cyl 1.8 L Engine[Std on ES,Wgn] +85
4 cyl 2.4 L Engine[Opt on DL Wgn] +40
Auto 3-Speed Transmission +115
Auto 4-Speed Transmission +155
AM/FM Stereo Tape +65
Air Conditioning +180
Aluminum/Alloy Wheels +75
Anti-Lock Brakes +150
Cruise Control +50
Luggage Rack +30
Power Door Locks +55
Power Steering[Opt on ES,Sdn] +55
Power Windows +60
Tilt Steering Wheel[Opt on ES] +35

TALON   1993

The Talon gets a new base model to attract bargain shoppers. The new Talon DL comes standard with a disappointing 92-horsepower engine. Geez, that's just a little more than the base Summit. The former base model is renamed the ES.

RATINGS (SCALE OF 1-10)

Overall	Safety	Reliability	Performance	Comfort	Value
N/A	N/A	8.1	8.4	6.8	4.4

Category F
2 Dr DL Hbk	2975	3965
2 Dr ES Hbk	3400	4530
2 Dr TSi Turbo Hbk	4040	5385
2 Dr TSi Turbo 4WD Hbk	4390	5855

OPTIONS FOR TALON

Auto 4-Speed Transmission +175
Air Conditioning +185
Aluminum/Alloy Wheels[Std on 4WD] +70
Anti-Lock Brakes +150
Compact Disc W/fm/tape +110
Cruise Control +45
Leather Seats +145
Power Door Locks +45
Power Steering[Opt on DL] +75
Power Windows +50
Premium Sound System +80
Sunroof +85

VISION   1993

Eagle receives its version of the Chrysler LH sedan in the form of the Vision. Available as an ESi or TSi, the Vision features cab-forward styling, dual airbags, V6 power, and available antilock brakes. TSi models are the sportier of the two, it comes equipped with a touring suspension, standard antilock brakes, a 214-horsepower engine, and sixteen-inch wheels.

RATINGS (SCALE OF 1-10)

Overall	Safety	Reliability	Performance	Comfort	Value
7.8	7.8	6.4	8.4	8.5	7.8

Category B
4 Dr ESi Sdn	3740	5120
4 Dr TSi Sdn	4185	5735

OPTIONS FOR VISION

AM/FM Compact Disc Player +70
Anti-Lock Brakes[Opt on ESi] +155
Climate Control for AC[Opt on ESi] +40
Cruise Control[Opt on ESi] +50
Dual Power Seats +85
Keyless Entry System +40
Leather Seats +150
Power Door Locks[Opt on ESi] +55

Don't forget to refer to the Mileage Adjustment Table at the back of this book!

EAGLE 93-91

Model Description	Trade-in Value	Market Value	Model Description	Trade-in Value	Market Value

Power Windows +65
Premium Sound System +90
Traction Control System +40

1992 EAGLE

PREMIER 1992

Exterior tweaks to the Premier include a new grille, tail lights and new paint.
Category C

4 Dr ES Sdn	1815	2630
4 Dr ES Limited Sdn	2340	3390
4 Dr LX Sdn	1635	2370

OPTIONS FOR PREMIER
Anti-Lock Brakes[Opt on ES,LX] +110
Cruise Control[Opt on LX] +40
Leather Seats[Opt on ES] +110
Power Door Locks[Opt on LX] +45
Power Drivers Seat[Opt on ES,LX] +55
Power Windows[Opt on ES,LX] +55

SUMMIT 1992

Cloth seats are now optional on base models for those who don't like the adhesive quality imparted by vinyl seats in the summer.
Category E

4 Dr DL Wgn	1890	2955
2 Dr ES Hbk	1555	2430
4 Dr ES Sdn	1605	2510
4 Dr LX Wgn	2070	3235
2 Dr STD Hbk	1400	2190
4 Dr STD Sdn	1490	2330
4 Dr STD 4WD Wgn	2155	3370

OPTIONS FOR SUMMIT
4 cyl 2.4 L Engine +35
Auto 3-Speed Transmission +100
Auto 4-Speed Transmission +130
Air Conditioning +145
Anti-Lock Brakes +120
Cruise Control +40
Power Door Locks +45
Power Windows +50

TALON 1992

The Talon is redesigned for 1992, getting a new grille, headlights, taillights and sheetmetal.

RATINGS (SCALE OF 1-10)

Overall	Safety	Reliability	Performance	Comfort	Value
N/A	N/A	7.2	8.4	6.8	3.3

Category F

2 Dr STD Hbk	2665	3650
2 Dr TSi Turbo Hbk	3230	4425
2 Dr TSi Turbo 4WD Hbk	3710	5080

OPTIONS FOR TALON
Auto 4-Speed Transmission +145
Air Conditioning +150
Anti-Lock Brakes +125
Cruise Control +40
Leather Seats +120
Power Door Locks +35
Power Windows +40
Sunroof +70

1991 EAGLE

PREMIER 1991

No changes for the Premier.
Category C

4 Dr ES Sdn	1530	2350
4 Dr ES Limited Sdn	1985	3050
4 Dr LX Sdn	1300	2000

OPTIONS FOR PREMIER
Leather Seats[Opt on ES] +90
Power Door Locks[Opt on LX] +35
Power Drivers Seat[Opt on ES,LX] +45
Power Windows[Opt on ES,LX] +45

SUMMIT 1991

No changes to the Summit.
Category E

2 Dr ES Hbk	1190	2015
4 Dr ES Sdn	1240	2100
2 Dr STD Hbk	1065	1805
4 Dr STD Sdn	1140	1930

OPTIONS FOR SUMMIT
Auto 3-Speed Transmission +80
Auto 4-Speed Transmission +100
Air Conditioning +120
Power Door Locks +35
Power Windows +40

TALON 1991

Antilock brakes are now available on the Talon.

RATINGS (SCALE OF 1-10)

Overall	Safety	Reliability	Performance	Comfort	Value
N/A	N/A	6.7	8.4	6.8	4.2

Category F

2 Dr STD Hbk	2340	3295
2 Dr TSi Turbo Hbk	2765	3895
2 Dr TSi Turbo 4WD Hbk	3165	4455

OPTIONS FOR TALON
Auto 4-Speed Transmission +115
Air Conditioning +125
Anti-Lock Brakes +100
Cruise Control +30
Leather Seats +95

Don't forget to refer to the Mileage Adjustment Table at the back of this book!

Model Description	Trade-in Value	Market Value
Power Door Locks +30		
Power Windows +35		
Sunroof +60		

1990 EAGLE

PREMIER 1990

The Premier's enthusiast-oriented ES model is introduced in 1990. Noticeably missing on this alleged sports sedan is a manual transmission. A power sunroof and CD player are added to the Premier's option list.

Category C

Model	Trade-in	Market
4 Dr ES Sdn	1265	2070
4 Dr ES Limited Sdn	1590	2610
4 Dr LX Sdn	1090	1785

OPTIONS FOR PREMIER

Air Conditioning[Opt on LX] +95
Leather Seats[Opt on ES] +75
Power Door Locks[Opt on ES,LX] +30
Power Drivers Seat[Opt on ES,LX] +35
Power Windows[Opt on ES,LX] +35

SUMMIT 1990

An ES sport model is added to the Summit lineup, as is a truly inexpensive base model. The LX model's three-speed automatic is replaced by a four-speed this year. All automatics get a shift-lock feature that prevents the car from being shifted out of "Park" unless the brake pedal is fully depressed.

Category E

Model	Trade-in	Market
4 Dr DL Sdn	810	1555
4 Dr ES Sdn	880	1695

Model Description	Trade-in Value	Market Value
4 Dr LX Sdn	1090	2100
4 Dr LX DOHC Sdn	1230	2365
4 Dr STD Sdn	690	1325

OPTIONS FOR SUMMIT

Auto 3-Speed Transmission +60
Auto 4-Speed Transmission +85
Air Conditioning +100
Power Door Locks +30
Power Windows +30

TALON 1990

A cool new sports coupe is offered through Eagle: it's called the Talon. Available with a turbo or normally aspirated engine, this little rocket redefines the inexpensive sports coupe. Available all-wheel drive and 190-horsepower distinguish the Talon from nearly everything else in this segment.

RATINGS (SCALE OF 1-10)

Overall	Safety	Reliability	Performance	Comfort	Value
N/A	N/A	4.9	8.4	6.8	5.6

Category F

Model	Trade-in	Market
2 Dr STD Hbk	1945	2820
2 Dr TSi Turbo Hbk	2360	3420
2 Dr TSi Turbo 4WD Hbk	2775	4020

OPTIONS FOR TALON

Auto 4-Speed Transmission +85
Air Conditioning +100
Cruise Control +25
Leather Seats +80
Power Windows +25

FORD 99

Model Description	Trade-in Value	Market Value	Model Description	Trade-in Value	Market Value

FORD USA

1997 Ford F-150

1999 FORD

CLUB WAGON/ECONOLINE 1999

RATINGS (SCALE OF 1-10)

Overall	Safety	Reliability	Performance	Comfort	Value
N/A	N/A	N/A	6.6	7.4	N/A

E-150
Category H

	Trade-in	Market
2 Dr STD Econoline	13460	15835

E-150 WAGON
Category H

	Trade-in	Market
2 Dr Chateau Club Wagon	17475	20560
2 Dr XL Pass. Van	15080	17740
2 Dr XLT Pass. Van	15445	18170

E-250
Category H

	Trade-in	Market
2 Dr STD Cargo Van	13225	15560
2 Dr STD Cargo Van Ext	14065	16545

E-350 SUPER DUTY
Category H

	Trade-in	Market
2 Dr STD Cargo Van	14690	17285
2 Dr STD Cargo Van Ext	14905	17540

F-350 SUPER DUTY WAGON
Category H

	Trade-in	Market
2 Dr E-350 Chateau Pass. Van	17860	21010
2 Dr XL Pass. Van	15275	17970
2 Dr XL Pass. Van Ext	15640	18400
2 Dr XLT Pass. Van	16155	19005
2 Dr XLT Pass. Van Ext	16595	19525

OPTIONS FOR CLUB WAGON/ECONOLINE
10 cyl 6.8 L Engine +500
8 cyl 4.6 L Engine +550
8 cyl 5.4 L Engine[Std on E-350] +720
8 cyl 7.3 L Turbodsl Engine +3070
AM/FM Stereo Tape +160
Air Conditioning[Std on XL, XLT, Chateau] +600
Aluminum/Alloy Wheels[Opt on XLT] +235
Anti-Lock Brakes[Std on XL, XLT, Chateau] +370
Cruise Control +140
Dual Air Conditioning +990
Keyless Entry System +130
Power Door Locks[Std on Chateau, XLT] +140
Power Driver's Seat +210
Power Mirrors +75
Power Windows[Std on Chateau, XLT] +140
Privacy Glass +125
Tilt Steering Wheel +135

CONTOUR 1999

All-speed traction control is a new option on V6 models equipped with ABS. Tropic Green and Medium Steel Blue replace Dark Green Satin, Light Denim Blue and Pacific Green on the color chart. The integrated child seat is dropped from the optional equipment list, as are the 15-inch wheel covers. The instrument panel receives a mild revision and the 10-way power seats become 6-way power seats thanks to the deletion of the power lumbar and recline adjustments. Ford increases rear seat room in the Contour for the third year in a row, desperately trying to shed this sedan's cramped car image.

RATINGS (SCALE OF 1-10)

Overall	Safety	Reliability	Performance	Comfort	Value
N/A	6.9	7.5	8.2	7.9	N/A

Category C

	Trade-in	Market
4 Dr LX Sdn	7615	9175
4 Dr SE Sdn	8665	10440
4 Dr SVT Sdn	13755	16575

OPTIONS FOR CONTOUR
6 cyl 2.5 L Engine[Opt on SE] +500
Auto 4-Speed Transmission +600
AM/FM Compact Disc Player +270
AM/FM Stereo Tape[Opt on LX] +120
Aluminum/Alloy Wheels[Std on SVT] +225
Anti-Lock Brakes[Std on SVT] +450
Cruise Control[Opt on LX] +155
Keyless Entry System[Std on SVT] +140
Leather Seats[Opt on SE] +450
Power Door Locks[Opt on LX] +185
Power Driver's Seat[Std on SVT] +220
Power Moonroof +510
Power Windows[Opt on LX] +230
Rear Window Defroster[Opt on LX] +125
Traction Control System[Opt on SE] +180

Don't forget to refer to the Mileage Adjustment Table at the back of this book!

Model Description	Trade-in Value	Market Value	Model Description	Trade-in Value	Market Value

CROWN VICTORIA 1999

Antilock brakes are now standard on Base and LX models. A stereo with cassette player is also newly standard on the Base model. Deep Wedgewood Blue, Light Blue and Harvest Gold are new exterior colors. Medium Wedgewood Blue, Light Denim Blue and Light Prairie Tan are no longer available.

RATINGS (SCALE OF 1-10)

Overall	Safety	Reliability	Performance	Comfort	Value
N/A	8.1	8.7	7.7	8.2	N/A

Category B

4 Dr LX Sdn	14040	16915
4 Dr STD Sdn	13450	16205

OPTIONS FOR CROWN VICTORIA

AM/FM Compact Disc Player +245
Aluminum/Alloy Wheels +245
Climate Control for AC +125
Dual Power Seats +280
Keyless Entry System[Std on LX] +130
Leather Seats +505
Power Driver's Seat[Std on LX] +230
Traction Control System +130

ESCORT 1999

Ford's entry-level car gets new colors, new interior fabrics, and revised options. An AM/FM stereo with cassette is now standard on the Escort SE. An interior trunk release is now standard on all models. The sedans and wagon get all-door remote keyless entry added to their standard equipment lists. An integrated child seat is no longer available.

RATINGS (SCALE OF 1-10)

Overall	Safety	Reliability	Performance	Comfort	Value
N/A	6.1	8.6	7.2	7.3	N/A

Category E

4 Dr LX Sdn	7045	8590
4 Dr SE Sdn	7655	9335
4 Dr SE Wgn	7855	9580
2 Dr ZX2 Cool Cpe	7600	9270
2 Dr ZX2 Hot Cpe	8320	10145

OPTIONS FOR ESCORT

Auto 4-Speed Transmission +600
AM/FM Stereo Tape[Std on SE,ZX2 Hot] +225
Air Conditioning[Std on SE,ZX2 Hot] +605
Aluminum/Alloy Wheels +245
Anti-Lock Brakes +500
Cruise Control +165
Fog Lights +110
Keyless Entry System[Std on SE,ZX2 Hot] +115
Power Door Locks +180
Power Moonroof +425
Power Windows +195

Rear Window Defroster[Std on SE,ZX2 Hot] +120
Tilt Steering Wheel +110

EXPEDITION 1999

Power output is improved for both Triton V8 engines on Ford's full-size sport-ute. Package content is added for both XLT and Eddie Bauer trim levels. Power adjustable accelerator and brake pedals have been added to the option list to make it easier for the vertically challenged to reach the stop and go pedals. An updated Command Trac four-wheel drive system allows automatic four-wheel drive operation when required. Spruce Green, Harvest Gold, Tropic Green and Deep Wedgewood Blue replace Light Prairie Tan, Vermont Green, Light Denim Blue and Pacific Green on the color chart.

RATINGS (SCALE OF 1-10)

Overall	Safety	Reliability	Performance	Comfort	Value
N/A	8.3	8.4	6.8	8.1	N/A

Category H

4 Dr Eddie Bauer Wgn	23650	27825
4 Dr Eddie Bauer 4WD Wgn	24670	29025
4 Dr XLT Wgn	19110	22485
4 Dr XLT 4WD Wgn	21395	25170

OPTIONS FOR EXPEDITION

8 cyl 5.4 L Engine[Opt on XLT,2WD] +720
Comfort/Convenience Group +1420
Aluminum/Alloy Wheels[Opt on XLT] +235
Auto Load Leveling +520
Camper/Towing Package +255
Compact Disc Changer +320
Dual Air Conditioning[Opt on XLT] +990
Fog Lights[Opt on XLT] +90
Heated Front Seats +250
Heated Power Mirrors +75
Leather Seats[Opt on XLT] +730
Privacy Glass[Opt on XLT] +125
Running Boards[Opt on XLT] +255
Third Seat[Opt on XLT] +470

EXPLORER 1999

The Explorer gets exterior revisions including new fog lamps, rocker panel moldings, wheel moldings, running boards and wheels. Harvest Gold, Chestnut, Deep Wedgewood, Spruce Green and Tropic Green replaces Light Prairie Tan, Desert Violet, Light Denim Blue, Pacific Green and Evergreen Frost on the color chart. New options include a reverse sensing system and rear load leveling. Side impact airbags are also newly available.

RATINGS (SCALE OF 1-10)

Overall	Safety	Reliability	Performance	Comfort	Value
N/A	7.8	8.8	7.8	7.3	N/A

Model Description	Trade-in Value	Market Value	Model Description	Trade-in Value	Market Value
Category G			2 Dr Lariat 4WD Std Cab SB	18205	21420
4 Dr Eddie Bauer Wgn	17610	20965	2 Dr Lariat Std Cab Stepside SB		
4 Dr Eddie Bauer 4WD Wgn	18530	22060		17165	20195
4 Dr Limited Wgn	18225	21695	2 Dr Lariat 4WD Std Cab Stepside SB		
4 Dr Limited 4WD Wgn	19645	23385		18765	22075
2 Dr Sport Utility	14235	16945	4 Dr Work Ext Cab LB	11450	13470
2 Dr Sport 4WD Utility	15205	18100	4 Dr Work 4WD Ext Cab LB	14360	16895
4 Dr XL Wgn	14790	17605	4 Dr Work Ext Cab SB	11375	13380
4 Dr XL 4WD Wgn	15195	18090	4 Dr Work 4WD Ext Cab SB	14285	16805
4 Dr XLS Wgn	15405	18340	2 Dr Work Std Cab LB	10090	11870
4 Dr XLS 4WD Wgn	16195	19280	2 Dr Work 4WD Std Cab LB	11410	13425
4 Dr XLT Wgn	16995	20235	2 Dr Work Std Cab SB	10025	11795
4 Dr XLT 4WD Wgn	18100	21545	2 Dr Work 4WD Std Cab SB	11395	13405
			4 Dr XL Ext Cab LB	13110	15425
			4 Dr XL 4WD Ext Cab LB	15430	18150
			4 Dr XL Ext Cab SB	13040	15340
			4 Dr XL 4WD Ext Cab SB	15350	18060
			4 Dr XL Ext Cab Stepside SB	13530	15915
			4 Dr XL 4WD Ext Cab Stepside SB		
				15850	18645
			2 Dr XL Std Cab LB	11480	13505
			2 Dr XL 4WD Std Cab LB	13455	15830
			2 Dr XL Std Cab SB	11420	13435
			2 Dr XL 4WD Std Cab SB	13365	15725
			2 Dr XL Std Cab Stepside SB	11490	13520
			2 Dr XL 4WD Std Cab Stepside SB		
				13725	16145
			4 Dr XLT Ext Cab LB	15320	18025
			4 Dr XLT 4WD Ext Cab LB	17495	20585
			4 Dr XLT Ext Cab SB	15245	17935
			4 Dr XLT 4WD Ext Cab SB	17325	20385
			4 Dr XLT Ext Cab Stepside SB	15740	18515
			4 Dr XLT 4WD Ext Cab Stepside SB		
				17835	20980
			2 Dr XLT Std Cab LB	13795	16230
			2 Dr XLT 4WD Std Cab LB	15355	18065
			2 Dr XLT Std Cab SB	13730	16155
			2 Dr XLT 4WD Std Cab SB	15260	17955
			2 Dr XLT Std Cab Stepside SB	14265	16785
			2 Dr XLT 4WD Std Cab Stepside SB		
				15805	18595

OPTIONS FOR EXPLORER

6 cyl 4.0 L SOHC Engine[Opt on Sport,XL,XLS,XLT] +400
8 cyl 5.0 L Engine +400
Auto 5-Speed Transmission[Opt on Sport,XL,XLS] +785
Sport Group +585
AM/FM Compact Disc Player[Opt on Sport,XL] +245
Aluminum/Alloy Wheels[Opt on XL] +245
Compact Disc Changer +385
Compact Disc W/fm/tape[Opt on Sport,XL,XLS,XLT] +355
Cruise Control[Opt on Sport,XL,XLS] +155
Fog Lights[Opt on Sport] +105
Keyless Entry System[Opt on Sport,XL,XLS] +150
Leather Seats[Std on Eddie Bauer,Limited] +575
Luggage Rack[Opt on XL] +115
Power Door Locks[Opt on XL] +170
Power Driver's Seat[Opt on Sport, XLT] +210
Power Mirrors[Opt on XL] +100
Power Moonroof +645
Power Windows[Opt on XL] +175
Privacy Glass[Opt on XL,XLS] +195
Running Boards[Std on Eddie Bauer,Limited] +285
Tilt Steering Wheel[Opt on XL,XLS] +130

F-SERIES PICKUP   1999

RATINGS (SCALE OF 1-10)

Overall	Safety	Reliability	Performance	Comfort	Value
N/A	N/A	N/A	6.6	7.8	N/A

F-150

Model Description	Trade-in Value	Market Value
Category H		
4 Dr Lariat Ext Cab LB	17440	20520
4 Dr Lariat 4WD Ext Cab LB	19790	23285
4 Dr Lariat Ext Cab SB	17360	20425
4 Dr Lariat 4WD Ext Cab SB	19710	23190
4 Dr Lariat Ext Cab Stepside SB		
	17855	21005
4 Dr Lariat 4WD Ext Cab Stepside SB		
	20140	23695
2 Dr Lariat Std Cab LB	16695	19640
2 Dr Lariat 4WD Std Cab LB	18315	21545
2 Dr Lariat Std Cab SB	16640	19575

F-150 SVT

Model Description	Trade-in Value	Market Value
Category H		
2 Dr Lightning Std Cab Stepside SB		
	22040	25930

F-250

Model Description	Trade-in Value	Market Value
Category H		
4 Dr Lariat Ext Cab SB	19055	22415
4 Dr Lariat 4WD Ext Cab SB	20655	24300
2 Dr Lariat Std Cab LB	17975	21145
2 Dr Lariat 4WD Std Cab LB	19820	23320

Model Description	Trade-in Value	Market Value	Model Description	Trade-in Value	Market Value
4 Dr Work Ext Cab SB	14650	17235	4 Dr Lariat 4WD Ext Cab LB	21435	25215
4 Dr Work 4WD Ext Cab SB	16120	18965	4 Dr Lariat Ext Cab SB	20000	23530
2 Dr Work Std Cab LB	12225	14385	4 Dr Lariat 4WD Ext Cab SB	21355	25125
2 Dr Work 4WD Std Cab LB	13530	15920	2 Dr Lariat Std Cab LB	17865	21020
4 Dr XL Ext Cab SB	16405	19300	2 Dr Lariat 4WD Std Cab LB	19685	23160
4 Dr XL 4WD Ext Cab SB	17345	20405	4 Dr XL Crew Cab LB	19125	22500
2 Dr XL Std Cab LB	14920	17555	4 Dr XL 4WD Crew Cab LB	21150	24880
2 Dr XL 4WD Std Cab LB	15625	18380	4 Dr XL Crew Cab SB	18945	22290
4 Dr XLT Ext Cab SB	18380	21625	4 Dr XL 4WD Crew Cab SB	21040	24755
4 Dr XLT 4WD Ext Cab SB	19505	22945	4 Dr XL Ext Cab LB	18305	21535
2 Dr XLT Std Cab LB	16290	19165	4 Dr XL 4WD Ext Cab LB	19875	23380
2 Dr XLT 4WD Std Cab LB	17580	20685	4 Dr XL Ext Cab SB	18115	21310

F-250 SUPER DUTY

Category H

Model Description	Trade-in Value	Market Value
4 Dr Lariat Crew Cab LB	20740	24400
4 Dr Lariat 4WD Crew Cab LB	23135	27215
4 Dr Lariat Crew Cab SB	20665	24310
4 Dr Lariat 4WD Crew Cab SB	23075	27145
4 Dr Lariat Ext Cab LB	17125	20145
4 Dr Lariat 4WD Ext Cab LB	18995	22345
4 Dr Lariat Ext Cab SB	17045	20050
4 Dr Lariat 4WD Ext Cab SB	18925	22265
2 Dr Lariat Std Cab LB	16580	19505
2 Dr Lariat 4WD Std Cab LB	18545	21815
4 Dr XL Crew Cab LB	19505	22945
4 Dr XL 4WD Crew Cab LB	21200	24940
4 Dr XL Crew Cab SB	19425	22850
4 Dr XL 4WD Crew Cab SB	21140	24870
4 Dr XL Ext Cab LB	16645	19580
4 Dr XL 4WD Ext Cab LB	18000	21175
4 Dr XL Ext Cab SB	16560	19480
4 Dr XL 4WD Ext Cab SB	17925	21090
2 Dr XL Std Cab LB	15785	18570
2 Dr XL 4WD Std Cab LB	17490	20575
4 Dr XLT Crew Cab LB	20025	23560
4 Dr XLT 4WD Crew Cab LB	22585	26570
4 Dr XLT Crew Cab SB	19945	23465
4 Dr XLT 4WD Crew Cab SB	22520	26495
4 Dr XLT Ext Cab LB	17625	20735
4 Dr XLT 4WD Ext Cab LB	19985	23510
4 Dr XLT Ext Cab SB	17510	20600
4 Dr XLT 4WD Ext Cab SB	19905	23420
2 Dr XLT Std Cab LB	16580	19505
2 Dr XLT 4WD Std Cab LB	17960	21130

F-350

Category H

Model Description	Trade-in Value	Market Value
4 Dr Lariat Crew Cab LB	20955	24650
4 Dr Lariat 4WD Crew Cab LB	22720	26730
4 Dr Lariat Crew Cab SB	20850	24530
4 Dr Lariat 4WD Crew Cab SB	22610	26600
4 Dr Lariat Ext Cab LB	20090	23635

Model Description	Trade-in Value	Market Value
4 Dr XL 4WD Ext Cab SB	19705	23180
2 Dr XL Std Cab LB	16135	18980
2 Dr XL 4WD Std Cab LB	18725	22030
4 Dr XLT Crew Cab LB	20250	23825
4 Dr XLT 4WD Crew Cab LB	22070	25965
4 Dr XLT Crew Cab SB	20075	23615
4 Dr XLT 4WD Crew Cab SB	21975	25850
4 Dr XLT Ext Cab LB	18915	22250
4 Dr XLT 4WD Ext Cab LB	20530	24155
4 Dr XLT Ext Cab SB	18795	22110
4 Dr XLT 4WD Ext Cab SB	20390	23990
2 Dr XLT Std Cab LB	16900	19885
2 Dr XLT 4WD Std Cab LB	18175	21385

OPTIONS FOR F-SERIES PICKUP

10 cyl 6.8 L Engine +500
8 cyl 4.6 L Engine[Std on F-150 4WD, F250, Lariat] +550
8 cyl 5.4 L Engine[Std on F-250 Super Duty, F-350] +720
8 cyl 7.3 L Turbodsl Engine +3070
Auto 4-Speed Transmission +735
AM/FM Compact Disc Player +230
Air Conditioning[Std on Lariat] +600
Aluminum/Alloy Wheels[Std on XLT] +235
Anti-Lock Brakes[Std on XLT, Lariat] +370
Camper/Towing Package +255
Chrome Wheels[Std on Lariat] +220
Cruise Control[Std on XLT, Lariat] +140
Fog Lights[Std on F-150 SVT, Lariat 4WD] +90
Keyless Entry System +130
Leather Seats +730
Power Door Locks[Std on XLT, Lariat] +140
Power Driver's Seat +210
Power Mirrors[Std on XLT, Lariat, F-150 SVT] +75
Power Windows[Std on XLT, Lariat, F-150 SVT] +140
Sliding Rear Window[Std on F-150 SVT] +85
Tilt Steering Wheel[Std on XLT, Lariat, F-150 SVT] +135
Trailer Hitch +120

MUSTANG   1999

Following on the heels of the '98 Camaro update, Ford gives its sports car fresh styling and more motor. The 3.8-liter V6 engine makes 190 horsepower and 220 foot-pounds of torque, putting it within spitting distance of the V6 Camaro. The SOHC V8 found in GT models gets an 16-percent increase in horsepower, and a new SVT Cobra model boasts 320 ponies and an independent rear suspension. Improvements to the V6 and GT suspension and steering gear, as well as a styling update, insure that this car will maintain its lead in the pony car wars.

RATINGS (SCALE OF 1-10)

Overall	Safety	Reliability	Performance	Comfort	Value
N/A	7	N/A	8.2	7.4	N/A

Category F

Model Description	Trade-in Value	Market Value
2 Dr Cobra Conv	21325	25690
2 Dr Cobra Cpe	18835	22690
2 Dr GT Conv	16205	19525
2 Dr GT Cpe	14785	17815
2 Dr STD Conv	13105	15790
2 Dr STD Cpe	11115	13390

OPTIONS FOR MUSTANG

Auto 4-Speed Transmission +600
Anti-Lock Brakes[Opt on STD] +505
Cruise Control[Std on Cobra] +155
Leather Seats +485
Power Driver's Seat[Opt on STD] +180
Rear Window Defroster[Std on Cobra] +125

RANGER   1999

The Ranger is "Built Ford Tough" according to its ads and we tend to agree. This year's changes include standard 15-inch silver styled wheels, a class III frame-mounted hitch receiver for V6 applications, and a spare tire access lock. All models get dual front cup holders and Dark Graphite has been added to the interior colors option list while Willow Green and Denim Blue have been removed as interior choices. Too bad for you folks who liked the splashy "Splash" model, it has been discontinued. Finally, a 3.0-liter V6 flexible fuel engine is available that is designed specifically for ethanol/gasoline fuel blends.

RATINGS (SCALE OF 1-10)

Overall	Safety	Reliability	Performance	Comfort	Value
N/A	N/A	N/A	7	7.8	N/A

Category G

Model Description	Trade-in Value	Market Value
2 Dr XL Ext Cab SB	8745	10410
2 Dr XL 4WD Ext Cab SB	11150	13275
2 Dr XL Ext Cab Stepside SB	9465	11265
2 Dr XL 4WD Ext Cab Stepside SB		
	11770	14010
2 Dr XL Std Cab LB	8195	9755
2 Dr XL 4WD Std Cab LB	10685	12720
2 Dr XL Std Cab SB	8050	9585
2 Dr XL 4WD Std Cab SB	10490	12490
2 Dr XL Std Cab Stepside SB	8530	10155
2 Dr XL 4WD Std Cab Stepside SB		
	11250	13395
2 Dr XLT Ext Cab SB	9635	11470
2 Dr XLT 4WD Ext Cab SB	12000	14285
2 Dr XLT Ext Cab Stepside SB	10280	12240
2 Dr XLT 4WD Ext Cab Stepside SB		
	12460	14835
2 Dr XLT Std Cab LB	9485	11290
2 Dr XLT 4WD Std Cab LB	10815	12875
2 Dr XLT Std Cab SB	8605	10245
2 Dr XLT 4WD Std Cab SB	10605	12625
2 Dr XLT Std Cab Stepside SB	10635	12660
2 Dr XLT 4WD Std Cab Stepside SB		
	11935	14210

OPTIONS FOR RANGER

4 Door Supercab (XLT only) +460
6 cyl 3.0 L Engine[Std on 4WD] +415
6 cyl 4.0 L Engine +750
Auto 4-Speed Transmission +810
Auto 5-Speed Transmission +835
AM/FM Compact Disc Player +245
Air Conditioning +605
Aluminum/Alloy Wheels[Std on XLT 4WD] +245
Anti-Lock Brakes[Std on XLT 4WD] +445
Bed Liner +210
Cruise Control +155
Fog Lights +105
Keyless Entry System +150
Power Door Locks +170
Power Mirrors +100
Power Windows +175
Sliding Rear Window +90
Tilt Steering Wheel +130

TAURUS   1999

Against all odds, the Taurus SHO pulls through for another model year. The light group and speed control are now optional on LX level cars. Chrome wheels on the SE models have been replaced with five-spoke aluminum wheels.

RATINGS (SCALE OF 1-10)

Overall	Safety	Reliability	Performance	Comfort	Value
N/A	7.8	7.9	8	7.9	N/A

Category C

Model Description	Trade-in Value	Market Value
4 Dr LX Sdn	9050	11065
4 Dr SE Sdn	10585	12755
4 Dr SE Wgn	10830	13050

Category F

Model Description	Trade-in Value	Market Value
4 Dr SHO Sdn	15380	18530

OPTIONS FOR TAURUS

6 cyl 3.0 L DOHC Engine +390
Aluminum/Alloy Wheels +225

Anti-Lock Brakes[Std on SHO] +450
Compact Disc Changer[Opt on SE] +355
Heated Power Mirrors[Opt on SE] +80
Keyless Entry System[Opt on LX] +140
Leather Seats[Opt on SE] +450
Power Door Locks[Opt on LX] +185
Power Driver's Seat +220
Power Moonroof[Opt on SE] +510

WINDSTAR 1999

Ford continues to battle it out with GM and Chrysler in the hotly contested minivan segment. This year the Windstar has been totally redesigned in yet another attempt to dethrone the hot pentastar prospects. The biggest news for '99, in addition to the completely new exterior and interior styling, is a left-hand sliding door. The second and third row seats are now on rollers for easier adjustment/interchangeability and the instrument panel has been redesigned for improved ergonomics. There's also a more powerful and cleaner-burning 3.8-liter V6 plus upgraded suspension, transmission, brakes and air conditioning components. Hot new options include side airbags and a trick reverse sensing system to keep you from banging into those short gas station poles.

RATINGS (SCALE OF 1-10)

Overall	Safety	Reliability	Performance	Comfort	Value
N/A	8.8	7.7	7	7.8	N/A

Category G
2 Dr LX Pass. Van	14545	17315
2 Dr SE Pass. Van	17600	20950
2 Dr SEL Pass. Van	19740	23500
2 Dr STD Cargo Van	11285	13435
2 Dr STD Pass. Van	11930	14205

OPTIONS FOR WINDSTAR

6 cyl 3.8 L Engine[Opt on STD] +275
Pwr Sliding Lh & Rh Doors +590
Air Conditioning[Opt on STD] +605
Aluminum/Alloy Wheels[Opt on LX] +245
Captain Chairs (4)[Opt on LX] +465
Compact Disc W/fm/tape[Std on SEL] +355
Cruise Control[Opt on STD] +155
Dual Air Conditioning[Opt on LX] +700
Keyless Entry System[Std on SE,SEL] +150
Leather Seats[Opt on SE] +575
Luggage Rack[Opt on LX] +115
Power Door Locks[Opt on STD] +170
Power Driver's Seat[Std on SE, SEL] +210
Power Mirrors[Opt on STD] +100
Power Windows[Opt on STD] +175
Privacy Glass[Std on SE,SEL] +195
Rear Window Defroster[Opt on STD] +125
Sliding Driver Side Door[Opt on LX,STD] +390
Tilt Steering Wheel[Opt on STD] +130

1998 FORD

CLUB WAGON/ECONOLINE 1998

New interior and exterior packages appear on the Club Wagon and Econoline vans.

RATINGS (SCALE OF 1-10)

Overall	Safety	Reliability	Performance	Comfort	Value
N/A	7.9	N/A	6.6	7.4	N/A

E-150
Category H
2 Dr Chateau Club Wagon	15685	18675
2 Dr STD Econoline	11695	13920
2 Dr XL Club Wagon	13100	15595
2 Dr XLT Club Wagon	13910	16560

E-250
Category H
2 Dr STD Econoline	11580	13785
2 Dr STD Econoline Ext	12035	14325

E-350
Category H
2 Dr Chateau Club Wagon	17200	20475
2 Dr STD Econoline	12495	14875
2 Dr STD Econoline Ext	12920	15380
2 Dr XL Club Wagon	14580	17360
2 Dr XL Club Wagon Ext	14985	17840
2 Dr XLT Club Wagon	14985	17840
2 Dr XLT Club Wagon Ext	15395	18325

OPTIONS FOR CLUB WAGON/ECONOLINE

10 cyl 6.8 L Engine +370
8 cyl 4.6 L Engine +400
8 cyl 5.4 L Engine[Std on E-350] +560
8 cyl 7.3 L Turbodsl Engine +2965
12 Passenger Seating[Std on XL,Club Wagon] +370
Air Conditioning[Std on Chateau, XL, XLT] +490
Aluminum/Alloy Wheels[Opt on XLT] +190
Anti-Lock Brakes[Std on Chateau, XL, XLT] +300
Cruise Control +115
Dual Air Conditioning +810
Keyless Entry System +105
Power Door Locks[Std on Chateau, XLT] +115
Power Driver's Seat +170
Power Mirrors +60
Power Windows[Std on Chateau, XLT] +115
Privacy Glass +100
Tilt Steering Wheel +110

CONTOUR 1998

A redesigned face gives this Ford more character, but the new taillight treatment is almost identical to the Contour's sibling, the Mercury Mystique. New alloy wheels and a slightly more commodious rear seat

FORD 98

Model Description	Trade-in Value	Market Value	Model Description	Trade-in Value	Market Value

debut. The outstanding SVT model provides the performance of a BMW 328i at the price of a Buick Century. Mid-year changes included a model consolidation, the addition of de-powered airbags, as well as improved handling and new wheels for the SVT.

RATINGS (SCALE OF 1-10)

Overall	Safety	Reliability	Performance	Comfort	Value
7.4	6.7	6.7	8.2	7.9	7.4

Category C
4 Dr LX Sdn	6695	8165
4 Dr SE Sdn	7710	9405
4 Dr STD Sdn	6395	7800
4 Dr SVT Sdn	11330	13815

OPTIONS FOR CONTOUR

6 cyl 2.5 L Engine[Std on SE, SVT] +415
Auto 4-Speed Transmission +500
AM/FM Compact Disc Player +220
Air Conditioning[Std on SVT] +490
Aluminum/Alloy Wheels[Opt on GL, LX] +180
Anti-Lock Brakes[Std on SVT] +370
Cruise Control[Std on SVT] +130
Keyless Entry System[Std on SVT] +115
Leather Seats[Std on SVT] +365
Power Door Locks[Opt on GL, LX] +150
Power Driver's Seat[Std on SVT] +180
Power Moonroof +415
Power Windows[Std on SVT] +190
Rear Window Defroster[Std on SE, SVT] +100
Traction Control System[Opt on SE] +150

CROWN VICTORIA   1998

A formal roofline graces this favorite of police officers and taxi Driver's. To further add to the Crown Victoria's driving excitement, the power steering and suspension have been improved.

RATINGS (SCALE OF 1-10)

Overall	Safety	Reliability	Performance	Comfort	Value
8.2	8.1	8.6	7.7	8.2	8.4

Category B
4 Dr LX Sdn	12835	15465
4 Dr STD Sdn	12290	14805

OPTIONS FOR CROWN VICTORIA

Aluminum/Alloy Wheels +200
Anti-Lock Brakes +420
Climate Control for AC +105
Dual Power Seats +230
Keyless Entry System[Std on LX] +105
Leather Seats +410
Power Driver's Seat[Std on LX] +190
Traction Control System +105

ESCORT   1998

Packages are reshuffled on Ford's entry-level cars. Available this year as sedans, wagons or stylish coupes, the Ford Escort now qualifies as a low emissions vehicle, thanks to the car's split-port induction 2.0-liter four-cylinder engine.

RATINGS (SCALE OF 1-10)

Overall	Safety	Reliability	Performance	Comfort	Value
7.3	6.1	8.5	7.2	7.3	7.2

Category E
4 Dr LX Sdn	6015	7425
4 Dr SE Sdn	6785	8375
4 Dr SE Wgn	6940	8565
2 Dr ZX2 Cool Cpe	6540	8075
2 Dr ZX2 Hot Cpe	6690	8260

OPTIONS FOR ESCORT

Auto 4-Speed Transmission +475
Air Conditioning[Std on SE] +495
Aluminum/Alloy Wheels +200
Anti-Lock Brakes +410
Cruise Control +135
Keyless Entry System[Std on SE] +95
Luggage Rack +80
Power Door Locks +145
Power Mirrors[Std on SE] +65
Power Moonroof +350
Power Windows +160
Premium Sound System +200
Rear Window Defroster[Std on SE] +100
Rear Window Wiper +75
Tilt Steering Wheel +90

EXPEDITION   1998

After an insanely successful first year, the Ford Expedition pounds its way into 1998 without changes.

RATINGS (SCALE OF 1-10)

Overall	Safety	Reliability	Performance	Comfort	Value
7.5	8.1	7.9	6.8	7.9	7

Category H
4 Dr Eddie Bauer Wgn	18740	22310
4 Dr Eddie Bauer 4WD Wgn	20635	24565
4 Dr XLT Wgn	18115	21565
4 Dr XLT 4WD Wgn	19910	23705

OPTIONS FOR EXPEDITION

8 cyl 5.4 L Engine +560
Aluminum/Alloy Wheels[Opt on XLT] +190
Camper/Towing Package +205
Compact Disc Changer +265
Compact Disc W/fm/tape +190
Cruise Control[Opt on XLT] +115
Dual Air Conditioning +810
Fog Lights[Opt on XLT] +75

Don't forget to refer to the Mileage Adjustment Table at the back of this book!

FORD 98

Model Description	Trade-in Value	Market Value	Model Description	Trade-in Value	Market Value

Heated Front Seats +205
Heated Power Mirrors +60
Leather Seats[Opt on XLT] +595
Power Driver's Seat[Opt on XLT] +170
Privacy Glass[Opt on XLT] +100
Running Boards +210
Third Seat +385

EXPLORER 1998

The Ford Explorer gets a restyled tailgate for 1998.

RATINGS (SCALE OF 1-10)

Overall	Safety	Reliability	Performance	Comfort	Value
7.4	7.7	7.9	7.8	7.1	6.7

Category G

	Trade-in	Market
4 Dr Eddie Bauer Wgn	15080	17950
4 Dr Eddie Bauer 4WD Wgn	15905	18935
4 Dr Limited Wgn	17045	20290
4 Dr Limited 4WD Wgn	18105	21555
2 Dr Sport Utility	12550	14940
2 Dr Sport 4WD Utility	13820	16450
4 Dr XL Wgn	13355	15900
4 Dr XL 4WD Wgn	14135	16825
4 Dr XLT Wgn	14585	17365
4 Dr XLT 4WD Wgn	15441	18380

OPTIONS FOR EXPLORER

6 cyl 4.0 L SOHC Engine[Opt on Sport, XLT] +330
8 cyl 5.0 L Engine +545
Auto 4-Speed Transmission +610
Auto 5-Speed Transmission[Std on Eddie Bauer, Limited] +655
Aluminum/Alloy Wheels[Opt on XL] +200
Climate Control for AC[Std on Limited] +120
Compact Disc Changer +315
Compact Disc W/fm/tape[Std on Limited] +290
Cruise Control[Opt on Sport, XL] +125
Dual Power Seats[Std on Limited] +235
Fog Lights[Std on Limited] +90
Keyless Entry System[Std on Limited] +120
Leather Seats[Std on Limited] +470
Power Driver's Seat[Opt on Sport, XLT] +170
Power Moonroof +525
Rear Heater[Std on Limited] +125
Rear Window Defroster[Opt on Sport, XL] +105
Rear Window Wiper[Opt on Sport, XL] +95
Running Boards[Std on Limited] +235
Tilt Steering Wheel[Opt on XL] +105
Tutone Paint[Opt on XLT] +160

F-SERIES PICKUP 1998

The 1998 F-150 celebrates its 50th Anniversary with a small decal on the windshield. Other changes include making the locking tailgate standard on XLT and Lariat trims, optional on XL and Standard models. Fog lights become optional this year on all four-wheel drive models except for the Lariat, which gets them standard.

An STX package featuring 17-inch tires, aluminum wheels, and color-keyed grille debuts as an option for the XLT 2WD. The Lariat receives a color-keyed steering column, leather-wrapped steering wheel, and outside power signal mirrors. Silver Metallic paint replaces Silver Frost paint, and Light Denim Blue replaces Portofino Blue.

RATINGS (SCALE OF 1-10)

Overall	Safety	Reliability	Performance	Comfort	Value
N/A	7.4	8.5	6.6	7.8	N/A

F-150

Category H

	Trade-in	Market
2 Dr Lariat Ext Cab LB	13560	16145
2 Dr Lariat 4WD Ext Cab LB	15900	18930
2 Dr Lariat Ext Cab SB	13465	16030
2 Dr Lariat 4WD Ext Cab SB	15840	18860
2 Dr Lariat Ext Cab Stepside SB	13900	16545
2 Dr Lariat 4WD Ext Cab Stepside SB	16185	19270
2 Dr Lariat Std Cab LB	12400	14760
2 Dr Lariat 4WD Std Cab LB	15230	18130
2 Dr Lariat Std Cab SB	12250	14585
2 Dr Lariat 4WD Std Cab SB	15160	18045
2 Dr Lariat Std Cab Stepside SB	12690	15105
2 Dr Lariat 4WD Std Cab Stepside SB	15545	18505
2 Dr STD Ext Cab LB	10925	13005
2 Dr STD 4WD Ext Cab LB	13270	15800
2 Dr STD Ext Cab SB	10795	12850
2 Dr STD 4WD Ext Cab SB	13085	15575
2 Dr STD Std Cab LB	10315	12280
2 Dr STD 4WD Std Cab LB	12525	14910
2 Dr STD Std Cab SB	10245	12195
2 Dr STD 4WD Std Cab SB	12455	14830
2 Dr XL Ext Cab LB	10980	13070
2 Dr XL 4WD Ext Cab LB	13425	15985
2 Dr XL Ext Cab SB	10790	12845
2 Dr XL 4WD Ext Cab SB	13350	15895
2 Dr XL Ext Cab Stepside SB	11090	13205
2 Dr XL 4WD Ext Cab Stepside SB	13780	16405
2 Dr XL Std Cab LB	10205	12150
2 Dr XL 4WD Std Cab LB	12685	15100
2 Dr XL Std Cab SB	10135	12065
2 Dr XL 4WD Std Cab SB	12535	14925
2 Dr XL Std Cab Stepside SB	10605	12625
2 Dr XL 4WD Std Cab Stepside SB	13080	15570
2 Dr XLT Ext Cab LB	12245	14580

Model Description	Trade-in Value	Market Value
2 Dr XLT 4WD Ext Cab LB	14770	17585
2 Dr XLT Ext Cab SB	12165	14480
2 Dr XLT 4WD Ext Cab SB	14670	17465
2 Dr XLT Ext Cab Stepside SB	12585	14985
2 Dr XLT 4WD Ext Cab Stepside SB	15110	17990
2 Dr XLT Std Cab LB	11195	13330
2 Dr XLT 4WD Std Cab LB	13315	15850
2 Dr XLT Std Cab SB	11130	13250
2 Dr XLT 4WD Std Cab SB	13250	15775
2 Dr XLT Std Cab Stepside SB	11195	13325
2 Dr XLT 4WD Std Cab Stepside SB	13050	15535

F-250

Category H

Model Description	Trade-in Value	Market Value
2 Dr Lariat Ext Cab SB	16010	19060
2 Dr Lariat 4WD Ext Cab SB	17040	20285
2 Dr Lariat Std Cab LB	15030	17890
2 Dr Lariat 4WD Std Cab LB	16770	19965
2 Dr STD Ext Cab SB	13585	16170
2 Dr STD 4WD Ext Cab SB	15115	17995
2 Dr STD Std Cab LB	12480	14855
2 Dr STD 4WD Std Cab LB	14135	16825
2 Dr XL Ext Cab SB	13585	16170
2 Dr XL 4WD Ext Cab SB	15345	18270
2 Dr XL Std Cab LB	12300	14645
2 Dr XL 4WD Std Cab LB	14075	16755
2 Dr XLT Ext Cab SB	14975	17830
2 Dr XLT 4WD Ext Cab SB	16795	19995
2 Dr XLT Std Cab LB	13560	16145
2 Dr XLT 4WD Std Cab LB	15330	18250

OPTIONS FOR F-SERIES PICKUP

8 cyl 4.6 L Engine[Std on F-150 4WD, F-250, Lariat] +400
8 cyl 5.4 L Engine +560
Auto 4-Speed Transmission +610
AM/FM Compact Disc Player +190
Air Conditioning +490
Aluminum/Alloy Wheels[Std on Lariat] +190
Anti-Lock Brakes[Std on Lariat] +300
Camper/Towing Package +205
Chrome Wheels[Std on Lariat] +180
Cruise Control +115
Fog Lights[Std on Lariat] +75
Keyless Entry System +105
Leather Steering Wheel[Opt on XLT] +40
Power Driver's Seat +170
Power Mirrors[Std on Lariat, XLT Stepside] +60
Skid Plates +65
Sliding Rear Window +70
Tilt Steering Wheel +110

MUSTANG 1998

The Mustang gains standard equipment, such as power windows and door locks, air conditioning, and premium sound. Options are shuffled as well, making it easier to choose the car you want. GT models get a slight boost in power.

RATINGS (SCALE OF 1-10)

Overall	Safety	Reliability	Performance	Comfort	Value
6.9	6.7	7.8	8.8	7.3	3.7

Category F

Model Description	Trade-in Value	Market Value
2 Dr Cobra Conv	17680	21560
2 Dr Cobra Cpe	15955	19460
2 Dr GT Conv	13155	16040
2 Dr GT Cpe	11535	14065
2 Dr STD Conv	11415	13920
2 Dr STD Cpe	9805	11960

OPTIONS FOR MUSTANG

Auto 4-Speed Transmission +500
Anti-Lock Brakes[Std on Cobra] +415
Cruise Control[Std on Cobra] +125
Leather Seats +395
Power Driver's Seat[Opt on STD] +150
Rear Window Defroster[Std on Cobra] +100

RANGER 1998

The Ranger gets new sheetmetal, a new grille and revised headlamps. The wheelbase on regular cab models has been stretched to provide more cabin room and the displacement of the base engine has been increased. A short- and long-arm (SLA) suspension replaces the Twin-I-Beam suspension found on last year's models. A four-door Ranger join the lineup mid-year.

RATINGS (SCALE OF 1-10)

Overall	Safety	Reliability	Performance	Comfort	Value
N/A	N/A	8.7	7.2	7.3	N/A

Category G

Model Description	Trade-in Value	Market Value
2 Dr Splash Ext Cab Stepside SB	10015	11925
2 Dr Splash 4WD Ext Cab Stepside SB	12080	14380
2 Dr Splash Std Cab Stepside SB	9330	11110
2 Dr Splash 4WD Std Cab Stepside SB	11360	13525
2 Dr XL Ext Cab SB	7885	9385
2 Dr XL 4WD Ext Cab SB	9850	11725
2 Dr XL Ext Cab Stepside SB	8545	10170
2 Dr XL 4WD Ext Cab Stepside SB	10645	12670

Model Description	Trade-in Value	Market Value	Model Description	Trade-in Value	Market Value
2 Dr XL Std Cab LB	7175	8540			
2 Dr XL 4WD Std Cab LB	9385	11170			
2 Dr XL Std Cab SB	6990	8320			
2 Dr XL 4WD Std Cab SB	9140	10880			
2 Dr XL Std Cab Stepside SB	7445	8865			
2 Dr XL 4WD Std Cab Stepside SB	9560	11380			
2 Dr XLT Ext Cab SB	8795	10470			
2 Dr XLT 4WD Ext Cab SB	10500	12500			
2 Dr XLT Ext Cab Stepside SB	9215	10970			
2 Dr XLT 4WD Ext Cab Stepside SB	10850	12915			
2 Dr XLT Std Cab LB	7630	9085			
2 Dr XLT 4WD Std Cab LB	10190	12130			
2 Dr XLT Std Cab SB	7470	8890			
2 Dr XLT 4WD Std Cab SB	9990	11895			
2 Dr XLT Std Cab Stepside SB	8000	9525			
2 Dr XLT 4WD Std Cab Stepside SB	10435	12420			

OPTIONS FOR RANGER

6 cyl 3.0 L Engine[Std on 4WD, Splash 2WD Ext Cab] +305
6 cyl 4.0 L Engine +550
Auto 4-Speed Transmission +675
Auto 5-Speed Transmission +695
AM/FM Compact Disc Player +200
Air Conditioning +495
Aluminum/Alloy Wheels[Opt on XL, XLT, Ext Cab] +200
Anti-Lock Brakes +365
Bed Liner +170
Chrome Wheels[Opt on XLT] +105
Cruise Control +125
Fog Lights +90
Keyless Entry System +120
Power Door Locks +140
Power Mirrors[Opt on XLT] +80
Power Windows +145
Sliding Rear Window[Opt on XL, XLT, Std Cab, 2WD] +70
Tilt Steering Wheel +105

TAURUS   1998

A mild facelift, revised trim levels and fewer options are the only changes to Ford's mid-size sedan.

RATINGS (SCALE OF 1-10)

Overall	Safety	Reliability	Performance	Comfort	Value
7.9	7.9	8.1	8	8	7.4

Category C
4 Dr LX Sdn				9075	11070
4 Dr SE Sdn				9535	11625
4 Dr SE Wgn				9745	11885

Category F
4 Dr SHO Sdn				13140	16025

OPTIONS FOR TAURUS

6 cyl 3.0 L DOHC Engine[Opt on LX, SE] +305
Aluminum/Alloy Wheels +180
Anti-Lock Brakes[Std on SHO] +370
Chrome Wheels[Opt on SE] +370
Climate Control for AC[Opt on SE] +100
Compact Disc Changer[Opt on SE] +290
Dual Power Seats[Opt on SE] +360
Heated Power Mirrors[Opt on SE] +65
Keyless Entry System[Opt on LX, Wgn] +115
Leather Seats +365
Power Door Locks[Opt on LX] +150
Power Driver's Seat +180
Power Moonroof[Opt on SE] +415

WINDSTAR   1998

Ford widens the driver's door as a stop-gap measure until the 1999 Windstar arrives with a fourth door. Subtle styling revisions and a new Limited model round out the changes for 1998.

RATINGS (SCALE OF 1-10)

Overall	Safety	Reliability	Performance	Comfort	Value
7.1	8.1	6.3	6.8	7.3	6.9

Category G
2 Dr GL Pass. Van				10510	12515
2 Dr LX Pass. Van				13320	15860
2 Dr Limited Pass. Van				14940	17785
2 Dr STD Cargo Van				7820	9310
2 Dr STD Pass. Van				9960	11855

OPTIONS FOR WINDSTAR

6 cyl 3.8 L Engine[Std on Limited, LX] +255
AM/FM Compact Disc Player +200
Air Conditioning[Std on LX] +495
Aluminum/Alloy Wheels[Opt on GL] +200
Captain Chairs (4)[Opt on GL, LX] +380
Cruise Control[Opt on GL, STD] +125
Dual Air Conditioning[Opt on GL, LX] +575
JBL Sound System +465
Keyless Entry System +120
Leather Seats[Opt on LX] +470
Power Door Locks[Opt on GL, STD] +140
Power Driver's Seat[Opt on GL] +170
Power Mirrors[Opt on GL, STD] +80
Power Windows[Opt on GL, STD] +145
Privacy Glass +160
Rear Window Defroster[Std on Limited] +105
Tilt Steering Wheel[Opt on GL, STD] +105
Traction Control System +165

1997 FORD

AEROSTAR   1997

Ford's aging minivan gets a 5-speed automatic transmission this year. The sound systems are upgraded and the seats are restyled as well.

Don't forget to refer to the Mileage Adjustment Table at the back of this book!

FORD 97

Model Description	Trade-in Value	Market Value	Model Description	Trade-in Value	Market Value

RATINGS (SCALE OF 1-10)

Overall	Safety	Reliability	Performance	Comfort	Value
7.3	5.8	7.7	6.8	7.5	8.5

Category G

	Trade-in	Market
2 Dr STD Cargo Van	6285	7570
2 Dr XLT Pass. Van	7615	9175
2 Dr XLT Pass. Van Ext	8015	9655
2 Dr XLT 4WD Pass. Van Ext	9355	11270

OPTIONS FOR AEROSTAR

6 cyl 4.0 L Engine[Opt on 2WD] +415
AM/FM Compact Disc Player +160
AM/FM Stereo Tape +110
Air Conditioning[Opt on STD] +405
Aluminum/Alloy Wheels +165
Captain Chairs (4) +310
Child Seat (1) +85
Cruise Control +105
Dual Air Conditioning +470
Luggage Rack +80
Power Door Locks +115
Power Windows +120
Running Boards +190

ASPIRE   1997

This Kia-built entry-level Ford gets a higher final drive ratio on models equipped with an automatic transmission. New wheel covers, paint choices and interior trim are the only other changes.

RATINGS (SCALE OF 1-10)

Overall	Safety	Reliability	Performance	Comfort	Value
6.9	6.6	8.7	7.2	7.3	4.9

Category E

	Trade-in	Market
2 Dr STD Hbk	3640	4605
4 Dr STD Hbk	3855	4880

OPTIONS FOR ASPIRE

Auto 3-Speed Transmission +330
AM/FM Stereo Tape +150
Air Conditioning +405
Anti-Lock Brakes +335
Power Steering +125
Rear Window Defroster +80

CLUB WAGON/ECONOLINE 1997

More power? Ford's full-size vans are now the only ones in the segment to offer V10 power. Multiple overhead-cam engines also debut in models across the board. Econoline vans get standard four-wheel ABS this year.

RATINGS (SCALE OF 1-10)

Overall	Safety	Reliability	Performance	Comfort	Value
N/A	7.9	8.9	6.6	7.4	N/A

E-150

Category H

	Trade-in	Market
2 Dr Chateau Club Wagon	14205	16910
2 Dr STD Econoline	10620	12640
2 Dr XL Club Wagon	11195	13330
2 Dr XLT Club Wagon	12465	14840

E-250

Category H

	Trade-in	Market
2 Dr STD Cargo Van	8770	10440
2 Dr STD Cargo Van Ext	10285	12245
2 Dr STD Econoline	10785	12840
2 Dr STD Econoline Ext	11240	13380

E-350

Category H

	Trade-in	Market
2 Dr Chateau Club Wagon	14015	16685
2 Dr STD Econoline	10140	12070
2 Dr STD Econoline Ext	10540	12550
2 Dr XL Club Wagon	11770	14010
2 Dr XL Club Wagon Ext	12180	14500
2 Dr XLT Club Wagon	12285	14625
2 Dr XLT Club Wagon Ext	12590	14990

OPTIONS FOR CLUB WAGON/ECONOLINE

10 cyl 6.8 L Engine +210
8 cyl 4.6 L Engine +295
8 cyl 5.4 L Engine[Std on E-350] +410
8 cyl 7.3 L Turbodsl Engine +2095
AM/FM Stereo Tape[Std on Chateau] +105
Air Conditioning[Std on Chateau,XLT] +400
Aluminum/Alloy Wheels[Opt on XL,XLT] +155
Anti-Lock Brakes[Opt on STD] +245
Camper/Towing Package +170
Chrome Bumpers[Std on Chateau,XLT] +85
Cruise Control[Std on Chateau] +95
Dual Air Conditioning +660
Keyless Entry System +85
Limited Slip Diff +130
Power Door Locks[Std on Chateau,XLT] +95
Power Driver's Seat +140
Power Windows[Std on Chateau,XLT] +95
Velour/Cloth Seats[Std on Chateau,XLT] +65

CONTOUR   1997

The addition of a Sport Package for the GL and LX models and the inclusion of a standard trunk light are the only changes for the 1997 Contour.

RATINGS (SCALE OF 1-10)

Overall	Safety	Reliability	Performance	Comfort	Value
7.5	6.8	7.1	8.2	7.9	7.3

Category C

	Trade-in	Market
4 Dr GL Sdn	5910	7295
4 Dr LX Sdn	6115	7550
4 Dr SE Sdn	7065	8725

Don't forget to refer to the Mileage Adjustment Table at the back of this book!

Model Description	Trade-in Value	Market Value

OPTIONS FOR CONTOUR
6 cyl 2.5 L Engine[Std on SE] +455
Auto 4-Speed Transmission +410
AM/FM Compact Disc Player +180
Air Conditioning +400
Aluminum/Alloy Wheels[Std on SE] +150
Anti-Lock Brakes +300
Cruise Control +105
Keyless Entry System +95
Leather Seats +300
Power Door Locks +125
Power Driver's Seat +145
Power Moonroof +340
Power Windows +155
Rear Spoiler[Opt on GL] +85
Traction Control System +120

CROWN VICTORIA   1997

After a mild facelift last year, the Crown Vic soldiers on with a few color changes, improved power steering, and the addition of rear air suspension to the handling package.

RATINGS (SCALE OF 1-10)

Overall	Safety	Reliability	Performance	Comfort	Value
8	7.9	7.7	7.7	8.2	8.3

Category B
4 Dr LX Sdn	10605	12930
4 Dr STD Sdn	10165	12395

OPTIONS FOR CROWN VICTORIA
Handling/Performance Pkg +550
AM/FM Stereo Tape +85
Aluminum/Alloy Wheels +165
Anti-Lock Brakes +340
Climate Control for AC +85
Cruise Control +110
Dual Power Seats +190
Keyless Entry System +85
Leather Seats +335
Power Door Locks +125
Premium Sound System +195
Traction Control System +85
Trip Computer +195

ESCORT   1997

The Ford Escort is totally redesigned this year with improvements across the board. The most noticeable improvements are in the powertrain and ride quality. New sheetmetal gives the Escort a rounder, more aerodynamic appearance as well. To the chagrin of bargain-basement enthusiasts, the GT hatchback version is dropped.

RATINGS (SCALE OF 1-10)

Overall	Safety	Reliability	Performance	Comfort	Value
7.1	6.1	8.5	7.2	7.3	6.2

Model Description	Trade-in Value	Market Value

Category E
4 Dr LX Sdn	5255	6650
4 Dr LX Wgn	5470	6925
4 Dr STD Sdn	5250	6645

OPTIONS FOR ESCORT
Auto 4-Speed Transmission +370
AM/FM Stereo Tape +150
Air Conditioning +405
Aluminum/Alloy Wheels +165
Anti-Lock Brakes +335
Child Seat (1) +55
Compact Disc Changer +250
Cruise Control +110
Keyless Entry System +80
Luggage Rack +65
Power Door Locks +120
Power Windows +130
Tilt Steering Wheel +75

EXPEDITION   1997

Ford's replacement for the aging Bronco is the all-new Expedition. Based on the hugely successful 1997 F-150 platform, this full-size sport-utility vehicle is poised to do battle with the wildly popular Chevrolet Tahoe and GMC Yukon. Ford has priced the Expedition aggressively and stands to steal some sales from GM customers who have been told that they'll have to wait four months for their full-size SUV.

RATINGS (SCALE OF 1-10)

Overall	Safety	Reliability	Performance	Comfort	Value
7.1	8.1	7.4	6.8	7.9	5.5

Category H
4 Dr Eddie Bauer Wgn	16945	20170
4 Dr Eddie Bauer 4WD Wgn	18560	22095
4 Dr XLT Wgn	16605	19770
4 Dr XLT 4WD Wgn	18370	21870

OPTIONS FOR EXPEDITION
8 cyl 5.4 L Engine +410
Aluminum/Alloy Wheels[Opt on XLT] +155
Camper/Towing Package +170
Chrome Wheels +145
Compact Disc W/fm/tape +155
Cruise Control[Opt on XLT] +95
Dual Air Conditioning +660
Leather Seats[Opt on XLT] +485
Limited Slip Diff +130
Luggage Rack[Opt on XLT] +75
Power Driver's Seat[Opt on XLT] +140
Power Moonroof +480
Running Boards +170
Skid Plates +55
Third Seat +315

FORD 97

Model Description	Trade-in Value	Market Value	Model Description	Trade-in Value	Market Value

EXPLORER 1997

Ford's best-selling Explorer receives a few appreciated improvements this year. A new SOHC V6 engine is now available, providing nearly as much power as the 5.0-liter V8. Also new is a five-speed automatic transmission, the first ever offered by an American auto manufacturer, which is standard on V6 models equipped with automatic.

RATINGS (SCALE OF 1-10)

Overall	Safety	Reliability	Performance	Comfort	Value
7.1	7.6	7.7	7.8	7.1	5.5

Category G

	Trade-in	Market
4 Dr Eddie Bauer Wgn	13465	16220
4 Dr Eddie Bauer 4WD Wgn	14235	17150
4 Dr Limited Wgn	14560	17545
4 Dr Limited 4WD Wgn	15245	18370
2 Dr Sport Utility	11475	13825
2 Dr Sport 4WD Utility	12305	14825
2 Dr XL Utility	10820	13035
2 Dr XL 4WD Utility	11640	14025
4 Dr XL Wgn	11775	14185
4 Dr XL 4WD Wgn	12520	15085
4 Dr XLT Wgn	12950	15600
4 Dr XLT 4WD Wgn	13735	16550

OPTIONS FOR EXPLORER

6 cyl 4.0 L SOHC Engine[Opt on Sport,XL,XLT] +215
8 cyl 5.0 L Engine +610
Auto 4-Speed Transmission +500
Auto 5-Speed Transmission[Opt on Sport,XL,XLT] +535
AM/FM Stereo Tape[Std on Eddie Bauer] +110
Camper/Towing Package +150
Child Seat (1) +85
Chrome Wheels[Opt on Sport] +85
Climate Control for AC[Std on Limited] +95
Compact Disc Changer +255
Cruise Control[Opt on XL] +105
Dual Power Seats[Opt on Sport,XLT] +190
JBL Sound System[Std on Limited] +380
Keyless Entry System[Std on Limited] +100
Leather Seats[Std on Limited] +385
Limited Slip Diff +135
Luggage Rack[Opt on Sport,XL,XLT] +80
Power Door Locks[Opt on XL] +115
Power Moonroof +430
Power Windows[Opt on XL] +120
Running Boards[Std on Limited] +190

F-SERIES PICKUP 1997

Everything is new (except for Heavy Duty models, which retain last year's chassis and body style). New engines, new sheetmetal, and a new suspension compliment dual airbags and class-leading side impact protection in this user-friendly heavy hauler. All SuperCab models get a third door for easy access to the rear compartment.

RATINGS (SCALE OF 1-10)

Overall	Safety	Reliability	Performance	Comfort	Value
N/A	7.4	8	6.6	7.8	N/A

F-150

Category H

	Trade-in	Market
2 Dr Lariat Ext Cab LB	12670	15085
2 Dr Lariat 4WD Ext Cab LB	13900	16550
2 Dr Lariat Ext Cab SB	12590	14990
2 Dr Lariat 4WD Ext Cab SB	13760	16380
2 Dr Lariat Ext Cab Stepside SB	12980	15455
2 Dr Lariat 4WD Ext Cab Stepside SB	14180	16880
2 Dr Lariat Std Cab LB	11735	13970
2 Dr Lariat 4WD Std Cab LB	13350	15895
2 Dr Lariat Std Cab SB	11650	13870
2 Dr Lariat 4WD Std Cab SB	13220	15740
2 Dr Lariat Std Cab Stepside SB	12080	14380
2 Dr Lariat 4WD Std Cab Stepside SB	13675	16280
2 Dr STD Ext Cab LB	10090	12010
2 Dr STD 4WD Ext Cab LB	11325	13485
2 Dr STD Ext Cab SB	10000	11905
2 Dr STD 4WD Ext Cab SB	11175	13305
2 Dr STD Std Cab LB	9435	11230
2 Dr STD 4WD Std Cab LB	10645	12670
2 Dr STD Std Cab SB	9355	11135
2 Dr STD 4WD Std Cab SB	10505	12505
2 Dr XL Ext Cab LB	9985	11885
2 Dr XL 4WD Ext Cab LB	11670	13895
2 Dr XL Ext Cab SB	9885	11770
2 Dr XL 4WD Ext Cab SB	11550	13750
2 Dr XL Ext Cab Stepside SB	10210	12155
2 Dr XL 4WD Ext Cab Stepside SB	11855	14115
2 Dr XL Std Cab LB	9340	11120
2 Dr XL 4WD Std Cab LB	11275	13425
2 Dr XL Std Cab SB	9265	11030
2 Dr XL 4WD Std Cab SB	11170	13300
2 Dr XL Std Cab Stepside SB	9685	11530
2 Dr XL 4WD Std Cab Stepside SB	11650	13870
2 Dr XLT Ext Cab LB	10985	13075
2 Dr XLT 4WD Ext Cab LB	13415	15970
2 Dr XLT Ext Cab SB	10895	12970
2 Dr XLT 4WD Ext Cab SB	13335	15875
2 Dr XLT Ext Cab Stepside SB	11250	13395

Model Description	Trade-in Value	Market Value
2 Dr XLT 4WD Ext Cab Stepside SB		
	13715	16325
2 Dr XLT Std Cab LB	10110	12035
2 Dr XLT 4WD Std Cab LB	12325	14675
2 Dr XLT Std Cab SB	10005	11910
2 Dr XLT 4WD Std Cab SB	12225	14555
2 Dr XLT Std Cab Stepside SB	10405	12385
2 Dr XLT 4WD Std Cab Stepside SB		
	12500	14880

F-250

Category H

Model Description	Trade-in Value	Market Value
2 Dr Lariat Ext Cab SB	14335	17065
2 Dr Lariat 4WD Ext Cab SB	10050	11965
2 Dr Lariat Std Cab LB	13460	16025
2 Dr Lariat 4WD Std Cab LB	15030	17895
2 Dr STD Ext Cab SB	12750	15180
2 Dr STD 4WD Ext Cab SB	14340	17070
2 Dr STD Std Cab LB	11250	13390
2 Dr STD 4WD Std Cab LB	13275	15805
2 Dr XL Ext Cab SB	12420	14785
2 Dr XL 4WD Ext Cab SB	13535	16115
2 Dr XL Std Cab LB	10995	13090
2 Dr XL 4WD Std Cab LB	12715	15135
4 Dr XL Crew Cab SB HD	13470	16035
4 Dr XL 4WD Crew Cab SB HD	15160	18050
2 Dr XL Ext Cab LB HD	12625	15030
2 Dr XL 4WD Ext Cab LB HD	14365	17100
2 Dr XL Ext Cab SB HD	12195	14520
2 Dr XL 4WD Ext Cab SB HD	13700	16310
2 Dr XL Std Cab LB HD	11350	13510
2 Dr XL 4WD Std Cab LB HD	13060	15550
2 Dr XLT Ext Cab SB	13040	15525
2 Dr XLT 4WD Ext Cab SB	14380	17120
2 Dr XLT Std Cab LB	11875	14135
2 Dr XLT 4WD Std Cab LB	13530	16105
4 Dr XLT Crew Cab SB HD	15190	18085
4 Dr XLT 4WD Crew Cab SB HD	16970	20200
2 Dr XLT Ext Cab LB HD	13610	16205
2 Dr XLT 4WD Ext Cab LB HD	15290	18200
2 Dr XLT Ext Cab SB HD	13530	16110
2 Dr XLT 4WD Ext Cab SB HD	15345	18265
2 Dr XLT Std Cab LB HD	12540	14930
2 Dr XLT 4WD Std Cab LB HD	13770	16390

F-350

Category H

Model Description	Trade-in Value	Market Value
4 Dr XL Crew Cab LB	14990	17845
4 Dr XL 4WD Crew Cab LB	16665	19840
2 Dr XL Ext Cab LB	14145	16840
2 Dr XL Std Cab LB	12850	15295
2 Dr XL 4WD Std Cab LB	14725	17530
4 Dr XLT Crew Cab LB	16255	19350

Model Description	Trade-in Value	Market Value
4 Dr XLT 4WD Crew Cab LB	17810	21205
2 Dr XLT Ext Cab LB	14650	17440
2 Dr XLT 4WD Std Cab LB	16440	19570

OPTIONS FOR F-SERIES PICKUP

8 cyl 4.6 L Engine +295
8 cyl 5.4 L Engine +410
8 cyl 7.3 L Turbodsl Engine +2095
8 cyl 7.5 L Engine +195
Auto 4-Speed Transmission +455
Off-Road Equipment Group +360
Air Conditioning[Opt on F-150,F-250] +400
Aluminum/Alloy Wheels[Std on Lariat] +155
Anti-Lock Brakes[Std on Lariat] +245
Camper/Towing Package +170
Chrome Wheels[Opt on XL,XLT] +145
Compact Disc W/fm/tape +155
Cruise Control[Opt on F-150,F-250] +95
Dual Rear Wheels +410
Keyless Entry System +85
Limited Slip Diff +130
Power Driver's Seat +140
Rear Step Bumper +75
Skid Plates +55
Tutone Paint +125

MUSTANG   1997

While messing around with the rest of their models, Ford decided to take it easy with changes to the Mustang. GT models and base convertibles get new interior color options, and 'Stangs equipped with an automatic transmission (what fun) get a thicker shift lever. New 17-inch aluminum wheels are optional on the GT. Lastly, the Passive Anti-Theft System has been introduced to all Mustangs in an attempt decrease this vehicle's extremely high theft rating.

RATINGS (SCALE OF 1-10)

Overall	Safety	Reliability	Performance	Comfort	Value
6.9	7	8.3	8.8	7.3	3

Category F

Model Description	Trade-in Value	Market Value
2 Dr Cobra Conv	16175	19725
2 Dr Cobra Cpe	14385	17545
2 Dr GT Conv	11655	14215
2 Dr GT Cpe	10080	12290
2 Dr STD Conv	9920	12100
2 Dr STD Cpe	7960	9710

OPTIONS FOR MUSTANG

Auto 4-Speed Transmission +410
Air Conditioning[Std on Cobra] +415
Aluminum/Alloy Wheels[Opt on STD] +150
Anti-Lock Brakes[Std on Cobra] +335
Compact Disc W/fm/tape +250
Cruise Control[Std on Cobra] +105
Keyless Entry System[Std on Cobra] +90
Leather Seats +325

Don't forget to refer to the Mileage Adjustment Table at the back of this book!

Model Description	Trade-in Value	Market Value

Limited Slip Diff[Std on Cobra] +170
Power Door Locks[Std on Cobra,Conv] +100
Power Driver's Seat[Std on Cobra] +120
Power Windows[Std on Cobra,Conv] +110
Premium Sound System +185
Rear Spoiler[Opt on STD,Cpe] +120

PROBE   1997

Ford adds a GTS Sport Appearance Package to the GT's option sheet. The package includes a rear spoiler, racing stripes and 16-inch chrome wheels.

RATINGS (SCALE OF 1-10)

Overall	Safety	Reliability	Performance	Comfort	Value
N/A	7.1	7.6	9	7.4	N/A

Category E

	Trade-in	Market
2 Dr GT Hbk	7635	9665
2 Dr STD Hbk	6525	8260

OPTIONS FOR PROBE

Auto 4-Speed Transmission +450
AM/FM Compact Disc Player +225
Air Conditioning +405
Aluminum/Alloy Wheels[Std on GT] +165
Anti-Lock Brakes +335
Chrome Wheels +195
Cruise Control +110
Keyless Entry System +80
Leather Seats +430
Power Door Locks +120
Power Driver's Seat +150
Power Sunroof +305
Power Windows +130

RANGER   1997

Ford introduces its brand-new five-speed automatic transmission to the Ranger lineup. Available with the V6 engines, the five-speed automatic is designed to improve the Ranger's acceleration, towing, and hill climbing ability.

RATINGS (SCALE OF 1-10)

Overall	Safety	Reliability	Performance	Comfort	Value
N/A	6.7	8.9	7.2	7.3	N/A

Category G

	Trade-in	Market
2 Dr STX 4WD Ext Cab SB	9775	11775
2 Dr STX 4WD Std Cab LB	9380	11300
2 Dr STX 4WD Std Cab SB	9165	11045
2 Dr Splash Ext Cab Stepside SB	9060	10915
2 Dr Splash 4WD Ext Cab Stepside SB	10925	13160
2 Dr Splash Std Cab Stepside SB	7290	8785
2 Dr Splash 4WD Std Cab Stepside SB	10340	12460

	Trade-in	Market
2 Dr XL Ext Cab SB	6970	8400
2 Dr XL 4WD Ext Cab SB	9585	11550
2 Dr XL Ext Cab Stepside SB	7435	8960
2 Dr XL 4WD Ext Cab Stepside SB	10070	12130
2 Dr XL Std Cab LB	6375	7680
2 Dr XL 4WD Std Cab LB	8475	10210
2 Dr XL Std Cab SB	5945	7160
2 Dr XL 4WD Std Cab SB	8430	10155
2 Dr XL Std Cab Stepside SB	6255	7535
2 Dr XL 4WD Std Cab Stepside SB	8935	10765
2 Dr XLT Ext Cab SB	7895	9510
2 Dr XLT 4WD Ext Cab SB	10095	12160
2 Dr XLT Ext Cab Stepside SB	7560	9110
2 Dr XLT 4WD Ext Cab Stepside SB	10385	12515
2 Dr XLT Std Cab LB	6650	8010
2 Dr XLT 4WD Std Cab LB	8895	10715
2 Dr XLT Std Cab SB	6560	7905
2 Dr XLT 4WD Std Cab SB	8715	10500
2 Dr XLT Std Cab Stepside SB	6815	8210
2 Dr XLT 4WD Std Cab Stepside SB	8965	10800

OPTIONS FOR RANGER

6 cyl 3.0 L Engine +345
6 cyl 4.0 L Engine +415
Auto 4-Speed Transmission +525
Auto 5-Speed Transmission +540
AM/FM Compact Disc Player +160
Air Conditioning +405
Aluminum/Alloy Wheels[Std on Splash] +165
Anti-Lock Brakes +295
Bed Liner +140
Chrome Wheels[Opt on XLT] +85
Cruise Control +105
Keyless Entry System +100
Limited Slip Diff +135
Power Door Locks +115
Power Driver's Seat +140
Power Steering[Std on Splash,STX,Ext Cab,4WD] +140
Power Windows +120

TAURUS   1997

After totally redesigning the Taurus for 1996, Ford is taking it slow with changes for '97. A few new exterior color choices are added and there are minor changes to a couple of optional equipment packages.

RATINGS (SCALE OF 1-10)

Overall	Safety	Reliability	Performance	Comfort	Value
8.1	7.8	7.7	8	8	9.1

Model Description	Trade-in Value	Market Value
Category C		
4 Dr G Sdn	7335	9055
4 Dr GL Sdn	7670	9470
4 Dr GL Wgn	7840	9680
4 Dr LX Sdn	8450	10430
4 Dr LX Wgn	8585	10600
Category F		
4 Dr SHO Sdn	11560	14095

OPTIONS FOR TAURUS

AM/FM Compact Disc Player +180
Aluminum/Alloy Wheels[Opt on G,GL] +150
Anti-Lock Brakes[Std on SHO] +300
Child Seat (1) +60
Chrome Wheels +290
Climate Control for AC +85
Cruise Control[Std on SHO] +105
Keyless Entry System +90
Leather Seats +300
Power Door Locks[Opt on G,GL] +125
Power Driver's Seat[Opt on GL] +145
Power Moonroof +320
Third Seat +85

THUNDERBIRD   1997

The Thunderbird receives few updates this year. A revised center console, a few new colors, and standard four-wheel disc brakes are the big news for 1997.

RATINGS (SCALE OF 1-10)

Overall	Safety	Reliability	Performance	Comfort	Value
7.6	7.9	7.8	8	7.9	6.2

Category C		
2 Dr LX Cpe	8500	10495

OPTIONS FOR THUNDERBIRD

8 cyl 4.6 L Engine +370
Aluminum/Alloy Wheels +150
Anti-Lock Brakes +300
Chrome Wheels +300
Compact Disc W/fm/tape +165
Keyless Entry System +95
Leather Seats +300
Power Driver's Seat +145
Power Moonroof +340
Premium Sound System +195
Traction Control System +120

WINDSTAR   1997

Not much is new for the 1997 Ford Windstar. Caught flatfooted by the Chrysler and GM minivans that feature sliding left-side doors, Ford has installed a tip forward driver's seat, on early release 1998 models, to give passengers the option of entering from the driver's side. Hmmm, seems like that won't be enough to satisfy the fickle buyers of the minivan market.

RATINGS (SCALE OF 1-10)

Overall	Safety	Reliability	Performance	Comfort	Value
7.6	8.4	7.5	6.8	7.3	8.1

Category G		
2 Dr GL Pass. Van	9520	11470
2 Dr LX Pass. Van	11915	14355

OPTIONS FOR WINDSTAR

6 cyl 3.8 L Engine[Std on LX] +205
AM/FM Compact Disc Player +160
Air Conditioning[Std on LX] +405
Aluminum/Alloy Wheels[Opt on GL] +165
Child Seats (2) +125
Cruise Control[Std on LX] +105
Dual Air Conditioning +470
Keyless Entry System +100
Leather Seats +385
Luggage Rack +80
Power Door Locks[Std on LX] +115
Power Windows[Std on LX] +120
Traction Control System +135

1996 FORD

AEROSTAR   1996

Smoother shifting transmission debuts, along with revised A/C controls and a new radio with visible controls. Solar tinted glass is standard.

RATINGS (SCALE OF 1-10)

Overall	Safety	Reliability	Performance	Comfort	Value
7.4	5.7	7.7	6.8	7.5	9.1

Category G		
2 Dr STD Cargo Van	5600	6915
2 Dr XLT Pass. Van	6320	7805
2 Dr XLT Pass. Van Ext	6730	8310
2 Dr XLT 4WD Pass. Van Ext	8815	10885

OPTIONS FOR AEROSTAR

6 cyl 4.0 L Engine[Opt on 2WD] +310
AM/FM Compact Disc Player +135
Air Conditioning[Opt on STD] +330
Aluminum/Alloy Wheels +135
Captain Chairs (4) +255
Child Seat (1) +70
Cruise Control[Opt on STD,Pass. Van] +85
Dual Air Conditioning +385
Luggage Rack +65
Power Door Locks +95
Power Windows +95

ASPIRE   1996

Korean-built minicompact loses the SE trim level and several items of standard and optional equipment. Four new colors debut.

Model Description	Trade-in Value	Market Value

RATINGS (SCALE OF 1-10)

Overall	Safety	Reliability	Performance	Comfort	Value
7.1	6.6	8.5	7.2	7.3	5.9

Category E
2 Dr STD Hbk	2745	3610
4 Dr STD Hbk	2935	3860

OPTIONS FOR ASPIRE
Auto 3-Speed Transmission +255
AM/FM Stereo Tape +125
Air Conditioning +330
Anti-Lock Brakes +275
Power Steering +105

BRONCO   1996

Trick new turn signal system is embedded in side view mirrors. Otherwise, minor trim changes mark the passing of the last Bronco.

RATINGS (SCALE OF 1-10)

Overall	Safety	Reliability	Performance	Comfort	Value
7.2	8	8.6	6.4	6.6	6.5

Category H
2 Dr Eddie Bauer 4WD Utility	12355	14890
2 Dr XL 4WD Utility	10630	12805
2 Dr XLT 4WD Utility	11085	13355

OPTIONS FOR BRONCO
8 cyl 5.8 L Engine +385
Auto 4-Speed Transmission[Opt on XL,XLT] +410
AM/FM Compact Disc Player +125
Air Conditioning[Opt on XL,XLT] +330
Camper/Towing Package +140
Chrome Wheels +120
Keyless Entry System +70
Leather Seats +400
Limited Slip Diff +105
Power Door Locks +75
Power Windows +75
Rear Window Defroster[Opt on XL,XLT] +60
Velour/Cloth Seats[Std on XLT] +55

CLUB WAGON/ECONOLINE 1996

For Club Wagon, the flip-out rear door glass is replaced by that of the fixed variety, four new colors are available, and E-150 models get plastic hubcaps. For Econoline, monster 14,050 GVWR E-350 van and van cutaway are introduced.

RATINGS (SCALE OF 1-10)

Overall	Safety	Reliability	Performance	Comfort	Value
N/A	7	8.5	6.4	7.8	N/A

E-150
Category H
2 Dr Chateau Club Wagon	12550	15120
2 Dr STD Econoline	9090	10950
2 Dr XL Club Wagon	9800	11805
2 Dr XL Econoline	9545	11500
2 Dr XLT Club Wagon	10960	13205

E-250
Category H
2 Dr STD Econoline	8335	10040
2 Dr STD Econoline Ext	9045	10895
2 Dr XL Econoline	8565	10320
2 Dr XL Econoline Ext	9355	11270

E-350
Category H
2 Dr Chateau Club Wagon	11560	13925
2 Dr STD Econoline	8140	9805
2 Dr STD Econoline Ext	8565	10320
2 Dr XL Club Wagon	9385	11305
2 Dr XL Club Wagon Ext	9640	11615
2 Dr XL Econoline	8830	10640
2 Dr XL Econoline Ext	9130	11000
2 Dr XLT Club Wagon	9795	11800
2 Dr XLT Club Wagon Ext	10085	12150

OPTIONS FOR CLUB WAGON/ECONOLINE
8 cyl 5.0 L Engine +230
8 cyl 5.8 L Engine +385
8 cyl 7.3 L Turbodsl Engine +1850
8 cyl 7.5 L Engine +335
Auto 4-Speed Transmission[Opt on E-250,E-350,STD] +120
AM/FM Stereo Tape[Std on Chateau] +85
Air Conditioning[Std on XLT] +330
Aluminum/Alloy Wheels[Std on Chateau] +125
Anti-Lock Brakes[Opt on Econoline,Econoline Ext] +200
Camper/Towing Package +140
Chrome Bumpers[Std on Chateau,XLT,E-150] +70
Cruise Control[Std on Chateau] +75
Dual Air Conditioning[Std on Chateau] +540
Keyless Entry System +70
Limited Slip Diff +105
Power Door Locks[Opt on STD, XL Club Wagon] +75
Power Driver's Seat +115
Power Windows[Opt on STD, XL Club Wagon] +75

CONTOUR   1996

Designers sculpt and adjust interior seating to make more leg and head room in the back seat. Five new colors are available and improvements to shift effort on manual transmission models make the 1996 Contour more competitive.

RATINGS (SCALE OF 1-10)

Overall	Safety	Reliability	Performance	Comfort	Value
7.2	6.8	6.5	8.2	7.9	6.6

Category C
4 Dr GL Sdn	5085	6520
4 Dr LX Sdn	5410	6935
4 Dr SE Sdn	5620	7205

Don't forget to refer to the Mileage Adjustment Table at the back of this book!

Model Description	Trade-in Value	Market Value

OPTIONS FOR CONTOUR
6 cyl 2.5 L Engine[Std on SE] +405
Auto 4-Speed Transmission +315
AM/FM Compact Disc Player +145
Air Conditioning +325
Anti-Lock Brakes +245
Keyless Entry System +75
Leather Seats +245
Power Door Locks +100
Power Driver's Seat +120
Power Moonroof +280
Power Windows +125

CROWN VICTORIA 1996

A new steering wheel and gas cap are standard, and some equipment has been dropped from the roster, including the JBL sound system and trailer towing package.

RATINGS (SCALE OF 1-10)

Overall	Safety	Reliability	Performance	Comfort	Value
7.9	7.7	7	7.7	8.2	8.8

Category B
4 Dr LX Sdn	8470	10590
4 Dr STD Sdn	8105	10130

OPTIONS FOR CROWN VICTORIA
Handling/Performance Pkg +420
Preferred Equipment Pkg 2 +485
Anti-Lock Brakes +280
Climate Control for AC +70
Cruise Control +90
Dual Power Seats +155
Keyless Entry System +70
Leather Seats +275
Power Door Locks +105
Premium Sound System +160
Traction Control System +70
Trip Computer +160

ESCORT 1996

Last year for the second-generation Escort. The 1.9-liter engine gets 100,000-mile tune-up interval. Automatic transmissions have lower final drive ratio when coupled with 1.9-liter engine to improve acceleration. Sport/Appearance Group available on four-door models. Ultra Violet decor no longer offered on GT. Integrated child safety seat, added during 1995 model year, continues for 1996 on sedan and wagon.

RATINGS (SCALE OF 1-10)

Overall	Safety	Reliability	Performance	Comfort	Value
7.1	6.6	8.3	6.8	7.3	6.5

Category E
2 Dr GT Hbk	4710	6195
2 Dr LX Hbk	3645	4795
4 Dr LX Hbk	3795	4995

4 Dr LX Sdn	3805	5005
4 Dr LX Wgn	3935	5175
2 Dr STD Hbk	3415	4495

OPTIONS FOR ESCORT
Auto 4-Speed Transmission +315
AM/FM Compact Disc Player +185
Air Conditioning +330
Anti-Lock Brakes +275
Child Seat (1) +45
Cruise Control +90
Luggage Rack +50
Power Door Locks +100
Power Moonroof +230
Power Steering[Std on GT] +105
Power Windows +105
Rear Spoiler[Opt on LX] +85
Tilt Steering Wheel +60

EXPLORER 1996

The long-awaited V8 AWD Explorers are available in XLT, Eddie Bauer or Limited Edition flavors. An integrated child safety seat is optional, and the Expedition model has been replaced by a Premium trim package for the Sport.

RATINGS (SCALE OF 1-10)

Overall	Safety	Reliability	Performance	Comfort	Value
6.8	7.4	7.1	7.6	7.1	4.9

Category G
4 Dr Eddie Bauer Wgn	12000	14815
4 Dr Eddie Bauer 4WD Wgn	12440	15360
4 Dr Limited Wgn	12600	15555
4 Dr Limited 4WD Wgn	13115	16190
2 Dr Sport Utility	9350	11545
2 Dr Sport 4WD Utility	10270	12680
2 Dr XL Utility	8395	10365
2 Dr XL 4WD Utility	9860	12170
4 Dr XL Wgn	10065	12425
4 Dr XL 4WD Wgn	10540	13010
4 Dr XLT Wgn	11015	13600
4 Dr XLT 4WD Wgn	11550	14260

OPTIONS FOR EXPLORER
8 cyl 5.0 L Engine +385
Auto 4-Speed Transmission[Opt on Sport,XL,XLT] +380
Premium Sport Pkg +970
AM/FM Stereo Tape[Std on Eddie Bauer] +90
Aluminum/Alloy Wheels +135
Camper/Towing Package +120
Child Seat (1) +70
Chrome Wheels[Opt on Sport] +70
Climate Control for AC[Std on Limited] +80
Compact Disc Changer +210
Cruise Control[Opt on XL] +85
Dual Power Seats[Opt on XLT] +155
JBL Sound System[Std on Limited] +310

Don't forget to refer to the Mileage Adjustment Table at the back of this book!

Model Description	Trade-in Value	Market Value	Model Description	Trade-in Value	Market Value
Keyless Entry System[Opt on Sport,XLT, Eddie Bauer] +80			2 Dr Special Ext Cab LB	6690	8060
Leather Seats[Std on Limited] +315			2 Dr Special Ext Cab SB	6520	7855
Limited Slip Diff +110			2 Dr Special Std Cab LB	5975	7200
Luggage Rack[Opt on Sport,XL,XLT] +65			2 Dr Special 4WD Std Cab LB	7615	9175
Power Door Locks[Opt on XL] +95			2 Dr Special Std Cab SB	5810	7000
Power Moonroof +350			2 Dr Special 4WD Std Cab SB	7460	8985
Power Windows[Opt on XL] +95			2 Dr XL Ext Cab LB	8255	9945
Running Boards[Std on Limited] +155			2 Dr XL 4WD Ext Cab LB	9700	11685

F-250 HEAVY DUTY — 1996

Category H

Model Description	Trade-in Value	Market Value
2 Dr XL Std Cab LB	10655	12835
2 Dr XLT Std Cab LB	11695	14090

OPTIONS FOR F-250 HEAVY DUTY

AM/FM Stereo Tape[Opt on XL] +85
Air Conditioning[Opt on XL] +330
Camper/Towing Package +140
Cruise Control[Opt on XL] +75
Tilt Steering Wheel[Opt on XL] +75
Velour/Cloth Seats[Opt on XL] +55

F-SERIES PICKUP — 1996

Until an all-new truck goes into production for release in the spring, we're stuck with the same old truck that's been on the road since 1980. The Lightning has been axed from the 1996 lineup. Two new F-250 models debut, and both F-250 and F-350 models receive improvements.

RATINGS (SCALE OF 1-10)

Overall	Safety	Reliability	Performance	Comfort	Value
N/A	6.6	7.7	6.8	7.4	N/A

F-150

Category H

Model Description	Trade-in Value	Market Value
2 Dr Eddie Bauer Ext Cab LB	9800	11805
2 Dr Eddie Bauer 4WD Ext Cab LB	11420	13760
2 Dr Eddie Bauer Ext Cab SB	9735	11730
2 Dr Eddie Bauer 4WD Ext Cab SB	11300	13615
2 Dr Eddie Bauer Ext Cab Stepside SB	10085	12150
2 Dr Eddie Bauer 4WD Ext Cab Stepside SB	11685	14080
2 Dr Eddie Bauer Std Cab LB	8655	10430
2 Dr Eddie Bauer 4WD Std Cab LB	10385	12515
2 Dr Eddie Bauer Std Cab SB	8600	10360
2 Dr Eddie Bauer 4WD Std Cab SB	10280	12385
2 Dr Eddie Bauer Std Cab Stepside SB	8970	10805
2 Dr Eddie Bauer 4WD Std Cab Stepside SB	10630	12810

Model Description	Trade-in Value	Market Value
2 Dr XL Ext Cab SB	8145	9815
2 Dr XL 4WD Ext Cab SB	9560	11520
2 Dr XL Ext Cab Stepside SB	8530	10275
2 Dr XL 4WD Ext Cab Stepside SB	9300	11205
2 Dr XL Std Cab LB	7180	8650
2 Dr XL 4WD Std Cab LB	9090	10950
2 Dr XL Std Cab SB	7125	8585
2 Dr XL 4WD Std Cab SB	9015	10860
2 Dr XL Std Cab Stepside SB	7570	9120
2 Dr XL 4WD Std Cab Stepside SB	9435	11365
2 Dr XLT Ext Cab LB	9625	11595
2 Dr XLT 4WD Ext Cab LB	10830	13050
2 Dr XLT Ext Cab SB	9545	11500
2 Dr XLT 4WD Ext Cab SB	10765	12970
2 Dr XLT Ext Cab Stepside SB	9875	11900
2 Dr XLT 4WD Ext Cab Stepside SB	11040	13300
2 Dr XLT Std Cab LB	8595	10355
2 Dr XLT 4WD Std Cab LB	10585	12750
2 Dr XLT Std Cab SB	8485	10220
2 Dr XLT 4WD Std Cab SB	10520	12675
2 Dr XLT Std Cab Stepside SB	8820	10625
2 Dr XLT 4WD Std Cab Stepside SB	10530	12685

F-250

Category H

Model Description	Trade-in Value	Market Value
4 Dr XL Crew Cab LB	13360	16095
4 Dr XL 4WD Crew Cab LB	15040	18120
2 Dr XL Ext Cab LB	10100	12170
2 Dr XL 4WD Ext Cab LB	12030	14495
2 Dr XL Ext Cab SB	9970	12010
2 Dr XL 4WD Ext Cab SB	12015	14475
2 Dr XL Std Cab LB	8090	9745
2 Dr XL 4WD Std Cab LB	10800	13010
4 Dr XLT Crew Cab LB	13915	16765
4 Dr XLT 4WD Crew Cab LB	15610	18805
2 Dr XLT Ext Cab LB	11070	13340
2 Dr XLT 4WD Ext Cab LB	12945	15595
2 Dr XLT Ext Cab SB	11015	13270
2 Dr XLT 4WD Ext Cab SB	12775	15390

Don't forget to refer to the Mileage Adjustment Table at the back of this book!

Model Description	Trade-in Value	Market Value	Model Description	Trade-in Value	Market Value
2 Dr XLT Std Cab LB	9875	11895	2 Dr GT Conv	9930	12570
2 Dr XLT 4WD Std Cab LB	11595	13970	2 Dr GT Cpe	8265	10460
F-350			2 Dr STD Conv	8510	10770
Category H			2 Dr STD Cpe	6965	8815
4 Dr XL Crew Cab LB	12535	15105			
4 Dr XL 4WD Crew Cab LB	14000	16865	*OPTIONS FOR MUSTANG*		
2 Dr XL Ext Cab LB	12270	14785	*Auto 4-Speed Transmission +315*		
2 Dr XL Std Cab LB	11390	13720	*Mystic Metallic Paint +315*		
2 Dr XL 4WD Std Cab LB	13020	15685	*Air Conditioning[Std on Cobra] +340*		
4 Dr XLT Crew Cab LB	13515	16285	*Anti-Lock Brakes[Std on Cobra] +275*		
4 Dr XLT 4WD Crew Cab LB	15025	18105	*Compact Disc W/fm/tape +205*		
2 Dr XLT Ext Cab LB	13210	15915	*Cruise Control[Std on Cobra] +85*		
2 Dr XLT Std Cab LB	12595	15175	*Keyless Entry System[Std on Cobra] +70*		
2 Dr XLT 4WD Std Cab LB	13460	16215	*Leather Seats +265*		

OPTIONS FOR F-SERIES PICKUP

8 cyl 5.0 L Engine +230
8 cyl 5.8 L Engine +385
8 cyl 7.3 L Turbodsl Engine +1850
8 cyl 7.5 L Engine +335
Auto 3-Speed Transmission +300
Auto 4-Speed Transmission +390
Air Conditioning[Opt on Special,XL] +330
Anti-Lock Brakes +200
Camper/Towing Package +140
Chrome Wheels[Opt on XL] +120
Compact Disc W/fm/tape +125
Cruise Control[Opt on Special,XL] +75
Dual Rear Wheels +335
Keyless Entry System +70
Limited Slip Diff +105
Power Door Locks[Opt on XL] +75
Power Driver's Seat +115
Power Windows[Opt on XL] +75
Rear Bench Seat +130
Skid Plates +45
Tilt Steering Wheel[Opt on Special,XL] +75

MUSTANG — 1996

After much anticipation among enthusiasts, Ford plugs a 4.6-liter modular V8 into its pony car. Too bad it doesn't make any more power than the old 5.0-liter motor it replaces. Suspension and steering upgrades compliment the new engine, which does live up to its promise in the limited-edition 305-horsepower Cobra. Base cars also get engine improvements, and all Mustangs get minor styling revisions. Collectors tip: The GTS model, a midyear 1995 V8 base Mustang, has been dropped. Buy one if you can find one.

RATINGS (SCALE OF 1-10)

Overall	Safety	Reliability	Performance	Comfort	Value
6.8	6.9	7.7	8.8	7.3	3.4

Category F

	Trade-in	Market
2 Dr Cobra Conv	13720	17365
2 Dr Cobra Cpe	11430	14470

Power Door Locks[Std on Cobra,Conv] +80
Power Driver's Seat[Std on Cobra] +100
Power Windows[Std on Cobra,Conv] +90
Premium Sound System +150
Rear Spoiler[Std on Cobra,Conv] +100

PROBE — 1996

Ford concentrates on the SE and GT trim levels this year, revising and simplifying options lists and making minor cosmetic and trim revisions.

RATINGS (SCALE OF 1-10)

Overall	Safety	Reliability	Performance	Comfort	Value
6.9	7.1	7.5	9	7.4	3.5

Category E

	Trade-in	Market
2 Dr GT Hbk	6265	8245
2 Dr SE Hbk	5385	7085
2 Dr STD Hbk	5175	6810

OPTIONS FOR PROBE

Auto 4-Speed Transmission +315
AM/FM Compact Disc Player +185
Air Conditioning +330
Anti-Lock Brakes +275
Chrome Wheels +155
Cruise Control +90
Keyless Entry System +65
Leather Seats +355
Power Door Locks +100
Power Driver's Seat +125
Power Sunroof +250
Power Windows +105
Tilt Steering Wheel +60

RANGER — 1996

An optional passenger-side airbag is available, and it comes with a switch that will disable the system if a child seat is installed in the truck. Cool, huh? Super Cab models get standard privacy glass, Splash models lose that putrid green tape stripe, and the Flareside box from the Splash is now available on two-wheel drive, four-cylinder XL and XLT models.

Don't forget to refer to the Mileage Adjustment Table at the back of this book!

FORD 96

Model Description	Trade-in Value	Market Value	Model Description	Trade-in Value	Market Value

RATINGS (SCALE OF 1-10)

Overall	Safety	Reliability	Performance	Comfort	Value
N/A	6.7	8.7	7.2	7.3	N/A

Category G

Model	Trade-in	Market
2 Dr STX 4WD Ext Cab SB	8175	10095
2 Dr STX 4WD Std Cab LB	8240	10175
2 Dr STX 4WD Std Cab SB	8165	10080
2 Dr Splash Ext Cab Stepside SB	7535	9305
2 Dr Splash 4WD Ext Cab Stepside SB	9690	11965
2 Dr Splash Std Cab Stepside SB	6825	8425
2 Dr Splash 4WD Std Cab Stepside SB	8940	11035
2 Dr XL Ext Cab SB	6310	7790
2 Dr XL 4WD Ext Cab SB	8355	10315
2 Dr XL Ext Cab Stepside SB	6510	8035
2 Dr XL 4WD Ext Cab Stepside SB	8840	10915
2 Dr XL Std Cab LB	5275	6515
2 Dr XL 4WD Std Cab LB	7105	8770
2 Dr XL Std Cab SB	5190	6410
2 Dr XL 4WD Std Cab SB	7025	8670
2 Dr XL Std Cab Stepside SB	5190	6405
2 Dr XL 4WD Std Cab Stepside SB	7430	9170
2 Dr XLT Ext Cab SB	6480	8000
2 Dr XLT 4WD Ext Cab SB	8380	10345
2 Dr XLT Ext Cab Stepside SB	6710	8285
2 Dr XLT 4WD Ext Cab Stepside SB	8865	10945
2 Dr XLT Std Cab LB	5690	7025
2 Dr XLT 4WD Std Cab LB	7990	9865
2 Dr XLT Std Cab SB	5605	6920
2 Dr XLT 4WD Std Cab SB	7890	9740
2 Dr XLT Std Cab Stepside SB	5650	6975
2 Dr XLT 4WD Std Cab Stepside SB	8045	9935

OPTIONS FOR RANGER
6 cyl 3.0 L Engine +290
6 cyl 4.0 L Engine +310
Auto 4-Speed Transmission +420
AM/FM Compact Disc Player +135
Air Conditioning +330
Anti-Lock Brakes[Opt on 2WD] +245
Bed Liner +115
Chrome Wheels[Opt on XL,XLT] +70
Cruise Control +85
Dual Air Bag Restraints +175
Keyless Entry System +80
Limited Slip Diff +110
Power Door Locks +95
Power Driver's Seat +115
Power Steering[Std on Splash,STX,Ext Cab,4WD] +115
Power Windows +95

TAURUS 1996

All-new Taurus debuts in sedan and wagon format, available in GL, LX and SHO trim levels. New or substantially revised engines and suspensions improve the performance of the Taurus, while several functional innovations make the car easier and more enjoyable to drive.

RATINGS (SCALE OF 1-10)

Overall	Safety	Reliability	Performance	Comfort	Value
7.7	7.6	6.3	8	8	8.8

Category C

Model	Trade-in	Market
4 Dr G Sdn	5990	7680
4 Dr GL Sdn	6435	8250
4 Dr GL Wgn	6605	8465
4 Dr LX Sdn	7285	9340
4 Dr LX Wgn	7525	9650

Category F

4 Dr SHO Sdn	9845	12465

OPTIONS FOR TAURUS
AM/FM Compact Disc Player +145
Anti-Lock Brakes[Std on SHO] +245
Child Seat (1) +50
Chrome Wheels[Opt on LX] +245
Climate Control for AC +70
Cruise Control[Std on SHO] +85
Keyless Entry System +70
Leather Seats[Opt on LX] +245
Power Door Locks[Opt on GL] +100
Power Driver's Seat[Opt on GL] +120
Power Moonroof +265
Premium Sound System +160
Third Seat +70

THUNDERBIRD 1996

Revised styling greatly improves the look of the Thunderbird for 1996. The Super Coupe is deleted, replaced by a Sport Package for the V8 model. Base V6 engines have been upgraded, and go 100,000 miles between tune-ups. Equipment rosters have been shuffled.

RATINGS (SCALE OF 1-10)

Overall	Safety	Reliability	Performance	Comfort	Value
7.4	7.7	7	8	7.9	6.6

Category C

2 Dr LX Cpe	7105	9110

OPTIONS FOR THUNDERBIRD
Preferred Equipment Pkg 2 +365
AM/FM Compact Disc Player +145

Don't forget to refer to the Mileage Adjustment Table at the back of this book!

EDMUND'S® USED CARS & TRUCKS   www.edmunds.com   199

Model Description	Trade-in Value	Market Value	Model Description	Trade-in Value	Market Value

Anti-Lock Brakes +245
Climate Control for AC +70
Keyless Entry System +75
Leather Seats +245
Power Driver's Seat +120
Power Moonroof +280
Premium Sound System +160
Traction Control System +100

WINDSTAR 1996

Holy Smokes! That's just what the front tires will be doing, unless you find one with the optional traction control system. Ford boosted output on the 3.8-liter V6 from 155 to 200 horsepower. Trim and equipment have been revised, and four-wheel disc brakes come with traction control or the tow package. A new integrated child safety seat has been added to the options list. Tune-ups happen every 100,000 miles.

RATINGS (SCALE OF 1-10)

Overall	Safety	Reliability	Performance	Comfort	Value
7.4	8.2	6.4	6.8	7.3	8.5

Category G
2 Dr GL Pass. Van	7960	9825
2 Dr LX Pass. Van	9900	12225
2 Dr STD Cargo Van	6045	7465

OPTIONS FOR WINDSTAR
6 cyl 3.8 L Engine[Std on LX] +175
AM/FM Compact Disc Player +135
Air Conditioning[Std on LX] +330
Child Seats (2) +105
Cruise Control +85
Dual Air Conditioning +385
Keyless Entry System +80
Luggage Rack +65
Power Door Locks[Std on LX] +95
Power Windows[Std on LX] +95
Traction Control System +110

1995 FORD

AEROSTAR 1995

The XL and Eddie Bauer trim levels are dropped; only the XLT remains. The AWD system is available only in extended-length versions. Antilock brakes become standard for the Aerostar.

RATINGS (SCALE OF 1-10)

Overall	Safety	Reliability	Performance	Comfort	Value
7.2	6.1	7.4	6.6	7.5	8.5

Category G
2 Dr STD Cargo Van	4055	5135
2 Dr XLT Pass. Van	5465	6920
2 Dr XLT Pass. Van Ext	6010	7605
2 Dr XLT 4WD Pass. Van Ext	7155	9060

OPTIONS FOR AEROSTAR
6 cyl 4.0 L Engine[Opt on 2WD] +255
AM/FM Stereo Tape[Std on 4WD] +75
Air Conditioning[Opt on STD] +270
Camper/Towing Package +100
Captain Chairs (4) +205
Child Seat (1) +55
Cruise Control[Opt on STD] +70
Dual Air Conditioning +315
Luggage Rack +50
Power Door Locks[Std on 4WD] +75
Power Windows[Std on 4WD] +80

ASPIRE 1995

Commonly referred to as the Expire, the latest runabout from Ford has little to offer but economy. Available as a two- or four-door hatchback, the Aspire comes with dual airbags and available antilock brakes.

RATINGS (SCALE OF 1-10)

Overall	Safety	Reliability	Performance	Comfort	Value
7.4	7.3	7.9	7.2	7.3	7.3

Category E
2 Dr SE Hbk	2900	3975
2 Dr STD Hbk	2335	3200
4 Dr STD Hbk	2545	3485

OPTIONS FOR ASPIRE
Auto 3-Speed Transmission +190
AM/FM Compact Disc Player +150
Air Conditioning +270
Anti-Lock Brakes +225
Power Steering +85
Premium Sound System +110
Rear Window Defroster +55

BRONCO 1995

An available Sport Package and new exterior styling for the Eddie Bauer model are the sole changes for 1995.

RATINGS (SCALE OF 1-10)

Overall	Safety	Reliability	Performance	Comfort	Value
7.2	8.8	7.3	6.4	6.6	7

Category H
2 Dr Eddie Bauer 4WD Utility	10820	13360
2 Dr XL 4WD Utility	9360	11555
2 Dr XLT 4WD Utility	9695	11970

OPTIONS FOR BRONCO
8 cyl 5.8 L Engine +305
Auto 4-Speed Transmission[Opt on XL,XLT] +345
AM/FM Compact Disc Player +105
Air Conditioning[Opt on XL,XLT] +270
Camper/Towing Package +115
Chrome Wheels +100
Keyless Entry System +55

Don't forget to refer to the Mileage Adjustment Table at the back of this book!

FORD 95

Model Description	Trade-in Value	Market Value	Model Description	Trade-in Value	Market Value

Leather Seats +325
Limited Slip Diff +85
Power Door Locks +60
Power Windows +65
Velour/Cloth Seats +45

Limited Slip Diff +85
Power Door Locks[Opt on STD, XL] +60
Power Driver's Seat +95
Power Windows[Opt on STD, XL] +65
Velour/Cloth Seats[Std on XL] +45

CLUB WAGON/ECONOLINE 1995

The optional diesel engine gets a turbocharger. Heavy-duty versions of the van receive the driver airbag that became standard on light-duty models in 1992.

RATINGS (SCALE OF 1-10)

Overall	Safety	Reliability	Performance	Comfort	Value
N/A	7.7	8.3	6.4	7.8	N/A

E-150

Category H

2 Dr Chateau Club Wagon	8580	10590
2 Dr STD Econoline	6810	8410
2 Dr XL Club Wagon	7405	9140
2 Dr XL Econoline	7135	8810
2 Dr XLT Club Wagon	8055	9945

E-250

Category H

2 Dr STD Econoline	6570	8110
2 Dr STD Econoline Ext	6855	8460
2 Dr XL Econoline	6955	8585
2 Dr XL Econoline Ext	7430	9170

E-350

Category H

2 Dr Chateau Club Wagon	8510	10505
2 Dr STD Econoline	6745	8325
2 Dr STD Econoline Ext	7110	8775
2 Dr XL Club Wagon	7320	9040
2 Dr XL Club Wagon Ext	7755	9575
2 Dr XL Econoline	6795	8390
2 Dr XL Econoline Ext	7175	8855
2 Dr XLT Club Wagon	7990	9865
2 Dr XLT Club Wagon Ext	8360	10320

OPTIONS FOR CLUB WAGON/ECONOLINE

8 cyl 5.0 L Engine +200
8 cyl 5.8 L Engine +305
8 cyl 7.3 L Turbodsl Engine +1480
8 cyl 7.5 L Engine +290
Auto 4-Speed Transmission[Opt on E-250, E-350] +100
AM/FM Stereo Tape[Std on Chateau] +70
Air Conditioning[Opt on STD,XL] +270
Anti-Lock Brakes[Std on Club Wagon, Club Wagon Ext] +165
Camper/Towing Package[Opt on E-150, E-250,
*   Club Wagon] +115*
Chrome Bumpers +60
Cruise Control[Std on Chateau] +60
Dual Air Conditioning +440
Keyless Entry System +55

CONTOUR 1995

The Contour replaces the much-maligned Tempo in an attempt to compete with European and Japanese compacts. Based on the European Mondeo, the Contour has front-wheel drive and dual airbags. Traction control and antilock brakes are available on all models, as is a V6 engine that produces an impressive 170 horsepower.

RATINGS (SCALE OF 1-10)

Overall	Safety	Reliability	Performance	Comfort	Value
7.1	7	5.3	8.2	7.9	7.1

Category C

4 Dr GL Sdn	4110	5480
4 Dr LX Sdn	4405	5870
4 Dr SE Sdn	4720	6290

OPTIONS FOR CONTOUR

6 cyl 2.5 L Engine[Std on SE] +320
Auto 4-Speed Transmission +270
Air Conditioning +265
Anti-Lock Brakes +200
Compact Disc W/fm/tape +110
Cruise Control +70
Keyless Entry System +60
Leather Seats +200
Power Door Locks +80
Power Driver's Seat +100
Power Moonroof +225
Power Windows +105
Premium Sound System +130

CROWN VICTORIA 1995

New grille, trunk lid, wheels, and bumpers freshen the Crown Victoria's styling. Rear window defroster and heated outside mirrors move from the options list to the standard equipment roster. A new interior includes a revised stereo, backlit door switches, restyled instrument panel, and a fresh climate control system.

RATINGS (SCALE OF 1-10)

Overall	Safety	Reliability	Performance	Comfort	Value
7.4	8.1	5.4	7.7	8.2	7.4

Category B

4 Dr LX Sdn	7135	9145
4 Dr STD Sdn	6885	8830

OPTIONS FOR CROWN VICTORIA

Handling/Performance Pkg +280
AM/FM Stereo Tape +60
Aluminum/Alloy Wheels +110

Don't forget to refer to the Mileage Adjustment Table at the back of this book!

Model Description	Trade-in Value	Market Value	Model Description	Trade-in Value	Market Value

Anti-Lock Brakes +230
Camper/Towing Package +125
Climate Control for AC +55
Cruise Control +75
Dual Power Seats +125
Keyless Entry System +55
Leather Seats +225
Power Door Locks +85
Premium Sound System +130
Traction Control System +60

ESCORT   1995

A passenger airbag is now available but the motorized seatbelts mysteriously remain. A more powerful, optional air conditioner appears in the revised instrument panel. An integrated child seat is available on sedans and wagons.

RATINGS (SCALE OF 1-10)

Overall	Safety	Reliability	Performance	Comfort	Value
6.7	6.9	6.9	6.8	7.3	5.5

Category E

2 Dr GT Hbk	3900	5340
2 Dr LX Hbk	2820	3860
4 Dr LX Hbk	2920	4000
4 Dr LX Sdn	3050	4175
4 Dr LX Wgn	3090	4230
2 Dr STD Hbk	2565	3515

OPTIONS FOR ESCORT

Auto 4-Speed Transmission +270
AM/FM Compact Disc Player +150
Air Conditioning +270
Anti-Lock Brakes +225
Child Seat (1) +35
Cruise Control +75
Luggage Rack +45
Power Door Locks +80
Power Moonroof +190
Power Steering[Std on GT] +85
Power Windows +85
Premium Sound System +110
Rear Spoiler[Opt on LX] +70
Tilt Steering Wheel +50

EXPLORER   1995

Dual airbags top the changes for the redesigned Explorer. Integrated child safety seats are optional on four-door models. Exterior changes include new sheetmetal, headlights, grille, taillights, and side moldings. The Control-Trac four-wheel-drive system automatically sends power to front wheels if it senses rear-wheel slippage. This feature can be locked in for full-time four-wheeling.

RATINGS (SCALE OF 1-10)

Overall	Safety	Reliability	Performance	Comfort	Value
7.3	8	6.3	7.6	7.1	7.6

Category G

4 Dr Eddie Bauer Wgn	9995	12655
4 Dr Eddie Bauer 4WD Wgn	10525	13320
2 Dr Expedition 4WD Utility	9655	12220
4 Dr Limited Wgn	10600	13420
4 Dr Limited 4WD Wgn	10955	13870
2 Dr Sport Utility	8025	10160
2 Dr Sport 4WD Utility	8770	11100
2 Dr XL Utility	7390	9355
2 Dr XL 4WD Utility	8055	10195
4 Dr XL Wgn	8420	10660
4 Dr XL 4WD Wgn	8615	10905
4 Dr XLT Wgn	9350	11835
4 Dr XLT 4WD Wgn	9800	12405

OPTIONS FOR EXPLORER

Auto 4-Speed Transmission[Opt on Sport,XL,XLT] +310
Preferred Equipment Pkg +270
AM/FM Stereo Tape[Opt on Sport,XL,XLT] +75
Aluminum/Alloy Wheels +110
Camper/Towing Package +100
Climate Control for AC[Std on Limited] +65
Compact Disc Changer +170
Cruise Control[Opt on XL] +70
Dual Power Seats[Opt on Sport,XLT] +125
JBL Sound System[Std on Limited] +255
Keyless Entry System[Opt on Sport,XLT, Eddie Bauer] +65
Leather Seats[Std on Limited] +255
Limited Slip Diff +90
Luggage Rack[Opt on Sport,XL,XLT] +50
Power Door Locks[Opt on XL] +75
Power Moonroof +290
Power Windows[Opt on XL] +80
Running Boards[Std on Limited] +130

F-SERIES PICKUP   1995

The Lightning model returns after a one-year hiatus and a new turbodiesel engine is made available.

RATINGS (SCALE OF 1-10)

Overall	Safety	Reliability	Performance	Comfort	Value
N/A	7.3	7.4	6.8	7.4	N/A

F-150

Category H

2 Dr Eddie Bauer Ext Cab LB	8495	10490
2 Dr Eddie Bauer 4WD Ext Cab LB		
	10045	12400
2 Dr Eddie Bauer Ext Cab SB	8410	10385
2 Dr Eddie Bauer 4WD Ext Cab SB		
	9980	12320

Model Description	Trade-in Value	Market Value
2 Dr Eddie Bauer Ext Cab Stepside SB		
	8775	10835
2 Dr Eddie Bauer 4WD Ext Cab Stepside SB		
	10325	12745
2 Dr Eddie Bauer Std Cab LB	7465	9215
2 Dr Eddie Bauer 4WD Std Cab LB		
	9270	11445
2 Dr Eddie Bauer Std Cab SB	7395	9130
2 Dr Eddie Bauer 4WD Std Cab SB		
	9190	11345
2 Dr Eddie Bauer Std Cab Stepside SB		
	7740	9555
2 Dr Eddie Bauer 4WD Std Cab Stepside SB		
	9545	11785
2 Dr Lightning Std Cab SB	9760	12050
2 Dr Special Ext Cab LB	5875	7255
2 Dr Special Ext Cab SB	5765	7115
2 Dr Special Std Cab LB	5115	6315
2 Dr Special 4WD Std Cab LB	6905	8525
2 Dr Special Std Cab SB	4975	6145
2 Dr Special 4WD Std Cab SB	6845	8450
2 Dr XL Ext Cab LB	7265	8970
2 Dr XL 4WD Ext Cab LB	8730	10780
2 Dr XL Ext Cab SB	7175	8860
2 Dr XL 4WD Ext Cab SB	8590	10605
2 Dr XL Ext Cab Stepside SB	7460	9210
2 Dr XL 4WD Ext Cab Stepside SB		
	8920	11015
2 Dr XL Std Cab LB	6565	8105
2 Dr XL 4WD Std Cab LB	7935	9795
2 Dr XL Std Cab SB	6465	7980
2 Dr XL 4WD Std Cab SB	7855	9700
2 Dr XL Std Cab Stepside SB	6850	8455
2 Dr XL 4WD Std Cab Stepside SB		
	8210	10135
2 Dr XLT Ext Cab LB	8115	10020
2 Dr XLT 4WD Ext Cab LB	9620	11875
2 Dr XLT Ext Cab SB	8050	9940
2 Dr XLT 4WD Ext Cab SB	9535	11770
2 Dr XLT Ext Cab Stepside SB	8395	10365
2 Dr XLT 4WD Ext Cab Stepside SB		
	9835	12140
2 Dr XLT Std Cab LB	7455	9205
2 Dr XLT 4WD Std Cab LB	8950	11050
2 Dr XLT Std Cab SB	7390	9125
2 Dr XLT 4WD Std Cab SB	8840	10915
2 Dr XLT Std Cab Stepside SB	7730	9545
2 Dr XLT 4WD Std Cab Stepside SB		
	9175	11330

F-250
Category H

Model Description	Trade-in Value	Market Value
2 Dr Special Ext Cab LB	8105	10005
2 Dr XL Ext Cab LB	8650	10680
2 Dr XL 4WD Ext Cab LB	9730	12010
2 Dr XL Std Cab LB	7735	9550
2 Dr XL 4WD Std Cab LB	9265	11440
2 Dr XLT Ext Cab LB	9190	11345
2 Dr XLT 4WD Ext Cab LB	10715	13230
2 Dr XLT Std Cab LB	7780	9605
2 Dr XLT 4WD Std Cab LB	9475	11700

F-350
Category H

Model Description	Trade-in Value	Market Value
4 Dr XL Crew Cab LB	10295	12710
4 Dr XL 4WD Crew Cab LB	11400	14075
2 Dr XL Ext Cab LB	10075	12440
2 Dr XL Std Cab LB	8935	11030
2 Dr XL 4WD Std Cab LB	10775	13305
4 Dr XLT Crew Cab LB	11835	14610
4 Dr XLT 4WD Crew Cab LB	13510	16680
2 Dr XLT Ext Cab LB	10725	13240
2 Dr XLT Std Cab LB	10225	12625
2 Dr XLT 4WD Std Cab LB	12055	14885

OPTIONS FOR F-SERIES PICKUP
8 cyl 5.0 L Engine +200
8 cyl 5.8 L Engine +305
8 cyl 7.3 L Turbodsl Engine +1480
8 cyl 7.5 L Engine +290
Auto 3-Speed Transmission +245
Auto 4-Speed Transmission[Std on Lightning] +320
AM/FM Compact Disc Player +105
Air Conditioning[Opt on Special,XL] +270
Camper/Towing Package +115
Chrome Wheels[Opt on XL] +100
Cruise Control[Opt on Special,XL] +60
Dual Rear Wheels +275
Keyless Entry System +55
Limited Slip Diff +85
Power Driver's Seat +95
Premium Sound System +130
Skid Plates +35

MUSTANG   1995

A power driver's seat moves from the standard equipment list to the options list. A powerful new stereo with a CD changer also debuts on the options list.

RATINGS (SCALE OF 1-10)

Overall	Safety	Reliability	Performance	Comfort	Value
6.8	7.3	6.4	8.8	7.3	4.4

Category F

Model Description	Trade-in Value	Market Value
2 Dr Cobra Conv	12035	15430
2 Dr Cobra Cpe	10540	13515

Model Description	Trade-in Value	Market Value
2 Dr GT Conv	8705	11160
2 Dr GT Cpe	7665	9830
2 Dr GTS Cpe	7150	9165
2 Dr STD Conv	7420	9510
2 Dr STD Cpe	6230	7985

OPTIONS FOR MUSTANG

Auto 4-Speed Transmission +260
Air Conditioning +275
Anti-Lock Brakes[Std on Cobra] +225
Compact Disc W/fm/tape +165
Cruise Control +70
Keyless Entry System +60
Leather Seats[Opt on GT] +215
Power Door Locks[Std on Cobra,GT,Conv] +65
Power Driver's Seat +80
Power Windows[Std on Cobra,GT,Conv] +75
Rear Spoiler[Opt on STD] +80

PROBE   1995

The SE Package becomes a trim level. Base and GT models receive new taillights. GTs receive 16-inch directional wheels. The rear-window wiper washer, four-way seat height adjuster and graphic equalizer have been deleted from the option list.

RATINGS (SCALE OF 1-10)

Overall	Safety	Reliability	Performance	Comfort	Value
6.9	7.8	7.1	9	7.4	3.3

Model Description	Trade-in Value	Market Value
Category E		
2 Dr SE Hbk	4700	6435
2 Dr STD Hbk	4490	6150
Category F		
2 Dr GT Hbk	5655	7250

OPTIONS FOR PROBE

Auto 4-Speed Transmission +260
AM/FM Compact Disc Player +150
Air Conditioning[Std on SE] +270
Anti-Lock Brakes +225
Chrome Wheels +195
Cruise Control[Std on SE] +70
Keyless Entry System +50
Leather Seats +215
Power Door Locks[Std on SE] +65
Power Driver's Seat +80
Power Sunroof +205
Power Windows[Std on SE] +75

RANGER   1995

A driver airbag and optional four-wheel antilock brakes are two of the features added to the safety equipment roster of the capable Ford Ranger. SuperCab models can now be had with a power driver's seat.

RATINGS (SCALE OF 1-10)

Overall	Safety	Reliability	Performance	Comfort	Value
N/A	6.7	8.5	7.2	7.3	N/A

Model Description	Trade-in Value	Market Value
Category G		
2 Dr STX 4WD Ext Cab SB	6915	8755
2 Dr STX 4WD Std Cab LB	6520	8250
2 Dr STX 4WD Std Cab SB	6365	8060
2 Dr Splash Ext Cab Stepside SB	6610	8365
2 Dr Splash 4WD Ext Cab Stepside SB	8150	10315
2 Dr Splash Std Cab Stepside SB	5855	7410
2 Dr Splash 4WD Std Cab Stepside SB	7890	9985
2 Dr XL Ext Cab SB	5670	7180
2 Dr XL 4WD Ext Cab SB	7195	9110
2 Dr XL Std Cab LB	4490	5685
2 Dr XL 4WD Std Cab LB	6330	8015
2 Dr XL Std Cab SB	4415	5590
2 Dr XL 4WD Std Cab SB	6285	7955
2 Dr XLT Ext Cab SB	5870	7430
2 Dr XLT 4WD Ext Cab SB	7130	9025
2 Dr XLT Std Cab LB	4765	6030
2 Dr XLT 4WD Std Cab LB	6930	8775
2 Dr XLT Std Cab SB	4695	5940
2 Dr XLT 4WD Std Cab SB	6835	8650
2 Dr XLT Std Cab Stepside SB	4700	5950

OPTIONS FOR RANGER

6 cyl 3.0 L Engine +235
6 cyl 4.0 L Engine +255
Auto 4-Speed Transmission +345
AM/FM Compact Disc Player +110
Air Conditioning +270
Anti-Lock Brakes[Opt on 2WD] +200
Chrome Wheels[Std on Splash] +55
Cruise Control +70
Limited Slip Diff[Std on Splash 4WD Ext Cab Stepside SB,STX 4WD Ext Cab SB,XLT 4WD Ext Cab SB] +90
Power Door Locks +75
Power Driver's Seat +95
Power Steering[Std on Splash,STX,Ext Cab,4WD] +95
Power Windows +80
Velour/Cloth Seats +70

TAURUS   1995

Sport edition model is introduced as an SE. The SE includes aluminum wheels, sport bucket seats, air conditioning, and a rear defroster. The base engine has been revised to decrease engine noise.

Model Description	Trade-in Value	Market Value	Model Description	Trade-in Value	Market Value

FORD 95-94

RATINGS (SCALE OF 1-10)

Overall	Safety	Reliability	Performance	Comfort	Value
7.6	7.4	6.8	8	7.8	8.2

Category C
4 Dr GL Sdn	4445	5925
4 Dr GL Wgn	4645	6195
4 Dr LX Sdn	5615	7485
4 Dr LX Wgn	5740	7655
4 Dr SE Sdn	4675	6230

Category F
4 Dr SHO Sdn	6350	8140

OPTIONS FOR TAURUS

6 cyl 3.0 L FLEX Engine +155
6 cyl 3.8 L Engine[Opt on GL,SE] +210
Auto 4-Speed Transmission[Opt on SHO] +260
Anti-Lock Brakes[Std on SHO] +200
Climate Control for AC[Opt on LX] +55
Compact Disc W/fm/tape +110
Cruise Control[Std on SHO] +70
Keyless Entry System[Std on SHO] +60
Leather Seats +200
Power Door Locks[Opt on GL] +80
Power Driver's Seat[Opt on GL] +100
Power Moonroof +215
Power Passenger Seat +90
Power Windows[Opt on GL] +105
Premium Sound System[Opt on LX] +130
Third Seat +55

THUNDERBIRD   1995

The trunk-mounted CD changer is deleted in favor of an in-dash CD-player. Variable-assist power steering is lost from the standard equipment list.

RATINGS (SCALE OF 1-10)

Overall	Safety	Reliability	Performance	Comfort	Value
7.8	8.7	.7.3	8	7.9	7.1

Category C
2 Dr LX Cpe	5855	7810

Category F
2 Dr SC Sprchgd Cpe	7720	9895

OPTIONS FOR THUNDERBIRD

8 cyl 4.6 L Engine +205
Auto 4-Speed Transmission[Opt on SC] +260
AM/FM Compact Disc Player +120
Anti-Lock Brakes[Opt on LX] +200
Climate Control for AC[Opt on LX] +55
Keyless Entry System +60
Leather Seats[Opt on LX] +200
Power Door Locks[Opt on LX] +65
Power Moonroof +215
Power Passenger Seat +90
Premium Sound System +125

WINDSTAR   1995

This year, Ford introduces its version of the front-wheel drive minivan. Designed to replace the archaic Aerostar, the Windstar offers an extensive standard equipment list. Dual airbags, antilock brakes, a four-speed automatic transmission, and V6 power are just a few of the things Windstar owners will find included on their vehicle. The Windstar has seating for seven that includes a unique integrated child seat: an attractive feature for a family with toddlers.

RATINGS (SCALE OF 1-10)

Overall	Safety	Reliability	Performance	Comfort	Value
7.2	8.9	5.9	6.6	7.3	7.1

Category G
2 Dr GL Pass. Van	6110	7735
1995.5 2 Dr GL Pass. Van	6135	7765
2 Dr LX Pass. Van	7715	9765
1995.5 2 Dr LX Pass. Van	7735	9790
2 Dr STD Cargo Van	4975	6300
1995.5 2 Dr STD Cargo Van	5020	6355

OPTIONS FOR WINDSTAR

6 cyl 3.8 L Engine[Opt on 1995.5] +140
AM/FM Compact Disc Player +110
Air Conditioning[Std on LX] +270
Child Seat (1) +55
Cruise Control[Std on LX] +70
Dual Air Conditioning +315
Keyless Entry System +65
Leather Seats +255
Luggage Rack +50
Power Door Locks[Std on LX] +75
Power Windows[Std on LX] +80

1994 FORD

AEROSTAR   1994

A high-mounted rear brake light is standard. No other changes to Ford's venerable minivan.

RATINGS (SCALE OF 1-10)

Overall	Safety	Reliability	Performance	Comfort	Value
7.1	6.2	7.7	6.6	7.5	7.4

Category G
2 Dr Eddie Bauer Pass. Van	5190	6740
2 Dr Eddie Bauer 4WD Pass. Van	6050	7860
2 Dr Eddie Bauer Pass. Van Ext	5610	7285
2 Dr Eddie Bauer 4WD Pass. Van Ext	6365	8265
2 Dr STD Cargo Van	2735	3550
2 Dr STD 4WD Cargo Van	3770	4895

Don't forget to refer to the Mileage Adjustment Table at the back of this book!

Model Description	Trade-in Value	Market Value
2 Dr STD Cargo Van Ext	3370	4375
2 Dr STD 4WD Cargo Van Ext	4485	5825
2 Dr Window Cargo Van	2705	3510
2 Dr Window 4WD Cargo Van	3830	4975
2 Dr Window Cargo Van Ext	3375	4380
2 Dr Window 4WD Cargo Van Ext	4485	5825
2 Dr XL Pass. Van	3720	4830
2 Dr XL 4WD Pass. Van	4695	6095
2 Dr XL Pass. Van Ext	4115	5345
2 Dr XL 4WD Pass. Van Ext	5055	6565
2 Dr XL Plus Pass. Van	3995	5190
2 Dr XL Plus 4WD Pass. Van	4720	6130
2 Dr XL Plus Pass. Van Ext	4375	5685
2 Dr XL Plus 4WD Pass. Van Ext	5500	7140
2 Dr XLT Pass. Van	4565	5930
2 Dr XLT 4WD Pass. Van	5275	6850
2 Dr XLT Pass. Van Ext	4840	6285
2 Dr XLT 4WD Pass. Van Ext	5630	7310

OPTIONS FOR AEROSTAR

6 cyl 4.0 L Engine[Std on Cargo Van,4WD, Eddie Bauer Pass. Van Ext] +125
Auto 4-Speed Transmission[Std on Eddie Bauer, XLT,4WD] +205
AM/FM Stereo Tape +60
Air Conditioning[Std on XLT] +220
Captain Chairs (4) +170
Child Seat (1) +45
Cruise Control[Std on Eddie Bauer,XLT] +55
Dual Air Conditioning[Std on Eddie Bauer] +255
Leather Seats +210
Luggage Rack[Std on Eddie Bauer] +45
Power Door Locks[Std on Eddie Bauer] +65
Power Windows[Std on Eddie Bauer] +65
Premium Sound System[Opt on XLT] +95
Trip Computer[Opt on XLT] +40

ASPIRE   1994

Ford introduces the Aspire as a replacement for the aging Festiva. This little econobox has a 1.3-liter inline-four that produces a measly 63 horsepower. The Aspire is available with a five-speed manual or a three-speed automatic transmission.

RATINGS (SCALE OF 1-10)

Overall	Safety	Reliability	Performance	Comfort	Value
7	7.3	6.9	7.2	7.3	6.3

Category E
2 Dr SE Hbk	2385	3405
2 Dr STD Hbk	1825	2610
4 Dr STD Hbk	1775	2535

OPTIONS FOR ASPIRE

Auto 3-Speed Transmission +160
AM/FM Compact Disc Player +125

Air Conditioning +220
Anti-Lock Brakes +180
Power Steering +70
Premium Sound System +90
Rear Window Defroster +45

BRONCO   1994

The 1994 Bronco receives a driver airbag and door guard beams. ABS now works in two-wheel drive and four-wheel drive.

RATINGS (SCALE OF 1-10)

Overall	Safety	Reliability	Performance	Comfort	Value
6.9	8.8	6	6.4	6.6	6.9

Category H
2 Dr Eddie Bauer 4WD Utility	8755	11085
2 Dr XL 4WD Utility	8115	10270
2 Dr XLT 4WD Utility	8305	10515

OPTIONS FOR BRONCO

8 cyl 5.8 L Engine +235
Auto 4-Speed Transmission[Opt on XL,XLT] +255
AM/FM Compact Disc Player +85
Air Conditioning[Opt on XL,XLT] +220
Camper/Towing Package +90
Chrome Wheels +80
Keyless Entry System +45
Leather Seats +265
Limited Slip Diff +70
Power Door Locks +50
Power Windows +50
Swing Out Tire Carrier +45

CLUB WAGON/ECONOLINE 1994

Four-wheel antilock brakes replace previous rear-wheel antilock brakes.

RATINGS (SCALE OF 1-10)

Overall	Safety	Reliability	Performance	Comfort	Value
N/A	7.8	8.5	6.4	7.8	N/A

E-150

Category H
2 Dr Chateau Club Wagon	7775	9840
2 Dr STD Econoline	5820	7365
2 Dr XL Club Wagon	6420	8125
2 Dr XL Econoline	6115	7740
2 Dr XLT Club Wagon	7005	8870

E-250

Category H
2 Dr STD Econoline	5485	6940
2 Dr STD Econoline Ext	5670	7180
2 Dr XL Econoline	5860	7420

Don't forget to refer to the Mileage Adjustment Table at the back of this book!

Model Description	Trade-in Value	Market Value

E-350

Category H

Model Description	Trade-in Value	Market Value
2 Dr Chateau Club Wagon	7690	9735
2 Dr STD Econoline	6100	7720
2 Dr STD Econoline Ext	6365	8055
2 Dr XL Club Wagon	6835	8655
2 Dr XL Club Wagon Ext	7080	8960
2 Dr XL Econoline	6255	7920
2 Dr XLT Club Wagon	6980	8835
2 Dr XLT Club Wagon Ext	7205	9120

OPTIONS FOR CLUB WAGON/ECONOLINE

8 cyl 5.0 L Engine +165
8 cyl 5.8 L Engine +235
8 cyl 7.3 L Dsl Engine +695
8 cyl 7.5 L Engine +245
Auto 4-Speed Transmission[Std on Chateau,Club Wagon Ext,E-150 XL Club Wagon,E-150 XLT Club Wagon] +80
AM/FM Stereo Tape[Std on Chateau] +60
Air Conditioning[Std on Chateau,E-150 XLT Club Wagon] +220
Anti-Lock Brakes[Opt on STD,Econoline] +135
Camper/Towing Package[Std on E-350 STD Econoline, E-350 Club Wagon,E-350 Club Wagon Ext] +90
Chrome Bumpers[Opt on STD] +45
Cruise Control +50
Dual Air Conditioning +360
Limited Slip Diff +70
Power Door Locks[Opt on STD] +50
Power Driver's Seat[Std on Chateau] +75
Power Passenger Seat +70
Power Windows[Opt on STD, XL] +50
Premium Sound System +105
Velour/Cloth Seats[Opt on STD, XL Club Wagon] +35

CROWN VICTORIA 1994

A passenger airbag is now standard. Air conditioning gets CFC-free refrigerant.

RATINGS (SCALE OF 1-10)

Overall	Safety	Reliability	Performance	Comfort	Value
7.9	7.8	7	7.7	8.2	8.6

Category B

Model	Trade-in Value	Market Value
4 Dr LX Sdn	5515	7255
4 Dr S Sdn	5325	7005
4 Dr STD Sdn	5345	7030

OPTIONS FOR CROWN VICTORIA

Preferred Equipment Pkg +225
AM/FM Stereo Tape +50
Aluminum/Alloy Wheels +90
Anti-Lock Brakes +185
Climate Control for AC +45
Cruise Control[Std on S] +60
Keyless Entry System +45
Leather Seats +185
Power Door Locks +70

Premium Sound System +105
Traction Control System +50

ESCORT 1994

A driver airbag debuts on all models. Antilock brakes are now available on the GT. The LX-E sedan is dropped from the lineup.

RATINGS (SCALE OF 1-10)

Overall	Safety	Reliability	Performance	Comfort	Value
6.9	6.2	8	6.8	7.6	5.9

Category E

Model	Trade-in Value	Market Value
2 Dr GT Hbk	3100	4430
2 Dr LX Hbk	2220	3170
4 Dr LX Hbk	2450	3500
4 Dr LX Sdn	2435	3480
4 Dr LX Wgn	2550	3640
2 Dr STD Hbk	2175	3105

OPTIONS FOR ESCORT

Auto 4-Speed Transmission +215
AM/FM Compact Disc Player +125
Air Conditioning +220
Anti-Lock Brakes +180
Cruise Control +60
Luggage Rack +35
Power Door Locks +65
Power Moonroof +155
Power Steering[Std on GT] +70
Power Windows +70
Premium Sound System +90
Rear Spoiler[Opt on LX] +60

EXPLORER 1994

New wheels and a power equipment group for the Eddie Bauer model are the only changes to this year's Explorer.

RATINGS (SCALE OF 1-10)

Overall	Safety	Reliability	Performance	Comfort	Value
6.8	5.2	5.5	7.4	8.3	7.4

Category G

Model	Trade-in Value	Market Value
2 Dr Eddie Bauer Utility	6560	8520
2 Dr Eddie Bauer 4WD Utility	7020	9115
4 Dr Eddie Bauer Wgn	6780	8805
4 Dr Eddie Bauer 4WD Wgn	7445	9670
4 Dr Limited Wgn	7740	10050
4 Dr Limited 4WD Wgn	8330	10820
2 Dr Sport Utility	6200	8055
2 Dr Sport 4WD Utility	6405	8320
2 Dr XL Utility	5570	7235
2 Dr XL 4WD Utility	6020	7815
4 Dr XL Wgn	6380	8285
4 Dr XL 4WD Wgn	6535	8485

Model Description	Trade-in Value	Market Value
4 Dr XLT Wgn	6655	8645
4 Dr XLT 4WD Wgn	7090	9210

OPTIONS FOR EXPLORER

Auto 4-Speed Transmission[Std on Limited] +245
Air Conditioning[Std on Limited] +220
Camper/Towing Package +80
Compact Disc W/fm/tape +130
Cruise Control[Opt on Sport,XL] +55
JBL Sound System +210
Keyless Entry System[Std on Limited] +55
Leather Seats[Std on Limited] +210
Limited Slip Diff +75
Luggage Rack[Opt on Sport,XL, XLT Wgn] +45
Power Door Locks[Opt on Sport,XL] +65
Power Windows[Opt on Sport,XL] +65
Running Boards +105

F-SERIES PICKUP   1994

A driver airbag becomes part of the standard equipment list on the light-duty trucks. Side-door beams and a high-mounted third taillight round out the safety changes for this year. New options include a CD player and a unique tri-fold seat that turns into a center armrest.

RATINGS (SCALE OF 1-10)

Overall	Safety	Reliability	Performance	Comfort	Value
N/A	7.1	6.9	6.8	7.4	N/A

F-150
Category H

Model Description	Trade-in Value	Market Value
2 Dr Eddie Bauer Ext Cab LB	6650	8415
2 Dr Lightning Std Cab SB	8740	11065
2 Dr S Ext Cab LB	4880	6175
2 Dr S Ext Cab SB	4690	5935
2 Dr S Std Cab LB	5255	6655
2 Dr S 4WD Std Cab LB	6545	8285
2 Dr S Std Cab SB	4405	5575
2 Dr S 4WD Std Cab SB	6420	8125
2 Dr XL Ext Cab LB	6215	7865
2 Dr XL 4WD Ext Cab LB	6930	8775
2 Dr XL Ext Cab SB	6135	7765
2 Dr XL 4WD Ext Cab SB	6865	8690
2 Dr XL Ext Cab Stepside SB	6465	8185
2 Dr XL 4WD Ext Cab Stepside SB	7145	9045
2 Dr XL Std Cab LB	5490	6950
2 Dr XL 4WD Std Cab LB	6575	8320
2 Dr XL Std Cab SB	5380	6810
2 Dr XL 4WD Std Cab SB	6520	8255
2 Dr XL Std Cab Stepside SB	5615	7110
2 Dr XL 4WD Std Cab Stepside SB	6750	8545
2 Dr XLT Ext Cab LB	6985	8840
2 Dr XLT 4WD Ext Cab LB	7660	9695

Model Description	Trade-in Value	Market Value
2 Dr XLT Ext Cab SB	6930	8770
2 Dr XLT 4WD Ext Cab SB	7505	9500
2 Dr XLT Ext Cab Stepside SB	7195	9110
2 Dr XLT 4WD Ext Cab Stepside SB	7785	9855
2 Dr XLT Std Cab LB	6155	7790
2 Dr XLT 4WD Std Cab LB	7135	9030
2 Dr XLT Std Cab SB	6065	7675
2 Dr XLT 4WD Std Cab SB	7005	8870
2 Dr XLT Std Cab Stepside SB	6325	8005
2 Dr XLT 4WD Std Cab Stepside SB	7350	9305

F-250
Category H

Model Description	Trade-in Value	Market Value
2 Dr S Ext Cab LB	7115	9005
2 Dr XL Ext Cab LB	7535	9540
2 Dr XL 4WD Ext Cab LB	9295	11765
2 Dr XL Std Cab LB	6910	8745
2 Dr XL 4WD Std Cab LB	8105	10260
2 Dr XLT Ext Cab LB	8520	10785
2 Dr XLT 4WD Ext Cab LB	9845	12460
2 Dr XLT Std Cab LB	7455	9435
2 Dr XLT 4WD Std Cab LB	8905	11270

F-350
Category H

Model Description	Trade-in Value	Market Value
4 Dr XL Crew Cab LB	9015	11410
4 Dr XL 4WD Crew Cab LB	10035	12705
2 Dr XL Ext Cab LB	8070	10215
2 Dr XL Std Cab LB	8330	10545
2 Dr XL 4WD Std Cab LB	9395	11890
4 Dr XLT Crew Cab LB	9610	12165
4 Dr XLT 4WD Crew Cab LB	10570	13380
2 Dr XLT Ext Cab LB	8780	11115
2 Dr XLT Std Cab LB	9200	11645
2 Dr XLT 4WD Std Cab LB	9990	12645

OPTIONS FOR F-SERIES PICKUP

8 cyl 5.0 L Engine +165
8 cyl 5.8 L Engine +235
8 cyl 7.3 L Dsl Engine +695
8 cyl 7.3 L Turbodsl Engine +1040
8 cyl 7.5 L Engine +245
Auto 3-Speed Transmission +190
Auto 4-Speed Transmission[Std on Lightning] +255
AM/FM Compact Disc Player +85
Air Conditioning[Opt on S,XL] +220
Camper/Towing Package +90
Cruise Control[Opt on S,XL] +50
Dual Rear Wheels +225
Keyless Entry System +45
Power Door Locks[Std on F-250,F-350,Eddie Bauer,Lightning] +50
Power Driver's Seat +75

Power Windows[Std on F-250, F-350, Eddie Bauer, Lightning] +50
Premium Sound System +105
Rear Step Bumper +40

MUSTANG 1994

New sheetmetal for the venerable pony. The LX model and hatchback are dropped. The base Mustang gets a 3.8-liter V6, and GT models receive a boost in horsepower. Four-wheel disc brakes are standard on both Mustangs and ABS finally becomes an available option. A passenger airbag, power driver's seat, and tilt steering wheel become standard in 1994. Convertibles are available with a removable hardtop.

RATINGS (SCALE OF 1-10)

Overall	Safety	Reliability	Performance	Comfort	Value
7	7.4	6.9	8.8	7.3	4.8

Category F
2 Dr Cobra Conv	10960	14420
2 Dr Cobra Cpe	9240	12155
2 Dr GT Conv	7770	10225
2 Dr GT Cpe	6880	9055
2 Dr STD Conv	6580	8660
2 Dr STD Cpe	5465	7190

OPTIONS FOR MUSTANG
Auto 4-Speed Transmission +215
Air Conditioning +225
Anti-Lock Brakes[Std on Cobra] +185
Compact Disc W/fm/tape +135
Cruise Control +55
Keyless Entry System +50
Leather Seats[Opt on GT,STD,Cpe] +175
Power Door Locks[Opt on STD Cpe] +55
Power Windows[Opt on STD Cpe] +60
Premium Sound System +100
Rear Spoiler[Opt on STD] +65

PROBE 1994

Dual airbags are now standard on all Probes. A Sport Appearance Package is available for base models.

RATINGS (SCALE OF 1-10)

Overall	Safety	Reliability	Performance	Comfort	Value
7	7.8	7.2	9	7.4	3.4

Category E
2 Dr SE Hbk	3285	4695
2 Dr STD Hbk	3425	4890
Category F
2 Dr GT Hbk	4550	5990

OPTIONS FOR PROBE
Auto 4-Speed Transmission +215
AM/FM Compact Disc Player +125
Air Conditioning +220
Anti-Lock Brakes +180

Cruise Control +55
Keyless Entry System +45
Leather Seats +175
Power Door Locks +55
Power Driver's Seat +65
Power Sunroof +165
Power Windows +60

RANGER 1994

Side-impact door beams are installed on the Ranger to protect occupants. The Splash model is now available as a SuperCab. Look out, the Splash 2WD holds the road better than most sport coupes.

RATINGS (SCALE OF 1-10)

Overall	Safety	Reliability	Performance	Comfort	Value
N/A	4.9	7.9	7.2	7.3	N/A

Category G
2 Dr STX Ext Cab SB	5260	6830
2 Dr STX 4WD Ext Cab SB	6515	8460
2 Dr STX Std Cab LB	4705	6110
2 Dr STX 4WD Std Cab LB	6170	8015
2 Dr STX Std Cab SB	4535	5890
2 Dr STX 4WD Std Cab SB	5790	7520
2 Dr Splash Ext Cab Stepside SB		
	5985	7770
2 Dr Splash 4WD Ext Cab Stepside SB		
	7440	9665
2 Dr Splash Std Cab Stepside SB		
	4920	6390
2 Dr Splash 4WD Std Cab Stepside SB		
	6620	8595
2 Dr XL Ext Cab SB	4880	6335
2 Dr XL 4WD Ext Cab SB	6420	8335
2 Dr XL Std Cab LB	4535	5890
2 Dr XL 4WD Std Cab LB	5845	7590
2 Dr XL Std Cab SB	4360	5660
2 Dr XL 4WD Std Cab SB	5665	7355
2 Dr XLT Ext Cab SB	5105	6630
2 Dr XLT 4WD Ext Cab SB	6560	8520
2 Dr XLT Std Cab LB	4160	5405
2 Dr XLT 4WD Std Cab LB	6005	7800
2 Dr XLT Std Cab SB	4060	5275
2 Dr XLT 4WD Std Cab SB	5880	7635

OPTIONS FOR RANGER
6 cyl 3.0 L Engine +165
6 cyl 4.0 L Engine +125
Auto 4-Speed Transmission +270
AM/FM Compact Disc Player +90
Air Conditioning +220
Cruise Control +55
Limited Slip Diff +75
Power Door Locks +65
Power Steering[Std on Splash,STX,Ext Cab,4WD] +75

Don't forget to refer to the Mileage Adjustment Table at the back of this book!

Model Description	Trade-in Value	Market Value	Model Description	Trade-in Value	Market Value

Power Windows +65
Premium Sound System +95

TAURUS 1994

The passenger airbag is finally a standard equipment item. GL models receive 15-inch wheels and all Tauruses get a new steering wheel. Cellular phones are a new option.

RATINGS (SCALE OF 1-10)

Overall	Safety	Reliability	Performance	Comfort	Value
7.8	7.3	7.1	8	7.8	8.7

Category C

4 Dr GL Sdn	3795	5130
4 Dr GL Wgn	3975	5370
4 Dr LX Sdn	4705	6355
4 Dr LX Wgn	4870	6580

Category F

4 Dr SHO Sdn	5380	7080

OPTIONS FOR TAURUS

6 cyl 3.8 L Engine[Opt on GL,LX] +150
Auto 4-Speed Transmission[Opt on SHO] +215
Flex Fuel Option +280
Air Conditioning[Std on LX,SHO] +220
Anti-Lock Brakes[Std on SHO] +165
Climate Control for AC[Opt on LX] +45
Compact Disc W/fm/tape +90
Cruise Control[Std on SHO] +55
Keyless Entry System +50
Leather Seats[Std on SHO] +165
Power Door Locks[Std on LX,SHO] +65
Power Driver's Seat[Opt on GL,Wgn] +80
Power Moonroof +175
Power Passenger Seat +75
Power Windows[Std on LX,SHO] +85
Premium Sound System +105
Third Seat +45

TEMPO 1994

CFC-free air conditioning refrigerant and redesigned seatbelts are the only changes this year. The Tempo is mercifully retired after this model year in favor of the new Contour.

RATINGS (SCALE OF 1-10)

Overall	Safety	Reliability	Performance	Comfort	Value
6.9	5.2	7.5	7.6	7.1	7

Category C

2 Dr GL Sdn	2345	3170
4 Dr GL Sdn	2440	3295
4 Dr LX Sdn	2745	3710

OPTIONS FOR TEMPO

6 cyl 3.0 L Engine +185
Auto 3-Speed Transmission +145
AM/FM Stereo Tape +45

Air Bag Restraint +130
Air Conditioning +220
Cruise Control +55
Power Door Locks[Opt on GL] +65
Power Driver's Seat +80
Power Windows +85

THUNDERBIRD 1994

Dual airbags make their first appearance on the Thunderbird. An optional 4.6-liter V8 replaces last year's 5.0-liter V8. Dual cupholders complement the center console and the airbags are housed in a restyled dashboard.

RATINGS (SCALE OF 1-10)

Overall	Safety	Reliability	Performance	Comfort	Value
7.4	8.7	6.9	8	7.9	5.7

Category C

2 Dr LX Cpe	4810	6500

Category F

2 Dr SC Sprchgd Cpe	6460	8500

OPTIONS FOR THUNDERBIRD

8 cyl 4.6 L Engine +155
Auto 4-Speed Transmission[Opt on SC] +215
Anti-Lock Brakes[Opt on LX] +165
Climate Control for AC[Opt on LX] +45
Compact Disc Changer +130
Cruise Control[Opt on SC] +55
Keyless Entry System +50
Leather Seats +165
Power Door Locks[Opt on SC] +55
Power Driver's Seat[Opt on SC] +65
Power Moonroof +175
Power Passenger Seat +75
Premium Sound System +100
Traction Control System +65

1993 FORD

AEROSTAR 1993

An integrated child seat is introduced as an option.

RATINGS (SCALE OF 1-10)

Overall	Safety	Reliability	Performance	Comfort	Value
7	6.2	6.7	6.6	7.5	8.2

Category G

2 Dr Eddie Bauer Pass. Van	3970	5295
2 Dr Eddie Bauer 4WD Pass. Van		
	5115	6820
2 Dr Eddie Bauer Pass. Van Ext		
	4500	6000
2 Dr Eddie Bauer 4WD Pass. Van Ext		
	4995	6660
2 Dr STD Cargo Van	2090	2785
2 Dr STD 4WD Cargo Van	2610	3480

Don't forget to refer to the Mileage Adjustment Table at the back of this book!

Model Description	Trade-in Value	Market Value	Model Description	Trade-in Value	Market Value
2 Dr STD 4WD Cargo Van Ext	3490	4655			
2 Dr STD Cargo Van Ext	2830	3770			
2 Dr Window Cargo Van	2020	2695			
2 Dr Window 4WD Cargo Van	2825	3765			
2 Dr XL Pass. Van	2815	3755			
2 Dr XL 4WD Pass. Van	3550	4735			
2 Dr XL Pass. Van Ext	3085	4110			
2 Dr XL 4WD Pass. Van Ext	4055	5405			
2 Dr XL Plus Pass. Van	2930	3905			
2 Dr XL Plus 4WD Pass. Van	3785	5045			
2 Dr XL Plus Pass. Van Ext	3250	4330			
2 Dr XLT Pass. Van	3940	5250			
2 Dr XLT Pass. Van Ext	4200	5600			
2 Dr XLT 4WD Pass. Van Ext	4385	5845			
2 Dr XLT Plus Pass. Van	3475	4635			
2 Dr XLT Plus 4WD Pass. Van	3820	5090			

OPTIONS FOR AEROSTAR
6 cyl 4.0 L Engine[Std on 4WD, Eddie Bauer] +105
Auto 4-Speed Transmission[Std on Eddie Bauer,XLT, XLT Plus,4WD] +170
AM/FM Stereo Tape +50
Air Conditioning[Std on XLT,XLT Plus,Eddie Bauer] +180
Aluminum/Alloy Wheels[Std on Eddie Bauer] +75
Captain Chairs (4)[Opt on XL,XL Plus,XLT,XLT Plus, Pass. Van Ext] +140
Child Seat (1) +35
Chrome Wheels +40
Cruise Control[Opt on STD,XL,XL Plus] +45
Dual Air Conditioning[Std on Eddie Bauer] +210
Leather Seats +170
Luggage Rack[Std on Eddie Bauer] +35
Power Door Locks[Std on Eddie Bauer] +50
Power Windows[Std on Eddie Bauer] +55
Premium Sound System[Std on Eddie Bauer] +75
Trip Computer[Std on Eddie Bauer] +35

BRONCO   1993
Four-wheel antilock brakes introduced on the 1993 Bronco.

RATINGS (SCALE OF 1-10)

Overall	Safety	Reliability	Performance	Comfort	Value
6.4	6.4	5.7	6.4	6.6	6.8

Category H
2 Dr Eddie Bauer 4WD Utility	7550	9555
2 Dr STD 4WD Utility	6785	8590
2 Dr XLT 4WD Utility	7055	8930

OPTIONS FOR BRONCO
8 cyl 5.8 L Engine +195
Auto 4-Speed Transmission[Opt on STD,XLT] +205
AM/FM Stereo Tape +45
Air Conditioning[Opt on STD,XLT] +180
Aluminum/Alloy Wheels[Opt on XLT] +70
Camper/Towing Package +75

Leather Seats +215
Limited Slip Diff +55
Power Door Locks +40
Power Driver's Seat +60
Power Windows +40
Swing Out Tire Carrier[Std on XLT] +40
Velour/Cloth Seats[Std on Eddie Bauer] +30

CLUB WAGON/ECONOLINE 1993
No changes to the recently redesigned Ford Club Wagon.

RATINGS (SCALE OF 1-10)

Overall	Safety	Reliability	Performance	Comfort	Value
N/A	7.8	8.3	6.4	7.8	N/A

E-150
Category H
2 Dr Chateau Club Wagon	6475	8195
2 Dr Custom Club Wagon	5535	7005
2 Dr STD Econoline	5230	6620
2 Dr XL Econoline	5515	6980
2 Dr XLT Club Wagon	5735	7260
2 Dr XLT Super Club Wagon Ext	5805	7345

E-250
Category H
2 Dr STD Econoline	4465	5655
2 Dr STD Econoline Ext	4660	5900
2 Dr XL Econoline	4965	6285
2 Dr XL Econoline Ext	5075	6425

E-350
Category H
2 Dr Custom Club Wagon	6545	8285
2 Dr Custom Super Club Wagon Ext	5635	7130
2 Dr STD Econoline	4825	6105
2 Dr STD Econoline Ext	5170	6545
2 Dr XL Econoline	5100	6455
2 Dr XL Econoline Ext	5290	6695
2 Dr XLT Super Club Wagon Ext	5915	7490

OPTIONS FOR CLUB WAGON/ECONOLINE
8 cyl 5.0 L Engine +135
8 cyl 5.8 L Engine +195
8 cyl 7.3 L Dsl Engine +595
8 cyl 7.5 L Engine +220
Auto 4-Speed Transmission[Std on Chateau,Custom, XLT] +65
Club Wagon Seat/Bed Pkg +225
Seat/bed Combination +225
AM/FM Stereo Tape[Std on Chateau] +45
Air Conditioning[Std on Chateau] +180
Aluminum/Alloy Wheels[Std on Chateau] +70
Camper/Towing Package[Opt on Custom,STD,XL] +75
Chrome Bumpers[Std on Chateau,XLT,XLT Super] +40

FORD 93

Model Description	Trade-in Value	Market Value	Model Description	Trade-in Value	Market Value

Cruise Control[Std on Chateau] +40
Limited Slip Diff +55
Power Door Locks[Std on Chateau,XLT,XLT Super] +40
Power Driver's Seat[Std on Chateau] +60
Power Windows[Std on Chateau,XLT,XLT Super] +40
Velour/Cloth Seats[Opt on E-250,Custom,Custom Super,STD,XL] +30

CROWN VICTORIA 1993

The touring sedan is no longer available. Front-end styling changes include the addition of a grille. Cupholders finally appear in the dashboard. An express-down feature shows up for the driver's side window. An electronic overdrive lock-out debuts on the automatic transmission and a traction control system is available with the antilock brakes option. A 10-disc CD changer and an auto-dimming mirror are new options.

RATINGS (SCALE OF 1-10)

Overall	Safety	Reliability	Performance	Comfort	Value
7.6	6.8	6.8	7.5	8.2	8.5

Category B
4 Dr LX Sdn	4455	6100
4 Dr STD Sdn	4390	6015

OPTIONS FOR CROWN VICTORIA

AM/FM Stereo Tape +40
Air Bag Restraint[Opt on LX] +185
Aluminum/Alloy Wheels +75
Anti-Lock Brakes +155
Climate Control for AC +40
Compact Disc Changer +100
Cruise Control +50
Dual Power Seats +85
Keyless Entry System +40
Leather Seats +150
Power Door Locks +55
Premium Sound System +90
Traction Control System +40
Trip Computer +85

ESCORT 1993

Minor styling changes to all trim-levels include new taillights and grille. GT models receive a new spoiler and wheels. The LX models receive body-color spoilers.

RATINGS (SCALE OF 1-10)

Overall	Safety	Reliability	Performance	Comfort	Value
6.5	4.6	7	6.8	7.6	6.3

Category E
2 Dr GT Hbk	2380	3550
2 Dr LX Hbk	1805	2695
4 Dr LX Hbk	1935	2885
4 Dr LX Sdn	1995	2975
4 Dr LX Wgn	2105	3140
4 Dr LX-E Sdn	2180	3255
2 Dr STD Hbk	1745	2605

OPTIONS FOR ESCORT

Auto 4-Speed Transmission +165
AM/FM Stereo Tape[Opt on LX,STD] +65
Air Conditioning +180
Cruise Control +50
Luggage Rack +30
Power Door Locks +55
Power Moonroof +125
Power Steering[Opt on LX,STD] +55
Power Windows +60
Premium Sound System +70
Rear Spoiler[Opt on LX] +50

EXPLORER 1993

A new steering wheel and instrument panel freshen the Explorer's interior. New wheels are the only exterior changes. Explorers gain four-wheel antilock brakes that work in both two- and four-wheel-drive modes.

RATINGS (SCALE OF 1-10)

Overall	Safety	Reliability	Performance	Comfort	Value
6.4	4.2	4.9	7.4	8.3	7.4

Category G
2 Dr Eddie Bauer Utility	5425	7235
2 Dr Eddie Bauer 4WD Utility	6020	8025
4 Dr Eddie Bauer Wgn	5735	7645
4 Dr Eddie Bauer 4WD Wgn	6430	8575
4 Dr Limited Wgn	6475	8635
4 Dr Limited 4WD Wgn	6755	9005
2 Dr Sport Utility	4735	6310
2 Dr Sport 4WD Utility	5200	6930
2 Dr XL Utility	4625	6165
2 Dr XL 4WD Utility	5060	6745
4 Dr XL Wgn	5025	6700
4 Dr XL 4WD Wgn	5585	7445
4 Dr XLT Wgn	5685	7580
4 Dr XLT 4WD Wgn	6210	8280

OPTIONS FOR EXPLORER

Auto 4-Speed Transmission[Std on Limited] +200
AM/FM Compact Disc Player +70
Air Conditioning[Std on Limited] +180
Aluminum/Alloy Wheels[Opt on XL] +75
Camper/Towing Package +65
Cruise Control[Opt on Sport,XL] +45
Dual Power Seats[Opt on XLT] +85
Keyless Entry System +45
Leather Seats[Std on Limited] +170
Limited Slip Diff +60
Luggage Rack[Opt on Sport,XL,XLT] +35
Power Door Locks[Opt on Sport,XL] +50
Power Windows[Opt on Sport,XL] +55
Premium Sound System +75

Don't forget to refer to the Mileage Adjustment Table at the back of this book!

Model Description	Trade-in Value	Market Value
Running Boards +85		
Sunroof +65		

F-SERIES PICKUP 1993

No changes for the 1993 F-Series.

RATINGS (SCALE OF 1-10)

Overall	Safety	Reliability	Performance	Comfort	Value
N/A	5.4	6.8	6.8	7.4	N/A

F-150

Category H

Model Description	Trade-in Value	Market Value
2 Dr Lightning Std Cab SB	7665	9705
2 Dr S Std Cab LB	3880	4910
2 Dr S 4WD Std Cab LB	5275	6680
2 Dr S Std Cab SB	3745	4740
2 Dr S 4WD Std Cab SB	5150	6520
2 Dr XL Ext Cab LB	5405	6840
2 Dr XL 4WD Ext Cab LB	6320	8000
2 Dr XL Ext Cab SB	5300	6710
2 Dr XL 4WD Ext Cab SB	6250	7910
2 Dr XL Ext Cab Stepside SB	5510	6975
2 Dr XL 4WD Ext Cab Stepside SB	6580	8330
2 Dr XL Std Cab LB	5105	6460
2 Dr XL 4WD Std Cab LB	5920	7495
2 Dr XL Std Cab SB	4995	6325
2 Dr XL 4WD Std Cab SB	5820	7365
2 Dr XL Std Cab Stepside SB	5270	6670
2 Dr XL 4WD Std Cab Stepside SB	6070	7685
2 Dr XLT Ext Cab LB	5560	7035
2 Dr XLT 4WD Ext Cab LB	6960	8810
2 Dr XLT Ext Cab SB	5455	6905
2 Dr XLT 4WD Ext Cab SB	6855	8675
2 Dr XLT Ext Cab Stepside SB	5745	7270
2 Dr XLT 4WD Ext Cab Stepside SB	7155	9055
2 Dr XLT Std Cab LB	5245	6640
2 Dr XLT 4WD Std Cab LB	6280	7950
2 Dr XLT Std Cab SB	5140	6505
2 Dr XLT 4WD Std Cab SB	6220	7875
2 Dr XLT Std Cab Stepside SB	5465	6920
2 Dr XLT 4WD Std Cab Stepside SB	6610	8365

F-250

Category H

Model Description	Trade-in Value	Market Value
2 Dr XL Ext Cab LB	6405	8105
2 Dr XL 4WD Ext Cab LB	7690	9735
2 Dr XL Std Cab LB	6140	7770
2 Dr XL 4WD Std Cab LB	7365	9325
2 Dr XLT Ext Cab LB	7170	9075
2 Dr XLT 4WD Ext Cab LB	8590	10875
2 Dr XLT Std Cab LB	6145	7780
2 Dr XLT 4WD Std Cab LB	7320	9265

F-350

Category H

Model Description	Trade-in Value	Market Value
4 Dr XL Crew Cab LB	7905	10005
4 Dr XL 4WD Crew Cab LB	8830	11180
2 Dr XL Ext Cab LB	7495	9485
2 Dr XL Std Cab LB	7030	8900
2 Dr XL 4WD Std Cab LB	8235	10425
2 Dr XL 4WD Std Cab SB	7760	9820
4 Dr XLT Crew Cab LB	8385	10615
4 Dr XLT 4WD Crew Cab LB	9145	11575
2 Dr XLT Ext Cab LB	7755	9815
2 Dr XLT Std Cab LB	7820	9900
2 Dr XLT 4WD Std Cab LB	8155	10320

OPTIONS FOR F-SERIES PICKUP

8 cyl 5.0 L Engine +135
8 cyl 5.8 L Engine +195
8 cyl 7.3 L Dsl Engine +595
8 cyl 7.3 L Turbodsl Engine +830
8 cyl 7.5 L Engine +220
4-Speed Transmission +25
Auto 3-Speed Transmission +155
Auto 4-Speed Transmission[Std on Lightning] +205
AM/FM Stereo Tape[Std on XLT] +45
Air Conditioning[Opt on Lightning,S,XL,XLT] +180
Aluminum/Alloy Wheels[Std on Lightning] +70
Camper/Towing Package +75
Cruise Control[Opt on XL, XLT] +40
Dual Rear Wheels +185
Limited Slip Diff[Std on Lightning] +55
Power Door Locks[Opt on XL, XLT] +40
Power Windows[Opt on XL, XLT] +40
Rear Step Bumper +35
Sliding Rear Window +25

FESTIVA • 1993

No changes to the 1993 Festiva.

RATINGS (SCALE OF 1-10)

Overall	Safety	Reliability	Performance	Comfort	Value
6.1	4.6	7.5	6.2	6.9	5.1

Category E

Model Description	Trade-in Value	Market Value
2 Dr GL Hbk	1675	2500
2 Dr L Hbk	1565	2335

OPTIONS FOR FESTIVA

Auto 3-Speed Transmission +115
AM/FM Stereo Tape +65
Air Conditioning +180
Rear Spoiler +50
Rear Window Defroster +35
Sunroof +75

Model Description	Trade-in Value	Market Value	Model Description	Trade-in Value	Market Value

MUSTANG 1993

The Cobra is introduced to the lineup. Two hundred forty-five horsepower, a beefy suspension, and four-wheel disc brakes distinguish it from other Mustangs. Improved stereos grace all Mustangs this year.

RATINGS (SCALE OF 1-10)

Overall	Safety	Reliability	Performance	Comfort	Value
N/A	N/A	7.1	7.8	6.3	3.9

Category C
2 Dr LX Conv	3590	4985
2 Dr LX Cpe	2530	3515
2 Dr LX Hbk	2835	3935

Category F
2 Dr Cobra Hbk	7710	10280
2 Dr GT Conv	6160	8210
2 Dr GT Hbk	5475	7300
2 Dr LX 5.0 Conv	5330	7105
2 Dr LX 5.0 Cpe	4430	5905
2 Dr LX 5.0 Hbk	4610	6145

OPTIONS FOR MUSTANG

Auto 4-Speed Transmission +135
AM/FM Compact Disc Player +80
Air Conditioning +180
Aluminum/Alloy Wheels[Opt on LX] +65
Chrome Wheels +130
Cruise Control +45
Leather Seats +145
Power Door Locks[Std on Conv] +45
Power Driver's Seat +55
Power Windows[Std on Conv] +50
Rear Spoiler[Opt on Conv] +55
Sunroof +80

PROBE 1993

A driver airbag becomes standard on the restyled Probe. The Probe's wheelbase stretches four inches and its curb weight jumps 100 pounds. The slow-selling LX model is dropped. Four-cylinder engines in the base model are good for 115 horsepower; GT models get a twin-cam 2.5-liter V6 engine that makes 164. Antilock brakes become optional for all Probes.

RATINGS (SCALE OF 1-10)

Overall	Safety	Reliability	Performance	Comfort	Value
6.7	6	6.7	9	7.4	4.2

Category C
2 Dr STD Hbk	2950	4095

Category F
2 Dr GT Hbk	3650	4865

OPTIONS FOR PROBE

Auto 4-Speed Transmission +165
AM/FM Compact Disc Player +80
Air Conditioning +180
Aluminum/Alloy Wheels[Std on GT] +65
Anti-Lock Brakes +135
Cruise Control +45
Keyless Entry System +40
Leather Seats +135
Power Door Locks +45
Power Driver's Seat[Std on GT] +65
Power Sunroof +150
Power Windows +50

RANGER 1993

The classy-looking Ranger Splash is introduced in 1993, offering the first flareside cargo box in the small pickup class. The rest of the Ranger lineup gets new sheetmetal.

RATINGS (SCALE OF 1-10)

Overall	Safety	Reliability	Performance	Comfort	Value
N/A	5	8.1	7.2	7.3	N/A

Category G
2 Dr STX Ext Cab SB	4345	5795
2 Dr STX 4WD Ext Cab SB	5670	7560
2 Dr STX Std Cab LB	3790	5050
2 Dr STX 4WD Std Cab LB	5180	6905
2 Dr STX Std Cab SB	3610	4810
2 Dr STX 4WD Std Cab SB	5080	6770
2 Dr Splash Std Cab Stepside SB	4135	5515
2 Dr Splash 4WD Std Cab Stepside SB	5720	7625
2 Dr Sport Std Cab LB	3295	4395
2 Dr Sport 4WD Std Cab LB	4850	6465
2 Dr Sport Std Cab SB	3135	4180
2 Dr Sport 4WD Std Cab SB	4705	6275
2 Dr XL Ext Cab SB	3745	4995
2 Dr XL 4WD Ext Cab SB	4835	6445
2 Dr XL Std Cab LB	3330	4440
2 Dr XL 4WD Std Cab LB	4905	6540
2 Dr XL Std Cab SB	3285	4380
2 Dr XL 4WD Std Cab SB	4785	6380
2 Dr XLT Ext Cab SB	4015	5350
2 Dr XLT 4WD Ext Cab SB	5425	7230
2 Dr XLT Std Cab LB	3565	4750
2 Dr XLT 4WD Std Cab LB	5065	6755
2 Dr XLT Std Cab SB	3490	4655
2 Dr XLT 4WD Std Cab SB	5000	6665

OPTIONS FOR RANGER

6 cyl 3.0 L Engine +145
6 cyl 4.0 L Engine +105

Model Description	Trade-in Value	Market Value	Model Description	Trade-in Value	Market Value

Auto 4-Speed Transmission +220
AM/FM Compact Disc Player +70
Air Conditioning +180
Aluminum/Alloy Wheels[Std on Splash] +75
Cruise Control +45
Limited Slip Diff +60
Power Door Locks +50
Power Steering[Opt on XL 2WD Std Cab] +60
Power Windows +55
Premium Sound System +75

TAURUS   1993

SHOs finally receive an optional automatic transmission. The base L model is dropped in favor of the new entry-level Taurus GL. Body-color bumpers and side moldings are now standard.

RATINGS (SCALE OF 1-10)

Overall	Safety	Reliability	Performance	Comfort	Value
7.2	6.4	5.2	8	7.8	8.6

Category C
4 Dr GL Sdn				2730	3795
4 Dr GL Wgn				2825	3925
4 Dr LX Sdn				3465	4815
4 Dr LX Wgn				3660	5080

Category F
4 Dr SHO Sdn				4255	5670

OPTIONS FOR TAURUS

6 cyl 3.0 L FLEX Engine +165
6 cyl 3.8 L Engine +125
Auto 4-Speed Transmission[Opt on SHO] +145
AM/FM Compact Disc Player +80
Air Conditioning[Opt on GL] +180
Aluminum/Alloy Wheels[Opt on GL] +65
Anti-Lock Brakes[Std on SHO] +135
Climate Control for AC[Opt on LX] +35
Cruise Control[Std on SHO] +45
Dual Air Bag Restraints +110
Dual Power Seats +130
Leather Seats +135
Power Door Locks[Opt on GL] +55
Power Moonroof +145
Power Windows[Opt on GL] +70
Premium Sound System +80
Third Seat +35

TEMPO   1993

Say goodbye to the GLS. GL and LX Tempos have removable cupholders and a leather-wrapped shift knob. A driver airbag is optional on both models.

RATINGS (SCALE OF 1-10)

Overall	Safety	Reliability	Performance	Comfort	Value
6.6	4.4	7.1	7.6	7.1	6.8

Category C
2 Dr GL Sdn				1820	2525
4 Dr GL Sdn				1900	2640
4 Dr LX Sdn				2245	3120

OPTIONS FOR TEMPO

6 cyl 3.0 L Engine +155
Auto 3-Speed Transmission +125
AM/FM Stereo Tape +35
Air Bag Restraint +105
Air Conditioning +180
Aluminum/Alloy Wheels +65
Cruise Control +45
Power Door Locks[Opt on GL] +55
Power Driver's Seat +65
Power Windows +70

THUNDERBIRD   1993

Base and Sport models are discontinued. Restyled alloy wheels and a new steering wheel complete the changes to the 1993 Thunderbird.

RATINGS (SCALE OF 1-10)

Overall	Safety	Reliability	Performance	Comfort	Value
6.9	5.7	7	6.8	8	6.9

Category C
2 Dr LX Cpe				3710	5155

Category F
2 Dr SC Sprchgd Cpe				5280	7035

OPTIONS FOR THUNDERBIRD

8 cyl 5.0 L Engine +255
Auto 4-Speed Transmission[Opt on SC] +135
AM/FM Compact Disc Player +80
Aluminum/Alloy Wheels[Opt on LX] +65
Anti-Lock Brakes +135
Climate Control for AC +35
Cruise Control[Opt on SC] +45
Keyless Entry System +40
Leather Seats +135
Power Door Locks[Opt on SC] +45
Power Driver's Seat +55
Power Moonroof +145
Power Passenger Seat +60
Premium Sound System +80

1992 FORD

AEROSTAR   1992

A driver airbag becomes standard on passenger and cargo models. A new dashboard includes redesigned climate controls. On automatics, the shift lever moves from the floor to the column. High-back front bucket seats are now standard for all trim levels. Leather seats are available for the Eddie Bauer model. Outboard rear-seat passengers get a shoulder belt. A new grille and headlights appear on the exterior.

Don't forget to refer to the Mileage Adjustment Table at the back of this book!

Model Description	Trade-in Value	Market Value

RATINGS (SCALE OF 1-10)

Overall	Safety	Reliability	Performance	Comfort	Value
7	6.2	6.6	6.6	7.5	8.1

Category G

Model Description	Trade-in Value	Market Value
2 Dr Eddie Bauer Pass. Van	2785	3815
2 Dr Eddie Bauer 4WD Pass. Van	3580	4905
2 Dr Eddie Bauer Pass. Van Ext	3275	4485
2 Dr Eddie Bauer 4WD Pass. Van Ext	4075	5585
2 Dr STD Cargo Van	1750	2395
2 Dr STD 4WD Cargo Van	2150	2945
2 Dr STD Cargo Van Ext	2360	3230
2 Dr STD 4WD Cargo Van Ext	2705	3705
2 Dr XL Pass. Van	2520	3450
2 Dr XL 4WD Pass. Van	3060	4190
2 Dr XL Pass. Van Ext	2750	3770
2 Dr XL 4WD Pass. Van Ext	3285	4500
2 Dr XLT Pass. Van	2760	3780
2 Dr XLT 4WD Pass. Van	3360	4600
2 Dr XLT Pass. Van Ext	3195	4380
2 Dr XLT 4WD Pass. Van Ext	3805	5215

OPTIONS FOR AEROSTAR
6 cyl 4.0 L Engine[Std on 4WD] +100
Auto 4-Speed Transmission[Opt on 2WD] +135
Plus Pkg +175
Seat/Bed Combination +170
Air Conditioning[Std on XLT] +145
Captain Chairs (4) +115
Cruise Control[Opt on STD,XL] +40
Dual Air Conditioning[Opt on XL,XLT] +170
Power Door Locks[Opt on STD,XL] +40
Power Windows[Opt on STD,XL] +45

BRONCO   1992

Freshened front-end styling and the addition of the XLT and Eddie Bauer models are the main changes for 1992.

RATINGS (SCALE OF 1-10)

Overall	Safety	Reliability	Performance	Comfort	Value
6.2	5.6	5.5	6.4	6.6	6.7

Category H

Model Description	Trade-in Value	Market Value
2 Dr Custom 4WD Utility	5685	7380
2 Dr Eddie Bauer 4WD Utility	6000	7795
2 Dr XLT 4WD Utility	5885	7645

OPTIONS FOR BRONCO
8 cyl 5.0 L Engine[Opt on Custom,XLT] +105
8 cyl 5.8 L Engine +155
Auto 4-Speed Transmission +165
Air Conditioning[Opt on Custom,XLT] +145
Camper/Towing Package +60

Cruise Control[Opt on Custom,XLT] +35
Limited Slip Diff +45
Power Door Locks +35
Power Windows +35

CLUB WAGON/ECONOLINE 1992

Fully redesigned, Ford's full-size van receives a new body, lights, suspension and fuel tank. New safety features include a driver's side airbag and a high-mounted third brake light.

RATINGS (SCALE OF 1-10)

Overall	Safety	Reliability	Performance	Comfort	Value
N/A	7	7.9	6.4	7.8	N/A

E-150

Category H

Model Description	Trade-in Value	Market Value
2 Dr Chateau Club Wagon	5045	6550
2 Dr STD Club Wagon	4175	5420
2 Dr STD Econoline	3985	5175
2 Dr XL Econoline	4400	5715
2 Dr XLT Club Wagon	4715	6125

E-250

Category H

Model Description	Trade-in Value	Market Value
2 Dr STD Econoline	3630	4715
2 Dr STD Econoline Ext	3790	4920
2 Dr XL Econoline	3850	5000
2 Dr XL Econoline Ext	4125	5360

E-350

Category H

Model Description	Trade-in Value	Market Value
2 Dr Chateau Club Wagon Ext	4665	6060
2 Dr STD Club Wagon	4440	5765
2 Dr STD Econoline	3990	5185
2 Dr STD Econoline Ext	4160	5405
2 Dr Super Club Wagon Ext	3845	4995
2 Dr XL Dsl Econoline	4485	5825
2 Dr XL Econoline Ext	4250	5520
2 Dr XLT Club Wagon Ext	4545	5905
2 Dr XLT Pass. Van	4360	5665

OPTIONS FOR CLUB WAGON/ECONOLINE
8 cyl 5.0 L Engine +105
8 cyl 5.8 L Engine +155
8 cyl 7.3 L Dsl Engine +465
8 cyl 7.5 L Engine +175
Auto 4-Speed Transmission[Std on E-150 Club Wagon] +55
Seat/Bed Combination +145
Seat/Bed Pkg +180
XLT Trim Pkg +160
Air Conditioning +145
Camper/Towing Package[Std on E-150 Econoline Ext,
*   E-350 Econoline, E-350 Econoline Ext] +60*
Cruise Control +35
Dual Air Conditioning +240

Don't forget to refer to the Mileage Adjustment Table at the back of this book!

FORD 92

Model Description	Trade-in Value	Market Value	Model Description	Trade-in Value	Market Value

Power Door Locks +35
Power Driver's Seat +50
Power Windows +35

CROWN VICTORIA 1992

After a total redesign, the corny LTD moniker is dropped from name and the station wagon body style is deleted from the Crown Vic's lineup. Suspension improvements include gas-charged shock absorbers and rear stabilizer bars. Antilock brakes are optional but four-wheel disc brakes are standard.

RATINGS (SCALE OF 1-10)

Overall	Safety	Reliability	Performance	Comfort	Value
7.2	6.8	5.8	7.5	8.2	7.8

Category B
4 Dr LX Sdn	3505	5010
4 Dr STD Sdn	3265	4665
4 Dr Touring Sdn	3900	5570

OPTIONS FOR CROWN VICTORIA

Anti-Lock Brakes[Std on Touring] +125
Cruise Control[Std on Touring] +40
JBL Sound System +100
Leather Seats +125
Power Driver's Seat[Std on Touring] +55
Power Passenger Seat[Opt on LX] +60
Trip Computer +70

ESCORT 1992

A notchback sedan is introduced as an LX-E trim-level; it offers four-wheel disc brakes, the GT engine, and GT interior touches. The Pony Comfort Group option makes air conditioning and power steering available on the base model.

RATINGS (SCALE OF 1-10)

Overall	Safety	Reliability	Performance	Comfort	Value
6.3	4.5	6.9	6.8	7.6	5.8

Category E
2 Dr GT Hbk	1775	2775
2 Dr LX Hbk	1285	2005
4 Dr LX Hbk	1395	2180
4 Dr LX Sdn	1540	2405
4 Dr LX Wgn	1660	2590
4 Dr LX-E Sdn	1720	2690
2 Dr Pony Hbk	1350	2110

OPTIONS FOR ESCORT

Auto 4-Speed Transmission +130
Air Conditioning +145
Cruise Control +40
Power Door Locks +45

Power Steering[Opt on LX,Pony] +45
Power Windows +50

EXPLORER 1992

A 3.55 axle replaces last year's 3.27 on four-wheel drive models. A one-touch-down driver's window becomes standard on all Explorers equipped with power windows. Eddie Bauer models receive color-keyed alloy wheels. A tilt-open sunroof is now available without an option package.

RATINGS (SCALE OF 1-10)

Overall	Safety	Reliability	Performance	Comfort	Value
6.2	4.3	4.8	7.4	8.3*	6

Category G
2 Dr Eddie Bauer Utility	4090	5600
2 Dr Eddie Bauer 4WD Utility	4875	6680
4 Dr Eddie Bauer Wgn	4535	6210
4 Dr Eddie Bauer 4WD Wgn	5060	6930
2 Dr Sport Utility	3860	5290
2 Dr Sport 4WD Utility	4445	6090
2 Dr XL Utility	3675	5035
2 Dr XL 4WD Utility	4285	5870
4 Dr XL Wgn	4210	5770
4 Dr XL 4WD Wgn	4725	6475
4 Dr XLT Wgn	4635	6350
4 Dr XLT 4WD Wgn	5025	6885

OPTIONS FOR EXPLORER

Auto 4-Speed Transmission +160
AM/FM Compact Disc Player +60
Air Conditioning +145
Camper/Towing Package +55
Cruise Control[Std on Eddie Bauer, XLT] +40
Flip-Up Sunroof +60
Leather Seats +140
Limited Slip Diff +50
Power Door Locks[Std on Eddie Bauer, XLT] +40
Power Driver's Seat[Opt on XLT] +50
Power Windows[Std on Eddie Bauer, XLT] +45

F-SERIES PICKUP 1992

New front sheetmetal, a redesigned dashboard, and the return of the Flareside mark the changes for the 1992 F-Series. Climate controls are simplified and stereo controls are moved closer to the driver.

RATINGS (SCALE OF 1-10)

Overall	Safety	Reliability	Performance	Comfort	Value
N/A	5.6	7.1	6.8	7.4	N/A

F-150

Category H
2 Dr S Ext Cab LB	3810	4950
2 Dr S Ext Cab SB	3730	4845

Model Description	Trade-in Value	Market Value
2 Dr S Std Cab LB	3340	4340
2 Dr S 4WD Std Cab LB	4520	5870
2 Dr S Std Cab SB	3280	4260
2 Dr S 4WD Std Cab SB	4395	5710
2 Dr STD Ext Cab LB	4495	5840
2 Dr STD 4WD Ext Cab LB	5530	7185
2 Dr STD Ext Cab SB	4395	5710
2 Dr STD 4WD Ext Cab SB	5450	7080
2 Dr STD Ext Cab Stepside SB	4775	6200
2 Dr STD 4WD Ext Cab Stepside SB	5830	7570
2 Dr STD Std Cab LB	4275	5555
2 Dr STD 4WD Std Cab LB	5275	6850
2 Dr STD Std Cab SB	4195	5445
2 Dr STD 4WD Std Cab SB	5155	6695
2 Dr STD Std Cab Stepside SB	4430	5750
2 Dr STD 4WD Std Cab Stepside SB	5450	7080
2 Dr XL Ext Cab LB	4630	6015
2 Dr XL 4WD Ext Cab LB	5805	7540
2 Dr XL Ext Cab SB	4510	5860
2 Dr XL 4WD Ext Cab SB	5735	7450
2 Dr XL Ext Cab Stepside SB	4755	6175
2 Dr XL 4WD Ext Cab Stepside SB	5980	7765
2 Dr XL Std Cab LB	4425	5745
2 Dr XL 4WD Std Cab LB	5380	6985
2 Dr XL Std Cab SB	4385	5695
2 Dr XL 4WD Std Cab SB	5300	6885
2 Dr XL Std Cab Stepside SB	4585	5955
2 Dr XL 4WD Std Cab Stepside SB	5550	7205
2 Dr XLT Lariat Ext Cab LB	4990	6480
2 Dr XLT Lariat 4WD Ext Cab LB	5865	7615
2 Dr XLT Lariat Ext Cab SB	4900	6365
2 Dr XLT Lariat 4WD Ext Cab SB	5790	7520
2 Dr XLT Lariat Ext Cab Stepside SB	5130	6665
2 Dr XLT Lariat 4WD Ext Cab Stepside SB	6075	7890
2 Dr XLT Lariat Std Cab LB	4760	6180
2 Dr XLT Lariat 4WD Std Cab LB	6285	8160
2 Dr XLT Lariat Std Cab SB	4660	6050
2 Dr XLT Lariat 4WD Std Cab SB	5425	7045
2 Dr XLT Lariat Std Cab Stepside SB	4865	6315
2 Dr XLT Lariat 4WD Std Cab Stepside SB	5655	7345

F-250

Category H

Model Description	Trade-in Value	Market Value
2 Dr STD Ext Cab LB	5535	7190
2 Dr STD 4WD Ext Cab LB	6570	8530
2 Dr STD Std Cab LB	5280	6855
2 Dr STD 4WD Std Cab LB	5970	7755
2 Dr XLT Lariat Ext Cab LB	6120	7950
2 Dr XLT Lariat 4WD Ext Cab LB	7080	9195
2 Dr XLT Lariat Std Cab LB	5800	7535
2 Dr XLT Lariat 4WD Std Cab LB	6765	8785

F-350

Category H

Model Description	Trade-in Value	Market Value
4 Dr STD Crew Cab LB	6300	8185
4 Dr STD 4WD Crew Cab LB	6820	8860
2 Dr STD Ext Cab LB	5560	7220
2 Dr STD Std Cab LB	5850	7600
2 Dr STD 4WD Std Cab LB	6655	8640
4 Dr XLT Lariat Crew Cab LB	6525	8475
4 Dr XLT Lariat 4WD Crew Cab LB	7105	9230
2 Dr XLT Lariat Ext Cab LB	6770	8790
2 Dr XLT Lariat Std Cab LB	6385	8290
2 Dr XLT Lariat 4WD Std Cab LB	6920	8990

OPTIONS FOR F-SERIES PICKUP

8 cyl 5.0 L Engine +105
8 cyl 5.8 L Engine +155
8 cyl 7.3 L Dsl Engine +465
8 cyl 7.5 L Engine +175
Auto 3-Speed Transmission +145
Auto 4-Speed Transmission +165
Nite Trim Pkg +210
Air Conditioning +145
Camper/Towing Package +60
Cruise Control +35
Dual Rear Wheels +150
Limited Slip Diff +45
Power Door Locks +35
Power Windows +35

FESTIVA   1992

The GL gets alloy wheels. Sport trim and a spoiler are part of the GL's optional Sport Package.

RATINGS (SCALE OF 1-10)

Overall	Safety	Reliability	Performance	Comfort	Value
6.1	4.6	7.9	6.2	6.9	5

Category E

Model Description	Trade-in Value	Market Value
2 Dr GL Hbk	1375	2145
2 Dr L Hbk	1270	1985

FORD 92

Model Description	Trade-in Value	Market Value	Model Description	Trade-in Value	Market Value

OPTIONS FOR FESTIVA
Auto 3-Speed Transmission +95
Air Conditioning +145
Sunroof +65

MUSTANG 1992

LX models receive color-keyed body side moldings and bumper rub strips. All models get a new dome lamp.

RATINGS (SCALE OF 1-10)

Overall	Safety	Reliability	Performance	Comfort	Value
N/A	N/A	7.2	7.8	6.3	4.6

Category C
2 Dr LX Conv	3370	4885
2 Dr LX Cpe	2210	3200
2 Dr LX Hbk	2355	3415

Category F
2 Dr GT Conv	5315	7280
2 Dr GT Hbk	4860	6660
2 Dr LX 5.0 Conv	4275	5855
2 Dr LX 5.0 Cpe	3750	5140
2 Dr LX 5.0 Hbk	3910	5355

OPTIONS FOR MUSTANG
Auto 4-Speed Transmission +105
Air Conditioning +145
Cruise Control +40
Leather Seats +120
Power Door Locks[Std on Conv] +35
Power Driver's Seat +45
Power Windows[Std on Conv] +40
Sunroof +65

PROBE 1992

The Sport Option Package becomes available for the LX model. A rear window defroster, interval wipers, power mirrors, tinted glass, and a tilt steering wheel are no longer standard on the GT or LX.

Category E
2 Dr GL Hbk	2020	3160
2 Dr LX Hbk	2295	3585

Category F
2 Dr GT Turbo Hbk	2765	3785

OPTIONS FOR PROBE
Auto 4-Speed Transmission +130
Air Conditioning +145
Anti-Lock Brakes +120
Cruise Control +40
Leather Seats +120
Power Door Locks +35
Power Driver's Seat +45
Power Windows +40
Sunroof +65

RANGER 1992

No changes to the 1992 Ford Ranger.

Category G
2 Dr Custom Std Cab LB	2615	3585
2 Dr Custom 4WD Std Cab LB	3885	5325
2 Dr Custom Std Cab SB	2415	3305
2 Dr Custom 4WD Std Cab SB	3765	5160
2 Dr S Std Cab SB	2155	2950
2 Dr STD Ext Cab SB	2940	4030
2 Dr STD 4WD Ext Cab SB	4135	5665
2 Dr STX Ext Cab SB	3380	4630
2 Dr STX 4WD Ext Cab SB	4335	5935
2 Dr STX Std Cab LB	2780	3810
2 Dr STX 4WD Std Cab LB	4225	5785
2 Dr STX Std Cab SB	2705	3705
2 Dr STX 4WD Std Cab SB	4060	5565
2 Dr Sport Std Cab LB	2630	3600
2 Dr Sport 4WD Std Cab LB	3800	5205
2 Dr Sport Std Cab SB	2400	3285
2 Dr Sport 4WD Std Cab SB	3665	5020
2 Dr XLT Ext Cab SB	3330	4565
2 Dr XLT 4WD Ext Cab SB	4385	6010
2 Dr XLT Std Cab LB	2795	3830
2 Dr XLT 4WD Std Cab LB	4150	5685
2 Dr XLT Std Cab SB	2765	3785
2 Dr XLT 4WD Std Cab SB	3955	5420

OPTIONS FOR RANGER
6 cyl 2.9 L Engine +100
6 cyl 3.0 L Engine[Std on STX] +140
6 cyl 4.0 L Engine +100
Auto 4-Speed Transmission +170
Chrome Rally Bar Pkg +170
Chrome Sport Appear Pkg +155
Air Conditioning +145
Cruise Control[Opt on Custom,Sport,STD,XLT,4WD] +40
Limited Slip Diff +50
Power Door Locks +40
Power Driver's Seat +50
Power Windows +45

TAURUS 1992

A passenger airbag is now optional. Interior changes include a new dash. Restyled sheetmetal replaces everything but the doors. Antilock brakes are standard on the SHO and optional on other models. The SHO receives distinctive front-end styling. Wagons get an optional remote lift gate release.

RATINGS (SCALE OF 1-10)

Overall	Safety	Reliability	Performance	Comfort	Value
7.2	6.6	5.7	8	7.8	8.1

Don't forget to refer to the Mileage Adjustment Table at the back of this book!

Model Description	Trade-in Value	Market Value
Category C		
4 Dr GL Sdn	2180	3160
4 Dr GL Wgn	2315	3355
4 Dr L Sdn	1975	2860
4 Dr L Wgn	2100	3040
4 Dr LX Sdn	3050	4420
4 Dr LX Wgn	3200	4635
Category F		
4 Dr SHO Sdn	3685	5045

OPTIONS FOR TAURUS

6 cyl 3.8 L Engine[Opt on GL] +90
AM/FM Compact Disc Player +65
Air Conditioning[Std on LX,SHO] +145
Anti-Lock Brakes[Std on SHO] +110
Cruise Control[Std on SHO] +40
Dual Air Bag Restraints +90
Leather Seats +110
Power Door Locks[Std on LX,SHO] +45
Power Driver's Seat[Std on LX,SHO] +55
Power Moonroof +115
Power Windows[Std on LX,SHO] +55

TEMPO   1992

V6 power becomes available but the four-wheel drive option departs. Rear stabilizer bars are added to V6 models and sequential-port fuel injection appears on all Tempos. The GLS model receives fog lamps, alloy wheels and 15-inch tires.

RATINGS (SCALE OF 1-10)

Overall	Safety	Reliability	Performance	Comfort	Value
6.4	4.4	6.6	7.6	7.1	6.3

	Trade-in Value	Market Value
Category C		
2 Dr GL Sdn	1565	2270
4 Dr GL Sdn	1640	2380
2 Dr GLS Sdn	1695	2460
4 Dr GLS Sdn	1730	2510
4 Dr LX Sdn	1815	2630

OPTIONS FOR TEMPO

6 cyl 3.0 L Engine[Std on GLS] +125
Auto 3-Speed Transmission +100
Air Bag Restraint +85
Air Conditioning[Std on GLS] +145
Cruise Control +40
Power Door Locks[Std on LX] +45
Power Driver's Seat +55
Power Windows +55

THUNDERBIRD   1992

A V8 engine is available on the Base and LX Thunderbird; standard on the new Sport. The Sport has alloy wheels and V8 fender badges.

RATINGS (SCALE OF 1-10)

Overall	Safety	Reliability	Performance	Comfort	Value
6.8	5.7	6.5	6.8	8	6.9

	Trade-in Value	Market Value
Category C		
2 Dr LX Cpe	3385	4910
2 Dr STD Cpe	3045	4415
2 Dr Sport Cpe	3335	4835
Category F		
2 Dr SC Sprchgd Cpe	4470	6120

OPTIONS FOR THUNDERBIRD

8 cyl 5.0 L Engine[Std on Sport] +200
Auto 4-Speed Transmission[Opt on SC] +105
AM/FM Compact Disc Player +65
Anti-Lock Brakes[Std on SC] +110
Cruise Control[Opt on STD] +40
JBL Sound System +90
Leather Seats +110
Power Door Locks[Std on LX] +35
Power Driver's Seat[Std on LX] +45
Power Moonroof +115
Power Passenger Seat +50

1991 FORD

AEROSTAR   1991

A new sport appearance package debuts on XL and XLT models; it includes running boards and a front air dam. The towing harness is upgraded and a door ajar dummy-light appears for rear doors. The Eddie Bauer trim-level is added this year.

RATINGS (SCALE OF 1-10)

Overall	Safety	Reliability	Performance	Comfort	Value
6.4	4.4	5.7	6.6	7.3	8.1

	Trade-in Value	Market Value
Category G		
2 Dr Eddie Bauer Pass. Van	2410	3445
2 Dr Eddie Bauer 4WD Pass. Van	3265	4665
2 Dr Eddie Bauer Pass. Van Ext	2900	4145
2 Dr Eddie Bauer 4WD Pass. Van Ext	3690	5270
2 Dr STD Cargo Van	1570	2240
2 Dr STD 4WD Cargo Van	1965	2805
2 Dr STD Cargo Van Ext	2070	2960
2 Dr STD 4WD Cargo Van Ext	2435	3475
2 Dr STD Pass. Van	2205	3150
2 Dr XL Pass. Van	2210	3160
2 Dr XL 4WD Pass. Van	2585	3690
2 Dr XL Pass. Van Ext	2455	3510
2 Dr XL 4WD Pass. Van Ext	2735	3905
2 Dr XLT Pass. Van	2365	3380
2 Dr XLT 4WD Pass. Van	2785	3975

Don't forget to refer to the Mileage Adjustment Table at the back of this book!

Model Description	Trade-in Value	Market Value	Model Description	Trade-in Value	Market Value
2 Dr XLT Pass. Van Ext	2780	3970	2 Dr STD Econoline Ext	3020	4140
2 Dr XLT 4WD Pass. Van Ext	2960	4225	2 Dr XLT Club Wagon	3905	5350

OPTIONS FOR AEROSTAR

6 cyl 4.0 L Engine[Opt on 2WD] +90
Auto 4-Speed Transmission[Opt on XL,XLT] +100
Seat/Bed Combination +130
Air Conditioning[Std on Eddie Bauer, XLT] +120
Camper/Towing Package +45
Captain Chairs (4) +90
Cruise Control[Std on Eddie Bauer, XLT] +30
Dual Air Conditioning[Opt on STD,XL,XLT] +140
Power Door Locks +35
Power Windows +35

BRONCO 1991

A four-speed automatic transmission replaces the three-speed unit. A silver-anniversary edition is available.

Category H

	Trade-in	Market
2 Dr Custom 4WD Utility	4675	6405
2 Dr Eddie Bauer 4WD Utility	5215	7145
2 Dr Slvr Anniversary 4WD Utility	5105	6990
2 Dr XLT 4WD Utility	4790	6565
2 Dr XLT Nite 4WD Utility	4980	6820

OPTIONS FOR BRONCO

8 cyl 5.0 L Engine[Opt on Custom,XLT] +85
8 cyl 5.8 L Engine +120
Auto 4-Speed Transmission[Std on Slvr Anniversary] +135
Air Conditioning[Opt on Custom] +120
Camper/Towing Package +50
Cruise Control[Opt on Custom] +30
Limited Slip Diff +40
Power Door Locks[Opt on Custom] +30
Power Windows[Opt on Custom] +30

CLUB WAGON/ECONOLINE 1991

The short wheelbase model is dropped but a Heavy Duty workhorse becomes available. Optional 15-inch deep-dish wheels are available for those who want that "sporty" full-size van look.

E-150

Category H

	Trade-in	Market
2 Dr STD Econoline	2825	3870
2 Dr STD Econoline Ext	2980	4085
2 Dr XL Econoline	3120	4275
2 Dr XL Econoline Ext	3275	4485
2 Dr XLT Club Wagon	3825	5240

E-250

Category H

	Trade-in	Market
2 Dr STD Club Wagon	3520	4820
2 Dr STD Econoline	2915	3995

E-350

Category H

	Trade-in	Market
2 Dr STD Econoline	3105	4255
2 Dr STD Econoline Ext	3240	4435
2 Dr Super Club Wagon Ext	3105	4255
2 Dr XLT Club Wagon Ext	3240	4440

OPTIONS FOR CLUB WAGON/ECONOLINE

8 cyl 5.0 L Engine +85
8 cyl 5.8 L Engine +120
8 cyl 7.3 L Dsl Engine +350
8 cyl 7.5 L Engine +125
Auto 4-Speed Transmission[Std on E-150 XLT
* Club Wagon] +45*
Air Conditioning +120
Camper/Towing Package[Std on E-250 XLT Club Wagon] +50
Cruise Control[Std on E-250 XLT Club Wagon] +30
Dual Air Conditioning[Std on E-250 XLT Club Wagon] +195
Power Door Locks[Std on E-250 XLT Club Wagon] +30
Power Driver's Seat +40
Power Windows[Std on E-250 XLT Club Wagon] +30

CROWN VICTORIA 1991

No changes to the 1991 Crown Victoria.

Category B

	Trade-in	Market
4 Dr Cntry Squire Wgn	2255	3315
4 Dr Cntry Squire LX Wgn	2490	3660
4 Dr LX Sdn	2350	3455
4 Dr LX Wgn	2405	3535
4 Dr S Sdn	1960	2880
4 Dr STD Sdn	2035	2995
4 Dr STD Wgn	2190	3220

OPTIONS FOR CROWN VICTORIA

Cruise Control +30
Leather Seats +100
Power Door Locks +40
Power Driver's Seat +45
Power Passenger Seat +50

ESCORT 1991

A totally redesigned Escort bows in 1991. New engines, sheetmetal and interiors round out the changes.

RATINGS (SCALE OF 1-10)

Overall	Safety	Reliability	Performance	Comfort	Value
6	4.4	5.5	6.8	7.6	5.6

Category E

	Trade-in	Market
2 Dr GT Hbk	1390	2355
2 Dr LX Hbk	1125	1905
4 Dr LX Hbk	1190	2020
4 Dr LX Wgn	1280	2170
2 Dr Pony Hbk	1035	1750

Model Description	Trade-in Value	Market Value	Model Description	Trade-in Value	Market Value

OPTIONS FOR ESCORT

Auto 4-Speed Transmission +110
Air Conditioning +120
Cruise Control +35
Power Door Locks +35
Power Steering[Std on GT] +40

EXPLORER   1991

New model introduced to replace aging Bronco II. The Explorer is one of the bigger compact sport utilities and comes in two- or four-door models. A 4.0-liter V6 engine powers two- and four-wheel-drive models. Part-time four-wheel drive can be engaged with the push of a button.

RATINGS (SCALE OF 1-10)

Overall	Safety	Reliability	Performance	Comfort	Value
6	4.2	4.1	7.4	8.3	5.9

Category G

	Trade-in	Market
2 Dr Eddie Bauer Utility	3655	5220
2 Dr Eddie Bauer 4WD Utility	4045	5780
4 Dr Eddie Bauer Wgn	4130	5900
4 Dr Eddie Bauer 4WD Wgn	4510	6440
2 Dr Sport Utility	3195	4565
2 Dr Sport 4WD Utility	3780	5400
2 Dr XL Utility	3020	4315
2 Dr XL 4WD Utility	3630	5185
4 Dr XL Wgn	3735	5335
4 Dr XL 4WD Wgn	3950	5645
4 Dr XLT Wgn	3960	5660
4 Dr XLT 4WD Wgn	4290	6130

OPTIONS FOR EXPLORER

Auto 4-Speed Transmission +130
AM/FM Compact Disc Player +50
Air Conditioning +120
Camper/Towing Package +45
Cruise Control[Opt on Sport,XL] +30
JBL Sound System +115
Leather Seats +115
Power Door Locks[Opt on Sport,XL] +35
Power Driver's Seat +40
Power Windows[Opt on Sport,XL] +35
Sunroof +45

F-SERIES PICKUP   1991

A Nite Appearance Package is offered and the 5.0-liter engine is now available with the four-speed automatic transmission. F-250 and 350s receive auto-locking hubs. Ford's touch-drive transfer case replaces the older, floor-mounted system.

F-150

Category H

	Trade-in	Market
2 Dr S Std Cab LB	2655	3640
2 Dr S Std Cab SB	2705	3705
2 Dr STD Ext Cab LB	3680	5040
2 Dr STD 4WD Ext Cab LB	4680	6410
2 Dr STD Ext Cab SB	3620	4960
2 Dr STD 4WD Ext Cab SB	4655	6380
2 Dr STD Std Cab LB	3290	4505
2 Dr STD 4WD Std Cab LB	4500	6165
2 Dr STD Std Cab SB	3200	4385
2 Dr STD 4WD Std Cab SB	4400	6030
2 Dr XL Ext Cab LB	3750	5140
2 Dr XL 4WD Ext Cab LB	5045	6910
2 Dr XL Ext Cab SB	3665	5020
2 Dr XL 4WD Ext Cab SB	5010	6865
2 Dr XL Std Cab LB	3560	4880
2 Dr XL 4WD Std Cab LB	4300	5890
2 Dr XL Std Cab SB	3450	4725
2 Dr XL 4WD Std Cab SB	4185	5735
2 Dr XLT Lariat Ext Cab LB	4025	5515
2 Dr XLT Lariat 4WD Ext Cab LB	5245	7185
2 Dr XLT Lariat Ext Cab SB	3975	5445
2 Dr XLT Lariat 4WD Ext Cab SB	5130	7025
2 Dr XLT Lariat Std Cab LB	3735	5115
2 Dr XLT Lariat 4WD Std Cab LB	4635	6350
2 Dr XLT Lariat Std Cab SB	3645	4990
2 Dr XLT Lariat 4WD Std Cab SB	4540	6220

F-250

Category H

	Trade-in	Market
2 Dr STD Ext Cab LB	4705	6445
2 Dr STD 4WD Ext Cab LB	5480	7505
2 Dr STD Std Cab LB	4595	6295
2 Dr STD 4WD Std Cab LB	4645	6365
2 Dr XL Ext Cab LB	5065	6935
2 Dr XL 4WD Ext Cab LB	5615	7695
2 Dr XL Std Cab LB	4730	6480
2 Dr XL 4WD Std Cab LB	5060	6930
2 Dr XLT Lariat Ext Cab LB	5115	7010
2 Dr XLT Lariat 4WD Ext Cab LB	5930	8120
2 Dr XLT Lariat Std Cab LB	4855	6650
2 Dr XLT Lariat 4WD Std Cab LB	5480	7505

F-350

Category H

	Trade-in	Market
4 Dr STD Crew Cab LB	4870	6670
4 Dr STD 4WD Crew Cab LB	5050	6920
2 Dr STD Ext Cab LB	4390	6015
2 Dr STD Std Cab LB	5135	7035
2 Dr STD 4WD Std Cab LB	5460	7480

Model Description	Trade-in Value	Market Value
2 Dr XL 4WD Std Cab LB	5905	8090
4 Dr XLT Lariat Crew Cab LB	5375	7365
4 Dr XLT Lariat 4WD Crew Cab LB	5835	7990
2 Dr XLT Lariat Ext Cab LB	4935	6760
2 Dr XLT Lariat Std Cab LB	4580	6275
2 Dr XLT Lariat 4WD Std Cab LB	5155	7065

OPTIONS FOR F-SERIES PICKUP

8 cyl 5.0 L Engine +85
8 cyl 5.8 L Engine +120
8 cyl 7.3 L Dsl Engine +350
8 cyl 7.5 L Engine +125
Auto 3-Speed Transmission +115
Auto 4-Speed Transmission +135
Air Conditioning +120
Camper/Towing Package +50
Cruise Control +30
Dual Rear Wheels +120
Limited Slip Diff +40
Power Door Locks +30
Power Windows +30

FESTIVA 1991

The L Plus model is dropped. The LX is renamed GL and gets body-color bumpers and color-keyed wheels in the process.

RATINGS (SCALE OF 1-10)

Overall	Safety	Reliability	Performance	Comfort	Value
5.9	4.6	6.9	6.2	6.9	5

	Trade-in	Market
Category E		
2 Dr GL Hbk	880	1490
2 Dr L Hbk	775	1315

OPTIONS FOR FESTIVA

Auto 3-Speed Transmission +75
Air Conditioning +120

MUSTANG 1991

New wheels appear on the GT and LX 5.0 Mustangs.

RATINGS (SCALE OF 1-10)

Overall	Safety	Reliability	Performance	Comfort	Value
N/A	N/A	6.2	7.8	6.3	4.1

	Trade-in	Market
Category C		
2 Dr LX Cpe	1570	2415
2 Dr LX Hbk	1740	2675
Category F		
2 Dr GT Conv	4485	6320
2 Dr GT Hbk	4200	5915
2 Dr LX 5.0 Conv	3840	5410
2 Dr LX 5.0 Cpe	3310	4660
2 Dr LX 5.0 Hbk	3445	4855

OPTIONS FOR MUSTANG

Auto 4-Speed Transmission +90
Air Conditioning +120
Cruise Control +30
Flip-Up Sunroof +55
Leather Seats +90
Power Door Locks[Std on Conv] +30
Power Windows[Std on Conv] +35

PROBE 1991

All Probes get revised front and rear styling. GT models lose their body-side cladding resulting in a cleaner look.

	Trade-in	Market
Category E		
2 Dr GL Hbk	1515	2570
2 Dr LX Hbk	1770	3000
Category F		
2 Dr GT Turbo Hbk	2405	3390

OPTIONS FOR PROBE

Auto 4-Speed Transmission +110
Air Conditioning +120
Anti-Lock Brakes +100
Cruise Control +30
Flip-Up Sunroof +50
Power Door Locks +30
Power Driver's Seat +35
Power Windows +35

RANGER 1991

Ford introduces a Sport model to the Ranger stable. Equipped with an optional V6 engine, alloy wheels, and snazzy graphics, the Ranger Sport promises to be one of the hottest vehicles in the high-school parking lot.

	Trade-in	Market
Category G		
2 Dr Custom Ext Cab SB	2550	3640
2 Dr Custom 4WD Ext Cab SB	3575	5110
2 Dr Custom Std Cab LB	2345	3350
2 Dr Custom 4WD Std Cab LB	3150	4500
2 Dr Custom Std Cab SB	2035	2910
2 Dr Custom 4WD Std Cab SB	3105	4435
2 Dr S Std Cab SB	1885	2695
2 Dr STX Ext Cab SB	2830	4040
2 Dr STX 4WD Ext Cab SB	3775	5395
2 Dr STX Std Cab LB	2315	3305
2 Dr STX 4WD Std Cab LB	3445	4920
2 Dr STX Std Cab SB	2205	3150
2 Dr STX 4WD Std Cab SB	3410	4870
2 Dr Sport Std Cab LB	2100	3000
2 Dr Sport 4WD Std Cab LB	3135	4480
2 Dr Sport Std Cab SB	2035	2905
2 Dr Sport 4WD Std Cab SB	2925	4175
2 Dr XLT Ext Cab SB	2645	3775
2 Dr XLT 4WD Ext Cab SB	3765	5380

Don't forget to refer to the Mileage Adjustment Table at the back of this book!

FORD 91-90

Model Description	Trade-in Value	Market Value
2 Dr XLT Std Cab LB	2325	3320
2 Dr XLT 4WD Std Cab LB	3350	4785
2 Dr XLT Std Cab SB	2260	3225
2 Dr XLT 4WD Std Cab SB	3240	4625

OPTIONS FOR RANGER
6 cyl 2.9 L Engine +75
6 cyl 3.0 L Engine +105
6 cyl 4.0 L Engine +90
Auto 4-Speed Transmission +135
Sport Appearance Pkg +115
Air Conditioning +120
Cruise Control +30
Limited Slip Diff +40
Power Door Locks +35

TAURUS   1991

Sequential multi-port fuel injection systems are added to the Taurus.

Model Description	Trade-in Value	Market Value
Category C		
4 Dr GL Sdn	1640	2520
4 Dr GL Wgn	1845	2840
4 Dr L Sdn	1415	2175
4 Dr L Wgn	1515	2330
4 Dr LX Sdn	2325	3580
4 Dr LX Wgn	2445	3760
Category F		
4 Dr SHO Sdn	2860	4025

OPTIONS FOR TAURUS
6 cyl 3.0 L Engine[Std on LX,SHO,Wgn] +100
6 cyl 3.8 L Engine +80
Air Conditioning[Opt on GL,L] +120
Anti-Lock Brakes[Opt on GL,L] +90
Cruise Control[Std on SHO] +30
JBL Sound System +75
Leather Seats +90
Power Door Locks[Opt on GL,L] +35
Power Driver's Seat[Opt on GL,L] +45
Power Sunroof +100
Power Windows[Opt on GL,L] +45

TEMPO   1991

No significant changes for the 1991 Tempo.

RATINGS (SCALE OF 1-10)

Overall	Safety	Reliability	Performance	Comfort	Value
6.5	4.5	6.5	7.2	7.1	7.3

Model Description	Trade-in Value	Market Value
Category C		
2 Dr GL Sdn	1200	1845
4 Dr GL Sdn	1295	1990
2 Dr GLS Sdn	1405	2165
4 Dr GLS Sdn	1485	2285
2 Dr L Sdn	990	1520
4 Dr L Sdn	1280	1970

Model Description	Trade-in Value	Market Value
4 Dr LX Sdn	1510	2325
4 Dr STD 4WD Sdn	1620	2495

OPTIONS FOR TEMPO
Auto 3-Speed Transmission[Std on STD] +85
Air Conditioning +120
Cruise Control +30
Power Door Locks[Std on LX] +35
Power Driver's Seat +45
Power Windows[Std on LX] +45

THUNDERBIRD   1991

No changes for the 1991 Thunderbird.

RATINGS (SCALE OF 1-10)

Overall	Safety	Reliability	Performance	Comfort	Value
6.7	5.6	6.1	6.8	8	6.8

Model Description	Trade-in Value	Market Value
Category C		
2 Dr LX Cpe	2515	3870
2 Dr STD Cpe	2365	3635
Category F		
2 Dr SC Sprchgd Cpe	3820	5380

OPTIONS FOR THUNDERBIRD
8 cyl 5.0 L Engine +165
Anti-Lock Brakes[Std on SC] +90
Cruise Control[Opt on STD] +30
Leather Seats +90
Power Door Locks[Opt on STD] +35
Power Driver's Seat[Opt on STD] +45
Power Moonroof +95

1990 FORD

AEROSTAR   1990

Rear-wheel antilock brakes and full-time all-wheel drive become available. A 4.0-liter V6 is also available. An under-seat locking storage compartment is now standard on the Aerostar and will store small valuables.

RATINGS (SCALE OF 1-10)

Overall	Safety	Reliability	Performance	Comfort	Value
6.1	4	5	6.6	7.3	7.6

Model Description	Trade-in Value	Market Value
Category G		
2 Dr Eddie Bauer Pass. Van	2040	3090
2 Dr Eddie Bauer 4WD Pass. Van		
	2345	3555
2 Dr Eddie Bauer Pass. Van Ext		
	2425	3675
2 Dr Eddie Bauer 4WD Pass. Van Ext		
	2650	4015
2 Dr STD Cargo Van	1430	2170
2 Dr STD Cargo Van Ext	1675	2540
2 Dr STD Pass. Van	1560	2360
2 Dr STD 4WD Pass. Van	1965	2980

Don't forget to refer to the Mileage Adjustment Table at the back of this book!

Model Description	Trade-in Value	Market Value
2 Dr STD Pass. Van Ext	2230	3380
2 Dr STD 4WD Pass. Van Ext	2385	3610
2 Dr XL Pass. Van	1685	2550
2 Dr XL 4WD Pass. Van	2175	3295
2 Dr XL Pass. Van Ext	1975	2990
2 Dr XL 4WD Pass. Van Ext	2145	3250
2 Dr XLT Pass. Van	1880	2850
2 Dr XLT 4WD Pass. Van	2180	3305
2 Dr XLT Pass. Van Ext	2355	3570
2 Dr XLT 4WD Pass. Van Ext	2445	3705

OPTIONS FOR AEROSTAR
6 cyl 4.0 L Engine[Opt on 2WD] +75
Auto 4-Speed Transmission[Opt on 2WD] +80
Air Conditioning[Opt on STD,Cargo Van,XL,XLT] +100
Camper/Towing Package +35
Captain Chairs (4) +75
Cruise Control[Std on Eddie Bauer] +25
Dual Air Conditioning[Opt on STD,XL,XLT] +115
Power Door Locks[Std on Eddie Bauer] +30
Power Windows[Std on Eddie Bauer] +30

BRONCO 1990

No changes for 1990.

Category H	Trade-in	Market
2 Dr Custom 4WD Utility	3990	5540
2 Dr Eddie Bauer 4WD Utility	4620	6415
2 Dr XLT 4WD Utility	4230	5875

OPTIONS FOR BRONCO
8 cyl 5.0 L Engine[Opt on Custom,XLT] +70
8 cyl 5.8 L Engine +100
Auto 4-Speed Transmission +110
Air Conditioning[Opt on Custom,XLT] +100
Camper/Towing Package +40
Limited Slip Diff +30

BRONCO II 1990

New floor mats appear on the Eddie Bauer trim level. Louder horn debuts.

Category G	Trade-in	Market
2 Dr Eddie Bauer Utility	2315	3505
2 Dr Eddie Bauer 4WD Utility	2800	4245
2 Dr Sport Utility	2300	3485
2 Dr Sport 4WD Utility	2625	3980
2 Dr XL Utility	2085	3160
2 Dr XL 4WD Utility	2370	3590
2 Dr XLT Utility	2215	3355
2 Dr XLT 4WD Utility	2455	3720

OPTIONS FOR BRONCO II
Auto 4-Speed Transmission +115
Air Conditioning[Std on Eddie Bauer] +100
Cruise Control[Std on Eddie Bauer] +25
Power Door Locks[Std on Eddie Bauer] +30
Power Windows[Std on Eddie Bauer] +30

CLUB WAGON/ECONOLINE 1990

No changes for 1990.

E-150

Category H	Trade-in	Market
2 Dr STD Club Wagon	2885	4005
2 Dr STD Econoline	2160	3000
2 Dr STD Econoline Ext	2505	3480
2 Dr XL Econoline	2400	3335
2 Dr XL Econoline Ext	2770	3850
2 Dr XLT Club Wagon	3420	4750

E-250

Category H	Trade-in	Market
2 Dr STD Club Wagon	2825	3925
2 Dr STD Econoline	2475	3440
2 Dr STD Econoline Ext	2555	3550
2 Dr XL Econoline	2525	3510
2 Dr XL Econoline Ext	2680	3720
2 Dr XLT Club Wagon	3375	4685

E-350

Category H	Trade-in	Market
2 Dr STD Club Wagon Ext	2925	4065
2 Dr STD Econoline	2565	3565
2 Dr STD Econoline Ext	2665	3700
2 Dr XL Dsl Econoline	3440	4775
2 Dr XL Econoline Ext	2940	4080
2 Dr XLT Club Wagon Ext	2820	3915

OPTIONS FOR CLUB WAGON/ECONOLINE
8 cyl 5.0 L Engine +70
8 cyl 5.8 L Engine +100
8 cyl 7.3 L Dsl Engine +290
8 cyl 7.5 L Engine +100
Auto 4-Speed Transmission[Std on E-150 STD Club Wagon,E-150 XLT Club Wagon] +30
RV Converter Pkg +140
Air Conditioning +100
Camper/Towing Package +40
Dual Air Conditioning +160

CROWN VICTORIA 1990

A driver airbag becomes standard and the instrument panel is redesigned.

Category B	Trade-in	Market
4 Dr Cntry Squire Wgn	2030	3125
4 Dr Cntry Squire LX Wgn	2080	3200
4 Dr LX Sdn	1920	2950
4 Dr LX Wgn	2000	3080
4 Dr STD Sdn	1715	2635
4 Dr STD Wgn	1760	2710

OPTIONS FOR CROWN VICTORIA
Cruise Control +25
Leather Seats +80

Don't forget to refer to the Mileage Adjustment Table at the back of this book!

Model Description	Trade-in Value	Market Value
Power Door Locks +30		
Power Driver's Seat +40		

ESCORT 1990

No changes.
Category E

Model Description	Trade-in Value	Market Value
2 Dr GT Hbk	900	1730
2 Dr LX Hbk	780	1500
4 Dr LX Hbk	830	1595
4 Dr LX Wgn	855	1645
2 Dr Pony Hbk	750	1440

OPTIONS FOR ESCORT
Auto 3-Speed Transmission +65
Air Conditioning +100
Cruise Control +25

F-SERIES PICKUP 1990

No major changes for the 1990 F-series.

F-150

Category H

Model Description	Trade-in Value	Market Value
2 Dr S Std Cab LB	2435	3385
2 Dr S Std Cab SB	2340	3250
2 Dr STD Ext Cab LB	3205	4450
2 Dr STD 4WD Ext Cab LB	4275	5935
2 Dr STD Ext Cab SB	3105	4310
2 Dr STD 4WD Ext Cab SB	4215	5855
2 Dr STD Std Cab LB	2970	4125
2 Dr STD 4WD Std Cab LB	3985	5535
2 Dr STD Std Cab SB	2885	4010
2 Dr STD 4WD Std Cab SB	3900	5420
2 Dr XL Ext Cab LB	3450	4790
2 Dr XL 4WD Ext Cab LB	4310	5985
2 Dr XL Ext Cab SB	3350	4650
2 Dr XL 4WD Ext Cab SB	4220	5860
2 Dr XL Std Cab LB	3055	4245
2 Dr XL 4WD Std Cab LB	3910	5430
2 Dr XL Std Cab SB	2965	4120
2 Dr XL 4WD Std Cab SB	3845	5340
2 Dr XLT Lariat Ext Cab LB	3825	5315
2 Dr XLT Lariat 4WD Ext Cab LB	4520	6280
2 Dr XLT Lariat Ext Cab SB	3750	5210
2 Dr XLT Lariat 4WD Ext Cab SB	4430	6155
2 Dr XLT Lariat Std Cab LB	3400	4725
2 Dr XLT Lariat 4WD Std Cab LB	4155	5770
2 Dr XLT Lariat Std Cab SB	3335	4635
2 Dr XLT Lariat 4WD Std Cab SB	4100	5695

F-250

Category H

Model Description	Trade-in Value	Market Value
2 Dr STD Ext Cab LB	4430	6155
2 Dr STD 4WD Ext Cab LB	5225	7260
2 Dr STD Std Cab LB	3850	5350
2 Dr STD 4WD Std Cab LB	4435	6160
2 Dr XL Ext Cab LB	4485	6230
2 Dr XL 4WD Ext Cab LB	5020	6970
2 Dr XL Std Cab LB	4060	5640
2 Dr XL 4WD Std Cab LB	4340	6025
2 Dr XLT Lariat Ext Cab LB	4890	6790
2 Dr XLT Lariat 4WD Ext Cab LB	5420	7525
2 Dr XLT Lariat Std Cab LB	4265	5925
2 Dr XLT Lariat 4WD Std Cab LB	4865	6755

F-350

Category H

Model Description	Trade-in Value	Market Value
4 Dr STD Crew Cab LB	3865	5370
4 Dr STD 4WD Crew Cab LB	5615	7800
2 Dr STD Ext Cab LB	3555	4935
2 Dr STD Std Cab LB	3275	4550
2 Dr STD 4WD Std Cab LB	3585	4980
4 Dr XL Crew Cab LB	4630	6430
4 Dr XL 4WD Crew Cab LB	4910	6820
2 Dr XL Ext Cab LB	5210	7235
2 Dr XL Std Cab LB	4325	6005
2 Dr XL 4WD Std Cab LB	5495	7635
4 Dr XLT Lariat Crew Cab LB	4505	6255
4 Dr XLT Lariat 4WD Crew Cab LB	5045	7010
2 Dr XLT Lariat Ext Cab LB	4265	5925
2 Dr XLT Lariat Std Cab LB	3975	5520
2 Dr XLT Lariat 4WD Std Cab LB	4265	5925

OPTIONS FOR F-SERIES PICKUP
8 cyl 5.0 L Engine +70
8 cyl 5.8 L Engine +100
8 cyl 7.3 L Dsl Engine +290
8 cyl 7.5 L Engine +100
Auto 3-Speed Transmission +85
Auto 4-Speed Transmission +110
Sport Appearance Pkg +120
Suspension Pkg +95
Air Conditioning +100
Camper/Towing Package +40
Dual Rear Wheels +100
Limited Slip Diff +30

FESTIVA 1990

A five-speed manual transmission and fuel injection becomes standard. New seat cushions and a restyled grille are the only other changes.

Don't forget to refer to the Mileage Adjustment Table at the back of this book!

FORD 90

Model Description	Trade-in Value	Market Value	Model Description	Trade-in Value	Market Value

RATINGS (SCALE OF 1-10)

Overall	Safety	Reliability	Performance	Comfort	Value
6	4.6	7.1	6.2	6.9	5.4

Model Description	Trade-in Value	Market Value
Category E		
2 Dr L Hbk	680	1305
2 Dr L Plus Hbk	720	1385
2 Dr LX Hbk	815	1570

OPTIONS FOR FESTIVA

Auto 3-Speed Transmission +65
Air Conditioning +100
Sunroof +40

MUSTANG   1990

A driver airbag becomes standard. Knee bolsters and a leather-wrapped steering wheel complete interior changes. The exterior receives clear coat paint.

RATINGS (SCALE OF 1-10)

Overall	Safety	Reliability	Performance	Comfort	Value
N/A	N/A	6.5	7.8	6.3	3.5

Model Description	Trade-in Value	Market Value
Category F		
2 Dr GT Conv	3825	5545
2 Dr GT Hbk	3435	4980
2 Dr LX 5.0 Conv	3270	4740
2 Dr LX 5.0 Cpe	2765	4010
2 Dr LX 5.0 Hbk	2945	4270
2 Dr LX Limited Conv	3285	4760

OPTIONS FOR MUSTANG

Auto 4-Speed Transmission +75
Air Conditioning +95
Cruise Control +25
Leather Seats +80
Power Windows[Opt on Cpe,Hbk] +25
Sunroof +45

PROBE   1990

A multitude of engine choices are available with the addition of the 3.0-liter V6 to the LX models. Antilock brakes become standard on the GT and optional on the LX. An automatic transmission becomes available on the GT.

Model Description	Trade-in Value	Market Value
Category E		
2 Dr GL Hbk	1225	2355
2 Dr LX Hbk	1305	2510
Category F		
2 Dr GT Turbo Hbk	1860	2695

OPTIONS FOR PROBE

Auto 4-Speed Transmission +90
Air Conditioning +100
Anti-Lock Brakes +80
Cruise Control +25
Flip-Up Sunroof +40
Leather Seats +80

Power Driver's Seat +30
Power Windows +25

RANGER   1990

No changes for the Ford Ranger.

Model Description	Trade-in Value	Market Value
Category G		
2 Dr S Std Cab LB	1695	2565
2 Dr S 4WD Std Cab LB	2435	3690
2 Dr S Std Cab SB	1585	2400
2 Dr S 4WD Std Cab SB	2325	3520
2 Dr STD Ext Cab SB	1990	3015
2 Dr STD 4WD Ext Cab SB	2950	4470
2 Dr STD Std Cab LB	1615	2445
2 Dr STD 4WD Std Cab LB	2380	3605
2 Dr STD Std Cab SB	1510	2285
2 Dr STD 4WD Std Cab SB	2360	3575
2 Dr STX 4WD Ext Cab SB	3180	4815
2 Dr STX 4WD Std Cab LB	2670	4045
2 Dr STX 4WD Std Cab SB	2565	3885
2 Dr Sport Ext Cab SB	2045	3095
2 Dr Sport 4WD Ext Cab SB	2890	4375
2 Dr Sport Std Cab LB	1700	2575
2 Dr Sport 4WD Std Cab LB	2490	3770
2 Dr Sport Std Cab SB	1625	2460
2 Dr Sport 4WD Std Cab SB	2410	3650
2 Dr XLT Ext Cab SB	2265	3435
2 Dr XLT 4WD Ext Cab SB	3105	4705
2 Dr XLT Std Cab LB	1815	2750
2 Dr XLT 4WD Std Cab LB	2615	3960
2 Dr XLT Std Cab SB	1770	2685
2 Dr XLT 4WD Std Cab SB	2515	3810

OPTIONS FOR RANGER

6 cyl 2.9 L Engine +80
6 cyl 4.0 L Engine +75
Auto 4-Speed Transmission +110
Ranger Sport Appear Pkg +95
Air Conditioning +100
Cruise Control +25
Power Door Locks +30
Power Windows +30

TAURUS   1990

Antilock brakes are available for all Tauruses. A driver airbag debuts this year.

Model Description	Trade-in Value	Market Value
Category C		
4 Dr GL Sdn	1275	2090
4 Dr GL Wgn	1395	2285
4 Dr L Sdn	1160	1905
4 Dr L Wgn	1285	2105
4 Dr LX Sdn	1590	2610
4 Dr LX Wgn	1730	2840
Category F		
4 Dr SHO Sdn	2355	3410

Don't forget to refer to the Mileage Adjustment Table at the back of this book!

FORD 90

Model Description	Trade-in Value	Market Value	Model Description	Trade-in Value	Market Value

OPTIONS FOR TAURUS

6 cyl 3.0 L Engine[Std on LX,SHO,Wgn] +85
6 cyl 3.8 L Engine +80
Air Conditioning[Std on LX,SHO] +95
Anti-Lock Brakes[Std on SHO] +75
Cruise Control[Std on SHO] +25
Leather Seats +75
Power Door Locks[Std on LX,SHO] +30
Power Driver's Seat[Std on LX,SHO] +35
Power Sunroof +80
Power Windows[Std on LX,SHO] +35

TEMPO   1990

Rear shoulder belts become standard on the 1990 Tempo.

RATINGS (SCALE OF 1-10)

Overall	Safety	Reliability	Performance	Comfort	Value
6.4	4.5	6	7.2	7.1	7.3

Category C
2 Dr GL Sdn	1070	1755
4 Dr GL Sdn	1115	1830
2 Dr GLS Sdn	1140	1870
4 Dr GLS Sdn	1220	2000
4 Dr LX Sdn	1270	2080
4 Dr STD 4WD Sdn	1320	2165

OPTIONS FOR TEMPO

Auto 3-Speed Transmission[Std on STD] +70
Sport Appearance Pkg +145

Air Conditioning +95
Cruise Control +25
Power Door Locks[Std on LX] +30
Power Driver's Seat +35
Power Windows +35

THUNDERBIRD   1990

Thirty-fifth anniversary model. No changes.

RATINGS (SCALE OF 1-10)

Overall	Safety	Reliability	Performance	Comfort	Value
6.2	5.6	5.6	6.8	8	5

Category C
2 Dr LX Cpe	2205	3615
2 Dr STD Cpe	1960	3210

Category F
2 Dr SC Sprchgd Cpe	3080	4460

OPTIONS FOR THUNDERBIRD

Auto 4-Speed Transmission[Opt on SC] +70
Anti-Lock Brakes[Std on SC] +75
Cruise Control[Std on LX] +25
JBL Sound System +60
Leather Seats +75
Power Driver's Seat[Std on LX] +30
Power Passenger Seat +35
Power Sunroof +80

Don't forget to refer to the Mileage Adjustment Table at the back of this book!

GEO 97

Model Description	Trade-in Value	Market Value	Model Description	Trade-in Value	Market Value

GEO

Japan

1994 Geo Prizm

1997 GEO

METRO 1997

Geo drops the base sedan variant of the Metro for 1997. A new convenience package is available on LSi models, and the LSi hatchback comes with the larger 1.3-liter engine standard. Two new colors debut.

RATINGS (SCALE OF 1-10)

Overall	Safety	Reliability	Performance	Comfort	Value
6.1	6.3	7.1	6.6	6.4	4.3

Category E
2 Dr LSi Hbk	3790	4795
4 Dr LSi Sdn	4010	5075
2 Dr STD Hbk	3510	4445

OPTIONS FOR METRO
Auto 3-Speed Transmission +300
Air Conditioning +405
Anti-Lock Brakes +335
Compact Disc W/fm/tape +290
Power Door Locks +120
Power Steering +125
Rear Window Defroster +80

PRIZM 1997

The Prizm is essentially carried over for 1997, sporting new door trim panels, standard power steering, new exterior colors, and strengthened side-impact protection.

RATINGS (SCALE OF 1-10)

Overall	Safety	Reliability	Performance	Comfort	Value
7	6.5	8.5	8	7.8	4.4

Category E
4 Dr LSi Sdn	6290	7965
4 Dr STD Sdn	5995	7590

OPTIONS FOR PRIZM
4 cyl 1.8 L Engine +175
Auto 3-Speed Transmission +250
Auto 4-Speed Transmission +400
Air Conditioning +405
Aluminum/Alloy Wheels +165
Anti-Lock Brakes +335
Child Seat (1) +55
Compact Disc W/fm/tape +290
Cruise Control +110
Leather Seats +430
Power Door Locks +120
Power Sunroof +305
Power Windows +130
Rear Window Defroster +80

TRACKER 1997

After a heavy makeover for 1996, changes for 1997 are limited. Convertibles get a standard fold-and-stow rear bench seat along with an enhanced evaporative emissions system. All Trackers can be painted Sunset Red Metallic or Azurite Blue Metallic for the first time. Prices have been at or near 1996 levels in an effort to make the Tracker more attractive to folks shopping Kia Sportage, Toyota RAV4 and Honda CR-V.

RATINGS (SCALE OF 1-10)

Overall	Safety	Reliability	Performance	Comfort	Value
6.1	5.5	8.6	6.4	6.8	3.2

Category G
4 Dr LSi Wgn	6675	8040
4 Dr LSi 4WD Wgn	7120	8580
2 Dr STD Conv	5895	7100
2 Dr STD 4WD Conv	6415	7730
4 Dr STD Wgn	6345	7645
4 Dr STD 4WD Wgn	6780	8170

OPTIONS FOR TRACKER
Auto 3-Speed Transmission +315
Auto 4-Speed Transmission +475
Air Conditioning +405
Aluminum/Alloy Wheels +165
Anti-Lock Brakes +295
Auto Locking Hubs (4WD) +125
Compact Disc W/fm/tape +240
Cruise Control +105
Power Door Locks +115
Power Steering[Std on LSi,Wgn,4WD] +140
Power Windows +120
Skid Plates +65

GEO 96-95

Model Description	Trade-in Value	Market Value	Model Description	Trade-in Value	Market Value

1996 GEO

METRO 1996

A zoned rear window defroster clears the center of the Metro's tiny rear backlight first, base coupes get dual exterior mirrors, and LSi coupes get cool hubcaps and body-color bumpers that keep it from looking like a refugee from some third-world country.

RATINGS (SCALE OF 1-10)

Overall	Safety	Reliability	Performance	Comfort	Value
6.3	6.5	7.7	6.6	6.4	4.3

Category E
2 Dr LSi Hbk	3080	4050
4 Dr LSi Sdn	3215	4230
2 Dr STD Hbk	2860	3760
4 Dr STD Sdn	2995	3940

OPTIONS FOR METRO
4 cyl 1.3 L Engine[Opt on Hbk] +140
Auto 3-Speed Transmission +190
Air Conditioning +330
Anti-Lock Brakes +275
Compact Disc W/fm/tape +235
Power Door Locks +100
Power Steering +105

PRIZM 1996

An integrated child safety seat is optional on the LSi, and daytime running lights debut, making the Prizm more visible to other motorists, and radar-toting police officers. Three new exterior colors and added equipment to the base model round out the changes to this excellent compact.

RATINGS (SCALE OF 1-10)

Overall	Safety	Reliability	Performance	Comfort	Value
7.3	6.6	9.1	8	7.8	4.9

Category E
4 Dr LSi Sdn	5365	7060
4 Dr STD Sdn	5080	6685

OPTIONS FOR PRIZM
4 cyl 1.8 L Engine +135
Auto 3-Speed Transmission +190
Auto 4-Speed Transmission +305
Air Conditioning +330
Anti-Lock Brakes +275
Child Seat (1) +45
Compact Disc W/fm/tape +235
Cruise Control +90
Leather Seats +355
Power Door Locks +100
Power Steering +105
Power Sunroof +250
Power Windows +105

TRACKER 1996

A new four-door model joins the lineup, and dual airbags are standard on all Trackers. Four-wheel antilock brakes are optional. Revised styling freshens the new exterior, and daytime running lights make the Tracker more conspicuous to motorists. In a switch from tradition, tasteful exterior colors are newly available. Cruise control is a new convenience option.

RATINGS (SCALE OF 1-10)

Overall	Safety	Reliability	Performance	Comfort	Value
6.1	5.4	8.1	6.4	6.8	3.7

Category G
2 Dr LSi Conv	5420	6690
2 Dr LSi 4WD Conv	5845	7215
4 Dr LSi Wgn	5690	7025
4 Dr LSi 4WD Wgn	6160	7605
2 Dr STD Conv	4925	6080
2 Dr STD 4WD Conv	5325	6575
4 Dr STD Wgn	5390	6655
4 Dr STD 4WD Wgn	5860	7235

OPTIONS FOR TRACKER
Auto 3-Speed Transmission +235
Auto 4-Speed Transmission +305
Air Conditioning +330
Aluminum/Alloy Wheels +135
Anti-Lock Brakes +245
Auto Locking Hubs (4WD) +105
Compact Disc W/fm/tape +195
Cruise Control +85
Power Door Locks +95
Power Steering[Std on Wgn,LSi 4WD Conv] +115
Power Windows +95
Skid Plates +55

1995 GEO

METRO 1995

All-new car is larger than previous model, and comes as a two-door hatchback or four-door sedan in base or LSi trim. Dual airbags are standard. ABS is optional on all models. Hatchbacks get the carryover 1.0-liter three-cylinder motor. Optional on LSi hatchback and standard on sedans is a 70-horsepower, 1.3-liter four-cylinder engine. Daytime running lights are standard.

RATINGS (SCALE OF 1-10)

Overall	Safety	Reliability	Performance	Comfort	Value
6.3	7	7	6.6	6.4	4.7

Category E
2 Dr LSi Hbk	2570	3520
4 Dr LSi Sdn	2710	3710

Don't forget to refer to the Mileage Adjustment Table at the back of this book!

Model Description	Trade-in Value	Market Value
2 Dr STD Hbk	2375	3250
4 Dr STD Sdn	2510	3435

OPTIONS FOR METRO
4 cyl 1.3 L Engine[Opt on Hbk] +120
Auto 3-Speed Transmission +165
Air Conditioning +270
Anti-Lock Brakes +225
Compact Disc W/fm/tape +190
Power Door Locks +80
Power Steering +85
Rear Window Defroster +55

PRIZM 1995

Base 1.6-liter engine loses horsepower. All models get new wheelcovers, and leather is newly optional on LSi.

RATINGS (SCALE OF 1-10)

Overall	Safety	Reliability	Performance	Comfort	Value
7.3	7	8.1	8	7.8	5.4

Category E
4 Dr LSi Sdn	4475	6130
4 Dr STD Sdn	4220	5780

OPTIONS FOR PRIZM
4 cyl 1.8 L Engine +215
Auto 3-Speed Transmission +165
Auto 4-Speed Transmission +265
Air Conditioning +270
Aluminum/Alloy Wheels +110
Anti-Lock Brakes +225
Compact Disc W/fm/tape +190
Cruise Control +75
Leather Seats +290
Power Door Locks +80
Power Steering +85
Power Sunroof +205
Power Windows +85

TRACKER 1995

All 4WD models and Massachusetts-bound Trackers get 95-horsepower engine. Convertible top has been redesigned for easier operation. Expressions Packages offer color-coordinated tops and wheels.

RATINGS (SCALE OF 1-10)

Overall	Safety	Reliability	Performance	Comfort	Value
5.5	2.7	7.8	6.2	7	3.6

Category G
2 Dr LSi 4WD Conv	4275	5410
2 Dr LSi 4WD Utility	4730	5990
2 Dr STD Conv	3785	4790
2 Dr STD 4WD Conv	4125	5220
2 Dr STD 4WD Utility	4410	5580

OPTIONS FOR TRACKER
Auto 3-Speed Transmission +195
Air Conditioning +270
Aluminum/Alloy Wheels +110
Compact Disc W/fm/tape +160
Skid Plates +45

1994 GEO

METRO 1994

Convertible is dropped as is LSi trim level. CFC-free refrigerant is added to air conditioning systems.

RATINGS (SCALE OF 1-10)

Overall	Safety	Reliability	Performance	Comfort	Value
N/A	N/A	7.4	6.6	7.1	4.2

Category E
2 Dr STD Hbk	1790	2555
4 Dr STD Hbk	1855	2650
2 Dr XFi Hbk	1615	2310

OPTIONS FOR METRO
Auto 3-Speed Transmission +135
AM/FM Stereo Tape +80
Air Conditioning +220
Rear Window Defroster +45

PRIZM 1994

Passenger airbag is added. Air conditioners get CFC-free coolant.

RATINGS (SCALE OF 1-10)

Overall	Safety	Reliability	Performance	Comfort	Value
7.2	7	7.7	8	7.8	5.3

Category E
4 Dr LSi Sdn	3485	4980
4 Dr STD Sdn	3265	4665

OPTIONS FOR PRIZM
4 cyl 1.8 L Engine +125
Auto 3-Speed Transmission +135
Auto 4-Speed Transmission +220
Air Conditioning +220
Aluminum/Alloy Wheels +90
Anti-Lock Brakes +180
Compact Disc W/fm/tape +155
Cruise Control +60
Leather Seats +235
Power Door Locks +65
Power Steering +70
Power Sunroof +165
Power Windows +70
Premium Sound System +90

Don't forget to refer to the Mileage Adjustment Table at the back of this book!

GEO 94-93

Model Description	Trade-in Value	Market Value	Model Description	Trade-in Value	Market Value

TRACKER   1994

Trackers sold in California and New York get 95-horsepower version of 1.6-liter engine to clear emissions hurdles. Four-wheel-drive models trade on-/off-road tires for better riding all-season type rubber. Alloy wheels have been restyled. Center console gets cupholders. Interior fabrics are new. Optional is a CD/cassette player.

RATINGS (SCALE OF 1-10)

Overall	Safety	Reliability	Performance	Comfort	Value
5.2	2.3	6.9	6.2	7	3.6

Category G

2 Dr LSi 4WD Conv	3645	4735
2 Dr LSi 4WD Utility	4090	5310
2 Dr STD Conv	3050	3960
2 Dr STD 4WD Conv	3390	4405
2 Dr STD 4WD Utility	3820	4960

OPTIONS FOR TRACKER

Auto 3-Speed Transmission +165
Air Conditioning +220
Aluminum/Alloy Wheels +90
Compact Disc W/fm/tape +130
Luggage Rack +45
Power Steering[Opt on STD] +75
Skid Plates +35

1993 GEO

METRO   1993

Automatic door locks are added. Convertibles can have an optional CD player.

RATINGS (SCALE OF 1-10)

Overall	Safety	Reliability	Performance	Comfort	Value
N/A	N/A	7.9	6.6	7.1	4.7

Category E

2 Dr LSi Conv	1925	2875
2 Dr LSi Hbk	1650	2465
4 Dr LSi Hbk	1740	2595
2 Dr STD Hbk	1525	2275
4 Dr STD Hbk	1580	2355
2 Dr XFi Hbk	1340	2000

OPTIONS FOR METRO

Auto 3-Speed Transmission +110
AM/FM Stereo Tape +65
Air Conditioning +180
Rear Window Defroster[Std on LSi] +35

PRIZM   1993

Totally redesigned and available in base or LSi trim in sedan configuration. A driver airbag is standard. ABS is available. Still based on Toyota Corolla design. Standard engine is a 108-horsepower, DOHC 1.6-liter engine. Available on LSi models is a twin-cam 1.8-liter engine making 115 horsepower.

RATINGS (SCALE OF 1-10)

Overall	Safety	Reliability	Performance	Comfort	Value
7.1	5.8	8.1	8	7.8	5.7

Category E

4 Dr LSi Sdn	2805	4185
4 Dr STD Sdn	2625	3915

OPTIONS FOR PRIZM

4 cyl 1.8 L Engine +85
Auto 3-Speed Transmission +110
Auto 4-Speed Transmission +175
AM/FM Compact Disc Player +100
Air Conditioning +180
Aluminum/Alloy Wheels +75
Anti-Lock Brakes +150
Cruise Control +50
Power Door Locks +55
Power Steering +55
Power Sunroof +135
Power Windows +60
Rear Window Defroster +35

STORM   1993

Hatchback model is dropped. Base engine loses five horsepower, but peak torque is made at lower rpm. Base models can be equipped with alloys. A CD player is optional.

RATINGS (SCALE OF 1-10)

Overall	Safety	Reliability	Performance	Comfort	Value
N/A	N/A	N/A	N/A	N/A	3.3

Category E

2 Dr GSi Cpe	2785	4160
2 Dr STD Cpe	2420	3615

OPTIONS FOR STORM

Auto 3-Speed Transmission +120
Auto 4-Speed Transmission +165
AM/FM Compact Disc Player +100
Air Conditioning +180
Aluminum/Alloy Wheels[Opt on STD] +75

TRACKER   1993

Radios get revised controls.

RATINGS (SCALE OF 1-10)

Overall	Safety	Reliability	Performance	Comfort	Value
5.3	2.5	7.5	6.2	7	3.4

Category G

2 Dr LSi 4WD Conv	3015	4020
2 Dr LSi 4WD Utility	3295	4390
2 Dr STD Conv	2655	3540

Don't forget to refer to the Mileage Adjustment Table at the back of this book!

Model Description	Trade-in Value	Market Value
2 Dr STD 4WD Conv	2900	3865
2 Dr STD 4WD Utility	3115	4150

OPTIONS FOR TRACKER
Auto 3-Speed Transmission +135
AM/FM Stereo Tape +50
Air Conditioning +180
Aluminum/Alloy Wheels +75
Power Steering +60

1992 GEO

METRO 1992

Styling is revised front and rear. A new instrument panel is installed. New wheelcovers are installed on base and LSi models. Four-door hatchbacks get child safety rear-door locks.

RATINGS (SCALE OF 1-10)

Overall	Safety	Reliability	Performance	Comfort	Value
N/A	N/A	7.2	6.6	7.1	4.5

Category E
2 Dr LSi Conv	1675	2620
2 Dr LSi Hbk	1275	1995
4 Dr LSi Hbk	1330	2075
2 Dr STD Hbk	1215	1895
4 Dr STD Hbk	1265	1980
2 Dr XFi Hbk	1050	1640

OPTIONS FOR METRO
Auto 3-Speed Transmission +90
Air Conditioning +145

PRIZM 1992

Four-door hatchback is dropped.
Category E
4 Dr GSi Sdn	2515	3930
4 Dr LSi Sdn	2205	3445
4 Dr STD Sdn	2060	3220

OPTIONS FOR PRIZM
Auto 3-Speed Transmission +90
Auto 4-Speed Transmission +140
Air Conditioning[Opt on STD] +145
Cruise Control +40
Power Door Locks[Std on LSi] +45
Power Sunroof +110
Power Windows +50

STORM 1992

Styling is revised front and rear. GSi models get new 1.8-liter engine making 140 horsepower.

RATINGS (SCALE OF 1-10)

Overall	Safety	Reliability	Performance	Comfort	Value
N/A	N/A	N/A	N/A	N/A	4.8

Model Description	Trade-in Value	Market Value
Category E		
2 Dr 2+2 Cpe	1845	2880
2 Dr GSi Cpe	2145	3350
2 Dr STD Hbk	1650	2580

OPTIONS FOR STORM
Auto 3-Speed Transmission +100
Auto 4-Speed Transmission +135
Air Conditioning +145

TRACKER 1992

Dashboard is slightly revised and a tilt steering column is a new option. Center console includes cupholders. New seat fabrics and cloth bolsters are added.

RATINGS (SCALE OF 1-10)

Overall	Safety	Reliability	Performance	Comfort	Value
5.5	2.4	7.9	6.2	7	3.8

Category G
2 Dr LSi 4WD Conv	2560	3510
2 Dr LSi 4WD Utility	2750	3770
2 Dr STD Conv	2240	3070
2 Dr STD 4WD Conv	2480	3400
2 Dr STD 4WD Utility	2635	3610

OPTIONS FOR TRACKER
Auto 3-Speed Transmission +105
Air Conditioning +145

1991 GEO

METRO 1991

LSi Convertible debuts, and includes driver airbag and larger tires. Convertible seats only two.

RATINGS (SCALE OF 1-10)

Overall	Safety	Reliability	Performance	Comfort	Value
N/A	N/A	7.6	6.6	7.1	4.6

Category E
2 Dr LSi Conv	1380	2340
2 Dr LSi Hbk	1040	1760
4 Dr LSi Hbk	1105	1870
2 Dr STD Hbk	920	1560
4 Dr STD Hbk	1000	1695
2 Dr XFi Hbk	810	1375

OPTIONS FOR METRO
Auto 3-Speed Transmission +70
Air Conditioning +120

PRIZM 1991

Horsepower is up to 102 on base models and 130 on GSi models.
Category E
4 Dr GSi Hbk	1905	3225
4 Dr GSi Sdn	1960	3320

Don't forget to refer to the Mileage Adjustment Table at the back of this book!

Model Description	Trade-in Value	Market Value
4 Dr STD Hbk	1470	2495
4 Dr STD Sdn	1540	2610

OPTIONS FOR PRIZM
Auto 3-Speed Transmission +70
Auto 4-Speed Transmission +115
LSi Pkg +195
Air Conditioning +120
Cruise Control +35
Power Door Locks +35
Power Sunroof +90
Power Windows +40

STORM 1991

A funky-looking three-door hatchback joins the lineup with squared-off rear styling like that found on the Honda Civic. New hatchback is available only in base trim.

RATINGS (SCALE OF 1-10)

Overall	Safety	Reliability	Performance	Comfort	Value
N/A	N/A	N/A	N/A	N/A	3.8

Category E

	Trade-in	Market
2 Dr 2+2 Cpe	1320	2235
2 Dr GSi Cpe	1535	2600
2 Dr STD Hbk	1155	1955

OPTIONS FOR STORM
Auto 3-Speed Transmission +80
Auto 4-Speed Transmission +110
Air Conditioning +120

TRACKER 1991

Rear antilock brakes are standard, and work only in 2WD. Four-wheel drive LSi models get auto-locking front hubs.

RATINGS (SCALE OF 1-10)

Overall	Safety	Reliability	Performance	Comfort	Value
5.5	2.3	7.5	6.2	7	4.3

Category G

	Trade-in	Market
2 Dr LSi 4WD Conv	2175	3105
2 Dr LSi 4WD Utility	2270	3240
2 Dr STD Conv	1840	2625
2 Dr STD 4WD Conv	2120	3030
2 Dr STD 4WD Utility	2210	3155

OPTIONS FOR TRACKER
Auto 3-Speed Transmission +85
Air Conditioning +120

1990 GEO

METRO 1990

Passive front seatbelts are added, and automatics get a new brake/transmission shift interlock. Fuel sipper strippo model is now called XFi and gets 53 mpg in the city. XFi engine makes only 49 horsepower. Four-door hatch is now available in base trim.

RATINGS (SCALE OF 1-10)

Overall	Safety	Reliability	Performance	Comfort	Value
N/A	N/A	7.4	6.6	7.1	4.5

Category E

	Trade-in	Market
2 Dr LSi Conv	1040	2000
2 Dr LSi Hbk	740	1420
4 Dr LSi Hbk	785	1510
2 Dr STD Hbk	640	1235
4 Dr STD Hbk	695	1335
2 Dr XFi Hbk	595	1140

OPTIONS FOR METRO
Auto 3-Speed Transmission +55
Air Conditioning +100

PRIZM 1990

Sporty GSi models added to lineup, powered by a 115-horsepower version of standard DOHC 1.6-liter engine. GSi trim adds body-color bumpers, power steering, four-wheel disc brakes and a tachometer.

Category E

	Trade-in	Market
4 Dr GSi Hbk	1400	2695
4 Dr GSi Sdn	1450	2785
4 Dr STD Hbk	1065	2050
4 Dr STD Sdn	1090	2100

OPTIONS FOR PRIZM
Auto 3-Speed Transmission +50
Auto 4-Speed Transmission +95
Air Conditioning +100
Cruise Control +25
Power Door Locks +30
Power Sunroof +75
Power Windows +30

STORM 1990

Small sport coupe based on Isuzu Impulse. Sold in base or GSi trim. Driver airbag is standard. Base models have 95 horsepower; GSi models are boosted to 130 horsepower.

Model Description	Trade-in Value	Market Value

RATINGS (SCALE OF 1-10)

Overall	Safety	Reliability	Performance	Comfort	Value
N/A	N/A	N/A	N/A	N/A	3.4

Category E

2 Dr 2+2 Cpe	935	1795
2 Dr GSi Cpe	1160	2230

OPTIONS FOR STORM
Auto 3-Speed Transmission +65
Auto 4-Speed Transmission +90
Air Conditioning +100

TRACKER   1990

Production moved to Canada, and Trackers are sold nationwide. Convertible gets LSi trim level. Air conditioning and automatic transmission are now optional on all Trackers.

Model Description	Trade-in Value	Market Value

RATINGS (SCALE OF 1-10)

Overall	Safety	Reliability	Performance	Comfort	Value
5.6	2.3	7.1	6.2	7	5.2

Category G

2 Dr LSi 4WD Conv	1810	2740
2 Dr LSi 4WD Utility	1900	2880
2 Dr STD 4WD Conv	1600	2425
2 Dr STD 4WD Utility	1715	2595

OPTIONS FOR TRACKER
Auto 3-Speed Transmission +70
Air Conditioning +100

GMC 99

Model Description	Trade-in Value	Market Value	Model Description	Trade-in Value	Market Value

GMC   USA

1995 GMC Suburban

1999 GMC

ENVOY   1999

After its debut as General Motors' high-end compact SUV last year, the GMC Envoy gets equipment upgrades for '99. A new mini-module for the driver's airbag allows for steering-wheel radio controls, and the turn-signal stalk now incorporates a flash-to-pass headlamp feature. Heated, eight-way power front seating is improved, thanks to available two-position memory for the driver and power recliners. A liftgate ajar telltale resides in the instrument cluster, and the outside rearview mirrors have been redesigned, featuring electrochromic dimming and power folding capability. GM's advanced AutoTrac active transfer case is now standard, while a new, shift lever-mounted button selects a Tow/Haul mode to optimize transmission shift points. There are three new metallic exterior paint colors: Topaz gold, Meadow green and Indigo blue.

RATINGS (SCALE OF 1-10)

Overall	Safety	Reliability	Performance	Comfort	Value
N/A	7.3	8.5	N/A	N/A	N/A

Category G

4 Dr STD 4WD Wgn	20910	24890

JIMMY   1999

There are three new colors and revised outside mirrors, but most changes to the '99 Jimmy are inside. You'll find new power-seating features, redundant radio controls and a mini-module depowered airbag in the steering wheel, as well as a new Bose premium sound system and six-disc CD changer. A vehicle content theft alarm, flash-to-pass headlamp feature, and liftgate ajar

warning lamp have also been added. Four-wheel-drive versions get the new AutoTrac active transfer case and four-door models gain a Tow/Haul mode for the transmission. Finally, the optional Z85 Euro-Ride suspension has been retuned.

RATINGS (SCALE OF 1-10)

Overall	Safety	Reliability	Performance	Comfort	Value
N/A	7.2	N/A	8	7.9	N/A

Category G

2 Dr SL Utility	13640	16240
2 Dr SL 4WD Utility	14900	17740
4 Dr SL Wgn	14375	17115
4 Dr SL 4WD Wgn	15160	18045
4 Dr SLE Wgn	15970	19010
4 Dr SLE 4WD Wgn	16515	19660
2 Dr SLS Sport Utility	14390	17130
2 Dr SLS Sport 4WD Utility	15315	18235
4 Dr SLT Wgn	16900	20120
4 Dr SLT 4WD Wgn	18200	21665

OPTIONS FOR JIMMY

AM/FM Compact Disc Player +245
Aluminum/Alloy Wheels[Opt on SL] +245
Cruise Control[Opt on SLS Sport] +155
Keyless Entry System[Std on SLT] +150
Luggage Rack[Opt on SL] +115
Power Door Locks[Std on SLE,SLT] +170
Power Drivers Seat[Std on SLE, SLT] +210
Power Windows[Std on SLE,SLT] +175
Rear Window Defroster[Std on SLE,SLT] +125
Rear Window Wiper[Std on SLE,SLT] +115
Tilt Steering Wheel[Std on SLE,SLT] +130

SAFARI   1999

RATINGS (SCALE OF 1-10)

Overall	Safety	Reliability	Performance	Comfort	Value
N/A	7.2	8.5	N/A	6.1	N/A

SAFARI CARGO

Category G

2 Dr SL Cargo Van Ext	11215	13350
2 Dr SL 4WD Cargo Van Ext	14590	17370

SAFARI PASSENGER

Category G

2 Dr SL Pass. Van Ext	12330	14680
2 Dr SL 4WD Pass. Van Ext	13875	16515
2 Dr SLE Pass. Van Ext	13545	16125
2 Dr SLE 4WD Pass. Van Ext	15480	18430
2 Dr SLT Pass. Van Ext	14195	16900
2 Dr SLT 4WD Pass. Van Ext	16535	19685

OPTIONS FOR SAFARI

AM/FM Stereo Tape[Std on SLE] +170
Aluminum/Alloy Wheels[Std on SLT] +245

Don't forget to refer to the Mileage Adjustment Table at the back of this book!

Model Description	Trade-in Value	Market Value
Cruise Control[Std on SLE,SLT] +155		
Dual Air Conditioning +700		
Power Door Locks[Std on SLE,SLT] +170		
Power Mirrors[Opt on SL] +100		
Power Windows[Std on SLE,SLT] +175		
Privacy Glass[Std on SLE,SLT] +195		
Rear Window Defroster +125		
Rear Window Wiper +115		
Tilt Steering Wheel[Std on SLE,SLT] +130		

SAVANA 1999

GMC's full-size van gets two new exterior colors, one new interior color and automatic transmission enhancements.

RATINGS (SCALE OF 1-10)

Overall	Safety	Reliability	Performance	Comfort	Value
N/A	N/A	N/A	4.8	6.5	N/A

Category H

	Trade-in	Market
2 Dr G15 SLE Pass. Van	17305	20360
2 Dr G25 SLE Pass. Van	18815	22135
2 Dr G25 SLE Pass. Van Ext	20760	24425
2 Dr G25 STD Pass. Van	15725	18500
2 Dr G15 Cargo Van	13880	16330
2 Dr G25 Cargo Van	14040	16515
2 Dr G25 Cargo Van Ext	14200	16705
2 Dr G15 Pass. Van	15220	17905
2 Dr G25 Pass. Van Ext	16815	19785

OPTIONS FOR SAVANA

8 cyl 5.0 L Engine +365
8 cyl 5.7 L Engine[Std on G25, G35] +750
8 cyl 6.5 L Turbodsl Engine +2115
8 cyl 7.4 L Engine +445
15 Passenger Seating +615
AM/FM Compact Disc Player +230
Air Conditioning[Opt on Cargo Van, Cargo Van Ext] +600
Aluminum/Alloy Wheels +235
Cruise Control[Opt on STD] +140
Dual Air Conditioning +990
Keyless Entry System +130
Power Door Locks[Opt on STD] +140
Power Drivers Seat +210
Power Windows[Opt on STD] +140
Privacy Glass +125
Rear Heater +160
Tilt Steering Wheel[Opt on STD] +135

SIERRA PICKUP 1999

C/K 1500

Category H

	Trade-in	Market
2 Dr C1500 SL Ext Cab Stepside SB		
	14915	17545
2 Dr C1500 SL Std Cab Stepside SB		
	13245	15585
2 Dr C1500 SLE Ext Cab SB	16695	19640
2 Dr C1500 SLE Ext Cab Stepside SB		
	17385	20450
2 Dr C1500 SLE Std Cab Stepside SB		
	15120	17790
2 Dr C1500 SLT Ext Cab LB	17330	20390
2 Dr C1500 SLT Ext Cab SB	17240	20280
2 Dr C1500 SLT Ext Cab Stepside SB		
	17895	21055
2 Dr K1500 SL 4WD Ext Cab Stepside SB		
	17335	20395
2 Dr K1500 SL 4WD Std Cab Stepside SB		
	15540	18280
2 Dr K1500 SLE 4WD Ext Cab SB	18435	21690
2 Dr K1500 SLE 4WD Ext Cab Stepside SB		
	19460	22895
2 Dr K1500 SLE 4WD Std Cab Stepside SB		
	17105	20125
2 Dr K1500 SLT 4WD Ext Cab LB	19310	22720
2 Dr K1500 SLT 4WD Ext Cab SB	19215	22605
2 Dr K1500 SLT 4WD Ext Cab Stepside SB		
	19720	23200

C/K 2500

Category H

	Trade-in	Market
2 Dr K2500 HD SL 4WD Ext Cab LB		
	18360	21600
2 Dr K2500 HD SL 4WD Ext Cab SB		
	18090	21280
2 Dr K2500 HD SLE 4WD Ext Cab LB		
	20785	24455
2 Dr K2500 HD SLE 4WD Ext Cab SB		
	20485	24100
2 Dr K2500 HD SLT 4WD Ext Cab LB		
	21010	24715
2 Dr K2500 HD SLT 4WD Ext Cab SB		
	20795	24465
4 Dr K2500 SLE 4WD Crew Cab SB		
	22255	26185
4 Dr K2500 SLT 4WD Crew Cab SB		
	22795	26815
2 Dr K2500 SLT 4WD Ext Cab LB	21600	25410
2 Dr K2500 SLT 4WD Ext Cab SB	21405	25185
4 Dr K2500 STD 4WD Crew Cab SB		
	20415	24020

C/K 3500

Category H

	Trade-in	Market
4 Dr C3500 SL Crew Cab LB	19370	22790
4 Dr C3500 SL Crew Cab SB	18870	22200
2 Dr C3500 SL Ext Cab LB	17735	20865
2 Dr C3500 SL Std Cab LB	16445	19345
4 Dr C3500 SLE Crew Cab LB	20360	23950
4 Dr C3500 SLE Crew Cab SB	20735	24395

Don't forget to refer to the Mileage Adjustment Table at the back of this book!

Model Description	Trade-in Value	Market Value
2 Dr C3500 SLE Ext Cab LB	19415	22840
2 Dr C3500 SLE Std Cab LB	17660	20775
4 Dr C3500 SLT Crew Cab LB	20925	24615
4 Dr C3500 SLT Crew Cab SB	22220	26140
2 Dr C3500 SLT Ext Cab LB	20845	24525
2 Dr C3500 SLT Std Cab LB	18655	21945
4 Dr K3500 SL 4WD Crew Cab LB	21065	24785
4 Dr K3500 SL 4WD Crew Cab SB	21330	25095
4 Dr K3500 SLE 4WD Crew Cab LB	22130	26035
4 Dr K3500 SLE 4WD Crew Cab SB	22350	26295
4 Dr K3500 SLT 4WD Crew Cab LB	22590	26575
4 Dr K3500 SLT 4WD Crew Cab SB	23845	28050

SIERRA 1500

Category H

Model Description	Trade-in Value	Market Value
2 Dr SL Ext Cab LB	14920	17550
2 Dr SL 4WD Ext Cab LB	17050	20060
2 Dr SL Ext Cab SB	14695	17290
2 Dr SL 4WD Ext Cab SB	16930	19915
2 Dr SL Std Cab LB	12350	14530
2 Dr SL 4WD Std Cab LB	14255	16770
2 Dr SL Std Cab SB	12265	14430
2 Dr SL 4WD Std Cab SB	14045	16525
2 Dr SLE Ext Cab LB	16975	19970
2 Dr SLE 4WD Ext Cab LB	19055	22415
2 Dr SLE Ext Cab SB	16880	19860
2 Dr SLE 4WD Ext Cab SB	18945	22290
2 Dr SLE Std Cab LB	14660	17245
2 Dr SLE 4WD Std Cab LB	17015	20020
2 Dr SLE Std Cab SB	14585	17160
2 Dr SLE 4WD Std Cab SB	16925	19910

SIERRA 2500

Category H

Model Description	Trade-in Value	Market Value
2 Dr SL 4WD Ext Cab LB	20190	23750
2 Dr SL 4WD Ext Cab SB	20005	23535
2 Dr SL 4WD Std Cab LB	17955	21125
2 Dr SLE 4WD Ext Cab LB	21390	25165
2 Dr SLE 4WD Ext Cab SB	21170	24905
2 Dr SLE 4WD Std Cab LB	19395	22815

OPTIONS FOR SIERRA PICKUP

8 cyl 4.8 L Engine[Opt on Std Cab] +440
8 cyl 5.3 L Engine[Std on Sierra 2500] +755
8 cyl 5.7 L Engine[Opt on C1500 SLE,K1500 SLE] +750
8 cyl 6.0 L Engine +370
8 cyl 6.5 L Turbodsl Engine +2115
8 cyl 7.4 L Engine +445
Auto 4-Speed Transmission[Opt on Std Cab] +735
AM/FM Compact Disc Player +230

Air Conditioning[Std on SLE, SLT] +600
Aluminum/Alloy Wheels[Std on SLT] +235
Bed Liner +165
Camper/Towing Package +255
Cruise Control[Std on SLE, SLT] +140
Keyless Entry System[Std on SLE, SLT] +130
Power Door Locks[Std on SLE, SLT] +140
Power Drivers Seat +210
Privacy Glass +125
Skid Plates +80
Sliding Rear Window +85

SONOMA   1999

The '99 Sonoma touts four new exterior colors, a new steering wheel with mini-module depowered airbag, and larger, more robust outside rearview mirrors, with the uplevel power mirror gaining a heated feature. AutoTrac, GM's electronic push-button two-speed transfer case, is now standard on four-wheel-drive models, and all Sonomas get a content theft alarm with remote keyless entry as well as a flash-to-pass headlamp feature for the smart stalk. Serious four-wheelers can now order composite skid plates.

RATINGS (SCALE OF 1-10)

Overall	Safety	Reliability	Performance	Comfort	Value
N/A	N/A	N/A	6.6	8.1	N/A

Category G

Model Description	Trade-in Value	Market Value
2 Dr SL Std Cab LB	8675	10330
2 Dr SL 4WD Std Cab LB	11470	13655
2 Dr SL Std Cab SB	8490	10105
2 Dr SL 4WD Std Cab SB	11330	13490
2 Dr SLE Ext Cab SB	10275	12230
2 Dr SLE 4WD Ext Cab SB	13410	15965
2 Dr SLE Std Cab SB	10430	12415
2 Dr SLE 4WD Std Cab SB	12145	14460
2 Dr SLS Sport Ext Cab SB	9340	11120
2 Dr SLS Sport 4WD Ext Cab SB	12035	14330
2 Dr SLS Sport Ext Cab Stepside SB	9750	11605
2 Dr SLS Sport 4WD Ext Cab Stepside SB	12470	14845
2 Dr SLS Sport Std Cab LB	9015	10730
2 Dr SLS Sport 4WD Std Cab LB	11550	13750
2 Dr SLS Sport Std Cab SB	8835	10515
2 Dr SLS Sport 4WD Std Cab SB	11380	13545
2 Dr SLS Sport Std Cab Stepside SB	9185	10935
2 Dr SLS Sport 4WD Std Cab Stepside SB	12300	14640

OPTIONS FOR SONOMA

6 cyl 4.3 L Engine[Opt on 2WD] +805
6 cyl 4.3 L Vortec Engine +680

Don't forget to refer to the Mileage Adjustment Table at the back of this book!

GMC 99-98

Model Description	Trade-in Value	Market Value	Model Description	Trade-in Value	Market Value

Auto 4-Speed Transmission +790
ZR2 Highrider Suspension +1215
AM/FM Compact Disc Player +245
Air Conditioning +605
Aluminum/Alloy Wheels +245
Cruise Control +155
Hinged Third Door (PU) +255
Keyless Entry System +150
Power Door Locks +170
Power Windows +175
Sliding Rear Window +90
Sport Suspension +345
Tilt Steering Wheel +130

SUBURBAN 1999

A couple of new colors are the only modifications to the Suburban.

RATINGS (SCALE OF 1-10)

Overall	Safety	Reliability	Performance	Comfort	Value
N/A	8.4	8.1	7	7.9	N/A

Category H

	Trade-in	Market
4 Dr C1500 Wgn	18545	21815
4 Dr C2500 Wgn	19475	22910
4 Dr K1500 4WD Wgn	20565	24195
4 Dr K2500 4WD Wgn	21735	25570

OPTIONS FOR SUBURBAN

8 cyl 6.5 L Turbodsl Engine[Opt on 2500] +2115
8 cyl 7.4 L Engine[Opt on 2500] +445
SLE Pkg +2295
SLT Pkg +2670
AM/FM Compact Disc Player +230
Air Conditioning +600
Aluminum/Alloy Wheels +235
Automatic Dimming Mirror +105
Camper/Towing Package +255
Cruise Control +140
Dual Air Conditioning +990
Heated Front Seats +250
Keyless Entry System +130
Leather Seats +730
Power Drivers Seat +210
Power Mirrors +75
Power Windows +140
Privacy Glass +125
Rear Heater +160
Rear Window Defroster +115
Rear Window Wiper +90
Running Boards +255
Tilt Steering Wheel +135

YUKON 1999

More new colors are added as Yukon cruises into 1999.

RATINGS (SCALE OF 1-10)

Overall	Safety	Reliability	Performance	Comfort	Value
N/A	N/A	N/A	7.4	8	N/A

Category H

	Trade-in	Market
4 Dr SLE Wgn	19945	23465
4 Dr SLE 4WD Wgn	22590	26575
4 Dr SLT Wgn	21165	24900
4 Dr SLT 4WD Wgn	22795	26820

OPTIONS FOR YUKON

AM/FM Compact Disc Player +230
Camper/Towing Package +255
Dual Air Conditioning[Opt on SLE] +990
Heated Front Seats +250
Running Boards +255

YUKON DENALI 1999

General Motors brand managers came up with an idea to dress up the GMC Yukon, fill it full of luxury touches and give it a special name to toss their hat into the luxury SUV arena. Enter the 1999 GMC Yukon Denali, with loads of unique features and exclusive exterior paint colors- until, that is, GM decided to spin-off a clone for Cadillac called the Escalade.

RATINGS (SCALE OF 1-10)

Overall	Safety	Reliability	Performance	Comfort	Value
N/A	N/A	N/A	7.4	8	N/A

Category H

	Trade-in	Market
4 Dr Denali 4WD Wgn	24030	28270

1998 GMC

ENVOY 1998

GMC is introduces its finest luxury compact SUV to date: the Envoy.

RATINGS (SCALE OF 1-10)

Overall	Safety	Reliability	Performance	Comfort	Value
N/A	7.1	7.4	N/A	N/A	N/A

Category G

	Trade-in	Market
4 Dr STD 4WD Wgn	19000	22620

JIMMY 1998

A revised interior contains dual second-generation airbags, improved climate controls and available premium sound systems. Outside, the front bumper, grille and headlights are new. Side cladding is restyled and SLT models have new alloy wheels. Fresh colors inside and out sum up the changes.

RATINGS (SCALE OF 1-10)

Overall	Safety	Reliability	Performance	Comfort	Value
7.6	7.3	8	8	7.9	6.9

Category G

	Trade-in	Market
2 Dr SL Utility	11935	14210
2 Dr SL 4WD Utility	12700	15120

Don't forget to refer to the Mileage Adjustment Table at the back of this book!

Model Description	Trade-in Value	Market Value	Model Description	Trade-in Value	Market Value
4 Dr SL Wgn	12680	15095			
4 Dr SL 4WD Wgn	13435	15995			
4 Dr SLE Wgn	14450	17205			
4 Dr SLE 4WD Wgn	15200	18095			
2 Dr SLS Sport Utility	13460	16025			
2 Dr SLS Sport 4WD Utility	14255	16970			
4 Dr SLS Sport Wgn	14320	17045			
4 Dr SLS Sport 4WD Wgn	15075	17945			
4 Dr SLT Wgn	15090	17965			
4 Dr SLT 4WD Wgn	15855	18875			

OPTIONS FOR JIMMY

AM/FM Compact Disc Player +200
Aluminum/Alloy Wheels[Opt on SL] +200
Cruise Control[Opt on SL] +125
Heated Front Seats +160
Keyless Entry System[Std on SLE, SLT] +120
Luggage Rack[Opt on SL] +95
Power Door Locks[Opt on SL] +140
Power Drivers Seat[Std on SLE, SLT] +170
Power Mirrors[Opt on SL] +80
Power Moonroof +525
Power Windows[Opt on SL] +145
Rear Window Defroster[Opt on SL] +105
Rear Window Wiper[Opt on SL] +95
Tilt Steering Wheel[Opt on SL] +105

SAFARI   1998

New colors, a theft deterrent system and automatic transmission refinements are the changes to the Safari. This van is one of the few GM models that retains full-power airbags for 1998.

RATINGS (SCALE OF 1-10)

Overall	Safety	Reliability	Performance	Comfort	Value
7.4	7.1	8	7	6.5	8.6

Category G

Model Description	Trade-in Value	Market Value
2 Dr SL Cargo Van Ext	10000	11905
2 Dr SL 4WD Cargo Van Ext	12265	14600
2 Dr SLE Pass. Van Ext	12540	14930
2 Dr SLE 4WD Pass. Van Ext	14015	16685
2 Dr SLT Pass. Van Ext	13635	16235
2 Dr SLT 4WD Pass. Van Ext	14730	17535
2 Dr SLX Pass. Van Ext	11295	13445
2 Dr SLX 4WD Pass. Van Ext	12890	15345

OPTIONS FOR SAFARI

8 Passenger Seating[Opt on SLX] +240
AM/FM Compact Disc Player[Std on SLT] +200
Aluminum/Alloy Wheels[Std on SLT] +200
Cruise Control[Opt on SL, SLX] +125
Dual Air Conditioning +575
Dual Power Seats +235
Keyless Entry System[Std on SLT] +120
Leather Seats +470
Power Door Locks[Opt on SL, SLX] +140

Power Drivers Seat[Std on SLT] +170
Power Mirrors[Std on SLT] +80
Power Windows[Opt on SL, SLX] +145
Premium Sound System +210
Privacy Glass[Opt on SL, SLX] +160
Rear Heater +125
Rear Window Defroster +105
Rear Window Wiper +95
Tilt Steering Wheel[Opt on SL, SLX] +105

SAVANA   1998

New colors, transmission enhancements, more power for the diesel engine, revised uplevel stereos and the addition of a PassLock theft deterrent system mark the changes for 1998. A mini-module driver's airbag is new, but it and the passenger airbag still deploy at full-force levels.

Category H

Model Description	Trade-in Value	Market Value
2 Dr G15 Cargo Van	12350	14700
2 Dr G15 Pass. Van	14300	17025
2 Dr G15 SLE Pass. Van	15920	18950
2 Dr G25 Cargo Van	12580	14975
2 Dr G25 Cargo Van Ext	12785	15220
2 Dr G25 Pass. Van	15005	17865
2 Dr G25 Pass. Van Ext	15750	18750
2 Dr G25 SLE Pass. Van	15555	18520
2 Dr G25 SLE Pass. Van Ext	16305	19410

OPTIONS FOR SAVANA

8 cyl 5.0 L Engine +305
8 cyl 5.7 L Engine[Std on G25 Pass. Van, G25 Pass. Van Ext., G35] +615
8 cyl 6.5 L Turbodsl Engine +1845
8 cyl 7.4 L Engine +370
15 Passenger Seating +505
AM/FM Compact Disc Player +190
Air Conditioning[Opt on Cargo Van, Cargo Van Ext] +490
Aluminum/Alloy Wheels +190
Cruise Control[Opt on STD] +115
Dual Air Conditioning +810
Keyless Entry System +105
Power Door Locks[Opt on STD] +115
Power Drivers Seat +170
Power Windows[Opt on STD] +115
Privacy Glass +100
Rear Heater +130
Tilt Steering Wheel[Opt on STD] +110

SIERRA PICKUP   1998

With an all-new Sierra just one year away, changes are minimal. Diesel engines make more power and torque, extended cab models get rear heater ducts, a PassLock theft deterrent system is standard, 1500-series trucks get reduced rolling resistance tires and three new colors debut. Second generation airbags are standard.

Model Description	Trade-in Value	Market Value

RATINGS (SCALE OF 1-10)

Overall	Safety	Reliability	Performance	Comfort	Value
N/A	N/A	7.5	6.6	8.3	N/A

SIERRA 1500
Category H

Model	Trade-in	Market
2 Dr C1500 SL Ext Cab LB	12105	14410
2 Dr C1500 SL Ext Cab SB	11910	14180
2 Dr C1500 SL Std Cab LB	11045	13150
2 Dr C1500 SL Std Cab SB	10970	13060
2 Dr C1500 SL Std Cab Stepside SB	11485	13675
2 Dr C1500 SLE Ext Cab LB	13070	15560
2 Dr C1500 SLE Ext Cab SB	12915	15375
2 Dr C1500 SLE Ext Cab Stepside SB	13345	15885
2 Dr C1500 SLE Std Cab LB	11740	13975
2 Dr C1500 SLE Std Cab SB	11630	13845
2 Dr C1500 SLE Std Cab Stepside SB	12105	14410
2 Dr C1500 SLT Ext Cab LB	13620	16215
2 Dr C1500 SLT Ext Cab SB	13525	16100
2 Dr C1500 SLT Ext Cab Stepside SB	14110	16795
2 Dr C1500 SLT Std Cab LB	13190	15705
2 Dr C1500 SLT Std Cab SB	13120	15620
2 Dr C1500 SLT Std Cab Stepside SB	13635	16230
2 Dr C1500 Special Std Cab LB	10800	12855
2 Dr C1500 Special Std Cab SB	10725	12765
2 Dr K1500 SL 4WD Ext Cab LB	14315	17040
2 Dr K1500 SL 4WD Ext Cab SB	14230	16940
2 Dr K1500 SL 4WD Std Cab LB	13200	15715
2 Dr K1500 SL 4WD Std Cab SB	13125	15625
2 Dr K1500 SL 4WD Std Cab Stepside SB	13625	16220
2 Dr K1500 SLE 4WD Ext Cab LB	15740	18740
2 Dr K1500 SLE 4WD Ext Cab SB	15655	18635
2 Dr K1500 SLE 4WD Ext Cab Stepside SB	16090	19155
2 Dr K1500 SLE 4WD Std Cab LB	14200	16905
2 Dr K1500 SLE 4WD Std Cab SB	14245	16960
2 Dr K1500 SLE 4WD Std Cab Stepside SB	14535	17305
2 Dr K1500 SLT 4WD Ext Cab LB	16690	19870
2 Dr K1500 SLT 4WD Ext Cab Stepside SB	17285	20580
2 Dr K1500 SLT 4WD Std Cab LB	15210	18105
2 Dr K1500 SLT 4WD Std Cab SB	15130	18010
2 Dr K1500 SLT 4WD Std Cab Stepside SB	15890	18915
2 Dr K1500 Special 4WD Std Cab LB	13140	15645
2 Dr K1500 Special 4WD Std Cab SB	13025	15505

SIERRA 2500
Category H

Model	Trade-in	Market
2 Dr C2500 SL Ext Cab SB	13630	16225
2 Dr C2500 SL Std Cab LB	11670	13890
2 Dr C2500 SLE Ext Cab SB	15105	17980
2 Dr C2500 SLE Std Cab LB	14285	17005
2 Dr C2500 SLT Ext Cab SB	16535	19685
2 Dr C2500 SLT Std Cab LB	14995	17850
2 Dr K2500 HD SL 4WD Ext Cab LB	14805	17625
2 Dr K2500 HD SL 4WD Ext Cab SB	14610	17395
2 Dr K2500 HD SL 4WD Std Cab LB	13660	16260
2 Dr K2500 HD SLE 4WD Ext Cab LB	15865	18885
2 Dr K2500 HD SLE 4WD Ext Cab SB	15655	18635
2 Dr K2500 HD SLE 4WD Std Cab LB	15170	18060
2 Dr K2500 HD SLT 4WD Ext Cab LB	17800	21190
2 Dr K2500 HD SLT 4WD Ext Cab SB	17625	20985
2 Dr K2500 HD SLT 4WD Std Cab LB	16565	19720

SIERRA 3500
Category H

Model	Trade-in	Market
4 Dr C3500 SL Crew Cab LB	16810	20010
2 Dr C3500 SL Ext Cab LB	16565	19720
2 Dr C3500 SL Std Cab LB	14780	17595
4 Dr C3500 SLE Crew Cab LB	17915	21325
2 Dr C3500 SLE Ext Cab LB	17550	20890
2 Dr C3500 SLE Std Cab LB	16245	19340
4 Dr C3500 SLT Crew Cab LB	18925	22530
2 Dr C3500 SLT Ext Cab LB	18035	21470
2 Dr C3500 SLT Std Cab LB	16975	20210
4 Dr K3500 SL 4WD Crew Cab LB	19230	22895
2 Dr K3500 SL 4WD Ext Cab LB	18310	21800
2 Dr K3500 SL 4WD Std Cab LB	16295	19400
4 Dr K3500 SLE 4WD Crew Cab LB	19525	23245
2 Dr K3500 SLE 4WD Ext Cab LB	18440	21950
2 Dr K3500 SLE 4WD Std Cab LB	16960	20190
4 Dr K3500 SLT 4WD Crew Cab LB	20355	24235

Don't forget to refer to the Mileage Adjustment Table at the back of this book!

Model Description	Trade-in Value	Market Value	Model Description	Trade-in Value	Market Value
2 Dr K3500 SLT 4WD Ext Cab LB	19350	23035	2 Dr SLS Sport Std Cab SB	7925	9435
2 Dr K3500 SLT 4WD Std Cab LB	17895	21305	2 Dr SLS Sport 4WD Std Cab SB	10340	12310
			2 Dr SLS Sport Std Cab Stepside SB		
				8360	9950
			2 Dr SLS Sport 4WD Std Cab Stepside SB		
				10985	13080

OPTIONS FOR SIERRA PICKUP

8 cyl 5.0 L Engine[Std on C1500 Ext Cab, C2500, K1500 4WD Ext Cab] +305
8 cyl 5.7 L Engine[Opt on C1500, C2500, K1500] +615
8 cyl 6.5 L Turbodsl Engine +1845
8 cyl 7.4 L Engine +370
Auto 4-Speed Transmission[Std on C1500 Ext Cab Stepside] +595
AM/FM Compact Disc Player +190
Air Conditioning[Std on SLE, SLT] +490
Aluminum/Alloy Wheels[Std on SLT] +190
Bed Liner +135
Camper/Towing Package +205
Cruise Control[Std on SLE, SLT] +115
Dual Rear Wheels[Std on Ext Cab] +500
Hinged Third Door (PU) +255
Keyless Entry System[Opt on SLE] +105
Power Door Locks[Std on SLE, SLT] +115
Power Drivers Seat[Opt on SLE] +170
Privacy Glass +100
Rear Window Defroster +95
Sliding Rear Window +70
Tilt Steering Wheel[Std on SLE, SLT] +110

OPTIONS FOR SONOMA

6 cyl 4.3 L Engine[Opt on 2WD] +670
6 cyl 4.3 L Vortec Engine +495
Auto 4-Speed Transmission +655
Highrider Suspension Pkg +930
AM/FM Compact Disc Player +200
Air Conditioning +495
Aluminum/Alloy Wheels[Std on SLE] +200
Cruise Control +125
Heavy Duty Suspension[Opt on SL, Std Cab, 4WD] +85
Hinged Third Door (PU) +205
Keyless Entry System +120
Power Door Locks +140
Power Mirrors +80
Power Windows +145
Premium Sound System +210
Sliding Rear Window +70
Sport Suspension +285
Tilt Steering Wheel +105

SONOMA   1998

Styling is re-tuned inside and out, resulting in a sleeker look and better interior ergonomics. Dual second-generation airbags are standard, and seats are upgraded for improved comfort and appearance. Four-wheel disc brakes are standard on 4WD models and uplevel stereos are new for 1998. New colors inside and out round out the changes.

RATINGS (SCALE OF 1-10)

Overall	Safety	Reliability	Performance	Comfort	Value
N/A	N/A	7.3	6.6	8.1	N/A

Category G

2 Dr SL Std Cab LB	7685	9150
2 Dr SL 4WD Std Cab LB	10390	12370
2 Dr SL Std Cab SB	7585	9030
2 Dr SL 4WD Std Cab SB	10205	12150
2 Dr SLE Ext Cab SB	9250	11010
2 Dr SLE 4WD Ext Cab SB	11715	13945
2 Dr SLE Std Cab SB	7860	9355
2 Dr SLE 4WD Std Cab SB	10645	12675
2 Dr SLS Sport Ext Cab SB	8595	10230
2 Dr SLS Sport 4WD Ext Cab SB	11040	13145
2 Dr SLS Sport Ext Cab Stepside SB		
	8945	10650
2 Dr SLS Sport 4WD Ext Cab Stepside SB		
	11485	13670
2 Dr SLS Sport Std Cab LB	8080	9620
2 Dr SLS Sport 4WD Std Cab LB	10510	12510

SUBURBAN   1998

De-powered second-generation airbags protect front seat occupants for 1998. A new innovation called carpeted floor mats finally appears inside the big 'Burban. Standard equipment now includes PassLock theft deterrent system, electrochromic rearview mirror, and automatic four-wheel drive on K-series models.

RATINGS (SCALE OF 1-10)

Overall	Safety	Reliability	Performance	Comfort	Value
7.6	8.3	7.5	7.2	7.9	7.3

Category H

4 Dr C1500 Wgn	16355	19470
4 Dr C2500 Wgn	16855	20065
4 Dr K1500 4WD Wgn	18020	21455
4 Dr K2500 4WD Wgn	19325	23005

OPTIONS FOR SUBURBAN

8 cyl 6.5 L Turbodsl Engine[Opt on 2500] +1845
8 cyl 7.4 L Engine[Opt on 2500] +370
SLE Pkg +2010
SLT Pkg +2360
Air Conditioning +490
Aluminum/Alloy Wheels +190
Camper/Towing Package +205
Compact Disc W/fm/tape +190
Cruise Control +115
Dual Air Conditioning +810
Heated Front Seats +205
Keyless Entry System +105

Don't forget to refer to the Mileage Adjustment Table at the back of this book!

Model Description	Trade-in Value	Market Value
Leather Seats +595		
Power Drivers Seat +170		
Power Mirrors +60		
Power Windows +115		
Privacy Glass +100		
Rear Heater +130		
Rear Window Defroster +95		
Rear Window Wiper +75		
Running Boards +210		
Tilt Steering Wheel +110		

YUKON 1998

The two-door model gets the ax this year. Rear seat passengers are cooled by a newly optional rear air conditioning system. A host of new standard features has been added, including carpeted floor mats. Three new colors spruce up the outside a bit, and second-generation airbags are standard inside.

RATINGS (SCALE OF 1-10)

Overall	Safety	Reliability	Performance	Comfort	Value
7.7	8.4	7.4	7.4	8	7.3

Category H

	Trade-in	Market
4 Dr SLE Wgn	18035	21470
4 Dr SLE 4WD Wgn	19490	23205
4 Dr SLT Wgn	18935	22540
4 Dr SLT 4WD Wgn	20320	24190

OPTIONS FOR YUKON
Luxury Convenience Group +525
Compact Disc W/fm/tape[Opt on SLE] +190
Dual Air Conditioning[Opt on SLE] +810
Heated Front Seats +205
Running Boards +210

1997 GMC

JIMMY 1997

Highrider off-road package deleted as GMC realigns Jimmy as luxury sport-ute. Instead, buyers can opt for a Gold Edition in one of four colors. New options include a power sunroof and HomeLink universal transmitter. In a fit of good taste, Radar Purple and Bright Teal paint colors are replaced by Fairway Green and Smoky Caramel.

RATINGS (SCALE OF 1-10)

Overall	Safety	Reliability	Performance	Comfort	Value
7.1	5.1	7.7	8	7.9	6.9

Category G

	Trade-in	Market
2 Dr SL Utility	11195	13490
2 Dr SL 4WD Utility	12045	14515
4 Dr SL Wgn	11600	13975
4 Dr SL 4WD Wgn	12350	14880
4 Dr SLE Wgn	12485	15045

	Trade-in	Market
4 Dr SLE 4WD Wgn	13230	15940
2 Dr SLS Sport Utility	12220	14725
2 Dr SLS Sport 4WD Utility	12765	15380
4 Dr SLS Sport Wgn	12620	15205
4 Dr SLS Sport 4WD Wgn	13230	15940
4 Dr SLT Wgn	13585	16370
4 Dr SLT 4WD Wgn	14075	16960

OPTIONS FOR JIMMY
AM/FM Compact Disc Player +160
Aluminum/Alloy Wheels[Opt on SL] +165
Camper/Towing Package +150
Cruise Control[Std on SLE,SLS Sport,SLT] +105
Keyless Entry System[Std on SLT] +100
Luggage Rack[Std on SLE,SLS Sport,SLT] +80
Power Door Locks[Std on SLE,SLS Sport,SLT] +115
Power Drivers Seat[Std on SLT] +140
Power Moonroof +430
Power Windows[Std on SLE,SLS Sport,SLT] +120
Premium Sound System[Std on SLT] +170
Skid Plates +65
Swing Out Tire Carrier +95

SAFARI 1997

Illuminated entry and daytime running lights debut this year, along with a couple of new colors and automatic transmission improvements. SLT models can be equipped with leather seating, and a HomeLink three-channel transmitter is optional. Speed-sensitive power steering makes parking easier.

RATINGS (SCALE OF 1-10)

Overall	Safety	Reliability	Performance	Comfort	Value
7.3	7	7.4	7	6.5	8.5

Category G

	Trade-in	Market
2 Dr SL Cargo Van Ext	8210	9890
2 Dr SL 4WD Cargo Van Ext	9915	11945
2 Dr SLE Pass. Van Ext	10995	13245
2 Dr SLE 4WD Pass. Van Ext	11655	14045
2 Dr SLT Pass. Van Ext	11525	13885
2 Dr SLT 4WD Pass. Van Ext	12505	15065
2 Dr SLX Pass. Van Ext	9795	11800
2 Dr SLX 4WD Pass. Van Ext	10970	13215

OPTIONS FOR SAFARI
Aluminum/Alloy Wheels[Std on SLT] +165
Camper/Towing Package +150
Chrome Wheels +85
Compact Disc W/fm/tape +240
Cruise Control[Opt on SL, SLX] +105
Dual Air Conditioning +470
Dual Power Seats +190
Keyless Entry System[Std on SLT] +100
Leather Seats +385
Luggage Rack[Std on SLT] +80
Power Door Locks[Opt on SL,SLX] +115

Don't forget to refer to the Mileage Adjustment Table at the back of this book!

Model Description	Trade-in Value	Market Value	Model Description	Trade-in Value	Market Value

Power Drivers Seat[Std on SLT] +140
Power Windows[Opt on SL,SLX] +120

SAVANA   1997

G3500 models get dual airbags, while daytime running lights are a new standard feature. Speed-sensitive steering reduces effort at low speeds. Chrome-plated wheels are a new option. Remote keyless entry key fobs are redesigned, and automatic transmissions provide better fuel economy and smoother shifts.

Category H

Model	Trade-in	Market
2 Dr 1500 Cargo Van	13155	15660
2 Dr 1500 Pass. Van	13970	16630
2 Dr 1500 SLE Pass. Van	14490	17250
2 Dr 2500 Cargo Van	13370	15915
2 Dr 2500 Cargo Van Ext	13640	16240
2 Dr 2500 Pass. Van	14245	16960
2 Dr 2500 Pass. Van Ext	14475	17235
2 Dr 2500 RV Cargo Van	12650	15060
2 Dr 2500 RV Cargo Van Ext	13165	15670
2 Dr 3500 Cargo Van Ext	13870	16510
2 Dr 3500 Pass. Van	14375	17115
2 Dr 3500 Pass. Van Ext	14625	17410
2 Dr 3500 SLE Pass. Van	14750	17560
2 Dr 3500 SLE Pass. Van Ext	14940	17785

OPTIONS FOR SAVANA

8 cyl 5.0 L Engine +250
8 cyl 5.7 L Engine[Std on G35] +520
8 cyl 6.5 L Turbodsl Engine +1535
8 cyl 7.4 L Engine +300
Air Conditioning[Opt on Cargo Van,Cargo Van Ext] +400
Aluminum/Alloy Wheels +155
Camper/Towing Package +170
Chrome Bumpers[Std on SLE] +85
Chrome Wheels +145
Compact Disc W/fm/tape +155
Cruise Control[Std on SLE] +95
Dual Air Conditioning[Opt on G15 Savana] +660
Dual Power Seats +230
Keyless Entry System +85
Locking Differential +125
Power Door Locks[Std on SLE] +95
Power Windows[Std on SLE] +95

SIERRA PICKUP   1997

A passenger airbag is added, along with speed sensitive steering that reduces low-speed effort. K1500 models have a tighter turning radius for better maneuverability. Automatic transmissions are refined to provide smoother shifts and improved efficiency. Three new paint colors debut.

RATINGS (SCALE OF 1-10)

Overall	Safety	Reliability	Performance	Comfort	Value
N/A	N/A	7.5	N/A	N/A	N/A

SIERRA 1500

Category H

Model	Trade-in	Market
2 Dr C1500 GT Std Cab SB	11285	13435
2 Dr C1500 SL Ext Cab LB	11125	13245
2 Dr C1500 SL Ext Cab SB	11020	13120
2 Dr C1500 SL Ext Cab Stepside SB	11585	13790
2 Dr C1500 SL Std Cab LB	10215	12160
2 Dr C1500 SL Std Cab SB	10120	12050
2 Dr C1500 SL Std Cab Stepside SB	10560	12570
2 Dr C1500 SLE Ext Cab LB	11665	13885
2 Dr C1500 SLE Ext Cab SB	11545	13745
2 Dr C1500 SLE Ext Cab Stepside SB	12110	14415
2 Dr C1500 SLE Std Cab LB	10855	12925
2 Dr C1500 SLE Std Cab SB	10710	12750
2 Dr C1500 SLE Std Cab Stepside SB	11345	13505
2 Dr C1500 SLT Ext Cab LB	13030	15510
2 Dr C1500 SLT Ext Cab SB	12890	15345
2 Dr C1500 SLT Ext Cab Stepside SB	13245	15765
2 Dr C1500 SLT Std Cab LB	12310	14655
2 Dr C1500 SLT Std Cab SB	12220	14550
2 Dr C1500 SLT Std Cab Stepside SB	12635	15040
2 Dr C1500 Special Std Cab LB	9320	11095
2 Dr C1500 Special Std Cab SB	9190	10940
2 Dr K1500 SL 4WD Ext Cab LB	12930	15395
2 Dr K1500 SL 4WD Ext Cab SB	12755	15185
2 Dr K1500 SL 4WD Ext Cab Stepside SB	13235	15755
2 Dr K1500 SL 4WD Std Cab LB	12095	14400
2 Dr K1500 SL 4WD Std Cab SB	11990	14275
2 Dr K1500 SL 4WD Std Cab Stepside SB	12520	14905
2 Dr K1500 SLE 4WD Ext Cab LB	14315	17040
2 Dr K1500 SLE 4WD Ext Cab SB	14185	16885
2 Dr K1500 SLE 4WD Ext Cab Stepside SB	14610	17390
2 Dr K1500 SLE 4WD Std Cab LB	13245	15765
2 Dr K1500 SLE 4WD Std Cab SB	13090	15585
2 Dr K1500 SLE 4WD Std Cab Stepside SB	13580	16165
2 Dr K1500 SLT 4WD Ext Cab LB	15055	17920
2 Dr K1500 SLT 4WD Ext Cab SB	14975	17825
2 Dr K1500 SLT 4WD Ext Cab Stepside SB	15305	18220
2 Dr K1500 SLT 4WD Std Cab LB	13985	16650
2 Dr K1500 SLT 4WD Std Cab SB	13885	16530

Don't forget to refer to the Mileage Adjustment Table at the back of this book!

GMC 97

Model Description	Trade-in Value	Market Value	Model Description	Trade-in Value	Market Value

Model Description	Trade-in Value	Market Value
2 Dr K1500 SLT 4WD Std Cab Stepside SB		
	14305	17030
2 Dr K1500 Special 4WD Std Cab LB		
	11800	14045
2 Dr K1500 Special 4WD Std Cab SB		
	11720	13955

SIERRA 2500

Category H

Model Description	Trade-in Value	Market Value
2 Dr C2500 SL Ext Cab SB	13345	15885
2 Dr C2500 SL Std Cab LB	12325	14675
2 Dr C2500 SLE Ext Cab SB	13765	16385
2 Dr C2500 SLE Std Cab LB	12840	15285
2 Dr C2500 SLT Ext Cab SB	14395	17135
2 Dr C2500 SLT Std Cab LB	13610	16200
2 Dr K2500 HD SL 4WD Ext Cab LB		
	14110	16800
2 Dr K2500 HD SL 4WD Ext Cab SB		
	13900	16550
2 Dr K2500 HD SL 4WD Std Cab LB		
	12720	15145
2 Dr K2500 HD SLE 4WD Ext Cab LB		
	14775	17590
2 Dr K2500 HD SLE 4WD Ext Cab SB		
	14570	17345
2 Dr K2500 HD SLE 4WD Std Cab LB		
	13595	16185
2 Dr K2500 HD SLT 4WD Ext Cab LB		
	15685	18675
2 Dr K2500 HD SLT 4WD Ext Cab SB		
	15380	18310
2 Dr K2500 HD SLT 4WD Std Cab LB		
	14770	17585

SIERRA 3500

Category H

Model Description	Trade-in Value	Market Value
4 Dr C3500 SL Crew Cab LB	16105	19170
2 Dr C3500 SL Ext Cab LB	15140	18025
2 Dr C3500 SL Std Cab LB	14150	16845
4 Dr C3500 SLE Crew Cab LB	17530	20870
2 Dr C3500 SLE Ext Cab LB	16615	19780
2 Dr C3500 SLE Std Cab LB	14970	17820
4 Dr C3500 SLT Crew Cab LB	17705	21075
2 Dr C3500 SLT Ext Cab LB	17220	20500
2 Dr C3500 SLT Std Cab LB	15630	18605
4 Dr K3500 SL 4WD Crew Cab LB	16865	20080
2 Dr K3500 SL 4WD Ext Cab LB	16085	19150
2 Dr K3500 SL 4WD Std Cab LB	15270	18180
4 Dr K3500 SLE 4WD Crew Cab LB		
	18240	21715
2 Dr K3500 SLE 4WD Ext Cab LB	17470	20800
2 Dr K3500 SLE 4WD Std Cab LB	15655	18635

Model Description	Trade-in Value	Market Value
4 Dr K3500 SLT 4WD Crew Cab LB		
	18820	22405
2 Dr K3500 SLT 4WD Ext Cab LB	18160	21620
2 Dr K3500 SLT 4WD Std Cab LB	16645	19815

OPTIONS FOR SIERRA PICKUP

8 cyl 5.0 L Engine +250
8 cyl 5.7 L Engine +520
8 cyl 6.5 L Turbodsl Engine +1535
8 cyl 7.4 L Engine +300
Auto 4-Speed Transmission +485
AM/FM Compact Disc Player +155
Air Conditioning[Opt on SL,Special] +400
Aluminum/Alloy Wheels[Std on SLT] +155
Bed Liner +110
Camper/Towing Package +170
Chrome Wheels[Std on GT] +145
Compact Disc W/fm/tape +155
Cruise Control[Opt on SL,Special] +95
Dual Rear Wheels +410
Hinged Third Door (PU) +205
Keyless Entry System[Opt on SLE] +85
Locking Differential +125
Power Door Locks[Opt on GT,SL] +95
Power Drivers Seat[Opt on SLE] +140
Rear Step Bumper +75
Skid Plates +55

SONOMA   1997

Nothing much. Changes are limited to new colors, availability of the Sport Suspension on extended cab models, engine and transmission improvements, lighter-weight plug-in half shafts for 4WD Sonomas, and console-mounted shifter for trucks equipped with a center console and bucket seats.

RATINGS (SCALE OF 1-10)

Overall	Safety	Reliability	Performance	Comfort	Value
N/A	4.9	6.8	6.6	8.1	N/A

Category G

Model Description	Trade-in Value	Market Value
2 Dr SL Std Cab LB	6860	8265
2 Dr SL 4WD Std Cab LB	9615	11585
2 Dr SL Std Cab SB	6640	8000
2 Dr SL 4WD Std Cab SB	9450	11385
2 Dr SLE Ext Cab SB	7690	9265
2 Dr SLE 4WD Ext Cab SB	10900	13130
2 Dr SLE Ext Cab Stepside SB	8020	9660
2 Dr SLE 4WD Ext Cab Stepside SB		
	11250	13555
2 Dr SLE Std Cab SB	7945	9575
2 Dr SLE 4WD Std Cab SB	9670	11650
2 Dr SLE Std Cab Stepside SB	8280	9975
2 Dr SLE 4WD Std Cab Stepside SB		
	10415	12550
2 Dr SLS Sport Ext Cab SB	7005	8440

Don't forget to refer to the Mileage Adjustment Table at the back of this book!

Model Description	Trade-in Value	Market Value
2 Dr SLS Sport Ext Cab Stepside SB	7480	9010
2 Dr SLS Sport 4WD Ext Cab Stepside SB	10840	13060
2 Dr SLS Sport Std Cab LB	7390	8905
2 Dr SLS Sport 4WD Std Cab LB	9430	11360
2 Dr SLS Sport Std Cab SB	7300	8795
2 Dr SLS Sport 4WD Std Cab SB	9250	11145
2 Dr SLS Sport Std Cab Stepside SB	7655	9225
2 Dr SLS Sport 4WD Std Cab Stepside SB	10140	12215

OPTIONS FOR SONOMA
6 cyl 4.3 L Engine +495
6 cyl 4.3 L Vortec Engine +380
Auto 4-Speed Transmission +535
Highrider Suspension Pkg +875
AM/FM Compact Disc Player +160
AM/FM Stereo Tape +110
Air Conditioning +405
Aluminum/Alloy Wheels[Std on SLE] +165
Cruise Control +105
Power Door Locks +115
Power Windows +120
Tilt Steering Wheel +85
Tutone Paint[Opt on SLS Sport] +130

SUBURBAN   1997

GMC has added a passenger side airbag and a power lock switch in the cargo compartment. SLE and SLT trim now includes rear heat and air conditioning, as well as remote keyless entry. Uplevel SLT trim also includes a combination CD and cassette player stereo system. All Suburbans receive speed-sensitive power steering, and 4WD models have a tighter turning circle. Two new colors freshen the dated exterior design this year.

RATINGS (SCALE OF 1-10)

Overall	Safety	Reliability	Performance	Comfort	Value
7.5	8.3	7	7.2	7.9	7.1

Category H
	Trade-in	Market
4 Dr C1500 Wgn	15515	18470
4 Dr C2500 Wgn	16750	19940
4 Dr K1500 4WD Wgn	17055	20305
4 Dr K2500 4WD Wgn	18360	21855

OPTIONS FOR SUBURBAN
8 cyl 6.5 L Turbodsl Engine +1535
8 cyl 7.4 L Engine +300
Folding Center/Rear Seats +595
SLE Pkg +1670
SLT Pkg +1815
Air Conditioning +400
Aluminum/Alloy Wheels +155

Camper/Towing Package +170
Compact Disc W/fm/tape +155
Cruise Control +95
Dual Air Conditioning +660
Keyless Entry System +85
Leather Seats +485
Luggage Rack +75
Power Drivers Seat +140
Power Windows +95
Running Boards +170
Skid Plates +55

YUKON   1997

Dual airbags, speed-sensitive steering and a tighter turning circle for 4WD models. A power lock switch is added to the cargo compartment, and SLT models have a standard CD/cassette combo stereo. Remote keyless entry is standard on four-door models, and on SLE and SLT two-door models. Newly optional on four-door models is a rear air conditioning unit.

RATINGS (SCALE OF 1-10)

Overall	Safety	Reliability	Performance	Comfort	Value
7.6	8	7.3	7.4	8	7.2

Category H
	Trade-in	Market
2 Dr SL Utility	13695	16305
2 Dr SL 4WD Utility	15020	17880
2 Dr SLE Utility	15870	18895
2 Dr SLE 4WD Utility	16570	19725
4 Dr SLE Wgn	16970	20200
4 Dr SLE 4WD Wgn	18210	21680
2 Dr SLT Utility	16725	19910
2 Dr SLT 4WD Utility	17635	20995
4 Dr SLT Wgn	17930	21345
4 Dr SLT 4WD Wgn	19360	23050

OPTIONS FOR YUKON
8 cyl 6.5 L Turbodsl Engine +1535
Air Conditioning[Opt on SL] +400
Aluminum/Alloy Wheels[Opt on SL] +155
Camper/Towing Package +170
Compact Disc W/fm/tape[Std on SLT] +155
Cruise Control[Opt on SL] +95
Dual Air Conditioning +660
Keyless Entry System[Opt on SL ,SLE] +85
Power Drivers Seat[Std on SLT] +140
Running Boards +170
Skid Plates +55

1996 GMC

JIMMY   1996

GMC's popular compact sport utility gets a super-duper optional off-road package called Highrider, as well as an available five-speed transmission. Either of these are available on two-door models only. All Jimmys

GMC 96

Model Description	Trade-in Value	Market Value	Model Description	Trade-in Value	Market Value

receive glow-in-the-day headlights and long-life engine coolant. Spark plugs last 100,000 miles. All-wheel drive, which became optional in mid-1995, continues. Conspicuously absent is a passenger airbag.

RATINGS (SCALE OF 1-10)

Overall	Safety	Reliability	Performance	Comfort	Value
6.5	4.9	7.1	8	7.9	4.8

Category G

	Trade-in Value	Market Value
2 Dr SL 4WD Utility	10350	12775
2 Dr SL Utility	9355	11550
4 Dr SL Wgn	10520	12990
4 Dr SL 4WD Wgn	10945	13510
4 Dr SLE Wgn	10740	13260
4 Dr SLE 4WD Wgn	11505	14205
2 Dr SLS Utility	10135	12510
2 Dr SLS 4WD Utility	10935	13500
4 Dr SLS Wgn	10690	13195
4 Dr SLS 4WD Wgn	11345	14005
4 Dr SLT Wgn	11155	13770
4 Dr SLT 4WD Wgn	11865	14650
2 Dr STD Utility	8845	10920
2 Dr STD 4WD Utility	9760	12050
4 Dr STD Wgn	9640	11900
4 Dr STD 4WD Wgn	10430	12875

OPTIONS FOR JIMMY

AM/FM Compact Disc Player +135
Aluminum/Alloy Wheels[Opt on SL,STD] +135
Camper/Towing Package +120
Cruise Control[Opt on STD] +85
Keyless Entry System[Std on SLT] +80
Limited Slip Diff +110
Luggage Rack[Opt on STD] +65
Power Door Locks[Opt on STD] +95
Power Drivers Seat[Std on SLT] +115
Power Windows[Opt on STD] +95
Premium Sound System[Std on SLT] +140
Skid Plates +55
Swing Out Tire Carrier +80

SAFARI   1996

An all-new interior debuts with dual airbags, more leg and foot room, and a host of other features. Important among them are the availability of dual integrated child seats and a child-proof lock on the right side sliding door. Under seat heat ducts help warm the rear passengers, and new audio systems include a radio that can be tuned independently by rear seat passengers without disturbing the listening pleasure, or program, that the front occupants are enjoying.

RATINGS (SCALE OF 1-10)

Overall	Safety	Reliability	Performance	Comfort	Value
7.3	6.9	7.5	7	6.5	8.4

Category G

	Trade-in Value	Market Value
2 Dr SL Cargo Van Ext	7405	9140
2 Dr SL 4WD Cargo Van Ext	8075	9970
2 Dr SLE Pass. Van Ext	8505	10500
2 Dr SLE 4WD Pass. Van Ext	9745	12030
2 Dr SLT Pass. Van Ext	9820	12125
2 Dr SLT 4WD Pass. Van Ext	10375	12810
2 Dr SLX Pass. Van Ext	7810	9645
2 Dr SLX 4WD Pass. Van Ext	8560	10565
2 Dr STD Pass. Van Ext	8425	10400
2 Dr STD 4WD Pass. Van Ext	9000	11110

OPTIONS FOR SAFARI

Aluminum/Alloy Wheels[Std on SLT] +135
Camper/Towing Package +120
Chrome Wheels +70
Compact Disc W/fm/tape +195
Cruise Control[Opt on SL] +85
Dual Air Conditioning +385
Keyless Entry System[Opt on SLE] +80
Luggage Rack[Std on SLT] +65
Power Door Locks[Opt on SL,STD] +95
Power Drivers Seat[Std on SLT] +115
Power Passenger Seat +110
Power Windows[Opt on SL] +95

SAVANA   1996

Category H

	Trade-in Value	Market Value
2 Dr 1500 Cargo Van	11600	13975
2 Dr 1500 Pass. Van	13105	15790

OPTIONS FOR SAVANA

8 cyl 5.0 L Engine +230
8 cyl 5.7 L Engine[Std on G35 Savana,G25 Savana] +410
8 cyl 6.5 L Turbodsl Engine +1340
8 cyl 7.4 L Engine +245
Air Conditioning[Opt on Cargo Van,Cargo Van Ext] +330
Aluminum/Alloy Wheels +125
Camper/Towing Package +140
Chrome Bumpers +70
Compact Disc W/fm/tape +125
Cruise Control +75
Dual Air Conditioning +540
Power Door Locks +75
Power Drivers Seat +115
Power Passenger Seat +105
Power Windows +75

SIERRA PICKUP   1996

Extended-cab models get a trick new side-access panel on the passenger side of the truck. Engines are dramatically improved across the board, daytime running lights debut, and long-life engine coolant gets changed about the same time you make your last

---

Don't forget to refer to the Mileage Adjustment Table at the back of this book!

payment. Spark plugs last 100,000 miles. Passenger car tires on 1500 models improve the ride and make the Sierra quieter. Heat ducts keep rear passengers' tootsies warm on extended cab models. Four-wheel-drive models get optional electronic shift-on-the-fly, and illuminated entry is a nice new touch.

RATINGS (SCALE OF 1-10)

Overall	Safety	Reliability	Performance	Comfort	Value
N/A	N/A	6.8	N/A	N/A	N/A

SIERRA 1500

Category H

Model Description	Trade-in Value	Market Value
2 Dr C1500 SL Ext Cab LB	9975	12020
2 Dr C1500 SL Ext Cab SB	9880	11905
2 Dr C1500 SL Ext Cab Stepside SB	10300	12410
2 Dr C1500 SL Std Cab LB	8330	10035
2 Dr C1500 SL Std Cab SB	8240	9930
2 Dr C1500 SL Std Cab Stepside SB	8640	10410
2 Dr C1500 SLE Ext Cab LB	11030	13290
2 Dr C1500 SLE Ext Cab SB	10960	13205
2 Dr C1500 SLE Ext Cab Stepside SB	11380	13710
2 Dr C1500 SLE Std Cab LB	10460	12605
2 Dr C1500 SLE Std Cab SB	10350	12470
2 Dr C1500 SLE Std Cab Stepside SB	10770	12975
2 Dr C1500 SLT Ext Cab LB	11850	14275
2 Dr C1500 SLT Ext Cab SB	11780	14190
2 Dr C1500 SLT Ext Cab Stepside SB	12195	14690
2 Dr C1500 SLT Std Cab LB	11000	13255
2 Dr C1500 SLT Std Cab SB	10905	13140
2 Dr C1500 SLT Std Cab Stepside SB	11300	13615
2 Dr C1500 Special Std Cab LB	7515	9055
2 Dr C1500 Special Std Cab SB	7430	8950
2 Dr K1500 SL 4WD Ext Cab LB	11020	13275
2 Dr K1500 SL 4WD Ext Cab SB	10875	13100
2 Dr K1500 SL 4WD Ext Cab Stepside SB	11795	14210
2 Dr K1500 SL 4WD Std Cab LB	10170	12250
2 Dr K1500 SL 4WD Std Cab SB	10055	12115
2 Dr K1500 SL 4WD Std Cab Stepside SB	10570	12735
2 Dr K1500 SLE 4WD Ext Cab LB	12715	15320
2 Dr K1500 SLE 4WD Ext Cab SB	12640	15230
2 Dr K1500 SLE 4WD Ext Cab Stepside SB	13065	15740
2 Dr K1500 SLE 4WD Std Cab LB	11625	14005

Model Description	Trade-in Value	Market Value
2 Dr K1500 SLE 4WD Std Cab SB	11475	13825
2 Dr K1500 SLE 4WD Std Cab Stepside SB	12185	14680
2 Dr K1500 SLT 4WD Ext Cab LB	13460	16215
2 Dr K1500 SLT 4WD Ext Cab SB	13420	16170
2 Dr K1500 SLT 4WD Ext Cab Stepside SB	13925	16780
2 Dr K1500 SLT 4WD Std Cab LB	12625	15210
2 Dr K1500 SLT 4WD Std Cab SB	12520	15085
2 Dr K1500 SLT 4WD Std Cab Stepside SB	12945	15595
2 Dr K1500 Special 4WD Std Cab LB	8825	10630
2 Dr K1500 Special 4WD Std Cab SB	8685	10465

SIERRA 2500

Category H

Model Description	Trade-in Value	Market Value
2 Dr C2500 SL Ext Cab LB	11600	13975
2 Dr C2500 SL Ext Cab SB	11365	13690
2 Dr C2500 SL Std Cab LB	10405	12535
2 Dr C2500 SLE Ext Cab LB	12265	14780
2 Dr C2500 SLE Ext Cab SB	12100	14580
2 Dr C2500 SLE Std Cab LB	10995	13245
2 Dr C2500 SLT Ext Cab SB	12785	15405
2 Dr C2500 SLT Std Cab LB	11855	14285
2 Dr K2500 SL 4WD Ext Cab LB	13125	15815
2 Dr K2500 SL 4WD Ext Cab SB	12965	15620
2 Dr K2500 SL 4WD Std Cab LB	12275	14790
2 Dr K2500 SLE 4WD Ext Cab LB	14270	17195
2 Dr K2500 SLE 4WD Ext Cab SB	13825	16655
2 Dr K2500 SLE 4WD Std Cab LB	12165	14655
2 Dr K2500 SLT 4WD Ext Cab LB	14630	17625
2 Dr K2500 SLT 4WD Std Cab LB	13520	16290

SIERRA 3500

Category H

Model Description	Trade-in Value	Market Value
4 Dr C3500 SL Crew Cab LB	14465	17430
2 Dr C3500 SL Ext Cab LB	13645	16440
2 Dr C3500 SL Std Cab LB	12910	15555
4 Dr C3500 SLE Crew Cab LB	15185	18295
2 Dr C3500 SLE Ext Cab LB	14315	17245
4 Dr C3500 SLT Crew Cab LB	16415	19775
2 Dr C3500 SLT Ext Cab LB	15465	18630
2 Dr C3500 SLT Std Cab LB	14820	17855
4 Dr K3500 SL 4WD Crew Cab LB	16360	19710
2 Dr K3500 SL 4WD Ext Cab LB	15480	18650
2 Dr K3500 SL 4WD Std Cab LB	13825	16655
4 Dr K3500 SLE 4WD Crew Cab LB	16040	19325
2 Dr K3500 SLE 4WD Ext Cab LB	15100	18195
2 Dr K3500 SLE 4WD Std Cab LB	14560	17540

Model Description	Trade-in Value	Market Value
4 Dr K3500 SLT 4WD Crew Cab LB		
	17085	20585
2 Dr K3500 SLT 4WD Ext Cab LB	16235	19560
2 Dr K3500 SLT 4WD Std Cab LB	15565	18755

OPTIONS FOR SIERRA PICKUP

8 cyl 5.0 L Engine +230
8 cyl 5.7 L Engine +410
8 cyl 6.5 L Turbodsl Engine +1340
8 cyl 7.4 L Engine +245
Auto 4-Speed Transmission +390
Air Conditioning[Std on SLE,SLT] +330
Aluminum/Alloy Wheels[Std on SLT] +125
Bed Liner +90
Camper/Towing Package +140
Chrome Bumpers[Opt on SL] +70
Chrome Wheels +120
Compact Disc W/fm/tape +125
Cruise Control[Std on SLE,SLT] +75
Dual Rear Wheels +335
Hinged Third Door (PU) +170
Keyless Entry System[Opt on SLE] +70
Locking Differential +100
Power Door Locks[Opt on SL] +75
Power Drivers Seat[Opt on SLE] +115
Rear Step Bumper +60
Skid Plates +45

SONOMA   1996

Extended-cab models get an optional driver's side rear access panel. All Sonomas are now equipped with four-wheel ABS. A new sport suspension provides sporty handling, and a snazzy Sportside box ends Ford's reign as lord of compact stepsides. A new five-speed transmission improves shifter location and operation when equipped with the base four-cylinder. Still missing is the availability of a passenger airbag.

RATINGS (SCALE OF 1-10)

Overall	Safety	Reliability	Performance	Comfort	Value
N/A	5	6.3	6.6	8.1	N/A

Category G

2 Dr SL Std Cab LB	6060	7480
2 Dr SL 4WD Std Cab LB	8000	9875
2 Dr SL Std Cab SB	5875	7255
2 Dr SL 4WD Std Cab SB	7810	9645
2 Dr SLE Ext Cab SB	7165	8845
2 Dr SLE 4WD Ext Cab SB	9165	11315
2 Dr SLE Ext Cab Stepside SB	7445	9190
2 Dr SLE 4WD Ext Cab Stepside SB		
	9570	11815
2 Dr SLE Std Cab SB	7295	9005
2 Dr SLE 4WD Std Cab SB	8965	11070
2 Dr SLS Sport Ext Cab SB	6135	7575
2 Dr SLS Sport 4WD Ext Cab SB	8580	10595

Model Description	Trade-in Value	Market Value
2 Dr SLS Sport Ext Cab Stepside SB		
	6460	7975
2 Dr SLS Sport 4WD Ext Cab Stepside SB		
	8900	10990
2 Dr SLS Sport Std Cab LB	5830	7195
2 Dr SLS Sport 4WD Std Cab LB	8365	10330
2 Dr SLS Sport Std Cab SB	5675	7005
2 Dr SLS Sport 4WD Std Cab SB	8100	10000
2 Dr SLS Sport Std Cab Stepside SB		
	6440	7950
2 Dr SLS Sport 4WD Std Cab Stepside SB		
	8880	10965

OPTIONS FOR SONOMA

6 cyl 4.3 L Engine +400
6 cyl 4.3 L Vortec Engine +305
Auto 4-Speed Transmission +430
Highrider Suspension Pkg +695
AM/FM Compact Disc Player +135
Air Conditioning +330
Aluminum/Alloy Wheels[Std on SLE] +135
Camper/Towing Package +120
Cruise Control +85
Hinged Third Door (PU) +140
Keyless Entry System +80
Limited Slip Diff +110
Power Door Locks +95
Power Windows +95
Premium Sound System +140
Skid Plates +55
Tutone Paint[Opt on SLS Sport] +105

SUBURBAN   1996

Giant SUV gets daytime running lights to make it more visible to other drivers. This is akin to installing field lighting on the bow of the Queen Mary. New V8s, quieter tires, and long-life spark plugs and coolant make the Suburban more satisfying to skipper. Rear passengers get warmer faster, thanks to new rear-seat heat ducting. Illuminated entry is newly standard, and electronic 4WD controls are a new option.

RATINGS (SCALE OF 1-10)

Overall	Safety	Reliability	Performance	Comfort	Value
7.2	6.8	6.7	7.2	7.9	7.6

Category H

4 Dr C1500 Wgn	14825	17860
4 Dr C2500 Wgn	15525	18705
4 Dr K1500 4WD Wgn	16350	19700
4 Dr K2500 4WD Wgn	17205	20730

OPTIONS FOR SUBURBAN

8 cyl 6.5 L Turbodsl Engine +1340
8 cyl 7.4 L Engine +245
Folding Center/Rear Seats +475
SLE Pkg +1005

Don't forget to refer to the Mileage Adjustment Table at the back of this book!

Model Description	Trade-in Value	Market Value	Model Description	Trade-in Value	Market Value
SLT Pkg +1540			2 Dr SLE 4WD Utility	15455	18620
Air Conditioning +330			4 Dr SLE Wgn	15645	18850
Camper/Towing Package[Std on C2500] +140			4 Dr SLE 4WD Wgn	16540	19930
Compact Disc W/fm/tape +125			2 Dr SLT Utility	15085	18175
Cruise Control +75			2 Dr SLT 4WD Utility	15835	19080
Dual Air Conditioning +540			4 Dr SLT Wgn	16710	20135
Keyless Entry System +70			4 Dr SLT 4WD Wgn	17510	21095
Leather Seats +400					
Luggage Rack +60					
Power Door Locks +75					

OPTIONS FOR YUKON
8 cyl 6.5 L Turbodsl Engine +1340
Air Conditioning[Opt on SL] +330
Aluminum/Alloy Wheels[Opt on SL] +125
Camper/Towing Package +140
Compact Disc W/fm/tape +125
Cruise Control[Opt on SL] +75
Keyless Entry System[Opt on SL,SLE] +70
Power Drivers Seat[Opt on SLE, SLT] +115
Rear Window Defroster[Opt on SL] +60
Running Boards +140
Skid Plates +45

Power Drivers Seat +115
Power Windows +75
Skid Plates +45

VANDURA/RALLY WAGON 1996

RALLY WAGON

Category H

Model	Trade-in	Market
2 Dr G35 Rally Wagon	9555	11510
2 Dr G35 Rally Wagon Ext	10165	12245
2 Dr G35 STX Rally Wagon	10690	12880
2 Dr G35 STX Rally Wagon Ext	11120	13400

VANDURA

Category H

Model	Trade-in	Market
2 Dr G35 Vandura	8320	10025
2 Dr G35 Vandura Ext	8895	10715

OPTIONS FOR VANDURA/RALLY WAGON
8 cyl 6.5 L Dsl Engine +670
8 cyl 7.4 L Engine +245
AM/FM Compact Disc Player +125
Air Conditioning[Opt on STD] +330
Camper/Towing Package +140
Chrome Bumpers[Opt on Vandura, Vandura Ext] +70
Cruise Control[Opt on STD] +75
Dual Air Conditioning +540
Keyless Entry System +70
Power Door Locks[Opt on STD] +75
Power Windows[Opt on STD] +75
Premium Sound System +155

YUKON   1996

Just what we need: a two-wheel-drive two-door Yukon. A new 5700 Vortec V8 gets long-life coolant and spark plugs, as well as a hefty bump in power and torque. Passenger car tires on less stout Yukons result in a softer, quieter ride. Rear heat ducts, illuminated entry, and height-adjustable seat belts debut. Four-wheel-drive models get a newly optional electronic shift mechanism.

RATINGS (SCALE OF 1-10)

Overall	Safety	Reliability	Performance	Comfort	Value
7.4	7.1	6.9	7.4	8	7.6

Category H

Model	Trade-in	Market
2 Dr SL Utility	13895	16740
2 Dr SL 4WD Utility	14695	17705
2 Dr SLE Utility	14710	17725

1995 GMC

JIMMY   1995

All-new SUV appears based on revamped Sonoma. Four-wheel-drive models have electronic transfer case as standard equipment. Spare tire on four-door models is mounted beneath cargo bay instead of in it. Five different suspension packages are available. One engine, a 195-horsepower 4.3-liter V6, is available. All-wheel drive is optional. Driver airbag and air conditioning are standard equipment.

RATINGS (SCALE OF 1-10)

Overall	Safety	Reliability	Performance	Comfort	Value
6.6	5.3	5.8	8	7.9	6.1

Category G

Model	Trade-in	Market
2 Dr SL Utility	7590	9610
2 Dr SL 4WD Utility	8545	10815
4 Dr SLE Wgn	8775	11110
4 Dr SLE 4WD Wgn	9585	12135
2 Dr SLS Utility	8155	10320
2 Dr SLS 4WD Utility	8875	11235
4 Dr SLS Wgn	8775	11110
4 Dr SLS 4WD Wgn	9565	12105
4 Dr SLT Wgn	9450	11960
4 Dr SLT 4WD Wgn	10110	12795
2 Dr STD Utility	7065	8940
2 Dr STD 4WD Utility	7930	10040
4 Dr STD Wgn	7915	10020
4 Dr STD 4WD Wgn	8720	11040

OPTIONS FOR JIMMY
AM/FM Compact Disc Player +110
Camper/Towing Package +100

Model Description	Trade-in Value	Market Value	Model Description	Trade-in Value	Market Value

Cruise Control[Opt on STD] +70
Keyless Entry System[Std on SLT] +65
Limited Slip Diff +90
Luggage Rack[Opt on STD] +50
Power Door Locks[Opt on STD] +75
Power Drivers Seat[Std on SLT] +95
Power Windows[Opt on STD] +80
Premium Sound System[Std on SLT Wgn] +115
Skid Plates +45
Swing Out Tire Carrier +65

SAFARI   1995

Front sheetmetal is restyled. Regular-length versions are dropped from the lineup, leaving only the extended model. Multileaf steel springs replace single-leaf plastic springs. One engine is available, the 190-horsepower, 4.3-liter V6. Air conditioning is newly standard, and remote keyless entry is a new option.

RATINGS (SCALE OF 1-10)

Overall	Safety	Reliability	Performance	Comfort	Value
7	6	6.3	7.2	6.6	8.9

Category G

Model	Trade-in	Market
2 Dr SL Cargo Van Ext	6525	8260
2 Dr SL 4WD Cargo Van Ext	6705	8490
2 Dr SLE Pass. Van Ext	7015	8880
2 Dr SLE 4WD Pass. Van Ext	7200	9115
2 Dr SLT Pass. Van Ext	7340	9290
2 Dr SLT 4WD Pass. Van Ext	7855	9940
2 Dr SLX Pass. Van Ext	6745	8535
2 Dr SLX 4WD Pass. Van Ext	7155	9055
2 Dr STD Pass. Van Ext	6350	8040
2 Dr STD 4WD Pass. Van Ext	7025	8895

OPTIONS FOR SAFARI

AM/FM Compact Disc Player +110
Camper/Towing Package +100
Cruise Control[Opt on SLT] +70
Dual Air Conditioning +315
Keyless Entry System[Std on SLT] +65
Limited Slip Diff +90
Luggage Rack +50
Power Door Locks[Std on SLE,SLT] +75
Power Drivers Seat +95
Power Windows[Std on SLT] +80
Premium Sound System +115

SIERRA PICKUP   1995

New interior with driver airbag (models under 8,500 lb. GVWR) and standard four-wheel ABS debut. Sport package is dropped. New dashboard features modular design with controls that are much easier to read and use. Power mirrors and remote keyless entry are new options. Uplevel radios come with automatic volume controls that raise or lower volume depending on vehicle speed.

RATINGS (SCALE OF 1-10)

Overall	Safety	Reliability	Performance	Comfort	Value
N/A	N/A	5.7	N/A	N/A	N/A

SIERRA 1500

Category H

Model	Trade-in	Market
2 Dr C1500 SL Ext Cab LB	8955	11055
2 Dr C1500 SL Ext Cab SB	8780	10840
2 Dr C1500 SL Ext Cab Stepside SB	9075	11205
2 Dr C1500 SL Std Cab LB	7695	9500
2 Dr C1500 SL Std Cab SB	7580	9360
2 Dr C1500 SL Std Cab Stepside SB	7940	9805
2 Dr C1500 SLE Ext Cab LB	9615	11870
2 Dr C1500 SLE Ext Cab SB	9535	11770
2 Dr C1500 SLE Ext Cab Stepside SB	9815	12120
2 Dr C1500 SLE Std Cab LB	8735	10785
2 Dr C1500 SLE Std Cab SB	8620	10645
2 Dr C1500 SLE Std Cab Stepside SB	8990	11100
2 Dr C1500 SLT Ext Cab LB	10180	12570
2 Dr C1500 SLT Ext Cab SB	10120	12495
2 Dr C1500 SLT Ext Cab Stepside SB	10390	12830
2 Dr C1500 Special Std Cab LB	6300	7775
2 Dr C1500 Special Std Cab SB	6185	7635
2 Dr K1500 SL 4WD Ext Cab LB	9925	12255
2 Dr K1500 SL 4WD Ext Cab SB	9875	12190
2 Dr K1500 SL 4WD Ext Cab Stepside SB	10240	12645
2 Dr K1500 SL 4WD Std Cab LB	9280	11455
2 Dr K1500 SL 4WD Std Cab SB	9195	11350
2 Dr K1500 SL 4WD Std Cab Stepside SB	9625	11880
2 Dr K1500 SLE 4WD Ext Cab LB	10605	13095
2 Dr K1500 SLE 4WD Ext Cab SB	10455	12905
2 Dr K1500 SLE 4WD Ext Cab Stepside SB	10915	13475
2 Dr K1500 SLE 4WD Std Cab LB	10050	12410
2 Dr K1500 SLE 4WD Std Cab SB	9965	12300
2 Dr K1500 SLE 4WD Std Cab Stepside SB	10405	12845
2 Dr K1500 SLS 4WD Ext Cab SB	10020	12370
2 Dr K1500 SLS 4WD Ext Cab Stepside SB	10435	12880
2 Dr K1500 SLT 4WD Ext Cab LB	11635	14365
2 Dr K1500 SLT 4WD Ext Cab SB	11570	14285
2 Dr K1500 SLT 4WD Ext Cab Stepside SB	11875	14660

Don't forget to refer to the Mileage Adjustment Table at the back of this book!

Model Description	Trade-in Value	Market Value
2 Dr K1500 Special 4WD Std Cab LB	7825	9660
2 Dr K1500 Special 4WD Std Cab SB	7730	9545

SIERRA 2500

Category H

Model Description	Trade-in Value	Market Value
2 Dr C2500 SL Ext Cab LB	9485	11710
2 Dr C2500 SL Ext Cab SB	9325	11515
2 Dr C2500 SL Std Cab LB	8250	10185
2 Dr C2500 SLE Ext Cab LB	10435	12880
2 Dr C2500 SLE Ext Cab SB	10225	12625
2 Dr C2500 SLE Std Cab LB	9105	11240
2 Dr C2500 SLT Ext Cab LB	11190	13815
2 Dr C2500 SLT Ext Cab SB	11035	13625
2 Dr K2500 SL 4WD Ext Cab LB	11030	13620
2 Dr K2500 SL 4WD Ext Cab SB	10930	13495
2 Dr K2500 SL 4WD Std Cab LB	9775	12070
2 Dr K2500 SLE 4WD Ext Cab LB	11850	14630
2 Dr K2500 SLE 4WD Ext Cab SB	11690	14435
2 Dr K2500 SLE 4WD Std Cab LB	10640	13135
2 Dr K2500 SLT 4WD Ext Cab LB	12695	15670
2 Dr K2500 SLT 4WD Ext Cab SB	12485	15415

SIERRA 3500

Category H

Model Description	Trade-in Value	Market Value
4 Dr C3500 SL Crew Cab LB	12175	15030
2 Dr C3500 SL Ext Cab LB	11180	13805
2 Dr C3500 SL Std Cab LB	10155	12535
4 Dr C3500 SLE Crew Cab LB	13190	16285
2 Dr C3500 SLE Ext Cab LB	12180	15040
2 Dr C3500 SLE Std Cab LB	11545	14255
2 Dr C3500 SLT Ext Cab LB	12480	15405
4 Dr K3500 SL 4WD Crew Cab LB	13975	17255
2 Dr K3500 SL 4WD Ext Cab LB	12100	14940
2 Dr K3500 SL 4WD Std Cab LB	10810	13345
4 Dr K3500 SLE 4WD Crew Cab LB	12440	15355
2 Dr K3500 SLE 4WD Ext Cab LB	13130	16210
2 Dr K3500 SLE 4WD Std Cab LB	10945	13510
2 Dr K3500 SLT 4WD Ext Cab LB	13230	16335

OPTIONS FOR SIERRA PICKUP

8 cyl 5.0 L Engine +200
8 cyl 5.7 L Engine +250
8 cyl 6.5 L Turbodsl Engine +1055
8 cyl 7.4 L Engine +185
Auto 4-Speed Transmission +305
Air Conditioning[Std on SLE , SLT] +270
Bed Liner +75
Camper/Towing Package +115
Chrome Bumpers[Opt on C1500,K1500] +60
Chrome Wheels +100
Compact Disc W/fm/tape +105
Cruise Control[Std on SLE,SLT] +60

Dual Rear Wheels +275
Keyless Entry System[Opt on SL,SLE] +55
Limited Slip Diff +85
Locking Differential +85
Power Door Locks[Std on SLE,SLT] +60
Power Drivers Seat[Opt on SLE] +95
Premium Sound System +130
Rear Step Bumper +50
Skid Plates +35

SONOMA   1995

Driver airbag is added, and daytime running lights are standard. Highrider off-road package can be ordered on the Club Coupe. Power window and lock buttons are illuminated at night. Remote keyless entry is a new option. A single key operates both the door locks and the ignition. A manual transmission can now be ordered with the 191-horsepower, 4.3-liter V6.

RATINGS (SCALE OF 1-10)

Overall	Safety	Reliability	Performance	Comfort	Value
N/A	4.9	5.7	6.6	8.1	N/A

Category G

Model Description	Trade-in Value	Market Value
2 Dr SL Std Cab LB	5005	6335
2 Dr SL 4WD Std Cab LB	6925	8765
2 Dr SL Std Cab SB	4855	6145
2 Dr SL 4WD Std Cab SB	6755	8550
2 Dr SLE Ext Cab SB	6150	7785
2 Dr SLE 4WD Ext Cab SB	8325	10540
2 Dr SLE Std Cab SB	5288	6695
2 Dr SLE 4WD Std Cab SB	7120	9015
2 Dr SLS Ext Cab SB	5730	7255
2 Dr SLS 4WD Ext Cab SB	8175	10350
2 Dr SLS Std Cab LB	5255	6655
2 Dr SLS 4WD Std Cab LB	7160	9065
2 Dr SLS Std Cab SB	5185	6565
2 Dr SLS 4WD Std Cab SB	6990	8850

OPTIONS FOR SONOMA

6 cyl 4.3 L Engine +265
6 cyl 4.3 L CPI Engine +275
Auto 4-Speed Transmission +335
Highrider Suspension Pkg +570
AM/FM Compact Disc Player +110
Air Conditioning +270
Anti-Lock Brakes[Opt on 2WD] +200
Camper/Towing Package +100
Cruise Control +70
Keyless Entry System +65
Limited Slip Diff +90
Power Door Locks +75
Power Windows +80
Premium Sound System +115
Rear Step Bumper[Opt on SL] +50
Skid Plates +45
Velour/Cloth Seats +70

Model Description	Trade-in Value	Market Value

SUBURBAN 1995

New interior with driver airbag debuts. New dashboard features modular design with controls that are much easier to read and use. 1500 models can now be ordered with turbodiesel engine. Brake/transmission shift interlock is added to automatic transmission. Seats and door panels are revised. New console on models with bucket seats features pivoting writing surface, along with rear cupholders and storage drawer. Uplevel radios come with automatic volume controls that raise or lower the volume depending on vehicle speed.

RATINGS (SCALE OF 1-10)

Overall	Safety	Reliability	Performance	Comfort	Value
6.9	7.1	5.1	7	7.9	7.5

Category H

	Trade-in	Market
4 Dr C1500 Wgn	12395	15300
4 Dr C2500 Wgn	13175	16265
4 Dr K1500 4WD Wgn	14000	17285
4 Dr K2500 4WD Wgn	14875	18365

OPTIONS FOR SUBURBAN

8 cyl 6.5 L Turbodsl Engine +1055
8 cyl 7.4 L Engine +185
Folding Center/Rear Seats +390
SLE Pkg +1100
SLT Pkg +1300
Air Conditioning +270
Camper/Towing Package[Std on C2500] +115
Compact Disc W/fm/tape +105
Cruise Control +60
Dual Air Conditioning +440
Keyless Entry System +55
Leather Seats +325
Luggage Rack +50
Power Door Locks +60
Power Drivers Seat +95
Power Windows +65
Skid Plates +35

VANDURA/RALLY WAGON 1995

No changes.

RALLY WAGON

Category H

	Trade-in	Market
2 Dr G25 Rally Wagon	7360	9085
2 Dr G25 STX Rally Wagon	7915	9770
2 Dr G35 Rally Wagon	8420	10395
2 Dr G35 Rally Wagon Ext	8860	10940
2 Dr G35 STX Rally Wagon	8665	10695
2 Dr G35 STX Rally Wagon Ext	9185	11340

VANDURA

Category H

	Trade-in	Market
2 Dr G15 Vandura	7555	9325
2 Dr G15 Vandura Ext	7685	9490
2 Dr G25 Vandura	8485	10475
2 Dr G25 Vandura Ext	8560	10565
2 Dr G35 Vandura	7365	9095
2 Dr G35 Vandura Ext	7500	9260

OPTIONS FOR VANDURA/RALLY WAGON

8 cyl 5.0 L Engine +200
8 cyl 5.7 L Engine[Opt on G25] +250
8 cyl 6.5 L Dsl Engine +740
8 cyl 7.4 L Engine +185
AM/FM Compact Disc Player +105
Air Conditioning[Std on STX] +270
Camper/Towing Package +115
Chrome Bumpers[Opt on G15, Vandura, Vandura Ext] +60
Cruise Control[Std on STX] +60
Dual Air Conditioning +440
Keyless Entry System +55
Limited Slip Diff +85
Power Door Locks[Std on STX] +60
Power Windows[Std on STX] +65
Premium Sound System +130

YUKON 1995

New interior with driver airbag debuts. New dashboard features modular design with controls that are much easier to read and use. New four-door model is added midyear, nicely sized between Jimmy and Suburban. New model is offered only in SLE or SLT trim with a 5.7-liter V8 and an automatic transmission in either 2WD or 4WD. Brake/transmission shift interlock is added to automatic transmission. New console on models with bucket seats features pivoting writing surface, along with rear cupholders and storage drawer.

RATINGS (SCALE OF 1-10)

Overall	Safety	Reliability	Performance	Comfort	Value
7.2	7.8	5.6	7.2	8	7.6

Category H

	Trade-in	Market
2 Dr SLE 4WD Utility	13005	16055
4 Dr SLE Wgn	13300	16420
4 Dr SLE 4WD Wgn	14120	17430
2 Dr SLT 4WD Utility	13630	16830
4 Dr SLT Wgn	13830	17075
4 Dr SLT 4WD Wgn	15850	19570
2 Dr STD 4WD Utility	11755	14510

OPTIONS FOR YUKON

8 cyl 6.5 L Turbodsl Engine +1055
Auto 4-Speed Transmission[Std on Wgn] +305
Air Conditioning[Opt on STD] +270
Camper/Towing Package +115
Compact Disc W/fm/tape +105
Cruise Control[Opt on STD] +60
Keyless Entry System[Opt on SLE] +55
Power Door Locks[Opt on STD] +60
Power Drivers Seat[Opt on SLE] +95

GMC 95-94

Model Description	Trade-in Value	Market Value	Model Description	Trade-in Value	Market Value

Running Boards +115
Skid Plates +35

1994 GMC

S15 JIMMY — 1994

Side-door guard beams and a high-mounted center brake light are added. Front bench seat is now standard on four-door models.

RATINGS (SCALE OF 1-10)

Overall	Safety	Reliability	Performance	Comfort	Value
6	5.1	6.6	6.8	7.1	4.6

Category G

	Trade-in	Market
2 Dr SLE Utility	5790	7520
2 Dr SLE 4WD Utility	6185	8030
4 Dr SLE Wgn	6305	8190
4 Dr SLE 4WD Wgn	6665	8655
2 Dr SLS Utility	5230	6790
2 Dr SLS 4WD Utility	5480	7115
4 Dr SLS Wgn	6025	7825
4 Dr SLS 4WD Wgn	6355	8255
2 Dr SLT Utility	6120	7945
2 Dr SLT 4WD Utility	6420	8335
4 Dr SLT Wgn	6680	8675
4 Dr SLT 4WD Wgn	6925	8995
2 Dr STD Utility	5580	7245
2 Dr STD 4WD Utility	5890	7650
4 Dr STD Wgn	6220	8075
4 Dr STD 4WD Wgn	6460	8390

OPTIONS FOR S15 JIMMY

6 cyl 4.3 L CPI Engine +155
Auto 4-Speed Transmission +245
AM/FM Compact Disc Player +90
Air Conditioning[Opt on SLS,STD] +220
Camper/Towing Package +80
Cruise Control[Std on SLE,SLT] +55
Keyless Entry System[Std on SLT] +55
Limited Slip Diff +75
Luggage Rack[Std on SLE,SLT] +45
Power Door Locks[Std on SLT, SLE] +65
Power Drivers Seat[Opt on SLE,SLS,STD] +75
Power Windows[Std on SLT,SLE Wgn] +65
Premium Sound System +95
Skid Plates +35

SAFARI — 1994

Driver airbag is made standard. Side-door guard beams are stronger, and air conditioners use CFC-free refrigerant. A high-mount center brake light is added. Analog gauges get new graphics, and carpet is treated with Scotchgard.

RATINGS (SCALE OF 1-10)

Overall	Safety	Reliability	Performance	Comfort	Value
7	5.8	6.2	7.2	6.6	9.3

Category G

	Trade-in	Market
2 Dr SLE Pass. Van	5230	6790
2 Dr SLE Pass. Van Ext	5915	7685
2 Dr SLE 4WD Pass. Van Ext	6505	8445
2 Dr SLT Pass. Van	5445	7070
2 Dr SLT Pass. Van Ext	6075	7890
2 Dr SLT 4WD Pass. Van Ext	6685	8685
2 Dr SLX Pass. Van	4965	6445
2 Dr SLX 4WD Pass. Van Ext	6220	8080
2 Dr SLX Pass. Van Ext	5555	7215
2 Dr STD Cargo Van	4035	5240
2 Dr STD 4WD Cargo Van	4715	6125
2 Dr STD Cargo Van Ext	4645	6035
2 Dr STD 4WD Cargo Van Ext	5335	6930
2 Dr STD Pass. Van	4815	6250
2 Dr STD Pass. Van	5455	7085
2 Dr STD Pass. Van Ext	5350	6950
2 Dr STD 4WD Pass. Van Ext	6220	8080

OPTIONS FOR SAFARI

6 cyl 4.3 L CPI Engine[Std on 4WD] +155
AM/FM Compact Disc Player +90
Air Conditioning +220
Camper/Towing Package +80
Chrome Bumpers +45
Cruise Control[Std on SLT] +55
Dual Air Conditioning +255
Keyless Entry System +55
Limited Slip Diff +75
Luggage Rack[Std on SLT Pass. Van] +45
Power Drivers Seat +75
Power Windows[Std on SLT] +65
Premium Sound System +95

SIERRA PICKUP — 1994

Grilles are restyled, side-door guard beams are added, and a third brake light is installed. Leather seats are included in new SLT package. Front seatback on Club Coupe models gets memory feature to improve entry and exit to rear seat. A 6.5-liter diesel replaces last year's 6.2-liter unit.

RATINGS (SCALE OF 1-10)

Overall	Safety	Reliability	Performance	Comfort	Value
N/A	N/A	7.3	N/A	N/A	N/A

SIERRA 1500

Category H

	Trade-in	Market
2 Dr C1500 Ext Cab LB	7530	9530
2 Dr C1500 Std Cab LB	6705	8485
2 Dr C1500 Std Cab SB	6755	8550

Model Description	Trade-in Value	Market Value	Model Description	Trade-in Value	Market Value
2 Dr C1500 Std Cab Stepside SB			**SIERRA 2500**		
	6975	8830	Category H		
2 Dr C1500 SL Ext Cab LB	7635	9665	2 Dr C2500 Ext Cab LB	8645	10940
2 Dr C1500 SL Ext Cab SB	7550	9555	2 Dr C2500 Ext Cab SB	8570	10845
2 Dr C1500 SL Ext Cab Stepside SB			2 Dr C2500 Std Cab LB	7595	9615
	7845	9930	2 Dr C2500 SL Ext Cab LB	8720	11040
2 Dr C1500 SL Std Cab LB	7005	8870	2 Dr C2500 SL Ext Cab SB	8605	10895
2 Dr C1500 SL Std Cab SB	6945	8790	2 Dr C2500 SL Std Cab LB	7725	9780
2 Dr C1500 SL Std Cab Stepside SB			2 Dr C2500 SLE Ext Cab LB	8735	11055
	7230	9150	2 Dr C2500 SLE Ext Cab SB	8580	10860
2 Dr C1500 SLE Ext Cab LB	7930	10035	2 Dr C2500 SLE Std Cab LB	7925	10030
2 Dr C1500 SLE Ext Cab SB	7865	9955	2 Dr K2500 4WD Ext Cab LB	9470	11990
2 Dr C1500 SLE Ext Cab Stepside SB			2 Dr K2500 4WD Ext Cab SB	9365	11855
	8115	10270	2 Dr K2500 4WD Std Cab LB	8235	10425
2 Dr C1500 SLE Std Cab LB	7105	8995	2 Dr K2500 SL 4WD Ext Cab LB	9695	12275
2 Dr C1500 SLE Std Cab SB	6990	8850	2 Dr K2500 SL 4WD Ext Cab SB	9615	12170
2 Dr C1500 SLE Std Cab Stepside SB			2 Dr K2500 SL 4WD Std Cab LB	8470	10720
	7330	9280	2 Dr K2500 SLE 4WD Ext Cab LB	10030	12695
2 Dr C1500 SLT Ext Cab SB	8060	10205	2 Dr K2500 SLE 4WD Ext Cab SB	9840	12455
2 Dr C1500 SLT Ext Cab Stepside SB			2 Dr K2500 SLE 4WD Std Cab LB	9075	11485
	8415	10655	**SIERRA 3500**		
2 Dr C1500 Special Std Cab LB	5685	7195	Category H		
2 Dr C1500 Special Std Cab SB	5530	7000	2 Dr C3500 Ext Cab LB	8510	10775
2 Dr K1500 4WD Ext Cab LB	8665	10970	2 Dr C3500 Std Cab LB	8855	11210
2 Dr K1500 4WD Ext Cab SB	8560	10835	2 Dr C3500 SL Ext Cab LB	10265	12995
2 Dr K1500 4WD Ext Cab Stepside SB			2 Dr C3500 SL Std Cab LB	9130	11555
	8860	11215	2 Dr C3500 SLE Ext Cab LB	10360	13115
2 Dr K1500 4WD Std Cab LB	7880	9975	2 Dr C3500 SLE Std Cab LB	9500	12025
2 Dr K1500 4WD Std Cab SB	7815	9890	2 Dr K3500 4WD Std Cab LB	9690	12265
2 Dr K1500 4WD Std Cab Stepside SB			2 Dr K3500 SL 4WD Std Cab LB	10260	12985
	8140	10305	2 Dr K3500 SLE 4WD Std Cab LB	10620	13445
2 Dr K1500 SL 4WD Std Cab LB	8640	10935			
2 Dr K1500 SL 4WD Std Cab SB	8555	10830	**OPTIONS FOR SIERRA PICKUP**		
2 Dr K1500 SL 4WD Std Cab Stepside SB			8 cyl 5.0 L Engine +165		
	8870	11225	8 cyl 5.7 L Engine +195		
2 Dr K1500 SLE 4WD Ext Cab LB	9290	11760	8 cyl 6.5 L Dsl Engine +735		
2 Dr K1500 SLE 4WD Ext Cab SB	9220	11670	8 cyl 6.5 L Turbodsl Engine +845		
2 Dr K1500 SLE 4WD Ext Cab Stepside SB			8 cyl 7.4 L Engine +160		
	9710	12290	Auto 4-Speed Transmission +250		
2 Dr K1500 SLE 4WD Std Cab LB	8365	10590	Deluxe Two Tone +340		
2 Dr K1500 SLE 4WD Std Cab SB	8280	10480	Air Conditioning[Std on SLE] +220		
2 Dr K1500 SLE 4WD Std Cab Stepside SB			Aluminum/Alloy Wheels +85		
	8615	10905	Bed Liner +60		
2 Dr K1500 SLT 4WD Ext Cab LB	9855	12475	Camper/Towing Package +90		
2 Dr K1500 SLT 4WD Ext Cab SB	9735	12320	Chrome Bumpers +45		
2 Dr K1500 SLT 4WD Ext Cab Stepside SB			Chrome Wheels +80		
	10120	12810	Cruise Control[Std on SLT] +50		
2 Dr K1500 Special 4WD Std Cab LB			Dual Rear Wheels[Opt on Crew Cab,Std Cab] +225		
	6860	8685	Limited Slip Diff +70		
2 Dr K1500 Special 4WD Std Cab SB			Locking Differential +70		
	6760	8555	Power Door Locks[Std on SLT] +50		
			Power Drivers Seat[Std on SLT] +75		
			Power Windows[Std on SLT] +50		
			Premium Sound System[Std on SLT] +105		

Don't forget to refer to the Mileage Adjustment Table at the back of this book!

GMC 94

Model Description	Trade-in Value	Market Value	Model Description	Trade-in Value	Market Value

Rear Step Bumper +40
Skid Plates +30

SONOMA 1994

All-new truck debuts with more powerful engines and available four-wheel ABS. Side-door guard beams are standard. Rear ABS is standard on four-cylinder models; V6 trucks get the new four-wheel ABS system that works in both two- and four-wheel drive. Highrider package is for serious off-roaders. Available only on regular-cab shortbed models, the Highrider includes four-inch wider track, three-inch height increase, off-road suspension and tires, wheel flares, and thick skid plates. Base engine is 118-horse, 2.2-liter four cylinder. Standard on 4WD models is a 165-horsepower, 4.3-liter V6. Optional on all models is a 195-horsepower, high-output 4.3-liter V6.

RATINGS (SCALE OF 1-10)

Overall	Safety	Reliability	Performance	Comfort	Value
N/A	4.9	6.5	6.6	8.1	N/A

Category G

2 Dr SL Std Cab LB	4305	5590
2 Dr SL 4WD Std Cab LB	5905	7670
2 Dr SL Std Cab SB	4195	5450
2 Dr SL 4WD Std Cab SB	5755	7475
2 Dr SLE Ext Cab SB	4795	6225
2 Dr SLE 4WD Ext Cab SB	6430	8350
2 Dr SLE Std Cab LB	4535	5890
2 Dr SLE 4WD Std Cab LB	6083	7900
2 Dr SLE Std Cab SB	4425	5745
2 Dr SLS Ext Cab SB	4720	6130
2 Dr SLS 4WD Ext Cab SB	6460	8390
2 Dr SLS Std Cab SB	4470	5805
2 Dr SLS 4WD Std Cab SB	6195	8045

OPTIONS FOR SONOMA

6 cyl 4.3 L Engine +235
6 cyl 4.3 L CPI Engine +155
Auto 4-Speed Transmission +255
AM/FM Compact Disc Player +90
Air Conditioning +220
Aluminum/Alloy Wheels +90
Anti-Lock Brakes[Opt on 2WD] +160
Camper/Towing Package +80
Cruise Control +55
Limited Slip Diff +75
Power Door Locks +65
Power Windows +65
Premium Sound System +95
Skid Plates +35

SUBURBAN 1994

Side-door guard beams are added, as well as a high-mounted center brake light. A turbocharged diesel is newly optional on 2500 models. A new grille appears.

RATINGS (SCALE OF 1-10)

Overall	Safety	Reliability	Performance	Comfort	Value
6.8	6.6	6.7	7	7.5	6.3

Category H

4 Dr C1500 Wgn	10350	13100
4 Dr C2500 Wgn	11180	14155
4 Dr K1500 4WD Wgn	11955	15135
4 Dr K2500 4WD Wgn	12800	16205

OPTIONS FOR SUBURBAN

8 cyl 6.5 L Turbodsl Engine +845
8 cyl 7.4 L Engine +160
SLE Decor Group +500
AM/FM Stereo Tape +60
Air Conditioning +220
Camper/Towing Package +90
Cruise Control +50
Dual Air Conditioning +360
Leather Seats +265
Limited Slip Diff +70
Luggage Rack +40
Power Door Locks +50
Power Drivers Seat +75
Power Mirrors +30
Power Windows +50
Premium Sound System +105
Skid Plates +30

VANDURA/RALLY WAGON 1994

Driver airbag is added to all models under 8,500-lb. GVWR. Side-door guard beams are installed in front doors and a high-mounted center brake light is added.

RALLY WAGON

Category H

2 Dr G25 Rally Wagon	6730	8520
2 Dr G25 STX Rally Wagon	7250	9180
2 Dr G35 Rally Wagon	7230	9150
2 Dr G35 Rally Wagon Ext	7350	9305

VANDURA

Category H

2 Dr G15 Vandura	6245	7905
2 Dr G15 Vandura Ext	6390	8090
2 Dr G25 Vandura	7055	8930
2 Dr G25 Vandura Ext	7215	9135
2 Dr G35 Vandura	6120	7745
2 Dr G35 Vandura Ext	6365	8055

OPTIONS FOR VANDURA/RALLY WAGON

8 cyl 5.0 L Engine +165
8 cyl 5.7 L Engine[Opt on G25, Vandura] +195

Model Description	Trade-in Value	Market Value	Model Description	Trade-in Value	Market Value

GMC 94-93

8 cyl 6.2 L Turbodsl Engine +455
8 cyl 6.5 L Dsl Engine +735
8 cyl 7.4 L Engine +160
AM/FM Compact Disc Player +85
Air Conditioning[Std on STX] +220
Camper/Towing Package +90
Captain Chairs (2)[Std on STX] +150
Chrome Bumpers[Opt on G15,Vandura,Vandura Ext] +45
Cruise Control +50
Dual Air Conditioning +360
Keyless Entry System +45
Leather Seats +265
Limited Slip Diff +70
Power Door Locks +50
Power Windows +50
Premium Sound System +105

YUKON   1994

Air conditioning receives CFC-free coolant. Side-door guard beams are added. A new grille appears, and models equipped with a decor package get composite headlamps. A turbocharged diesel is newly optional. Third brake light is added.

Category H
2 Dr SLE 4WD Utility	9815	12425
2 Dr STD 4WD Utility	9480	12000
2 Dr Sport 4WD Utility	9910	12545

OPTIONS FOR YUKON

8 cyl 6.5 L Turbodsl Engine +845
Auto 4-Speed Transmission +245
AM/FM Stereo Tape[Std on Sport] +60
Air Conditioning[Std on Sport] +220
Camper/Towing Package +90
Cruise Control[Std on Sport] +50
Luggage Rack +40
Power Door Locks[Std on Sport] +50
Power Drivers Seat +75
Power Windows[Std on Sport] +50
Premium Sound System +105
Skid Plates +30
Tilt Steering Wheel[Std on Sport] +50

1993 GMC

S15 JIMMY   1993

Two-door model available in SLT trim. Four-door models get monochromatic paint scheme in SLS trim. V6 engines get internal balance shaft designed to reduce vibration. Automatic transmission receives electronic shift controls and second-gear start feature. Manual lumbar adjusters are newly standard on front seats. Typhoon can be ordered in white as well as black.

RATINGS (SCALE OF 1-10)

Overall	Safety	Reliability	Performance	Comfort	Value
5.9	5.1	6.1	6.8	7.1	4.3

Category G
2 Dr SLE Utility	4660	6210
2 Dr SLE 4WD Utility	5125	6835
4 Dr SLE Wgn	4795	6395
4 Dr SLE 4WD Wgn	5275	7035
2 Dr SLS Utility	4440	5920
2 Dr SLS 4WD Utility	4855	6470
4 Dr SLS 4WD Wgn	5405	7205
2 Dr SLT Utility	4965	6620
2 Dr SLT 4WD Utility	5320	7090
4 Dr SLT Wgn	5215	6955
4 Dr SLT 4WD Wgn	5687	7580
2 Dr STD Utility	4290	5720
2 Dr STD 4WD Utility	4660	6210

OPTIONS FOR S15 JIMMY

6 cyl 4.3 L CPI Engine +110
Auto 4-Speed Transmission +205
AM/FM Compact Disc Player +70
Air Conditioning[Std on SLT Wgn] +180
Aluminum/Alloy Wheels[Opt on SLE,STD] +75
Camper/Towing Package +65
Cruise Control[Std on SLT Wgn] +45
Keyless Entry System[Std on SLT Wgn] +45
Leather Seats[Std on SLT] +170
Limited Slip Diff +60
Luggage Rack[Std on SLT Wgn] +35
Power Door Locks[Std on SLT Wgn] +50
Power Drivers Seat[Std on SLT] +60
Power Windows[Std on SLT Wgn] +55
Premium Sound System +75

SAFARI   1993

Base 4.3-liter V6 gets 15 additional horsepower. Automatic transmission gets electronic shift controls and second-gear start feature. New speedometer reads to 100 mph. Driver airbag is offered as an option midyear.

RATINGS (SCALE OF 1-10)

Overall	Safety	Reliability	Performance	Comfort	Value
6.6	4	6.3	7.2	6.6	9.1

Category G
2 Dr GT Sport Pass. Van Ext	3775	5035
2 Dr SLE Pass. Van	3995	5325
2 Dr SLE 4WD Pass. Van	4665	6220
2 Dr SLE 4WD Pass. Van Ext	5263	7020
2 Dr SLE Pass. Van Ext	4720	6295
2 Dr SLT Pass. Van	4165	5555
2 Dr SLT 4WD Pass. Van	5055	6740
2 Dr SLT Pass. Van Ext	4805	6405

Model Description	Trade-in Value	Market Value
2 Dr SLT 4WD Pass. Van Ext	5695	7590
2 Dr STD Cargo Van	2950	3935
2 Dr STD Cargo Van Ext	3555	4740
2 Dr STD 4WD Cargo Van Ext	4420	5890
2 Dr STD Pass. Van	3945	5260
2 Dr STD 4WD Pass. Van	4665	6220
2 Dr STD Pass. Van Ext	4370	5825
2 Dr STD 4WD Pass. Van Ext	5215	6950

OPTIONS FOR SAFARI

6 cyl 4.3 L CPI Engine[Std on 4WD] +110
AM/FM Compact Disc Player +70
Air Bag Restraint[Std on Cargo Van Ext] +110
Air Conditioning +180
Aluminum/Alloy Wheels +75
Camper/Towing Package +65
Chrome Bumpers +35
Cruise Control +45
Dual Air Conditioning +210
Limited Slip Diff +60
Luggage Rack +35
Power Door Locks +50
Power Drivers Seat +60
Power Windows +55
Premium Sound System +75

SIERRA PICKUP   1993

Solar-Ray tinted glass is made standard. Cloth interior surfaces are now protected by Scotchgard fabric protection. Automatic transmissions get electronic shift controls. Base V6 gets five additional horsepower.

RATINGS (SCALE OF 1-10)

Overall	Safety	Reliability	Performance	Comfort	Value
N/A	N/A	7.4	N/A	N/A	N/A

SIERRA 1500

Category H

Model Description	Trade-in Value	Market Value
2 Dr C1500 Ext Cab LB	6175	7815
2 Dr C1500 Ext Cab SB	6070	7685
2 Dr C1500 Ext Cab Stepside SB	6280	7950
2 Dr C1500 Std Cab LB	5755	7285
2 Dr C1500 Std Cab SB	5665	7170
2 Dr C1500 Std Cab Stepside SB	5980	7570
2 Dr C1500 SLE Ext Cab LB	6575	8325
2 Dr C1500 SLE Ext Cab SB	6515	8245
2 Dr C1500 SLE Ext Cab Stepside SB	6935	8780
2 Dr C1500 SLE Std Cab LB	6260	7925
2 Dr C1500 SLE Std Cab SB	6160	7795
2 Dr C1500 SLE Std Cab Stepside SB	6440	8155
2 Dr C1500 SLX Ext Cab LB	6310	7990

Model Description	Trade-in Value	Market Value
2 Dr C1500 SLX Ext Cab SB	6235	7895
2 Dr C1500 SLX Ext Cab Stepside SB	6490	8215
2 Dr C1500 SLX Std Cab SB	5850	7405
2 Dr C1500 Special Std Cab LB	5240	6635
2 Dr K1500 4WD Ext Cab LB	7375	9335
2 Dr K1500 4WD Ext Cab SB	7295	9235
2 Dr K1500 4WD Std Cab LB	6705	8490
2 Dr K1500 4WD Std Cab SB	6520	8255
2 Dr K1500 SLE 4WD Ext Cab LB	7935	10045
2 Dr K1500 SLE 4WD Ext Cab SB	7840	9925
2 Dr K1500 SLE 4WD Ext Cab Stepside SB	8230	10420
2 Dr K1500 SLE 4WD Std Cab LB	7215	9135
2 Dr K1500 SLE 4WD Std Cab SB	7135	9030
2 Dr K1500 SLE 4WD Std Cab Stepside SB	7325	9270
2 Dr K1500 SLX 4WD Ext Cab LB	7940	10050
2 Dr K1500 SLX 4WD Ext Cab SB	7790	9860
2 Dr K1500 Special 4WD Std Cab LB	6245	7905
2 Dr K1500 Sport 4WD Std Cab SB	7210	9125
2 Dr STD 4WD Std Cab Stepside SB	7010	8875

SIERRA 2500

Category H

Model Description	Trade-in Value	Market Value
2 Dr C2500 Ext Cab LB	7260	9190
2 Dr C2500 Ext Cab SB	7195	9110
2 Dr C2500 Std Cab LB	6400	8100
2 Dr C2500 SLE Ext Cab LB	7280	9215
2 Dr C2500 SLE Ext Cab SB	7195	9110
2 Dr C2500 SLE Std Cab LB	6580	8330
2 Dr C2500 SLX Ext Cab LB	7035	8905
2 Dr C2500 SLX Ext Cab SB	7195	9105
2 Dr C2500 SLX Std Cab LB	6365	8055
2 Dr K2500 4WD Ext Cab LB	7995	10120
2 Dr K2500 4WD Ext Cab SB	7860	9950
2 Dr K2500 4WD Std Cab SB	7210	9125
2 Dr K2500 SLE 4WD Ext Cab LB	8210	10395
2 Dr K2500 SLE 4WD Ext Cab SB	8135	10300
2 Dr K2500 SLE 4WD Std Cab LB	7115	9005
2 Dr K2500 SLX 4WD Ext Cab LB	8115	10270
2 Dr K2500 SLX 4WD Ext Cab SB	7945	10060
2 Dr K2500 SLX 4WD Std Cab LB	7150	9050

SIERRA 3500

Category H

Model Description	Trade-in Value	Market Value
4 Dr C3500 Crew Cab LB	8540	10810
2 Dr C3500 Ext Cab LB	7855	9945
2 Dr C3500 Std Cab LB	7420	9390
4 Dr C3500 SLE Crew Cab LB	9575	12120

Don't forget to refer to the Mileage Adjustment Table at the back of this book!

Model Description	Trade-in Value	Market Value	Model Description	Trade-in Value	Market Value
2 Dr C3500 SLE Ext Cab LB	8255	10450	2 Dr STD 4WD Ext Cab SB	5185	6915
2 Dr C3500 SLE Std Cab LB	7705	9750	2 Dr STD Std Cab LB	3305	4405
2 Dr C3500 SLX Ext Cab LB	8100	10255	2 Dr STD 4WD Std Cab LB	4310	5745
2 Dr C3500 SLX Std Cab LB	7540	9545	2 Dr STD Std Cab SB	3140	4185
2 Dr K3500 4WD Std Cab LB	8735	11055	2 Dr STD 4WD Std Cab SB	4540	6055
2 Dr K3500 SL Turbodsl 4WD Ext Cab LB			2 Dr Special Std Cab SB	3040	4050
	9519	12050	2 Dr Special 4WD Std Cab SB	4405	5870
2 Dr K3500 SLE 4WD Std Cab LB	8490	10745			

OPTIONS FOR SIERRA PICKUP

8 cyl 5.0 L Engine +135
8 cyl 5.7 L Engine +190
8 cyl 6.2 L Dsl Engine +475
8 cyl 6.5 L Turbodsl Engine +625
8 cyl 7.4 L Engine +175
Auto 4-Speed Transmission +200
SLE Decor Pkg +180
Sport Handling Pkg +195
AM/FM Stereo Tape +45
Air Conditioning[Std on SL] +180
Aluminum/Alloy Wheels +70
Bed Liner +50
Camper/Towing Package +75
Cruise Control +40
Dual Rear Wheels +185
Limited Slip Diff +55
Locking Differential +55
Power Door Locks +40
Power Drivers Seat +60
Power Windows +40
Premium Sound System +85
Rear Step Bumper +35

SONOMA 1993

V6 engines get internal balance shaft designed to reduce vibration. Automatic transmission gets electronic shift controls. Syclone dropped.

RATINGS (SCALE OF 1-10)

Overall	Safety	Reliability	Performance	Comfort	Value
N/A	3.2	6.6	7.2	7	N/A

Category G

2 Dr SLE Ext Cab SB	4075	5435
2 Dr SLE 4WD Ext Cab SB	5520	7360
2 Dr SLE Std Cab LB	3490	4650
2 Dr SLE 4WD Std Cab LB	4690	6250
2 Dr SLE Std Cab SB	3410	4545
2 Dr SLE 4WD Std Cab SB	4570	6095
2 Dr SLS Ext Cab SB	4015	5350
2 Dr SLS 4WD Ext Cab SB	5380	7175
2 Dr SLS Std Cab LB	3425	4565
2 Dr SLS 4WD Std Cab LB	4500	6000
2 Dr SLS Std Cab SB	3350	4465
2 Dr SLS 4WD Std Cab SB	4400	5865
2 Dr STD Ext Cab SB	3900	5200

OPTIONS FOR SONOMA

6 cyl 2.8 L Engine +85
6 cyl 4.3 L Engine +140
6 cyl 4.3 L CPI Engine +110
Auto 4-Speed Transmission +200
AM/FM Stereo[Opt on Special] +40
AM/FM Stereo Tape +50
Air Conditioning +180
Aluminum/Alloy Wheels +75
Cruise Control +45
Power Mirrors[Std on SLE] +30
Power Steering[Opt on 2WD] +60
Tilt Steering Wheel +40

SUBURBAN 1993

No changes.

RATINGS (SCALE OF 1-10)

Overall	Safety	Reliability	Performance	Comfort	Value
7	6.8	6.9	7	7.5	6.7

Category H

4 Dr C1500 Wgn	8825	11170
4 Dr C2500 Wgn	9740	12330
4 Dr K1500 4WD Wgn	10380	13140
4 Dr K2500 4WD Wgn	11160	14125

OPTIONS FOR SUBURBAN

8 cyl 7.4 L Engine +175
SLE Pkg +300
AM/FM Stereo Tape +45
Air Conditioning +180
Aluminum/Alloy Wheels +70
Camper/Towing Package +75
Cruise Control +40
Dual Air Conditioning +295
Leather Seats +215
Luggage Rack +35
Power Door Locks +40
Power Drivers Seat +60
Power Passenger Seat +55
Power Windows +40
Premium Sound System +85

TYPHOON 1993

Typhoon can be ordered in white as well as black.

Category I

2 Dr STD Turbo 4WD Utility	11915	15675

GMC 93-92

Model Description	Trade-in Value	Market Value	Model Description	Trade-in Value	Market Value

OPTIONS FOR TYPHOON
AM/FM Compact Disc Player +30
Luggage Rack +30

VANDURA/RALLY WAGON 1993

Solar-Ray tinted glass and Scotchgard fabric protectant are both standard. Four-wheel ABS is a new standard feature. Remote keyless entry joins the options list.

RALLY WAGON
Category H

	Trade-in	Market
2 Dr G15 Rally Wagon	4790	6065
2 Dr G15 Rally Wagon Ext	4865	6160
2 Dr G15 STX Rally Wagon	5330	6745
2 Dr G25 Rally Wagon Ext	6125	7755
2 Dr G25 STX Rally Wagon Ext	6690	8470
2 Dr G35 Rally Wagon Ext	6285	7955

VANDURA
Category H

	Trade-in	Market
2 Dr G15 Vandura	4660	5900
2 Dr G15 Vandura Ext	4750	6010
2 Dr G25 Vandura	5465	6915
2 Dr G25 Vandura Ext	5270	6670
2 Dr G35 Vandura Ext	5560	7040

OPTIONS FOR VANDURA/RALLY WAGON
8 cyl 5.0 L Engine +135
8 cyl 5.7 L Engine[Std on G35] +190
8 cyl 6.2 L Dsl Engine +475
8 cyl 7.4 L Engine +175
AM/FM Compact Disc Player +70
Air Conditioning +180
Aluminum/Alloy Wheels +70
Camper/Towing Package +75
Chrome Bumpers[Opt on Vandura, Vandura Ext] +40
Cruise Control +40
Dual Air Conditioning +295
Keyless Entry System +40
Power Door Locks +40
Power Windows +40
Premium Sound System +85

YUKON 1993

No changes.
Category H

	Trade-in	Market
2 Dr SLE 4WD Utility	8865	11220
2 Dr STD 4WD Utility	8255	10445
2 Dr Sport GT 4WD Utility	9275	11740

OPTIONS FOR YUKON
Auto 4-Speed Transmission +200
AM/FM Stereo Tape[Opt on STD] +45
Air Conditioning[Opt on STD] +180
Aluminum/Alloy Wheels[Opt on STD] +70
Camper/Towing Package +75
Cruise Control[Opt on STD] +40
Luggage Rack +35

Power Door Locks +40
Power Drivers Seat +60
Power Windows +40
Premium Sound System +85

1992 GMC

S15 JIMMY 1992

Four-wheel ABS is standard on all models. Electronic-shift transfer case is added to options list; comes standard with SLT trim. A high-performance, 4.3-liter V6 debuts with 40 additional horsepower, bringing total output to 200 ponies. Bucket seats are redesigned, a new speedometer is installed, and a four-spoke steering wheel is added.

RATINGS (SCALE OF 1-10)

Overall	Safety	Reliability	Performance	Comfort	Value
5.8	3.9	6.2	6.8	7.1	4.9

Category G

	Trade-in	Market
2 Dr SLE Utility	3485	4775
2 Dr SLE 4WD Utility	3800	5205
4 Dr SLE Wgn	3865	5295
4 Dr SLE 4WD Wgn	4295	5885
4 Dr SLT Wgn	4130	5655
4 Dr SLT 4WD Wgn	4375	5995
2 Dr STD Utility	3360	4605
2 Dr STD 4WD Utility	3715	5090
4 Dr STD Wgn	3815	5225
4 Dr STD 4WD Wgn	4195	5745

OPTIONS FOR S15 JIMMY
Auto 4-Speed Transmission +165
Air Conditioning +145
Camper/Towing Package +55
Cruise Control +40
Leather Seats +140
Limited Slip Diff +50
Power Door Locks +40
Power Windows +45

SAFARI 1992

Dutch rear door treatment is available. With Dutch doors, a rear washer/wiper and rear defogger can be ordered. All-wheel-drive models get high-output, 200-horsepower V6 standard. Engine is optional on 2WD models.

RATINGS (SCALE OF 1-10)

Overall	Safety	Reliability	Performance	Comfort	Value
6.5	4.1	6.6	7.2	6.6	8.1

Category G

	Trade-in	Market
2 Dr SLE Pass. Van	3240	4435
2 Dr SLE 4WD Pass. Van	4005	5485
2 Dr SLE Pass. Van Ext	3810	5220

Don't forget to refer to the Mileage Adjustment Table at the back of this book!

Model Description	Trade-in Value	Market Value
2 Dr SLT Pass. Van	3210	4395
2 Dr SLT 4WD Pass. Van	4000	5480
2 Dr SLT Pass. Van Ext	3815	5225
2 Dr SLT 4WD Pass. Van Ext	4635	6350
2 Dr STD Cargo Van	2490	3410
2 Dr STD Cargo Van Ext	2975	4075
2 Dr STD 4WD Cargo Van Ext	3655	5010
2 Dr STD Pass. Van	3290	4505
2 Dr STD 4WD Pass. Van	4010	5490
2 Dr STD Pass. Van Ext	3560	4880
2 Dr STD 4WD Pass. Van Ext	4225	5790

OPTIONS FOR SAFARI

6 cyl 4.3 L CPI Engine[Std on 4WD] +95
Air Conditioning +145
Camper/Towing Package +55
Cruise Control +40
Dual Air Conditioning +170
Power Door Locks +40
Power Drivers Seat +50
Power Windows +45

SIERRA PICKUP 1992

Extended-cab models get Sportside box option. Crew Cab model is all-new, sporting same engineering and styling as rest of Sierra line. Front buckets have been redesigned. Standard gauge cluster is restyled. Integral head restraints are added for outboard passengers. A new turbocharged, 6.5-liter diesel V8 is optional in C/K 2500 and regular-cab C/K 3500 models. Four-speed manual transmission is dropped.

RATINGS (SCALE OF 1-10)

Overall	Safety	Reliability	Performance	Comfort	Value
N/A	N/A	6.8	N/A	N/A	N/A

SIERRA 1500

Category H

Model Description	Trade-in Value	Market Value
2 Dr C1500 Ext Cab LB	5400	7010
2 Dr C1500 Ext Cab SB	5380	6990
2 Dr C1500 Ext Cab Stepside SB	5560	7220
2 Dr C1500 Std Cab LB	5035	6540
2 Dr C1500 Std Cab SB	4975	6460
2 Dr C1500 SLE Ext Cab LB	5875	7630
2 Dr C1500 SLE Ext Cab SB	5790	7520
2 Dr C1500 SLE Ext Cab Stepside SB	6190	8040
2 Dr C1500 SLE Std Cab LB	5250	6820
2 Dr C1500 SLE Std Cab SB	5185	6735
2 Dr C1500 SLE Std Cab Stepside SB	5400	7010
2 Dr C1500 SLX Ext Cab LB	5410	7025
2 Dr C1500 SLX Ext Cab SB	5295	6875
2 Dr C1500 SLX Ext Cab Stepside SB	5580	7245
2 Dr C1500 SLX Std Cab LB	5010	6505
2 Dr C1500 SLX Std Cab SB	4895	6355
2 Dr C1500 SLX Std Cab Stepside SB	5150	6690
2 Dr C1500 Special Std Cab LB	4065	5280
2 Dr K1500 4WD Ext Cab LB	6820	8860
2 Dr K1500 4WD Ext Cab SB	6760	8780
2 Dr K1500 4WD Ext Cab Stepside SB	6915	8980
2 Dr K1500 4WD Std Cab LB	5880	7635
2 Dr K1500 4WD Std Cab SB	5820	7560
2 Dr K1500 4WD Std Cab Stepside SB	6160	8000
2 Dr K1500 SLE 4WD Ext Cab LB	7150	9285
2 Dr K1500 SLE 4WD Ext Cab SB	7080	9195
2 Dr K1500 SLE 4WD Ext Cab Stepside SB	7360	9560
2 Dr K1500 SLE 4WD Std Cab LB	6090	7910
2 Dr K1500 SLE 4WD Std Cab SB	6000	7790
2 Dr K1500 SLE 4WD Std Cab Stepside SB	6240	8105
2 Dr K1500 SLX 4WD Ext Cab LB	6780	8805
2 Dr K1500 SLX 4WD Ext Cab SB	6705	8705
2 Dr K1500 SLX 4WD Ext Cab Stepside SB	7030	9130
2 Dr K1500 SLX 4WD Std Cab LB	6100	7925
2 Dr K1500 SLX 4WD Std Cab SB	5990	7780
2 Dr K1500 SLX 4WD Std Cab Stepside SB	6315	8200
2 Dr K1500 Special 4WD Std Cab LB	5480	7115

SIERRA 2500

Category H

Model Description	Trade-in Value	Market Value
2 Dr C2500 Ext Cab LB	5700	7405
2 Dr C2500 Ext Cab SB	5700	7400
2 Dr C2500 Std Cab LB	5040	6545
2 Dr C2500 SLE Ext Cab LB	5995	7785
2 Dr C2500 SLE Ext Cab SB	5920	7690
2 Dr C2500 SLE Std Cab LB	5215	6770
2 Dr C2500 SLX Ext Cab LB	5735	7445
2 Dr C2500 SLX Ext Cab SB	5780	7505
2 Dr C2500 SLX Std Cab LB	4955	6435
2 Dr K2500 4WD Ext Cab LB	7455	9680
2 Dr K2500 4WD Ext Cab SB	7055	9160
2 Dr K2500 4WD Std Cab LB	6355	8255
2 Dr K2500 SLE 4WD Ext Cab LB	7450	9675
2 Dr K2500 SLE 4WD Ext Cab SB	7275	9445
2 Dr K2500 SLE 4WD Std Cab LB	6170	8015
2 Dr K2500 SLX 4WD Ext Cab LB	6975	9060

Don't forget to refer to the Mileage Adjustment Table at the back of this book!

Model Description	Trade-in Value	Market Value
2 Dr K2500 SLX 4WD Ext Cab SB	6845	8890
2 Dr K2500 SLX 4WD Std Cab LB	5755	7475

SIERRA 3500

Category H

Model Description	Trade-in Value	Market Value
4 Dr C3500 Crew Cab LB	6630	8610
2 Dr C3500 Ext Cab LB	5935	7705
2 Dr C3500 SLE Ext Cab LB	7275	9445
2 Dr C3500 SLX Ext Cab LB	6770	8795
2 Dr K3500 4WD Ext Cab LB	8160	10600

OPTIONS FOR SIERRA PICKUP

8 cyl 5.0 L Engine +105
8 cyl 5.7 L Engine +150
8 cyl 6.2 L Dsl Engine +375
8 cyl 6.5 L Turbodsl Engine +480
8 cyl 7.4 L Engine +135
Auto 4-Speed Transmission +160
SLE Pkg +165
Sport Handling Pkg +155
Air Conditioning +145
Camper/Towing Package +60
Cruise Control +35
Dual Rear Wheels +150
Limited Slip Diff +45
Power Door Locks +35
Power Windows +35

SONOMA   1992

New GT model debuts, available on regular-cab shortbed 2WD models and including many Syclone styling cues along with high-output, 4.3-liter V6. Front bucket seats are redesigned, integral head restraints are added, and Club Coupes can be equipped with leather seats. New speedometer and four-spoke steering wheel are installed. Premium sound system with CD player is added to options list. Four-wheel-drive models can be equipped with an electronic-shift transfer case.

RATINGS (SCALE OF 1-10)

Overall	Safety	Reliability	Performance	Comfort	Value
N/A	3	6.6	7.2	7	N/A

Category G

Model Description	Trade-in Value	Market Value
2 Dr GT Std Cab SB	4875	6675
2 Dr SLE Ext Cab SB	3370	4615
2 Dr SLE 4WD Ext Cab SB	4240	5810
2 Dr SLE Std Cab LB	2795	3830
2 Dr SLE 4WD Std Cab LB	3655	5005
2 Dr SLE Std Cab SB	2745	3760
2 Dr SLE 4WD Std Cab SB	3605	4935
2 Dr STD Ext Cab SB	3225	4420
2 Dr STD 4WD Ext Cab SB	4280	5860
2 Dr STD Std Cab LB	2750	3765
2 Dr STD 4WD Std Cab LB	3695	5060
2 Dr STD Std Cab SB	2670	3660

Model Description	Trade-in Value	Market Value
2 Dr STD 4WD Std Cab SB	3760	5150
2 Dr Special Std Cab SB	2510	3435
2 Dr Special 4WD Std Cab SB	3670	5030

OPTIONS FOR SONOMA

6 cyl 2.8 L Engine +70
6 cyl 4.3 L Engine +110
Auto 4-Speed Transmission[Std on GT,Syclone] +160
Air Conditioning[Std on GT] +145
Camper/Towing Package +55
Cruise Control[Opt on SLE,STD] +40
Limited Slip Diff[Opt on SLE,STD] +50
Power Door Locks[Opt on SLE,STD] +40
Power Windows[Opt on SLE,STD] +45

SUBURBAN   1992

All-new design debuts based on platform and styling of Sierra. Cargo space and towing capacity are up. ABS works on all four wheels even in 4WD. Tailgate glass is lifted up instead of powered down. No diesel is offered. GM's Instatrac 4WD system is standard on K models.

RATINGS (SCALE OF 1-10)

Overall	Safety	Reliability	Performance	Comfort	Value
6.8	6.6	6.3	7	7.5	6.6

Category H

Model Description	Trade-in Value	Market Value
4 Dr C1500 Wgn	7750	10065
4 Dr C2500 Wgn	8440	10960
4 Dr K1500 4WD Wgn	8380	10885
4 Dr K2500 4WD Wgn	8995	11680

OPTIONS FOR SUBURBAN

8 cyl 7.4 L Engine +135
SLE Pkg +355
Air Conditioning +145
Camper/Towing Package +60
Cruise Control +35
Dual Air Conditioning +240
Limited Slip Diff +45
Power Door Locks +35
Power Drivers Seat +50
Power Windows +35

TYPHOON   1992

Typhoon blows into town, featuring Syclone powertrain wrapped in two-door Jimmy body.

Category I

Model Description	Trade-in Value	Market Value
2 Dr STD Turbo 4WD Utility	10740	14135

OPTIONS FOR TYPHOON

Ground Effects Package +30

VANDURA/RALLY WAGON 1992

Minor suspension modifications improve the ride.

GMC 92-91

Model Description	Trade-in Value	Market Value	Model Description	Trade-in Value	Market Value

RALLY WAGON

Category H

Model	Trade-in	Market
2 Dr G15 Rally Wagon	4135	5370
2 Dr G15 Rally Wagon Ext	4325	5620
2 Dr G15 STX Rally Wagon	4765	6190
2 Dr G25 Rally Wagon Ext	4930	6405
2 Dr G25 STX Rally Wagon Ext	5215	6775

VANDURA

Category H

Model	Trade-in	Market
2 Dr G15 Vandura	3775	4905
2 Dr G15 Vandura Ext	3930	5105
2 Dr G25 Vandura	4270	5545
2 Dr G25 Vandura Ext	4170	5415

OPTIONS FOR VANDURA/RALLY WAGON

8 cyl 5.0 L Engine +105
8 cyl 5.7 L Engine[Opt on G15,G25,Vandura] +150
8 cyl 6.2 L Dsl Engine +375
8 cyl 7.4 L Engine +135
Air Conditioning +145
Camper/Towing Package +60
Cruise Control +35
Dual Air Conditioning +240
Limited Slip Diff +45
Power Door Locks +35
Power Windows +35

YUKON 1992

Totally redesigned and based on same platform and sheetmetal as Sierra pickup, the old Jimmy becomes the Yukon to differentiate it from the Sonoma-based Jimmy. Six-passenger seating is standard. Cargo area gets fixed metal roof rather than fiberglass shell. Four-wheel ABS is standard and works in 4WD. New Sport appearance package includes two-tone paint and wheelwell flares. Diesel option is dropped. Five-speed manual is standard transmission. An automatic is optional. Shift-on-the-fly 4WD is standard.

Category H

Model	Trade-in	Market
2 Dr SLE 4WD Utility	7605	9880
2 Dr STD 4WD Utility	7175	9320
2 Dr Sport 4WD Utility	7495	9735

OPTIONS FOR YUKON

Auto 4-Speed Transmission +160
SLE Pkg +220
Sport Handling Pkg +290
Air Conditioning +145
Camper/Towing Package +60
Cruise Control +35
Limited Slip Diff +45
Power Door Locks +35
Power Drivers Seat +50
Power Windows +35

1991 GMC

JIMMY 1991

Throttle-body fuel injection is improved, and more powerful alternator is standard.

Category H

Model	Trade-in	Market
2 Dr STD 4WD Utility	3700	5070

OPTIONS FOR JIMMY

8 cyl 6.2 L Dsl Engine +345
Auto 4-Speed Transmission +130
Air Conditioning +120
Camper/Towing Package +50
Cruise Control +30
Limited Slip Diff +40
Power Door Locks +30
Power Windows +30

R35 PICKUP 1991

Category H

Model	Trade-in	Market
4 Dr SLE Crew Cab LB	5450	7465
4 Dr STD Crew Cab LB	5075	6950

OPTIONS FOR R35 PICKUP

8 cyl 6.2 L Dsl Engine +345
8 cyl 7.4 L Engine +115
Auto 4-Speed Transmission +130
Air Conditioning +120
Cruise Control +30
Dual Rear Wheels +120
Power Door Locks +30
Power Windows +30

S15 JIMMY 1991

Four-door models get new Gypsy package on the options list. It includes two-tone paint, alloy wheels and chrome trim. A heavy-duty battery is standard on all models, and 2WD Jimmys can be equipped with 15-inch alloy wheels. Front bench seat option will give four-door six passenger capacity. SLT Touring Package with softer suspension added midyear.

RATINGS (SCALE OF 1-10)

Overall	Safety	Reliability	Performance	Comfort	Value
5.5	3.7	5.4	6.8	7.1	4.3

Category G

Model	Trade-in	Market
2 Dr SLE Utility	2960	4230
2 Dr SLE 4WD Utility	3380	4825
4 Dr SLE 4WD Wgn	3895	5565
2 Dr SLS Utility	2950	4215
2 Dr SLS 4WD Utility	3275	4675
4 Dr SLS Wgn	3115	4450
4 Dr SLS 4WD Wgn	3460	4940
4 Dr SLT 4WD Wgn	4115	5875
2 Dr STD Utility	2725	3890

Don't forget to refer to the Mileage Adjustment Table at the back of this book!

Model Description	Trade-in Value	Market Value
2 Dr STD 4WD Utility	2980	4255
4 Dr STD 4WD Wgn	2830	4045
4 Dr STD 4WD Wgn	3085	4410

OPTIONS FOR S15 JIMMY
Auto 4-Speed Transmission +130
Air Conditioning[Std on SLT] +120
Camper/Towing Package +45
Cruise Control[Std on SLT] +30
Limited Slip Diff +40
Power Door Locks[Std on SLT] +35
Power Windows[Std on SLT] +35

SAFARI   1991

Cargo models gain the 4.3-liter V6 as standard equipment. A new GT model is available with sport suspension, rally wheels, front air dam, fog lights, and a sport steering wheel. Side and rear windows now have swing-out glass. Extended-length models can now be ordered with the Sport Appearance Package. A high-output, 4.3-liter V6 option is expected midyear.

RATINGS (SCALE OF 1-10)

Overall	Safety	Reliability	Performance	Comfort	Value
6.3	3.9	6.2	7.2	6.6	7.7

Category G

Model Description	Trade-in Value	Market Value
2 Dr SLE Pass. Van	2660	3800
2 Dr SLE 4WD Pass. Van	3485	4975
2 Dr SLE Pass. Van Ext	2985	4265
2 Dr SLE 4WD Pass. Van Ext	4205	6005
2 Dr SLT Pass. Van	2800	4000
2 Dr SLT 4WD Pass. Van	3665	5235
2 Dr SLT Pass. Van Ext	3075	4395
2 Dr SLT 4WD Pass. Van Ext	3885	5550
2 Dr STD Cargo Van	2085	2980
2 Dr STD 4WD Cargo Van	2840	4055
2 Dr STD Cargo Van Ext	2425	3465
2 Dr STD 4WD Cargo Van Ext	3010	4300
2 Dr STD Pass. Van	2655	3790
2 Dr STD 4WD Pass. Van	3290	4700
2 Dr STD Pass. Van Ext	2980	4260
2 Dr STD 4WD Pass. Van Ext	3670	5245

OPTIONS FOR SAFARI
6 cyl 4.3 L HO Engine +60
Sport Handling Pkg +135
Air Conditioning +120
Camper/Towing Package +45
Cruise Control +30
Dual Air Conditioning +140
Power Door Locks +35
Power Drivers Seat +40
Power Windows +35

SIERRA PICKUP   1991

7.4-liter V8 is reworked, and can be mated to four-speed automatic transmission. New gauge cluster includes a tachometer. Bucket seats are a new option. Air conditioners get a new recirculation mode. Two-wheel-drive models add tow hooks to the options list. Special gets new steering wheel and revised outside mirrors.

RATINGS (SCALE OF 1-10)

Overall	Safety	Reliability	Performance	Comfort	Value
N/A	N/A	6.3	N/A	N/A	N/A

SIERRA 1500

Category H

Model Description	Trade-in Value	Market Value
2 Dr C1500 Ext Cab LB	4670	6395
2 Dr C1500 Ext Cab SB	4590	6285
2 Dr C1500 Ext Cab Stepside SB	4755	6515
2 Dr C1500 Std Cab LB	4305	5895
2 Dr C1500 Std Cab SB	4240	5810
2 Dr C1500 Std Cab Stepside SB	4565	6255
2 Dr C1500 SLE Ext Cab LB	4925	6745
2 Dr C1500 SLE Ext Cab SB	4880	6685
2 Dr C1500 SLE Std Cab LB	4630	6340
2 Dr C1500 SLE Std Cab SB	4530	6205
2 Dr C1500 SLE Std Cab Stepside SB	4745	6500
2 Dr C1500 SLX Ext Cab LB	4730	6480
2 Dr C1500 SLX Ext Cab SB	4645	6365
2 Dr C1500 SLX Std Cab LB	4185	5735
2 Dr C1500 SLX Std Cab SB	4135	5665
2 Dr C1500 SLX Std Cab Stepside SB	4400	6025
2 Dr K1500 4WD Ext Cab LB	5735	7855
2 Dr K1500 4WD Ext Cab SB	5645	7735
2 Dr K1500 4WD Std Cab LB	5145	7045
2 Dr K1500 4WD Std Cab SB	5040	6905
2 Dr K1500 4WD Std Cab Stepside SB	5400	7400
2 Dr K1500 SLE 4WD Ext Cab LB	5735	7855
2 Dr K1500 SLE 4WD Ext Cab SB	5670	7770
2 Dr K1500 SLE 4WD Std Cab LB	5485	7515
2 Dr K1500 SLE 4WD Std Cab SB	5410	7410
2 Dr K1500 SLE 4WD Std Cab Stepside SB	5635	7720
2 Dr K1500 SLX 4WD Ext Cab LB	5735	7855
2 Dr K1500 SLX 4WD Ext Cab SB	5680	7780
2 Dr K1500 SLX 4WD Std Cab LB	5195	7115
2 Dr K1500 SLX 4WD Std Cab SB	5095	6980
2 Dr K1500 SLX 4WD Std Cab Stepside SB	5375	7360

Model Description	Trade-in Value	Market Value	Model Description	Trade-in Value	Market Value
SIERRA 2500			*Category G*		
Category H			2 Dr SLE Ext Cab SB	2605	3720
2 Dr C2500 Ext Cab LB	4955	6785	2 Dr SLE 4WD Ext Cab SB	3480	4970
2 Dr C2500 Std Cab LB	4400	6025	2 Dr SLE Std Cab LB	2420	3460
2 Dr C2500 SLE Ext Cab LB	5280	7235	2 Dr SLE 4WD Std Cab LB	3370	4815
2 Dr C2500 SLE Ext Cab SB	5140	7040	2 Dr SLE Std Cab SB	2275	3250
2 Dr C2500 SLE Std Cab LB	4520	6195	2 Dr SLE 4WD Std Cab SB	3215	4590
2 Dr C2500 SLX Ext Cab LB	5715	7830	2 Dr STD Ext Cab SB	2515	3595
2 Dr C2500 SLX Std Cab LB	4440	6080	2 Dr STD 4WD Ext Cab SB	3415	4875
2 Dr K2500 4WD Std Cab LB	5440	7450	2 Dr STD Std Cab LB	1975	2820
2 Dr K2500 SLE 4WD Ext Cab LB	6170	8450	2 Dr STD 4WD Std Cab LB	3220	4600
2 Dr K2500 SLE 4WD Ext Cab SB	6035	8265	2 Dr STD Std Cab SB	1885	2695
2 Dr K2500 SLE 4WD Std Cab LB	5400	7395	2 Dr STD 4WD Std Cab SB	3140	4485
2 Dr K2500 SLX 4WD Ext Cab LB	6385	8745	2 Dr Special Std Cab SB	1550	2215
2 Dr K2500 SLX 4WD Ext Cab SB	6250	8560			
2 Dr K2500 SLX 4WD Std Cab LB	5250	7195			

SIERRA 3500

Category H

Model Description	Trade-in Value	Market Value
2 Dr C3500 Std Cab LB	5915	8100
2 Dr C3500 SLE Ext Cab LB	6825	9350
2 Dr C3500 SLE Std Cab LB	6225	8525
2 Dr K3500 4WD Ext Cab LB	6695	9170
2 Dr K3500 SLE 4WD Ext Cab LB	7735	10595

OPTIONS FOR SIERRA PICKUP

8 cyl 5.0 L Engine +85
8 cyl 5.7 L Engine +120
8 cyl 6.2 L Dsl Engine +345
8 cyl 7.4 L Engine +115
Auto 4-Speed Transmission +130
Sport Handling Pkg +125
Air Conditioning +120
Camper/Towing Package +50
Cruise Control +30
Dual Rear Wheels[Opt on C3500,SLE] +120
Limited Slip Diff +40
Power Door Locks +30
Power Windows +30

SONOMA 1991

Introduced in January, 1990, Sonoma is a S15 Pickup with a new name and an exterior facelift that includes a new grille, fresh trim and restyled wheels. Four-wheel drive models get the 4.3-liter V6 as standard equipment. High Sierra trim is dropped, and Sierra Classic trim is changed to SLE. Midyear, the base four-cylinder powerplant gets more horsepower.

RATINGS (SCALE OF 1-10)

Overall	Safety	Reliability	Performance	Comfort	Value
N/A	2.9	6	7.2	7	N/A

OPTIONS FOR SONOMA

6 cyl 2.8 L Engine +60
6 cyl 4.3 L Engine +90
Auto 4-Speed Transmission[Opt on SLE,STD] +130
Air Conditioning[Opt on SLE,Special,STD] +120
Camper/Towing Package +45
Cruise Control[Opt on SLE,STD] +30
Limited Slip Diff[Opt on SLE,STD] +40
Power Door Locks[Opt on SLE,STD] +35
Power Windows[Opt on SLE,STD] +35

SUBURBAN 1991

Manual transmission is dropped.

Category H

Model Description	Trade-in Value	Market Value
4 Dr R1500 Wgn	4850	6645
4 Dr R2500 Wgn	5545	7595
4 Dr V1500 4WD Wgn	5460	7480
4 Dr V2500 4WD Wgn	6120	8385

OPTIONS FOR SUBURBAN

8 cyl 6.2 L Dsl Engine +345
8 cyl 7.4 L Engine +115
SLE Pkg +240
Air Conditioning +120
Camper/Towing Package +50
Cruise Control +30
Dual Air Conditioning +195
Limited Slip Diff +40
Power Door Locks +30
Power Windows +30
Rear Bench Seat +45

SYCLONE 1991

This Sonoma pickup is an all-wheel-drive turbocharged V6 terror with a Corvette automatic transmission, four-wheel ABS and 280 horsepower. GMC says acceleration from zero to 60 is accomplished in 4.6 seconds.

Model Description	Trade-in Value	Market Value
Category I		
2 Dr STD Turbo 4WD Std Cab SB	10685	14250

V3500 PICKUP 1991

Category H		
4 Dr STD 4WD Crew Cab LB	6430	8810

OPTIONS FOR V3500 PICKUP
8 cyl 6.2 L Dsl Engine +345
8 cyl 7.4 L Engine +115
Auto 4-Speed Transmission +130
SLE Pkg - R&v Series +130
Air Conditioning +120
Power Door Locks +30
Power Windows +30

VANDURA/RALLY WAGON 1991

7.4-liter engine can be equipped with a four-speed automatic transmission.

RALLY WAGON

Category H		
2 Dr G15 Rally Wagon	4055	5555
2 Dr G15 Rally Wagon Ext	4025	5510
2 Dr G25 Rally Wagon	3855	5280
2 Dr G35 Rally Wagon Ext	3415	4680
2 Dr G35 STX Rally Wagon Ext	3805	5215

VANDURA

Category H		
2 Dr G15 Vandura	3135	4295
2 Dr G15 Vandura Ext	3065	4200
2 Dr G25 Vandura	3305	4525
2 Dr G25 Vandura Ext	3250	4450
2 Dr G35 Vandura	3600	4930
2 Dr G35 Vandura Ext	3490	4780

OPTIONS FOR VANDURA/RALLY WAGON
8 cyl 5.0 L Engine +85
8 cyl 5.7 L Engine[Opt on G25,G15] +120
8 cyl 6.2 L Dsl Engine +345
8 cyl 7.4 L Engine +115
Air Conditioning +120
Camper/Towing Package +50
Cruise Control +30
Dual Air Conditioning +195
Power Door Locks +30
Power Windows +30

1990 GMC

JIMMY 1990

Rear-wheel ABS that works only in 2WD is added.

Category H		
2 Dr STD 4WD Utility	3910	5430
2 Dr Sierra Classic 4WD Utility		
	4120	5720

OPTIONS FOR JIMMY
8 cyl 6.2 L Dsl Engine +290
Auto 4-Speed Transmission +105
Air Conditioning +100
Limited Slip Diff +30

S15 JIMMY 1990

A four-door model with standard four-wheel ABS is added to the lineup, and the 2.8-liter engine is dropped in favor of the more powerful 160-horsepower, 4.3-liter V6.

RATINGS (SCALE OF 1-10)

Overall	Safety	Reliability	Performance	Comfort	Value
5.9	3.9	5.7	6.8	7.1	6.2

Category G		
2 Dr Gypsy Utility	2435	3690
2 Dr Gypsy 4WD Utility	2880	4365
2 Dr STD Utility	2040	3090
2 Dr STD 4WD Utility	2770	4195
2 Dr Sierra Classic Utility	2390	3620
2 Dr Sierra Classic 4WD Utility		
	2845	4310

OPTIONS FOR S15 JIMMY
Auto 4-Speed Transmission +105
Air Conditioning +100
Camper/Towing Package +35
Cruise Control +25
Limited Slip Diff +35
Power Door Locks +30
Power Windows +30

S15 PICKUP 1990

Category G		
2 Dr EL Std Cab SB	1915	2900
2 Dr High Sierra Ext Cab SB	2540	3850
2 Dr High Sierra 4WD Ext Cab SB		
	3080	4665
2 Dr High Sierra Std Cab LB	2065	3125
2 Dr High Sierra Std Cab SB	1995	3025
2 Dr High Sierra 4WD Std Cab SB		
	3015	4570
2 Dr STD Ext Cab SB	2455	3720
2 Dr STD 4WD Ext Cab SB	2850	4320
2 Dr STD Std Cab LB	1975	2995
2 Dr STD Std Cab SB	1935	2935
2 Dr Sierra Classic Ext Cab SB		
	2530	3830
2 Dr Sierra Classic 4WD Ext Cab SB		
	3070	4650
2 Dr Sierra Classic Std Cab LB		
	1945	2945

Don't forget to refer to the Mileage Adjustment Table at the back of this book!

Model Description	Trade-in Value	Market Value
2 Dr Sierra Classic 4WD Std Cab LB	2530	3830
2 Dr Sierra Classic Std Cab SB	2045	3100
2 Dr Sierra Classic 4WD Std Cab SB	2465	3735

OPTIONS FOR S15 PICKUP
6 cyl 2.8 L Engine +45
6 cyl 4.3 L Engine +75
Auto 4-Speed Transmission +105
Air Conditioning +100
Camper/Towing Package +35
Cruise Control +25
Limited Slip Diff +35
Power Door Locks +30
Power Windows +30

SAFARI   1990

All-wheel drive is newly optional, and an extended body style is introduced. Standard engine on passenger models is a 150-horsepower 4.3-liter V6. The optional sport suspension, and the Sport Appearance Package, will not be available on AWD vans. Four-wheel ABS is standard on all but commercially purchased cargo vans.

RATINGS (SCALE OF 1-10)

Overall	Safety	Reliability	Performance	Comfort	Value
6.2	3.8	5.5	7.2	6.6	8.1

Category G

Model Description	Trade-in Value	Market Value
2 Dr SLE Pass. Van	2130	3225
2 Dr SLE 4WD Pass. Van	2860	4335
2 Dr SLE Pass. Van Ext	2505	3795
2 Dr SLE 4WD Pass. Van Ext	3150	4770
2 Dr SLT Pass. Van	2545	3855
2 Dr SLT 4WD Pass. Van	2925	4435
2 Dr SLT Pass. Van Ext	2800	4245
2 Dr SLT 4WD Pass. Van Ext	3110	4710
2 Dr SLX Pass. Van	2005	3040
2 Dr SLX 4WD Pass. Van	2705	4100
2 Dr SLX Pass. Van Ext	2370	3590
2 Dr SLX 4WD Pass. Van Ext	3090	4685
2 Dr STD Cargo Van	1610	2440
2 Dr STD 4WD Cargo Van	2330	3530
2 Dr STD Cargo Van Ext	1905	2890

OPTIONS FOR SAFARI
6 cyl 4.3 L Engine[Std on SLE,SLT,SLX,4WD] +75
GT Pkg +135
Air Conditioning +100
Camper/Towing Package +35
Cruise Control +25
Dual Air Conditioning +115
Power Door Locks +30

Power Drivers Seat +35
Power Windows +30

SIERRA PICKUP   1990

Stripped Special model is added to serve as a serious work truck. C/K 2500 Bonus Cab model dropped.

RATINGS (SCALE OF 1-10)

Overall	Safety	Reliability	Performance	Comfort	Value
N/A	N/A	6.4	N/A	N/A	N/A

SIERRA 1500

Category H

Model Description	Trade-in Value	Market Value
2 Dr C1500 Ext Cab LB	4400	6110
2 Dr C1500 Ext Cab SB	4330	6015
2 Dr C1500 Std Cab LB	3685	5115
2 Dr C1500 Std Cab SB	3630	5040
2 Dr C1500 Std Cab Stepside SB	3865	5370
2 Dr C1500 SLE Ext Cab LB	4615	6410
2 Dr C1500 SLE Ext Cab SB	4545	6315
2 Dr C1500 SLE Std Cab LB	4215	5855
2 Dr C1500 SLE Std Cab SB	4135	5740
2 Dr C1500 SLE Std Cab Stepside SB	4335	6020
2 Dr C1500 SLX Ext Cab LB	4485	6230
2 Dr C1500 SLX Ext Cab SB	4400	6110
2 Dr C1500 SLX Std Cab LB	3810	5295
2 Dr C1500 SLX Std Cab SB	3735	5185
2 Dr C1500 SLX Std Cab Stepside SB	3955	5495
2 Dr K1500 4WD Ext Cab LB	5250	7295
2 Dr K1500 4WD Ext Cab SB	5185	7200
2 Dr K1500 4WD Std Cab LB	4905	6815
2 Dr K1500 4WD Std Cab SB	4840	6720
2 Dr K1500 SLE 4WD Ext Cab LB	5250	7290
2 Dr K1500 SLE 4WD Ext Cab SB	5125	7115
2 Dr K1500 SLE 4WD Ext Cab Stepside SB	5330	7405
2 Dr K1500 SLE 4WD Std Cab LB	5020	6975
2 Dr K1500 SLE 4WD Std Cab SB	4935	6855
2 Dr K1500 SLE 4WD Std Cab Stepside SB	5165	7175
2 Dr K1500 SLX 4WD Ext Cab LB	5115	7105
2 Dr K1500 SLX 4WD Ext Cab SB	5010	6955
2 Dr K1500 SLX 4WD Std Cab LB	4710	6540
2 Dr K1500 SLX 4WD Std Cab SB	4600	6390
2 Dr K1500 Special 4WD Std Cab LB	4555	6325

GMC 90

Model Description	Trade-in Value	Market Value	Model Description	Trade-in Value	Market Value
SIERRA 2500			**OPTIONS FOR SUBURBAN**		
Category H			*8 cyl 6.2 L Dsl Engine +290*		
2 Dr C2500 Ext Cab LB	4400	6110	*8 cyl 7.4 L Engine +55*		
2 Dr C2500 Ext Cab SB	4330	6015	*Auto 4-Speed Transmission[Std on R15] +105*		
2 Dr C2500 Std Cab LB	4055	5630	*SLE Pkg +195*		
2 Dr C2500 SLE Ext Cab LB	4470	6210	*Air Conditioning +100*		
2 Dr C2500 SLE Ext Cab SB	4375	6075	*Camper/Towing Package +40*		
2 Dr C2500 SLE Std Cab LB	4025	5590	*Dual Air Conditioning +160*		
2 Dr C2500 SLX Std Cab LB	4305	5980	*Limited Slip Diff +30*		
2 Dr K2500 4WD Std Cab LB	4905	6810			

V3500 PICKUP · 1990

Model Description	Trade-in Value	Market Value
Category H		
4 Dr SLE 4WD Crew Cab LB	5405	7505
4 Dr STD 4WD Crew Cab LB	5385	7480

(continued SIERRA 2500)

Model Description	Trade-in Value	Market Value
2 Dr K2500 SLE 4WD Ext Cab LB	5305	7370
2 Dr K2500 SLE 4WD Ext Cab SB	5165	7175
2 Dr K2500 SLE 4WD Std Cab LB	4650	6455
2 Dr K2500 SLX 4WD Ext Cab LB	5590	7765
2 Dr K2500 SLX 4WD Ext Cab SB	5420	7530
2 Dr K2500 SLX 4WD Std Cab LB	4830	6710

OPTIONS FOR V3500 PICKUP
8 cyl 6.2 L Dsl Engine +290
8 cyl 7.4 L Engine +55
Auto 3-Speed Transmission +80
Air Conditioning +100
Limited Slip Diff +30

SIERRA 3500

Model Description	Trade-in Value	Market Value
Category H		
2 Dr C3500 Ext Cab LB	5805	8065
2 Dr C3500 Std Cab LB	4620	6420
2 Dr C3500 SLE Ext Cab LB	5905	8200
2 Dr C3500 SLE Std Cab LB	5355	7435
2 Dr C3500 SLX Ext Cab LB	5665	7865
2 Dr C3500 SLX Std Cab LB	5350	7430
2 Dr K3500 4WD Ext Cab LB	6125	8510
2 Dr K3500 4WD Std Cab LB	5350	7430
2 Dr K3500 SLE 4WD Ext Cab LB	6315	8770
2 Dr K3500 SLE 4WD Std Cab LB	6205	8620
2 Dr K3500 SLX 4WD Ext Cab LB	6665	9260

VANDURA/RALLY WAGON · 1990

No changes.

RALLY WAGON

Model Description	Trade-in Value	Market Value
Category H		
2 Dr G15 Rally Wagon	3610	5015
2 Dr G15 Rally Wagon Ext	3700	5140
2 Dr G25 Rally Wagon	3005	4175
2 Dr G25 STX Rally Wagon	3590	4990
2 Dr G35 Rally Wagon	3255	4520
2 Dr G35 STX Rally Wagon	3410	4735
2 Dr STD Pass. Van Ext	3145	4370

VANDURA

Model Description	Trade-in Value	Market Value
Category H		
2 Dr G15 Vandura	2450	3405
2 Dr G15 Vandura Ext	2385	3310
2 Dr G25 Vandura	2550	3545
2 Dr G25 Vandura Ext	2510	3485
2 Dr G35 Vandura	2795	3885
2 Dr G35 Vandura Ext	2730	3790

OPTIONS FOR SIERRA PICKUP
8 cyl 5.0 L Engine +70
8 cyl 5.7 L Engine +95
8 cyl 6.2 L Dsl Engine +290
Auto 3-Speed Transmission +75
Auto 4-Speed Transmission +105
Sport Handling Pkg +110
Air Conditioning +100
Camper/Towing Package +40
Dual Rear Wheels +100
Limited Slip Diff +30

OPTIONS FOR VANDURA/RALLY WAGON
8 cyl 5.0 L Engine +70
8 cyl 5.7 L Engine[Opt on G15, G25, Vandura] +95
8 cyl 6.2 L Dsl Engine +290
8 cyl 7.4 L Engine +55
Auto 4-Speed Transmission[Std on STX, Rally Wagon, Rally Wagon Ext] +30
Air Conditioning +100
Camper/Towing Package +40
Dual Air Conditioning +160

SUBURBAN · 1990

Rear-wheel ABS that works in 2WD only is added.

Model Description	Trade-in Value	Market Value
Category H		
4 Dr R1500 Wgn	4205	5840
4 Dr R2500 Wgn	4495	6245
4 Dr V1500 4WD Wgn	4855	6740
4 Dr V2500 4WD Wgn	5260	7305

Model Description	Trade-in Value	Market Value	Model Description	Trade-in Value	Market Value

HONDA 99

HONDA Japan

1993 Honda Civic

1999 HONDA

ACCORD 1999

The coupes remain unchanged after their recent overhaul, but the sedans receive new seat fabric, and the LX and EX sedans now feature foldaway side mirrors.

RATINGS (SCALE OF 1-10)

Overall	Safety	Reliability	Performance	Comfort	Value
N/A	7.1	8.9	7.6	8.3	N/A

Category E

4 Dr DX Sdn	10405	12535
2 Dr EX Cpe	14365	17305
4 Dr EX Sdn	14515	17490
2 Dr EX V6 Cpe	16400	19760
4 Dr EX V6 Sdn	16580	19975
2 Dr LX Cpe	12145	14635
4 Dr LX Sdn	12295	14815
2 Dr LX V6 Cpe	14185	17090
4 Dr LX V6 Sdn	14325	17260

OPTIONS FOR ACCORD
Auto 4-Speed Transmission[Std on EX V6,LX V6] +590
Air Conditioning[Opt on DX] +605
Aluminum/Alloy Wheels[Std on EX,EX V6] +245
Anti-Lock Brakes[Opt on LX] +500
Keyless Entry System[Opt on LX] +115
Leather Seats[Std on EX V6] +645
Power Drivers Seat[Opt on EX] +230

CIVIC 1999

The Civic gets new front and rear styling as well as an improved instrument panel. The DX trim gets a rear wiper and washer, a cargo cover and a low-fuel warning light. A hotrod Si model is introduced mid-year with a 160-hp VTEC engine.

RATINGS (SCALE OF 1-10)

Overall	Safety	Reliability	Performance	Comfort	Value
N/A	6.8	9	8.2	7.8	N/A

Category E

2 Dr CX Hbk	6725	8100
2 Dr DX Cpe	8410	10130
2 Dr DX Hbk	7975	9610
4 Dr DX Sdn	8565	10320
2 Dr EX Cpe	11065	13330
4 Dr EX Sdn	11255	13560
2 Dr HX Cpe	9305	11210
4 Dr LX Sdn	9810	11820
2 Dr SI Cpe	11320	13640
4 Dr VP Sdn	9070	10930

OPTIONS FOR CIVIC
Auto 4-Speed Transmission[Std on VP] +630
AM/FM Compact Disc Player[Opt on DX,LX] +340
Air Conditioning[Opt on CX,DX,HX] +605

CR-V 1999

The CR-V gains 20 horsepower, bringing the total output to 146. Automatic transmission models have a revised column shifter with an overdrive switch. The power window buttons are illuminated, the spare tire cover has been upgraded, and the front passenger seat is equipped with an armrest. Since Honda has effectively addressed all of our previous gripes with this year's changes, we'll have to get more creative with our complaints.

RATINGS (SCALE OF 1-10)

Overall	Safety	Reliability	Performance	Comfort	Value
N/A	N/A	N/A	8	8.5	N/A

Category G

4 Dr EX 4WD Wgn	13955	16615
4 Dr LX Wgn	12450	14820
4 Dr LX 4WD Wgn	13105	15600

OPTIONS FOR CR-V
Auto 4-Speed Transmission[Std on 2WD] +590
AM/FM Compact Disc Player[Std on EX] +245

PASSPORT 1999

Last year, the Passport and the identical Isuzu Rodeo were completely redesigned, so there are no new changes this year.

RATINGS (SCALE OF 1-10)

Overall	Safety	Reliability	Performance	Comfort	Value
N/A	7.6	N/A	6.6	7.3	N/A

Don't forget to refer to the Mileage Adjustment Table at the back of this book!

Model Description	Trade-in Value	Market Value
Category G		
4 Dr EX Wgn	17415	20735
4 Dr EX 4WD Wgn	18520	22050
4 Dr LX Wgn	14240	16955
4 Dr LX 4WD Wgn	15385	18315

OPTIONS FOR PASSPORT

Auto 4-Speed Transmission[Std on EX] +850
Leather Seats +575
Limited Slip Diff[Std on EX] +200
Swing Out Tire Carrier[Std on EX] +145

PRELUDE   1999

Prelude gets another five horsepower, bringing it up to 200 horsepower with the manual transmission and 195 horsepower with the automatic. A remote keyless entry system is added, as is an air filtration system, mesh-style grille and new interior color choices.

RATINGS (SCALE OF 1-10)

Overall	Safety	Reliability	Performance	Comfort	Value
N/A	N/A	N/A	8.6	6.9	N/A

Category F		
2 Dr STD Cpe	16035	18865
2 Dr Type SH Cpe	18180	21390

OPTIONS FOR PRELUDE

Auto 4-Speed Transmission +740

1998 HONDA

ACCORD   1998

Honda redesigns its best-seller for 1998. A 3.0-liter V6 engine makes its debut in LX V6 and EX V6 models, marking the first six-cylinder VTEC in the Honda lineup. The standard 2.3-liter four-banger is also re-engineered, as is the chassis. The new Accord is also larger, and the interior boasts more room inside than any of Accord's competitors.

RATINGS (SCALE OF 1-10)

Overall	Safety	Reliability	Performance	Comfort	Value
7.2	6.9	8.2	7.6	8.3	5

Category E		
4 Dr DX Sdn	9695	11680
2 Dr EX Cpe	13120	15810
4 Dr EX Sdn	13290	16010
2 Dr EX V6 Cpe	15250	18375
4 Dr EX V6 Sdn	15415	18570
2 Dr LX Cpe	11030	13290
4 Dr LX Sdn	11185	13475
2 Dr LX V6 Cpe	12875	15515
4 Dr LX V6 Sdn	13035	15705

OPTIONS FOR ACCORD

Auto 4-Speed Transmission[Std on EX V6, LX V6] +490
Air Conditioning[Opt on DX] +495
Aluminum/Alloy Wheels[Std on EX, EX V6] +200
Anti-Lock Brakes[Std on EX, EX V6, LX V6] +410
Leather Seats[Std on EX V6] +530
Power Drivers Seat[Std on EX V6, LX V6] +185

CIVIC   1998

Last year's best-selling small car gets minor revisions: select models get new wheelcovers, a rear hatch handle, and map lights.

RATINGS (SCALE OF 1-10)

Overall	Safety	Reliability	Performance	Comfort	Value
7.5	6.7	8.7	8.2	7.8	6

Category E		
2 Dr CX Hbk	6325	7620
2 Dr DX Cpe	8020	9665
2 Dr DX Hbk	7680	9250
4 Dr DX Sdn	8200	9880
2 Dr EX Cpe	10315	12430
4 Dr EX Sdn	10500	12650
2 Dr HX Cpe	8840	10650
4 Dr LX Sdn	9140	11010

OPTIONS FOR CIVIC

Auto 4-Speed Transmission +520
AM/FM Compact Disc Player +275
Air Conditioning[Std on EX, LX] +495
Power Steering[Opt on CX] +155

CR-V   1998

A manual transmission lowers the ante, making the CR-V a more attractive value than before. Also available is a front-wheel drive LX model, and the EX trim level now includes a CD player, anti-lock brakes, and remote keyless entry.

RATINGS (SCALE OF 1-10)

Overall	Safety	Reliability	Performance	Comfort	Value
N/A	7.3	8.5	7.8	8.5	N/A

Category G		
4 Dr EX 4WD Wgn	12980	15455
4 Dr LX Wgn	11665	13885
4 Dr LX 4WD Wgn	12270	14610

OPTIONS FOR CR-V

Auto 4-Speed Transmission[Std on 2WD] +490

ODYSSEY   1998

The engine is upgraded to a more sophisticated 2.3-liter, good for an extra 10 horsepower and seven foot-pounds of torque. New looks up front come from a revised bumper and grille, and the interior gets dressed in new fabric.

Don't forget to refer to the Mileage Adjustment Table at the back of this book!

Model Description	Trade-in Value	Market Value

RATINGS (SCALE OF 1-10)

Overall	Safety	Reliability	Performance	Comfort	Value
7.7	7.5	9.2	7.2	7.1	7.3

Category G

4 Dr EX Pass. Van	15805	18815
4 Dr LX Pass. Van	14160	16860

OPTIONS FOR ODYSSEY
6 Passenger Seating[Opt on LX] +315
Captain Chairs (4)[Opt on LX] +380

PASSPORT 1998

Like its Isuzu Rodeo counterpart, the Passport has been completely revised from top to bottom. The Passport gets modernized styling, a user-friendly interior, more powerful V6 and added room for passengers and cargo.

RATINGS (SCALE OF 1-10)

Overall	Safety	Reliability	Performance	Comfort	Value
7	7.3	7.1	6.6	7.3	6.6

Category G

4 Dr EX Wgn	15830	18845
4 Dr EX 4WD Wgn	16825	20030
4 Dr LX Wgn	12895	15350
4 Dr LX 4WD Wgn	13960	16620

OPTIONS FOR PASSPORT
Auto 4-Speed Transmission[Opt on LX] +705
Compact Disc W/fm/tape +290
Leather Seats +470
Limited Slip Diff[Opt on LX] +165
Swing Out Tire Carrier +120

PRELUDE 1998

The Prelude doesn't change for 1998, because you don't mess with success. (Pssst, buy this car!)

RATINGS (SCALE OF 1-10)

Overall	Safety	Reliability	Performance	Comfort	Value
N/A	N/A	8.8	8.6	6.9	4.2

Category F

2 Dr STD Cpe	13465	16030
2 Dr Type SH Cpe	15845	18865

OPTIONS FOR PRELUDE
Auto 4-Speed Transmission +615

1997 HONDA

ACCORD 1997

Changes to the ever-popular Accord include the deletion of antilock brakes on the LX five-speed models and the discontinuation of the EX coupes with leather. No other changes for the 1997 Accord.

Model Description	Trade-in Value	Market Value

RATINGS (SCALE OF 1-10)

Overall	Safety	Reliability	Performance	Comfort	Value
7.5	6.8	8.9	7.8	8	5.8

Category E

4 Dr DX Sdn	8330	10160
2 Dr EX Cpe	11300	13780
4 Dr EX Sdn	11495	14020
4 Dr EX Wgn	11970	14600
4 Dr EX V6 Sdn	13445	16395
2 Dr LX Cpe	9740	11875
4 Dr LX Sdn	9920	12095
4 Dr LX Wgn	10405	12690
4 Dr LX V6 Sdn	11560	14095
2 Dr Special Edition Cpe	10505	12810
4 Dr Special Edition Sdn	10705	13055
4 Dr Value Sdn	9305	11345

OPTIONS FOR ACCORD
Auto 4-Speed Transmission[Opt on DX,LX,EX Sdn, EX Cpe] +400
Air Conditioning[Opt on DX] +405
Aluminum/Alloy Wheels[Opt on LX] +165
Anti-Lock Brakes[Opt on LX] +335
Compact Disc W/fm/tape[Opt on EX,EX V6] +290
Leather Seats[Opt on EX] +430
Power Drivers Seat[Opt on EX] +150

CIVIC 1997

For some reason, Honda deletes the Civic EX Coupe five-speed with ABS model. Maybe they think that people who like to row their own gears don't worry about whether they can stop or not. DX models receive new wheel covers, all Civics get 14-inch wheels, and the LX sedan gets air conditioning.

RATINGS (SCALE OF 1-10)

Overall	Safety	Reliability	Performance	Comfort	Value
7	6.7	8.6	8.2	7.8	3.9

Category E

2 Dr CX Hbk	5905	7200
2 Dr DX Cpe	7420	9050
2 Dr DX Hbk	6980	8510
4 Dr DX Sdn	7595	9265
2 Dr EX Cpe	9070	11060
4 Dr EX Sdn	9250	11280
2 Dr HX Cpe	8250	10060
4 Dr LX Sdn	8405	10250

OPTIONS FOR CIVIC
Auto 4-Speed Transmission +450
AM/FM Compact Disc Player +225
Air Conditioning[Std on EX,LX] +405
Anti-Lock Brakes[Opt on Cpe] +335
Leather Seats +430

Don't forget to refer to the Mileage Adjustment Table at the back of this book!

Model Description	Trade-in Value	Market Value

Power Steering[Std on EX,HX,LX,DX,Sdn] +125
Rear Spoiler +105

CIVIC DEL SOL 1997

No changes to Honda's two-seater.

RATINGS (SCALE OF 1-10)

Overall	Safety	Reliability	Performance	Comfort	Value
N/A	N/A	N/A	N/A	N/A	4.1

Category F

2 Dr S Cpe	8270	9965
2 Dr Si Cpe	9585	11545
2 Dr VTEC Cpe	10155	12235

OPTIONS FOR CIVIC DEL SOL

Auto 4-Speed Transmission +445
Air Conditioning +415
Power Steering[Opt on S] +170

CR-V 1997

Priced competitively with mini-utes, the CR-V offers more passenger room and cargo capacity than its peers. The CR-V is available with antilock brakes.

RATINGS (SCALE OF 1-10)

Overall	Safety	Reliability	Performance	Comfort	Value
N/A	7.3	8.5	7.8	8.5	N/A

Category G

4 Dr STD 4WD Wgn	11245	13550

OPTIONS FOR CR-V

AM/FM Compact Disc Player +160
Aluminum/Alloy Wheels +165
Anti-Lock Brakes +295
Luggage Rack +80

ODYSSEY 1997

No changes for the 1997 Honda Odyssey.

RATINGS (SCALE OF 1-10)

Overall	Safety	Reliability	Performance	Comfort	Value
7.6	7.5	9.3	7.2	7.1	6.8

Category G

4 Dr EX Pass. Van	13980	16845
4 Dr LX Pass. Van	12540	15110

OPTIONS FOR ODYSSEY

AM/FM Compact Disc Player +160
Captain Chairs (4)[Opt on LX] +310
Luggage Rack +80

PASSPORT 1997

Honda drops the slow-selling DX four-cylinder Passport.

RATINGS (SCALE OF 1-10)

Overall	Safety	Reliability	Performance	Comfort	Value
7	6.8	8	6.6	7.1	6.6

Category G

4 Dr EX Wgn	13275	15995
4 Dr EX 4WD Wgn	14320	17250
4 Dr LX Wgn	10800	13015
4 Dr LX 4WD Wgn	11950	14400

OPTIONS FOR PASSPORT

Auto 4-Speed Transmission[Opt on LX,4WD] +545
Air Conditioning[Std on EX,4WD] +405
Limited Slip Diff[Opt on LX] +135

PRELUDE 1997

The Prelude is totally redesigned for 1997. A base model is available with a five-speed manual or four-speed automatic gearbox, but the top-of-the-line Type SH model, featuring Honda's new Active Torque Transfer System, can only be had as a manual. Both the base and Type SH Preludes feature last year's VTEC engine which produces 195-horsepower for 1997.

RATINGS (SCALE OF 1-10)

Overall	Safety	Reliability	Performance	Comfort	Value
N/A	N/A	8.6	8.6	6.9	2.6

Category F

2 Dr STD Cpe	12605	15185
2 Dr Type SH Cpe	14725	17740

1996 HONDA

ACCORD 1996

All Accords get revised styling, featuring new taillights and bumper covers. Wagons have a new roof rack, while sedans boast a new pass-through ski sack.

RATINGS (SCALE OF 1-10)

Overall	Safety	Reliability	Performance	Comfort	Value
7.3	6.8	8.8	7.8	8	5

Category E

4 Dr 25th Anniversary Sdn	8270	10340
4 Dr DX Sdn	7230	9040
2 Dr EX Cpe	9675	12095
4 Dr EX Sdn	10175	12720
4 Dr EX Wgn	10570	13215
4 Dr EX V6 Sdn	11450	14315
2 Dr LX Cpe	8330	10410
4 Dr LX Sdn	8795	10990
4 Dr LX Wgn	9065	11330
4 Dr LX V6 Sdn	9960	12450

OPTIONS FOR ACCORD

Auto 4-Speed Transmission[Opt on DX,LX,EX Cpe, EX Sdn] +325
Air Conditioning[Opt on DX] +330
Aluminum/Alloy Wheels[Opt on LX,LX V6] +135
Anti-Lock Brakes[Opt on LX] +275

Don't forget to refer to the Mileage Adjustment Table at the back of this book!

Compact Disc W/fm/tape +235
Leather Seats[Opt on EX] +355

CIVIC 1996

Keeping to their legendary four-year redesign schedule, Honda engineers have created a more powerful, and more contemporary Civic for 1996. This is a great car for those concerned about reliability and value, but who don't want to sacrifice style.

RATINGS (SCALE OF 1-10)

Overall	Safety	Reliability	Performance	Comfort	Value
7.1	6.7	8.4	8.2	7.8	4.4

Category E
2 Dr CX Hbk	5220	6525
2 Dr DX Cpe	6410	8010
2 Dr DX Hbk	5680	7100
4 Dr DX Sdn	6465	8085
2 Dr EX Cpe	8010	10015
4 Dr EX Sdn	8315	10395
2 Dr HX Cpe	7260	9075
4 Dr LX Sdn	7430	9290

OPTIONS FOR CIVIC
Auto 4-Speed Transmission +365
AM/FM Stereo Tape +125
Air Conditioning[Std on EX] +330
Aluminum/Alloy Wheels[Opt on DX] +135
Anti-Lock Brakes[Opt on LX,Cpe] +275
Compact Disc Changer +205
Power Steering[Std on EX,HX,LX,DX Sdn] +105
Rear Spoiler +85

CIVIC DEL SOL 1996

No changes to the 1996 del Sol.

RATINGS (SCALE OF 1-10)

Overall	Safety	Reliability	Performance	Comfort	Value
N/A	N/A	N/A	N/A	N/A	4

Category F
2 Dr S Cpe	7345	9065
2 Dr Si Cpe	8285	10230
2 Dr VTEC Cpe	9065	11195

OPTIONS FOR CIVIC DEL SOL
Auto 4-Speed Transmission +350
Air Conditioning +340
Power Steering[Opt on S] +140

ODYSSEY 1996

Minivan-wagon hybrid carries into 1996 sans changes.

RATINGS (SCALE OF 1-10)

Overall	Safety	Reliability	Performance	Comfort	Value
7.8	7.5	9.3	7.2	7.1	7.8

Category G
4 Dr EX Pass. Van	11790	14375
4 Dr LX Pass. Van	11110	13545

OPTIONS FOR ODYSSEY
Captain Chairs (4)[Opt on LX] +255

PASSPORT 1996

New wheels, dual airbags, available ABS, and a stronger V6 engine are the changes for the 1996 Isuzu Rodeo, er, we mean Passport.

RATINGS (SCALE OF 1-10)

Overall	Safety	Reliability	Performance	Comfort	Value
7.1	6.8	7.7	6.6	7.1	7.5

Category G
4 Dr DX Wgn	8210	10015
4 Dr EX Wgn	11590	14135
4 Dr EX 4WD Wgn	12130	14790
4 Dr LX Wgn	9640	11760
4 Dr LX 4WD Wgn	10815	13190

OPTIONS FOR PASSPORT
Auto 4-Speed Transmission[Opt on LX,4WD] +440
Air Conditioning[Std on EX,4WD] +330

PRELUDE 1996

This is the last year for the current-generation Prelude. All of the really exciting stuff happens in 1997.

RATINGS (SCALE OF 1-10)

Overall	Safety	Reliability	Performance	Comfort	Value
7.1	7.4	9.2	9	6.8	3.1

Category F
2 Dr S Cpe	9640	11900
2 Dr Si Cpe	10920	13480
2 Dr VTEC Cpe	12425	15335

OPTIONS FOR PRELUDE
Auto 4-Speed Transmission +325

1995 HONDA

ACCORD 1995

Finally, a V6 is offered in the midsized Honda! Unfortunately, it fails to improve performance figures because of the mandatory automatic transmission. V6 Accords gain different front styling as a result of the increased size of the engine bay. All V6 Accords come with standard antilock brakes.

RATINGS (SCALE OF 1-10)

Overall	Safety	Reliability	Performance	Comfort	Value
7.3	7.4	8.2	7.8	8	5

Model Description	Trade-in Value	Market Value
Category E		
4 Dr DX Sdn	6155	7995
2 Dr EX Cpe	8085	10500
4 Dr EX Sdn	8245	10705
4 Dr EX Wgn	8615	11190
4 Dr EX V6 Sdn	9275	12045
2 Dr LX Cpe	7030	9130
4 Dr LX Sdn	7165	9305
4 Dr LX Wgn	7410	9625
4 Dr LX V6 Sdn	8060	10465

OPTIONS FOR ACCORD

Auto 4-Speed Transmission[Opt on DX,LX,EX Cpe, EX Sdn] +245
Air Conditioning[Opt on DX] +270
Anti-Lock Brakes[Opt on LX] +225
Compact Disc W/fm/tape +190
Leather Seats[Std on EX V6] +290
Power Drivers Seat[Opt on EX] +100

CIVIC   1995

No changes for the last year of the current Civic.

RATINGS (SCALE OF 1-10)

Overall	Safety	Reliability	Performance	Comfort	Value
7.1	6.5	8.6	8	8	4.4

	Trade-in	Market
Category E		
2 Dr CX Hbk	4510	5855
2 Dr DX Cpe	5450	7075
2 Dr DX Hbk	5030	6530
4 Dr DX Sdn	5615	7290
2 Dr EX Cpe	6605	8575
4 Dr EX Sdn	6740	8750
4 Dr LX Sdn	5885	7640
2 Dr Si Hbk	5895	7655
2 Dr VX Hbk	5245	6810

OPTIONS FOR CIVIC

Auto 4-Speed Transmission +270
AM/FM Stereo Tape[Opt on DX] +100
Air Conditioning[Std on EX Sdn] +270
Aluminum/Alloy Wheels[Opt on EX] +110
Anti-Lock Brakes[Opt on LX,Cpe] +225
Power Steering[Opt on DX Hbk] +85
Premium Sound System +110
Rear Spoiler +70

CIVIC DEL SOL   1995

Antilock brakes are now standard on VTEC models. Power door locks are also new to the standard equipment lists of Si and VTEC models. All del Sols get a remote trunk release.

RATINGS (SCALE OF 1-10)

Overall	Safety	Reliability	Performance	Comfort	Value
N/A	N/A	N/A	N/A	N/A	4.5

Model Description	Trade-in Value	Market Value
Category F		
2 Dr S Cpe	6375	7970
2 Dr Si Cpe	7190	8990
2 Dr VTEC Cpe	8015	10020

OPTIONS FOR CIVIC DEL SOL

Auto 4-Speed Transmission +285
Air Conditioning +275
Power Steering[Opt on S] +115

ODYSSEY   1995

Honda finally gets its minivan in the form of the Odyssey. Unique to the Odyssey is five-door design that includes four passenger car-like swing-out doors. LX and EX models come standard with antilock brakes and dual airbags.

RATINGS (SCALE OF 1-10)

Overall	Safety	Reliability	Performance	Comfort	Value
7.5	8.2	8.9	7.2	7.1	6

	Trade-in	Market
Category G		
4 Dr EX Pass. Van	10380	12810
4 Dr LX Pass. Van	9580	11830

OPTIONS FOR ODYSSEY

Captain Chairs (4) +205
Luggage Rack[Opt on LX] +50

PASSPORT   1995

Midyear change gives the Passport a driver airbag.

RATINGS (SCALE OF 1-10)

Overall	Safety	Reliability	Performance	Comfort	Value
6.9	7	7.1	6.6	7.1	6.8

	Trade-in	Market
Category G		
4 Dr DX Wgn	6990	8630
1995.5 4 Dr DX Wgn	7091	8755
4 Dr EX 4WD Wgn	10690	12100
1995.5 4 Dr EX Wgn	9801	13335
1995.5 4 Dr EX 4WD Wgn	10773	13300
4 Dr LX Wgn	8290	10235
4 Dr LX 4WD Wgn	9385	11590
1995.5 4 Dr LX Wgn	8421	10400
1995.5 4 Dr LX 4WD Wgn	9477	11700

Auto 4-Speed Transmission +380
AM/FM Stereo Tape[Opt on DX] +75
Air Conditioning[Opt on DX,2WD] +270
Leather Seats +255
Limited Slip Diff[Opt on LX] +90
Luggage Rack +50
Running Boards +130

PRELUDE   1995

The ill-conceived Si 4WS is mercifully dropped from the Prelude lineup. The fourth-generation Prelude is nearing the end of its life. Few changes for 1995, except

---

Don't forget to refer to the Mileage Adjustment Table at the back of this book!

HONDA 95-94

Model Description	Trade-in Value	Market Value	Model Description	Trade-in Value	Market Value

the addition of air conditioning to the standard equipment list of S models.

RATINGS (SCALE OF 1-10)

Overall	Safety	Reliability	Performance	Comfort	Value
7.1	8.1	9.1	9	6.8	2.6

Category F

2 Dr S Cpe	8035	10045
2 Dr SE Cpe	9540	11925
2 Dr Si Cpe	9180	11475
2 Dr VTEC Cpe	10230	12785

OPTIONS FOR PRELUDE
Auto 4-Speed Transmission +245

1994 HONDA

ACCORD   1994

Once again, Honda's best-selling model is redesigned. Changes for 1994 make the vehicle more competitive with its midsize rival, the Ford Taurus. Shorter and wider than the previous generation Accord, the 1994 model is available in three trim levels. Antilock brakes are standard on the EX and are finally available on the LX and DX. New engines across the board improve horsepower figures for all Accords.

RATINGS (SCALE OF 1-10)

Overall	Safety	Reliability	Performance	Comfort	Value
7.3	7.5	8.2	7.8	8	4.8

Category E

2 Dr DX Cpe	5010	6680
4 Dr DX Sdn	5165	6885
2 Dr EX Cpe	6645	8860
4 Dr EX Sdn	6810	9080
4 Dr EX Wgn	6990	9320
2 Dr LX Cpe	5920	7890
4 Dr LX Sdn	6055	8070
4 Dr LX Wgn	6355	8470

OPTIONS FOR ACCORD
Auto 4-Speed Transmission +205
AM/FM Compact Disc Player +125
Air Conditioning[Opt on DX] +220
Anti-Lock Brakes[Std on EX] +180
Leather Seats +235

CIVIC   1994

The passenger airbag is now standard on all Civics. Antilock brakes are optional on the LX sedan, EX coupe and Si hatchback.

RATINGS (SCALE OF 1-10)

Overall	Safety	Reliability	Performance	Comfort	Value
7.3	6.3	7.9	8	8	6.3

Category E

2 Dr CX Hbk	3570	4760
2 Dr DX Cpe	4335	5780
2 Dr DX Hbk	3990	5320
4 Dr DX Sdn	4465	5950
2 Dr EX Cpe	5275	7030
4 Dr EX Sdn	5440	7250
4 Dr LX Sdn	4780	6375
2 Dr Si Hbk	4805	6405
2 Dr VX Hbk	4110	5480

OPTIONS FOR CIVIC
Auto 4-Speed Transmission +225
AM/FM Compact Disc Player +125
Air Conditioning[Std on EX Sdn] +220
Aluminum/Alloy Wheels[Std on VX] +90
Anti-Lock Brakes[Opt on LX,Si,Cpe] +180
Cruise Control[Opt on DX] +60
Leather Seats +235
Power Door Locks[Opt on VX] +65
Power Steering[Std on EX,LX,Si,Sdn] +70
Rear Spoiler +60

CIVIC DEL SOL   1994

VTEC technology makes its way to the del Sol, giving buyers a choice of three models. VTEC del Sols offer 35 more horsepower than the Si. A passenger airbag joins the standard equipment list for all models. VTEC del Sols gain performance-oriented upgrades that include a beefier suspension, larger tires and bigger brakes.

RATINGS (SCALE OF 1-10)

Overall	Safety	Reliability	Performance	Comfort	Value
N/A	N/A	N/A	N/A	N/A	4.3

Category F

2 Dr S Cpe	5450	6985
2 Dr Si Cpe	6230	7990
2 Dr VTEC Cpe	6750	8655

OPTIONS FOR CIVIC DEL SOL
Auto 4-Speed Transmission +240
AM/FM Stereo Tape[Opt on S] +60
Air Conditioning +225
Power Steering[Opt on S] +95

PASSPORT   1994

Honda loyalists waiting for the launch of a Honda sport utility should be thrilled with the Passport, until they discover that it's an Isuzu. Based on the highly successful Rodeo, the Honda Passport has very little to distinguish it from its less expensive twin. Two- and four-wheel-drive models are available in three trim levels ranging from the budget-minded DX to the top-end EX.

Don't forget to refer to the Mileage Adjustment Table at the back of this book!

Model Description	Trade-in Value	Market Value
4 Dr LX Wgn	5295	7250
2 Dr SE Cpe	6105	8365
4 Dr SE Sdn	6240	8550

RATINGS (SCALE OF 1-10)

Overall	Safety	Reliability	Performance	Comfort	Value
6.3	3.7	6.3	6.6	7.4	7.4

Category G

	Trade-in	Market
4 Dr DX Wgn	5295	6535
4 Dr EX 4WD Wgn	8865	10945
4 Dr LX Wgn	7445	9190
4 Dr LX 4WD Wgn	7710	9520

OPTIONS FOR PASSPORT

Auto 4-Speed Transmission +285
AM/FM Stereo Tape[Std on EX] +60
Air Conditioning[Opt on DX,2WD] +220
Luggage Rack +45

OPTIONS FOR ACCORD

Auto 4-Speed Transmission[Opt on DX,EX,LX] +170
AM/FM Stereo Tape[Opt on DX] +65
Air Conditioning[Opt on DX] +180
Aluminum/Alloy Wheels[Opt on LX] +75
Anti-Lock Brakes[Opt on LX] +150
Leather Seats[Std on SE] +195

PRELUDE 1994

Dual airbags are standard on all Preludes this year. Improved interior ergonomics, freshened front-end styling, and environmentally conscious CFC-free air conditioning are also welcome changes to this car.

RATINGS (SCALE OF 1-10)

Overall	Safety	Reliability	Performance	Comfort	Value
7.2	8.1	9	9	6.8	3

Category F

	Trade-in	Market
2 Dr S Cpe	6530	8370
2 Dr Si Cpe	7385	9465
2 Dr Si 4WS Cpe	7805	10005
2 Dr VTEC Cpe	8005	10265

OPTIONS FOR PRELUDE

Auto 4-Speed Transmission +205
Air Conditioning[Opt on S] +225
Aluminum/Alloy Wheels[Opt on S] +85
Rear Spoiler[Opt on Si] +65

1993 HONDA

ACCORD 1993

The SE model is re-introduced as the top-of-the-line Accord. A passenger airbag is added.

RATINGS (SCALE OF 1-10)

Overall	Safety	Reliability	Performance	Comfort	Value
N/A	N/A	8	8	8.4	4.8

Category E

	Trade-in	Market
4 Dr 10th Anniversary Sdn	5660	7755
2 Dr DX Cpe	4130	5660
4 Dr DX Sdn	4240	5810
2 Dr EX Cpe	5415	7415
4 Dr EX Sdn	5550	7600
4 Dr EX Wgn	5775	7910
2 Dr LX Cpe	4845	6635
4 Dr LX Sdn	4980	6820

CIVIC 1993

A coupe body style is added to the Civic stable. EX models get standard power steering and a sunroof. A passenger airbag is available on the EX coupe.

RATINGS (SCALE OF 1-10)

Overall	Safety	Reliability	Performance	Comfort	Value
6.8	5	8.1	8	8	4.8

Category E

	Trade-in	Market
2 Dr CX Hbk	3075	4210
2 Dr DX Cpe	3695	5060
2 Dr DX Hbk	3475	4760
4 Dr DX Sdn	3825	5240
2 Dr EX Cpe	4470	6125
4 Dr EX Sdn	4440	6085
4 Dr LX Sdn	3990	5465
2 Dr Si Hbk	4025	5515
2 Dr VX Hbk	3605	4935

OPTIONS FOR CIVIC

Auto 4-Speed Transmission +185
AM/FM Compact Disc Player +100
Air Conditioning +180
Aluminum/Alloy Wheels[Opt on EX] +75
Cruise Control[Opt on VX] +50
Dual Air Bag Restraints +115
Power Steering[Opt on DX Cpe] +55
Rear Spoiler +50

CIVIC DEL SOL 1993

The sun, that's what Honda wants you to think of when you picture this open-air replacement for the CRX. Poised to recapture some of the two-seater market from the Mazda Miata, the del Sol offers solid performance and value. Usable trunk space and improved body rigidity are the benefits the del Sol has over its rivals. We know, however, that the Miata's superior horsepower and rear-wheel drive will prove to be more fun in the long run.

RATINGS (SCALE OF 1-10)

Overall	Safety	Reliability	Performance	Comfort	Value
N/A	N/A	N/A	N/A	N/A	4.4

Don't forget to refer to the Mileage Adjustment Table at the back of this book!

Model Description	Trade-in Value	Market Value
Category F		
2 Dr S Cpe	4690	6090
2 Dr Si Cpe	5195	6745

OPTIONS FOR CIVIC DEL SOL

Auto 4-Speed Transmission +195
AM/FM Stereo Tape +45
Air Conditioning +185
Power Door Locks +45

PRELUDE   1993

More power, in the form of Honda's exclusive VTEC system, is available to the Prelude. A boost of 30 horsepower for top-end Preludes means that this car won't be the laughingstock of stoplight drags anymore.

RATINGS (SCALE OF 1-10)

Overall	Safety	Reliability	Performance	Comfort	Value
6.9	7	8.9	9	6.8	3

	Trade-in	Market
Category F		
2 Dr S Cpe	5805	7540
2 Dr Si Cpe	6420	8335
2 Dr Si 4WS Cpe	6815	8850
2 Dr VTEC Cpe	7080	9195

OPTIONS FOR PRELUDE

Auto 4-Speed Transmission +170
AM/FM Compact Disc Player +105
Air Conditioning[Opt on S] +185

1992 HONDA

ACCORD   1992

The SE model is dropped. The EX model gains antilock brakes with rear discs instead of drums. Horsepower is up in the EX sedans, 10 more than last year's 130. A driver airbag is added to the standard equipment list.

RATINGS (SCALE OF 1-10)

Overall	Safety	Reliability	Performance	Comfort	Value
N/A	N/A	7.4	8	8.4	5.7

	Trade-in	Market
Category E		
2 Dr DX Cpe	3440	4915
4 Dr DX Sdn	3505	5010
2 Dr EX Cpe	4450	6355
4 Dr EX Sdn	4530	6470
4 Dr EX Wgn	4730	6760
2 Dr LX Cpe	4020	5740
4 Dr LX Sdn	4105	5865
4 Dr LX Wgn	4345	6210

OPTIONS FOR ACCORD

Auto 4-Speed Transmission +135
Air Conditioning[Opt on DX] +145

CIVIC   1992

A driver airbag is standard on all new Civics. Unfortunately, the wagon body style is dropped from the lineup. VTEC power is available by way of the top-end EX model. All sedans now have power steering added to their standard equipment list.

RATINGS (SCALE OF 1-10)

Overall	Safety	Reliability	Performance	Comfort	Value
6.9	5	7.9	8	8	5.7

	Trade-in	Market
Category E		
2 Dr CX Hbk	2595	3705
2 Dr DX Hbk	2945	4210
4 Dr DX Sdn	3250	4640
4 Dr EX Sdn	3685	5265
4 Dr LX Sdn	3375	4820
2 Dr Si Hbk	3395	4850
2 Dr VX Hbk	3050	4355

OPTIONS FOR CIVIC

Auto 4-Speed Transmission +135
Air Conditioning +145

PRELUDE   1992

Totally redesigned for 1992, the fourth generation Prelude sports a driver airbag in all models and a standard passenger airbag on the Si 4WS. Antilock brakes are still available only on Si models.

RATINGS (SCALE OF 1-10)

Overall	Safety	Reliability	Performance	Comfort	Value
7.2	7	8.8	9	6.8	4.4

	Trade-in	Market
Category F		
2 Dr S Cpe	4910	6545
2 Dr Si Cpe	5425	7230

OPTIONS FOR PRELUDE

Auto 4-Speed Transmission +135
Air Conditioning[Opt on S] +150
Leather Seats +120

1991 HONDA

ACCORD   1991

Honda introduces a leather-trimmed SE model to the lineup to compete in the upscale market.

RATINGS (SCALE OF 1-10)

Overall	Safety	Reliability	Performance	Comfort	Value
N/A	N/A	6.9	8	8.4	6.5

	Trade-in	Market
Category E		
2 Dr DX Cpe	2865	4215
4 Dr DX Sdn	2950	4335
2 Dr EX Cpe	3745	5505

Don't forget to refer to the Mileage Adjustment Table at the back of this book!

HONDA 91-90

Model Description	Trade-in Value	Market Value	Model Description	Trade-in Value	Market Value

Model Description	Trade-in Value	Market Value
4 Dr EX Sdn	3835	5640
4 Dr EX Wgn	3905	5745
2 Dr LX Cpe	3310	4865
4 Dr LX Sdn	3365	4950
4 Dr LX Wgn	3545	5210
4 Dr SE Sdn	4385	6445

OPTIONS FOR ACCORD
Auto 4-Speed Transmission[Std on SE] +110
Air Conditioning[Opt on DX] +120
Cruise Control[Opt on DX] +35

CIVIC 1991

Few changes for Honda's popular subcompact. A complete redesign is expected for 1992.
Category E

	Trade-in Value	Market Value
2 Dr DX Hbk	2270	3340
4 Dr DX Sdn	2400	3530
4 Dr EX Sdn	2725	4005
4 Dr LX Sdn	2620	3855
2 Dr STD Hbk	2110	3100
4 Dr STD Wgn	2430	3575
4 Dr STD 4WD Wgn	2715	3990
2 Dr Si Hbk	2640	3885

OPTIONS FOR CIVIC
Auto 4-Speed Transmission +125
Air Conditioning +120
Cruise Control[Std on EX,LX] +35

CIVIC CRX 1991

This is the last year for the Honda CRX. Stiff competition from Toyota and Mazda are forcing this superb two-seater into obscurity. The CRX's large luggage storage and peppy performance will be missed.
Category E

	Trade-in Value	Market Value
2 Dr HF Cpe	2380	3500
2 Dr STD Cpe	2560	3765
2 Dr Si Cpe	2830	4165

OPTIONS FOR CIVIC CRX
Auto 4-Speed Transmission +90
Air Conditioning +120
Cruise Control +35

PRELUDE 1991

1991 is the last year for the third-generation Prelude, so no major changes in face of next year's redesign.
Category F

	Trade-in Value	Market Value
2 Dr 2.0 Si Cpe	3750	5065
2 Dr Si Cpe	4190	5660

OPTIONS FOR PRELUDE
Auto 4-Speed Transmission +110
Air Conditioning +125
Anti-Lock Brakes +100
Power Door Locks +30

1990 HONDA

ACCORD 1990

The Accord is entirely redesigned for 1990. Nearly five inches longer than the previous model, the 1990 Accord has considerably more interior space than last year's model.

RATINGS (SCALE OF 1-10)

Overall	Safety	Reliability	Performance	Comfort	Value
N/A	N/A	7.3	8	8.4	6.9

Category E

	Trade-in Value	Market Value
2 Dr DX Cpe	2515	3810
4 Dr DX Sdn	2585	3920
2 Dr EX Cpe	3110	4715
4 Dr EX Sdn	3180	4820
2 Dr LX Cpe	2830	4285
4 Dr LX Sdn	2895	4390

OPTIONS FOR ACCORD
Auto 4-Speed Transmission +90
Air Conditioning[Opt on DX] +100
Cruise Control[Opt on DX] +25

CIVIC 1990

New bumpers are given to the hatchbacks and sedans. New front and rear light combinations also appear on the 1990 Civic. A top-of-the-line EX version is added.
Category E

	Trade-in Value	Market Value
2 Dr DX Hbk	1935	2930
4 Dr DX Sdn	2015	3050
4 Dr EX Sdn	2305	3490
4 Dr LX Sdn	2175	3295
2 Dr STD Hbk	1840	2785
4 Dr STD Wgn	2000	3030
4 Dr STD 4WD Wgn	2265	3435
2 Dr Si Hbk	2120	3210

OPTIONS FOR CIVIC
Auto 4-Speed Transmission +100
Air Conditioning +100
Cruise Control[Std on EX,LX] +25

CIVIC CRX 1990

All CRXs are equipped with passive restraint seatbelts. New wheel covers are among the only other changes to this peppy little car.
Category E

	Trade-in Value	Market Value
2 Dr HF Cpe	1910	2895
2 Dr STD Cpe	2080	3155
2 Dr Si Cpe	2275	3450

Don't forget to refer to the Mileage Adjustment Table at the back of this book!

Model Description	Trade-in Value	Market Value	Model Description	Trade-in Value	Market Value

OPTIONS FOR CIVIC CRX
Auto 4-Speed Transmission +75
Air Conditioning +100
Cruise Control +25

PRELUDE   1990

Antilock brakes are finally available on Honda's pricey pocket rocket. Minor styling updates are the only other changes.
Category F

2 Dr S Cpe	3080	4165
2 Dr Si Cpe	3550	4795

OPTIONS FOR PRELUDE
Auto 4-Speed Transmission +90
4 Wheel Steering +130
Air Conditioning[Opt on S] +100
Anti-Lock Brakes +80

Don't forget to refer to the Mileage Adjustment Table at the back of this book!

HYUNDAI   S. Korea

1995 Hyundai Sonata

1999 HYUNDAI

ACCENT   1999

The L model has power steering standard, the GS and GL models have standard alloy wheels and a couple of new paint options are available. Hyundai's new, industry leading buyer assurance program is also worth taking note of.

RATINGS (SCALE OF 1-10)

Overall	Safety	Reliability	Performance	Comfort	Value
N/A	6.1	N/A	N/A	N/A	N/A

Category E
4 Dr GL Sdn	6700	8170
2 Dr GS Hbk	6315	7700
2 Dr L Hbk	5900	7195

OPTIONS FOR ACCENT
Auto 4-Speed Transmission +590
AM/FM Compact Disc Player +340
Air Conditioning +605
Flip-Up Sunroof +255
Keyless Entry System +115

ELANTRA   1999

The 1999 Elantra boasts a more powerful engine, styling changes and the best buyer assurance program of any car in this class.

RATINGS (SCALE OF 1-10)

Overall	Safety	Reliability	Performance	Comfort	Value
N/A	6.1	N/A	N/A	N/A	N/A

Category E
4 Dr GL Sdn	7360	8975
4 Dr GL Wgn	7775	9480
4 Dr GLS Sdn	7680	9365
4 Dr GLS Wgn	8145	9935

OPTIONS FOR ELANTRA
Auto 4-Speed Transmission[Std on 4 Dr GLS Wagon] +580
AM/FM Compact Disc Player +340
Aluminum/Alloy Wheels +245
Anti-Lock Brakes +500
Cruise Control +165
Keyless Entry System +115
Power Moonroof +425

SONATA   1999

Hyundai's Sonata is completely new and much-improved for 1999.
Category D
4 Dr GLS Sdn	10380	12660
4 Dr STD Sdn	9105	11105

OPTIONS FOR SONATA
Auto 4-Speed Transmission +590
AM/FM Compact Disc Player[Std on GLS] +390
Anti-Lock Brakes +670
Cruise Control[Std on GLS] +180
Keyless Entry System +235
Leather Seats[Opt on GLS] +820
Power Moonroof +620

TIBURON   1999

Nothing changes on the Tiburon for 1999, but the company's all-new, industry leading buyer assurance program is worth investigation.
Category E
2 Dr FX Hbk	9415	11480
2 Dr STD Hbk	8690	10600

OPTIONS FOR TIBURON
Auto 4-Speed Transmission +590
AM/FM Compact Disc Player +340
Air Conditioning +605
Aluminum/Alloy Wheels[Std on FX] +245
Anti-Lock Brakes +500
Cruise Control +165
Fog Lights[Std on FX] +110
Keyless Entry System +115
Leather Seats +645
Power Sunroof +455

1998 HYUNDAI

ACCENT   1998

The Accent GSi replaces the Accent GT this year. New front and rear fascias, and new engine mounts, which reduce engine vibration and harshness, are the only other changes to Hyundai's smallest car.

Model Description	Trade-in Value	Market Value

RATINGS (SCALE OF 1-10)

Overall	Safety	Reliability	Performance	Comfort	Value
N/A	6.1	N/A	N/A	N/A	N/A

Category E

4 Dr GL Sdn	5525	6820
2 Dr GS Hbk	5255	6485
2 Dr GSi Hbk	5720	7060
2 Dr L Hbk	4750	5865

OPTIONS FOR ACCENT

Auto 4-Speed Transmission +465
AM/FM Compact Disc Player +275
Air Conditioning +495
Anti-Lock Brakes +410
Flip-Up Sunroof +210
Keyless Entry System +95

ELANTRA   1998

No changes to the Elantra for 1998.

RATINGS (SCALE OF 1-10)

Overall	Safety	Reliability	Performance	Comfort	Value
N/A	6.1	N/A	N/A	N/A	N/A

Category E

4 Dr GLS Sdn	6490	8015
4 Dr GLS Wgn	6855	8465
4 Dr STD Sdn	5990	7395
4 Dr STD Wgn	6360	7850

OPTIONS FOR ELANTRA

Auto 4-Speed Transmission[Std on GLS Wgn] +490
AM/FM Compact Disc Player +275
Air Conditioning +495
Aluminum/Alloy Wheels +200
Anti-Lock Brakes +410
Cruise Control +135
Keyless Entry System +95
Power Moonroof +350

SONATA   1998

No changes to the Sonata for 1998.
Category D

4 Dr GL Sdn	7895	9745
4 Dr GL V6 Sdn	8390	10355
4 Dr GLS Sdn	8950	11050
4 Dr STD Sdn	7370	9100

OPTIONS FOR SONATA

Auto 4-Speed Transmission[Opt on STD] +490
Anti-Lock Brakes +550
Cruise Control[Std on GLS] +145
Keyless Entry System +190
Leather Seats +670
Power Moonroof +505

TIBURON   1998

Base Tiburons get the 2.0-liter 140-horsepower engine as standard equipment.
Category E

2 Dr FX Hbk	8205	10130
2 Dr STD Hbk	7325	9045

OPTIONS FOR TIBURON

Auto 4-Speed Transmission +490
Air Conditioning +495
Aluminum/Alloy Wheels[Std on FX] +200
Anti-Lock Brakes +410
Cruise Control +135
Fog Lights[Std on FX] +90
Keyless Entry System +95
Leather Seats +530
Power Sunroof +375

1997 HYUNDAI

ACCENT   1997

In the absence of truly ground-breaking improvement, Hyundai revises trim levels, adding GS hatchback and GL sedan mid-range models.

RATINGS (SCALE OF 1-10)

Overall	Safety	Reliability	Performance	Comfort	Value
N/A	5.9	N/A	N/A	N/A	N/A

Category E

4 Dr GL Sdn	4160	5400
2 Dr GS Hbk	3860	5015
2 Dr GT Hbk	4315	5605
2 Dr L Hbk	3730	4845

OPTIONS FOR ACCENT

Auto 4-Speed Transmission +380
AM/FM Compact Disc Player +225
AM/FM Stereo Tape +150
Air Conditioning +405
Anti-Lock Brakes +335
Flip-Up Sunroof +170
Keyless Entry System +80
Power Steering[Std on GT] +125
Rear Spoiler[Std on GT] +105

ELANTRA   1997

Elantra rolls into 1997 with zero changes, save for a slight price increase.

RATINGS (SCALE OF 1-10)

Overall	Safety	Reliability	Performance	Comfort	Value
N/A	5.8	N/A	N/A	N/A	N/A

Category E

4 Dr GLS Sdn	5510	7155
4 Dr GLS Wgn	5780	7505

Don't forget to refer to the Mileage Adjustment Table at the back of this book!

Model Description	Trade-in Value	Market Value
4 Dr STD Sdn	4955	6435
4 Dr STD Wgn	5260	6830

OPTIONS FOR ELANTRA

Auto 4-Speed Transmission[Opt on STD] +400
AM/FM Compact Disc Player +225
Air Conditioning +405
Aluminum/Alloy Wheels +165
Anti-Lock Brakes +335
Cruise Control +110
Keyless Entry System +80
Luggage Rack[Opt on GLS] +65
Power Moonroof +285
Rear Spoiler +105

SONATA   1997

Sheetmetal is all-new, and gives Sonata a more substantial look despite somewhat controversial retro-style front fascia and grille. Flush-fitting doors and restyled exterior mirrors help quiet the ride, while horn activation switches from spoke button to center steering wheel pad.

Category D

Model Description	Trade-in Value	Market Value
4 Dr GL Sdn	6695	8265
4 Dr GLS Sdn	7545	9315
4 Dr STD Sdn	6115	7550

OPTIONS FOR SONATA

6 cyl 3.0 L Engine[Opt on GL] +500
Auto 4-Speed Transmission[Opt on STD] +400
Anti-Lock Brakes +450
Compact Disc W/fm/tape +400
Cruise Control[Opt on GL] +120
Keyless Entry System +155
Leather Seats +545
Power Moonroof +415

TIBURON   1997

Loosely based on the 1993 HCD-II concept car, the Tiburon (Spanish for shark) debuts as a budget sport coupe that promises to gobble competitors such as the Toyota Paseo like so much chum.

Category E

Model Description	Trade-in Value	Market Value
2 Dr FX Hbk	6745	8760
2 Dr STD Hbk	6050	7855

OPTIONS FOR TIBURON

Auto 4-Speed Transmission +400
Air Conditioning +405
Aluminum/Alloy Wheels[Std on FX] +165
Anti-Lock Brakes +335
Center Console[Std on FX] +45
Compact Disc W/fm/tape +290
Cruise Control +110
Fog Lights[Std on FX] +75
Keyless Entry System +80
Leather Seats +430

Power Sunroof +305
Rear Spoiler[Std on FX] +105

1996 HYUNDAI

ACCENT   1996

Hyundai is painting the Accent in some new colors this year, and height-adjustable seatbelt anchors are standard. Front and rear center consoles with cupholders debut, and optional air conditioning is now CFC-free. A new, 105-horsepower GT hatch debuted midyear.

RATINGS (SCALE OF 1-10)

Overall	Safety	Reliability	Performance	Comfort	Value
N/A	5.8	N/A	N/A	N/A	N/A

Category E

Model Description	Trade-in Value	Market Value
2 Dr GT Hbk	3335	4510
2 Dr L Hbk	3020	4080
2 Dr STD Hbk	2830	3825
4 Dr STD Sdn	2980	4030

OPTIONS FOR ACCENT

Auto 4-Speed Transmission +305
AM/FM Compact Disc Player +185
Air Conditioning +330
Anti-Lock Brakes +275
Power Steering[Std on GT] +105
Rear Spoiler[Std on GT] +85
Sunroof +140

ELANTRA   1996

All-new Elantra is a slickly styled sedan or wagon featuring dual airbags, side-impact protection, and a more powerful engine. Pricing is up as well, pushing this Hyundai squarely into Dodge Neon and Honda Civic territory.

RATINGS (SCALE OF 1-10)

Overall	Safety	Reliability	Performance	Comfort	Value
N/A	5.8	N/A	N/A	N/A	N/A

Category E

Model Description	Trade-in Value	Market Value
4 Dr GLS Sdn	4415	5965
4 Dr GLS Wgn	4720	6380
4 Dr STD Sdn	4030	5445
4 Dr STD Wgn	4305	5820

OPTIONS FOR ELANTRA

Auto 4-Speed Transmission[Opt on STD,Sdn] +350
AM/FM Compact Disc Player +185
Air Conditioning +330
Aluminum/Alloy Wheels +135
Anti-Lock Brakes +275
Cruise Control +90
Rear Spoiler +85
Sunroof +140

Don't forget to refer to the Mileage Adjustment Table at the back of this book!

Model Description	Trade-in Value	Market Value

SONATA 1996

Noise, vibration and harshness are quelled with the addition of insulation to the floor and cowl, and liquid-filled V6 engine mounts. ABS is available as a stand-alone option on the GLS, and Steel Gray joins the color chart. Upgraded seat fabric comes in the base and GL models, while all Sonatas get CFC-free A/C.

Category D

Model Description	Trade-in Value	Market Value
4 Dr GL Sdn	5110	6550
4 Dr GL V6 Sdn	5380	6900
4 Dr GLS Sdn	5830	7475
4 Dr STD Sdn	4745	6085

OPTIONS FOR SONATA

Auto 4-Speed Transmission[Opt on STD] +325
Anti-Lock Brakes +365
Compact Disc W/fm/tape +325
Cruise Control[Std on GLS] +100
Leather Seats +445
Power Moonroof +340

1995 HYUNDAI

ACCENT 1995

Dramatically improved car replaces Excel in lineup. Dual airbags are standard, and ABS is optional. Power comes from the 1.5-liter Alpha engine which debuted in 1993 Scoupe.

Category E

Model Description	Trade-in Value	Market Value
2 Dr L Hbk	2400	3380
2 Dr STD Hbk	2215	3120
4 Dr STD Sdn	2355	3315

OPTIONS FOR ACCENT

Auto 4-Speed Transmission +285
AM/FM Stereo Tape +100
Air Conditioning +270
Anti-Lock Brakes +225
Power Steering +85
Sunroof +115

ELANTRA 1995

No changes.

Category E

Model Description	Trade-in Value	Market Value
4 Dr GLS Sdn	2790	3930
4 Dr SE Sdn	2510	3535
4 Dr STD Sdn	2400	3380

OPTIONS FOR ELANTRA

4 cyl 1.8 L Engine[Std on GLS] +215
Auto 4-Speed Transmission +240
AM/FM Stereo Tape[Std on GLS] +100
Air Conditioning +270
Aluminum/Alloy Wheels +110

Anti-Lock Brakes +225
Cruise Control +75
Power Moonroof +190
Premium Sound System +110
Rear Spoiler[Std on SE] +70

SCOUPE 1995

No changes.

Category E

Model Description	Trade-in Value	Market Value
2 Dr LS Cpe	2910	4100
2 Dr STD Cpe	2575	3630

OPTIONS FOR SCOUPE

Auto 4-Speed Transmission +225
AM/FM Compact Disc Player +150
Air Conditioning +270
Aluminum/Alloy Wheels[Opt on LS] +110
Flip-Up Sunroof +115
Power Steering[Std on LS] +85
Premium Sound System +110

SONATA 1995

Brand-new Sonata debuted in mid-1994. Dual airbags are standard. A 137-horsepower engine powers base and GL models while a 142-horsepower V6 is optional on midlevel GL and standard on GLS. Both engines are Mitsubishi-based designs. New car meets 1997 side-impact standards. Air conditioning and cassette stereo are standard on all models.

Category D

Model Description	Trade-in Value	Market Value
4 Dr GL Sdn	4015	5285
4 Dr GL V6 Sdn	4220	5550
4 Dr GLS Sdn	4580	6025
4 Dr STD Sdn	3680	4840

OPTIONS FOR SONATA

Auto 4-Speed Transmission[Opt on STD] +265
Anti-Lock Brakes +300
Compact Disc W/fm/tape +265
Cruise Control[Std on GLS] +80
Leather Seats +365
Power Moonroof +275
Power Sunroof +245

1994 HYUNDAI

ELANTRA 1994

Styling is updated, and a driver airbag is standard. ABS is optional on GLS models. CFC-free refrigerant replaces freon in Elantra's air conditioning system.

Category E

Model Description	Trade-in Value	Market Value
4 Dr GLS Sdn	2225	3320
4 Dr STD Sdn	1905	2840

OPTIONS FOR ELANTRA

4 cyl 1.8 L Engine[Opt on STD] +125
Auto 4-Speed Transmission +200

HYUNDAI 94-93

Model Description	Trade-in Value	Market Value	Model Description	Trade-in Value	Market Value

AM/FM Compact Disc Player +125
Air Conditioning +220
Aluminum/Alloy Wheels +90
Anti-Lock Brakes +180
Cruise Control +60
Power Sunroof +165

EXCEL   1994

Four-speed manual dropped from base car in favor of five-speed unit. Base sedan is discontinued. New interior fabrics and wheel covers spruce up the Excel. Air conditioners get CFC-free coolant.
Category E

4 Dr GL Sdn	1700	2540
2 Dr GS Hbk	1770	2645
2 Dr STD Hbk	1650	2465

OPTIONS FOR EXCEL

Auto 4-Speed Transmission +155
AM/FM Stereo Tape[Opt on STD] +80
Air Conditioning +220
Power Steering +70
Power Sunroof +165

SCOUPE   1994

Base and LS models receive new interior fabrics, wheel covers and revised trim molding. CFC-free refrigerant is added to the air conditioner.
Category E

2 Dr LS Cpe	2330	3480
2 Dr STD Cpe	2050	3060

OPTIONS FOR SCOUPE

Auto 4-Speed Transmission +185
AM/FM Compact Disc Player +125
Air Conditioning +220
Aluminum/Alloy Wheels +90
Flip-Up Sunroof +95
Power Steering[Std on LS] +70

SONATA   1994

No changes.
Category D

4 Dr GLS Sdn	2285	3045
4 Dr GLS V6 Sdn	2445	3260
4 Dr STD Sdn	2065	2755
4 Dr V6 Sdn	2225	2965

OPTIONS FOR SONATA

Auto 4-Speed Transmission[Opt on GLS,STD] +215
Aluminum/Alloy Wheels[Opt on GLS] +125
Anti-Lock Brakes +245
Compact Disc W/fm/tape +220
Cruise Control[Opt on STD, V6] +65
Leather Seats +300
Power Door Locks[Opt on STD, V6] +75
Power Sunroof +200
Power Windows[Opt on STD, V6] +75

1993 HYUNDAI

ELANTRA   1993

Base model gets a black grille, while GLS features a body-color piece. GLS also gets new wheelcovers and steering wheel. All automatic models and the five-speed GLS get a new 1.8-liter engine good for 124 horsepower.
Category E

4 Dr GLS Sdn	1680	2710
4 Dr STD Sdn	1525	2460

OPTIONS FOR ELANTRA

4 cyl 1.8 L Engine[Opt on STD] +85
Auto 4-Speed Transmission +160
AM/FM Stereo Tape[Opt on STD] +65
Air Conditioning +180
Aluminum/Alloy Wheels +75
Cruise Control +50
Power Sunroof +135

EXCEL   1993

Slight styling revisions update Excel.
Category E

4 Dr GL Sdn	1385	2235
2 Dr GS Hbk	1320	2125
2 Dr STD Hbk	1165	1880
4 Dr STD Sdn	1260	2030

OPTIONS FOR EXCEL

Auto 4-Speed Transmission +135
AM/FM Stereo Tape[Opt on STD] +65
Air Conditioning +180
Aluminum/Alloy Wheels +75
Power Steering +55
Sunroof +75

SCOUPE   1993

Styling updates, a new engine, and a new Turbo model summarize the big news for 1993. The new motor is a 1.5-liter SOHC four-cylinder designed and built by Hyundai. Called Alpha, the new engine makes 92 horsepower in base and LS Scoupes; 115 horsepower in Turbo format. Turbos are available only with a manual transmission. Dashboard is slightly revised and features rotary climate controls.
Category E

2 Dr LS Cpe	1760	2840
2 Dr STD Cpe	1545	2495
2 Dr STD Turbo Cpe	1840	2970

OPTIONS FOR SCOUPE

Auto 4-Speed Transmission +130
AM/FM Stereo Tape[Std on LS, Turbo] +65
Air Conditioning +180
Aluminum/Alloy Wheels[Std on Turbo] +75

Don't forget to refer to the Mileage Adjustment Table at the back of this book!

HYUNDAI 93-91

Model Description	Trade-in Value	Market Value	Model Description	Trade-in Value	Market Value

Power Steering[Std on LS, Turbo] +55
Sunroof +75

SONATA 1993

Front air intake is now body-color, and new wheelcovers debut.

Category D

4 Dr GLS Sdn	1965	2770
4 Dr STD Sdn	1720	2420

OPTIONS FOR SONATA

6 cyl 3.0 L Engine +175
Auto 4-Speed Transmission +165
AM/FM Compact Disc Player +115
Aluminum/Alloy Wheels +105
Anti-Lock Brakes +200
Cruise Control[Opt on STD] +55
Leather Seats +245
Power Door Locks[Opt on STD] +60
Power Sunroof +165
Power Windows[Opt on STD] +60

1992 HYUNDAI

ELANTRA 1992

Brand-new compact is slotted between Excel and Sonata. All models come standard with a 113-horsepower, 1.6-liter, twin-cam four-cylinder engine. Horsepower drops to 105 with the automatic transmission.

Category E

4 Dr GLS Sdn	1355	2380
4 Dr STD Sdn	1240	2175

OPTIONS FOR ELANTRA

Auto 4-Speed Transmission +115
Air Conditioning +145
Cruise Control +40
Power Sunroof +110

EXCEL 1992

GLS sedan dropped from lineup.

Category E

4 Dr GL Sdn	1085	1900
2 Dr GS Hbk	1030	1810
2 Dr STD Hbk	925	1620
4 Dr STD Sdn	990	1740

OPTIONS FOR EXCEL

Auto 4-Speed Transmission +105
Air Conditioning +145

SCOUPE 1992

No changes.

Category E

2 Dr LS Cpe	1395	2450
2 Dr STD Cpe	1250	2190

OPTIONS FOR SCOUPE

Auto 4-Speed Transmission +105
Air Conditioning +145
Cruise Control +40
Sunroof +65

SONATA 1992

Styling is tweaked, ABS is optional on GLS V6 models, and a new 2.0-liter, twin-cam engine replaces the less-powerful, 2.4-liter base unit.

Category D

4 Dr GLS Sdn	1610	2400
4 Dr STD Sdn	1510	2250

OPTIONS FOR SONATA

6 cyl 3.0 L Engine +250
Auto 4-Speed Transmission +135
Air Conditioning[Opt on STD] +155
Anti-Lock Brakes +165
Cruise Control[Opt on STD] +45
Power Door Locks[Opt on STD] +50
Power Moonroof +150
Power Windows[Opt on STD] +50

1991 HYUNDAI

EXCEL 1991

No changes.

Category E

4 Dr GL Sdn	790	1580
4 Dr GL SE Sdn	805	1610
4 Dr GLS Sdn	820	1640
2 Dr GS Hbk	775	1545
2 Dr GS SE Hbk	810	1620
2 Dr STD Hbk	655	1305
4 Dr STD Sdn	715	1425

OPTIONS FOR EXCEL

Auto 4-Speed Transmission +100
Air Conditioning +120

SCOUPE 1991

"Sports" coupe debuts based on Excel underpinnings. Car gets its own coupe styling, interior and Lotus-tuned suspension. Scoupe has a whopping 81 horsepower; a shorter final-drive ratio makes Scoupe slightly speedier than the slooooooow Excel.

Category E

2 Dr LS Cpe	870	1740
2 Dr SE Cpe	905	1805
2 Dr STD Cpe	735	1470

OPTIONS FOR SCOUPE

Auto 4-Speed Transmission +75
Air Conditioning +120
Cruise Control +35
Sunroof +50

Don't forget to refer to the Mileage Adjustment Table at the back of this book!

Model Description	Trade-in Value	Market Value
SONATA		**1991**
Child-proof rear door locks are added.		
Category D		
4 Dr GLS Sdn	1365	2070
4 Dr GLS SE Sdn	1490	2260
4 Dr STD Sdn	1245	1885

OPTIONS FOR SONATA
6 cyl 3.0 L Engine[Std on GLS SE] +110
Auto 4-Speed Transmission[Std on GLS SE] +105
Radio Option +195
Air Conditioning[Opt on STD] +125
Cruise Control[Opt on STD] +35
Power Door Locks[Opt on STD] +40
Power Windows[Opt on STD] +40

1990 HYUNDAI

Model Description	Trade-in Value	Market Value
EXCEL		**1990**

All-new Excel debuts. Engine is improved, with more horsepower and torque. Automatic transmission is redesigned, and manual transmission shifts more smoothly. For the first time, a tilt wheel is optional.

Category E

Model Description	Trade-in Value	Market Value
4 Dr GL Hbk	510	1160
4 Dr GL Sdn	565	1280

Model Description	Trade-in Value	Market Value
4 Dr GLS Sdn	595	1355
2 Dr GS Hbk	540	1225
2 Dr STD Hbk	475	1080
4 Dr STD Sdn	510	1160

OPTIONS FOR EXCEL
Auto 4-Speed Transmission +65
Air Conditioning +100

Model Description	Trade-in Value	Market Value
SONATA		**1990**

GLS gets new grille, upholstery and tinted glass. A V6 was added early in the model year. Premium sound and leather interior are offered for the first time. Automatic transmission gets an available power/normal shift selector.

Category D

Model Description	Trade-in Value	Market Value
4 Dr GLS Sdn	1065	1640
4 Dr GLS V6 Sdn	1170	1800
4 Dr STD Sdn	1000	1535
4 Dr V6 Sdn	1100	1690

OPTIONS FOR SONATA
Auto 4-Speed Transmission[Opt on GLS,STD] +85
Air Conditioning +105
Cruise Control[Opt on STD,V6] +30
Power Door Locks[Opt on STD,V6] +35
Power Windows[Opt on STD,V6] +35

Don't forget to refer to the Mileage Adjustment Table at the back of this book!

INFINITI 99-98

Model Description	Trade-in Value	Market Value	Model Description	Trade-in Value	Market Value

INFINITI   Japan

1993 Infiniti J30

1999 INFINITI

G20   1999

The G20 returns to the Infiniti lineup after a two-year hiatus. This entry-level compact is based on the European- and Japanese- market Primera, which has garnered a great deal of acclaim from the foreign automotive press.

RATINGS (SCALE OF 1-10)

Overall	Safety	Reliability	Performance	Comfort	Value
N/A	N/A	9.1	7.8	7.8	N/A

Category D
4 Dr STD Sdn   13400   15955
4 Dr Touring Sdn   14575   17350

OPTIONS FOR G20
Auto 4-Speed Transmission +590
Climate Control for AC[Opt on STD] +220
Heated Front Seats +300
Leather Seats +820
Leather Steering Wheel[Opt on STD] +80
Power Drivers Seat +220
Power Moonroof +620

I30   1999

Traction control is available as an option, the audio faceplate has been updated and an ignition immobilizer is offered on the I30.

RATINGS (SCALE OF 1-10)

Overall	Safety	Reliability	Performance	Comfort	Value
N/A	N/A	N/A	8.4	8	N/A

Category D
4 Dr STD Sdn   18125   21580
4 Dr Touring Sdn   19170   22820

OPTIONS FOR I30
Auto 4-Speed Transmission[Opt on Touring] +740
Infiniti Communicator +665
Automatic Dimming Mirror[Opt on STD] +180
Heated Front Seats +300
Leather Seats[Opt on STD] +820
Power Moonroof[Opt on STD] +620

Q45   1999

Several small exterior and interior enhancements have been added to the Q for 1999, including a new sunroof, revised front styling and the return of the analog clock.

RATINGS (SCALE OF 1-10)

Overall	Safety	Reliability	Performance	Comfort	Value
N/A	N/A	N/A	8.4	9	N/A

Category L
4 Dr STD Sdn   30735   34925
4 Dr Touring Sdn   31960   36320

OPTIONS FOR Q45
Infiniti Communicator +665
Compact Disc Changer +825
Heated Front Seats +355

QX4   1999

Infiniti's luxury sport-ute enters its third year with no major changes.

RATINGS (SCALE OF 1-10)

Overall	Safety	Reliability	Performance	Comfort	Value
N/A	N/A	N/A	7	7.3	N/A

Category G
4 Dr STD 4WD Wgn   21955   26135

OPTIONS FOR QX4
Infiniti Communicator +1180
Comrpact Disc Changer +385
Heated Front Seats +195
Power Moonroof +645

1998 INFINITI

I30   1998

Side-impact airbags make their way into the Infiniti I30, as do new headlamps, taillamps, center console and wheels.

RATINGS (SCALE OF 1-10)

Overall	Safety	Reliability	Performance	Comfort	Value
7.5	7.9	9.3	8.4	8	4.1

Don't forget to refer to the Mileage Adjustment Table at the back of this book!

Model Description	Trade-in Value	Market Value

Category D
| 4 Dr STD Sdn | 15720 | 18715 |
| 4 Dr Touring Sdn | 16735 | 19925 |

OPTIONS FOR I30
Auto 4-Speed Transmission[Opt on Touring] +615
Infiniti Communicator +550
Heated Front Seats[Opt on STD] +245
Heated Power Mirrors[Opt on STD] +50
Leather Seats[Opt on STD] +670
Power Moonroof[Opt on STD] +505

Q45 1998

The Q45 gets front seatbelt pretensioners. No other changes for Infiniti's flagship.

RATINGS (SCALE OF 1-10)

Overall	Safety	Reliability	Performance	Comfort	Value
N/A	N/A	9	8.4	9	5.3

Category J
| 4 Dr STD Sdn | 26210 | 31200 |
| 4 Dr Touring Sdn | 27140 | 32310 |

OPTIONS FOR Q45
Infiniti Communicator +550
Compact Disc Changer[Opt on STD] +560
Heated Front Seats[Opt on STD] +255

QX4 1998

No changes to the QX4.

RATINGS (SCALE OF 1-10)

Overall	Safety	Reliability	Performance	Comfort	Value
N/A	N/A	8.8	7	7.3	4.6

Category G
| 4 Dr STD 4WD Wgn | 20260 | 24120 |

OPTIONS FOR QX4
Compact Disc Changer +315
Heated Front Seats +160
Power Moonroof +525

1997 INFINITI

I30 1997

A few new paint colors are the only changes to the 1997 I30.

RATINGS (SCALE OF 1-10)

Overall	Safety	Reliability	Performance	Comfort	Value
7.5	7.5	9.3	8.4	8	4.1

Category D
| 4 Dr STD Sdn | 13405 | 16150 |
| 4 Dr Touring Sdn | 14300 | 17230 |

OPTIONS FOR I30
Auto 4-Speed Transmission +485
Heated Front Seats[Opt on STD] +200
Leather Seats[Opt on STD] +545
Limited Slip Diff[Opt on STD] +240
Power Moonroof[Opt on STD] +415

J30 1997

There are no changes to the 1997 Infiniti J30.

RATINGS (SCALE OF 1-10)

Overall	Safety	Reliability	Performance	Comfort	Value
7.7	7.6	9.7	8.4	8.5	4.4

Category J
4 Dr STD Sdn	14195	17105
1997.5 4 Dr STD Sdn	14860	17905
4 Dr Touring Sdn	14455	17415
1997.5 4 Dr Touring Sdn	14620	17615

Q45 1997

This totally redesigned luxury car has almost nothing in common with its predecessor. Power now comes via a 4.1-liter V-8 engine and is still delivered through the rear wheels. The Q45 no longer has aspirations to be a sports sedan; its prime duties now are interstate cruising.

RATINGS (SCALE OF 1-10)

Overall	Safety	Reliability	Performance	Comfort	Value
N/A	N/A	8.5	8.4	9	4

Category J
| 4 Dr STD Sdn | 21665 | 26100 |
| 4 Dr Touring Sdn | 22425 | 27020 |

OPTIONS FOR Q45
Heated Front Seats[Opt on STD] +210

QX4 1997

A version of Nissan's wonderful four-wheeler is introduced by Infiniti, aiming to compete with the Mercury Mountaineer, Acura SLX and Land Rover Discovery. Differences between the QX4 and the Pathfinder include the Q's full-time four-wheel drive system, a more luxurious interior, and some different sheetmetal.

RATINGS (SCALE OF 1-10)

Overall	Safety	Reliability	Performance	Comfort	Value
N/A	N/A	8.6	7	7.3	4.5

Category G
| 4 Dr STD 4WD Wgn | 18290 | 22035 |

OPTIONS FOR QX4
Heated Front Seats +130
Limited Slip Diff +135
Power Moonroof +430

1996 INFINITI

G20 — 1996

Emergency locking front and rear seatbelts have been installed, and fake wood is applied on models equipped with the Leather Appointment Package. This is the last year for the entry-level Infiniti.

RATINGS (SCALE OF 1-10)

Overall	Safety	Reliability	Performance	Comfort	Value
N/A	N/A	8.9	8.6	7.8	5.9

Category D

	Trade-in	Market
4 Dr STD Sdn	8190	10110
4 Dr Touring Sdn	9070	11200

OPTIONS FOR G20
Auto 4-Speed Transmission +405
Dual Power Seats[Opt on STD] +340
Keyless Entry System[Opt on STD] +125
Leather Seats[Opt on STD] +445
Power Moonroof[Opt on STD] +340

I30 — 1996

New luxo-sport sedan based on the Nissan Maxima arrived during 1995. Slotted between the G20 and the J30, the I30 competes with the Lexus ES 300, BMW 3-Series, and the new Acura TL-Series. If you like big chrome grilles, this is the car to buy.

RATINGS (SCALE OF 1-10)

Overall	Safety	Reliability	Performance	Comfort	Value
N/A	N/A	9.2	8.4	8	5

Category D

	Trade-in	Market
4 Dr STD Sdn	11095	13700
4 Dr Touring Sdn	12090	14930

OPTIONS FOR I30
Auto 4-Speed Transmission +370
Heated Front Seats[Opt on STD] +165
Leather Seats[Opt on STD] +445
Limited Slip Diff[Opt on STD] +195
Power Moonroof[Opt on STD] +340

J30 — 1996

Three new colors join the paint palette.

RATINGS (SCALE OF 1-10)

Overall	Safety	Reliability	Performance	Comfort	Value
7.7	7.6	9.8	8.4	8.5	4.4

Category J

	Trade-in	Market
4 Dr STD Sdn	12355	15065
4 Dr Touring Sdn	12835	15650

Q45 — 1996

Active suspension model is canceled, but two new exterior colors are available.

RATINGS (SCALE OF 1-10)

Overall	Safety	Reliability	Performance	Comfort	Value
N/A	N/A	9.2	8.6	9.1	5.7

Category J

	Trade-in	Market
4 Dr STD Sdn	15835	19310
4 Dr Touring Sdn	16440	20050

OPTIONS FOR Q45
Compact Disc W/fm/tape +325
Heated Front Seats +170
Traction Control System +480

1995 INFINITI

G20 — 1995

All-season tires are added to the G20. No other changes are made to the entry-level Infiniti.

RATINGS (SCALE OF 1-10)

Overall	Safety	Reliability	Performance	Comfort	Value
N/A	N/A	8.3	8.6	7.8	5.4

Category D

	Trade-in	Market
4 Dr STD Sdn	7325	9275
4 Dr Touring Sdn	8010	10140

OPTIONS FOR G20
Auto 4-Speed Transmission +330
Dual Power Seats +280
Keyless Entry System[Opt on STD] +105
Leather Seats[Opt on STD] +365
Power Moonroof[Opt on STD] +275

J30 — 1995

Redesigned taillights, power lumbar support for the driver's seat, and an anti-glare mirror mark the changes for the 1995 J30.

RATINGS (SCALE OF 1-10)

Overall	Safety	Reliability	Performance	Comfort	Value
7.9	8.3	9.4	8.4	8.5	4.9

Category J

	Trade-in	Market
4 Dr STD Sdn	11035	13625

OPTIONS FOR J30
Touring Pkg +520
Rear Spoiler +135

Q45 — 1995

Alloy wheels for the base model are about the only changes for the Q45.

Don't forget to refer to the Mileage Adjustment Table at the back of this book!

Model Description	Trade-in Value	Market Value

RATINGS (SCALE OF 1-10)

Overall	Safety	Reliability	Performance	Comfort	Value
N/A	N/A	8.8	8.6	9.1	5.6

Category J

	Trade-in	Market
4 Dr A Sdn	13480	16645
4 Dr STD Sdn	12760	15750

OPTIONS FOR Q45
Touring Pkg +480
Compact Disc Changer[Std on A] +305
Heated Front Seats[Std on A] +140
Traction Control System[Std on A] +390

1994 INFINITI

G20   1994

No changes to the G20.

RATINGS (SCALE OF 1-10)

Overall	Safety	Reliability	Performance	Comfort	Value
N/A	N/A	8.4	8.6	7.8	6.3

Category D

	Trade-in	Market
4 Dr STD Sdn	5695	7300

OPTIONS FOR G20
Auto 4-Speed Transmission +275
Dual Power Seats +230
Keyless Entry System +85
Leather Seats +300
Limited Slip Diff +130
Power Moonroof +225
Rear Spoiler +115

J30   1994

Heated front seats and the addition of two speakers further pamper passengers in the J30.

RATINGS (SCALE OF 1-10)

Overall	Safety	Reliability	Performance	Comfort	Value
7.7	8.3	9	8.4	8.5	4.3

Category J

	Trade-in	Market
4 Dr STD Sdn	9160	11450

OPTIONS FOR J30
Touring Pkg +555
Rear Spoiler +110

Q45   1994

A passenger airbag appears on the restyled 1994 Infiniti. Changes to the grille, bumpers and fog lights will distinguish this car from previous models.

RATINGS (SCALE OF 1-10)

Overall	Safety	Reliability	Performance	Comfort	Value
N/A	N/A	8	8.6	9.1	5.5

Model Description	Trade-in Value	Market Value

Category J

	Trade-in	Market
4 Dr A Sdn	11220	14025
4 Dr STD Sdn	10665	13330

OPTIONS FOR Q45
Touring Pkg +635
Heated Front Seats[Std on A] +115
Traction Control System[Std on A] +320

1993 INFINITI

G20   1993

Driver and passenger airbags are introduced as a midyear change to the G20.

RATINGS (SCALE OF 1-10)

Overall	Safety	Reliability	Performance	Comfort	Value
N/A	N/A	8.3	8.6	7.8	6.2

Category D

	Trade-in	Market
4 Dr STD Sdn	4755	6255

OPTIONS FOR G20
Auto 4-Speed Transmission +200
Dual Power Seats +185
Keyless Entry System +70
Leather Seats +245
Power Sunroof +165

J30   1993

A new introduction to the Infiniti lineup, the J30 really shakes things up. Love it or hate it, this car certainly turns heads. Powered by a 210-horsepower V6 gleaned from the Nissan 300ZX, the J30 is shifted by a four-speed automatic transmission. Dual airbags are standard on the J30, as are antilock brakes.

RATINGS (SCALE OF 1-10)

Overall	Safety	Reliability	Performance	Comfort	Value
7.6	8.3	9.1	8.4	8.5	3.8

Category J

	Trade-in	Market
4 Dr STD Sdn	7070	9180

OPTIONS FOR J30
Touring Pkg +385
Rear Spoiler +90

Q45   1993

Interior designers get a hold of the Q, sprucing and covering everything in beautiful new materials; even the clock on this car masquerades as a hand-crafted timepiece. Additional touches include map pockets to the front seat backs.

RATINGS (SCALE OF 1-10)

Overall	Safety	Reliability	Performance	Comfort	Value
N/A	N/A	8.7	9	8.4	5.4

Don't forget to refer to the Mileage Adjustment Table at the back of this book!

Model Description	Trade-in Value	Market Value
Category J		
4 Dr A Sdn	7930	10300
4 Dr STD Sdn	7545	9800

OPTIONS FOR Q45
Touring Pkg +605
Traction Control System +260

1992 INFINITI

G20   1992

New tires and an automatic transmission are introduced on Infiniti junior.

RATINGS (SCALE OF 1-10)

Overall	Safety	Reliability	Performance	Comfort	Value
N/A	N/A	8.1	8.6	7.8	6.2

Category D

	Trade-in	Market
4 Dr STD Sdn	4050	5400

OPTIONS FOR G20
Auto 4-Speed Transmission +160
Leather Seats +200
Power Sunroof +135

M30   1992

Unique, door opening system is introduced to the M30; this system enables both doors to be locked/unlocked from either door. This car is replaced by the more exotic looking J30 in 1993.

Category J

	Trade-in	Market
2 Dr STD Conv	7610	10010
2 Dr STD Cpe	5635	7415

Q45   1992

High-performance tires and new exterior colors are available on the 1992 Q45.

RATINGS (SCALE OF 1-10)

Overall	Safety	Reliability	Performance	Comfort	Value
N/A	N/A	8.5	9	8.4	5.9

Category J

	Trade-in	Market
4 Dr A Sdn	7305	9610
4 Dr STD Sdn	7005	9220

OPTIONS FOR Q45
Touring Pkg +450
Traction Control System +215

1991 INFINITI

G20   1991

Infiniti's entry-level sedan is the new G20. Based on the Japanese market Nissan Primera, but suitably well-dressed to call itself an Infiniti, the G20 is designed to lure not-yet-affluent car buyers into the Infiniti family.

RATINGS (SCALE OF 1-10)

Overall	Safety	Reliability	Performance	Comfort	Value
N/A	N/A	6.8	8.6	7.8	5.5

Category D

	Trade-in	Market
4 Dr STD Sdn	3545	4855

OPTIONS FOR G20
Auto 4-Speed Transmission +120
Leather Seats +165
Power Sunroof +110

M30   -   1991

No significant changes for the midsized offering from Infiniti.

Category J

	Trade-in	Market
2 Dr STD Conv	6450	8600
2 Dr STD Cpe	4695	6260

Q45   1991

Four-wheel steering is introduced to the Infiniti flagship. Full Active Suspension is available on the Q45, enabling the car to react much more quickly to changes in car position than a vehicle with conventional shock absorbers.

RATINGS (SCALE OF 1-10)

Overall	Safety	Reliability	Performance	Comfort	Value
N/A	N/A	7.5	9	8.4	5.8

Category J

	Trade-in	Market
4 Dr A Sdn	6540	8720
4 Dr STD Sdn	6300	8400

OPTIONS FOR Q45
Touring Pkg +370

1990 INFINITI

M30   1990

Based on a popular Japanese sedan, the M30 is introduced to the American market. Fans of the Maxima will appreciate the engine in the M30, which is lifted straight out of the Nissan parts bin. The rear-wheel

---

Don't forget to refer to the Mileage Adjustment Table at the back of this book!

INFINITI 90

Model Description	Trade-in Value	Market Value	Model Description	Trade-in Value	Market Value

drive, however, gives this car a distinct advantage over other Japanese luxury imports. Antilock brakes and an automatic transmission are standard on the M30.

Category J

	Trade-in	Market
2 Dr STD Cpe	3880	5245

Q45   1990

The flagship for Nissan's upmarket Infiniti division, the Q45 is the third entry into the growing Japanese luxury segment. Distinctive styling and a powerful, 270-horsepower V8 engine make this car desirable, as does the extensive standard equipment list and luxurious interior appointments.

RATINGS (SCALE OF 1-10)

Overall	Safety	Reliability	Performance	Comfort	Value
N/A	N/A	7.1	9	8.4	5

Category J

	Trade-in	Market
4 Dr STD Sdn	5490	7420

OPTIONS FOR Q45
Touring Pkg +305

Don't forget to refer to the Mileage Adjustment Table at the back of this book!

Model Description	Trade-in Value	Market Value

ISUZU   *Japan*

1996 Isuzu Oasis

1999 ISUZU

AMIGO   1999

Two body styles are available, hardtop or softtop, and an automatic transmission is now offered with the V6 engine.

Category G

2 Dr S Utility	11965	14245
2 Dr S V6 Utility	12640	15050
2 Dr S V6 4WD Utility	13285	15815

OPTIONS FOR AMIGO

Auto 4-Speed Transmission +575
AM/FM Compact Disc Player +245
Air Conditioning +605
Aluminum/Alloy Wheels +245
Fog Lights +105
Keyless Entry System +150
Power Door Locks +170
Power Mirrors +100
Power Windows +175

HOMBRE   1999

Hombres receive additional exterior colors and a new bumper fascia. A three-door spacecab model is now available.

RATINGS (SCALE OF 1-10)

Overall	Safety	Reliability	Performance	Comfort	Value
N/A	N/A	N/A	6.6	7.9	N/A

Category G

2 Dr S Std Cab SB	7600	9050
2 Dr XS Std Cab SB	8250	9820

OPTIONS FOR HOMBRE

Auto 4-Speed Transmission[Std on XS V6] +790
AM/FM Compact Disc Player +245
Air Conditioning +605
Aluminum/Alloy Wheels[Std on 4WD] +245
Cruise Control +155
Power Door Locks +170
Power Windows +175
Sliding Rear Window +90
Tilt Steering Wheel +130

RODEO   1999

Isuzu juggles minor standard and optional equipment for 1999, making items from last year's S V6 preferred equipment package standard on the LS, and last year's LS equipment standard on a new trim level called LSE.

RATINGS (SCALE OF 1-10)

Overall	Safety	Reliability	Performance	Comfort	Value
N/A	7.5	N/A	7.8	7.3	N/A

Category G

4 Dr LS Wgn	14790	17605
4 Dr LS 4WD Wgn	15690	18680
4 Dr LSE Wgn	16420	19550
4 Dr LSE 4WD Wgn	17405	20720
4 Dr S Wgn	11910	14180
4 Dr S V6 Wgn	12550	14940
4 Dr S V6 4WD Wgn	13500	16070

OPTIONS FOR RODEO

Auto 4-Speed Transmission[Std on LSE 4WD] +740
AM/FM Compact Disc Player +245
Air Conditioning[Std on LS,LSE] +605
Aluminum/Alloy Wheels[Std on LSE,LS 4WD] +245
Luggage Rack[Std on LS,LSE] +115
Swing Out Tire Carrier +145

TROOPER   1999

A gold trim package is added to the Trooper's option list and Torque on Demand is now standard with the automatic transmission.

RATINGS (SCALE OF 1-10)

Overall	Safety	Reliability	Performance	Comfort	Value
N/A	7.6	N/A	6.8	7.6	N/A

Category G

4 Dr S 4WD Wgn	16370	19490

OPTIONS FOR TROOPER

Auto 4-Speed Transmission +1145
Luxury Pkg +1260
AM/FM Compact Disc Player +245
Dual Power Seats +285
Heated Front Seats +195
Leather Seats +575
Limited Slip Diff +200

Don't forget to refer to the Mileage Adjustment Table at the back of this book!

ISUZU 99-98

Model Description	Trade-in Value	Market Value

Privacy Glass +195
Running Boards +285

VEHICROSS 1999

Isuzu imports its unique-looking, award-winning SUV to the U.S. in 1999.
Category G

2 Dr STD 4WD Utility	21670	25800

OPTIONS FOR VEHICROSS
Ironman Pkg +800

1998 ISUZU

AMIGO 1998

Isuzu reintroduces its convertible sport utility after a three-year hiatus. This model comes with a modest four-cylinder engine, but the powerful V6 from the Rodeo is available and turns this 4WD droptop into a screamer.
Category G

2 Dr S Utility	9720	11570
2 Dr S 4WD Utility	10200	12140
2 Dr S V6 4WD Utility	10785	12840

OPTIONS FOR AMIGO
AM/FM Compact Disc Player +200
Air Conditioning +495
Aluminum/Alloy Wheels +200
Cruise Control +125
Fog Lights +90
Keyless Entry System +120
Power Door Locks +140
Power Mirrors +80
Power Windows +145
Tilt Steering Wheel +105

HOMBRE 1998

Four-wheel drive arrives, finally. Also new are a theft deterrent system and dual airbags housed in a revised instrument panel, with a passenger-side airbag cutoff switch so the kiddies can ride up front.

RATINGS (SCALE OF 1-10)

Overall	Safety	Reliability	Performance	Comfort	Value
N/A	6.5	8.4	6.6	7.9	N/A

Category G

2 Dr S Std Cab SB	6820	8120
2 Dr XS Ext Cab SB	8480	10095
2 Dr XS 4WD Ext Cab SB	10540	12550
2 Dr XS Std Cab SB	7390	8800
2 Dr XS V6 Ext Cab SB	9435	11235

OPTIONS FOR HOMBRE
Auto 4-Speed Transmission[Std on XS V6] +620
AM/FM Compact Disc Player +200
Air Conditioning +495

Aluminum/Alloy Wheels[Std on S,4WD] +200
Cruise Control +125
Power Door Locks +140
Power Mirrors +80
Power Windows +145
Sliding Rear Window +70
Tilt Steering Wheel +105

OASIS 1998

The engine is upgraded to a more sophisticated 2.3-liter, good for an extra 10 horsepower and 7 foot-ponds of torque, and the transmission is revised. A tachometer is now standard, so you can better measure all that extra power.

RATINGS (SCALE OF 1-10)

Overall	Safety	Reliability	Performance	Comfort	Value
N/A	7.5	9.2	N/A	N/A	N/A

Category G

4 Dr LS Pass. Van	14360	17095
4 Dr S Pass. Van	12950	15415

OPTIONS FOR OASIS
Luggage Rack[Opt on S] +95

RODEO 1998

Though it may not look like it, Isuzu has completely revised the Rodeo from top to bottom, giving it more modern styling, a user-friendly interior, more V6 power, and added room for passengers and cargo.

RATINGS (SCALE OF 1-10)

Overall	Safety	Reliability	Performance	Comfort	Value
6.9	7.1	7.1	7.8	7.3	5.4

Category G

4 Dr LS Wgn	13615	16210
4 Dr LS 4WD Wgn	14370	17105
4 Dr S Wgn	10265	12220
4 Dr S V6 Wgn	10935	13015
4 Dr S V6 4WD Wgn	11835	14090

OPTIONS FOR RODEO
Auto 4-Speed Transmission[Std on LS] +615
AM/FM Compact Disc Player +200
Air Conditioning[Std on LS] +495
Cruise Control[Std on LS] +125
Fog Lights[Std on LS] +90
Heated Power Mirrors[Std on LS] +45
Keyless Entry System[Std on LS] +120
Power Door Locks[Std on LS] +140
Power Windows[Std on LS] +145
Swing Out Tire Carrier[Opt on S, S V6, 2WD] +120
Tilt Steering Wheel[Std on LS] +105

TROOPER 1998

A bigger and lighter engine provides huge improvements in horsepower and torque (up 13 and

---

Don't forget to refer to the Mileage Adjustment Table at the back of this book!

EDMUND'S® USED CARS & TRUCKS

ISUZU 98-97

Model Description	Trade-in Value	Market Value	Model Description	Trade-in Value	Market Value

22 percent, respectively). And the new Torque On Demand (TOD) drive system replaces conventional four-high mode for better performance on paved or slippery roads.

RATINGS (SCALE OF 1-10)

Overall	Safety	Reliability	Performance	Comfort	Value
7.5	7.5	8.7	6.8	7.8	6.9

Category G

4 Dr Luxury 4WD Wgn	17980	21405
4 Dr S 4WD Wgn	14995	17850

OPTIONS FOR TROOPER

Auto 4-Speed Transmission[Opt on S] +770
Leather Seating Pkg +515
Performance Pkg +1020
AM/FM Compact Disc Player +200
Compact Disc Changer[Opt on S] +315
Dual Power Seats[Opt on S] +235
Heated Front Seats[Opt on S] +160
Leather Seats[Opt on S] +470
Limited Slip Diff +165
Privacy Glass +160
Running Boards +235

1997 ISUZU

HOMBRE   1997

A Spacecab model debuts, with seating for five passengers and your choice of four-cylinder or V6 power. Other news includes two fresh paint colors and revised graphics.

RATINGS (SCALE OF 1-10)

Overall	Safety	Reliability	Performance	Comfort	Value
N/A	5.6	8.2	6.6	7.9	N/A

Category G

2 Dr S Std Cab SB	5695	6860
2 Dr XS Ext Cab SB	7285	8775
2 Dr XS Std Cab SB	6255	7535
2 Dr XS V6 Ext Cab SB	8075	9730

OPTIONS FOR HOMBRE

Auto 4-Speed Transmission[Opt on S,XS] +500
AM/FM Compact Disc Player +160
Air Conditioning +405
Cruise Control +105
Power Door Locks +115
Power Windows +120
Rear Step Bumper +70

OASIS   1997

Cruise control is added to the S model's standard equipment list, and four new colors are available.

RATINGS (SCALE OF 1-10)

Overall	Safety	Reliability	Performance	Comfort	Value
7.3	7.5	9.3	7.2	7.1	5.6

Category G

4 Dr LS Pass. Van	13095	15780
4 Dr S Pass. Van	11825	14245

OPTIONS FOR OASIS

AM/FM Compact Disc Player +160
Luggage Rack[Opt on S] +80

RODEO   1997

All 4WD models get a standard shift-on-the-fly transfer case, and improvements have been made to reduce noise, vibration and harshness.

RATINGS (SCALE OF 1-10)

Overall	Safety	Reliability	Performance	Comfort	Value
6.9	6.8	7.8	7	7.1	5.7

Category G

4 Dr LS Wgn	11600	13975
4 Dr LS 4WD Wgn	12350	14880
4 Dr S Wgn	9065	10920
4 Dr S V6 Wgn	9555	11510
4 Dr S V6 4WD Wgn	10310	12420

OPTIONS FOR RODEO

Auto 4-Speed Transmission[Opt on S V6,4WD] +545
Air Conditioning[Std on LS] +405
Aluminum/Alloy Wheels[Std on LS] +165
Anti-Lock Brakes +295
Compact Disc W/fm/tape +240
Cruise Control[Std on LS] +105
Keyless Entry System +100
Leather Seats +385
Limited Slip Diff +135
Luggage Rack[Std on LS] +80
Moonroof +175
Power Door Locks[Std on LS] +115
Power Windows[Std on LS] +120
Running Boards +190
Swing Out Tire Carrier[Opt on S] +95

TROOPER   1997

Antilock brakes are now standard on all models, and dealers get a wider profit margin to help increase sales. Despite delirious requests by a certain consumer group, Isuzu will not equip the Trooper with training wheels for 1997.

RATINGS (SCALE OF 1-10)

Overall	Safety	Reliability	Performance	Comfort	Value
7.3	7.1	8	6.8	7.6	7

Don't forget to refer to the Mileage Adjustment Table at the back of this book!

Model Description	Trade-in Value	Market Value
Category G		
4 Dr LS 4WD Wgn	14765	17790
4 Dr Limited 4WD Wgn	16460	19830
4 Dr S 4WD Wgn	11750	14155

OPTIONS FOR TROOPER
Auto 4-Speed Transmission[Opt on S] +630
Seat Pkg +465
AM/FM Compact Disc Player +160
Air Conditioning[Opt on S] +405
Alarm System[Opt on S] +140
Aluminum/Alloy Wheels[Opt on S] +165
Cruise Control[Opt on S] +105
Dual Power Seats[Opt on LS] +190
Heated Front Seats[Opt on LS] +130
Keyless Entry System[Opt on LS,S] +100
Leather Seats[Opt on LS] +385
Limited Slip Diff[Opt on LS,S] +135
Power Door Locks[Opt on S] +115
Power Moonroof[Opt on LS] +430
Power Windows[Opt on S] +120
Running Boards +190

1996 ISUZU

HOMBRE 1996

In a switch from history, Isuzu clones a Chevy S-10 and dumps its Japanese-built compact truck. Sheetmetal is unique to Isuzu, but everything else is pure General Motors.

RATINGS (SCALE OF 1-10)

Overall	Safety	Reliability	Performance	Comfort	Value
N/A	N/A	8	6.6	7.9	N/A

Category G		
2 Dr S Std Cab SB	4840	5900
2 Dr XS Std Cab SB	5120	6245

OPTIONS FOR HOMBRE
AM/FM Stereo Tape +90
Air Conditioning +330
Rear Step Bumper[Opt on S] +60

OASIS 1996

New Isuzu minivan is a clone of the Honda Odyssey, except for the grille, badging and wheels. The Isuzu offers a better warranty, too.

RATINGS (SCALE OF 1-10)

Overall	Safety	Reliability	Performance	Comfort	Value
N/A	N/A	9.3	7.2	7.1	6.6

Category G		
4 Dr LS Pass. Van	11225	13690
4 Dr S Pass. Van	9885	12050

OPTIONS FOR OASIS
AM/FM Compact Disc Player +135
Cruise Control[Opt on S] +85
Luggage Rack[Opt on S] +65

RODEO 1996

Finally, Isuzu's Rodeo can be equipped with four-wheel antilock brakes, and 4WD models get a standard shift-on-the-fly system. New style wheels debut, and the engine now makes 190 horsepower. Increased wheel track improves ride quality, and spare tire covers are redesigned.

RATINGS (SCALE OF 1-10)

Overall	Safety	Reliability	Performance	Comfort	Value
7	6.8	7.7	7	7.1	6.2

Category G		
4 Dr LS Wgn	10385	12665
4 Dr LS 4WD Wgn	11080	13510
4 Dr S Wgn	7930	9670
4 Dr S V6 Wgn	8295	10115
4 Dr S V6 4WD Wgn	8995	10970

OPTIONS FOR RODEO
Auto 4-Speed Transmission[Opt on S V6,4WD] +440
AM/FM Compact Disc Player +135
Air Conditioning[Std on LS] +330
Aluminum/Alloy Wheels[Std on LS] +135
Anti-Lock Brakes +245
Cruise Control[Std on LS] +85
Keyless Entry System +80
Leather Seats +315
Limited Slip Diff +110
Luggage Rack[Std on LS] +65
Moonroof +140
Power Door Locks[Std on LS] +95
Power Windows[Std on LS] +95
Running Boards +155
Swing Out Tire Carrier[Opt on S] +80

TROOPER 1996

More standard equipment, a horsepower boost for the SOHC V6 engine, and standard shift-on-the-fly debut for 1996.

RATINGS (SCALE OF 1-10)

Overall	Safety	Reliability	Performance	Comfort	Value
7.4	6.6	7.9	6.8	7.6	7.9

Category G		
4 Dr LS 4WD Wgn	12855	15675
4 Dr Limited 4WD Wgn	14970	18255
4 Dr S 4WD Wgn	10495	12800
4 Dr SE 4WD Wgn	14385	17545

ISUZU 96-94

Model Description	Trade-in Value	Market Value	Model Description	Trade-in Value	Market Value

OPTIONS FOR TROOPER
Auto 4-Speed Transmission[Opt on S] +505
Seat Pkg +540
AM/FM Compact Disc Player +135
Air Conditioning[Opt on S] +330
Aluminum/Alloy Wheels[Opt on S] +135
Anti-Lock Brakes[Opt on LS,S] +245
Cruise Control[Opt on S] +85
Dual Power Seats[Opt on LS] +155
Keyless Entry System[Std on SE] +80
Leather Seats[Opt on LS] +315
Limited Slip Diff[Std on SE] +110
Power Door Locks[Opt on S] +95
Power Moonroof[Opt on LS] +350
Power Windows[Opt on S] +95
Running Boards +155

1995 ISUZU

HALF TON PICKUP 1995

Spacecab, V6 power and automatic transmission are canceled for 1995. All that's left are four-cylinder regular-cab trucks in 2WD or 4WD. California didn't get any 1995 Pickups, thanks to strict emissions regulations.

Category G

2 Dr S Std Cab LB	3850	4750
2 Dr S Std Cab SB	3685	4550
2 Dr S 4WD Std Cab SB	5820	7185

OPTIONS FOR HALF TON PICKUP
Wheel Pkg +265
AM/FM Stereo Tape +75
Air Conditioning +270
Power Steering[Opt on 2WD] +95
Rear Step Bumper +50

RODEO 1995

S V6 models can be equipped with a Bright Package in conjunction with the Preferred Equipment Package. It includes lots of chrome trim and aluminum wheels.

RATINGS (SCALE OF 1-10)

Overall	Safety	Reliability	Performance	Comfort	Value
6.6	7	6.4	7	7.1	5.6

Category G

4 Dr LS Wgn	9135	11275
4 Dr LS 4WD Wgn	9835	12145
4 Dr S Wgn	6895	8515
4 Dr S 4WD Wgn	7770	9595
4 Dr S V6 Wgn	7345	9070

OPTIONS FOR RODEO
Auto 4-Speed Transmission[Opt on S,S V6,4WD] +355
Bright Pkg +350
Air Conditioning[Std on LS] +270

Aluminum/Alloy Wheels[Std on LS] +110
Anti-Lock Brakes +200
Compact Disc W/fm/tape +160
Cruise Control[Std on LS] +70
Dual Air Bag Restraints[Opt on S,S V6,2WD] +145
Keyless Entry System +65
Limited Slip Diff +90
Luggage Rack[Std on LS] +50
Power Door Locks[Std on LS] +75
Power Windows[Std on LS] +80
Running Boards +130
Sunroof +95
Swing Out Tire Carrier[Opt on S] +65

TROOPER 1995

Dual airbags are standard. Styling is revised. A new top-of-the-line trim level debuts. The Limited has a power sunroof, leather upholstery, heated seats, and wood grain trim. Suspensions have been reworked to provide a better ride.

RATINGS (SCALE OF 1-10)

Overall	Safety	Reliability	Performance	Comfort	Value
7.4	7.5	8.2	6.8	7.6	7

Category G

4 Dr LS 4WD Wgn	10175	12560
4 Dr Limited 4WD Wgn	11785	14550
2 Dr RS 4WD Utility	9945	12280
4 Dr S 4WD Wgn	8150	10060
4 Dr SE 4WD Wgn	11300	13950

OPTIONS FOR TROOPER
Auto 4-Speed Transmission[Opt on LS,RS,S] +380
AM/FM Compact Disc Player +110
Air Conditioning[Opt on S] +270
Aluminum/Alloy Wheels[Opt on S] +110
Anti-Lock Brakes[Opt on S] +200
Cruise Control[Opt on S] +70
Keyless Entry System[Opt on S] +65
Limited Slip Diff[Opt on S] +90
Power Door Locks[Opt on S] +75
Power Windows[Opt on S] +80
Premium Sound System[Opt on S] +115

1994 ISUZU

AMIGO 1994

Automatic transmission disappears from options list, and base 2.3-liter, four-cylinder engine is no longer available. Power steering, power outside mirrors, a center floor console, and 16-inch tires are all newly standard.

Category G

2 Dr S Utility	4715	5820
2 Dr S 4WD Utility	5295	6540

Don't forget to refer to the Mileage Adjustment Table at the back of this book!

Model Description	Trade-in Value	Market Value
2 Dr XS Utility	5380	6645
2 Dr XS 4WD Utility	5985	7390

OPTIONS FOR AMIGO
AM/FM Stereo Tape +60
Air Conditioning +220
Sunroof[Opt on S,2WD] +80

HALF TON PICKUP   1994

Vent windows are dropped. Models with 2.6-liter engine get standard power steering. Outside mirrors are revised.

Category G

Model Description	Trade-in Value	Market Value
2 Dr S Ext Cab SB	3935	4855
2 Dr S Std Cab LB	3355	4145
2 Dr S 4WD Std Cab SB	4855	5995
2 Dr S 2.6 Ext Cab SB	4020	4960
2 Dr S 2.6 Std Cab SB	3435	4240
2 Dr STD Std Cab SB	3200	3950

OPTIONS FOR HALF TON PICKUP
6 cyl 3.1 L Engine +235
Tire/Wheel Pkg +230
AM/FM Stereo Tape +60
Air Conditioning +220
Chrome Bumpers +45
Power Steering[Std on Ext Cab,4WD] +75
Rear Step Bumper +40

RODEO   1994

S model gets standard power steering. LS models are equipped with standard air conditioning. Front vent windows are dropped. All V6 models come with standard rear wiper/washer and tailgate spare tire carrier.

RATINGS (SCALE OF 1-10)

Overall	Safety	Reliability	Performance	Comfort	Value
6.1	3.7	6.3	7	7.4	6.2

Category G

Model Description	Trade-in Value	Market Value
4 Dr LS Wgn	7730	9545
4 Dr LS 4WD Wgn	8380	10345
4 Dr S Wgn	5525	6820
4 Dr S 4WD Wgn	6455	7970
4 Dr S V6 Wgn	5800	7160

OPTIONS FOR RODEO
Auto 4-Speed Transmission[Opt on S,S V6,4WD] +285
Air Conditioning[Std on LS] +220
Compact Disc W/fm/tape +130
Cruise Control[Std on LS] +55
Keyless Entry System +55
Limited Slip Diff +75
Luggage Rack[Std on LS] +45
Power Door Locks[Std on LS] +65
Power Windows[Std on LS] +65

Sunroof +80
Swing Out Tire Carrier[Opt on 2WD] +55

TROOPER   1994

Four-wheel ABS filters down to the Trooper S options sheet. Gray leather upholstery is a new options for the LS model, and it includes heated front seats with power adjustments. RS gets new alloys.

RATINGS (SCALE OF 1-10)

Overall	Safety	Reliability	Performance	Comfort	Value
7.3	4.2	8.5	7.8	7.8	8.3

Category G

Model Description	Trade-in Value	Market Value
4 Dr LS 4WD Wgn	8245	10180
2 Dr RS 4WD Utility	8005	9885
4 Dr S 4WD Wgn	6825	8425
4 Dr SE 4WD Wgn	9115	11250

OPTIONS FOR TROOPER
Auto 4-Speed Transmission[Std on SE] +315
AM/FM Compact Disc Player +90
Air Conditioning[Opt on S] +220
Anti-Lock Brakes[Opt on S] +160
Cruise Control[Opt on S] +55
Dual Power Seats[Opt on LS] +105
Heated Front Seats[Opt on LS] +70
Leather Seats[Opt on LS] +210
Limited Slip Diff[Opt on S] +75
Power Door Locks[Opt on S] +65
Power Sunroof[Opt on LS] +210
Power Windows[Opt on S] +65

1993 ISUZU

AMIGO   1993

Amigo gets a new grille.

Category G

Model Description	Trade-in Value	Market Value
2 Dr S Utility	3800	4870
2 Dr S 4WD Utility	4185	5365
2 Dr XS Utility	4405	5650
2 Dr XS 4WD Utility	4795	6150

OPTIONS FOR AMIGO
4 cyl 2.6 L Engine[Std on XS,4WD] +190
Auto 4-Speed Transmission +200
Amigo Tire/Wheel Pkg +180
AM/FM Stereo Tape +50
Air Conditioning +180
Aluminum/Alloy Wheels[Opt on S,2WD] +75
Sunroof +65

HALF TON PICKUP   1993

LS trim level dropped. Two models discontinued: one-ton Longbed and 4WD Spacecab. A new grille graces the front of the Pickup.

Don't forget to refer to the Mileage Adjustment Table at the back of this book!

Model Description	Trade-in Value	Market Value
Category G		
2 Dr S Ext Cab SB	3385	4340
2 Dr S Std Cab LB	2860	3665
2 Dr S Std Cab SB	2755	3530
2 Dr S 4WD Std Cab SB	4235	5430
2 Dr S 2.6 Std Cab SB	2845	3645

OPTIONS FOR HALF TON PICKUP
6 cyl 3.1 L Engine +190
Pick Up 4WD Bright Pkg +270
AM/FM Stereo Tape +50
Air Conditioning +180
Aluminum/Alloy Wheels +75
Power Steering[Std on S 2.6,Ext Cab,4WD] +60
Rear Step Bumper +30

RODEO 1993

More potent V6 engine filters into Rodeo from big brother Trooper for a horsepower boost of 55 ponies. A new grille is installed up front.

RATINGS (SCALE OF 1-10)

Overall	Safety	Reliability	Performance	Comfort	Value
6.4	4	7.6	7	7.4	6.2

	Trade-in	Market
Category G		
4 Dr LS Wgn	6230	7985
4 Dr LS 4WD Wgn	6755	8660
4 Dr S Wgn	4525	5800
4 Dr S 4WD Wgn	5290	6780
4 Dr S V6 Wgn	4760	6105

OPTIONS FOR RODEO
Auto 4-Speed Transmission +220
Rodeo Tire/Wheel Pkg +200
AM/FM Compact Disc Player +70
Air Conditioning +180
Aluminum/Alloy Wheels +75
Cruise Control[Std on LS] +45
Limited Slip Diff +60
Luggage Rack[Std on LS] +35
Sunroof +65

TROOPER 1993

A short-wheelbase two-door model joins the lineup in RS trim. Four-wheel ABS is optional on this stubby new model.

RATINGS (SCALE OF 1-10)

Overall	Safety	Reliability	Performance	Comfort	Value
6.8	4	8	7.8	7.8	6.4

	Trade-in	Market
Category G		
4 Dr LS 4WD Wgn	7075	9070
2 Dr RS 4WD Utility	6410	8220
4 Dr S 4WD Wgn	5900	7565

OPTIONS FOR TROOPER
Auto 4-Speed Transmission +260
AM/FM Compact Disc Player +70
Air Conditioning[Opt on S] +180
Aluminum/Alloy Wheels[Opt on S] +75
Cruise Control[Opt on S] +45
Limited Slip Diff[Opt on S] +60
Power Door Locks[Opt on S] +50
Power Sunroof +170
Power Windows[Opt on S] +55
Premium Sound System[Opt on S] +75

1992 ISUZU

AMIGO 1992

Those who hate shifting their own gears are in luck; an automatic is newly optional.

	Trade-in	Market
Category G		
2 Dr S Utility	2975	3915
2 Dr S 4WD Utility	3300	4340
2 Dr XS Utility	3575	4705
2 Dr XS 4WD Utility	3905	5140

OPTIONS FOR AMIGO
4 cyl 2.6 L Engine[Std on XS,4WD] +135
Auto 4-Speed Transmission +160
Air Conditioning +145
Sunroof +55

HALF TON PICKUP 1992

No changes.

	Trade-in	Market
Category G		
2 Dr LS Ext Cab SB	3255	4285
2 Dr S Ext Cab SB	2880	3790
2 Dr S Std Cab LB	2415	3180
2 Dr S Std Cab SB	2350	3090
2 Dr S 4WD Std Cab SB	3790	4985

OPTIONS FOR HALF TON PICKUP
4 cyl 2.6 L Engine[Std on LS,Ext Cab,4WD] +135
6 cyl 3.1 L Engine +75
Auto 4-Speed Transmission +160
Air Conditioning +145
Cruise Control +40
Power Door Locks +40
Power Windows +45

IMPULSE 1992

XS gets ten more horsepower, thanks to a larger 1.8-liter twin-cam engine.

	Trade-in	Market
Category E		
2 Dr XS Cpe	2540	3625

OPTIONS FOR IMPULSE
Impulse Rs Pkg +150
Air Conditioning[Std on RS] +145

Don't forget to refer to the Mileage Adjustment Table at the back of this book!

ISUZU 92-91

Model Description	Trade-in Value	Market Value

RODEO 1992

No changes.

RATINGS (SCALE OF 1-10)

Overall	Safety	Reliability	Performance	Comfort	Value
6.2	4.1	7	6.6	7.4	6.1

Category G

	Trade-in	Market
4 Dr LS Wgn	4935	6495
4 Dr LS 4WD Wgn	5510	7250
4 Dr LX 4WD Wgn	5650	7435
4 Dr S Wgn	3850	5065
4 Dr S 4WD Wgn	4570	6010
4 Dr S V6 Wgn	4060	5340
4 Dr XS Wgn	4260	5605
4 Dr XS 4WD Wgn	4800	6315

OPTIONS FOR RODEO
Auto 3-Speed Transmission +160
Auto 4-Speed Transmission +180
Air Conditioning +145
Cruise Control +40
Limited Slip Diff[Opt on LS] +50
Power Door Locks +40
Power Windows +45
Sunroof +55

STYLUS 1992

RS gets 10 more horsepower, thanks to a larger 1.8-liter twin-cam engine.

Category E

	Trade-in	Market
4 Dr RS Sdn	1655	2365
4 Dr S Sdn	1485	2120

OPTIONS FOR STYLUS
Auto 3-Speed Transmission +100
Air Conditioning +145
Cruise Control +40
Power Door Locks +45
Power Windows +50

TROOPER 1992

Beefy SUV moves upscale with total redesign that renders it longer, wider, taller and heavier. Four-wheel ABS is optional on LS models. A new Isuzu-designed 3.2-liter V6 powers Trooper; base models have an SOHC unit, while LS models get a DOHC engine good for 190 horsepower.

RATINGS (SCALE OF 1-10)

Overall	Safety	Reliability	Performance	Comfort	Value
6.9	4	8.4	7.8	7.8	6.4

Category G

	Trade-in	Market
4 Dr LS 4WD Wgn	6215	8175
4 Dr S 4WD Wgn	4835	6365

OPTIONS FOR TROOPER
Auto 4-Speed Transmission +205
Air Conditioning[Opt on S] +145
Anti-Lock Brakes[Std on S] +110
Limited Slip Diff[Opt on S] +50
Power Sunroof +140

1991 ISUZU

AMIGO 1991

Warranty changes from 3 years/36,000 miles to 3 years/50,000 miles. Rust coverage is extended to 6 years/100,000 miles from 3 years/unlimited mileage. New powertrain warranty is good for 5 years/60,000 miles. XS gets locking center console standard; item is optional on S. New paint colors, graphics and alloy wheels debut.

Category G

	Trade-in	Market
2 Dr S Utility	2500	3380
2 Dr S 4WD Utility	2810	3800
2 Dr XS Utility	3015	4075
2 Dr XS 4WD Utility	3310	4475

OPTIONS FOR AMIGO
4 cyl 2.6 L Engine[Std on XS,4WD] +85
Air Conditioning +120
Sunroof +45

HALF TON PICKUP 1991

Warranty changes from 3 years/36,000 miles to 3 years/50,000 miles. Rust coverage extended to 6 years/100,000 miles. New powertrain warranty is good for 5 years/60,000 miles. A 3.1-liter, GM V-6 is newly optional. Grille and tailgate graphics are revised with new lettering. LS models get standard sliding rear window. On 2WD with 2.6-liter engine, drums replace the rear discs.

Category G

	Trade-in	Market
2 Dr LS Ext Cab SB	2810	3800
2 Dr LS 4WD Std Cab SB	3480	4700
2 Dr S Ext Cab SB	2365	3195
2 Dr S Std Cab LB	2045	2765
2 Dr S Std Cab SB	1990	2690
2 Dr S 4WD Std Cab SB	2935	3965

OPTIONS FOR HALF TON PICKUP
4 cyl 2.6 L Engine[Std on LS,Ext Cab,4WD] +85
6 cyl 3.1 L Engine[Opt on S] +50
Auto 4-Speed Transmission +125
Power Pkg +115
Air Conditioning +120
Cruise Control +30
Power Door Locks +35
Power Windows +35

EDMUND'S® USED CARS & TRUCKS

Model Description	Trade-in Value	Market Value

IMPULSE 1991

New RS model debuts equipped with turbocharged engine and all-wheel drive, two items twin Geo Storm never received. RS turbo makes 160 horsepower and can be equipped with optional ABS. Also new is an aberration called Impulse XS hatchback. Warranty changes from 3 years/36,000 miles to 3 years/50,000 miles. Rust coverage is extended to 6 years/100,000 miles from 3 years/unlimited mileage. New powertrain warranty is good for 5 years/60,000 miles.

Category E

2 Dr RS Turbo 4WD Cpe	1880	2765
2 Dr XS Cpe	1695	2490
2 Dr XS Hbk	1545	2275

OPTIONS FOR IMPULSE

Auto 4-Speed Transmission +110
Air Conditioning +120
Cruise Control +35
Power Door Locks +35
Power Sunroof +90
Power Windows +40

ONE TON 1991

Category G

2 Dr S Std Cab LB	2360	3190

OPTIONS FOR ONE TON

Air Conditioning +120

RODEO 1991

New Pickup-based sport utility debuts. Built in Indiana. Available with two- or four-wheel-drive with either Isuzu-built four cylinder or GM-sourced V6. Rodeo features a long wheelbase for ride comfort and excellent rear seat legroom. Four-wheel disc brakes accompany V6 engines.

RATINGS (SCALE OF 1-10)

Overall	Safety	Reliability	Performance	Comfort	Value
6.1	4	6.9	6.6	7.4	5.6

Category G

4 Dr LS Wgn	3845	5195
4 Dr LS 4WD Wgn	4460	6025
4 Dr S Wgn	3080	4165
4 Dr S 4WD Wgn	3715	5020
4 Dr S V6 Wgn	3200	4405
4 Dr XS Wgn	3610	4875
4 Dr XS 4WD Wgn	4075	5510

OPTIONS FOR RODEO

Auto 4-Speed Transmission +140
Air Conditioning +120
Cruise Control +30
Power Door Locks +35

Power Windows +35
Sunroof +45

STYLUS 1991

New sedan based on Impulse running gear includes standard driver airbag. XS is quite a spry sport sedan with 130-horsepower, twin-cam 1.6-liter engine.

Category E

4 Dr S Sdn	1290	1895
4 Dr XS Sdn	1470	2165

OPTIONS FOR STYLUS

Auto 3-Speed Transmission +70
Air Conditioning +120
Cruise Control +35
Power Door Locks +35
Power Sunroof +90
Power Windows +40

TROOPER 1991

Warranty changes from 3 years/36,000 miles to 3 years/50,000 miles. Rust coverage is extended to 6 years/100,000 miles from 3 years/unlimited mileage. New powertrain warranty is good for 5 years/60,000 miles.

Category G

4 Dr LS 4WD Wgn	3955	5345
4 Dr S 4WD Wgn	3400	4595
4 Dr SE 4WD Wgn	4070	5500
4 Dr XS 4WD Wgn	3655	4940

OPTIONS FOR TROOPER

6 cyl 2.8 L Engine[Opt on S] +60
Auto 4-Speed Transmission +160
Air Conditioning +120
Camper/Towing Package[Opt on S] +45

1990 ISUZU

AMIGO 1990

A removable stereo is a new option.

Category G

2 Dr S Utility	2065	2865
2 Dr S 4WD Utility	2295	3190
2 Dr XS Utility	2360	3280
2 Dr XS 4WD Utility	2760	3830

OPTIONS FOR AMIGO

4 cyl 2.6 L Engine[Std on XS, 4WD] +75
Air Conditioning +100
Sunroof +35

HALF TON PICKUP 1990

Rear-wheel ABS debuts. System works only in 2WD.

Category G

2 Dr LS Ext Cab SB	2390	3320
2 Dr LS 4WD Ext Cab SB	2990	4155

Don't forget to refer to the Mileage Adjustment Table at the back of this book!

ISUZU 90

Model Description	Trade-in Value	Market Value
2 Dr LS Std Cab SB	2010	2795
2 Dr LS 4WD Std Cab SB	2615	3635
2 Dr S Ext Cab SB	1970	2735
2 Dr S Std Cab LB	1735	2410
2 Dr S Std Cab SB	1650	2295
2 Dr S 4WD Std Cab SB	2425	3365
2 Dr XS Ext Cab SB	2085	2895
2 Dr XS Std Cab SB	1715	2385
2 Dr XS 4WD Std Cab SB	2490	3455

OPTIONS FOR HALF TON PICKUP
4 cyl 2.6 L Engine[Std on LS,XS,Ext Cab,4WD] +75
Auto 4-Speed Transmission +100
Power Pkg +95
Air Conditioning +100
Cruise Control +25
Power Door Locks +30
Power Windows +30

IMPULSE   1990

Totally redesigned car carrying traditional Impulse styling cues. Identical in structure and engineering to Geo Storm. XS model has 130 horsepower normally aspirated motor and front-wheel drive. Driver airbag is standard.

Model Description	Trade-in Value	Market Value
Category E		
2 Dr XS Hbk	1420	2150

OPTIONS FOR IMPULSE
Auto 4-Speed Transmission +90
Air Conditioning +100
Cruise Control +25
Power Door Locks +30
Power Windows +30

TROOPER   1990

S model gets full carpeting, dual outside mirrors and improved instrumentation. XS model is available only with V6 engine. After one season, the short-wheelbase two-door model is dropped.

Category G		
4 Dr LS 4WD Wgn	3190	4430
4 Dr S 4WD Wgn	2815	3910
4 Dr XS 4WD Wgn	2990	4150

OPTIONS FOR TROOPER
6 cyl 2.8 L Engine[Opt on S] +45
Auto 4-Speed Transmission +135
Air Conditioning +100
Camper/Towing Package +35

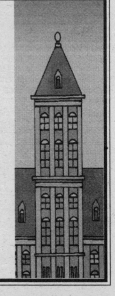
Don't forget to refer to the Mileage Adjustment Table at the back of this book!

JAGUAR — Britain

1995 Jaguar XJ12

Harman Kardon Sound Sys +1055
Traction Control System +875

1998 JAGUAR

XJ-SERIES — 1998

A new V8 engine, taken from the XK8 coupe and convertible, makes its way into the engine bay. A revised instrument panel greatly improves interior ergonomics. Cruise and satellite stereo controls are located on the steering wheel.

Category J

	Trade-in	Market
4 Dr Vanden Plas Sdn	36495	42435
4 Dr XJ8 Sdn	32425	37705
4 Dr XJ8L Sdn	34045	39590

Category L

	Trade-in	Market
4 Dr XJR Sprchgd Sdn	40180	47270

OPTIONS FOR XJ-SERIES
All Weather Pkg +765
Compact Disc Changer +560
Harman Kardon Sound Sys +860
Heated Seats +300
Traction Control System +715

XK-SERIES — 1998

The 1998 XK8 gets automatic on/off headlamps, an engine immobilizer feature as part of the security system, and a cellular phone keypad integrated into the stereo controls. Other changes include the addition of two new exterior colors.

Category J

	Trade-in	Market
2 Dr XK8 Conv	44395	51620
2 Dr XK8 Cpe	41050	47735

OPTIONS FOR XK-SERIES
Compact Disc Changer +560

1999 JAGUAR

XJ-SERIES — 1999

Jaguar's venerable XJ sedans enter '99 largely unchanged after a major workover in '98.

RATINGS (SCALE OF 1-10)

Overall	Safety	Reliability	Performance	Comfort	Value
N/A	N/A	N/A	8	7.8	N/A

Category J

	Trade-in	Market
4 Dr XJ8 Sdn	36920	42435
4 Dr Vanden Plas Sdn	41865	48120

Category L

	Trade-in	Market
4 Dr XJR Sprchgd Sdn	45690	53125

OPTIONS FOR XJ-SERIES
All Weather Pkg +1010
Compact Disc Changer[Std on Sprchgd] +685
Harman Kardon Sound Sys[Std on Sprchgd] +1055
Heated Seats[Std on Sprchgd] +365
Traction Control System[Std on Sprchgd] +875

XK-SERIES — 1999

The stunning XK returns for '99 with no significant changes.

RATINGS (SCALE OF 1-10)

Overall	Safety	Reliability	Performance	Comfort	Value
N/A	N/A	N/A	8.8	7.9	N/A

Category J

	Trade-in	Market
2 Dr XK8 Conv	46875	53880

OPTIONS FOR XK-SERIES
Chrome Wheels +1090
Compact Disc Changer +685

1997 JAGUAR

XJ-SERIES — 1997

The 1997 XJ-Series loses the V12 model that has been a mainstay of the Jaguar lineup for so many years. A long-wheelbase model becomes available this year, filling a niche between the XJ6 and the Vanden Plas. All models receive a contoured bench seat and three-point seatbelts for rear occupants. The XJ6 replaces last year's chrome-vane grille with a black-vane grille, and the convenience group becomes optional on this model. The XJR loses its rear passenger heater ducts.

Category J

	Trade-in	Market
4 Dr Vanden Plas Sdn	29445	34640
4 Dr XJ6 Sdn	25490	29990
4 Dr XJ6L Sdn	26990	31755

Don't forget to refer to the Mileage Adjustment Table at the back of this book!

Category L

4 Dr XJR Sprchgd Sdn	31750	37355

OPTIONS FOR XJ-SERIES
All Weather Pkg +1005
Chrome Wheels +730
Compact Disc Changer +455
Traction Control System +585

XK8   1997

An all-new Jaguar debuts this year, replacing the stodgy XJ-S. This new sports car boasts the first V-8 engine ever found in a Jag, as well as an all-new 5-speed manual transmission that features normal and sport modes. The XK8 is available in coupe and convertible forms, but Jaguar insiders expect a full 70% of sales to be of the convertible.

Category J

2 Dr XK8 Conv	38255	45005
2 Dr XK8 Cpe	33905	39890

OPTIONS FOR XK8
All-weather Pkg +1005
Compact Disc Changer +455
Harman Kardon Sound Sys +705
Traction Control System +585

1996 JAGUAR

XJ-SERIES   1996

On the XJ6, thicker side window glass insulates passengers from annoying wind noise and outside distractions. After a 20-year reign, the XJS coupe is put out to pasture. The only model offered for 1996 is the six-cylinder convertible; the most popular XJS in its unremarkable history. The changes for 1996 include new wheels, new bucket seats, additional chrome exterior trim, and an adjustable, wood-trimmed steering wheel.

Category J

4 Dr Vanden Plas Sdn	24490	29155
4 Dr XJ12 Sdn	27575	32825
4 Dr XJ6 Sdn	21355	25425
2 Dr XJS Conv	27565	32815

Category L

4 Dr XJR Sprchgd Sdn	27210	32390

OPTIONS FOR XJ-SERIES
All Weather Pkg +400
Chrome Wheels +595
Compact Disc Changer +375
Sport Suspension +170
Traction Control System +480

1995 JAGUAR

XJ-SERIES   1995

Horsepower is upped for naturally aspirated 4.0-liter engine, and inline-six and V12 engines. New sheetmetal showcases a more "traditional" Jaguar, ironic considering the amount of input Ford had into the creation of this car. XJS V12 models get new wheels and a plethora of standard equipment such as heated seats and a multi-disc CD changer. A supercharged XJR model is introduced.

Category J

4 Dr XJ12 Sdn	22760	27420
4 Dr XJ6 Sdn	16725	20150
4 Dr XJ6 Vanden Plas Sdn	19185	23115
2 Dr XJS Conv	21640	26070
2 Dr XJS Cpe	18135	21850
2 Dr XJS V12 Conv	24390	29385
2 Dr XJS V12 Cpe	20700	24940

Category L

4 Dr XJR Sprchgd Sdn	22425	27350

OPTIONS FOR XJ-SERIES
Luxury Pkg +415
AM/FM Compact Disc Player +145
Chrome Wheels +485
Compact Disc Changer +305
Limited Slip Diff +270
Power Sunroof +375
Rear Spoiler +135
Traction Control System +390

1994 JAGUAR

XJ-SERIES   1994

A passenger airbag joins the safety equipment roster. CFC-free air conditioning is added to the standard equipment list. For the XJS, a five-speed manual transmission is available as a new option for the 4.0-liter inline-six engine. An XJR-S derived XJ-S 6.0-liter V12 is available, they are differentiated by a rear spoiler, mirrors, grille, and alloy wheels. The XJ-12 is available with a 301-horsepower engine and a four-speed automatic transmission.

Category J

2 Dr XJS Cpe	14055	16935
4 Dr XJ6 Sdn	12145	14635
4 Dr XJ6 Vanden Plas Sdn	14050	16925
2 Dr XJS Conv	17575	21175
2 Dr XJS V12 Conv	20085	24200
2 Dr XJS V12 Cpe	16590	19985

Don't forget to refer to the Mileage Adjustment Table at the back of this book!

Model Description	Trade-in Value	Market Value

Model Description	Trade-in Value	Market Value

OPTIONS FOR XJ-SERIES
Sport Handling Pkg +275
AM/FM Compact Disc Player +120
Limited Slip Diff +220
Power Sunroof +305

1993 JAGUAR

XJ-SERIES 1993

The XJ6 loses the Sovereign model. Comfy power seats, integrated fog lights and new wheels mark the changes for Britain's most popular luxury sedan. ON the XJS, the V12 engine is dropped in favor of a 4.0-liter inline-six. Mercifully, a four-speed automatic transmission replaces the previous three-speed. A traction control system starts the car in second gear to limit wheel-spin on slippery surfaces.

Category J

Model	Trade-in	Market
4 Dr XJ6 Sdn	8915	11005
4 Dr XJ6 Vanden Plas Sdn	10660	13160
2 Dr XJS Conv	14785	18250
2 Dr XJS Cpe	11860	14645

OPTIONS FOR XJ-SERIES
Compact Disc Changer +205
Power Sunroof +250

1992 JAGUAR

XJ-SERIES 1992

The XJS gets a new grille and headlights. Two-driver memory is also available for the mirrors and driver's seat.

Category J

Model	Trade-in	Market
4 Dr XJ6 Sdn	7285	9340
4 Dr XJ6 Majestic Sdn	9175	11760
4 Dr XJ6 Sovereign Sdn	7545	9675
4 Dr XJ6 Vanden Plas Sdn	8620	11050
2 Dr XJS Conv	13015	16685
2 Dr XJS Cpe	10440	13385

1991 JAGUAR

XJ-SERIES 1991

Bigger engine is available on the XJS to compete with sportier competitors. A driver airbag is added to the standard equipment list.

Category J

Model	Trade-in	Market
4 Dr XJ6 Sdn	5900	7665
4 Dr XJ6 Sovereign Sdn	6485	8420
4 Dr XJ6 Vanden Plas Sdn	7345	9540
2 Dr XJS Conv	11525	14965
2 Dr XJS Cpe	8710	11310

1990 JAGUAR

XJ-SERIES 1990

Broadening appeal, Jaguar offers four trim-levels of their attractive XJ6 sedan. Analog gauges replace the digital dash that looked so out of place on last year's Jaguar. Engine power has been boosted and a new four-speed automatic transmission delivers the power to the wheels.

Category J

Model	Trade-in	Market
4 Dr XJ6 Sdn	5135	6845
4 Dr XJ6 Sovereign Sdn	5650	7530
4 Dr XJ6 Vanden Majestic Sdn	6935	9245
4 Dr XJ6 Vanden Plas Sdn	6585	8780
2 Dr XJS Conv	9925	13235
2 Dr XJS Cpe	7485	9980

OPTIONS FOR XJ-SERIES
Power Sunroof +135

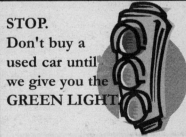
Don't forget to refer to the Mileage Adjustment Table at the back of this book!

JEEP 99

Model Description	Trade-in Value	Market Value	Model Description	Trade-in Value	Market Value

JEEP   USA

1997 Jeep Wrangler

1999 JEEP

CHEROKEE   1999

The Cherokee Sport gets a revised front fascia including body-colored grille and bumpers. New exterior colors include Forest Green and Desert Sand, to match the most common Cherokee surroundings.

RATINGS (SCALE OF 1-10)

Overall	Safety	Reliability	Performance	Comfort	Value
N/A	6.3	8.4	7.4	7	N/A

Category G
	Trade-in	Market
4 Dr Classic Wgn	13940	16595
4 Dr Classic 4WD Wgn	14805	17625
4 Dr Limited Wgn	15980	19025
4 Dr Limited 4WD Wgn	16760	19950
2 Dr SE Utility	11120	13240
2 Dr SE 4WD Utility	11800	14050
4 Dr SE Wgn	11700	13930
4 Dr SE 4WD Wgn	12447	14820
2 Dr Sport Utility	12155	14470
2 Dr Sport 4WD Utility	12770	15205
4 Dr Sport Wgn	12795	15235
4 Dr Sport 4WD Wgn	13480	16050

OPTIONS FOR CHEROKEE
6 cyl 4.0 L Engine[Opt on SE] +750
Auto 3-Speed Transmission +460
Auto 4-Speed Transmission[Opt on SE,Sport] +700
Air Conditioning[Std on Limited] +605
Aluminum/Alloy Wheels[Opt on SE,Sport] +245
Anti-Lock Brakes +445
Compact Disc W/fm/tape +355
Cruise Control[Std on Limited] +155
Fog Lights +105

Keyless Entry System[Std on Limited] +150
Power Door Locks[Std on Limited] +170
Power Drivers Seat[Std on Limited] +210
Power Mirrors[Opt on SE,Sport] +100
Power Windows[Std on Limited] +175
Rear Window Wiper[Opt on SE,Sport] +115
Tilt Steering Wheel[Std on Limited] +130

GRAND CHEROKEE   1999

A lot. The new-for-99 Grand Cherokee contains only 127 carryover parts from the current model, and gets a new powertrain, rear suspension, braking and steering systems, 4WD system, interior and exterior styling.

RATINGS (SCALE OF 1-10)

Overall	Safety	Reliability	Performance	Comfort	Value
N/A	N/A	8.3	7	7.6	N/A

Category G
	Trade-in	Market
4 Dr Laredo Wgn	17680	21045
4 Dr Laredo 4WD Wgn	18490	22010
4 Dr Limited Wgn	20390	24275
4 Dr Limited 4WD Wgn	21170	25205

OPTIONS FOR GRAND CHEROKEE
8 cyl 4.7 L Engine +785
QuadraDrive Transfer Case +735
AM/FM Compact Disc Player +245
Camper/Towing Package +220
Dual Power Seats[Opt on Laredo] +285
Fog Lights[Opt on Laredo] +105
Heated Front Seats +195
Leather Seats[Opt on Laredo] +575
Power Sunroof +580
Sunscreen Glass[Opt on Laredo] +275

WRANGLER   1999

The Wrangler's interior finally enters the '90s with rotary HVAC controls, replacing the old slider control system. The hard or soft top is available in Dark Tan, and new colors decorate both the exterior and the interior.

RATINGS (SCALE OF 1-10)

Overall	Safety	Reliability	Performance	Comfort	Value
N/A	7.1	8.3	7	5.6	N/A

Category G
	Trade-in	Market
2 Dr SE 4WD Utility	10985	13080
2 Dr Sahara 4WD Utility	14765	17575
2 Dr Sport 4WD Utility	12745	15170

OPTIONS FOR WRANGLER
Auto 3-Speed Transmission +460
Color Match Dual Roofs +1130
AM/FM Stereo Tape[Std on Sahara] +170
Air Conditioning +605
Aluminum/Alloy Wheels[Std on Sahara] +245
Anti-Lock Brakes +445

Don't forget to refer to the Mileage Adjustment Table at the back of this book!

Model Description	Trade-in Value	Market Value	Model Description	Trade-in Value	Market Value

Cruise Control +155
Hardtop Roof +585
Rear Window Defroster +125
Rear Window Wiper +115
Tilt Steering Wheel[Std on Sahara] +130

1998 JEEP

CHEROKEE 1998

Cherokee Classic and Limited replace the Cherokee Country. A new 2.5-liter four-cylinder engine is now the base engine for the SE, available with an optional three-speed automatic. New colors include Chili Pepper Red, Emerald Green and Deep Amethyst.

RATINGS (SCALE OF 1-10)

Overall	Safety	Reliability	Performance	Comfort	Value
6.9	6.1	7.5	7.4	7	6.3

Category G
4 Dr Classic Wgn	12650	15060
4 Dr Classic 4WD Wgn	13285	15815
4 Dr Limited Wgn	14645	17435
4 Dr Limited 4WD Wgn	15340	18260
2 Dr SE Utility	9650	11490
2 Dr SE 4WD Utility	10315	12280
4 Dr SE Wgn	10085	12005
4 Dr SE 4WD Wgn	10755	12805
2 Dr Sport Utility	10710	12750
2 Dr Sport 4WD Utility	11295	13445
4 Dr Sport Wgn	11180	13310
4 Dr Sport 4WD Wgn	11825	14080

OPTIONS FOR CHEROKEE

6 cyl 4.0 L Engine[Opt on SE] +550
Auto 3-Speed Transmission +410
Auto 4-Speed Transmission[Opt on SE, Sport] +580
Air Conditioning[Std on Limited] +495
Aluminum/Alloy Wheels[Opt on SE, Sport] +200
Anti-Lock Brakes +365
Auto Locking Hubs (4WD)[Opt on Utility] +155
Compact Disc W/fm/tape +290
Cruise Control[Std on Limited] +125
Fog Lights +90
Keyless Entry System[Std on Limited] +120
Leather Seats[Opt on Classic] +470
Power Door Locks[Std on Limited] +140
Power Drivers Seat[Std on Limited] +170
Power Mirrors[Opt on SE, Sport] +80
Power Windows[Std on Limited] +145
Rear Window Defroster[Std on Limited] +105
Rear Window Wiper[Opt on SE, Sport] +95
Sunscreen Glass[Opt on Sport] +225
Tilt Steering Wheel[Std on Limited] +105

GRAND CHEROKEE 1998

A 5.9-liter V8 making 245 horsepower and 345 foot-pounds torque powers the Grand Cherokee 5.9 Limited, making it the mightiest of all Jeeps. With the addition of the 5.9, the putrid Orvis model dies. Two new colors and "next-generation" airbags round out the changes.

RATINGS (SCALE OF 1-10)

Overall	Safety	Reliability	Performance	Comfort	Value
7.2	7.1	8.1	7	7.6	6.4

Category G
4 Dr 5.9 Limited 4WD Wgn	19650	23395
4 Dr Laredo Wgn	14375	17115
4 Dr Laredo 4WD Wgn	15135	18015
4 Dr Limited Wgn	17035	20280
4 Dr Limited 4WD Wgn	17750	21130
4 Dr TSi Wgn	16165	19245
4 Dr TSi 4WD Wgn	16850	20060

OPTIONS FOR GRAND CHEROKEE

8 cyl 5.2 L Engine +535
Camper/Towing Package +180
Compact Disc W/fm/tape[Opt on Laredo, TSi] +290
Dual Power Seats[Opt on Laredo, TSi] +235
Fog Lights[Opt on Laredo, TSi] +90
Heated Front Seats[Std on 5.9 Limited] +160
Heated Power Mirrors[Opt on Laredo, TSi] +45
Leather Seats[Opt on Laredo, TSi] +470
Locking Differential[Std on 5.9 Limited] +180
Power Sunroof[Std on 5.9 Limited] +470
Sunscreen Glass[Opt on Laredo, TSi] +225

WRANGLER 1998

Jeep has improved off-road capability by increasing the axle ratio offered with the 4.0-liter engine and revising the torsion bar for better steering. Optional this year are a tilting driver's seat, automatic speed control, a combination CD/cassette stereo, a new Smart Key Immobilizer theft deterrent system and two new colors.

RATINGS (SCALE OF 1-10)

Overall	Safety	Reliability	Performance	Comfort	Value
6.4	6.9	7.4	7	5.6	5.2

Category G
2 Dr SE 4WD Utility	9900	11785
2 Dr Sahara 4WD Utility	12900	15360
2 Dr Sport 4WD Utility	11550	13750

OPTIONS FOR WRANGLER

Auto 3-Speed Transmission +385
Color Match Dual Roofs +980
AM/FM Stereo Tape[Std on Sahara] +135

Don't forget to refer to the Mileage Adjustment Table at the back of this book!

JEEP 98-97

Model Description	Trade-in Value	Market Value	Model Description	Trade-in Value	Market Value

Air Conditioning +495
Aluminum/Alloy Wheels[Opt on Sport] +200
Anti-Lock Brakes +365
Compact Disc W/fm/tape +290
Cruise Control +125
Fog Lights[Opt on Sport] +90
Hardtop Roof +480
Rear Window Defroster +105
Rear Window Wiper +95
Tilt Steering Wheel[Std on Sahara] +105
Velour/Cloth Seats[Std on Sahara] +130

1997 JEEP

CHEROKEE 1997

A new interior sporting modern instrumentation debuts. Front and rear styling is refined, and the rear liftgate is now stamped from steel. Multi-plex wiring is designed to improve reliability of the electrical system, while a new paint process aims to polish the finish of all Cherokees.

RATINGS (SCALE OF 1-10)

Overall	Safety	Reliability	Performance	Comfort	Value
6.8	6	6.9	7.4	7	6.9

Category G

4 Dr Country Wgn	12195	14695
4 Dr Country 4WD Wgn	12795	15415
2 Dr SE Utility	8145	9815
2 Dr SE 4WD Utility	8800	10600
4 Dr SE Wgn	8570	10325
4 Dr SE 4WD Wgn	9220	11110
2 Dr Sport Utility	9145	11020
2 Dr Sport 4WD Utility	9730	11720
4 Dr Sport Wgn	9545	11500
4 Dr Sport 4WD Wgn	10205	12295

OPTIONS FOR CHEROKEE

6 cyl 4.0 L Engine[Opt on SE] +415
Auto 4-Speed Transmission[Std on Country] +475
Air Conditioning +405
Aluminum/Alloy Wheels[Std on Country] +165
Anti-Lock Brakes +295
Camper/Towing Package +150
Compact Disc W/fm/tape +240
Cruise Control +105
Keyless Entry System[Opt on Sport] +100
Leather Seats +385
Locking Differential +145
Luggage Rack[Std on Country] +80
Power Door Locks[Opt on Sport] +115
Power Drivers Seat +140
Power Windows[Opt on Sport] +120
Skid Plates +65

GRAND CHEROKEE 1997

Last year's integrated child safety seat has mysteriously disappeared from press kit and dealer order sheet radar. Other big news is the availability of the optional 5.2-liter V8 engine in 2WD models, and a six-cylinder that qualifies the JGC as a Transitional Low Emissions Vehicle (TLEV) in California. Refinements have been made to the ABS system, entry-level cassette stereo, and floor carpet fit. In January, a sporty TSi model debuted with monotone paint, special aluminum wheels, and other goodies.

RATINGS (SCALE OF 1-10)

Overall	Safety	Reliability	Performance	Comfort	Value
7.1	6.8	6.9	7	7.6	7

Category G

4 Dr Laredo Wgn	12735	15345
4 Dr Laredo 4WD Wgn	13390	16135
4 Dr Limited Wgn	14835	17875
4 Dr Limited 4WD Wgn	15485	18655
4 Dr TSi Wgn	12440	14985
4 Dr TSi 4WD Wgn	13145	15835

OPTIONS FOR GRAND CHEROKEE

8 cyl 5.2 L Engine +420
Camper/Towing Package +150
Compact Disc W/fm/tape +240
Dual Power Seats[Std on Limited] +190
Infinity Sound System[Std on Limited] +210
Leather Seats[Std on Limited] +385
Limited Slip Diff +135
Locking Differential +145
Power Sunroof +385
Skid Plates +65

WRANGLER 1997

Jeep has totally redesigned this American icon. A Quadra-coil suspension improves on and off-road manners; while dual airbags and optional antilock brakes increase the Wrangler's ability to keep occupants safe. Round, retro-style headlights add a nostalgic touch to this venerable ground-pounder. Fortunately, none of these refinements soften the Wrangler's tough exterior. A restyled interior includes integrated air vents, a glovebox, and car-like stereo controls and accessory switches.

RATINGS (SCALE OF 1-10)

Overall	Safety	Reliability	Performance	Comfort	Value
6.1	7.1	6.4	7	5.6	4.6

Category G

2 Dr SE 4WD Utility	8825	10635
2 Dr Sahara 4WD Utility	11365	13690
2 Dr Sport 4WD Utility	10265	12365

Don't forget to refer to the Mileage Adjustment Table at the back of this book!

JEEP 97-95

Model Description	Trade-in Value	Market Value	Model Description	Trade-in Value	Market Value

OPTIONS FOR WRANGLER

Auto 3-Speed Transmission +275
AM/FM Stereo Tape[Std on Sahara] +110
Air Conditioning +405
Aluminum/Alloy Wheels[Opt on Sport] +165
Anti-Lock Brakes +295
Bucket Seats[Opt on SE] +170
Hardtop Roof +390
Locking Differential +145
Power Steering[Opt on SE] +140
Velour/Cloth Seats[Std on Sahara] +105

1996 JEEP

CHEROKEE   1996

Perennial favorite rolls into 1996 with improved engines, new colors, upgraded Selec-Trac four-wheel-drive system, more standard equipment, and the same sheetmetal that it wore on introduction day in 1983.

RATINGS (SCALE OF 1-10)

Overall	Safety	Reliability	Performance	Comfort	Value
6.8	5.7	6.7	7.4	6.6	7.5

Category G
4 Dr Country Wgn	9385	11585
4 Dr Country 4WD Wgn	10075	12440
2 Dr SE Utility	6580	8125
2 Dr SE 4WD Utility	7495	9255
4 Dr SE Wgn	7175	8860
4 Dr SE 4WD Wgn	7960	9830
2 Dr Sport Utility	7810	9640
2 Dr Sport 4WD Utility	8305	10250
4 Dr Sport Wgn	8275	10215
4 Dr Sport 4WD Wgn	8760	10815

OPTIONS FOR CHEROKEE

6 cyl 4.0 L Engine[Opt on SE] +310
Auto 4-Speed Transmission +360
Off-Road Suspension Pkg +305
Air Conditioning +330
Aluminum/Alloy Wheels +135
Anti-Lock Brakes +245
Camper/Towing Package +120
Compact Disc W/fm/tape +195
Cruise Control +85
Keyless Entry System +80
Leather Seats +315
Limited Slip Diff +110
Locking Differential +120
Luggage Rack[Std on Country] +65
Power Door Locks +95
Power Drivers Seat +115
Power Windows +95
Skid Plates +55

GRAND CHEROKEE   1996

Jeep turns its flagship into an Explorer killer with dual airbags, revised styling, a better V6 engine, improved front suspension, and an upgraded Selec-Trac four-wheel-drive system. Interiors have been restyled, featuring new luxury doodads and an optional integrated child safety seat. Trim levels are two: Laredo and Limited. The gaudy Orvis continues as an option on the Limited. It's almost perfect; if they could just get rid of that pesky spare tire in the cargo hold.

RATINGS (SCALE OF 1-10)

Overall	Safety	Reliability	Performance	Comfort	Value
7.2	6.9	7.1	7	7.6	7.5

Category G
4 Dr Laredo Wgn	11025	13610
4 Dr Laredo 4WD Wgn	11795	14560
4 Dr Limited Wgn	12930	15960
4 Dr Limited 4WD Wgn	13650	16850

OPTIONS FOR GRAND CHEROKEE

8 cyl 5.2 L Engine +300
Camper/Towing Package +120
Child Seat (1) +70
Compact Disc W/fm/tape +195
Infinity Sound System[Opt on Laredo] +175
Leather Seats[Opt on Laredo] +315
Limited Slip Diff +110
Locking Differential +120
Power Sunroof +315
Skid Plates +55
Trip Computer[Opt on 2WD] +60

1995 JEEP

CHEROKEE   1995

Driver airbag is added on all models. SE model gets reclining bucket seats.

RATINGS (SCALE OF 1-10)

Overall	Safety	Reliability	Performance	Comfort	Value
6.6	6.3	6.2	7.4	6.6	6.6

Category G
4 Dr Country Wgn	7650	9685
4 Dr Country 4WD Wgn	7945	10055
2 Dr SE Utility	5495	6955
2 Dr SE 4WD Utility	6180	7825
4 Dr SE Wgn	6025	7625
4 Dr SE 4WD Wgn	6675	8450
2 Dr Sport Utility	6170	7810
2 Dr Sport 4WD Utility	6780	8580
4 Dr Sport Wgn	6580	8330
4 Dr Sport 4WD Wgn	7095	8980

Don't forget to refer to the Mileage Adjustment Table at the back of this book!

OPTIONS FOR CHEROKEE

6 cyl 4.0 L Engine[Opt on SE] +255
Auto 4-Speed Transmission +295
Off-Road Suspension Pkg +250
AM/FM Stereo Tape +75
Air Conditioning +270
Anti-Lock Brakes +200
Camper/Towing Package +100
Center Console[Std on Country] +55
Keyless Entry System +65
Leather Seats +255
Limited Slip Diff +90
Locking Differential +95
Luggage Rack[Std on Country] +50
Power Door Locks +75
Power Drivers Seat +95
Power Windows +80
Skid Plates +45

GRAND CHEROKEE — 1995

Rear disc brakes are added to all models. An Orvis trim package is added to the Limited 4WD. New options are an integrated child safety seat and a flip-up liftgate window. Optional V8 engine gets a torque increase. A 2WD Limited model is newly available. A power sunroof is added to the options list.

RATINGS (SCALE OF 1-10)

Overall	Safety	Reliability	Performance	Comfort	Value
7.2	6.8	7.6	7	7.8	6.7

	Trade-in	Market
Category G		
4 Dr Laredo Wgn	8900	11265
4 Dr Laredo 4WD Wgn	9585	12130
4 Dr Limited Wgn	10660	13495
4 Dr Limited 4WD Wgn	11425	14460
4 Dr SE Wgn	8100	10250
4 Dr SE 4WD Wgn	8795	11130

OPTIONS FOR GRAND CHEROKEE

8 cyl 5.2 L Engine +245
Up Country Suspension Grp +260
AM/FM Compact Disc Player +110
Camper/Towing Package +100
Child Seat (1) +55
Dual Power Seats +125
Infinity Sound System[Std on Limited] +140
Leather Seats[Std on Limited] +255
Limited Slip Diff +90
Locking Differential +95
Power Sunroof +260
Skid Plates +45

WRANGLER — 1995

S model can be equipped with new Rio Grande package. Renegade is dropped from lineup. An optional dome light can be attached to the optional sound bar.

RATINGS (SCALE OF 1-10)

Overall	Safety	Reliability	Performance	Comfort	Value
5.9	4.1	6.9	6.6	5.9	6

	Trade-in	Market
Category G		
2 Dr Rio Grande 4WD Utility	7270	9200
2 Dr S 4WD Utility	6875	8705
2 Dr SE 4WD Utility	7870	9960
2 Dr Sahara 4WD Utility	9795	12400

OPTIONS FOR WRANGLER

Auto 3-Speed Transmission +205
AM/FM Stereo Tape[Opt on S] +75
Air Conditioning +270
Aluminum/Alloy Wheels +110
Anti-Lock Brakes +200
Hardtop Roof +260
Locking Differential +95
Power Steering[Opt on S] +95
Velour/Cloth Seats[Opt on S] +70

1994 JEEP

CHEROKEE — 1994

Side-door guard beams have been added, and cente high-mounted brake light is new. Base model gets SE nomenclature.

RATINGS (SCALE OF 1-10)

Overall	Safety	Reliability	Performance	Comfort	Value
6.2	4.6	6.5	7.4	6.6	6.1

	Trade-in	Market
Category G		
2 Dr Country Utility	5700	7400
2 Dr Country 4WD Utility	6245	8110
4 Dr Country Wgn	6335	8230
4 Dr Country 4WD Wgn	6715	8720
2 Dr SE Utility	4310	5600
2 Dr SE 4WD Utility	4945	6420
4 Dr SE Wgn	4885	6345
4 Dr SE 4WD Wgn	5570	7235
2 Dr Sport Utility	5225	6785
2 Dr Sport 4WD Utility	5715	7420
4 Dr Sport Wgn	5585	7255
4 Dr Sport 4WD Wgn	6090	7910

OPTIONS FOR CHEROKEE

6 cyl 4.0 L Engine[Opt on SE] +125
Auto 4-Speed Transmission +245
AM/FM Stereo Tape +60
Air Conditioning +220
Anti-Lock Brakes +160
Camper/Towing Package +80
Cruise Control +55
Keyless Entry System +55
Leather Seats +210
Limited Slip Diff +75

Don't forget to refer to the Mileage Adjustment Table at the back of this book!

Model Description	Trade-in Value	Market Value
Locking Differential +80		
Luggage Rack[Std on Country] +45		
Power Door Locks +65		
Power Drivers Seat +75		
Power Windows +65		
Skid Plates +35		

GRAND CHEROKEE 1994

Side-door guard beams are added for 1994. Grand Wagoneer trim level is dropped. Base model is now called SE. Limited gets rear disc brakes.

RATINGS (SCALE OF 1-10)

Overall	Safety	Reliability	Performance	Comfort	Value
7	6.9	7.1	7	7.8	6

Category G

	Trade-in	Market
4 Dr Laredo Wgn	7240	9405
4 Dr Laredo 4WD Wgn	7775	10100
4 Dr Limited 4WD Wgn	9695	12590
4 Dr SE Wgn	6640	8625
4 Dr SE 4WD Wgn	7200	9350

OPTIONS FOR GRAND CHEROKEE

8 cyl 5.2 L Engine +190
Auto 4-Speed Transmission[Std on Limited,2WD] +245
Camper/Towing Package[Std on Limited] +80
Compact Disc W/fm/tape +130
Dual Power Seats +105
Infinity Sound System[Std on Limited] +115
Keyless Entry System[Opt on SE] +55
Leather Seats[Std on Limited] +210
Limited Slip Diff +75
Power Door Locks[Opt on SE] +65
Power Windows[Opt on SE] +65
Skid Plates +35
Trip Computer[Opt on Laredo] +40

WRANGLER 1994

The four-cylinder engine can be saddled with an automatic transmission this year. Base trim is now termed SE. Center high-mounted brake light is added.

RATINGS (SCALE OF 1-10)

Overall	Safety	Reliability	Performance	Comfort	Value
5.9	4	6.8	6.6	5.9	6

Category G

	Trade-in	Market
2 Dr Renegade 4WD Utility	8735	11345
2 Dr S 4WD Utility	5980	7765
2 Dr SE 4WD Utility	6940	9010
2 Dr Sahara 4WD Utility	8535	11085
2 Dr Sport 4WD Utility	7865	10215

OPTIONS FOR WRANGLER

Auto 3-Speed Transmission +170
AM/FM Stereo Tape[Opt on S,SE,Sport] +60
Air Conditioning +220
Anti-Lock Brakes +160

Model Description	Trade-in Value	Market Value
Chrome Bumpers +45		
Hardtop Roof +215		
Limited Slip Diff +75		
Locking Differential +80		
Power Steering[Opt on S,SE] +75		
Velour/Cloth Seats[Opt on SE,Sport] +60		

1993 JEEP

CHEROKEE 1993

Lineup is shuffled to make room for Grand Cherokee. Country trim replaces Limited. Base prices fall substantially, but models are decontented to achieve lower price.

RATINGS (SCALE OF 1-10)

Overall	Safety	Reliability	Performance	Comfort	Value
6.1	4.6	6.1	7.4	6.6	5.9

Category G

	Trade-in	Market
2 Dr Country Utility	4675	6230
2 Dr Country 4WD Utility	5310	7080
4 Dr Country Wgn	5050	6735
4 Dr Country 4WD Wgn	5650	7530
2 Dr STD Utility	3870	5160
2 Dr STD 4WD Utility	4349	5800
4 Dr STD Wgn	3990	5320
4 Dr STD 4WD Wgn	4620	6160
2 Dr Sport Utility	4125	5500
2 Dr Sport 4WD Utility	4688	6250
4 Dr Sport Wgn	4350	5800
4 Dr Sport 4WD Wgn	4900	6530

OPTIONS FOR CHEROKEE

6 cyl 4.0 L Engine[Opt on STD] +105
Auto 4-Speed Transmission +200
Off-road Suspension Pkg +170
AM/FM Stereo Tape +50
Air Conditioning +180
Aluminum/Alloy Wheels[Std on Country] +75
Anti-Lock Brakes +135
Camper/Towing Package +65
Cruise Control +45
Keyless Entry System +45
Luggage Rack[Std on Country] +35
Power Door Locks +50
Power Drivers Seat +60
Power Windows +55
Premium Sound System +75
Skid Plates +30
Swing Out Tire Carrier[Std on Sport 4WD Wgn] +45

GRAND CHEROKEE 1993

Introduced in April, 1992, Grand Cherokee gets a V8-engine option and a Grand Wagoneer model that includes the V8 and fake-wood siding. Late in the year, 2WD models in Base and Laredo trim are introduced.

Don't forget to refer to the Mileage Adjustment Table at the back of this book!

Model Description	Trade-in Value	Market Value

A driver airbag and ABS that works in 2WD or 4WD are standard.

RATINGS (SCALE OF 1-10)

Overall	Safety	Reliability	Performance	Comfort	Value
6.5	6.3	5.3	7	7.8	6

Category G

	Trade-in Value	Market Value
4 Dr Laredo Wgn	5955	7940
4 Dr Laredo 4WD Wgn	6495	8660
4 Dr Limited 4WD Wgn	7935	10580
4 Dr STD Wgn	5240	6985
4 Dr STD 4WD Wgn	5800	7730

OPTIONS FOR GRAND CHEROKEE

8 cyl 5.2 L Engine +195
Auto 4-Speed Transmission[Std on Limited,2WD] +195
Up Country Suspension Grp +175
AM/FM Compact Disc Player +70
Air Conditioning[Std on Limited] +180
Aluminum/Alloy Wheels[Std on Limited] +75
Camper/Towing Package +65
Cruise Control[Opt on STD] +45
Keyless Entry System[Std on Limited] +45
Leather Seats[Opt on Laredo] +170
Locking Differential +65
Luggage Rack[Opt on STD] +35
Power Door Locks[Std on Limited] +50
Power Drivers Seat[Opt on Laredo] +60
Power Passenger Seat[Opt on Laredo] +60
Power Windows[Std on Limited] +55
Premium Sound System[Std on Limited] +75
Skid Plates +30

GRAND WAGONEER 1993

Category G

	Trade-in Value	Market Value
4 Dr STD 4WD Wgn	7830	10440

OPTIONS FOR GRAND WAGONEER

AM/FM Compact Disc Player +70

WRANGLER 1993

ABS that works in both two- and four-wheel drive is newly optional with six-cylinder engines. Islander model disappears. Other changes include a stainless steel exhaust system, tamper-resistant odometer, and tinted plastic windows for the convertible. Sport package includes new graphics and five-spoke steel wheels.

RATINGS (SCALE OF 1-10)

Overall	Safety	Reliability	Performance	Comfort	Value
5.7	4.3	6.4	6.6	5.9	5.4

Category G

	Trade-in Value	Market Value
2 Dr Renegade 4WD Utility	7135	9510
2 Dr S 4WD Utility	5195	6925
2 Dr STD 4WD Utility	5925	7900
2 Dr Sahara 4WD Utility	6955	9275

OPTIONS FOR WRANGLER

6 cyl 4.0 L Engine[Opt on S,STD] +105
Auto 3-Speed Transmission +130
Sport Handling Pkg +265
AM/FM Stereo Tape +50
Air Conditioning +180
Aluminum/Alloy Wheels[Std on Renegade] +75
Anti-Lock Brakes +135
Hardtop Roof +175
Locking Differential +65
Power Steering[Opt on S,STD] +60

1992 JEEP

CHEROKEE 1992

Sport models gain a glass sunroof option, while Laredos get integral vent windows. All radios now have an integral digital clock. Leather upholstery is available on Laredo for the first time. Detachable cupholders are added to the center console.

RATINGS (SCALE OF 1-10)

Overall	Safety	Reliability	Performance	Comfort	Value
6.7	4.7	7	7.4	6.6	7.7

Category G

	Trade-in Value	Market Value
4 Dr Briarwood 4WD Wgn	5565	7620
2 Dr Laredo 4WD Utility	4385	6010
4 Dr Laredo Wgn	4005	5485
4 Dr Laredo 4WD Wgn	4455	6100
4 Dr Limited 4WD Wgn	5580	7645
2 Dr STD Utility	3335	4570
2 Dr STD 4WD Utility	3670	5030
4 Dr STD Wgn	3665	5020
4 Dr STD 4WD Wgn	4015	5500
2 Dr Sport 4WD Utility	3955	5420
4 Dr Sport Wgn	3985	5460
4 Dr Sport 4WD Wgn	4335	5940

OPTIONS FOR CHEROKEE

6 cyl 4.0 L Engine[Opt on Laredo,Sport,STD] +100
Auto 4-Speed Transmission[Opt on Laredo,Sport,STD] +160
Off Road Pkg +175
Sport Handling Pkg +140
AM/FM Compact Disc Player +60
Air Conditioning[Opt on Laredo,Sport,STD] +145
Anti-Lock Brakes +110
Camper/Towing Package +55
Leather Seats[Opt on Laredo,Sport,STD] +140
Locking Differential +55
Power Door Locks[Opt on Laredo,Sport,STD] +40
Power Drivers Seat[Opt on Laredo,Sport,STD] +50
Power Passenger Seat[Opt on Laredo,Sport,STD] +50
Power Windows[Opt on Laredo,Sport,STD] +45
Sunroof +55

Don't forget to refer to the Mileage Adjustment Table at the back of this book!

JEEP 92-91

Model Description	Trade-in Value	Market Value	Model Description	Trade-in Value	Market Value

COMANCHE 1992

Sport option group debuts. Radios have digital clocks. Detachable cupholders are added to center console.

Category G

	Trade-in	Market
2 Dr Eliminator 4WD Std Cab LB	3475	4760
2 Dr Eliminator 4WD Std Cab SB	3380	4630
2 Dr Pioneer 4WD Std Cab LB	3370	4615
2 Dr Pioneer 4WD Std Cab SB	3280	4490
2 Dr STD 4WD Std Cab LB	3155	4325
2 Dr STD 4WD Std Cab SB	3050	4180
2 Dr Sport 4WD Std Cab LB	3265	4470
2 Dr Sport 4WD Std Cab SB	3195	4375

OPTIONS FOR COMANCHE

6 cyl 4.0 L Engine +100
5-Speed Transmission +35
Auto 4-Speed Transmission +180
Off Road Pkg +175
Air Conditioning +145
Locking Differential +55
Power Steering +50

WRANGLER 1992

Three-point seatbelts anchored to the roll bar are added. New colors round out the changes.

RATINGS (SCALE OF 1-10)

Overall	Safety	Reliability	Performance	Comfort	Value
5.6	4.2	5.9	6.6	5.9	5.3

Category G

	Trade-in	Market
2 Dr Islander 4WD Utility	5330	7300
2 Dr Renegade 4WD Utility	5770	7905
2 Dr S 4WD Utility	4415	6050
2 Dr STD 4WD Utility	5075	6950
2 Dr Sahara 4WD Utility	5640	7725

OPTIONS FOR WRANGLER

6 cyl 4.0 L Engine +100
Auto 3-Speed Transmission +105
Air Conditioning +145
Hardtop Roof +140
Locking Differential +55
Rear Bench Seat[Opt on S] +75

1991 JEEP

CHEROKEE 1991

Two new models, the Sport four-door and top-of-the-line Briarwood, join the lineup. Child-proof rear door locks are added to four-door models. A security alarm system is a new option. Power is increased for both engines. An automatic transmission is no longer available with the base four-cylinder engine.

RATINGS (SCALE OF 1-10)

Overall	Safety	Reliability	Performance	Comfort	Value
6	4.1	5	7.4	6.6	7.1

Category G

	Trade-in	Market
4 Dr Briarwood 4WD Wgn	4870	6955
2 Dr Laredo 4WD Utility	3925	5610
4 Dr Laredo Wgn	3365	4810
4 Dr Laredo 4WD Wgn	4145	5920
4 Dr Limited 4WD Wgn	4910	7015
2 Dr STD Utility	2810	4015
2 Dr STD 4WD Utility	3250	4645
4 Dr STD Wgn	3020	4315
4 Dr STD 4WD Wgn	3440	4915
2 Dr Sport Utility	3080	4400
2 Dr Sport 4WD Utility	3375	4820
4 Dr Sport Wgn	3285	4690
4 Dr Sport 4WD Wgn	3590	5130

OPTIONS FOR CHEROKEE

6 cyl 4.0 L Engine[Opt on Laredo,Sport,STD] +90
Auto 4-Speed Transmission[Opt on Laredo,Sport,STD] +130
Cherokee Off Road Pkg +145
Air Conditioning[Opt on Laredo,Sport,STD] +120
Anti-Lock Brakes +90
Camper/Towing Package +45
Dual Power Seats[Opt on Laredo] +55
Leather Seats[Opt on Laredo,STD] +115
Limited Slip Diff +40
Power Door Locks[Opt on Laredo,Sport,STD] +35
Power Windows[Opt on Laredo,Sport,STD] +35
Sunroof +45

COMANCHE 1991

Power is increased for both engines, and five new colors are available.

Category G

	Trade-in	Market
2 Dr Eliminator Std Cab LB	2265	3235
2 Dr Pioneer Std Cab LB	2170	3100
2 Dr STD Std Cab LB	2065	2950

OPTIONS FOR COMANCHE

6 cyl 4.0 L Engine[Opt on Eliminator,STD] +90
5-Speed Transmission +30
Auto 3-Speed Transmission +120
Big Ton Pkg +110
Suspension Pkg +145
Air Conditioning +120
Limited Slip Diff +40
Power Steering +40

GRAND WAGONEER 1991

Five new exterior colors and one new interior color debut.

Model Description	Trade-in Value	Market Value
Category H		
4 Dr STD 4WD Wgn	5230	7165

OPTIONS FOR GRAND WAGONEER
Camper/Towing Package +50
Limited Slip Diff +40
Power Sunroof +210

WRANGLER 1991

New Renegade option replaces Laredo and adds fender flares, fog lights and alloy wheels. A new six-cylinder engine boosts horsepower substantially, from 112 with the old 4.2-liter unit to 180 with the new 4.0-liter motor. Four-cylinder models also get a slight bump in power. New seats with reclining backrests are new to all models except S. A sound bar is also available on all models except S.

RATINGS (SCALE OF 1-10)

Overall	Safety	Reliability	Performance	Comfort	Value
5.2	3.8	4.8	6.6	5.9	4.7

Category G		
2 Dr Islander 4WD Utility	4590	6555
2 Dr Renegade 4WD Utility	5075	7250
2 Dr S 4WD Utility	3835	5475
2 Dr STD 4WD Utility	4435	6335
2 Dr Sahara 4WD Utility	4955	7080

OPTIONS FOR WRANGLER
6 cyl 4.0 L Engine +90
Auto 3-Speed Transmission +85
Air Conditioning +120
Hardtop Roof +115
Limited Slip Diff +40
Power Steering +40

1990 JEEP

CHEROKEE 1990

AM/FM stereo is newly standard. Rear seats get three-point seatbelts, and an overhead console is a new option.

RATINGS (SCALE OF 1-10)

Overall	Safety	Reliability	Performance	Comfort	Value
6	3.8	4.9	7.4	6.6	7.5

Category G		
2 Dr Laredo 4WD Utility	3275	4965
4 Dr Laredo Wgn	2765	4190
4 Dr Laredo 4WD Wgn	3100	4700
2 Dr Limited 4WD Utility	3830	5800
4 Dr Limited 4WD Wgn	4015	6080
2 Dr Pioneer 4WD Utility	2995	4535
4 Dr Pioneer Wgn	2510	3805
4 Dr Pioneer 4WD Wgn	2838	4300

Model Description	Trade-in Value	Market Value
2 Dr STD Utility	2260	3425
2 Dr STD 4WD Utility	2890	4375
4 Dr STD Wgn	2315	3510
4 Dr STD 4WD Wgn	3020	4575
2 Dr Sport Utility	2450	3710
2 Dr Sport 4WD Utility	2995	4540

OPTIONS FOR CHEROKEE
6 cyl 4.0 L Engine[Opt on Sport,STD] +75
Auto 4-Speed Transmission[Std on Limited] +105
Off Road Pkg +115
AM/FM Compact Disc Player +40
Air Conditioning[Std on Limited] +100
Anti-Lock Brakes +70
Camper/Towing Package +35
Dual Power Seats[Opt on Laredo] +45
Limited Slip Diff +35
Power Door Locks[Std on Limited] +30
Power Windows[Std on Limited] +30
Sunroof +35

COMANCHE 1990

No changes.

Category G		
2 Dr Eliminator Std Cab SB	2105	3190
2 Dr Pioneer Std Cab LB	1790	2715
2 Dr Pioneer Std Cab SB	1750	2655
2 Dr STD Std Cab LB	1725	2615
2 Dr STD Std Cab SB	1685	2550

OPTIONS FOR COMANCHE
6 cyl 4.0 L Engine[Std on Eliminator] +75
Auto 3-Speed Transmission +115
Off Road Pkg +115
Air Conditioning +100
Limited Slip Diff +35
Power Steering[Std on Eliminator] +35

GRAND WAGONEER 1990

Rear seats get three-point seatbelts.

Category H		
4 Dr STD 4WD Wgn	4605	6395

OPTIONS FOR GRAND WAGONEER
Camper/Towing Package +40
Limited Slip Diff +30
Power Sunroof +170

WAGONEER 1990

Rear seats get three-point seatbelts.

Category G		
4 Dr Limited 4WD Wgn	3685	5585

OPTIONS FOR WAGONEER
Anti-Lock Brakes +70
Camper/Towing Package +35
Limited Slip Diff +35
Sunroof +35

Don't forget to refer to the Mileage Adjustment Table at the back of this book!

JEEP 90

Model Description	Trade-in Value	Market Value	Model Description	Trade-in Value	Market Value

WRANGLER 1990

Locking half doors are available for the first time. Order a hardtop and you'll get a new rear window wiper/washer. Front seats gain improved lateral support, and Sahara and Laredo models get a larger, 20-gallon fuel tank. S models have a wider variety of options.

RATINGS (SCALE OF 1-10)

Overall	Safety	Reliability	Performance	Comfort	Value
5.1	3.7	5.2	6.2	5.9	4.7

Category G

2 Dr Islander 4WD Utility	3975	6020
2 Dr Laredo 4WD Utility	4625	7010
2 Dr S 4WD Utility	3335	5055
2 Dr STD 4WD Utility	3830	5800
2 Dr Sahara 4WD Utility	4245	6435

OPTIONS FOR WRANGLER

6 cyl 4.2 L Engine[Std on Laredo] +55
Auto 3-Speed Transmission +70
Air Conditioning +100
Hardtop Roof[Std on Laredo] +95
Limited Slip Diff +35
Power Steering[Std on Laredo, Sahara] +35
Rear Bench Seat +50

KIA
S. Korea

1997 Kia Sephia

1999 KIA

SEPHIA — 1999

The Sephia was entirely redesigned in '98 and enters '99 essentially unchanged.

RATINGS (SCALE OF 1-10)

Overall	Safety	Reliability	Performance	Comfort	Value
N/A	N/A	N/A	5.8	6.4	N/A

Category E

	Trade-in	Market
4 Dr LS Sdn	6350	7745
4 Dr STD Sdn	6110	7450

OPTIONS FOR SEPHIA
Auto 4-Speed Transmission +720
AM/FM Compact Disc Player +340
Air Conditioning +605
Aluminum/Alloy Wheels +245
Anti-Lock Brakes +500
Cruise Control +165
Power Door Locks +180
Power Mirrors +80
Power Steering[Std on LS] +190
Power Windows +195

SPORTAGE — 1999

A new two-door convertible model joins the four-door Sportage in 1999. The convertible comes in either a 4x2 layout with automatic transmission or a 4x4 layout with five-speed manual transmission. It also boasts dual front airbags and a driver's side front knee bag.

Category G

	Trade-in	Market
4 Dr EX Wgn	10815	13030
4 Dr EX 4WD Wgn	10985	13235
2 Dr STD Conv	8880	10700

Model Description	Trade-in Value	Market Value
2 Dr STD 4WD Conv	9130	11000
4 Dr STD Wgn	9295	11200
4 Dr STD 4WD Wgn	9970	12015

OPTIONS FOR SPORTAGE
Auto 4-Speed Transmission +740
AM/FM Compact Disc Player[Std on EX] +245
Air Conditioning[Std on EX] +605
Aluminum/Alloy Wheels[Std on EX,4WD] +245
Anti-Lock Brakes +445
Leather Seats +575
Rear Window Wiper[Std on EX] +115

1998 KIA

SEPHIA — 1998

The Sephia is totally redesigned for 1998.

Category E

	Trade-in	Market
4 Dr LS Sdn	5670	7000
4 Dr STD Sdn	5235	6460

OPTIONS FOR SEPHIA
Auto 4-Speed Transmission +600
AM/FM Compact Disc Player +275
Air Conditioning +495
Aluminum/Alloy Wheels +200
Anti-Lock Brakes +410
Cruise Control +135
Power Door Locks +145
Power Mirrors +65
Power Steering[Std on LS] +155
Power Windows +160

SPORTAGE — 1998

There are lots of improvements this year for the Sportage, including a new grille, new alloy wheels, tilt steering wheel, passenger-side airbag, better brakes, improved air conditioning and four-wheel ABS that replaces last year's rear-wheel ABS.

Category G

	Trade-in	Market
4 Dr EX Wgn	9550	11645
4 Dr EX 4WD Wgn	10170	12400
4 Dr STD Wgn	8270	10085
4 Dr STD 4WD Wgn	8870	10820

OPTIONS FOR SPORTAGE
Auto 4-Speed Transmission +615
AM/FM Compact Disc Player[Std on EX] +200
Air Conditioning[Std on EX] +495
Aluminum/Alloy Wheels[Std on EX, 4WD] +200
Anti-Lock Brakes +365
Leather Seats +470

Don't forget to refer to the Mileage Adjustment Table at the back of this book!

KIA 97-95

Model Description	Trade-in Value	Market Value	Model Description	Trade-in Value	Market Value

1997 KIA

SEPHIA 1997

RS models get body-color bumpers this year, and a tan interior is newly available with black exterior paint.

Category E

4 Dr GS Sdn	4585	5955
4 Dr LS Sdn	4060	5275
4 Dr RS Sdn	3670	4765

OPTIONS FOR SEPHIA

Auto 4-Speed Transmission +455
AM/FM Compact Disc Player +225
AM/FM Stereo Tape[Std on GS] +150
Air Conditioning +405
Aluminum/Alloy Wheels +165
Anti-Lock Brakes +335
Power Steering[Opt on RS] +125
Premium Sound System +160

SPORTAGE 1997

An automatic transmission is offered on 2WD models, and the EX trim level is available in 2WD for the first time. Power door locks, a theft deterrent system, and a spare tire carrier are all standard on all Sportages for 1997. A new option is a CD player. Sportage gets a new grille. A tan interior can be combined with black paint for the first time. Base 2WD models lose their standard alloy wheels.

Category G

4 Dr EX Wgn	7850	9570
4 Dr EX 4WD Wgn	8065	9835
4 Dr STD Wgn	6760	8245
4 Dr STD 4WD Wgn	7320	8925

OPTIONS FOR SPORTAGE

Auto 4-Speed Transmission +500
AM/FM Compact Disc Player +160
Air Conditioning +405
Aluminum/Alloy Wheels[Std on EX,4WD] +165
Leather Seats +385
Luggage Rack[Std on EX] +80
Swing Out Tire Carrier[Std on EX,4WD] +95

1996 KIA

SEPHIA 1996

Styling and suspension tweaks, dual airbags, and new twin-cam motors appeared with the introduction of the 1995.5 Sephia. These improvements, along with interior revisions and improved equipment levels, make the Kia more competitive in the compact sedan marketplace. Sephia now meets 1997 side-impact standards, and GS models can be equipped with antilock brakes. Sephia comes with 5 year/60,000 mile powertrain coverage.

Category E

4 Dr GS Sdn	3700	5000
4 Dr LS Sdn	3315	4480
4 Dr RS Sdn	2980	4025

OPTIONS FOR SEPHIA

Auto 4-Speed Transmission +355
AM/FM Stereo Tape[Std on GS] +125
Air Conditioning +330
Anti-Lock Brakes +275
Power Steering[Opt on RS] +105
Premium Sound System +135

SPORTAGE 1996

The world's first knee airbag arrives in conjunction with a driver airbag, and a two-wheel drive edition is available this year. A spirited twin-cam engine arrived late in 1995, and cured Sportage's power ills.

Category G

4 Dr EX Wgn	6640	8300
4 Dr EX 4WD Wgn	7020	8770
4 Dr STD Wgn	6440	8055
4 Dr STD 4WD Wgn	6665	8330

OPTIONS FOR SPORTAGE

4 cyl 2.0 L DOHC Engine +305
Auto 4-Speed Transmission +415
AM/FM Stereo Tape +90
Air Conditioning +330
Leather Seats +315
Luggage Rack +65
Swing Out Tire Carrier +80

1995 KIA

SEPHIA 1995

Oh no, another Korean manufacturer trying to break into the American market. But wait, this one is actually worth considering; a lot of help from Mazda and Ford mean that this little upstart is actually making fairly reliable little cars. The Sephia has plenty of Mazda parts and Kia has a long history of building durable, cheap cars.

Category E

4 Dr GS Sdn	2800	3945
1995.5 4 Dr GS Sdn	2775	3910
4 Dr LS Sdn	2525	3555
1995.5 4 Dr LS Sdn	2185	3075
4 Dr RS Sdn	2275	3205
1995.5 4 Dr RS Sdn	2255	3175

OPTIONS FOR SEPHIA

4 cyl 1.6 L DOHC Engine +35
4 cyl 1.8 L Engine +215

Don't forget to refer to the Mileage Adjustment Table at the back of this book!

KIA 95-94

Model Description	Trade-in Value	Market Value
Auto 4-Speed Transmission +275		
AM/FM Stereo Tape[Std on GS] +100		
Air Conditioning +270		
Cruise Control[Opt on GS] +75		
Dual Air Bag Restraints +170		
Power Steering[Opt on RS,RS 1995.5] +85		
Premium Sound System +110		

SPORTAGE   1995

Another mini-SUV is introduced, competing with everything from the Jeep Cherokee to the Geo Tracker. The Sportage offers comfortable seating for four, ample storage space, and available four-wheel drive. Designed with Ford and Mazda, with suspension tuning by Lotus, the Sportage should provide a good deal of fun and durability.

Category G

Model Description	Trade-in Value	Market Value
4 Dr EX 4WD Wgn	6105	8035
4 Dr STD 4WD Wgn	5500	7240

OPTIONS FOR SPORTAGE

4 cyl 2.0 L DOHC Engine +245	
Auto 4-Speed Transmission +330	
AM/FM Stereo Tape +75	
Air Conditioning +270	

Model Description	Trade-in Value	Market Value
Leather Seats +255		
Luggage Rack +50		
Swing Out Tire Carrier +65		

1994 KIA

SEPHIA   1994

New subcompact sedan from South Korea based on 1990-1994 Mazda Protege platform and powered by a 1.6-liter, 88-horsepower four-cylinder engine. Sold only in the western and southwestern regions of the U.S.

Category E

Model Description	Trade-in Value	Market Value
4 Dr GS Sdn	2100	3130
4 Dr LS Sdn	1985	2960
4 Dr RS Sdn	1850	2765

OPTIONS FOR SEPHIA

Auto 4-Speed Transmission +205	
AM/FM Stereo Tape[Std on GS] +80	
Air Conditioning +220	
Cruise Control +60	
Power Steering[Opt on RS] +70	
Premium Sound System +90	

Don't forget to refer to the Mileage Adjustment Table at the back of this book!

LAND ROVER 99-97

Model Description	Trade-in Value	Market Value	Model Description	Trade-in Value	Market Value

LAND ROVER Britain

1996 Land Rover Discovery

1999 LAND ROVER

DISCOVERY   1999

The 1999 Discovery Series II, which will be introduced later in the year, brings the first engineering redesign since the vehicle's European introduction 11 years ago. Traction Control, Active Cornering Enhancement and Hill Descent Control will be standard features. In the interim, Land Rover is offering the Discovery SD, a $33,000 upgraded version of last year's Discovery.

RATINGS (SCALE OF 1-10)

Overall	Safety	Reliability	Performance	Comfort	Value
N/A	N/A	N/A	6.2	7	N/A

Category H

4 Dr SD AWD Wgn	25000	28410
4 Dr Series II AWD Wgn	23885	27140

OPTIONS FOR DISCOVERY
Performance Pkg +2145
Rear Seat Pkg +1295
Compact Disc Changer +320
Dual Air Conditioning +990
Dual Sunroof +1170
Heated Front Seats +250
Leather Seats[Std on SD] +730

RANGE ROVER   1999

Engine upgrades, new color schemes, traction control and standard side-mounted airbags are some of the additions to the 1999 Range Rovers, which will be introduced later in the year. For now, interim Range Rover models called the 4.0 and 4.0S are available.

RATINGS (SCALE OF 1-10)

Overall	Safety	Reliability	Performance	Comfort	Value
N/A	N/A	N/A	6.4	N/A	N/A

Category H

4 Dr 4.0 4WD Wgn	38805	44100
4 Dr 4.0 S 4WD Wgn	38805	44100
4 Dr 4.0 SE 4WD Wgn	39480	44860
4 Dr 4.6 HSE 4WD Wgn	44860	50975

OPTIONS FOR RANGE ROVER
Navigation System +2215

1998 LAND ROVER

DISCOVERY   1998

Changes to the Discovery include interior trim enhancements for the LE and LSE. The rearview mirror also features map lights for the first time.

Category H

4 Dr 50TH Anniversary 4WD Wgn	23190	26965
4 Dr LE 4WD Wgn	21575	25090
4 Dr LSE 4WD Wgn	22955	26690

OPTIONS FOR DISCOVERY
Compact Disc Changer[Opt on LE] +265
Dual Air Conditioning +810
Rear Jump Seats +610
Special Factory Paint +85

RANGE ROVER   1998

Range Rover models get a new Harmon Kardon audio system this year. Other changes include a new upholstery stitch pattern and a leather-wrapped gearshift knob.

Category H

4 Dr 4.0 SE 4WD Wgn	33485	38935
4 Dr 4.6 HSE 4WD Wgn	38135	44345
4 Dr 50TH Anniversary 4WD Wgn	33485	38935

OPTIONS FOR RANGE ROVER
Special Factory Paint +85

1997 LAND ROVER

DEFENDER 90   1997

After a one year hiatus, Defender 90 returns in convertible and hardtop bodystyles. A 4.0-liter V-8 engine is standard, mated to a ZF 4-speed automatic transmission. A redesigned center console includes cupholders, and hardtops have new interior trim. Convertibles get improved top sealing, while all Defender 90s are treated to fresh paint colors.

Model Description	Trade-in Value	Market Value
Category G		
2 Dr STD 4WD Conv	27465	34765
2 Dr STD 4WD Utility	25370	32115

DISCOVERY 1997

A diversity antenna is added, and all interiors are trimmed with polished burled walnut. The sunroof has darker tinting, the airbag system benefits from simplified operation, and engine management is improved. Three new exterior colors debut: Oxford Blue, Rioja Red and Charleston Green.

Model Description	Trade-in Value	Market Value
Category H		
4 Dr LSE 4WD Wgn	18820	21880
4 Dr SD 4WD Wgn	17765	20655
4 Dr SE 4WD Wgn	18815	21875
4 Dr SE7 4WD Wgn	19020	22120
4 Dr XD 4WD Wgn	18575	21600

OPTIONS FOR DISCOVERY
Auto 4-Speed Transmission[Std on SE,XD] +500
Leather Rear Jump Seats +490
Compact Disc Changer +215
Dual Power Seats[Opt on SD] +230
Leather Seats[Opt on SD] +485
Luggage Rack[Std on XD] +75
Rear Jump Seats[Std on SE7] +495

RANGE ROVER 1997

4.0 SE gets three new exterior colors (Oxford Blue, Rioja Red and White Gold, all matched to Saddle leather interior), a HomeLink transmitter, and jeweled wheel center caps. The 4.6 HSE gets three new exterior colors (British Racing Green, Monza Red, AA Yellow), one new interior color (Lightstone with contrasting piping), and a leather shift handle.

Model Description	Trade-in Value	Market Value
Category H		
4 Dr 4.0 SE 4WD Wgn	28670	33340
4 Dr 4.6 HSE 4WD Wgn	32915	38275

OPTIONS FOR RANGE ROVER
Kensington Interior Pkg +1505
Vitesse Pkg +1505

1996 LAND ROVER

DISCOVERY 1996

Three new trim levels, a revised engine that gets better around-town fuel economy, new colors, increased seat travel, and new power seats sum up the changes for 1996.

Model Description	Trade-in Value	Market Value
Category H		
4 Dr SD 4WD Wgn	15465	18195
4 Dr SE 4WD Wgn	16200	19060
4 Dr SE7 4WD Wgn	15965	18785

OPTIONS FOR DISCOVERY
Auto 4-Speed Transmission[Std on SE] +465
Compact Disc Changer +175
Compact Disc W/fm/tape +125
Leather Seats[Opt on SD] +400
Third Seat[Std on SE7] +255

RANGE ROVER 1996

Base 4.0 SE model is unchanged for 1996. A new, more powerful 4.6 HSE model debuts, giving buyers extra horsepower, fat wheels and tires, mud flaps, and chrome exhaust for a $7,000 premium over the 4.0 SE.

Model Description	Trade-in Value	Market Value
Category H		
4 Dr 4.0 SE 4WD Wgn	24045	28285
4 Dr 4.6 HSE 4WD Wgn	28060	33010

OPTIONS FOR RANGE ROVER
AM/FM Compact Disc Player +125

1995 LAND ROVER

DEFENDER 1995

Model Description	Trade-in Value	Market Value
Category G		
2 Dr STD 4WD Utility	17340	23120

OPTIONS FOR DEFENDER
Full Top & Safari Cage +460
Air Conditioning +270

DISCOVERY 1995

Model Description	Trade-in Value	Market Value
Category H		
4 Dr STD 4WD Wgn	12665	15075

OPTIONS FOR DISCOVERY
Auto 4-Speed Transmission +380
Jump Seat +290
Leather Jump Seat +320
Dual Air Conditioning +440
Leather Seats +325

RANGE ROVER 1995

Model Description	Trade-in Value	Market Value
Category H		
4 Dr 4.0 SE 4WD Wgn	18840	22430
4 Dr County Classic 4WD Wgn	18185	21645
4 Dr County LWB 4WD Wgn	18185	21645

OPTIONS FOR RANGE ROVER
Body Kit +660
Interior Trim/Light Stone +290

1994 LAND ROVER

DISCOVERY 1994

Model Description	Trade-in Value	Market Value
Category H		
4 Dr STD 4WD Wgn	11515	13875

Don't forget to refer to the Mileage Adjustment Table at the back of this book!

Model Description	Trade-in Value	Market Value

OPTIONS FOR DISCOVERY
Auto 4-Speed Transmission +300
Dual Air Conditioning +360
Leather Seats +265
Power Moonroof +265
Rear Jump Seats +270

RANGE ROVER 1994

Category H

Model Description	Trade-in Value	Market Value
4 Dr County LWB 4WD Wgn	14895	17945
4 Dr County SWB 4WD Wgn	12840	15465

OPTIONS FOR RANGE ROVER
Black Sable Edition +290

1993 LAND ROVER

RANGE ROVER 1993

Category H

Model Description	Trade-in Value	Market Value
4 Dr County 4WD Wgn	11070	13670
4 Dr LWB 4WD Wgn	12650	15615

OPTIONS FOR RANGE ROVER
Chrome Wheels +65
Compact Disc Changer +95
Running Boards +75

1992 LAND ROVER

RANGE ROVER 1992

Category H

Model Description	Trade-in Value	Market Value
4 Dr County 4WD Wgn	9600	12000
4 Dr LSE 4WD Wgn	10135	12665
4 Dr STD 4WD Wgn	9030	11285

OPTIONS FOR RANGE ROVER
Third Seat +115

1991 LAND ROVER

RANGE ROVER 1991

Category H

Model Description	Trade-in Value	Market Value
4 Dr County SE 4WD Wgn	8605	11180
4 Dr Great Divide 4WD Wgn	8010	10405
4 Dr STD 4WD Wgn	7625	9900

OPTIONS FOR RANGE ROVER
Power Sunroof[Opt on STD] +210

1990 LAND ROVER

RANGE ROVER 1990

Category H

Model Description	Trade-in Value	Market Value
4 Dr County 4WD Wgn	7420	9635
4 Dr STD 4WD Wgn	7180	9320

OPTIONS FOR RANGE ROVER
AM/FM Compact Disc Player +40
Power Sunroof +170

Don't forget to refer to the Mileage Adjustment Table at the back of this book!

LEXUS 99

Model Description	Trade-in Value	Market Value	Model Description	Trade-in Value	Market Value

LEXUS   Japan

1994 Lexus GS 300

1999 LEXUS

ES 300   1999

A new 3.0-liter V6 engine with VVTi (Variable Valve Timing with intelligence) gives the 1999 ES300 more horsepower, lower emissions and improved fuel economy. Optional Vehicle Skid Control (VSC) is available on the new ES as are one-touch open and close front windows and a one touch operated moonroof.

RATINGS (SCALE OF 1-10)

Overall	Safety	Reliability	Performance	Comfort	Value
N/A	8.5	9.4	8.2	8.8	N/A

Category J
4 Dr STD Sdn   21535   25640

OPTIONS FOR ES 300
Chrome Wheels +1090
Compact Disc Changer +685
Heated Front Seats +310
Leather Seats +865
Nakamichi Sound System +1030
Power Moonroof +695

GS   1999

The GS series was totally redesigned last year with improvements in performance and a completely new look. As a result, the 1999 model goes unchanged except for the addition of daytime running lights and standard floor mats.

RATINGS (SCALE OF 1-10)

Overall	Safety	Reliability	Performance	Comfort	Value
N/A	N/A	9.8	9.2	8.8	N/A

Category J
4 Dr GS300 Sdn   26980   32120
4 Dr GS400 Sdn   32640   38855

OPTIONS FOR GS
Navigation System +1855
Chrome Wheels +1090
Compact Disc Changer +685
Heated Front Seats +310
Leather Seats[Std on GS400] +865
Nakamichi Sound System +1030
Power Moonroof +695

LS 400   1999

After a number of improvements to the LS400 last year, the 1999 model sees only minor upgrades to interior trim levels. Daytime running lights are now standard equipment and Mystic Gold Metallic replaces Cashmere Beige.

RATINGS (SCALE OF 1-10)

Overall	Safety	Reliability	Performance	Comfort	Value
N/A	N/A	9.9	8.2	9.4	N/A

Category L
4 Dr STD Sdn   37815   42975

OPTIONS FOR LS 400
Navigation System +1665
Cellular Telephone +745
Chrome Wheels +1140
Compact Disc Changer +825
Heated Front Seats +355
Nakamichi Sound System +825
Power Moonroof +695

LX 470   1999

For 1999 the LX470 gets a redesigned roof rack, standard floor mats, and an optional Nakamichi audio system featuring a dash-mounted, single-feed six-disc CD changer.

RATINGS (SCALE OF 1-10)

Overall	Safety	Reliability	Performance	Comfort	Value
N/A	N/A	N/A	7	8	N/A

Category H
4 Dr STD 4WD Wgn   34960   41130

OPTIONS FOR LX 470
Convenience Pkg +790
Nakamichi Sound System +885
Power Moonroof +720

RX 300   1999

The RX300 is an all new car-based SUV from Lexus designed to compete in the luxury SUV segment.

Don't forget to refer to the Mileage Adjustment Table at the back of this book!

Model Description	Trade-in Value	Market Value

RATINGS (SCALE OF 1-10)

Overall	Safety	Reliability	Performance	Comfort	Value
N/A	N/A	N/A	7.8	8.3	N/A

Category H

	Trade-in	Market
4 Dr STD Wgn	24275	28560
4 Dr STD 4WD Wgn	23840	28050

OPTIONS FOR RX 300

Limited Pkg +600
Premium Pkg +565
Compact Disc Changer +320
Heated Front Seats +250
Leather Seats +730
Power Moonroof +720 *

SC   1999

The SC coupe gets minor enhancements this year including new, perforated leather inserts, larger brakes on the SC300, daytime running lights, and a new three-spoke steering wheel similar to the GS series sport sedans.

RATINGS (SCALE OF 1-10)

Overall	Safety	Reliability	Performance	Comfort	Value
N/A	N/A	N/A	8.6	7.9	N/A

Category J

	Trade-in	Market
2 Dr SC300 Cpe	29410	35010
2 Dr SC400 Cpe	34490	41060

OPTIONS FOR SC

Leather Seats [Std on SC400] +865
Nakamichi Sound System +1030
Power Moonroof +695
Traction Control System +875

1998 LEXUS

ES 300   1998

Side-impact airbags debut on Lexus's entry-level car, as does an engine immobilizer anti-theft system and an optional Nakamichi audio system. Reduced force front airbags are also new on all 1998 Lexus models.

RATINGS (SCALE OF 1-10)

Overall	Safety	Reliability	Performance	Comfort	Value
8.1	8.5	9.3	8.2	8.8	5.8

Category J

	Trade-in	Market
4 Dr STD Sdn	20445	24340

OPTIONS FOR ES 300

Chrome Wheels +890
Compact Disc Changer +560
Heated Front Seats +255
Leather Seats +705
Nakamichi Sound System +840

Power Moonroof +570
Traction Control System +715

GS   1998

A totally redesigned GS appears for 1998. Featuring the familiar inline-six engine of the previous model in the GS300 or an overhead cam V8 with continuously variable valve timing in the GS400, the new cars live up to the promise of providing serious fun in an elegant package.

RATINGS (SCALE OF 1-10)

Overall	Safety	Reliability	Performance	Comfort	Value
N/A	N/A	9.1	9.2	N/A	4.5

Category J

	Trade-in	Market
4 Dr GS300 Sdn	25475	30330
4 Dr GS400 Sdn	30340	36120

OPTIONS FOR GS

Navigation System +1380
Chrome Wheels +890
Compact Disc Changer +560
Heated Front Seats +255
Leather Seats +705
Nakamichi Sound System +840
Power Moonroof +570

LS 400   1998

Lexus further refines its flagship by introducing a new four-cam V8 engine that features continuously variable valve timing. Also new this year is a five-speed automatic transmission, Vehicle Skid Control (VSC) and a host of interior improvements.

RATINGS (SCALE OF 1-10)

Overall	Safety	Reliability	Performance	Comfort	Value
N/A	N/A	9.8	8.2	9.4	4.2

Category L

	Trade-in	Market
4 Dr STD Sdn	33355	37900

OPTIONS FOR LS 400

Navigation System +1380
Auto Load Leveling +680
Chrome Wheels +930
Compact Disc Changer +675
Heated Front Seats +290
Nakamichi Sound System +675
Power Moonroof +570

LX 470   1998

Lexus' new LX470 luxury SUV replaces the LX450, offering a completely new body design, a more powerful engine, a roomier interior and more standard perks.

Category H

	Trade-in	Market
4 Dr STD 4WD Wgn	33345	39225

Model Description	Trade-in Value	Market Value

OPTIONS FOR LX 470
Power Moonroof +590

SC 1998

The SC400 gets a new four-liter four-cam aluminum V8 engine this year, while the SC300 continues with the inline-six motor from last year. Both powerplants benefit from continuously variable valve timing technology. An engine immobilizer, depowered airbags and a sophisticated five-speed automatic transmission are standard this year as well. The SC300 loses its five-speed manual transmission.

RATINGS (SCALE OF 1-10)

Overall	Safety	Reliability	Performance	Comfort	Value
N/A	N/A	9.7	N/A	N/A	N/A

Category J
2 Dr SC300 Cpe	25275	30090
2 Dr SC400 Cpe	30430	36225

OPTIONS FOR SC
Leather Seats[Std on SC400] +705

1997 LEXUS

ES 300 1997

The entry-level Lexus has been totally redesigned this year, growing in nearly every dimension. Lexus manages to eke out more power from the ES300's 3.0-liter V-6 engine. No longer just a dressed-up Camry, the ES300 has finally come into its own.

RATINGS (SCALE OF 1-10)

Overall	Safety	Reliability	Performance	Comfort	Value
7.8	7.6	9.1	8.2	8.8	5.3

Category J
4 Dr STD Sdn	17755	21390

OPTIONS FOR ES 300
Chrome Wheels +730
Compact Disc Changer +455
Leather Seats +580
Power Moonroof +465
Traction Control System +585

LS 400 1997

Side-impact airbags are standard, yet, the price doesn't go up! Magic? You be the judge.

RATINGS (SCALE OF 1-10)

Overall	Safety	Reliability	Performance	Comfort	Value
N/A	N/A	9.7	8	9.4	5.5

Category L
4 Dr Coach Sdn	30035	34520
4 Dr STD Sdn	29140	33495

OPTIONS FOR LS 400
Drivers Memory System +400
Cellular Telephone +500
Chrome Wheels +760
Compact Disc Changer[Opt on STD] +550
Nakamichi Sound System +550
Power Moonroof[Opt on STD] +465
Traction Control System +700

LX 450 1997

There are no changes to the 1997 LX450.

Category G
4 Dr STD 4WD Wgn	26335	31725

OPTIONS FOR LX 450
F&R Locking Diff. Axles +450
Compact Disc Changer +255
Luggage Rack +80
Power Moonroof +430
Running Boards +190
Trailer Hitch +140

SC 1997

Minor interior and exterior enhancements update the look of the SC coupes.

RATINGS (SCALE OF 1-10)

Overall	Safety	Reliability	Performance	Comfort	Value
N/A	N/A	9.3	N/A	N/A	2.7

Category J
2 Dr SC300 Cpe	21800	26265
2 Dr SC400 Cpe	25095	30235

OPTIONS FOR SC
Leather Trim Pkg +375
Compact Disc Changer +455
Leather Seats[Std on SC400] +580
Power Moonroof +465
Rear Spoiler +200
Traction Control System +585

1996 LEXUS

ES 300 1996

Two new colors are available.

RATINGS (SCALE OF 1-10)

Overall	Safety	Reliability	Performance	Comfort	Value
7.9	7.7	9.4	8.4	8.1	5.8

Category J
4 Dr STD Sdn	14710	17940

OPTIONS FOR ES 300
Chrome Wheels +595
Compact Disc Changer +375
Leather Seats +470
Power Moonroof +380

Don't forget to refer to the Mileage Adjustment Table at the back of this book!

Model Description	Trade-in Value	Market Value

GS — 1996

A five-speed automatic transmission makes the GS 300 feel more sporty, while rear styling revisions and five new exterior colors update the suave exterior. 1997 side-impact standards are met this year, and the power moonroof features one-touch operation.

RATINGS (SCALE OF 1-10)

Overall	Safety	Reliability	Performance	Comfort	Value
N/A	N/A	9.7	8.6	N/A	4.6

Category J

	Trade-in	Market
4 Dr GS300 Sdn	18580	22655

OPTIONS FOR GS
Chrome Wheels +595
Compact Disc Changer +375
Leather Seats +470
Nakamichi Sound System +560
Power Moonroof +380
Traction Control System +480

LS 400 — 1996

Deep Jewel Green Pearl is newly available on the paint palette.

RATINGS (SCALE OF 1-10)

Overall	Safety	Reliability	Performance	Comfort	Value
N/A	N/A	9.3	8	9.4	5.4

Category L

	Trade-in	Market
4 Dr STD Sdn	23745	27935

OPTIONS FOR LS 400
Chrome Wheels +620
Compact Disc Changer +450
Nakamichi Sound System +450
Power Moonroof +380
Traction Control System +575

LX 450 — 1996

Lexus clones a Toyota Land Cruiser, puts some fancy wheels on it, and slathers leather and wood all over the interior to capitalize on the booming sport-ute market.

Category G

	Trade-in	Market
4 Dr STD 4WD Wgn	24125	29420

OPTIONS FOR LX 450
F&R Locking Differential +365
Compact Disc Changer +210
Luggage Rack +65
Power Moonroof +350
Running Boards +155

SC — 1996

SC300 boasts a larger options roster with the addition of a one-touch operation moonroof and electrochromatic rearview mirrors. The buttery V8 from the LS 400 is installed in the SC 400, and chrome wheels are available. Auto-dimming electrochromic inside and outside rearview mirrors are now standard, a new remote keyless entry system debuts, and the optional moonroof now features one-touch operation.

RATINGS (SCALE OF 1-10)

Overall	Safety	Reliability	Performance	Comfort	Value
N/A	N/A	9.1	N/A	N/A	3.7

Category J

	Trade-in	Market
2 Dr SC300 Cpe	19695	24020
2 Dr SC400 Cpe	22345	27250

OPTIONS FOR SC
Compact Disc Changer +375
Leather Seats[Std on SC400] +470
Power Moonroof +380

1995 LEXUS

ES 300 — 1995

Styling is freshened, and chrome wheels are available. Trunk-mounted CD changer is a new option.

RATINGS (SCALE OF 1-10)

Overall	Safety	Reliability	Performance	Comfort	Value
8	8.4	9.2	8.4	8.1	5.7

Category J

	Trade-in	Market
4 Dr STD Sdn	12325	15215

OPTIONS FOR ES 300
Chrome Wheels +485
Compact Disc Changer +305
Leather Seats +385
Power Moonroof +310

GS — 1995

No changes.

RATINGS (SCALE OF 1-10)

Overall	Safety	Reliability	Performance	Comfort	Value
N/A	N/A	9.7	8.6	N/A	6.1

Category J

	Trade-in	Market
4 Dr GS300 Sdn	15640	19305

OPTIONS FOR GS
Compact Disc Changer +305
Leather Seats +385
Nakamichi Sound System +460
Power Moonroof +310
Traction Control System +390

LS 400 — 1995

All-new car looks pretty much the same as it has for half a decade. The interior and trunk are larger, the engine more powerful, and the car is quicker than before. Six-disc CD changer is dash-mounted.

RATINGS (SCALE OF 1-10)

Overall	Safety	Reliability	Performance	Comfort	Value
N/A	N/A	9.3	8	9.4	6.3

Category L

	Trade-in	Market
4 Dr STD Sdn	20285	24145

OPTIONS FOR LS 400
AM/FM Compact Disc Player +300
Chrome Wheels +510
Compact Disc Changer +370
Nakamichi Sound System +370
Power Moonroof +310
Traction Control System +470

SC   1995

Revised styling and new wheels spruce up the look of these coupes. 1997 side-impact standards are met this year. A cupholder is added inside.

RATINGS (SCALE OF 1-10)

Overall	Safety	Reliability	Performance	Comfort	Value
N/A	N/A	8.9	N/A	N/A	4.9

Category J

	Trade-in	Market
2 Dr SC300 Cpe	15890	19620
2 Dr SC400 Cpe	18310	22605

OPTIONS FOR SC
Compact Disc Changer +305
Leather Seats[Std on SC400] +385
Power Moonroof +310
Rear Spoiler +135

1994 LEXUS

ES 300   1994

Passenger airbag added. New 3.0-liter engine has aluminum block and a few more horsepower. Several convenience features are now standard, including an outside temperature gauge.

RATINGS (SCALE OF 1-10)

Overall	Safety	Reliability	Performance	Comfort	Value
8	8.4	9.3	8.4	8.1	5.7

Category J

	Trade-in	Market
4 Dr STD Sdn	10415	13015

OPTIONS FOR ES 300
Cellular Telephone +485
Compact Disc Changer +250
Leather Seats +315
Power Moonroof +255

GS   1994

No changes.

RATINGS (SCALE OF 1-10)

Overall	Safety	Reliability	Performance	Comfort	Value
N/A	N/A	9.3	8.6	N/A	6.1

Category J

	Trade-in	Market
4 Dr GS300 Sdn	13560	16955

OPTIONS FOR GS
Compact Disc Changer +250
Leather Seats +315
Nakamichi Sound System +375
Power Moonroof +255
Traction Control System +320

LS 400   1994

Minor trim revisions.

RATINGS (SCALE OF 1-10)

Overall	Safety	Reliability	Performance	Comfort	Value
N/A	N/A	9.7	9	9.3	6.3

Category L

	Trade-in	Market
4 Dr STD Sdn	15490	18895

OPTIONS FOR LS 400
Electric Air Suspension +465
Memory System +220
Compact Disc Changer +300
Nakamichi Sound System +300
Power Moonroof +255
Traction Control System +385

SC   1994

Air conditioning is now CFC-free.

RATINGS (SCALE OF 1-10)

Overall	Safety	Reliability	Performance	Comfort	Value
N/A	N/A	8.9	N/A	N/A	4.9

Category J

	Trade-in	Market
2 Dr SC300 Cpe	13195	16495
2 Dr SC400 Cpe	15255	19070

OPTIONS FOR SC
Leather Seats[Std on SC400] +315
Leather Steering Wheel[Std on SC400] +25
Power Moonroof +255
Rear Spoiler +110

1993 LEXUS

ES 300   1993

A fuel cap tether and automatic-locking safety belt retractors are added.

RATINGS (SCALE OF 1-10)

Overall	Safety	Reliability	Performance	Comfort	Value
8.1	8.4	9.1	8.4	8.1	6.7

Don't forget to refer to the Mileage Adjustment Table at the back of this book!

Model Description	Trade-in Value	Market Value	Model Description	Trade-in Value	Market Value
Category J			*Category J*		
4 Dr STD Sdn	8195	10640	2 Dr SC300 Cpe	11530	14975
			2 Dr SC400 Cpe	12590	16350

OPTIONS FOR ES 300
Compact Disc Changer +205
Leather Seats +260
Power Moonroof +210

OPTIONS FOR SC
Compact Disc Changer +205
Leather Seats[Std on SC400] +260
Power Moonroof +210
Rear Spoiler +90

GS 1993

New sports sedan looks great, but fails to deliver much performance. Arrived late in 1993 with dual airbags, ABS and CFC-free air conditioning.

RATINGS (SCALE OF 1-10)

Overall	Safety	Reliability	Performance	Comfort	Value
N/A	N/A	9.3	N/A	N/A	6.4

Category J

4 Dr GS300 Sdn	11750	15260

OPTIONS FOR GS
Portable Plus Telephone +375
Cellular Telephone +400
Chrome Wheels +325
Compact Disc Changer +205
Leather Seats +260
Nakamichi Sound System +305
Power Moonroof +210
Traction Control System +260

LS 400 1993

Passenger airbag added. New alloy wheels debut. Brakes and tires are bigger. Styling is touched up, and interiors receive a host of upgrades. CFC-free air conditioning replaces Freon-based unit.

RATINGS (SCALE OF 1-10)

Overall	Safety	Reliability	Performance	Comfort	Value
N/A	N/A	9.9	9	9.3	4.6

Category L

4 Dr STD Sdn	13410	16555

OPTIONS FOR LS 400
Memory System +180
Cellular Telephone +225
Compact Disc Changer +245
Nakamichi Sound System +245
Power Moonroof +205
Traction Control System +315

SC 1993

Passenger airbag added. Automatic headlamp system debuts, and owners could pre-wire the car for use with a "Portable Plus" cellular phone.

RATINGS (SCALE OF 1-10)

Overall	Safety	Reliability	Performance	Comfort	Value
N/A	N/A	9.1	N/A	N/A	4.9

1992 LEXUS

ES 300 1992

Camry-based replacement for ES250. ABS and driver airbag are standard.

RATINGS (SCALE OF 1-10)

Overall	Safety	Reliability	Performance	Comfort	Value
7.8	7.4	8.9	8.4	8.1	6.1

Category J

4 Dr STD Sdn	7310	9615

OPTIONS FOR ES 300
Auto 4-Speed Transmission +160
AM/FM Compact Disc Player +80
Leather Seats +210
Power Moonroof +170

LS 400 1992

No changes.

RATINGS (SCALE OF 1-10)

Overall	Safety	Reliability	Performance	Comfort	Value
N/A	N/A	9.3	9	9.3	6.1

Category L

4 Dr STD Sdn	10805	13505

OPTIONS FOR LS 400
Memory System +145
AM/FM Compact Disc Player +165
Compact Disc Changer +200
Power Moonroof +170
Premium Sound System +175
Traction Control System +255

SC 1992

Introduced in June 1991, these sleek coupes feature standard ABS and driver airbag. Traction control is optional with automatic transmission. SC300 is powered by inline six-cylinder engine.

RATINGS (SCALE OF 1-10)

Overall	Safety	Reliability	Performance	Comfort	Value
N/A	N/A	8.3	N/A	N/A	5.3

Category J

2 Dr SC300 Cpe	9875	12995
2 Dr SC400 Cpe	11195	14725

Don't forget to refer to the Mileage Adjustment Table at the back of this book!

LEXUS 92-90

Model Description	Trade-in Value	Market Value	Model Description	Trade-in Value	Market Value

OPTIONS FOR SC
Leather Seats[Std on SC400] +210
Power Moonroof +170

1991 LEXUS

ES 250 — 1991

No changes.
Category D
4 Dr STD Sdn — 4725 — 6475

OPTIONS FOR ES 250
Auto 4-Speed Transmission +110
Compact Disc W/fm/tape +120
Leather Seats +165
Power Drivers Seat +45
Power Sunroof +110

LS 400 — 1991

No changes.

RATINGS (SCALE OF 1-10)

Overall	Safety	Reliability	Performance	Comfort	Value
N/A	N/A	9.2	9	9.3	5.5

Category L
4 Dr STD Sdn — 9150 — 11730

OPTIONS FOR LS 400
Air Suspension System +220
Memory System +120
AM/FM Compact Disc Player +135
Leather Seats +180
Nakamichi Sound System +165
Power Moonroof +140

Premium Sound System +145
Traction Control System +210

1990 LEXUS

ES 250 — 1990

Camry-based luxury compact meant to serve as entry-level car for new Lexus division. ABS and driver airbag are standard.
Category D
4 Dr STD Sdn — 4115 — 5715

OPTIONS FOR ES 250
Auto 4-Speed Transmission +90
Compact Disc W/fm/tape +95
Leather Seats +135
Power Drivers Seat +35
Power Sunroof +90

LS 400 — 1990

Brand-new flagship for brand-new Toyota luxury division. ABS and driver airbag are standard. Traction control is optional.

RATINGS (SCALE OF 1-10)

Overall	Safety	Reliability	Performance	Comfort	Value
N/A	N/A	8.8	9	9.3	4.2

Category L
4 Dr STD Sdn — 7835 — 10310

OPTIONS FOR LS 400
Air Suspension System +185
Memory System +100
AM/FM Compact Disc Player +110
Cellular Telephone +120
Compact Disc Changer +135
Leather Seats +145
Nakamichi Sound System +135
Power Sunroof +110
Traction Control System +170

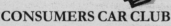

Don't forget to refer to the Mileage Adjustment Table at the back of this book!

Model Description	Trade-in Value	Market Value

Model Description	Trade-in Value	Market Value

LINCOLN · USA

1999 Lincoln Town Car

1999 LINCOLN

CONTINENTAL · 1999

Lincoln's luxury liner gets added safety in 1999 with the addition of standard side airbags for the driver and front passenger. There's also five new exterior colors, upgraded interior trim options, two new wheel designs and an improved audio system. Otherwise the Lincoln remains unchanged after its major rework in 1998.

RATINGS (SCALE OF 1-10)

Overall	Safety	Reliability	Performance	Comfort	Value
N/A	N/A	N/A	7.6	8.3	N/A

Category A
4 Dr STD Sdn · 22170 · 26085

OPTIONS FOR CONTINENTAL
Cellular Telephone +530
Chrome Wheels +750
Compact Disc Changer +590
Heated Front Seats +150
Power Moonroof +1010

RESCU Pkg +1060

NAVIGATOR · 1999

Into its second year, Lincoln's Navigator enters 1999 with more power, adjustable pedals, speed-sensitive stereo volume, and a hands-free cellular phone. Also, the optional third row seat is mounted on rollers this year for easy installation and removal.

RATINGS (SCALE OF 1-10)

Overall	Safety	Reliability	Performance	Comfort	Value
N/A	N/A	N/A	5.6	7.5	N/A

Category H
4 Dr STD Wgn · 28640 · 33690
4 Dr STD 4WD Wgn · 30111 · 35420

OPTIONS FOR NAVIGATOR
Chrome Wheels +220
Compact Disc Changer +320
Dual Air Conditioning +990
Limited Slip Diff[Opt on 2WD] +190
Power Moonroof +720

TOWN CAR · 1999

Standard side airbags improve the Town Car's ability to protect occupants and a new JBL audio system makes getting there even more fun.

RATINGS (SCALE OF 1-10)

Overall	Safety	Reliability	Performance	Comfort	Value
N/A	N/A	9.2	7.4	8.4	N/A

Category A
4 Dr Cartier Sdn · 23325 · 27440
4 Dr Executive Sdn · 21020 · 24730
4 Dr Signature Sdn · 22220 · 26140

OPTIONS FOR TOWN CAR
Cellular Telephone +530
Chrome Wheels[Std on Cartier] +750
Compact Disc Changer +590
Power Moonroof +1010

1998 LINCOLN

CONTINENTAL · 1998

Lincoln's front-wheel drive luxo-barge gets a bigger grille (just what it needs) and rounded corners. It also gets an interior freshening that replaces the digital clock with an analog timepiece.

RATINGS (SCALE OF 1-10)

Overall	Safety	Reliability	Performance	Comfort	Value
N/A	N/A	8.7	7.6	8.3	5

Category A
4 Dr STD Sdn · 17910 · 21325

OPTIONS FOR CONTINENTAL
RESCU Pkg +595
Chrome Wheels +610
Compact Disc Changer +480
Heated Front Seats +120
JBL Sound System +340
Power Moonroof +825

MARK VIII · 1998

No changes to Lincoln's muscle car.

Don't forget to refer to the Mileage Adjustment Table at the back of this book!

Model Description	Trade-in Value	Market Value

RATINGS (SCALE OF 1-10)

Overall	Safety	Reliability	Performance	Comfort	Value
N/A	N/A	8.6	8.4	7.9	4.5

Category A

2 Dr LSC Cpe	18585	22125
2 Dr STD Cpe	17885	21290

OPTIONS FOR MARK VIII

AM/FM Compact Disc Player +300
Chrome Wheels[Opt on STD] +610
Compact Disc Changer +480
Heated Front Seats +120
Power Moonroof +825

NAVIGATOR   1998

This all-new entrant into the luxury SUV market is the first truck ever sold by Lincoln. Based on the highly-acclaimed Ford Expedition, the Navigator is powered by a 5.4-liter SOHC V8 engine and has standard goodies that include illuminated running boards and a load-leveling air suspension. This truck also features one of the largest grilles this side of a Kenworth.

RATINGS (SCALE OF 1-10)

Overall	Safety	Reliability	Performance	Comfort	Value
N/A	N/A	8.5	5.4	7.5	N/A

Category H

4 Dr STD Wgn	24935	29685
4 Dr STD 4WD Wgn	26212	31205

OPTIONS FOR NAVIGATOR

Chrome Wheels +180
Compact Disc Changer +265
Dual Air Conditioning +810
Limited Slip Diff[Opt on 2WD] +155
Power Moonroof +590

TOWN CAR   1998

Lincoln redesigns its Town Car this year, making it lower, stiffer and faster. The interior is nicely improved as well, with softer seats and better positioned controls.

RATINGS (SCALE OF 1-10)

Overall	Safety	Reliability	Performance	Comfort	Value
N/A	N/A	8.4	7.4	8.4	5

Category A

4 Dr Cartier Sdn	21195	25235
4 Dr Executive Sdn	18665	22220
4 Dr Signature Sdn	19645	23385

OPTIONS FOR TOWN CAR

Chrome Wheels +610
Compact Disc Changer +480
Heated Front Seats[Std on Cartier] +120
JBL Sound System[Std on Cartier] +340
Leather Seats[Std on Cartier] +405

Power Moonroof +825
Traction Control System[Std on Cartier] +130

1997 LINCOLN

CONTINENTAL   1997

The changes to the 1997 Continental are minor this year. The first is the addition of a single-key locking system that locks the doors, glove box, and trunk with a turn of the wrist. The second is the addition of all-speed traction control. Lastly, the Continental receives a minor interior and exterior facelift.

RATINGS (SCALE OF 1-10)

Overall	Safety	Reliability	Performance	Comfort	Value
N/A	N/A	8.7	7.6	8.1	6.1

Category A

4 Dr STD Sdn	14595	17585

OPTIONS FOR CONTINENTAL

RESCU Pkg +645
Cellular Telephone +355
Chrome Wheels +500
Compact Disc Changer +395
Power Moonroof +675

MARK VIII   1997

Lincoln thoroughly updates this personal coupe, lighting the darn thing up like a Christmas tree in the process. The Mark now has high-intensity discharge front headlamps, cornering lamps, a neon rear applique, and puddle lamps. Wow, you'll see this thing from miles away. The hood, grille and interior have also been slightly redesigned.

RATINGS (SCALE OF 1-10)

Overall	Safety	Reliability	Performance	Comfort	Value
N/A	N/A	8.6	8.4	7.9	5.2

Category A

2 Dr LSC Cpe	16280	19610
2 Dr STD Cpe	15735	18960

OPTIONS FOR MARK VIII

AM/FM Compact Disc Player +245
Cellular Telephone +355
Chrome Wheels[Opt on STD] +500
Compact Disc Changer +395
Power Moonroof +675

TOWN CAR   1997

The Town Car's power steering has been improved. Watch out, Mario!

RATINGS (SCALE OF 1-10)

Overall	Safety	Reliability	Performance	Comfort	Value
7.7	8.2	8.1	7.4	8.4	6.3

Don't forget to refer to the Mileage Adjustment Table at the back of this book!

Model Description	Trade-in Value	Market Value
Category A		
4 Dr Cartier Sdn	17710	21335
4 Dr Executive Sdn	15705	18925
4 Dr Signature Sdn	16340	19690

OPTIONS FOR TOWN CAR
Cellular Telephone +355
Chrome Wheels +500
Compact Disc Changer +395
JBL Sound System[Std on Cartier] +275
Leather Seats[Std on Cartier] +330
Power Moonroof +675
Traction Control System[Std on Cartier] +105

1996 LINCOLN

CONTINENTAL 1996

The big news for Continental is an optional gee-whiz rescue unit that uses a Global Positioning Satellite to pinpoint your location for roadside assistance, medical, and law enforcement personnel in the event of an emergency. Likely the greatest safety advance since airbags and antilock brakes. Also new are run-flat Michelin tires, a 75th Diamond Anniversary Edition, and a standard anti-theft system. It's getting there.

RATINGS (SCALE OF 1-10)

Overall	Safety	Reliability	Performance	Comfort	Value
N/A	N/A	8.1	7.6	8.1	6.5

	Trade-in	Market
Category A		
4 Dr STD Sdn	12115	14775

OPTIONS FOR CONTINENTAL
Cellular Telephone +290
Chrome Wheels +410
Compact Disc Changer +320
JBL Sound System +225
Power Moonroof +550
Traction Control System +85

MARK VIII 1996

Last year's limited-edition LSC model goes full-time for 1996. Eight new colors are available, and borderless floor mats debut. A Touring Package and 75th Diamond Anniversary model are offered.

RATINGS (SCALE OF 1-10)

Overall	Safety	Reliability	Performance	Comfort	Value
N/A	N/A	8.7	8.4	7.9	5.7

	Trade-in	Market
Category A		
2 Dr LSC Cpe	13525	16495
2 Dr STD Cpe	12830	15645

OPTIONS FOR MARK VIII
Cellular Telephone +290
Chrome Wheels[Opt on STD] +410
Compact Disc Changer +320

Power Moonroof +550
Traction Control System +85

TOWN CAR 1996

Engine upgrades, new automatic climate controls, and real wood on the dashboard in Cartier models sum up the changes to the Town Car.

RATINGS (SCALE OF 1-10)

Overall	Safety	Reliability	Performance	Comfort	Value
7.6	8	7.5	7.4	8.4	6.7

	Trade-in	Market
Category A		
4 Dr Cartier Sdn	14475	17650
4 Dr Executive Sdn	12705	15495
4 Dr Signature Sdn	13270	16180

OPTIONS FOR TOWN CAR
Limousine Builder's Pkg +350
Cellular Telephone +290
Compact Disc Changer +320
JBL Sound System[Std on Cartier] +225
Leather Seats[Std on Cartier] +270
Power Moonroof +550
Traction Control System[Std on Cartier] +85

1995 LINCOLN

CONTINENTAL 1995

An all-new Continental is released with a V8 DOHC engine. A new suspension system that adjusts the shock absorbers to the prevailing driving conditions debuts, as does a memory seat system that will retain the seating preferences for two people. The new Continental has swoopier styling which is geared towards attracting a more youthful audience.

RATINGS (SCALE OF 1-10)

Overall	Safety	Reliability	Performance	Comfort	Value
N/A	N/A	8.1	7.6	8.1	5.7

	Trade-in	Market
Category A		
4 Dr STD Sdn	9585	11980

OPTIONS FOR CONTINENTAL
Cellular Telephone +235
Chrome Wheels +335
Compact Disc Changer +265
Power Moonroof +450
Traction Control System +70

MARK VIII 1995

Lincoln's premium touring coupe receives significant changes across the board. A new instrument panel houses a new stereo with larger buttons. A feature called retained accessory power makes an appearance on the Mark VIII, allowing passengers 10 seconds to close the window after the car is turned off.

Don't forget to refer to the Mileage Adjustment Table at the back of this book!

Model Description	Trade-in Value	Market Value

Model Description	Trade-in Value	Market Value

RATINGS (SCALE OF 1-10)

Overall	Safety	Reliability	Performance	Comfort	Value
N/A	N/A	7.8	8.4	7.9	6.1

Category A

	Trade-in	Market
2 Dr LSC Cpe	11040	13805
2 Dr STD Cpe	10910	13635

OPTIONS FOR MARK VIII
Cellular Telephone +235
Chrome Wheels +335
Compact Disc Changer +265
Power Moonroof +450
Traction Control System +70

TOWN CAR   1995

Exterior changes on the Town Car include new headlights, grille, taillights, bumpers, and bodyside molding. The outside mirrors have been moved forward slightly to increase visibility. An electronic steering switch selector allows the driver to select the type of steering effort they want. The instrument panel includes a redesigned two-spoke steering wheel, illuminated switches, and improved stereos with larger controls. Signature and Cartier models get steering wheel-mounted stereo and climate controls. A gate access unit integrated into the driver's side visor allows up to three frequencies to be programmed into its memory.

RATINGS (SCALE OF 1-10)

Overall	Safety	Reliability	Performance	Comfort	Value
7.7	8.7	6.5	7.4	8.4	7.7

Category A

	Trade-in	Market
4 Dr Cartier Sdn	11480	14350
4 Dr Executive Sdn	9980	12475
4 Dr Signature Sdn	10475	13090

OPTIONS FOR TOWN CAR
Cellular Telephone +235
Compact Disc Changer +265
JBL Sound System[Std on Cartier] +185
Leather Seats[Std on Cartier] +220
Power Moonroof +450
Traction Control System[Std on Cartier] +70

1994 LINCOLN

CONTINENTAL   1994

Suspension changes improve the Continental's ride. A memory feature on the remote keyless entry automatically adjusts the driver's seat to a pre-set position each time it's activated. Exterior changes include revised taillamps, grille and rocker moldings. A retractable trunk cord is standard on all Continentals; it is designed to keep the trunk from bouncing around when it has to be left open for large loads.

RATINGS (SCALE OF 1-10)

Overall	Safety	Reliability	Performance	Comfort	Value
N/A	N/A	6.3	7.6	7.6	6.4

Category A

	Trade-in	Market
4 Dr Executive Sdn	6510	8350
4 Dr Signature Sdn	6950	8910

OPTIONS FOR CONTINENTAL
AM/FM Compact Disc Player +135
Cellular Telephone +195
Keyless Entry System[Opt on Executive] +65
Power Moonroof +370
Power Passenger Seat[Opt on Executive] +80

MARK VIII   1994

Chrome wheels are now an available option on the Mark VIII. There is a memory feature for the seats and outside mirrors.

RATINGS (SCALE OF 1-10)

Overall	Safety	Reliability	Performance	Comfort	Value
N/A	N/A	8.7	8.4	7.9	6.1

Category A

	Trade-in	Market
2 Dr STD Cpe	8280	10615

OPTIONS FOR MARK VIII
AM/FM Compact Disc Player +135
Cellular Telephone +195
Chrome Wheels +275
Compact Disc Changer +215
Power Moonroof +370
Traction Control System +55

TOWN CAR   1994

A dual exhaust system on the Town Car is made standard this year, upping horsepower to 210. All models receive solar tinted glass. The Jack Nicklaus Special Edition has been dropped.

RATINGS (SCALE OF 1-10)

Overall	Safety	Reliability	Performance	Comfort	Value
N/A	N/A	7.7	7	8	7.1

Category A

	Trade-in	Market
4 Dr Cartier Sdn	8665	11110
4 Dr Executive Sdn	7400	9490
4 Dr Signature Sdn	7840	10050

OPTIONS FOR TOWN CAR
Cellular Telephone +195
Compact Disc Changer +215
JBL Sound System[Std on Cartier] +150
Keyless Entry System[Opt on Executive] +65
Leather Seats[Std on Cartier] +180

Don't forget to refer to the Mileage Adjustment Table at the back of this book!

Model Description	Trade-in Value	Market Value

Power Moonroof +370
Traction Control System +55

1993 LINCOLN

CONTINENTAL 1993

Bucket seats are available this year with a handy center console. The Signature series gets remote keyless entry, aluminum wheels, and the Comfort and Convenience Group added to its standard features list. Both models receive adjustable seatbelt anchor points.

RATINGS (SCALE OF 1-10)

Overall	Safety	Reliability	Performance	Comfort	Value
N/A	N/A	6.9	7.6	7.6	5.8

Category A
4 Dr Executive Sdn	4690	6335
4 Dr Signature Sdn	5060	6835

OPTIONS FOR CONTINENTAL
AM/FM Compact Disc Player +110
Cellular Telephone +160
Dual Power Seats[Opt on Executive] +85
Keyless Entry System[Opt on Executive] +55
Power Sunroof +310
Premium Sound System[Opt on Executive] +75

MARK VIII 1993

The Mark VIII debuts replacing the dated Mark VII. Based on the Thunderbird platform, the new Mark has a sportier feel than previous models. A twin-cam, 4.6-liter V8 produces 280 horsepower in the Mark VIII, and the transmission is an electronically controlled four-speed automatic.

RATINGS (SCALE OF 1-10)

Overall	Safety	Reliability	Performance	Comfort	Value
N/A	N/A	7.6	8.4	7.9	4.3

Category A
2 Dr STD Cpe	6575	8885

OPTIONS FOR MARK VIII
Cellular Telephone +160
Compact Disc Changer +175
Compact Disc W/fm/tape +145
Power Sunroof +310

TOWN CAR 1993

Styling changes and an optional Handling Package mark the differences in this year's Town Car. The formerly optional geometric aluminum wheels are made standard and the grille and headlights are slightly altered. The Handling Package consists of a firmer suspension and larger tires. The Executive series gains some features that were standard on the other models.

RATINGS (SCALE OF 1-10)

Overall	Safety	Reliability	Performance	Comfort	Value
N/A	N/A	8.2	7	8	6.6

Category A
4 Dr Cartier Sdn	6930	9365
4 Dr Executive Sdn	5930	8010
4 Dr Signature Sdn	6230	8420

OPTIONS FOR TOWN CAR
Cellular Telephone +160
Compact Disc Changer +175
Leather Seats[Std on Cartier] +150
Power Sunroof +310
Premium Sound System[Std on Cartier] +75

1992 LINCOLN

CONTINENTAL 1992

The passenger airbag is revived this year and two trim-levels are available, the Signature and the Executive. Several optional safety features debut this year, such as an electrochromatic rearview mirror and a remote keyless entry system with a panic button.

RATINGS (SCALE OF 1-10)

Overall	Safety	Reliability	Performance	Comfort	Value
N/A	N/A	6.5	7.6	7.6	5.7

Category A
4 Dr Executive Sdn	3755	5290
4 Dr Signature Sdn	4025	5670

OPTIONS FOR CONTINENTAL
Cellular Telephone +130
Compact Disc W/fm/tape +115
Power Moonroof +245

MARK VII 1992

The final year for the Mark VII, changes are limited to minor alterations of the interior.
Category A
2 Dr Bill Blass Cpe	5230	7365
2 Dr LSC Cpe	5340	7520

OPTIONS FOR MARK VII
AM/FM Compact Disc Player +90
Cellular Telephone +130
Power Moonroof +245

TOWN CAR 1992

Transmission adaptations include electronic shift controls, overdrive lockout, and a feature that won't allow the car to be shifted out of "Park" unless the brake is on.

Don't forget to refer to the Mileage Adjustment Table at the back of this book!

Model Description	Trade-in Value	Market Value	Model Description	Trade-in Value	Market Value

RATINGS (SCALE OF 1-10)

Overall	Safety	Reliability	Performance	Comfort	Value
N/A	N/A	7.3	7	8	6.9

Category A

	Trade-in	Market
4 Dr Cartier Sdn	5390	7590
4 Dr Executive Sdn	4675	6580
4 Dr Signature Sdn	4990	7030

OPTIONS FOR TOWN CAR
AM/FM Compact Disc Player +90
Cellular Telephone +130
JBL Sound System[Std on Cartier] +100
Leather Seats +120
Power Moonroof +245
Power Passenger Seat[Opt on Executive] +55

RATINGS (SCALE OF 1-10)

Overall	Safety	Reliability	Performance	Comfort	Value
N/A	N/A	6.3	7	8	6.9

Category A

	Trade-in	Market
4 Dr Cartier Sdn	4345	6295
4 Dr STD Sdn	3645	5285
4 Dr Signature Sdn	4010	5815

OPTIONS FOR TOWN CAR
AM/FM Compact Disc Player +75
Cellular Telephone +105
Leather Seats[Std on Cartier] +100
Power Passenger Seat[Opt on STD] +45
Power Sunroof +210
Traction Control System +30

1991 LINCOLN

CONTINENTAL 1991

A passenger airbag is available only in a portion of these cars since they ran out of propellant halfway through the production run.

RATINGS (SCALE OF 1-10)

Overall	Safety	Reliability	Performance	Comfort	Value
N/A	N/A	5.3	7.6	7.6	7.1

Category A

	Trade-in	Market
4 Dr STD Sdn	2930	4245
4 Dr Signature Sdn	3225	4670

OPTIONS FOR CONTINENTAL
AM/FM Compact Disc Player +75
Cellular Telephone +105
Power Passenger Seat[Opt on STD] +45
Power Sunroof +210

MARK VII 1991

No significant changes to the Mark VII.

Category A

	Trade-in	Market
2 Dr Bill Blass Cpe	4040	5855
2 Dr LSC Cpe	4055	5875

OPTIONS FOR MARK VII
AM/FM Compact Disc Player +75
Cellular Telephone +105
Power Sunroof +210

TOWN CAR 1991

An impressive 4.6-liter, overhead-cam V8 engine debuts in the Town Car. Offering 40 to 60 more horsepower, depending on the exhaust system, than the previous 5.0-liter V8. The new Town Car has quite a bit more pizzazz than many luxo-barges.

1990 LINCOLN

CONTINENTAL 1990

A serious-looking aerodynamic grille appears on the nose of the Continental and new taillamps illuminate the rear.

RATINGS (SCALE OF 1-10)

Overall	Safety	Reliability	Performance	Comfort	Value
N/A	N/A	4.4	7.6	7.6	6.9

Category A

	Trade-in	Market
4 Dr STD Sdn	2465	3735
4 Dr Signature Sdn	2705	4095

OPTIONS FOR CONTINENTAL
AM/FM Compact Disc Player +60
Cellular Telephone +85
Power Passenger Seat[Opt on STD] +35
Power Sunroof +170

MARK VII 1990

The Mark VII receives a standard driver airbag. The LSC receives new wheels.

Category A

	Trade-in	Market
2 Dr Bill Blass Cpe	3120	4725
2 Dr LSC Cpe	3135	4750

OPTIONS FOR MARK VII
AM/FM Compact Disc Player +60
Cellular Telephone +85
Leather Seats +80
Power Sunroof +170

TOWN CAR 1990

The Town Car gets new sheetmetal. Rounded edges and aerodynamic shapes produce a car that looks much more modern than its predecessor.

LINCOLN 90

Model Description	Trade-in Value	Market Value	Model Description	Trade-in Value	Market Value

RATINGS (SCALE OF 1-10)

Overall	Safety	Reliability	Performance	Comfort	Value
N/A	N/A	5.9	6.8	8	6.3

Category A

	Trade-in Value	Market Value
4 Dr Cartier Sdn	3560	5395
4 Dr STD Sdn	3065	4645
4 Dr Signature Sdn	3330	5040

OPTIONS FOR TOWN CAR

AM/FM Compact Disc Player +60
Anti-Lock Brakes +110
Cellular Telephone +85
Leather Seats[Std on Cartier] +80
Power Passenger Seat +35
Power Sunroof +170

MAZDA

Japan

1995 Mazda Millenia

1999 MAZDA

626 — 1999

After a major makeover in '98, the 626 slides into '99 with only one major change: a new height-adjustable seat for the driver.

RATINGS (SCALE OF 1-10)

Overall	Safety	Reliability	Performance	Comfort	Value
N/A	7.2	8.7	9	7.9	N/A

Category D

4 Dr ES Sdn	12560	14950
4 Dr ES V6 Sdn	13820	16450
4 Dr LX Sdn	10695	12730
4 Dr LX V6 Sdn	11950	14225

OPTIONS FOR 626

Auto 4-Speed Transmission[Std on ES] +590
Aluminum/Alloy Wheels[Std on ES V6] +345
Anti-Lock Brakes +670
Bose Sound System[Std on ES V6] +560
Power Moonroof[Std on ES V6] +620

B-SERIES — 1999

The B-Series now comes with a four-door option called the Cab Plus 4. Option packages have been consolidated and simplified this year to reduce buyer confusion. A class III frame mounted hitch receiver is available with V6 applications.

RATINGS (SCALE OF 1-10)

Overall	Safety	Reliability	Performance	Comfort	Value
N/A	N/A	N/A	6.8	7.4	N/A

Category G

2 Dr B2500 SE Ext Cab SB	10565	12575
4 Dr B2500 SE Ext Cab SB	10880	12955
2 Dr B2500 SE Std Cab SB	8970	10680
2 Dr B2500 SX Std Cab SB	6990	8320
2 Dr B2500 TL Std Cab SB	8875	10565
2 Dr B3000 SE Ext Cab SB	10585	12600
2 Dr B3000 SE 4WD Ext Cab SB	14280	17000
4 Dr B3000 SE Ext Cab SB	10985	13080
4 Dr B3000 SE 4WD Ext Cab SB	14625	17410
4 Dr B3000 TL Ext Cab SB	11530	13725
2 Dr B4000 SE Ext Cab SB	11115	13230
2 Dr B4000 SE 4WD Ext Cab SB	14850	17680
4 Dr B4000 SE Ext Cab SB	11480	13665
4 Dr B4000 SE 4WD Ext Cab SB	15180	18070
2 Dr B4000 SE Std Cab SB	9255	11020
4 Dr B4000 TL 4WD Ext Cab SB	15800	18810

OPTIONS FOR B-SERIES

Auto 4-Speed Transmission +810
Auto 5-Speed Transmission[Std on B4000 SE 2WD Cab Plus/Cab Plus 4] +835
Air Conditioning[Opt on B2500 SX] +605
Anti-Lock Brakes +445
Bed Liner[Std on B4000 SE, B4000 TL] +210
Cruise Control[Std on B4000 SE, B4000 TL] +155
Keyless Entry System +150
Power Door Locks +170
Power Mirrors +100
Power Windows +175
Sliding Rear Window[Std on B4000 SE, B4000 TL] +90
Tilt Steering Wheel[Std on B4000 SE, B4000 TL] +130

MIATA — 1999

Mazda cautiously redesigns the Miata, improving the car in every way without bumping up the price or diluting the car's personality. Very nice job.

RATINGS (SCALE OF 1-10)

Overall	Safety	Reliability	Performance	Comfort	Value
N/A	N/A	9	9	7.1	N/A

Category F

2 Dr MX-5 Conv	13030	15330
2 Dr MX-5 10TH Anniv. Conv	20495	24110

OPTIONS FOR MIATA

Auto 4-Speed Transmission +560
Leather Pkg +2700
Sports Pkg +580
Air Conditioning +620
Aluminum/Alloy Wheels[Opt on MX-5] +230
Anti-Lock Brakes +505
Cruise Control[Opt on MX-5] +155
Hardtop Roof +1010
Leather Seats[Opt on MX-5] +485
Limited Slip Diff[Opt on MX-5] +255

Don't forget to refer to the Mileage Adjustment Table at the back of this book!

Power Door Locks[Opt on MX-5] +150
Power Mirrors[Opt on MX-5] +95
Power Steering[Opt on MX-5] +255
Power Windows[Opt on MX-5] +165
Rear Spoiler[Opt on MX-5] +185
Sport Suspension[Opt on MX-5] +135

MILLENIA   1999

Revised front- and rear-end styling, plus an optional two-tone color scheme, separate the '99 Millenia from past models.

RATINGS (SCALE OF 1-10)

Overall	Safety	Reliability	Performance	Comfort	Value
N/A	8	N/A	8.2	7.9	N/A

Category D

4 Dr S Sdn	18070	21510
4 Dr STD Sdn	15920	18950

OPTIONS FOR MILLENIA

Bose Sound System[Std on S] +560
Heated Front Seats +300
Keyless Entry System[Std on S] +235
Leather Seats[Std on S] +820
Power Moonroof[Std on S] +620
Traction Control System[Std on S] +455

PROTEGE   1999

The Protege gets an extensive makeover for '99 that includes new exterior and interior styling, a more powerful engine lineup, additional luxury options, and five new colors.

RATINGS (SCALE OF 1-10)

Overall	Safety	Reliability	Performance	Comfort	Value
N/A	6.6	8.5	7.6	7.8	N/A

Category E

4 Dr DX Sdn	8010	9650
4 Dr ES Sdn	10210	12300
4 Dr LX Sdn	8860	10675

OPTIONS FOR PROTEGE

Auto 4-Speed Transmission +590
AM/FM Compact Disc Player[Opt on DX] +340
Air Conditioning[Std on ES] +605
Aluminum/Alloy Wheels +245
Anti-Lock Brakes +500
Keyless Entry System[Std on ES] +115
Power Moonroof +425

1998 MAZDA

626   1998

Mazda redesigns the 626, giving it more upscale styling, more powerful engines, a tighter body and increased cargo and people space while retaining the sedan's distinctive sporting nature.

RATINGS (SCALE OF 1-10)

Overall	Safety	Reliability	Performance	Comfort	Value
7.7	7	7.9	9	7.9	6.5

Category D

4 Dr DX Sdn	8490	10105
4 Dr ES Sdn	11840	14095
4 Dr LX Sdn	9595	11425
4 Dr LX V6 Sdn	10795	12850

OPTIONS FOR 626

Auto 4-Speed Transmission +490
AM/FM Compact Disc Player[Opt on DX] +320
Air Conditioning[Opt on DX] +515
Aluminum/Alloy Wheels[Std on ES] +280
Anti-Lock Brakes[Opt on LX] +550
Bose Sound System[Std on ES] +460
Keyless Entry System[Opt on LX] +190
Leather Seats[Opt on LX] +670
Power Drivers Seat[Std on ES] +180
Power Moonroof[Std on ES] +505

B-SERIES PICKUP   1998

Fresh styling, a revised front suspension, a larger regular cab, a more powerful 2.5-liter four-cylinder engine, a stiffer frame and a new 4WD system ensure that Mazda's compact truck will remain competitive through the end of the century.

RATINGS (SCALE OF 1-10)

Overall	Safety	Reliability	Performance	Comfort	Value
N/A	7.3	8.5	7.2	7.4	N/A

Category G

2 Dr B2500 SE Ext Cab SB	8120	9670
4 Dr B2500 SE Ext Cab SB	8465	10075
2 Dr B2500 SE Std Cab SB	7540	8975
2 Dr B2500 SX Std Cab SB	6695	7970
2 Dr B3000 SE Ext Cab SB	8920	10620
2 Dr B3000 SE 4WD Ext Cab SB	9210	10965
2 Dr B3000 SE 4WD Std Cab SB	9745	11605
2 Dr B3000 SX 4WD Std Cab SB	9235	10995
2 Dr B4000 SE Ext Cab SB	9385	11175
2 Dr B4000 SE 4WD Ext Cab SB	11075	13185

OPTIONS FOR B-SERIES PICKUP

Auto 4-Speed Transmission +655
Auto 5-Speed Transmission[Opt on B4000] +680
AM/FM Compact Disc Player +200
Air Conditioning +495
Aluminum/Alloy Wheels +200
Anti-Lock Brakes +365
Bed Liner +170
Cruise Control +125
Fog Lights +90

Don't forget to refer to the Mileage Adjustment Table at the back of this book!

Model Description	Trade-in Value	Market Value
Keyless Entry System +120		
Power Door Locks +140		
Power Mirrors +80		
Power Windows +145		
Sliding Rear Window +70		
Tilt Steering Wheel +105		

MILLENIA — 1998

Millenia carries over into 1998 with no changes.

RATINGS (SCALE OF 1-10)

Overall	Safety	Reliability	Performance	Comfort	Value
7.5	8	9	8.4	7.9	4.1

Category D		
4 Dr S Sdn	16320	19430
4 Dr STD Sdn	14465	17220

OPTIONS FOR MILLENIA

Premium Pkg +530
Bose Sound System[Std on S] +460
Dual Power Seats[Std on S] +510
Heated Front Seats +245
Heated Power Mirrors +50
Keyless Entry System[Std on S] +190
Leather Seats[Std on S] +670
Power Moonroof[Std on S] +505
Traction Control System[Std on S] +370

MPV — 1998

A CD player is now standard.

RATINGS (SCALE OF 1-10)

Overall	Safety	Reliability	Performance	Comfort	Value
7.4	7.7	8.4	7.6	7.6	5.6

Category G		
2 Dr ES Pass. Van	13855	16495
2 Dr ES 4WD Pass. Van	15020	17880
2 Dr LX Pass. Van	12270	14610
2 Dr LX 4WD Pass. Van	13470	16035

OPTIONS FOR MPV

Air Conditioning +495
Aluminum/Alloy Wheels[Std on ES,4WD] +200
Auto Load Leveling[Opt on LX] +135
Dual Air Conditioning +575
Keyless Entry System +120
Leather Seats[Opt on LX] +470
Power Moonroof +525
Privacy Glass +160

PROTEGE — 1998

A CD player is standard on ES and LX. It also comes on DX models equipped with an option package.

RATINGS (SCALE OF 1-10)

Overall	Safety	Reliability	Performance	Comfort	Value
N/A	N/A	8.4	8	7.4	5.4

Model Description	Trade-in Value	Market Value
Category E		
4 Dr DX Sdn	6795	8185
4 Dr ES Sdn	8605	10365
4 Dr LX Sdn	7580	9130

OPTIONS FOR PROTEGE

Auto 4-Speed Transmission +490
AM/FM Compact Disc Player[Opt on DX] +275
Air Conditioning[Std on ES] +495
Aluminum/Alloy Wheels +200
Anti-Lock Brakes +410
Keyless Entry System +95
Power Moonroof +350

1997 MAZDA

626 — 1997

LX V6 and ES models gain power and torque, while the four-cylinder LX gets a Lexus-like trim package that includes two-tone paint, chrome wheel covers, leather interior, and other creature comforts. Audio systems are revised and two new colors debut.

RATINGS (SCALE OF 1-10)

Overall	Safety	Reliability	Performance	Comfort	Value
7.6	7	8	8.8	8.1	5.9

Category D		
4 Dr DX Sdn	7335	8840
4 Dr ES Sdn	10815	13030
4 Dr LX Sdn	8265	9955
4 Dr LX V6 Sdn	9385	11310

OPTIONS FOR 626

Auto 4-Speed Transmission +390
AM/FM Stereo Tape[Opt on DX] +180
Air Conditioning[Opt on DX] +420
Aluminum/Alloy Wheels[Opt on LX] +230
Anti-Lock Brakes[Std on ES] +450
Chrome Wheels +265
Keyless Entry System[Std on ES] +155
Leather Seats[Std on ES] +545
Power Antenna[Std on ES] +60
Power Drivers Seat[Std on ES] +150
Power Moonroof[Std on ES] +415

B-SERIES PICKUP — 1997

The lineup is trimmed, leaving just B2300 and B4000 models available. SE-5 designation returns to bolster marketing efforts. B4000 pickups can be equipped with a new five-speed automatic transmission.

RATINGS (SCALE OF 1-10)

Overall	Safety	Reliability	Performance	Comfort	Value
N/A	6.5	8.7	7.2	7.3	N/A

Don't forget to refer to the Mileage Adjustment Table at the back of this book!

Model Description	Trade-in Value	Market Value	Model Description	Trade-in Value	Market Value
Category G					
2 Dr B2300 Std Cab SB	6280	7565			
2 Dr B2300 SE Ext Cab SB	7570	9120			
2 Dr B2300 SE Std Cab SB	6760	8145			
2 Dr B4000 4WD Ext Cab SB	9530	11480			
2 Dr B4000 4WD Std Cab SB	8725	10510			
2 Dr B4000 SE Ext Cab SB	8515	10260			
2 Dr B4000 SE 4WD Ext Cab SB	10210	12300			

OPTIONS FOR B-SERIES PICKUP

Auto 4-Speed Transmission +535
Auto 5-Speed Transmission +555
AM/FM Compact Disc Player +160
Air Conditioning +405
Aluminum/Alloy Wheels +165
Anti-Lock Brakes +295
Bed Liner +140
Compact Disc Changer +255
Cruise Control +105
Keyless Entry System +100
Limited Slip Diff +135
Power Door Locks +115
Power Steering[Std on B4000,B4000 SE,Ext Cab] +140
Power Windows +120
Premium Sound System +170
Rear Step Bumper[Opt on Ext Cab] +70

MIATA   1997

Mazda adds a Touring Package to the options list, consisting of alloy wheels, power steering, leather-wrapped steering wheel, power mirrors, power windows, and door map pockets. Midyear a new M-Edition debuts, sporting Marina Green paint and chromed alloy wheels. Summertime brings the limited-production STO-Edition, of which 1,500 were produced.

RATINGS (SCALE OF 1-10)

Overall	Safety	Reliability	Performance	Comfort	Value
7.3	6.3	9	9	7.1	5

	Trade-in	Market
Category F		
2 Dr MX-5 Conv	10170	12255
2 Dr MX-5 M-Edition Conv	11430	13770
2 Dr MX-5 STO Conv	10875	13100

OPTIONS FOR MIATA

Auto 4-Speed Transmission +440
Leather Pkg +1480
Air Conditioning[Opt on MX-5] +415
Aluminum/Alloy Wheels[Opt on MX-5] +150
Anti-Lock Brakes +335
Compact Disc W/fm/tape[Opt on MX-5] +250
Cruise Control[Opt on MX-5] +105
Hardtop Roof +675
Leather Seats[Opt on MX-5] +325
Limited Slip Diff[Opt on MX-5] +170
Power Steering[Opt on MX-5] +170

Power Windows[Opt on MX-5] +110
Rear Spoiler +120
Sport Suspension +90

MILLENIA   1997

Models equipped with leather are upgraded this year with an eight-way power passenger seat, 16-inch alloy wheels, and revised final drive ratio for better low-end response. S models also get the power passenger seat. All Millenias have a new rear-window-mounted diversity antenna, a new sound system with in-dash CD player, revised center console design, and Michelin tires.

RATINGS (SCALE OF 1-10)

Overall	Safety	Reliability	Performance	Comfort	Value
7.5	8	8.9	8.4	7.9	4.5

	Trade-in	Market
Category D		
4 Dr L Sdn	13835	16670
4 Dr S Sdn	14995	18065
4 Dr STD Sdn	13175	15875

OPTIONS FOR MILLENIA

Bose Sound System +375
Traction Control System[Std on S] +305

MPV   1997

Four-wheel ABS is standard across the board, and all but the LX 2WD model are dressed in dorky All-Sport exterior trim.

RATINGS (SCALE OF 1-10)

Overall	Safety	Reliability	Performance	Comfort	Value
7.4	7.7	8.3	7.6	7.6	6

	Trade-in	Market
Category G		
2 Dr ES Pass. Van	12120	14600
2 Dr ES 4WD Pass. Van	13350	16085
2 Dr LX Pass. Van	10810	13025
2 Dr LX 4WD Pass. Van	12060	14530

OPTIONS FOR MPV

Air Conditioning +405
Aluminum/Alloy Wheels[Std on ES,4WD] +165
Compact Disc W/fm/tape +240
Dual Air Conditioning +470
Keyless Entry System +100
Luggage Rack[Std on ES,4WD] +80
Power Moonroof +430

MX6   1997

All LS models get a rear spoiler.

RATINGS (SCALE OF 1-10)

Overall	Safety	Reliability	Performance	Comfort	Value
7.5	7.2	8.6	9	7.9	4.6

Don't forget to refer to the Mileage Adjustment Table at the back of this book!

Model Description	Trade-in Value	Market Value

Category F

Model Description	Trade-in Value	Market Value
2 Dr LS Cpe	10780	12990
2 Dr STD Cpe	8645	10415

OPTIONS FOR MX6

Auto 4-Speed Transmission +400
Air Conditioning[Std on LS] +415
Aluminum/Alloy Wheels[Std on LS] +150
Anti-Lock Brakes +335
Keyless Entry System[Std on LS] +90
Leather Seats +325
Power Drivers Seat +120
Power Sunroof[Std on LS] +335
Rear Spoiler[Std on LS] +120

PROTEGE   1997

Styling revisions inside and out update this roomy compact nicely.

RATINGS (SCALE OF 1-10)

Overall	Safety	Reliability	Performance	Comfort	Value
N/A	N/A	8.1	8	7.4	5.3

Category E

	Trade-in	Market
4 Dr DX Sdn	5905	7200
4 Dr ES Sdn	7390	9010
4 Dr LX Sdn	6645	8105

OPTIONS FOR PROTEGE

Auto 4-Speed Transmission +400
AM/FM Stereo Tape[Opt on DX] +150
Air Conditioning[Std on ES] +405
Aluminum/Alloy Wheels +165
Anti-Lock Brakes +335
Power Moonroof +285

1996 MAZDA

626   1996

Chrome is tacked on front and rear, and the hood is raised a bit to give the 626 a more substantial look. ABS is available as a stand alone option on LX and LX V6 models for the first time (formerly, you had to buy an option package), and side-impact protection meets 1997 standards.

RATINGS (SCALE OF 1-10)

Overall	Safety	Reliability	Performance	Comfort	Value
7.5	7.1	8.1	8.8	8.1	5.4

Category D

	Trade-in	Market
4 Dr DX Sdn	6365	7855
4 Dr ES Sdn	9085	11215
4 Dr LX Sdn	7095	8760
4 Dr LX V6 Sdn	8060	9950

OPTIONS FOR 626

Auto 4-Speed Transmission +325
AM/FM Stereo Tape[Opt on DX] +145

Air Conditioning[Opt on DX] +345
Anti-Lock Brakes[Std on ES] +365
Keyless Entry System[Std on ES] +125
Power Drivers Seat[Std on ES] +120
Power Moonroof[Std on ES] +340

B-SERIES PICKUP   1996

A passenger side airbag comes with SE Plus and LE trim levels, and it can be deactivated in the event that a rear facing child safety seat is installed. SE models also get new chrome bumpers.

RATINGS (SCALE OF 1-10)

Overall	Safety	Reliability	Performance	Comfort	Value
N/A	6.5	8.5	7.2	7.3	N/A

Category G

	Trade-in	Market
2 Dr B2300 Ext Cab SB	6490	7915
2 Dr B2300 Std Cab LB	5690	6940
2 Dr B2300 Std Cab SB	5560	6780
2 Dr B2300 4WD Std Cab SB	7775	9480
2 Dr B2300 SE Ext Cab SB	6835	8335
2 Dr B2300 SE Std Cab SB	6000	7315
2 Dr B3000 4WD Ext Cab SB	8530	10400
2 Dr B3000 SE Ext Cab SB	7255	8850
2 Dr B4000 LE Ext Cab SB	8510	10380
2 Dr B4000 LE 4WD Ext Cab SB	9510	11600
2 Dr B4000 SE 4WD Ext Cab SB	8885	10835
2 Dr B4000 SE 4WD Std Cab SB	8040	9805

OPTIONS FOR B-SERIES PICKUP

Auto 4-Speed Transmission +420
Air Conditioning[Std on B4000 LE] +330
Aluminum/Alloy Wheels[Std on B4000 LE] +135
Anti-Lock Brakes +245
Bed Liner +115
Compact Disc Changer +210
Cruise Control +85
Lighted Entry System +60
Power Door Locks +95
Power Windows +95
Premium Sound System +140
Rear Jump Seats[Std on B4000 LE] +90

MIATA   1996

Side-impact standards for 1997 are met a year early, and to offset the added weight, Mazda boosts power and torque.

RATINGS (SCALE OF 1-10)

Overall	Safety	Reliability	Performance	Comfort	Value
7.3	6.3	9.1	9	7.1	5

Category F

	Trade-in	Market
2 Dr MX-5 Conv	8445	10425
2 Dr MX-5 M-Edition Conv	9680	11950

Model Description	Trade-in Value	Market Value	Model Description	Trade-in Value	Market Value

OPTIONS FOR MIATA

Auto 4-Speed Transmission +370
Sensory Sound System +355
Air Conditioning[Opt on MX-5] +340
Aluminum/Alloy Wheels[Opt on MX-5] +125
Anti-Lock Brakes[Opt on MX-5] +275
Cruise Control[Opt on MX-5] +85
Hardtop Roof +550
Leather Seats[Opt on MX-5] +265
Limited Slip Diff[Opt on MX-5] +140
Power Steering[Opt on MX-5] +140
Power Windows[Opt on MX-5] +90
Rear Spoiler +100
Sport Suspension +75

MILLENIA   1996

The Millenia S gets revised bright-finish alloy wheels.

RATINGS (SCALE OF 1-10)

Overall	Safety	Reliability	Performance	Comfort	Value
7.5	8	8.8	8.4	7.9	4.5

Category D

4 Dr L Sdn	11850	14630
4 Dr S Sdn	12670	15645
4 Dr STD Sdn	11395	14065

OPTIONS FOR MILLENIA

Bose Sound System +305
Traction Control System[Std on S] +245

MPV   1996

New styling up front, a fourth door on the driver's side, and a revised instrument panel with dual airbags sum up the changes to Mazda's attempt at a minivan.

RATINGS (SCALE OF 1-10)

Overall	Safety	Reliability	Performance	Comfort	Value
7.5	7.7	8.3	7.6	7.6	6.2

Category G

2 Dr DX Pass. Van	8095	9870
2 Dr ES Pass. Van	10205	12445
2 Dr ES 4WD Pass. Van	11300	13780
2 Dr LX Pass. Van	9235	11265
2 Dr LX 4WD Pass. Van	10285	12545

OPTIONS FOR MPV

AM/FM Compact Disc Player +135
Air Conditioning +330
Aluminum/Alloy Wheels[Opt on 2WD] +135
Dual Air Conditioning +385
Keyless Entry System +80
Power Moonroof +350

MX6   1996

No changes for 1995.

RATINGS (SCALE OF 1-10)

Overall	Safety	Reliability	Performance	Comfort	Value
7.3	7.2	8.5	9	7.9	4.1

Category F

2 Dr LS Cpe	9240	11405
2 Dr M-Edition Cpe	9690	11965
2 Dr STD Cpe	7665	9460

OPTIONS FOR MX6

Auto 4-Speed Transmission +325
Air Conditioning[Opt on STD] +340
Aluminum/Alloy Wheels[Opt on STD] +125
Anti-Lock Brakes[Opt on LS,STD] +275
Keyless Entry System[Opt on STD] +70
Leather Seats[Opt on LS] +265
Power Drivers Seat[Opt on LS] +100
Power Sunroof[Opt on STD] +275
Rear Spoiler[Opt on LS,STD] +100

PROTEGE   1996

No changes for 1996.

RATINGS (SCALE OF 1-10)

Overall	Safety	Reliability	Performance	Comfort	Value
N/A	N/A	8	8	7.4	5.8

Category E

4 Dr DX Sdn	5390	6735
4 Dr ES Sdn	6575	8220
4 Dr LX Sdn	5910	7385

OPTIONS FOR PROTEGE

Auto 4-Speed Transmission +325
AM/FM Stereo Tape[Opt on DX] +125
Air Conditioning[Std on ES] +330
Anti-Lock Brakes +275
Keyless Entry System +65
Power Moonroof +230

1995 MAZDA

626   1995

ES gets remote keyless entry, which is available on LX and LX-V6 models. New wheels and wheelcovers are added across the board.

RATINGS (SCALE OF 1-10)

Overall	Safety	Reliability	Performance	Comfort	Value
7.7	7.7	7.4	8.8	8.1	6.3

Category D

4 Dr DX Sdn	4975	6300
4 Dr ES Sdn	6995	8855
4 Dr LX Sdn	5675	7185
4 Dr LX V6 Sdn	6440	8155

Don't forget to refer to the Mileage Adjustment Table at the back of this book!

MAZDA 95

Model Description	Trade-in Value	Market Value	Model Description	Trade-in Value	Market Value

OPTIONS FOR 626
Auto 4-Speed Transmission +265
AM/FM Stereo Tape[Opt on DX] +120
Air Conditioning[Opt on DX] +280
Aluminum/Alloy Wheels[Opt on LX] +155
Anti-Lock Brakes[Std on ES] +300
Keyless Entry System[Std on ES] +105
Power Drivers Seat[Std on ES] +100
Power Moonroof[Std on ES] +275

929 1995

Leather seats, wood trim and remote keyless entry are standard. Final year for sleek executive sedan.

RATINGS (SCALE OF 1-10)

Overall	Safety	Reliability	Performance	Comfort	Value
N/A	N/A	8.5	8.2	8.4	3.8

Category D
4 Dr STD Sdn | | | | 9300 | 11775

OPTIONS FOR 929
Limited Slip Diff +160

B-SERIES PICKUP 1995

Redesigned dashboard with driver airbag debuts. Four-wheel ABS is standard on 4WD and 2WD B4000 models.

RATINGS (SCALE OF 1-10)

Overall	Safety	Reliability	Performance	Comfort	Value
N/A	6.7	8.5	7.2	7.3	N/A

Category G
2 Dr B2300 Ext Cab SB		5540	6840
2 Dr B2300 Std Cab LB		4850	5990
2 Dr B2300 Std Cab SB		4675	5770
2 Dr B2300 4WD Std Cab SB		6640	8195
2 Dr B2300 SE Ext Cab SB		5835	7205
2 Dr B2300 SE Std Cab SB		5085	6275
2 Dr B3000 SE Ext Cab SB		6150	7590
2 Dr B3000 SE 4WD Ext Cab SB		6940	8570
2 Dr B3000 SE Std Cab SB		5465	6745
2 Dr B4000 LE Ext Cab SB		6705	8275
2 Dr B4000 LE 4WD Ext Cab SB		8350	10310
2 Dr B4000 SE Ext Cab SB		6515	8045
2 Dr B4000 SE 4WD Ext Cab SB		7910	9765
2 Dr B4000 SE 4WD Std Cab SB		7225	8920

OPTIONS FOR B-SERIES PICKUP
Auto 4-Speed Transmission +345
AM/FM Stereo Tape[Opt on B2300] +75
Air Conditioning[Std on B4000 LE] +270
Aluminum/Alloy Wheels +110
Auto Locking Hubs (4WD)[Std on B4000 SE] +85
Bed Liner +95
Compact Disc Changer +170
Cruise Control +70

Keyless Entry System +65
Limited Slip Diff +90
Power Door Locks +75
Power Drivers Seat +95
Power Steering[Std on SE,LE,Ext Cab,4WD] +95
Power Windows +80
Premium Sound System +115

MIATA 1995

Option packages are revised, and a gorgeous M-Edition with Merlot Mica paint, tan top, tan leather interior, and 15-inch BBS rims is available.

RATINGS (SCALE OF 1-10)

Overall	Safety	Reliability	Performance	Comfort	Value
7.3	6.9	8	9	7.1	5.4

Category F
2 Dr MX-5 Conv		7060	8825
2 Dr MX-5 M-Edition Conv		8210	10260

OPTIONS FOR MIATA
Auto 4-Speed Transmission +280
Leather Pkg +735
Sensory Sound System +290
Air Conditioning[Opt on MX-5] +275
Aluminum/Alloy Wheels[Opt on MX-5] +100
Anti-Lock Brakes[Opt on MX-5] +225
Compact Disc W/fm/tape +165
Cruise Control[Opt on MX-5] +70
Hardtop Roof +450
Limited Slip Diff +115
Power Steering[Opt on MX-5] +115
Power Windows[Opt on MX-5] +75
Rear Spoiler +80
Sport Seats +155
Sport Suspension +60

MILLENIA 1995

Luxury-oriented model that was to be in Mazda's aborted upscale Amati luxury division. Positioned to do battle with entry-level Lexus, Infiniti and BMW models. S models have 2.3-liter V6 with Miller-cycle technology and 210 horsepower. Dual airbags and ABS are standard on all models. The Millenia S adds traction control.

RATINGS (SCALE OF 1-10)

Overall	Safety	Reliability	Performance	Comfort	Value
7.4	8	8.3	8.4	7.9	4.4

Category D
4 Dr S Sdn		9295	11765
4 Dr STD Sdn		8295	10500

OPTIONS FOR MILLENIA
Bose Sound System +250
Compact Disc Changer +225
Keyless Entry System[Std on S] +105

MAZDA 95-94

Model Description	Trade-in Value	Market Value	Model Description	Trade-in Value	Market Value

Leather Seats[Std on S] +365
Power Moonroof[Std on S] +275
Power Passenger Seat[Std on S] +125
Traction Control System[Std on S] +200

MPV　　1995

New lineup includes L, LX and LXE trim levels. All come with seven-passenger seating. Four-cylinder engine has been dropped.

RATINGS (SCALE OF 1-10)

Overall	Safety	Reliability	Performance	Comfort	Value
7.5	6.5	8.9	7.8	7.6	6.5

Category G
	Trade-in	Market
2 Dr L Pass. Van	7010	8655
2 Dr LX Pass. Van	7450	9200
2 Dr LX 4WD Pass. Van	8215	10140
2 Dr LXE Pass. Van	8610	10630
2 Dr LXE 4WD Pass. Van	9355	11550

OPTIONS FOR MPV
Air Conditioning +270
Aluminum/Alloy Wheels +110
Camper/Towing Package[Opt on LX] +100
Dual Air Conditioning +315
Keyless Entry System +65
Power Moonroof +290

MX3　　1995

GS model, and its cool 1.8-liter, V6 engine, vanishes. ABS is available only with manual transmission.
Category E
	Trade-in	Market
2 Dr STD Hbk	4840	6285

OPTIONS FOR MX3
Auto 4-Speed Transmission +265
Air Conditioning +270
Aluminum/Alloy Wheels +110
Anti-Lock Brakes +225
Cruise Control +75
Power Door Locks +80
Power Sunroof +205
Power Windows +85

MX6　　1995

No changes for 1995.

RATINGS (SCALE OF 1-10)

Overall	Safety	Reliability	Performance	Comfort	Value
7.4	7.9	8.3	9	7.9	4

Category F
	Trade-in	Market
2 Dr LS Cpe	7165	8955
2 Dr STD Cpe	5735	7170

OPTIONS FOR MX6
Auto 4-Speed Transmission +265
Air Conditioning[Std on LS] +275

Aluminum/Alloy Wheels +100
Anti-Lock Brakes +225
Keyless Entry System +60
Leather Seats +215
Power Sunroof[Std on LS] +225
Rear Spoiler +80

PROTEGE　　1995

Totally redesigned, the Protege grows substantially in interior volume. Has 10 more cubic feet of volume than Honda Civic. Dual airbags are finally added. ABS is standard on ES trim level; optional on LX.

RATINGS (SCALE OF 1-10)

Overall	Safety	Reliability	Performance	Comfort	Value
N/A	N/A	6.8	8	7.4	5.6

Category E
	Trade-in	Market
4 Dr DX Sdn	3965	5150
4 Dr ES Sdn	5125	6655
4 Dr LX Sdn	4405	5720

OPTIONS FOR PROTEGE
Auto 4-Speed Transmission +265
AM/FM Stereo Tape[Opt on DX] +100
Air Conditioning[Std on ES] +270
Aluminum/Alloy Wheels +110
Anti-Lock Brakes[Opt on LX] +225
Power Moonroof +190

RX-7　　1995

CFC-free refrigerant is added to air conditioner. Touring package ousted. Red leather option dumped. Last year for RX-7.
Category F
	Trade-in	Market
2 Dr STD Turbo Rotary Cpe	15465	19330

OPTIONS FOR RX-7
Auto 4-Speed Transmission +295
Leather Seats +215
Power Sunroof +225
Rear Spoiler +80
Sport Suspension +60

1994 MAZDA

323　　1994

No changes. Final year for homely, slow-selling hatchback.

RATINGS (SCALE OF 1-10)

Overall	Safety	Reliability	Performance	Comfort	Value
6.2	4.3	7.2	6.8	7	5.8

Category E
	Trade-in	Market
2 Dr STD Hbk	2340	3120

Don't forget to refer to the Mileage Adjustment Table at the back of this book!

OPTIONS FOR 323

Auto 4-Speed Transmission +205
AM/FM Stereo Tape +80
Air Conditioning +220
Power Steering +70

626   1994

Passenger airbag added. LX-V6 debuts. Four-cylinder models get new Ford transmission for smoother shifting than previous Mazda unit. ABS becomes standard on ES trim level, as well as leather seats and power sunroof.

RATINGS (SCALE OF 1-10)

Overall	Safety	Reliability	Performance	Comfort	Value
7.6	7.9	8	8.8	8.1	5.2

Category D

	Trade-in	Market
4 Dr DX Sdn	3945	5060
4 Dr ES Sdn	5665	7265
4 Dr LX Sdn	4490	5755
4 Dr LX V6 Sdn	5130	6575

OPTIONS FOR 626

Auto 4-Speed Transmission +220
Air Conditioning[Opt on DX] +230
Aluminum/Alloy Wheels +125
Anti-Lock Brakes[Std on ES] +245
Cruise Control[Opt on DX] +65
Power Door Locks[Opt on DX] +75
Power Drivers Seat[Std on ES] +80
Power Moonroof[Std on ES] +225
Power Windows[Opt on DX] +75

929   1994

Trimmed to one model. Console cupholder added, height-adjustable seatbelts debut, and a limited-slip differential is included with the Cold Package. Premium Package adds remote keyless entry. New alloy wheels are standard.

RATINGS (SCALE OF 1-10)

Overall	Safety	Reliability	Performance	Comfort	Value
N/A	N/A	8	8.2	8.4	5.4

Category D

	Trade-in	Market
4 Dr STD Sdn	7335	9405

OPTIONS FOR 929

Premium Pkg +490
Cellular Telephone +255
Compact Disc Changer +180
Leather Seats +300
Power Passenger Seat +100

B-SERIES PICKUP   1994

Mazda revises the styling of Ford's Ranger, slaps its name on the tailgate, and has a new compact pickup to sell. Base, SE and LE trim levels are offered in two- or four-wheel drive and two bodystyles.

RATINGS (SCALE OF 1-10)

Overall	Safety	Reliability	Performance	Comfort	Value
N/A	4.9	7.9	7.2	7.3	N/A

Category G

	Trade-in	Market
2 Dr B2300 Ext Cab SB	4920	6075
2 Dr B2300 Std Cab SB	3905	4820
2 Dr B2300 SE Std Cab SB	4295	5300
2 Dr B3000 Ext Cab SB	5245	6475
2 Dr B3000 4WD Ext Cab SB	6230	7690
2 Dr B3000 4WD Std Cab SB	5550	6850
2 Dr B3000 SE Ext Cab SB	5555	6855
2 Dr B3000 SE Std Cab LB	4740	5850
2 Dr B3000 SE Std Cab SB	4550	5615
2 Dr B4000 LE Ext Cab SB	5875	7255
2 Dr B4000 LE 4WD Ext Cab SB	6940	8565
2 Dr B4000 SE 4WD Ext Cab SB	6550	8085
2 Dr B4000 SE Std Cab LB	5180	6395
2 Dr B4000 SE 4WD Std Cab SB	5765	7120

OPTIONS FOR B-SERIES PICKUP

Auto 4-Speed Transmission[Std on B4000 LE] +395
AM/FM Compact Disc Player +90
Air Conditioning +220
Aluminum/Alloy Wheels +90
Bed Liner +75
Power Door Locks[Std on B4000 LE] +65
Power Steering[Opt on B2300 Std Cab SB] +75
Power Windows[Std on B4000 LE] +65

MIATA   1994

Dual airbags arrive, and a 1.8-liter four cylinder making 128 horsepower replaces the original 1.6-liter engine. Sharp new alloy wheels debut. Optional automatic gets electronic shift controls. Larger diameter disc brakes are standard. Bigger gas tank added. New R package debuts with sportier suspension. Superman Blue replaced by Montego Blue. M-Edition is painted Montego Blue with chromed alloys.

RATINGS (SCALE OF 1-10)

Overall	Safety	Reliability	Performance	Comfort	Value
7.5	6.9	8.5	9	7.1	5.9

Category F

	Trade-in	Market
2 Dr MX-5 Conv	6020	7720
2 Dr MX-5 M-Edition Conv	6915	8865

OPTIONS FOR MIATA

Auto 4-Speed Transmission +180
Air Conditioning[Opt on MX-5] +225
Aluminum/Alloy Wheels[Opt on MX-5] +85
Anti-Lock Brakes +185
Compact Disc W/fm/tape +135
Cruise Control[Opt on MX-5] +55
Hardtop Roof +370
Leather Seats[Opt on MX-5] +175

Don't forget to refer to the Mileage Adjustment Table at the back of this book!

Model Description	Trade-in Value	Market Value
Limited Slip Diff[Opt on MX-5] +90		
Power Steering[Opt on MX-5] +95		
Power Windows[Opt on MX-5] +60		
Rear Spoiler +65		
Sport Suspension +50		

MPV 1994

Side-door impact beams are added. Four-wheel disc brakes are new. Standard tire size increases.

RATINGS (SCALE OF 1-10)

Overall	Safety	Reliability	Performance	Comfort	Value
7.2	6.3	7.8	7.8	7.6	6.3

Category G

	Trade-in	Market
2 Dr STD Pass. Van	5865	7240
2 Dr STD 4WD Pass. Van	6760	8345

OPTIONS FOR MPV

6 cyl 3.0 L Engine[Opt on 2WD] +165
Luxury Pkg +285
7 Passenger Seating[Opt on 2WD] +140
AM/FM Compact Disc Player +90
Air Conditioning +220
Aluminum/Alloy Wheels +90
Camper/Towing Package +80
Cruise Control +55
Dual Air Conditioning +255
Keyless Entry System +55
Leather Seats +210
Power Door Locks +65
Power Moonroof +235
Power Windows +65

MX3 1994

Base model gets more power, and a passenger airbag is added. ABS can be ordered on base models for the first time. Can't get ABS on GS with automatic transmission. Base cars can be equipped with power sunroof. Both models get new wheels.

Category E

	Trade-in	Market
2 Dr GS Hbk	5170	6895
2 Dr STD Hbk	4030	5370

OPTIONS FOR MX3

Auto 4-Speed Transmission +240
Air Conditioning +220
Aluminum/Alloy Wheels +90
Anti-Lock Brakes +180
Cruise Control +60
Power Door Locks +65
Power Sunroof +165
Power Windows +70

MX6 1994

Passenger airbag debuts. Air conditioning and power sunroof become standard on LS.

RATINGS (SCALE OF 1-10)

Overall	Safety	Reliability	Performance	Comfort	Value
7.2	7.9	7.7	9	7.9	3.3

Category F

	Trade-in	Market
2 Dr LS Cpe	6240	8000
2 Dr STD Cpe	4885	6260

OPTIONS FOR MX6

Auto 4-Speed Transmission +220
Air Conditioning[Std on LS] +225
Aluminum/Alloy Wheels +85
Anti-Lock Brakes +185
Leather Seats +175
Power Drivers Seat +65
Power Sunroof[Std on LS] +185
Rear Spoiler +65

NAVAJO 1994

Restyled alloy wheels are new. Since Ford won't give Mazda a four-door version of Explorer to sell, this is final year for Navajo as Mazda picks up its toys and goes home to pout.

RATINGS (SCALE OF 1-10)

Overall	Safety	Reliability	Performance	Comfort	Value
7.2	5.7	5.9	7.6	8.3	8.4

Category G

	Trade-in	Market
2 Dr DX 4WD Utility	6030	7445
2 Dr LX 4WD Utility	6475	7995

OPTIONS FOR NAVAJO

Auto 4-Speed Transmission +245
AM/FM Compact Disc Player +90
Air Conditioning +220
Camper/Towing Package +80
Cruise Control +55
Leather Seats +210
Limited Slip Diff +75
Luggage Rack +45
Moonroof +95
Power Drivers Seat +75

PROTEGE 1994

Minor styling revisions include new grille, headlamps, hood and front fascia.

RATINGS (SCALE OF 1-10)

Overall	Safety	Reliability	Performance	Comfort	Value
N/A	N/A	6.8	8.2	7.4	5

Category E

	Trade-in	Market
4 Dr DX Sdn	3030	4040
4 Dr LX Sdn	3430	4570
4 Dr Special Sdn	2850	3800

OPTIONS FOR PROTEGE

Auto 4-Speed Transmission +210
AM/FM Stereo Tape[Opt on DX] +80

MAZDA 94-93

Model Description	Trade-in Value	Market Value

Air Conditioning +220
Aluminum/Alloy Wheels +90
Power Door Locks[Opt on DX] +65
Power Sunroof +165
Power Windows[Opt on DX] +70
Tilt Steering Wheel[Opt on DX] +40

RX-7 — 1994

Dual airbags appear, and softer suspension settings are available. Seatbacks get map pockets, and power windows have a driver express-down feature.

Category F

2 Dr STD Turbo Rotary Cpe	12665	16240

OPTIONS FOR RX-7
Auto 4-Speed Transmission +245
R-2 Pkg +405
Touring Pkg +345
AM/FM Compact Disc Player +130
Bose Sound System +145
Leather Seats +175
Power Moonroof +175
Rear Spoiler +65
Sport Suspension +50

1993 MAZDA

323 — 1993

No changes.

RATINGS (SCALE OF 1-10)

Overall	Safety	Reliability	Performance	Comfort	Value
6.3	4.3	7.9	6.8	7	5.7

Category E

2 Dr SE Hbk	2140	2930
2 Dr STD Hbk	1960	2685

OPTIONS FOR 323
Auto 4-Speed Transmission +160
AM/FM Stereo Tape +65
Air Conditioning +180
Power Steering +55

626 — 1993

Completely redesigned for 1993. First import-badged car to be classified domestic by EPA. Driver airbag is standard, and ABS is optional. Top-end ES model gets 2.5-liter V6 engine. DX and LX powered by four-cylinder motor.

RATINGS (SCALE OF 1-10)

Overall	Safety	Reliability	Performance	Comfort	Value
7.1	6.1	7.5	8.8	8.1	5.1

Category D

4 Dr DX Sdn	3220	4235
4 Dr ES Sdn	4465	5875
4 Dr LX Sdn	3585	4715

Model Description	Trade-in Value	Market Value

OPTIONS FOR 626
Auto 4-Speed Transmission +175
AM/FM Compact Disc Player +115
Air Conditioning[Opt on DX] +190
Alarm System[Opt on LX] +115
Aluminum/Alloy Wheels[Opt on LX] +105
Anti-Lock Brakes +200
Compact Disc W/fm/tape +180
Cruise Control[Opt on DX] +55
Leather Seats +245
Power Door Locks[Opt on DX] +60
Power Drivers Seat +65
Power Moonroof +185
Power Windows[Opt on DX] +60

929 — 1993

Glass moonroof replaces steel offering. Revised alloy wheels, optional wood trim and optional power passenger's seat are new for 1993.

RATINGS (SCALE OF 1-10)

Overall	Safety	Reliability	Performance	Comfort	Value
N/A	N/A	8	8.2	8.4	5.4

Category D

4 Dr STD Sdn	6040	7950

OPTIONS FOR 929
Premium Pkg +310
Compact Disc Changer +150
Leather Seats +245
Power Passenger Seat +80
Premium Sound System +85

B-SERIES PICKUP — 1993

No changes.

Category G

2 Dr B2200 Ext Cab SB	3685	4725
2 Dr B2200 Std Cab LB	3000	3845
2 Dr B2200 Std Cab SB	2920	3745
2 Dr B2600i Ext Cab SB	4040	5180
2 Dr B2600i 4WD Ext Cab SB	5340	6845
2 Dr B2600i 4WD Std Cab SB	4825	6185

OPTIONS FOR B-SERIES PICKUP
Auto 4-Speed Transmission +180
AM/FM Stereo Tape +50
Air Conditioning +180
Aluminum/Alloy Wheels +75
Bed Liner +60
Chrome Wheels +40
Power Steering[Std on B2600i,Ext Cab] +60
Rear Step Bumper +30

MIATA — 1993

Limited Edition available with black paint and red leather interior; just 1,500 were produced. Yellow dropped from paint roster. Tan roof and leather interior optional

---

Don't forget to refer to the Mileage Adjustment Table at the back of this book!

Model Description	Trade-in Value	Market Value

on red and white cars. A 130-watt Sensory°Sound System is newly optional.

RATINGS (SCALE OF 1-10)

Overall	Safety	Reliability	Performance	Comfort	Value
7.3	6.2	8.6	8.8	7.1	5.9

Category F
2 Dr MX-5 Conv	5430	7050
2 Dr MX-5 Limited Conv	5785	7510

OPTIONS FOR MIATA
Auto 4-Speed Transmission +170
AM/FM Compact Disc Player +105
Air Conditioning[Opt on MX-5] +185
Aluminum/Alloy Wheels[Opt on MX-5] +70
Anti-Lock Brakes[Opt on MX-5] +150
Cruise Control[Opt on MX-5] +45
Hardtop Roof +300
Leather Seats[Opt on MX-5] +145
Limited Slip Diff[Opt on MX-5] +75
Power Steering[Opt on MX-5] +75
Power Windows[Opt on MX-5] +50

MPV　　1993

Keyless entry system added to options list. Driver airbag added midyear.

RATINGS (SCALE OF 1-10)

Overall	Safety	Reliability	Performance	Comfort	Value
7	5.3	8.1	7.8	7.6	6.2

Category G
2 Dr STD Pass. Van	4650	5960
2 Dr STD 4WD Pass. Van	5475	7020

OPTIONS FOR MPV
6 cyl 3.0 L Engine[Opt on 2WD] +145
Air Conditioning +180
Aluminum/Alloy Wheels[Opt on 2WD] +75
Camper/Towing Package +65
Compact Disc W/fm/tape +105
Cruise Control +45
Dual Air Conditioning +210
Keyless Entry System +45
Leather Seats +170
Power Door Locks +50
Power Moonroof +190
Power Windows +55

MX3　　1993

A cassette stereo is made standard, and Laguna Blue Metallic is a new color.
Category E
2 Dr GS Hbk	4015	5500
2 Dr STD Hbk	3085	4225
2 Dr Special Hbk	4185	5730

OPTIONS FOR MX3
Auto 4-Speed Transmission +160
AM/FM Compact Disc Player +100
Air Conditioning +180
Aluminum/Alloy Wheels[Opt on STD] +75
Anti-Lock Brakes +150
Cruise Control[Opt on GS] +50
Power Door Locks[Opt on GS,STD] +55
Power Sunroof[Opt on GS] +135
Power Windows[Opt on GS,STD] +60

MX6　　1993

All-new this year, sporting dramatically swept bodywork and a speedy LS model with 2.5-liter V6 engine. EPA says MX-6 is a domestic car. Driver airbag standard, while ABS is optional.

RATINGS (SCALE OF 1-10)

Overall	Safety	Reliability	Performance	Comfort	Value
N/A	N/A	7	9	7.9	4.7

Category F
2 Dr LS Cpe	4945	6420
2 Dr STD Cpe	3840	4990

OPTIONS FOR MX6
Auto 4-Speed Transmission +180
AM/FM Compact Disc Player +105
Air Conditioning +185
Aluminum/Alloy Wheels[Std on LS] +70
Anti-Lock Brakes +150
Leather Seats +145
Power Drivers Seat +55
Power Sunroof +150
Rear Spoiler +55

NAVAJO　　1993

Four-wheel ABS is newly standard.

RATINGS (SCALE OF 1-10)

Overall	Safety	Reliability	Performance	Comfort	Value
7	5	4.9	7.6	8.3	9.3

Category G
2 Dr DX 4WD Utility	4645	5955
2 Dr LX 4WD Utility	5095	6530

OPTIONS FOR NAVAJO
Auto 4-Speed Transmission +200
Navajo LX Leather Pkg +460
AM/FM Compact Disc Player +70
Air Conditioning +180
Camper/Towing Package +65
Cruise Control +45
Leather Seats +170
Luggage Rack +35
Power Drivers Seat +60
Sunroof +65

MAZDA 93-92

Model Description	Trade-in Value	Market Value

PROTEGE 1993

Trim and equipment revisions.

RATINGS (SCALE OF 1-10)

Overall	Safety	Reliability	Performance	Comfort	Value
N/A	N/A	7.7	8.2	7.4	5.6

Category E
4 Dr DX Sdn	2635	3610
4 Dr LX Sdn	2920	4000

OPTIONS FOR PROTEGE
Auto 4-Speed Transmission +160
AM/FM Stereo Tape[Opt on LX] +65
Air Conditioning +180
Aluminum/Alloy Wheels +75
Power Sunroof +135
Tilt Steering Wheel[Opt on DX] +35

RX-7 1993

All-new supercar designed with a singular purpose: speed. Convertible dropped. 2+2 version canceled. Twin-turbo rotary engine is standard. Driver airbag and ABS are standard.

Category F
2 Dr STD Turbo Rotary Cpe	10585	13745

OPTIONS FOR RX-7
Auto 4-Speed Transmission +190
R-1 Pkg +270
Touring Pkg +260
AM/FM Compact Disc Player +105
Bose Sound System +120
Leather Seats +145
Power Sunroof +150
Premium Sound System +80
Rear Spoiler +55

1992 MAZDA

323 1992

New taillights debut.

RATINGS (SCALE OF 1-10)

Overall	Safety	Reliability	Performance	Comfort	Value
6.3	4.3	7.7	6.8	7	5.6

Category E
2 Dr SE Hbk	1660	2370
2 Dr STD Hbk	1530	2185

OPTIONS FOR 323
Auto 4-Speed Transmission +125
Air Conditioning +145
Power Steering +45

626 1992

Touring Sedan is dropped.

Model Description	Trade-in Value	Market Value

Category D
4 Dr DX Sdn	2500	3330
4 Dr LX Sdn	2785	3710

OPTIONS FOR 626
Auto 4-Speed Transmission +140
Air Conditioning +155
Anti-Lock Brakes +165
Power Moonroof +150

929 1992

Completely redesigned. Dual airbags and antilock brakes are standard.

RATINGS (SCALE OF 1-10)

Overall	Safety	Reliability	Performance	Comfort	Value
N/A	N/A	7.3	8.2	8.4	5.8

Category D
4 Dr STD Sdn	5150	6865

OPTIONS FOR 929
Compact Disc Changer +120
Leather Seats +200
Power Moonroof +150
Power Passenger Seat +65

B-SERIES PICKUP 1992

New steering wheel and minor trim changes. Extended-cab models get new rear lap/shoulder seatbelts.

Category G
2 Dr B2200 Ext Cab SB	3165	4165
2 Dr B2200 Std Cab LB	2545	3350
2 Dr B2200 Std Cab SB	2460	3240
2 Dr B2600i Ext Cab SB	3410	4485
2 Dr B2600i 4WD Ext Cab SB	4685	6165
2 Dr B2600i Std Cab SB	2665	3505
2 Dr B2600i 4WD Std Cab SB	3995	5255

OPTIONS FOR B-SERIES PICKUP
Auto 4-Speed Transmission +145
Air Conditioning +145
Power Steering[Std on B2600i,Ext Cab] +50

MIATA 1992

Silver paint dropped in favor of yellow and black. Remote trunk release added. Optional hardtop gets rear window defogger. Brilliant Black special edition available.

RATINGS (SCALE OF 1-10)

Overall	Safety	Reliability	Performance	Comfort	Value
7	6.2	8.5	8.8	7.1	4.3

Category F
2 Dr MX-5 Conv	4770	6360

Don't forget to refer to the Mileage Adjustment Table at the back of this book!

Model Description	Trade-in Value	Market Value	Model Description	Trade-in Value	Market Value

OPTIONS FOR MIATA

Auto 4-Speed Transmission +135
Pkg C +140
AM/FM Compact Disc Player +85
Air Conditioning +150
Anti-Lock Brakes +125
Hardtop Roof +245
Leather Seats +120
Limited Slip Diff +60
Power Steering +60
Power Windows +40

MPV 1992

Eight-passenger seating and power moonroof added to options list. Five-speed manual transmission dropped. V6 engine gets five additional horsepower. New alloy wheels debut.

RATINGS (SCALE OF 1-10)

Overall	Safety	Reliability	Performance	Comfort	Value
7.2	4.9	7.5	7.8	7.6	8.4

Category G
2 Dr STD Pass. Van — 3765 — 4955
2 Dr STD 4WD Pass. Van — 4610 — 6065

OPTIONS FOR MPV

6 cyl 3.0 L Engine[Opt on 2WD] +140
Luxury Pkg +240
AM/FM Compact Disc Player +60
Air Conditioning +145
Camper/Towing Package +55
Dual Air Conditioning +170
Leather Seats +140
Power Door Locks +40
Power Moonroof +155
Power Windows +45

MX3 1992

All-new sport coupe takes over where Honda CRX left off. A 1.8-liter V6 engine, the industry's smallest, is standard on GS models. ABS optional on GS.

Category E
2 Dr GS Hbk — 3170 — 4525
2 Dr STD Hbk — 2415 — 3450

OPTIONS FOR MX3

Auto 4-Speed Transmission +125
AM/FM Compact Disc Player +80
Air Conditioning +145
Anti-Lock Brakes +120
Power Door Locks +45
Power Sunroof +110
Power Windows +50

MX6 1992

No changes.
Category F
2 Dr DX Cpe — 2725 — 3630
2 Dr LX Cpe — 2940 — 3920

OPTIONS FOR MX6

Auto 4-Speed Transmission +140
AM/FM Compact Disc Player +85
Air Conditioning +150
Anti-Lock Brakes +125
Power Sunroof +120

NAVAJO 1992

A base model joins the lineup, called DX. Upper trim level becomes LX. Two-wheel drive is now available in either trim level.

RATINGS (SCALE OF 1-10)

Overall	Safety	Reliability	Performance	Comfort	Value
6.4	5.1	4.8	7.6	8.3	6.4

Category G
2 Dr DX Utility — 3385 — 4455
2 Dr DX 4WD Utility — 4015 — 5285
2 Dr LX Utility — 3825 — 5030
2 Dr LX 4WD Utility — 4380 — 5760

OPTIONS FOR NAVAJO

Auto 4-Speed Transmission +155
Air Conditioning +145
Camper/Towing Package +55
Leather Seats +140
Moonroof +65
Power Drivers Seat +50

PROTEGE 1992

New taillights are added, and the all-wheel-drive model is dropped.

RATINGS (SCALE OF 1-10)

Overall	Safety	Reliability	Performance	Comfort	Value
N/A	N/A	7.6	8.2	7.4	5.5

Category E
4 Dr DX Sdn — 2115 — 3020
4 Dr LX Sdn — 2310 — 3300

OPTIONS FOR PROTEGE

Auto 4-Speed Transmission +125
Air Conditioning +145
Power Steering[Opt on DX] +45
Power Sunroof +110

1991 MAZDA

323 — 1991

No changes.

RATINGS (SCALE OF 1-10)

Overall	Safety	Reliability	Performance	Comfort	Value
6	4.3	7	6.8	7	5

Category E

	Trade-in	Market
2 Dr SE Hbk	1450	2130
2 Dr STD Hbk	1335	1965

OPTIONS FOR 323
Auto 4-Speed Transmission +105
Air Conditioning +120
Power Steering +40

626 — 1991

New option packages added.
Category D

	Trade-in	Market
4 Dr DX Sdn	2105	2885
4 Dr GT Turbo Hbk	2760	3780
4 Dr LE Sdn	2660	3645
4 Dr LX Hbk	2410	3300
4 Dr LX Sdn	2370	3245

OPTIONS FOR 626
Auto 4-Speed Transmission +105
Air Conditioning[Std on LE] +125
Anti-Lock Brakes +135
Power Sunroof[Std on LE] +110

929 — 1991

Lace alloys standard on all models. Two new option packages are available.
Category D

	Trade-in	Market
4 Dr S Sdn	3525	4830
4 Dr STD Sdn	3330	4560

OPTIONS FOR 929
Compact Disc W/fm/tape +120
Leather Seats +165
Power Passenger Seat +55

B-SERIES PICKUP — 1991

Four-wheel-drive models get new grille and fender flares. Regular-cab models get headrest.
Category G

	Trade-in	Market
2 Dr B2200 Ext Cab SB	2775	3750
2 Dr B2200 Std Cab LB	2165	2925
2 Dr B2200 Std Cab SB	2105	2845
2 Dr B2600i Ext Cab SB	2940	3970
2 Dr B2600i 4WD Ext Cab SB	4050	5470
2 Dr B2600i Std Cab SB	2355	3180
2 Dr B2600i 4WD Std Cab SB	3460	4675

OPTIONS FOR B-SERIES PICKUP
Auto 4-Speed Transmission +115
Air Conditioning +120
Power Steering[Std on B2600i,Ext Cab] +40

MIATA — 1991

Special edition painted British Racing Green; 4,000 units produced. ABS is a new option.

RATINGS (SCALE OF 1-10)

Overall	Safety	Reliability	Performance	Comfort	Value
6.9	6	7.7	8.8	7.1	4.9

Category F

	Trade-in	Market
2 Dr MX-5 Conv	4065	5490
2 Dr MX-5 Special Conv	4385	5925

OPTIONS FOR MIATA
Auto 4-Speed Transmission +85
Air Conditioning[Opt on MX-5] +125
Anti-Lock Brakes +100
Hardtop Roof +200
Limited Slip Diff[Opt on MX-5] +50
Power Steering[Opt on MX-5] +50
Power Windows[Opt on MX-5] +35

MPV — 1991

Luxury package with lace alloy wheels, leather seats and two-tone paint debuts.

RATINGS (SCALE OF 1-10)

Overall	Safety	Reliability	Performance	Comfort	Value
7	4.7	6.4	7.8	7.6	8.3

Category G

	Trade-in	Market
2 Dr STD Cargo Van	2390	3230
2 Dr STD Pass. Van	3215	4345
2 Dr STD 4WD Pass. Van	3865	5225

OPTIONS FOR MPV
6 cyl 3.0 L Engine[Opt on 2WD] +105
Auto 4-Speed Transmission[Std on Cargo Van,4WD] +105
Value Pkg +255
AM/FM Compact Disc Player +50
Air Conditioning +120
Camper/Towing Package[Opt on 2WD] +45
Dual Air Conditioning +140
Leather Seats +115
Power Door Locks +35
Power Windows +35

MX6 — 1991

GT 4WS dropped.
Category F

	Trade-in	Market
2 Dr DX Cpe	2355	3180
2 Dr GT Turbo Cpe	2745	3710
2 Dr LE Cpe	2920	3945
2 Dr LX Cpe	2555	3450

Don't forget to refer to the Mileage Adjustment Table at the back of this book!

MAZDA 91-90

Model Description	Trade-in Value	Market Value	Model Description	Trade-in Value	Market Value

OPTIONS FOR MX6
Auto 4-Speed Transmission +105
AM/FM Compact Disc Player +70
Air Conditioning[Std on LE] +125
Anti-Lock Brakes +100
Power Sunroof[Std on LE] +100

NAVAJO   1991

Reskinned two-door Ford Explorer gives Mazda its first sport-utility vehicle. Single trim level with 4WD and rear antilock brakes available.

RATINGS (SCALE OF 1-10)

Overall	Safety	Reliability	Performance	Comfort	Value
6.3	5	4.1	7.6	8.3	6.4

Category G
2 Dr STD 4WD Utility — 3500 — 4730

OPTIONS FOR NAVAJO
Auto 4-Speed Transmission +130
Air Conditioning +120
Camper/Towing Package +45
Leather Seats +115
Sunroof +45

PROTEGE   1991

No changes.

RATINGS (SCALE OF 1-10)

Overall	Safety	Reliability	Performance	Comfort	Value
N/A	N/A	7.2	8.2	7.4	5

Category E
4 Dr DX Sdn — 1780 — 2620
4 Dr LX Sdn — 1930 — 2840

OPTIONS FOR PROTEGE
Auto 4-Speed Transmission +105
Air Conditioning +120
Power Steering[Opt on DX] +40
Power Sunroof +90

RX-7   1991

Lineup trimmed to three models: base, Turbo and convertible. ABS is standard on Turbo. A driver airbag is standard on the convertible.

Category F
2 Dr STD Rotary Conv — 5705 — 7710
2 Dr STD Rotary Cpe — 3770 — 5095

OPTIONS FOR RX-7
Auto 4-Speed Transmission +110
Leather Seats[Std on Conv] +95
Power Sunroof[Opt on STD] +100

1990 MAZDA

323   1990

Completely redesigned, 323 is available as hatchback only.

RATINGS (SCALE OF 1-10)

Overall	Safety	Reliability	Performance	Comfort	Value
6	4.3	6.3	6.8	7	5.4

Category E
2 Dr SE Hbk — 1285 — 1950
2 Dr STD Hbk — 1205 — 1825

OPTIONS FOR 323
Auto 4-Speed Transmission +85
Air Conditioning +100
Power Steering +30

626   1990

Some production moved to Michigan plant that produces MX-6 and Ford Probe. A new grille, alloy wheels, taillights, upholstery, and steering wheel debut.

Category D
4 Dr DX Sdn — 1885 — 2615
4 Dr GT Turbo Hbk — 2300 — 3195
4 Dr LX Hbk — 2075 — 2880
4 Dr LX Sdn — 2045 — 2840

OPTIONS FOR 626
Auto 4-Speed Transmission +90
AM/FM Compact Disc Player +65
Air Conditioning +105
Anti-Lock Brakes +110
Power Sunroof +90

929   1990

A new sport version called 929 S arrives with more power, upgraded suspension and standard ABS. A new grille, new bumpers and lower bodyside molding are added. All 929s get two-tone paint.

Category D
4 Dr S Sdn — 2845 — 3950
4 Dr STD Sdn — 2705 — 3760

OPTIONS FOR 929
AM/FM Compact Disc Player +65
Anti-Lock Brakes[Std on S] +110
Leather Seats +135

B-SERIES PICKUP   1990

New five-spoke alloys debut on options list. 2.6-liter engine is optional on 2WD models. Rear wheel ABS now standard. LE-5 replaces LX model.

MAZDA 90

Model Description	Trade-in Value	Market Value
Category G		
2 Dr B2200 Ext Cab SB	2365	3285
2 Dr B2200 Std Cab LB	1950	2710
2 Dr B2200 Std Cab SB	1895	2630
2 Dr B2600i Ext Cab SB	2565	3565
2 Dr B2600i 4WD Ext Cab SB	3405	4730
2 Dr B2600i Std Cab SB	1985	2755
2 Dr B2600i 4WD Std Cab SB	2950	4095

OPTIONS FOR B-SERIES PICKUP

Auto 4-Speed Transmission +85
LE5 Luxury Pkg +100
Air Conditioning +100
Power Steering[Opt on B2200] +35

MIATA 1990

The love affair begins. 116 horsepower from 1.6-liter inline four. Driver airbag is standard. Available in red, white, blue and silver.

RATINGS (SCALE OF 1-10)

Overall	Safety	Reliability	Performance	Comfort	Value
7.3	5.6	8.2	8.8	7.1	6.9

	Trade-in	Market
Category F		
2 Dr MX-5 Conv	3520	4760

OPTIONS FOR MIATA

Auto 4-Speed Transmission +90
AM/FM Compact Disc Player +60
Air Conditioning +100
Hardtop Roof +165
Limited Slip Diff +40
Power Steering +40
Power Windows +25

MPV 1990

A dual-range five-speed manual transmission is new.

RATINGS (SCALE OF 1-10)

Overall	Safety	Reliability	Performance	Comfort	Value
6.6	4.7	6.2	7.8	7.6	6.9

	Trade-in	Market
Category G		
2 Dr LX Pass. Van	2885	4010
2 Dr STD Cargo Van	1845	2560
2 Dr STD Pass. Van	2495	3465
2 Dr STD 4WD Pass. Van	3110	4320

OPTIONS FOR MPV

6 cyl 3.0 L Engine[Std on 4WD] +110
Auto 4-Speed Transmission[Std on LX] +80
AM/FM Compact Disc Player +40
Air Conditioning +100
Camper/Towing Package[Opt on 2WD] +35
Dual Air Conditioning +115
Power Door Locks[Std on LX] +30
Power Windows[Std on LX] +30

MX6 1990

No changes.

Model Description	Trade-in Value	Market Value
Category F		
2 Dr 4WS Turbo Cpe	2580	3485
2 Dr DX Cpe	1960	2650
2 Dr GT Turbo Cpe	2370	3205
2 Dr LX Cpe	2215	2995

OPTIONS FOR MX6

Auto 4-Speed Transmission +90
AM/FM Compact Disc Player +60
Air Conditioning +100
Anti-Lock Brakes +80
Power Sunroof[Std on 4WS] +80

PROTEGE 1990

Formerly the 323 sedan, this redesigned model is available in two trim levels.

RATINGS (SCALE OF 1-10)

Overall	Safety	Reliability	Performance	Comfort	Value
N/A	N/A	7	8.2	7.4	5.9

	Trade-in	Market
Category E		
4 Dr LX Sdn	1625	2460
4 Dr SE Sdn	1465	2220
4 Dr STD 4WD Sdn	1685	2550

OPTIONS FOR PROTEGE

Auto 4-Speed Transmission +90
Air Conditioning +100
Power Steering[Opt on SE] +30
Power Sunroof +75

RX-7 1990

No changes.

	Trade-in	Market
Category F		
2 Dr 2+2 GXL Rotary Cpe	3360	4545
2 Dr GTU Rotary Cpe	3020	4080
2 Dr GTUs Rotary Cpe	3080	4165
2 Dr GXL Rotary Cpe	3360	4545
2 Dr STD Rotary Conv	4935	6665
2 Dr Turbo Rotary Cpe	3830	5175

OPTIONS FOR RX-7

Auto 3-Speed Transmission +90
Auto 4-Speed Transmission +90
AM/FM Compact Disc Player +60
Air Conditioning[Opt on GTU,GTUs,STD] +100
Leather Seats[Std on STD] +80
Power Sunroof[Opt on GTU] +80

Don't forget to refer to the Mileage Adjustment Table at the back of this book!

MERCEDES-BENZ 99

Model Description	Trade-in Value	Market Value	Model Description	Trade-in Value	Market Value

MERCEDES Germany

1997 Mercedes-Benz C230

1999 MERCEDES-BENZ

C-CLASS   1999

The SLK's 2.3-liter supercharged engine gets dropped into the C-Class, replacing the normally-aspirated engine of the last C230. Performance has been turned up a notch. In addition, leather seating surfaces are now standard across the C-Class line.

RATINGS (SCALE OF 1-10)

Overall	Safety	Reliability	Performance	Comfort	Value
N/A	8.5	9	8.6	8.1	N/A

Category L

	Trade-in	Market
4 Dr C230 Komp Sdn	21820	25370
4 Dr C280 Sdn	26045	30285
4 Dr C43 Sdn	37560	43675

OPTIONS FOR C-CLASS
Full Leather Seat Trim +980
Option Pkg C1 +630
Bose Sound System[Opt on Kompressor] +410
Dual Power Seats[Opt on Kompressor] +575
Heated Front Seats[Std on C43] +355
Leather Seats[Opt on Kompressor] +900
Power Moonroof[Std on C43] +695
Telescopic Steering Whl[Std on C43] +135
Traction Control System[Std on C43] +1050

CLK320   1999

These guys are still on a roll. Last year, Mercedes introduced an all-new sport coupe that is an amalgamation of C- and SLK-Class technologies, available this year with a larger engine in the CLK 430 model, and now they're rolling out the CLK 320 Cabriolet, a convertible version of the fabulous little car.

RATINGS (SCALE OF 1-10)

Overall	Safety	Reliability	Performance	Comfort	Value
N/A	N/A	N/A	8.4	8	N/A

Category L

	Trade-in	Market
2 Dr STD Conv	42690	49640
2 Dr STD Cpe	34845	40520

OPTIONS FOR CLK320
Compact Disc Changer +825
Heated Front Seats +355
Power Moonroof +695
Traction Control System +1050
Xenon Headlamps +680

CLK430   1999

These guys are still on a roll. Last year, Mercedes introduced an all-new sport coupe that is an amalgamation of C- and SLK-Class technologies, available this year with a larger engine in the CLK 430 model, and now they're rolling out the CLK 320 Cabriolet, a convertible version of the fabulous little car.

RATINGS (SCALE OF 1-10)

Overall	Safety	Reliability	Performance	Comfort	Value
N/A	N/A	N/A	8.6	8	N/A

Category J

	Trade-in	Market
2 Dr STD Cpe	38350	44080

OPTIONS FOR CLK430
Option Pkg K4 +745
Compact Disc Changer +685
Heated Front Seats +310
Power Moonroof +695
Xenon Headlamps +610

E-CLASS   1999

More airbags find room in the E-Class, which now features a full curtain side airbag protection system. The E300 Turbodiesel and E320 wagon are enhanced with leather seat inserts, and all E-Class cars get fiber-optic technology in their sound system/optional telephone unit. A performance-oriented E55 model is also available, bringing with it a fire-breathing V8.

RATINGS (SCALE OF 1-10)

Overall	Safety	Reliability	Performance	Comfort	Value
N/A	N/A	8.7	9.4	8.6	N/A

Category L

	Trade-in	Market
4 Dr E320 Sdn	34085	39635
4 Dr E55 Sdn	60405	70240
4 Dr E430 Sdn	37735	43875
4 Dr E300TD Turbodsl Sdn	28855	33550
4 Dr E320 Wgn	34505	40120

Don't forget to refer to the Mileage Adjustment Table at the back of this book!

Model Description	Trade-in Value	Market Value	Model Description	Trade-in Value	Market Value

OPTIONS FOR E-CLASS

Elect. Stability Program +740
Option Pkg E1 +700
Parktronic System +720
Pkg K2 +625
Sport Pkg E3 +1160
Bose Sound System[Std on E430, E55] +410
Compact Disc Changer +825
Heated Front Seats[Std on E55] +355
Leather Seats[Opt on Wgn, Turbodsl] +900
Power Moonroof[Std on E55] +695
Traction Control System[Opt on Turbodsl, E320 Sedan] +1050
Xenon Headlamps[Std on E55] +680

M-CLASS 1999

Mercedes expands its M-Class with the addition of the more powerful and luxurious ML430 and gives the 320 more standard equipment.

RATINGS (SCALE OF 1-10)

Overall	Safety	Reliability	Performance	Comfort	Value
N/A	N/A	N/A	7.8	8.1	N/A

Category G
4 Dr ML320 4WD Wgn — 25000 30120
Category H
4 Dr ML430 4WD Wgn — 32735 37200

OPTIONS FOR M-CLASS

M1 Option Pkg +730
M4 Option Pkg +750
Power Skyview Roof +1770
Bose Sound System +520
Compact Disc Changer +320
Dual Power Seats[Std on ML430] +285
Heated Front Seats +195
Leather Seats[Std on ML430] +575
Power Moonroof +645
Privacy Glass[Std on ML430] +195
Trip Computer[Std on ML430] +110

S-CLASS 1999

The folks at the three-pointed star unleash an S-Class Mercedes that offers freshened styling, unstoppable engines and a host of luxuries. A limited-production Grand Edition S500 also debuts.

RATINGS (SCALE OF 1-10)

Overall	Safety	Reliability	Performance	Comfort	Value
N/A	N/A	N/A	8	9	N/A

Category L
4 Dr S320 LWB Sdn — 44030 51200
4 Dr S420 Sdn — 46980 54625
4 Dr S500 Sdn — 56960 66235
4 Dr S320 SWB Sdn — 41895 48715

OPTIONS FOR S-CLASS

Adapt Damping System +1490
Four Place Power Seating +3640
Grand Edition Pkg +885
Parktronic System +640
Power Rear Seat Adjusters +1150
Compact Disc Changer[Std on S600] +825
Dual Air Conditioning[Std on S600] +1390
Heated Front Seats[Std on S500, S600] +355
Traction Control System[Std on S600] +1050
Xenon Headlamps[Std on S500, S600] +680

SL-CLASS 1999

The SL500 gets a brand-spankin'-new 5.0-liter V8 that delivers better performance than ever before. Both SL models get side view mirrors from the SLK, body-colored door handles and new side molding, new taillights, new exterior colors, a new instrument panel, new shifter and shift gate, and a new four-spoke steering wheel.

RATINGS (SCALE OF 1-10)

Overall	Safety	Reliability	Performance	Comfort	Value
N/A	N/A	N/A	9.6	7.9	N/A

Category J
2 Dr SL500 STD Conv — 57090 65620

OPTIONS FOR SL-CLASS

Removable Panorama Roof +2730
SL1 Sport Option Pkg +3675
Heated Front Seats[Std on SL600] +310
Xenon Headlamps[Std on SL600] +610

SLK230 1999

This year, Mercedes gives the SLK a standard five-speed manual transmission, optional Sport Package, a new-generation stereo with cassette that uses fiber-optic technology, and integrated controls for a cellular phone.

RATINGS (SCALE OF 1-10)

Overall	Safety	Reliability	Performance	Comfort	Value
N/A	N/A	N/A	8	7.9	N/A

Category J
2 Dr STD Sprchgd Conv — 29230 33595
2 Dr Sport Sprchgd Conv — 31495 36200

OPTIONS FOR SLK230

Auto 5-Speed Transmission +665
Heated Front Seats +310

1998 MERCEDES-BENZ

C-CLASS 1998

The C280 is the lucky recipient of Mercedes' new V-type engine technology, receiving a 2.8-liter unit for the engine bay. BabySmart car seats, Brake Assist and

---

Don't forget to refer to the Mileage Adjustment Table at the back of this book!

MERCEDES-BENZ 98

Model Description	Trade-in Value	Market Value	Model Description	Trade-in Value	Market Value

side airbags also debut on the C-Class this year. For the C43, think BMW M3 without all the fun of a stick shift. The C43 is fast and stylish, but the automatic transmission robs plenty of the fun.

RATINGS (SCALE OF 1-10)

Overall	Safety	Reliability	Performance	Comfort	Value
7.9	8.5	8.9	8.6	8.1	5.2

Category L

	Trade-in	Market
4 Dr C230 Sdn	18980	22330
4 Dr C280 Sdn	21755	25595
4 Dr C43 Sdn	35715	42020

OPTIONS FOR C-CLASS

Bose Sound System[Opt on C230] +335
Compact Disc Changer +675
Dual Power Seats[Opt on C230] +470
Heated Front Seats +290
Leather Seats +735
Power Moonroof +570
Sport Suspension +100
Telescopic Steering Whl +110
Traction Control System +860

CLK320 1998

These guys are on a roll. Right after introducing their SUV, Mercedes is rolling out an all-new sport coupe that is an amalgamation of C- and SLK-Class technologies. The CLK is infused with the same 3.2-liter V6 that has made its way into the ML320 and E320. Those who have spent an obscene amount of money on the BMW 840Ci must be scratching their heads at this one; the CLK costs less than $40,000.

Category L

	Trade-in	Market
2 Dr STD Cpe	30115	35430

OPTIONS FOR CLK320

K2 Option Pkg +520
K4 Option Pkg +990
Compact Disc Changer +675
Heated Front Seats +290
Power Moonroof +570

E-CLASS 1998

All-wheel drive comes to the Mercedes' E-Class lineup via the E320 sedan and all-new E320 wagon. Like the rest of Mercedes' model lineup, E-Class cars formerly powered by an inline-six engine now receive a more fuel efficient V6 unit that is also supposed to improve the cars' low-end torque. The 1998 E-Class cars receive the benefit of BabySmart airbags which are able to detect the presence of a Mercedes' car seat in the front passenger seat and disable the front passenger airbag. Brake Assist is also a new feature, which aids drivers' stopping distance in a panic stop situation.

RATINGS (SCALE OF 1-10)

Overall	Safety	Reliability	Performance	Comfort	Value
N/A	N/A	9.1	9.4	8.6	5.3

Category L

	Trade-in	Market
4 Dr E300TD Turbodsl Sdn	27330	32150
4 Dr E320 Sdn	30620	36025
4 Dr E320 Wgn	31105	36595
4 Dr E320 4WD Wgn	34185	40220
4 Dr E430 Sdn	33365	39250

OPTIONS FOR E-CLASS

Option Pkg E1 +900
Parktronic System +600
Pkg K2 +520
Sport Pkg E3 +2190
Bose Sound System[Std on E430] +335
Compact Disc Changer +675
Leather Seats[Opt on E300TD,Wgn] +735
Luggage Rack +185
Metallic Paint +365
Power Moonroof +570

M-CLASS 1998

Mercedes enters the sport-ute fray with the introduction of the ML320. Designed from a clean sheet of paper, the ML320 offers the best of the car and truck worlds.

RATINGS (SCALE OF 1-10)

Overall	Safety	Reliability	Performance	Comfort	Value
N/A	N/A	7.6	7.2	8.1	N/A

Category G

	Trade-in	Market
4 Dr ML320 4WD Wgn	22675	27655

OPTIONS FOR M-CLASS

M1 Option Pkg +960
M4 Option Pkg +500
Automatic Dimming Mirror +105
Bose Sound System +425
Dual Power Seats +235
Heated Front Seats +160
Leather Seats +470
Power Moonroof +525
Privacy Glass +160
Trip Computer +90

S-CLASS 1998

The uber-Mercedes are not changed much in anticipation of the cars' imminent replacement. Brake Assist and BabySmart appear in the lineup, but the S320s don't receive the V6 engines that have empowered lesser Mercedes, like the C280 and E320.

Category L

	Trade-in	Market
4 Dr S320 LWB Sdn	39790	46810
4 Dr S320 SWB Sdn	38050	44765
4 Dr S420 Sdn	41730	49095
4 Dr S500 Sdn	48910	57540

Don't forget to refer to the Mileage Adjustment Table at the back of this book!

Model Description	Trade-in Value	Market Value	Model Description	Trade-in Value	Market Value

OPTIONS FOR S-CLASS
Adapt Damping System +1395
Four Place Power Seating +3405
Parktronic System +600
Power Rear Seat Adjusters +1075
Auto Load Leveling[Std on S500,S600] +680
Compact Disc Changer[Std on S600] +675
Dual Air Conditioning[Std on S600] +1140
Headlight Washers[Opt on S320 SWB] +195
Heated Front Seats[Std on S500,S600] +290
Traction Control System[Std on S600] +860
Xenon Headlamps[Std on S500,S600] +555

SL-CLASS 1998

The bargain basement, ha ha, SL320 has been discontinued this year, leaving only the wallet busting SL500 and SL600. The big news is the $10,000 price reduction of the SL500; this car cost only $79,900 when new.

Category J

2 Dr SL500 Conv	51675	60085
2 Dr SL500 SL1 Sport Conv	54300	63140
2 Dr SL600 Conv	68620	79790

OPTIONS FOR SL-CLASS
Adapt Damping System +2695
Removable Panorama Roof +2210
Heated Front Seats[Opt on SL500] +255
Traction Control System +715

SLK230 1998

Mercedes-Benz releases an all-new retractable-hardtop roadster. Powered by a supercharged 2.3-liter engine, which is hooked to a five-speed automatic transmission, the SLK races to 60 mph in just over seven seconds.

Category J

2 Dr STD Sprchgd Conv	27080	31490

OPTIONS FOR SLK230
Compact Disc Changer +560
Heated Front Seats +255

1997 MERCEDES-BENZ

C-CLASS 1997

The C220 is replaced by a more powerful C230. The C36 gains more horsepower. All C-Class models have redesigned headlamps.

RATINGS (SCALE OF 1-10)

Overall	Safety	Reliability	Performance	Comfort	Value
7.6	7.5	8.8	8.6	8.1	5.2

Category L

4 Dr C230 Sdn	17960	21130
4 Dr C280 Sdn	20515	24135
4 Dr C36 Sdn	22730	26740

OPTIONS FOR C-CLASS
Bose Sound System[Opt on C230] +275
Cellular Telephone +500
Compact Disc Changer +550
Dual Power Seats[Opt on C230] +385
Leather Seats[Std on C36] +600
Limited Slip Diff +660
Power Moonroof[Std on C36] +465
Sport Suspension +80
Telescopic Steering Whl +90
Traction Control System +700

E-CLASS 1997

The Mercedes-Benz E300D and E320 receive the driver-adaptable five-speed automatic transmission. The E-Class also has a smart sensor to determine if anyone is sitting in the passenger seat and to determine whether or not to deploy the air bag. The E420 can be had with a Sport Package.

RATINGS (SCALE OF 1-10)

Overall	Safety	Reliability	Performance	Comfort	Value
N/A	N/A	8.9	9.4	8.6	5.1

Category L

4 Dr E300D Dsl Sdn	25970	30555
4 Dr E320 Sdn	28010	32955
4 Dr E420 Sdn	30665	36075

OPTIONS FOR E-CLASS
Option Pkg E4 +735
Sport Pkg E6 +1400
Bose Sound System[Std on E420] +275
Cellular Telephone +500
Chrome Wheels +760
Compact Disc Changer +550
Compact Disc W/fm/tape +320
Leather Seats[Opt on E300D] +600
Limited Slip Diff[Opt on E320] +660
Power Moonroof +465

S-CLASS 1997

It's a big year for the big Benz. After a few years of relatively minor changes, the S-Class gets its share of the fun that has been flying around the Stuttgart design studios. Side impact air bags debut in all S-Class cars this year. S-Class coupes get new front bumpers. All cars get new alloy wheels. A Parktronic system is available for those who aren't comfortable parking their $100,000 car in a narrow space. Mercedes' outstanding Automatic Slip Reduction (ASR) traction control system is finally available on the S320s. Lastly,

MERCEDES-BENZ 97-96

Model Description	Trade-in Value	Market Value	Model Description	Trade-in Value	Market Value

a rain sensor system is now standard on all models. (It adjusts the speed of the wipers to the intensity of the rain.)

Category L

4 Dr S320 LWB Sdn	35335	41570
4 Dr S320 SWB Sdn	33985	39980
4 Dr S420 Sdn	37885	44570
2 Dr S500 Cpe	49790	58575
4 Dr S500 Sdn	44260	52070
2 Dr S600 Cpe	63320	74495

OPTIONS FOR S-CLASS

Adapt Damping System +1120
Four Place Power Seating +2740
Parktronic System +480
Power Rear Seat Adjusters +865
Auto Load Leveling[Opt on S320,S420] +555
Traction Control System[Opt on S420,S500] +700

SL-CLASS   1997

A Panorama hardtop is now available, and it helps improve top-up visibility. ASR traction control is now standard on the SL320. A rain sensor is now standard on all models as well.

Category J

2 Dr SL320 Conv	41365	48665
2 Dr SL500 Conv	47060	55365
2 Dr SL500 SL1 Sport Conv	49570	58315
2 Dr SL600 Conv	62860	73950

OPTIONS FOR SL-CLASS

Adapt Damping System +2170
Removable Panorama Roof +1755
Sl1 Sport Pkg +2250
Traction Control System[Opt on SL500] +585

1996 MERCEDES-BENZ

C-CLASS   1996

An infrared remote security system, dual cupholders in the console, a delayed headlamp dousing system, and reconfigured option packages mark the changes to the baby Benz.

RATINGS (SCALE OF 1-10)

Overall	Safety	Reliability	Performance	Comfort	Value
7.7	7.4	8.5	8.6	8.1	5.7

Category L

4 Dr C220 Sdn	15885	18910
4 Dr C280 Sdn	18520	22050
4 Dr C36 Sdn	27480	32715

OPTIONS FOR C-CLASS

Bose Sound System[Opt on C220] +225
Cellular Telephone +410
Compact Disc Changer +450

Leather Seats[Std on C36] +490
Limited Slip Diff +540
Power Moonroof[Std on C36] +380
Power Passenger Seat +185
Telescopic Steering Whl[Std on C36] +75
Traction Control System +575

E-CLASS   1996

All-new and sporting a face anybody's mother could love, the E-Class comes in three flavors: E300 Diesel, E320 and E420. A new front suspension and larger wheels and tires provide better handling response, while optional gas-discharge headlamps mark new technology. Side-impact airbags are included in the doors of all E-Class models. E420's can be had with ESP, which is a new safety system that makes sure the E420 is under control at all times. The E420 also gets a new five-speed transmission.

RATINGS (SCALE OF 1-10)

Overall	Safety	Reliability	Performance	Comfort	Value
N/A	N/A	8.6	9.4	8.6	5.1

Category L

4 Dr E300D Dsl Sdn	22720	27050
4 Dr E320 Sdn	25475	30325

OPTIONS FOR E-CLASS

Bose Sound System +225
Cellular Telephone +410
Compact Disc Changer +450
Leather Seats[Std on E320] +490
Limited Slip Diff +540
Power Moonroof +380

G320   1996

Category G

4 Dr STD 4WD Wgn	12270	16140

OPTIONS FOR G320

Auxiliary Seats +1135
Motion Detector +330
Programmable Heater +1390

S-CLASS   1996

No cosmetic improvements to the S-Class this year; everything new is under the skin. ESP is standard on the S600 and optional on all other models. ESP is a safety system designed to help the driver keep the S-Class under control at all times. V8 and V12 versions get a new five-speed automatic, and all models get a standard power glass sunroof and smog-sensing climate control system. The S350 Turbodiesel is history.

Category L

4 Dr S320 LWB Sdn	30610	36440
4 Dr S320 SWB Sdn	29680	35335
4 Dr S420 Sdn	32590	38795

Don't forget to refer to the Mileage Adjustment Table at the back of this book!

Model Description	Trade-in Value	Market Value
2 Dr S500 Cpe	44315	52755
4 Dr S500 Sdn	36290	43200
2 Dr S600 Cpe	55130	65630
4 Dr S600 Sdn	53515	63710

OPTIONS FOR S-CLASS
Adapt Damping System +995
Elect. Stability Program +755
Four Place Power Seating +1910
Rear Axle Level Control +360
Cellular Telephone +410
Power Moonroof +380

SL-CLASS   1996

Tweaked styling and new alloys freshen the exterior of the SL roadster. Underneath, ESP keeps drivers on track in lousy driving conditions. It comes standard on the SL600; can be ordered for the SL320 and SL500. Side airbags are standard across the board. A five-speed automatic is included with SL500 and SL600. Cool gas-discharge headlamps are not available on the SL320.

Category J

Model	Trade-in	Market
2 Dr SL320 Conv	36135	43020
2 Dr SL500 Conv	41415	49305
2 Dr SL600 Conv	53780	64025

OPTIONS FOR SL-CLASS
Adapt Damping System +1695
Slip Control +485
Cellular Telephone +730

1995 MERCEDES-BENZ

C-CLASS   1995

The AMG-prepared C36 is introduced to the C-Class family. This little mighty mouse runs circles around its lesser siblings and gives BMW M3 owners something to think about. Only 300 copies of the C36 are available in 1995; get one if you can.

RATINGS (SCALE OF 1-10)

Overall	Safety	Reliability	Performance	Comfort	Value
7.4	7.5	8.6	8.6	8.1	4.3

Category L

Model	Trade-in	Market
4 Dr C220 Sdn	14085	17175
4 Dr C280 Sdn	15845	19325
4 Dr C36 Sdn	24885	30350

OPTIONS FOR C-CLASS
Option Pkg C1 +540
Bose Sound System[Opt on C220] +185
Leather Seats[Std on C36] +400
Limited Slip Diff +440
Power Moonroof +310

Power Passenger Seat[Opt on C220] +150
Telescopic Steering Whl +60
Traction Control System +470

E-CLASS   1995

No changes for the last year of this rendition of the E-Class.

RATINGS (SCALE OF 1-10)

Overall	Safety	Reliability	Performance	Comfort	Value
N/A	N/A	8.3	8.8	8.4	5

Category L

Model	Trade-in	Market
4 Dr E300D Dsl Sdn	17230	21010
2 Dr E320 Conv	33175	40460
2 Dr E320 Cpe	25600	31220
4 Dr E320 Sdn	20275	24725
4 Dr E320 Wgn	20625	25150
4 Dr E420 Sdn	22100	26950

OPTIONS FOR E-CLASS
Option Pkg E1 +755
Sportline Pkg +360
Cellular Telephone +335
Compact Disc Changer +370
Leather Seats[Opt on E300D,Wgn] +400
Limited Slip Diff +440
Premium Sound System[Std on E420,Cpe] +325
Telescopic Steering Whl[Opt on E300D,Wgn] +60

G320   1995

Category G

Model	Trade-in	Market
4 Dr STD 4WD Wgn	7950	10600

OPTIONS FOR G320
Auxiliary Folding Seats +925
Programmable Heater +1140

S-CLASS   1995

Minuscule exterior changes and a drop in price are about the only changes to the S-Class.

Category L

Model	Trade-in	Market
4 Dr S320 LWB Sdn	26960	32880
4 Dr S320 SWB Sdn	25980	31685
4 Dr S420 Sdn	28610	34890
2 Dr S500 Cpe	37280	45465
4 Dr S500 Sdn	31260	38120
2 Dr S600 Cpe	46445	56640
4 Dr S600 Sdn	42690	52060

OPTIONS FOR S-CLASS
Adapt Damping System +855
Four Place Power Seating +1565
Rear Axle Level Control +290
Cellular Telephone +335
Power Moonroof +310

Don't forget to refer to the Mileage Adjustment Table at the back of this book!

Model Description	Trade-in Value	Market Value

SL-CLASS 1995

Traction control is now standard on the SL320. Price cuts are the only other change for the Mercedes roadster.

Category J

Model Description	Trade-in Value	Market Value
2 Dr SL320 Conv	32880	39615
2 Dr SL500 Conv	38100	45905
2 Dr SL600 Conv	46610	56155

OPTIONS FOR SL-CLASS

Adapt Damping System +1365
Slip Control +545
Cellular Telephone +595

1994 MERCEDES-BENZ

C-CLASS 1994

This peppy replacement for the 190 is long-awaited. Longer and wider than the 190, the C-Class gives rear seat passengers more room. Standard on the C-Class are dual airbags, a wood-trimmed interior, four-wheel antilock brakes and a power sunroof. The C-Class cars are available in four- or six-cylinder flavors with a standard automatic transmission.

RATINGS (SCALE OF 1-10)

Overall	Safety	Reliability	Performance	Comfort	Value
7.8	7.4	8.7	8.6	8.1	6.1

Category L

Model Description	Trade-in Value	Market Value
4 Dr C220 Sdn	12185	15230
4 Dr C280 Sdn	13855	17320

OPTIONS FOR C-CLASS

Leather Seats +330
Limited Slip Diff +360
Power Moonroof +255
Power Passenger Seat[Opt on C220] +125
Premium Sound System +265
Traction Control System +385

E-CLASS 1994

In an effort at simplification, Mercedes renames its 300-Class, now calling it the E-Class. Like the new C-Class, the numeral after the E indicates the engine's size. Pretty cool, huh? Coupe, convertible, sedan and wagon body styles are still offered.

RATINGS (SCALE OF 1-10)

Overall	Safety	Reliability	Performance	Comfort	Value
N/A	N/A	8.3	8.8	8.4	5

Category L

Model Description	Trade-in Value	Market Value
2 Dr E320 Conv	28660	35825
2 Dr E320 Cpe	21730	27165
4 Dr E320 Sdn	16750	20935
4 Dr E320 Wgn	17120	21400
4 Dr E420 Sdn	18250	22810
4 Dr E500 Sdn	27360	34200

OPTIONS FOR E-CLASS

Sportline Pkg +400
Leather Seats[Opt on Wgn] +330
Premium Sound System[Opt on E320 STD Sdn] +265
Sport Suspension +45
Tilt Steering Wheel[Opt on Wgn] +90
Traction Control System[Std on E500] +385

S-CLASS 1994

The big Benz gains Mercedes's new alphanumeric nomenclature that makes it easier to identify the vehicle family and engine size. Fuel economy is improved for the S-Class, and all but the S600 switch to H-rated tires for increased traction in inclement weather.

Category L

Model Description	Trade-in Value	Market Value
4 Dr S320 Sdn	22555	28195
4 Dr S350D Turbodsl Sdn	20130	25160
4 Dr S420 Sdn	24100	30125
2 Dr S500 Cpe	30380	37975
4 Dr S500 Sdn	26065	32580
2 Dr S600 Cpe	39930	49915
4 Dr S600 Sdn	34255	42820

OPTIONS FOR S-CLASS

Adapt Damping System +675
Four Place Seating +1340
Level Control Suspension +235
Rear Power Seatback +285
Cellular Telephone[Opt on S500] +275
Power Sunroof +250
Traction Control System[Opt on S320,S420] +385

SL-CLASS 1994

The SL300 becomes the SL320 as a new powerplant slips into the engine bay. Offering the same horsepower as the previous engine, the SL320 throws out considerably more torque than last year's model. A Bose stereo is added to the standard equipment lists of the entire SL-Class.

Category J

Model Description	Trade-in Value	Market Value
2 Dr SL320 Conv	28620	34480
2 Dr SL500 Conv	33505	40365
2 Dr SL600 Conv	39310	47360

OPTIONS FOR SL-CLASS

Adapt Damping System +1100
Traction Control System[Opt on SL320] +320

MERCEDES-BENZ 93-92

Model Description	Trade-in Value	Market Value	Model Description	Trade-in Value	Market Value

1993 MERCEDES-BENZ

190   1993

No changes for the little Mercedes that could; still a good car at a relatively good price. A new model replaces the 190 for 1994.

Category L

	Trade-in	Market
4 Dr 190E Sdn	7940	10050
4 Dr 190E 2.6 Sdn	9190	11635

OPTIONS FOR 190

Auto 4-Speed Transmission +200
190E 2.6 Sportline Pkg +350
Cellular Telephone +225
Compact Disc W/fm/tape +145
Dual Power Seats[Opt on STD] +170
Leather Seats +270
Limited Slip Diff +295
Power Sunroof +205
Sport Suspension +35
Traction Control System +315

300   1993

All but the turbo models receive a larger engine. A driver airbag is finally standard on the 300-Class Mercedes. A 300 CE cabriolet model is brought into the fold; it has a power top and a pop-up roll bar similar to the one found on the SL-roadsters.

Category L

	Trade-in	Market
2 Dr 300CE Conv	27260	34505
2 Dr 300CE Cpe	18975	24020
4 Dr 300D Turbodsl Sdn	12325	15600
4 Dr 300E Sdn	13585	17195
4 Dr 300E 2.8 Sdn	12350	15635
4 Dr 300SD Turbodsl Sdn	18635	23590
4 Dr 300SE Sdn	19180	24280
2 Dr 300SL Conv	25430	32190
4 Dr 300TE Wgn	13985	17700

OPTIONS FOR 300

Auto 5-Speed Transmission[Opt on 300SL] +245
300E Sportline Pkg +380
Adapt Damping System +705
CE Sportline Pkg +235
Four Place Seating +1160
Power Rear Seat Back +230
Rear Axle Level Cntrl Sus +190
AM/FM Compact Disc Player +200
Cellular Telephone +225
Leather Seats[Opt on 300D,300TE,2.8] +270
Power Moonroof +205
Premium Sound System[Opt on 300D,2.8] +215
Sport Suspension +35
Third Seat +245
Traction Control System +315

400   1993

The 400SE becomes the 400SEL in order to compete with the longer wheelbase sedans from BMW.

Category L

	Trade-in	Market
4 Dr 400E Sdn	14800	18735
4 Dr 400SEL Sdn	20400	25820

OPTIONS FOR 400

Adapt Damping System +610
Four Place Seating +1160
Power Rear Seat Back +230
Rear Axle Level Cntrl Sus +190
Cellular Telephone +225
Compact Disc Changer +245
Power Moonroof +205
Traction Control System +315

500   1993

No changes to 500-Series models.

Category L

	Trade-in	Market
4 Dr 500E Sdn	26570	33630
4 Dr 500SEL Sdn	23410	29630
2 Dr 500SL Conv	29550	37405

OPTIONS FOR 500

Adapt Damping System +600
Four Place Seating +1160
Cellular Telephone +225
Power Moonroof +205

1992 MERCEDES-BENZ

190   1992

A sportline package is now available on the six-cylinder 190E 2.6. The package consists of go-fast goodies like V-rated tires, a sport-tuned suspension and quicker steering.

Category L

	Trade-in	Market
4 Dr 190E Sdn	6785	8810
4 Dr 190E 2.6 Sdn	7835	10175

OPTIONS FOR 190

Auto 4-Speed Transmission +160
Sportline Pack +225
Auto Load Leveling +205
Dual Power Seats +140
Leather Seats +220
Power Sunroof +165

300   1992

No changes for 1992.

Category L

	Trade-in	Market
2 Dr 300CE Cpe	14590	18950
4 Dr 300D Turbodsl Sdn	10465	13590
4 Dr 300E Sdn	11135	14460
4 Dr 300E 4matic 4WD Sdn	11805	15330

Don't forget to refer to the Mileage Adjustment Table at the back of this book!

Model Description	Trade-in Value	Market Value
4 Dr 300SD Turbodsl Sdn	16715	21710
4 Dr 300SE Sdn	17395	22590
2 Dr 300SL Conv	23115	30020
4 Dr 300TE Wgn	11590	15055
4 Dr 300TE 4matic 4WD Wgn	12455	16175

OPTIONS FOR 300

Auto 4-Speed Transmission[Opt on 300SL] +180
Adapt Damping System +560
Four Place Seating Pkg +920
Rear Power Seats +185
Sportline Pkg +295
Alarm System[Opt on 300D,300E STD Sdn] +105
Auto Load Leveling[Std on 300TE] +205
Dual Air Bag Restraints[Std on 300SD,300SL] +120
Leather Seats[Opt on 300D,300TE,300E STD Sdn] +220
Power Sunroof +165
Premium Sound System[Opt on 300D,300E STD Sdn] +175
Third Seat +200

400   1992

A new model is introduced to the lineup of midsize Mercedes: the 400E. It offers V8 power, a first in this line of cars, and comes standard with an automatic transmission. Dual airbags are now standard on these pricey sedans, as are neat features like traction control, a five-speed automatic transmission, heated front seats, double paned side-windows, and a self-leveling system.

Category L

Model Description	Trade-in Value	Market Value
4 Dr 400E Sdn	12590	16350
4 Dr 400SE Sdn	18230	23675

OPTIONS FOR 400

Adapt Damping System +485
Four Place Seating Pkg +920
Power Seatback Recliner +185
Auto Load Leveling +205
Power Passenger Seat +80
Power Sunroof +165
Traction Control System +255

500   1992

A new 500E model is introduced to the Mercedes top-drawer lineup.

Category L

Model Description	Trade-in Value	Market Value
4 Dr 500E Sdn	23245	30190
4 Dr 500SEL Sdn	19670	25545
2 Dr 500SL Conv	26740	34730

OPTIONS FOR 500

Adapt Damping System +535
Four Place Seating +855
Air Bag Restraint[Std on 500E] +110
Cellular Telephone +180
Power Moonroof +170

1991 MERCEDES-BENZ

190   1991

A four-cylinder gas powered model is reintroduced to the 190 lineup.

Category L

Model Description	Trade-in Value	Market Value
4 Dr 190E Sdn	5945	7825
4 Dr 190E 2.6 Sdn	6970	9170

OPTIONS FOR 190

Auto 4-Speed Transmission +130
Dual Power Seats[Opt on STD] +115
Leather Seats +180
Limited Slip Diff +195
Power Drivers Seat +70
Power Sunroof +135
Traction Control System +210

300   1991

No major changes for this recently overhauled Mercedes.

Category L

Model Description	Trade-in Value	Market Value
2 Dr 300CE Cpe	12720	16735
4 Dr 300D Turbodsl Sdn	8430	11095
4 Dr 300E Sdn	9760	12840
4 Dr 300E 2.6 Sdn	8855	11650
4 Dr 300E 4matic 4WD Sdn	10190	13410
4 Dr 300SE Sdn	10810	14225
4 Dr 300SEL Sdn	11050	14540
2 Dr 300SL Conv	21290	28015
4 Dr 300TE Wgn	10115	13310
4 Dr 300TE 4matic 4WD Wgn	10855	14280

OPTIONS FOR 300

Auto 4-Speed Transmission[Opt on 300SL] +145
Adapt Damping System +560
Four Place Seating Pkg +455
Dual Air Bag Restraints[Std on 300SL] +100
Leather Seats[Opt on 300D,2.6,300E STD Sdn] +180
Power Sunroof +135
Premium Sound System[Opt on 300D,2.6,300E STD Sdn] +145
Third Seat +165

350   1991

No changes.

Category L

Model Description	Trade-in Value	Market Value
4 Dr 350SD Turbodsl Sdn	11935	15705
4 Dr 350SDL Turbodsl Sdn	12240	16105

OPTIONS FOR 350

Four Place Seating Pkg +455
Leather Seats +180
Power Sunroof +135

Don't forget to refer to the Mileage Adjustment Table at the back of this book!

Model Description	Trade-in Value	Market Value

420 — 1991

No changes.
Category L

Model Description	Trade-in Value	Market Value
4 Dr 420SEL Sdn	12100	15920

OPTIONS FOR 420
Four Place Seating Pkg +455
Power Sunroof +135

500 — 1991

We wait in anticipation as Mercedes readies its new flagship. Unfortunately, there are no major changes in the interim.
Category L

2 Dr 500SL Conv	24675	32465

OPTIONS FOR 500
Adapt Damping System +560

560 — 1991

We wait in anticipation as Mercedes readies its new flagship. Unfortunately, there are no major changes in the interim.
Category L

2 Dr 560SEC Cpe	16705	21975
4 Dr 560SEL Sdn	12355	16260

OPTIONS FOR 560
Four Place Seating Pkg +350

1990 MERCEDES-BENZ

190 — 1990

No changes for the baby Benz.
Category L

4 Dr 190E Sdn	5380	7175

OPTIONS FOR 190
Auto 4-Speed Transmission +110
Dual Power Seats +95
Leather Seats +145
Power Sunroof +110

300 — 1990

Big changes for the midsized offering from Mercedes. The 260 is now called the Mercedes 300E 2.6 to indicate that it is indeed a 300 and not a 190. The 300CE gains a boost in horsepower by adding two more valves per cylinder. The central locking system will now handily close the windows and sunroof as well as lock the doors. The interior has been made more luxurious by adding more leather and wood to everything. SL Roadster is completely redesigned.
Category L

2 Dr 300CE Cpe	11265	15020
4 Dr 300D Turbodsl Sdn	7240	9655

4 Dr 300E Sdn	8460	11280
4 Dr 300E 2.6 Sdn	7525	10030
4 Dr 300SE Sdn	9345	12460
4 Dr 300SEL Sdn	9475	12635
2 Dr 300SL Conv	20055	26740
4 Dr 300TE Wgn	8770	11690

OPTIONS FOR 300
Auto 4-Speed Transmission[Opt on 300SL,300TE STD Wgn] +120
Four Place Seating Pkg +370
Air Bag Restraint[Std on 300SEL,300SL,2.6] +75
Alarm System[Opt on 2.6] +70
Leather Seats[Opt on 300D,300TE,2.6] +145
Power Drivers Seat[Opt on 300D,2.6] +60
Power Passenger Seat[Opt on 2.6] +55
Power Sunroof[Opt on 300TE] +110
Premium Sound System[Opt on 300E STD Sdn] +120
Third Seat +135

350 — 1990

Category L

4 Dr 350SDL Turbodsl Sdn	11930	15910

OPTIONS FOR 350
Four Place Seating Pkg +370

420 — 1990

No major changes for 1990.
Category L

4 Dr 420SEL Sdn	10300	13735

OPTIONS FOR 420
Four Place Seating Pkg +370

500 — 1990

Goodness gracious, the roadsters sure look different than last year. Appealing to a more youthful audience, Mercedes ditched the long, sedate look in favor of an aerodynamic, almost racy sports car. Available with a 320-horsepower V8, this car is the most powerful in its class. The convertible top is entirely automatic and a pop-up roll bar will protect occupants in the event of a roll-over accident.
Category L

2 Dr 500SL Conv	23275	31035

560 — 1990

The 560 coupe and sedan receive no changes.
Category L

2 Dr 560SEC Cpe	14395	19190
4 Dr 560SEL Sdn	11485	15310

OPTIONS FOR 560
Four Place Seating Pkg +285

Don't forget to refer to the Mileage Adjustment Table at the back of this book!

MERCURY 99

Model Description	Trade-in Value	Market Value	Model Description	Trade-in Value	Market Value

MERCURY   USA

1995 Mercury Sable

1999 MERCURY

COUGAR   1999

Mercury reintroduces the Cougar this year after a one-year hiatus that saw the departure of most of Ford Motor Co.'s personal coupes. The new model is built on the Mondeo global platform that is also the basis for the Ford Contour and Mercury Mystique. This new coupe is powered by the same engine choices as the Contour/Mystique, which means that buyers can choose between a zippy Zetec four-cylinder and a high-revving Duratec V6.

RATINGS (SCALE OF 1-10)

Overall	Safety	Reliability	Performance	Comfort	Value
N/A	N/A	8.4	7.2	7.1	N/A

Category C
2 Dr I4 Cpe	11400	13735
2 Dr V6 Cpe	11995	14450

OPTIONS FOR COUGAR
Auto 4-Speed Transmission +600
AM/FM Compact Disc Player +270
Anti-Lock Brakes +450
Cruise Control +155
Keyless Entry System +140
Leather Seats +450
Power Drivers Seat +220
Traction Control System +180

GRAND MARQUIS   1999

Not much. This traditional American sedan got a revised rear suspension and exterior styling last year. This year all it gets are some new color options.

RATINGS (SCALE OF 1-10)

Overall	Safety	Reliability	Performance	Comfort	Value
N/A	8.3	8.7	7.6	8.3	N/A

Category B
4 Dr GS Sdn	14340	17280
4 Dr LS Sdn	14690	17700

OPTIONS FOR GRAND MARQUIS
AM/FM Compact Disc Player +245
Aluminum/Alloy Wheels +245
Anti-Lock Brakes +510
Dual Power Seats +280
Keyless Entry System[Std on LS] +130
Leather Seats +505
Traction Control System +130

MOUNTAINEER   1999

For '99 the Mountaineer gets optional rear load leveling and a reverse parking aid. It also receives a new seat design.

RATINGS (SCALE OF 1-10)

Overall	Safety	Reliability	Performance	Comfort	Value
N/A	N/A	N/A	7.4	7.3	N/A

Category H
4 Dr STD Wgn	17490	20575
4 Dr STD 4WD Wgn	18750	22060

OPTIONS FOR MOUNTAINEER
8 cyl 5.0 L Engine +365
Alarm System +145
Chrome Wheels +220
Climate Control for AC +435
Compact Disc W/fm/tape +230
Dual Power Seats +345
Keyless Entry System +130
Leather Seats +730
Power Drivers Seat +210
Power Moonroof +720

MYSTIQUE   1999

The Mystique gets a revised instrument panel and redesigned front seats this year. A six-way power adjustable seat is now standard on the LS model and all Mystiques benefit from a revised suspension and larger fuel tank. Medium Steel Blue replaces Light Denim Blue as an exterior color. A final note to family-oriented shoppers: the optional integrated child safety seat is no longer available.

RATINGS (SCALE OF 1-10)

Overall	Safety	Reliability	Performance	Comfort	Value
N/A	6.9	7.5	N/A	N/A	N/A

Category C
4 Dr GS Sdn	8940	10770
4 Dr LS Sdn	10150	12230

Don't forget to refer to the Mileage Adjustment Table at the back of this book!

Model Description	Trade-in Value	Market Value

Model Description	Trade-in Value	Market Value

OPTIONS FOR MYSTIQUE

Auto 4-Speed Transmission +600
AM/FM Compact Disc Player +270
Aluminum/Alloy Wheels[Std on LS] +225
Anti-Lock Brakes +450
Keyless Entry System[Std on LS] +140
Power Drivers Seat[Std on LS] +220
Power Moonroof +510

SABLE   1999

Still smarting from that 1996 "redesign" that had many longtime Sable fans running to the competition, Mercury performed some minor cosmetic surgery in '98 to help soften the Sable's front end. This year's changes are limited to new wheel designs, a revised gauge cluster and interior console, as well as suspension alterations designed to improve overall ride quality. The particulate filtration system has been deleted from this year's models.

RATINGS (SCALE OF 1-10)

Overall	Safety	Reliability	Performance	Comfort	Value
N/A	7.8	7.9	7.8	8.1	N/A

Category C

4 Dr GS Sdn	10585	12750
4 Dr LS Sdn	11455	13800
4 Dr LS Wgn	12385	14920

OPTIONS FOR SABLE

6 cyl 3.0 L DOHC Engine +390
Aluminum/Alloy Wheels[Std on LS] +225
Anti-Lock Brakes +450
Climate Control for AC +125
Compact Disc Changer +355
Dual Power Seats +440
Keyless Entry System[Std on LS] +140
Leather Seats +450
Power Drivers Seat[Std on LS] +220
Power Moonroof +510

TRACER   1999

The Tracer gets a new sport wagon model to help extend its appeal to young buyers. The LS Sport Wagon model comes standard with leather seating surfaces and 15-inch wheels. Other changes include a standard interior trunk release on all sedans. A remote, keyless entry and AM/FM cassette player is standard on LS models.

RATINGS (SCALE OF 1-10)

Overall	Safety	Reliability	Performance	Comfort	Value
N/A	6.3	8.6	6.6	7.3	N/A

Category E

4 Dr GS Sdn	6645	8105
4 Dr LS Sdn	7505	9150
4 Dr LS Wgn	7850	9575

OPTIONS FOR TRACER

Auto 4-Speed Transmission +600
AM/FM Stereo Tape[Std on LS] +225
Air Conditioning[Std on LS] +605
Aluminum/Alloy Wheels +245
Anti-Lock Brakes +500
Cruise Control +165
Keyless Entry System[Std on LS] +115
Power Door Locks +180
Power Mirrors[Std on LS] +80
Power Windows +195
Tilt Steering Wheel +110

VILLAGER   1999

The Mercury Villager is completely redesigned for '99. Improvements range from a more powerful engine to a larger interior to a second sliding door on the driver's side. New styling features include larger headlights and a distinctive front grille. Inside, ergonomics have been addressed with easier to reach controls and an innovative storage shelf located behind the third seat.

RATINGS (SCALE OF 1-10)

Overall	Safety	Reliability	Performance	Comfort	Value
N/A	N/A	8.6	6.8	7.4	N/A

Category G

2 Dr Estate Pass. Van	17320	20620
2 Dr STD Pass. Van	15235	18135
2 Dr Sport Pass. Van	17515	20850

OPTIONS FOR VILLAGER

Aluminum/Alloy Wheels[Opt on STD] +245
Anti-Lock Brakes +445
Climate Control for AC +145
Compact Disc W/fm/tape +355
Dual Air Conditioning +700
Dual Power Seats +285
Keyless Entry System +150
Leather Seats +575
Power Drivers Seat +210
Power Moonroof +645
Privacy Glass +195

1998 MERCURY

GRAND MARQUIS   1998

Vive le Grand Marquis! The last of the American rear-drive sedans gets substantial improvements this year, including a new instrument panel, new steering gear and an improved ride, thanks to a Watt's linkage suspension. All-speed traction control debuts this year as well.

RATINGS (SCALE OF 1-10)

Overall	Safety	Reliability	Performance	Comfort	Value
8.2	8.3	8.5	7.6	8.3	8.4

Don't forget to refer to the Mileage Adjustment Table at the back of this book!

Model Description	Trade-in Value	Market Value	Model Description	Trade-in Value	Market Value
Category B			*Category C*		
4 Dr GS Sdn	12745	15355	4 Dr GS Sdn	7810	9525
4 Dr LS Sdn	13075	15755	4 Dr LS Sdn	8835	10775

OPTIONS FOR GRAND MARQUIS
AM/FM Compact Disc Player +200
Aluminum/Alloy Wheels +200
Anti-Lock Brakes +420
Climate Control for AC +105
Dual Power Seats +230
Keyless Entry System[Opt on GS] +105
Leather Seats +410
Traction Control System +105

MOUNTAINEER 1998

The Mountaineer gets minor front and rear styling tweaks as it enters its second year of production. In addition, a new model, with full-time four-wheel drive, receives the SOHC V6 and five-speed automatic transmission that became available on the Explorer last year.

RATINGS (SCALE OF 1-10)

Overall	Safety	Reliability	Performance	Comfort	Value
N/A	N/A	8.4	6.6	7.3	8.2

Category H		
4 Dr STD Wgn	15055	17920
4 Dr STD 4WD Wgn	16105	19175

OPTIONS FOR MOUNTAINEER
8 cyl 5.0 L Engine +305
Chrome Wheels +180
Climate Control for AC +355
Compact Disc Changer +265
Compact Disc W/fm/tape +190
Dual Power Seats +280
Keyless Entry System +105
Leather Seats +595
Power Drivers Seat +170
Power Moonroof +590
Running Boards +210

MYSTIQUE 1998

The 1998 Mystique receives a freshened interior and exterior that includes new wheels and a new front end. Mechanical enhancements include 100,000-mile maintenance intervals for the 2.0-liter Zetec engine, improved manual transmission shifter feel, improved NVH and improved air conditioning performance. New interior pieces are intended to distinguish the Mystique from its otherwise-identical twin, the Ford Contour.

RATINGS (SCALE OF 1-10)

Overall	Safety	Reliability	Performance	Comfort	Value
7.4	6.7	6.7	8.2	7.9	7.5

OPTIONS FOR MYSTIQUE
Auto 4-Speed Transmission +500
AM/FM Compact Disc Player +220
Aluminum/Alloy Wheels[Opt on GS] +180
Anti-Lock Brakes +370
Keyless Entry System[Opt on GS] +115
Leather Seats +365
Power Drivers Seat[Opt on GS] +180
Power Moonroof +415

SABLE 1998

A mild facelift and fewer options are the only change to Mercury's mid-size sedan.

RATINGS (SCALE OF 1-10)

Overall	Safety	Reliability	Performance	Comfort	Value
8.1	7.9	8.1	7.8	8.1	8.6

Category C		
4 Dr GS Sdn	9260	11295
4 Dr LS Sdn	9880	12050
4 Dr LS Wgn	10850	13230

OPTIONS FOR SABLE
6 cyl 3.0 L DOHC Engine +305
Aluminum/Alloy Wheels[Opt on GS] +180
Anti-Lock Brakes +370
Chrome Wheels +370
Climate Control for AC +100
Compact Disc Changer +290
Dual Power Seats +360
Heated Power Mirrors +65
Keyless Entry System[Opt on GS] +115
Leather Seats +365
Power Drivers Seat[Opt on GS] +180
Power Moonroof +415

TRACER 1998

No changes to Mercury's recently redesigned entry-level car.

RATINGS (SCALE OF 1-10)

Overall	Safety	Reliability	Performance	Comfort	Value
7.4	6.3	8.5	6.6	7.3	8.2

Category E		
4 Dr GS Sdn	5930	7320
4 Dr LS Sdn	6615	8165
4 Dr LS Wgn	6905	8525

OPTIONS FOR TRACER
Auto 4-Speed Transmission +500
Air Conditioning[Opt on GS] +495
Aluminum/Alloy Wheels +200
Anti-Lock Brakes +410
Cruise Control +135

Don't forget to refer to the Mileage Adjustment Table at the back of this book!

MERCURY 98-97

Model Description	Trade-in Value	Market Value	Model Description	Trade-in Value	Market Value

Keyless Entry System[Opt on GS] +95
Power Door Locks +145
Power Mirrors[Opt on GS] +65
Power Windows +160
Rear Window Defroster[Opt on GS] +100
Tilt Steering Wheel +90

VILLAGER   1998

No changes to the 1998 Villager as Mercury readies a replacement.

RATINGS (SCALE OF 1-10)

Overall	Safety	Reliability	Performance	Comfort	Value
7.7	7.3	8.2	6.8	7.5	8.7

Category G

	Trade-in	Market
2 Dr GS Pass. Van	11510	13700
2 Dr LS Pass. Van	13400	15950
2 Dr Nautica Pass. Van	15230	18130

OPTIONS FOR VILLAGER

7 Passenger Seating[Opt on GS] +315
Air Conditioning[Opt on GS] +495
Aluminum/Alloy Wheels[Opt on GS, LS] +200
Anti-Lock Brakes[Opt on GS] +365
Climate Control for AC +120
Compact Disc W/fm/tape +290
Cruise Control +125
Dual Air Conditioning +575
Dual Power Seats +235
Keyless Entry System +120
Leather Seats[Opt on LS] +470
Power Door Locks[Opt on GS] +140
Power Drivers Seat +170
Power Mirrors[Opt on GS] +80
Power Moonroof +525
Power Windows[Opt on GS] +145
Premium Sound System +210
Privacy Glass[Opt on GS] +160
Rear Window Defroster[Opt on GS] +105

1997 MERCURY

COUGAR XR7   1997

This is it, your last chance to own a brand new Cougar. That's right folks, after 1997 Mercury chops its personal coupe. To commemorate the occasion, which coincides with Cougar's 30th birthday, Mercury will give you the chance to buy a special anniversary edition replete with plenty of badges, a special interior and a few luxury doo-dads.

RATINGS (SCALE OF 1-10)

Overall	Safety	Reliability	Performance	Comfort	Value
7.6	7.9	8.2	8	7.8	6.3

Category C

	Trade-in	Market
2 Dr XR7 Cpe	9080	11210

OPTIONS FOR COUGAR XR7

8 cyl 4.6 L Engine +370
AM/FM Compact Disc Player +180
Aluminum/Alloy Wheels +150
Anti-Lock Brakes +300
Cruise Control +105
Dual Power Seats +295
Keyless Entry System +95
Power Door Locks +125
Power Drivers Seat +145
Power Moonroof +340
Premium Sound System +195
Sport Suspension +105
Traction Control System +120

GRAND MARQUIS   1997

After a mild facelift last year, the Grand Marquis soldiers on with a few color changes, improved power steering and the addition of rear air suspension to the handling package.

RATINGS (SCALE OF 1-10)

Overall	Safety	Reliability	Performance	Comfort	Value
8	7.9	7.7	7.6	8.3	8.3

Category B

	Trade-in	Market
4 Dr GS Sdn	10940	13340
4 Dr LS Sdn	11435	13945

OPTIONS FOR GRAND MARQUIS

Aluminum/Alloy Wheels +165
Anti-Lock Brakes +340
Cruise Control +110
Keyless Entry System +85
Leather Seats +335
Power Door Locks +125
Premium Sound System +195
Traction Control System +85
Trip Computer +195

MOUNTAINEER   1997

The all-new Mercury Mountaineer is yet another entrant into the booming luxury sport-utility market. Based on the wildly successful Ford Explorer, the Mountaineer is intended to appeal to outdoor sophisticates rather than true roughnecks. Distinguishing characteristics of the Mountaineer include four-wheel antilock brakes, a pushrod V8 engine and optional all-wheel drive.

RATINGS (SCALE OF 1-10)

Overall	Safety	Reliability	Performance	Comfort	Value
N/A	N/A	8	7.6	7.3	8.6

Category H

	Trade-in	Market
4 Dr STD Wgn	13690	16295
4 Dr STD 4WD Wgn	14500	17260

Don't forget to refer to the Mileage Adjustment Table at the back of this book!

MERCURY 97

Model Description	Trade-in Value	Market Value
4 Dr LS Sdn	8355	10315
4 Dr LS Wgn	9235	11400

OPTIONS FOR SABLE
Leather Bucket Seats +495
AM/FM Stereo Tape[Opt on GS] +80
Aluminum/Alloy Wheels[Opt on GS] +150
Anti-Lock Brakes +300
Child Seat (1) +60
Chrome Wheels +300
Compact Disc Changer +235
Cruise Control +105
Keyless Entry System +95
Leather Seats[Opt on GS] +300
Power Door Locks[Opt on GS] +125
Power Moonroof +340

TRACER 1997

The Mercury Tracer is totally redesigned this year with enhancements across the board. The most noticeable improvements are in the powertrain and in the ride quality. New sheetmetal gives the Tracer a rounder, more aerodynamic appearance as well. The speedy LTS sedan is discontinued.

RATINGS (SCALE OF 1-10)

Overall	Safety	Reliability	Performance	Comfort	Value
7	6.3	8.3	7.2	7.3	6.1

Category E
4 Dr GS Sdn	5070	6420
4 Dr LS Sdn	5670	7175
4 Dr LS Wgn	5950	7530

OPTIONS FOR TRACER
Auto 4-Speed Transmission +385
AM/FM Stereo Tape +150
Air Conditioning +405
Aluminum/Alloy Wheels +165
Anti-Lock Brakes +335
Child Seat (1) +55
Compact Disc Changer +250
Cruise Control +110
Keyless Entry System +80
Power Door Locks +120
Power Windows +130

VILLAGER 1997

The Villager adds some luxury equipment such as rear passenger air conditioning and quad seating to distinguish it from the mechanically identical Nissan Quest.

RATINGS (SCALE OF 1-10)

Overall	Safety	Reliability	Performance	Comfort	Value
7.4	7.2	7.6	6.8	7.5	8.1

OPTIONS FOR MOUNTAINEER
Camper/Towing Package +170
Child Seat (1) +100
Compact Disc Changer +215
Compact Disc W/fm/tape +155
Keyless Entry System +85
Leather Seats +485
Luggage Rack +75
Power Drivers Seat +140
Power Moonroof +480
Running Boards +170

MYSTIQUE 1997

The addition of a Spree Package for the GS model and the inclusion of a tilt steering wheel and standard trunk light are the only changes for the 1997 Mystique.

RATINGS (SCALE OF 1-10)

Overall	Safety	Reliability	Performance	Comfort	Value
7.5	6.8	7.1	8.2	7.9	7.4

Category C
4 Dr GS Sdn	6000	7405
4 Dr LS Sdn	6925	8550
4 Dr STD Sdn	5850	7220

OPTIONS FOR MYSTIQUE
6 cyl 2.5 L Engine +455
Auto 4-Speed Transmission +410
AM/FM Compact Disc Player +180
AM/FM Stereo Tape[Std on LS] +80
Air Conditioning +400
Aluminum/Alloy Wheels[Opt on GS] +150
Anti-Lock Brakes +300
Cruise Control +105
Keyless Entry System +95
Leather Seats +300
Power Door Locks +125
Power Drivers Seat[Opt on GS] +145
Power Moonroof +340
Power Windows +155
Premium Sound System +195

SABLE 1997

The 1997 Sable LS can now be had with Ford's outstanding Mach audio system. Other changes, occurring at the end of the 1996 model year, include the addition of a mass airflow sensor to the Vulcan V6, and improvements to the Duratec V6 to improve responsiveness.

RATINGS (SCALE OF 1-10)

Overall	Safety	Reliability	Performance	Comfort	Value
8	7.8	7.5	7.8	8.1	9

Category C
4 Dr GS Sdn	7715	9525
4 Dr GS Wgn	8640	10665

Don't forget to refer to the Mileage Adjustment Table at the back of this book!

Category G
Model Description	Trade-in Value	Market Value
2 Dr GS Pass. Van	10225	12320
2 Dr LS Pass. Van	12035	14500
2 Dr Nautica Pass. Van	13530	16300

OPTIONS FOR VILLAGER

7 Passenger Seating[Opt on GS] +260
Air Conditioning[Opt on GS Cargo Van] +405
Aluminum/Alloy Wheels[Opt on GS] +165
Anti-Lock Brakes[Opt on GS] +295
Captain Chairs (4)[Opt on LS] +310
Child Seats (2) +125
Compact Disc W/fm/tape +240
Cruise Control +105
Dual Air Conditioning +470
Dual Power Seats +190
Keyless Entry System +100
Leather Seats[Opt on LS] +385
Luggage Rack[Opt on GS] +80
Power Door Locks[Opt on GS Cargo Van] +115
Power Drivers Seat +140
Power Moonroof +430
Power Windows[Opt on GS Cargo Van] +120
Premium Sound System +170

1996 MERCURY

COUGAR 1996

New styling and powertrain improvements highlight the 1996 Cougar. Some formerly standard equipment is now optional. New options include a revamped cruise control system and a Total Anti-theft System. Four new colors debut.

RATINGS (SCALE OF 1-10)
Overall	Safety	Reliability	Performance	Comfort	Value
N/A	7.9	7.9	8	N/A	6.6

Category C
	Trade-in	Market
2 Dr XR7 Cpe	7375	9455

OPTIONS FOR COUGAR

AM/FM Compact Disc Player +145
Anti-Lock Brakes +245
Chrome Wheels +245
Cruise Control +85
Keyless Entry System +75
Leather Seats +245
Power Door Locks +100
Power Drivers Seat +120
Power Moonroof +280
Power Passenger Seat +110
Premium Sound System +160
Traction Control System +100

GRAND MARQUIS 1996

This distant descendant of the Turnpike Cruiser gets engine and transmission upgrades, a new steering wheel and a new gas cap design. Passenger power lumbar support has been deleted.

RATINGS (SCALE OF 1-10)
Overall	Safety	Reliability	Performance	Comfort	Value
7.8	7.7	6.9	7.6	8.3	8.7

Category B
	Trade-in	Market
4 Dr GS Sdn	8985	11230
4 Dr LS Sdn	9410	11760

OPTIONS FOR GRAND MARQUIS

Anti-Lock Brakes +280
Cruise Control +90
Keyless Entry System +70
Leather Steering Wheel +35
Power Door Locks +105
Power Passenger Seat +135
Premium Sound System +160

MYSTIQUE 1996

More rear seat room is the big story for Mystique in 1996. Gearshift effort has been improved on manual transmissions, a new Sport Appearance Package is available, and five new colors are on the palette. Alloy wheels have been restyled on LS models.

RATINGS (SCALE OF 1-10)
Overall	Safety	Reliability	Performance	Comfort	Value
7.2	6.8	6.5	8.2	7.9	6.8

Category C
	Trade-in	Market
4 Dr GS Sdn	5270	6755
4 Dr LS Sdn	5915	7585

OPTIONS FOR MYSTIQUE

6 cyl 2.5 L Engine +405
Auto 4-Speed Transmission +315
AM/FM Compact Disc Player +145
Air Conditioning +325
Anti-Lock Brakes +245
Cruise Control +85
Keyless Entry System +75
Leather Seats +245
Power Antenna[Opt on GS] +35
Power Door Locks +100
Power Drivers Seat[Opt on GS] +120
Power Moonroof +280
Power Windows +125

SABLE 1996

Fresh off the drawing boards for 1996, and it seems the drawing boards were poorly lit. Styling is heavy-handed and homely, but definitely not dull. Otherwise, the new Sable is an excellent car, powered by new engines, suspended by new components, and innovative in nearly every way. Longer and wider sedan and wagon bodystyles are offered in GS and LS trim.

MERCURY 96-95

Model Description	Trade-in Value	Market Value	Model Description	Trade-in Value	Market Value

RATINGS (SCALE OF 1-10)

Overall	Safety	Reliability	Performance	Comfort	Value
7.8	7.7	6.5	7.8	8.1	8.8

Category C

	Trade-in	Market
4 Dr G Sdn	6275	8045
4 Dr GS Sdn	6400	8205
4 Dr GS Wgn	6965	8930
4 Dr LS Sdn	7160	9180
4 Dr LS Wgn	7825	10030

OPTIONS FOR SABLE

Preferred Equipment Pkg +295
AM/FM Stereo Tape[Std on LS] +65
Anti-Lock Brakes +245
Child Seat (1) +50
Chrome Wheels +245
Compact Disc Changer +195
Cruise Control +85
Keyless Entry System +75
Leather Seats +245
Power Door Locks[Opt on GS] +100
Power Drivers Seat[Opt on GS] +120
Power Moonroof +280

TRACER   1996

Automatic transmission modifications make base Tracers more responsive, and the standard 1.9-liter engine now goes 100,000 miles between tune-ups. Last year's integrated child seat continues, and Trio models are now available in all colors, including a new one called Toreador Red.

RATINGS (SCALE OF 1-10)

Overall	Safety	Reliability	Performance	Comfort	Value
7.2	6.8	8.3	7.6	7.1	6.4

Category E

	Trade-in	Market
4 Dr LTS Sdn	5525	7270
4 Dr STD Sdn	4495	5915
4 Dr STD Wgn	4675	6150

OPTIONS FOR TRACER

Auto 4-Speed Transmission +315
AM/FM Compact Disc Player +185
Air Conditioning +330
Anti-Lock Brakes +275
Child Seat (1) +45
Cruise Control[Opt on STD] +90
Luggage Rack +50
Power Door Locks +100
Power Moonroof +230
Power Windows +105

VILLAGER   1996

A passenger-side airbag is installed in a redesigned dashboard for 1996, and fresh front and rear styling updates this versatile van. Villager also gets an optional integrated child seat, automatic climate control system, and remote keyless entry system. Substantial trim and functional changes make Villager competitive once again.

RATINGS (SCALE OF 1-10)

Overall	Safety	Reliability	Performance	Comfort	Value
7.3	7	6.8	6.8	7.5	8.5

Category G

	Trade-in	Market
2 Dr GS Pass. Van	8620	10640
2 Dr LS Pass. Van	10100	12470
2 Dr Nautica Pass. Van	11215	13845

OPTIONS FOR VILLAGER

7 Passenger Seating[Opt on GS] +210
Air Conditioning[Opt on GS Cargo Van] +330
Captain Chairs (4)[Opt on LS] +255
Child Seats (2) +105
Compact Disc W/fm/tape +195
Cruise Control +85
Dual Air Conditioning +385
Keyless Entry System +80
Leather Seats[Opt on LS] +315
Luggage Rack[Opt on GS] +65
Power Door Locks[Opt on GS Cargo Van] +95
Power Drivers Seat +115
Power Moonroof +350
Power Passenger Seat +110
Power Windows[Opt on GS Cargo Van] +95
Premium Sound System +140

1995 MERCURY

COUGAR   1995

A Sport Appearance Package is offered to spruce up the Cougar with BBS wheels and a luggage rack. Unfortunately, the trunk-mounted CD-changer is deleted from the option list. Antilock brakes and a traction-lock axle are available as separate options for the first time this year.

RATINGS (SCALE OF 1-10)

Overall	Safety	Reliability	Performance	Comfort	Value
N/A	8.7	7.3	8	N/A	7.1

Category C

	Trade-in	Market
2 Dr XR7 Cpe	5820	7760

OPTIONS FOR COUGAR

8 cyl 4.6 L Engine +205
AM/FM Compact Disc Player +120
Anti-Lock Brakes +200
Climate Control for AC +55
Cruise Control +70
Keyless Entry System +60
Leather Seats +200
Power Door Locks +80
Power Drivers Seat +100

Don't forget to refer to the Mileage Adjustment Table at the back of this book!

MERCURY 95

Model Description	Trade-in Value	Market Value	Model Description	Trade-in Value	Market Value

Power Moonroof +225
Power Passenger Seat +90
Premium Sound System +130

GRAND MARQUIS 1995

Updated styling and an increased number of convenience features improve upon last year's model. A battery saver shuts off power to accessories or lights 10 minutes after the ignition is switched off. The mast antenna has been replaced by an integrated rear window antenna. Interior updates include a 12-volt outlet in a redesigned dashboard. Enlarged stereo controls improve ease of operation and bigger gauges improve the instrument panel.

RATINGS (SCALE OF 1-10)

Overall	Safety	Reliability	Performance	Comfort	Value
7.6	8.1	5.4	7.6	8.3	8.7

Category B

	Trade-in	Market
4 Dr GS Sdn	7235	9275
4 Dr LS Sdn	7505	9620

OPTIONS FOR GRAND MARQUIS

Anti-Lock Brakes +230
Climate Control for AC +55
Cruise Control +75
Keyless Entry System +55
Leather Seats +225
Power Door Locks +85
Power Passenger Seat +110
Power Sunroof +375
Premium Sound System +130

MYSTIQUE 1995

Introduced to replace the aging Topaz, the Mystique is a virtual twin to the Ford Contour. Euro-styling combined with German engineering results in a $20,000 American car that can compete with import sedans that cost nearly twice as much. You may choose between two trim levels, the base GS or the more luxurious LS. A 170-horsepower V6 engine is optional.

RATINGS (SCALE OF 1-10)

Overall	Safety	Reliability	Performance	Comfort	Value
7.1	7	5.3	8.2	7.9	7.2

Category C

	Trade-in	Market
4 Dr GS Sdn	4490	5985
4 Dr LS Sdn	4740	6325

OPTIONS FOR MYSTIQUE

6 cyl 2.5 L Engine +320
Auto 4-Speed Transmission +270
AM/FM Compact Disc Player +120
Air Conditioning +265
Anti-Lock Brakes +200
Cruise Control +70
Keyless Entry System +60

Leather Seats +200
Power Door Locks +80
Power Drivers Seat[Opt on GS] +100
Power Moonroof +225
Power Windows +105
Premium Sound System +130

SABLE 1995

Last year for the Sable in its current form. New cylinder heads and crankshafts are intended to decrease engine noise by reducing vibration. Solar control window glass makes a brief appearance on the sedan and wagon.

RATINGS (SCALE OF 1-10)

Overall	Safety	Reliability	Performance	Comfort	Value
7.9	7.4	7.4	8	7.8	8.7

Category C

	Trade-in	Market
4 Dr GS Sdn	4855	6470
4 Dr GS Wgn	5440	7250
4 Dr LS Sdn	5585	7445
4 Dr LS Wgn	6120	8160

OPTIONS FOR SABLE

6 cyl 3.8 L Engine +210
AM/FM Compact Disc Player +120
Anti-Lock Brakes[Opt on GS] +200
Chrome Wheels +200
Cruise Control +70
Dual Power Seats +195
Keyless Entry System +60
Leather Seats +200
Power Door Locks[Opt on GS] +80
Power Moonroof +225
Power Windows[Opt on GS] +105

TRACER 1995

A passenger airbag is finally available for the Tracer. Unfortunately, some engineering genius decided to retain the annoying motorized shoulder belts. An integrated child seat is introduced as an optional safety feature. The Trio package is introduced, designed to give budget shoppers the option of purchasing some of the more popular LTS features such as the spoiler, aluminum wheels and leather-wrapped steering wheel.

RATINGS (SCALE OF 1-10)

Overall	Safety	Reliability	Performance	Comfort	Value
7.2	7.2	7.7	7.6	7.1	6.4

Category E

	Trade-in	Market
4 Dr LTS Sdn	4335	5940
4 Dr STD Sdn	3695	5065
4 Dr STD Wgn	3835	5250

Don't forget to refer to the Mileage Adjustment Table at the back of this book!

Model Description	Trade-in Value	Market Value

OPTIONS FOR TRACER
Auto 4-Speed Transmission +270
AM/FM Compact Disc Player +150
Air Conditioning +270
Anti-Lock Brakes +225
Child Seat (1) +35
Cruise Control[Opt on STD] +75
Luggage Rack +45
Power Door Locks +80
Power Moonroof +190
Power Windows +85

VILLAGER   1995
No changes for the Villager.

RATINGS (SCALE OF 1-10)

Overall	Safety	Reliability	Performance	Comfort	Value
7.2	7	6	6.8	7.1	9

Category G

	Trade-in	Market
2 Dr GS Pass. Van	6555	8295
2 Dr LS Pass. Van	8115	10270
2 Dr Nautica Pass. Van	8890	11255

OPTIONS FOR VILLAGER
Super Sound +285
7 Passenger Seating[Opt on GS] +170
Air Conditioning[Opt on GS Cargo Van] +270
Captain Chairs (4)[Opt on LS] +205
Compact Disc W/fm/tape +160
Cruise Control[Opt on GS Cargo Van] +70
Keyless Entry System +65
Leather Seats[Opt on LS] +255
Luggage Rack[Opt on GS] +50
Power Door Locks[Opt on GS Cargo Van] +75
Power Drivers Seat +95
Power Moonroof +290
Power Passenger Seat +90
Power Windows[Opt on GS Cargo Van] +80
Premium Sound System +115

1994 MERCURY

CAPRI   1994
A passenger airbag is added. A new suspension on the XR2 improves handling. Both trim levels get a freshened exterior. Slow sales make this the final year for this car.

Category F

	Trade-in	Market
2 Dr STD Conv	3820	5025
2 Dr XR2 Turbo Conv	4565	6005

OPTIONS FOR CAPRI
Auto 4-Speed Transmission +215
AM/FM Stereo Tape[Opt on STD] +60
Air Conditioning +225
Aluminum/Alloy Wheels +85
Cruise Control +55

Leather Seats +175
Power Door Locks +55

COUGAR   1994
Dual airbags are finally available on the Cougar. The standard four-speed automatic transmission gains electronic shift controls and an overdrive lockout switch. Optional traction control joins the lineup of safety features. Updated front and rear fascias, taillamps and headlights round out the changes.

RATINGS (SCALE OF 1-10)

Overall	Safety	Reliability	Performance	Comfort	Value
N/A	8.7	7.6	8	N/A	7.5

Category C

	Trade-in	Market
2 Dr XR7 Cpe	4890	6605

OPTIONS FOR COUGAR
8 cyl 4.6 L Engine +155
Aluminum/Alloy Wheels +80
Anti-Lock Brakes +165
Climate Control for AC +45
Compact Disc Changer +130
Cruise Control +55
Keyless Entry System +50
Leather Seats +165
Power Door Locks +65
Power Drivers Seat +80
Power Moonroof +185
Power Passenger Seat +75
Premium Sound System +105
Traction Control System +65

GRAND MARQUIS   1994
The Grand Marquis passes the stringent 1997 side-impact standards this year. Wire-spoke wheelcovers are now part of the standard equipment package.

RATINGS (SCALE OF 1-10)

Overall	Safety	Reliability	Performance	Comfort	Value
7.8	7.8	6.9	7.6	8.3	8.6

Category B

	Trade-in	Market
4 Dr GS Sdn	5950	7830
4 Dr LS Sdn	6260	8240

OPTIONS FOR GRAND MARQUIS
Anti-Lock Brakes +185
Cruise Control +60
Keyless Entry System +45
Leather Seats +185
Power Door Locks +70
Power Passenger Seat +90
Premium Sound System +105
Rear Window Defroster +45
Traction Control System +50

MERCURY 94

Model Description	Trade-in Value	Market Value

SABLE 1994

Rear window defroster becomes standard equipment on the sedan and wagon. The wagon gets a standard rear window wiper as well. CFC-free air conditioning is introduced to the Sable.

RATINGS (SCALE OF 1-10)

Overall	Safety	Reliability	Performance	Comfort	Value
7.7	7.3	6.7	8	7.8	8.7

Category C

	Trade-in	Market
4 Dr GS Sdn	3910	5285
4 Dr GS Wgn	4445	6010
4 Dr LS Sdn	4535	6125
4 Dr LS Wgn	4900	6620

OPTIONS FOR SABLE

6 cyl 3.8 L Engine +150
AM/FM Compact Disc Player +100
Anti-Lock Brakes[Opt on GS] +165
Cruise Control +55
Keyless Entry System +50
Leather Seats +165
Power Door Locks +65
Power Drivers Seat[Opt on GS] +80
Power Moonroof +155
Power Passenger Seat +75
Power Windows[Opt on GS] +85

TOPAZ 1994

The Topaz receives CFC-free air conditioning. This will be the last year for the Topaz; Mercury is replacing it with an all-new compact called the Mystique.

RATINGS (SCALE OF 1-10)

Overall	Safety	Reliability	Performance	Comfort	Value
6.9	5.4	7.5	7.6	7.1	7

Category C

	Trade-in	Market
2 Dr GS Sdn	2385	3220
4 Dr GS Sdn	2530	3420

OPTIONS FOR TOPAZ

6 cyl 3.0 L Engine +185
Auto 3-Speed Transmission +145
AM/FM Stereo Tape +45
Air Bag Restraint +130
Air Conditioning +220
Cruise Control +55
Power Door Locks +65
Power Drivers Seat +80
Power Windows +85
Tilt Steering Wheel +40

TRACER 1994

A driver's side airbag is introduced on all models. New alloy wheels and optional antilock brakes show up on the LTS.

RATINGS (SCALE OF 1-10)

Overall	Safety	Reliability	Performance	Comfort	Value
6.9	6.2	7.5	7.6	7.1	6.3

Category E

	Trade-in	Market
4 Dr LTS Sdn	3345	4780
4 Dr STD Sdn	2865	4090
4 Dr STD Wgn	2985	4265

OPTIONS FOR TRACER

Auto 4-Speed Transmission +215
AM/FM Compact Disc Player +125
Air Conditioning +220
Anti-Lock Brakes +180
Cruise Control[Opt on STD] +60
Luggage Rack +35
Power Door Locks +65
Power Moonroof +155
Power Windows +70
Premium Sound System +90

VILLAGER 1994

A driver airbag is installed in the Villager and a special edition luxury model debuts. Borrowing the name of an upscale men's clothier, the Nautica edition of the Villager includes such niceties as two-tone paint, alloy wheels and leather upholstery; all tastefully done in blue and white befitting a nautical theme.

RATINGS (SCALE OF 1-10)

Overall	Safety	Reliability	Performance	Comfort	Value
7.4	7.3	7.2	6.8	7.1	8.5

Category G

	Trade-in	Market
2 Dr GS Pass. Van	5565	7225
2 Dr LS Pass. Van	6720	8730
2 Dr Nautica Pass. Van	7225	9380

OPTIONS FOR VILLAGER

7 Passenger Seating[Opt on GS] +140
Air Conditioning[Opt on GS Cargo Van] +220
Captain Chairs (4)[Opt on LS] +170
Compact Disc W/fm/tape +130
Cruise Control[Opt on GS Cargo Van] +55
Dual Air Conditioning +255
Keyless Entry System +55
Leather Seats[Opt on LS] +210
Luggage Rack[Opt on GS] +45
Power Door Locks[Opt on GS Cargo Van] +65
Power Drivers Seat +75
Power Moonroof +235
Power Passenger Seat +75
Power Windows[Opt on GS Cargo Van] +65
Premium Sound System +95

1993 MERCURY

CAPRI 1993

A new radio is introduced as the only change on the 1993 Capri.

Category F

	Trade-in Value	Market Value
2 Dr STD Conv	2775	3700
2 Dr XR2 Turbo Conv	3640	4850

OPTIONS FOR CAPRI

Auto 4-Speed Transmission +165
AM/FM Stereo Tape[Opt on STD] +45
Air Conditioning[Opt on STD] +185
Aluminum/Alloy Wheels[Opt on STD] +70
Cruise Control[Opt on STD] +45
Hardtop Roof +300
Leather Seats +145
Premium Sound System +80

COUGAR 1993

The LS trim level is dropped in favor of the XR-7. The XR-7 is decontented for 1993, losing the V8 engine, optional limited-slip axle and antilock brakes from the standard equipment lists. Split-fold rear seats are no longer available.

RATINGS (SCALE OF 1-10)

Overall	Safety	Reliability	Performance	Comfort	Value
7	5.7	7.1	6.8	7.8	7.4

Category C

	Trade-in Value	Market Value
2 Dr XR7 Cpe	3870	5375

OPTIONS FOR COUGAR

8 cyl 5.0 L Engine +255
AM/FM Compact Disc Player +80
Aluminum/Alloy Wheels +65
Anti-Lock Brakes +135
Cruise Control +45
Dual Power Seats +130
Keyless Entry System +40
Leather Seats +135
Power Door Locks +55
Power Moonroof +150
Premium Sound System +85

GRAND MARQUIS 1993

A passenger airbag, an overdrive-lockout selector on the automatic gearshift, a stainless steel exhaust system, an express-down driver's window, and dual front cupholders appear on the Grand Marquis's extensive standard equipment list this year.

RATINGS (SCALE OF 1-10)

Overall	Safety	Reliability	Performance	Comfort	Value
7.6	6.8	6.8	7.4	8.3	8.5

Category B

	Trade-in Value	Market Value
4 Dr GS Sdn	4835	6625
4 Dr LS Sdn	5065	6940

OPTIONS FOR GRAND MARQUIS

Aluminum/Alloy Wheels +75
Anti-Lock Brakes +155
Cruise Control +50
Keyless Entry System +40
Leather Seats +150
Power Door Locks +55
Power Passenger Seat +75
Premium Sound System +90
Traction Control System +40

SABLE 1993

The lower body-side cladding and bumpers become body colored for 1993. Bucket seats become an option on both body styles.

RATINGS (SCALE OF 1-10)

Overall	Safety	Reliability	Performance	Comfort	Value
7.2	6.9	4.9	8	7.8	8.2

Category C

	Trade-in Value	Market Value
4 Dr GS Sdn	3010	4180
4 Dr GS Wgn	3455	4800
4 Dr LS Sdn	3555	4935
4 Dr LS Wgn	3895	5410

OPTIONS FOR SABLE

6 cyl 3.8 L Engine +125
AM/FM Compact Disc Player +80
Aluminum/Alloy Wheels +65
Anti-Lock Brakes +135
Cruise Control +45
Keyless Entry System +40
Leather Seats +135
Power Door Locks +55
Power Drivers Seat +65
Power Passenger Seat +60
Power Sunroof +150
Power Windows[Opt on GS] +70
Premium Sound System +85

TOPAZ 1993

Mercury offers only one trim level for the Topaz this year: the lowly GS.

RATINGS (SCALE OF 1-10)

Overall	Safety	Reliability	Performance	Comfort	Value
6.7	4.5	7.3	7.6	7.1	6.8

Category C

	Trade-in Value	Market Value
2 Dr GS Sdn	1945	2700
4 Dr GS Sdn	2095	2910

OPTIONS FOR TOPAZ

6 cyl 3.0 L Engine +155
Auto 3-Speed Transmission +125

MERCURY 93-92

Model Description	Trade-in Value	Market Value	Model Description	Trade-in Value	Market Value

AM/FM Stereo Tape +35
Air Bag Restraint +105
Air Conditioning +180
Aluminum/Alloy Wheels +65
Cruise Control +45
Power Door Locks +55
Power Drivers Seat +65
Power Windows +70
Premium Sound System +85

TRACER — 1993

Beefy stabilizer arms on all trim levels improve handling. Base models receive a new fascia and the LTS receives a one-piece spoiler. All models get new interior fabrics and tail lamps.

RATINGS (SCALE OF 1-10)

Overall	Safety	Reliability	Performance	Comfort	Value
6.4	4.7	7	7.6	7.1	5.8

Category E
4 Dr LTS Sdn	2665	3980
4 Dr STD Sdn	2240	3345
4 Dr STD Wgn	2370	3535

OPTIONS FOR TRACER

Auto 4-Speed Transmission +165
AM/FM Stereo Tape[Opt on STD] +65
Air Conditioning +180
Cruise Control[Opt on STD] +50
Luggage Rack +30
Power Door Locks +55
Power Moonroof +125
Power Steering[Std on LTS,Wgn] +55
Power Windows +60

VILLAGER — 1993

Mercury joins the minivan fray by introducing a vehicle designed jointly with Nissan. Attractive styling and standard features such as antilock brakes are certainly commendable, but the absence of airbags would lead us toward another model.

RATINGS (SCALE OF 1-10)

Overall	Safety	Reliability	Performance	Comfort	Value
6.2	5.5	4.5	6.8	7.1	7.3

Category G
2 Dr GS Pass. Van	4315	5755
2 Dr LS Pass. Van	5485	7310

OPTIONS FOR VILLAGER

Air Conditioning[Opt on GS Cargo Van] +180
Aluminum/Alloy Wheels +75
Captain Chairs (4) +140
Compact Disc W/fm/tape +105
Cruise Control[Opt on GS Cargo Van] +45
Keyless Entry System +45
Leather Seats +170

Luggage Rack[Opt on GS] +35
Power Door Locks[Opt on GS Cargo Van] +50
Power Drivers Seat +60
Power Passenger Seat +60
Power Sunroof +170
Power Windows[Opt on GS Cargo Van] +55
Trip Computer +35

1992 MERCURY

CAPRI — 1992

The XR2 receives 15-inch wheels, new tires and updated cabin trim. Power door locks are no longer available but cruise control is added to the options list.

Category F
2 Dr STD Conv	2375	3255
2 Dr XR2 Turbo Conv	2905	3980

OPTIONS FOR CAPRI

Auto 4-Speed Transmission +130
Air Conditioning[Opt on STD] +150
Hardtop Roof +245
Leather Seats +120

COUGAR — 1992

The 25th anniversary edition debuts. A unique LS model becomes available this year equipped with 5.0-liter V8 engine, monochromatic colors, BBS aluminum wheels, and special trim. White sidewall tires and the anti-theft system are no longer available.

RATINGS (SCALE OF 1-10)

Overall	Safety	Reliability	Performance	Comfort	Value
6.8	5.7	7	6.8	7.8	6.9

Category C
2 Dr LS Cpe	2855	4140
2 Dr XR7 Cpe	3325	4820

OPTIONS FOR COUGAR

8 cyl 5.0 L Engine[Opt on LS] +200
AM/FM Compact Disc Player +65
Anti-Lock Brakes[Opt on LS] +110
Leather Seats +110
Power Door Locks +45
Power Drivers Seat +55
Power Moonroof +125
Power Passenger Seat +50

GRAND MARQUIS — 1992

New sheetmetal debuts on the Grand Marquis. Rounded styling and two additional inches in length give the car a sleeker appearance. The old V8 engine is replaced with a 4.6-liter V8 that makes between 40 and 60 more horsepower, depending on the exhaust system. A new passenger airbag is added to the options list. Antilock brakes are available in the

---

Don't forget to refer to the Mileage Adjustment Table at the back of this book!

Model Description	Trade-in Value	Market Value	Model Description	Trade-in Value	Market Value

MERCURY 92-91

performance and handling package. The wagon is discontinued.

RATINGS (SCALE OF 1-10)

Overall	Safety	Reliability	Performance	Comfort	Value
N/A	6.8	5.8	7.4	N/A	7.8

Category B

4 Dr GS Sdn	3740	5340
4 Dr LS Sdn	3960	5655

OPTIONS FOR GRAND MARQUIS
Anti-Lock Brakes +125
Dual Air Bag Restraints +90
Leather Seats +125
Power Door Locks +45
Power Drivers Seat +55
Power Passenger Seat +60

SABLE   1992

Sable gets dual airbags for front seat occupants. New sheetmetal does little to change the looks of the car. Fifteen-inch wheels replace last year's 14-inchers. Additional radio controls have been placed near the steering wheel and the power window buttons have been moved to the armrest. Variable-assist power steering becomes standard and the heated windshield is dropped from the options list.

RATINGS (SCALE OF 1-10)

Overall	Safety	Reliability	Performance	Comfort	Value
7.2	6.7	5.5	8	7.8	8

Category C

4 Dr GS Sdn	2335	3385
4 Dr GS Wgn	2610	3785
4 Dr LS Sdn	2810	4075
4 Dr LS Wgn	3045	4415

OPTIONS FOR SABLE
6 cyl 3.8 L Engine +100
Anti-Lock Brakes +110
Leather Seats +110
Power Door Locks +45
Power Drivers Seat +55
Power Moonroof +125
Power Passenger Seat +50
Power Windows[Opt on GS] +55

TOPAZ   1992

V6 is available for those who need a little more horsepower. Unfortunately the all-wheel-drive system is dropped from the option list.

RATINGS (SCALE OF 1-10)

Overall	Safety	Reliability	Performance	Comfort	Value
6.7	4.5	6.6	7.6	7.1	7.5

Category C

2 Dr GS Sdn	1775	2570
4 Dr GS Sdn	1880	2725
4 Dr LS Sdn	2125	3080
4 Dr LTS Sdn	2300	3335
2 Dr XR5 Sdn	1925	2790

OPTIONS FOR TOPAZ
6 cyl 3.0 L Engine[Opt on GS,LS] +125
Auto 3-Speed Transmission +100
Air Bag Restraint +85
Air Conditioning[Opt on GS,LS] +145
Power Door Locks[Opt on GS,XR5] +45
Power Drivers Seat[Std on LTS] +55
Power Windows[Opt on GS] +55

TRACER   1992

No changes.

RATINGS (SCALE OF 1-10)

Overall	Safety	Reliability	Performance	Comfort	Value
6.5	4.6	7.6	7.6	7.1	5.8

Category E

4 Dr LTS Sdn	1935	3020
4 Dr STD Sdn	1565	2445
4 Dr STD Wgn	1700	2655

OPTIONS FOR TRACER
Auto 4-Speed Transmission +130
Air Conditioning +145
Power Door Locks +45
Power Moonroof +105
Power Steering[Std on LTS,Wgn] +45
Power Windows +50

1991 MERCURY

CAPRI   1991

This Australian-built convertible is based on the Mazda 323 platform. The 1.6-liter engine is available in turbo or regularly aspirated versions good for either 132 or 100 horsepower. An optional lift-off hardtop with a rear window defroster and interior lights is also available.

Category F

2 Dr STD Conv	1930	2715
2 Dr XR2 Turbo Conv	2405	3390

OPTIONS FOR CAPRI
Auto 4-Speed Transmission +110
Air Conditioning[Opt on STD] +125
Hardtop Roof +200
Power Door Locks[Opt on STD] +30

COUGAR   1991

No significant changes to the Mercury Cougar.

Don't forget to refer to the Mileage Adjustment Table at the back of this book!

Model Description	Trade-in Value	Market Value

RATINGS (SCALE OF 1-10)

Overall	Safety	Reliability	Performance	Comfort	Value
6.7	5.7	6.5	6.8	7.8	6.8

Category C

	Trade-in	Market
2 Dr LS Cpe	2345	3605
2 Dr XR7 Cpe	2705	4165

OPTIONS FOR COUGAR

8 cyl 5.0 L Engine[Opt on LS] +165
Anti-Lock Brakes[Opt on LS] +90
Leather Seats +90
Power Door Locks +35
Power Drivers Seat +45
Power Passenger Seat +40
Power Sunroof +100

GRAND MARQUIS   1991

No major changes to the 1991 Grand Marquis.

Category B

	Trade-in	Market
4 Dr Colony Park GS Wgn	2175	3200
4 Dr Colony Park LS Wgn	2365	3475
4 Dr GS Sdn	2535	3725
4 Dr LS Sdn	2735	4020

OPTIONS FOR GRAND MARQUIS

Auto Load Leveling +25
Leather Seats +100
Power Door Locks +40
Power Drivers Seat +45
Power Passenger Seat +50

SABLE   1991

No significant changes to the 1991 Sable.

Category C

	Trade-in	Market
4 Dr GS Sdn	1830	2815
4 Dr GS Wgn	2115	3255
4 Dr LS Sdn	2145	3300
4 Dr LS Wgn	2340	3600

OPTIONS FOR SABLE

6 cyl 3.8 L Engine +80
Anti-Lock Brakes +90
Leather Seats +90
Power Door Locks +35
Power Drivers Seat +45
Power Passenger Seat +40
Power Sunroof +100
Power Windows[Opt on GS] +45

TOPAZ   1991

No changes for the 1991 Topaz.

RATINGS (SCALE OF 1-10)

Overall	Safety	Reliability	Performance	Comfort	Value
6.6	4.6	6.8	7.2	7.1	7.3

Model Description	Trade-in Value	Market Value

Category C

	Trade-in	Market
2 Dr GS Sdn	1365	2100
4 Dr GS Sdn	1455	2235
4 Dr GS 4WD Sdn	1570	2415
4 Dr LS Sdn	1575	2425
4 Dr LTS Sdn	1850	2845
2 Dr XR5 Sdn	1500	2305

OPTIONS FOR TOPAZ

Auto 3-Speed Transmission +85
Air Bag Restraint +70
Air Conditioning[Std on LTS] +120
Power Door Locks[Opt on GS,XR5] +35
Power Drivers Seat[Std on LTS] +45
Power Windows[Opt on GS] +45

TRACER   1991

Tracer receives a mighty makeover. Base notchback and wagon body styles share the Escort's base engine, but the up-level LTS receives a much more powerful Mazda DOHC engine that produces 127 horsepower.

RATINGS (SCALE OF 1-10)

Overall	Safety	Reliability	Performance	Comfort	Value
6.2	4.5	6	7.6	7.1	5.6

Category E

	Trade-in	Market
4 Dr LTS Sdn	1600	2710
4 Dr STD Sdn	1295	2195
4 Dr STD Wgn	1300	2205

OPTIONS FOR TRACER

Auto 4-Speed Transmission +110
Air Conditioning +120
Power Door Locks +35
Power Steering[Std on LTS,Wgn] +40
Power Sunroof +90
Power Windows +40

1990 MERCURY

COUGAR   1990

Contoured front headrests are introduced on the Cougar. Front and rear styling is updated.

RATINGS (SCALE OF 1-10)

Overall	Safety	Reliability	Performance	Comfort	Value
6.2	5.6	5.8	6.8	7.8	5

Category C

	Trade-in	Market
2 Dr LS Cpe	1835	3005
2 Dr XR7 Sprchgd Cpe	2180	3575

OPTIONS FOR COUGAR

Auto 4-Speed Transmission[Std on LS] +65
Anti-Lock Brakes[Opt on LS] +75
Leather Seats +75
Power Door Locks +30
Power Drivers Seat +35

Don't forget to refer to the Mileage Adjustment Table at the back of this book!

Model Description	Trade-in Value	Market Value	Model Description	Trade-in Value	Market Value
Power Passenger Seat +35			Leather Seats +75		
Power Sunroof +80			Power Door Locks +30		

GRAND MARQUIS 1990

A driver airbag and tilt steering wheel are added to the standard features list.

Category B

	Trade-in	Market
4 Dr Colony Park GS Wgn	1895	2915
4 Dr Colony Park LS Wgn	2080	3200
4 Dr GS Sdn	2140	3295
4 Dr LS Sdn	2345	3605

OPTIONS FOR GRAND MARQUIS

Leather Seats +80
Power Door Locks +30
Power Drivers Seat +40
Power Passenger Seat +40

SABLE 1990

Standard driver airbag and knee bolsters improve crash protection. Antilock brakes are optional on the sedan and a CD player is optional for both body styles. The tilt steering wheel becomes standard.

Category C

	Trade-in	Market
4 Dr GS Sdn	1435	2355
4 Dr GS Wgn	1600	2620
4 Dr LS Sdn	1655	2710
4 Dr LS Wgn	1845	3025

OPTIONS FOR SABLE

6 cyl 3.8 L Engine +80
Anti-Lock Brakes +75

Power Drivers Seat +35
Power Passenger Seat +35
Power Sunroof +80
Power Windows[Opt on GS] +35

TOPAZ 1990

No changes.

RATINGS (SCALE OF 1-10)

Overall	Safety	Reliability	Performance	Comfort	Value
6.4	4.6	6	7.2	7.1	7.3

Category C

	Trade-in	Market
2 Dr GS Sdn	1120	1835
4 Dr GS Sdn	1160	1905
4 Dr GS 4WD Sdn	1280	2100
4 Dr LS Sdn	1325	2175
4 Dr LS 4WD Sdn	1435	2350
4 Dr LTS Sdn	1505	2470
4 Dr LTS 4WD Sdn	1555	2550
2 Dr XR5 Sdn	1165	1910

OPTIONS FOR TOPAZ

Auto 3-Speed Transmission[Std on 4WD] +65
Air Bag Restraint +60
Air Conditioning[Std on LTS] +95
Power Door Locks[Opt on GS,XR5] +30
Power Drivers Seat[Std on LTS] +35
Power Windows[Opt on GS,XR5] +35

MITSUBISHI 99

Model Description	Trade-in Value	Market Value	Model Description	Trade-in Value	Market Value

MITSUBISHI Japan

1994 Mitsubishi Diamante

1999 MITSUBISHI

3000GT 1999

The 1999 3000GT sees some styling changes and a few choice pieces of standard equipment, including antilock brakes and a power sunroof for the SL.

RATINGS (SCALE OF 1-10)

Overall	Safety	Reliability	Performance	Comfort	Value
N/A	N/A	N/A	8.8	6.6	N/A

Category F
2 Dr SL Cpe — 20785 24455
2 Dr STD Cpe — 15855 18655

OPTIONS FOR 3000GT
Auto 4-Speed Transmission +670
AM/FM Compact Disc Player +355

DIAMANTE 1999

Only one Diamante model is available, replacing the ES and LS models. Mitsubishi also adds some new standard features, options and exterior colors to this top-level model.

RATINGS (SCALE OF 1-10)

Overall	Safety	Reliability	Performance	Comfort	Value
N/A	N/A	N/A	7.4	7.5	N/A

Category D
4 Dr STD Sdn — 14695 17490

OPTIONS FOR DIAMANTE
Aluminum/Alloy Wheels +345
Dual Power Seats +625
Fog Lights +175
Infinity Sound System +315

Leather Seats +820
Power Drivers Seat +220
Power Moonroof +620

ECLIPSE 1999

For 1999, the Eclipse gets a host of new standard equipment, and there is a new Sports Value Option Package for buyers of the GS.

RATINGS (SCALE OF 1-10)

Overall	Safety	Reliability	Performance	Comfort	Value
N/A	6.8	N/A	8.4	6.6	N/A

Category F
2 Dr GS Hbk — 11475 13500
2 Dr GS-T Turbo Hbk — 14510 17070
2 Dr GSX Turbo 4WD Hbk — 16245 19110
2 Dr RS Hbk — 9955 11710

OPTIONS FOR ECLIPSE
Auto 4-Speed Transmission +595
AM/FM Compact Disc Player[Opt on GS, RS] +355
Air Conditioning[Opt on GS,RS] +620
Aluminum/Alloy Wheels[Std on GSX] +230
Anti-Lock Brakes[Std on GSX] +505
Cruise Control[Opt on GS,RS] +155
Keyless Entry System[Opt on GS,RS] +130
Leather Seats[Std on GSX] +485
Power Door Locks[Opt on GS,RS] +150
Power Moonroof[Opt on GS,RS] +480
Power Windows[Opt on GS,RS] +165

ECLIPSE SPYDER 1999

Sundance Plum Pearl exterior paint replaces Magenta Gray Pearl, black leather interior replaces the gray, and the GS-T model gets white-faced instrumentation.

RATINGS (SCALE OF 1-10)

Overall	Safety	Reliability	Performance	Comfort	Value
N/A	N/A	N/A	8.4	6.6	N/A

Category F
2 Dr Spyder GS Conv — 15200 17885
2 Dr Spyder GS-T Turbo Conv — 17190 20225

OPTIONS FOR ECLIPSE SPYDER
Auto 4-Speed Transmission +590
Anti-Lock Brakes +505
Cruise Control[Opt on Spyder GS] +155
Infinity Sound System[Opt on Spyder GS] +480
Keyless Entry System[Opt on Spyder GS] +130
Leather Seats[Opt on Spyder GS] +485

GALANT 1999

The all-new '99 Galant lineup features a new V6 engine option, more standard equipment and a GTZ model with a sport-tuned suspension.

Don't forget to refer to the Mileage Adjustment Table at the back of this book!

Model Description	Trade-in Value	Market Value

Model Description	Trade-in Value	Market Value

RATINGS (SCALE OF 1-10)

Overall	Safety	Reliability	Performance	Comfort	Value
N/A	7.3	8	7.4	7.9	N/A

Category D

Model	Trade-in	Market
4 Dr DE Sdn	10330	12300
4 Dr ES Sdn	11380	13545
4 Dr ES V6 Sdn	13225	15745
4 Dr GTZ Sdn	15920	18950
4 Dr LS Sdn	15765	18765

OPTIONS FOR GALANT

Auto 4-Speed Transmission[Opt on ES] +575
AM/FM Compact Disc Player +390
Aluminum/Alloy Wheels[Std on GTZ,LS] +345
Anti-Lock Brakes[Opt on ES] +670
Leather Seats[Std on GTZ,LS] +820
Power Moonroof[Std on GTZ,LS] +620
Side Air Bag Restraint[Std on GTZ,LS] +220

MIRAGE   1999

A new rear deck lid and taillamps, new seat fabric and some different exterior colors premier on the Mirage. The LS trim level also gets a few interior enhancements.

RATINGS (SCALE OF 1-10)

Overall	Safety	Reliability	Performance	Comfort	Value
N/A	N/A	N/A	7.4	6.4	N/A

Category E

Model	Trade-in	Market
2 Dr DE Cpe	6465	7790
4 Dr DE Sdn	6620	7975
2 Dr LS Cpe	8085	9740
4 Dr LS Sdn	8295	9995

OPTIONS FOR MIRAGE

Auto 4-Speed Transmission +535
AM/FM Compact Disc Player[Std on LS Coupe] +340
Air Conditioning[Std on LS Coupe] +605
Aluminum/Alloy Wheels[Std on Cpe] +245
Anti-Lock Brakes +500
Cruise Control +165
Keyless Entry System +115
Power Door Locks +180
Power Mirrors +80
Power Moonroof +425
Power Windows +195
Tilt Steering Wheel[Std on LS] +110

MONTERO   1999

Nothing changes on the Montero this year, but one less paint color is available.

RATINGS (SCALE OF 1-10)

Overall	Safety	Reliability	Performance	Comfort	Value
N/A	N/A	N/A	6.6	7.5	N/A

Category G

Model	Trade-in	Market
4 Dr STD 4WD Wgn	18765	22335

OPTIONS FOR MONTERO

Premium Pkg +620
AM/FM Compact Disc Player +245
Alarm System +210
Chrome Wheels +125
Compact Disc Changer +385
Heated Front Seats +195
Infinity Sound System +320
Keyless Entry System +150
Leather Seats +575
Power Drivers Seat +210
Power Moonroof +645

MONTERO SPORT   1999

A new Limited model joins the Montero Sport lineup and with it comes a powerful new V6 engine.

Category G

Model	Trade-in	Market
4 Dr ES Wgn	13665	16265
4 Dr LS Wgn	16605	19765
4 Dr LS 4WD Wgn	17505	20840
4 Dr Limited Wgn	18685	22245
4 Dr Limited 4WD Wgn	19545	23270
4 Dr XLS Wgn	17730	21110
4 Dr XLS 4WD Wgn	18585	22125

OPTIONS FOR MONTERO SPORT

Auto 4-Speed Transmission[Opt on LS] +635
AM/FM Compact Disc Player[Opt on LS, XLS] +245
Keyless Entry System[Std on Limited,XLS] +150
Power Moonroof[Std on Limited] +645

1998 MITSUBISHI

3000GT   1998

SL and VR-4 models get a standard power sunroof this year.

RATINGS (SCALE OF 1-10)

Overall	Safety	Reliability	Performance	Comfort	Value
N/A	N/A	7.8	8.8	6.6	N/A

Category F

Model	Trade-in	Market
2 Dr SL Gpe	18705	22270
2 Dr STD Cpe	14105	16790

OPTIONS FOR 3000GT

Auto 4-Speed Transmission[Opt on STD, SL] +555
Anti-Lock Brakes[Opt on SL] +415
Compact Disc W/fm/tapo[Opt on STD] +305
Fog Lights[Opt on STD] +110
Leather Seats[Opt on STD] +395

DIAMANTE   1998

All Diamantes get standard ABS and remote keyless entry for 1998.

Don't forget to refer to the Mileage Adjustment Table at the back of this book!

Model Description	Trade-in Value	Market Value

RATINGS (SCALE OF 1-10)

Overall	Safety	Reliability	Performance	Comfort	Value
N/A	N/A	8.6	7.4	7.5	4

Category D
4 Dr ES Sdn	13890	16535
4 Dr LS Sdn	16380	19500

OPTIONS FOR DIAMANTE

Luxury Group +1620
Aluminum/Alloy Wheels[Opt on ES] +280
Chrome Wheels +325
Dual Power Seats +510
Fog Lights[Opt on ES] +145
Infinity Sound System +260
Leather Seats[Opt on ES] +670
Power Drivers Seat[Opt on ES] +180
Power Moonroof[Opt on ES] +505

ECLIPSE   1998

The GSX gets a standard sunroof, power driver's seat and remote keyless entry.

RATINGS (SCALE OF 1-10)

Overall	Safety	Reliability	Performance	Comfort	Value
6.4	6.4	6.3	8.4	6.6	4.2

Category F
2 Dr GS Hbk	10685	12720
2 Dr GS-T Turbo Hbk	13420	15975
2 Dr GSX Turbo 4WD Hbk	14790	17610
2 Dr RS Hbk	9235	10995

OPTIONS FOR ECLIPSE

Auto 4-Speed Transmission +475
AM/FM Compact Disc Player[Opt on GS, RS] +290
Air Conditioning[Opt on GS, RS] +505
Aluminum/Alloy Wheels[Opt on GS, RS] +185
Anti-Lock Brakes +415
Cruise Control[Opt on GS, RS, Spyder GS] +125
Infinity Sound System +390
Keyless Entry System[Std on GSX, Spyder GS-T] +110
Leather Seats[Std on GSX, Spyder GS-T] +395
Power Door Locks[Opt on GS, RS] +120
Power Moonroof[Std on GSX] +395
Power Windows[Opt on GS, RS] +135

ECLIPSE SPYDER   1998

Eclipse Spyder GS gets air conditioning, AM/FM stereo with CD player and wheel locks. The Spyder GS-T is now flashier than ever before thanks to standard 16-inch chrome-plated alloy wheels. All models have a fresh black interior appearance with gray cloth.

RATINGS (SCALE OF 1-10)

Overall	Safety	Reliability	Performance	Comfort	Value
N/A	N/A	6.3	N/A	N/A	N/A

Category F
2 Dr Spyder GS Conv	13165	15670
2 Dr Spyder GS-T Turbo Conv	15785	18790

OPTIONS FOR ECLIPSE SPYDER

Cruise Control[Opt on Spyder GS] +125
Rear Spoiler[Opt on Spyder GS] +150

GALANT   1998

Solar tinted glass makes it harder to tan in the new Galant. The ES gets a standard manual transmission, and the ES and LS have a new black grille with chrome accents. The LS also benefits from standard antilock brakes. All models have a new heavy-duty starter and battery.

RATINGS (SCALE OF 1-10)

Overall	Safety	Reliability	Performance	Comfort	Value
7.4	6.5	7.8	8	8.3	6.5

Category D
4 Dr DE Sdn	8045	9580
4 Dr ES Sdn	9230	10990
4 Dr LS Sdn	11635	13850

OPTIONS FOR GALANT

Auto 4-Speed Transmission[Std on LS] +505
AM/FM Compact Disc Player +320
Air Conditioning[Opt on DE] +515
Aluminum/Alloy Wheels[Opt on ES] +280
Anti-Lock Brakes[Opt on ES] +550
Fog Lights[Opt on ES] +145
Leather Seats[Opt on ES] +670
Power Moonroof[Opt on ES] +505

MIRAGE   1998

Some new colors to choose from and a new heavy duty starter and battery make the Mirage more reliable.

RATINGS (SCALE OF 1-10)

Overall	Safety	Reliability	Performance	Comfort	Value
N/A	N/A	7.8	7.4	6.4	5.4

Category E
2 Dr DE Cpe	5880	7085
4 Dr DE Sdn	6040	7280
2 Dr LS Cpe	7070	8520
4 Dr LS Sdn	7285	8775

OPTIONS FOR MIRAGE

Auto 4-Speed Transmission +430
AM/FM Compact Disc Player[Opt on Sdn] +275
Air Conditioning[Opt on DE, Sdn] +495
Anti-Lock Brakes +410
Cruise Control +135
Keyless Entry System +95
Power Door Locks +145
Power Mirrors +65
Power Moonroof +350

Don't forget to refer to the Mileage Adjustment Table at the back of this book!

Power Windows +160
Tilt Steering Wheel[Opt on DE] +90

MONTERO 1998

A revised front bumper and grille, new fenders and new rear quarter panels mark the exterior changes. Inside is a new steering wheel, while the standard equipment list now includes ABS, air conditioning, third row seats and alloy wheels.

Category G

4 Dr STD 4WD Wgn	16043	19100

OPTIONS FOR MONTERO

Premium Pkg +490
AM/FM Compact Disc Player +200
Chrome Wheels +105
Compact Disc Changer +315
Heated Front Seats +160
Infinity Sound System +260
Keyless Entry System +120
Leather Seats +470
Power Drivers Seat +170
Power Moonroof +525

MONTERO SPORT 1998

Montero Sports get lots of features added to their option packages, and 4WD models now come with standard ABS.

RATINGS (SCALE OF 1-10)

Overall	Safety	Reliability	Performance	Comfort	Value
N/A	N/A	8.4	6	7.5	N/A

Category G

4 Dr ES Wgn	12245	14575
4 Dr LS Wgn	13525	16100
4 Dr LS 4WD Wgn	14400	17140
4 Dr XLS Wgn	16170	19250
4 Dr XLS 4WD Wgn	17175	20445

OPTIONS FOR MONTERO SPORT

Auto 4-Speed Transmission[Std on XLS, 2WD] +530
Appearance Pkg +730
AM/FM Compact Disc Player +200
Air Conditioning[Std on XLS] +495
Aluminum/Alloy Wheels[Opt on LS] +200
Cruise Control[Opt on LS] +125
Keyless Entry System +120
Limited Slip Diff[Opt on LS, 2WD] +165
Power Door Locks[Opt on LS] +140
Power Mirrors +80
Power Moonroof[Opt on LS] +525
Power Windows[Opt on LS] +145
Rear Heater[Opt on LS] +125
Tutone Paint[Opt on LS] +160

3000GT 1997

A value-leader base model is introduced. It has less than stellar performance and we think that it's embarrassing that this car is in the same lineup as the earth-scorching VR-4.

RATINGS (SCALE OF 1-10)

Overall	Safety	Reliability	Performance	Comfort	Value
N/A	7.9	7.7	8.8	6.6	N/A

Category F

2 Dr SL Cpe	17010	20495
2 Dr STD Cpe	12590	15170
2 Dr VR-4 Turbo 4WD Cpe	21225	25570

OPTIONS FOR 3000GT

Auto 4-Speed Transmission +450
Anti-Lock Brakes[Opt on SL] +335
Compact Disc W/fm/tape[Opt on STD] +250
Keyless Entry System[Std on VR-4] +90
Leather Seats[Opt on STD] +325
Power Sunroof +335

DIAMANTE 1997

After a one-year hiatus, the Diamante returns to the Mitusbishi lineup sporting clean, crisp styling, a full-load of luxury features, and a lower price. The old car barely registered on near-luxury car buyers' radar; this new one deserves consideration and a close inspection.

RATINGS (SCALE OF 1-10)

Overall	Safety	Reliability	Performance	Comfort	Value
N/A	N/A	8.5	7.4	7.5	3.9

Category D

4 Dr ES Sdn	11460	13810
4 Dr LS Sdn	13565	16345

OPTIONS FOR DIAMANTE

Luxury Group +700
Aluminum/Alloy Wheels[Opt on ES] +230
Anti-Lock Brakes +450
Fog Lights[Opt on ES] +120
Infinity Sound System +210
Keyless Entry System +155
Leather Seats[Opt on ES] +545
Leather Steering Wheel[Opt on ES] +55
Power Drivers Seat[Opt on ES] +150
Power Moonroof +415

ECLIPSE 1997

Revised styling makes the attractive Eclipse drop-dead gorgeous. New interior fabrics and paint colors debut as well. Antilock brakes are now available on the GS

Model Description	Trade-in Value	Market Value

Model Description	Trade-in Value	Market Value

model, and a CD player joins its standard equipment list. Two new exterior colors, new seat fabrics and a new interior color combination round out the changes.

RATINGS (SCALE OF 1-10)

Overall	Safety	Reliability	Performance	Comfort	Value
6.6	6.5	6.3	8.4	6.6	5

Category F

2 Dr GS Hbk	9355	11270
2 Dr GS-T Turbo Hbk	11530	13890
2 Dr GSX Turbo 4WD Hbk	12075	14550
2 Dr RS Hbk	8185	9860
2 Dr STD Hbk	7905	9525

OPTIONS FOR ECLIPSE

Auto 4-Speed Transmission +375
Air Conditioning[Opt on GS,RS,Spyder GS,STD] +415
Aluminum/Alloy Wheels[Opt on GS,RS] +150
Anti-Lock Brakes +335
Compact Disc W/fm/tape[Opt on GS,Spyder GS] +250
Keyless Entry System[Std on Spyder GS-T] +90
Leather Seats[Std on Spyder GS-T] +325
Power Door Locks[Opt on GS,RS] +100
Power Drivers Seat[Opt on GSX] +120
Power Moonroof +320
Power Windows[Opt on GS,RS] +110

ECLIPSE SPYDER   1997

The 1997 Spyder gets revised front and rear styling. Anti-lock brakes are now available on the GS model. Two new exterior colors, new seat fabrics, and a new interior color combination round out the changes.

RATINGS (SCALE OF 1-10)

Overall	Safety	Reliability	Performance	Comfort	Value
N/A	N/A	6.3	N/A	N/A	N/A

Category F

2 Dr Spyder GS Conv	11290	13600
2 Dr Spyder GS-T Turbo Conv	13385	16125

OPTIONS FOR ECLIPSE SPYDER

Air Conditioning[Opt on Spyder GS] +415
Cruise Control[Opt on Spyder GS] +105
Rear Spoiler[Opt on Spyder GS] +120

GALANT   1997

Mitsubishi shuffles the Galant lineup, replacing the S sedan with a base model called the DE. Front and rear fascias have been redesigned, and the interiors of all models have been upgraded by the addition of more ergonomically correct center armrests, upgraded upholstery, additional sound deadening material, and a new steering wheel.

RATINGS (SCALE OF 1-10)

Overall	Safety	Reliability	Performance	Comfort	Value
7.1	6.5	7.4	8	8.3	5.3

Category D

4 Dr DE Sdn	7140	8600
4 Dr ES Sdn	7670	9240
4 Dr LS Sdn	9680	11665

OPTIONS FOR GALANT

Auto 4-Speed Transmission[Opt on DE] +435
AM/FM Compact Disc Player +260
Air Conditioning[Opt on DE] +420
Aluminum/Alloy Wheels[Opt on ES] +230
Anti-Lock Brakes +450
Fog Lights[Opt on ES] +120
Keyless Entry System[Opt on ES] +155
Leather Seats[Opt on ES] +545
Power Moonroof[Opt on ES] +415

MIRAGE   1997

The Mirage is totally redesigned for 1997, sharing little with the model it replaces. Mitsubishi claims that interior size has been increased and that NVH have been reduced.

RATINGS (SCALE OF 1-10)

Overall	Safety	Reliability	Performance	Comfort	Value
N/A	N/A	8.3	7.4	6.4	5.4

Category E

2 Dr DE Cpe	5235	6385
4 Dr DE Sdn	5390	6575
2 Dr LS Cpe	6100	7440
4 Dr LS Sdn	6275	7655

OPTIONS FOR MIRAGE

Auto 4-Speed Transmission +345
Air Conditioning +405
Aluminum/Alloy Wheels[Opt on Sdn] +165
Anti-Lock Brakes +335
Compact Disc W/fm/tape +290
Cruise Control +110
Keyless Entry System +80
Power Door Locks +120
Power Moonroof +285
Power Steering[Opt on DE Cpe] +125
Power Windows +130

MONTERO   1997

The pricey Montero moves further up-market in anticipation of the Montero Sport's arrival to these shores. This year sees the deletion of the LS with a manual transmission, and the addition of a more powerful V6 engine. Leather seats are now available on the LS as well as the SR.

RATINGS (SCALE OF 1-10)

Overall	Safety	Reliability	Performance	Comfort	Value
N/A	N/A	N/A	N/A	N/A	3.5

Model Description	Trade-in Value	Market Value

Category G

4 Dr LS 4WD Wgn	13135	15825
4 Dr SR 4WD Wgn	16345	19690

OPTIONS FOR MONTERO

Air Conditioning[Opt on LS] +405
Alarm System +140
Aluminum/Alloy Wheels[Opt on LS] +165
Anti-Lock Brakes +295
Chrome Wheels +85
Heated Front Seats +130
Keyless Entry System +100
Leather Seats[Opt on LS] +385
Luggage Rack +80
Power Drivers Seat[Opt on LS] +140
Power Moonroof[Opt on LS] +430
Running Boards +190
Third Seat +355
Trailer Hitch +140

MONTERO SPORT 1997

This all-new entry from Mitsubishi is poised to steal sales in the ever-growing midsized sport-utility segment. Based on the same floorpan as the full-sized Montero, the Montero Sport is shorter in length, lighter in weight, and generally more nimble than its big brother.

RATINGS (SCALE OF 1-10)

Overall	Safety	Reliability	Performance	Comfort	Value
N/A	N/A	8.1	6	7.5	N/A

Category G

4 Dr ES Wgn	10270	12375
4 Dr LS Wgn	11895	14330
4 Dr LS 4WD Wgn	12510	15070
4 Dr XLS 4WD Wgn	15570	18760

OPTIONS FOR MONTERO SPORT

Auto 4-Speed Transmission[Std on XLS,2WD] +450
Appearance Pkg +745
LS Appearance Pkg +745
Premium Pkg +645
Air Conditioning[Std on XLS] +405
Aluminum/Alloy Wheels[Opt on LS] +165
Anti-Lock Brakes +295
Compact Disc W/fm/tape +240
Cruise Control[Opt on LS] +105
Infinity Sound System[Opt on LS] +210
Leather Seats[Opt on LS] +385
Limited Slip Diff +135
Luggage Rack +80
Power Door Locks[Opt on LS] +115
Power Moonroof[Opt on LS] +430
Power Windows[Opt on LS] +120
Rear Heater +100
Rear Window Wiper[Opt on ES] +75

1996 MITSUBISHI

3000GT 1996

Base model gets new cloth interior, while upper trim levels receive a choice of black or tan leather. Remote keyless entry gets panic feature, and several new colors are available.

RATINGS (SCALE OF 1-10)

Overall	Safety	Reliability	Performance	Comfort	Value
N/A	7.9	7.6	8.8	6.6	N/A

Category F

2 Dr SL Cpe	14465	17855
2 Dr STD Cpe	11990	14800
2 Dr VR-4 Turbo 4WD Cpe	19400	23950

OPTIONS FOR 3000GT

Auto 4-Speed Transmission +355
Chrome Wheels[Opt on SL] +235
Compact Disc Changer +260
Power Sunroof +275

DIAMANTE 1996

The only Diamantes sold this year were for fleet sales. So unless you see one at a rental car auction, chances are not good that you'll find a used 1996 model.

Category D

4 Dr ES Sdn	9005	11115

ECLIPSE 1996

Three new colors debut, audio systems are revised, and RS models can be ordered with a rear spoiler. Remote keyless entry systems get a new panic feature.

RATINGS (SCALE OF 1-10)

Overall	Safety	Reliability	Performance	Comfort	Value
6.6	6.5	6.3	8.4	6.6	5

Category F

2 Dr GS Hbk	7965	9835
2 Dr GS-T Turbo Hbk	9580	11830
2 Dr GSX Turbo 4WD Hbk	10655	13155
2 Dr RS Hbk	6990	8630
2 Dr STD Hbk	7000	8645
2 Dr Spyder GS Conv	10455	12910
2 Dr Spyder GS-T Turbo Conv	11590	14310

OPTIONS FOR ECLIPSE

Auto 4-Speed Transmission +305
Air Conditioning[Std on GS-T,GSX] +340
Aluminum/Alloy Wheels[Std on GS-T,GSX] +125
Anti-Lock Brakes +275
Cruise Control[Std on GS-T,GSX] +85
Keyless Entry System[Opt on GS,GSX,Spyder GS] +70
Leather Seats[Std on GSX,GS-T Turbo Conv] +265
Power Drivers Seat[Std on GSX] +100

Don't forget to refer to the Mileage Adjustment Table at the back of this book!

MITSUBISHI 96-95

Model Description	Trade-in Value	Market Value	Model Description	Trade-in Value	Market Value

Power Sunroof +275
Rear Window Wiper[Opt on GS] +60

GALANT 1996

A Homelink transmitter is available, and a panic feature debuts on keyless entry systems. New two-tone interiors debut, and four fresh exterior colors join the palette. Other changes include new wheelcovers, expanded availability of alloy wheels, and a heavy duty defroster with timer. LS models have standard leather seating and antilock brakes are available across the line.

RATINGS (SCALE OF 1-10)

Overall	Safety	Reliability	Performance	Comfort	Value
7.2	6.5	7.3	8	8.3	5.8

Category D
4 Dr ES Sdn	6960	8595
4 Dr LS Sdn	8535	10540
4 Dr S Sdn	6470	7985

OPTIONS FOR GALANT

Auto 4-Speed Transmission[Opt on S] +360
AM/FM Compact Disc Player +210
AM/FM Stereo Tape[Opt on S] +145
Air Conditioning[Opt on S] +345
Aluminum/Alloy Wheels[Opt on ES] +190
Anti-Lock Brakes +365
Cruise Control[Opt on S] +100
Keyless Entry System +125
Power Door Locks[Opt on S] +110
Power Moonroof[Opt on ES] +340
Power Windows[Opt on S] +110

MIGHTY MAX PICKUP 1996

No changes this year, the Mighty Max's last.
Category G
2 Dr STD Std Cab SB	7155	8725

OPTIONS FOR MIGHTY MAX PICKUP

Auto 4-Speed Transmission +575
AM/FM Stereo Tape +90
Air Conditioning +330
Power Steering +115
Rear Step Bumper +60

MIRAGE 1996

Four colors debut, and the Preferred Equipment Packages are revised a bit.

RATINGS (SCALE OF 1-10)

Overall	Safety	Reliability	Performance	Comfort	Value
6.6	5.3	8.1	8.2	7	4.6

Category E
2 Dr LS Cpe	4470	5585
2 Dr S Cpe	3730	4665
4 Dr S Sdn	3920	4900

OPTIONS FOR MIRAGE

Auto 3-Speed Transmission[Opt on Cpe] +220
Auto 4-Speed Transmission +265
AM/FM Compact Disc Player +185
AM/FM Stereo Tape[Opt on S] +125
Air Conditioning +330
Power Steering[Std on LS,Sdn] +105

MONTERO 1996

Refinements result in a better SUV this year. A passenger airbag has been installed, optional side steps make it easier to clamber aboard, and split-fold second row seats increase versatility. New colors, new seat fabrics and better audio systems round out the package.

RATINGS (SCALE OF 1-10)

Overall	Safety	Reliability	Performance	Comfort	Value
N/A	N/A	N/A	N/A	N/A	3.8

Category G
4 Dr LS 4WD Wgn	11700	14270
4 Dr SR 4WD Wgn	14140	17240

OPTIONS FOR MONTERO

Auto 4-Speed Transmission[Opt on LS] +360
Leather/Wood Pkg +305
Air Conditioning[Opt on LS] +330
Aluminum/Alloy Wheels[Opt on LS] +135
Anti-Lock Brakes[Opt on LS] +245
Chrome Wheels +70
Compact Disc Changer +210
Keyless Entry System[Opt on LS] +80
Leather Seats +315
Luggage Rack +65
Power Moonroof[Opt on LS] +350
Power Sunroof +315
Running Boards +155
Trailer Hitch +115

1995 MITSUBISHI

3000GT 1995

The VR-4 gains chrome-plated alloy wheels as standard equipment.

RATINGS (SCALE OF 1-10)

Overall	Safety	Reliability	Performance	Comfort	Value
N/A	8.7	7.5	8.8	6.6	N/A

Category F
2 Dr SL Cpe	12390	15485
2 Dr STD Cpe	10270	12835
2 Dr Spyder SL Conv	18045	22555
2 Dr VR-4 Turbo 4WD Cpe	16185	20230

OPTIONS FOR 3000GT

Auto 4-Speed Transmission[Opt on SL,STD] +290
Chrome Wheels[Opt on SL] +195

Don't forget to refer to the Mileage Adjustment Table at the back of this book!

MITSUBISHI 95

Model Description	Trade-in Value	Market Value	Model Description	Trade-in Value	Market Value

Compact Disc Changer[Opt on SL,STD,VR-4] +215
Power Sunroof +225

DIAMANTE 1995

The base Diamante sedan is sent out to pasture, available only to fleet purchasers such as rental car agencies. No other changes for the Mitsubishi flagship.

RATINGS (SCALE OF 1-10)

Overall	Safety	Reliability	Performance	Comfort	Value
7.3	7	8.2	8.4	8.4	4.3

Category D
4 Dr ES Sdn	7210	9130
4 Dr LS Sdn	8685	10990
4 Dr STD Wgn	7105	8990

OPTIONS FOR DIAMANTE
Compact Disc Changer +225
Power Moonroof +275
Power Passenger Seat +125
Traction Control System +200

ECLIPSE 1995

Radically redesigned, the new Eclipse sports bulging shoulders and no-nonsense looks, particularly in GSX guise. Engine ratings are improved for all models, while the turbocharged GS-T and GSX produce a mighty 210 horsepower at 6,000 rpm. Antilock brakes are optional on all models. Dual airbags are finally standard on the Eclipse.

RATINGS (SCALE OF 1-10)

Overall	Safety	Reliability	Performance	Comfort	Value
6.4	6.9	5.7	8.4	6.6	4.2

Category F
2 Dr GS Hbk	6560	8200
2 Dr GS-T Turbo Hbk	7830	9785
2 Dr GSX Turbo 4WD Hbk	8965	11205
2 Dr RS Hbk	6095	7620

OPTIONS FOR ECLIPSE
Auto 4-Speed Transmission +250
AM/FM Compact Disc Player +160
Air Conditioning[Opt on GS,RS] +275
Aluminum/Alloy Wheels[Opt on GS,RS] +100
Cruise Control[Opt on GS] +70
Infinity Sound System[Opt on GS] +215
Leather Seats[Std on GSX] +215
Power Door Locks[Opt on GS] +65
Power Drivers Seat[Std on GSX] +80
Power Sunroof +225
Power Windows[Opt on GS] +75

EXPO 1995

This is the last year for the Expo.
Category E
4 Dr STD Hbk	5300	6880

OPTIONS FOR EXPO
AM/FM Stereo Tape +100
Air Conditioning +270
Anti-Lock Brakes +225
Cruise Control +75
Luggage Rack +45
Power Door Locks +80
Power Windows +85

GALANT 1995

The much anticipated V6 engine never transpired in the 1995 Galant due to the increased costs and complexity involved in making the model. The 1995 Galants are available in three trim-levels, all with the 141-horsepower four-cylinder.

RATINGS (SCALE OF 1-10)

Overall	Safety	Reliability	Performance	Comfort	Value
6.8	7	6.7	8	8.3	4.1

Category D
4 Dr ES Sdn	5840	7390
4 Dr LS Sdn	6520	8250
4 Dr S Sdn	4750	6015

OPTIONS FOR GALANT
Auto 4-Speed Transmission[Opt on S] +295
AM/FM Compact Disc Player +175
Air Conditioning[Opt on S] +280
Aluminum/Alloy Wheels[Opt on ES] +155
Anti-Lock Brakes +300
Cruise Control[Opt on S] +80
Keyless Entry System +105
Leather Seats +365
Power Door Locks[Opt on S] +90
Power Drivers Seat +100
Power Windows[Opt on S] +90

MIGHTY MAX PICKUP 1995

The Mighty Max line is drastically reduced. Remaining is a four-cylinder two-wheel-drive regular-cab model.
Category G
2 Dr STD Std Cab SB	4075	5030

OPTIONS FOR MIGHTY MAX PICKUP
Auto 4-Speed Transmission +305
AM/FM Stereo Tape +75
Air Conditioning +270
Power Steering +95
Rear Step Bumper +50

MIRAGE 1995

The often changing Mitsubishi Mirage is once again revised, this time with dual airbags. LS versions get bigger alloy wheels.

Don't forget to refer to the Mileage Adjustment Table at the back of this book!

Model Description	Trade-in Value	Market Value	Model Description	Trade-in Value	Market Value

RATINGS (SCALE OF 1-10)

Overall	Safety	Reliability	Performance	Comfort	Value
6.8	5.8	7.7	8.2	7	5.2

Category E

	Trade-in	Market
2 Dr ES Cpe	3635	4720
4 Dr ES Sdn	3810	4945
2 Dr LS Cpe	4075	5295
2 Dr S Cpe	3145	4085
4 Dr S Sdn	3295	4280

OPTIONS FOR MIRAGE
Auto 3-Speed Transmission[Opt on Cpe] +245
Auto 4-Speed Transmission +175
AM/FM Compact Disc Player +150
AM/FM Stereo Tape[Opt on S] +100
Air Conditioning +270
Bucket Seats +40
Cruise Control[Opt on ES] +75
Power Door Locks +80
Power Steering[Std on ES,LS,Sdn] +85
Power Windows +85
Tinted Glass[Opt on S] +35

MONTERO   1995

The Montero LS gets a more powerful V6 that offers a 26-horsepower boost over last year's marginal 151-horsepower rating. Towing capacity increases to 5,000 pounds for all models. Tricky, electronic shock absorbers return to the Montero SR's standard equipment list, letting drivers choose between soft, medium or hard setting depending on their preferences.

RATINGS (SCALE OF 1-10)

Overall	Safety	Reliability	Performance	Comfort	Value
N/A	N/A	N/A	N/A	N/A	4.3

Category G

	Trade-in	Market
4 Dr LS 4WD Wgn	10490	12950
4 Dr SR 4WD Wgn	12345	15240

OPTIONS FOR MONTERO
Auto 4-Speed Transmission[Opt on LS] +280
Leather/Wood Pkg +485
Anti-Lock Brakes[Opt on LS] +200
Chrome Wheels +55
Compact Disc W/fm/tape +160
Keyless Entry System[Opt on LS] +65
Leather Seats +255
Luggage Rack +50
Power Drivers Seat +95
Power Sunroof[Opt on LS] +260

1994 MITSUBISHI

3000GT   1994

The 3000GT gets a passenger airbag. The 3000GT VR-4 gets a totally unnecessary 20 extra horsepower. But, hey, you won't find us complaining. To harness the extra power, the VR-4 switches to a six-speed manual gearbox. Freshened styling and CFC-free air conditioning round out the changes for all models.

RATINGS (SCALE OF 1-10)

Overall	Safety	Reliability	Performance	Comfort	Value
N/A	8.7	7.5	8.8	6.6	N/A

Category F

	Trade-in	Market
2 Dr SL Cpe	9375	12020
2 Dr STD Cpe	7925	10160
2 Dr VR-4 Turbo 4WD Cpe	12890	16525

OPTIONS FOR 3000GT
Auto 4-Speed Transmission +240
Compact Disc Changer +175
Leather Seats[Opt on SL] +175
Sunroof +105

DIAMANTE   1994

A passenger airbag and CFC-free air conditioning make the Diamante much friendlier to its passengers and the environment. A five-door wagon model introduced late last year comes with the 175-horsepower engine that is standard in the ES sedan. New wood trim and an upgraded Infinity stereo debut on the 1994 Diamante.

RATINGS (SCALE OF 1-10)

Overall	Safety	Reliability	Performance	Comfort	Value
7	6.8	7.5	8.4	8.4	3.8

Category D

	Trade-in	Market
4 Dr ES Sdn	6235	7995
4 Dr LS Sdn	7345	9415
4 Dr STD Wgn	5730	7345

OPTIONS FOR DIAMANTE
AM/FM Compact Disc Player +140
Anti-Lock Brakes[Std on LS] +245
Infinity Sound System[Opt on ES] +115
Keyless Entry System[Std on LS] +85
Leather Seats[Std on LS] +300
Power Drivers Seat[Std on LS] +80
Power Passenger Seat[Opt on ES] +100
Power Sunroof +200
Traction Control System +165

Model Description	Trade-in Value	Market Value

ECLIPSE 1994

Last year for the current edition of the Diamond Star sport coupe. Turbo engines gain a minimal boost in horsepower. Several of the models get more standard equipment in an attempt to increase sales in this edition's final year.

RATINGS (SCALE OF 1-10)

Overall	Safety	Reliability	Performance	Comfort	Value
N/A	N/A	8	8.4	6.8	3.9

Category F

	Trade-in	Market
2 Dr GS Turbo Hbk	5300	6795
2 Dr GS 1.8 Hbk	4535	5815
2 Dr GS 2.0 Hbk	4740	6075

OPTIONS FOR ECLIPSE

Auto 4-Speed Transmission +205
Air Conditioning[Opt on GS 1.8] +225
Anti-Lock Brakes[Opt on GS] +185
Compact Disc W/fm/tape[Opt on GS 2.0] +135
Cruise Control[Opt on GS 1.8] +55
Keyless Entry System[Std on GS 2.0] +50
Leather Seats +175
Power Door Locks[Std on GS,GSX] +55
Power Windows[Std on GS,GSX] +60
Sunroof +105

EXPO 1994

The Expo and LRV receive a driver airbag this year. Unfortunately, the Expo loses its up-level SP model, but base models do receive better standard equipment as a result. LRVs are available only as two-wheel-drive models in 1994; the AWD has been axed. This is the last year for the Expo LRV, although it will live on as the Eagle Summit wagon.

Category E

	Trade-in	Market
2 Dr LRV 1.8 Hbk	3655	4875
2 Dr LRV 2.4 Hbk	3845	5125
2 Dr LRV Sport Hbk	4840	6455
4 Dr STD Hbk	4030	5375

OPTIONS FOR EXPO

Auto 4-Speed Transmission +190
AM/FM Stereo Tape +80
Air Conditioning +220
Aluminum/Alloy Wheels +90
Anti-Lock Brakes +180
Cruise Control +60
Keyless Entry System +45
Luggage Rack +35
Power Door Locks +65
Power Sunroof +165
Power Windows +70

GALANT 1994

Dual airbags debut on this totally redesigned sedan. Four trim-levels are offered, ranging from the low-level S to the luxury ES and sporty GS models. An automatic transmission is standard on the ES and LS models. GS Galants come with a twin-cam engine rated at 160 horsepower.

RATINGS (SCALE OF 1-10)

Overall	Safety	Reliability	Performance	Comfort	Value
7	7	6.9	8	8.3	4.7

Category D

	Trade-in	Market
4 Dr ES Sdn	4655	5970
4 Dr GS Sdn	5665	7265
4 Dr LS Sdn	5095	6530
4 Dr S Sdn	3960	5075

OPTIONS FOR GALANT

Auto 4-Speed Transmission[Opt on GS,S] +230
Air Conditioning[Opt on S] +230
Anti-Lock Brakes +245
Compact Disc W/fm/tape[Std on GS] +220
Keyless Entry System +85

MIGHTY MAX PICKUP 1994

The Mighty Max gains a few safety features such as a high-mounted rear stop light and side-impact door guard beams. The vehicle is otherwise unchanged.

Category G

	Trade-in	Market
2 Dr STD Ext Cab SB	3875	4780
2 Dr STD Std Cab SB	3340	4120
2 Dr STD 4WD Std Cab SB	4875	6015

OPTIONS FOR MIGHTY MAX PICKUP

Auto 4-Speed Transmission +220
AM/FM Stereo Tape +60
Air Conditioning +220
Limited Slip Diff +75
Power Steering[Std on 4WD] +75
Rear Step Bumper +40
Sliding Rear Window +30
Velour/Cloth Seats[Std on 4WD] +60

MIRAGE 1994

The Mirage finally gains a standard driver airbag, but the LS loses its optional antilock brakes. The LS coupe gets the 1.8-liter engine that was formerly available only on the LS and ES sedans. S and ES coupes get power steering added to their standard equipment lists, and LS sedans get alloy wheels.

RATINGS (SCALE OF 1-10)

Overall	Safety	Reliability	Performance	Comfort	Value
N/A	N/A	7.8	8.2	7	5.7

Don't forget to refer to the Mileage Adjustment Table at the back of this book!

Model Description	Trade-in Value	Market Value
Category E		
2 Dr ES Cpe	2560	3410
4 Dr ES Sdn	2770	3690
2 Dr LS Cpe	3200	4265
4 Dr LS Sdn	3370	4490
2 Dr S Cpe	2350	3130
4 Dr S Sdn	2510	3345

OPTIONS FOR MIRAGE

Auto 3-Speed Transmission +130
Auto 4-Speed Transmission[Opt on ES,Cpe] +170
AM/FM Compact Disc Player +125
AM/FM Stereo Tape[Std on LS] +80
Air Conditioning +220
Cruise Control[Opt on ES] +60
Keyless Entry System[Opt on LS] +45
Power Door Locks[Std on LS] +65
Power Windows[Std on LS] +70
Tilt Steering Wheel[Opt on ES] +40

MONTERO   1994

Deciding to go the luxury sport-ute route, Mitsubishi drops its entry-level Monteros. The remaining models are the luxury-oriented LS and sporty SR. A driver airbag is standard on the 1994 Montero. Antilock brakes move from the standard equipment list to the option list of both trucks. CFC-free air conditioning, a third-row bench seat, heated outside mirrors, and a leather-wrapped steering wheel become standard equipment. SR models finally receive a gutsier engine to move this scale-tipping SUV around; a 215-horsepower V6 engine is now standard on that model.

RATINGS (SCALE OF 1-10)

Overall	Safety	Reliability	Performance	Comfort	Value
N/A	N/A	N/A	N/A	N/A	4.3

Category G		
4 Dr LS 4WD Wgn	8735	10785
4 Dr SR 4WD Wgn	10390	12825

OPTIONS FOR MONTERO

Auto 4-Speed Transmission[Opt on LS] +235
Air Conditioning[Opt on LS] +220
Aluminum/Alloy Wheels +90
Anti-Lock Brakes[Opt on LS] +160
Chrome Wheels +45
Compact Disc W/fm/tape +130
Keyless Entry System[Opt on LS] +55
Leather Seats +210
Limited Slip Diff +75
Luggage Rack +45
Power Drivers Seat +75
Power Sunroof +210
Running Boards +105

1993 MITSUBISHI

3000GT   1993

Leather makes its way into the top-of-the-line VR-4. Base models get bigger and better standard equipment lists that include air conditioning, power windows, power door locks, and cruise control (to name a few).

RATINGS (SCALE OF 1-10)

Overall	Safety	Reliability	Performance	Comfort	Value
N/A	6.9	7.4	8.8	6.6	N/A

Category F		
2 Dr SL Cpe	7660	9945
2 Dr STD Cpe	6440	8365
2 Dr VR-4 Turbo 4WD Cpe	9945	12915

OPTIONS FOR 3000GT

Auto 4-Speed Transmission +190
Compact Disc Changer +140
Leather Seats[Opt on SL] +145
Sunroof +85

DIAMANTE   1993

Base models are now called ES and gain cruise control, a power trunk opener and steering wheel mounted stereo controls.

RATINGS (SCALE OF 1-10)

Overall	Safety	Reliability	Performance	Comfort	Value
N/A	N/A	7	8.4	8.4	3.7

Category D		
4 Dr ES Sdn	4825	6350
4 Dr ES Wgn	4980	6550
4 Dr LS Sdn	5960	7840

OPTIONS FOR DIAMANTE

Diamante Euro Handling Pkg +375
Diamante Leather Seat Pkg +195
AM/FM Compact Disc Player +115
Aluminum/Alloy Wheels[Opt on ES] +105
Anti-Lock Brakes[Opt on ES] +200
Keyless Entry System[Opt on ES] +70
Leather Seats[Opt on ES] +245
Power Drivers Seat[Opt on ES] +65
Power Sunroof +165
Premium Sound System[Opt on ES] +85
Traction Control System +135

ECLIPSE   1993

The GS model gets a rear spoiler. GSX Eclipses now have standard antilock brakes. Some interior changes include new seat stitching and a new manual shift knob. Exterior changes are limited to new wheels and optional graphics.

Don't forget to refer to the Mileage Adjustment Table at the back of this book!

Model Description	Trade-in Value	Market Value		Model Description	Trade-in Value	Market Value

RATINGS (SCALE OF 1-10)

Overall	Safety	Reliability	Performance	Comfort	Value
N/A	N/A	7.6	8.4	6.8	4.2

Category F

2 Dr GS 2.0 Hbk	3775	4905
2 Dr GSX Turbo 4WD Hbk	5180	6730

OPTIONS FOR ECLIPSE

Auto 4-Speed Transmission +165
Air Conditioning +185
Aluminum/Alloy Wheels +70
Cruise Control +45
Keyless Entry System +40
Leather Seats +145
Power Door Locks +45
Power Windows +50
Premium Sound System +80
Rear Window Wiper +35
Sunroof +85

EXPO   1993

Mitsubishi increases the number of valves on the Expo's 2.4-liter engine, improving horsepower by 12 percent. Sport and AWD Sport Expo LRVs get the larger 2.4-liter engine found on the Expo. More equipment is now standard on the LRV Sport models.

Category E

2 Dr LRV Hbk	2805	3840
2 Dr LRV Sport Hbk	3635	4980
4 Dr SP Hbk	3790	5195
4 Dr STD Hbk	3105	4250

OPTIONS FOR EXPO

Auto 4-Speed Transmission +155
AM/FM Stereo Tape[Std on SP] +65
Air Conditioning +180
Anti-Lock Brakes +150
Cruise Control[Std on SP] +50
Luggage Rack +30
Power Door Locks[Std on SP] +55
Power Sunroof +135
Power Windows[Std on SP] +60
Premium Sound System +70

GALANT   1993

Sporty VR-4 model goes the way of the buffalo. GS and GSR models are combined into the previously named luxury LS. The former LS model is now the ES model. Base Galants are now called S models. Confused? So are we. All 1993 Galants use the SOHC 2.0-liter engine, which makes 121-horsepower this year with the addition of an extra two valves per cylinder.

RATINGS (SCALE OF 1-10)

Overall	Safety	Reliability	Performance	Comfort	Value
N/A	N/A	8.6	7.4	7.9	5.8

Category D

4 Dr ES Sdn	3355	4415
4 Dr LS Sdn	3935	5180
4 Dr S Sdn	2880	3790

OPTIONS FOR GALANT

Auto 4-Speed Transmission[Opt on S] +345
AM/FM Compact Disc Player +115
Air Conditioning +190
Aluminum/Alloy Wheels[Opt on ES] +105
Cruise Control[Opt on S] +55
Power Door Locks[Opt on S] +60
Power Sunroof +165
Power Windows[Opt on S] +60
Premium Sound System +85

MIGHTY MAX PICKUP   1993

The Mighty Max is unchanged for 1993.

Category G

2 Dr STD Std Cab SB	2725	3495
2 Dr STD 4WD Std Cab SB	4680	5995

OPTIONS FOR MIGHTY MAX PICKUP

Auto 4-Speed Transmission +185
AM/FM Stereo Tape +50
Air Conditioning +180
Bed Liner +60
Chrome Wheels +40
Limited Slip Diff +60
Power Steering[Std on 4WD] +60
Sliding Rear Window +25

MIRAGE   1993

The Mirage is totally redesigned this year, gaining size but losing weight. A coupe and sedan are offered in Base, S, ES and LS trim-levels. A five-speed manual transmission is standard on all vehicles, although an automatic is available on all Mirages except the S coupe. Antilock brakes make their first appearance on the Mirage, becoming an available option on the LS sedan.

RATINGS (SCALE OF 1-10)

Overall	Safety	Reliability	Performance	Comfort	Value
N/A	N/A	6.5	8.2	7	6.6

Category E

2 Dr ES Cpe	2090	2865
4 Dr ES Sdn	2230	3055
2 Dr LS Cpe	2420	3315
4 Dr LS Sdn	2600	3565
2 Dr S Cpe	2005	2745
4 Dr S Sdn	2170	2975

OPTIONS FOR MIRAGE

Auto 3-Speed Transmission +105
Auto 4-Speed Transmission +145
Air Conditioning +180

Don't forget to refer to the Mileage Adjustment Table at the back of this book!

MITSUBISHI 93-92

Model Description	Trade-in Value	Market Value	Model Description	Trade-in Value	Market Value

Aluminum/Alloy Wheels[Opt on Sdn] +75
Anti-Lock Brakes +150
Compact Disc W/fm/tape +130
Cruise Control[Opt on ES] +50
Power Door Locks[Opt on ES,S,LS,Cpe] +55
Power Steering[Opt on S,ES Cpe] +55
Power Windows[Opt on ES,S,LS,Cpe] +60
Tilt Steering Wheel[Opt on ES] +35

MONTERO   1993

Shift-on-the-fly four-wheel drive is introduced to the 1993 Montero. Antilock brakes become standard equipment for the SR and optional for the RS; they were formerly standard only on the LS. Top-of-the-line Monteros may now be ordered with a leather and wood package, for those who really want to get down and dirty.

RATINGS (SCALE OF 1-10)

Overall	Safety	Reliability	Performance	Comfort	Value
N/A	N/A	N/A	N/A	N/A	4.2

Category G
4 Dr LS 4WD Wgn | | | | 7010 | 8990
4 Dr RS 4WD Wgn | | | | 6815 | 8740
4 Dr SR 4WD Wgn | | | | 7245 | 9290
4 Dr STD 4WD Wgn | | | | 6660 | 8540

OPTIONS FOR MONTERO
Auto 4-Speed Transmission[Std on LS,SR] +185
Montero Lthr & Wood Pkg +260
AM/FM Compact Disc Player +70
Air Conditioning +180
Cruise Control[Opt on RS] +45
Fog Lights[Std on STD] +30
Leather Seats +170
Limited Slip Diff +60
Luggage Rack +35
Power Door Locks[Opt on RS] +50
Power Sunroof +170
Power Windows[Opt on RS] +55

PRECIS   1993

No changes for the last year of this little hatchback.
Category E
2 Dr STD Hbk | | | | 1385 | 1900

OPTIONS FOR PRECIS
Auto 4-Speed Transmission +145
AM/FM Stereo Tape +65
Air Conditioning +180
Power Steering +55

1992 MITSUBISHI

3000GT   1992

New paint. That's the only change for the highly touted 3000GT.

RATINGS (SCALE OF 1-10)

Overall	Safety	Reliability	Performance	Comfort	Value
N/A	6.9	7.4	8.8	6.6	N/A

Category F
2 Dr SL Cpe | 6445 | 8595
2 Dr STD Cpe | 5125 | 6835
2 Dr VR-4 Turbo 4WD Cpe | 8465 | 11285

OPTIONS FOR 3000GT
Auto 4-Speed Transmission +150
Air Conditioning[Opt on STD] +150
Anti-Lock Brakes[Opt on STD] +125
Compact Disc W/fm/tape +90
Leather Seats +120
Sunroof +70

DIAMANTE   1992

As a replacement for the low-tech Sigma, the Diamante offers V6 power delivering 175-horsepower in the base model, 202-horsepower in the LS. Antilock brakes are standard on the LS and optional on the base, and a driver airbag is standard on both models. A Euro Handling Package and an electronically controlled suspension that includes traction control is an available option on the LS.

RATINGS (SCALE OF 1-10)

Overall	Safety	Reliability	Performance	Comfort	Value
N/A	N/A	7.1	8.4	8.4	4.2

Category D
4 Dr LS Sdn | 4570 | 6095
4 Dr STD Sdn | 3950 | 5265

OPTIONS FOR DIAMANTE
Euro Handling Pkg +300
Luxury Pkg +140
AM/FM Compact Disc Player +95
Anti-Lock Brakes[Std on LS] +165
Leather Seats +200
Power Passenger Seat +65
Power Sunroof +135

ECLIPSE   1992

Freshened front-end styling includes aero headlights and a new air dam. The GS-X model loses leather trim from its options list.

RATINGS (SCALE OF 1-10)

Overall	Safety	Reliability	Performance	Comfort	Value
N/A	N/A	7.8	8.4	6.8	3.3

Category F
2 Dr GS Hbk | 3020 | 4025
2 Dr GS Turbo Hbk | 3410 | 4545
2 Dr GSX Turbo 4WD Hbk | 3955 | 5270
2 Dr STD Hbk | 2740 | 3650

Don't forget to refer to the Mileage Adjustment Table at the back of this book!

Model Description	Trade-in Value	Market Value

OPTIONS FOR ECLIPSE

Auto 4-Speed Transmission +125
Air Conditioning[Std on GSX] +150
Anti-Lock Brakes +125
Power Door Locks[Opt on GS] +35
Power Steering[Opt on STD] +60
Power Windows[Opt on GS] +40
Sunroof +70

EXPO   1992

Mitsubishi creates a van/station wagon hybrid. Designed to compete with everything from the Dodge Caravan to the Subaru Legacy wagon, the Expo seats seven while the Expo LRV seats five. Three models are available including a Sport all-wheel drive, a logical choice for residents of bad-weather states.

Category E

2 Dr LRV Hbk	2245	3210
2 Dr LRV Sport Hbk	2805	4010
4 Dr SP Hbk	2985	4265
4 Dr SP 4WD Hbk	3695	5280

OPTIONS FOR EXPO

Auto 4-Speed Transmission +125
Air Conditioning +145
Anti-Lock Brakes +120
Power Door Locks +45
Power Sunroof +110
Power Windows +50

GALANT   1992

The GS-X model is discontinued in favor of ultra-high performance VR-4. A 195-horsepower engine lurks under its sedate exterior. Standard antilock brakes, four-wheel steering, and leather seating surfaces are a few of the standard equipment items found on this very competent sedan. A Euro Handling Package and an Electronically Controlled Suspension are available options on the LS model.

RATINGS (SCALE OF 1-10)

Overall	Safety	Reliability	Performance	Comfort	Value
N/A	N/A	7.9	7.4	7.9	5.2

Category D

4 Dr GS Sdn	3010	4010
4 Dr GSR Sdn	3250	4330
4 Dr LS Sdn	2830	3775
4 Dr STD Sdn	2185	2915
4 Dr VR-4 Turbo 4WD Sdn	4465	5955

OPTIONS FOR GALANT

Auto 4-Speed Transmission[Opt on GS, STD] +200
AM/FM Compact Disc Player +95
Air Conditioning[Std on VR4] +155
Anti-Lock Brakes[Std on VR4] +165
Leather Seats +200

Power Door Locks[Opt on STD] +50
Power Sunroof +135
Power Windows[Opt on STD] +50

MIGHTY MAX PICKUP   1992

Safety-interlocks are now standard on manual transmission models, requiring the clutch to be fully depressed before the vehicle will start. The automatic transmission also gets a shift-interlock, requiring the brake to be depressed before the car can be shifted out of park. Two-wheel-drive Mighty Max models lose their rear-wheel antilock brakes.

Category G

2 Dr Mighty Max Std Cab SB	2235	2940
2 Dr Mighty Max 4WD Std Cab SB		
	3205	4215

OPTIONS FOR MIGHTY MAX PICKUP

Auto 4-Speed Transmission +140
Air Conditioning +145
Limited Slip Diff +50
Power Steering[Std on 4WD] +50

MIRAGE   1992

Base models finally lose the sticky vinyl interior in favor of full-cloth seats. LS models receive minor exterior trim changes.

Category E

4 Dr GS Sdn	1945	2775
4 Dr LS Sdn	1660	2370
2 Dr STD Hbk	1460	2085
4 Dr STD Sdn	1575	2250
2 Dr VL Hbk	1490	2125

OPTIONS FOR MIRAGE

Auto 3-Speed Transmission +95
Auto 4-Speed Transmission +115
Air Conditioning +145
Power Steering[Std on GS] +45

MONTERO   1992

An all-new Montero is introduced. The new Montero features new wheels, a new grille, more interesting sheetmetal, more curves around the edges, and a very serious-looking blackout treatment on the formerly chrome accessories. Horsepower is upped but only enough to keep pace with its 125-pound weight gain. Antilock brakes are standard on the LS and optional on the SR model, working in both two- and four-wheel-drive mode.

RATINGS (SCALE OF 1-10)

Overall	Safety	Reliability	Performance	Comfort	Value
N/A	N/A	N/A	N/A	N/A	5.2

Don't forget to refer to the Mileage Adjustment Table at the back of this book!

Model Description	Trade-in Value	Market Value
Category G		
4 Dr LS 4WD Wgn	6125	8060
4 Dr RS 4WD Wgn	6035	7940
4 Dr SR 4WD Wgn	6720	8845
4 Dr STD 4WD Wgn	5770	7590

OPTIONS FOR MONTERO
Auto 4-Speed Transmission[Std on LS,SR] +145
Air Conditioning +145
Anti-Lock Brakes[Opt on SR] +110
Compact Disc W/fm/tape +85
Leather Seats +140
Limited Slip Diff[Opt on SR] +50
Power Door Locks[Opt on RS] +40
Power Sunroof +140
Power Windows[Opt on RS] +45

PRECIS 1992

The bargain-basement Precis gets a nose job.

Model Description	Trade-in Value	Market Value
Category E		
2 Dr STD Hbk	1205	1720

OPTIONS FOR PRECIS
Auto 4-Speed Transmission +120
Air Conditioning +145
Power Steering +45

1991 MITSUBISHI

3000GT 1991

Dumping the Starion in favor of the 3000GT is one of the better decisions made by Mitsubishi this decade. Gorgeous styling, exceptional handling, and available all-wheel drive characterize the improvements the 3000GT has over Mitsubishi's previous sports cars. A driver airbag is standard on all models; antilock brakes are standard on the SL and VR-4 models.

RATINGS (SCALE OF 1-10)

Overall	Safety	Reliability	Performance	Comfort	Value
N/A	6.8	6.9	8.8	6.6	N/A

Model Description	Trade-in Value	Market Value
Category F		
2 Dr SL Cpe	5265	7115
2 Dr STD Cpe	3980	5380
2 Dr VR-4 Turbo 4WD Cpe	7290	9850

OPTIONS FOR 3000GT
Auto 4-Speed Transmission +120
Anti-Lock Brakes[Opt on STD] +100
Compact Disc W/fm/tape +75
Leather Seats +95
Power Windows[Opt on STD] +35

ECLIPSE 1991

Antilock brakes are offered on the GS-T and GSX models.

RATINGS (SCALE OF 1-10)

Overall	Safety	Reliability	Performance	Comfort	Value
N/A	N/A	7.3	8.4	6.8	4.2

Model Description	Trade-in Value	Market Value
Category F		
2 Dr GS Hbk	2480	3350
2 Dr GS Turbo Hbk	2795	3780
2 Dr GSX Turbo 4WD Hbk	3230	4365
2 Dr STD Hbk	2265	3060

OPTIONS FOR ECLIPSE
4 cyl 2.0 L 16V Engine +130
Auto 3-Speed Transmission +95
Auto 4-Speed Transmission +100
Turbo Pkg +440
Air Conditioning +125
Anti-Lock Brakes +100
Power Door Locks +30
Power Steering[Opt on STD] +50
Power Windows +35

GALANT 1991

A sporty GSR model is added to the lineup.

RATINGS (SCALE OF 1-10)

Overall	Safety	Reliability	Performance	Comfort	Value
N/A	N/A	7.6	7.4	7.9	5.2

Model Description	Trade-in Value	Market Value
Category D		
4 Dr GS Sdn	2580	3535
4 Dr GSR Sdn	2820	3860
4 Dr GSX 4WD Sdn	3175	4350
4 Dr LS Sdn	2340	3205
4 Dr STD Sdn	2005	2745
4 Dr VR-4 Turbo 4WD Sdn	3520	4825

OPTIONS FOR GALANT
Auto 4-Speed Transmission[Opt on GS,STD] +160
AM/FM Compact Disc Player +75
Air Conditioning[Std on VR4] +125
Anti-Lock Brakes[Opt on GS,GSX] +135
Power Door Locks[Opt on STD] +40
Power Sunroof +110
Power Windows[Opt on STD] +40

MIGHTY MAX PICKUP 1991

A Special Edition Package is added to the option list, featuring wide-spoke wheels, upgraded seats, better carpet, and a tachometer for four-wheel-drive models.

Model Description	Trade-in Value	Market Value
Category G		
2 Dr Mighty Max Std Cab SB	1960	2650
2 Dr Mighty Max 4WD Std Cab SB	2885	3900

OPTIONS FOR MIGHTY MAX PICKUP
Auto 3-Speed Transmission +110
Air Conditioning +120
Anti-Lock Brakes +90

Don't forget to refer to the Mileage Adjustment Table at the back of this book!

Model Description	Trade-in Value	Market Value

Limited Slip Diff +40
Power Steering[Std on 4WD] +40

MIRAGE 1991

No changes for the Mirage.
Category E

Model	Trade-in	Market
4 Dr GS Sdn	1655	2435
4 Dr LS Sdn	1485	2185
2 Dr STD Hbk	1340	1970
4 Dr STD Sdn	1425	2095

OPTIONS FOR MIRAGE
Auto 3-Speed Transmission +80
Auto 4-Speed Transmission +95
Air Conditioning +120
Power Door Locks +35
Power Windows +40

MONTERO 1991

The slow-selling two-door Montero is dropped in favor of the popular four-door. Base models are no longer available with an automatic transmission. RS models now come standard with an automatic. The top-end LS model is available with a manual or automatic transmission.
Category G

Model	Trade-in	Market
4 Dr LS 4WD Wgn	4565	6170
4 Dr RS 4WD Wgn	4360	5890
4 Dr STD 4WD Wgn	4080	5515

OPTIONS FOR MONTERO
Auto 4-Speed Transmission[Opt on LS] +105
Air Conditioning +120
Power Sunroof +115
Power Windows[Opt on RS] +35
Theft Deterrent System +55

PRECIS 1991

No changes for the Hyundai-twin.
Category E

Model	Trade-in	Market
2 Dr RS Hbk	1220	1795
2 Dr STD Hbk	1115	1640

OPTIONS FOR PRECIS
Auto 4-Speed Transmission +90
Air Conditioning +120
Power Steering +40

1990 MITSUBISHI

ECLIPSE 1990

The first car created by the Chrysler-Mitsubishi partnership, the Eclipse is available as a sporty hatchback with three available engines. Four-wheel disc brakes are standard on all models.

RATINGS (SCALE OF 1-10)

Overall	Safety	Reliability	Performance	Comfort	Value
N/A	N/A	5.7	8.4	6.8	3.6

Category F

Model	Trade-in	Market
2 Dr GS Hbk	2260	3055
2 Dr GS Turbo Hbk	2430	3285
2 Dr GSX Turbo 4WD Hbk	2900	3920
2 Dr STD Hbk	2035	2750

OPTIONS FOR ECLIPSE
4 cyl 2.0 L 16V Engine +105
Auto 4-Speed Transmission +75
Air Conditioning +100
Power Steering[Opt on STD] +40
Power Windows +25
Sunroof +50

GALANT 1990

Mitsubishi's highly acclaimed all-wheel-drive system is introduced to the American market sedan in the GS-X model. GS-X models have the same 135-horsepower engine as the GS. No other changes for the 1990 Galant.

RATINGS (SCALE OF 1-10)

Overall	Safety	Reliability	Performance	Comfort	Value
N/A	N/A	7.8	7.4	7.9	5.2

Category D

Model	Trade-in	Market
4 Dr GS Sdn	2070	2875
4 Dr GSX 4WD Sdn	2180	3025
4 Dr LS Sdn	1805	2510
4 Dr STD Sdn	1665	2315

OPTIONS FOR GALANT
Auto 4-Speed Transmission[Std on LS] +125
Air Conditioning +105
Anti-Lock Brakes +110
Power Door Locks[Opt on STD] +35
Power Sunroof +90
Power Windows[Opt on STD] +35

MIGHTY MAX PICKUP 1990

New four-cylinder and V6 engines are available in the 1990 Mighty Max, producing greater horsepower and torque. Models are otherwise unchanged.
Category G

Model	Trade-in	Market
2 Dr Mighty Max Std Cab SB	1810	2515
2 Dr Mighty Max 4WD Std Cab SB	2550	3545

OPTIONS FOR MIGHTY MAX PICKUP
Auto 4-Speed Transmission +90
Air Conditioning +100
Power Steering[Std on 4WD] +35

Don't forget to refer to the Mileage Adjustment Table at the back of this book!

Model Description	Trade-in Value	Market Value	Model Description	Trade-in Value	Market Value

MIRAGE 1990

The turbocharged model is dropped, no other changes for the Mirage.

Category E

4 Dr EXE Special ED Sdn	1385	2100
4 Dr RS Sdn	1250	1895
2 Dr STD Hbk	1155	1750
4 Dr STD Sdn	1200	1815
2 Dr VL Hbk	910	1375

OPTIONS FOR MIRAGE
Auto 3-Speed Transmission +55
Auto 4-Speed Transmission +55
Air Conditioning[Opt on RS,STD,VL] +100
Power Steering[Opt on RS,STD] +30

MONTERO 1990

No major changes for the Montero.

Category G

4 Dr LS 4WD Wgn	3825	5310
4 Dr RS 4WD Wgn	3525	4895
2 Dr SP 4WD Utility	3325	4615
4 Dr STD 4WD Wgn	3260	4525

OPTIONS FOR MONTERO
Auto 4-Speed Transmission[Std on LS,Sport] +100
Air Conditioning +100
Power Sunroof +95
Power Windows[Std on LS] +30

PRECIS 1990

New sheetmetal for Mitsubishi's econobox. This year the Precis is available as a base model or uplevel RS and LS.

Category E

2 Dr LS Hbk	1035	1570
2 Dr RS Hbk	935	1415
2 Dr STD Hbk	740	1120

OPTIONS FOR PRECIS
Auto 4-Speed Transmission +70
Air Conditioning +100
Power Steering +30
Power Sunroof +75

SIGMA 1990

Mitsubishi's answer to the Accord and Camry is the updated Sigma. For 1990 it receives a 3.0-liter V6 engine as standard equipment. Antilock brakes are available as a standalone option on the Sigma for the first time. Delayed accessory power allows the driver to close windows and the sunroof for up to 30 seconds after the ignition is turned off.

Category D

4 Dr Luxury Sdn	2145	2980

OPTIONS FOR SIGMA
Eurotech Pkg +250
Anti-Lock Brakes +110
Leather Seats +135
Power Sunroof +90

VANWAGON 1990

Category G

2 Dr STD Cargo Van	1510	2095
2 Dr STD Pass. Van	2295	3185

OPTIONS FOR VANWAGON
LS Pkg +100
Air Conditioning +100
Dual Air Conditioning +115
Power Steering +35
Power Sunroof +95
Power Windows +30

Don't forget to refer to the Mileage Adjustment Table at the back of this book!

NISSAN 99

Model Description	Trade-in Value	Market Value	Model Description	Trade-in Value	Market Value

NISSAN Japan

1996 Nissan 300ZX

1999 NISSAN

ALTIMA 1999

All 1999 models get two new exterior colors, improved speakers and a new head unit for the three-in-one stereo combo. The GLE trim level gets alloy wheels added to its standard equipment list, and all alloy wheels now have a bright finish instead of a painted finish. All SE trim levels are now called SE Limited (SE-L) models and come with additional equipment.

RATINGS (SCALE OF 1-10)

Overall	Safety	Reliability	Performance	Comfort	Value
N/A	N/A	N/A	8	7.8	N/A

Category D
4 Dr GLE Sdn	12905	15365
4 Dr GXE Sdn	10875	12945
4 Dr SE Sdn	12095	14400
4 Dr SE Limited Sdn	13315	15850
4 Dr XE Sdn	9305	11075

OPTIONS FOR ALTIMA
Auto 4-Speed Transmission[Std on GLE] +590
Air Conditioning[Opt on XE] +630
Cruise Control[Opt on XE] +180
Keyless Entry System[Opt on GXE] +235
Leather Seats[Std on GLE] +820
Power Drivers Seat[Std on GLE] +220
Power Moonroof +620

FRONTIER 1999

Two new King Cab models debut with a powerful V6 engine under the hood, and new standard and optional equipment is available.

RATINGS (SCALE OF 1-10)

Overall	Safety	Reliability	Performance	Comfort	Value
N/A	N/A	N/A	6	7.3	N/A

Category G
2 Dr SE Ext Cab SB	11265	13410
2 Dr SE 4WD Ext Cab SB	13825	16460
2 Dr XE Ext Cab SB	9615	11445
2 Dr XE 4WD Ext Cab SB	12195	14520
2 Dr XE Std Cab SB	8585	10220
2 Dr XE 4WD Std Cab SB	11180	13310
2 Dr XE V6 4WD Ext Cab SB	13120	15620

OPTIONS FOR FRONTIER
Auto 4-Speed Transmission +775
Air Conditioning[Std on SE] +605
Aluminum/Alloy Wheels[Std on SE] +245
Bed Liner +210
Compact Disc W/fm/tape +355
Cruise Control +155
Keyless Entry System +150
Power Door Locks +170
Power Mirrors +100
Power Windows +175
Sliding Rear Window[Std on SE] +90
Tilt Steering Wheel[Std on SE] +130

MAXIMA 1999

Traction Control is now available on models with automatic transmissions and, in addition to minor interior enhancements, four new colors debut. The SE trim level has been renamed SE-Limited (SE-L) and offers new standard features.

RATINGS (SCALE OF 1-10)

Overall	Safety	Reliability	Performance	Comfort	Value
N/A	7.5	9.1	8	7.8	N/A

Category D
4 Dr GLE Sdn	16280	19380
4 Dr GXE Sdn	13060	15550
4 Dr SE Sdn	15215	18115
4 Dr SE Limited Sdn	16020	19070

OPTIONS FOR MAXIMA
Auto 4-Speed Transmission[Std on GLE] +925
Aluminum/Alloy Wheels[Opt on GXE] +345
Anti-Lock Brakes +670
Bose Sound System[Std on GLE] +560
Compact Disc W/fm/tape[Opt on GXE] +595
Dual Power Seats[Std on GLE] +625
Heated Front Seats +300
Keyless Entry System[Std on GLE] +235
Leather Seats[Std on GLE] +820
Power Drivers Seat +220
Power Moonroof +620
Side Air Bag Restraint +220

Don't forget to refer to the Mileage Adjustment Table at the back of this book!

NISSAN 99-98

Model Description	Trade-in Value	Market Value	Model Description	Trade-in Value	Market Value

PATHFINDER 1999

Only the LE trim level sees change in 1999, with new body-color fender flares and SE-style alloy wheels, tires and tubular step rails.

RATINGS (SCALE OF 1-10)

Overall	Safety	Reliability	Performance	Comfort	Value
N/A	7	8.7	7.4	8.3	N/A

Category G

4 Dr LE Wgn	19615	23350
4 Dr LE 4WD Wgn	20740	24690
4 Dr SE 4WD Wgn	18330	21820
1999.5 4 Dr SE Limited 4WD Wgn	18675	22230
4 Dr XE Wgn	15790	18800
4 Dr XE 4WD Wgn	16835	20040
1999.5 4 Dr XE 4WD Wgn	17215	20495

OPTIONS FOR PATHFINDER

Auto 4-Speed Transmission[Std on LE] +765
Aluminum/Alloy Wheels[Opt on XE] +245
Bose Sound System[Std on LE] +520
Compact Disc W/fm/tape[Std on LE] +355
Cruise Control[Opt on XE] +155
Dual Power Seats +285
Fog Lights[Opt on XE] +105
Heated Front Seats[Std on LE 4WD] +195
Keyless Entry System[Opt on XE] +150
Leather Seats[Std on LE, SE Limited] +575
Limited Slip Diff[Std on LE 4WD] +200
Power Door Locks[Opt on XE] +170
Power Moonroof +645
Power Windows[Opt on XE] +175

QUEST 1999

Nissan redesigns its minivan for 1999 and adds a new SE trim level, standard driver-side sliding rear door and a more powerful engine.

RATINGS (SCALE OF 1-10)

Overall	Safety	Reliability	Performance	Comfort	Value
N/A	N/A	8.6	6.8	7.5	N/A

Category G

2 Dr GLE Pass. Van	17685	21055
2 Dr GXE Pass. Van	16120	19190
2 Dr SE Pass. Van	16970	20205

OPTIONS FOR QUEST

Compact Disc W/fm/tape +355
Dual Air Conditioning[Opt on GXE] +700
Dual Power Seats[Opt on SE] +285
Leather Seats[Std on GLE] +575
Power Moonroof +645

SENTRA 1999

Fresh front-end styling, a Limited Edition Option Package for GXE models, and some new paint colors constitute the changes for 1999. Nissan also renamed the SE trim level the SE-Limited (SE-L) and added more features.

RATINGS (SCALE OF 1-10)

Overall	Safety	Reliability	Performance	Comfort	Value
N/A	6.4	N/A	6.4	6.9	N/A

Category E

4 Dr GXE Sdn	8720	10505
4 Dr SE Sdn	10020	12070
4 Dr SE Limited Sdn	10180	12265
4 Dr XE Sdn	7735	9320

OPTIONS FOR SENTRA

Auto 4-Speed Transmission +590
AM/FM Compact Disc Player[Opt on GXE,SE] +340
Air Conditioning[Opt on XE] +605
Anti-Lock Brakes +500
Keyless Entry System[Std on SE Limited] +115
Power Moonroof +425

1998 NISSAN

200SX 1998

Exterior enhancements include new headlights, taillights, front and rear bumpers and revised grille. Three new colors are available for 1998.

RATINGS (SCALE OF 1-10)

Overall	Safety	Reliability	Performance	Comfort	Value
N/A	6.6	8.6	7.8	6.8	N/A

Category F

2 Dr SE Cpe	8310	9895
2 Dr SE-R Cpe	9510	11320
2 Dr STD Cpe	7585	9030

OPTIONS FOR 200SX

Auto 4-Speed Transmission +490
AM/FM Compact Disc Player[Opt on STD] +290
Air Conditioning[Opt on STD] +505
Anti-Lock Brakes +415
Keyless Entry System +110
Power Moonroof +395

240SX 1998

No changes to Nissan's sporty coupe.

RATINGS (SCALE OF 1-10)

Overall	Safety	Reliability	Performance	Comfort	Value
6.8	6.5	8.7	8.4	7.6	2.7

Category F

2 Dr LE Cpe	13180	15690
2 Dr SE Cpe	11295	13445
2 Dr STD Cpe	9805	11675

Don't forget to refer to the Mileage Adjustment Table at the back of this book!

NISSAN 98

Model Description	Trade-in Value	Market Value	Model Description	Trade-in Value	Market Value

OPTIONS FOR 240SX

Auto 4-Speed Transmission +490
AM/FM Compact Disc Player +290
Air Conditioning[Opt on STD] +505
Aluminum/Alloy Wheels[Opt on STD] +185
Anti-Lock Brakes +415
Cruise Control[Opt on STD] +125
Power Door Locks[Opt on STD] +120
Power Mirrors[Opt on STD] +75
Power Moonroof[Std on LE] +395
Tilt Steering Wheel[Opt on STD] +110

ALTIMA 1998

Altima is totally, and unnecessarily, redesigned for 1998. The Altima's new look is more wedge-shaped, with a trunk that looks like it has met the business end of a band saw. Standard equipment is up, including a CD player on every model except the XE.

RATINGS (SCALE OF 1-10)

Overall	Safety	Reliability	Performance	Comfort	Value
N/A	N/A	9	8	7.8	N/A

Category D

	Trade-in	Market
4 Dr GLE Sdn	11385	13555
4 Dr GXE Sdn	9570	11395
4 Dr SE Sdn	10485	12480
4 Dr XE Sdn	8175	9730

OPTIONS FOR ALTIMA

Auto 4-Speed Transmission[Std on GLE] +490
Air Conditioning[Opt on XE] +515
Aluminum/Alloy Wheels[Std on SE] +280
Anti-Lock Brakes +550
Compact Disc W/fm/tape[Opt on GXE] +490
Cruise Control[Opt on XE] +145
Keyless Entry System[Opt on GXE] +190
Leather Seats[Opt on SE] +670
Power Drivers Seat[Std on GLE] +180
Power Moonroof +505

FRONTIER 1998

Nissan introduces an all-new truck for 1998. This model, named the Frontier, is larger than the model it replaces, and has improved interior ergonomics.

RATINGS (SCALE OF 1-10)

Overall	Safety	Reliability	Performance	Comfort	Value
N/A	N/A	8.9	6	7.3	N/A

Category G

	Trade-in	Market
2 Dr SE Ext Cab SB	10250	12205
2 Dr SE 4WD Ext Cab SB	12265	14600
2 Dr STD Std Cab SB	7080	8430
2 Dr XE Ext Cab SB	8570	10200
2 Dr XE 4WD Ext Cab SB	10735	12780
2 Dr XE Std Cab SB	7685	9150
2 Dr XE 4WD Std Cab SB	9790	11655

OPTIONS FOR FRONTIER

Auto 4-Speed Transmission[Opt on 2WD] +645
Aluminum/Alloy Wheels[Std on SE, XE 2WD Ext Cab SB] +200
Bed Liner[Opt on STD, XE, 2WD] +170
Compact Disc W/fm/tape[Opt on XE] +290
Cruise Control[Opt on XE] +125
Keyless Entry System[Opt on XE] +120
Power Door Locks[Opt on XE] +140
Power Mirrors[Opt on XE] +80
Power Windows[Opt on XE] +145
Sliding Rear Window[Opt on XE] +70
Tilt Steering Wheel[Opt on XE] +105

MAXIMA 1998

Side-impact airbags are added to the optional equipment lists of the SE and GLE models. Sterling Mist is a new color choice for this sporty sedan.

RATINGS (SCALE OF 1-10)

Overall	Safety	Reliability	Performance	Comfort	Value
7.3	7.5	9	8	7.8	4.1

Category D

	Trade-in	Market
4 Dr GLE Sdn	14165	16865
4 Dr GXE Sdn	11535	13730
4 Dr SE Sdn	13425	15985

OPTIONS FOR MAXIMA

Auto 4-Speed Transmission[Std on GLE] +845
Aluminum/Alloy Wheels[Opt on GXE] +280
Anti-Lock Brakes +550
Bose Sound System +460
Climate Control for AC[Opt on SE] +180
Compact Disc W/fm/tape[Opt on GXE] +490
Dual Power Seats[Opt on SE] +510
Heated Front Seats +245
Keyless Entry System[Std on GLE] +190
Leather Seats[Opt on SE] +670
Power Drivers Seat +180
Power Moonroof +505
Side Air Bag Restraint +180

PATHFINDER 1998

The only changes to the 1998 Pathfinder include chrome bumpers for the XE model, the addition of air conditioning to XE and SE standard equipment lists and additions to the XE Sport Package equipment.

RATINGS (SCALE OF 1-10)

Overall	Safety	Reliability	Performance	Comfort	Value
7	7	8.8	7.4	8.3	3.5

Category G

	Trade-in	Market
4 Dr LE Wgn	17030	20275
4 Dr LE 4WD Wgn	18125	21575
4 Dr SE 4WD Wgn	15590	18560

Don't forget to refer to the Mileage Adjustment Table at the back of this book!

Model Description	Trade-in Value	Market Value
4 Dr XE Wgn	13335	15875
4 Dr XE 4WD Wgn	14315	17040

OPTIONS FOR PATHFINDER

Auto 4-Speed Transmission[Std on LE] +615
Aluminum/Alloy Wheels[Opt on XE] +200
Bose Sound System[Opt on SE] +425
Compact Disc W/fm/tape[Opt on SE] +290
Cruise Control[Opt on XE] +125
Dual Power Seats +235
Fog Lights[Opt on XE] +90
Heated Front Seats[Opt on SE] +160
Heated Power Mirrors[Opt on XE] +45
Keyless Entry System[Opt on XE] +120
Leather Seats[Opt on SE] +470
Limited Slip Diff[Std on LE] +165
Power Door Locks[Opt on XE] +140
Power Moonroof +525
Power Windows[Opt on XE] +145

QUEST   1998

No changes to the 1998 Quest.

RATINGS (SCALE OF 1-10)

Overall	Safety	Reliability	Performance	Comfort	Value
7.5	6.8	8.2	6.2	7.5	8.7

Category G

	Trade-in	Market
2 Dr GXE Pass. Van	14105	16790
2 Dr XE Pass. Van	11850	14110

OPTIONS FOR QUEST

Aluminum/Alloy Wheels[Opt on XE] +200
Anti-Lock Brakes[Opt on XE] +365
Captain Chairs (4)[Opt on XE] +380
Climate Control for AC +120
Compact Disc W/fm/tape[Opt on XE] +290
Dual Air Conditioning[Opt on XE] +575
Dual Power Seats +235
Leather Seats +470
Power Moonroof +525

SENTRA   1998

A new Sentra SE debuts, sporting the same 140-horespower engine and styling cues found in the 200SX SE-R coupe. Other changes include an exterior freshening that features new front and rear fascias.

RATINGS (SCALE OF 1-10)

Overall	Safety	Reliability	Performance	Comfort	Value
6.7	6.3	8.7	6.4	6.9	5.4

Category E

	Trade-in	Market
4 Dr GLE Sdn	8400	10120
4 Dr GXE Sdn	7640	9205
4 Dr SE Sdn	8855	10670
4 Dr STD Sdn	6130	7385
4 Dr XE Sdn	6840	8240

OPTIONS FOR SENTRA

Auto 4-Speed Transmission +490
Air Conditioning[Opt on STD] +495
Anti-Lock Brakes +410
Compact Disc W/fm/tape[Std on GLE] +350
Keyless Entry System[Opt on SE] +95
Power Moonroof +350

1997 NISSAN

200SX   1997

A spoiler is now standard on all models. An additional exterior color is the only other change for 1997.

RATINGS (SCALE OF 1-10)

Overall	Safety	Reliability	Performance	Comfort	Value
6.9	6.6	7.7	7.8	6.8	5.5

Category F

	Trade-in	Market
2 Dr SE Cpe	7220	8700
2 Dr SE-R Cpe	8550	10300
2 Dr STD Cpe	6390	7700

OPTIONS FOR 200SX

Auto 4-Speed Transmission +400
AM/FM Compact Disc Player +235
AM/FM Stereo Tape[Opt on STD] +105
Air Conditioning[Opt on STD] +415
Anti-Lock Brakes +335
Compact Disc Changer +320
Power Moonroof +320

240SX   1997

Extensive exterior changes update the look of the 240SX. A luxury model is introduced midyear.

RATINGS (SCALE OF 1-10)

Overall	Safety	Reliability	Performance	Comfort	Value
6.7	6.5	8.5	8.4	7.6	2.6

Category F

	Trade-in	Market
2 Dr LE Cpe	11650	14035
2 Dr SE Cpe	10435	12575
2 Dr STD Cpe	8800	10600

OPTIONS FOR 240SX

Auto 4-Speed Transmission +410
Air Conditioning[Opt on STD] +415
Aluminum/Alloy Wheels[Opt on STD] +150
Anti-Lock Brakes +335
Cruise Control[Opt on STD] +105
Leather Seats[Opt on SE] +325
Limited Slip Diff +170
Power Door Locks[Opt on STD] +100
Power Mirrors[Opt on STD] +60
Power Moonroof[Std on LE] +320

Don't forget to refer to the Mileage Adjustment Table at the back of this book!

Model Description	Trade-in Value	Market Value

ALTIMA 1997

1997 models are virtually identical to 1996 models, except for the addition of new emissions equipment.

RATINGS (SCALE OF 1-10)

Overall	Safety	Reliability	Performance	Comfort	Value
7.3	7	8.5	8	7.5	5.4

Category D

	Trade-in Value	Market Value
4 Dr GLE Sdn	10085	12150
1997.5 4 Dr GLE Sdn	10293	12400
4 Dr GXE Sdn	8075	9730
1997.5 4 Dr GXE Sdn	8315	10020
4 Dr SE Sdn	8885	10705
1997.5 4 Dr SE Sdn	9055	10910
4 Dr XE Sdn	7255	8740
1997.5 4 Dr XE Sdn	7440	8965

OPTIONS FOR ALTIMA

Auto 4-Speed Transmission[Std on GLE] +395
Air Conditioning[Opt on GXE,XE] +420
Aluminum/Alloy Wheels[Opt on GXE] +230
Anti-Lock Brakes +450
Compact Disc W/fm/tape[Std on GLE] +400
Cruise Control[Opt on GXE,XE] +120
Keyless Entry System +155
Leather Seats[Std on GLE] +545
Leather Steering Wheel[Opt on GLE] +55
Power Moonroof[Std on GLE] +415
Rear Spoiler[Std on SE] +215

MAXIMA 1997

The Nissan Maxima gets a new grille, headlights, bumpers and taillights. New alloy wheels and fog lights on the SE, new wheel covers on the GXE, and new aluminum wheels on the GLE round out the changes.

RATINGS (SCALE OF 1-10)

Overall	Safety	Reliability	Performance	Comfort	Value
7.2	7.1	8.9	8	7.8	4

Category D

	Trade-in Value	Market Value
4 Dr GLE Sdn	12385	14920
4 Dr GXE Sdn	9970	12010
4 Dr SE Sdn	11310	13625

OPTIONS FOR MAXIMA

Auto 4-Speed Transmission[Std on GLE] +690
Aluminum/Alloy Wheels[Opt on GXE] +230
Anti-Lock Brakes +450
Bose Sound System +375
Climate Control for AC[Opt on SE] +150
Compact Disc W/fm/tape[Opt on GXE] +400
Dual Power Seats[Opt on SE] +420
Heated Front Seats +200
Keyless Entry System[Std on GLE] +155
Leather Seats[Opt on SE] +545
Power Moonroof +415

PATHFINDER 1997

Changes to the 1997 Nissan Pathfinder include storage pockets added at all doors, a new exterior color and an available Bose sound system.

RATINGS (SCALE OF 1-10)

Overall	Safety	Reliability	Performance	Comfort	Value
7	7	8.5	7.4	8.3	3.9

Category G

	Trade-in Value	Market Value
4 Dr LE Wgn	14830	17870
4 Dr LE 4WD Wgn	15540	18720
4 Dr SE 4WD Wgn	13400	16145
4 Dr XE Wgn	10930	13170
4 Dr XE 4WD Wgn	11740	14145

OPTIONS FOR PATHFINDER

Auto 4-Speed Transmission[Std on LE] +500
Air Conditioning[Std on LE] +405
Aluminum/Alloy Wheels[Opt on SE] +165
Bose Sound System[Opt on SE] +345
Climate Control for AC[Opt on SE] +95
Cruise Control[Opt on XE] +105
Dual Power Seats +190
Fog Lights[Opt on XE] +70
Heated Front Seats[Opt on SE] +130
Keyless Entry System[Opt on XE] +100
Leather Seats[Opt on SE] +385
Limited Slip Diff[Std on LE] +135
Luggage Rack[Opt on XE] +80
Power Door Locks[Opt on XE] +115
Power Moonroof +430
Power Windows[Opt on XE] +120
Swing Out Tire Carrier +95

QUEST 1997

A few new colors are the only changes to the 1997 Quest.

RATINGS (SCALE OF 1-10)

Overall	Safety	Reliability	Performance	Comfort	Value
7.2	6.8	7.6	6.2	7.5	8.1

Category G

	Trade-in Value	Market Value
2 Dr GXE Pass. Van	12975	15635
2 Dr XE Pass. Van	10910	13145

OPTIONS FOR QUEST

Aluminum/Alloy Wheels[Opt on XE] +165
Anti-Lock Brakes[Opt on XE] +295
Captain Chairs (4)[Opt on XE] +310
Child Seat (1) +85
Compact Disc W/fm/tape +240
Cruise Control[Opt on XE] +105
Dual Air Conditioning[Opt on XE] +470
Keyless Entry System[Opt on XE] +100
Leather Seats +385
Luggage Rack[Opt on XE] +80
Power Door Locks[Opt on XE] +115

Don't forget to refer to the Mileage Adjustment Table at the back of this book!

Model Description	Trade-in Value	Market Value

Model Description	Trade-in Value	Market Value

Power Moonroof +430
Power Windows[Opt on XE] +120
Steer. Whl. Radio Cntrls[Opt on XE] +80

SENTRA   1997

The base model is now simply called "Base" instead of S. Nissan works to quiet the Sentra's interior by using a bigger muffler and reducing the number of suspension-mounting points.

RATINGS (SCALE OF 1-10)

Overall	Safety	Reliability	Performance	Comfort	Value
6.6	6.1	7.6	6.4	6.9	5.8

Category E

	Trade-in	Market
4 Dr GLE Sdn	7320	8925
4 Dr GXE Sdn	6740	8220
4 Dr STD Sdn	5250	6405
4 Dr XE Sdn	6070	7405

OPTIONS FOR SENTRA

Auto 4-Speed Transmission +360
AM/FM Compact Disc Player +225
Air Conditioning[Opt on STD] +405
Alarm System[Opt on GXE] +200
Anti-Lock Brakes +335
Power Moonroof +285
Rear Spoiler +105

TRUCK   1997
HALF TON

Category G

	Trade-in	Market
2 Dr STD Std Cab SB	5805	6995
2 Dr XE Std Cab SB	6555	7900
2 Dr XE 4WD Std Cab SB	8685	10465

KING CAB

Category G

	Trade-in	Market
2 Dr SE Ext Cab SB	9295	11200
2 Dr SE 4WD Ext Cab SB	11200	13495
2 Dr XE Ext Cab SB	7505	9040
2 Dr XE 4WD Ext Cab SB	9435	11365

OPTIONS FOR TRUCK

AM/FM Stereo Tape[Std on SE] +110
Air Conditioning[Std on SE] +405
Aluminum/Alloy Wheels[Std on SE] +165
Bed Liner[Std on SE] +140
Power Steering[Opt on STD] +140

1996 NISSAN

200SX   1996

Body-color door handles and outside mirrors are newly standard on SE and SE-R models.

RATINGS (SCALE OF 1-10)

Overall	Safety	Reliability	Performance	Comfort	Value
6.9	6.5	7.5	7.8	6.8	6

Category F

	Trade-in	Market
2 Dr SE Cpe	6385	7885
2 Dr SE-R Cpe	7470	9225
2 Dr STD Cpe	5765	7120

OPTIONS FOR 200SX

Auto 4-Speed Transmission +310
AM/FM Stereo Tape[Opt on STD] +85
Air Conditioning[Opt on STD] +340
Anti-Lock Brakes +275
Power Moonroof +265
Rear Spoiler[Opt on SE] +100

240SX   1996

Sporty new fabrics and a new grille are the only changes to the attractive 240SX.

RATINGS (SCALE OF 1-10)

Overall	Safety	Reliability	Performance	Comfort	Value
7	6.5	8.3	8.4	7.6	4

Category F

	Trade-in	Market
2 Dr SE Cpe	8950	11050
2 Dr STD Cpe	7645	9440

OPTIONS FOR 240SX

Auto 4-Speed Transmission +325
Air Conditioning[Std on SE] +340
Aluminum/Alloy Wheels[Std on SE] +125
Anti-Lock Brakes +275
Cruise Control[Std on SE] +85
Keyless Entry System +70
Leather Seats +265
Limited Slip Diff +140
Power Door Locks[Std on SE] +80
Power Sunroof +275
Steer. Whl. Radio Cntrls +70

300ZX   1996

It's the end of the world as we know it. The final Z-car is produced for 1996.

RATINGS (SCALE OF 1-10)

Overall	Safety	Reliability	Performance	Comfort	Value
N/A	N/A	N/A	N/A	N/A	4.2

Category F

	Trade-in	Market
2 Dr 2+2 Cpe	16255	20070
2 Dr STD Conv	18955	23400
2 Dr STD Cpe	15735	19425
2 Dr STD Turbo Cpe	18485	22820

OPTIONS FOR 300ZX

Auto 4-Speed Transmission +365
Glass Panel T-tops[Std on 2+2, Turbo] +400
Leather Seats[Std on Conv] +265
Power Drivers Seat[Std on Turbo] +100

EDMUND'S® USED CARS & TRUCKS

Model Description	Trade-in Value	Market Value

ALTIMA 1996

New wheelcovers, power lock logic and fresh GXE upholstery update this hot-selling sedan.

RATINGS (SCALE OF 1-10)

Overall	Safety	Reliability	Performance	Comfort	Value
7.4	7	8.8	8	7.5	5.9

Category D

	Trade-in	Market
4 Dr GLE Sdn	9115	11255
4 Dr GXE Sdn	6790	8385
4 Dr SE Sdn	7800	9630
4 Dr XE Sdn	5915	7300

OPTIONS FOR ALTIMA

Auto 4-Speed Transmission[Std on GLE] +335
AM/FM Stereo Tape[Std on SE] +145
Air Conditioning[Opt on GXE,XE] +345
Anti-Lock Brakes +365
Cruise Control[Opt on GXE,XE] +100
Leather Seats +445
Power Moonroof +340

MAXIMA 1996

All new for 1995, the excellent Maxima receives few changes for 1996. A four-way power passenger seat is available, a new center console cupholder will hold a Big Gulp, and two new colors grace the Maxima's decidedly dull flanks. Taillights are as ugly as ever.

RATINGS (SCALE OF 1-10)

Overall	Safety	Reliability	Performance	Comfort	Value
7.2	7.1	8.9	8	7.8	4

Category D

	Trade-in	Market
4 Dr GLE Sdn	10715	13230
4 Dr GXE Sdn	8755	10810
4 Dr SE Sdn	9735	12020

OPTIONS FOR MAXIMA

Auto 4-Speed Transmission[Std on GLE] +515
Aluminum/Alloy Wheels[Opt on GXE] +190
Anti-Lock Brakes +365
Bose Sound System +305
Climate Control for AC[Opt on SE] +120
Compact Disc W/fm/tape[Opt on GXE] +325
Heated Front Seats +165
Keyless Entry System[Std on GLE] +125
Leather Seats[Opt on SE] +445
Power Moonroof +340

PATHFINDER 1996

Outstanding new Pathfinder debuts with dual airbags and great styling. Engine output is up, but the Pathfinder is still not going to win any drag races. The new interior is open, airy, and much more comfortable than most of its competitors.

RATINGS (SCALE OF 1-10)

Overall	Safety	Reliability	Performance	Comfort	Value
7.4	6.8	7.5	7.4	8.3	7

Category G

	Trade-in	Market
4 Dr LE Wgn	13200	16100
4 Dr LE 4WD Wgn	13980	17050
4 Dr SE 4WD Wgn	12145	14810
4 Dr XE Wgn	9625	11740
4 Dr XE 4WD Wgn	10440	12730

OPTIONS FOR PATHFINDER

Auto 4-Speed Transmission[Std on LE] +405
Air Conditioning[Std on LE] +330
Climate Control for AC[Opt on SE] +80
Cruise Control[Opt on XE] +85
Dual Power Seats +155
Fog Lights[Opt on XE] +60
Heated Front Seats[Opt on SE] +105
Keyless Entry System[Opt on XE] +80
Leather Seats[Opt on SE] +315
Limited Slip Diff[Std on LE] +110
Luggage Rack[Opt on XE] +65
Power Door Locks[Opt on XE] +95
Power Moonroof +350
Power Windows[Opt on XE] +95
Swing Out Tire Carrier +80

QUEST 1996

Substantial upgrades include dual airbags, integrated child safety seats, side-impact protection meeting 1997 passenger car standards, revamped fabrics, new colors, freshened styling, and a cool, in-dash six-disc CD changer. The Quest is still in the hunt.

RATINGS (SCALE OF 1-10)

Overall	Safety	Reliability	Performance	Comfort	Value
7.1	6.6	6.8	6.2	7.5	8.5

Category G

	Trade-in	Market
2 Dr GXE Pass. Van	11215	13675
2 Dr XE Pass. Van	9555	11655

OPTIONS FOR QUEST

Aluminum/Alloy Wheels[Opt on XE] +135
Anti-Lock Brakes[Opt on XE] +245
Child Seat (1) +70
Climate Control for AC +80
Cruise Control[Opt on XE] +85
Dual Air Conditioning[Opt on XE] +385
Keyless Entry System[Opt on XE] +80
Leather Seats +315
Luggage Rack[Opt on XE] +65
Power Door Locks[Opt on XE] +95
Power Passenger Seat +110
Power Windows[Opt on XE] +95
Privacy Glass[Opt on XE] +110

Don't forget to refer to the Mileage Adjustment Table at the back of this book!

NISSAN 96-95

Model Description	Trade-in Value	Market Value	Model Description	Trade-in Value	Market Value

SENTRA 1996

Prices have crept up, making the Sentra a hard sell against the Neon, Prizm and Cavalier. Still, you may be able to find a good deal on a former rental vehicle. We've seen tons of them at the Alamo rental lots.

RATINGS (SCALE OF 1-10)

Overall	Safety	Reliability	Performance	Comfort	Value
6.7	6.2	7.7	6.4	6.9	6.2

Category E
4 Dr GLE Sdn	6470	8090
4 Dr GXE Sdn	5970	7460
4 Dr STD Sdn	4615	5770
4 Dr XE Sdn	5540	6925

OPTIONS FOR SENTRA
Auto 4-Speed Transmission +325
AM/FM Stereo Tape[Opt on STD] +125
Air Conditioning[Opt on STD] +330
Anti-Lock Brakes +275

TRUCK 1996

No changes for the Truck.

RATINGS (SCALE OF 1-10)

Overall	Safety	Reliability	Performance	Comfort	Value
N/A	5.2	7.5	6	6.1	N/A

HALF TON

Category G
2 Dr STD Std Cab SB	5170	6305
2 Dr XE Std Cab SB	5835	7115
2 Dr XE 4WD Std Cab SB	7600	9270

KING CAB

Category G
2 Dr SE Ext Cab SB	8280	10100
2 Dr SE 4WD Ext Cab SB	9990	12180
2 Dr XE Ext Cab SB	6785	8275
2 Dr XE 4WD Ext Cab SB	8440	10295

OPTIONS FOR TRUCK
Auto 4-Speed Transmission +405
AM/FM Stereo Tape +90
Air Conditioning[Std on SE] +330
Aluminum/Alloy Wheels[Std on SE] +135
Center Console[Std on 2WD] +65
Chrome Bumpers[Std on SE] +65
Chrome Wheels +70
Cruise Control[Std on SE] +85
Flip-Up Sunroof[Opt on 4WD] +135
Power Steering[Opt on STD] +115
Power Windows[Opt on 4WD] +95
Privacy Glass[Std on SE] +110
Tilt Steering Wheel[Opt on Half Ton] +70

1995 NISSAN

200SX 1995

A Sentra derived 200SX is introduced to the sporting public. Basically a two-door version of the redesigned Sentra, the 200SX comes equipped with dual airbags. The 200SX has two available powerplants, a 1.6-liter four-cylinder that produces 115-horsepower or a 2.0-liter four that is good for 140 ponies.

RATINGS (SCALE OF 1-10)

Overall	Safety	Reliability	Performance	Comfort	Value
7.1	7.2	8.1	7.8	6.8	5.5

Category F
2 Dr SE Cpe	5555	6945
2 Dr SE-R Cpe	6350	7940
2 Dr STD Cpe	4880	6100

OPTIONS FOR 200SX
Auto 4-Speed Transmission +265
AM/FM Stereo Tape[Opt on STD] +70
Air Conditioning[Opt on STD] +275
Anti-Lock Brakes +225
Power Moonroof +215
Rear Spoiler[Opt on SE] +80

240SX 1995

Totally redesigned, the 240SX loses its hatchback and convertible body styles. Available as a base or SE model, the 240 uses the same engine as the previous generation model. Dual airbags are standard on the new 240SX as are side door beams that help the car meet federal side-impact standards.

RATINGS (SCALE OF 1-10)

Overall	Safety	Reliability	Performance	Comfort	Value
6.8	7.1	7.3	8.4	7.6	3.5

Category F
2 Dr SE Cpe	6835	8545
2 Dr STD Cpe	5890	7365

OPTIONS FOR 240SX
Auto 4-Speed Transmission +280
Air Conditioning[Std on SE] +275
Aluminum/Alloy Wheels[Std on SE] +100
Anti-Lock Brakes +225
Cruise Control[Std on SE] +70
Leather Seats +215
Leather Steering Wheel[Opt on SE] +50
Limited Slip Diff +115
Power Door Locks[Std on SE] +65
Power Moonroof +215

300ZX 1995

No changes for the 300ZX.

Model Description	Trade-in Value	Market Value

RATINGS (SCALE OF 1-10)

Overall	Safety	Reliability	Performance	Comfort	Value
N/A	N/A	N/A	N/A	N/A	4.1

Category F

2 Dr 2+2 Cpe	14120	17650
2 Dr STD Conv	16865	21080
2 Dr STD Cpe	13710	17140
2 Dr STD Turbo Cpe	15905	19880

OPTIONS FOR 300ZX

Auto 4-Speed Transmission +295
Glass Panel T-tops[Std on 2+2, Turbo] +325
Leather Seats[Std on Conv] +215
Power Drivers Seat[Opt on STD Cpe] +80

ALTIMA 1995

Minor exterior tweaks to the grille, taillights and wheels are the only changes for this attractive compact from Tennessee.

RATINGS (SCALE OF 1-10)

Overall	Safety	Reliability	Performance	Comfort	Value
7.4	7.7	7.9	8	7.5	5.8

Category D

4 Dr GLE Sdn	7095	8980
4 Dr GXE Sdn	5465	6915
4 Dr SE Sdn	6220	7875
4 Dr XE Sdn	5055	6400

OPTIONS FOR ALTIMA

Auto 4-Speed Transmission[Std on GLE] +275
Air Conditioning[Opt on GXE,XE] +280
Anti-Lock Brakes +300
Cruise Control[Opt on GXE,XE] +80
Power Moonroof[Opt on GXE] +275

MAXIMA 1995

Wow, what a beauty. The redesigned Maxima bows with an aerodynamic shape and a lengthened wheelbase. The new Maxima is available as a budget-minded GXE, sporty SE or luxurious GLE. All Maximas get the 190-horsepower engine previously exclusive to the SE.

RATINGS (SCALE OF 1-10)

Overall	Safety	Reliability	Performance	Comfort	Value
7.4	7.7	8.5	8	7.8	5

Category D

4 Dr GLE Sdn	8655	10955
4 Dr GXE Sdn	7140	9035
4 Dr SE Sdn	8150	10315

OPTIONS FOR MAXIMA

Auto 4-Speed Transmission[Std on GLE] +430
Aluminum/Alloy Wheels[Opt on GXE] +155
Anti-Lock Brakes +300

Climate Control for AC[Opt on SE] +100
Compact Disc W/fm/tape[Std on GLE] +265
Heated Front Seats +135
Keyless Entry System[Std on GLE] +105
Leather Seats[Std on GLE] +365
Power Drivers Seat[Std on GLE] +100
Power Moonroof +275
Rear Spoiler[Std on SE] +145

PATHFINDER 1995

Whoopee. A two-wheel-drive version of Nissan's ancient sport utility is now available in LE flavor.

RATINGS (SCALE OF 1-10)

Overall	Safety	Reliability	Performance	Comfort	Value
6.7	4.3	9.1	7.6	7.5	4.8

Category G

4 Dr LE Wgn	10880	13435
4 Dr LE 4WD Wgn	11685	14425
4 Dr SE 4WD Wgn	10135	12515
4 Dr XE Wgn	8150	10060
4 Dr XE 4WD Wgn	8910	11000

OPTIONS FOR PATHFINDER

Auto 4-Speed Transmission[Std on LE] +400
Air Conditioning[Std on LE] +270
Camper/Towing Package +100
Compact Disc W/fm/tape[Opt on SE] +160
Cruise Control[Opt on XE] +70
Fog Lights[Opt on XE] +50
Heated Front Seats[Opt on SE] +85
Intermittent Wipers[Opt on XE] +30
Keyless Entry System[Opt on XE] +65
Leather Seats[Opt on SE] +255
Limited Slip Diff[Std on LE] +90
Power Door Locks[Opt on XE] +75
Power Windows[Opt on XE] +80
Swing Out Tire Carrier[Opt on XE] +65

QUEST 1995

GXE models get standard captain's chairs for second-row occupants. The Extra Performance Package is renamed the Handling Package. No other significant changes for the Quest.

RATINGS (SCALE OF 1-10)

Overall	Safety	Reliability	Performance	Comfort	Value
7	6.5	6	6.2	7.1	9

Category G

2 Dr GXE Pass. Van	9240	11410
2 Dr XE Pass. Van	8025	9905

OPTIONS FOR QUEST

Anti-Lock Brakes[Opt on XE] +200
Cruise Control[Opt on XE] +70
Dual Air Conditioning[Opt on XE] +315
Keyless Entry System +65

Model Description	Trade-in Value	Market Value	Model Description	Trade-in Value	Market Value
Leather Seats +255			Air Conditioning[Std on SE V6] +270		
Lighted Entry System +50			Chrome Bumpers[Std on SE V6] +55		
Luggage Rack[Opt on XE] +50			Chrome Wheels[Std on XE V6,King Cab XE		
Power Door Locks[Opt on XE] +75			4WD Ext Cab SB] +55		
Power Moonroof +290			Cruise Control[Opt on XE V6] +70		
Power Passenger Seat +90			Flip-Up Sunroof +110		
Power Windows[Opt on XE] +80			Limited Slip Diff[Opt on XE V6] +90		
Privacy Glass[Opt on XE] +90			Power Door Locks +75		
			Power Steering[Std on HD,SE V6,XE V4,4WD] +95		
			Power Windows +80		
			Rear Step Bumper[Opt on STD] +50		
			Tilt Steering Wheel[Opt on XE V6] +60		

SENTRA   1995

An all-new Sentra is released featuring aero styling and a stubby trunk. The 1995 Sentra is available only as a four-door sedan, the two-door model now being called the 200SX. Increased interior space is the most noticeable feature of the redesign. The engines remain unchanged from previous models.

RATINGS (SCALE OF 1-10)

Overall	Safety	Reliability	Performance	Comfort	Value
N/A	N/A	7.4	6.4	6.9	5.6

Category E

	Trade-in	Market
4 Dr GLE Sdn	5145	6685
4 Dr GXE Sdn	4705	6110
4 Dr STD Sdn	3775	4900
4 Dr XE Sdn	4425	5745

OPTIONS FOR SENTRA

Auto 4-Speed Transmission +265
Air Conditioning[Opt on STD] +270
Anti-Lock Brakes +225

TRUCK   1995

The two-wheel-drive Nissan trucks finally get rear-wheel antilock brakes.

RATINGS (SCALE OF 1-10)

Overall	Safety	Reliability	Performance	Comfort	Value
N/A	4.3	8.6	6	6.1	N/A

HALF TON

Category G

	Trade-in	Market
2 Dr HD Std Cab LB	5255	6490
2 Dr STD Std Cab SB	4400	5435
2 Dr XE Std Cab SB	4930	6085
2 Dr XE 4WD Std Cab SB	6795	8390

KING CAB

Category G

	Trade-in	Market
2 Dr SE V6 4WD Ext Cab SB	8670	10705
2 Dr XE Ext Cab SB	5900	7285
2 Dr XE 4WD Ext Cab SB	7530	9295
2 Dr XE V6 Ext Cab SB	6385	7885
2 Dr XE V6 4WD Ext Cab SB	7920	9780

OPTIONS FOR TRUCK

Auto 4-Speed Transmission +385
AM/FM Stereo Tape[Std on SE V6] +75

1994 NISSAN

240SX   1994

A convertible body style is the sole offering this year as the coupe is set for a complete redesign.

RATINGS (SCALE OF 1-10)

Overall	Safety	Reliability	Performance	Comfort	Value
N/A	N/A	8	8	7.3	3.4

Category F

	Trade-in	Market
2 Dr SE Conv	6940	8900

OPTIONS FOR 240SX

Air Conditioning +225

300ZX   1994

A passenger airbag is a new safety feature on the 300ZX, which allows the use of manual seatbelts. Remote keyless entry is another new feature for the 300ZX.

RATINGS (SCALE OF 1-10)

Overall	Safety	Reliability	Performance	Comfort	Value
N/A	N/A	N/A	N/A	N/A	3.6

Category F

	Trade-in	Market
2 Dr 2+2 Cpe	11285	14470
2 Dr STD Conv	13105	16800
2 Dr STD Cpe	10780	13820
2 Dr STD Turbo Cpe	12100	15510

OPTIONS FOR 300ZX

Auto 4-Speed Transmission +265
Alarm System +50
Compact Disc W/fm/tape +135
Glass Panel T-tops[Opt on STD] +265
Leather Seats[Std on Conv] +175

ALTIMA   1994

A passenger-side airbag is added to this hot-selling Tennessee-built compact. SE models gain a standard sunroof and GLEs have it as an available option.

Model Description	Trade-in Value	Market Value

RATINGS (SCALE OF 1-10)

Overall	Safety	Reliability	Performance	Comfort	Value
7.5	7.7	8.4	8	7.5	5.8

Category D

	Trade-in	Market
4 Dr GLE Sdn	5910	7575
4 Dr GXE Sdn	4720	6050
4 Dr SE Sdn	5245	6725
4 Dr XE Sdn	4210	5395

OPTIONS FOR ALTIMA

Auto 4-Speed Transmission[Std on GLE] +240
Air Conditioning[Opt on GXE,XE] +230
Aluminum/Alloy Wheels[Opt on GXE] +125
Anti-Lock Brakes +245
Compact Disc W/fm/tape +220
Cruise Control[Opt on GXE,XE] +65
Leather Seats +300
Power Antenna[Opt on GXE] +30
Power Sunroof[Opt on GXE] +200
Premium Sound System +100

MAXIMA 1994

No changes for the 1994 Maxima.

RATINGS (SCALE OF 1-10)

Overall	Safety	Reliability	Performance	Comfort	Value
N/A	N/A	8.1	8.8	7.9	4.3

Category D

	Trade-in	Market
4 Dr GXE Sdn	6100	7820
4 Dr SE Sdn	6560	8410

OPTIONS FOR MAXIMA

Auto 4-Speed Transmission[Opt on SE] +255
AM/FM Compact Disc Player +140
Anti-Lock Brakes +245
Bose Sound System[Std on SE] +205
Climate Control for AC +80
Leather Seats +300
Power Drivers Seat +80
Power Passenger Seat +100
Power Sunroof +200

PATHFINDER 1994

The LE model is introduced for the country-club crowd. Standard equipment on the LE includes leather upholstery, heated seats, a CD player, and a luggage rack. All 1994 Pathfinders sport a redesigned dashboard and instrument panel. SE models get new alloy wheels and a sunroof.

RATINGS (SCALE OF 1-10)

Overall	Safety	Reliability	Performance	Comfort	Value
6.5	4.2	8.3	7.6	7.5	4.7

Category G

	Trade-in	Market
4 Dr LE 4WD Wgn	9665	11930
4 Dr SE 4WD Wgn	8175	10095
4 Dr XE Wgn	6770	8360
4 Dr XE 4WD Wgn	7480	9235

OPTIONS FOR PATHFINDER

Auto 4-Speed Transmission[Std on LE] +335
Air Conditioning[Std on LE] +220
Alarm System[Opt on XE] +75
Cruise Control[Opt on XE] +55
Fog Lights[Opt on XE] +40
Heated Front Seats +70
Leather Seats[Opt on SE] +210
Limited Slip Diff[Std on LE] +75
Luggage Rack[Opt on SE] +45
Power Door Locks[Opt on XE] +65
Power Windows[Opt on XE] +65
Theft Deterrent System[Opt on XE] +100

QUEST 1994

The Quest gets a driver airbag added to its standard equipment list for 1994. GXE models can now be had with a premium audio package that includes a CD player.

RATINGS (SCALE OF 1-10)

Overall	Safety	Reliability	Performance	Comfort	Value
7.1	6.8	6.9	6.2	7.1	8.5

Category G

	Trade-in	Market
2 Dr GXE Pass. Van	7385	9120
2 Dr XE Pass. Van	6660	8220

OPTIONS FOR QUEST

Aluminum/Alloy Wheels +90
Anti-Lock Brakes[Opt on XE] +160
Camper/Towing Package +80
Captain Chairs (2) +140
Compact Disc W/fm/tape +130
Cruise Control[Opt on XE] +55
Dual Air Conditioning[Opt on XE] +255
Keyless Entry System +55
Leather Seats +210
Lighted Entry System +40
Luggage Rack[Opt on XE] +45
Power Door Locks[Opt on XE] +65
Power Moonroof +235
Power Passenger Seat +75
Power Windows[Opt on XE] +65

SENTRA 1994

CFC-free coolant is now standard on vehicles equipped with air conditioning. XE models get more standard equipment that includes air conditioning, cruise control and a stereo with cassette player.

RATINGS (SCALE OF 1-10)

Overall	Safety	Reliability	Performance	Comfort	Value
N/A	N/A	8.2	7.2	7.9	5.6

Don't forget to refer to the Mileage Adjustment Table at the back of this book!

Model Description	Trade-in Value	Market Value
Category E		
2 Dr E Sdn	2775	3700
4 Dr E Sdn	2895	3860
4 Dr GXE Sdn	3605	4805
1994.5 2 Dr Limited Sdn	3415	4555
1994.5 4 Dr Limited Sdn	3575	4765
2 Dr SE Sdn	3425	4565
2 Dr SE-R Sdn	3825	5100
2 Dr XE Sdn	3300	4400
4 Dr XE Sdn	3455	4605

OPTIONS FOR SENTRA

Auto 4-Speed Transmission +250
AM/FM Stereo Tape[Opt on E,SE] +80
Air Bag Restraint[Std on GXE] +155
Air Conditioning[Opt on E,SE,SE-R] +220
Aluminum/Alloy Wheels[Std on GXE,SE-R] +90
Anti-Lock Brakes +180
Cruise Control[Opt on SE,SE-R] +60
Power Steering[Opt on E] +70
Power Sunroof +165
Tilt Steering Wheel[Opt on E] +40

TRUCK   1994

The Nissan pickup gets a redesigned dashboard and a new model for 1994. The new model is called the XE.

RATINGS (SCALE OF 1-10)

Overall	Safety	Reliability	Performance	Comfort	Value
N/A	4.3	7.9	6	6.1	N/A

HALF TON

Category G		
2 Dr STD Std Cab SB	3890	4800
2 Dr V6 Std Cab LB	4695	5795
2 Dr XE Std Cab SB	4435	5475
2 Dr XE 4WD Std Cab SB	6170	7620

KING CAB

Category G		
2 Dr SE V6 Ext Cab SB	5860	7235
2 Dr SE V6 4WD Ext Cab SB	7185	8870
2 Dr XE Ext Cab SB	5075	6265
2 Dr XE 4WD Ext Cab SB	6555	8090
2 Dr XE V6 4WD Ext Cab SB	6845	8450

OPTIONS FOR TRUCK

Auto 4-Speed Transmission +310
Sport Handling Pkg +310
AM/FM Stereo Tape[Std on SE V6,XE Std Cab SB] +60
Air Conditioning +220
Aluminum/Alloy Wheels +90
Bed Liner +75
Chrome Bumpers[Std on SE V6] +45
Chrome Wheels[Std on SE V6] +45
Cruise Control[Opt on XE V6] +55
Flip-Up Sunroof +90

Limited Slip Diff +75
Power Door Locks +65
Power Steering[Std on SE V6,XE V6,4WD] +75
Power Windows +65
Rear Jump Seats[Opt on XE] +60
Sliding Rear Window[Opt on STD] +30
Tilt Steering Wheel[Opt on XE V6] +50

1993 NISSAN

240SX   1993

The luxury-oriented LE is dropped from the 240SX lineup due to poor sales. Don't worry, those with a penchant for leather can still get their kicks in a cowhide-equipped SE model. Half of the 240SXs produced this year have CFC-free air conditioning.

RATINGS (SCALE OF 1-10)

Overall	Safety	Reliability	Performance	Comfort	Value
N/A	N/A	8.2	8	7.3	4

Category F		
2 Dr SE Conv	5995	7785
2 Dr SE Cpe	4090	5310
2 Dr SE Hbk	4360	5665
2 Dr STD Cpe	3420	4440
2 Dr STD Hbk	3640	4730

OPTIONS FOR 240SX

Auto 4-Speed Transmission[Std on Conv] +185
Air Conditioning +185
Anti-Lock Brakes +150
Flip-Up Sunroof +90
Leather Seats +145
Limited Slip Diff +75
Power Sunroof +150
Sport Suspension +40

300ZX   1993

The first chop-top Z-car debuts this year. A basket handle behind the seats reduces body flex in the 300ZX and gives the seatbelts an anchor point. No changes for the other models.

RATINGS (SCALE OF 1-10)

Overall	Safety	Reliability	Performance	Comfort	Value
N/A	N/A	N/A	N/A	N/A	3.1

Category F		
2 Dr 2+2 Cpe	9425	12240
2 Dr STD Conv	11790	15310
2 Dr STD Cpe	9050	11755
2 Dr STD Turbo Cpe	10740	13950

OPTIONS FOR 300ZX

Auto 4-Speed Transmission +215
AM/FM Stereo Tape[Opt on Cpe] +45
Glass Panel T-tops[Std on 2+2,Turbo] +220

Don't forget to refer to the Mileage Adjustment Table at the back of this book!

Model Description	Trade-in Value	Market Value

Leather Seats +145
Premium Sound System[Std on 2+2, Turbo] +80

ALTIMA 1993

The Infiniti-inspired Altima replaces the aging Stanza. Swooping sheetmetal, a longer wheelbase, and increased cabin size distinguish the Altima from its lackluster predecessor. The Altima is powered by a twin-cam four-cylinder that produces 150 horsepower. A driver airbag is standard on the Altima, as are motorized seatbelts.

RATINGS (SCALE OF 1-10)

Overall	Safety	Reliability	Performance	Comfort	Value
N/A	N/A	7.7	8	7.5	6.2

Category D

4 Dr GLE Sdn	4980	6550
4 Dr GXE Sdn	3810	5010
4 Dr SE Sdn	4360	5740
4 Dr XE Sdn	3490	4590

OPTIONS FOR ALTIMA

Auto 4-Speed Transmission[Std on GLE] +185
Air Conditioning[Opt on GXE,XE] +190
Alarm System[Opt on SE] +115
Anti-Lock Brakes +200
Compact Disc W/fm/tape[Opt on SE] +180
Cruise Control[Opt on GXE,XE] +55
Leather Seats +245
Power Antenna[Opt on GXE] +25
Power Moonroof +185
Theft Deterrent System +105

MAXIMA 1993

The driver airbag is now standard on Nissan's front-wheel drive midsize sedan. Both cars have CFC-free air conditioning and SE models get a trick new stereo, compliments of Bose.

RATINGS (SCALE OF 1-10)

Overall	Safety	Reliability	Performance	Comfort	Value
N/A	N/A	7.8	8.8	7.9	5.6

Category D

4 Dr GXE Sdn	5235	6885
4 Dr SE Sdn	5565	7325

OPTIONS FOR MAXIMA

Auto 4-Speed Transmission[Opt on SE] +210
Luxury Pkg +105
Anti-Lock Brakes +200
Bose Sound System[Std on SE] +170
Climate Control for AC +65
Compact Disc W/fm/tape +180
Dual Power Seats +185
Leather Seats +245
Power Sunroof +165

NX 1993

The 2000 gets a standard T-top. New interior fabrics mark the only other changes for the NX line.

RATINGS (SCALE OF 1-10)

Overall	Safety	Reliability	Performance	Comfort	Value
N/A	N/A	N/A	N/A	N/A	4.6

Category E

2 Dr 1600 Cpe	2905	3980
2 Dr 2000 Cpe	3770	5165

OPTIONS FOR NX

Auto 4-Speed Transmission +185
AM/FM Stereo Tape[Opt on 1600] +65
Air Conditioning +180
Anti-Lock Brakes +150
Cruise Control +50
Power Door Locks +55
Power Windows +60
T-Bar Roof[Opt on 1600] +200

PATHFINDER 1993

CFC-free air conditioning is standard and side-impact door beams are introduced to protect occupants. The Pathfinder's standard stereo gets its wattage increased and the SE's leather seats are now heated. How cozy.

RATINGS (SCALE OF 1-10)

Overall	Safety	Reliability	Performance	Comfort	Value
6.5	4.3	8.9	7.6	6.8	4.8

Category G

4 Dr SE 4WD Wgn	7060	9050
4 Dr XE Wgn	5930	7605
4 Dr XE 4WD Wgn	6615	8480

OPTIONS FOR PATHFINDER

Auto 4-Speed Transmission +280
Sport Handling Pkg +260
Air Conditioning[Opt on XE] +180
Aluminum/Alloy Wheels +75
Heated Front Seats +60
Leather Seats +170
Limited Slip Diff +60
Luggage Rack +35
Power Door Locks[Opt on XE] +50
Power Windows[Opt on XE] +55
Sunroof +65

QUEST 1993

After messing around with the Axxess and Nissan Van, Nissan finally gets it right on this joint project with Mercury. The Quest is a front-engine, front-wheel-drive minivan that is built alongside the Villager at the Ford plant in Avon Lake, Ohio. The Quest is powered by a 3.0-liter V6 engine that produces 150-horsepower. The Quest seats seven and has standard air

Don't forget to refer to the Mileage Adjustment Table at the back of this book!

Model Description	Trade-in Value	Market Value

conditioning, a tilt steering wheel, and a stereo with cassette. Antilock brakes are optional on the Quest.

RATINGS (SCALE OF 1-10)

Overall	Safety	Reliability	Performance	Comfort	Value
6.1	5	5	6.2	7.1	7.4

Category G
2 Dr GXE Pass. Van	6265	8030
2 Dr STD Cargo Van	5110	6550
2 Dr XE Pass. Van	5430	6960

OPTIONS FOR QUEST
7 Passenger Seating[Opt on XE] +115
AM/FM Stereo Tape[Std on XE] +50
Aluminum/Alloy Wheels[Opt on XE] +75
Anti-Lock Brakes +135
Cruise Control[Opt on XE] +45
Dual Air Conditioning[Opt on XE] +210
Keyless Entry System +45
Leather Seats +170
Lighted Entry System +30
Luggage Rack[Opt on XE] +35
Power Door Locks[Opt on XE] +50
Power Passenger Seat +60
Power Sunroof +170
Power Windows[Opt on XE] +55
Premium Sound System[Opt on XE] +75

SENTRA 1993

A driver airbag is now standard on the GXE model. Base models ditch the Flintstone transmissions, gaining a standard five-speed manual or optional four-speed automatic in place of the archaic four-speed manual and three-speed automatic that was formerly available. All Sentras receive minor nose work that includes a redesigned grille, headlights and front fascia.

RATINGS (SCALE OF 1-10)

Overall	Safety	Reliability	Performance	Comfort	Value
N/A	N/A	8.4	7.2	7.9	4.5

Category E
2 Dr E Sdn	2340	3205
4 Dr E Sdn	2445	3350
4 Dr GXE Sdn	3095	4240
2 Dr SE Sdn	2685	3675
2 Dr SE-R Sdn	3165	4335
2 Dr XE Sdn	2575	3530
4 Dr XE Sdn	2695	3695

OPTIONS FOR SENTRA
Auto 4-Speed Transmission +210
AM/FM Stereo Tape[Std on GXE] +65
Air Bag Restraint[Std on GXE] +130
Air Conditioning[Std on GXE] +180
Anti-Lock Brakes +150
Cruise Control[Std on GXE] +50

Power Steering[Opt on E] +55
Power Sunroof +135

TRUCK 1993

CFC-free air conditioning debuts. No other changes to this mini-bruiser.

RATINGS (SCALE OF 1-10)

Overall	Safety	Reliability	Performance	Comfort	Value
N/A	4.3	8.1	6	6.5	N/A

HALF TON

Category G
2 Dr STD Std Cab LB	3465	4440
2 Dr STD Std Cab SB	3305	4240
2 Dr STD 4WD Std Cab SB	5025	6445

KING CAB

Category G
2 Dr SE Ext Cab SB	4890	6270
2 Dr SE 4WD Ext Cab SB	5985	7675
2 Dr STD Ext Cab SB	4340	5565
2 Dr STD 4WD Ext Cab SB	5305	6800

OPTIONS FOR TRUCK
6 cyl 3.0 L Engine +145
Auto 4-Speed Transmission +220
2WD Sport Pkg +195
4WD Sport Pkg +185
AM/FM Stereo Tape[Std on SE,4WD] +50
Air Conditioning +180
Aluminum/Alloy Wheels +75
Bed Liner +60
Camper/Towing Package +65
Chrome Bumpers[Std on SE] +35
Chrome Wheels[Std on King Cab,4WD] +40
Flip-Up Sunroof +75
Limited Slip Diff +60
Power Door Locks +50
Power Steering[Std on King Cab,4WD] +60
Power Windows +55

1992 NISSAN

240SX 1992

Nissan chops the top off the 240SX, adding a convertible to this versatile line of cars. Antilock brakes are made available on the LE model.

RATINGS (SCALE OF 1-10)

Overall	Safety	Reliability	Performance	Comfort	Value
N/A	N/A	8.3	8	7.3	4

Category F
2 Dr LE Hbk	4035	5380
2 Dr SE Conv	5065	6755
2 Dr SE Cpe	3565	4755
2 Dr SE Hbk	3740	4985

NISSAN 92

Model Description	Trade-in Value	Market Value
2 Dr STD Cpe	3070	4095
2 Dr STD Hbk	3260	4345

OPTIONS FOR 240SX
Auto 4-Speed Transmission[Std on Conv] +150
Air Conditioning[Std on LE] +150
Anti-Lock Brakes +125
Flip-Up Sunroof +70
Leather Seats[Opt on SE] +120
Limited Slip Diff +60
Power Sunroof +120

300ZX 1992

The driver airbag is moved to the standard equipment list this year. No other changes to this fine car.

RATINGS (SCALE OF 1-10)

Overall	Safety	Reliability	Performance	Comfort	Value
N/A	N/A	N/A	N/A	N/A	3.5

Category F
2 Dr 2+2 Cpe	7575	10100
2 Dr STD Cpe	7320	9760
2 Dr STD Turbo Cpe	9180	12240

OPTIONS FOR 300ZX
Auto 4-Speed Transmission +170
Bose Sound System[Std on 2+2,Turbo] +95
Glass Panel T-tops[Std on Turbo] +180
Leather Seats +120
Power Drivers Seat[Std on 2+2,Turbo] +45

MAXIMA 1992

The Maxima gets an available driver airbag and a bigger engine for the SE. The SE's new engine is a DOHC, 190-horsepower V6. Unfortunately, the SE loses its standard sunroof. All Maximas receive a new grille and taillights for 1992.

RATINGS (SCALE OF 1-10)

Overall	Safety	Reliability	Performance	Comfort	Value
N/A	N/A	7.5	8.8	7.9	6.4

Category D
4 Dr GXE Sdn	4510	6015
4 Dr SE Sdn	4765	6350

OPTIONS FOR MAXIMA
Auto 4-Speed Transmission[Opt on SE] +170
Luxury Pkg +160
Air Bag Restraint +100
Anti-Lock Brakes +165
Bose Sound System[Std on SE] +135
Climate Control for AC +55
Dual Power Seats +150
Leather Seats +200
Power Sunroof +135

NX 1992

The optional T-tops are now available on the 1600. The NX 2000 is available this year with a power package that adds power windows, power door locks and cruise control.

RATINGS (SCALE OF 1-10)

Overall	Safety	Reliability	Performance	Comfort	Value
N/A	N/A	N/A	N/A	N/A	4.5

Category E
2 Dr 1600 Cpe	2365	3380
2 Dr 2000 Cpe	2995	4280

OPTIONS FOR NX
Auto 4-Speed Transmission +150
Air Conditioning +145
Anti-Lock Brakes +120
Power Door Locks +45
Power Windows +50
T-Tops (solid/Colored) +160

PATHFINDER 1992

Safari Green paint is a new exterior color choice for this aging veteran of the sport-ute wars. No other changes are made.

RATINGS (SCALE OF 1-10)

Overall	Safety	Reliability	Performance	Comfort	Value
6.7	4.3	8.7	7.6	6.8	6.2

Category G
4 Dr SE 4WD Wgn	6305	8295
4 Dr XE Wgn	5045	6640
4 Dr XE 4WD Wgn	5805	7635

OPTIONS FOR PATHFINDER
Auto 4-Speed Transmission +205
AM/FM Compact Disc Player +60
Air Conditioning[Opt on XE] +145
Flip-Up Sunroof +60
Leather Seats +140
Limited Slip Diff +50
Power Door Locks[Opt on XE] +40
Power Windows[Opt on XE] +45

SENTRA 1992

A passenger's side vanity mirror and black body-side moldings are now standard on the two-door Sentra. The Value Option Package (includes air conditioning, cruise control, and a stereo) is extended to the SE Sentras this year.

RATINGS (SCALE OF 1-10)

Overall	Safety	Reliability	Performance	Comfort	Value
N/A	N/A	8.1	7.2	7.9	4.9

Don't forget to refer to the Mileage Adjustment Table at the back of this book!

Model Description	Trade-in Value	Market Value
Category E		
2 Dr E Sdn	1990	2840
4 Dr E Sdn	2085	2980
4 Dr GXE Sdn	2560	3655
2 Dr SE Sdn	2340	3345
2 Dr SE-R Sdn	2605	3720
2 Dr XE Sdn	2200	3145
4 Dr XE Sdn	2265	3235

OPTIONS FOR SENTRA

Auto 4-Speed Transmission +150
Air Conditioning[Std on GXE] +145
Anti-Lock Brakes +120
Power Steering[Opt on E] +45
Power Sunroof +110

STANZA   1992

A sporty SE model joins the roster of available Stanzas this year. Distinguished by a blacked-out grille, fog lights, rear spoiler, and leather-wrapped steering wheel and shift knob, the SE is attempting to draw in customers who want more from their compact family sedan.

Category E

Model Description	Trade-in Value	Market Value
4 Dr GXE Sdn	2875	4110
4 Dr SE Sdn	3090	4415
4 Dr XE Sdn	2315	3310

OPTIONS FOR STANZA

Auto 4-Speed Transmission[Std on GXE] +160
Air Conditioning[Opt on XE] +145
Anti-Lock Brakes +120
Power Door Locks[Opt on XE] +45
Power Sunroof +110
Power Windows[Opt on XE] +50

TRUCK   1992

No changes for the Nissan Pickup.

RATINGS (SCALE OF 1-10)

Overall	Safety	Reliability	Performance	Comfort	Value
N/A	4	7.9	6	6.5	N/A

HALF TON

Category G

Model Description	Trade-in Value	Market Value
2 Dr STD Std Cab LB	3040	4000
2 Dr STD Std Cab SB	2895	3810
2 Dr STD 4WD Std Cab SB	4275	5625

KING CAB

Category G

Model Description	Trade-in Value	Market Value
2 Dr SE Ext Cab SB	4265	5615
2 Dr SE 4WD Ext Cab SB	5280	6950
2 Dr STD Ext Cab SB	3660	4815
2 Dr STD 4WD Ext Cab SB	4630	6095

OPTIONS FOR TRUCK

6 cyl 3.0 L Engine +140
Auto 4-Speed Transmission +165
Air Conditioning +145
Flip-Up Sunroof +60
Limited Slip Diff +50
Power Door Locks +40
Power Steering[Std on SE,4WD] +50
Power Windows +45

1991 NISSAN

240SX   1991

More gadgets for the Nissan sport coupe. Four-wheel steering and antilock brakes are the latest additions to Nissan's spry pocket-rocket. The 2.4-liter DOHC inline-four produces 15 more horsepower than last year.

RATINGS (SCALE OF 1-10)

Overall	Safety	Reliability	Performance	Comfort	Value
N/A	N/A	7.6	8	7.3	4.4

Category F

Model Description	Trade-in Value	Market Value
2 Dr LE Hbk	3410	4610
2 Dr Limited Hbk	3585	4845
2 Dr SE Cpe	3045	4115
2 Dr SE Hbk	3230	4365
2 Dr STD Cpe	2630	3555
2 Dr STD Hbk	2805	3790

OPTIONS FOR 240SX

Auto 4-Speed Transmission +120
Air Conditioning[Opt on SE,STD] +125
Anti-Lock Brakes +100
Flip-Up Sunroof +60
Leather Seats[Opt on SE] +95
Power Sunroof +100

300ZX   1991

The 300ZX is available with the four-wheel steering and antilock brakes. A driver airbag joins the options list this year.

RATINGS (SCALE OF 1-10)

Overall	Safety	Reliability	Performance	Comfort	Value
N/A	N/A	N/A	N/A	N/A	3.9

Category F

Model Description	Trade-in Value	Market Value
2 Dr 2+2 Cpe	6545	8845
2 Dr STD Cpe	6245	8440
2 Dr STD Turbo Cpe	7930	10715

OPTIONS FOR 300ZX

Auto 4-Speed Transmission +120
Air Bag Restraint +75
Bose Sound System +80
Glass Panel T-tops +145

Don't forget to refer to the Mileage Adjustment Table at the back of this book!

NISSAN 91

Model Description	Trade-in Value	Market Value	Model Description	Trade-in Value	Market Value

Leather Seats +95
Power Drivers Seat +35

MAXIMA 1991

Antilock brakes are added to the options list of the capable Maxima.

RATINGS (SCALE OF 1-10)

Overall	Safety	Reliability	Performance	Comfort	Value
N/A	N/A	7.3	8.8	7.9	6.9

Category D
4 Dr GXE Sdn	3655	5005
4 Dr SE Sdn	3980	5450

OPTIONS FOR MAXIMA

Auto 4-Speed Transmission[Opt on SE] +140
Anti-Lock Brakes +135
Bose Sound System[Std on SE] +110
Compact Disc W/fm/tape +120
Leather Seats +165
Power Drivers Seat +45
Power Sunroof[Std on SE] +110

NX 1991

The replacement for the Nissan Pulsar appears in the guise of the NX twins. Available with the same engines found in the Nissan Sentra, the NX duo are designed to be a sportier alternative to their pedestrian cousins. Both models feature a driver airbag, a two-door body style and front-wheel drive. Antilock brakes are available on the NX 2000 equipped with a manual transmission.

RATINGS (SCALE OF 1-10)

Overall	Safety	Reliability	Performance	Comfort	Value
N/A	N/A	N/A	N/A	N/A	4.9

Category E
2 Dr 1600 Cpe	2095	3080
2 Dr 2000 Cpe	2575	3785

OPTIONS FOR NX

Auto 4-Speed Transmission +120
Air Conditioning +120
Anti-Lock Brakes +100
T-Tops (solid/Colored) +130

PATHFINDER 1991

The two-door version of Nissan's sport-utility wagon is dropped in favor of the much better selling four-door. Reaching a new level of refinement, Nissan makes leather seating surfaces available on the top-end SE model. All '91 Pathfinders get rear-wheel antilock brakes.

RATINGS (SCALE OF 1-10)

Overall	Safety	Reliability	Performance	Comfort	Value
6.6	4.2	8.1	7.6	6.8	6.5

Category G
4 Dr SE 4WD Wgn	5630	7605
4 Dr XE Wgn	4370	5905
4 Dr XE 4WD Wgn	5220	7055

OPTIONS FOR PATHFINDER

Auto 4-Speed Transmission +160
AM/FM Compact Disc Player +50
Air Conditioning[Opt on XE] +120
Leather Seats +115
Limited Slip Diff +40
Power Door Locks[Opt on XE] +35
Power Windows[Opt on XE] +35
Sunroof +45

SENTRA 1991

The Nissan Sentra is totally redesigned for 1991. Edges are smoothed out and corners are rounded, giving the '91 Sentra a more substantial feel. A racy SE-R is introduced with an outstanding little 140-horsepower engine. All other Sentras get a 110-horsepower engine that is about average for this class. A four-speed automatic transmission is available on all Sentras but the SE-R.

RATINGS (SCALE OF 1-10)

Overall	Safety	Reliability	Performance	Comfort	Value
N/A	N/A	7.1	7.2	7.9	5.9

Category E
2 Dr E Sdn	1680	2470
4 Dr E Sdn	1720	2530
4 Dr GXE Sdn	2145	3155
2 Dr SE Sdn	1980	2910
2 Dr SE-R Sdn	2240	3295
2 Dr XE Sdn	1900	2795
4 Dr XE Sdn	1970	2895

OPTIONS FOR SENTRA

Auto 3-Speed Transmission +130
Auto 4-Speed Transmission +105
Air Conditioning[Std on GXE] +120
Anti-Lock Brakes +100
Power Steering[Opt on E] +40
Power Sunroof +90

STANZA 1991

Four-wheel antilock brakes are a new option on the Stanza GXE. No other changes for the recently redesigned sedan from Nissan.

Category E
4 Dr GXE Sdn	2470	3630
4 Dr XE Sdn	2075	3055

OPTIONS FOR STANZA

Auto 4-Speed Transmission +110
Air Conditioning[Opt on XE] +120
Anti-Lock Brakes +100

NISSAN 91-90

Model Description	Trade-in Value	Market Value	Model Description	Trade-in Value	Market Value

Power Door Locks[Opt on XE] +35
Power Sunroof +90
Power Windows[Opt on XE] +40

TRUCK 1991

The regular cab six-cylinder four-wheel-drive model is dropped. The remaining Nissan four-wheel drives are equipped with rear-wheel antilock brakes.

RATINGS (SCALE OF 1-10)

Overall	Safety	Reliability	Performance	Comfort	Value
N/A	3.9	7.5	6	6.5	N/A

HALF TON
Category G

2 Dr STD Std Cab LB	2515	3400
2 Dr STD Std Cab SB	2385	3220
2 Dr STD 4WD Std Cab SB	3665	4955

KING CAB
Category G

2 Dr SE Ext Cab SB	3550	4800
2 Dr SE 4WD Ext Cab SB	4680	6325
2 Dr STD Ext Cab SB	3040	4110
2 Dr STD 4WD Ext Cab SB	4055	5480

OPTIONS FOR TRUCK
6 cyl 3.0 L Engine[Std on King Cab,LB] +105
Auto 4-Speed Transmission +130
Chrome Pkg +120
Air Conditioning +120
Limited Slip Diff +40
Power Door Locks +35
Power Steering[Std on King Cab,4WD] +40
Power Windows +35
Sunroof +45

1990 NISSAN

240SX 1990

After last year's amazing innovations the designers at Nissan decided not to mess with the 240SX, offering a standard power antenna and an upgraded stereo as the only modifications.

RATINGS (SCALE OF 1-10)

Overall	Safety	Reliability	Performance	Comfort	Value
N/A	N/A	7.7	8	7.3	3.8

Category F

2 Dr SE Hbk	2595	3505
2 Dr XE Cpe	2410	3260

OPTIONS FOR 240SX
Auto 4-Speed Transmission +100
Air Conditioning +100
Anti-Lock Brakes +80

Power Sunroof +80
Power Windows +25

300ZX 1990

Cutting-edge styling and exceptional performance launch the new 300ZX onto our top-ten list of all-time favorite sports cars. Available as a two-seater or a two-plus-two, the 300ZX can move its occupants hither and yon with alacrity. An available turbo engine in the two-seater makes the 300ZX even more fun.

RATINGS (SCALE OF 1-10)

Overall	Safety	Reliability	Performance	Comfort	Value
N/A	N/A	N/A	N/A	N/A	3.3

Category F

2 Dr GS Cpe	6190	8365
2 Dr GS 2+2 Cpe	5930	8015
2 Dr STD Turbo Cpe	7450	10065

OPTIONS FOR 300ZX
Auto 4-Speed Transmission +100
Electronics Pkg +110
Leather Seats +80
Power Drivers Seat +30

AXXESS 1990

What's that? This is the most frequently asked question regarding the Axxess. The Axxess replaces the now defunct Stanza wagon and is sandwiched between minivans and compact station wagons in size and utility. The Axxess offers interesting features such as available four-wheel drive and dual sliding passenger doors that allow the middle-row passengers an entrance or exit from either side of the vehicle.

Category G

2 Dr SE Pass. Van	2505	3475
2 Dr SE 4WD Pass. Van	2510	3485
2 Dr XE Pass. Van	2150	2985
2 Dr XE 4WD Pass. Van	2295	3185

OPTIONS FOR AXXESS
Auto 4-Speed Transmission[Opt on XE] +90
Air Conditioning[Opt on XE] +100
Power Sunroof[Opt on XE] +95
Power Windows[Opt on XE] +30

MAXIMA 1990

The radio is upgraded and there are a few more colors available for the 1990 Maxima.

RATINGS (SCALE OF 1-10)

Overall	Safety	Reliability	Performance	Comfort	Value
N/A	N/A	8	8.8	7.9	5.1

Category D

4 Dr GXE Sdn	3145	4365
4 Dr SE Sdn	3435	4770

Don't forget to refer to the Mileage Adjustment Table at the back of this book!

NISSAN 90

Model Description	Trade-in Value	Market Value	Model Description	Trade-in Value	Market Value

OPTIONS FOR MAXIMA

Auto 4-Speed Transmission[Opt on SE] +115
Electronics Pkg +125
AM/FM Compact Disc Player +65
Anti-Lock Brakes +110
Bose Sound System[Std on SE] +90
Leather Seats +135
Power Drivers Seat +35
Power Passenger Seat +45
Power Sunroof[Std on SE] +90

PATHFINDER   1990

Nissan joins the four-door sport-ute frenzy by adding two doors to the popular Pathfinder. No other changes are made this year.

RATINGS (SCALE OF 1-10)

Overall	Safety	Reliability	Performance	Comfort	Value
6.3	3.8	7.1	7.6	6.8	6

Category G
2 Dr SE 4WD Utility	4420	6140
4 Dr SE 4WD Wgn	4610	6400
4 Dr XE 4WD Wgn	4210	5845

OPTIONS FOR PATHFINDER

Auto 4-Speed Transmission +130
Power Plus Pkg +170
Sport Handling Pkg +100
Air Conditioning[Opt on XE] +100
Limited Slip Diff[Opt on Wgn] +35
Power Door Locks[Opt on XE] +30
Power Windows[Opt on XE] +30
Sunroof[Opt on Wgn] +35

PULSAR   1990

No changes for 1990.
Category E
2 Dr NX XE Cpe	1480	2240

OPTIONS FOR PULSAR

Auto 3-Speed Transmission +65
Air Conditioning +100

SENTRA   1990

The bargain-basement Sentra E has been dropped from the model list. No other changes are made.
Category E
2 Dr SE Cpe	1655	2505
2 Dr STD Sdn	1185	1795
2 Dr XE Cpe	1615	2450
2 Dr XE Sdn	1355	2055
4 Dr XE Sdn	1430	2165
4 Dr XE Wgn	1455	2205

OPTIONS FOR SENTRA

Auto 3-Speed Transmission +80
Air Conditioning +100

Power Steering +30
Sunroof[Opt on XE] +40

STANZA   1990

An all-new Stanza debuts in 1990. The new Stanza has the same engine as the sporty 240SX but continues with a tired suspension and uninteresting styling. Better luck next time.
Category E
4 Dr GXE Sdn	2005	3035
4 Dr XE Sdn	1750	2650

OPTIONS FOR STANZA

Auto 4-Speed Transmission +100
Air Conditioning[Opt on XE] +100
Anti-Lock Brakes +80
Power Door Locks[Opt on XE] +30
Power Sunroof +75
Power Windows[Opt on XE] +30

TRUCK   1990

No significant changes for the Nissan pickup.

RATINGS (SCALE OF 1-10)

Overall	Safety	Reliability	Performance	Comfort	Value
N/A	3.9	6.5	6	6.5	N/A

HALF TON

Category G
2 Dr STD Std Cab LB	2185	3035
2 Dr STD Std Cab SB	2050	2850
2 Dr STD 4WD Std Cab SB	3115	4325

KING CAB

Category G
2 Dr SE Ext Cab SB	3005	4175
2 Dr SE 4WD Ext Cab SB	3940	5470
2 Dr STD Ext Cab SB	2495	3465
2 Dr STD 4WD Ext Cab SB	3400	4725

OPTIONS FOR TRUCK

6 cyl 3.0 L Engine[Std on King Cab] +110
Auto 4-Speed Transmission +115
Black Value Pkg +110
Chrome Value Pkg +120
Air Conditioning +100
Flip-Up Sunroof +40
Limited Slip Diff +35
Power Door Locks +30
Power Steering[Std on King Cab, 4WD, LB] +35
Power Windows +30
Sunroof +35

VAN   1990

Category G
2 Dr GXE Pass. Van	2460	3415
2 Dr XE Pass. Van	2265	3150

OLDSMOBILE 99

Model Description	Trade-in Value	Market Value	Model Description	Trade-in Value	Market Value

OLDSMOBILE USA

1996 Oldsmobile Achieva

1999 OLDSMOBILE

ALERO 1999

Oldsmobile has dropped the slow-selling Achieva in favor of this new clean-sheet design patterned after the successful Intrigue midsize sedan. Available in both two- and four-door configurations with three well-equipped trim levels the Alero represents a quantum leap forward over previous small Olds models.

RATINGS (SCALE OF 1-10)

Overall	Safety	Reliability	Performance	Comfort	Value
N/A	N/A	N/A	7.6	8	N/A

Category C

2 Dr GL Cpe	11105	13380
4 Dr GL Sdn	11300	13615
2 Dr GLS Cpe	12070	14545
4 Dr GLS Sdn	12220	14725
2 Dr GX Cpe	9865	11885
4 Dr GX Sdn	10025	12080

OPTIONS FOR ALERO
6 cyl 3.4 L Engine[Opt on GL] +445
Aluminum/Alloy Wheels[Opt on GL] +225
Compact Disc W/fm/tape[Std on GLS] +250
Cruise Control[Opt on GX] +155
Keyless Entry System[Opt on GL] +140
Power Drivers Seat[Opt on GL] +220
Power Moonroof +510

AURORA 1999

It's the status quo again in Auroraville, except this year Olds has added two more hydraulic engine mounts (for a total of three to better isolate engine vibrations.

Other than that, a few new colors have been added (Galaxy Silver, Copper Nightmist and Dark Bronzemist).

RATINGS (SCALE OF 1-10)

Overall	Safety	Reliability	Performance	Comfort	Value
N/A	7.1	N/A	8.8	9	N/A

Category B

4 Dr STD Sdn	20420	24605

OPTIONS FOR AURORA
Bose Sound System +495
Chrome Wheels +510
Heated Front Seats +230
Power Moonroof +725

BRAVADA 1999

In the wake of last year's restyle, Bravada sees feature refinements for '99. The driver-side airbag has been redesigned into a mini-module to permit a clearer view of the instruments, while the turn signal stalk now provides a flash-to-pass feature. A telltale warning lamp has been added to alert the driver when the tailgate lift glass is ajar. And an anti-theft alarm system is now standard. There's also an option package that combines a driver-side memory seat and a power passenger-side seat, as well as sound system upgrades across the board.

RATINGS (SCALE OF 1-10)

Overall	Safety	Reliability	Performance	Comfort	Value
N/A	7.3	N/A	8	8	N/A

Category G

4 Dr STD 4WD Wgn	18160	21615

OPTIONS FOR BRAVADA
Bose Sound System +520
Heated Front Seats +195
Power Moonroof +645

CUTLASS 1999

No changes to Oldsmobile's fresh-in-'97 bread-and butter sedan, except for two new colors, Bronze Mist and Dark Cherry, and the addition of a Gold Package.

RATINGS (SCALE OF 1-10)

Overall	Safety	Reliability	Performance	Comfort	Value
N/A	7.5	8.6	N/A	8.3	N/A

Category C

4 Dr GL Sdn	10545	12705
4 Dr GLS Sdn	11775	14190

OPTIONS FOR CUTLASS
Aluminum/Alloy Wheels[Opt on GL] +225
Compact Disc W/fm/tape +250
Keyless Entry System[Opt on GL] +140
Power Drivers Seat[Opt on GL] +220
Power Mirrors[Opt on GL] +85

Model Description	Trade-in Value	Market Value

Power Moonroof +510
Power Windows[Opt on GL] +230

EIGHTY EIGHT   1999

Nothing, unless you count the fact the Eighty-Eight gets two new exterior colors, Champagne and Evergreen, and the LS model gets the option of white-stripe 16-inch tires. Oh, wait. Oldsmobile is celebrating the nameplate's golden anniversary with a special 50th Anniversary Edition Eighty Eight. It has 16-inch aluminum wheels fitted with 215/65SR blackwalls, a highly contented leather interior package and special badging finished in, what else? gold.

RATINGS (SCALE OF 1-10)

Overall	Safety	Reliability	Performance	Comfort	Value
N/A	7.6	8.9	8.6	8.5	N/A

Category B

	Trade-in	Market
4 Dr 50TH Anniversary Sdn	14245	17160
4 Dr LS Sdn	13390	16135
4 Dr STD Sdn	12575	15150

OPTIONS FOR EIGHTY EIGHT

Aluminum/Alloy Wheels[Opt on STD] +245
Compact Disc W/fm/tape[Opt on LS,STD] +285
Dual Power Seats[Opt on LS] +280
Keyless Entry System[Opt on STD] +130
Leather Seats[Std on 50TH Anniversary] +505

INTRIGUE   1999

Last year, Oldsmobile dumped the stodgy Cutlass Supreme for the Intrigue; a suave, sophisticated sporty sedan designed to take on the best of the imports. For '99 Olds is dumping the 3800 Series II V6 that powers the Intrigue for an all-new, 24-valve 3.5-liter twin cam V6. Until production of the 3.5 liter (a design based on the Aurora V8) can be ramped up to meet the Intrigue build schedule, the new 215-horsepower engine will come standard only in the new top-line GLS model, and optional in the base GX and mid-line GL series. Full function traction control is now available in models equipped with the new powerplant. Minor feature revisions, one new color and new badging rounds out the changes this year.

RATINGS (SCALE OF 1-10)

Overall	Safety	Reliability	Performance	Comfort	Value
N/A	N/A	N/A	8.2	8	N/A

Category B

	Trade-in	Market
4 Dr GL Sdn	12560	15135
4 Dr GLS Sdn	13490	16255
4 Dr GX Sdn	11950	14395

OPTIONS FOR INTRIGUE

6 cyl 3.5 L Engine[Std on GLS] +290
Bose Sound System +495

Model Description	Trade-in Value	Market Value

Chrome Wheels +510
Compact Disc W/fm/tape[Std on GLS] +285
Keyless Entry System[Opt on GX] +130
Leather Seats[Std on GLS] +505
Power Drivers Seat[Opt on GX] +230
Power Moonroof +725

SILHOUETTE   1999

Olds is headlining its Premiere Edition, a loaded-up model that debuted in mid-'98 with a standard integrated video entertainment system in back. But other news for 1999 includes a horsepower and torque increase for Silhouette's 3.4-liter V6, plus the addition of a theft-deterrent system and heated outside rearview mirrors as standard equipment. And if four new exterior colors (Sky, Ruby, Silvermist and Cypress) weren't enough, then consider the availability of a new Gold Package (but only if you must).

RATINGS (SCALE OF 1-10)

Overall	Safety	Reliability	Performance	Comfort	Value
N/A	8	8.5	7.8	7.9	N/A

Category G

	Trade-in	Market
4 Dr GL Pass. Van Ext	15632	18610
4 Dr GLS Pass. Van Ext	17005	20245
4 Dr GS Pass. Van	16105	19175
4 Dr Premiere Pass. Van Ext	17835	21235

OPTIONS FOR SILHOUETTE

Aluminum/Alloy Wheels[Opt on GL,GS] +245
Captain Chairs (4)[Opt on GL,GS] +465
Compact Disc W/fm/tape[Std on Premiere] +355
Dual Air Conditioning[Opt on GL] +700
Keyless Entry System[Opt on GL] +150
Leather Seats[Std on GLS,Premiere] +575
Traction Control System[Opt on GL,GS] +200

1998 OLDSMOBILE

ACHIEVA   1998

Oldsmobile limited sales of the Achieva to fleets for 1998, so if you're considering one, it's probably a former rental car.

Category C

	Trade-in	Market
4 Dr SL Sdn	8030	9795

AURORA   1998

Status quo in Auroraville, but second-generation airbags have been added.

RATINGS (SCALE OF 1-10)

Overall	Safety	Reliability	Performance	Comfort	Value
8.4	7.1	8.4	8.8	9	8.7

Category A

	Trade-in	Market
4 Dr STD Sdn	16185	19270

Don't forget to refer to the Mileage Adjustment Table at the back of this book!

OLDSMOBILE 98

OPTIONS FOR AURORA

Bose Sound System +355
Chrome Wheels +610
Heated Front Seats +120
Power Moonroof +825

BRAVADA — 1998

Front styling is revised, and new body-side cladding alters the Bravada's profile. Inside, dual second generation airbags are housed in a new dashboard. A heated driver's side exterior mirror is newly standard, while heated front seats have been added to the options roster. Battery rundown protection and a theft deterrent system are new standard features.

RATINGS (SCALE OF 1-10)

Overall	Safety	Reliability	Performance	Comfort	Value
7.7	7.1	7.4	8	8	8.1

Category G

4 Dr STD 4WD Wgn	15855	18875

OPTIONS FOR BRAVADA

Compact Disc W/fm/tape +290
Heated Front Seats +160
Power Moonroof +525

CUTLASS — 1998

No changes to Oldsmobile's fresh bread-and-butter sedan, except for the addition of second-generation airbags.

RATINGS (SCALE OF 1-10)

Overall	Safety	Reliability	Performance	Comfort	Value
7.9	7.5	8.2	8.4	8.3	7.3

Category C

4 Dr GL Sdn	9625	11740
4 Dr GLS Sdn	10570	12890

OPTIONS FOR CUTLASS

Aluminum/Alloy Wheels[Opt on GL] +180
Compact Disc W/fm/tape +200
Keyless Entry System[Opt on GL] +115
Power Drivers Seat[Opt on GL] +180
Power Mirrors[Opt on GL] +70
Power Moonroof +415
Power Windows[Opt on GL] +190

EIGHTY EIGHT — 1998

Virtually nothing, unless you find a new fuel cap, better access to rear seat belts, new ABS wheel-speed sensors and a couple of new colors intriguing. Second-generation airbags are standard.

RATINGS (SCALE OF 1-10)

Overall	Safety	Reliability	Performance	Comfort	Value
8.4	7.6	8.6	8.6	8.5	8.8

Category B

4 Dr LS Sdn	11530	13890
4 Dr STD Sdn	10190	12275

OPTIONS FOR EIGHTY EIGHT

Aluminum/Alloy Wheels[Std on LS] +200
Compact Disc W/fm/tape +235
Dual Power Seats +230
Keyless Entry System[Std on LS] +105
Leather Seats +410

INTRIGUE — 1998

Oldsmobile dumps the stodgy Cutlass Supreme for the Intrigue: a suave, sophisticated, sporty sedan designed to take on the best of the imports. Too bad refinement issues exist. Second-generation airbags are standard equipment.

RATINGS (SCALE OF 1-10)

Overall	Safety	Reliability	Performance	Comfort	Value
N/A	N/A	8.3	8.2	8	N/A

Category B

4 Dr GL Sdn	12115	14595
4 Dr GLS Sdn	12615	15200
4 Dr STD Sdn	11685	14080

OPTIONS FOR INTRIGUE

Bose Sound System +405
Chrome Wheels +415
Compact Disc W/fm/tape[Std on GLS] +235
Keyless Entry System[Opt on STD] +105
Leather Seats[Opt on GL] +410
Power Drivers Seat[Std on GL] +190
Power Moonroof +590

LSS — 1998

New colors, improved ABS, a revised electrochromic rearview mirror, second-generation airbags and a redesigned fuel cap are the major changes for 1998.

RATINGS (SCALE OF 1-10)

Overall	Safety	Reliability	Performance	Comfort	Value
8.4	7.6	8.6	8.4	8.6	8.8

Category C

4 Dr STD Sdn	12460	15200

OPTIONS FOR LSS

Chrome Wheels +370
Power Moonroof +415

REGENCY — 1998

Minor changes to this retirement village special for '98. The ABS is upgraded, it's easier to get at the rear seat belts, colors are revised and the "unleaded fuel only" label is removed from the inside of the fuel door.

Don't forget to refer to the Mileage Adjustment Table at the back of this book!

OLDSMOBILE 98-97

Model Description	Trade-in Value	Market Value	Model Description	Trade-in Value	Market Value

RATINGS (SCALE OF 1-10)

Overall	Safety	Reliability	Performance	Comfort	Value
N/A	7.6	8.7	8.6	N/A	N/A

Category A

4 Dr STD Sdn	11980	14260

OPTIONS FOR REGENCY
Power Moonroof +825

SILHOUETTE   1998

Side-impact airbags are standard for front seat passengers, and Oldsmobile is building more short-wheelbase vans with dual sliding doors. Front airbags get second generation technology, which results in slower deployment speeds. Midyear, a Premiere Edition debuted, loaded with standard features including a TV/VCP setup in back.

RATINGS (SCALE OF 1-10)

Overall	Safety	Reliability	Performance	Comfort	Value
7.6	7.8	7.4	7.8	7.9	6.9

Category G

2 Dr GL Pass. Van Ext	13103	15600
2 Dr GLS Pass. Van Ext	14735	17540
2 Dr GS Pass. Van	13510	16085
2 Dr Premiere Pass. Van Ext	15350	18275

OPTIONS FOR SILHOUETTE
Aluminum/Alloy Wheels[Opt on GL, GS] +200
Auto Load Leveling[Opt on GL, GS] +135
Captain Chairs (2) +310
Compact Disc W/fm/tape[Std on Premiere] +290
Dual Air Conditioning[Opt on GL, GLS] +575
Dual Power Seats[Opt on GL] +235
Keyless Entry System[Opt on GL] +120
Leather Seats +470
Privacy Glass[Opt on GL] +160
Traction Control System[Std on Premiere] +165

1997 OLDSMOBILE

ACHIEVA   1997

Side-impact standards are met, and standard equipment lists are enhanced. Series II Coupe gets new alloy wheels, and the lineup has been simplified.

RATINGS (SCALE OF 1-10)

Overall	Safety	Reliability	Performance	Comfort	Value
7.7	7.5	8.3	8.4	7.6	6.7

Category C

2 Dr SC Series I Cpe	6428	7935
2 Dr SC Series II Cpe	6685	8255
4 Dr SL Series I Sdn	6460	8100
4 Dr SL Series II Sdn	6561	8505

OPTIONS FOR ACHIEVA
6 cyl 3.1 L Engine +215
Compact Disc W/fm/tape +165
Cruise Control[Opt on SL Series I] +105
Keyless Entry System +95
Leather Steering Wheel[Opt on SL Series II] +50
Power Drivers Seat +145
Power Moonroof +340
Power Windows[Opt on SC Series I,SL Series I] +155
Rear Spoiler[Opt on SL Series II] +85

AURORA   1997

Larger front brakes, an in-dash CD player for the Bose sound system, a tilt-down right-hand exterior mirror for backing assistance, an integrated rearview mirror compass, and a three-channel garage door opener are added this year.

RATINGS (SCALE OF 1-10)

Overall	Safety	Reliability	Performance	Comfort	Value
8.3	7.1	8	8.8	9	8.5

Category A

4 Dr STD Sdn	13615	16405

OPTIONS FOR AURORA
Bose Sound System +290
Chrome Wheels +500
Compact Disc Changer +395
Heated Front Seats +100
Power Moonroof +675

BRAVADA   1997

Bravada drops the split-tailgate arrangement at the rear in favor of a top-hinged liftgate with separately lifting glass. So, tailgate parties aren't as convenient, but loading cargo sure is easier. Also new to the options list is a power tilt and slide sunroof. Included with the hole in the roof are a mini-overhead console, a pop-up wind deflector, and a sun shade. Rear disc brakes replace the former drums, combining with the front discs to provide better stopping ability.

RATINGS (SCALE OF 1-10)

Overall	Safety	Reliability	Performance	Comfort	Value
7.1	5.3	7.2	8	8	6.8

Category G

4 Dr STD 4WD Wgn	14325	17255

OPTIONS FOR BRAVADA
AM/FM Compact Disc Player +160
Camper/Towing Package +150
Gold Package +185
Power Moonroof +430

CUTLASS   1997

Oldsmobile retires the Ciera and introduces the Cutlass, based on the same platform as Chevy's new Malibu.

Don't forget to refer to the Mileage Adjustment Table at the back of this book!

Model Description	Trade-in Value	Market Value

Cutlass is more upscale that its Chevrolet counterpart, offering a slightly more powerful V-6 engine on all models, and a sunroof option, standard leather interior, and larger wheels on the GLS.

RATINGS (SCALE OF 1-10)

Overall	Safety	Reliability	Performance	Comfort	Value
7.8	7.5	7.6	8.4	8.3	7.1

Category C

	Trade-in	Market
4 Dr GLS Sdn	9165	11310
4 Dr STD Sdn	8365	10325

OPTIONS FOR CUTLASS

Aluminum/Alloy Wheels[Opt on STD] +150
Compact Disc W/fm/tape +165
Keyless Entry System[Opt on STD] +95
Power Drivers Seat[Opt on STD] +145
Power Moonroof +340
Power Windows[Opt on STD] +155

CUTLASS SUPREME   1997

Alloy wheels and a power trunk release are added to the standard equipment list, while coupes gain side-impact protection that meets federal safety standards. The 3.4-liter DOHC V-6 engine is dropped from the options list.

RATINGS (SCALE OF 1-10)

Overall	Safety	Reliability	Performance	Comfort	Value
7.9	7.6	8	8.2	8.3	7.6

Category C

	Trade-in	Market
2 Dr SL Series I Cpe	8730	10775
4 Dr SL Series I Sdn	8890	10975
2 Dr SL Series II Cpe	9050	11175
4 Dr SL Series II Sdn	9225	11390
2 Dr SL Series III Cpe	9285	11460
4 Dr SL Series III Sdn	9475	11695

OPTIONS FOR CUTLASS SUPREME

Compact Disc W/fm/tape +165
Keyless Entry System[Opt on SL Series I] +95
Power Drivers Seat[Opt on SL Series I] +145
Power Moonroof +340

EIGHTY EIGHT   1997

Side-impact protection is upgraded to federal safety standards, interiors are improved, and new Oldsmobile logos adorn the body.

RATINGS (SCALE OF 1-10)

Overall	Safety	Reliability	Performance	Comfort	Value
8.3	7.6	8.6	8.6	8.5	8.3

Category B

	Trade-in	Market
4 Dr LS Sdn	9935	12115
4 Dr STD Sdn	9375	11430

OPTIONS FOR EIGHTY EIGHT

Aluminum/Alloy Wheels[Std on LS] +165
Compact Disc W/fm/tape +190
Dual Power Seats +190
Leather Seats +335

LSS   1997

Minor changes accompany Oldsmobile's euro-flavored sedan into 1997. The center console and shifter are new, and other interior upgrades have been made. New, more prominent badging has been added to the exterior. Finally, the final-drive ratio has been changed to 2.93:1 from 2.97:1.

RATINGS (SCALE OF 1-10)

Overall	Safety	Reliability	Performance	Comfort	Value
8.3	7.6	8.6	8.4	8.6	8.3

Category C

	Trade-in	Market
4 Dr STD Sdn	11190	13815

OPTIONS FOR LSS

Chrome Wheels +300
Power Moonroof +340

REGENCY   1997

New name for an old concept. Look closely...see the old Eighty Eight before 1996's restyle? Regency takes over where the Ninety Eight left off, satisfying traditional Oldsmobile buyers.

RATINGS (SCALE OF 1-10)

Overall	Safety	Reliability	Performance	Comfort	Value
N/A	N/A	8.7	8.6	N/A	N/A

Category A

	Trade-in	Market
4 Dr STD Sdn	9350	11265

OPTIONS FOR REGENCY

Power Moonroof +675

SILHOUETTE   1997

Completely redesigned, the new Silhouette comes in several trim levels and two sizes, each with a healthy load of standard equipment.

RATINGS (SCALE OF 1-10)

Overall	Safety	Reliability	Performance	Comfort	Value
7.4	7	7.5	7.8	7.9	6.8

Category G

	Trade-in	Market
2 Dr GL Pass. Van Ext	11585	13960
2 Dr GLS Pass. Van Ext	13240	15950
2 Dr STD Pass. Van	11025	13285
2 Dr STD Pass. Van Ext	11345	13670

OPTIONS FOR SILHOUETTE

Aluminum/Alloy Wheels[Opt on GL] +165
Auto Load Leveling[Opt on GL] +110
Child Seats (2) +125

Don't forget to refer to the Mileage Adjustment Table at the back of this book!

Model Description	Trade-in Value	Market Value	Model Description	Trade-in Value	Market Value

Compact Disc W/fm/tape +240
Dual Air Conditioning[Opt on GL] +470
Leather Seats +385
Power Moonroof +430
Privacy Glass[Opt on STD] +130
Sliding Driver Side Door +260
Traction Control System[Opt on GL] +135

1996 OLDSMOBILE

ACHIEVA 1996

Substantial upgrades make the Achieva palatable for 1996. A new interior with dual airbags, standard air conditioning, a new base engine, daytime running lights, a theft-deterrent system and optional traction control make this Oldsmobile an excellent value in the compact class.

RATINGS (SCALE OF 1-10)

Overall	Safety	Reliability	Performance	Comfort	Value
7.4	7.1	6.7	8.4	7.6	7.2

Category C
2 Dr SC Series I Cpe   5085   6520
2 Dr SC Series II Cpe   5303   6800
2 Dr SC Series III Cpe   5570   7140
4 Dr SL Series II Sdn   5150   6600
4 Dr SL Series III Sdn   5705   7315

OPTIONS FOR ACHIEVA
6 cyl 3.1 L Engine +185
Auto 4-Speed Transmission[Opt on SC Series II, SL Series II] +320
Compact Disc W/fm/tape +135
Cruise Control[Opt on SC Series II, SL Series II] +85
Keyless Entry System +75
Power Drivers Seat +120
Power Sunroof +275

AURORA 1996

Daytime running lights are added, and looking through the backlight won't make your eyes water from distortions anymore. We knew it was only a matter of time before some goofball decided chrome wheels and a gold package would look great on the otherwise classy Aurora. The new Oldsmobile? What's that? When do we get the fake convertible roof, guys?

RATINGS (SCALE OF 1-10)

Overall	Safety	Reliability	Performance	Comfort	Value
8	7	7.7	8.8	9	7.3

Category A
4 Dr STD Sdn   11910   14520

OPTIONS FOR AURORA
Bose Sound System +240
Chrome Wheels +410

Compact Disc Changer +320
Heated Front Seats +80
Power Moonroof +550

BRAVADA 1996

Nice truck, but how many luxury SUV's do we really need? The only thing different about the Bravada to differentiate it from the Chevy Blazer and GMC Jimmy are the seats, front styling, trim — and the price tag.

RATINGS (SCALE OF 1-10)

Overall	Safety	Reliability	Performance	Comfort	Value
6.7	4.9	6.8	8	8	5.8

Category G
4 Dr STD 4WD Wgn   12420   15330

OPTIONS FOR BRAVADA
AM/FM Compact Disc Player +135
Camper/Towing Package +120
Gold Package +150

CIERA 1996

Bestseller prepares for retirement at the end of the year, receiving badge revisions, some additional standard equipment and an improved, optional V6 engine.

RATINGS (SCALE OF 1-10)

Overall	Safety	Reliability	Performance	Comfort	Value
7.5	6.5	7.3	7.4	7.6	8.5

Category C
4 Dr SL Wgn   5790   7420
4 Dr SL Series I Sdn   5830   7475
4 Dr SL Series II Sdn   6155   7890

OPTIONS FOR CIERA
6 cyl 3.1 L Engine[Opt on SL Series I] +185
AM/FM Compact Disc Player +145
Cruise Control[Std on SL Series II] +85
Keyless Entry System +75
Luggage Rack +45
Power Drivers Seat +120
Power Windows[Std on SL Series II] +125
Third Seat +70

CUTLASS SUPREME 1996

The convertible has been retired. The sedan and coupe enjoy their last year in production, receiving engine upgrades for 1996.

RATINGS (SCALE OF 1-10)

Overall	Safety	Reliability	Performance	Comfort	Value
7.9	7.6	7.8	8.2	8.3	7.5

Category C
2 Dr SL Cpe   7135   9150
2 Dr SL Series I Cpe   7275   9325
4 Dr SL Series I Sdn   7450   9550

Don't forget to refer to the Mileage Adjustment Table at the back of this book!

OLDSMOBILE 96-95

Model Description	Trade-in Value	Market Value
2 Dr SL Series II Cpe	7332	9400
4 Dr SL Series II Sdn	7485	9595
2 Dr SL Series III Cpe	7394	9480
4 Dr SL Series III Sdn	7225	9265
2 Dr SL Series IV Cpe	7485	9595
4 Dr SL Series IV Sdn	7630	9785

OPTIONS FOR CUTLASS SUPREME

6 cyl 3.4 L Engine +495
Compact Disc W/fm/tape[Std on SL Series IV] +135
Keyless Entry System[Opt on SL Series II,
*   SL Series I Sdn] +75*
Leather Seats[Opt on SL Series I] +245
Power Drivers Seat[Std on SL Series IV] +120
Power Moonroof +280
Rear Spoiler +70

EIGHTY EIGHT   1996

Royale designation dropped, and the Eighty Eight gets fresh Aurora-inspired styling front and rear. Standard equipment levels go up, and daytime running lights are added.

RATINGS (SCALE OF 1-10)

Overall	Safety	Reliability	Performance	Comfort	Value
8.2	7.5	8	8.6	8.5	8.3

Category B
4 Dr LS Sdn	8700	10875
4 Dr LSS Sdn	9225	11530
4 Dr LSS Sprchgd Sdn	9670	12090
4 Dr STD Sdn	7950	9940

OPTIONS FOR EIGHTY EIGHT

Chrome Wheels +280
Compact Disc W/fm/tape +155
Cruise Control[Opt on STD] +90
Leather Seats[Std on LSS] +275
Power Drivers Seat[Opt on STD] +125
Power Moonroof +395
Traction Control System[Opt on LS] +70

NINETY-EIGHT   1996

Supercharged engine dropped from this model, and daytime running lamps have been added. Don't expect a 1997 Ninety Eight.

RATINGS (SCALE OF 1-10)

Overall	Safety	Reliability	Performance	Comfort	Value
8	7.5	8.4	7.9	8.1	8.3

Category A
4 Dr Series I Sdn	11025	13445
4 Dr Series II Sdn	11520	14045

OPTIONS FOR NINETY-EIGHT

Compact Disc W/fm/tape +260
Power Sunroof +570
Traction Control System[Opt on Series I] +85

SILHOUETTE   1996

New 180-horsepower 3.4-liter V6 makes the Silhouette even better able to imitate Japan's bullet train.

RATINGS (SCALE OF 1-10)

Overall	Safety	Reliability	Performance	Comfort	Value
7.4	6.4	7.8	7.2	7.3	8.5

Category G
2 Dr Series I Pass. Van	9270	11445
2 Dr Series II Pass. Van	9700	11975

OPTIONS FOR SILHOUETTE

AM/FM Compact Disc Player +135
Auto Load Leveling +90
Child Seats (2) +105
Dual Air Conditioning +385
Power Sliding Door[Opt on Series I] +160

1995 OLDSMOBILE

ACHIEVA   1995

Fewer options and powertrains are available; SOHC and high-output Quad 4 engines are gone. Standard engine makes 150 horsepower this year, up from 115 in 1994. A V6 is optional. Air conditioning is standard.

RATINGS (SCALE OF 1-10)

Overall	Safety	Reliability	Performance	Comfort	Value
7.6	6.6	7.8	8.4	7.9	7.1

Category C
4 Dr S Sdn	3865	5150
2 Dr S Series I Cpe	3790	5055
2 Dr S Series II Cpe	4325	5770

OPTIONS FOR ACHIEVA

6 cyl 3.1 L Engine +160
Auto 3-Speed Transmission +185
Auto 4-Speed Transmission[Std on S Series II] +250
AM/FM Stereo Tape[Std on S Series II] +55
Air Conditioning[Std on S Series II] +265
Cruise Control[Std on S Series II] +70
Keyless Entry System +60
Power Windows[Std on S Series II] +105
Rear Spoiler +60

AURORA   1995

World-class V8 front-drive luxury sedan features cutting-edge styling, dual airbags, ABS and traction control.

RATINGS (SCALE OF 1-10)

Overall	Safety	Reliability	Performance	Comfort	Value
8	7.8	7.5	8.8	9	7.1

Category A
4 Dr STD Sdn	9265	11580

Don't forget to refer to the Mileage Adjustment Table at the back of this book!

EDMUND'S® USED CARS & TRUCKS

Model Description	Trade-in Value	Market Value	Model Description	Trade-in Value	Market Value

OPTIONS FOR AURORA

Bose Sound System +195
Heated Front Seats +65
Power Moonroof +450

CIERA 1995

Offered in a single trim level this year. Rear defroster and cassette player are standard. Brake/transmission shift interlock is new.

RATINGS (SCALE OF 1-10)

Overall	Safety	Reliability	Performance	Comfort	Value
7.7	7.1	7.4	7.4	7.6	8.9

Category C

4 Dr SL Sdn	4755	6340
4 Dr SL Wgn	5320	7090

OPTIONS FOR CIERA

6 cyl 3.1 L Engine[Opt on Sdn] +160
AM/FM Stereo Tape[Opt on Wgn] +55
Aluminum/Alloy Wheels +100
Cruise Control[Opt on Wgn] +70
Keyless Entry System +60
Luggage Rack +40
Power Drivers Seat +100
Power Windows +105
Third Seat +55
Woodgrain Applique +100

CUTLASS SUPREME 1995

Redesigned dashboard equipped with dual airbags debuts. Single trim level offered this year. Front bench seat is no longer available. Front seatbelts are mounted to door pillars instead of doors. Air conditioning, power windows, power locks, tilt steering, and cassette player are standard on all models.

RATINGS (SCALE OF 1-10)

Overall	Safety	Reliability	Performance	Comfort	Value
7.9	8.1	6.8	8.2	8.3	7.9

Category C

2 Dr S Cpe	6340	8455
4 Dr S Sdn	6455	8605
2 Dr STD Conv	7900	10530

OPTIONS FOR CUTLASS SUPREME

6 cyl 3.4 L Engine +405
Compact Disc W/fm/tape +110
Cruise Control[Opt on Sdn] +70
Keyless Entry System[Opt on Sdn] +60
Leather Seats[Opt on S] +200
Power Drivers Seat[Opt on S] +100
Power Moonroof +225

EIGHTY-EIGHT ROYALE 1995

Engine upgraded to 3800 Series II status, and supercharged 3.8-liter V6 is a new option on LSS models. New on-board navigation system called Guidestar was a $1,995 option, originally available only in California.

RATINGS (SCALE OF 1-10)

Overall	Safety	Reliability	Performance	Comfort	Value
N/A	8.3	7.2	8.5	N/A	N/A

Category B

4 Dr LS Sdn	7100	9100
4 Dr LSS Sdn	7275	9330
4 Dr LSS Sprchgd Sdn	7540	9665
4 Dr STD Sdn	6480	8305

OPTIONS FOR EIGHTY-EIGHT ROYALE

Compact Disc W/fm/tape +125
Cruise Control[Opt on STD] +75
Leather Seats[Std on LSS] +225
Power Drivers Seat[Opt on STD] +105
Traction Control System[Std on LSS] +60

NINETY-EIGHT 1995

Engine upgraded to 3800 Series II status. Alloy wheels are standard. Flash-to-pass is new standard feature.

RATINGS (SCALE OF 1-10)

Overall	Safety	Reliability	Performance	Comfort	Value
7.8	8.2	7.3	7.9	8.1	7.6

Category A

4 Dr STD Sdn	8650	10815

OPTIONS FOR NINETY-EIGHT

Compact Disc W/fm/tape +215
Keyless Entry System +80
Power Moonroof +450
Traction Control System +70

SILHOUETTE 1995

3.1-liter V6 engine dropped in favor of more powerful 3.8-liter V6.

RATINGS (SCALE OF 1-10)

Overall	Safety	Reliability	Performance	Comfort	Value
7	6.6	5.9	7.2	7.3	7.8

Category G

2 Dr STD Pass. Van	7035	8905

OPTIONS FOR SILHOUETTE

AM/FM Compact Disc Player +110
Child Seats (2) +85
Dual Air Conditioning +315
Keyless Entry System +65
Leather Seats +255
Power Drivers Seat +95
Traction Control System +90

Don't forget to refer to the Mileage Adjustment Table at the back of this book!

1994 OLDSMOBILE

ACHIEVA 1994

Driver airbag debuts. 3.1-liter V6 replaces 3.3-liter V6 on options sheet. Hot-rod SCX gone from lineup.

RATINGS (SCALE OF 1-10)

Overall	Safety	Reliability	Performance	Comfort	Value
7.6	6.5	8	8.4	7.9	7.1

Category C

2 Dr S Cpe	3240	4380
4 Dr S Sdn	3315	4480
2 Dr SC Cpe	4180	5650
4 Dr SL Sdn	4235	5720

OPTIONS FOR ACHIEVA

6 cyl 3.1 L Engine +140
Auto 3-Speed Transmission +150
Auto 4-Speed Transmission +205
AM/FM Stereo Tape[Opt on S] +45
Air Conditioning[Opt on S] +220
Astro Roof +180
Cruise Control[Opt on S] +55
Leather Seats +165
Power Drivers Seat +80
Power Mirrors[Opt on S] +30
Power Windows +85

BRAVADA 1994

New Special Edition model has gold trim. Doors get guard beams. Shock absorbers are softened for a better ride.

RATINGS (SCALE OF 1-10)

Overall	Safety	Reliability	Performance	Comfort	Value
6.1	5	6.5	6.8	7.1	5.2

Category G

4 Dr STD 4WD Wgn	7280	9455
4 Dr Special Edition 4WD Wgn	7565	9825

OPTIONS FOR BRAVADA

AM/FM Compact Disc Player +90
Camper/Towing Package[Opt on STD] +80
Electronic Gauges[Opt on STD] +70
Gold Package[Opt on STD] +100
Leather Seats[Opt on STD] +210
Swing Out Tire Carrier[Opt on STD] +55

CUTLASS CIERA 1994

Driver airbag and ABS standard for all models. Four-cylinder engine back in base models, producing 120 horsepower. A 3.1-liter V6 replaces last year's 3.3-liter V6. Variable-assist steering is a new option on sedans. SL replaced by Special Edition models.

RATINGS (SCALE OF 1-10)

Overall	Safety	Reliability	Performance	Comfort	Value
7.3	7.1	6.1	7.4	7.6	8.3

Category C

4 Dr S Sdn	4075	5505
4 Dr S Wgn	4255	5755
4 Dr Special Edition Sdn	4300	5810
4 Dr Special Edition Wgn	4525	6115

OPTIONS FOR CUTLASS CIERA

6 cyl 3.1 L Engine[Opt on S Sdn] +140
AM/FM Stereo Tape[Opt on S] +45
Cruise Control[Opt on S] +55
Keyless Entry System +50
Leather Seats +165
Power Drivers Seat[Opt on S] +80
Power Windows[Opt on S] +85
Premium Sound System +105
Third Seat[Opt on S] +45
Woodgrain Applique +85

CUTLASS SUPREME 1994

Driver airbag added and ABS is made standard on all models. International Series dropped. Special Editions are on sale, carrying one-price stickers and a healthy load of standard equipment. 3.1-liter V6 makes 20 more horsepower. 3.4-liter V6 makes 15 more horsepower. New standard features include tilt steering, intermittent wipers, Pass-Key theft deterrent system, and rear defogger.

RATINGS (SCALE OF 1-10)

Overall	Safety	Reliability	Performance	Comfort	Value
7.7	7.4	6.5	8.2	8	8.4

Category C

2 Dr S Cpe	4960	6705
4 Dr S Sdn	4900	6620
2 Dr STD Conv	6765	9145
2 Dr Special Edition Cpe	5300	7165
4 Dr Special Edition Sdn	5185	7005

OPTIONS FOR CUTLASS SUPREME

6 cyl 3.4 L Engine +360
Climate Control for AC[Opt on S Cpe] +45
Cruise Control[Opt on S] +55
Keyless Entry System +50
Leather Seats[Std on STD] +165
Lighted Entry System[Opt on STD] +40
Power Drivers Seat[Std on STD] +80
Power Moonroof +185
Power Passenger Seat +75
Power Windows[Opt on S] +85
Premium Sound System +105

Don't forget to refer to the Mileage Adjustment Table at the back of this book!

Model Description	Trade-in Value	Market Value

EIGHTY-EIGHT ROYALE 1994

Passenger airbag is housed in a new dashboard featuring more compact layout and new four-spoke steering wheel. Grille is body-color. Headlamps and turn signals are restyled. Traction control system can now reduce engine power as well as apply brakes to slipping wheel. New Special Edition model is available.

RATINGS (SCALE OF 1-10)

Overall	Safety	Reliability	Performance	Comfort	Value
N/A	8.3	7.7	8.3	N/A	N/A

Category B
4 Dr LS Sdn	5880	7735
4 Dr LSS Sdn	6005	7900
4 Dr STD Sdn	5445	7165
4 Dr Special Edition Sdn	5675	7470

OPTIONS FOR EIGHTY-EIGHT ROYALE

Compact Disc W/fm/tape +105
Cruise Control[Opt on STD] +60
Keyless Entry System +45
Leather Seats[Std on LS Special Edit.] +185
Power Drivers Seat[Opt on LS,STD] +85
Traction Control System +50

NINETY-EIGHT 1994

Passenger airbag is housed in a new dashboard featuring more compact layout. Touring Sedan is dropped, and a Special Edition is added. Supercharged engine is now available on the Elite, and it gains horsepower and torque. Traction control system can now reduce engine power as well as apply brakes to slipping wheel. There is an additional inch of seat travel. The grille and headlamps are restyled.

RATINGS (SCALE OF 1-10)

Overall	Safety	Reliability	Performance	Comfort	Value
8.1	8.3	7.7	7.7	8.1	8.5

Category A
4 Dr Elite Sdn	6625	8490
4 Dr STD Sdn	6435	8250
4 Dr Special Edition Sdn	6550	8395

OPTIONS FOR NINETY-EIGHT

Astro Roof +380
Compact Disc W/fm/tape +175
Keyless Entry System[Opt on STD] +65
Leather Seats[Opt on Elite, STD] +180
Power Passenger Seat[Opt on STD] +80
Traction Control System +55

SILHOUETTE 1994

Driver airbag added to standard equipment list. Traction control and integrated child seats are new options. Power sliding side door debuts. New Special Edition model is available.

RATINGS (SCALE OF 1-10)

Overall	Safety	Reliability	Performance	Comfort	Value
7	6.5	5.9	7.2	7.3	8.3

Category G
2 Dr STD Pass. Van	5845	7595
2 Dr Special Edition Pass. Van		
	6065	7880

OPTIONS FOR SILHOUETTE

6 cyl 3.8 L Engine[Opt on STD] +110
Auto 4-Speed Transmission[Opt on STD] +55
AM/FM Compact Disc Player +90
AM/FM Stereo Tape[Opt on STD] +60
Child Seats (2) +70
Cruise Control[Opt on STD] +55
Keyless Entry System +55
Leather Seats +210
Luggage Rack[Opt on STD] +45
Power Door Locks[Opt on STD] +65
Power Drivers Seat +75
Power Windows[Opt on STD] +65
Traction Control System +75

1993 OLDSMOBILE

ACHIEVA 1993

All four-cylinder engines lose five horsepower, thanks to emissions regulations. They also get new engine mounts and other revisions aimed at making them smoother and quieter. Battery rundown protection is new standard feature.

RATINGS (SCALE OF 1-10)

Overall	Safety	Reliability	Performance	Comfort	Value
7	4.3	7.6	8.4	7.9	6.9

Category C
2 Dr S Cpe	2510	3490
4 Dr S Sdn	2571	3575
2 Dr SL Cpe	2934	4080
4 Dr SL Sdn	2970	4125

OPTIONS FOR ACHIEVA

4 cyl 2.3 L Quad 4 Engine +90
6 cyl 3.3 L Engine[Opt on S,Sdn] +120
Auto 3-Speed Transmission[Opt on S] +125
Achieva SC Performance Pkg +315
Achieva SCX Performance Pkg +480
AM/FM Stereo Tape[Opt on S] +35
Air Conditioning +180
Aluminum/Alloy Wheels +65
Cruise Control +45
Keyless Entry System +40
Power Drivers Seat +65
Power Windows +70

OLDSMOBILE 93

Model Description	Trade-in Value	Market Value

BRAVADA 1993

Electronic shift controls added to transmission. Gold Package is new option. Driver's seat gets six-way power adjustment. Both front seats gain power lumbar adjusters. Sun visors get extender panels, and a new overhead console with compass is added.

RATINGS (SCALE OF 1-10)

Overall	Safety	Reliability	Performance	Comfort	Value
6.3	5.1	7	6.8	7.1	5.6

Category G
4 Dr STD 4WD Wgn — 6090 — 8120

OPTIONS FOR BRAVADA

AM/FM Compact Disc Player +70
Camper/Towing Package +65
Electronic Gauges +55
Leather Seats +170
Swing Out Tire Carrier +45

CUTLASS CIERA 1993

Driver airbag is standard on SL; optional on S. Four-cylinder engine dropped in favor of standard V6 power. Air conditioning also makes the standard equipment list. SL sedans get a trunk cargo net; SL wagons get a cargo cover. Leather is new option on base model.

RATINGS (SCALE OF 1-10)

Overall	Safety	Reliability	Performance	Comfort	Value
7.4	6.1	6.9	7.4	7.6	8.8

Category C
4 Dr S Sdn — 3120 — 4335
4 Dr S Cruiser Wgn — 3230 — 4490
4 Dr SL Sdn — 3505 — 4865
4 Dr SL Cruiser Wgn — 3650 — 5065

OPTIONS FOR CUTLASS CIERA

6 cyl 3.3 L Engine[Opt on S,S Cruiser] +120
Auto 4-Speed Transmission[Std on SL Cruiser] +45
AM/FM Stereo Tape[Opt on S,S Cruiser] +35
Air Bag Restraint[Opt on S,S Cruiser] +105
Aluminum/Alloy Wheels +65
Cruise Control +45
Keyless Entry System +40
Leather Seats +135
Power Drivers Seat +65
Power Windows +70
Premium Sound System +85
Third Seat[Opt on S Cruiser] +35
Woodgrain Applique +70

CUTLASS SUPREME 1993

3.4-liter, twin-cam engine now available in convertible, but can't be ordered with five-speed transmission anymore. International Series gets new alloys, and all models are equipped with automatic power door locks.

RATINGS (SCALE OF 1-10)

Overall	Safety	Reliability	Performance	Comfort	Value
7.2	5.3	6.9	8.2	8	7.8

Category C
2 Dr International Cpe — 5135 — 7135
4 Dr International Sdn — 5035 — 6990
2 Dr S Cpe — 3965 — 5505
4 Dr S Sdn — 3890 — 5400
2 Dr STD Conv — 5845 — 8120
2 Dr Special Cpe — 4220 — 5860
4 Dr Special Sdn — 4140 — 5750

OPTIONS FOR CUTLASS SUPREME

6 cyl 3.4 L Engine[Opt on S,STD] +300
Auto 4-Speed Transmission[Opt on S] +40
AM/FM Stereo Tape[Opt on S] +35
Aluminum/Alloy Wheels[Opt on S] +65
Anti-Lock Brakes[Opt on S,STD] +135
Climate Control for AC[Opt on S,STD] +35
Cruise Control[Opt on S,STD] +45
Leather Seats +135
Power Drivers Seat[Opt on S,STD] +65
Power Sunroof +150
Power Windows[Std on Special,STD] +70
Premium Sound System +85
Steer. Whl. Radio Cntrls[Opt on S,STD] +35

EIGHTY-EIGHT ROYALE 1993

ABS is standard on all models. Engine makes more torque. LSS gets new alloy wheels and variable-assist power steering.

RATINGS (SCALE OF 1-10)

Overall	Safety	Reliability	Performance	Comfort	Value
N/A	6.8	7.1	8.3	N/A	N/A

Category B
4 Dr LS Sdn — 4930 — 6750
4 Dr STD Sdn — 4575 — 6265

OPTIONS FOR EIGHTY-EIGHT ROYALE

LSS Pkg +255
AM/FM Stereo Tape[Std on LS] +40
Aluminum/Alloy Wheels +75
Auto Load Leveling +40
Cruise Control[Std on LS] +50
Leather Seats +150
Power Door Locks[Std on LS] +55
Power Drivers Seat +70
Premium Sound System +90
Traction Control System +40

NINETY-EIGHT 1993

Base V6 makes more torque. Touring Sedan gets body-color grille and headlight trim. Base model loses standard cassette player.

Don't forget to refer to the Mileage Adjustment Table at the back of this book!

Model Description	Trade-in Value	Market Value

RATINGS (SCALE OF 1-10)

Overall	Safety	Reliability	Performance	Comfort	Value
N/A	N/A	7.3	7.7	7.7	8.4

Category A

	Trade-in	Market
4 Dr Regency Sdn	5200	7025
4 Dr Regency Elite Sdn	5670	7660
4 Dr Regency Touring Sdn	6140	8295
4 Dr Special Sdn	5380	7270

OPTIONS FOR NINETY-EIGHT

AM/FM Stereo Tape[Opt on Regency] +30
Aluminum/Alloy Wheels[Opt on Regency] +100
Keyless Entry System[Opt on Regency] +55
Leather Seats[Opt on Regency,Regency Elite] +150
Power Passenger Seat +65
Power Sunroof +310
Premium Sound System[Std on Regency Touring] +75
Steer. Whl. Radio Cntrls[Opt on Regency] +40

SILHOUETTE   1993

Subtle restyle includes front and rear fascias, as well as alloy wheels. Optional V6 makes more power.

RATINGS (SCALE OF 1-10)

Overall	Safety	Reliability	Performance	Comfort	Value
7	5.6	6.5	7.2	7.3	8.3

Category G

	Trade-in	Market
2 Dr STD Pass. Van	4275	5705

OPTIONS FOR SILHOUETTE

6 cyl 3.8 L Engine +125
Auto 4-Speed Transmission +110
AM/FM Compact Disc Player +70
Auto Load Leveling +50
Cruise Control +45
Dual Air Conditioning +210
Leather Seats +170
Luggage Rack +35
Power Door Locks +50
Power Drivers Seat +60
Power Windows +55
Sunroof +65

1992 OLDSMOBILE

ACHIEVA   1992

Cutlass Calais replacement. SCX coupe is hot-rod of the bunch, featuring a 190-horsepower Quad 4 engine. ABS is standard. Computer Command Ride is optional on SL and SC, and allows driver to select one of three suspension settings.

RATINGS (SCALE OF 1-10)

Overall	Safety	Reliability	Performance	Comfort	Value
6.9	4.4	7.1	8.4	7.9	6.8

Category C

	Trade-in	Market
2 Dr S Cpe	2250	3265
4 Dr S Sdn	2220	3220
2 Dr SCX Cpe	2615	3790
2 Dr SL Cpe	2425	3515
4 Dr SL Sdn	2465	3575

OPTIONS FOR ACHIEVA

4 cyl 2.3 L Quad 4 Engine[Opt on S] +75
6 cyl 3.3 L Engine +100
Auto 3-Speed Transmission[Opt on S] +100
Sport Performance Pkg +235
Air Conditioning +145
Power Drivers Seat +55
Power Windows +55

BRAVADA   1992

CD player and outside spare tire carrier are new options. New speedometer placed in dashboard. Midyear, a 200-horsepower V6 is added.

RATINGS (SCALE OF 1-10)

Overall	Safety	Reliability	Performance	Comfort	Value
5.8	3.8	6.7	6.4	7.1	5

Category G

	Trade-in	Market
4 Dr STD 4WD Wgn	5080	6960

OPTIONS FOR BRAVADA

AM/FM Compact Disc Player +60
Camper/Towing Package +55
Leather Seats +140
Swing Out Tire Carrier +35

CUSTOM CRUISER   1992

A more powerful 5.7-liter V8 is newly optional.

Category C

	Trade-in	Market
4 Dr STD Wgn	4075	5905

OPTIONS FOR CUSTOM CRUISER

8 cyl 5.7 L Engine +45
Power Door Locks +45
Power Drivers Seat +55
Power Windows +55

CUTLASS CIERA   1992

Coupe and base sedan are given the axe. Automatic door locks made standard.

RATINGS (SCALE OF 1-10)

Overall	Safety	Reliability	Performance	Comfort	Value
7	4.7	6.7	7.4	7.6	8.7

Category C

	Trade-in	Market
4 Dr S Sdn	2385	3455
4 Dr S Cruiser Wgn	2430	3520
4 Dr SL Sdn	2765	4010
4 Dr SL Cruiser Wgn	2875	4165

Model Description	Trade-in Value	Market Value

OPTIONS FOR CUTLASS CIERA
6 cyl 3.3 L Engine[Opt on S,S Cruiser] +100
Auto 4-Speed Transmission[Std on SL Cruiser] +35
Air Conditioning[Opt on S,S Cruiser] +145
Leather Seats +110
Power Drivers Seat[Opt on S] +55
Power Windows +55
Third Seat[Opt on S Cruiser] +30

CUTLASS SUPREME   1992

Styling is updated front and rear. Four-cylinder engine dropped. International Series models get 3.4-liter twin-cam engine, heads-up instrument display and ABS standard. Sedans get folding rear seatback. Alloys are standard on SL models.

RATINGS (SCALE OF 1-10)

Overall	Safety	Reliability	Performance	Comfort	Value
7.4	5.4	7	8.2	8	8.3

Category C
2 Dr International Cpe	3460	5015
4 Dr International Sdn	3390	4910
2 Dr S Cpe	3115	4515
4 Dr S Sdn	3030	4390
2 Dr STD Conv	4535	6575

OPTIONS FOR CUTLASS SUPREME
6 cyl 3.4 L Engine +220
Auto 4-Speed Transmission[Std on STD] +30
Anti-Lock Brakes[Opt on S,STD] +110
Astro Roof +120
Auto Load Leveling +45
Keyless Entry System[Opt on S,STD] +35
Leather Seats +110
Power Door Locks[Opt on S,STD] +45
Power Windows[Std on STD] +55

EIGHTY-EIGHT ROYALE   1992

Redesigned and based on Ninety-Eight platform. Available only as a sedan; coupe dropped from lineup. Driver airbag is standard. LS models have standard ABS; this feature is optional on base models. 3.8-liter V6 makes 170 horsepower. Passenger and cargo volume are both up. Traction control is optional on LS models. Midyear, an LSS model debuted with FE3 suspension, alloy wheels and bucket seats.

RATINGS (SCALE OF 1-10)

Overall	Safety	Reliability	Performance	Comfort	Value
N/A	6.8	6.9	8.3	N/A	N/A

Category B
4 Dr LS Sdn	3820	5455
4 Dr STD Sdn	3610	5160

OPTIONS FOR EIGHTY-EIGHT ROYALE
LSS Pkg +250
Anti-Lock Brakes[Std on LS] +125

Auto Load Leveling +35
Leather Seats +125
Power Door Locks[Std on LS] +45
Power Drivers Seat +55
Power Passenger Seat +60
Traction Control System +30

NINETY-EIGHT   1992

Supercharged engine is optional on Touring Sedan. Traction control is optional on any model.

RATINGS (SCALE OF 1-10)

Overall	Safety	Reliability	Performance	Comfort	Value
N/A	N/A	7	7.7	7.7	7.9

Category A
4 Dr Regency Sdn	4020	5660
4 Dr Regency Elite Sdn	4300	6055
4 Dr Regency Touring Sdn	4775	6725

OPTIONS FOR NINETY-EIGHT
AM/FM Compact Disc Player +90
Astro Roof +255
Dual Power Seats +70
Leather Seats[Std on Regency Touring] +120
Traction Control System +40

SILHOUETTE   1992

Newly optional 165-horsepower, 3.8-liter V6 is highly recommended. ABS is made standard. Larger wheels and tires are standard. New options include sunroof, remote keyless entry and rear climate controls.

RATINGS (SCALE OF 1-10)

Overall	Safety	Reliability	Performance	Comfort	Value
7	5.7	6.6	7.2	7.3	8.3

Category G
2 Dr STD Pass. Van	3575	4895

OPTIONS FOR SILHOUETTE
6 cyl 3.8 L Engine +120
Auto 4-Speed Transmission +35
AM/FM Compact Disc Player +60
Auto Load Leveling +40
Dual Air Conditioning +170
Leather Seats +140
Power Door Locks +40
Power Windows +45

TORONADO   1992

Trofeo gets firmer suspension and bigger wheels and tires.

Category B
2 Dr STD Cpe	4190	5985
2 Dr Trofeo Cpe	4740	6775

OPTIONS FOR TORONADO
Visual Info System +205
AM/FM Compact Disc Player +60

Don't forget to refer to the Mileage Adjustment Table at the back of this book!

OLDSMOBILE 92-91

Model Description	Trade-in Value	Market Value	Model Description	Trade-in Value	Market Value

Astro Roof +230
Leather Seats[Opt on STD] +125
Power Passenger Seat[Opt on STD] +60

1991 OLDSMOBILE

BRAVADA 1991

Olds markets a gussied-up S10 Blazer. Features all-wheel drive and four-wheel ABS. Remote keyless entry is standard.

RATINGS (SCALE OF 1-10)

Overall	Safety	Reliability	Performance	Comfort	Value
5.5	3.6	5.8	6.4	7.1	4.5

Category G
4 Dr STD 4WD Wgn — 4390 — 6270

OPTIONS FOR BRAVADA
Camper/Towing Package +45
Leather Seats +115

CUSTOM CRUISER 1991

Behemoth wagon based on same chassis and bodywork as Caprice and Roadmaster joins lineup. Features eight-passenger seating, glass Vista Roof treatment, ABS and driver airbag. Leather is optional.
Category C
4 Dr STD Wgn — 2650 — 4075

OPTIONS FOR CUSTOM CRUISER
Leather Seats +90
Power Door Locks +35
Power Drivers Seat +45
Power Passenger Seat +40
Power Windows +45

CUTLASS CALAIS 1991

Quad 442 gets performance tires. International Series has standard ABS.
Category C

	Trade-in	Market
2 Dr International Cpe	2400	3690
4 Dr International Sdn	2500	3845
2 Dr S Cpe	1900	2925
4 Dr S Sdn	1950	3000
2 Dr SL Cpe	2225	3425
4 Dr SL Sdn	2300	3540
2 Dr STD Cpe	1880	2895
4 Dr STD Sdn	1980	3045

OPTIONS FOR CUTLASS CALAIS
4 cyl 2.3 L Quad 4 Engine[Opt on S,STD] +95
6 cyl 3.3 L Engine +95
Auto 3-Speed Transmission[Std on SL] +80
Quad 442 Performance Pkg +255
Air Conditioning[Opt on S,STD] +120
Leather Seats +90
Power Door Locks +35

Power Drivers Seat +45
Power Windows +45

CUTLASS CIERA 1991

No changes.

RATINGS (SCALE OF 1-10)

Overall	Safety	Reliability	Performance	Comfort	Value
6.8	4.6	5.9	7.4	7.6	8.3

Category C

	Trade-in	Market
2 Dr S Cpe	1850	2845
4 Dr S Sdn	1930	2970
4 Dr S Cruiser Wgn	2000	3075
4 Dr SL Sdn	2235	3435
4 Dr SL Cruiser Wgn	2300	3535
4 Dr STD Sdn	1855	2850

OPTIONS FOR CUTLASS CIERA
6 cyl 3.3 L Engine[Std on SL,SL Cruiser] +95
Auto 4-Speed Transmission[Opt on S,SL] +30
Sport Appearance Pkg +120
Air Conditioning[Std on SL,SL Cruiser] +120
Leather Seats +90
Power Door Locks +35
Power Drivers Seat +45
Power Windows +45
Third Seat[Opt on S Cruiser] +25

CUTLASS SUPREME 1991

3.4-liter, twin-cam V6 debuts on options list, equipped with a five-speed in coupes and an automatic in sedans.

RATINGS (SCALE OF 1-10)

Overall	Safety	Reliability	Performance	Comfort	Value
7.2	5.3	6.3	8.2	8	8.1

Category C

	Trade-in	Market
2 Dr International Cpe	2705	4160
4 Dr International Sdn	2625	4040
2 Dr SL Cpe	2430	3735
4 Dr SL Sdn	2380	3665
2 Dr STD Conv	3620	5570
2 Dr STD Cpe	2205	3390
4 Dr STD Sdn	2115	3250

OPTIONS FOR CUTLASS SUPREME
6 cyl 3.1 L Engine[Std on International,SL,Conv] +80
6 cyl 3.4 L Engine +110
Anti-Lock Brakes +90
Leather Seats +90
Power Door Locks[Opt on SL,STD] +35
Power Drivers Seat +45
Power Sunroof +100
Power Windows[Std on Conv] +45

Power Drivers Seat +45
Power Windows +45

Don't forget to refer to the Mileage Adjustment Table at the back of this book!

EIGHTY-EIGHT ROYALE — 1991

No changes.
Category B

Model Description	Trade-in Value	Market Value
2 Dr Brougham Cpe	2870	4220
4 Dr Brougham Sdn	3010	4425
2 Dr STD Cpe	2350	3455
4 Dr STD Sdn	2460	3615

OPTIONS FOR EIGHTY-EIGHT ROYALE
Touring Suspension +115
Air Bag Restraint +125
Anti-Lock Brakes +100
Leather Seats +100
Power Door Locks +40
Power Drivers Seat[Opt on STD] +45
Power Passenger Seat +50
Power Windows +45

NINETY-EIGHT — 1991

Total redesign gives Ninety-Eight nine inches of additional length. Automatic load leveling, ABS, child-proof rear door locks, driver airbag, and automatic climate controls are standard. Touring Sedan again available.

RATINGS (SCALE OF 1-10)

Overall	Safety	Reliability	Performance	Comfort	Value
N/A	N/A	6.9	7.7	7.7	8

Category A

	Trade-in	Market
4 Dr Regency Elite Sdn	3520	5100
4 Dr Touring Sdn	4035	5850

OPTIONS FOR NINETY-EIGHT
AM/FM Compact Disc Player +75
Astro Roof +210
Leather Seats[Std on Touring] +100
Power Passenger Seat[Std on Touring] +45

SILHOUETTE — 1991

No changes.

RATINGS (SCALE OF 1-10)

Overall	Safety	Reliability	Performance	Comfort	Value
6.7	4.8	6.8	6.8	7.3	7.7

Category G

	Trade-in	Market
2 Dr STD Pass. Van	2890	4130

OPTIONS FOR SILHOUETTE
AM/FM Compact Disc Player +50
Auto Load Leveling +35
Leather Seats +115
Power Door Locks +35
Power Drivers Seat +40
Power Windows +35

TORONADO — 1991

Remote keyless entry standard. Hands-free mobile phone is optional.
Category B

	Trade-in	Market
2 Dr STD Cpe	3290	4835
2 Dr Trofeo Cpe	3705	5445

OPTIONS FOR TORONADO
Visual Info System +145
AM/FM Compact Disc Player +50
Leather Seats[Opt on STD] +100
Power Sunroof +170

1990 OLDSMOBILE

CUSTOM CRUISER — 1990

No changes for 1990.
Category B

	Trade-in	Market
4 Dr STD Wgn	1730	2665

OPTIONS FOR CUSTOM CRUISER
Power Door Locks +30
Power Drivers Seat +40
Power Passenger Seat +40
Power Windows +35

CUTLASS CALAIS — 1990

New Quad 442 option includes high-output Quad 4 engine, sport suspension, and manual transmission. Remote keyless entry and a CD player are new options.
Category C

	Trade-in	Market
2 Dr International Cpe	1545	2535
4 Dr International Sdn	1695	2780
2 Dr S Cpe	1430	2345
4 Dr S Sdn	1515	2485
2 Dr SL Cpe	1580	2590
4 Dr SL Sdn	1640	2685
2 Dr STD Cpe	1360	2230
4 Dr STD Sdn	1405	2305

OPTIONS FOR CUTLASS CALAIS
4 cyl 2.3 L Quad 4 Engine[Std on SL] +75
6 cyl 3.3 L Engine +75
Auto 3-Speed Transmission[Std on SL] +65
Quad 442 Pkg +205
Air Conditioning[Opt on S,SL,STD] +95
Leather Seats +75
Power Door Locks +30
Power Drivers Seat +35
Power Windows +35
Sunroof +45

OLDSMOBILE 90

CUTLASS CIERA 1990

2.8-liter V6 option disappears. Manual transmission dropped. Door-mounted passive seatbelts are added for front seat passengers. Seats have been upgraded.

RATINGS (SCALE OF 1-10)

Overall	Safety	Reliability	Performance	Comfort	Value
6.5	4.4	5.7	7.4	7.6	7.5

Category C

2 Dr International Cpe	1655	2715
4 Dr International Sdn	1755	2875
2 Dr S Cpe	1225	2010
4 Dr S Sdn	1405	2305
4 Dr S Cruiser Wgn	1350	2210
4 Dr SL Sdn	1700	2785
4 Dr SL Cruiser Wgn	1710	2800
4 Dr STD Sdn	1435	2350

OPTIONS FOR CUTLASS CIERA

6 cyl 3.3 L Engine[Opt on S,S Cruiser,STD] +75
Air Conditioning[Opt on S,S Cruiser,STD] +95
Dual Power Seats +70
Leather Seats +75
Power Door Locks +30
Power Sunroof +80
Power Windows +35

CUTLASS SUPREME 1990

A sedan joins the lineup. International Series gets high-output Quad 4 engine, teamed with five-speed manual transmission.

RATINGS (SCALE OF 1-10)

Overall	Safety	Reliability	Performance	Comfort	Value
6.7	4.7	4.5	8.2	8	8

Category C

2 Dr International Cpe	2110	3455
4 Dr International Sdn	2175	3565
2 Dr SL Cpe	1975	3235
4 Dr SL Sdn	2060	3375
2 Dr STD Conv	2685	4400
2 Dr STD Cpe	1810	2970
4 Dr STD Sdn	1755	2880

OPTIONS FOR CUTLASS SUPREME

6 cyl 3.1 L Engine[Std on SL,Conv] +75
Anti-Lock Brakes +75
Astro Roof +80
Leather Seats +75
Power Door Locks[Opt on SL,STD] +30
Power Drivers Seat[Opt on SL,STD] +35
Power Windows[Std on Conv] +35

EIGHTY-EIGHT ROYALE 1990

Minor styling updates front and rear. A power auto-down driver's window, and remote keyless entry are new options.

Category B

2 Dr Brougham Cpe	2285	3520
4 Dr Brougham Sdn	2405	3700
2 Dr STD Cpe	2080	3205
4 Dr STD Sdn	2200	3385

OPTIONS FOR EIGHTY-EIGHT ROYALE

Touring Ride & Handling Pkg +95
Air Bag Restraint +100
Anti-Lock Brakes +85
Leather Seats +80
Power Door Locks +30
Power Drivers Seat +40
Power Passenger Seat +40
Power Windows +35

NINETY-EIGHT 1990

Minor styling updates front and rear. Express-down feature for the power driver's window is standard this year. Optional astroroof has an express-open feature. Remote keyless entry is a new option. Center armrest is redesigned to accommodate optional CD player.

Category A

4 Dr Regency Sdn	2305	3495
4 Dr Regency Brougham Sdn	2400	3635
4 Dr Touring Sdn	3165	4795

OPTIONS FOR NINETY-EIGHT

AM/FM Compact Disc Player +60
Air Bag Restraint +100
Anti-Lock Brakes[Std on Touring] +110
Astro Roof +170
Leather Seats[Std on Touring] +80
Power Passenger Seat[Std on Touring] +35

SILHOUETTE 1990

Underpowered minivan with lots of standard equipment. 3.1-liter V6 offers a measly 120 horsepower.

RATINGS (SCALE OF 1-10)

Overall	Safety	Reliability	Performance	Comfort	Value
6.3	4.6	5.7	6.8	7.3	7.1

Category G

2 Dr STD Pass. Van	2385	3610

OPTIONS FOR SILHOUETTE

Leather Seats +95
Power Door Locks +30
Power Drivers Seat +35
Power Windows +30

Don't forget to refer to the Mileage Adjustment Table at the back of this book!

Model Description	Trade-in Value	Market Value	Model Description	Trade-in Value	Market Value

TORONADO 1990

Redesigned inside and out. Car is more than a foot longer than last year. Trunk is 2.5 cubic feet larger. Driver airbag is a new option on base models; standard on Trofeo. Dash features full analog gauges. Suspension is revamped and features automatic load leveling.

Category B

	Trade-in	Market
2 Dr STD Cpe	2540	3905
2 Dr Trofeo Cpe	2905	4465

OPTIONS FOR TORONADO
Visual Information Center +160
AM/FM Compact Disc Player +40
Anti-Lock Brakes[Opt on STD] +85
Astro Roof +155
Bose Sound System +80
Leather Seats[Opt on STD] +80

Don't forget to refer to the Mileage Adjustment Table at the back of this book!

Model Description	Trade-in Value	Market Value	Model Description	Trade-in Value	Market Value

PLYMOUTH 99

PLYMOUTH USA

1995 Plymouth Neon

1999 PLYMOUTH

BREEZE   1999

Power windows, locks and mirrors, along with floor mats and a driver's seat height adjuster are now standard on the Breeze. In addition, the suspension has been revised for a more pleasant ride. What more could you ask? Oh yeah: the Noise, Vibration and Harshness levels have also been reduced.

RATINGS (SCALE OF 1-10)

Overall	Safety	Reliability	Performance	Comfort	Value
N/A	6.4	N/A	6.6	7.1	N/A

Category C

4 Dr Expresso Sdn	8810	10615
4 Dr STD Sdn	8460	10195

OPTIONS FOR BREEZE

4 cyl 2.4 L Engine +335
Auto 4-Speed Transmission +775
AM/FM Compact Disc Player +270
Aluminum/Alloy Wheels +225
Anti-Lock Brakes +450
Cruise Control +155
Keyless Entry System +140

NEON   1999

The Neon is now based on the same platform as the Viper. No, just kidding. Nothing's changed for '99.

RATINGS (SCALE OF 1-10)

Overall	Safety	Reliability	Performance	Comfort	Value
N/A	6	7.6	7.4	7.6	N/A

Category E

2 Dr Competition Cpe	6810	8305
4 Dr Competition Sdn	7025	8565
2 Dr Expresso Cpe	7240	8830
4 Dr Expresso Sdn	7410	9035
2 Dr Highline Cpe	6985	8520
4 Dr Highline Sdn	7150	8720

OPTIONS FOR NEON

4 cyl 2.0 L DOHC Engine[Opt on Highline] +110
Auto 3-Speed Transmission +445
Competition Pkg +1115
AM/FM Compact Disc Player +340
Air Conditioning[Std on Expresso] +605
Aluminum/Alloy Wheels +245
Anti-Lock Brakes +500
Cruise Control +165
Keyless Entry System +115
Power Door Locks +180
Power Mirrors +80
Power Windows +195
Rear Window Defroster[Opt on Competition] +120
Tilt Steering Wheel +110

PROWLER   1999

A brand-new 3.5-liter engine under the hood creates performance more fitting a hot rod. Also new for '99 is one more color option: Prowler Yellow.

RATINGS (SCALE OF 1-10)

Overall	Safety	Reliability	Performance	Comfort	Value
N/A	N/A	N/A	8.6	7.6	N/A

Category F

2 Dr STD Conv	35590	42880

OPTIONS FOR PROWLER

Chrome Wheels +430

VOYAGER   1999

SE trim levels get body-colored door and liftgate handles, as well as a body-colored front grille. All models add a cargo net between the front seats, and the new exterior color this year is Light Cypress Green.

RATINGS (SCALE OF 1-10)

Overall	Safety	Reliability	Performance	Comfort	Value
N/A	6.4	8.8	6.6	7.4	N/A

Category G

2 Dr Expresso Pass. Van	13640	16240
2 Dr Grand Pass. Van	12850	15300
2 Dr Grand Expresso Pass. Van	14670	17465
2 Dr Grand SE Pass. Van	14406	17150
2 Dr SE Pass. Van	13350	15895
2 Dr STD Pass. Van	11844	14100

Don't forget to refer to the Mileage Adjustment Table at the back of this book!

Model Description	Trade-in Value	Market Value
Model Description	Trade-in Value	Market Value

OPTIONS FOR VOYAGER

6 cyl 3.0 L Engine[Opt on STD] +415
6 cyl 3.3 L Engine +715
6 cyl 3.8 L Engine +275
Auto 4-Speed Transmission[Opt on STD] +150
Air Conditioning[Opt on Grand,STD] +605
Aluminum/Alloy Wheels +245
Anti-Lock Brakes[Opt on Grand,STD] +445
Compact Disc W/fm/tape[Opt on Grand SE,SE] +355
Cruise Control[Opt on Grand,STD] +155
Keyless Entry System +150
Power Door Locks +170
Power Windows +175
Rear Window Defroster[Opt on Grand,STD] +125
Sliding Driver Side Door[Opt on STD] +390
Sunscreen Glass[Std on Expresso,Grand Expresso] +275
Tilt Steering Wheel[Opt on Grand,STD] +130

1998 PLYMOUTH

BREEZE 1998

Availability of a 2.4-liter engine brings 150 horsepower and 167 foot-pounds of torque, and that's just what the Breeze needs to live up to its name. Both engines can meet California emissions regulations, and new engine mounts helps make them quieter. An Expresso package adds some aesthetic changes, a power sunroof is now optional and there are six new colors to choose from.

RATINGS (SCALE OF 1-10)

Overall	Safety	Reliability	Performance	Comfort	Value
N/A	6.3	7.5	6.6	7.1	N/A

Category C

4 Dr Expresso Sdn	7820	9535
4 Dr STD Sdn	7410	9035

OPTIONS FOR BREEZE

4 cyl 2.4 L Engine +275
Auto 4-Speed Transmission +645
AM/FM Compact Disc Player +220
Aluminum/Alloy Wheels +180
Anti-Lock Brakes +370
Cruise Control +130
Keyless Entry System +115
Power Door Locks +150
Power Sunroof +410
Power Windows +190

NEON 1998

California and other emission-regulating states get an LEV (Low Emission Vehicle) engine calibration. Also changed this year are ABS, a new ignition key lock and the addition of four new colors.

RATINGS (SCALE OF 1-10)

Overall	Safety	Reliability	Performance	Comfort	Value
7.1	6.1	7.7	7.4	7.6	6.8

Category E

2 Dr Competition Cpe	6475	7995
4 Dr Competition Sdn	6585	8130
2 Dr Expresso Cpe	6840	8445
4 Dr Expresso Sdn	7045	8695
2 Dr Highline Cpe	6335	7820
4 Dr Highline Sdn	6490	8010
4 Dr Style Sdn	6915	8535

OPTIONS FOR NEON

Auto 3-Speed Transmission +370
Competition Pkg +965
AM/FM Compact Disc Player +275
Air Conditioning[Std on Expresso, Style] +495
Aluminum/Alloy Wheels[Std on Style] +200
Anti-Lock Brakes +410
Cruise Control +135
Keyless Entry System +95
Power Door Locks +145
Power Mirrors +65
Power Moonroof +350
Power Windows +160
Rear Window Defroster[Opt on Competition] +100
Tilt Steering Wheel +90

VOYAGER 1998

Expresso Decor Package, four new exterior colors and "next generation" depowered airbags.

RATINGS (SCALE OF 1-10)

Overall	Safety	Reliability	Performance	Comfort	Value
7.5	6.3	8	6.6	7.4	9.2

Category G

2 Dr Expresso Pass. Van	11850	14105
2 Dr Grand Pass. Van	11420	13595
2 Dr Grand Expresso Pass. Van	12820	15260
2 Dr Grand SE Pass. Van	12410	14775
2 Dr SE Pass. Van	11365	13530
2 Dr STD Pass. Van	10145	12075

OPTIONS FOR VOYAGER

6 cyl 3.0 L Engine[Opt on STD] +305
6 cyl 3.3 L Engine +210
6 cyl 3.3 L FLEX Engine +125
Auto 4-Speed Transmission[Opt on Grand,STD] +155
Air Conditioning[Opt on Grand, Grand SE, SE, STD] +495
Aluminum/Alloy Wheels +200
Anti-Lock Brakes[Opt on Grand, STD] +365
Compact Disc W/fm/tape[Opt on Grand SE,SE] +290
Cruise Control[Opt on Grand, STD] +125
Keyless Entry System +120
Power Door Locks +140
Power Mirrors[Opt on Grand, STD] +80

Don't forget to refer to the Mileage Adjustment Table at the back of this book!

Model Description	Trade-in Value	Market Value	Model Description	Trade-in Value	Market Value

PLYMOUTH 98-96

Power Windows +145
Rear Window Defroster[Opt on Grand, Grand SE, SE, STD] +105
Sliding Driver Side Door[Opt on STD] +320
Sunscreen Glass[Opt on Grand, Grand SE, SE, STD] +225
Tilt Steering Wheel[Opt on Grand, STD] +105

1997 PLYMOUTH

BREEZE   1997

Plymouth is inching the Breeze up-market in both price and content. This year sees a fairly sizable price hike and the addition of luxury options such as an in-dash CD changer. Changes to the standard equipment list brings a nicer center console, improved basic stereos, and increased flow rear seat heater ducts.

RATINGS (SCALE OF 1-10)

Overall	Safety	Reliability	Performance	Comfort	Value
N/A	N/A	6.3	6.6	7.1	6.7

Category C
4 Dr STD Sdn   6480   8000

OPTIONS FOR BREEZE
Auto 4-Speed Transmission +510
AM/FM Compact Disc Player +180
Aluminum/Alloy Wheels +150
Anti-Lock Brakes +300
Child Seat (1) +60
Cruise Control +105
Keyless Entry System +95
Power Door Locks +125
Power Windows +155

NEON   1997

1997 Neons are made quieter with the addition of a structural oil pan. Other changes include new optional radios, a new seat fabric, new wheels and wheel covers, and a few new paint colors.

RATINGS (SCALE OF 1-10)

Overall	Safety	Reliability	Performance	Comfort	Value
6.9	6	7.1	7.4	7.6	6.6

Category E
2 Dr Expresso Cpe   5585   7070
4 Dr Expresso Sdn   5740   7265
2 Dr Highline Cpe   5460   6910
4 Dr Highline Sdn   5650   7150
2 Dr STD Cpe   5190   6570
4 Dr STD Sdn   5320   6735

OPTIONS FOR NEON
4 cyl 2.0 L DOHC Engine +75
Auto 3-Speed Transmission +290
Competition Pkg +625
AM/FM Compact Disc Player +225

Air Conditioning[Opt on STD] +405
Aluminum/Alloy Wheels +165
Anti-Lock Brakes +335
Child Seat (1) +55
Keyless Entry System +80
Power Door Locks +120
Power Moonroof +285
Power Windows +130

PROWLER   1997

Category K
2 Dr STD Conv   33490   39865

VOYAGER   1997

For 1997, the Plymouth minivans receive a cornucopia of changes. This year brings new wheel covers, improved antilock braking systems, an accident response system that unlocks the doors and turns on the interior lights if the air bags deploy, better radios, a quieter interior, and more optional equipment for Base and SE models.

RATINGS (SCALE OF 1-10)

Overall	Safety	Reliability	Performance	Comfort	Value
6.9	6	6.4	6.6	7.4	8

Category G
2 Dr Grand Pass. Van   9520   11470
2 Dr Grand SE Pass. Van   10304   12415
2 Dr SE Pass. Van   9085   10945
2 Dr STD Pass. Van   8070   9725

OPTIONS FOR VOYAGER
6 cyl 3.0 L Engine +345
6 cyl 3.3 L Engine +460
Auto 4-Speed Transmission[Opt on Grand,STD] +120
7 Passenger Seating[Opt on STD] +260
Air Conditioning +405
Aluminum/Alloy Wheels +165
Anti-Lock Brakes[Opt on Grand,STD] +295
Auto Load Leveling +110
Captain Chairs (4) +310
Child Seats (2) +125
Compact Disc W/fm/tape +240
Cruise Control[Opt on Grand,STD] +105
Dual Air Conditioning +470
Keyless Entry System +100
Luggage Rack +80
Power Door Locks +115
Power Drivers Seat +140
Power Windows +120
Sliding Driver Side Door +260

1996 PLYMOUTH

BREEZE   1996

The Breeze is introduced this year as Chrysler Corporation's bargain-basement midsize sedan.

Don't forget to refer to the Mileage Adjustment Table at the back of this book!

PLYMOUTH 96-95

Model Description	Trade-in Value	Market Value	Model Description	Trade-in Value	Market Value

Nicely equipped with air conditioning and a decent stereo, the Breeze has a surprising amount of interior room.

RATINGS (SCALE OF 1-10)

Overall	Safety	Reliability	Performance	Comfort	Value
N/A	N/A	5.3	6.6	7.1	6.2

Category C

	Trade-in	Market
4 Dr STD Sdn	5440	6975

OPTIONS FOR BREEZE

Auto 4-Speed Transmission +425
Anti-Lock Brakes +245
Child Seat (1) +50
Compact Disc W/fm/tape +135
Keyless Entry System +75
Power Door Locks +100
Power Sunroof +275
Power Windows +125

NEON   1996

Antilock brakes are optional across the line, and base models get more standard equipment for 1996. A value-packed Expresso package is aimed at twenty-something first-time buyers. A base coupe is newly available, and all Neons are supposedly quieter than last year. A power moonroof joins the options list, and a remote keyless entry system with panic alarm is available.

RATINGS (SCALE OF 1-10)

Overall	Safety	Reliability	Performance	Comfort	Value
6.6	5.9	6.3	7.4	7.6	5.9

Category E

	Trade-in	Market
2 Dr Highline Cpe	4570	6015
4 Dr Highline Sdn	4715	6205
2 Dr STD Cpe	4265	5610
4 Dr STD Sdn	4415	5810
2 Dr Sport Cpe	4995	6570
4 Dr Sport Sdn	5115	6730

OPTIONS FOR NEON

4 cyl 2.0 L DOHC Engine +60
Auto 3-Speed Transmission +240
Competition Pkg +415
AM/FM Compact Disc Player +185
Air Conditioning +330
Aluminum/Alloy Wheels +135
Anti-Lock Brakes +275
Child Seat (1) +45
Cruise Control +90
Keyless Entry System +65
Power Door Locks[Std on Sport] +100
Power Moonroof +230
Power Windows +105
Rear Spoiler +85
Tilt Steering Wheel[Std on Sport] +60

VOYAGER   1996

Chrysler's stylists and engineers have achieved what many thought was impossible: they substantially improved upon their original formula in every way. Interior comfort is top-notch, and the left-hand passenger door is an industry first.

RATINGS (SCALE OF 1-10)

Overall	Safety	Reliability	Performance	Comfort	Value
6.7	5.8	5	6.6	7.4	8.8

Category G

	Trade-in	Market
2 Dr Grand Pass. Van	8215	10145
2 Dr Grand SE Pass. Van	9290	11470
2 Dr SE Pass. Van	8185	10105
2 Dr STD Pass. Van	7150	8825

OPTIONS FOR VOYAGER

6 cyl 3.0 L Engine[Std on Grand] +290
6 cyl 3.3 L Engine +350
7 Passenger Seating[Opt on STD] +210
Air Conditioning +330
Aluminum/Alloy Wheels +135
Anti-Lock Brakes[Opt on Grand,STD] +245
Captain Chairs (4) +255
Child Seats (2) +105
Compact Disc W/fm/tape +195
Cruise Control[Opt on Grand,STD] +85
Dual Air Conditioning +385
Keyless Entry System +80
Luggage Rack +65
Power Door Locks +95
Power Windows +95
Premium Sound System +140
Sliding Driver Side Door +215

1995 PLYMOUTH

ACCLAIM   1995

The Acclaim is into the home stretch of its career.

RATINGS (SCALE OF 1-10)

Overall	Safety	Reliability	Performance	Comfort	Value
7	6.7	7.5	6.8	7.4	6.6

Category C

	Trade-in	Market
4 Dr STD Sdn	3950	5265

OPTIONS FOR ACCLAIM

6 cyl 3.0 L Engine +265
Aluminum/Alloy Wheels +100
Power Door Locks +80
Power Drivers Seat +100
Power Windows +105

NEON   1995

The all-new Neon is introduced as Plymouth's entry in the compact car class. Roomy, cute and quick are three

PLYMOUTH 95-94

Model Description	Trade-in Value	Market Value	Model Description	Trade-in Value	Market Value

of the best adjectives we can find for this car. Unfortunately, Chrysler Corporation is still grappling with reliability and noise issues. The Neon is available in coupe and sedan bodystyles in three trim-levels. Safety equipment includes standard dual airbags, optional antilock brakes and an optional integrated child seat.

RATINGS (SCALE OF 1-10)

Overall	Safety	Reliability	Performance	Comfort	Value
6.5	5.6	4.8	7.4	7.6	6.9

Category E
2 Dr Highline Cpe	3645	4990
4 Dr Highline Sdn	3780	5175
4 Dr STD Sdn	3260	4465
2 Dr Sport Cpe	3980	5450
4 Dr Sport Sdn	4095	5610

OPTIONS FOR NEON
4 cyl 2.0 L DOHC Engine[Std on Sport] +55
Auto 3-Speed Transmission +200
AM/FM Compact Disc Player +150
Air Conditioning +270
Anti-Lock Brakes[Std on Sport] +225
Child Seat (1) +35
Cruise Control +75
Power Door Locks[Std on Sport] +80
Power Windows +85
Tilt Steering Wheel[Std on Sport] +50

VOYAGER   1995

A 3.3-liter V6 natural gas engine is available this year. Plymouth introduces a snazzy Rallye package for those trying to disguise the fact that they are driving a minivan.

RATINGS (SCALE OF 1-10)

Overall	Safety	Reliability	Performance	Comfort	Value
7.7	8.2	6.4	7.4	8.3	8.4

Category G
2 Dr Grand Pass. Van	5990	7585
2 Dr Grand LE Pass. Van	7625	9650
2 Dr Grand LE 4WD Pass. Van	7976	10100
2 Dr Grand SE Pass. Van	6910	8745
2 Dr Grand SE 4WD Pass. Van	7260	9190
2 Dr LE Pass. Van	6855	8680
2 Dr SE Pass. Van	5775	7310
2 Dr STD Pass. Van	4825	6105

OPTIONS FOR VOYAGER
6 cyl 3.0 L Engine[Opt on STD] +235
6 cyl 3.3 L Engine[Opt on LE,SE,STD] +75
6 cyl 3.8 L Engine +140
Auto 4-Speed Transmission[Opt on SE,STD] +65
7 Passenger Seating[Opt on STD] +170
Air Conditioning[Std on Grand LE,LE] +270
Anti-Lock Brakes[Std on Grand LE,LE,4WD] +200

Captain Chairs (4) +205
Child Seats (2) +85
Compact Disc W/fm/tape +160
Cruise Control[Opt on Grand,STD] +70
Dual Air Conditioning +315
Keyless Entry System[Opt on Grand SE,SE] +65
Leather Seats +255
Luggage Rack +50
Power Door Locks[Std on Grand LE,LE] +75
Power Drivers Seat +95
Power Windows +80
Trip Computer[Opt on Grand SE] +50

1994 PLYMOUTH

ACCLAIM   1994

The Acclaim gains a motorized passenger seatbelt. The flexible-fuel model is now available to retail customers.

RATINGS (SCALE OF 1-10)

Overall	Safety	Reliability	Performance	Comfort	Value
7.2	6.6	7.8	6.8	7.4	7.4

Category C
4 Dr STD Sdn	3010	4070

OPTIONS FOR ACCLAIM
6 cyl 3.0 L Engine +185
Auto 4-Speed Transmission +45
AM/FM Stereo Tape +45
Air Conditioning +220
Anti-Lock Brakes +165
Cruise Control +55
Power Door Locks +65
Power Drivers Seat +80
Power Windows +85
Rear Window Defroster +45
Tilt Steering Wheel +40

COLT   1994

A driver's airbag is now standard on the Colt. CFC-free air conditioning optional.

RATINGS (SCALE OF 1-10)

Overall	Safety	Reliability	Performance	Comfort	Value
6.6	5.5	7.4	8	7.4	4.7

Category E
2 Dr GL Sdn	2935	4190
4 Dr GL Sdn	3030	4330
4 Dr SE Wgn	3515	5020
2 Dr STD Sdn	2645	3780
4 Dr STD Sdn	2795	3990
4 Dr STD Wgn	2960	4225

OPTIONS FOR COLT
4 cyl 1.8 L Engine[Opt on GL Sdn] +125
4 cyl 2.4 L Engine[Opt on STD Wgn] +50

Don't forget to refer to the Mileage Adjustment Table at the back of this book!

Model Description	Trade-in Value	Market Value	Model Description	Trade-in Value	Market Value

Auto 3-Speed Transmission +140
Auto 4-Speed Transmission +190
AM/FM Stereo Tape +80
Air Conditioning +220
Aluminum/Alloy Wheels +90
Anti-Lock Brakes +180
Cruise Control +60
Keyless Entry System +45
Power Door Locks[Std on SE] +65
Power Windows +70
Rear Window Wiper[Std on SE,4WD] +35

LASER   1994

The final year for the Laser brings automatic-locking retractors for rear seats, making them more compatible for child seats.

RATINGS (SCALE OF 1-10)

Overall	Safety	Reliability	Performance	Comfort	Value
N/A	N/A	7.5	8.4	6.8	4

Category C
2 Dr RS Hbk   3975   5370
2 Dr STD Hbk   3450   4665

OPTIONS FOR LASER

Auto 4-Speed Transmission +215
AM/FM Compact Disc Player +100
Air Conditioning +220
Aluminum/Alloy Wheels[Opt on 2WD] +80
Anti-Lock Brakes +165
Cruise Control +55
Power Door Locks +65
Power Windows +85
Premium Sound System +105
Rear Spoiler[Std on RS] +50
Rear Window Wiper +40
Sunroof +100

SUNDANCE   1994

The Sundance gets a motorized passenger shoulder belt and CFC-free air conditioning.

RATINGS (SCALE OF 1-10)

Overall	Safety	Reliability	Performance	Comfort	Value
6.4	6.5	6.7	7.2	6.8	5

Category E
2 Dr Duster Hbk   2595   3705
4 Dr Duster Hbk   2690   3840
2 Dr STD Hbk   2555   3650
4 Dr STD Hbk   2620   3740

OPTIONS FOR SUNDANCE

4 cyl 2.5 L Engine[Opt on STD] +80
6 cyl 3.0 L Engine +220
Auto 3-Speed Transmission +155
Auto 4-Speed Transmission +200

AM/FM Compact Disc Player +125
Air Conditioning +220
Aluminum/Alloy Wheels +90
Anti-Lock Brakes +180
Cruise Control +60
Power Door Locks +65
Power Drivers Seat +85
Power Windows +70
Premium Sound System +90

VOYAGER   1994

New safety features include a passenger airbag and side-impact door beams that meet federal 1997 passenger car standards. Other changes include a new dashboard, optional integrated child seats and new body moldings.

RATINGS (SCALE OF 1-10)

Overall	Safety	Reliability	Performance	Comfort	Value
7.5	8.2	5.9	7.4	8.3	7.8

Category G
2 Dr Grand Pass. Van   4615   5995
2 Dr Grand LE Pass. Van   6050   7855
2 Dr Grand LE 4WD Pass. Van   6820   8855
2 Dr Grand SE Pass. Van   5415   7030
2 Dr Grand SE 4WD Pass. Van   5985   7775
2 Dr LE Pass. Van   5550   7210
2 Dr SE Pass. Van   4625   6005
2 Dr STD Pass. Van   3740   4855

OPTIONS FOR VOYAGER

6 cyl 3.0 L Engine[Opt on STD] +165
6 cyl 3.3 L Engine +30
6 cyl 3.8 L Engine +110
Auto 3-Speed Transmission[Opt on STD] +165
Auto 4-Speed Transmission[Opt on Grand,LE,SE,STD] +95
7 Passenger Seating[Std on Grand SE,SE] +140
AM/FM Compact Disc Player +90
AM/FM Stereo Tape[Opt on Grand,STD] +60
Air Conditioning[Std on Grand LE,LE] +220
Aluminum/Alloy Wheels +90
Anti-Lock Brakes[Std on 4WD] +160
Captain Chairs (4) +170
Child Seats (2) +70
Cruise Control[Opt on Grand,STD] +55
Dual Air Conditioning +255
Infinity Sound System +115
Keyless Entry System[Opt on Grand SE,SE] +55
Leather Seats +210
Luggage Rack +45
Power Door Locks[Std on Grand LE,LE] +65
Power Drivers Seat +75
Power Windows[Std on LE] +65

1993 PLYMOUTH

ACCLAIM 1993

The Acclaim is now available to fleet purchasers as a flexible-fuel vehicle, able to run on a fuel mix that is 85 percent methanol.

RATINGS (SCALE OF 1-10)

Overall	Safety	Reliability	Performance	Comfort	Value
7.1	6.1	8	6.8	7.4	7.4

Category C
	Trade-in	Market
4 Dr STD Sdn	2230	3100

OPTIONS FOR ACCLAIM

6 cyl 3.0 L Engine +155
Auto 3-Speed Transmission +125
Auto 4-Speed Transmission +155
AM/FM Stereo Tape +35
Air Conditioning +180
Aluminum/Alloy Wheels +65
Anti-Lock Brakes +135
Cruise Control +45
Power Door Locks +55
Power Drivers Seat +65
Power Windows +70

COLT 1993

The Colt is redesigned for 1993. The hatchback is dropped in favor of two- and four-door notchback styles and the GL model is equipped with a 113-horsepower engine that is optional on the base.

RATINGS (SCALE OF 1-10)

Overall	Safety	Reliability	Performance	Comfort	Value
N/A	N/A	6	8	7.4	6.6

Category E
	Trade-in	Market
2 Dr GL Sdn	2225	3320
4 Dr GL Sdn	2325	3470
4 Dr SE Wgn	2900	4325
2 Dr STD Sdn	2040	3045
4 Dr STD Sdn	2155	3220
4 Dr STD Wgn	2320	3465

OPTIONS FOR COLT

4 cyl 1.8 L Engine[Std on GL, Wgn] +85
4 cyl 2.4 L Engine[Std on SE] +40
Auto 3-Speed Transmission +115
Auto 4-Speed Transmission +155
AM/FM Stereo Tape +65
Air Conditioning +180
Aluminum/Alloy Wheels +75
Anti-Lock Brakes +150
Cruise Control +50
Keyless Entry System +35
Power Door Locks +55
Power Steering[Opt on GL, Sdn] +55

Power Windows +60
Rear Window Wiper +30

LASER 1993

The all-wheel drive Laser is now available with an automatic transmission. New alloy wheels are introduced to all but the base Laser. A gold package is available for those of you wanting the ever-popular midlife crisis look.

RATINGS (SCALE OF 1-10)

Overall	Safety	Reliability	Performance	Comfort	Value
N/A	N/A	7.3	8.4	6.8	4.2

Category C
	Trade-in	Market
2 Dr RS Hbk	3110	4320
2 Dr RS Turbo Hbk	3490	4845
2 Dr STD Hbk	2835	3940

OPTIONS FOR LASER

Auto 4-Speed Transmission +175
Air Conditioning +180
Aluminum/Alloy Wheels[Opt on 2WD] +65
Anti-Lock Brakes +135
Compact Disc W/fm/tape +75
Cruise Control +45
Power Door Locks +55
Power Windows +70
Premium Sound System +85
Sunroof +80

SUNDANCE 1993

The Sundance is available with antilock brakes in 1993.

RATINGS (SCALE OF 1-10)

Overall	Safety	Reliability	Performance	Comfort	Value
6.6	6.5	7.5	7.2	6.8	5

Category E
	Trade-in	Market
2 Dr Duster Hbk	2105	3140
4 Dr Duster Hbk	2195	3275
2 Dr STD Hbk	1985	2960
4 Dr STD Hbk	2010	3000

OPTIONS FOR SUNDANCE

4 cyl 2.5 L Engine[Opt on STD] +65
6 cyl 3.0 L Engine +155
Auto 3-Speed Transmission +125
Auto 4-Speed Transmission +155
AM/FM Compact Disc Player +100
Air Conditioning +180
Aluminum/Alloy Wheels +75
Anti-Lock Brakes +150
Cruise Control +50
Power Door Locks +55
Power Drivers Seat +70
Power Windows +60
Premium Sound System +70

Don't forget to refer to the Mileage Adjustment Table at the back of this book!

PLYMOUTH 93-92

Model Description	Trade-in Value	Market Value	Model Description	Trade-in Value	Market Value

VOYAGER 1993

Front shoulder belts are now height adjustable on the Voyager. All-wheel drive models gain new exterior and interior options.

RATINGS (SCALE OF 1-10)

Overall	Safety	Reliability	Performance	Comfort	Value
6.9	6	4.7	7.4	8.3	8.2

Category G

2 Dr Grand Pass. Van	3520	4695
2 Dr Grand LE Pass. Van	4780	6375
2 Dr Grand LE 4WD Pass. Van	5315	7085
2 Dr Grand SE Pass. Van	4075	5430
2 Dr Grand SE 4WD Pass. Van	4550	6065
2 Dr LE Pass. Van	4425	5900
2 Dr LE 4WD Pass. Van	5130	6840
2 Dr SE Pass. Van	3505	4675
2 Dr SE 4WD Pass. Van	4345	5795
2 Dr STD Pass. Van	2885	3845

OPTIONS FOR VOYAGER

6 cyl 3.0 L Engine[Opt on SE,STD] +145
6 cyl 3.3 L Engine[Std on Grand LE,Grand SE,4WD] +95
Auto 3-Speed Transmission +135
Auto 4-Speed Transmission +55
7 Passenger Seating +115
AM/FM Compact Disc Player +70
Air Conditioning[Std on Grand LE,LE] +180
Aluminum/Alloy Wheels +75
Anti-Lock Brakes +135
Captain Chairs (4) +140
Child Seats (2) +55
Cruise Control[Std on Grand LE,LE] +45
Dual Air Conditioning +210
Luggage Rack +35
Power Door Locks[Std on Grand LE] +50
Power Drivers Seat +60
Power Windows[Std on LE] +55
Premium Sound System +75
Velour/Cloth Seats[Opt on STD] +45
Woodgrain Applique +75

1992 PLYMOUTH

ACCLAIM 1992

Plymouth trims the fat, offering the Acclaim in only one trim level for 1992. The remaining Acclaim can be had with four-cylinder or V6 power.

RATINGS (SCALE OF 1-10)

Overall	Safety	Reliability	Performance	Comfort	Value
7	6	7.3	6.8	7.4	7.7

Category C

4 Dr STD Sdn	1775	2575

OPTIONS FOR ACCLAIM

6 cyl 3.0 L Engine +125
Auto 3-Speed Transmission +100
Auto 4-Speed Transmission +115
Air Conditioning +145
Anti-Lock Brakes +110
Power Door Locks +45
Power Drivers Seat +55
Power Windows +55

COLT 1992

Factory options list is pared in a cost-savings measure. A 113-horsepower engine is standard and a 118-horsepower engine is optional.

Category E

2 Dr GL Hbk	1805	2820
4 Dr SE Wgn	2415	3770
2 Dr STD Hbk	1700	2655
4 Dr STD Wgn	1930	3015
4 Dr STD 4WD Wgn	2265	3540

OPTIONS FOR COLT

4 cyl 2.4 L Engine +35
Auto 3-Speed Transmission +100
Auto 4-Speed Transmission +130
Air Conditioning +145
Anti-Lock Brakes +120
Power Door Locks +45
Power Windows +50

LASER 1992

The Laser gains all-wheel drive as an option that greatly improves handling. Front and rear styling changes include headlights, taillamps, and a new rear spoiler on turbo models.

RATINGS (SCALE OF 1-10)

Overall	Safety	Reliability	Performance	Comfort	Value
N/A	N/A	7.1	8.4	6.8	3.2

Category C

2 Dr RS Hbk	2315	3355
2 Dr RS Turbo Hbk	2680	3885
2 Dr RS Turbo 4WD Hbk	3190	4625
2 Dr STD Hbk	2400	3475

OPTIONS FOR LASER

Auto 4-Speed Transmission +135
Air Conditioning +145
Anti-Lock Brakes +110
Power Door Locks +45
Power Windows +55
Sunroof +65

SUNDANCE 1992

The RS trim level is dropped due to poor sales. No other changes to the Sundance.

Don't forget to refer to the Mileage Adjustment Table at the back of this book!

Model Description	Trade-in Value	Market Value

Model Description	Trade-in Value	Market Value

RATINGS (SCALE OF 1-10)

Overall	Safety	Reliability	Performance	Comfort	Value
6.3	5.7	6.4	7.2	6.8	5.4

Category E

2 Dr America Hbk	1500	2345
4 Dr America Hbk	1565	2445
2 Dr Duster Hbk	1710	2670
4 Dr Duster Hbk	1735	2710
2 Dr Highline Hbk	1625	2540
4 Dr Highline Hbk	1705	2665

OPTIONS FOR SUNDANCE

4 cyl 2.5 L Engine[Std on Duster] +50
6 cyl 3.0 L Engine +135
Auto 3-Speed Transmission +100
Auto 4-Speed Transmission +125
AM/FM Compact Disc Player +80
Air Conditioning +145
Power Door Locks +45
Power Drivers Seat +55
Power Windows +50
Sunroof +65

VOYAGER   1992

The driver airbag first seen on the 1991 model becomes standard in 1992. An integrated child seat is available for those with toddlers.

RATINGS (SCALE OF 1-10)

Overall	Safety	Reliability	Performance	Comfort	Value
6.6	5.3	3.9	7.4	8.3	8.1

Category G

2 Dr Grand Pass. Van	2975	4075
2 Dr Grand LE Pass. Van	3855	5280
2 Dr Grand LE 4WD Pass. Van	4235	5800
2 Dr Grand SE Pass. Van	3215	4405
2 Dr Grand SE 4WD Pass. Van	3785	5185
2 Dr LE Pass. Van	3515	4815
2 Dr LE 4WD Pass. Van	4195	5745
2 Dr LX Pass. Van	3480	4765
2 Dr LX 4WD Pass. Van	4435	6075
2 Dr SE Pass. Van	2880	3945
2 Dr SE 4WD Pass. Van	3630	4975
2 Dr STD Pass. Van	2450	3355

OPTIONS FOR VOYAGER

6 cyl 3.0 L Engine[Opt on SE,STD] +140
6 cyl 3.3 L Engine[Std on Grand LE,Grand SE,4WD] +70
Auto 3-Speed Transmission +105
Auto 4-Speed Transmission +30
7 Passenger Seating[Opt on STD] +95
Air Conditioning[Std on Grand LE,LE,LX] +145
Power Door Locks[Std on Grand LE,LE,LX] +40
Power Windows +45

ACCLAIM   1991

Four-wheel antilock brakes are introduced as an option on the 1991 Acclaim.

RATINGS (SCALE OF 1-10)

Overall	Safety	Reliability	Performance	Comfort	Value
6.9	5.8	6.2	6.8	7.4	8.2

Category C

4 Dr LE Sdn	1890	2910
4 Dr LX Sdn	2120	3265
4 Dr STD Sdn	1345	2070

OPTIONS FOR ACCLAIM

6 cyl 3.0 L Engine[Std on LX] +100
Auto 3-Speed Transmission[Opt on STD] +80
Auto 4-Speed Transmission[Opt on LE] +55
Air Conditioning +120
Anti-Lock Brakes +90
Power Door Locks +35
Power Drivers Seat +45
Power Windows +45

COLT   1991

No changes to the Colt.

Category E

2 Dr GL Hbk	1145	1940
2 Dr STD Hbk	1005	1705
4 Dr Vista Wgn	1545	2615
4 Dr Vista 4WD Wgn	1795	3045

OPTIONS FOR COLT

Auto 3-Speed Transmission +80
Air Conditioning +120
Power Door Locks +35
Power Steering[Std on 4WD] +40
Power Windows +40

LASER   1991

No major changes for the '91 Laser.

RATINGS (SCALE OF 1-10)

Overall	Safety	Reliability	Performance	Comfort	Value
N/A	N/A	6.7	8.4	6.8	3.2

Category C

2 Dr RS Hbk	1870	2880
2 Dr RS Turbo Hbk	2180	3350
2 Dr STD Hbk	1725	2650

OPTIONS FOR LASER

Auto 4-Speed Transmission +100
Air Conditioning +120
Anti-Lock Brakes +90
Power Door Locks +35

Don't forget to refer to the Mileage Adjustment Table at the back of this book!

EDMUND'S® USED CARS & TRUCKS   www.edmunds.com   439

PLYMOUTH 91-90

Model Description	Trade-in Value	Market Value	Model Description	Trade-in Value	Market Value

Power Windows +45
Sunroof +55

SUNDANCE 1991

No major changes to the bargain-basement Sundance.

RATINGS (SCALE OF 1-10)

Overall	Safety	Reliability	Performance	Comfort	Value
6.3	5.6	5.7	7.4	6.8	5.8

Category E

	Trade-in	Market
2 Dr America Hbk	1175	1990
4 Dr America Hbk	1225	2075
2 Dr Highline Hbk	1305	2210
4 Dr Highline Hbk	1365	2310
2 Dr RS Hbk	1435	2430
2 Dr RS Turbo Hbk	1490	2525
4 Dr RS Hbk	1480	2505
4 Dr RS Turbo Hbk	1545	2620

OPTIONS FOR SUNDANCE

4 cyl 2.5 L Engine[Std on RS] +40
Auto 3-Speed Transmission +80
Air Conditioning +120
Power Door Locks +35
Power Drivers Seat +45
Power Windows +40
Sunroof +50

VOYAGER 1991

Big changes for the all-new Plymouth Voyager. New sheetmetal, available antilock brakes and optional all-wheel drive are new features for the Voyager. A driver airbag also debuts on the Voyager. An LX model joins the Voyager lineup sporting a front air dam, fog lights and alloy wheels.

RATINGS (SCALE OF 1-10)

Overall	Safety	Reliability	Performance	Comfort	Value
6.6	4.8	3.7	7.4	8.3	8.6

Category G

	Trade-in	Market
2 Dr Grand LE Pass. Van	3055	4365
2 Dr Grand LE 4WD Pass. Van	3405	4865
2 Dr Grand SE Pass. Van	2575	3680
2 Dr Grand SE 4WD Pass. Van	3095	4420
2 Dr LE Pass. Van	2795	3995
2 Dr LE 4WD Pass. Van	3155	4505
2 Dr LX Pass. Van	2795	3990
2 Dr LX 4WD Pass. Van	3295	4705
2 Dr SE Pass. Van	2305	3295
2 Dr SE 4WD Pass. Van	2775	3965
2 Dr STD Pass. Van	2050	2930

OPTIONS FOR VOYAGER

6 cyl 3.0 L Engine[Std on LX] +105
6 cyl 3.3 L Engine[Std on Grand LE, Grand SE, 4WD] +85

Auto 4-Speed Transmission[Std on Grand LE, Grand SE, LX, 4WD] +25
Luxury Pkg +170
7 Passenger Seating[Opt on STD] +75
Air Bag Restraint[Std on STD] +75
Air Conditioning[Std on Grand LE, LE, LX] +120
Anti-Lock Brakes +90
Captain Chairs (4) +90
Dual Air Conditioning +140
Leather Seats +115
Power Door Locks[Std on Grand LE, LE, LX] +35
Power Drivers Seat +40
Power Windows +35

1990 PLYMOUTH

ACCLAIM 1990

The 1990 Acclaim gains a driver's side airbag and available V6 power in all of its models.

RATINGS (SCALE OF 1-10)

Overall	Safety	Reliability	Performance	Comfort	Value
7	5.6	6.9	6.8	7.4	8.1

Category C

	Trade-in	Market
4 Dr LE Sdn	1225	2005
4 Dr LE Turbo Sdn	1325	2170
4 Dr LX Sdn	1625	2665
4 Dr STD Sdn	1070	1750
4 Dr STD Turbo Sdn	1185	1940

OPTIONS FOR ACCLAIM

6 cyl 3.0 L Engine[Std on LX] +85
Auto 3-Speed Transmission[Std on LX] +70
Auto 4-Speed Transmission[Std on LX] +75
Air Conditioning +95
Power Door Locks +30
Power Drivers Seat +35
Power Windows +30
Sunroof +40

COLT 1990

No changes for 1990.

Category E

	Trade-in	Market
4 Dr DL 4WD Wgn	1545	2970
2 Dr GL Hbk	750	1445
2 Dr GT Hbk	965	1855
2 Dr STD Hbk	820	1580
4 Dr STD Wgn	1325	2550
4 Dr STD 4WD Wgn	1425	2745

OPTIONS FOR COLT

Auto 3-Speed Transmission +60
Auto 4-Speed Transmission +80
Performance Pkg +185
Sport Appearance Pkg +100
Air Conditioning +100

Don't forget to refer to the Mileage Adjustment Table at the back of this book!

Power Door Locks +30
Power Windows +30

HORIZON 1990

No changes for 1990.
Category E

4 Dr America Hbk	630	1210

OPTIONS FOR HORIZON
Auto 3-Speed Transmission +60
Air Conditioning +100
Power Steering +30

LASER 1990

Based on the Mitsubishi Eclipse, the Laser is designed to compete with the Probe, MX-6 and Daytona. A 92-horsepower powerplant is standard on Base and RS models, but the RS can be had with DOHC 2.0-liter four-cylinder engine that makes 135 horsepower.

RATINGS (SCALE OF 1-10)

Overall	Safety	Reliability	Performance	Comfort	Value
N/A	N/A	4.2	8.4	6.8	2.6

Category C

2 Dr RS Hbk	1460	2395
2 Dr RS Turbo Hbk	1710	2800
2 Dr STD Hbk	1400	2295

OPTIONS FOR LASER
4 cyl 2.0 L Engine +105
Auto 4-Speed Transmission +85
Air Conditioning +95
Power Door Locks +30
Power Windows +35
Sunroof +45

SUNDANCE 1990

A driver airbag becomes standard on all Sundances. The dashboard is slightly changed and it includes a better stereo.

RATINGS (SCALE OF 1-10)

Overall	Safety	Reliability	Performance	Comfort	Value
6.5	5.5	6.3	7.4	6.8	6.7

Category E

2 Dr RS Hbk	1000	1925
2 Dr RS Turbo Hbk	1070	2060
4 Dr RS Hbk	1045	2005
4 Dr RS Turbo Hbk	1095	2110
2 Dr STD Hbk	955	1835
2 Dr STD Turbo Hbk	1025	1975
4 Dr STD Hbk	1005	1935
4 Dr STD Turbo Hbk	1070	2055

OPTIONS FOR SUNDANCE
4 cyl 2.5 L Engine[Std on RS Hbk] +35
Auto 3-Speed Transmission +65
Air Conditioning +100
Power Door Locks +30
Power Drivers Seat +35
Power Windows +30
Sunroof +40

VOYAGER 1990

The Voyager and Grand Voyager get a 20-gallon fuel tank and the Grand Voyager gets a larger V6 engine.
Category G

2 Dr Grand LE Pass. Van	2315	3505
2 Dr Grand SE Pass. Van	2045	3100
2 Dr LE Pass. Van	1915	2900
2 Dr LE Turbo Pass. Van	1990	3015
2 Dr LX Pass. Van	1920	2910
2 Dr LX Turbo Pass. Van	2045	3100
2 Dr SE Pass. Van	1685	2550
2 Dr SE Turbo Pass. Van	1750	2655
2 Dr STD Pass. Van	1530	2320
2 Dr STD Turbo Pass. Van	1600	2425

OPTIONS FOR VOYAGER
6 cyl 3.0 L Engine[Std on LX] +110
Auto 3-Speed Transmission +70
Auto 4-Speed Transmission[Opt on LE,SE] +90
7 Passenger Seating[Opt on SE,STD] +65
Air Conditioning[Std on Grand LE,LE,LX] +100
Dual Air Conditioning +115
Leather Seats +95
Power Door Locks[Std on Grand LE,LE,LX] +30
Power Drivers Seat +35
Power Sunroof +95
Power Windows[Std on Grand LE,LE,LX] +30

Don't forget to refer to the Mileage Adjustment Table at the back of this book!

PONTIAC 99

Model Description	Trade-in Value	Market Value	Model Description	Trade-in Value	Market Value

PONTIAC USA

1996 Pontiac Firebird Coupe

1999 PONTIAC

BONNEVILLE 1999

All the '99 model year has to offer the rapidly aging Bonneville is a couple of new exterior colors and the availability of GM's dealer-installed OnStar mobile communications system.

RATINGS (SCALE OF 1-10)

Overall	Safety	Reliability	Performance	Comfort	Value
N/A	7.6	8.8	8.4	7.8	N/A

Category B.

	Trade-in	Market
4 Dr SE Sdn	12555	15125
4 Dr SLE Sdn	13250	15965
4 Dr SSE Sdn	16355	19705
4 Dr SSEi Sprchgd Sdn	17440	21010

OPTIONS FOR BONNEVILLE

AM/FM Compact Disc Player[Opt on SE,SLE] +245
Aluminum/Alloy Wheels[Opt on SE] +245
Chrome Wheels +510
Keyless Entry System[Opt on SE] +130
Power Drivers Seat[Opt on SE] +230
Power Mirrors[Opt on SE] +75
Power Moonroof +725
Premium Sound System[Opt on SE] +295
Traction Control System[Opt on SE,SLE] +130

FIREBIRD 1999

After last year's freshening, Firebird gets minor revisions and a few new standard items. Electronic traction control is now available on all models, with a bigger gas tank and an oil life monitor standard. A Torsen limited-slip rear axle comes with V8 models (and V6 cars with the performance package), while an eight-speaker Delco-

Monsoon sound system goes into the convertible. A power-steering cooler is now available for V8s, and a Hurst shifter is optional on the six-speed manual transmission. The Ram Air WS6 package now sports dual outlet exhaust, and two new exterior colors debut, Pewter and Medium Blue metallic.

RATINGS (SCALE OF 1-10)

Overall	Safety	Reliability	Performance	Comfort	Value
N/A	8	N/A	N/A	7.3	N/A

Category F

	Trade-in	Market
2 Dr Formula Cpe	15085	18175
2 Dr STD Conv	15740	18965
2 Dr STD Cpe	12555	15125
2 Dr Trans Am Conv	19380	23350
2 Dr Trans Am Cpe	16665	20080

OPTIONS FOR FIREBIRD

Auto 4-Speed Transmission[Opt on STD] +600
30th Anniversary Pkg +1165
AutoCross Performance Pkg +870
Ram Air Performance Pkg +2330
Sport Appearance Pkg +770
Chrome Wheels +430
Glass Panel T-tops[Std on Trans Am] +730
Keyless Entry System[Std on Trans Am,Conv] +130
Leather Seats[Std on Trans Am] +485
Power Door Locks[Opt on Base Coupe] +150
Power Drivers Seat[Std on Trans Am,Conv] +180
Power Mirrors[Opt on Base Coupe] +95
Power Windows[Opt on Base Coupe] +165
Traction Control System +320

GRAND AM 1999

New for 1999, the Grand Am offers a host of standard and optional equipment as well as a completely redesigned exterior.

RATINGS (SCALE OF 1-10)

Overall	Safety	Reliability	Performance	Comfort	Value
N/A	7.3	8.8	7.8	8	N/A

Category C

	Trade-in	Market
2 Dr GT Cpe	12120	14600
4 Dr GT Sdn	12305	14825
2 Dr GT1 Cpe	13090	15770
4 Dr GT1 Sdn	13270	15990
2 Dr SE Cpe	10295	12405
4 Dr SE Sdn	10460	12600
2 Dr SE1 Cpe	10875	13105
4 Dr SE1 Sdn	11045	13310
2 Dr SE2 Cpe	11210	13505
4 Dr SE2 Sdn	11385	13715

OPTIONS FOR GRAND AM

6 cyl 3.4 L Engine[Opt on SE1] +445
AM/FM Compact Disc Player[Std on GT1,SE2] +270

Don't forget to refer to the Mileage Adjustment Table at the back of this book!

PONTIAC 99

Model Description	Trade-in Value	Market Value	Model Description	Trade-in Value	Market Value

Cruise Control[Opt on SE] +155
Keyless Entry System[Std on GT1,SE2] +140
Leather Seats +450
Power Drivers Seat +220
Power Moonroof[Std on GT1] +510

GRAND PRIX   1999

The Grand Prix gets more muscle for '99 with low-restriction air-induction components giving the naturally aspirated 3.8-liter V6 five more horsepower, to 200. This engine is standard on the GT (sedan and coupe) and optional on the SE sedan. A traction control indicator and on/off button are now standard on GTP models. Minor revisions are in order inside, with front-door courtesy lamps and a six-speaker sound system now standard, with an eight-speaker Bose audio unit and OnStar mobile communications system optional. Outside, a rear deck spoiler is standard on the GT model, and two colors have been added to the 1999 exterior paint chart.

RATINGS (SCALE OF 1-10)

Overall	Safety	Reliability	Performance	Comfort	Value
N/A	7.7	8.5	8.8	7.9	N/A

Category C

			Trade-in	Market
2 Dr GT Cpe			13100	15785
4 Dr GT Sdn			13270	15990
2 Dr GTP Sprchgd Cpe			14990	18060
4 Dr GTP Sprchgd Sdn			15145	18245
4 Dr SE Sdn			12025	14485

OPTIONS FOR GRAND PRIX

6 cyl 3.8 L Engine[Std on GT] +305
AM/FM Compact Disc Player[Std on GTP] +270
Aluminum/Alloy Wheels[Opt on SE] +225
Climate Control for AC[Opt on GT] +125
Cruise Control[Opt on SE] +155
Heads-up Display +185
Keyless Entry System[Std on GTP] +140
Leather Seats +450
Power Drivers Seat[Std on GTP] +220
Power Moonroof +510
Trip Computer[Opt on GT] +140

MONTANA   1999

After a ground-up redesign in 1997, the entire line gets a name change this year, from Trans Sport to Montana (the name pulled from '98's sporty trim package). Regular-wheelbase models come with one or two sliding doors, while extended wheelbase vans get two only with a right-side power sliding door option. Side-impact airbags are standard, as are 15-inch 215-70R white-letter puncture sealant tires. New two-tone paint jobs are available and four new exterior colors are offered, as are options for front-row leather seats and an overhead video system. Better still, a special sport performance package adds cast aluminum wheels, traction control and a specially tuned sport suspension for soccer dads (and moms) who are sport sedan wannabees.

RATINGS (SCALE OF 1-10)

Overall	Safety	Reliability	Performance	Comfort	Value
N/A	8	8.5	7.8	7.9	N/A

Category G

			Trade-in	Market
4 Dr STD Pass. Van Ext			14845	17670

OPTIONS FOR MONTANA

Aluminum/Alloy Wheels +245
Captain Chairs (4) +465
Compact Disc W/fm/tape +355
Dual Air Conditioning +700
Keyless Entry System +150
Leather Seats +575
Power Drivers Seat +210
Power Sliding Door +290
Power Windows +175
Privacy Glass +195
Traction Control System +200

SUNFIRE   1999

After Sunfire coupes got a rear spoiler last year, this year it's the sedan's turn, only as an option. The top-line 2.4-liter twin-cam engine is revised to improve breathing, including new fuel injectors, injection rails, exhaust manifold and catalytic converter. Fern Green Metallic is added to the paint color chart.

RATINGS (SCALE OF 1-10)

Overall	Safety	Reliability	Performance	Comfort	Value
N/A	6.8	9	6.8	7.1	N/A

Category E

			Trade-in	Market
2 Dr GT Conv			11655	14215
2 Dr GT Cpe			9920	12095
2 Dr SE Cpe			7420	9050
4 Dr SE Sdn			7590	9255

OPTIONS FOR SUNFIRE

4 cyl 2.4 L Engine[Std on GT] +335
Auto 3-Speed Transmission +445
Auto 4-Speed Transmission[Std on Conv] +600
AM/FM Compact Disc Player[Std on GT] +340
Air Conditioning[Std on GT] +605
Aluminum/Alloy Wheels[Std on GT] +245
Cruise Control[Std on Conv] +165
Keyless Entry System[Std on Conv] +115
Power Door Locks[Std on Conv] +180
Power Mirrors[Std on Conv] +80
Power Moonroof +425
Power Windows[Std on Conv] +195
Premium Sound System +245
Rear Window Defroster[Std on GT] +120
Tilt Steering Wheel[Std on GT] +110

PONTIAC 98

Model Description	Trade-in Value	Market Value	Model Description	Trade-in Value	Market Value

1998 PONTIAC

BONNEVILLE 1998

Second-generation airbags are standard, the SE comes with a standard decklid spoiler, and the SSE gets more standard equipment. New colors freshen the rapidly aging Bonneville.

RATINGS (SCALE OF 1-10)

Overall	Safety	Reliability	Performance	Comfort	Value
8.2	7.6	8.6	8.4	7.8	8.8

Category B

	Trade-in	Market
4 Dr SE Sdn	10910	13145
4 Dr SLE Sdn	11505	13860
4 Dr SSE Sdn	13925	16780
4 Dr SSEi Sprchgd Sdn	14580	17565

OPTIONS FOR BONNEVILLE

AM/FM Compact Disc Player[Opt on SE, SLE] +200
Aluminum/Alloy Wheels[Opt on SE] +200
Chrome Wheels +415
Dual Power Seats[Opt on SE, SLE] +230
Keyless Entry System[Opt on SE] +105
Power Drivers Seat[Opt on SE] +190
Power Mirrors[Opt on SE] +60
Power Moonroof +590
Premium Sound System[Opt on SE] +240
Traction Control System[Opt on SE, SLE] +105

FIREBIRD 1998

Firebirds get a minor restyle that is most evident from the front end. Also on tap for Formula and Trans Am models is a de-tuned Corvette engine making 305 horsepower without Ram Air induction. Base models can be equipped with a new Sport Appearance Package, and two new exterior colors debut. Second-generation airbags are standard.

RATINGS (SCALE OF 1-10)

Overall	Safety	Reliability	Performance	Comfort	Value
N/A	8	8	N/A	7.3	4.1

Category F

	Trade-in	Market
2 Dr Formula Cpe	13470	16425
2 Dr STD Conv	14030	17110
2 Dr STD Cpe	10785	13150
2 Dr Trans Am Conv	17270	21060
2 Dr Trans Am Cpe	15045	18345

OPTIONS FOR FIREBIRD

Auto 4-Speed Transmission[Opt on STD] +500
AutoCross Performance Pkg +720
Performance Handling Pkg +1905
Performance/Handling Pkg +1905
Sport Appearance Pkg +610
Chrome Wheels +355

Glass Panel T-tops[Std on Trans Am] +595
Keyless Entry System[Std on Trans Am, Conv] +110
Leather Seats[Std on Trans Am] +395
Power Door Locks[Opt on STD Cpe] +120
Power Drivers Seat[Std on Trans Am] +150
Power Mirrors[Opt on STD Cpe] +75
Power Windows[Opt on STD Cpe] +135
Traction Control System +260

GRAND AM 1998

Second generation airbags are newly standard, and option groups are simplified.

RATINGS (SCALE OF 1-10)

Overall	Safety	Reliability	Performance	Comfort	Value
7.6	7.3	8.6	8.2	7.4	6.3

Category C

	Trade-in	Market
2 Dr GT Cpe	8825	10765
4 Dr GT Sdn	8975	10945
2 Dr SE Cpe	7625	9300
4 Dr SE Sdn	7835	9555

OPTIONS FOR GRAND AM

6 cyl 3.1 L Engine +275
Auto 4-Speed Transmission +500
AM/FM Compact Disc Player +220
Aluminum/Alloy Wheels[Opt on SE] +180
Cruise Control +130
Keyless Entry System +115
Leather Seats +365
Power Drivers Seat +180
Power Mirrors +70
Power Moonroof +415
Power Windows +190
Premium Sound System +240
Rear Window Defroster +100
Tilt Steering Wheel[Opt on SE] +95
Traction Control System +150

GRAND PRIX 1998

Supercharged GTP models get traction control, and new colors are available inside and out. Second-generation airbags debut as standard equipment.

RATINGS (SCALE OF 1-10)

Overall	Safety	Reliability	Performance	Comfort	Value
8.3	7.7	8.5	8.8	7.9	8.7

Category C

	Trade-in	Market
2 Dr GT Cpe	12035	14675
4 Dr GT Sdn	12205	14885
2 Dr GTP Sprchgd Cpe	12855	15675
4 Dr GTP Sprchgd Sdn	12995	15850
4 Dr SE Sdn	10885	13275

OPTIONS FOR GRAND PRIX

6 cyl 3.8 L Engine[Opt on SE] +265
AM/FM Compact Disc Player +220

Model Description	Trade-in Value	Market Value
Aluminum/Alloy Wheels[Opt on SE]	+180	
Climate Control for AC	+100	
Cruise Control[Opt on SE]	+130	
Heads-up Display	+150	
Keyless Entry System	+115	
Leather Seats	+365	
Power Drivers Seat	+180	
Power Moonroof	+415	
Premium Sound System[Opt on SE]	+240	
Trip Computer[Std on GTP]	+115	

SUNFIRE 1998

All coupes have a rear spoiler, a new six-speaker sound system is available, the base four-cylinder gets some additional low-end punch, and Topaz Gold Metallic is added to the paint color chart. Second-generation airbags are added as standard equipment.

RATINGS (SCALE OF 1-10)

Overall	Safety	Reliability	Performance	Comfort	Value
7.2	6.8	8.5	6.8	7.1	6.8

Category E

	Trade-in	Market
2 Dr GT Cpe	8420	10395
2 Dr SE Conv	9380	11580
2 Dr SE Cpe	6660	8220
4 Dr SE Sdn	6810	8410

OPTIONS FOR SUNFIRE

4 cyl 2.4 L Engine[Opt on SE]	+275
Auto 3-Speed Transmission	+370
Auto 4-Speed Transmission[Std on Conv]	+500
AM/FM Compact Disc Player[Std on GT, Conv]	+275
Air Conditioning[Std on GT, Conv]	+495
Aluminum/Alloy Wheels[Opt on SE]	+200
Cruise Control[Std on Conv]	+135
Keyless Entry System	+95
Power Door Locks	+145
Power Mirrors	+65
Power Moonroof	+350
Power Windows	+160
Premium Sound System	+200
Rear Window Defroster[Std on GT, Conv]	+100
Tilt Steering Wheel[Std on GT, Conv]	+90

TRANS SPORT 1998

Short-wheelbase models get the dual sliding doors and power sliding door options. Side-impact airbags are standard, and a white two-tone paint job is new. Second generation airbags are standard for front seat occupants.

RATINGS (SCALE OF 1-10)

Overall	Safety	Reliability	Performance	Comfort	Value
7.5	7.9	7.4	7.6	7.9	6.9

Category G

	Trade-in	Market
2 Dr Montana Pass. Van	12935	15400
2 Dr Montana Pass. Van Ext	13356	15900

	Trade-in	Market
2 Dr STD Pass. Van	12020	14310
2 Dr STD Pass. Van Ext	12449	14820

OPTIONS FOR TRANS SPORT

Aluminum/Alloy Wheels[Opt on STD]	+200
Auto Load Leveling[Opt on STD]	+135
Captain Chairs (4)	+380
Compact Disc W/fm/tape	+290
Cruise Control[Std on Pass. Van Ext]	+125
Dual Air Conditioning	+575
Dual Power Seats	+235
Keyless Entry System	+120
Leather Seats	+470
Power Drivers Seat	+170
Power Windows	+145
Premium Sound System	+210
Privacy Glass	+160
Rear Window Defroster	+105
Sliding Driver Side Door[Std on Montana, Pass. Van Ext]	+320
Traction Control System[Opt on STD]	+165

1997 PONTIAC

BONNEVILLE 1997

Changes for 1997 are few. Supercharged Bonnevilles get a new transmission, a new Delco/Bose premium sound system is optional on the SSE, and the EYE CUE head-up display has a new motorized adjustment feature. Two new exterior colors, a new interior color and a new interior fabric liven the aging Bonneville visually.

RATINGS (SCALE OF 1-10)

Overall	Safety	Reliability	Performance	Comfort	Value
8	7.5	8.2	8.4	7.8	8.2

Category B

	Trade-in	Market
4 Dr SE Sdn	9030	11015
4 Dr SE Sprchgd Sdn	9465	11540
4 Dr SSE Sdn	11555	14090
4 Dr SSEi Sprchgd Sdn	11970	14600

OPTIONS FOR BONNEVILLE

Computer Command Ride Pkg	+420
Aluminum/Alloy Wheels[Opt on SE]	+165
Chrome Wheels	+340
Compact Disc W/fm/tape	+190
Dual Power Seats	+190
Keyless Entry System[Opt on SE]	+85
Leather Seats	+335
Power Moonroof	+485
Premium Sound System[Opt on SE]	+195
Steer. Whl. Radio Cntrls[Opt on SE]	+65
Traction Control System	+85

Don't forget to refer to the Mileage Adjustment Table at the back of this book!

PONTIAC 97

Model Description	Trade-in Value	Market Value	Model Description	Trade-in Value	Market Value

FIREBIRD 1997

Pontiac upgrades the Firebird in several ways for 1997. Performance freaks will appreciate the addition of Ram Air induction to the options list of the Formula and Trans Am convertibles. Audiophiles will be blown away by the newly optional 500-watt Monsoon sound system. Luxury intenders can get power seats swathed in leather this year. Safety-conscious buyers will find daytime running lights. Additional cosmetic and comfort items keep the fourth-generation Firebird fresh for its fifth year.

RATINGS (SCALE OF 1-10)

Overall	Safety	Reliability	Performance	Comfort	Value
N/A	7.8	7.1	N/A	7.3	4

Category F

2 Dr Formula Conv	13980	17050
2 Dr Formula Cpe	11535	14065
2 Dr STD Conv	12015	14650
2 Dr STD Cpe	9035	11020
2 Dr Trans Am Conv	14850	18110
2 Dr Trans Am Cpe	13840	16880

OPTIONS FOR FIREBIRD

Auto 4-Speed Transmission[Opt on STD] +410
Performance Handling Pkg +1390
Performance Pkg +590
Sport Appearance Pkg +675
AM/FM Compact Disc Player +235
Chrome Wheels +290
Cruise Control[Std on Trans Am,Conv] +105
Glass Panel T-tops +490
Keyless Entry System[Opt on Formula,STD] +90
Leather Seats +325
Power Door Locks[Std on Trans Am,Conv] +100
Power Drivers Seat +120
Power Windows[Std on Trans Am,Conv] +110
Steer. Whl. Radio Cntrls[Opt on Formula,STD] +85
Traction Control System +215

GRAND AM 1997

Very minimal changes this year as Pontiac concentrates on Grand Prix and Trans Sport launches. Air conditioning is now standard. Also, three new colors are added.

RATINGS (SCALE OF 1-10)

Overall	Safety	Reliability	Performance	Comfort	Value
7.5	7.2	7.9	8.2	7.4	6.6

Category C

2 Dr GT Cpe	7560	9335
4 Dr GT Sdn	7695	9500
2 Dr SE Cpe	6770	8355
4 Dr SE Sdn	6890	8505

OPTIONS FOR GRAND AM

6 cyl 3.1 L Engine +215
Auto 4-Speed Transmission +405
Aluminum/Alloy Wheels[Opt on SE] +150
Compact Disc W/fm/tape +165
Cruise Control +105
Keyless Entry System +95
Leather Seats +300
Power Drivers Seat +145
Power Moonroof +340
Power Windows +155
Premium Sound System +195

GRAND PRIX 1997

Pontiac redesigns the Grand Prix for 1997, giving buyers slick new styling, a longer and wider wheelbase, and available supercharged V6 power on GT models. Traction control, antilock brakes, dual airbags and side-impact protection are standard. Optional is a built-in child safety seat.

RATINGS (SCALE OF 1-10)

Overall	Safety	Reliability	Performance	Comfort	Value
8	7.7	8.2	8.8	7.9	7.6

Category C

2 Dr GT Cpe	10695	13205
4 Dr GT Sdn	10915	13475
2 Dr GTP Sprchgd Cpe	11325	13980
4 Dr GTP Sprchgd Sdn	11520	14220
4 Dr SE Sdn	9395	11600

OPTIONS FOR GRAND PRIX

6 cyl 3.8 L Engine[Opt on SE] +210
Aluminum/Alloy Wheels[Opt on SE] +150
Child Seat (1) +60
Climate Control for AC +85
Compact Disc W/fm/tape +165
Cruise Control[Opt on SE,Cpe] +105
Keyless Entry System +95
Leather Seats +300
Power Drivers Seat +145
Power Moonroof +340
Premium Sound System +195
Trip Computer[Std on GTP] +95

SUNFIRE 1997

SE Convertible gets a higher level of standard equipment, including an automatic transmission. Coupes get a new front seatbelt guide loop, and a new Sports Interior trim debuts called Patina/Redondo cloth.

RATINGS (SCALE OF 1-10)

Overall	Safety	Reliability	Performance	Comfort	Value
6.6	6.6	7.5	6.8	7.1	5.1

Category E

2 Dr GT Cpe	6695	8475
2 Dr SE Conv	7910	10010

Don't forget to refer to the Mileage Adjustment Table at the back of this book!

Model Description	Trade-in Value	Market Value
2 Dr SE Cpe	5755	7285
4 Dr SE Sdn	5930	7505

OPTIONS FOR SUNFIRE

4 cyl 2.4 L Engine[Opt on SE] +215
Auto 3-Speed Transmission +275
Auto 4-Speed Transmission[Std on Conv] +405
AM/FM Compact Disc Player +225
Air Conditioning[Std on Conv] +405
Aluminum/Alloy Wheels[Opt on SE] +165
Cruise Control[Std on Conv] +110
Keyless Entry System +80
Overhead Console[Std on Conv] +55
Power Door Locks +120
Power Moonroof +285
Power Windows +130
Premium Sound System +160
Rear Spoiler[Std on GT,Conv] +105
Tilt Steering Wheel[Std on GT,Conv] +75

TRANS SPORT   1997

After years of taking it on the chin, Pontiac redesigns the Trans Sport and lands one squarely in Chrysler's face. This van is good-looking, loaded with features and fun to drive. Wait. Did we say fun to drive?

RATINGS (SCALE OF 1-10)

Overall	Safety	Reliability	Performance	Comfort	Value
7.4	7.2	7.5	7.6	7.9	6.8

Category G

	Trade-in	Market
2 Dr SE Pass. Van	11585	13960
2 Dr SE Pass. Van Ext	12015	14475

OPTIONS FOR TRANS SPORT

7 Passenger Seating[Opt on Pass. Van] +260
Aluminum/Alloy Wheels +165
Auto Load Leveling +110
Captain Chairs (4) +310
Child Seats (2) +125
Compact Disc W/fm/tape +240
Cruise Control +105
Dual Power Seats +190
Keyless Entry System +100
Leather Seats +385
Luggage Rack +80
Power Windows +120
Premium Sound System +170
Rear Heater +100
Sliding Driver Side Door +260

1996 PONTIAC

BONNEVILLE   1996

The Series II V6 has been supercharged for 1996, pumping out 240 horsepower. Styling front and rear has been tweaked, and daytime running lights debut.

RATINGS (SCALE OF 1-10)

Overall	Safety	Reliability	Performance	Comfort	Value
7.9	7.5	7.8	8.4	7.8	8.2

Category B

	Trade-in	Market
4 Dr SE Sdn	7945	9930
4 Dr SE Sprchgd Sdn	8330	10410
4 Dr SLE Sdn	8445	10555
4 Dr SSE Sdn	10090	12615
4 Dr SSE Sprchgd Sdn	10645	13305

OPTIONS FOR BONNEVILLE

Computer Command Ride Pkg +370
SSEi Supercharger Pkg +450
Chrome Wheels +280
Climate Control for AC[Opt on SE] +70
Compact Disc W/fm/tape +155
Keyless Entry System[Opt on SE] +70
Leather Seats +275
Power Drivers Seat[Opt on SE] +125
Power Moonroof +395
Power Passenger Seat +135
Premium Sound System[Opt on SE] +160
Traction Control System +70

FIREBIRD   1996

A new standard V6 makes 40 more horsepower than the old one. The LT1 V8 also makes more power, particularly when equipped with Ram Air induction. A new color livens up the exterior, as if it needed it.

RATINGS (SCALE OF 1-10)

Overall	Safety	Reliability	Performance	Comfort	Value
N/A	8	7.3	N/A	7.3	4.3

Category F

	Trade-in	Market
2 Dr Formula Conv	11770	14900
2 Dr Formula Cpe	10035	12705
2 Dr STD Conv	9075	11490
2 Dr STD Cpe	7525	9525
2 Dr Trans Am Conv	12435	15740
2 Dr Trans Am Cpe	10335	13080

OPTIONS FOR FIREBIRD

Auto 4-Speed Transmission +305
Performance Handling Pkg +1045
AM/FM Compact Disc Player +195
Air Conditioning[Opt on STD Cpe] +340
Chrome Wheels +235
Cruise Control[Std on Trans Am,Conv] +85
Glass Panel T-tops +400
Keyless Entry System[Opt on Formula,STD,Cpe] +70
Leather Seats +265
Power Door Locks[Std on Trans Am,Conv] +80
Power Drivers Seat +100
Power Windows[Std on Trans Am,Conv] +90
Premium Sound System[Std on Trans Am,Conv] +150
Steer. Whl. Radio Cntrls[Opt on Formula,STD,Cpe] +70

GRAND AM 1996

New styling, a new base engine, and ... what's this? Dual airbags and body-mounted seatbelts? Will wonders never cease?

RATINGS (SCALE OF 1-10)

Overall	Safety	Reliability	Performance	Comfort	Value
7.3	6.9	6.8	8.2	7.4	7

Category C

2 Dr GT Cpe	6620	8490
4 Dr GT Sdn	6800	8715
2 Dr SE Cpe	5630	7215
4 Dr SE Sdn	5845	7495

OPTIONS FOR GRAND AM

6 cyl 3.1 L Engine +185
Auto 4-Speed Transmission +305
Air Conditioning[Opt on SE] +325
Compact Disc W/fm/tape +135
Cruise Control +85
Keyless Entry System +75
Leather Seats +245
Power Drivers Seat +120
Power Moonroof +280
Power Windows +125
Premium Sound System +160

GRAND PRIX 1996

Minor trim and powertrain improvements to the only car in GM's stable that still has those stupid door-mounted seatbelts. Do yourself a favor. Buy the 1997 GP.

RATINGS (SCALE OF 1-10)

Overall	Safety	Reliability	Performance	Comfort	Value
7.7	7.2	8	8	7.3	8

Category C

4 Dr GT Sdn	7875	10095
2 Dr GTP Cpe	8335	10685
2 Dr SE Cpe	7215	9250
4 Dr SE Sdn	7005	8980

OPTIONS FOR GRAND PRIX

GT Performance Pkg +370
AM/FM Compact Disc Player +145
Aluminum/Alloy Wheels[Opt on SE] +120
Anti-Lock Brakes[Opt on SE] +245
Cruise Control[Opt on GT,Sdn] +85
Keyless Entry System +75
Leather Seats +245
Power Drivers Seat +120
Power Moonroof +280
Premium Sound System +160
Sport Suspension[Opt on SE] +85
Trip Computer +75

SUNFIRE 1996

Traction control, remote keyless entry and steering wheel radio controls are newly available. Old Quad 4 engine dumped in favor of new 2.4-liter twin-cam engine. Two new paint choices spiff up the exterior.

RATINGS (SCALE OF 1-10)

Overall	Safety	Reliability	Performance	Comfort	Value
6.6	6.4	6.7	6.8	7.1	6

Category E

2 Dr GT Cpe	5835	7680
2 Dr SE Conv	6500	8550
2 Dr SE Cpe	4840	6370
4 Dr SE Sdn	4995	6575

OPTIONS FOR SUNFIRE

4 cyl 2.4 L Engine[Opt on SE] +140
Auto 3-Speed Transmission[Std on Conv] +210
Auto 4-Speed Transmission +250
AM/FM Compact Disc Player +185
Air Conditioning[Std on Conv] +330
Cruise Control +90
Keyless Entry System +65
Power Door Locks +100
Power Sunroof +250
Power Windows +105
Premium Sound System +135

TRANS SPORT 1996

A 180-horsepower 3.4-liter V6 replaces last year's pathetic base engine as well as the optional 3.8-liter V6. Front air conditioning is standard equipment for 1996.

RATINGS (SCALE OF 1-10)

Overall	Safety	Reliability	Performance	Comfort	Value
7.4	6.5	7.6	7.2	7.1	8.5

Category G

2 Dr SE Pass. Van	8190	10110

OPTIONS FOR TRANS SPORT

7 Passenger Seating +210
Air Conditioning +330
Auto Load Leveling +90
Child Seats (2) +105
Cruise Control +85
Dual Air Conditioning +385
Keyless Entry System +80
Leather Seats +315
Power Door Locks +95
Power Drivers Seat +115
Power Sliding Door +160
Power Windows +95
Premium Sound System +140
Traction Control System +110

Don't forget to refer to the Mileage Adjustment Table at the back of this book!

1995 PONTIAC

BONNEVILLE 1995

Base engine is upgraded to 3800 Series II status, gaining 35 horsepower in the process. SE models with the SLE package can be ordered with the supercharged 3.8-liter V6. Computer Command Ride is made available on SE models.

RATINGS (SCALE OF 1-10)

Overall	Safety	Reliability	Performance	Comfort	Value
7.9	8.3	7.3	8.4	7.8	7.9

Category B

4 Dr SE Sdn	6705	8595
4 Dr SE Sprchgd Sdn	6860	8795
4 Dr SSE Sdn	8035	10300
4 Dr SSEi Sprchgd Sdn	8195	10505

OPTIONS FOR BONNEVILLE

Articulating Lthr Seats +360
Climate Control for AC +55
Dual Power Seats +125
Keyless Entry System +55
Leather Seats +225
Power Moonroof +325
Premium Sound System[Opt on SE] +130
Steer. Whl. Radio Cntrls +45

FIREBIRD 1995

Traction control is added as an option on Formula and Trans Am. Trans Am GT is dropped from lineup. Californians get a 3.8-liter V6 equipped with an automatic transmission on base models instead of the 3.4-liter V6. The new engine meets strict emissions standards in that state, and makes 40 additional horsepower.

RATINGS (SCALE OF 1-10)

Overall	Safety	Reliability	Performance	Comfort	Value
N/A	8.7	6.9	N/A	7.3	4.4

Category F

2 Dr Formula Conv	9900	12695
2 Dr Formula Cpe	7880	10105
2 Dr STD Conv	7720	9895
2 Dr STD Cpe	6330	8115
2 Dr Trans Am Conv	10840	13895
2 Dr Trans Am Cpe	8810	11295

OPTIONS FOR FIREBIRD

Auto 4-Speed Transmission +255
AM/FM Compact Disc Player +160
Air Conditioning[Std on Trans Am,Conv] +275
Cruise Control[Std on Trans Am,Conv] +70
Glass Panel T-tops +325
Keyless Entry System[Opt on Formula,STD] +60
Leather Seats[Opt on Formula,STD] +215
Power Door Locks[Std on Trans Am,Conv] +65
Power Windows[Std on Trans Am,Conv] +75
Premium Sound System[Opt on Formula,STD] +125
Steer. Whl. Radio Cntrls +60
Traction Control System +145

GRAND AM 1995

Base engine upgraded to a 150-horsepower version of the Quad 4. High-output Quad 4 motor is dropped from the GT, which now uses the same standard and optional powerplants as the SE. Variable-effort power steering is a new option on GT models, rear suspensions are redesigned, and SE models get restyled wheelcovers and alloy wheels.

RATINGS (SCALE OF 1-10)

Overall	Safety	Reliability	Performance	Comfort	Value
7.2	6.6	7.8	8.2	7.3	6

Category C

2 Dr GT Cpe	5170	6895
4 Dr GT Sdn	5350	7135
2 Dr SE Cpe	4315	5755
4 Dr SE Sdn	4440	5920

OPTIONS FOR GRAND AM

6 cyl 3.1 L Engine +160
Auto 3-Speed Transmission +185
Auto 4-Speed Transmission +250
AM/FM Compact Disc Player +120
Air Conditioning[Opt on SE] +265
Cruise Control +70
Keyless Entry System +60
Leather Seats +200
Power Drivers Seat +100
Power Moonroof +225
Power Windows +105
Premium Sound System +130

GRAND PRIX 1995

Brake/transmission shift interlock is added. GT coupe dropped in favor of GTP Package. GT sedan continues. Variable-effort steering is added to GTP and GT. New alloys debut on GT and GTP. Coupes can be equipped with a White Appearance Package, which includes color-keyed alloys and special pinstriping. Floor consoles are redesigned on models with bucket seats.

RATINGS (SCALE OF 1-10)

Overall	Safety	Reliability	Performance	Comfort	Value
7.6	7.6	7.3	8	7.3	7.9

Category C

4 Dr GT Sdn	6255	8340
2 Dr GTP Cpe	6580	8775
2 Dr SE Cpe	6100	8130
4 Dr SE Sdn	5935	7910

Don't forget to refer to the Mileage Adjustment Table at the back of this book!

OPTIONS FOR GRAND PRIX

AM/FM Compact Disc Player +120
Anti-Lock Brakes[Opt on SE] +200
Cruise Control +70
Keyless Entry System +60
Leather Seats +200
Power Drivers Seat +100
Power Moonroof +225
Premium Sound System +130
Sport Suspension[Opt on SE] +70
Trip Computer +60

SUNFIRE   1995

All-new replacement for aged Sunbird comes in SE coupe or sedan, and GT coupe trim levels. An SE convertible debuted midyear. Dual airbags, ABS, tilt steering and tachometer are standard. Base engine is a 2.2-liter four cylinder good for 120 horsepower. GT models get a 150-horsepower Quad 4 engine, which is optional on SE. Order the four-speed automatic transmission, and you'll get traction control.

RATINGS (SCALE OF 1-10)

Overall	Safety	Reliability	Performance	Comfort	Value
7	7.1	6.8	6.8	7.1	7.1

Category E

	Trade-in	Market
2 Dr GT Cpe	4885	6690
2 Dr SE Conv	5535	7580
2 Dr SE Cpe	4075	5585
4 Dr SE Sdn	4170	5715

OPTIONS FOR SUNFIRE

4 cyl 2.3 L Quad 4 Engine[Opt on SE] +130
Auto 3-Speed Transmission[Std on Conv] +165
Auto 4-Speed Transmission[Opt on GT only] +155
AM/FM Compact Disc Player +150
Air Conditioning +270
Cruise Control +75
Power Door Locks +80
Power Sunroof +205
Power Windows +85
Premium Sound System +110
Tilt Steering Wheel[Std on GT,Conv] +50

TRANS SPORT   1995

A brake/transmission shift interlock is added. New overhead console includes outside temperature gauge, compass and storage bin.

RATINGS (SCALE OF 1-10)

Overall	Safety	Reliability	Performance	Comfort	Value
7	6.8	5.8	7.2	7.1	8.3

Category G

	Trade-in	Market
2 Dr SE Pass. Van	5915	7490

OPTIONS FOR TRANS SPORT

6 cyl 3.8 L Engine +140
Auto 4-Speed Transmission +65
7 Passenger Seating +170
AM/FM Compact Disc Player +110
Air Conditioning +270
Auto Load Leveling +75
Child Seats (2) +85
Cruise Control +70
Dual Air Conditioning +315
Keyless Entry System +65
Leather Seats +255
Luggage Rack +50
Power Door Locks +75
Power Windows +80
Premium Sound System +115
Traction Control System +90

1994 PONTIAC

BONNEVILLE   1994

Dual airbags are standard. SE and SSE trim levels are available. Californians get SLE model. SSEi is an option package on SSE. Supercharged engine in SSEi package gets 20 more horsepower. Automatic transmission gains "Normal" and "Performance" shift modes when hooked to supercharged engine. Traction control gains ability to retard engine power as well as apply brakes to slow spinning wheel(s). Get traction control on the SSE, and you can opt for Computer Command Ride, a suspension package that automatically adjusts the suspension to meet the demands of the driver.

RATINGS (SCALE OF 1-10)

Overall	Safety	Reliability	Performance	Comfort	Value
8.2	8.4	8	8.2	7.8	8.5

Category B

	Trade-in	Market
4 Dr SE Sdn	5305	6980
4 Dr SSE Sdn	6745	8875
4 Dr SSEi Sprchgd Sdn	6960	9155

OPTIONS FOR BONNEVILLE

Compact Disc W/fm/tape +105
Cruise Control[Opt on SE] +60
Keyless Entry System +45
Leather Seats +185
Power Drivers Seat[Opt on SE] +85
Power Moonroof +265
Power Passenger Seat +90
Premium Sound System[Opt on SE] +105
Sport Suspension +80
Traction Control System +50

Model Description	Trade-in Value	Market Value

FIREBIRD 1994

Trans Am GT debuts. Six-speed transmission is saddled with a first-to-fourth skip shift feature designed to improve fuel economy. Automatic is new electronically controlled unit with the V8 engine, and it features "Normal" and "Performance" modes. Remote keyless entry, cassette player, and leather-wrapped steering wheel move from the Trans Am standard equipment list to the options sheet. T/A also loses Batwing rear spoiler to GT, taking Formula's more subdued rear treatment. Convertible debuts at midyear.

RATINGS (SCALE OF 1-10)

Overall	Safety	Reliability	Performance	Comfort	Value
N/A	8.7	7.2	N/A	7.3	4.9

Category F

2 Dr Formula Conv	8055	10600
2 Dr Formula Cpe	7035	9255
2 Dr STD Conv	6680	8790
2 Dr STD Cpe	5375	7070
2 Dr Trans Am Cpe	7410	9750
2 Dr Trans Am 25th Anniv. Cpe	8560	11260
2 Dr Trans Am GT Conv	8875	11680
2 Dr Trans Am GT Cpe	7885	10375

OPTIONS FOR FIREBIRD

Auto 4-Speed Transmission +195
Air Conditioning[Opt on STD Cpe] +225
Compact Disc W/fm/tape +135
Cruise Control[Opt on Formula Cpe,STD Cpe] +55
Glass Panel T-tops +265
Keyless Entry System[Opt on Formula,STD,Trans Am] +50
Leather Seats[Std on Trans Am GT Conv] +175
Power Door Locks[Opt on Formula Cpe,STD Cpe] +55
Power Drivers Seat +65
Power Windows[Opt on STD Cpe,Formula Cpe] +60
Premium Sound System[Opt on Formula,STD,Trans Am] +100
Steer. Whl. Radio Cntrls +50

GRAND AM 1994

Driver airbag added. A 3.1-liter V6 replaces last year's optional 3.3-liter V6. Four-speed automatic debuts; standard with V6 and optional on four-cylinder models.

RATINGS (SCALE OF 1-10)

Overall	Safety	Reliability	Performance	Comfort	Value
7.1	6.5	7.7	8.2	7.3	6

Category C

2 Dr GT Cpe	4355	5885
4 Dr GT Sdn	4445	6005
2 Dr SE Cpe	3595	4855
4 Dr SE Sdn	3705	5010

OPTIONS FOR GRAND AM

6 cyl 3.1 L Engine +140
Auto 3-Speed Transmission +150
Auto 4-Speed Transmission +205
AM/FM Compact Disc Player +100
Air Conditioning[Opt on SE] +220
Cruise Control +55
Keyless Entry System +50
Leather Seats +165
Power Drivers Seat +80
Power Windows +85
Premium Sound System +105

GRAND PRIX 1994

Interior is redesigned to accommodate dual airbags. LE and STE sedans are dropped; GT and GTP become option packages on SE coupe. A GT package is available on SE sedan, and includes 3.4-liter V6, alloys, low-profile tires, ABS, and sport suspension. Front seatbelts are anchored to pillars instead of doors on sedan; coupe retains door-mounted belts. 3.1-liter V6 is up 20 horsepower. Twin-cam 3.4-liter V6 is up ten horsepower. Five-speed manual and three-speed automatic transmissions are dropped in favor of four-speed automatic. Coupes gain standard equipment, including 16-inch alloys, cruise, and leather-wrapped steering wheel with integral radio controls.

RATINGS (SCALE OF 1-10)

Overall	Safety	Reliability	Performance	Comfort	Value
7.7	7.8	6.9	8	7.3	8.3

Category C

2 Dr SE Cpe	5090	6875
4 Dr SE Sdn	4925	6655

OPTIONS FOR GRAND PRIX

6 cyl 3.4 L Engine +310
GT Performance Pkg +445
AM/FM Compact Disc Player +100
AM/FM Stereo Tape[Opt on Sdn] +45
Anti-Lock Brakes +165
Cruise Control[Opt on Sdn] +55
Keyless Entry System +50
Leather Seats +165
Power Drivers Seat +80
Power Sunroof +185
Premium Sound System +105
Sport Suspension +55
Trip Computer +50

SUNBIRD 1994

GT coupe, SE convertible and SE sedan vanish. Surviving are LE models and an SE coupe that comes standard with the GT's old body work. Convertibles get alloys and rear spoiler standard. SE comes with a 3.1-liter V6 standard.

Don't forget to refer to the Mileage Adjustment Table at the back of this book!

Model Description	Trade-in Value	Market Value

RATINGS (SCALE OF 1-10)

Overall	Safety	Reliability	Performance	Comfort	Value
6.5	5.5	7.5	6.6	6.8	5.9

Category E

	Trade-in	Market
2 Dr LE Conv	4140	5915
2 Dr LE Cpe	2765	3950
4 Dr LE Sdn	2915	4165
2 Dr SE Cpe	3480	4970

OPTIONS FOR SUNBIRD

6 cyl 3.1 L Engine[Opt on LE] +200
Auto 3-Speed Transmission +135
AM/FM Compact Disc Player +125
Air Conditioning +220
Aluminum/Alloy Wheels +90
Cruise Control +60
Power Windows[Std on Conv] +70
Sunroof +95

TRANS SPORT   1994

Driver airbag debuts and new front styling improves doorstop looks. Dashboard gets styling tweak to shorten visual acreage on top. A power sliding side door and integrated child seats are newly optional. Automatic power door locks are added, and rear seats gain a fold-and-stow feature. Traction control is made available at midyear; requires 3.8-liter engine.

RATINGS (SCALE OF 1-10)

Overall	Safety	Reliability	Performance	Comfort	Value
7	6.7	5.8	7.2	7.1	8.3

Category G

	Trade-in	Market
2 Dr SE Pass. Van	4985	6470

OPTIONS FOR TRANS SPORT

6 cyl 3.8 L Engine +110
7 Passenger Seating +140
AM/FM Compact Disc Player +90
Air Conditioning +220
Auto Load Leveling +60
Child Seats (2) +70
Cruise Control +55
Dual Air Conditioning +255
Keyless Entry System +55
Leather Seats +210
Luggage Rack +45
Power Door Locks +65
Power Drivers Seat +75
Power Windows +65
Premium Sound System +95
Traction Control System +75

BONNEVILLE   1993

SSE gets supercharged engine option. ABS is standard on all models. Sport Luxury Edition (SLE) for SE includes chrome grille, decklid spoiler, cross-lace alloy wheels, bigger tires, leather seats, and performance-oriented transaxle ratio.

RATINGS (SCALE OF 1-10)

Overall	Safety	Reliability	Performance	Comfort	Value
7.7	7.3	7.3	8.2	7.8	8

Category B

	Trade-in	Market
4 Dr SE Sdn	4250	5825
4 Dr SSE Sdn	5210	7140
4 Dr SSE Sprchgd Sdn	5360	7345
4 Dr SSEi Sprchgd Sdn	5705	7815

OPTIONS FOR BONNEVILLE

Aluminum/Alloy Wheels[Opt on SE] +75
Climate Control for AC[Opt on SSE] +40
Cruise Control[Opt on SE] +50
Keyless Entry System[Opt on SSEi] +40
Leather Seats[Std on SSEi] +150
Power Drivers Seat[Opt on SE] +70
Power Sunroof +250
Premium Sound System[Opt on SE] +90

FIREBIRD   1993

Brand new car debuts, marking first redesign since 1982. Base, Formula and Trans Am trim levels are available. Base car powered by 160-horsepower 3.4-liter V6. Formula and T/A get 5.7-liter V8 worth 275 horsepower. Formula and T/A get a standard six-speed manual transmission. Dual airbags and ABS are standard.

RATINGS (SCALE OF 1-10)

Overall	Safety	Reliability	Performance	Comfort	Value
N/A	8.7	7	N/A	7.3	3.8

Category F

	Trade-in	Market
2 Dr Formula Cpe	6060	8080
2 Dr STD Cpe	5015	6685
2 Dr Trans Am Cpe	6575	8765

OPTIONS FOR FIREBIRD

Auto 4-Speed Transmission +135
AM/FM Compact Disc Player +105
Air Conditioning[Opt on STD] +185
Cruise Control[Std on Trans Am] +45
Keyless Entry System[Opt on STD] +40
Leather Seats[Std on Trans Am] +145
Power Door Locks[Std on Trans Am] +45
Power Drivers Seat +55
Power Windows[Std on Trans Am] +50
Premium Sound System[Opt on STD] +80

GRAND AM   1993

Four-cylinder engines lose five horsepower, but gain modifications designed to reduce engine noise. Climate controls are revised, instrument panel graphics are revised on the SE, and battery-saver protection is added.

RATINGS (SCALE OF 1-10)

Overall	Safety	Reliability	Performance	Comfort	Value
6.7	4.3	7.1	8.2	7.3	6.7

Category C

2 Dr GT Cpe	3440	4775
4 Dr GT Sdn	3540	4915
2 Dr SE Cpe	2925	4060
4 Dr SE Sdn	3085	4285

OPTIONS FOR GRAND AM

4 cyl 2.3 L Quad 4 Engine[Opt on SE] +90
6 cyl 3.3 L Engine +120
Auto 3-Speed Transmission +125
AM/FM Compact Disc Player +80
Air Conditioning +180
Aluminum/Alloy Wheels[Opt on SE] +65
Cruise Control +45
Power Drivers Seat +65
Power Windows +70
Premium Sound System +85

GRAND PRIX   1993

An electronically-controlled four-speed automatic is optional on LE sedan and SE coupe. A Sport Appearance Package for the LE sedan includes aero body panels, heads-up display, and bucket seats with console. Automatic door locks are standard. Chime added to warn driver if turn signal has been left on.

RATINGS (SCALE OF 1-10)

Overall	Safety	Reliability	Performance	Comfort	Value
7.2	5.4	7.3	8	7	8.3

Category C

2 Dr GT Cpe	4330	6015
4 Dr LE Sdn	3480	4835
2 Dr SE Cpe	4095	5685
4 Dr SE Sdn	3945	5480
4 Dr STE Sdn	4610	6405

OPTIONS FOR GRAND PRIX

6 cyl 3.4 L Engine +225
Auto 4-Speed Transmission[Opt on LE,SE] +50
Aero Performance Pkg +430
AM/FM Compact Disc Player +80
Aluminum/Alloy Wheels[Opt on LE,SE Cpe] +65
Anti-Lock Brakes[Opt on LE,SE] +135
Cruise Control[Opt on LE,SE] +45
Keyless Entry System[Std on STE] +40
Leather Seats +135

Power Sunroof +150
Power Windows[Opt on LE,SE] +70
Premium Sound System[Opt on LE,SE] +85

LE MANS   1993

New front styling and revised taillights debut. New moldings and wheelcovers complete the minor makeover.

Category E

2 Dr SE Cpe	1600	2390
4 Dr SE Sdn	1665	2485
2 Dr Value Leader Cpe	1285	1915

OPTIONS FOR LE MANS

Auto 3-Speed Transmission +105
AM/FM Stereo Tape +65
Air Conditioning +180
Power Steering +55
Sunroof +75

SUNBIRD   1993

Base models can be equipped with a V6, and midline coupe gets Sport Appearance Package, which includes GT styling.

RATINGS (SCALE OF 1-10)

Overall	Safety	Reliability	Performance	Comfort	Value
6.4	5.4	6.6	6.6	6.8	6.7

Category E

2 Dr LE Cpe	2180	3255
4 Dr LE Sdn	2260	3370
2 Dr SE Conv	3170	4730
2 Dr SE Cpe	2355	3515
4 Dr SE Sdn	2515	3750

OPTIONS FOR SUNBIRD

6 cyl 3.1 L Engine[Std on GT] +135
Auto 3-Speed Transmission +110
AM/FM Compact Disc Player +100
Air Conditioning +180
Aluminum/Alloy Wheels[Std on GT] +75
Cruise Control +50
Power Windows[Std on Conv] +60
Rear Spoiler[Std on GT] +50
Sunroof +75
Tilt Steering Wheel +35

TRANS SPORT   1993

GT model canceled. SE is only trim level. Leather seats and steering wheel controls for the radio have been added to the options sheet. Climate controls are bigger. Sunroof becomes optional midyear.

RATINGS (SCALE OF 1-10)

Overall	Safety	Reliability	Performance	Comfort	Value
6.9	5.6	6.1	7.2	7.1	8.3

Don't forget to refer to the Mileage Adjustment Table at the back of this book!

Model Description	Trade-in Value	Market Value
Category G		
2 Dr SE Pass. Van	3925	5230

OPTIONS FOR TRANS SPORT
6 cyl 3.8 L Engine +125
AM/FM Compact Disc Player +70
Air Conditioning +180
Aluminum/Alloy Wheels +75
Cruise Control +45
Dual Air Conditioning +210
Keyless Entry System +45
Leather Seats +170
Luggage Rack +35
Power Door Locks +50
Power Drivers Seat +60
Power Windows +55
Premium Sound System +75

Model Description	Trade-in Value	Market Value
Category F		
2 Dr Formula Cpe	4145	5675
2 Dr STD Conv	4290	5880
2 Dr STD Cpe	3395	4650
2 Dr Trans Am Conv	6250	8565
2 Dr Trans Am Cpe	4615	6325

OPTIONS FOR FIREBIRD
8 cyl 5.0 L Engine[Opt on STD] +65
8 cyl 5.0 L TPI Engine[Opt on Formula] +135
8 cyl 5.7 L Engine[Std on Trans Am GTA] +80
Auto 4-Speed Transmission +95
AM/FM Compact Disc Player +85
Air Conditioning[Opt on STD] +150
Glass Panel T-tops +180
Leather Seats +120
Limited Slip Diff[Opt on Formula,STD] +60
Power Door Locks[Std on Trans Am GTA] +35
Power Windows[Std on Trans Am GTA] +40

1992 PONTIAC

BONNEVILLE 1992

Earns restyle that swaps stodgy, three-box design theme for flowing lines reminiscent of the Jaguar XJ6. LE trim level dies. 3.8-liter V6 gets five additional horsepower. SSEi has a supercharged V6 worth 205 horsepower and standard traction control. Traction control is optional on other Bonnevilles. ABS is standard on SSE and SSEi; optional on SE with Sport Appearance Package. A passenger airbag is standard on SSEi, optional on SSE. A heads-up display is standard on SSEi and optional on SSE.

RATINGS (SCALE OF 1-10)

Overall	Safety	Reliability	Performance	Comfort	Value
7.4	6.6	6.3	8.2	7.8	7.9

Category B		
4 Dr SE Sdn	3490	4985
4 Dr SSE Sdn	4025	5750
4 Dr SSE Sprchgd Sdn	4190	5985
4 Dr SSEi Sprchgd Sdn	4700	6715

OPTIONS FOR BONNEVILLE
Premium Equipment Pkg +165
Anti-Lock Brakes[Opt on SE] +125
Leather Seats +125
Power Drivers Seat[Opt on SE] +55
Power Moonroof +175
Power Sunroof +205

FIREBIRD 1992

Pontiac takes great pains to reduce the number of squeaks and rattles in the Firebird. Body has been stiffened for a tighter feel. Performance Equipment Group is available on Formula and Trans Am coupes, and boosts tuned-port 5.0-liter to 230 horsepower.

GRAND AM 1992

Redesign nets Grand Am swoopy look, standard ABS and optional V6 power. Car is now based on same platform as Chevy Corsica/Beretta. SE and GT models are available. Standard engine is a 120-horsepower SOHC engine. GT gets 180-horsepower Quad 4. Optional on both is a 3.3-liter V6. Hook an automatic to the Quad 4 engine and horsepower drops to 160.

RATINGS (SCALE OF 1-10)

Overall	Safety	Reliability	Performance	Comfort	Value
6.3	4.1	6.2	8.2	7.3	5.7

Category C		
2 Dr GT Cpe	2815	4080
4 Dr GT Sdn	2920	4230
2 Dr SE Cpe	2470	3580
4 Dr SE Sdn	2550	3695

OPTIONS FOR GRAND AM
6 cyl 3.3 L Engine +100
Auto 3-Speed Transmission +100
AM/FM Compact Disc Player +65
Air Conditioning +145
Power Drivers Seat +55
Power Windows +55

GRAND PRIX 1992

All sedans get STE light-bar front styling treatment. Base 160-horsepower Quad 4 motor replaced by 140-horsepower 3.1-liter V6. GTP coupe still has 210-horsepower twin-cam V6 standard. ABS is standard on GT, GTP, and STE; optional on LE and SE. Base SE coupes can be dressed in GT lower-body extensions.

RATINGS (SCALE OF 1-10)

Overall	Safety	Reliability	Performance	Comfort	Value
7.1	5.4	7.2	8	7	8

Don't forget to refer to the Mileage Adjustment Table at the back of this book!

Model Description	Trade-in Value	Market Value
Category C		
2 Dr GT Cpe	3705	5370
4 Dr LE Sdn	2865	4155
2 Dr SE Cpe	3215	4660
4 Dr SE Sdn	3050	4420
4 Dr STE Sdn	3865	5600

OPTIONS FOR GRAND PRIX

6 cyl 3.4 L Engine +180
Auto 4-Speed Transmission[Opt on LE,SE] +35
Aero Performance Pkg +395
Anti-Lock Brakes[Opt on LE,SE] +110
Leather Seats +110
Power Door Locks[Opt on LE,SE] +45
Power Drivers Seat[Std on STE] +55
Power Sunroof +125
Power Windows[Opt on LE,SE] +55

LE MANS 1992

LE designation swapped for SE nomenclature. Coupe gets amber turn signals.

Category E		
2 Dr SE Cpe	1215	1900
4 Dr SE Sdn	1275	1995
2 Dr Value Leader Cpe	960	1500

OPTIONS FOR LE MANS

Auto 3-Speed Transmission +85
Air Conditioning +145
Sunroof +65

SUNBIRD 1992

ABS is standard. LE designation extended to base coupe and sedan. 2.0-liter four-cylinder engine gets 15 more horsepower. Brake/transmission shift interlock is added. Fuel capacity jumps to 15.2 gallons. Automatic door locks lock doors when automatic is shifted from "Park" or manually shifted car begins moving forward. Convertible gets glass rear window at midyear.

RATINGS (SCALE OF 1-10)

Overall	Safety	Reliability	Performance	Comfort	Value
6	5.3	6.3	6.6	6.8	5.2

Category E		
2 Dr GT Cpe	2510	3920
2 Dr LE Cpe	1895	2960
4 Dr LE Sdn	1945	3040
2 Dr SE Conv	2545	3980
2 Dr SE Cpe	1975	3085
4 Dr SE Sdn	2045	3195

OPTIONS FOR SUNBIRD

6 cyl 3.1 L Engine[Opt on SE] +110
Auto 3-Speed Transmission +90
AM/FM Compact Disc Player +80
Air Conditioning +145

Power Windows[Std on Conv] +50
Sunroof +65

TRANS SPORT 1992

ABS is standard. SE becomes base model; new top-of-the-line is the GT. GT gets a standard 3.8-liter V6 good for 165 horsepower. SE retains old 3.1-liter, but offers the bigger motor as an option. 15-inch wheels replace 14-inch wheels on both models. Remote keyless entry and rear climate controls are added to the options list.

RATINGS (SCALE OF 1-10)

Overall	Safety	Reliability	Performance	Comfort	Value
6.9	5.7	6.2	7.2	7.1	8.2

Category G		
2 Dr GT Pass. Van	4045	5540
2 Dr SE Pass. Van	3145	4310

OPTIONS FOR TRANS SPORT

6 cyl 3.8 L Engine[Opt on SE] +120
7 Passenger Seating +95
AM/FM Compact Disc Player +60
Air Conditioning[Opt on SE] +145
Auto Load Leveling[Opt on SE] +40
Dual Air Conditioning +170
Power Door Locks +40
Power Drivers Seat +50
Power Windows +45

1991 PONTIAC

6000 1991

No changes.

Category C		
4 Dr LE Sdn	1890	2905
4 Dr LE Wgn	2210	3400
4 Dr SE Sdn	2155	3315

OPTIONS FOR 6000

6 cyl 3.1 L Engine[Std on SE,Wgn] +80
Auto 4-Speed Transmission[Std on SE,Wgn] +30
Air Conditioning[Std on SE,Wgn] +120
Power Door Locks[Opt on LE] +35
Power Drivers Seat +45
Power Windows[Opt on LE] +45

BONNEVILLE 1991

Brake/transmission shift interlock is added.

Category B		
4 Dr LE Sdn	2585	3800
4 Dr SE Sdn	2755	4050
4 Dr SSE Sdn	3310	4870

OPTIONS FOR BONNEVILLE

Anti-Lock Brakes[Std on SSE] +100
Leather Seats +100
Power Door Locks[Opt on LE] +40

Don't forget to refer to the Mileage Adjustment Table at the back of this book!

Model Description	Trade-in Value	Market Value
Power Drivers Seat[Opt on LE] +45		
Power Moonroof +145		
Power Windows[Opt on LE] +45		

FIREBIRD 1991

Top level V8 engines get more horsepower. Front and rear styling is freshened. Rocker panel extensions are restyled. Base coupes get new Sport Appearance Package.

Category F

	Trade-in	Market
2 Dr Formula Cpe	3395	4780
2 Dr STD Cpe	2730	3845
2 Dr Trans Am Conv	4810	6775
2 Dr Trans Am Cpe	3790	5335
2 Dr Trans Am GTA Cpe	4085	5755

OPTIONS FOR FIREBIRD

8 cyl 5.0 L Engine[Opt on STD] +50
8 cyl 5.7 L Engine[Std on Trans Am GTA] +70
Auto 4-Speed Transmission[Std on STD Conv] +75
AM/FM Compact Disc Player +70
Air Conditioning[Opt on STD] +125
Leather Seats +95
Limited Slip Diff[Opt on Formula,STD] +50
Power Door Locks[Std on Trans Am GTA] +30
Power Windows[Std on Trans Am GTA] +35
T-Tops (solid/Colored) +140

GRAND AM 1991

ABS is standard on SE. Larger, vented front rotors increase stopping ability on SE. LE with Sport Performance Package adds several SE goodies, like high-output Quad 4 engine, alloy wheels, exterior trim, and a revised suspension.

Category C

	Trade-in	Market
2 Dr LE Cpe	1760	2705
4 Dr LE Sdn	1900	2920
2 Dr SE Cpe	2035	3130
4 Dr SE Sdn	2095	3225
2 Dr STD Cpe	1665	2560
4 Dr STD Sdn	1735	2670

OPTIONS FOR GRAND AM

4 cyl 2.3 L Quad 4 Engine[Opt on LE] +95
Auto 3-Speed Transmission +80
Sport Performance Pkg +130
AM/FM Compact Disc Player +55
Air Conditioning[Std on SE] +120
Power Door Locks[Opt on LE] +35
Power Drivers Seat +45
Power Windows[Opt on LE] +45
Sunroof +55

GRAND PRIX 1991

LE and Turbo coupes dropped; GT coupe added. A twin-cam V6 with five-speed transmission is optional.

RATINGS (SCALE OF 1-10)

Overall	Safety	Reliability	Performance	Comfort	Value
6.8	5.2	5.8	8	7	8.1

Category C

	Trade-in	Market
2 Dr GT Cpe	2885	4435
4 Dr LE Sdn	2245	3455
2 Dr SE Cpe	2550	3925
4 Dr SE Sdn	2405	3700
4 Dr STE Sdn	3190	4905

OPTIONS FOR GRAND PRIX

6 cyl 3.1 L Engine[Opt on LE,SE] +80
6 cyl 3.4 L Engine +140
Auto 4-Speed Transmission[Opt on LE,SE] +30
Aero Performance Pkg +345
Anti-Lock Brakes +90
Leather Seats +90
Power Door Locks[Opt on LE,SE] +35
Power Drivers Seat[Opt on LE,SE] +45
Power Sunroof +100
Power Windows[Opt on LE,SE] +45

LE MANS 1991

Sporty GSE dropped.

Category E

	Trade-in	Market
2 Dr LE Cpe	895	1515
4 Dr LE Sdn	960	1625
2 Dr Value Leader Cpe	740	1255

OPTIONS FOR LE MANS

Auto 3-Speed Transmission +65
Air Conditioning +120
Power Steering +40
Sunroof +50

SUNBIRD 1991

Turbo engine dropped in favor of 3.1-liter V6. Six-cylinder makes 25 fewer horsepower than previous turbo. GT gets new alloys.

RATINGS (SCALE OF 1-10)

Overall	Safety	Reliability	Performance	Comfort	Value
5.9	4.4	6.6	6.6	6.8	5.2

Category E

	Trade-in	Market
2 Dr GT Cpe	2035	3450
2 Dr LE Conv	2075	3520
2 Dr LE Cpe	1310	2220
4 Dr LE Sdn	1370	2325
2 Dr SE Cpe	1630	2765
2 Dr STD Cpe	1185	2005
4 Dr STD Sdn	1265	2145

OPTIONS FOR SUNBIRD

6 cyl 3.1 L Engine[Std on GT] +100
Auto 3-Speed Transmission +70
AM/FM Compact Disc Player +65

Don't forget to refer to the Mileage Adjustment Table at the back of this book!

Air Conditioning +120
Power Door Locks[Std on Conv] +35
Power Windows[Std on Conv] +40
Sunroof +50

TRANS SPORT 1991

No changes.

RATINGS (SCALE OF 1-10)

Overall	Safety	Reliability	Performance	Comfort	Value
6.6	4.8	6.5	6.8	7.1	7.7

Category G

	Trade-in	Market
2 Dr SE Pass. Van	3005	4295
2 Dr STD Pass. Van	2745	3925

OPTIONS FOR TRANS SPORT
7 Passenger Seating +75
Air Conditioning[Std on SE] +120
Power Door Locks +35
Power Drivers Seat +40
Power Windows +35

1990 PONTIAC

6000 1990

STE dropped. S/E gains all-wheel drive option. 3.1-liter V6 replaces 2.8-liter V6, and makes more power. Air conditioning standard on all except LE sedan.

Category C

	Trade-in	Market
4 Dr LE Sdn	1405	2305
4 Dr LE Wgn	1500	2460
4 Dr SE Sdn	1750	2870
4 Dr SE 4WD Sdn	1935	3170
4 Dr SE Wgn	1785	2925

OPTIONS FOR 6000
6 cyl 3.1 L Engine[Std on SE, Wgn] +75
Air Conditioning[Std on SE, Wgn] +95
Power Door Locks[Opt on LE] +30
Power Drivers Seat +35
Power Windows[Opt on LE] +35

BONNEVILLE 1990

Front body/frame structure is redesigned. SSE gets new grille. LE and SE get new taillights. Remote keyless entry is new option. Power windows come with driver's express-down window. SE gets rear spoiler, fog lights and power trunk release standard. Alloy wheels are new. Bench seat is replaced by a 55/45 split bench.

Category B

	Trade-in	Market
4 Dr LE Sdn	1815	2790
4 Dr SE Sdn	2190	3370
4 Dr SSE Sdn	2725	4195

OPTIONS FOR BONNEVILLE
Anti-Lock Brakes[Std on SSE] +85
Leather Seats +80
Power Door Locks[Opt on LE] +30
Power Drivers Seat[Std on SSE] +40
Power Passenger Seat[Std on SSE] +40
Power Sunroof +135
Power Windows[Opt on LE] +35

FIREBIRD 1990

Driver airbag is added. A 3.1-liter V6 replaces the 2.8-liter V6. All models get dual body-color mirrors. Base cars get new interior trim. Some dashboard switchgear has been modified.

Category F

	Trade-in	Market
2 Dr Formula Cpe	2815	4080
2 Dr STD Cpe	2105	3055
2 Dr Trans Am Cpe	3215	4660

OPTIONS FOR FIREBIRD
8 cyl 5.0 L Engine[Opt on STD] +60
8 cyl 5.7 L Engine[Std on Trans Am GTA] +65
Auto 4-Speed Transmission +65
AM/FM Compact Disc Player +60
Air Conditioning[Opt on STD] +100
Leather Seats +80
Limited Slip Diff[Opt on Formula] +40
Power Windows[Std on Trans Am GTA] +25
T-Tops (solid/Colored) +115

GRAND AM 1990

Turbocharged engine dumped in favor of high-output Quad 4 motor. It is standard on SE model. Base Quad 4 engine is up ten horsepower this year. Express-down power windows are optional. SE gets 16-inch alloys.

Category C

	Trade-in	Market
2 Dr LE Cpe	1270	2085
4 Dr LE Sdn	1325	2170
2 Dr SE Cpe	1680	2750
4 Dr SE Sdn	1720	2820

OPTIONS FOR GRAND AM
4 cyl 2.3 L Quad 4 Engine[Opt on LE] +75
Auto 3-Speed Transmission +65
Air Conditioning[Opt on LE] +95
Power Door Locks[Opt on LE] +30
Power Drivers Seat +35
Power Windows[Opt on LE] +35
Sunroof +45

GRAND PRIX 1990

Sedan debuts, in LE and STE trim. STE includes remote keyless entry. Turbo coupe becomes regular production model. 2.8-liter V6 dumped in favor of 3.1-liter V6. A Quad 4 engine is available for the first time, and is standard on LE. STE sedan and SE coupe get smoother V6 power.

Don't forget to refer to the Mileage Adjustment Table at the back of this book!

Model Description	Trade-in Value	Market Value

RATINGS (SCALE OF 1-10)

Overall	Safety	Reliability	Performance	Comfort	Value
6.3	4.6	3.9	8	7	8

Category C

Model Description	Trade-in Value	Market Value
2 Dr LE Cpe	1730	2835
4 Dr LE Sdn	1600	2620
2 Dr SE Cpe	2135	3500
2 Dr SE Turbo Cpe	2460	4030
4 Dr STE Sdn	2340	3840
4 Dr STE Turbo Sdn	2600	4260

OPTIONS FOR GRAND PRIX

6 cyl 3.1 L Engine[Opt on LE] +75
Auto 4-Speed Transmission +60
Anti-Lock Brakes +75
Leather Seats +75
Power Door Locks[Opt on LE] +30
Power Drivers Seat[Opt on LE] +35
Power Sunroof +80
Power Windows[Opt on LE] +35

LE MANS   1990

SE sedan dropped from lineup. Motorized seatbelts appear. GSE gets quicker steering. Cars with 1.6-liter engine get better brakes. Suspensions retuned for better performance and quieter ride.

Category E

Model Description	Trade-in Value	Market Value
2 Dr GSE Cpe	880	1695
2 Dr LE Cpe	640	1235
4 Dr LE Sdn	705	1355
2 Dr Value Leader Cpe	570	1095

OPTIONS FOR LE MANS

Auto 3-Speed Transmission +55
Air Conditioning[Std on GSE] +100
Sunroof +40

SUNBIRD   1990

GT convertible switches to LE trim in cost-cutting move. SE and GT get new front styling. Passive restraint seatbelts are added. Turbo option dropped for SE model; is included in a sports package for LE convertible, along with GT suspension and steering.

RATINGS (SCALE OF 1-10)

Overall	Safety	Reliability	Performance	Comfort	Value
6.3	4.6	7.2	6.6	6.8	6.1

Category E

Model Description	Trade-in Value	Market Value
2 Dr GT Cpe	1380	2655
2 Dr GT Turbo Cpe	1455	2795
2 Dr LE Conv	1410	2710
2 Dr LE Turbo Conv	1230	2370
2 Dr LE Cpe	945	1815
4 Dr LE Sdn	1000	1920
2 Dr SE Cpe	1060	2040

OPTIONS FOR SUNBIRD

Auto 3-Speed Transmission +55
Air Conditioning +100
Power Door Locks +30
Power Steering[Std on GT,SE,Conv] +30
Power Windows +30
Sunroof +40

TRANS SPORT   1990

Weak-kneed minivan debuts with pathetic 120-horsepower V6 and plastic composite body panels. Load-leveling suspension is standard. Seating is modular in style, providing space for up to seven occupants.

RATINGS (SCALE OF 1-10)

Overall	Safety	Reliability	Performance	Comfort	Value
6.2	4.6	5.5	6.8	7.1	7.1

Category G

Model Description	Trade-in Value	Market Value
2 Dr SE Pass. Van	2560	3875
2 Dr STD Pass. Van	2355	3570

OPTIONS FOR TRANS SPORT

7 Passenger Seating +65
Air Conditioning[Std on SE] +100
Power Door Locks +30
Power Drivers Seat +35
Power Windows +30

Don't forget to refer to the Mileage Adjustment Table at the back of this book!

PORSCHE 99-98

Model Description	Trade-in Value	Market Value	Model Description	Trade-in Value	Market Value

PORSCHE   Germany

1997 Porsche 911

1999 PORSCHE

911   1999

Everything just got better with the totally redesigned 911, internally named the 996. The 911 Coupe, Cabriolet and Carrera 4 (available as either a coupe or cabrio) are all available for the 1999 model year.

RATINGS (SCALE OF 1-10)

Overall	Safety	Reliability	Performance	Comfort	Value
N/A	N/A	N/A	9	7	N/A

Category J

	Trade-in	Market
2 Dr Carrera Conv	59520	68415
2 Dr Carrera Cpe	52355	60180

OPTIONS FOR 911

Auto Manual Transmission +2525
Aluminum & Chrome Pkg +1435
Carbon/Alum. Brake Shiftr +650
Carbon/Lthr Steer Wheel +1225
Digital Sound Radio +870
F&R Aero Spoilers Kit +5205
Front & Rear Aero Kit +5890
Leather Dashboard Pkg +2160
Leather Interior Trim +2375
Litronic Headlamps +790
PCM Info/Navigation Systm +2615
Rear Window Washer +795
Rootwood Steering Wheel +1375
Sport Classic Wheels +1880
Sport Design Radial Whls +1965
Targa Wheels +685
Technology Alloy Wheels +1320
Turbo Look Alloy Wheels +880
AM/FM Compact Disc Player +325
Compact Disc Changer +685

Dual Power Seats +550
Hardtop Roof +2175
Heated Front Seats +310
Limited Slip Diff[Opt on Carrera] +605
Onboard Computer +325
Premium Sound System +970
Special Factory Paint +1245
Traction Control System[Opt on Carrera] +875

BOXSTER   1999

The Boxster is slowly adding features and options. This year, a Classic Package includes metallic paint and all-leather seats, and adds special highlights to the interior. The gas tank is increased from a 12.5- to a 14.1- gallon capacity, and gas-discharge Litronic headlights are optional. All the features in the Sport Package are individually optional this year, and 18-inch wheels are now available.

RATINGS (SCALE OF 1-10)

Overall	Safety	Reliability	Performance	Comfort	Value
N/A	N/A	N/A	9.2	7.8	N/A

Category J

	Trade-in	Market
2 Dr STD Conv	33149	38100

OPTIONS FOR BOXSTER

Auto Manual Transmission +2370
Boxster Design Wheels +1095
Leather Seat/Interior Trm +1470
Light Alloy Turbo Wheels +2020
Special Leather Seat Trim +1750
Sport Classic Wheels +1840
Sport Design Wheels +3080
Sport Handling Pkg +1515
Technic Sport Pkg +1010
AM/FM Compact Disc Player +325
Compact Disc Changer +685
Cruise Control +355
Heated Front Seats +310
Onboard Computer +325

1998 PORSCHE

911   1998

The current-generation 911 goes the way of the dodo at year's end, when it will be replaced by the next evolutionary step toward the perfect driving machine.

Category J

	Trade-in	Market
2 Dr Carrera Conv	53467	62175
2 Dr Carrera S Cpe	41105	52300
2 Dr Targa Cpe	44978	55355

OPTIONS FOR 911

5-Spoke Cast Alloy Wheels +885
Aero Kit +4330
Digital Sound Radio Equip +1275
F&R Aero Spoilers Kit +4055

Don't forget to refer to the Mileage Adjustment Table at the back of this book!

Model Description	Trade-in Value	Market Value
Hi-Fi Sound Radio Equip. +570		
Leather Door Panels +1160		
Leather Interior Trim +2450		
Leather/Vinyl Inter. Trim +950		
Litronic Headlamps +945		
Rear Window Washer +665		
Rootwood Steering Wheel +1140		
Special Chassis +985		
Special Leather Int. Trim +2880		
Sport Chassis W/18" Whls +1510		
Sport Classic Wheels +1255		
Targa Wheels +865		
Technology Alloy Wheels +1540		
Technology Pressure Whls. +1095		
Wood Dash +3995		
AM/FM Compact Disc Player +265		
Compact Disc Changer +560		
Dual Power Seats +450		
Hardtop Roof[Opt on Cabriolet] +1780		
Heated Front Seats +255		
Leather Seats +705		
Limited Slip Diff[Std on Carrera 4S, 4WD] +495		
Onboard Computer +265		
Premium Sound System +790		
Special Factory Paint +1020		
Traction Control System[Opt on 2WD] +715		

BOXSTER 1998

Side air bags are standard for 1998.

Category J

	Trade-in	Market
2 Dr STD Conv	31490	36615

OPTIONS FOR BOXSTER

Boxster Design Wheels +910
Leather Seat/Interior Trim +1220
Special Leather Seat Trim +1455
Sport Classic Wheels +1530
Sport Handling Pkg +1235
Technic Sport Pkg +740
AM/FM Compact Disc Player +265
Compact Disc Changer +560
Cruise Control +290
Heated Front Seats +255
Onboard Computer +265

1997 PORSCHE

911 1997

The only change to this year's Porsche 911 is the availability of a Porsche-engineered child seat that will deactivate the passenger airbag when it is in place.

Category J

	Trade-in	Market
2 Dr Carrera Conv	46770	55025
2 Dr Carrera Cpe	39880	46915
2 Dr Targa Cpe	43665	51370
2 Dr Turbo 4WD Cpe	77450	91120

OPTIONS FOR 911

17 Inch Cup Design Wheels +725
17 Inch Targa Wheels +1190
5 Spoke Light Alloy Whls +690
Aero Kit +3535
Aluminum/Chrome Pkg +1040
Carbon/Alloy Brake and Shifter +415
Carbon/Lth Steering Wheel +790
Digital Sound Radio +575
Hi-Fi Sound Radio +465
Leather Door Panels +950
Leather Headliner +785
Leather Interior Trim +2005
Leather Sun Visors +425
Pearlescent White Paint +6150
Technology Wheels +1620
Wood Dash +2185
AM/FM Compact Disc Player +215
Compact Disc Changer +455
Dual Power Seats[Std on Turbo, Turbo S] +365
Hardtop Roof +1455
Heated Front Seats[Std on Turbo S] +210
Leather Seats[Std on Turbo, Turbo S] +580
Limited Slip Diff[Opt on Targa, 2WD] +405
Onboard Computer[Std on Turbo, Turbo S] +220

BOXSTER 1997

This all-new roadster is introduced to compete in the revitalized midpriced sports car category. The Boxster features a 2.5-liter six-cylinder engine, a five-speed manual or five-speed Tiptronic transmission, and a power top that closes in an impressive 12 seconds.

Category J

	Trade-in	Market
2 Dr STD Conv	30280	35625

OPTIONS FOR BOXSTER

Aerokit +2860
Boxster-design Wheels +665
Color Keyed Rear Spoiler +785
Leather Seat Trim +1085
Rain Sensing Windshield +750
Special Leather Seat Trim +1290
Sport Classic Wheels +1350
Sport Handling Pkg +1635
Compact Disc Changer[Opt on STD] +455
Compact Disc W/fm/tape +395
Cruise Control +235
Hardtop Roof +1455
Heated Front Seats +210
Onboard Computer[Opt on STD] +220
Traction Control System +585

1996 PORSCHE

911 1996

Trick Targa model joins the lineup, and power is up in midrange revs. New Carrera 4S model provides Turbo looks without Turbo price or performance. Bigger

---

Don't forget to refer to the Mileage Adjustment Table at the back of this book!

Model Description	Trade-in Value	Market Value

wheels are standard across the line, as well as Litronic headlights. New stereos and exterior colors compliment one new interior color this year. Remote keyless entry system gets an immobilizer feature.

Category J

Model Description	Trade-in Value	Market Value
2 Dr Carrera Conv	41540	49455
2 Dr Carrera Cpe	33920	40380
2 Dr Carrera 4WD Cpe	40745	48505
2 Dr Carrera 4S 4WD Cpe	43250	51490
2 Dr STD Turbo 4WD Cpe	65280	77715
2 Dr Targa Cpe	37715	44895

OPTIONS FOR 911

5 Spoke Light Alloy Whls +555
Color To Sample Leather +2480
Digital Sound System +440
Door Panel Pkg +710
Hi-fi Sound +375
Leather Door Panels +765
Pearl White Metallic Pnt. +4420
Pearlescent White Paint +4940
Seat Pkg +735
Steering Wheel Pkg +490
Technology Wheels +720
Wood Dash +1760
AM/FM Compact Disc Player +175
Compact Disc Changer +375
Dual Power Seats[Std on STD] +300
Heated Front Seats +170
Leather Seats[Std on STD] +470
Limited Slip Diff[Opt on 2WD] +330
Onboard Computer +180
Premium Sound System +530

1995 PORSCHE

911 — 1995

Category J

Model Description	Trade-in Value	Market Value
2 Dr Carrera Conv	37255	44885
2 Dr Carrera Cpe	28895	34815

OPTIONS FOR 911

5 Spoke Light Alloy Whls +455
Active Brake Differential +300
Color To Sample Paint +825
Digital Sound Radio Equip +685
Door Panel Pkg +625
Hi-fi Sound W/amplifier +305
Rootwood Door Trim Pnl +480
Leather Door Panels +625
Leather Headliner +650
Rootwood Dashboard +1435
Pearlescent White Paint +4040
Pressure Cast Alloy Whls +455
Seat Pkg +575
Steering Wheel Pkg +400
Telephone Handset Kit +315
Wood Dash +1435

AM/FM Compact Disc Player +145
Compact Disc Changer +305
Dual Power Seats +245
Heated Front Seats +140
Leather Seats +385
Limited Slip Diff[Opt on 2WD] +270
Onboard Computer +145
Rear Window Wiper +115

968 — 1995

Category J

Model Description	Trade-in Value	Market Value
2 Dr STD Conv	20800	25060
2 Dr STD Cpe	16855	20305

OPTIONS FOR 968

17 Inch 5-Spoke Wheels +455
Compact Disc Changer +305
Compact Disc W/fm/tape +265
Heated Front Seats +140
Leather Seats +385
Limited Slip Diff +270
Power Drivers Seat +115
Power Passenger Seat +110

1994 PORSCHE

911 — 1994

Porsche modernizes the 911, updating and improving the car without killing its character. A more aerodynamic body and various tweaks to the engine and suspension make this old favorite even better.

Category J

Model Description	Trade-in Value	Market Value
2 Dr America Roadster Conv	25855	31155
2 Dr Cabriolet Conv	28090	33845
2 Dr Carrera Cpe	25505	30730
2 Dr Carrera Turbo Cpe	41835	50405
2 Dr RS America Cpe	22870	27555
2 Dr Speedster Conv	30625	36895
2 Dr Targa Cpe	26665	32125
2 Dr Wide Body Cpe	25965	31285

OPTIONS FOR 911

5-spoke 17 Inch Wheels +380
Boot Cover +710
Leather Headliner +375
Rootwood Dashboard +1195
Special Leather Console +725
AM/FM Compact Disc Player +120
Air Conditioning[Std on Cabriolet,Carrera,Targa, Wide Body] +755
Climate Control for AC[Opt on RS America,Speedster] +75
Compact Disc Changer +250
Cruise Control[Opt on Speedster] +130
Hardtop Roof +795
Headlight Washers[Opt on Targa] +65
Heated Front Seats +115
Limited Slip Diff[Std on Turbo] +220
Onboard Computer[Std on Turbo] +120

Don't forget to refer to the Mileage Adjustment Table at the back of this book!

Model Description	Trade-in Value	Market Value
Power Drivers Seat +90		
Power Passenger Seat +90		
Power Sunroof[Opt on RS America] +305		
Rear Window Wiper[Std on Turbo] +90		

968 — 1994

Category J

Model Description	Trade-in Value	Market Value
2 Dr Cabriolet Conv	17075	20570
2 Dr STD Cpe	13805	16630

OPTIONS FOR 968

5-Spoke 17-Inch Wheels +380
Leather Boot Cover +710
Rootwood Pkg +660
Sport Chassis +555
AM/FM Compact Disc Player +120
Compact Disc Changer +250
Heated Front Seats +115
Leather Seats +315
Limited Slip Diff +220
Power Drivers Seat +90
Power Passenger Seat +90
Premium Sound System +355

1993 PORSCHE

911 — 1993

Category J

Model Description	Trade-in Value	Market Value
2 Dr Cabriolet Conv	25710	31740
2 Dr Carrera Cpe	23105	28525
2 Dr RS America Cpe	20930	25835
2 Dr Targa Cpe	24625	30405

OPTIONS FOR 911

Leather Interior Trim +525
AM/FM Compact Disc Player +95
Air Conditioning[Std on Cabriolet Conv,Carrera 4WD Cpe] +620
Climate Control for AC[Opt on RS America] +60
Compact Disc Changer +205
Dual Power Seats +165
Hardtop Roof +650
Headlight Washers[Opt on Carrera] +55
Heated Front Seats +95
Leather Seats[Opt on Cabriolet] +260
Limited Slip Diff +180
Onboard Computer +95
Power Sunroof[Std on Carrera] +250

968 — 1993

Category J

Model Description	Trade-in Value	Market Value
2 Dr STD Cpe	11700	14440

OPTIONS FOR 968

5-Spoke 17-Inch Wheels +310
968 Special Chassis +450
Leather Piping All Seats +325
Lthr Interior W/Blck Belt +1230

Lthr Interior W/Lthr Belt +775
Metallic Paint To Sample +380
Painted Rims +240
Special Leather Upholstry +870
Compact Disc Changer +205
Heated Front Seats +95
Leather Seats +260
Limited Slip Diff +180
Sport Seats +165

1992 PORSCHE

911 — 1992

Category J

Model Description	Trade-in Value	Market Value
2 Dr Cabriolet Conv	21560	27645
2 Dr Carrera Cpe	18580	23820
2 Dr STD Turbo Cpe	34290	43965
2 Dr Targa Cpe	17540	22490

OPTIONS FOR 911

Lthr Instrument Housing +155
Rear Window Washing Systm +140
Special Leather Seat Trim +710
AM/FM Compact Disc Player +80
Compact Disc Changer +165
Dual Power Seats[Std on STD] +135
Hardtop Roof +530
Leather Seats[Opt on America Roadster] +210
Limited Slip Diff +145

968 — 1992

944 replacement arrives, sporting 928-inspired front end and the most powerful (naturally aspirated) 4-cylinder engine available anywhere.

Category J

Model Description	Trade-in Value	Market Value
2 Dr Cabriolet Conv	13380	17150
2 Dr STD Cpe	10000	12820

OPTIONS FOR 968

AM/FM Compact Disc Player +80
Compact Disc Changer +165
Leather Seats +210
Limited Slip Diff +145
Power Drivers Seat +60
Power Passenger Seat +60

1991 PORSCHE

911 — 1991

Category J

Model Description	Trade-in Value	Market Value
2 Dr Carrera Cpe	17795	23110
2 Dr Carrera 4 4WD Cpe	18815	24430
2 Dr Carrera 4 Cabrio 4WD Conv	22330	28995
2 Dr Carrera 4 Targa 4WD Cpe	20960	27220
2 Dr Carrera Cabrio Conv	19795	25705

Don't forget to refer to the Mileage Adjustment Table at the back of this book!

Model Description	Trade-in Value	Market Value
2 Dr Carrera Targa Cpe	18120	23530
2 Dr STD Turbo Cpe	25635	33290

OPTIONS FOR 911

All Leather Interior +1425
Car Color Rims +145
Forged Alloy Wheels +235
Leather Boot Cover +330
Leather Headliner +150
Leather Instr Panel +200
AM/FM Compact Disc Player +65
Compact Disc W/fm/tape +120
Leather Seats[Std on STD] +170
Limited Slip Diff +120
Power Drivers Seat[Std on STD] +50
Power Passenger Seat[Std on STD] +50

928 — 1991

Category J

Model Description	Trade-in Value	Market Value
2 Dr STD Cpe	16235	21085

OPTIONS FOR 928

All Leather Interior +1425
Passenger Memory Seat +145
Pwr Lumbar Supports +160

944 S2 — 1991

Category F

Model Description	Trade-in Value	Market Value
2 Dr Cabriolet Conv	11295	15060
2 Dr STD Cpe	8495	11330

OPTIONS FOR 944 S2

16-Inch Disc Wheels +295
Sport Chassis +290
AM/FM Compact Disc Player +70
Dual Power Seats +125
Leather Seats +95
Limited Slip Diff +50

1990 PORSCHE

911 — 1990

Category J

Model Description	Trade-in Value	Market Value
2 Dr Carrera Cpe	16150	21530
2 Dr Carrera 4 4WD Cpe	17640	23525
2 Dr Carrera 4 Targa 4WD	20735	27645
2 Dr Carrera Cabrio Conv	18260	24345
2 Dr Carrera Targa	17395	23195

OPTIONS FOR 911

Forged Alloy Wheels +190
Leather Boot Cover +270
Leather Headliner +125
Leather Instrument Panel +165
Supple Leather Seat Trim +355
AM/FM Compact Disc Player +55
Leather Seats +140
Limited Slip Diff +100

Power Drivers Seat +40
Power Passenger Seat +40

928 — 1990

Category J

Model Description	Trade-in Value	Market Value
2 Dr STD Cpe	13045	17390

OPTIONS FOR 928

All Leather Interior +670
Passenger Positrol Seats +115
AM/FM Compact Disc Player +55

944 S2 — 1990

Category F

Model Description	Trade-in Value	Market Value
2 Dr Cabriolet Conv	10010	13715
2 Dr STD Cpe	8050	11030

OPTIONS FOR 944 S2

16-Inch Disc Wheels +235
Sport Chassis +240
AM/FM Compact Disc Player +60
Leather Seats +80
Limited Slip Diff +40
Power Drivers Seat +30
Power Passenger Seat +35

SAAB 99-98

Model Description	Trade-in Value	Market Value	Model Description	Trade-in Value	Market Value

SAAB   Sweden

1997 Saab 900 Convertible

1999 SAAB

9-3   1999

Saab changed about 1,000 suspension, steering and interior pieces on the 900 and decided to change the car's name to the 9-3, giving it a mild exterior freshening to boot. Around mid-year, a high-output version of its 2.0-liter turbo four-cylinder (making an amazing 200 horsepower) becomes the standard engine in the uplevel SE five-door and SE Convertible models equipped with a manual transmission. All SE's also get new five-spoke 16-inch alloy wheels. All five-speed manual 9-3s get revised gearbox ratios and a numerically higher (4.05:1) final drive ratio for better off-the-line feel. A revised 9-3 interior headliner provides more padding for increased protection in the event of a crash. And five-door SE variants add an integrated driver-seat armrest and a centrally located cupholder that swings out from the instrument panel.

RATINGS (SCALE OF 1-10)

Overall	Safety	Reliability	Performance	Comfort	Value
N/A	8.1	8.7	8	7.8	N/A

Category J

	Trade-in	Market
2 Dr SE Turbo Conv	28090	32290
4 Dr SE Turbo Hbk	19520	22435
2 Dr SE HO Turbo Conv	26975	31005
4 Dr SE HO Turbo Hbk	19255	22130
2 Dr STD Turbo Conv	23460	26965
2 Dr STD Turbo Hbk	15834	18200
4 Dr STD Turbo Hbk	16141	18555
2 Dr Viggen Turbo Hbk	26425	30375

OPTIONS FOR 9-3

Auto 4-Speed Transmission +755
Styling Value Pkg +1820
Compact Disc Changer +685
Heated Front Seats +310
Leather Seats[Std on SE,SE HO,Viggen,Conv] +865
Power Moonroof[Opt on STD] +695

9-5   1999

Saab's replacement for the 9000 line of cars is finally here, and it's called the 9-5. Available as a sedan with a turbocharged four-cylinder or turbocharged V6 engine, the 9-5 is designed to compete against conventional cars like the BMW 5-Series and Infiniti I30.

RATINGS (SCALE OF 1-10)

Overall	Safety	Reliability	Performance	Comfort	Value
N/A	N/A	8.8	7.8	8.3	N/A

Category J

	Trade-in	Market
4 Dr SE Turbo Sdn	22055	25350
4 Dr SE V6 Turbo Sdn	23845	27410
4 Dr STD Turbo Sdn	18035	20730

OPTIONS FOR 9-5

Auto 4-Speed Transmission[Std on SE V6,V6 Turbo Wagon] +795
Power Ventilated Seats +655
Styling Value Pkg +1715
Heated Seats +365
Leather Seats[Opt on STD,STD Turbo Wagon] +865
Power Moonroof[Opt on STD] +695

1998 SAAB

900   1998

The Saab 900 three-door hatchback gets the same turbocharged engine as the SE models this year. Other changes include the addition of body-color front and rear bumpers.

RATINGS (SCALE OF 1-10)

Overall	Safety	Reliability	Performance	Comfort	Value
7.4	7	7.7	8.6	7.9	6

Category J

	Trade-in	Market
2 Dr S Conv	19070	22175
4 Dr S Hbk	14485	16845
2 Dr S Turbo Hbk	14820	17230
2 Dr SE Turbo Conv	22850	26570
2 Dr SE Turbo Hbk	16940	19695
4 Dr SE Turbo Hbk	17115	19900

OPTIONS FOR 900

Auto 4-Speed Transmission +625
Leather Seats[Std on SE, Conv] +705
Power Moonroof[Opt on S] +570

Don't forget to refer to the Mileage Adjustment Table at the back of this book!

Model Description	Trade-in Value	Market Value

9000 — 1998

No changes to the aging 9000.

RATINGS (SCALE OF 1-10)

Overall	Safety	Reliability	Performance	Comfort	Value
7.8	7.4	8.5	8.8	8.4	6.1

Category J

	Trade-in	Market
4 Dr CSE Turbo Hbk	18740	21790

OPTIONS FOR 9000
Auto 4-Speed Transmission +640

1997 SAAB

900 — 1997

No significant changes for the 1997 Saab 900.

RATINGS (SCALE OF 1-10)

Overall	Safety	Reliability	Performance	Comfort	Value
7.5	6.9	7	8.6	7.9	7.1

Category J

	Trade-in	Market
2 Dr S Conv	16745	19700
2 Dr S Hbk	12930	15210
4 Dr S Hbk	13105	15415
2 Dr SE Turbo Conv	19580	23035
2 Dr SE Turbo Hbk	14525	17090
4 Dr SE Turbo Hbk	14745	17345
2 Dr SE Talladega Turbo Conv	20020	23555
2 Dr SE Talladega Turbo Hbk	14780	17390
4 Dr SE Talladega Turbo Hbk	15010	17660
2 Dr SE V6 Conv	18890	22225
4 Dr SE V6 Hbk	15225	17910

OPTIONS FOR 900
Auto 4-Speed Transmission[Std on SE V6] +505
Child Seats (2) +125
Leather Seats[Opt on S Hbk] +580
Power Moonroof[Opt on S] +465

9000 — 1997

No changes to this aging model.

RATINGS (SCALE OF 1-10)

Overall	Safety	Reliability	Performance	Comfort	Value
7.7	7.4	8	8.8	8.4	6.1

Category J

	Trade-in	Market
4 Dr Aero Turbo Hbk	19035	22395
4 Dr CS Turbo Hbk	14250	16765
4 Dr CSE Turbo Hbk	16150	19000
4 Dr CSE Anniversary Turbo Hbk	16720	19670
4 Dr CSE V6 Hbk	16805	19770

OPTIONS FOR 9000
Auto 4-Speed Transmission[Std on CSE V6] +525
Dual Power Seats[Opt on CS] +365
Leather Seats[Opt on CS] +580
Power Moonroof[Opt on CS] +465

1996 SAAB

900 — 1996

The popular Saab 900 SE five-door is available this year with the amazing turbocharged four-cylinder engine. An automatic transmission is now optional on turbos. V6 models come only with an automatic. Adjustable driver's lumbar support is now standard on all 900 models.

RATINGS (SCALE OF 1-10)

Overall	Safety	Reliability	Performance	Comfort	Value
7.3	6.9	6.7	8.6	7.9	6.5

Category J

	Trade-in	Market
2 Dr S Conv	15090	17965
2 Dr S Hbk	10590	12610
4 Dr S Hbk	10785	12840
2 Dr SE Turbo Conv	17080	20335
2 Dr SE Turbo Hbk	12845	15290
4 Dr SE Turbo Hbk	13040	15525
2 Dr SE V6 Conv	16690	19870
4 Dr SE V6 Hbk	12415	14780

OPTIONS FOR 900
Auto 4-Speed Transmission[Opt on S,SE] +400
Child Seats (2) +100
Leather Seats[Std on SE,SE V6,Conv] +470
Power Moonroof[Opt on S] +380

9000 — 1996

The 9000 sedans are dropped, leaving only the hatchback bodystyle. Cupholders for rear seat passengers, new upholstery for the CS, and new three-spoke alloy wheels for the CS and CSE round out the major developments for this year's model.

RATINGS (SCALE OF 1-10)

Overall	Safety	Reliability	Performance	Comfort	Value
7.9	7.5	8.2	8.8	8.4	6.7

Category J

	Trade-in	Market
4 Dr Aero Turbo Hbk	15420	18360
4 Dr CS Turbo Hbk	10830	12895
4 Dr CSE Turbo Hbk	12380	14740
4 Dr CSE V6 Hbk	13435	15995

OPTIONS FOR 9000
Auto 4-Speed Transmission[Opt on CS,CSE] +420
Dual Power Seats[Opt on CS] +300
Leather Seats[Opt on CS] +470
Power Moonroof[Opt on CS] +380

Don't forget to refer to the Mileage Adjustment Table at the back of this book!

1995 SAAB

900 — 1995

Daytime Running Lights (DRLs) are now standard on the 900.

RATINGS (SCALE OF 1-10)

Overall	Safety	Reliability	Performance	Comfort	Value
6.7	7.3	5.7	8.6	7.9	4.1

Category J

	Trade-in	Market
2 Dr S Conv	12905	15550
2 Dr S Hbk	8835	10645
4 Dr S Hbk	9025	10875
2 Dr SE Conv	14385	17330
2 Dr SE Turbo Conv	14620	17615
2 Dr SE Turbo Hbk	10990	13240
4 Dr SE Hbk	10525	12680

OPTIONS FOR 900

Auto 4-Speed Transmission +330
AM/FM Compact Disc Player +145
Aluminum/Alloy Wheels[Std on SE,Conv] +125
Compact Disc Changer[Opt on Hbk] +305
Leather Seats[Std on SE,Conv] +385
Power Moonroof[Opt on S] +310

9000 — 1995

Saab adds a light-pressure turbo and a V6 to their large-car engine roster. V6 cars come only with an automatic transmission. Daytime running lights (DRLs) become standard on all 9000s this year.

RATINGS (SCALE OF 1-10)

Overall	Safety	Reliability	Performance	Comfort	Value
8	8.2	8	8.8	8.4	6.7

Category J

	Trade-in	Market
4 Dr Aero Turbo Hbk	13640	16435
4 Dr CDE Sdn	11105	13380
4 Dr CS Turbo Hbk	9815	11825
4 Dr CSE Hbk	11235	13535
4 Dr CSE Turbo Hbk	11630	14015

OPTIONS FOR 9000

Auto 4-Speed Transmission[Opt on Aero,CS,Turbo] +345
Leather Seats[Opt on CS] +385
Power Moonroof[Opt on CS] +310

1994 SAAB

900 — 1994

A totally new Saab is introduced with a little help from GM. The new 900 is available as two-door and four-door hatchbacks or a two-door convertible. The 900SE four-door features a V6 engine that was developed by GM for use in its Opels. Saab gets a new optional automatic transmission as well that offers three types of driving modes: sport, winter and economy. Saab's very cool black panel instrument cluster and dual airbags debut on this vehicle as well.

RATINGS (SCALE OF 1-10)

Overall	Safety	Reliability	Performance	Comfort	Value
6.5	7.1	5.1	8.6	7.9	3.6

Category J

	Trade-in	Market
2 Dr Commemorative Turbo Conv	12100	14580
2 Dr S Conv	9870	11890
2 Dr S Hbk	7265	8750
4 Dr S Hbk	7410	8930
2 Dr SE Turbo Hbk	9230	11120
4 Dr SE Hbk	8325	10030
2 Dr STD Turbo Conv	11355	13680

OPTIONS FOR 900

6 cyl 2.5 L Engine[Opt on S] +630
Auto 3-Speed Transmission +195
Auto 4-Speed Transmission +245
Aluminum/Alloy Wheels[Opt on S Hbk] +100
Child Seats (2) +70
Compact Disc W/fm/tape[Opt on S] +215
Leather Seats[Opt on S] +315
Power Drivers Seat[Opt on S Hbk,SE Hbk] +90
Power Moonroof[Opt on S] +255
Power Passenger Seat[Opt on SE Hbk,S Hbk] +90
Power Sunroof +305
Traction Control System[Opt on S] +320

9000 — 1994

Dual airbags for the 9000! CS models get front and rear fog lights. Unfortunately, traction control is dropped for all models.

RATINGS (SCALE OF 1-10)

Overall	Safety	Reliability	Performance	Comfort	Value
7.6	7.9	6.6	8.8	8.4	6.1

Category J

	Trade-in	Market
4 Dr Aero Turbo Hbk	11020	13280
4 Dr CD Turbo Sdn	9245	11140
4 Dr CDE Sdn	8680	10460
4 Dr CDE Turbo Sdn	9655	11635
4 Dr CS Hbk	7945	9570
4 Dr CS Turbo Hbk	8630	10400
4 Dr CSE Hbk	8555	10310
4 Dr CSE Turbo Hbk	9385	11305

OPTIONS FOR 9000

Auto 4-Speed Transmission +260
Compact Disc W/fm/tape +215
Leather Seats[Opt on CD,CS] +315
Power Moonroof[Opt on CD] +255

Don't forget to refer to the Mileage Adjustment Table at the back of this book!

SAAB 94-92

Model Description	Trade-in Value	Market Value	Model Description	Trade-in Value	Market Value

Rear Spoiler[Opt on CSE] +110
Traction Control System +320

1993 SAAB

900 — 1993

Base 900 models replace the 900S. The equipment that was standard on the 900S is now part of a preferred equipment package. The convertible can now get a blue or tan top.

RATINGS (SCALE OF 1-10)

Overall	Safety	Reliability	Performance	Comfort	Value
N/A	N/A	7.7	8.4	7.5	4.1

Category D
2 Dr Commemorative Turbo Hbk	7495	9990
2 Dr S Conv	7875	10500
2 Dr S Hbk	5235	7100
4 Dr S Sdn	5410	7215
2 Dr S Luxury Hbk	5515	7350
4 Dr S Luxury Sdn	5560	7415
2 Dr STD Turbo Conv	8740	11650
2 Dr STD Turbo Hbk	7375	9835

OPTIONS FOR 900
Auto 3-Speed Transmission +155

9000 — 1993

New nomenclature reflects Saab's current identity crisis. Base models are now called the CS and CD; luxury models are called CSE and CDE. Hatchbacks get more sedan-like styling that increases their length by four inches. A new Aero hatchback enters the lineup. The Aero is the fastest vehicle in the large-car class. It is powered by a 225-horsepower version of the inline-four found in the other turbo models, and it offers exceptional handling.

RATINGS (SCALE OF 1-10)

Overall	Safety	Reliability	Performance	Comfort	Value
7.6	6.4	6.4	8.8	8.4	8

Category J
4 Dr Aero Turbo Hbk	8935	11030
4 Dr CD Sdn	6545	8080
4 Dr CD Turbo Sdn	6820	8420
4 Dr CDE Sdn	7385	9115
4 Dr CDE Turbo Sdn	7730	9545
4 Dr CS Hbk	6460	7975
4 Dr CS Turbo Hbk	6700	8270
4 Dr CSE Hbk	7065	8720
4 Dr CSE Turbo Hbk	7400	9135

OPTIONS FOR 9000
Auto 4-Speed Transmission[Std on CD Sdn] +205
Leather Seats[Opt on CD,CS] +260
Power Sunroof[Opt on CD,CS] +250

1992 SAAB

900 — 1992

Saab Turbo SPG is dropped from the 900 lineup. Base models gain power windows and power/heated outside mirrors. 900S models get new alloy wheels and convertibles get freshened exterior and interior styling. Turbo models get new wheels, tires and a compact disc player.

RATINGS (SCALE OF 1-10)

Overall	Safety	Reliability	Performance	Comfort	Value
N/A	N/A	7.7	8.4	7.5	3.6

Category D
2 Dr S Conv	6655	8990
2 Dr S Hbk	4600	6215
4 Dr S Sdn	4535	6125
2 Dr STD Turbo Conv	7495	10130
2 Dr STD Hbk	4300	5810
2 Dr STD Turbo Hbk	6285	8495
4 Dr STD Sdn	4245	5735

OPTIONS FOR 900
Auto 3-Speed Transmission +120
Auto 4-Speed Transmission +120

9000 — 1992

A limited-edition Griffin Edition is introduced as the *crème de la crème* 9000 for 1992. It is available only as a four-door turbo sedan. All turbo models get traction control for 1992. All Saab 9000s get a sunroof as well.

RATINGS (SCALE OF 1-10)

Overall	Safety	Reliability	Performance	Comfort	Value
7.3	6.5	6.6	8.8	8.4	6.4

Category D
4 Dr CD Sdn	5295	7155
4 Dr CD Turbo Sdn	5795	7830
4 Dr S Hbk	5050	6825
4 Dr STD Hbk	4565	6170
4 Dr STD Turbo Hbk	4890	6605

Category J
4 Dr CD Griffin Turbo Sdn	5700	7310

OPTIONS FOR 9000
Auto 4-Speed Transmission[Std on CD] +160

SAAB 91-90

Model Description	Trade-in Value	Market Value	Model Description	Trade-in Value	Market Value

1991 SAAB

900 — 1991

The Turbo sedan is dropped from the 900 lineup.

RATINGS (SCALE OF 1-10)

Overall	Safety	Reliability	Performance	Comfort	Value
N/A	N/A	7	8.4	7.5	3.5

Category D

	Trade-in	Market
2 Dr S Conv	6330	8670
2 Dr S Hbk	3860	5285
4 Dr S Sdn	3725	5105
2 Dr STD Hbk	3075	4210
4 Dr STD Sdn	3010	4125

OPTIONS FOR 900

Auto 3-Speed Transmission +85

9000 — 1991

Turbo CD Sedan is introduced.

RATINGS (SCALE OF 1-10)

Overall	Safety	Reliability	Performance	Comfort	Value
7.6	6.7	7.4	8.8	8.4	6.9

Category D

	Trade-in	Market
4 Dr CD Sdn	4280	5865
4 Dr CD Turbo Sdn	4630	6345
4 Dr S Hbk	4105	5625
4 Dr STD Hbk	3665	5020
4 Dr STD Turbo Hbk	3960	5425

OPTIONS FOR 9000

Auto 4-Speed Transmission[Std on CD] +115

1990 SAAB

900 — 1990

A driver airbag is added to the standard equipment list.

RATINGS (SCALE OF 1-10)

Overall	Safety	Reliability	Performance	Comfort	Value
N/A	N/A	7.1	8.4	7.5	3.4

Category D

	Trade-in	Market
2 Dr S Hbk	2900	4025
4 Dr S Sdn	2880	4000
2 Dr SPG Turbo Hbk	4520	6280
2 Dr STD Turbo Conv	5590	7765
2 Dr STD Hbk	2400	3330
2 Dr STD Turbo Hbk	4225	5870
4 Dr STD Sdn	2320	3220

OPTIONS FOR 900

Auto 3-Speed Transmission +70

9000 — 1990

A new turbocharger is added to Turbo models.

RATINGS (SCALE OF 1-10)

Overall	Safety	Reliability	Performance	Comfort	Value
7.4	6.7	6.9	8.4	8.4	6.8

Category D

	Trade-in	Market
4 Dr CD Turbo Sdn	3510	4875
4 Dr S Hbk	2820	3915
4 Dr S Sdn	3090	4295
4 Dr STD Turbo Hbk	3275	4550

OPTIONS FOR 9000

Auto 4-Speed Transmission +95
Leather Pkg +95
Leather Seats[Opt on S] +135
Power Sunroof[Opt on S Hbk] +90

Don't forget to refer to the Mileage Adjustment Table at the back of this book!

Model Description	Trade-in Value	Market Value	Model Description	Trade-in Value	Market Value

SATURN 99

SATURN　　USA

1998 Saturn SL2

1999 SATURN

SC   1999

Saturn continues on its refinement theme for 1999. Refined powertrain performance, interior upgrades and new wheel selections top the list of changes for SC1 and SC2 models. New this year on all coupes is a standard driver's-side third door to improve access to the rear seats. Improvements to both the single- and dual-overhead cam engines (including new pistons, connecting rods and crankshafts) are designed to reduce noise, vibration and harshness while improving fuel economy about one mpg across the board. The SC2 gets redesigned standard wheel covers and new optional 15-inch aluminum wheels. Interior cloth fabrics have been revised, the capacity of the windshield washer solvent bottle has been increased to one gallon, and there's a new Green exterior paint. In a move backward, all Coupes will revert to rear drum brakes, replacing the once-available rear discs on SC2 with ABS.

RATINGS (SCALE OF 1-10)

Overall	Safety	Reliability	Performance	Comfort	Value
N/A	N/A	8.6	7.8	N/A	N/A

Category E

2 Dr SC1 Cpe	8255	10070
3 Dr SC1 Cpe	8445	10300
2 Dr SC2 Cpe	9535	11630
3 Dr SC2 Cpe	9760	11905

OPTIONS FOR SC

Auto 4-Speed Transmission +635
AM/FM Compact Disc Player +340
Air Conditioning[Std on SC2] +605

Aluminum/Alloy Wheels +245
Cruise Control +165
Keyless Entry System +115
Leather Seats +645
Power Door Locks +180
Power Mirrors +80
Power Sunroof +455
Power Windows +195
Premium Sound System +245
Traction Control System +35

SL   1999

Powertrain components in both the single- and dual-overhead cam engines (such as pistons, connecting rods, crankshaft and timing chain) have been revised to reduce noise, vibration and harshness, while returning an increase of about one mpg across the board. Three new exterior colors debut: Dark Blue on SL, Green and Blackberry on SL1 and SL2. Front seatbelts have been repositioned, and the windshield washer solvent bottle's capacity has been upped to one full gallon. Sadly, Saturn has moved to rear drum brakes on all models, replacing the rear discs that had been available on SL2s with ABS.

RATINGS (SCALE OF 1-10)

Overall	Safety	Reliability	Performance	Comfort	Value
N/A	7.4	8.7	7.8	7	N/A

Category E

4 Dr SL1 Sdn	7762	9465
4 Dr SL2 Sdn	8693	10600
4 Dr STD Sdn	7545	9200

OPTIONS FOR SL

Auto 4-Speed Transmission +635
AM/FM Compact Disc Player +340
Air Conditioning[Std on SL2] +605
Aluminum/Alloy Wheels +245
Anti-Lock Brakes +500
Cruise Control +165
Keyless Entry System +115
Leather Seats +645
Power Door Locks +180
Power Mirrors +80
Power Sunroof +455
Power Windows +195
Premium Sound System +245
Traction Control System +35

SW   1999

As with the rest of the 1999 Saturn line, SW models are sure to benefit from revised powertrain components in both the single- and dual-overhead cam engines. The pistons, connecting rods, crankshaft and timing chain in these motors have been redesigned to reduce noise, vibration and harshness, while returning an increase of about one mpg across the board. Wagons have a

Don't forget to refer to the Mileage Adjustment Table at the back of this book!

SATURN 99-98

Model Description	Trade-in Value	Market Value	Model Description	Trade-in Value	Market Value

new Green exterior color. The only other changes are repositioned front seatbelts for easier access and increased windshield washer solvent bottle capacity, which is now one full gallon.

RATINGS (SCALE OF 1-10)

Overall	Safety	Reliability	Performance	Comfort	Value
N/A	7.4	8.7	7.8	N/A	N/A

Category E

4 Dr STD Wgn	9405	11470
4 Dr STD Wgn	9515	11605

OPTIONS FOR SW

Auto 4-Speed Transmission +635
AM/FM Compact Disc Player +340
Air Conditioning[Std on SW2] +605
Aluminum/Alloy Wheels +245
Anti-Lock Brakes +500
Cruise Control +165
Keyless Entry System +115
Leather Seats +645
Power Door Locks +180
Power Mirrors +80
Power Windows +195
Premium Sound System +245
Traction Control System +35

1998 SATURN

SC   1998

Refinement is the name of the game for 1998. Improvements to the suspension, transmission and engine blocks are designed to smooth the ride, reduce noise, increase durability and provide slick shifts. Second-generation airbags deploy with less force than the old ones. A child seatbelt comfort guide has been added in the back seat, and SC1 models have a new wheel design. Dark Blue is the single new color.

RATINGS (SCALE OF 1-10)

Overall	Safety	Reliability	Performance	Comfort	Value
N/A	N/A	8.6	7.8	7	7.8

Category E

2 Dr SC1 Cpe	7285	8995
2 Dr SC2 Cpe	8565	10575

OPTIONS FOR SC

Auto 4-Speed Transmission +530
AM/FM Compact Disc Player +275
Air Conditioning[Opt on SC1] +495
Aluminum/Alloy Wheels +200
Anti-Lock Brakes +410
Cruise Control +135
Keyless Entry System +95
Leather Seats +530
Power Door Locks +145
Power Mirrors +65

Power Sunroof +375
Power Windows +160
Premium Sound System +200
Traction Control System +30

SL   1998

Minor trim modifications, reduced force airbags, and hardware improvements to stifle unwanted noise, vibration and harshness are on tap for 1998.

RATINGS (SCALE OF 1-10)

Overall	Safety	Reliability	Performance	Comfort	Value
7.9	7.4	8.7	8.2	7.4	8

Category E

4 Dr SL1 Sdn	6980	8615
4 Dr SL2 Sdn	7790	9615
4 Dr STD Sdn	6775	8365

OPTIONS FOR SL

Auto 4-Speed Transmission +530
AM/FM Compact Disc Player +275
Air Conditioning[Std on SL2] +495
Aluminum/Alloy Wheels +200
Anti-Lock Brakes +410
Cruise Control +135
Keyless Entry System +95
Leather Seats +530
Power Door Locks +145
Power Mirrors +65
Power Sunroof +375
Power Windows +160
Premium Sound System +200
Traction Control System +30

SW   1998

1998 brings fresh colors, revised fabrics, redesigned wheels, reduced force airbags and more attempts at reducing noise and vibration levels.

RATINGS (SCALE OF 1-10)

Overall	Safety	Reliability	Performance	Comfort	Value
7.9	7.4	8.7	7.8	7.5	8.1

Category E

4 Dr SW1 Wgn	8590	10605
4 Dr SW2 Wgn	8730	10775

OPTIONS FOR SW

Auto 4-Speed Transmission +530
AM/FM Compact Disc Player +275
Air Conditioning[Opt on SW1] +495
Aluminum/Alloy Wheels +200
Anti-Lock Brakes +410
Cruise Control +135
Keyless Entry System +95
Leather Seats +530
Power Door Locks +145
Power Mirrors +65
Power Windows +160

Don't forget to refer to the Mileage Adjustment Table at the back of this book!

SATURN 98-96

Model Description	Trade-in Value	Market Value	Model Description	Trade-in Value	Market Value

Premium Sound System +200
Traction Control System +30

1997 SATURN

SC   1997

Saturn restyles its sport coupe, moving it to the SL/SW platform in the process. The result is a larger, roomier and heavier car. Dashboard is carried over, but interior trim is new. Newly optional is an in-dash CD player. More steps are taken to reduce noise, vibration and harshness.

RATINGS (SCALE OF 1-10)

Overall	Safety	Reliability	Performance	Comfort	Value
N/A	N/A	7.4	7.8	7	8.9

Category E

2 Dr SC1 Cpe	6235	7895
2 Dr SC2 Cpe	7215	9135

OPTIONS FOR SC

Auto 4-Speed Transmission +395
AM/FM Compact Disc Player +225
Air Conditioning +405
Aluminum/Alloy Wheels +165
Anti-Lock Brakes +335
Cruise Control +110
Leather Seats +430
Power Door Locks +120
Power Sunroof +305
Power Windows +130
Premium Sound System +160
Rear Spoiler[Opt on SC1] +105

SL   1997

Once again, Saturn attempts to quell noise, vibration, and harshness (NVH) with improved engine mounts, revised torque struts, thicker dash mat, and non-asbestos organic front brake pads. Other changes are limited to new colors, an optional in-dash CD player, a panic mode for the security system, and a low-fuel indicator.

RATINGS (SCALE OF 1-10)

Overall	Safety	Reliability	Performance	Comfort	Value
7.9	7.2	7.5	8.2	7.4	9

Category E

4 Dr SL1 Sdn	6310	7990
4 Dr SL2 Sdn	6906	8745
4 Dr STD Sdn	6050	7660

OPTIONS FOR SL

Auto 4-Speed Transmission +415
AM/FM Compact Disc Player +225
Air Conditioning +405
Aluminum/Alloy Wheels +165
Anti-Lock Brakes +335

Cruise Control +110
Keyless Entry System +80
Leather Seats +430
Power Door Locks +120
Power Sunroof +305
Power Windows +130
Premium Sound System +160
Traction Control System +25

SW   1997

Once again, Saturn attempts to quell noise, vibration, and harshness (NVH) with improved engine mounts, revised torque struts, thicker dash mat, and non-asbestos organic front brake pads. Other changes are limited to a new color, an optional in-dash CD player, a panic mode for the security system, and a low-fuel indicator.

RATINGS (SCALE OF 1-10)

Overall	Safety	Reliability	Performance	Comfort	Value
7.8	7.2	7.5	7.8	7.5	9.1

Category E

4 Dr SW1 Wgn	7050	8925
4 Dr SW2 Wgn	7235	9160

OPTIONS FOR SW

Auto 4-Speed Transmission +415
AM/FM Compact Disc Player +225
Air Conditioning +405
Aluminum/Alloy Wheels +165
Anti-Lock Brakes +335
Cruise Control +110
Keyless Entry System +80
Leather Seats +430
Power Door Locks +120
Power Windows +130
Premium Sound System +160

1996 SATURN

SC   1996

Coupe carries over in anticipation of all-new styling to arrive for 1997. Traction control can now be ordered with the manual transmission and antilock brake system.

RATINGS (SCALE OF 1-10)

Overall	Safety	Reliability	Performance	Comfort	Value
7.5	6.5	7.8	8.5	7.1	7.5

Category E

2 Dr SC1 Cpe	5315	6995
2 Dr SC2 Cpe	5970	7855

OPTIONS FOR SC

Auto 4-Speed Transmission +320
AM/FM Stereo Tape +125
Air Conditioning +330

Don't forget to refer to the Mileage Adjustment Table at the back of this book!

SATURN 96-95

Model Description	Trade-in Value	Market Value	Model Description	Trade-in Value	Market Value

Aluminum/Alloy Wheels +135
Anti-Lock Brakes +275
Compact Disc Changer +205
Cruise Control +90
Keyless Entry System +65
Leather Seats +355
Power Door Locks +100
Power Sunroof +250
Power Windows +105
Premium Sound System +135

SL   1996

New bodywork and interior improvements make the SL an excellent value in the compact sedan class. SL's meet 1997 side-impact standards for the first time. A five-speed and traction control are no longer mutually exclusive items. The back seat is actually livable this year. Daytime running lights are standard, and rain water won't leak all over your stuff anymore when you open the trunk.

RATINGS (SCALE OF 1-10)

Overall	Safety	Reliability	Performance	Comfort	Value
7.7	7.3	7.9	8.2	7.4	7.7

Category E
4 Dr SL1 Sdn	5360	7055
4 Dr SL2 Sdn	5700	7500
4 Dr STD Sdn	5200	6845

OPTIONS FOR SL

Auto 4-Speed Transmission +320
AM/FM Compact Disc Player +185
Air Conditioning +330
Aluminum/Alloy Wheels +135
Anti-Lock Brakes +275
Cruise Control +90
Keyless Entry System +65
Leather Seats +355
Power Door Locks +100
Power Sunroof +250
Power Windows +105
Premium Sound System +135

SW   1996

Sporty wagon gets more conventional, but more attractive, plastic panels for 1996. Wagon meets 1997 side-impact standards this year, and five-speed models can be equipped with traction control. The rear seat is more comfortable, and head room is improved. Daytime running lights debut. Avoid new purple color, unless you want the kids calling your car the Barneymobile in front of friends and relatives.

RATINGS (SCALE OF 1-10)

Overall	Safety	Reliability	Performance	Comfort	Value
7.7	7.3	7.9	7.8	7.5	7.8

Category E
4 Dr SW1 Wgn	6065	7980
4 Dr SW2 Wgn	6280	8265

OPTIONS FOR SW

Auto 4-Speed Transmission +320
AM/FM Stereo Tape +125
Air Conditioning +330
Aluminum/Alloy Wheels +135
Anti-Lock Brakes +275
Cruise Control +90
Keyless Entry System +65
Leather Seats +355
Power Door Locks +100
Power Windows +105
Premium Sound System +135

1995 SATURN

SC   1995

Dashboard is redesigned and now contains two airbags. Base engine is rated at 100 horsepower, up 15 from last year. With the automatic transmission, traction control is included with optional ABS. Styling is cleaned up front and rear. Manual three-point front seatbelts replace automatic type. SC1 gets new bucket seats.

RATINGS (SCALE OF 1-10)

Overall	Safety	Reliability	Performance	Comfort	Value
7.4	7.1	7.1	8.5	7.1	7.4

Category E
2 Dr SC1 Cpe	4400	6030
2 Dr SC2 Cpe	4830	6615

OPTIONS FOR SC

Auto 4-Speed Transmission +270
AM/FM Stereo Tape +100
Air Conditioning +270
Aluminum/Alloy Wheels +110
Anti-Lock Brakes +225
Cruise Control +75
Keyless Entry System +50
Leather Seats +290
Power Door Locks +80
Power Sunroof +205
Power Windows +85
Premium Sound System +110

SL   1995

Dashboard is redesigned and now contains two airbags. Base engine is rated at 100 horsepower, up 15 from last year. With the automatic transmission, traction control is included with optional ABS. Styling is cleaned up front and rear. Manual three-point front seatbelts replace automatic type.

Don't forget to refer to the Mileage Adjustment Table at the back of this book!

Model Description	Trade-in Value	Market Value

RATINGS (SCALE OF 1-10)

Overall	Safety	Reliability	Performance	Comfort	Value
7.5	7.1	7.3	8.2	7.5	7.6

Category E

4 Dr SL1 Sdn	4115	5635
4 Dr SL2 Sdn	4440	6080
4 Dr STD Sdn	3925	5380

OPTIONS FOR SL

Auto 4-Speed Transmission +270
AM/FM Stereo Tape +100
Air Conditioning +270
Aluminum/Alloy Wheels +110
Anti-Lock Brakes +225
Compact Disc Changer +170
Cruise Control +75
Leather Seats +290
Power Door Locks +80
Power Mirrors +35
Power Sunroof +205
Power Windows +85
Premium Sound System +110

SW   1995

Dashboard is redesigned and now contains two airbags. Base engine is rated at 100 horsepower, up 15 from last year. With the automatic transmission, traction control is included with optional ABS. Styling is cleaned up front and rear. Manual three-point front seatbelts replace automatic type.

RATINGS (SCALE OF 1-10)

Overall	Safety	Reliability	Performance	Comfort	Value
7.5	7.1	7.3	7.8	7.5	7.8

Category E

4 Dr SW1 Wgn	4710	6455
4 Dr SW2 Wgn	4890	6700

OPTIONS FOR SW

Auto 4-Speed Transmission +270
AM/FM Stereo Tape +100
Air Conditioning +270
Aluminum/Alloy Wheels +110
Anti-Lock Brakes +225
Cruise Control +75
Leather Seats +290
Power Door Locks +80
Power Windows +85
Premium Sound System +110

1994 SATURN

SC   1994

CFC-free refrigerant is added to air conditioning system. Automatic transmission's "Performance" mode is recalibrated to give smoother shifts. New central

---

Model Description	Trade-in Value	Market Value

unlocking feature on power door locks allows all doors to be unlocked with a twist of the key. New alloy wheels are optional on SC1.

RATINGS (SCALE OF 1-10)

Overall	Safety	Reliability	Performance	Comfort	Value
7.1	5.5	7.5	8.3	7.3	6.9

Category E

2 Dr SC1 Cpe	3520	5025
2 Dr SC2 Cpe	3845	5495

OPTIONS FOR SC

Auto 4-Speed Transmission +220
AM/FM Compact Disc Player +125
Air Conditioning +220
Aluminum/Alloy Wheels +90
Anti-Lock Brakes +180
Cruise Control +60
Leather Seats +235
Power Door Locks +65
Power Sunroof +165
Power Windows +70
Premium Sound System +90

SL   1994

CFC-free refrigerant is added to air conditioning system. Automatic transmission's "Performance" mode is recalibrated to give smoother shifts. New central unlocking feature on power door locks allows all doors to be unlocked with a twist of the key. New alloy wheels are optional on SL2.

RATINGS (SCALE OF 1-10)

Overall	Safety	Reliability	Performance	Comfort	Value
7.3	5.5	8.1	8	7.6	7.1

Category E

4 Dr SL1 Sdn	3275	4680
4 Dr SL2 Sdn	3520	5025
4 Dr STD Sdn	3070	4385

OPTIONS FOR SL

Auto 4-Speed Transmission +220
AM/FM Compact Disc Player +125
Air Conditioning +220
Aluminum/Alloy Wheels +90
Anti-Lock Brakes +180
Cruise Control +60
Leather Seats +235
Power Door Locks +65
Power Sunroof +165
Power Windows +70
Premium Sound System +90

SW   1994

CFC-free refrigerant is added to air conditioning system. Automatic transmission's "Performance" mode is recalibrated to give smoother shifts. New central

---

Don't forget to refer to the Mileage Adjustment Table at the back of this book!

unlocking feature on power door locks allows all doors to be unlocked with a twist of the key. New alloy wheels are optional on SW2.

RATINGS (SCALE OF 1-10)

Overall	Safety	Reliability	Performance	Comfort	Value
7.2	5.5	8.1	7.4	7.6	7.2

Category E

4 Dr SW1 Wgn	3740	5340
4 Dr SW2 Wgn	3895	5565

OPTIONS FOR SW

Auto 4-Speed Transmission +220
AM/FM Compact Disc Player +125
AM/FM Stereo Tape +80
Air Conditioning +220
Aluminum/Alloy Wheels +90
Anti-Lock Brakes +180
Cruise Control +60
Leather Seats +235
Power Door Locks +65
Power Windows +70
Premium Sound System +90

1993 SATURN

SC   1993

Driver airbag added. Cars with ABS and automatic transmission can be ordered with traction control. SC coupe equipped with same 85-horsepower 1.9-liter engine as in SL.

RATINGS (SCALE OF 1-10)

• Overall	Safety	Reliability	Performance	Comfort	Value
7	5.3	7.1	8.3	7.3	6.8

Category E

2 Dr SC1 Cpe	2940	4385
2 Dr SC2 Cpe	3150	4705

OPTIONS FOR SC

Auto 4-Speed Transmission +170
AM/FM Compact Disc Player +100
AM/FM Stereo Tape +65
Air Conditioning +180
Aluminum/Alloy Wheels[Opt on SC1] +75
Anti-Lock Brakes +150
Cruise Control +50
Leather Seats +195
Power Door Locks +55
Power Sunroof +135
Power Windows +60
Premium Sound System +70

SL   1993

Driver airbag added. SL2 gets new front fascia and optional fog lights. Cars with ABS and automatic transmission can be ordered with traction control. SL2 suspension provides softer ride.

RATINGS (SCALE OF 1-10)

Overall	Safety	Reliability	Performance	Comfort	Value
7.1	5.3	7.5	8	7.6	7.1

Category E

4 Dr SL1 Sdn	2560	3820
4 Dr SL2 Sdn	2855	4260
4 Dr STD Sdn	2410	3600

OPTIONS FOR SL

Auto 4-Speed Transmission +170
AM/FM Compact Disc Player +100
Air Conditioning +180
Aluminum/Alloy Wheels[Opt on SL1] +75
Anti-Lock Brakes +150
Cruise Control +50
Leather Seats +195
Power Door Locks +55
Power Moonroof +125
Power Sunroof +135
Power Windows +60
Premium Sound System +70

SW   1993

Driver airbag added, and is standard on SW. Cars with ABS and automatic transmission can be ordered with traction control. New station wagon model comes in SW1 and SW2 trim, and rear wiper/washer and defogger are standard. SW1 equipped with same 85-horsepower 1.9-liter engine as in SL. SW2 gets twin-cam 124-horsepower engine and SL2's sport suspension.

RATINGS (SCALE OF 1-10)

Overall	Safety	Reliability	Performance	Comfort	Value
7	5.3	7.5	7.4	7.6	7.2

Category E

4 Dr SW1 Wgn	2995	4470
4 Dr SW2 Wgn	3225	4810

OPTIONS FOR SW

Auto 4-Speed Transmission +170
AM/FM Compact Disc Player +100
Air Conditioning +180
Aluminum/Alloy Wheels +75
Anti-Lock Brakes +150
Cruise Control +50
Power Door Locks +55
Power Windows +60
Premium Sound System +70

Don't forget to refer to the Mileage Adjustment Table at the back of this book!

Model Description	Trade-in Value	Market Value	Model Description	Trade-in Value	Market Value

1992 SATURN

SC 1992

New engine and transmission mounting system supposedly cuts down on noise and vibration. Passenger compartment gets added acoustic insulation. Alloy wheels are redesigned.

RATINGS (SCALE OF 1-10)

Overall	Safety	Reliability	Performance	Comfort	Value
6.6	4.4	7.3	8.6	7.3	5.3

Category E

	Trade-in	Market
2 Dr SC2 Cpe	2485	3880

OPTIONS FOR SC

Auto 4-Speed Transmission +160
AM/FM Compact Disc Player +80
Air Bag Restraint +105
Air Conditioning +145
Anti-Lock Brakes +120
Leather Seats +155
Power Door Locks +45
Power Sunroof +110
Power Windows +50

SL 1992

New engine and transmission mounting system supposedly cuts down on noise and vibration. Passenger compartment gets added acoustic insulation. Leather and a rear deck spoiler are new for SL2 models. Alloy wheels are redesigned.

RATINGS (SCALE OF 1-10)

Overall	Safety	Reliability	Performance	Comfort	Value
6.5	4.4	7.2	8	7.6	5.5

Category E

	Trade-in	Market
4 Dr SL1 Sdn	2100	3285
4 Dr SL2 Sdn	2315	3615
4 Dr STD Sdn	1875	2930

OPTIONS FOR SL

Auto 4-Speed Transmission +130
Air Bag Restraint +105
Air Conditioning +145
Anti-Lock Brakes +120
Leather Seats +155
Power Door Locks +45
Power Sunroof +110
Power Windows +50

1991 SATURN

SC 1991

Saturn coupe comes with a dual overhead cam engine, sport-tuned suspension, alloy wheels, and speed rated tires. All body panels except hood, roof and trunk lid are made of plastic composite materials on all models, and ABS is optional.

RATINGS (SCALE OF 1-10)

Overall	Safety	Reliability	Performance	Comfort	Value
6.4	3.5	7.6	8.6	7.3	5.2

Category E

	Trade-in	Market
2 Dr SC2 Cpe	2055	3480

OPTIONS FOR SC

Auto 4-Speed Transmission +100
AM/FM Compact Disc Player +65
Air Conditioning +120
Anti-Lock Brakes +100
Power Door Locks +35
Power Sunroof +90
Power Windows +40

SL 1991

Featuring an underpowered 1.9-liter engine and uninspired ergonomics, first Saturn sedan isn't all it's cracked up to be. The SL is very basic, with manual steering and transmission. Variable-effort steering, adjustable steering column, tachometer, and remote fuel door and trunk lid releases are standard on SL1. SL2 adds more powerful engine, sport-tuned suspension, alloy wheels, body-color bumpers, and speed-rated tires. All body panels except hood, roof and trunk lid are made of plastic composite materials on all models, and ABS is optional.

RATINGS (SCALE OF 1-10)

Overall	Safety	Reliability	Performance	Comfort	Value
6.4	3.5	7.5	8	7.6	5.4

Category E

	Trade-in	Market
4 Dr SL1 Sdn	1665	2825
4 Dr SL2 Sdn	1800	3055
4 Dr STD Sdn	1435	2430

OPTIONS FOR SL

Auto 4-Speed Transmission +100
AM/FM Compact Disc Player +65
Air Conditioning +120
Anti-Lock Brakes +100
Power Door Locks +35
Power Sunroof +90
Power Windows +40

Don't forget to refer to the Mileage Adjustment Table at the back of this book!

SUBARU   **Japan**

1997 Subaru Legacy

1999 SUBARU

FORESTER   1999

This year, Forester's engine makes more torque and the automatic transmission has been improved. L and S models have longer lists of standard equipment and two new colors are available.

RATINGS (SCALE OF 1-10)

Overall	Safety	Reliability	Performance	Comfort	Value
N/A	N/A	N/A	7	7.5	N/A

Category G

4 Dr L 4WD Wgn	14345	17080
4 Dr S 4WD Wgn	16230	19320
4 Dr STD 4WD Wgn	13295	15830

OPTIONS FOR FORESTER
Auto 4-Speed Transmission +590
AM/FM Compact Disc Player +245
Aluminum/Alloy Wheels[Std on S] +245
Cruise Control[Std on S] +155
Keyless Entry System +150
Leather Seats +575

IMPREZA   1999

More horsepower, more torque and a more efficient automatic transmission is the big news this year. Multi-reflector halogen headlights are new and Outback Sport gets a revised grille. The 2.5 RS gets silver alloy wheels, a new front bumper, white gauge faces and more torque, as well as an upgraded leather-wrapped steering wheel and shift knob. Two new colors are available for 1999.

RATINGS (SCALE OF 1-10)

Overall	Safety	Reliability	Performance	Comfort	Value
N/A	6.8	9.1	7.8	7.4	N/A

Category E

2 Dr L 4WD Cpe	10855	13080
4 Dr L 4WD Sdn	11010	13265
4 Dr L 4WD Wgn	11160	13445
4 Dr Outback Sport 4WD Wgn	12295	14815
2 Dr RS 4WD Cpe	13560	16335

OPTIONS FOR IMPREZA
Auto 4-Speed Transmission +580
AM/FM Compact Disc Player +340
Aluminum/Alloy Wheels[Std on RS] +245
Cruise Control +165
Keyless Entry System +115

LEGACY   1999

Subaru celebrates 30 years of selling cars in the United States by adding special editions to the Legacy lineup. The L sedan and wagon are available with a package of goodies that includes power moonroof, alloy wheels, rear spoiler or roof rack, body-color trim, power antenna, and seat height adjuster. New colors include Sandstone Metallic and Winestone Pearl. The 2.5GT Limited is newly available with a manual transmission, while all 2.5GT, Limited and Outback models receive standard remote keyless entry.

RATINGS (SCALE OF 1-10)

Overall	Safety	Reliability	Performance	Comfort	Value
N/A	7.4	8.3	7.6	7.5	N/A

Category D

4 Dr 30TH Anniversary 4WD Sdn	12745	15175
4 Dr Brighton 4WD Wgn	11065	13175
4 Dr GT 4WD Sdn	14580	17355
4 Dr GT 4WD Wgn	14950	17795
4 Dr GT Ltd. 30th Ann 4WD Sdn	15060	17930
4 Dr L 4WD Sdn	11665	13885
4 Dr L 4WD Wgn	12350	14700
4 Dr Limited 30TH ANN 4WD Sdn	14135	16825
4 Dr Outback 4WD Wgn	15065	17935
4 Dr Outback Ltd 30th 4WD Wgn	15490	18440

OPTIONS FOR LEGACY
Auto 4-Speed Transmission +590
30th Ann. Edition L Pkg +740
AM/FM Compact Disc Player[Std on GT Lim 30th An,
Outback Lim 30th An, SUS Lim 30th An] +390
Aluminum/Alloy Wheels[Opt on Brighton,L] +345
Dual Sunroof +885
Fog Lights[Opt on Brighton, L] +175
Heated Front Seats[Opt on Outback] +300
Keyless Entry System[Opt on Brighton, L] +235
Leather Seats[Opt on 30TH Anniversary,GT,Outback] +820

Don't forget to refer to the Mileage Adjustment Table at the back of this book!

SUBARU 98-97

Model Description	Trade-in Value	Market Value	Model Description	Trade-in Value	Market Value

1998 SUBARU

FORESTER 1998

Subaru attacks the mini-SUV market head-on with the Forester, which actually constitutes an SUV body on an Impreza platform with a Legacy engine under the hood. The most car-like of the mini-utes, Forester is also the most powerful. Airbags remain the full power variety, despite new rules allowing lower deployment speeds.

RATINGS (SCALE OF 1-10)

Overall	Safety	Reliability	Performance	Comfort	Value
N/A	N/A	8.5	7	7.5	N/A

Category G

4 Dr 4WD Wgn	12825	15270
4 Dr S 4WD Wgn	14435	17185
4 Dr STD 4WD Wgn	11930	14205

OPTIONS FOR FORESTER

Auto 4-Speed Transmission +485
AM/FM Compact Disc Player +200
Aluminum/Alloy Wheels[Std on S] +200
Cruise Control[Std on S] +125
Heated Front Seats +160
Heated Power Mirrors +45
Keyless Entry System +120
Leather Seats +470

IMPREZA 1998

Impreza gets a new dashboard and revised door panels. The entry-level Brighton coupe is dropped, and the high-end 2.5RS coupe is added. No depowered airbags here.

RATINGS (SCALE OF 1-10)

Overall	Safety	Reliability	Performance	Comfort	Value
7.6	6.8	9	7.8	7.4	6.9

Category E

2 Dr L 4WD Cpe	9460	11400
4 Dr L 4WD Sdn	9655	11630
4 Dr L 4WD Wgn	9820	11830
4 Dr Outback Sport 4WD Wgn	10985	13235
2 Dr RS 4WD Cpe	12125	14610

OPTIONS FOR IMPREZA

Auto 4-Speed Transmission +490
AM/FM Compact Disc Player +275
Aluminum/Alloy Wheels[Std on RS] +200
Cruise Control +135
Fog Lights[Std on RS] +90
Keyless Entry System +95

LEGACY 1998

Prices remain stable while equipment is shuffled and the LSi model is dropped. All Legacy sedans and wagons except the Outback sport the grille and multi-reflector halogen lights found on the 2.5GT. A new Limited model joins the 2.5GT lineup, and a dual power moonroof package is available for the Outback Limited wagon. Outbacks get new alloy wheels, an overhead console and longer splash guards, while mid-year Outback Limiteds with revised trim and added content were dubbed 30th Anniversary models. The cold weather package has heated windshield wiper nozzles this year instead of an engine block heater. The Brighton wagon's stereo loses half its wattage, Limited models have a standard CD player and the base Outback comes with a Weatherband radio. Full power airbags continue, despite new government rules allowing automakers to install reduced force bags to better protect small adults.

RATINGS (SCALE OF 1-10)

Overall	Safety	Reliability	Performance	Comfort	Value
7.5	7.3	7.8	7.6	7.5	7.2

Category D

4 Dr Brighton 4WD Wgn	9530	11345
4 Dr GT 4WD Sdn	13425	15985
4 Dr GT 4WD Wgn	13820	16450
4 Dr GT Limited 4WD Sdn	14255	16970
4 Dr L 4WD Sdn	11215	13350
4 Dr L 4WD Wgn	11485	13675
4 Dr Outback 4WD Wgn	13940	16595
4 Dr Outback Limited 4WD Wgn	14345	17075

OPTIONS FOR LEGACY

Auto 4-Speed Transmission[Std on GT Limited] +490
AM/FM Compact Disc Player[Std on Limited] +320
Aluminum/Alloy Wheels[Opt on Brighton, L] +280
Cruise Control[Opt on Brighton] +145
Dual Sunroof[Opt on Outback Limited] +725
Fog Lights[Opt on Brighton, L] +145
Heated Front Seats[Opt on Outback] +245
Heated Power Mirrors[Opt on Outback] +50
Keyless Entry System +190
Leather Seats[Opt on GT, Outback] +670

1997 SUBARU

IMPREZA 1997

Imprezas receive a facelifted front end that includes a Hemi-sized hood scoop. A new Outback Sport Wagon debuts, with nearly six-inches of additional ground clearance, fog lights, and a slightly raised roof. LX model disappears, which means only the Outback is equipped with ABS. Power and torque for both Impreza engines is up for 1997, and some new colors are available. HVAC controls are revised.

Model Description	Trade-in Value	Market Value

RATINGS (SCALE OF 1-10)

Overall	Safety	Reliability	Performance	Comfort	Value
7.4	6.8	9.1	7.8	7.4	5.9

Category E

Model	Trade-in	Market
2 Dr Brighton 4WD Cpe	7775	9480
2 Dr L 4WD Cpe	8410	10255
4 Dr L 4WD Sdn	8695	10605
4 Dr L 4WD Wgn	9070	11060
4 Dr Outback Sport 4WD Wgn	10080	12295

OPTIONS FOR IMPREZA

4 cyl 2.2 L Engine[Opt on Brighton] +100
Auto 4-Speed Transmission +400
AM/FM Compact Disc Player +225
Aluminum/Alloy Wheels +165
Compact Disc Changer +250
Cruise Control +110
Fog Lights[Std on L 4WD Cpe] +75
Keyless Entry System +80
Luggage Rack[Opt on L] +65
Rear Spoiler[Opt on Brighton,Sdn] +105

LEGACY   1997

Front-wheel drive models are given the ax as Subaru returns to its all-wheel drive roots. Power and torque are up marginally with the base 2.2-liter engine. The 2.5-liter motor (also stronger this year and now available with a manual transmission) is now the only engine mated to the Outback . L models gain cruise control, anti-lock brakes, and power door locks as standard equipment. GT's get a manual transmission, larger tires, and revised styling. The Outback lineup is expanded with the introduction of a Limited model, which includes a leather interior, new alloy wheels, fresh exterior colors, and woodgrain interior trim.

RATINGS (SCALE OF 1-10)

Overall	Safety	Reliability	Performance	Comfort	Value
7.3	7.2	7.2	7.6	7.5	7.1

Category D

Model	Trade-in	Market
4 Dr Brighton 4WD Wgn	8605	10370
4 Dr GT 4WD Sdn	11540	13905
4 Dr GT 4WD Wgn	11850	14280
4 Dr L 4WD Sdn	8780	10580
4 Dr L 4WD Wgn	10275	12380
4 Dr LSi 4WD Sdn	11805	14225
4 Dr LSi 4WD Wgn	12680	15275
4 Dr Outback 4WD Sdn	12990	15650
4 Dr Outback 4WD Wgn	11910	14350
4 Dr Outback Limited 4WD Wgn	12755	15365

OPTIONS FOR LEGACY

Auto 4-Speed Transmission[Std on LSi] +400
AM/FM Compact Disc Player +260
Alarm System[Std on LSi] +260

Aluminum/Alloy Wheels[Opt on Brighton,L] +230
Compact Disc Changer[Std on LSi] +335
Compact Disc W/fm/tape +400
Cruise Control[Opt on Brighton] +120
Heated Front Seats[Opt on Outback] +200
Keyless Entry System +155
Leather Seats[Opt on GT,Outback] +545
Luggage Rack[Opt on Brighton,L,LSi] +135

1996 SUBARU

IMPREZA   1996

The formerly optional 2.2-liter engine is standard across the board, except in the new budget-minded Brighton AWD Coupe. A new grille accompanies the bigger engine, and a five-speed is available as well.

RATINGS (SCALE OF 1-10)

Overall	Safety	Reliability	Performance	Comfort	Value
7.3	6.6	9	7.8	7.4	5.9

Category E

Model	Trade-in	Market
2 Dr Brighton 4WD Cpe	6150	7685
2 Dr L 4WD Cpe	6815	8520
4 Dr L 4WD Sdn	7155	8945
4 Dr L 4WD Wgn	7442	9300
2 Dr LX 4WD Cpe	8145	10180
4 Dr LX 4WD Sdn	8270	10335
4 Dr LX 4WD Wgn	8450	10565
4 Dr Outback 4WD Wgn	8985	11230

OPTIONS FOR IMPREZA

Auto 4-Speed Transmission[Opt on L,Outback,Cpe] +325
AM/FM Compact Disc Player +185
Aluminum/Alloy Wheels[Std on LX 4WD Cpe] +135
Anti-Lock Brakes[Opt on L] +275
Compact Disc Changer +205
Cruise Control +90
Luggage Rack[Opt on L,LX] +50

LEGACY   1996

A new sport model debuts, with a larger, more powerful engine. The 2.5GT is available in sedan or wagon format. The luxury-oriented LSi model also gets the new motor. A knobby-tired, raised-roof Outback wagon appears, offering 7.3 inches of ground clearance and an optional 2.5-liter engine. Designed specifically for American consumers, the Outback provides a car-like ride with light-duty off-road ability.

RATINGS (SCALE OF 1-10)

Overall	Safety	Reliability	Performance	Comfort	Value
7.7	7.4	7.9	7.4	7.5	8.3

Category D

Model	Trade-in	Market
4 Dr Brighton 4WD Wgn	6970	8605
4 Dr GT 4WD Sdn	10515	12980

Don't forget to refer to the Mileage Adjustment Table at the back of this book!

Model Description	Trade-in Value	Market Value
4 Dr GT 4WD Wgn	10775	13305
4 Dr L 4WD Sdn	7730	9545
4 Dr L 4WD Wgn	8635	10660
4 Dr LS 4WD Sdn	9645	11910
4 Dr LS 4WD Wgn	9830	12135
4 Dr LSi 4WD Sdn	10795	13330
4 Dr LSi 4WD Wgn	10965	13540
4 Dr Outback 4WD Wgn	10645	13145

OPTIONS FOR LEGACY

4 cyl 2.5 L DOHC Engine[Std on GT,LSi] +75
Auto 4-Speed Transmission[Std on GT,LS,LSi] +305
Aluminum/Alloy Wheels[Opt on L] +190
Anti-Lock Brakes[Opt on L] +365
Compact Disc W/fm/tape +325
Cruise Control[Opt on Brighton,L] +100
Heated Front Seats +165
Keyless Entry System +125
Luggage Rack[Opt on Brighton] +110

SVX   1996

Umm ... the L model gets standard solar-reduction glass this year. Whoopee.

Category F

	Trade-in	Market
2 Dr L 4WD Cpe	10880	13435
2 Dr LSi 4WD Cpe	13205	16300

OPTIONS FOR SVX

AM/FM Compact Disc Player +195

1995 SUBARU

IMPREZA   1995

An Impreza coupe and an Outback Wagon are added to Subaru's subcompact line of cars in an attempt to broaden their appeal with sporting and outdoor enthusiasts. Top-of-the-line LX model is introduced, replacing the LS trim-level, with an available 2.2-liter engine taken from the Legacy. Unfortunately it is available only with an automatic transmission.

RATINGS (SCALE OF 1-10)

Overall	Safety	Reliability	Performance	Comfort	Value
7.4	7.3	7.9	7.8	7.4	6.8

Category E

	Trade-in	Market
2 Dr L 4WD Cpe	5190	6740
4 Dr L 4WD Sdn	5280	6855
4 Dr L 4WD Wgn	5470	7105
4 Dr L Special Edit. 4WD Sdn	5890	7650
4 Dr L Special Edit. 4WD Wgn	6385	8295
2 Dr LX 4WD Cpe	6285	8160
4 Dr LX 4WD Sdn	6455	8380
4 Dr LX 4WD Wgn	6710	8715

Model Description	Trade-in Value	Market Value
4 Dr Outback 4WD Wgn	7065	9175
4 Dr Outback Spec. Ed. 4WD Wgn	7140	9275

OPTIONS FOR IMPREZA

4 cyl 2.2 L Engine[Std on LX] +320
Auto 4-Speed Transmission[Std on L Spec. Edition,LX,L Special Edit. 4WD Sdn] +265
4-WD Active Safety Group +595
AM/FM Compact Disc Player +150
Air Conditioning[Opt on STD,L 4WD Cpe] +270
Aluminum/Alloy Wheels[Std on LX 4WD Sdn] +110
Anti-Lock Brakes[Opt on L] +225
Cruise Control +75
Luggage Rack[Opt on L,L Special Edit.,LX] +45

LEGACY   1995

New sheetmetal freshens the flanks of one of our favorite compact sedans and wagons. Unfortunately the turbocharged engine has been dropped, leaving the Legacy with a rather anemic 2.2-liter four-cylinder that produces a meager 135 horsepower. The "value leader" Brighton wagon is introduced for budding naturalists. It includes all-wheel drive, air conditioning and a stereo with cassette. The Outback Wagon is also introduced as an alternative to the burgeoning SUV market.

RATINGS (SCALE OF 1-10)

Overall	Safety	Reliability	Performance	Comfort	Value
7.4	7.7	7.7	7.4	7.5	6.5

Category D

	Trade-in	Market
4 Dr Brighton 4WD Wgn	6125	7755
4 Dr L Sdn	6110	7735
4 Dr L 4WD Sdn	6815	8625
4 Dr L 4WD Wgn	6875	8705
4 Dr LS 4WD Sdn	8150	10315
4 Dr LS 4WD Wgn	8420	10660
4 Dr LSi 4WD Sdn	7940	10050
4 Dr LSi 4WD Wgn	8770	11100
4 Dr Outback 4WD Wgn	8295	10500
4 Dr STD Sdn	5745	7275

OPTIONS FOR LEGACY

Auto 4-Speed Transmission[Std on LS,LSi] +265
AM/FM Compact Disc Player[Std on LSi] +175
Air Conditioning[Opt on STD] +280
Aluminum/Alloy Wheels[Opt on Brighton,L,STD] +155
Anti-Lock Brakes[Opt on L] +300
Compact Disc Changer +225
Cruise Control[Opt on Brighton,L,STD] +80
Luggage Rack[Std on LSi,Outback] +90
Power Antenna[Opt on L] +40
Power Moonroof[Opt on L] +275

Model Description	Trade-in Value	Market Value

SVX 1995

Dual airbags are extended to the base model.

Category F

	Trade-in Value	Market Value
2 Dr L Cpe	8190	10235
2 Dr L 4WD Cpe	8920	11150
2 Dr LS Cpe	9130	11415
2 Dr LSi 4WD Cpe	11065	13830

1994 SUBARU

IMPREZA 1994

A passenger airbag joins the driver's airbag on all models. LS Imprezas have standard antilock brakes, automatic transmission and sunroof.

RATINGS (SCALE OF 1-10)

Overall	Safety	Reliability	Performance	Comfort	Value
7.4	6.8	8.6	7.6	7.4	6.8

Category E

	Trade-in Value	Market Value
4 Dr L 4WD Sdn	4170	5560
4 Dr L 4WD Wgn	4310	5745
4 Dr LS 4WD Sdn	5000	6665
4 Dr LS 4WD Wgn	5170	6890

OPTIONS FOR IMPREZA

Auto 4-Speed Transmission[Std on LS] +220
AM/FM Stereo Tape[Std on LS] +80
Air Conditioning[Std on LS] +220
Anti-Lock Brakes[Std on LS] +180
Dual Air Bag Restraints[Std on LS] +140
Power Door Locks[Std on LS] +65
Power Sunroof[Std on LS] +165
Power Windows[Std on LS] +70

JUSTY 1994

Continuously variable transmission is no longer available. Base models gain a standard rear-window defroster. Last year for the Justy runabout.

Category E

	Trade-in Value	Market Value
2 Dr DL Hbk	2110	2810

OPTIONS FOR JUSTY

Air Conditioning +220

LEGACY 1994

Antilock brakes become optional on the L sedan.

RATINGS (SCALE OF 1-10)

Overall	Safety	Reliability	Performance	Comfort	Value
N/A	N/A	8.2	8.3	7.8	6.5

Category D

	Trade-in Value	Market Value
4 Dr L Sdn	3730	4780
4 Dr L 4WD Sdn	4290	5500
4 Dr L 4WD Wgn	5310	6810
4 Dr LS Sdn	5080	6515
4 Dr LS 4WD Sdn	5690	7295
4 Dr LS 4WD Wgn	5970	7655
4 Dr LSi 4WD Sdn	6155	7890
4 Dr LSi 4WD Wgn	6595	8455
4 Dr Sport Turbo 4WD Sdn	6195	7945

OPTIONS FOR LEGACY

Auto 4-Speed Transmission[Opt on L] +220
AM/FM Compact Disc Player +140
Air Conditioning[Opt on L] +230
Aluminum/Alloy Wheels[Opt on L] +125
Anti-Lock Brakes[Opt on L] +245
Cruise Control[Opt on L] +65
Graphic Equalizer[Opt on L] +50
Keyless Entry System +85
Luggage Rack +75
Power Door Locks[Opt on L] +75
Power Moonroof[Opt on L,LS 4WD Sdn] +225
Power Windows[Opt on L] +75
Premium Sound System +100

LOYALE 1994

The Loyale is available only in the wagon bodystyle and is seeing its last year as the Impreza is set to take over the duties of all-wheel drive subcompact in Subaru's lineup.

Category D

	Trade-in Value	Market Value
4 Dr STD 4WD Wgn	4135	5300

OPTIONS FOR LOYALE

Auto 3-Speed Transmission +150
AM/FM Stereo Tape +95
Cruise Control +65
Luggage Rack +75

SVX 1994

Subaru introduces two-wheel drive "value leaders" to the SVX lineup called the L and LS. These new SVXs offer the same 3.3-liter Flat-6 found in the LSi, and antilock brakes are standard on the LS . A passenger airbag becomes standard on the uplevel LS and LSi models.

Category F

	Trade-in Value	Market Value
2 Dr L Cpe	6875	8815
2 Dr LS Cpe	8060	10335
2 Dr LSi 4WD Cpe	8890	11395

OPTIONS FOR SVX

Dual Air Bag Restraints[Opt on L] +135

1993 SUBARU

IMPREZA 1993

Designed as a replacement for the aging Loyale, the Impreza is a subcompact available as a sedan or

Model Description	Trade-in Value	Market Value

wagon. A driver airbag and available antilock brakes are important safety features included on the Impreza that never found their way to the Loyale. The Impreza is powered by a 1.8-liter 118-horsepower engine. Front-wheel drive and full-time all-wheel drive models are offered.

RATINGS (SCALE OF 1-10)

Overall	Safety	Reliability	Performance	Comfort	Value
N/A	N/A	8.8	7.6	7.4	6.8

Category E

Model Description	Trade-in Value	Market Value
4 Dr L Sdn	2950	4040
4 Dr L 4WD Sdn	3280	4495
4 Dr L 4WD Wgn	3370	4615
4 Dr LS Sdn	3455	4730
4 Dr LS 4WD Sdn	3695	5065
4 Dr LS 4WD Wgn	3820	5235
4 Dr STD Sdn	2820	3865

OPTIONS FOR IMPREZA
Auto 4-Speed Transmission[Opt on L] +180
AM/FM Stereo Tape +65
Air Conditioning[Opt on STD] +180
Aluminum/Alloy Wheels +75

JUSTY 1993

The base Justy gets a larger engine that increases horsepower to GL standards.

Category E

Model Description	Trade-in Value	Market Value
2 Dr GL Hbk	1845	2530
4 Dr GL Hbk	1990	2725
2 Dr STD Hbk	1650	2260

OPTIONS FOR JUSTY
Auto 3-Speed Transmission[Opt on 4WD] +95
AM/FM Stereo Tape +65
Air Conditioning +180

LEGACY 1993

A driver airbag is now standard on all Legacys. Touring wagons and LSi wagons were introduced in 1992 as upscale versions of the Legacy. Commendably, antilock brakes are now standard on all Legacys except the L models. Several new trim-levels of the Legacy are available for 1993. Based on the L wagon, these models are geared to appeal to different groups of outdoor enthusiasts such as skiers, beach combers and campers. The standard equipment lists of these models reflects the differences in their target market, such as heated seats and a ski rack on the Alpine model.

RATINGS (SCALE OF 1-10)

Overall	Safety	Reliability	Performance	Comfort	Value
N/A	N/A	7.8	8.3	7.8	6.4

Category D

Model Description	Trade-in Value	Market Value
4 Dr L Sdn	3330	4380
4 Dr L 4WD Sdn	3865	5085
4 Dr L 4WD Wgn	4095	5385
4 Dr LS Sdn	4085	5375
4 Dr LS 4WD Sdn	4620	6080
4 Dr LS 4WD Wgn	4975	6545
4 Dr LSi 4WD Sdn	5305	6980
4 Dr LSi 4WD Wgn	5400	7105
4 Dr Sport Turbo 4WD Sdn	5345	7030
4 Dr Touring Turbo 4WD Wgn	5425	7140

OPTIONS FOR LEGACY
Auto 4-Speed Transmission[Opt on L,Sport] +180
Anti-Lock Brakes[Opt on L Wgn] +200
Compact Disc W/fm/tape[Opt on LS] +180
Cruise Control[Opt on L Wgn] +55
Luggage Rack[Std on L] +60

LOYALE 1993

New colors are the only changes to the Loyale.

Category D

Model Description	Trade-in Value	Market Value
4 Dr FWD Sdn	2435	3205
4 Dr FWD Wgn	2735	3600
4 Dr STD 4WD Sdn	3050	4015
4 Dr STD 4WD Wgn	3410	4485

OPTIONS FOR LOYALE
Auto 3-Speed Transmission +125
AM/FM Stereo Tape +80
Luggage Rack +60

1992 SUBARU

JUSTY 1992

The Subaru Justy is unchanged.

Category E

Model Description	Trade-in Value	Market Value
2 Dr GL Hbk	1370	1955
2 Dr STD Hbk	1305	1865

OPTIONS FOR JUSTY
Air Conditioning +145

LEGACY 1992

A driver airbag is now standard on the Legacy LS and LSi; it is optional on L model. A trunk pass-through opening in the rear seats, rear heater ducts, and cupholders integrated into the dashboard give more utility to the passengers.

RATINGS (SCALE OF 1-10)

Overall	Safety	Reliability	Performance	Comfort	Value
N/A	N/A	7.1	8.3	7.8	5.7

Don't forget to refer to the Mileage Adjustment Table at the back of this book!

Model Description	Trade-in Value	Market Value

Category D

Model Description	Trade-in Value	Market Value
4 Dr L Sdn	2725	3635
4 Dr L 4WD Sdn	3055	4070
4 Dr L 4WD Wgn	3400	4530
4 Dr LS Sdn	3120	4160
4 Dr LS 4WD Sdn	3925	5235
4 Dr LS 4WD Wgn	4095	5460
4 Dr LSi Sdn	3565	4750
4 Dr LSi 4WD Sdn	4020	5360
4 Dr Sport Turbo 4WD Sdn	4495	5990

OPTIONS FOR LEGACY
Auto 4-Speed Transmission[Opt on L,Sport] +140
Air Bag Restraint[Std on Sport,LS Sdn] +100
Air Conditioning[Opt on L] +155
Anti-Lock Brakes[Opt on L] +165
Compact Disc W/fm/tape[Opt on L] +145
Power Door Locks[Opt on L] +50
Power Windows[Opt on L] +50

LOYALE — 1992

Still no changes for the Loyale.

Category D

Model Description	Trade-in Value	Market Value
4 Dr STD Sdn	1975	2635
4 Dr STD 4WD Sdn	2665	3550
4 Dr STD Wgn	2395	3195
4 Dr STD 4WD Wgn	2880	3840

OPTIONS FOR LOYALE
Auto 3-Speed Transmission +100

SVX — 1992

Subaru replaces the odd XT6 with the equally unusual SVX. Performance numbers are quite good with the standard 3.3-liter Flat-6 engine and standard all-wheel drive. The strange two-piece side windows, designed to decrease interior turbulence when the window is opened, leave something to be desired. Antilock brakes and a driver airbag are standard.

Category F

Model Description	Trade-in Value	Market Value
2 Dr STD 4WD Cpe	5730	7640

OPTIONS FOR SVX
Compact Disc W/fm/tape +90
Leather Seats +120
Power Drivers Seat +45
Power Sunroof +120

1991 SUBARU

JUSTY — 1991

The Subaru Justy is unchanged.

Category E

Model Description	Trade-in Value	Market Value
2 Dr GL Hbk	1035	1520
2 Dr GL 4WD Hbk	1345	1975
4 Dr GL 4WD Hbk	1485	2185

OPTIONS FOR JUSTY
Auto 3-Speed Transmission +80
Air Conditioning +120

LEGACY — 1991

Turbo power is now available on the Legacy Sport sedan. The boosted engine produces 160-horsepower and 180 ft-lbs. of torque; not too shabby for a family hauler.

RATINGS (SCALE OF 1-10)

Overall	Safety	Reliability	Performance	Comfort	Value
N/A	N/A	6.5	8.3	7.8	6.2

Category D

Model Description	Trade-in Value	Market Value
4 Dr L Sdn	2230	3055
4 Dr L 4WD Sdn	2605	3570
4 Dr L Wgn	2380	3260
4 Dr L 4WD Wgn	2785	3815
4 Dr LS Sdn	2735	3745
4 Dr LS 4WD Sdn	3115	4265
4 Dr LS 4WD Wgn	3230	4425
4 Dr LSi Sdn	2880	3945
4 Dr LSi 4WD Sdn	3330	4560
4 Dr Sport Turbo 4WD Sdn	3615	4950

OPTIONS FOR LEGACY
Auto 4-Speed Transmission[Std on LSi] +115
Air Conditioning[Opt on L] +125
Anti-Lock Brakes[Opt on L,L Plus] +135
Power Windows[Std on L Plus,LS,LSi,Sport,L 4WD Wgn] +40

LOYALE — 1991

No changes to the ever-popular Loyale.

Category D

Model Description	Trade-in Value	Market Value
4 Dr STD Sdn	1725	2360
4 Dr STD 4WD Sdn	2215	3035
4 Dr STD Wgn	1985	2720
4 Dr STD 4WD Wgn	2385	3265

OPTIONS FOR LOYALE
Auto 3-Speed Transmission +80
Sunroof +65

XT — 1991

The car with the weirdest steering wheel in the world enters its final year of production with no changes.

Category F

Model Description	Trade-in Value	Market Value
2 Dr GL Cpe	1505	2035
2 Dr XT6 Cpe	1845	2495
2 Dr XT6 4WD Cpe	2285	3085

OPTIONS FOR XT
Auto 4-Speed Transmission[Opt on GL,4WD] +115
Air Conditioning[Opt on GL] +125

Don't forget to refer to the Mileage Adjustment Table at the back of this book!

Model Description	Trade-in Value	Market Value

1990 SUBARU

JUSTY 1990

Goodness, gracious, great gobs of gimmickry: the Subaru's ECVT (gearless automatic transmission) is available with the four-wheel drive Justy. We can't imagine where you would take this car for repairs, but we are certain that the one mechanic in the world who can fix it lives in a very expensive house. Fuel-injection technology trickles down to the Justy, increasing horsepower by a whopping 15 percent. That brings the Justy up to a tire-smokin' 70-horsepower for those of you keeping track.

Category E

Model Description	Trade-in Value	Market Value
2 Dr DL Hbk	880	1335
2 Dr GL Hbk	920	1395
2 Dr GL 4WD Hbk	1195	1810
4 Dr GL 4WD Hbk	1255	1905

OPTIONS FOR JUSTY
Auto 3-Speed Transmission +65
Air Conditioning +100

LEGACY 1990

The Legacy is an entirely new line that is geared toward a more traditional audience than the Coupe/Sedan/Wagon. The Legacy is the largest vehicle produced by Subaru and is available as a sedan or wagon. A multi-valve engine is offered for the first time on a Subaru, as are the optional antilock brakes.

RATINGS (SCALE OF 1-10)

Overall	Safety	Reliability	Performance	Comfort	Value
N/A	N/A	5.8	8.3	7.8	5.7

Category D

Model Description	Trade-in Value	Market Value
4 Dr L Sdn	1780	2470
4 Dr L 4WD Sdn	2220	3085

Model Description	Trade-in Value	Market Value
4 Dr L Wgn	1900	2640
4 Dr L 4WD Wgn	2455	3410
4 Dr LS Sdn	2115	2935
4 Dr LS 4WD Sdn	2480	3445
4 Dr LS 4WD Wgn	2820	3915
4 Dr STD Sdn	2295	3185

OPTIONS FOR LEGACY
Auto 4-Speed Transmission +90
Air Conditioning[Std on LS] +105
Anti-Lock Brakes[Opt on L,Wgn,4WD] +110

LOYALE 1990

Subaru's popular Sedan/Wagon/Coupe line is renamed in a move toward traditional vehicle marketing. No other changes for this line of cars.

Category D

Model Description	Trade-in Value	Market Value
2 Dr STD Hbk	1225	1700
2 Dr STD 4WD Hbk	1445	2005
4 Dr STD Sdn	1255	1740
4 Dr STD 4WD Sdn	1640	2280
4 Dr STD Wgn	1420	1975
4 Dr STD 4WD Wgn	1835	2550
4 Dr STD Turbo 4WD Wgn	2010	2790

OPTIONS FOR LOYALE
Auto 3-Speed Transmission +85
Auto 4-Speed Transmission[Opt on Wgn] +75
Air Conditioning[Opt on Hbk,2WD,Non-turbo models] +105
Auto Locking Hubs (4WD) +70
Power Door Locks[Opt on 2WD,STD 4WD Wgn] +35
Power Windows[Opt on 2WD,STD 4WD Wgn] +35

Don't forget to refer to the Mileage Adjustment Table at the back of this book!

Model Description	Trade-in Value	Market Value

Model Description	Trade-in Value	Market Value

SUZUKI   Japan

1998 Suzuki Esteem

1999 SUZUKI

ESTEEM   1999

A restyled front end with multi-reflector headlights and an overall smoother body distinguishes the 1999 Esteem line from its predecessors. Base GL models now come with the 14-inch wheels that were standard on GLX models. Interior surfaces have been upgraded and a Clarion AM/FM cassette is now available. But the exciting news comes in the form of an all-new, 1.8-liter inline four that makes 122 horsepower.

RATINGS (SCALE OF 1-10)

Overall	Safety	Reliability	Performance	Comfort	Value
N/A	N/A	N/A	6.2	7	N/A

Category E
4 Dr GL Sdn	7575	9125
4 Dr GL Wgn	7670	9240
4 Dr GLX Sdn	8160	9830
4 Dr GLX Wgn	8350	10060

OPTIONS FOR ESTEEM
4 cyl 1.8 L Engine +370
Auto 4-Speed Transmission +740
Anti-Lock Brakes +500
Cruise Control +165

GRAND VITARA   1999

The Grand Vitara is a completely new design from Suzuki. Grand Vitara offers plenty of passenger room and a standard V6 engine.

RATINGS (SCALE OF 1-10)

Overall	Safety	Reliability	Performance	Comfort	Value
N/A	N/A	N/A	7.2	7.4	N/A

Category G
4 Dr JLX 4WD Hardtop	12095	14400
4 Dr JS Hardtop	11400	13570

OPTIONS FOR GRAND VITARA
Auto 4-Speed Transmission +740
Aluminum/Alloy Wheels +245
Anti-Lock Brakes +445

SWIFT   1999

With the exception of some color changes, the Suzuki Swift remains unchanged for '99.

RATINGS (SCALE OF 1-10)

Overall	Safety	Reliability	Performance	Comfort	Value
N/A	N/A	N/A	6.4	6.4	N/A

Category E
2 Dr STD Hbk	5510	6640

OPTIONS FOR SWIFT
Auto 3-Speed Transmission +480
AM/FM Stereo Tape +225
Air Conditioning +605

VITARA   1999

The Vitara is an all-new model that replaces the Sidekick as Suzuki's entry into the mini SUV class.

RATINGS (SCALE OF 1-10)

Overall	Safety	Reliability	Performance	Comfort	Value
N/A	N/A	N/A	6.6	7.4	N/A

Category G
4 Dr JX 4WD Wgn	11630	13845

OPTIONS FOR VITARA
Auto 4-Speed Transmission +740
Air Conditioning +605
Cruise Control +155
Keyless Entry System +150

1998 SUZUKI

ESTEEM   1998

A wagon adds diversity to the Esteem lineup.
Category E
4 Dr GL Sdn	6435	7755
4 Dr GL Wgn	6695	8065
4 Dr GL SE Wgn	7340	8845
4 Dr GLX Sdn	7165	8630
4 Dr GLX Wgn	7310	8805
4 Dr GLX SE Wgn	7880	9495

OPTIONS FOR ESTEEM
Auto 4-Speed Transmission[Opt on GL, GLX] +615
Anti-Lock Brakes +410
Cruise Control +135

Don't forget to refer to the Mileage Adjustment Table at the back of this book!

Model Description	Trade-in Value	Market Value

SIDEKICK 1998

A couple of new colors debut.

RATINGS (SCALE OF 1-10)

Overall	Safety	Reliability	Performance	Comfort	Value
6.3	5.5	8.9	6.4	6.6	4.2

Category G
4 Dr JS Wgn	7690	9155
2 Dr JX 4WD Conv	7800	9285
4 Dr JX 4WD Wgn	8105	9645
4 Dr JX FLT 4WD Wgn	9010	10725
2 Dr JX SE 4WD Conv	7835	9325
4 Dr Sport JLX 4WD Wgn	10120	12045
4 Dr Sport JS Wgn	8110	9655
4 Dr Sport JX 4WD Wgn	9610	11445
4 Dr Sport JX SE 4WD Wgn	9945	11835

OPTIONS FOR SIDEKICK
Auto 3-Speed Transmission +370
Auto 4-Speed Transmission +605
Air Conditioning[Opt on JS, JX] +495
Anti-Lock Brakes[Std on Sport JLX] +365

SWIFT 1998

Swift's engine makes nine more horsepower this year, and one more pound of torque.

RATINGS (SCALE OF 1-10)

Overall	Safety	Reliability	Performance	Comfort	Value
6.5	6.3	8.3	6.4	6.4	4.9

Category E
2 Dr STD Hbk	4760	5735

OPTIONS FOR SWIFT
Auto 3-Speed Transmission +400
Air Conditioning +495
Anti-Lock Brakes +410

X-90 1998

The VIN number is new for 1998.

Category G
2 Dr SE 4WD Utility	7360	8760
2 Dr STD 4WD Utility	6890	8205

OPTIONS FOR X-90
AM/FM Stereo Tape[Opt on 2WD] +135
Air Conditioning[Std on SE] +495

1997 SUZUKI

ESTEEM 1997

No changes to the economical Esteem.
Category E
4 Dr GL Sdn	5635	6870
4 Dr GLX Sdn	6050	7375

OPTIONS FOR ESTEEM
Auto 4-Speed Transmission +500
Anti-Lock Brakes +335
Cruise Control +110

SIDEKICK 1997

A JS Sport 2WD model is added to the Sidekick lineup. It has a DOHC engine that makes 120 horsepower at 6500 rpm. There are no changes to the rest of the Sidekick line.

RATINGS (SCALE OF 1-10)

Overall	Safety	Reliability	Performance	Comfort	Value
6	5.5	8.6	6.4	6.6	3.1

Category G
4 Dr JS Wgn	6905	8320
2 Dr JX 4WD Conv	6640	8000
4 Dr JX 4WD Wgn	7325	8830
4 Dr Sport JLX 4WD Wgn	9550	11510
4 Dr Sport JS Wgn	7545	9090
4 Dr Sport JX 4WD Wgn	9105	10970

OPTIONS FOR SIDEKICK
Auto 3-Speed Transmission +300
Auto 4-Speed Transmission +490
AM/FM Stereo Tape[Opt on Conv] +110
Air Conditioning[Opt on JS,JX] +405
Anti-Lock Brakes[Std on Sport JLX] +295

SWIFT 1997

New paint colors (Victory Red and Bright Teal Metallic) and new seat coverings are the only changes to the 1996 Swift.

RATINGS (SCALE OF 1-10)

Overall	Safety	Reliability	Performance	Comfort	Value
6.4	6.3	8.1	6.4	6.4	4.8

Category E
2 Dr STD Hbk	4250	5185

OPTIONS FOR SWIFT
Auto 3-Speed Transmission +325
AM/FM Stereo Tape +150
Air Conditioning +405
Anti-Lock Brakes +335

X-90 1997

No changes to Suzuki's interesting alternative to AWD vehicles.
Category G
2 Dr STD 4WD Utility	6170	7435

OPTIONS FOR X-90
Auto 4-Speed Transmission +475
AM/FM Stereo Tape[Opt on 2WD] +110
Air Conditioning +405

Don't forget to refer to the Mileage Adjustment Table at the back of this book!

Anti-Lock Brakes +295
Cruise Control +105

1996 SUZUKI

ESTEEM 1996

New for 1996 are daytime running lights, standard air conditioning and body-color bumpers on the GL.

Category E

4 Dr GL Sdn	4375	5470
4 Dr GLX Sdn	4810	6010

OPTIONS FOR ESTEEM

Auto 4-Speed Transmission +405
AM/FM Stereo Tape[Opt on GL] +125
Anti-Lock Brakes +275
Cruise Control +90

SIDEKICK 1996

Lots of changes to this mini SUV: the 16-valve, 95-horsepower engine is available across the board (except in the Sport), and dual airbags are housed in a revised instrument panel. New fabrics, colors and styling revisions update the Sidekick nicely. All-new for 1996 is a Sport variant, equipped with lots of exclusive standard equipment, a 120-horsepower twin-cam motor, a wider track, two-tone paint and a dorky chrome grille.

RATINGS (SCALE OF 1-10)

Overall	Safety	Reliability	Performance	Comfort	Value
6	5.4	8	6.4	6.6	3.6

Category G

2 Dr JX 4WD Conv	5750	7010
4 Dr JX 4WD Wgn	6240	7610
4 Dr Sport JLX 4WD Wgn	8205	10010
4 Dr Sport JX 4WD Wgn	7305	8910

OPTIONS FOR SIDEKICK

Auto 3-Speed Transmission +240
Auto 4-Speed Transmission +395
Air Conditioning[Opt on JS,JX] +330
Anti-Lock Brakes[Opt on JS,JX] +245

SWIFT 1996

Oh boy. Two new colors and new seat fabrics. Whoopee.

RATINGS (SCALE OF 1-10)

Overall	Safety	Reliability	Performance	Comfort	Value
6.4	6.3	8	6.4	6.4	4.8

Category E

2 Dr STD Hbk	3300	4125

OPTIONS FOR SWIFT

Auto 3-Speed Transmission +260
AM/FM Stereo Tape +125

Air Conditioning +330
Anti-Lock Brakes +275

X-90 1996

Based on Sidekick platform, this new concept features a two-seat cockpit, T-top roof, conventional trunk, and available four-wheel drive. Loaded with standard equipment, the X-90 is an interesting vehicle indeed.

Category G

2 Dr STD 4WD Utility	5675	6920

OPTIONS FOR X-90

Auto 4-Speed Transmission +385
Air Conditioning +330

1995 SUZUKI

ESTEEM 1995

The 1995 Esteem is Suzuki's latest entry in the hotly contested subcompact car market. The Esteem has standard antilock brakes and dual airbags but is saddled with a 1.6-liter engine. Competition from Toyota, Geo and Honda is stiff, but low resale values may make this car worthwhile.

Category E

4 Dr GL Sdn	3795	4930
4 Dr GLX Sdn	4160	5405

OPTIONS FOR ESTEEM

Auto 4-Speed Transmission +330
Air Conditioning +270
Anti-Lock Brakes +225
Cruise Control +75

SIDEKICK 1995

The convertible model gets a new top.

RATINGS (SCALE OF 1-10)

Overall	Safety	Reliability	Performance	Comfort	Value
5.7	2.7	8	6.6	6.6	4.6

Category G

4 Dr JLX 4WD Wgn	5790	7150
4 Dr JS Wgn	4295	5300
2 Dr JX 4WD Conv	4630	5715
4 Dr JX 4WD Wgn	5165	6375

OPTIONS FOR SIDEKICK

Auto 3-Speed Transmission +200
Auto 4-Speed Transmission +300
Air Conditioning +270
Luggage Rack +50

SWIFT 1995

The sedan is dropped and dual airbags are added. Antilock brakes become a much appreciated option. The two-door GT hatchback has also been dropped.

Don't forget to refer to the Mileage Adjustment Table at the back of this book!

Model Description	Trade-in Value	Market Value

RATINGS (SCALE OF 1-10)

Overall	Safety	Reliability	Performance	Comfort	Value
6.4	6.9	7.8	6.4	6.4	4.7

Category E

	Trade-in	Market
2 Dr STD Hbk	2610	3385

OPTIONS FOR SWIFT

Auto 3-Speed Transmission +380
AM/FM Stereo Tape +100
Air Conditioning +270
Anti-Lock Brakes +225

1994 SUZUKI

SAMURAI 1994

Another Samurai commits Hari-Kari; the two-wheel drive model is no longer available. Other changes are limited to the addition of a high-mounted rear brake light.

Category G

	Trade-in	Market
2 Dr JL 4WD Conv	3245	4005

OPTIONS FOR SAMURAI

Air Conditioning +220

SIDEKICK 1994

All Sidekicks get an alarm and a tilt steering wheel as standard equipment this year. A high-mounted rear brake light is a new safety item found on all Sidekicks.

RATINGS (SCALE OF 1-10)

Overall	Safety	Reliability	Performance	Comfort	Value
5.2	2.3	6.8	6.6	6.6	3.5

Category G

	Trade-in	Market
4 Dr JLX 4WD Wgn	5005	6180
4 Dr JS Wgn	4005	4945
2 Dr JX 4WD Conv	4205	5190
4 Dr JX 4WD Wgn	4700	5800

OPTIONS FOR SIDEKICK

Auto 3-Speed Transmission +165
Auto 4-Speed Transmission +275
Air Conditioning +220
Flip-Up Sunroof +90

SWIFT 1994

The GA hatchback gets a cargo cover and both GA models get a right sideview mirror. Will wonders never cease?

Category E

	Trade-in	Market
2 Dr GA Hbk	2020	2690
4 Dr GA Sdn	2260	3015
4 Dr GS Sdn	2355	3140
2 Dr GT Hbk	2260	3010

OPTIONS FOR SWIFT

Auto 3-Speed Transmission +175
AM/FM Stereo Tape[Opt on GA] +80
Air Conditioning +220

1993 SUZUKI

SAMURAI 1993

When are they going to retire this thing? The Samurai continues unchanged.

Category G

	Trade-in	Market
2 Dr JL 4WD Conv	2440	3130

OPTIONS FOR SAMURAI

AM/FM Stereo Tape +50
Air Conditioning +180

SIDEKICK 1993

No changes for the Sidekick.

RATINGS (SCALE OF 1-10)

Overall	Safety	Reliability	Performance	Comfort	Value
5.3	2.5	7.5	6.6	6.6	3.5

Category G

	Trade-in	Market
4 Dr JLX 4WD Wgn	3985	5105
2 Dr JX 4WD Conv	3180	4075
4 Dr JX 4WD Wgn	3875	4970

OPTIONS FOR SIDEKICK

Auto 3-Speed Transmission +135
Auto 4-Speed Transmission +205
AM/FM Stereo Tape[Opt on Conv] +50
Air Conditioning +180
Hardtop Roof +175

SWIFT 1993

The doors lock when the Swift reaches speeds of 8 mph or more; apparently Suzuki thinks that anyone crazy enough to buy this car won't be able to figure out how to do this on their own.

Category E

	Trade-in	Market
2 Dr GA Hbk	1590	2180
4 Dr GA Sdn	1760	2410
4 Dr GS Sdn	1735	2375
2 Dr GT Hbk	1925	2640

OPTIONS FOR SWIFT

Auto 3-Speed Transmission +135
AM/FM Stereo Tape[Opt on GA] +65
Air Conditioning +180

Don't forget to refer to the Mileage Adjustment Table at the back of this book!

1992 SUZUKI

SAMURAI 1992

The Samurai loses a trim-level, making it available only as a two-wheel drive JA or four-wheel drive JL. The JL model loses its back seat.

Category G

	Trade-in	Market
2 Dr JL 4WD Conv	2300	3025

OPTIONS FOR SAMURAI
AM/FM Stereo Tape +40
Air Conditioning +145

SIDEKICK 1992

Four-door models receive an increase of 15 horsepower and a four-speed automatic transmission. All Sidekicks get a redesigned instrument panel.

RATINGS (SCALE OF 1-10)

Overall	Safety	Reliability	Performance	Comfort	Value
5.4	2.4	7.8	6.6	6.6	3.8

Category G

	Trade-in	Market
4 Dr JLX 4WD Wgn	3675	4835
2 Dr JX 4WD Conv	2960	3895
4 Dr JX 4WD Wgn	3555	4680

OPTIONS FOR SIDEKICK
Auto 3-Speed Transmission +155
Air Conditioning +145
Hardtop Roof +140
Leather Seats +140

SWIFT 1992

All Swifts get a redesigned front and rear fascia as well as a new dashboard. GS sedans receive power steering and new hub caps.

Category E

	Trade-in	Market
2 Dr GA Hbk	1300	1855
4 Dr GA Sdn	1440	2055
4 Dr GS Sdn	1490	2130
2 Dr GT Hbk	1435	2050

OPTIONS FOR SWIFT
Auto 3-Speed Transmission +110
Air Conditioning +145

1991 SUZUKI

SAMURAI 1991

The Samurai receives a freshened front-end that includes a new grille.

Category G

	Trade-in	Market
2 Dr JL 4WD Conv	1890	2550
2 Dr STD Conv	1395	1885

OPTIONS FOR SAMURAI
Js Option +145
Air Conditioning +120

SIDEKICK 1991

A four-door Sidekick is introduced, offering more passenger and cargo room.

RATINGS (SCALE OF 1-10)

Overall	Safety	Reliability	Performance	Comfort	Value
5.4	2.3	7.1	6.6	6.6	4.3

Category G

	Trade-in	Market
2 Dr JL 4WD Conv	2390	3230
4 Dr JLX 4WD Wgn	3035	4100
2 Dr JS Conv	1975	2665
2 Dr JX 4WD Conv	2595	3505
4 Dr JX 4WD Wgn	2785	3765

OPTIONS FOR SIDEKICK
Auto 3-Speed Transmission +90
AM/FM Stereo Tape[Opt on JL,JS] +35
Air Conditioning +120
Chrome Wheels +25

SWIFT 1991

A GS sedan is introduced to the Swift lineup, offering first-time buyers a touch more luxury than is found in the base model.

Category E

	Trade-in	Market
2 Dr GA Hbk	1065	1565
4 Dr GA Sdn	1230	1810
4 Dr GS Sdn	1300	1910

OPTIONS FOR SWIFT
Auto 3-Speed Transmission +90
AM/FM Stereo Tape[Opt on GA] +45
Air Conditioning +120

1990 SUZUKI

SAMURAI 1990

No changes to the Samurai.

Category G

	Trade-in	Market
2 Dr JL 4WD Conv	1685	2340

OPTIONS FOR SAMURAI
Air Conditioning +100

SIDEKICK 1990

No changes for the mini sport-ute from Suzuki.

RATINGS (SCALE OF 1-10)

Overall	Safety	Reliability	Performance	Comfort	Value
5.4	2.3	7.5	6.6	6.6	4.2

Don't forget to refer to the Mileage Adjustment Table at the back of this book!

Model Description	Trade-in Value	Market Value	Model Description	Trade-in Value	Market Value
Category G			2 Dr GL Hbk	945	1435
2 Dr JLX 4WD Conv	1925	2675	4 Dr GL Sdn	1080	1635
2 Dr JX 4WD Conv	1835	2550	2 Dr GLX Hbk	1075	1625
			4 Dr GS Sdn	1080	1640

OPTIONS FOR SIDEKICK
Auto 3-Speed Transmission +75
Air Conditioning +100

OPTIONS FOR SWIFT
Auto 3-Speed Transmission +75
Air Conditioning +100

SWIFT 1990

A base hatchback, called the GA, and a sedan are introduced for 1990. The GTi is renamed the GT after a run-in with the people at Volkswagen.

Category E		
2 Dr GA Hbk	925	1400
4 Dr GA Sdn	1050	1590

Don't forget to refer to the Mileage Adjustment Table at the back of this book!

TOYOTA 99

Model Description	Trade-in Value	Market Value	Model Description	Trade-in Value	Market Value

TOYOTA
Japan

1994 Toyota Corolla

1999 TOYOTA

4RUNNER 1999

The 4Runner receives a number of upgrades this year, starting with a new and improved four-wheel drive system equipped with a center differential and featuring a full-time 4WD mode in addition to the current two-high, four-high and four-low modes. New exterior features include a front bumper redesign, multi-reflector headlamps, and an enhanced sport package with fender flares and a hood scoop on the SR5 model. Inside, a new center console/cupholder design will improve beverage-carrying capacity of the 4Runner and an automatic climate control system will be featured on the Limited models.

RATINGS (SCALE OF 1-10)

Overall	Safety	Reliability	Performance	Comfort	Value
N/A	7.8	9.4	6.6	6.9	N/A

Category G

	Trade-in	Market
4 Dr Limited Wgn	22110	26320
4 Dr Limited 4WD Wgn	23700	28215
4 Dr SR5 Wgn	17905	21315
4 Dr SR5 4WD Wgn	19790	23560
4 Dr STD Wgn	13530	16110
4 Dr STD 4WD Wgn	15234	18135

OPTIONS FOR 4RUNNER

Auto 4-Speed Transmission[Opt on STD,SR5 V6 4WD] +665
Black Elite Pkg +655
Sport Handling Pkg +630
Air Conditioning[Std on Limited] +605
Aluminum/Alloy Wheels[Std on Limited] +245
Anti-Lock Brakes[Std on Limited,SR5] +445
Compact Disc Changer +385

Compact Disc W/fm/tape +355
Cruise Control[Opt on STD] +155
Fog Lights[Std on Limited] +105
Keyless Entry System[Std on Limited] +150
Leather Seats[Opt on SR5] +575
Power Door Locks[Std on Limited] +170
Power Mirrors[Opt on STD] +100
Power Moonroof +645
Power Windows[Std on Limited] +175
Privacy Glass[Opt on STD] +195
Rear Window Defroster[Opt on STD] +125
Rear Window Wiper[Opt on STD] +115
Running Boards[Std on Limited] +285
Tilt Steering Wheel[Opt on STD] +130

AVALON 1999

After a body makeover and safety improvements (side airbags) last year, the Avalon heads into '99 with only minor updates. Daytime running lights with auto-off color-keyed foglamp covers and dual heated color keyed power mirrors are new this year. A new three-in-one ETR/cassette/CD sound system is optional on the XL model and Lunar Mist metallic replaces Golden Sand metallic.

RATINGS (SCALE OF 1-10)

Overall	Safety	Reliability	Performance	Comfort	Value
N/A	N/A	N/A	8.2	8.4	N/A

Category D

	Trade-in	Market
4 Dr XL Sdn	15690	18675
4 Dr XLS Sdn	18305	21790

OPTIONS FOR AVALON

Aluminum/Alloy Wheels[Opt on XL] +345
Compact Disc W/fm/tape[Opt on XL] +595
Heated Front Seats +300
Leather Seats +820
Power Moonroof +620
Traction Control System +455

CAMRY 1999

If it ain't broken, don't fix (or change) it. The Camry is already Toyota's best-selling car so changes to the '99 are minimal. Two new audio systems are available and both include three-in-one ETR/cassette/CD features. Also available are daytime running lights with auto-off. Vintage Red Pearl, Sable Pearl, and Woodland Pearl replace Sunfire Red Pearl, Ruby Red and Classic Green Pearl.

RATINGS (SCALE OF 1-10)

Overall	Safety	Reliability	Performance	Comfort	Value
N/A	7.9	8.7	8.6	8.1	N/A

Category D

	Trade-in	Market
4 Dr CE Sdn	10785	12840
4 Dr LE Sdn	12860	15310

Don't forget to refer to the Mileage Adjustment Table at the back of this book!

Model Description	Trade-in Value	Market Value
4 Dr LE V6 Sdn	13776	16400
4 Dr XLE Sdn	14305	17030
4 Dr XLE V6 Sdn	15260	18165

OPTIONS FOR CAMRY

Auto 4-Speed Transmission[Opt on CE] +590
Black Elite Pkg +605
Air Conditioning[Opt on CE] +630
Aluminum/Alloy Wheels[Std on XLE,XLE V6] +345
Anti-Lock Brakes[Opt on CE,LE] +670
Compact Disc W/fm/tape +595
Cruise Control[Opt on CE] +180
Keyless Entry System[Std on XLE,XLE V6] +235
Leather Seats +820
Power Door Locks[Opt on CE] +200
Power Drivers Seat +220
Power Mirrors[Opt on CE] +115
Power Moonroof +620
Power Windows[Opt on CE] +200
Side Air Bag Restraint +220
Traction Control System +455

CAMRY SOLARA   1999

This all-new coupe is based on the Camry platform. Designed jointly by the Toyota Motor Corporation in Japan and the Toyota Technical Center in Ann Arbor, Michigan, the Solara is targeted at consumers who want the style of a sports car but the room and comfort of a larger, more practical vehicle.

RATINGS (SCALE OF 1-10)

Overall	Safety	Reliability	Performance	Comfort	Value
N/A	N/A	N/A	8.6	8.1	N/A

Category D	Trade-in	Market
2 Dr SE Cpe	12995	15470
2 Dr SE V6 Cpe	14420	17170
2 Dr SLE Cpe	16820	20025

OPTIONS FOR CAMRY SOLARA

Auto 4-Speed Transmission[Std on SLE] +590
Aluminum/Alloy Wheels[Std on SLE] +345
Anti-Lock Brakes[Opt on SE] +670
Compact Disc W/fm/tape +595
Keyless Entry System[Std on SLE] +235
Power Drivers Seat[Std on SLE] +220
Power Moonroof +620
Side Air Bag Restraint +220
Traction Control System +455

CELICA   1999

The Celica GT Sport Coupe has been discontinued along with the color Galaxy Blue Metallic.

RATINGS (SCALE OF 1-10)

Overall	Safety	Reliability	Performance	Comfort	Value
N/A	N/A	N/A	8.2	7.6	N/A

Category D	Trade-in	Market
2 Dr GT Conv	16945	20175
2 Dr GT Hbk	14870	17705

OPTIONS FOR CELICA

Auto 4-Speed Transmission +590
Aluminum/Alloy Wheels[Std on Conv] +345
Anti-Lock Brakes +670
Compact Disc W/fm/tape[Std on Conv] +595
Leather Seats +820
Power Moonroof +620

COROLLA   1999

A major makeover in '98 means only minor updates to the Corolla in '99. The VE model will feature a Deluxe AM/FM ETR four-speaker audio system as standard equipment. A Touring Package will be standard equipment on the Corolla LE model. Five new exterior colors include Silver Stream Opal, Venetian Red Pearl, Dark Emerald Pearl, Aqua Blue Metallic and Twilight Blue Pearl.

RATINGS (SCALE OF 1-10)

Overall	Safety	Reliability	Performance	Comfort	Value
N/A	7.2	9.6	7.6	8.1	N/A

Category E	Trade-in	Market
4 Dr CE Sdn	8515	10260
4 Dr LE Sdn	9915	11945
4 Dr VE Sdn	8165	9840

OPTIONS FOR COROLLA

Auto 3-Speed Transmission +370
Auto 4-Speed Transmission +590
AM/FM Compact Disc Player +340
Air Conditioning[Std on LE] +605
Aluminum/Alloy Wheels +245
Anti-Lock Brakes +500
Cruise Control +165
Keyless Entry System +115
Power Door Locks[Std on LE] +180
Power Moonroof +425
Power Windows[Std on LE] +195
Rear Window Defroster[Opt on VE] +120
Side Air Bag Restraint +190

LAND CRUISER   1999

The Land Cruiser was reintroduced in '98 with major upgrades. As such, it enters '99 completely unchanged.

RATINGS (SCALE OF 1-10)

Overall	Safety	Reliability	Performance	Comfort	Value
N/A	N/A	N/A	7	7.9	N/A

Category G	Trade-in	Market
4 Dr STD 4WD Wgn	30255	36015

OPTIONS FOR LAND CRUISER

Convenience Pkg +580
Third Seat Pkg +840

Don't forget to refer to the Mileage Adjustment Table at the back of this book!

TOYOTA 99

Model Description	Trade-in Value	Market Value	Model Description	Trade-in Value	Market Value

Dual Air Conditioning +700
Leather Seats +575
Locking Differential +220
Power Moonroof +645
Running Boards +285
Third Seat +535

RAV4   1999

Toyota promises minor upgrades for it's mini-SUV in '99. Leather seats and color-keyed body cladding are now available as part of the "L Special Edition" package. Color-keyed mirrors and door handles can also be had this year and the spare tire is now a full-size steel wheel with a soft cover.

RATINGS (SCALE OF 1-10)

Overall	Safety	Reliability	Performance	Comfort	Value
N/A	6.6	8.3	7	6.4	N/A

Category G

	Trade-in	Market
4 Dr STD Wgn	12100	14405
4 Dr STD 4WD Wgn	12760	15190
4 Dr "L" Special Edition 4WD Wgn	13930	16585

OPTIONS FOR RAV4

Auto 4-Speed Transmission +775
AM/FM Compact Disc Player +245
Air Conditioning[Opt on STD] +605
Aluminum/Alloy Wheels[Opt on STD] +245
Anti-Lock Brakes +445
Cruise Control[Opt on STD] +155
Power Door Locks[Opt on STD] +170
Power Mirrors[Opt on STD] +100
Power Windows[Opt on STD] +175

SIENNA   1999

Entering its second full model year of production at Toyota's Kentucky plant, the Sienna minivan gets a right side power sliding door. An engine immobilizer system has been added to the keyless-entry security system and all Siennas will be equipped with daytime running lights. Selected models have a full size spare tire and Woodland Pearl replaces Classic Green Pearl as an exterior color option.

RATINGS (SCALE OF 1-10)

Overall	Safety	Reliability	Performance	Comfort	Value
N/A	N/A	N/A	7	7.9	N/A

Category G

	Trade-in	Market
2 Dr CE Pass. Van	16540	19690
4 Dr LE Pass. Van	17445	20765
4 Dr XLE Pass. Van	19275	22945

OPTIONS FOR SIENNA

AM/FM Compact Disc Player[Std on XLE] +245
Aluminum/Alloy Wheels[Std on XLE] +245
Captain Chairs (4)[Std on XLE] +465
Cruise Control[Opt on CE] +155

Dual Air Conditioning[Opt on CE] +700
Keyless Entry System[Std on XLE] +150
Leather Seats +575
Power Door Locks[Opt on CE] +170
Power Mirrors[Opt on CE] +100
Power Moonroof +645
Power Sliding Door +290
Power Windows[Opt on CE] +175
Privacy Glass[Opt on CE] +195
Rear Window Defroster[Opt on CE] +125

TACOMA   1999

Toyota adds new front seat belt pretensioners and force limiters. Newly optional on Xtra Cab models is an AM/FM four-speaker CD audio system while 4x4s get 15"x7" inch steel wheels. The PreRunner adds a regular cab option to its model mix. Natural White, Imperial Jade Mica and Horizon Blue Metallic replace White, Copper Canyon Mica, Evergreen Pearl, and Cool Steel Metallic as color options.

RATINGS (SCALE OF 1-10)

Overall	Safety	Reliability	Performance	Comfort	Value
N/A	N/A	N/A	7.2	7	N/A

Category G

	Trade-in	Market
2 Dr Limited 4WD Ext Cab SB	16860	20070
2 Dr Prerunner Ext Cab SB	12720	15140
2 Dr Prerunner Std Cab SB	10964	13050
2 Dr Prerunner V6 Ext Cab SB	13340	15880
2 Dr SR5 Ext Cab SB	12430	14800
2 Dr SR5 4WD Ext Cab SB	13975	16635
2 Dr SR5 V6 Ext Cab SB	13320	15855
2 Dr SR5 V6 4WD Ext Cab SB	14635	17425
2 Dr STD Ext Cab SB	11555	13755
2 Dr STD 4WD Ext Cab SB	12980	15450
2 Dr STD Std Cab SB	9925	11815
2 Dr STD 4WD Std Cab SB	11730	13965
2 Dr V6 Ext Cab SB	11665	13885
2 Dr V6 4WD Ext Cab SB	13530	16105

OPTIONS FOR TACOMA

Auto 4-Speed Transmission[Std on Prerunner, Prerunner V6] +630
TRD Off-Road Pkg +705
AM/FM Compact Disc Player[Std on Limited] +245
Air Conditioning[Opt on Limited,STD,V6] +605
Aluminum/Alloy Wheels[Std on Limited] +245
Anti-Lock Brakes +445
Auto Locking Hubs (4WD)[Std on Limited] +190
Bed Liner +210
Cruise Control[Std on Limited] +155
Flip-Up Sunroof +245
Keyless Entry System +150
Power Door Locks[Std on Limited] +170
Power Steering[Opt on STD 4 cyl.] +210
Power Windows[Std on Limited] +175

Don't forget to refer to the Mileage Adjustment Table at the back of this book!

TOYOTA 99-98

Model Description	Trade-in Value	Market Value	Model Description	Trade-in Value	Market Value

Sliding Rear Window[Std on Limited,SR5] +90
Tilt Steering Wheel[Std on Limited] +130

1998 TOYOTA

4RUNNER   1998

For 1998, the Toyota 4Runner gets rotary HVAC controls, a new four-spoke steering wheel and revised audio control head units.

RATINGS (SCALE OF 1-10)

Overall	Safety	Reliability	Performance	Comfort	Value
6.8	7.8	9.3	6.6	6.9	3.6

Category G

4 Dr Limited Wgn	20465	24365
4 Dr Limited 4WD Wgn	21750	25895
4 Dr SR5 Wgn	16220	19310
4 Dr SR5 4WD Wgn	17514	20850
4 Dr STD Wgn	12815	15255
4 Dr STD 4WD Wgn	13715	16330

OPTIONS FOR 4RUNNER

Auto 4-Speed Transmission[Std on Limited, SR5 2WD] +555
Black Elite Pkg +565
Elite Pkg +560
Sports Pkg +480
Air Conditioning[Std on Limited] +495
Aluminum/Alloy Wheels[Std on Limited] +200
Anti-Lock Brakes[Opt on STD] +365
Compact Disc Changer +315
Compact Disc W/fm/tape +290
Cruise Control[Std on Limited] +125
Fog Lights +90
Keyless Entry System +120
Leather Seats[Opt on SR5] +470
Power Door Locks[Opt on STD] +140
Power Mirrors[Opt on STD] +80
Power Moonroof +525
Power Windows[Std on Limited] +145
Privacy Glass[Opt on STD] +160
Rear Window Defroster[Opt on STD] +105
Rear Window Wiper[Opt on STD] +95
Running Boards[Opt on SR5,STD] +235
Tilt Steering Wheel[Opt on STD] +105

AVALON   1998

The Avalon gets side-impact airbags, new headlights and taillamps, a new grille, a new trunk lid and pretensioner seatbelts with force limiters.

RATINGS (SCALE OF 1-10)

Overall	Safety	Reliability	Performance	Comfort	Value
8	8.8	8.8	8.2	8.4	5.7

Category D

4 Dr XL Sdn	14760	17575
4 Dr XLS Sdn	15900	18925

OPTIONS FOR AVALON

Leather Bucket Seat Pkg +480
AM/FM Compact Disc Player[Opt on XL] +320
Aluminum/Alloy Wheels[Opt on XL] +280
Dual Power Seats[Opt on XL] +510
Heated Front Seats +245
Heated Power Mirrors[Opt on XL] +50
Leather Seats +670
Power Moonroof +505
Traction Control System +370

CAMRY   1998

Side-impact airbags debut on the recently redesigned Camry. Depowered front airbags further enhance this car's ability to protect its occupant in a crash. An engine immobilizer feature is now part of the theft-deterrent package.

RATINGS (SCALE OF 1-10)

Overall	Safety	Reliability	Performance	Comfort	Value
7.4	7.9	8.5	8.6	8.1	4

Category D

4 Dr CE Sdn	9465	11270
4 Dr CE V6 Sdn	10170	12110
4 Dr LE Sdn	11680	13905
4 Dr LE V6 Sdn	12580	14975
4 Dr XLE Sdn	13521	16100
4 Dr XLE V6 Sdn	14335	17065

OPTIONS FOR CAMRY

Auto 4-Speed Transmission[Opt on CE] +490
Black Elite Pkg +505
AM/FM Compact Disc Player[Std on XLE, XLE V6] +320
Air Conditioning[Opt on CE, CE V6] +515
Aluminum/Alloy Wheels[Std on XLE, XLE V6] +280
Anti-Lock Brakes[Opt on CE 4 cyl.] +550
Cruise Control[Opt on CE, CE V6] +145
Keyless Entry System[Std on XLE, XLE V6] +190
Leather Seats +670
Power Door Locks[Opt on CE, CE V6] +165
Power Drivers Seat +180
Power Mirrors[Opt on CE, CE V6] +95
Power Moonroof +505
Power Windows[Opt on CE, CE V6] +165
Side Air Bag Restraint +180
Traction Control System +370

CELICA   1998

Celica ST is eliminated. GT's get more standard features and one new color: Caribbean Green Metallic.

RATINGS (SCALE OF 1-10)

Overall	Safety	Reliability	Performance	Comfort	Value
N/A	N/A	9.7	8.2	7.6	N/A

Don't forget to refer to the Mileage Adjustment Table at the back of this book!

Model Description	Trade-in Value	Market Value	Model Description	Trade-in Value	Market Value

Category F

2 Dr GT Conv	15125	18005
2 Dr GT Cpe	13415	15970
2 Dr GT Hbk	13885	16530

OPTIONS FOR CELICA

Aluminum/Alloy Wheels[Std on Conv] +185
Compact Disc W/fm/tape[Opt on Hbk] +305
Leather Steering Wheel +90
Power Moonroof +395
Rear Spoiler[Opt on Cpe] +150

COROLLA   1998

The Toyota Corolla is completely redesigned this year with a new engine, new sheetmetal and a new standard for safety in compact cars: optional front passenger side-impact airbags.

RATINGS (SCALE OF 1-10)

Overall	Safety	Reliability	Performance	Comfort	Value
7.5	7.2	9.4	7.6	8.1	5.4

Category E

4 Dr CE Sdn	8165	9840
4 Dr LE Sdn	8945	10775
4 Dr VE Sdn	7460	8990

OPTIONS FOR COROLLA

Auto 3-Speed Transmission +305
Auto 4-Speed Transmission +490
AM/FM Compact Disc Player +275
Air Conditioning[Opt on VE] +495
Aluminum/Alloy Wheels +200
Anti-Lock Brakes +410
Cruise Control +135
Keyless Entry System +95
Power Door Locks[Opt on CE] +145
Power Moonroof +350
Power Windows[Opt on CE] +160
Rear Window Defroster[Opt on VE] +100
Side Air Bag Restraint +155
Tachometer[Opt on CE] +45

LAND CRUISER   1998

For 1998, Land Cruiser gets a more powerful V8 engine, standard ABS, an increase in structural rigidity, an improved suspension system, increased passenger and cargo room and a slew of new colors.

Category G

4 Dr STD 4WD Wgn	27970	33295

OPTIONS FOR LAND CRUISER

Convenience Pkg +470
Third Seat Pkg +675
Leather Seats +470
Locking Differential +180
Power Moonroof +525
Running Boards +235
Third Seat +435

RAV4   1998

Toyota's jellybean enters its third year of production with minor changes to the grille, headlights, taillamps and interior. Four-door RAV4s get new seat fabric. A late-year introduction of the new RAV4 convertible makes this sport-ute more appealing for those who live in the sunbelt.

RATINGS (SCALE OF 1-10)

Overall	Safety	Reliability	Performance	Comfort	Value
N/A	6.6	8.2	7	6.4	N/A

Category G

4 Dr 'L' Special Ed. Wgn	12995	15470
2 Dr STD Conv	11130	13250
2 Dr STD 4WD Conv	11780	14025
2 Dr STD Utility	10515	12515
2 Dr STD 4WD Utility	11665	13885
4 Dr STD Wgn	11840	14095
4 Dr STD 4WD Wgn	12255	14590

OPTIONS FOR RAV4

Auto 4-Speed Transmission +645
Luxury Pkg +1260
AM/FM Compact Disc Player +200
Air Conditioning +495
Aluminum/Alloy Wheels +200
Anti-Lock Brakes +365
Cruise Control +125
Keyless Entry System +120
Power Door Locks +140
Power Mirrors +80
Power Windows +145
Tilt Steering Wheel[Std on Wgn] +105

SIENNA   1998

A new minivan from Toyota brings some innovation to the family truckster market. A powerful 194-horsepower V6 engine rests under the hood of all models. Safety equipment includes standard anti-lock brakes, low tire pressure warning systems and five mph front and rear bumpers. Sienna boasts outstanding crash test scores.

RATINGS (SCALE OF 1-10)

Overall	Safety	Reliability	Performance	Comfort	Value
N/A	N/A	8.7	7	7.9	N/A

Category G

2 Dr CE Pass. Van	14060	16740
2 Dr LE Pass. Van	15450	18390
2 Dr XLE Pass. Van	17100	20355

OPTIONS FOR SIENNA

AM/FM Compact Disc Player[Std on XLE] +200
Aluminum/Alloy Wheels[Opt on LE] +200
Captain Chairs (4)[Opt on LE] +380
Cruise Control[Opt on CE] +125

Don't forget to refer to the Mileage Adjustment Table at the back of this book!

TOYOTA 98

Model Description	Trade-in Value	Market Value	Model Description	Trade-in Value	Market Value

Dual Air Conditioning[Opt on CE] +575
Heated Power Mirrors[Std on XLE] +45
Keyless Entry System[Std on XLE] +120
Leather Seats +470
Power Door Locks[Opt on CE] +140
Power Mirrors[Opt on CE] +80
Power Moonroof +525
Power Windows[Opt on CE] +145
Privacy Glass[Opt on CE] +160
Rear Window Defroster[Opt on CE] +105
Sliding Driver Side Door +320

T100   1998

No changes to Toyota's full-size truck.

RATINGS (SCALE OF 1-10)

Overall	Safety	Reliability	Performance	Comfort	Value
N/A	N/A	9.3	7	7.5	N/A

Category H
2 Dr DX Ext Cab SB	11655	13710
2 Dr DX 4WD Ext Cab SB	13670	16080
2 Dr SR5 Ext Cab SB	13820	16260
2 Dr SR5 4WD Ext Cab SB	15865	18665
2 Dr STD Std Cab LB	9960	11720

OPTIONS FOR T100

Auto 4-Speed Transmission +555
AM/FM Compact Disc Player +190
Air Conditioning +490
Aluminum/Alloy Wheels +190
Anti-Lock Brakes +300
Bed Liner +135
Cruise Control +115
Keyless Entry System +105
Power Door Locks +115
Power Mirrors +60
Power Windows +115
Privacy Glass[Opt on DX] +100
Sliding Rear Window[Std on SR5] +70
Tilt Steering Wheel[Std on SR5] +110
Velour/Cloth Seats[Opt on STD] +80

TACOMA   1998

The 1998 four-wheel drive Tacomas receive fresh front-end styling that makes them more closely resemble their two-wheel drive brothers. A new option package appears for 1998 as well; the TRD (no, not short for "turd") Off-Road Package for extended cab models is designed to make the Tacoma appeal to would-be Baja 1000 racers. On the safety front, Toyota introduces a passenger's side airbag that can be deactivated with a cut-off switch, making the Tacoma somewhat safer for children and short adults. Toyota also offers a new Tacoma PreRunner for 1998, billing it as a two-wheel drive truck with four-wheel drive performance.

RATINGS (SCALE OF 1-10)

Overall	Safety	Reliability	Performance	Comfort	Value
N/A	7.1	9.5	7.2	7	N/A

Category G
2 Dr Limited 4WD Ext Cab SB	14935	17780
2 Dr Prerunner Ext Cab SB	10375	12350
2 Dr Prerunner V6 Ext Cab SB	10960	13045
2 Dr SR5 Ext Cab SB	10715	12755
2 Dr SR5 4WD Ext Cab SB	13395	15945
2 Dr SR5 V6 Ext Cab SB	10950	13035
2 Dr SR5 V6 4WD Ext Cab SB	13710	16320
2 Dr STD Ext Cab SB	9075	10805
2 Dr STD 4WD Ext Cab SB	11930	14205
2 Dr STD Std Cab SB	8260	9835
2 Dr STD 4WD Std Cab SB	10685	12720
2 Dr V6 Ext Cab SB	10180	12120
2 Dr V6 4WD Ext Cab SB	12455	14825

OPTIONS FOR TACOMA

Auto 4-Speed Transmission[Std on Prerunner,
    Prerunner V6] +510
TRD Off-Road Pkg +750
AM/FM Compact Disc Player +200
Air Conditioning[Opt on Limited, STD, V6] +495
Aluminum/Alloy Wheels[Std on Limited] +200
Anti-Lock Brakes +365
Auto Locking Hubs (4WD)[Std on Limited] +155
Bed Liner +170
Cruise Control[Std on Limited] +125
Flip-Up Sunroof +200
Keyless Entry System +120
Power Door Locks[Std on Limited] +140
Power Steering[Opt on STD 4 cyl.] +170
Power Windows[Std on Limited] +145
Sliding Rear Window[Opt on STD, V6] +70
Tilt Steering Wheel[Std on Limited] +105

TERCEL   1998

For 1998, the Tercel is available exclusively as a two-door CE model with additional standard features like color-keyed grille and bumpers, rear seat headrests, AM/FM stereo with cassette, air conditioning, digital clock and power steering.

RATINGS (SCALE OF 1-10)

Overall	Safety	Reliability	Performance	Comfort	Value
6.9	6.1	9.3	6.6	7	5.5

Category E
2 Dr CE Sdn	6070	7315

OPTIONS FOR TERCEL

Auto 3-Speed Transmission +305
AM/FM Compact Disc Player +275
Anti-Lock Brakes +410
Keyless Entry System +95
Power Door Locks +145

Don't forget to refer to the Mileage Adjustment Table at the back of this book!

TOYOTA 98-97

Model Description	Trade-in Value	Market Value	Model Description	Trade-in Value	Market Value

Power Windows +160
Rear Window Defroster +100

1997 TOYOTA

4RUNNER 1997

Toyota's hot-selling redesign receives minor changes. The most noticeable is the addition of the 2WD Limited to the model lineup. SR5 models receive new interior fabrics.

RATINGS (SCALE OF 1-10)

Overall	Safety	Reliability	Performance	Comfort	Value
6.9	7.8	9.3	6.6	6.9	4.1

Category G
4 Dr Limited Wgn	18280	22025
4 Dr Limited 4WD Wgn	19405	23380
4 Dr SR5 Wgn	14380	17325
4 Dr SR5 4WD Wgn	15590	18785
4 Dr STD Wgn	11305	13620
4 Dr STD 4WD Wgn	12284	14800

OPTIONS FOR 4RUNNER
Auto 4-Speed Transmission[Opt on STD,SR5 4WD Wgn] +450
Elite Pkg +550
Walnut Wood Dash +400
Air Conditioning[Opt on SR5,STD] +405
Aluminum/Alloy Wheels[Opt on SR5,STD] +165
Anti-Lock Brakes[Opt on SR5,STD] +295
Compact Disc W/fm/tape +240
Cruise Control[Opt on SR5,STD] +105
Keyless Entry System +100
Leather Seats[Opt on SR5,STD] +385
Locking Differential +145
Luggage Rack +80
Power Door Locks[Opt on STD] +115
Power Moonroof +430
Power Windows[Opt on SR5,STD] +120
Rear Heater +100
Running Boards[Opt on SR5,STD] +190

AVALON 1997

More power, more torque, and added standard features make the Avalon one of the most appealing full-sized sedans

RATINGS (SCALE OF 1-10)

Overall	Safety	Reliability	Performance	Comfort	Value
8.2	8	8.7	8.2	8.4	7.9

Category D
4 Dr XL Sdn	12210	14710
4 Dr XLS Sdn	13565	16345

OPTIONS FOR AVALON
Power Bench Seat +410
Aluminum/Alloy Wheels[Opt on XL] +230
Compact Disc W/fm/tape +400
Dual Power Seats[Opt on XL] +420
Leather Seats +545
Power Moonroof +415
Traction Control System +305

CAMRY 1997

Toyota plays the market conservatively with the all-new Camry, giving consumers exactly what they want; a roomy, attractive, feature-laden car with available V6 performance and the promise of excellent reliability as well as resale value. The Camry is the new standard for midsized sedans.

RATINGS (SCALE OF 1-10)

Overall	Safety	Reliability	Performance	Comfort	Value
7.5	7.4	8.2	8.6	8.1	5

Category D
4 Dr CE Sdn	8575	10330
4 Dr CE V6 Sdn	9650	11625
4 Dr LE Sdn	10595	12765
4 Dr LE V6 Sdn	11540	13905
4 Dr XLE Sdn	12220	14725
4 Dr XLE V6 Sdn	13149	15845

OPTIONS FOR CAMRY
Auto 4-Speed Transmission[Opt on CE] +400
6-disc CD Autochanger +400
Elite Pkg +665
Air Conditioning[Opt on CE,CE V6] +420
Aluminum/Alloy Wheels[Std on XLE,XLE V6] +230
Anti-Lock Brakes[Opt on CE] +450
Child Seat (1) +75
Compact Disc W/fm/tape +400
Cruise Control[Opt on CE,CE V6] +120
Keyless Entry System[Std on XLE,XLE V6] +155
Leather Seats +545
Power Door Locks[Opt on CE,CE V6] +135
Power Moonroof +415
Power Windows[Opt on CE,CE V6] +135
Traction Control System +305

CELICA 1997

GT Coupe is gone, and Fiesta Blue Metallic can be specified for cars equipped with black sport cloth interior.

RATINGS (SCALE OF 1-10)

Overall	Safety	Reliability	Performance	Comfort	Value
N/A	N/A	9.5	8.2	7.6	4.3

Category F
2 Dr GT Conv	13110	15795
2 Dr GT Hbk	11815	14235

Don't forget to refer to the Mileage Adjustment Table at the back of this book!

Model Description	Trade-in Value	Market Value
2 Dr GT Limited Edit. Conv	14100	16990
2 Dr ST Cpe	9740	11735
2 Dr ST Hbk	10435	12570
2 Dr ST Limited Edit. Hbk	11195	13490

OPTIONS FOR CELICA
Auto 4-Speed Transmission +405
Air Conditioning[Opt on GT,ST] +415
Aluminum/Alloy Wheels[Opt on GT,ST] +150
Anti-Lock Brakes +335
Compact Disc W/fm/tape[Opt on GT] +250
Cruise Control[Opt on GT,ST] +105
Leather Seats +325
Power Door Locks[Opt on ST] +100
Power Moonroof +320
Power Windows[Opt on ST] +110
Premium Sound System +185
Sport Suspension +90

COROLLA   1997
The Classic Edition (CE) debuts and the slow-selling DX Wagon gets the ax.

RATINGS (SCALE OF 1-10)

Overall	Safety	Reliability	Performance	Comfort	Value
7.1	6.5	8.9	7.4	8.1	4.4

Category E

4 Dr CE Sdn	7210	8790
4 Dr DX Sdn	7280	8875
4 Dr STD Sdn	6870	8380

OPTIONS FOR COROLLA
Auto 3-Speed Transmission +250
Auto 4-Speed Transmission +400
Air Conditioning[Std on CE] +405
Aluminum/Alloy Wheels +165
Anti-Lock Brakes +335
Child Seat (1) +55
Compact Disc W/fm/tape +290
Cruise Control +110
Power Door Locks[Opt on DX] +120
Power Sunroof +305
Power Windows[Opt on DX] +130

LAND CRUISER   1997
The Black Package is discontinued, but black paint becomes an available color choice. A 40th-Anniversary Package lets buyers slather their Cruiser in leather and choose one of two unique paint schemes.

Category G

4 Dr 40th Anniv. Ltd. 4WD Wgn	25895	31200
4 Dr STD 4WD Wgn	22775	27440

OPTIONS FOR LAND CRUISER
Burlwood Dash +400
Convenience Pkg +400
Leather Trim Pkg +1390
Third Seat Pkg +600

Aluminum/Alloy Wheels +165
Compact Disc Changer +255
Compact Disc W/fm/tape +240
Dual Power Seats[Opt on STD] +190
Keyless Entry System +100
Leather Seats[Opt on STD] +385
Locking Differential +145
Luggage Rack +80
Power Moonroof +430
Running Boards +190
Third Seat[Opt on STD] +355

PASEO   1997
For some reason, Toyota product planners took a look at the cheap convertible market and thought, "Hmmm...a convertible Tercel with fancy styling will just kill the Sunfire SE Convertible's sales and make us rich." Coupes get dual-visor vanity mirrors, fresh door trim and rotary-heater controls.

RATINGS (SCALE OF 1-10)

Overall	Safety	Reliability	Performance	Comfort	Value
6.8	6.6	9.5	7	6.9	4.2

Category E

2 Dr STD Conv	8320	10150
2 Dr STD Cpe	7340	8955

OPTIONS FOR PASEO
Auto 4-Speed Transmission +400
AM/FM Compact Disc Player +225
Air Conditioning +405
Aluminum/Alloy Wheels +165
Anti-Lock Brakes +335
Cruise Control +110
Flip-Up Sunroof +170
Power Door Locks +120
Power Windows +130

PREVIA   1997

RATINGS (SCALE OF 1-10)

Overall	Safety	Reliability	Performance	Comfort	Value
7.4	6.7	8.7	7.7	7.3	6.7

Category G

2 Dr DX Sprchgd Pass. Van	11645	14030
2 Dr DX Sprchgd 4WD Pass. Van	12525	15090
2 Dr LE Sprchgd Pass. Van	13980	16845
2 Dr LE Sprchgd 4WD Pass. Van	14255	17175

OPTIONS FOR PREVIA
Aluminum/Alloy Wheels +165
Anti-Lock Brakes +295
Captain Chairs (4) +310
Compact Disc W/fm/tape +240
Cruise Control[Opt on DX] +105
Dual Air Conditioning[Opt on DX] +470
Keyless Entry System +100
Leather Seats +385

Don't forget to refer to the Mileage Adjustment Table at the back of this book!

Luggage Rack +80
Power Door Locks[Opt on DX] +115
Power Moonroof +430
Power Windows[Opt on DX] +120
Premium Sound System +170
Running Boards +190

RAV4 1997

New fabric debuts on the two-door RAV, and a sunroof is finally available on the four-door. Improvements have also been made by using sound deadening material in the dash area, reducing engine noise in the passenger compartment.

RATINGS (SCALE OF 1-10)

Overall	Safety	Reliability	Performance	Comfort	Value
N/A	6.8	9.2	7	6.4	N/A

Category G

2 Dr STD Utility	9860	11880
2 Dr STD 4WD Utility	10465	12610
4 Dr STD Wgn	10430	12565
4 Dr STD 4WD Wgn	11145	13425

OPTIONS FOR RAV4

Auto 4-Speed Transmission +525
AM/FM Compact Disc Player +160
Air Conditioning +405
Aluminum/Alloy Wheels +165
Anti-Lock Brakes +295
Cruise Control +105
Keyless Entry System +100
Leather Seats +385
Power Door Locks +115
Power Moonroof +430
Power Windows +120
Tilt Steering Wheel +85

SUPRA 1997

Turbo models get the six-speed manual transmission back, but the bigger news details massive price cuts. Turbos with automatics are $12,000 dollars less expensive than last year! All Supras commemorate the nameplate's 15th anniversary with a rear spoiler, premium sound and special badging. Despite price cuts, equipment levels are enhanced across the board.

Category F

2 Dr STD Hbk	19850	23915
2 Dr STD Turbo Hbk	22205	26750

OPTIONS FOR SUPRA

6-Speed Transmission +855
Auto 4-Speed Transmission[Std on Turbo] +450
Sport Roof +1855
Compact Disc Changer +320
Compact Disc W/fm/tape[Std on Turbo] +250
Keyless Entry System +90

Leather Seats[Std on Turbo] +325
Power Drivers Seat[Std on Turbo] +120

T100 1997

Two new colors debut and the optional wheel and tire packages are larger this year. Standard models get radio pre-wiring, midlevel models get fabric door trim panels, and SR5 models get chrome wheel arches.

RATINGS (SCALE OF 1-10)

Overall	Safety	Reliability	Performance	Comfort	Value
N/A	6.4	9.2	7	7.5	N/A

Category H

2 Dr SR5 Ext Cab SB	12035	14330
2 Dr SR5 4WD Ext Cab SB	13689	16300
2 Dr STD Ext Cab SB	11000	13095
2 Dr STD 4WD Ext Cab SB	12265	14600
2 Dr STD Std Cab LB	7805	9290

OPTIONS FOR T100

Auto 4-Speed Transmission +450
AM/FM Compact Disc Player +155
Air Conditioning +400
Aluminum/Alloy Wheels +155
Anti-Lock Brakes +245
Bed Liner +110
Chrome Wheels +145
Cruise Control +95
Keyless Entry System +85
Power Door Locks +95
Power Windows +95
Premium Sound System +190
Rear Step Bumper +75
Running Boards +170
Velour/Cloth Seats[Opt on Std Cab] +65

TACOMA 1997

The 1997 Tacoma receives several new value packages that make optioning the truck easier. A locking rear-wheel differential is now available on all 4WD models. Bucket seats can be had on all Xtracab Tacomas this year; not just the SR5. Two-wheel drive models have new headlamps and a new grille that make the vehicle look more like the T100.

RATINGS (SCALE OF 1-10)

Overall	Safety	Reliability	Performance	Comfort	Value
N/A	5.7	9.4	7.2	7	N/A

Category G

2 Dr SR5 4WD Ext Cab SB	11985	14440
2 Dr STD Ext Cab SB	8295	9995
2 Dr STD 4WD Ext Cab SB	10585	12755
2 Dr STD Std Cab SB	7435	8955
2 Dr STD 4WD Std Cab SB	9810	11820
2 Dr V6 Ext Cab SB	9510	11455

Don't forget to refer to the Mileage Adjustment Table at the back of this book!

Model Description	Trade-in Value	Market Value
2 Dr V6 4WD Ext Cab SB	11115	13390
2 Dr V6 4WD Std Cab SB	10610	12785

OPTIONS FOR TACOMA

Auto 4-Speed Transmission +425
Air Conditioning +405
Aluminum/Alloy Wheels[Std on SR5] +165
Anti-Lock Brakes +295
Auto Locking Hubs (4WD)[Std on SR5] +125
Bed Liner +140
Compact Disc W/fm/tape +240
Cruise Control +105
Power Door Locks +115
Power Steering[Std on SR5,V6,4WD] +140
Power Windows +120
Rear Step Bumper[Std on V6,Ext Cab,4WD] +70
Running Boards +190

TERCEL   1997

Standard and DX trim levels are shelved in favor of CE trim for all Tercels. All models have upgraded cloth trim, new rotary heater controls, a trip odometer, and a storage console. New wheelcovers adorn standard 14-inch wheels.

RATINGS (SCALE OF 1-10)

Overall	Safety	Reliability	Performance	Comfort	Value
6.9	6.1	9.2	6.6	7	5.5

Category E

2 Dr CE Sdn	5680	6925
4 Dr CE Sdn	5965	7275
2 Dr Limited Edition Sdn	6025	7350

OPTIONS FOR TERCEL

Auto 3-Speed Transmission +255
Auto 4-Speed Transmission +350
AM/FM Compact Disc Player +225
Air Conditioning +405
Anti-Lock Brakes +335
Keyless Entry System +80
Power Door Locks +120
Power Steering +125
Power Windows +130

1996 TOYOTA

4RUNNER   1996

A cool new 4Runner with a potent V6, big bruiser styling, and lots more interior room debuts. This thing annihilates most compact off-road vehicles.

RATINGS (SCALE OF 1-10)

Overall	Safety	Reliability	Performance	Comfort	Value
6.9	7.7	8.8	6.6	6.9	4.5

Category G

4 Dr Limited 4WD Wgn	17620	21485
4 Dr SR5 Wgn	13500	16465
4 Dr SR5 4WD Wgn	14439	17610
4 Dr STD Wgn	10580	12900
4 Dr STD 4WD Wgn	11470	13985

OPTIONS FOR 4RUNNER

Auto 4-Speed Transmission[Opt on STD,SR5 4WD Wgn] +365
Walnut Wood Dash +320
Air Conditioning[Opt on SR5,STD] +330
Aluminum/Alloy Wheels[Opt on SR5,STD] +135
Anti-Lock Brakes[Opt on STD] +245
Compact Disc W/fm/tape +195
Cruise Control[Opt on SR5,STD] +85
Keyless Entry System +80
Leather Seats[Opt on SR5] +315 *
Locking Differential +120
Luggage Rack +65
Power Door Locks[Opt on STD] +95
Power Moonroof +350
Power Windows[Opt on 2WD] +95
Rear Heater +80
Running Boards +155
Trailer Hitch +115

AVALON   1996

No changes as cloud car floats into its second year.

RATINGS (SCALE OF 1-10)

Overall	Safety	Reliability	Performance	Comfort	Value
8.1	7.6	8.3	8.2	8.4	7.8

Category D

4 Dr XL Sdn	11155	13770
4 Dr XLS Sdn	12205	15070

OPTIONS FOR AVALON

Power Bench Seat +325
Aluminum/Alloy Wheels[Opt on XL] +190
Anti-Lock Brakes[Opt on XL] +365
Compact Disc W/fm/tape +325
Dual Power Seats[Opt on XL] +340
Leather Seats +445
Power Moonroof +340
Premium Sound System[Opt on XL] +150

CAMRY   1996

The 1996 Camry remains virtually unchanged from last year's model. Minor engine adjustments mean that the four-cylinder is fully compliant with all On-Board Diagnostic standards, and is now certified as a Transitional Low Emission Vehicle powerplant. Additionally, the interior of the DX line gets a new seat fabric, the LE Sedan is available with a leather package, and the Wagon can now be ordered with power-operated driver and passenger seats.

Don't forget to refer to the Mileage Adjustment Table at the back of this book!

TOYOTA 96

Model Description	Trade-in Value	Market Value	Model Description	Trade-in Value	Market Value

RATINGS (SCALE OF 1-10)

Overall	Safety	Reliability	Performance	Comfort	Value
7.6	6.6	8.6	8.6	8.4	5.9

Category D

Model Description	Trade-in Value	Market Value
4 Dr Collector Sdn	11540	14245
2 Dr DX Cpe	7365	9095
4 Dr DX Sdn	7525	9290
2 Dr LE Cpe	9080	11210
4 Dr LE Sdn	9305	11490
4 Dr LE Wgn	9590	11840
2 Dr LE V6 Cpe	9560	11805
4 Dr LE V6 Sdn	9760	12050
4 Dr LE V6 Wgn	10150	12530
2 Dr SE Cpe	10805	13340
4 Dr SE Sdn	11160	13780
4 Dr XLE Sdn	11085	13685
4 Dr XLE V6 Sdn	11270	13915

OPTIONS FOR CAMRY

Auto 4-Speed Transmission[Opt on DX] +325
Air Conditioning[Opt on DX] +345
Anti-Lock Brakes[Std on XLE,XLE V6] +365
Compact Disc W/fm/tape[Std on Collector] +325
Cruise Control[Opt on DX] +100
Keyless Entry System +125
Leather Seats[Std on Collector] +445
Power Door Locks[Opt on DX] +110
Power Drivers Seat[Opt on LE,LE V6] +120
Power Moonroof +340
Power Passenger Seat +150
Power Windows[Opt on DX] +110
Premium Sound System +150

CELICA   1996

Minor front end freshening doesn't help much. A new spoiler, new wheelcovers, two new colors, and revised fabrics debut this year.

RATINGS (SCALE OF 1-10)

Overall	Safety	Reliability	Performance	Comfort	Value
N/A	N/A	9.2	8.2	7.6	4.3

Category F

Model Description	Trade-in Value	Market Value
2 Dr GT Conv	11635	14365
2 Dr GT Cpe	9435	11650
2 Dr GT Hbk	10220	12620
2 Dr GT 25th Anniv. Conv	12375	15280
2 Dr ST Cpe	8750	10805
2 Dr ST Hbk	9035	11155
2 Dr ST 25th Anniv. Hbk	10240	12640

OPTIONS FOR CELICA

Auto 4-Speed Transmission +325
Leather Sport Pkg +430
Air Conditioning[Opt on GT,ST] +340
Anti-Lock Brakes +275

Compact Disc W/fm/tape[Opt on GT] +205
Cruise Control[Opt on GT,ST] +85
Keyless Entry System +70
Leather Seats +265
Power Door Locks[Opt on ST] +80
Power Moonroof[Opt on GT,ST] +265
Power Windows[Opt on ST] +90
Premium Sound System +150
Sport Suspension +75

COROLLA   1996

The Toyota Corolla heads into 1996 with a redesigned front and rear fascia, three new colors, new wheel covers, an optional integrated child seat, and a revised interior. Additionally, the five-speed manual transmission has been revised for a better feel and more positive gear engagement.

RATINGS (SCALE OF 1-10)

Overall	Safety	Reliability	Performance	Comfort	Value
7.3	6.5	9.2	7.4	8.1	5.1

Category E

Model Description	Trade-in Value	Market Value
4 Dr DX Sdn	6450	8065
4 Dr DX Wgn	6805	8505
4 Dr STD Sdn	6175	7720

OPTIONS FOR COROLLA

Auto 3-Speed Transmission +195
Auto 4-Speed Transmission +325
Air Conditioning +330
Anti-Lock Brakes +275
Child Seat (1) +45
Cruise Control +90
Keyless Entry System +65
Power Door Locks +100
Power Sunroof +250
Power Windows +105

LAND CRUISER   1996

The Black Paint Package debuts, for those who enjoy spending long hours maintaining the finish on their truck.

Category G

Model Description	Trade-in Value	Market Value
4 Dr STD 4WD Wgn	19450	23720

OPTIONS FOR LAND CRUISER

Burlwood Dash +320
Leather Trim Pkg +1240
Third Seat Pkg +610
Compact Disc Changer +210
Compact Disc W/fm/tape +195
Dual Power Seats +155
Keyless Entry System +80
Leather Seats +315
Power Moonroof +350
Running Boards +155
Third Seat +290

TOYOTA 96

Model Description	Trade-in Value	Market Value	Model Description	Trade-in Value	Market Value

PASEO 1996

All new Paseo looks like last year's car, but is much improved. It now meets 1997 passenger car safety standards, and has a split-fold rear seat.

RATINGS (SCALE OF 1-10)

Overall	Safety	Reliability	Performance	Comfort	Value
6.8	6.6	9.4	7	6.9	4.2

Category E
2 Dr STD Cpe	6200	7755

OPTIONS FOR PASEO

Auto 4-Speed Transmission +325
AM/FM Stereo Tape +125
Air Conditioning +330
Rear Spoiler +85
Rear Window Defroster +65

PREVIA 1996

Supercharged engines for everyone!

RATINGS (SCALE OF 1-10)

Overall	Safety	Reliability	Performance	Comfort	Value
7.6	6.8	8.8	7.7	7.3	7.2

Category G
2 Dr DX Sprchgd Pass. Van	9720	11855
2 Dr DX Sprchgd 4WD Pass. Van	11185	13645
2 Dr LE Sprchgd Pass. Van	12915	15750
2 Dr LE Sprchgd 4WD Pass. Van	13845	16885

OPTIONS FOR PREVIA

Aluminum/Alloy Wheels +135
Anti-Lock Brakes +245
Captain Chairs (4) +255
Compact Disc W/fm/tape +195
Cruise Control[Opt on DX] +85
Dual Air Conditioning[Opt on DX] +385
Keyless Entry System +80
Leather Seats +315
Luggage Rack +65
Power Door Locks[Opt on DX] +95
Power Moonroof +350
Power Windows[Opt on DX] +95
Premium Sound System +140
Running Boards +155

RAV4 1996

A cool new mini-ute based on passenger car mechanicals debuts this year. Available as a two-door or four-door, the RAV4 has a gutsy powerplant and cute-as-can-be styling. We like the RAV, but think that the Jeep Cherokee offers more bang-for-the-buck.

RATINGS (SCALE OF 1-10)

Overall	Safety	Reliability	Performance	Comfort	Value
N/A	N/A	9	7	6.4	N/A

Category G
2 Dr STD Utility	8610	10500
2 Dr STD 4WD Utility	9285	11325
4 Dr STD Wgn	9125	11130
4 Dr STD 4WD Wgn	9985	12175

OPTIONS FOR RAV4

Auto 4-Speed Transmission +425
AM/FM Compact Disc Player +135
Air Conditioning +330
Aluminum/Alloy Wheels +135
Anti-Lock Brakes +245
Cruise Control +85
Keyless Entry System +80
Luggage Rack +65
Power Door Locks +95
Power Windows +95

SUPRA 1996

Manual transmission Turbo models are history, thanks to stringent emission regulations. Don't worry, they're back for 1997.

Category F
2 Dr STD Hbk	16500	20370
2 Dr STD Turbo Hbk	19940	24615

OPTIONS FOR SUPRA

Auto 4-Speed Transmission[Std on Turbo] +365
Sport Roof +1010
Compact Disc Changer +260
Compact Disc W/fm/tape +205
Dual Power Seats +345
Keyless Entry System +70
Leather Seats +265
Limited Slip Diff[Std on Turbo] +140

T100 1996

Essentially a carryover, but DX models are scrapped. Strangely, regular cabs can't be equipped with cruise control anymore. A new shade of red is offered, and tan interiors are offered in a wider variety of trucks.

RATINGS (SCALE OF 1-10)

Overall	Safety	Reliability	Performance	Comfort	Value
N/A	6.5	8.7	7	7.5	N/A

Category H
2 Dr SR5 Ext Cab SB	10175	12260
2 Dr SR5 4WD Ext Cab SB	11805	14225
2 Dr STD Ext Cab SB	8910	10735
2 Dr STD 4WD Ext Cab SB	10265	12365
2 Dr STD Std Cab LB	7240	8725

OPTIONS FOR T100

Auto 4-Speed Transmission +360
AM/FM Compact Disc Player +125
Air Conditioning +330
Aluminum/Alloy Wheels +125

Don't forget to refer to the Mileage Adjustment Table at the back of this book!

Model Description	Trade-in Value	Market Value	Model Description	Trade-in Value	Market Value

Anti-Lock Brakes +200
Bed Liner +90
Chrome Wheels +120
Cruise Control +75
Keyless Entry System +70
Power Door Locks +75
Power Windows +75
Premium Sound System +155
Rear Step Bumper +60
Running Boards +140
Velour/Cloth Seats[Opt on Std Cab] +55

TACOMA   1996

Regular Cab 4WD models can be equipped with a new Off-Road Package.

RATINGS (SCALE OF 1-10)

Overall	Safety	Reliability	Performance	Comfort	Value
N/A	5.7	8.8	7.2	7	N/A

Category G		
2 Dr SR5 4WD Ext Cab SB	10945	13345
2 Dr STD Ext Cab SB	7395	9020
2 Dr STD 4WD Ext Cab SB	9875	12040
2 Dr STD Std Cab SB	6565	8005
2 Dr STD 4WD Std Cab SB	9050	11035
2 Dr V6 Ext Cab SB	8665	10570
2 Dr V6 4WD Ext Cab SB	10210	12450
2 Dr V6 4WD Std Cab SB	9350	11405

OPTIONS FOR TACOMA

Auto 4-Speed Transmission +340
Off Road Pkg +545
Wheel Pkg +395
AM/FM Compact Disc Player +135
Air Conditioning +330
Aluminum/Alloy Wheels +135
Anti-Lock Brakes +245
Auto Locking Hubs (4WD)[Std on SR5] +105
Bed Liner +115
Cruise Control +85
Keyless Entry System +80
Power Door Locks +95
Power Steering[Std on SR5,V6,4WD] +115
Power Windows +95
Rear Step Bumper +60
Running Boards +155

TERCEL   1996

Base cars can be equipped with fabric seats, and a ... ha,ha,ha ... "Sports" package is available.

RATINGS (SCALE OF 1-10)

Overall	Safety	Reliability	Performance	Comfort	Value
6.8	6.1	8.9	6.6	7	5.4

Category E		
2 Dr DX Sdn	5245	6555
4 Dr DX Sdn	5555	6945
2 Dr STD Sdn	4740	5925

OPTIONS FOR TERCEL

Auto 3-Speed Transmission +280
Auto 4-Speed Transmission +280
AM/FM Compact Disc Player +185
Air Conditioning +330
Anti-Lock Brakes +275
Electric Sunroof +165
Keyless Entry System +65
Power Door Locks +100
Power Steering +105
Power Windows +105
Rear Window Defroster +65

1995 TOYOTA

4RUNNER   1995

V6 models get new tape stripes. Whoo-hoo!

RATINGS (SCALE OF 1-10)

Overall	Safety	Reliability	Performance	Comfort	Value
6.3	3.9	9.1	7	7	4.4

Category G		
4 Dr Limited 4WD Wgn	12490	15420
4 Dr SR5 Wgn	9965	12300
4 Dr SR5 4WD Wgn	10925	13485
4 Dr SR5 V6 4WD Wgn	11745	14500

OPTIONS FOR 4RUNNER

Auto 4-Speed Transmission[Std on 2WD] +345
Value Pkg +315
Air Conditioning[Std on Limited] +270
Anti-Lock Brakes +200
Compact Disc W/fm/tape +160
Cruise Control[Std on Limited] +70
Leather Seats[Opt on SR5 V6] +255
Luggage Rack[Std on Limited] +50
Power Door Locks[Std on Limited] +75
Power Moonroof +290
Power Windows[Opt on SR5 V6,2WD] +80
Premium Sound System +115
Rear Heater +65
Running Boards +130

AVALON   1995

Marginally larger than the Camry, the Avalon is a true six-passenger sedan set to conquer Buick LeSabre and Ford Crown Victoria. Dual airbags, power windows, power mirrors, and power locks are standard. ABS is optional. Mechanicals are mostly Camry-based.

TOYOTA 95

Model Description	Trade-in Value	Market Value	Model Description	Trade-in Value	Market Value

RATINGS (SCALE OF 1-10)

Overall	Safety	Reliability	Performance	Comfort	Value
8	8.3	8.5	8.2	8.4	6.6

Category D
4 Dr XL Sdn	9110	11530
4 Dr XLS Sdn	10075	12750

OPTIONS FOR AVALON

Power Bench Seat +260
Aluminum/Alloy Wheels[Opt on XL] +155
Anti-Lock Brakes[Opt on XL] +300
Compact Disc W/fm/tape +265
Dual Power Seats +280
Leather Seats +365
Power Moonroof +275
Premium Sound System[Opt on XL] +125

CAMRY   1995

Front and rear styling is updated, ABS is standard on XLE model, and Camry now meets 1997 side-impact protection standards. DX wagon dumped from lineup.

RATINGS (SCALE OF 1-10)

Overall	Safety	Reliability	Performance	Comfort	Value
7.9	7.4	9.1	8.6	8.4	6.1

Category D
2 Dr DX Cpe	6430	8140
4 Dr DX Sdn	6630	8390
2 Dr LE Cpe	7420	9395
4 Dr LE Sdn	7585	9600
4 Dr LE Wgn	7810	9885
2 Dr LE V6 Cpe	8115	10275
4 Dr LE V6 Sdn	8285	10490
4 Dr LE V6 Wgn	8735	11060
2 Dr SE Cpe	8485	10740
4 Dr SE Sdn	8690	11000
4 Dr XLE Sdn	8820	11165
4 Dr XLE V6 Sdn	9555	12095

OPTIONS FOR CAMRY

Auto 4-Speed Transmission[Opt on DX] +265
Elite Pkg +420
Air Conditioning[Opt on DX] +280
Anti-Lock Brakes[Std on XLE,XLE V6] +300
Compact Disc W/fm/tape +265
Cruise Control[Opt on DX] +80
Leather Seats +365
Power Door Locks[Opt on DX] +90
Power Drivers Seat[Std on XLE,XLE V6] +100
Power Moonroof +275
Power Passenger Seat +125
Power Windows[Opt on DX] +90
Premium Sound System +125

CELICA   1995

GT convertible returns to lineup, available in red, white, blue or black.

RATINGS (SCALE OF 1-10)

Overall	Safety	Reliability	Performance	Comfort	Value
N/A	N/A	8.9	8.2	7.6	4.3

Category F
2 Dr GT Conv	10210	12760
2 Dr GT Cpe	8470	10590
2 Dr GT Hbk	9160	11450
2 Dr ST Cpe	7230	9040
2 Dr ST Hbk	7795	9745

OPTIONS FOR CELICA

Auto 4-Speed Transmission +265
Air Conditioning +275
Anti-Lock Brakes +225
Compact Disc W/fm/tape +165
Cruise Control +70
Leather Seats +215
Power Door Locks[Opt on ST] +65
Power Moonroof +215
Power Windows[Opt on ST] +75
Premium Sound System +125
Sport Suspension +60

COROLLA   1995

1.8-liter engine loses ten horsepower to meet stricter emissions regulations. Torque is up, though. DX models get new interior fabric.

RATINGS (SCALE OF 1-10)

Overall	Safety	Reliability	Performance	Comfort	Value
7.1	7	8.1	7.4	8.1	5.1

Category E
4 Dr DX Sdn	5300	6880
4 Dr DX Wgn	5845	7590
4 Dr LE Sdn	6545	8500
4 Dr STD Sdn	4985	6475

OPTIONS FOR COROLLA

Auto 3-Speed Transmission +165
Auto 4-Speed Transmission[Opt on DX] +215
AM/FM Compact Disc Player +150
Air Conditioning[Std on LE] +270
Aluminum/Alloy Wheels +110
Anti-Lock Brakes +225
Cruise Control[Opt on DX] +75
Power Door Locks[Opt on DX] +80
Power Sunroof +205
Power Windows[Opt on DX] +85
Premium Sound System +110

TOYOTA 95

Model Description	Trade-in Value	Market Value	Model Description	Trade-in Value	Market Value

LAND CRUISER 1995

Redesigned dashboard carries dual airbags, and ABS is now standard. Revised grille carries Toyota logo rather than nameplate.

Category G

4 Dr STD 4WD Wgn	17410	21495

OPTIONS FOR LAND CRUISER

Leather Trim Pkg +775
Third Seat Pkg +365
Compact Disc Changer +170
Compact Disc W/fm/tape +160
Dual Power Seats +125
Leather Seats +255
Locking Differential +95
Luggage Rack +50
Power Moonroof +290
Running Boards +130
Third Seat +240

PASEO 1995

Several states with strict emissions laws get detuned Paseo for 1995.

RATINGS (SCALE OF 1-10)

Overall	Safety	Reliability	Performance	Comfort	Value
6.8	5.9	9.3	7.8	7.1	4.1

Category E

2 Dr STD Cpe	5155	6695

OPTIONS FOR PASEO

Auto 4-Speed Transmission +265
AM/FM Stereo Tape +100
Air Conditioning +270

PICKUP 1995

No changes.

HALF TON

Category G

2 Dr DX Ext Cab SB	7025	8675
2 Dr DX 4WD Ext Cab SB	8600	10615
2 Dr DX Std Cab SB	5355	6610
2 Dr DX 4WD Std Cab SB	7300	9010
2 Dr DX V6 Ext Cab SB	7555	9330
2 Dr DX V6 4WD Ext Cab SB	9075	11205
2 Dr DX V6 4WD Std Cab SB	7835	9675
2 Dr SR5 Ext Cab SB	8420	10390
2 Dr SR5 4WD Ext Cab SB	9560	11800
2 Dr STD Std Cab SB	4930	6090

OPTIONS FOR PICKUP

Auto 4-Speed Transmission +315
AM/FM Stereo Tape +75
Air Conditioning +270
Aluminum/Alloy Wheels +110

Anti-Lock Brakes +200
Auto Locking Hubs (4WD) +85
Bed Liner +95
Chrome Wheels +55
Cruise Control +70
Intermittent Wipers[Opt on DX] +30
Power Door Locks +75
Power Steering[Opt on DX,STD] +95
Power Windows +80
Premium Sound System +115
Rear Step Bumper +50
Running Boards +130

PREVIA 1995

Seatback map pockets and an illuminated driver's visor vanity mirror are standard on all models.

RATINGS (SCALE OF 1-10)

Overall	Safety	Reliability	Performance	Comfort	Value
7.7	7.4	8.4	7.7	7.3	7.6

Category G

2 Dr DX Pass. Van	8675	10710
2 Dr DX Sprchgd Pass. Van	9065	11195
2 Dr DX 4WD Pass. Van	9540	11775
2 Dr DX Sprchgd 4WD Pass. Van	9785	12080
2 Dr LE Pass. Van	10635	13130
2 Dr LE Sprchgd Pass. Van	10840	13385
2 Dr LE 4WD Pass. Van	11135	13750
2 Dr LE Sprchgd 4WD Pass. Van	12145	14990

OPTIONS FOR PREVIA

Dual Moonroofs +450
Aluminum/Alloy Wheels +110
Anti-Lock Brakes +200
Captain Chairs (2) +170
Compact Disc W/fm/tape +160
Cruise Control[Opt on DX] +70
Dual Air Conditioning[Opt on DX] +315
Leather Seats +255
Luggage Rack +50
Power Door Locks[Opt on DX] +75
Power Moonroof +290
Power Windows[Opt on DX] +80
Premium Sound System +115
Running Boards +130

SUPRA 1995

No changes.

Category F

2 Dr STD Hbk	15510	19385
2 Dr STD Turbo Hbk	17565	21955

OPTIONS FOR SUPRA

Auto 4-Speed Transmission +345
Sport Roof +380
Compact Disc W/fm/tape +165
Leather Seats +215

Don't forget to refer to the Mileage Adjustment Table at the back of this book!

Model Description	Trade-in Value	Market Value

Limited Slip Diff[Std on Turbo] +115
Power Drivers Seat[Std on Turbo] +80

T100   1995

The 1995 T100 adds an extended-cab body style to fill out this midsized truck's lineup. A much more powerful DOHC V6 engine is introduced this year as are four-wheel antilock brakes. The antilock brakes are available only on DX and Xtracab models equipped V6 engine.

RATINGS (SCALE OF 1-10)

Overall	Safety	Reliability	Performance	Comfort	Value
N/A	7.1	9	7	7.5	N/A

Category H

Model	Trade-in	Market
2 Dr DX Ext Cab SB	8150	9940
2 Dr DX 4WD Ext Cab SB	9320	11365
2 Dr DX Std Cab LB	7340	8950
2 Dr DX 4WD Std Cab LB	8185	9980
2 Dr DX 1 Ton Std Cab LB	7710	9405
2 Dr SR5 Ext Cab SB	8510	10375
2 Dr SR5 4WD Ext Cab SB	10000	12195
2 Dr STD Std Cab LB	5730	6985
2 Dr V6 Std Cab LB	6655	8115

OPTIONS FOR T100

Auto 4-Speed Transmission +295
AM/FM Compact Disc Player +105
Air Conditioning +270
Aluminum/Alloy Wheels +105
Anti-Lock Brakes +165
Bed Liner +75
Chrome Wheels +100
Cruise Control +60
Power Door Locks +60
Power Windows +65
Premium Sound System +130
Rear Step Bumper +50
Running Boards +115
Velour/Cloth Seats[Opt on STD] +45

TACOMA   1995

Toyota puts a city on wheels. No. New compact pickup with a real name debuted in March, 1995. Optional four-wheel ABS, a driver airbag, and potent new engines are highlights of the new design. Rack and pinion steering replaces the old recirculating ball-type on the old truck. Front seatbelts are height adjustable.

RATINGS (SCALE OF 1-10)

Overall	Safety	Reliability	Performance	Comfort	Value
N/A	6.3	8.7	7.2	7	N/A

Category G

Model	Trade-in	Market
2 Dr SR5 4WD Ext Cab SB	10575	13055
2 Dr STD Ext Cab SB	7055	8710
2 Dr STD 4WD Ext Cab SB	8930	11025
2 Dr STD Std Cab SB	6210	7665
2 Dr STD 4WD Std Cab SB	8240	10175
2 Dr V6 Ext Cab SB	7470	9220
2 Dr V6 4WD Ext Cab SB	9585	11835
2 Dr V6 4WD Std Cab SB	8600	10620

OPTIONS FOR TACOMA

Auto 4-Speed Transmission +280
Wheel Pkg +325
AM/FM Stereo Tape +75
Air Conditioning +270
Anti-Lock Brakes +200
Auto Locking Hubs (4WD) +85
Bed Liner +95
Chrome Bumpers[Std on SR5] +55
Cruise Control +70
Power Door Locks +75
Power Windows +80

TERCEL   1995

Redesigned, but based on 1991-1994 generation. Coupe and sedan body styles. Coupe available in Standard and DX trim; sedan comes in DX flavor only. Dual airbags are standard. Height-adjustable seat belts are new. Car now meets 1997 side-impact standards. Engine is more powerful than before.

RATINGS (SCALE OF 1-10)

Overall	Safety	Reliability	Performance	Comfort	Value
6.9	6.7	9	6.6	7	5.4

Category E

Model	Trade-in	Market
2 Dr DX Sdn	4300	5585
4 Dr DX Sdn	4585	5955
2 Dr STD Sdn	4005	5200

OPTIONS FOR TERCEL

Auto 3-Speed Transmission +230
Auto 4-Speed Transmission +235
AM/FM Compact Disc Player +150
Air Conditioning +270
Anti-Lock Brakes +225
Power Door Locks +80
Power Steering +85
Power Windows +85

1994 TOYOTA

4RUNNER   1994

Four-wheel ABS available on models with V6 engine. Side-door guard beams added. Air conditioners get CFC-free refrigerant. Optional leather can be had in new Oak color.

Don't forget to refer to the Mileage Adjustment Table at the back of this book!

TOYOTA 94

Model Description	Trade-in Value	Market Value	Model Description	Trade-in Value	Market Value

RATINGS (SCALE OF 1-10)

Overall	Safety	Reliability	Performance	Comfort	Value
6.1	3.9	8.5	7	7	4.2

Category G

4 Dr SR5 4WD Wgn	9625	11885
4 Dr SR5 V6 Wgn	9415	11625
4 Dr SR5 V6 4WD Wgn	9985	12325

OPTIONS FOR 4RUNNER

Auto 4-Speed Transmission[Std on 2WD] +290
Air Conditioning +220
Anti-Lock Brakes +160
Compact Disc W/fm/tape +130
Cruise Control +55
Leather Seats +210
Luggage Rack +45
Power Door Locks +65
Power Moonroof +235
Power Windows +65
Premium Sound System +95
Rear Heater +55
Running Boards +105

CAMRY   1994

Coupe body style debuts in DX, LE and SE form. All Camrys get passenger airbag. V6 engine is tweaked for more power. New fuzzy logic controls govern automatic transmission. SE models get standard power windows, locks, mirrors and cruise control.

RATINGS (SCALE OF 1-10)

Overall	Safety	Reliability	Performance	Comfort	Value
7.9	7.3	8.4	8.6	8.4	6.6

Category D

2 Dr DX Cpe	5300	6795
4 Dr DX Sdn	5485	7030
4 Dr DX Wgn	5590	7165
2 Dr LE Cpe	6180	7920
4 Dr LE Sdn	6390	8190
4 Dr LE Wgn	6495	8325
2 Dr LE V6 Cpe	6890	8835
4 Dr LE V6 Sdn	7140	9155
4 Dr LE V6 Wgn	7290	9345
2 Dr SE Cpe	6805	8725
4 Dr SE Sdn	7295	9355
4 Dr XLE Sdn	7450	9550
4 Dr XLE V6 Sdn	7735	9915

OPTIONS FOR CAMRY

Auto 4-Speed Transmission[Opt on DX Sdn,DX Cpe] +220
Elite Pkg +315
Air Conditioning[Opt on DX] +230
Anti-Lock Brakes +245
Compact Disc W/fm/tape +220
Cruise Control[Opt on DX] +65
Leather Seats +300

Power Door Locks[Opt on DX] +75
Power Drivers Seat[Opt on LE,LE V6] +80
Power Moonroof[Std on XLE,XLE V6] +225
Premium Sound System +100

CELICA   1994

Redesigned coupe and liftback debut. Turbocharged All-Trac is gone. ST and GT are only trim levels. Dual airbags are standard; ABS is optional. Power mirrors and driver's seat height adjuster are standard.

RATINGS (SCALE OF 1-10)

Overall	Safety	Reliability	Performance	Comfort	Value
N/A	N/A	9.3	8.2	7.6	5.2

Category F

2 Dr GT Cpe	6600	8460
2 Dr GT Hbk	7120	9130
2 Dr ST Cpe	5560	7130
2 Dr ST Hbk	6110	7835

OPTIONS FOR CELICA

Auto 4-Speed Transmission +220
Air Conditioning +225
Anti-Lock Brakes +185
Compact Disc W/fm/tape +135
Cruise Control +55
Leather Seats +175
Power Door Locks[Opt on ST] +55
Power Drivers Seat +65
Power Sunroof +185
Power Windows[Opt on ST] +60
Premium Sound System +100
Sport Suspension +50

COROLLA   1994

Passenger airbag added. Passenger seatbelts have automatic locking retractors. CFC-free refrigerant is added to air conditioning system.

RATINGS (SCALE OF 1-10)

Overall	Safety	Reliability	Performance	Comfort	Value
7.1	6.9	7.7	7.4	8.1	5.5

Category E

4 Dr DX Sdn	4510	6015
4 Dr DX Wgn	5035	6715
4 Dr LE Sdn	5330	7105
4 Dr STD Sdn	4145	5525

OPTIONS FOR COROLLA

Auto 3-Speed Transmission +135
Auto 4-Speed Transmission[Opt on DX] +220
AM/FM Compact Disc Player +125
Air Conditioning[Std on LE] +220
Aluminum/Alloy Wheels +90
Anti-Lock Brakes +180
Cruise Control[Opt on DX] +60
Power Door Locks[Opt on DX] +65

Don't forget to refer to the Mileage Adjustment Table at the back of this book!

TOYOTA 94

Model Description	Trade-in Value	Market Value	Model Description	Trade-in Value	Market Value

Power Sunroof +165
Power Windows[Opt on DX] +70
Premium Sound System +90

LAND CRUISER 1994

Standard sound system has nine speakers instead of five. Passenger seatbelts have automatic locking retractors.

Category G

4 Dr STD 4WD Wgn	16065	19835

OPTIONS FOR LAND CRUISER
Leather Trim Pkg +570
Third Rear Seat Pkg +380
Anti-Lock Brakes +160
Compact Disc W/fm/tape +130
Leather Seats +210
Limited Slip Diff +75
Luggage Rack +45
Power Drivers Seat +75
Power Moonroof +235
Power Passenger Seat +75
Running Boards +105
Third Seat +195

MR2 1994

Passenger airbag debuts. ABS made standard. Taillights are revised, and the suspension gets further fine-tuning. Base models get standard air conditioning (made standard last year on turbo), which is CFC-free on both models.

Category F

2 Dr STD Cpe	8355	10710

OPTIONS FOR MR2
Auto 4-Speed Transmission +220
Anti-Lock Brakes +185
Compact Disc W/fm/tape +135
Cruise Control[Std on Turbo] +55
Flip-Up Sunroof +110
Leather Seats +175
Limited Slip Diff +90
Power Door Locks[Std on Turbo] +55
Power Windows[Std on Turbo] +60
Premium Sound System[Std on Turbo] +100
T-Bar Roof[Std on Turbo] +235

PASEO 1994

CFC-free A/C added. Passenger seatbelts get automatic locking retractors.

RATINGS (SCALE OF 1-10)

Overall	Safety	Reliability	Performance	Comfort	Value
7.2	5.9	8.9	7.8	7.1	6.1

Category E

2 Dr STD Cpe	4210	5615

OPTIONS FOR PASEO
Auto 4-Speed Transmission +220
AM/FM Stereo Tape +80
Air Conditioning +220
Anti-Lock Brakes +180
Cruise Control +60
Pop-Up Moonroof +110

PICKUP 1994

Longbed models dropped. Side-door guard beams have been added.

RATINGS (SCALE OF 1-10)

Overall	Safety	Reliability	Performance	Comfort	Value
N/A	4.5	9.2	7.1	7.1	N/A

HALF TON

Category G

2 Dr DX Ext Cab SB	5880	7260
2 Dr DX 4WD Ext Cab SB	7800	9630
2 Dr DX Std Cab SB	4790	5915
2 Dr DX 4WD Std Cab SB	6385	7880
2 Dr DX V6 Ext Cab SB	6525	8055
2 Dr DX V6 4WD Ext Cab SB	8255	10190
2 Dr DX V6 4WD Std Cab SB	6725	8300
2 Dr SR5 V6 Ext Cab SB	7150	8825
2 Dr SR5 V6 4WD Ext Cab SB	8930	11025
2 Dr STD Std Cab SB	4760	5875

OPTIONS FOR PICKUP
Auto 4-Speed Transmission +265
AM/FM Stereo Tape +60
Air Conditioning +220
Anti-Lock Rear Brakes[Std on SR5 V6] +75
Auto Locking Hubs (4WD)[Opt on DX V6] +70
Bed Liner +75
Cruise Control +55
Power Door Locks +65
Power Steering[Opt on DX,STD] +75
Power Windows +65
Premium Sound System +95
Rear Jump Seats +60
Rear Step Bumper +40
Running Boards +105
Tilt Steering Wheel[Std on SR5 V6] +50

PREVIA 1994

Passenger airbag added. Supercharged engine included on S/C models. Manual transmission is dropped. CFC-free air conditioning is new. Leather is available on LE models. New front bucket seats are installed.

RATINGS (SCALE OF 1-10)

Overall	Safety	Reliability	Performance	Comfort	Value
7.6	7.4	8.5	7.7	7.3	7.2

Model Description	Trade-in Value	Market Value
Category G		
2 Dr DX Pass. Van	6780	8370
2 Dr DX 4WD Pass. Van	7580	9360
2 Dr LE Pass. Van	8165	10085
2 Dr LE 4WD Pass. Van	8735	10785

OPTIONS FOR PREVIA
Dual Moonroofs +425
Anti-Lock Brakes +160
Captain Chairs (2) +140
Compact Disc W/fm/tape +130
Cruise Control[Opt on DX] +55
Dual Air Conditioning[Opt on DX] +255
Leather Seats +210
Luggage Rack +45
Power Door Locks[Opt on DX] +65
Power Moonroof +235
Power Windows[Opt on DX] +65
Premium Sound System +95
Running Boards +105

SUPRA　　　　　　　　　　1994
Base model gets revised final-drive ratio for improved launch.

Category F

Model Description	Trade-in Value	Market Value
2 Dr STD Hbk	12730	16320
2 Dr STD Turbo Hbk	15770	20220

OPTIONS FOR SUPRA
Auto 4-Speed Transmission +245
Sport Roof +300
Compact Disc W/fm/tape +135
Leather Seats +175
Limited Slip Diff[Std on Turbo] +90

T100　　　　　　　　　　　1994
Driver airbag is added, and base models get four-cylinder engine. Side-door guard beams are installed, and beds get cargo tie-down hooks. Formerly standard rear ABS is now optional on base and DX trucks.

RATINGS (SCALE OF 1-10)

Overall	Safety	Reliability	Performance	Comfort	Value
N/A	6.9	8.9	6.8	7.5	N/A

Category H

Model Description	Trade-in Value	Market Value
2 Dr DX Std Cab LB	6140	7580
2 Dr DX 4WD Std Cab LB	7195	8880
2 Dr DX 1 Ton Std Cab LB	6540	8075
2 Dr SR5 Std Cab LB	6705	8280
2 Dr SR5 4WD Std Cab LB	7470	9225
2 Dr STD Std Cab LB	4965	6130

OPTIONS FOR T100
Auto 4-Speed Transmission +245
AM/FM Compact Disc Player +85
Air Conditioning +220
Anti-Lock Rear Brakes[Std on SR5] +70

Bed Liner +60
Cruise Control +50
Power Door Locks +50
Power Windows +50
Premium Sound System +105
Rear Step Bumper +40

TERCEL　　　　　　　　　　1994
CFC-free refrigerant added to optional A/C. Passenger seatbelts get automatic locking retractors. LE sedan is dropped.

RATINGS (SCALE OF 1-10)

Overall	Safety	Reliability	Performance	Comfort	Value
N/A	N/A	9	7.2	7.1	5.3

Category E

Model Description	Trade-in Value	Market Value
2 Dr DX Sdn	3340	4450
4 Dr DX Sdn	3610	4815
2 Dr STD Sdn	3190	4250

OPTIONS FOR TERCEL
Auto 3-Speed Transmission +135
AM/FM Stereo Tape +80
Air Conditioning +220
Anti-Lock Brakes +180
Power Steering +70

1993 TOYOTA

4RUNNER　　　　　　　　　1993
Two-door model is dropped from lineup, a victim of import tariffs. Four-wheel drive models come standard with 4WDemand system. Alloy wheels available only on V6 models, and now include chrome package.

RATINGS (SCALE OF 1-10)

Overall	Safety	Reliability	Performance	Comfort	Value
6.3	3.9	8.9	7	7	4.8

Category G

Model Description	Trade-in Value	Market Value
4 Dr SR5 4WD Wgn	8180	10490
4 Dr SR5 V6 Wgn	7415	9505
4 Dr SR5 V6 4WD Wgn	8665	11110

OPTIONS FOR 4RUNNER
Auto 4-Speed Transmission[Opt on 4WD] +235
Air Conditioning +180
Aluminum/Alloy Wheels +75
Anti-Lock Rear Brakes[Opt on SR5] +60
Compact Disc W/fm/tape +105
Cruise Control +45
Leather Seats +170
Luggage Rack +35
Power Door Locks +50
Power Moonroof +190
Power Windows +55
Premium Sound System +75

Don't forget to refer to the Mileage Adjustment Table at the back of this book!

TOYOTA 93

Model Description	Trade-in Value	Market Value	Model Description	Trade-in Value	Market Value

Rear Heater +45
Running Boards +85

CAMRY   1993

DX models get color-keyed bodyside moldings. Oak is a new interior color.

RATINGS (SCALE OF 1-10)

Overall	Safety	Reliability	Performance	Comfort	Value
N/A	N/A	8.8	8.6	8.4	6.5

Category D

Model	Trade-in	Market
4 Dr DX Sdn	5095	6705
4 Dr DX Wgn	5145	6770
4 Dr DX V6 Sdn	5445	7165
4 Dr LE Sdn	5550	7305
4 Dr LE Wgn	5960	7845
4 Dr LE V6 Sdn	5930	7800
4 Dr LE V6 Wgn	6310	8300
4 Dr SE Sdn	6190	8145
4 Dr XLE Sdn	6245	8220
4 Dr XLE V6 Sdn	6540	8605

OPTIONS FOR CAMRY

Auto 4-Speed Transmission[Opt on SE,DX Sdn] +180
AM/FM Compact Disc Player +115
Air Conditioning[Opt on DX,DX V6] +190
Anti-Lock Brakes +200
Cruise Control[Opt on DX,DX V6,SE] +55
Leather Seats +245
Power Door Locks[Opt on SE] +60
Power Moonroof[Std on XLE,XLE V6] +185
Power Windows[Opt on SE] +60
Premium Sound System +85

CELICA   1993

ABS is standard on All-Trac model; optional for first time on GT convertible.

Category F

Model	Trade-in	Market
2 Dr GT Conv	7060	9170
2 Dr GT Cpe	4875	6330
2 Dr GT Hbk	5145	6685
2 Dr GT-S Hbk	5535	7190
2 Dr ST Cpe	4690	6090

OPTIONS FOR CELICA

Auto 4-Speed Transmission +175
Air Conditioning[Std on STD] +185
Aluminum/Alloy Wheels[Opt on GT] +70
Anti-Lock Brakes[Std on STD] +150
Cruise Control[Std on STD] +45
Leather Seats[Std on STD] +145
Power Door Locks[Std on STD] +45
Power Drivers Seat[Std on STD] +55
Power Sunroof[Std on STD,Conv] +150
Power Windows[Std on STD] +50

COROLLA   1993

All-new Corolla arrives with driver airbag. Sedan and wagon body styles available. All-Trac wagon dies. Interior volume increases enough to move Corolla out of subcompact classification. Height-adjustable seat belts are standard. ABS optional on all models.

RATINGS (SCALE OF 1-10)

Overall	Safety	Reliability	Performance	Comfort	Value
7.1	5.7	8.3	7.4	8.1	5.9

Category E

Model	Trade-in	Market
4 Dr DX Sdn	3495	4785
4 Dr DX Wgn	3720	5095
4 Dr LE Sdn	4055	5555
4 Dr STD Sdn	3075	4210

OPTIONS FOR COROLLA

Auto 3-Speed Transmission +110
Auto 4-Speed Transmission[Opt on DX] +180
AM/FM Stereo Tape +65
Air Conditioning[Std on LE] +180
Aluminum/Alloy Wheels +75
Anti-Lock Brakes +150
Cruise Control[Opt on DX] +50
Power Door Locks[Opt on DX] +55
Power Sunroof +135
Power Windows[Opt on DX] +60

LAND CRUISER   1993

New 4.5-liter inline six pumps out 57 more horsepower than last year's engine; output is up to 212. Air conditioning and cruise control are added to the standard equipment list. Front and rear differential locks are newly optional. New leather package is available. Side-door guard beams added.

Category G

Model	Trade-in	Market
4 Dr STD 4WD Wgn	12585	16135

OPTIONS FOR LAND CRUISER

Leather Trim Pkg +455
Alarm System +60
Aluminum/Alloy Wheels +75
Anti-Lock Brakes +135
Compact Disc Changer +115
Compact Disc W/fm/tape +105
Dual Power Seats +85
Leather Seats +170
Locking Differential +65
Luggage Rack +35
Power Moonroof +190
Running Boards +85
Third Seat +160

MR2   1993

Suspension revisions aim to cure quirky cornering characteristics. All Turbos come with a standard T-bar

---

Don't forget to refer to the Mileage Adjustment Table at the back of this book!

Model Description	Trade-in Value	Market Value	Model Description	Trade-in Value	Market Value
			2 Dr SR5 V6 4WD Ext Cab SB	7100	9100
			2 Dr STD Std Cab SB	3825	4905

roof. Base MR2s get V-rated tires, and alloy wheels have been redesigned. An eight-speaker stereo, air conditioning, cruise, power windows, and power door locks are all newly standard on Turbo.

Category F

2 Dr STD Cpe	6355	8250
2 Dr STD Turbo Cpe	7345	9540

OPTIONS FOR MR2
Auto 4-Speed Transmission +180
Air Conditioning +185
Anti-Lock Brakes +150
Compact Disc W/fm/tape +110
Cruise Control[Std on Turbo] +45
Leather Seats +145
Limited Slip Diff +75
Power Door Locks[Std on Turbo] +45
Power Windows[Std on Turbo] +50
Premium Sound System +80
T-Tops (solid/Colored)[Std on Turbo] +210

PASEO   1993

Driver airbag added, and ABS is now optional. Interior fabrics are revised. Two new colors.

RATINGS (SCALE OF 1-10)

Overall	Safety	Reliability	Performance	Comfort	Value
7.1	5.9	9	7.8	7.1	5.5

Category E

2 Dr STD Cpe	3435	4705

OPTIONS FOR PASEO
Auto 4-Speed Transmission +180
AM/FM Stereo Tape +65
Air Conditioning +180
Aluminum/Alloy Wheels +75
Anti-Lock Brakes +150
Cruise Control +50
Moonroof +85

PICKUP   1993

One-ton and 4WD longbed dropped.

RATINGS (SCALE OF 1-10)

Overall	Safety	Reliability	Performance	Comfort	Value
N/A	4.4	8.7	7.1	7.1	N/A

HALF TON
Category G

2 Dr Deluxe Ext Cab SB	4570	5860
2 Dr Deluxe 4WD Ext Cab SB	6150	7885
2 Dr Deluxe Std Cab LB	4035	5170
2 Dr Deluxe Std Cab SB	3965	5085
2 Dr Deluxe 4WD Std Cab SB	5537	7100
2 Dr Deluxe V6 Ext Cab SB	4990	6400
2 Dr Deluxe V6 4WD Ext Cab SB	6405	8210
2 Dr SR5 V6 Ext Cab SB	5965	7650

OPTIONS FOR PICKUP
6 cyl 3.0 L Engine[Opt on Deluxe] +145
Auto 4-Speed Transmission +210
AM/FM Stereo Tape +50
Air Conditioning +180
Aluminum/Alloy Wheels +75
Anti-Lock Rear Brakes[Std on SR5 V6] +60
Auto Locking Hubs (4WD) +55
Bed Liner +60
Cruise Control +45
Power Door Locks +50
Power Steering[Opt on Deluxe,STD] +60
Power Windows +55
Premium Sound System +75
Rear Step Bumper +30
Velour/Cloth Seats[Opt on STD] +45

PREVIA   1993

All Previas seat seven instead of five. Only 2WD DX can be equipped with manual transmission. All-Tracs and 2WD LE get rear disc brakes.

RATINGS (SCALE OF 1-10)

Overall	Safety	Reliability	Performance	Comfort	Value
7	5.4	8.8	7.5	7.3	5.9

Category G

2 Dr Deluxe Pass. Van	5490	7040
2 Dr Deluxe 4WD Pass. Van	5915	7585
2 Dr LE Pass. Van	6975	8945
2 Dr LE 4WD Pass. Van	7410	9500

OPTIONS FOR PREVIA
Auto 4-Speed Transmission[Std on LE,4WD] +180
Aluminum/Alloy Wheels +75
Anti-Lock Brakes +135
Captain Chairs (2) +115
Compact Disc W/fm/tape +105
Cruise Control[Std on LE] +45
Dual Air Conditioning[Std on LE] +210
Luggage Rack +35
Power Door Locks[Std on LE] +50
Power Sunroof +170
Power Windows[Std on LE] +55

SUPRA   1993

Debuted in summer 1993. All-new car features dual airbags and ABS. Twin Turbo model has 320 horsepower and traction control.

Category F

2 Dr STD Hbk	11175	14515
2 Dr STD Turbo Hbk	13720	17820

OPTIONS FOR SUPRA
Auto 4-Speed Transmission +200
AM/FM Compact Disc Player +105

Leather Seats +145
Limited Slip Diff[Std on Turbo] +75
Power Sunroof +150
T-Tops (solid/Colored) +210

T100   1993

New full-size Toyota pickup designed to battle Chevy C/K, Ford F-Series and Dodge Ram. 150-horsepower V6 is only powerplant. One-ton model handles 2,570 lbs.

RATINGS (SCALE OF 1-10)

Overall	Safety	Reliability	Performance	Comfort	Value
N/A	N/A	8.8	6.8	7.5	N/A

Category H

2 Dr 1 Ton Std Cab LB	5145	6515
2 Dr SR5 Std Cab LB	4857	6150
2 Dr SR5 4WD Std Cab LB	6195	7840
2 Dr STD Std Cab LB	4266	5400
2 Dr STD 4WD Std Cab LB	5990	7585

OPTIONS FOR T100

Auto 4-Speed Transmission +200
AM/FM Compact Disc Player +70
Air Conditioning +180
Aluminum/Alloy Wheels +70
Bed Liner +50
Cruise Control +40
Power Door Locks +40
Power Windows +40
Premium Sound System +85
Rear Step Bumper +35

TERCEL   1993

Driver airbag added, and ABS is optional for first time. Sedans get height-adjustable seatbelts. Exteriors get a new grille. DX models get body-color bumpers and moldings. Airbag is housed in new steering wheel. LE gets standard power steering.

RATINGS (SCALE OF 1-10)

Overall	Safety	Reliability	Performance	Comfort	Value
N/A	N/A	8.5	7.2	7.1	5.2

Category E

2 Dr DX Sdn	2630	3600
4 Dr DX Sdn	2765	3790
4 Dr LE Sdn	2880	3945
2 Dr STD Sdn	2590	3550

OPTIONS FOR TERCEL

Auto 3-Speed Transmission +110
AM/FM Stereo Tape +65
Air Conditioning +180
Anti-Lock Brakes +150
Power Steering +55

4RUNNER   1992

New grille, front bumper and aero headlights debut. Power steering and a rear wiper/washer are standard on all models. Spare tire is moved underneath body of truck. Leather seats are newly optional on four-door models with a V6 engine.

RATINGS (SCALE OF 1-10)

Overall	Safety	Reliability	Performance	Comfort	Value
6.3	3.9	8.4	7	7	5.1

Category G

2 Dr SR5 4WD Utility	7005	9215
4 Dr SR5 Wgn	6900	9080
4 Dr SR5 4WD Wgn	7360	9685

OPTIONS FOR 4RUNNER

6 cyl 3.0 L Engine[Std on Utility,2WD] +140
Auto 4-Speed Transmission[Opt on 4WD] +200
Air Conditioning +145
Anti-Lock Rear Brakes +50
Auto Locking Hubs (4WD) +45
Compact Disc W/fm/tape +85
Leather Seats +140
Power Door Locks +40
Power Sunroof +140
Power Windows +45

CAMRY   1992

Redesign nets a driver airbag, larger engines, more interior volume and a sporty SE model. All-Trac has been dropped. ABS is optional across all trim levels and body styles.

RATINGS (SCALE OF 1-10)

Overall	Safety	Reliability	Performance	Comfort	Value
N/A	N/A	8.2	8.6	8.4	6.9

Category D

4 Dr Deluxe Sdn	4225	5635
4 Dr Deluxe Wgn	4350	5800
4 Dr LE Sdn	4650	6200
4 Dr LE Wgn	5295	7060
4 Dr SE Sdn	5230	6970
4 Dr XLE Sdn	5410	7210

OPTIONS FOR CAMRY

6 cyl 3.0 L Engine[Std on SE] +250
Auto 4-Speed Transmission[Std on LE,XLE,Wgn] +145
Bicentennial Pkg +230
Air Conditioning[Opt on Deluxe] +155
Anti-Lock Brakes +165
Compact Disc W/fm/tape +145
Leather Seats +200

Model Description	Trade-in Value	Market Value

Power Door Locks[Opt on SE] +50
Power Moonroof[Std on XLE] +150
Power Windows[Opt on SE] +50

CELICA 1992

Subtle restyling, larger wheels and tires, and wider availability of ABS.

Category F

Model Description	Trade-in Value	Market Value
2 Dr GT Conv	5935	7910
2 Dr GT Cpe	4090	5450
2 Dr GT Hbk	4405	5875
2 Dr GT-S Hbk	4945	6595
2 Dr ST Cpe	3910	5215

OPTIONS FOR CELICA

Auto 4-Speed Transmission +130
Air Conditioning +150
Anti-Lock Brakes +125
Compact Disc W/fm/tape +90
Leather Seats +120
Power Door Locks[Std on STD] +35
Power Drivers Seat +45
Power Sunroof +120
Power Windows[Std on STD] +40

COROLLA 1992

LE sedan comes with an automatic only. Coupe body style is dropped.

Category E

Model Description	Trade-in Value	Market Value
4 Dr Deluxe Sdn	2775	3965
4 Dr Deluxe Wgn	2855	4080
4 Dr Deluxe 4WD Wgn	3580	5115
4 Dr LE Sdn	2970	4245
4 Dr STD Sdn	2470	3525

OPTIONS FOR COROLLA

Auto 3-Speed Transmission +90
Auto 4-Speed Transmission[Std on LE] +145
Air Conditioning +145
Power Door Locks +45
Power Steering[Std on LE] +45
Power Sunroof +110
Power Windows +50

CRESSIDA 1992

No changes.

Category D

Model Description	Trade-in Value	Market Value
4 Dr STD Sdn	5315	7085

OPTIONS FOR CRESSIDA

Anti-Lock Brakes +165
Dual Power Seats +150
Leather Seats +200
Power Moonroof +150

LAND CRUISER 1992

Power windows, locks and outside mirrors are standard this year.

Category G

Model Description	Trade-in Value	Market Value
4 Dr STD 4WD Wgn	10765	14165

OPTIONS FOR LAND CRUISER

Air Conditioning +145
Compact Disc W/fm/tape +85
Leather Seats +140
Power Sunroof +140
Third Seat +130

MR2 1992

ABS is optional.

Category F

Model Description	Trade-in Value	Market Value
2 Dr STD Cpe	4975	6630
2 Dr STD Turbo Cpe	6440	8585

OPTIONS FOR MR2

Auto 4-Speed Transmission +145
Air Conditioning +150
Anti-Lock Brakes +125
Compact Disc W/fm/tape +90
Leather Seats +120
Power Door Locks +35
Power Windows +40
T-Tops (solid/Colored) +170

PASEO 1992

Sporty version of the Tercel offers more horsepower, stiffer suspension, and racier bodywork than its more pedestrian counterpart.

RATINGS (SCALE OF 1-10)

Overall	Safety	Reliability	Performance	Comfort	Value
6.3	3.6	8.6	7.8	7.1	4.3

Category E

Model Description	Trade-in Value	Market Value
2 Dr STD Cpe	2820	4025

OPTIONS FOR PASEO

Auto 4-Speed Transmission +145
Air Conditioning +145
Moonroof +70

PICKUP 1992

New front grille debuts. Storage compartment is added to dashboard. Two-wheel drive models get full wheelcovers. Four-wheel drive models get new steel wheels and passenger assist grip.

RATINGS (SCALE OF 1-10)

Overall	Safety	Reliability	Performance	Comfort	Value
N/A	3.7	8.9	7.1	7.1	N/A

Don't forget to refer to the Mileage Adjustment Table at the back of this book!

Model Description	Trade-in Value	Market Value

HALF TON

Category G

Model Description	Trade-in Value	Market Value
2 Dr Deluxe Ext Cab SB	4145	5455
2 Dr Deluxe 4WD Ext Cab SB	5515	7255
2 Dr Deluxe Std Cab LB	3610	4750
2 Dr Deluxe 4WD Std Cab LB	5290	6960
2 Dr Deluxe Std Cab SB	3540	4660
2 Dr Deluxe 4WD Std Cab SB	5215	6860
2 Dr SR5 Ext Cab SB	5470	7200
2 Dr SR5 4WD Ext Cab SB	6384	8400
2 Dr STD Std Cab SB	3415	4495

OPTIONS FOR PICKUP

6 cyl 3.0 L Engine[Opt on Deluxe] +140
Auto 4-Speed Transmission +160
Air Conditioning +145
Anti-Lock Brakes[Std on SR5] +110
Auto Locking Hubs (4WD)[Std on SR5] +45
Power Door Locks +40
Power Steering[Std on One Ton, SR5] +50
Power Windows +45

PREVIA   1992

Driver airbag is added, and with new knee bolsters under the dash and a third brake light, the 1992 Previa becomes the first minivan to meet passenger car safety requirements, including standards for roof crush and side-impact protection. ABS is newly optional on DX models. LE models get standard power windows, locks and mirrors.

RATINGS (SCALE OF 1-10)

Overall	Safety	Reliability	Performance	Comfort	Value
6.9	5.2	8.2	7.5	7.3	6.1

Category G

	Trade-in	Market
2 Dr Deluxe Pass. Van	4510	5935
2 Dr Deluxe 4WD Pass. Van	5010	6590
2 Dr LE Pass. Van	5785	7615
2 Dr LE 4WD Pass. Van	6015	7915

OPTIONS FOR PREVIA

Auto 4-Speed Transmission[Std on LE] +150
Anti-Lock Brakes +110
Captain Chairs (2) +90
Dual Air Conditioning[Std on LE] +170
Power Door Locks[Std on LE] +40
Power Windows[Std on LE] +45

SUPRA   1992

Automatic transmission gets revised shift points.
Category F

	Trade-in	Market
2 Dr STD Hbk	5690	7590
2 Dr STD Turbo Hbk	6020	8025

OPTIONS FOR SUPRA

Auto 4-Speed Transmission +135
AM/FM Compact Disc Player +85
Anti-Lock Brakes[Std on Turbo] +125
Leather Seats +120
Limited Slip Diff[Std on Turbo] +60
Solid Targa Top +165

TERCEL   1992

No changes.

RATINGS (SCALE OF 1-10)

Overall	Safety	Reliability	Performance	Comfort	Value
N/A	N/A	8.5	7.2	7.1	5.1

Category E

	Trade-in	Market
2 Dr DX Sdn	2285	3265
4 Dr DX Sdn	2415	3450
4 Dr LE Sdn	2530	3615
2 Dr STD Sdn	2145	3065

OPTIONS FOR TERCEL

Auto 3-Speed Transmission +90
Air Conditioning +145
Power Steering +45

1991 TOYOTA

4RUNNER   1991

No changes.

RATINGS (SCALE OF 1-10)

Overall	Safety	Reliability	Performance	Comfort	Value
6.1	3.9	8.1	7	7	4.7

Category G

	Trade-in	Market
2 Dr SR5 4WD Utility	6235	8425
4 Dr SR5 Wgn	5940	8025
4 Dr SR5 4WD Wgn	6425	8685
4 Dr SR5 V6 4WD Wgn	6475	8750

OPTIONS FOR 4RUNNER

6 cyl 3.0 L Engine[Opt on SR5] +105
Auto 4-Speed Transmission[Std on 2WD] +140
Air Conditioning +120
Anti-Lock Brakes[Opt on SR5] +90
Compact Disc W/fm/tape +70
Power Door Locks +35
Power Moonroof +130
Power Windows +35

CAMRY   1991

No changes.
Category D

	Trade-in	Market
4 Dr Deluxe Sdn	3070	4205
4 Dr Deluxe 4WD Sdn	3575	4900
4 Dr Deluxe Wgn	3210	4400
4 Dr LE Sdn	3445	4720

Don't forget to refer to the Mileage Adjustment Table at the back of this book!

Model Description	Trade-in Value	Market Value
4 Dr LE 4WD Sdn	3660	5015
4 Dr LE Wgn	3845	5265
4 Dr LE V6 Sdn	3670	5025
4 Dr STD Sdn	2790	3820

OPTIONS FOR CAMRY
6 cyl 2.5 L Engine[Opt on Deluxe] +190
Auto 4-Speed Transmission[Std on LE,LE V6, Wgn,4WD] +100
Air Conditioning[Std on LE V6,LE Wgn] +125
Anti-Lock Brakes +135
Leather Seats +165
Power Door Locks[Std on LE V6,LE Wgn] +40
Power Drivers Seat +45
Power Sunroof +110
Power Windows[Std on LE V6,LE Wgn] +40

CELICA   1991
Driver airbag added.
Category F

Model	Trade-in	Market
2 Dr GT Conv	5215	7050
2 Dr GT Cpe	3385	4575
2 Dr GT Hbk	3610	4875
2 Dr GT-S Hbk	3950	5335
2 Dr ST Cpe	3180	4295
2 Dr STD Turbo 4WD Hbk	4275	5775

OPTIONS FOR CELICA
Auto 4-Speed Transmission +100
Air Conditioning +125
Anti-Lock Brakes +100
Compact Disc W/fm/tape +75
Leather Seats +95
Power Door Locks[Std on STD] +30
Power Sunroof +100
Power Windows[Std on STD] +35

COROLLA   1991
All-Trac sedan dropped.
Category E

Model	Trade-in	Market
4 Dr Deluxe Sdn	2300	3385
4 Dr Deluxe Wgn	2375	3490
4 Dr Deluxe 4WD Wgn	2925	4300
2 Dr GT-S Cpe	2505	3685
4 Dr LE Sdn	2560	3765
2 Dr SR5 Cpe	2690	3955
4 Dr STD Sdn	2090	3070

OPTIONS FOR COROLLA
Auto 3-Speed Transmission +70
Auto 4-Speed Transmission +105
Air Conditioning +120
Power Door Locks +35
Power Steering[Std on GT-S,LE] +40
Power Sunroof +90
Power Windows +40

CRESSIDA   1991
No changes.
Category D

Model	Trade-in	Market
4 Dr Luxury Sdn	4555	6240

OPTIONS FOR CRESSIDA
Anti-Lock Brakes +135
Leather Seats +165
Power Drivers Seat +45
Power Passenger Seat +55
Power Sunroof +110

LAND CRUISER   1991
All-new design debuted in March, 1990. Features permanent 4WD. Coil springs replace leaf springs. 4.0-liter inline six makes 155 horsepower. Optional third seat allows truck to carry seven passengers.
Category G

Model	Trade-in	Market
4 Dr STD 4WD Wgn	9295	12560

OPTIONS FOR LAND CRUISER
Air Conditioning +120
Compact Disc W/fm/tape +70
Power Door Locks +35
Power Sunroof +115
Power Windows +35
Third Seat +105

MR2   1991
Back after one-year hiatus. Ferrari styling themes, driver airbag and optional turbocharged power make this one a winner.
Category F

Model	Trade-in	Market
2 Dr STD Cpe	4140	5595
2 Dr STD Turbo Cpe	4715	6370

OPTIONS FOR MR2
Auto 4-Speed Transmission +110
Air Conditioning +125
Anti-Lock Brakes +100
Compact Disc W/fm/tape +75
Leather Seats +95
Power Door Locks +30
Power Windows +35

PICKUP   1991
Wider availability of shift-on-the-fly 4WD and rear ABS. All engines have fuel injection. Four-speed manual transmission dropped. SR5 trim available only with V6 engine, and SR5s get new graphics and seat fabric.

RATINGS (SCALE OF 1-10)
Overall	Safety	Reliability	Performance	Comfort	Value
N/A	3.7	8.7	7.1	7.1	N/A

Model Description	Trade-in Value	Market Value

HALF TON

Category G

Model Description	Trade-in Value	Market Value
2 Dr Deluxe Ext Cab SB	3680	4970
2 Dr Deluxe 4WD Ext Cab SB	5115	6915
2 Dr Deluxe Std Cab LB	3450	4665
2 Dr Deluxe 4WD Std Cab LB	4605	6225
2 Dr Deluxe Std Cab SB	3385	4575
2 Dr Deluxe 4WD Std Cab SB	4550	6150
2 Dr SR5 Ext Cab SB	4805	6495
2 Dr SR5 4WD Ext Cab SB	5765	7790
2 Dr STD Std Cab SB	3110	4200

ONE TON

Category G

	Trade-in Value	Market Value
2 Dr STD Std Cab LB	3635	4915

OPTIONS FOR PICKUP
6 cyl 3.0 L Engine[Opt on Deluxe] +105
Auto 4-Speed Transmission +125
Air Conditioning +120
Anti-Lock Brakes +90
Auto Locking Hubs (4WD)[Std on SR5] +40
Power Door Locks +35
Power Steering[Std on One Ton, SR5] +40
Power Windows +35

PREVIA　　　　　　　　1991

Replaced Van in March, 1990. Employs midengine design driving the rear or all four wheels. ABS is optional on LE models.

RATINGS (SCALE OF 1-10)

Overall	Safety	Reliability	Performance	Comfort	Value
6.8	4.1	7	7.5	7.3	7.9

Category G

	Trade-in Value	Market Value
2 Dr Deluxe Pass. Van	3835	5180
2 Dr Deluxe 4WD Pass. Van	4260	5760
2 Dr LE Pass. Van	4960	6700
2 Dr LE 4WD Pass. Van	5275	7125

OPTIONS FOR PREVIA
Auto 4-Speed Transmission[Std on LE] +115
7 Passenger Seating[Std on LE] +75
Air Conditioning +120
Anti-Lock Brakes +90
Captain Chairs (4) +90
Dual Air Conditioning[Std on LE] +140
Power Door Locks[Std on LE] +35
Power Windows +35

SUPRA　　　　　　　　1991

ABS made standard on Turbo.

Category F

	Trade-in Value	Market Value
2 Dr STD Hbk	4980	6730
2 Dr STD Turbo Hbk	5230	7070

OPTIONS FOR SUPRA
Auto 4-Speed Transmission +110
Sport Handling Pkg +115
AM/FM Compact Disc Player +70
Anti-Lock Brakes[Std on Turbo] +100
Leather Seats +95
Power Drivers Seat +35
Power Sunroof +100
Solid Targa Top +135

TERCEL　　　　　　　　1991

Redesigned Tercel available in coupe and sedan versions only.

RATINGS (SCALE OF 1-10)

Overall	Safety	Reliability	Performance	Comfort	Value
N/A	N/A	8.5	7.2	7.1	4.6

Category E

	Trade-in Value	Market Value
2 Dr DX Sdn	1960	2885
4 Dr DX Sdn	2110	3100
4 Dr LE Sdn	2205	3245
2 Dr STD Sdn	1730	2545

OPTIONS FOR TERCEL
Auto 3-Speed Transmission +70
Air Conditioning +120
Power Steering[Opt on DX] +40

1990 TOYOTA

4RUNNER　　　　　　　　1990

Introduced in mid-1989, the 1990 4Runner is based on the 1989 Pickup. Rear ABS is standard, but works only in 2WD. Removable rear roof section disappears. Shift-on-the-fly 4WD is now optional. Two- and four-door models are available.

RATINGS (SCALE OF 1-10)

Overall	Safety	Reliability	Performance	Comfort	Value
6	3.9	7.7	7	7	4.6

Category G

	Trade-in Value	Market Value
2 Dr SR5 4WD Utility	5305	7365
4 Dr SR5 Wgn	5035	6995
4 Dr SR5 4WD Wgn	5495	7630
2 Dr SR5 V6 4WD Utility	5575	7745
4 Dr SR5 V6 Wgn	5150	7155
4 Dr SR5 V6 4WD Wgn	5770	8015

OPTIONS FOR 4RUNNER
Auto 4-Speed Transmission[Std on 2WD] +135
Compact Disc/Power Pkg +165
Air Conditioning +100
Anti-Lock Brakes[Std on SR5 V6,2WD] +70
Auto Locking Hubs (4WD) +30
Compact Disc W/fm/tape +60
Power Door Locks +30

Model Description	Trade-in Value	Market Value
Power Moonroof +105		
Power Windows[Opt on SR5,Wgn] +30		

CAMRY 1990

Base models get new seat fabric and dual cupholders. V6 models get more power. Optional split-folding rear seats are available on Deluxe.

Category D

Model Description	Trade-in Value	Market Value
4 Dr Deluxe Sdn	2525	3505
4 Dr Deluxe 4WD Sdn	2870	3990
4 Dr Deluxe Wgn	2715	3770
4 Dr LE Sdn	2770	3850
4 Dr LE 4WD Sdn	3220	4470
4 Dr LE Wgn	3385	4700
4 Dr STD Sdn	2445	3395

OPTIONS FOR CAMRY

6 cyl 2.5 L Engine[Opt on Deluxe,Sdn] +135
Auto 4-Speed Transmission[Std on LE,Wgn] +90
Air Conditioning[Std on LE Wgn] +105
Anti-Lock Brakes +110
Leather Seats +135
Power Door Locks[Opt on Deluxe,Sdn] +35
Power Drivers Seat +35
Power Sunroof +90
Power Windows[Opt on Deluxe,Sdn] +35

CELICA 1990

Completely redesigned for 1990. GT-S engine is larger. All-Trac Turbo still for sale. Audio systems are substantially upgraded.

Category F

Model Description	Trade-in Value	Market Value
2 Dr GT Cpe	2935	3965
2 Dr GT Hbk	3230	4365
2 Dr GT-S Hbk	3590	4850
2 Dr ST Cpe	2675	3615
2 Dr STD Turbo 4WD Hbk	3925	5305

OPTIONS FOR CELICA

Auto 4-Speed Transmission +85
Air Conditioning +100
Compact Disc W/fm/tape +60
Leather Seats +80
Power Drivers Seat +30
Power Sunroof +80
Power Windows[Std on STD] +25

COROLLA 1990

Fuel injection standard on all Corollas. GT-S model gets more horsepower. All other Corollas get 100-horsepower engine.

Category E

Model Description	Trade-in Value	Market Value
4 Dr Deluxe Sdn	1905	2890
4 Dr Deluxe Wgn	1945	2950
4 Dr Deluxe 4WD Wgn	2395	3630
2 Dr GT-S Cpe	2145	3250
4 Dr LE Sdn	2080	3155
2 Dr SR5 Cpe	2315	3505
4 Dr SR5 4WD Wgn	2605	3945
4 Dr STD Sdn	1735	2630

OPTIONS FOR COROLLA

Auto 3-Speed Transmission +60
Auto 4-Speed Transmission +90
Air Conditioning +100
Power Door Locks +30
Power Sunroof +75
Power Windows +30

CRESSIDA 1990

No changes.

Category D

Model Description	Trade-in Value	Market Value
4 Dr Luxury Sdn	3795	5270

OPTIONS FOR CRESSIDA

Anti-Lock Brakes +110
Leather Seats +135
Power Drivers Seat +35
Power Sunroof +90

LAND CRUISER 1990

No changes.

Category G

Model Description	Trade-in Value	Market Value
4 Dr STD 4WD Wgn	6260	8695

OPTIONS FOR LAND CRUISER

Air Conditioning +100
Power Door Locks +30
Power Windows +30

PICKUP 1990

SR5 V6 models get rear wheel ABS standard. This feature is optional on SR5 four-cylinder trucks.

RATINGS (SCALE OF 1-10)

Overall	Safety	Reliability	Performance	Comfort	Value
N/A	3.7	8.6	7.1	7.1	N/A

HALF TON

Category G

Model Description	Trade-in Value	Market Value
2 Dr Deluxe Ext Cab SB	3170	4405
2 Dr Deluxe 4WD Ext Cab SB	4600	6390
2 Dr Deluxe Std Cab LB	2880	4000
2 Dr Deluxe 4WD Std Cab LB	3785	5255
2 Dr Deluxe Std Cab SB	2775	3855
2 Dr Deluxe 4WD Std Cab SB	3720	5170
2 Dr SR5 Ext Cab SB	3915	5440
2 Dr SR5 4WD Ext Cab SB	4845	6730
2 Dr SR5 Std Cab LB	3210	4460
2 Dr SR5 4WD Std Cab SB	4235	5880
2 Dr STD Std Cab SB	2665	3700

Don't forget to refer to the Mileage Adjustment Table at the back of this book!

Model Description	Trade-in Value	Market Value

OPTIONS FOR PICKUP
6 cyl 3.0 L Engine[Std on One Ton] +110
Auto 4-Speed Transmission +100
Air Conditioning +100
Anti-Lock Brakes +70
Auto Locking Hubs (4WD) +30
Power Door Locks +30
Power Steering[Std on One Ton] +35
Power Windows +30

SUPRA   1990

Driver airbag added. ABS is optional.
Category F

Model Description	Trade-in Value	Market Value
2 Dr STD Hbk	4120	5565
2 Dr STD Turbo Hbk	4680	6325

OPTIONS FOR SUPRA
Auto 4-Speed Transmission +90
Sport Handling Pkg +95
AM/FM Compact Disc Player +60

Anti-Lock Brakes +80
Leather Seats +80
Power Drivers Seat +30
Solid Targa Top +110

TERCEL   1990

Four-door hatchback model dropped, and two-door Deluxe hatchback axed. Passive restraints added, and automatic transmissions get shift interlock.
Category E

Model Description	Trade-in Value	Market Value
2 Dr Base Hbk	1285	1950
2 Dr Deluxe Cpe	1520	2305
2 Dr EZ Hbk	1325	2010
2 Dr STD Cpe	1400	2120
2 Dr STD Hbk	1455	2205

OPTIONS FOR TERCEL
Auto 3-Speed Transmission +55
Air Conditioning +100
Power Steering[Opt on STD] +30

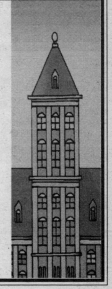
Don't forget to refer to the Mileage Adjustment Table at the back of this book!

Model Description	Trade-in Value	Market Value

VOLKSWAGEN Germany

1996 Volkswagen Cabrio

1999 VOLKSWAGEN

CABRIO 1999

Volkswagen imparts new Euro-styling on the '99 Cabrios, making them more aerodynamic and adding twin headlights that show interior elements through the lens. Cabrio interiors also receive makeovers.

RATINGS (SCALE OF 1-10)

Overall	Safety	Reliability	Performance	Comfort	Value
N/A	N/A	N/A	7.8	6.4	N/A

Category F
2 Dr GL Conv	13455	15645
2 Dr GLS Conv	15523	18050

OPTIONS FOR CABRIO
Auto 4-Speed Transmission +645
Air Conditioning[Opt on GL] +620
Aluminum/Alloy Wheels[Opt on GL,NEW GL] +230
Cruise Control[Opt on GL,NEW GL] +155
Heated Front Seats[Std on NEW GLS] +285
Keyless Entry System +130
Power Windows[Opt on GL,NEW GL] +165
Side Air Bag Restraint[Opt on GL,GLS] +290

EUROVAN 1999

After a five-year hiatus, the funky EuroVan passenger van returns to the U.S. with a six-cylinder engine, structural improvements and new safety features.

RATINGS (SCALE OF 1-10)

Overall	Safety	Reliability	Performance	Comfort	Value
N/A	N/A	N/A	6.2	6.4	N/A

Category G
2 Dr GLS Pass. Van	18030	21720
2 Dr MV Pass. Van	18885	22755

OPTIONS FOR EUROVAN
Weekender Pkg +2585
Heated Front Seats +195
Power Moonroof +645

GOLF 1999

The four-cylinder GTI is dropped in favor of a four-door Wolfsburg Edition during the final year for the current Golf.

RATINGS (SCALE OF 1-10)

Overall	Safety	Reliability	Performance	Comfort	Value
N/A	6.3	N/A	8	7.6	N/A

Category E
4 Dr GL Hbk	10110	12180
2 Dr GTI VR6 Hbk	13220	15925
4 Dr Wolfsburg Hbk	10965	13210

OPTIONS FOR GOLF
Auto 4-Speed Transmission +645
AM/FM Compact Disc Player +340
Air Conditioning[Opt on GL] +605
Anti-Lock Brakes[Std on VR6] +500
Leather Seats +645
Power Moonroof[Std on VR6] +425
Side Air Bag Restraint +190

GTI 1999

VW's all-new GTI arrives in 1999 with new interior and exterior designs and more powerful engines.

Category F
2 Dr NEW GLS Hbk	12775	14855
2 Dr NEW GLX Hbk	15805	18380

OPTIONS FOR GTI
Auto 4-Speed Transmission +645
AM/FM Compact Disc Player +355
Heated Front Seats[Std on NEW GLX] +285
Leather Seats[Std on NEW GLX] +485

JETTA 1999

Volkswagen trims model availability, killing the GLS and GT in favor of the Wolfsburg Edition.

RATINGS (SCALE OF 1-10)

Overall	Safety	Reliability	Performance	Comfort	Value
N/A	6.3	N/A	8.6	7.6	N/A

Category D
4 Dr GL Sdn	10865	12635
4 Dr GLX Sdn	15925	18515
4 Dr TDI Turbodsl Sdn	11585	13470
4 Dr Wolfsburg Sdn	12670	14730

VOLKSWAGEN 99-98

Model Description	Trade-in Value	Market Value	Model Description	Trade-in Value	Market Value

OPTIONS FOR JETTA

Auto 4-Speed Transmission +645
Air Conditioning[Opt on GL,TDI] +630
Aluminum/Alloy Wheels[Opt on GL,TDI] +345
Anti-Lock Brakes[Std on GLX] +670
Cruise Control[Opt on GL] +180
Leather Seats +820
Power Moonroof[Std on GLX] +620
Side Air Bag Restraint +220

NEW BEETLE   1999

A high-performance turbo model debuts this year. A small spoiler over the rear window is the only exterior telltale that the Slug Bug next to you has the 150-horsepower 1.8-liter turbocharged inline-four from the larger Passat sedan under the hood.

RATINGS (SCALE OF 1-10)

Overall	Safety	Reliability	Performance	Comfort	Value
N/A	N/A	N/A	6.8	7.9	N/A

Category E
2 Dr GL Sdn	12960	15615
2 Dr GLS Sdn	13695	16500
2 Dr GLS Turbo Sdn	14660	17660
2 Dr GLS TDI Turbodsl Sdn	14075	16960
2 Dr GLX Turbo Sdn	16020	19300

OPTIONS FOR NEW BEETLE

Auto 4-Speed Transmission +645
Aluminum/Alloy Wheels[Std on GLX] +245
Power Moonroof[Std on GLX] +425

NEW GOLF   1999

VW's all-new Golf arrives in 1999 with new interior and exterior designs and more powerful engines.

RATINGS (SCALE OF 1-10)

Overall	Safety	Reliability	Performance	Comfort	Value
N/A	N/A	N/A	8	7.9	N/A

Category E
2 Dr NEW GL Hbk	11360	13685
4 Dr NEW GLS Hbk	11575	13945

OPTIONS FOR NEW GOLF

Auto 4-Speed Transmission +645
Aluminum/Alloy Wheels +245
Power Moonroof +425

NEW JETTA   1999

VW's all-new 1999 Jetta arrives with bigger engines, updated styling and new standard equipment.

RATINGS (SCALE OF 1-10)

Overall	Safety	Reliability	Performance	Comfort	Value
N/A	N/A	N/A	8	7.6	N/A

Category D
4 Dr NEW GL Sdn	12150	14125
4 Dr NEW GL TDI Turbodsl Sdn	12880	14975
4 Dr NEW GLS Sdn	13320	15490
4 Dr NEW GLS TDI Turbodsl Sdn	14490	16850
4 Dr NEW GLS VR6 Sdn	14685	17075
4 Dr NEW GLX VR6 Sdn	16050	18665

OPTIONS FOR NEW JETTA

Auto 4-Speed Transmission +645
Aluminum/Alloy Wheels[Std on NEW GLX VR6] +345
Power Moonroof[Std on NEW GLX VR6] +620

PASSAT   1999

After promising the availability of all-wheel drive this year, Volkswagen, in a last-minute product change, has cancelled the Synchro all-wheel drive option on all Passats for 1999 and will not be offering the GLS wagon with a V6 engine.

RATINGS (SCALE OF 1-10)

Overall	Safety	Reliability	Performance	Comfort	Value
N/A	N/A	8.8	8.6	8.3	N/A

Category D
4 Dr GLS Turbo Sdn	15190	17660
4 Dr GLS Turbo Wgn	15827	18400
4 Dr GLS V6 Sdn	16095	18715
4 Dr GLX Sdn	19055	22155

OPTIONS FOR PASSAT

Auto Manual Transmission[Std on GLX] +795
AM/FM Compact Disc Player +390
Aluminum/Alloy Wheels +345
Power Moonroof[Std on GLX] +620

1998 VOLKSWAGEN

CABRIO   1998

The Highline trim designation is replaced by more sensible GLS nomenclature, though we'd prefer to see something like GTI grace the rear flanks of this drop-top. New GLS models gets a power top, making the Cabrio easier to live with. Optional are side impact airbags mounted inside the seats. Newly standard on both base and GLS are door pocket liners, a trunk cargo net and sport seats with height adjustment. Still no much-needed power boost.

RATINGS (SCALE OF 1-10)

Overall	Safety	Reliability	Performance	Comfort	Value
7	5.9	9	7.8	6.4	5.7

Category F
2 Dr GL Conv	12055	14180
2 Dr GLS Conv	14220	16730

Don't forget to refer to the Mileage Adjustment Table at the back of this book!

VOLKSWAGEN 98

Model Description	Trade-in Value	Market Value	Model Description	Trade-in Value	Market Value

OPTIONS FOR CABRIO

Auto 4-Speed Transmission +535
Air Conditioning[Opt on GL] +505
Aluminum/Alloy Wheels[Opt on GL] +185
Compact Disc Changer +390
Cruise Control[Opt on GL] +125
Heated Front Seats +235
Heated Power Mirrors[Opt on GL] +135
Keyless Entry System +110
Power Windows[Opt on GL] +135
Side Air Bag Restraint +240

GOLF   1998

All Golfs get standard remote keyless entry. GL has revised wheel covers.

RATINGS (SCALE OF 1-10)

Overall	Safety	Reliability	Performance	Comfort	Value
7.3	6.3	8.2	8.6	7.6	6

Category E
4 Dr GL Hbk	8745	10665
2 Dr GTI Hbk	9805	11955
4 Dr K2 Hbk	8885	10835
4 Dr Wolfsburg Hbk	9300	11340

Category F
2 Dr GTI VR6 Hbk	12080	14210

OPTIONS FOR GOLF

Auto 4-Speed Transmission +535
AM/FM Stereo Tape[Opt on GL] +185
Air Conditioning[Opt on GL, K2] +495
Leather Seats +395
Power Moonroof[Opt on GL,K2] +350
Power Windows[Opt on Wolfsburg] +160

JETTA   1998

The TDI has finally arrived. New wheel covers and colors spruce up the exterior for another year, while remote keyless entry makes it easier to lock and unlock the Jetta. GLX models have new one-touch up power windows with pinch protection.

RATINGS (SCALE OF 1-10)

Overall	Safety	Reliability	Performance	Comfort	Value
7.3	6.3	8.2	8.6	7.6	6

Category D
4 Dr GL Sdn	9580	11270
4 Dr GLS Sdn	11435	13455
4 Dr GLX Sdn	13980	16445
4 Dr GT Sdn	9875	11615
4 Dr K2 Sdn	9730	11445
4 Dr TDI Turbodsl Sdn	10070	11845
4 Dr Wolfsburg Sdn	10850	12765

OPTIONS FOR JETTA

Auto 4-Speed Transmission +545
Air Conditioning[Opt on GL, GT, TDI] +515
Aluminum/Alloy Wheels[Opt on GL, TDI] +280
Anti-Lock Brakes[Std on GLX] +550
Bose Sound System[Std on GLS] +460
Compact Disc Changer[Std on Wolfsburg] +410
Cruise Control[Std on GLS, GLX, TDI] +145
Heated Front Seats +245
Heated Power Mirrors[Std on GLS, GLX] +50
Leather Seats +670
Power Moonroof[Std on GLX, Wolfsburg] +505
Power Windows[Std on GLS, GLX] +165
Side Air Bag Restraint +180

NEW BEETLE   1998

Volkswagen attempts to revive a legend using retro styling touches wrapped around Golf underpinnings.

RATINGS (SCALE OF 1-10)

Overall	Safety	Reliability	Performance	Comfort	Value
N/A	8.3	8.3	N/A	N/A	N/A

Category E
2 Dr STD Sdn	12100	14755
2 Dr TDI Turbodsl Sdn	12315	15020

OPTIONS FOR NEW BEETLE

Auto 4-Speed Transmission +565
Aluminum/Alloy Wheels +200
Anti-Lock Brakes +410
Compact Disc Changer +305
Cruise Control[Std on TDI] +135
Fog Lights +90
Heated Front Seats +90
Power Windows +160

PASSAT   1998

An all-new Passat arrives wearing stylish sheetmetal over a stretched Audi A4 platform. Engine choices include a spunky turbocharged four or a silky V6.

RATINGS (SCALE OF 1-10)

Overall	Safety	Reliability	Performance	Comfort	Value
7.9	8.4	8.1	8.6	8.3	6.1

Category D
4 Dr GLS Turbo Sdn	13575	15970
4 Dr GLS Turbo Wgn	14281	16800
4 Dr GLS V6 Sdn	14550	17115
4 Dr GLX Sdn	15565	18310

OPTIONS FOR PASSAT

Heated Front Seats[Std on GLX] +245
Leather Seats[Std on GLX] +670
Power Moonroof[Std on GLX] +505

Don't forget to refer to the Mileage Adjustment Table at the back of this book!

1997 VOLKSWAGEN

CABRIO 1997

Cabrio comes in two trim levels for 1997: Base and Highline. Base models are decontented versions of last year's car, priced a couple thousand dollars lower to entice young drivers. Highline models have standard alloy wheels, fog lights and leather seats. Engines have a redesigned cylinder head resulting in quieter operation.

RATINGS (SCALE OF 1-10)

Overall	Safety	Reliability	Performance	Comfort	Value
6.9	5.9	8.7	7.8	6.4	5.6

Category F
2 Dr Highline Conv	12490	14870
2 Dr STD Conv	10905	12985

OPTIONS FOR CABRIO
Auto 4-Speed Transmission +440
Air Conditioning[Opt on STD] +415
Aluminum/Alloy Wheels[Opt on STD] +150
Compact Disc Changer +320
Cruise Control[Opt on STD] +105
Heated Front Seats +190
Power Windows[Opt on STD] +110

EUROVAN 1997

Category G
2 Dr Campmobile Pass. Van	16200	20510

OPTIONS FOR EUROVAN
AM/FM Stereo Tape +110

GOLF 1997

GTI VR6 gets a lowered suspension for improved handling, and a redesigned cylinder head quiets GL and GTI models. A K2 edition debuted in December, 1996, sporting heated front seats, premium sound, and a rack with either skis or a snowboard attached. Spring, 1997, brought a slick Trek model with alloys and a bike up top.

RATINGS (SCALE OF 1-10)

Overall	Safety	Reliability	Performance	Comfort	Value
7.1	5.9	7.9	8.6	7.6	5.3

Category E
2 Dr GL Hbk	7370	9210
4 Dr GL Hbk	7440	9300
2 Dr GTI Hbk	8750	10935
4 Dr K2 Hbk	7680	9600
4 Dr Trek Hbk	7610	9515

Category F
2 Dr GTI VR6 Hbk	11155	13280

OPTIONS FOR GOLF
Auto 4-Speed Transmission +440
AM/FM Stereo Tape[Opt on GL,Trek] +150
Air Conditioning[Opt on GL,K2,Trek] +405
Leather Seats +325
Power Moonroof[Opt on GL,K2,Trek] +285

JETTA 1997

Wolfsburg models are gone, and the Jetta GT arrives sporting the look of the GLX without that darn expensive VR6 engine. Trek gets alloy wheels. GL, GLS, Trek and GT run more quietly, thanks to a new cylinder head design.

RATINGS (SCALE OF 1-10)

Overall	Safety	Reliability	Performance	Comfort	Value
7.1	5.9	7.9	8.6	7.6	5.3

Category D
4 Dr GL Sdn	8610	10375
4 Dr GLS Sdn	10190	12280
4 Dr GLX Sdn	12210	14710
4 Dr GT Sdn	8875	10695
4 Dr TDI Turbodsl Sdn	9205	11090
4 Dr Trek Sdn	8760	10555

OPTIONS FOR JETTA
Auto 4-Speed Transmission +445
AM/FM Compact Disc Player +260
Air Conditioning[Std on GLS,GLX] +420
Aluminum/Alloy Wheels[Opt on GL] +230
Anti-Lock Brakes[Std on GLX] +450
Bose Sound System[Opt on GLS] +375
Cruise Control[Opt on GL,GT,Trek] +120
Heated Front Seats +200
Heated Power Mirrors[Opt on Trek] +40
Leather Seats +545
Power Moonroof[Std on GLX] +415
Power Windows[Opt on Trek] +135

PASSAT 1997

GLS model vanishes from radar as Volkswagen prepares for launch of all-new Passat in mid-1997.

RATINGS (SCALE OF 1-10)

Overall	Safety	Reliability	Performance	Comfort	Value
6.7	7.2	7.7	7.8	8	3

Category D
4 Dr GLX Sdn	11390	13725
4 Dr GLX Wgn	11990	14445
4 Dr TDI Turbodsl Sdn	11020	13275

OPTIONS FOR PASSAT
Auto 4-Speed Transmission +440
Anti-Lock Brakes[Opt on TDI] +450
Compact Disc Changer +335
Heated Front Seats +200

Don't forget to refer to the Mileage Adjustment Table at the back of this book!

Leather Seats +545
Power Moonroof +415

1996 VOLKSWAGEN

CABRIO 1996

Daytime running lights and new body-color side moldings alter the exterior appearance of the 1996 Cabrio. A new color scheme also livens things up. Central locking and unlocking switch is dash mounted.

RATINGS (SCALE OF 1-10)

Overall	Safety	Reliability	Performance	Comfort	Value
7	5.9	9	7.8	6.4	5.9

Category F

	Trade-in	Market
2 Dr STD Conv	10040	11950

OPTIONS FOR CABRIO

Auto 4-Speed Transmission +340
Air Conditioning +340
Aluminum/Alloy Wheels +125
Leather Seats +265

GOLF 1996

The Golf Sport becomes the GTI, powered by a 2.0-liter four-cylinder with alloys, sport seats, and smoke-tinted taillights. GTI VR6 continues, with firmer front suspension, three new colors, and new "Pininfarina" style alloy wheels. Black leather seats are newly optional on GTI VR6. Automatic transmissions are smoother this year.

RATINGS (SCALE OF 1-10)

Overall	Safety	Reliability	Performance	Comfort	Value
7	5.8	7.3	8.6	7.6	5.7

Category E

	Trade-in	Market
4 Dr GL Hbk	6625	8495

OPTIONS FOR GOLF

Auto 4-Speed Transmission +355
AM/FM Stereo Tape +125
Air Conditioning +330
Anti-Lock Brakes +275
Compact Disc Changer +205
Power Moonroof +230

GTI 1996

Category E

	Trade-in	Market
2 Dr STD Hbk	8100	10385

Category F

	Trade-in	Market
2 Dr VR6 Hbk	9820	11690

OPTIONS FOR GTI

Auto 4-Speed Transmission +355
Compact Disc Changer +205
Leather Seats +265

JETTA 1996

A new grille is added up front. GLX models get a firmer front suspension and new "Bugatti" style wheels. New colors sum up the changes.

RATINGS (SCALE OF 1-10)

Overall	Safety	Reliability	Performance	Comfort	Value
7	5.8	7.3	8.6	7.6	5.7

Category D

	Trade-in	Market
4 Dr City Sdn	6670	8340
4 Dr GL Sdn	7120	8900
4 Dr GLS Sdn	8205	10255
4 Dr GLX Sdn	10190	12740
4 Dr Trek Limited Ed. Sdn	7855	9820
4 Dr Wolfsburg Sdn	7180	8975

OPTIONS FOR JETTA

Auto 4-Speed Transmission +355
AM/FM Compact Disc Player[Std on TDI] +210
Air Conditioning[Std on GLS,GLX] +345
Aluminum/Alloy Wheels[Opt on GL] +190
Anti-Lock Brakes[Std on GLX] +365
Bose Sound System[Opt on GLS] +305
Cruise Control[Std on GLS,GLX] +100
Heated Front Seats +165
Leather Seats +445
Power Moonroof[Std on GLX,Wolfsburg] +340

PASSAT 1996

Daytime running lights debut, two new colors are added to the palette, and a new price-leader GLS model powered by a 2.0-liter, 115-horsepower, four-cylinder engine is introduced. Midyear, a Turbo Direct Injection (TDI) diesel model appears in sedan and wagon form.

RATINGS (SCALE OF 1-10)

Overall	Safety	Reliability	Performance	Comfort	Value
6.8	7.2	7.5	7.8	8	3.4

Category D

	Trade-in	Market
4 Dr GLS Sdn	7905	9880
4 Dr GLX Sdn	9530	11910
4 Dr GLX Wgn	10195	12745
4 Dr TDI Turbodsl Sdn	9235	11545

OPTIONS FOR PASSAT

Auto 4-Speed Transmission +325
Anti-Lock Brakes[Std on GLX] +365
Compact Disc Changer +270
Heated Front Seats +165
Leather Seats +445
Power Moonroof +340

Don't forget to refer to the Mileage Adjustment Table at the back of this book!

VOLKSWAGEN 95

Model Description	Trade-in Value	Market Value	Model Description	Trade-in Value	Market Value

1995 VOLKSWAGEN

CABRIO 1995

Dual airbags, ABS, and 115-horsepower engine are standard on this Golf derivative. Manual top only.

RATINGS (SCALE OF 1-10)

Overall	Safety	Reliability	Performance	Comfort	Value
6.4	5.9	6.8	7.8	6.4	4.9

Category F
2 Dr STD Conv — 8885 10835

OPTIONS FOR CABRIO
Auto 4-Speed Transmission +290
Air Conditioning +275
Aluminum/Alloy Wheels +100
Compact Disc Changer +215
Leather Seats +215

EUROVAN 1995

Category G
2 Dr Camp Mobile Pass. Van — 11645 15525

OPTIONS FOR EUROVAN
Auto 4-Speed Transmission +330

GOLF 1995

GTI VR6 debuts, with 2.8-liter V6, ABS, and traction control. Entry-level City trim level introduced for four-door models. Two-door Golf switches from GL to Sport designation, and includes spoked alloy wheels and blacked out taillights. Golf meets 1997 side-impact standards. Front seatbelts have height adjusters and emergency tensioners. Daytime running lights are standard on all Golf models.

RATINGS (SCALE OF 1-10)

Overall	Safety	Reliability	Performance	Comfort	Value
6.6	6	5.7	8.6	7.6	5.1

Category E
4 Dr Celebration Hbk — 5575 7145
4 Dr City Hbk — 5645 7240
2 Dr GL Hbk — 5785 7415
4 Dr GL Hbk — 6050 7755
4 Dr STD Hbk — 5690 7295
2 Dr Sport Hbk — 6445 8260
Category F
2 Dr GTI VR6 Hbk — 8565 10445

OPTIONS FOR GOLF
Auto 4-Speed Transmission +290
AM/FM Stereo Tape[Opt on City,STD] +100
Air Conditioning[Std on GTIVR6,GL,Sport] +270
Aluminum/Alloy Wheels[Opt on GL] +110
Anti-Lock Brakes[Std on GTIVR6] +225

Compact Disc Changer +170
Power Moonroof[Std on GTIVR6,Sport] +190
Premium Sound System +110

JETTA 1995

Entry-level City trim level introduced. Jetta meets 1997 side-impact standards. Front seatbelts have height adjusters and emergency tensioners. Daytime running lights are standard on all Jetta models.

RATINGS (SCALE OF 1-10)

Overall	Safety	Reliability	Performance	Comfort	Value
6.6	6	5.7	8.6	7.6	5.1

Category D
4 Dr Celebration Sdn — 5875 7435
4 Dr City Sdn — 5560 7035
4 Dr GL Sdn — 6125 7755
4 Dr GLS Sdn — 6990 8845
4 Dr GLX Sdn — 8570 10845
4 Dr STD Sdn — 5790 7330

OPTIONS FOR JETTA
Auto 4-Speed Transmission +290
AM/FM Stereo Tape[Std on GL,GLS,GLX] +120
Air Conditioning[Std on GL,GLS,GLX,STD] +280
Alarm System[Opt on Celebration] +175
Anti-Lock Brakes[Std on GLX] +300
Compact Disc Changer +225
Leather Seats +365
Power Moonroof[Std on GLS,GLX] +275

PASSAT 1995

Reskinned for 1995, VW adds dual airbags, three-point seatbelts, and side-impact protection that meets 1997 safety standards. Climate control system gains dust and pollen filter. GLX is only trim level.

RATINGS (SCALE OF 1-10)

Overall	Safety	Reliability	Performance	Comfort	Value
6.8	7.7	6.7	7.8	8	3.8

Category D
4 Dr GLS Sdn — 6820 8630
4 Dr GLX Sdn — 8035 10170
4 Dr GLX Wgn — 8404 10635

OPTIONS FOR PASSAT
Auto 4-Speed Transmission +265
Anti-Lock Brakes[Opt on GLS] +300
Compact Disc Changer +225
Heated Front Seats +135
Leather Seats +365
Power Moonroof +275

Don't forget to refer to the Mileage Adjustment Table at the back of this book!

VOLKSWAGEN 94-93

Model Description	Trade-in Value	Market Value	Model Description	Trade-in Value	Market Value

1994 VOLKSWAGEN

CORRADO 1994

Adaptive dual-mode automatic transmission debuts. Meets 1997 side-impact standards. Speed-activated spoiler rises at 55 mph instead of 45 mph.

Category F

	Trade-in	Market
2 Dr SLC Cpe	8225	10280

GOLF 1994

Two-door GL debuts. ABS is optional. Dual airbags are phased in shortly after 1994 production begins.

RATINGS (SCALE OF 1-10)

Overall	Safety	Reliability	Performance	Comfort	Value
6.6	5.9	5	8.6	7.6	6

Category E

	Trade-in	Market
2 Dr GL Hbk	4160	5545
4 Dr GL Hbk	4575	6100
2 Dr Limited Hbk	4600	6135

OPTIONS FOR GOLF

Auto 4-Speed Transmission +240
AM/FM Stereo Tape +80
Air Conditioning +220
Aluminum/Alloy Wheels +90
Anti-Lock Brakes +180
Dual Air Bag Restraints +140
Power Moonroof +155

JETTA 1994

GLS and GLX models arrive this year. ABS is optional on GL and GLS; standard on GLX. Dual airbags are phased in shortly after 1994 production begins. GLX features 2.8-liter V6 and traction control.

RATINGS (SCALE OF 1-10)

Overall	Safety	Reliability	Performance	Comfort	Value
6.6	5.9	5	8.6	7.6	6

Category D

	Trade-in	Market
4 Dr GL Sdn	5105	6630
4 Dr GLS Sdn	5645	7330
4 Dr GLX Sdn	7560	9815
4 Dr Limited Edition Sdn	4845	6290

OPTIONS FOR JETTA

Auto 4-Speed Transmission +255
AM/FM Stereo Tape[Opt on GL] +95
Air Conditioning[Std on GLS,GLX] +230
Aluminum/Alloy Wheels[Std on GLX] +125
Anti-Lock Brakes[Std on GLX] +245
Compact Disc Changer +180
Cruise Control[Std on GLS,GLX] +65
Dual Air Bag Restraints +170
Leather Seats +300

Power Moonroof +225
Premium Sound System +100

PASSAT 1994

GL dropped, leaving only the V6 GLX. ABS and traction control are standard. Adaptive dual-mode transmission debuts.

RATINGS (SCALE OF 1-10)

Overall	Safety	Reliability	Performance	Comfort	Value
6.6	4.9	8.1	7.8	8	4.4

Category D

	Trade-in	Market
4 Dr GLX Sdn	6455	8380
4 Dr GLX Wgn	6905	8965

OPTIONS FOR PASSAT

Auto 4-Speed Transmission +240
Compact Disc Changer +180
Heated Front Seats +110
Leather Seats +300

1993 VOLKSWAGEN

CABRIOLET 1993

Carat replaced by Classic. Base models get leatherette upholstery option. Audio systems are upgraded, and CD player joins options list.

Category F

	Trade-in	Market
2 Dr Classic Conv	5835	7575
2 Dr STD Conv	5590	7260

OPTIONS FOR CABRIOLET

Auto 3-Speed Transmission +135
Air Conditioning[Opt on STD] +185
Compact Disc Changer +140

CORRADO 1993

In mid-1992, supercharged four-cylinder engine was replaced by 2.8-liter V6. V6 model designated SLC. ABS and traction control are standard. BBS wheels dumped in favor of five-spoke VW design. Fuel capacity up four gallons, and front styling is tweaked. A/C is CFC-free. Radio turns off with ignition switch.

Category F

	Trade-in	Market
2 Dr SLC Cpe	7125	9250

OPTIONS FOR CORRADO

Auto 4-Speed Transmission +195
Heated Front Seats +85
Leather Seats +145
Power Sunroof +150

EUROVAN 1993

The EuroVan is introduced as a replacement for the aging Vanagon. Major differences over the previous generation Volkswagen van are the switch to a front-

---

Don't forget to refer to the Mileage Adjustment Table at the back of this book!

Model Description	Trade-in Value	Market Value

engine/front-wheel drive platform. Antilock brakes are available on the EuroVan, and it has a 2.5-liter four-cylinder engine that produces 109-horsepower. A five-speed manual transmission is standard, a four-speed automatic is optional.

Category G

	Trade-in	Market
2 Dr CL Pass. Van	4250	6075
2 Dr GL Pass. Van	5815	8305
2 Dr MV Pass. Van	6305	9010

OPTIONS FOR EUROVAN

Auto 4-Speed Transmission +200
Weekender Pkg +565
AM/FM Stereo Tape[Opt on CL] +50
Anti-Lock Brakes +135
Cruise Control +45
Dual Air Conditioning[Opt on CL] +210
Power Door Locks +50
Power Windows +55

FOX 1993

Air conditioning is standard. Five-speed transmission replaces four-speed unit on Base coupe. Base model gets wheelcovers, dual outside mirrors, body-color bumpers and bigger tires. GL model gets upgraded interior trim.

Category E

	Trade-in	Market
2 Dr Wolfsburg Sdn	1810	2480
4 Dr Wolfsburg GL Sdn	2050	2810

OPTIONS FOR FOX

AM/FM Stereo Tape +65

GOLF 1993

All new Golf debuts, but a strike at the assembly plant in Mexico restricts sales to Southern California and parts of New England.

Category E

	Trade-in	Market
4 Dr GL Hbk	3730	5110

OPTIONS FOR GOLF

Auto 4-Speed Transmission +195
AM/FM Stereo Tape +65
Air Conditioning +180
Power Sunroof +135

JETTA 1993

All new Jetta debuts, but a strike at the assembly plant in Mexico restricts sales to Southern California and parts of New England.

Category D

	Trade-in	Market
4 Dr GL Sdn	4405	5875

OPTIONS FOR JETTA

Auto 4-Speed Transmission +195
AM/FM Stereo Tape +80
Air Conditioning +190
Power Sunroof +165

PASSAT 1993

GLX trim level introduced, with 2.8-liter V6, ABS and traction control. Fog lamps and six-spoke alloys indicate GLX model. CL trim dropped. GL gets suspension modifications. All models get trip computer and CFC-free air conditioning.

RATINGS (SCALE OF 1-10)

Overall	Safety	Reliability	Performance	Comfort	Value
6.1	4.7	6.6	7.8	8	3.4

Category D

	Trade-in	Market
4 Dr GL Sdn	4250	5665
4 Dr GLX Sdn	5520	7360
4 Dr GLX Wgn	5780	7705

OPTIONS FOR PASSAT

Auto 4-Speed Transmission +195
Leather Seats +245
Power Sunroof[Opt on GL] +165

1992 VOLKSWAGEN

CABRIOLET 1992

Etienne Aigner edition dropped. Three-point seatbelts are added to the back seat. Base model gets full wheelcovers. Radio turns off with ignition switch.

Category F

	Trade-in	Market
2 Dr Carat Conv	5075	6765
2 Dr STD Conv	4550	6065
2 Dr Wolfsburg Class. Conv	4590	6120

OPTIONS FOR CABRIOLET

Auto 3-Speed Transmission +100
Auto 4-Speed Transmission +100
Power Convertible Top +155
Air Conditioning[Opt on Carat,STD] +150

CORRADO 1992

No changes.

Category F

	Trade-in	Market
2 Dr SLC Cpe	6010	8015
2 Dr STD Sprchgd Cpe	5635	7515

OPTIONS FOR CORRADO

Auto 4-Speed Transmission +145
Anti-Lock Brakes[Opt on STD] +125
Leather Seats +120
Power Sunroof +120

FOX 1992

Radio turns off with ignition switch.

Category E

	Trade-in	Market
4 Dr GL Sdn	1600	2285
2 Dr STD Sdn	1250	1785

Don't forget to refer to the Mileage Adjustment Table at the back of this book!

VOLKSWAGEN 92-91

Model Description	Trade-in Value	Market Value	Model Description	Trade-in Value	Market Value

OPTIONS FOR FOX
Air Conditioning[Std on GL] +145

GOLF 1992

Radio turns off with ignition switch.
Category E

2 Dr GL Hbk	2420	3455
4 Dr GL Hbk	2580	3685

Category F

2 Dr GTI Hbk	3530	4705
2 Dr GTI 16V Hbk	3965	5285

OPTIONS FOR GOLF
Auto 3-Speed Transmission +100
Air Conditioning +145
Sunroof +65

JETTA 1992

ECOdiesel debuts, featuring turbocharging and fewer pollutants. Two-door model dropped. GL models get new wheelcovers. Radio turns off with ignition switch.
Category D

4 Dr Carat Sdn	3155	4265
4 Dr GL Sdn	2870	3875
4 Dr GL ECO Dsl Sdn	2605	3520
4 Dr GLI Sdn	3725	5035

OPTIONS FOR JETTA
Auto 3-Speed Transmission +100
Air Conditioning +155
Aluminum/Alloy Wheels[Opt on GL] +85
Anti-Lock Brakes +165
Power Windows[Opt on GLI] +50
Sunroof +80

PASSAT 1992

New entry-level CL trim level introduced.

RATINGS (SCALE OF 1-10)

Overall	Safety	Reliability	Performance	Comfort	Value
6.2	4.4	7.1	7.4	8	4.3

Category D

4 Dr CL Sdn	3205	4335
4 Dr GL Sdn	3325	4495
4 Dr GL Wgn	3515	4745

OPTIONS FOR PASSAT
Auto 4-Speed Transmission +145
Air Conditioning[Opt on CL] +155
Aluminum/Alloy Wheels +85
Anti-Lock Brakes +165
Compact Disc Changer +120
Leather Seats +200
Power Sunroof +135

1991 VOLKSWAGEN

CABRIOLET 1991

Airbag added to steering wheel. Etienne Aigner edition debuts.
Category F

2 Dr STD Conv	3740	4985

OPTIONS FOR CABRIOLET
Auto 3-Speed Transmission +75
Air Conditioning +125
Leather Seats +95

CORRADO 1991

BBS alloy wheels are added as standard equipment.
Category F

2 Dr STD Sprchgd Cpe	4490	5985

OPTIONS FOR CORRADO
Auto 4-Speed Transmission +115
Anti-Lock Brakes +100
Leather Seats +95
Power Sunroof +100

FOX 1991

Restyled front end features flush headlamps. Wagon dropped. Lineup trimmed to Base coupe and GL sedan.
Category E

4 Dr GL Sdn	1385	2035
2 Dr STD Sdn	1050	1540

OPTIONS FOR FOX
Air Conditioning +120

GOLF 1991

BBS wheels added to GTI 16V as standard equipment.
Category E

2 Dr GL Hbk	1880	2765
4 Dr GL Hbk	2035	2995

Category F

2 Dr GTI Hbk	3010	4010
2 Dr GTI 16V Hbk	3385	4510

OPTIONS FOR GOLF
Auto 3-Speed Transmission +75
Air Conditioning +120
Sunroof +50

JETTA 1991

GLI 16V gets standard BBS alloys.
Category D

4 Dr Carat Sdn	2720	3725
2 Dr GL Dsl Sdn	1935	2650
2 Dr GL Sdn	2380	3260
4 Dr GL Sdn	2465	3375

Don't forget to refer to the Mileage Adjustment Table at the back of this book!

Model Description	Trade-in Value	Market Value
4 Dr GL Dsl Sdn	2065	2830
4 Dr GLI 16V Sdn	3260	4465

OPTIONS FOR JETTA

Auto 3-Speed Transmission +75
Air Conditioning +125
Anti-Lock Brakes +135
Power Windows[Std on Carat] +40
Sunroof +65

PASSAT 1991

No changes.

RATINGS (SCALE OF 1-10)

Overall	Safety	Reliability	Performance	Comfort	Value
6.5	4.4	7.2	7.4	8	5.3

Category D

	Trade-in Value	Market Value
4 Dr GL Sdn	2695	3690
4 Dr GL Wgn	2765	3785

OPTIONS FOR PASSAT

Auto 4-Speed Transmission +115
Anti-Lock Brakes +135
Leather Seats +165
Power Door Locks +40
Power Sunroof +110
Power Windows +40

VANAGON 1991

No changes. Final year for Vanagon.
Category G

	Trade-in Value	Market Value
2 Dr Carat Pass. Van	4710	7360
2 Dr GL Pass. Van	4750	7420
2 Dr GL Camper Pass. Van	5245	8195
2 Dr Multi Pass. Van	3655	5710
2 Dr STD Pass. Van	3245	5070

OPTIONS FOR VANAGON

Auto 3-Speed Transmission +80
Auto 4-Speed Transmission +80
Air Conditioning[Opt on STD,Syncro] +120
Power Door Locks[Std on Carat,GL Syncro,Multi] +35
Power Windows[Std on Carat,GL Syncro,Multi] +35

1990 VOLKSWAGEN

CABRIOLET 1990

No changes.
Category F

	Trade-in Value	Market Value
2 Dr STD Conv	3280	4490

OPTIONS FOR CABRIOLET

Auto 3-Speed Transmission +60
Air Conditioning +100

CORRADO 1990

Scirroco replacement moves slightly upscale, featuring supercharged Golf engine, optional ABS, and motorized seatbelts.
Category F

	Trade-in Value	Market Value
2 Dr STD Sprchgd Cpe	3850	5275

OPTIONS FOR CORRADO

Anti-Lock Brakes +80
Leather Seats +80
Power Sunroof +80

FOX 1990

No changes.
Category E

	Trade-in Value	Market Value
4 Dr GL Sdn	1015	1560
2 Dr GL Wgn	1145	1765
2 Dr GL Sport Sdn	1045	1605
2 Dr STD Sdn	940	1450

OPTIONS FOR FOX

Air Conditioning +100
Sunroof +40

GOLF 1990

Lineup trimmed to Base and GL models. GTI drops Golf designation. Lower cost GTI debuts with 105-horsepower eight-valve engine and rear drum brakes.
Category E

	Trade-in Value	Market Value
2 Dr GL Hbk	1435	2205
4 Dr GL Hbk	1605	2470

Category F

	Trade-in Value	Market Value
2 Dr GTI Hbk	2345	3210

OPTIONS FOR GOLF

Auto 3-Speed Transmission +65
Air Conditioning +100
Power Steering[Opt on GL] +30
Sunroof +40

JETTA 1990

No changes.
Category D

	Trade-in Value	Market Value
4 Dr Carat Sdn	2185	3035
2 Dr GL Sdn	2030	2820
4 Dr GL Sdn	2140	2970
4 Dr GLI 16V Sdn	2815	3910
4 Dr STD Dsl Sdn	1690	2350

OPTIONS FOR JETTA

Auto 3-Speed Transmission +60
Air Conditioning +105
Anti-Lock Brakes +110
Power Windows +35
Sunroof +50

Don't forget to refer to the Mileage Adjustment Table at the back of this book!

VOLKSWAGEN 90

Model Description	Trade-in Value	Market Value

PASSAT 1990

Delayed Quantum replacement debuts. Sedan and wagon are available in GL trim, with 134-horsepower engine. ABS is optional.

RATINGS (SCALE OF 1-10)

Overall	Safety	Reliability	Performance	Comfort	Value
6.1	4.3	6.8	7.4	8	4.2

Category D

	Trade-in	Market
4 Dr GL Sdn	2445	3395
4 Dr GL Wgn	2485	3450

OPTIONS FOR PASSAT

Auto 4-Speed Transmission[Opt on Sdn] +95
Anti-Lock Brakes +110
Leather Seats +135

Power Door Locks +35
Power Sunroof +90
Power Windows +35

VANAGON 1990

No changes.

Category G

	Trade-in	Market
2 Dr Carat Pass. Van	4195	6770
2 Dr GL Pass. Van	3785	6105
2 Dr GL Camper Pass. Van	4780	7710
2 Dr Multi Van Pass. Van	3555	5735
2 Dr STD Pass. Van	2835	4570

OPTIONS FOR VANAGON

Auto 3-Speed Transmission[Std on Carat,Multi Van] +65
Air Conditioning[Opt on Multi Van,STD] +100
Power Door Locks[Opt on GL,GL Camper,STD] +30
Power Windows[Opt on GL,GL Camper,STD] +30

Don't forget to refer to the Mileage Adjustment Table at the back of this book!

VOLVO 99-98

VOLVO Sweden

1997 Volvo 960

1999 VOLVO

70-SERIES 1999

Volvo's first all-wheel drive sedan debuts, vehicle options and color choices have been simplified, and S70/V70 models get new standard equipment.

RATINGS (SCALE OF 1-10)

Overall	Safety	Reliability	Performance	Comfort	Value
N/A	9.5	8.8	7.8	8.1	N/A

Category L
4 Dr GLT Turbo Sdn	19490	22665
4 Dr GLT Turbo Wgn	20345	23655
4 Dr R Turbo 4WD Wgn	27075	31485
4 Dr STD Sdn	17805	20705
4 Dr STD Turbo 4WD Sdn	21549	25060
4 Dr STD Wgn	18791	21850
4 Dr STD Turbo 4WD Wgn	22545	26215
4 Dr T-5 Turbo Sdn	21629	25150
4 Dr T-5 Turbo Wgn	22605	26285
4 Dr XC Turbo 4WD Wgn	23815	27690

OPTIONS FOR 70-SERIES
Auto 4-Speed Transmission[Std on GLT,R,XC,4WD] +720
Climate Control for AC[Opt on STD] +230
Compact Disc W/fm/tape[Std on R,T-5] +480
Dual Power Seats[Std on R,T-5] +575
Heated Front Seats[Std on R,XC,4] +355
Leather Seats[Std on R] +900
Power Moonroof[Std on R] +695
Traction Control System[Std on R,XC,4WD] +1050
Trip Computer[Opt on GLT,STD] +205

C70 1999

Volvo offers a light pressure turbocharged engine in the coupe to entice consumers looking for a lower-priced ticket. Both coupes and convertibles get a bit of new standard and optional equipment.

RATINGS (SCALE OF 1-10)

Overall	Safety	Reliability	Performance	Comfort	Value
N/A	N/A	N/A	8.4	7.9	N/A

Category L
2 Dr HT Turbo Cpe	26905	31285
2 Dr LT Turbo Conv	30655	35650
2 Dr LT Turbo Cpe	25730	29920

OPTIONS FOR C70
Auto 4-Speed Transmission[Std on LT] +720
Dolby Pro Logic Radio +985
Heated Front Seats +355
Traction Control System +1050
Trip Computer[Std on HT] +205

S80 1999

This long overdue redesign of the S90 counts several firsts to its credit: first with a transverse inline six, first with fully integrated GSM phone, first to carry an environmental specification (Europe only at introduction), and the S80 boasts the world's smallest manual transmission. Whoo-hoo!

RATINGS (SCALE OF 1-10)

Overall	Safety	Reliability	Performance	Comfort	Value
N/A	N/A	N/A	8.4	8.6	N/A

Category L
4 Dr 2.9 Sdn	23690	27545
4 Dr T-6 Turbo Sdn	27610	32105

OPTIONS FOR S80
Navigation System +1845
Compact Disc Changer +825
Heated Front Seats[Std on T-6] +355
Leather Seats +900
Power Moonroof +695

1998 VOLVO

C70 1998

Volvo performs a slam-dunk with its first new coupe in years; the convertible is somewhat less thrilling. Modeled on the S70 chassis, the C70 shares sheetmetal with the S70 from the windshield forward, and is powered by the same set of turbocharged powerplants.

Category L
2 Dr STD Turbo Cpe	24440	28750

Don't forget to refer to the Mileage Adjustment Table at the back of this book!

Model Description	Trade-in Value	Market Value

Model Description	Trade-in Value	Market Value

OPTIONS FOR C70

Auto 4-Speed Transmission +600
Heated Front Seats +290
Traction Control System +860

S70 1998

Volvo's 850 sedan gets a new name, new nose, body-color trim, stronger side-impact protection, more powerful turbo engines, redesigned interior, and revised suspension. A great car has been made better.

RATINGS (SCALE OF 1-10)

Overall	Safety	Reliability	Performance	Comfort	Value
8.6	9.5	8.6	8.4	8.4	8.1

Category L

	Trade-in	Market
4 Dr GLT Turbo Sdn	18580	21860
4 Dr GT Sdn	16329	19210
4 Dr STD Sdn	15639	18400
4 Dr T-5 Turbo Sdn	19678	23150

OPTIONS FOR S70

Auto 4-Speed Transmission[Std on GLT] +600
Aluminum/Alloy Wheels[Opt on STD] +260
Compact Disc W/fm/tape[Std on T-5] +390
Dual Power Seats[Std on T-5] +470
Heated Front Seats +290
Leather Seats +735
Sport Suspension +100
Traction Control System +860
Trip Computer[Std on T-5] +170

S90 1998

Absolutely nothing changes on this aged warhorse.

RATINGS (SCALE OF 1-10)

Overall	Safety	Reliability	Performance	Comfort	Value
N/A	N/A	9.3	7.8	8.1	6.6

Category L

	Trade-in	Market
4 Dr STD Sdn	18945	22285

OPTIONS FOR S90

Compact Disc W/fm/tape +390
Heated Front Seats +290

V70 1998

Volvo's 850 wagon gets a new name, new nose, body-color trim, stronger side-impact protection, more powerful turbo engines, redesigned interior and revised suspension. A great car has been made better. All-wheel drive versions arrive to battle luxury SUVs.

RATINGS (SCALE OF 1-10)

Overall	Safety	Reliability	Performance	Comfort	Value
N/A	N/A	8.6	8	8.4	8.3

Category L

	Trade-in	Market
4 Dr GLT Turbo Wgn	19890	23400
4 Dr GT Wgn	18175	21380
4 Dr R Turbo 4WD Wgn	22885	26925
4 Dr STD Wgn	17185	20220
4 Dr STD Turbo 4WD Wgn	19145	22525
4 Dr T-5 Turbo Wgn	18365	24600
4 Dr XC Turbo 4WD Wgn	21065	24785

OPTIONS FOR V70

Auto 4-Speed Transmission[Std on GLT, R, XC, 4WD] +600
Aluminum/Alloy Wheels[Opt on STD] +260
Auto Load Leveling[Std on R, XC, 4WD] +680
Compact Disc W/fm/tape[Std on T-5] +390
Dual Power Seats[Std on R, T-5, XC] +470
Heated Front Seats[Std on R, XC, 4WD] +290
Leather Seats[Std on R, XC] +735
Power Drivers Seat[Std on GLT, GT, 4WD] +290
Power Moonroof[Opt on STD, XC] +570
Sport Suspension +100
Traction Control System[Std on R, XC, 4WD] +860
Trip Computer[Std on R, T-5, XC] +170

V90 1998

Absolutely nothing changes on this aged warhorse.

RATINGS (SCALE OF 1-10)

Overall	Safety	Reliability	Performance	Comfort	Value
N/A	N/A	9	7.8	8.3	6.6

Category L

	Trade-in	Market
4 Dr STD Wgn	19955	23480

OPTIONS FOR V90

Auto Load Leveling +680
Compact Disc W/fm/tape +390
Heated Front Seats +290

1997 VOLVO

850 1997

Looking for the Turbo? Inexplicably, Volvo tossed two decades of tradition and the Turbo nameplate out the door. The Turbo is now known as the T-5. GLT models get a new engine that makes 22 more horsepower than last year, and peak torque at a low 1,800 rpm. Base and GLT models meet Transitional Low Emission Vehicle (TLEV) regulations this year.

RATINGS (SCALE OF 1-10)

Overall	Safety	Reliability	Performance	Comfort	Value
8.4	8.6	8.3	8.8	8.3	8

Category L

	Trade-in	Market
4 Dr GLT Turbo Sdn	16240	19105
4 Dr GLT Turbo Wgn	17940	21105
4 Dr R Turbo Sdn	19220	22610

Don't forget to refer to the Mileage Adjustment Table at the back of this book!

Model Description	Trade-in Value	Market Value
4 Dr R Turbo Wgn	20755	24420
4 Dr STD Sdn	14100	16590
4 Dr STD Wgn	15300	18000
4 Dr T-5 Turbo Sdn	17805	20945
4 Dr T-5 Turbo Wgn	19250	22645

OPTIONS FOR 850

Auto 4-Speed Transmission[Opt on STD] +490
Grand Touring Pkg +500
Wood Trim Pkg +405
Aluminum/Alloy Wheels[Opt on STD] +210
Auto Load Leveling[Std on R] +555
Compact Disc W/fm/tape[Std on R,T-5] +320
Dual Power Seats[Std on R,T-5] +385
Keyless Entry System[Opt on STD] +125
Leather Seats[Std on R] +600
Power Moonroof[Opt on STD] +465
Sport Suspension[Std on R] +80
Traction Control System[Std on R] +700
Trip Computer[Std on R,T-5] +140

960 — 1997

Automatic load leveling joins the options list for the wagon, while tailored leather seating is no longer available on the wagon.

RATINGS (SCALE OF 1-10)

Overall	Safety	Reliability	Performance	Comfort	Value
8.1	8.5	8.4	8.8	8	6.9

Category L
4 Dr STD Sdn	16165	19015
4 Dr STD Wgn	17355	20420

OPTIONS FOR 960

Auto Load Leveling +555
Compact Disc W/fm/tape +320

S90 — 1997

Midyear, Volvo went and switched names for the 960. The sedan is now known as S90, while the wagon is now the V90.

RATINGS (SCALE OF 1-10)

Overall	Safety	Reliability	Performance	Comfort	Value
N/A	N/A	N/A	N/A	N/A	7.2

Category L
4 Dr STD Sdn	16900	19880

V90 — 1997

Midyear, Volvo went and switched names for the 960. The sedan is now known as S90, while the wagon is now the V90.

RATINGS (SCALE OF 1-10)

Overall	Safety	Reliability	Performance	Comfort	Value
N/A	N/A	N/A	N/A	N/A	7.2

Category L
4 Dr STD Wgn	18690	21990

1996 VOLVO

850 — 1996

This year all Volvo 850s are equipped with front seat side-impact airbags, optional traction control (TRACS), and a life insurance policy that pays $250,000 to the estate of any occupant who loses their life in the 850 as the result of an accident.

RATINGS (SCALE OF 1-10)

Overall	Safety	Reliability	Performance	Comfort	Value
8.4	8.6	8.1	8.6	8.3	8.4

Category L
4 Dr GLT Sdn	13385	15935
4 Dr GLT Wgn	14215	16925
4 Dr Platinum Ltd. Ed. Turbo Sdn		
	15395	18330
4 Dr Platinum Ltd. Ed. Turbo Wgn		
	16382	19500
4 Dr R Turbo Sdn	17085	20340
4 Dr R Turbo Wgn	18100	21545
4 Dr STD Sdn	12280	14620
4 Dr STD Turbo Sdn	13900	16545
4 Dr STD Wgn	13140	15640
4 Dr STD Turbo Wgn	15085	17960

OPTIONS FOR 850

Auto 4-Speed Transmission[Opt on GLT,Non-turbo models] +395
Grand Touring Pkg +455
Aluminum/Alloy Wheels[Opt on STD Sdn,STD Wgn] +175
Auto Load Leveling[Opt on GLT,STD] +455
Dual Power Seats[Std on R] +315
Keyless Entry System[Opt on STD Wgn,STD Sdn] +100
Leather Seats[Opt on GLT,STD] +490
Sport Suspension[Std on R] +65
Traction Control System[Opt on GLT,STD] +575
Trip Computer[Opt on Non-turbo models] +115

960 — 1996

This year all Volvo 960s are equipped with front seat side-impact airbags, a multi-step power door locking system that increases driver safety when entering the vehicle in parking lots, and a life insurance policy that pays $250,000 to the estate of any occupant who loses their life in the 960 as a result of a car accident.

RATINGS (SCALE OF 1-10)

Overall	Safety	Reliability	Performance	Comfort	Value
8.2	8.5	8.2	8.8	8	7.3

Don't forget to refer to the Mileage Adjustment Table at the back of this book!

VOLVO 96-94

Model Description	Trade-in Value	Market Value	Model Description	Trade-in Value	Market Value

Category L

4 Dr STD Sdn	14595	17375
4 Dr STD Wgn	15490	18440

OPTIONS FOR 960
AM/FM Compact Disc Player +365

1995 VOLVO

850 — 1995

Side airbags are standard on all 850 Turbos this year; optional on other 850s. All models get Turbo's rounded front styling.

RATINGS (SCALE OF 1-10)

Overall	Safety	Reliability	Performance	Comfort	Value
8.3	8.5	7.8	8.6	8.3	8.4

Category L

4 Dr GLT Sdn	11165	13615
4 Dr GLT Wgn	11973	14600
4 Dr STD Sdn	10015	12215
4 Dr STD Turbo Sdn	11865	14470
4 Dr STD Wgn	10947	13350
4 Dr STD Turbo Wgn	12720	15515
4 Dr T-5R Turbo Sdn	13202	16100
4 Dr T-5R Turbo Wgn	13945	17005

OPTIONS FOR 850
Auto 4-Speed Transmission[Std on T-5R,Turbo] +295
Grand Lux Pkg +380
Grand Touring Pkg +280
Aluminum/Alloy Wheels[Std on GLT,T-5R,Turbo] +140
Climate Control for AC[Std on T-5R,Turbo] +105
Compact Disc W/fm/tape +215
Keyless Entry System[Std on GLT,T-5R,Turbo] +80
Leather Seats[Std on T-5R,STD Turbo Sdn] +400
Power Drivers Seat[Std on GLT,T-5R,Turbo] +160
Power Passenger Seat[Opt on STD,GLT Wgn] +150
Side Air Bag Restraint[Std on T-5R,Turbo,GLT Sdn] +165
Traction Control System[Std on T-5R] +470
Trip Computer[Opt on GLT] +90

940 — 1995

Daytime running lights debut. Level I and Level II trim is dropped in favor of less confusing base and Turbo designations.

RATINGS (SCALE OF 1-10)

Overall	Safety	Reliability	Performance	Comfort	Value
7.8	8	7.5	8	7.9	7.5

Category L

4 Dr STD Sdn	10190	12425
4 Dr STD Turbo Sdn	11530	14060
4 Dr STD Wgn	10900	13290
4 Dr STD Turbo Wgn	12645	15420

OPTIONS FOR 940
Aluminum/Alloy Wheels +140
Leather Seats +400
Power Drivers Seat +160
Power Moonroof +310

960 — 1995

Substantially revised with new sheetmetal and detuned powertrain. Horsepower is down to 181 from 201, thanks to emissions standards. Daytime running lights are added. The dashboard is softened with more curves and contours. Suspensions are revised, and larger tires are standard. Other new standard equipment includes remote locking, an alarm system, headlight wipers and washers, and wood interior trim.

RATINGS (SCALE OF 1-10)

Overall	Safety	Reliability	Performance	Comfort	Value
7.9	8.2	7.2	8.8	8	7.3

Category L

4 Dr STD Sdn	11395	13895
4 Dr STD Wgn	12295	14995

OPTIONS FOR 960
Compact Disc Changer +370
Leather Seats +400

1994 VOLVO

850 — 1994

Turbo model debuts with 222-horsepower 2.3-liter five-cylinder engine, and a wagon body style is introduced with standard integrated child seat. Turbo is available in either sedan or wagon format. Warranty is upped to 4 years/50,000 miles.

RATINGS (SCALE OF 1-10)

Overall	Safety	Reliability	Performance	Comfort	Value
8.3	8.5	7.7	8.6	8.3	8.4

Category L

4 Dr GLT Sdn	8550	10685
4 Dr GLTS Sdn	9202	11500
4 Dr GLTS Wgn	10125	12655
4 Dr STD Turbo Sdn	10330	12910
4 Dr STD Turbo Wgn	11260	14075

OPTIONS FOR 850
Auto 4-Speed Transmission[Opt on GLT,GLTS,Sdn] +245
Aluminum/Alloy Wheels[Std on GLTS,Wgn] +115
Auto Load Leveling +305
Climate Control for AC[Std on STD] +85
Leather Seats[Opt on GLT,GLTS,Sdn] +330
Power Drivers Seat[Std on GLTS,Wgn] +130
Power Passenger Seat +125
Sport Suspension +45

Don't forget to refer to the Mileage Adjustment Table at the back of this book!

VOLVO 94-93

Model Description	Trade-in Value	Market Value	Model Description	Trade-in Value	Market Value

Traction Control System +385
Trip Computer[Std on STD] +75

940 — 1994

940 gets passenger airbag. Level I 940s have 114-horsepower 2.3-liter engine; equip a 940 with Level II trim and you get a turbocharged version of this engine.

RATINGS (SCALE OF 1-10)

Overall	Safety	Reliability	Performance	Comfort	Value
7.9	8.2	7.7	8	8	7.4

Category L

	Trade-in	Market
4 Dr STD Sdn	7810	9765
4 Dr STD Turbo Sdn	9060	11325
4 Dr STD Wgn	8900	11125
4 Dr STD Turbo Wgn	9945	12430

OPTIONS FOR 940

Aluminum/Alloy Wheels[Std on Turbo] +115
Leather Seats[Std on Turbo] +330
Power Drivers Seat[Std on Turbo] +130
Power Passenger Seat +125
Power Sunroof[Std on Turbo] +250

960 — 1994

Base 960 is heavily decontented, and is available only in sedan format. Level II 960 adds leather, moonroof and other nice stuff.

RATINGS (SCALE OF 1-10)

Overall	Safety	Reliability	Performance	Comfort	Value
8	8.4	7.4	8.8	8.1	7.2

Category L

	Trade-in	Market
4 Dr Level II Sdn	9295	11620
4 Dr Level II Wgn	10267	12835
4 Dr STD Sdn	8740	10925

OPTIONS FOR 960

Aluminum/Alloy Wheels[Opt on STD] +115
Compact Disc Changer +300
Compact Disc W/fm/tape +175
Leather Seats[Opt on STD] +330
Power Moonroof +255
Power Passenger Seat[Std on Wgn] +125
Premium Sound System +265

1993 VOLVO

240 — 1993

GL model dropped, again. Metallic paint doesn't cost extra this year, air conditioning gets CFC-free refrigerant, and plush floormats are standard.

Category L

	Trade-in	Market
4 Dr STD Sdn	6715	8500
4 Dr STD Wgn	7150	9050

OPTIONS FOR 240

Auto 4-Speed Transmission +150
Aluminum/Alloy Wheels +95
Heated Front Seats +105
Leather Seats +270
Limited Slip Diff +295

850 — 1993

740 replacement arrives with 168-horsepower inline five-cylinder engine. Dual airbags and ABS are standard. Automatic transmission has "Economy" and "Sport" shift modes, as well as a winter second-gear start feature. Car meets 1997 side-impact standards, traction control is optional, and sedans have standard integrated child safety seats. Wagon not available.

RATINGS (SCALE OF 1-10)

Overall	Safety	Reliability	Performance	Comfort	Value
8.1	8.6	7.5	8.6	8.3	7.3

Category L

	Trade-in	Market
4 Dr GLT Sdn	7495	9490
4 Dr GLTS Sdn	7710	9760

OPTIONS FOR 850

Auto 4-Speed Transmission +170
Keyless Entry System[Opt on GLT] +55
Leather Seats[Opt on GLT] +270
Traction Control System +315
Trip Computer +60

940 — 1993

Wagons have integrated child seats. All stereos have anti-theft feature, and air conditioning is free of CFCs. Wagons have an extra four gallons of fuel capacity and a revised rear seat. 940 GL dropped, but a base sedan and wagon continue.

RATINGS (SCALE OF 1-10)

Overall	Safety	Reliability	Performance	Comfort	Value
7.5	7.6	7.4	8	8	6.7

Category L

	Trade-in	Market
4 Dr S Sdn	6960	8810
4 Dr S Wgn	7470	9455
4 Dr STD Sdn	6725	8510
4 Dr STD Turbo Sdn	7590	9605
4 Dr STD Wgn	7395	9360
4 Dr STD Turbo Wgn	8385	10615

OPTIONS FOR 940

Aluminum/Alloy Wheels[Std on S,Sdn,Turbo] +95
Power Passenger Seat +100

960 — 1993

960 gets passenger airbag. Wagons have integrated child seats. All stereos have anti-theft feature, and air

VOLVO 93-91

Model Description	Trade-in Value	Market Value	Model Description	Trade-in Value	Market Value

conditioning is free of CFCs. Wagons have an extra four gallons of fuel capacity and a revised rear seat.

RATINGS (SCALE OF 1-10)

Overall	Safety	Reliability	Performance	Comfort	Value
7.7	7.6	7.3	8.8	8.1	6.7

Category L

	Trade-in	Market
4 Dr STD Sdn	7670	9710
4 Dr STD Wgn	8373	10600

1992 VOLVO

240   1992

ABS is newly standard. GL model returns as top-of-the-line, and adds a sunroof and heated mirrors, among other items, over the base car. GL grille is chrome rather than matte black.

Category L

	Trade-in	Market
4 Dr GL Sdn	6120	7950
4 Dr STD Sdn	5490	7130
4 Dr STD Wgn	6195	8045

OPTIONS FOR 240

Auto 4-Speed Transmission +120
Anti-Lock Brakes[Std on Wgn] +190
Heated Front Seats[Std on GL] +85
Leather Seats +220
Limited Slip Diff[Std on GL] +240

740   1992

ABS is standard across the board. A locking differential is newly standard. Turbo sedan and 780 coupe have been dropped. Turbo wagon continues.

Category L

	Trade-in	Market
4 Dr GL Wgn	6445	8370
4 Dr STD Sdn	6180	8025
4 Dr STD Wgn	6395	8305
4 Dr STD Turbo Wgn	6830	8870

OPTIONS FOR 740

Aluminum/Alloy Wheels[Std on Turbo] +75
Leather Seats +220

940   1992

940 GLE, and its twin-cam engine, is discontinued for 1992.

RATINGS (SCALE OF 1-10)

Overall	Safety	Reliability	Performance	Comfort	Value
N/A	N/A	7.7	8	8	7.2

Category L

	Trade-in	Market
4 Dr GL Sdn	5885	7640
4 Dr STD Turbo Sdn	6220	8075

OPTIONS FOR 940

Aluminum/Alloy Wheels[Opt on GL] +75
Leather Seats[Opt on GL] +220
Power Drivers Seat[Opt on GL] +85
Power Passenger Seat +80

960   1992

960 model replaces 940 SE in lineup; is powered by 2.9-liter twin-cam inline-six good for 201 horsepower.

RATINGS (SCALE OF 1-10)

Overall	Safety	Reliability	Performance	Comfort	Value
N/A	N/A	7.7	8.8	8.1	7.1

Category L

	Trade-in	Market
4 Dr STD Sdn	6595	8565
4 Dr STD Wgn	7238	9400

1991 VOLVO

240   1991

SE wagon added to lineup. DL trim dropped, leaving base trim.

Category L

	Trade-in	Market
4 Dr SE Wgn	5330	7015
4 Dr STD Sdn	4745	6245
4 Dr STD Wgn	5075	6680

OPTIONS FOR 240

Auto 4-Speed Transmission[Std on SE] +100
Anti-Lock Brakes[Std on SE] +155
Leather Seats[Std on SE] +180
Sunroof +85

740   1991

DOHC motor dropped from lineup.

Category L

	Trade-in	Market
4 Dr SE Turbo Sdn	5660	7450
4 Dr SE Turbo Wgn	6140	8080
4 Dr STD Sdn	4680	6160
4 Dr STD Turbo Sdn	5160	6790
4 Dr STD Wgn	4970	6540
4 Dr STD Turbo Wgn	5440	7155

OPTIONS FOR 740

Auto 4-Speed Transmission[Std on SE,Non-turbo models] +100
Anti-Lock Brakes[Std on SE, Turbo] +155
Leather Seats +180
Limited Slip Diff[Std on SE, Turbo] +195
Sunroof +85

940   1991

New series of cars is basically renamed 760 series from last year. Base GLEs have twin-cam engine. Turbos and SE Turbos have slightly more powerful 162-horsepower engine.

Don't forget to refer to the Mileage Adjustment Table at the back of this book!

Model Description	Trade-in Value	Market Value

RATINGS (SCALE OF 1-10)

Overall	Safety	Reliability	Performance	Comfort	Value
N/A	N/A	7.1	8	8	7.8

Category L

	Trade-in	Market
4 Dr GLE Sdn	5565	7325
4 Dr GLE Wgn	5928	7800
4 Dr SE Turbo Sdn	5955	7840
4 Dr SE Turbo Wgn	6395	8415
4 Dr STD Turbo Sdn	5575	7340
4 Dr STD Turbo Wgn	6076	8000

OPTIONS FOR 940
Leather Seats[Opt on GLE] +180

1990 VOLVO

240   1990

A driver airbag and knee bolsters are standard this year on all models. 240GL dropped, and a base 240 is added below the 240DL. Wagons get a new tailgate with flush-mounted glass.

Category L

	Trade-in	Market
4 Dr DL Sdn	3740	4985
4 Dr DL Wgn	4075	5435
4 Dr STD Sdn	3275	4365
4 Dr STD Wgn	3565	4755

OPTIONS FOR 240
Auto 4-Speed Transmission +80
■ Sunroof +70

740   1990

740 GL gets driver airbag, and all 740s have new sheetmetal that closely resembles 760. New Generation III turbo engine is introduced.

Category L

	Trade-in	Market
4 Dr GL Sdn	3715	4950
4 Dr GL Wgn	4040	5385
4 Dr GLE Sdn	4053	5400
4 Dr GLE Wgn	4390	5850
4 Dr STD Sdn	3302	4400
4 Dr STD Turbo Sdn	4135	5515
4 Dr STD Wgn	3725	4965
4 Dr STD Turbo Wgn	4625	6165

OPTIONS FOR 740
Auto 4-Speed Transmission +75
Anti-Lock Brakes[Std on GLE, Turbo] +130
Leather Seats +145

760   1990

New Generation III turbo engine is introduced.

Category L

	Trade-in	Market
4 Dr GLE Sdn	4055	5410
4 Dr GLE Turbo Sdn	4580	6105
4 Dr GLE Turbo Wgn	4955	6605

OPTIONS FOR 760
Leather Seats[Opt on Sdn] +145

780   1990

New Generation III turbo engine is introduced.

Category L

	Trade-in	Market
2 Dr STD Turbo Cpe	6755	9005

8V	8-valve
12V	12-valve
16V	16-valve
24V	24-valve
2WD	two-wheel drive
4WD	four-wheel drive
ABS	antilock braking system
A/C	air conditioning
ALR	automatic locking retractor
Amp	ampere
AS	all-season
ASR	automatic slip regulation
AT	automatic
Auto	automatic
AWD	all-wheel drive
BSW	black sidewall
Cass.	cassette
CD	compact disc
CFC	chloroflourocarbon
Conv.	convertible
Cpe	coupe
Cu. Ft.	cubic foot (feet)
Cyl.	cylinder
DOHC	dual overhead cam
DRL	daytime running light(s)
DRW	dual rear wheels
DSC	dynamic stability control
EDL	electronic differential lock
EFI	electronic fuel injection
ELR	emergency locking retractor
EQ	equalizer
ETR	electronically-tuned radio
Ext.	extended
ft-lbs.	foot-pounds (measurement of torque)
FWD	front-wheel drive
Gal.	gallon(s)
GAWR	gross axle weight rating
GVW	gross vehicle weight
GVWR	gross vehicle weight rating
GPS	global positioning satellite
Hbk.	hatchback
HD	heavy duty
Hp	horsepower
HUD	heads-up display
HVAC	heating, ventilation and air conditioning
I-4	inline four
I-5	inline five
I-6	inline six
L	liter
LB	longbed
lb(s).	pound(s)
LCD	liquid crystal display
LED	light emitting diode
LEV	low emission vehicle
LH	left hand
LWB	long wheelbase
M&S	mud and snow
mpg	miles per gallon
mph	miles per hour
MPI	multi-port injection
MSRP	manufacturer's suggested retail price
N/A	not available OR not applicable
NC	no charge
NHTSA	National Highway and Traffic Safety Administration
NVH	noise, vibration and harshness
OD	overdrive
OHC	overhead cam
OHV	overhead valve
Opt.	option OR optional
OWL	outline white-letter
Pass.	passenger
Pkg.	package
PRNDL	Park, Reverse, Neutral, Drive, Low
RBL	raised black-letter
Reg.	regular
RH	right hand
r/l	right and left
rpm	revolutions per minute
RWD	rear-wheel drive
SB	shortbed
SBR	steel-belted radial
Sdn	sedan
SFI	sequential fuel injection
SLA	short/long arm
SMPI	sequential multi-port injection
SOHC	single overhead cam
SPI	sequential port injection
SRW	single rear wheels
Std.	standard
SUV	sport utility vehicle
SWB	short wheelbase
TDI	turbocharged direct injection
TOD	torque on demand
V6	V-type six
V8	V-type eight
V10	V-type ten
V12	V-type twelve
VR	v-rated
VSC	vehicle skid control
VTEC	variable valve timing and lift electronic control
VVT-i	variable valve timing, intelligence
Wgn.	wagon
WOL	white outline-letter
WS	work series
WSW	white sidewall
W/T	work truck
X-cab	extended cab

Frequently Asked Questions

Edmunds.com solicits email queries from consumers who visit our Web site at http://www.edmunds.com. Below are 20 commonly asked questions regarding used cars and the buying process.

1. How do I determine a fair price for a used car?

Edmunds.com publishes a Market Value, which is based on average asking and transaction prices by dealers and private owners nationwide. As a buyer or seller, you'll want to get as close to Market Value as possible.

2. How can I determine what a dealer paid for a used car at auction or in trade?

Unless the dealer discloses this amount honestly, you can't determine an exact "invoice" price. However, by pushing for the best deal you will find the point where the dealer firms up on price. When this happens, you've gotten about as low as you can go; any lower and the dealer figures it would be better to just hang on to the car.

3. Do you have pricing for used cars more than a decade old?

No, we do not. After a decade on the road, most cars have depreciated to the point where fluctuations in values are slight and do not have much impact on the transaction price. Older models will sell easily and for top-dollar if they are in excellent condition. Specialty models are covered by a variety of guides that you can buy in your local bookstore, or you can consult the classifieds in such publications as AutoWeek, Hemmings Motor News, and The DuPont Registry. Online used-car classifieds include clasifieds2000.com and traderonline.com.

4. Why does Edmunds.com's used-car pricing differ from other price guides?

Each guide uses different sources to determine pricing. You must keep in mind that these publications, and Edmunds.com, are to be considered guides. The values contained within are not absolute; they are intended to give the user a range of values to consider when determining a fair price. Used-car values depend on mileage, vehicle condition, geographic location, model popularity, seasonal demand, and even color.

Keep in mind that the dealer will use whatever pricing guide works to their advantage in the deal. By providing pricing that favors the dealer, other guides make big bucks on subscriptions to industry personnel. Some even publish two different pricing guides; one for consumers, and one for dealers. Rarely do dealers use values found at Edmunds.com. We believe that speaks volumes about the fairness of our published pricing to the consumer.

The most important thing to remember about buying, selling, or trading a used car is this: a used car is only worth as much as somebody is willing to pay for it.

5. How often is Edmunds.com's used-car pricing updated?

We update our used-car pricing quarterly.

6. The new model year rollout is occurring. How will this affect used-car values?

When you buy a new car, and it doesn't matter if it's an Acura or a Chevy, it depreciates the second it is titled in your name. Why? It has become a used car. Used cars age and accumulate mileage, and as they age and accumulate mileage they lose value. This is a constant process. Almost all used cars lose their value at a relatively steady rate, it's just that some makes, like Acura, lose value at a slower rate then other makes, like Chevy.

Just because our value guides are published quarterly doesn't mean that a car isn't losing value during that quarter. Used-car prices are never static. That's why we tell people that used-car values supplied by ANY publication are to be used simply as a guide to help you determine a fair price.

Because used-car prices are not static, the introduction of a new model year doesn't alter them much, if at all. Depreciation of used cars is almost always a steady, predictable process. Factor in climate, geographic region, supply and demand, etc., and that's where you get most of the fluctuation. Other factors, such as the release of a redesigned, and less expensive, new model and the whole Acura SLX/Isuzu Trooper rollover scare from a few years ago, can further alter valuations. And what would happen to Expedition/Suburban values if gas prices ever doubled? They'd drop in the toilet.

The bottom line is that the introduction of new model-year vehicles generally doesn't alter used-vehicle pricing much, if at all.

7. How do manufacturer-certified used-car programs affect used-car values?

Remember that our data samples include several sources, including advertised and selling prices from dealers who sell manufacturer-certified used cars. However, our data is also representative of a given vehicle in average condition, and most manufacturer-certified used cars are in good to excellent condition. Furthermore, the dealership spends anywhere from $500 to $1,000 to certify a used car to manufacturer specification. If you are shopping for a manufacturer-certified used car, you will need to take vehicle condition and the costs associated with the certification process into account when trying to determine a fair price.

8. Why won't the dealer give me wholesale value for my trade-in?

When a dealership takes a car in on trade, it is responsible for the car. Before the trade-in can be sold, it must be inspected and often repaired. Sometimes, emissions work is necessary. All this inspection and repair work costs the dealership money. If the trade is in good condition and has low miles, the dealer will put the car on the used-car lot for retail price. When the car sells, it is rarely for retail price, so the profit margin is shaved. The less you accept for the trade-in, the more room the dealer has to make a deal with a prospective buyer, and the more money the dealer will make, thanks to increased profit margins.

If the car doesn't sell, if it has high miles, or it is in poor condition, the dealer will have to wholesale it. The dealer will likely sell the car for below wholesale value at the auction, and expects to recoup some of the money spent reconditioning and inspecting the car. If the dealer offered you wholesale price when you traded in the car, he wouldn't make the money back in the event that the trade-in went to auction.

Regardless of the condition of your car, the dealer will anticipate taking the car to auction, and will leave room to make money in that event. Your best bet is to sell your car on your own to a private party, and forget about trading in.

9. Is it fair for a dealer to ask if my trade has ever been wrecked, or damaged in any way?

Certainly. If you were buying a car from a used-car dealer, you'd want to know the same thing, wouldn't you?

10. When is the best time to purchase a car from a dealer?

There's as much advice about when to visit a dealer as there are days in a year. Some say that Mondays are good because business is slower on Monday than on the weekend. Some say holidays like Thanksgiving are good for the same reason: nobody else will be there, and the sales team will be hungry for a sale. Others advise to go when it's raining or snowing; after all, who wants to look at a car and get wet? Then there's the advice that the end of the month is the best time because the dealership needs to make its "quota" of car sales and will be more willing to cut a deal. Still others advise not to buy a car until the end of the model year, or in slow months like August or December when people are busy thinking about going back to school or shopping for Christmas gifts rather than buying a new car.

Our advice is don't buy a car until you're ready. That's usually the best time. By then you have saved enough for a substantial down payment, and you've had plenty of time to do your research for the lowest interest rate, and you know all the current incentives and rebates. There is no way to tell when is the best time to buy other than personal need.

If a dealer has already made his target sales for the month, you're not going to have any advantage by showing up on the 31st of the month. While there may be something to say for going to a dealership on a weekday near the end of the month on Thanksgiving at five o'clock during a raging blizzard, your best bet is to track incentives and rebates, don't buy hot new models, and do your research first.

11. I want to pay cash for my car. Do I have an advantage?

Not necessarily. You must remember that no matter how you pay for your car, it's all cash to the dealer. In the old days when dealers carried your note, you could save money by paying cash because there was no risk to the dealer. Today, dealerships finance through one of several lending institutions (banks, credit unions, or the automaker's captive financing division) that pay them cash when the contract is presented. In fact, if dealerships do the financing on your behalf, they tend to make more money on your contract in the form of a reserve; anywhere from a one-half to a one point spread on the interest. For example, if the published rate is 8.75 percent, the lender to dealer rate may be discounted to 8 percent; the .75 percent is the reserve held by the dealer as additional profit. This may not sound like much, but it adds up to hundreds of thousands of dollars a year at larger dealerships. This is the reason you should always arrange financing before going to the dealership, and then ask the dealer if they can beat your pre-approved rate. In most cases, they cannot, because of the reserve.

Paying cash is an advantage if you suffer from poor credit or bankruptcy, because it allows you to avoid the higher interest rates charged on loans to people with past credit problems. The bottom line is that if you think you can invest your money at a higher return than the interest rate of the car loan, you could actually save money by not paying cash.

12. Can I negotiate price at Saturn, Daewoo and no-haggle dealerships?

You cannot negotiate price on used cars at Saturn dealerships, but you can haggle over your trade-in and shop aggressively for the lowest-rate financing to keep costs down. Daewoo dealers also use a one-price philosophy, but the company wants to expand quickly and sell lots of cars, so the climate is favorable for negotiation.

No-haggle dealerships might wiggle a little on price, but if they're smart, they'll tell you to get lost. If you want to duke it out over $100, why would you shop at a no-haggle dealership wasting their time and yours? Think about this. If the no-haggle dealer caves and drops the price to sell you the car, you're gonna tell your buddies, and they're gonna tell their buddies, and pretty soon the whole town will be haggling over cars with the no-haggle dealer, and the no-haggle dealer isn't a no-haggle dealer anymore. Get it?

13. Who sets the residual value for a lease?

The financing institution that is handling the lease for the dealership sets the residual value, which can be affected by market forces and vehicle popularity. When shopping leases, it is important to shop different financing institutions for the highest residual value and the lowest interest rate.

14. Why don't you have a listing for the late-model used car I want to buy or sell?

To generate an accurate value for any given used car, there must be enough used examples on the market to include in the sample. Most often, the reason we don't provide a listing is because there aren't enough examples to generate an accurate value. For special interest models, such as anniversary models, try consulting a specialty-car value guide at your local bookstore, or contact a dealer who specializes in these types of cars for information.

15. Why did the used car I'm considering take a nasty drop in the ratings recently?

Edmunds.com updates used-car ratings annually, usually early in the summer. We also tend to modify the formulas that create the ratings, in an effort to make the ratings more accurate. If you find that the rating has changed recently, it's only because fresh data is available and we've finished our annual update.

Keep in mind that pricing is different from ratings. Pricing is updated quarterly throughout the year; ratings are updated once per year.

16. How much does an extended warranty cost the warranty company?

The cost of an extended warranty is based upon the degree of probability that any given vehicle will require repairs during the extended warranty period. Reliability records and repair cost information for a vehicle are evaluated to forecast potential future repair costs, and the extended warranty company will then charge a premium adequate enough to cover the potential cost of repairing the vehicle during the warranty period, while still making a profit. It is important to note that the cost of an extended warranty includes administrative costs for handling paperwork and claims, and insurance to guarantee that claims will be paid.

Extended warranty costs are based on averages, so the cost of applying an extended warranty to any given make and model of car can vary from consumer to consumer. Let's say you bought a $1,000 extended warranty for two identical Brand X vehicles: Car A and Car B. During the extended warranty period, Car A never breaks, so the extended warranty is never used. At the same time, Car B suffers bills amounting to $1,200 for transmission and valve problems. Profit on the warranty sold for Car A will counterbalance the loss suffered on Car B. Extended warranty companies sell thousands of warranties annually, and are able to make a profit when the actual loss experience is lower than the forecast potential for future repair. In other words, when sales exceed overhead the company makes money.

17. What is a secret warranty, and how can I find out if any exist for my car?

A secret warranty, actually called a technical service bulletin (TSB), is a notice that dealer service departments receive from manufacturers regarding suggested repairs to solve common complaints. The dealer is instructed to replace or repair these parts free of charge while the vehicle is under warranty or if the customer complains about a problem while the car is under warranty, but the TSB repair is not available at the time of the complaint. By law, TSB repairs covering emissions equipment are free of charge to the customer for up to 100,000 miles. If a TSB has been issued for your vehicle, but your situation does not meet any of the three listed criteria, then you are responsible for the cost of the repairs. You can get a list of TSBs for your car by contacting the National Highway Traffic Safety Administration (NHTSA) at www.nhtsa.dot.gov and conducting a search for the information.

18. What's the difference between a demo car and a program car?

A demo car is one used by the dealership as a demonstrator to potential buyers. Often, dealership personnel will use the car as personal transportation. A program car is a former rental car, purchased at auction by the dealership. Either type of car is more likely to have been abused than a used car offered for sale by a private owner.

19. When should a car be considered used?

Technically, a vehicle is considered used if it has been titled. However, some dealers can rack up hundreds or thousands of miles on a new car without titling it. In these cases, the ethical definition of a used car should include any car used for extensive demonstration or personal use by dealership staff members. The only miles a new car should have on the odometer when purchased are those put on during previous test drives by prospective buyers (at dealerships where demonstrators are not used), and any miles driven during a dealer trade, within a reasonable limit. If the new car you're considering has more than 300 miles on the odometer, you should question how the car accumulated so many miles, and request a discount for the excessive mileage. We think a discount amounting to a dime a mile is a fair charge for wear and tear inflicted by the dealership.

A car should not be considered used if it is a brand-new leftover from a previous model year. However, it should be discounted, because many manufacturers offer dealers incentives designed to help the dealer lower prices and clear out old stock.

20. What is a trim level?

Most cars and trucks on the market today are available in various levels of trim with various levels of standard equipment. To distinguish between base models and better appointed or sporty models, manufacturers will add a numeric or alphabetic designation after the model name. For example, the Ford Taurus is sold in LX, SE and SHO trim levels. Similarly, the Nissan Maxima is sold in GXE, SE and GLE trim levels. Not all trim-level designations appear after the model name. Acura sells a 3.2TL and a 3.5RL. BMW's 3 Series model comes in several alphanumeric trim levels: 318ti, 323i, 323is, 323iC, 328i, 328is, 328iC and M3.

BUYER'S DECISION GUIDES
SCHEDULED RELEASE DATES
FOR 2000/2001*

VOL. 34/35		RELEASE DATE	COVER DATE
N3402	NEW CARS:Prices & Reviews[American & Import]	JUN 00	SUMMER 00
S3402	NEW TRUCKS:Prices & Reviews[American & Import]	JUN 00	SUMMER 00
U3403	USED CARS & TRUCKS:Prices & Ratings	JUL 00	FALL 00
N3403	NEW CARS:Prices & Reviews[American & Import]	SEPT 00	FALL 00
S3403	NEW TRUCKS:Prices & Reviews[American & Import]	SEPT 00	FALL 00
U3404	USED CARS & TRUCKS:Prices & Ratings	OCT 00	WINTER 00
N3404	NEW CARS:Prices & Reviews[American & Import]	DEC 00	WINTER 01
S3404	NEW TRUCKS:Prices & Reviews[American & Import]	DEC 00	WINTER 01
U3501	USED CARS & TRUCKS:Prices & Ratings	JAN 01	SPRING 01
N3501	NEW CARS:Prices & Reviews[American & Import]	MAR 01	SPRING 01
S3501	NEW TRUCKS:Prices & Reviews[American & Import]	MAR 01	SPRING 01
U3502	USED CARS & TRUCKS:Prices & Ratings	APR 01	SUMMER 01

*Subject to Change

 **SINGLE COPIES / ORDER FORM**

Please send me:

☐ **USED CARS & TRUCKS: PRICES & RATINGS** *(includes S&H)* **$14.99**

☐ **NEW CARS**
 —American & Import *(includes S&H)*.. **$14.99**

☐ **NEW TRUCKS [PICKUPS, VANS & SPORT UTILITIES]**
 —American & Import *(includes S&H)*.. **$14.99**

Name _____

Address _____

City, State, Zip _____

Phone _____

PAYMENT: __ MASTERCARD   __ VISA   __ CHECK or MONEY ORDER $_____

Make check or money order payable to:

Edmunds.com, Inc.   *P.O.Box 338, Shrub Oaks, NY 10588*

*For more information or to order by phone, call **(914) 962-6297***

Credit Card # _____ Exp. Date: _____

Cardholder Name: _____

Signature _____

Prices above include shipping within the U.S. and Canada only. Other countries, please add $7.00 to the price ($14.99+7.00) per book (via air mail) and $2.00 to the price ($14.99+2.00) per book (surface mail). Please pay through an American Bank or with American Currency. Rates subject to change without notice.

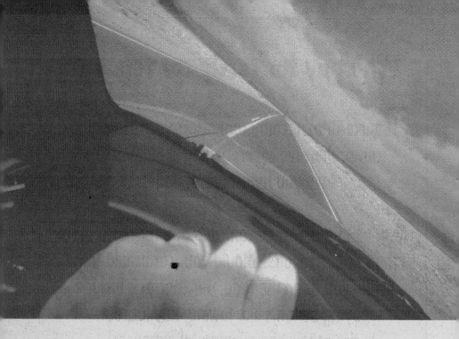

You Drive, You Decide...

Announcing an innovative type of "auto show" where you can test drive cars and experience all things automotive in one comfortable, convenient and entertaining location!

EdmundsLIVE is the industry's first automotive event of its kind. With over 50 of the industry's top vehicles on site, EdmundsLIVE enables you to research and compare vehicles in a no-pressure, sales-free environment. Come to this exciting event where you can attend informational workshops on car-related issues, receive information on specific models and test drive any number of the vehicles we have to offer on our eight specially designed tracks.

Sound good? Thousands of others agree, which is why a reservation for the EdmundsLIVE event is required. Reservations are made on a first-come, first-served basis, so don't delay. Click on the Edmunds-LIVE link on our homepage at www.edmunds.com to make your reservation NOW!

TOYOTA CAMRY

THE CLARK KENT OF FAMILY SEDANS

CHRISTIAN J.
WARDLAW
Editor-in-Chief

Lois Lane hasn't a clue who Clark Kent is, despite the fact that they work together at the Daily Planet and are buddies outside of the office. Lois knows Clark as a conservative, rather dull, but friendly sort who avoids the fast lane. She has based her assessment of Clark on the clothes he wears, the way he carries himself, and the way he behaves. What Lois doesn't realize, however, is that beneath the over-starched button-down oxford, too-short chinos, and boyish wire-rimmed spectacles is a pair of the wildest pajamas on Earth. Clark is really Superman, able to leap tall buildings in a single bound. Lois has the hots for Superman, but not Clark, though they are one and the same.

Toyota has redesigned the Camry for 1997, and after a drive in a CE V-6 equipped with a manual transmission, we've determined that this new sedan is the Clark Kent of family haulers. Conservatively styled, the new Camry goes about its business with little fanfare and utter competence. But drop down a gear, put your foot into it, and the Camry V-6 dons a red cape and flexes its considerable muscle, endearing itself to closet enthusiasts forced by necessity into an everyday sedan.

Several Camry models were on hand during a recent ride-and-drive in Chicago, but we selected the CE V-6 because it is the one members of our staff favor. Want an automatic transmission with your V-6? You'll need to step into an LE model for an additional $1,115, though you'll also get body-color exterior mirrors, cruise control, a cassette player, upgraded cloth for the interior, and a 6-way adjustable driver's seat for that price. Toyota says the LE model will account for 60% of sales volume, with V-6 models a small portion of that mix. If we have anything to say about it, more buyers will pony up the cash for the 3.0-liter V-6 engine, because it's a beauty.

Power and torque are up for all engines this year thanks to exhaust system modifications. The silky smooth V-6 under the hood of our maroon test car boasted 194 horsepower at 5200 rpm, and 209 lb./ft. of torque at 4400 rpm. Acceleration with the manual transmission is astonishing. We informally clocked the CE from zero to 60 mph in less than 8 seconds. Brakes are a bit touchy to the uninitiated, but once accustomed to the grabby pedal, the Camry stops smoothly and quickly. Body roll is evident in corners, but the Camry hangs on well and warns the driver when traction is reaching the limit of adhesion. Steering feedback is excellent, and feels perfectly weighted through an ideally sized tilt steering wheel. Ride comfort is a tad on the firm side, but its taut nature never results in discomfort. In short, the Camry operates in an unruffled, dignified manner, but is a willing playmate so long as the game isn't overly aggressive.

Inside, a logically organized two-tone dashboard greets passengers. Subdued tones and shapes lack personality, but make the Camry's cabin a relaxing place to spend time. Design and build quality exude attention to detail. Seats are comfortable front and rear, offering just the right mix of support and comfort. Folks with long legs or torsos might find the rear quarters a bit cramped, however. Climate controls blend two rotary knobs, a couple of push-buttons, and a slide lever to create a perfect example of ergonomic design. Gauges are large and legible, with clear markings and excellent nighttime lighting. Our test car was equipped with an AM/FM stereo with 4 speakers, and we implore Toyota to dump their

"scan" feature on the stereo face in favor of a tuning knob. Do that, or give passengers more than a couple of seconds to determine if the station "scan" has found is one they'd like to listen to for a while. Cupholders are mounted one in front of the other on the center console, and have slick plastic covers to hide them when not in use. A Super Size Sprite won't fit.

Standard surprise-and-delight features include sunvisor extensions, an auxiliary power point mounted on the dash, an overhead console for either sunglasses or a garage door opener, a tissue holder, and rear seat heat ducts.

Not all is rosy inside the new Camry. While the padded dashboard

offers nicely textured high-quality vinyl surfaces, plastic interior trim is far too shiny for a $21,000 Toyota. We noticed wind noise around the A-pillars and exterior mirrors, but the stereo compensated nicely. Visors can be unclipped too easily, smacking unsuspecting front seat occupants abruptly in the head. Finally, rear seat passengers get roof-mounted assist straps, but the front seat passenger does without. A consolation prize is in place, however. A perfectly sized and located door grip is provided for the front passenger, just like those in fine German sedans.

Outside, the new Camry is cloaked in rather dull sheetmetal, but we certainly prefer this cautious styling approach to the overly ovoid Ford Taurus and Mercury Sable. Boring, maybe, but it will wear well and won't induce fits of buyer's remorse after getting it home and looking at it in the driveway day after day. Composed of fewer parts, the front bumper assembly is lighter and stronger than last year. Bumpers front and rear can sustain a 5 mph impact. Headlight assemblies are simplified too, to save money and assembly time. We like the thin rear taillights and simple greenhouse, which has a radio antenna embedded in the rear glass of LE and XLE models. The front of the car resembles a Plymouth Breeze, a less than prestigious distinc-

tion. Oddly, the CE gets very attractive uni-directional spoked wheelcovers, while the LE makes do with flat bolt-on discs that only cheapen the appearance of the car. Pop the trunk, and you'll find a nicely finished cargo area with a low liftover.

Safety-conscious moms and dads will be pleased to hear that the 1997 Camry meets all safety standards mandated through the end of the decade, including Europe's off-set crash rules. New this year is an integrated child seat, available on models that are not equipped with leather upholstery. Opting for the child seat means you give up the 60 portion of the 60/40 split folding rear seat. Other important factoids about the 1997 Camry include the addition of more sound insulation, a standard full-size spare tire, a larger glovebox, standard antilock brakes on all models but the CE 4-cylinder, and optional traction control on LE and XLE V-6 models.

What's missing from the Camry? Not a thing, aside from a tuning knob on the stereo. Toyota offers consumers a dependable, reliable, comfortable, roomy, safe, and fun-to-drive sedan in the Camry. Ford or Honda may be trumpeting 1996 best-selling car honors this January, but a year from now, we think Toyota will have the race all wrapped up. Anybody in the market for a mid-sized sedan between $20-25,000 cannot afford to rule out a visit to a Toyota dealer for a test drive in the all-new Camry. Think of it as Clark Kent with his glasses off and his shirt unbuttoned just enough to see a bit of a big, red, S. ■

Base Price of Test Vehicle: $19,668 (including destination charge)
Options on Test Vehicle: Power Package (power windows, power door locks, power exterior mirrors, courtesy lighting), air conditioning, variable intermittent wipers
Price of Test Vehicle: $21,473

BMW 323is
BIGGER IS DEFINITELY BETTER

B. GRANT
WHITMORE

We like 'em, but we know they aren't cool. We're talking about the 4-cylinder Bimmers that used to populate the lowest levels of the 3-Series ranks. With the exception of the 318ti (hatchbacks are allowed to have 4-pot engines) the 318 lineup seemed like some sort of internal combustion rip-off. The cars looked like BMWs. They smelled like BMWs. They even shifted and steered like BMWs. They just didn't go like BMWs.

People buy BMWs because they like to drive. Sure, BMWs are also safe and luxurious, but let's face it, Volvo is the maker that we think of when safety issues come to mind, and Mercedes-Benz is the maker for buyers who value luxury over performance. This brings us back to BMW's target audience: drivers. One thing that drivers like to do is go fast. The previous 318is coupe isn't up to snuff in that department. Equipped with a 1.9-liter 4-cylinder engine that makes 138 horsepower and 133 lb./ft. of torque, the 1997 318is is fair game for any high school punk in a Dodge Neon. Equally embarrassing is the fact that the Neon, priced nearly $15,000 less than the 318is, is a match for the BMW in the stoplight drags. If you own last year's entry-level BMW coupe don't even think about what that kid in a Camaro could do to your pride.

BMW solved that problem this year by dropping a 2.5-liter inline 6-

cylinder motor into the engine bay of the bottom-rung 3-Series coupe and convertible. The sedan and hatchback still make do with the same 1.9-liter engine as last year. The two extra cylinders and added displacement make all the difference in the world for this car. Infused with 30 more horsepower and 48 more lb./ft. of torque than the 4-cylinder engine, the new 323is has earned the right to wear BMW's prominent propeller badge on its hood. BMW claims that acceleration times have improved by 1.5 seconds over last year's car. That means it takes 5-speed models 7.1 seconds to reach 60 mph. An important note is that this engine is not the one previously used in BMWs such as the 325is coupe and 525i sedan. This engine differs from the earlier 2.5-liter engine of 1995. It uses the same bore as the 328i (84 mm) but a different stroke (75 mm). BMW departed from their usual scheme of using the engine's displacement numbers to denote the car's trim level to keep customers from confusing this car with the earlier model.

The 323is got more than a new engine this year; door-mounted side-

impact airbags and rear passenger adjustable headrests were also added. Additional standard equipment features include leatherette upholstery, split-folding rear seats, multi-information display with outside temperature gauge and freeze warning, cruise control, AM/FM stereo with cassette and 10 speakers, dual zone climate controls, central door and trunk locking, powerful 4-wheel disc brakes with anti-lock, and all season traction control. The only option on our comfortable 323is tester was the Sport Package which includes 16x7-inch alloy wheels shod with 225/50ZR-16 performance tires, a sport suspension, and fog lights.

Fun to drive does not begin to describe how each of our staff members

felt about this car after spending just a few hours behind the wheel of BMW's cheapest 6-cylinder model. Greg Anderson, Edmund's newest automotive editor, liked the 323is's power delivery and clutch take-up, thinking that they were smooth as silk. He cites an occasion when he crested a ridge just outside of metro Denver and passed a Douglas County Sheriff's car headed in the opposite direction. As he sped past the peace officer, he looked down at the speedo

A magnificent strut-type front suspension and central link rear suspension combine to give the 323is one of the best rides on the road. Every dip and undulation of the road is felt in a manner that lets the driver know exactly what is happening to the car without causing any discomfort to the occupants. Perfectly weighted rack-and-pinion steering works well with the 323is's nearly ideal 50.2 front/49.8 rear weight bias to ensure effortless direction changes.

The BMW 323 is also available in a sporty drop-top version.

to see how fast he was going. His eyes nearly popped out of his head when he noticed that the dial was registering triple digits. Fortunately the police officer had other intentions and did not turn around to ticket Anderson. Afterward, Anderson claimed that he had no idea how fast he was travelling and that the 323is felt as solid at 100 mph as most cars do at 50. Having been awhile since last driving a BMW, this writer had forgotten how easy it is to tackle winding roads at high speeds. With the traction control turned off the 323is hangs its tail out gently and easily, never threatening to send the car down the road arse-end forward.

Our only gripes about the 323is concern its busy dashboard, cheap interior materials, and the contortions required of passengers trying to access the rear seat. The myriad climate and audio controls are piled on top of each other and create a cluttered center stack. Interior materials are also a bit lean in a car that pushes through the $30,000 price barrier. If Audi can fill their $23,000 1.8T with sumptuous faux-leather upholstery and nicely grained dashboard plastic why can't

BMW do the same with their entry-level cars? Our final complaint is about the 323is's small rear seat further exacerbated by the difficulty that passengers have accessing it. Requiring a step-twist-plop sort of motion for entry, the back seat of this coupe is going to win few fans. BMW could address this concern for us by dropping the new engine into the 318i sedan. This wouldn't increase rear passenger space, the coupe and sedan have the same interior dimensions, but the extra doors would make it easier for rear seat passengers to get in and out of the car.

Nearing the end of its life in this iteration, the entry-level BMW coupe has become the perfect example of what a sports coupe should be. It is compact, powerful, fun, and well mannered. It does not pick buyers' pockets at the dealership or at the gas pump. There are plenty of sports coupes on the market that offer a good ride at a reasonable price. We think, however, that this particular car is the one to purchase if you place more emphasis on fun than on luxury.

Vehicle tested: 1998 BMW 323is Coupe

Base Price: $29,270 (includes destination charge)

Options on Test Vehicle: Sport Package (Fog Lights, Sport Suspension, 16-inch Alloy Wheels, and P255/50ZR-16 Performance Tires).

Price of Vehicle as Tested: $ 30,260 (includes destination charge)

Notes

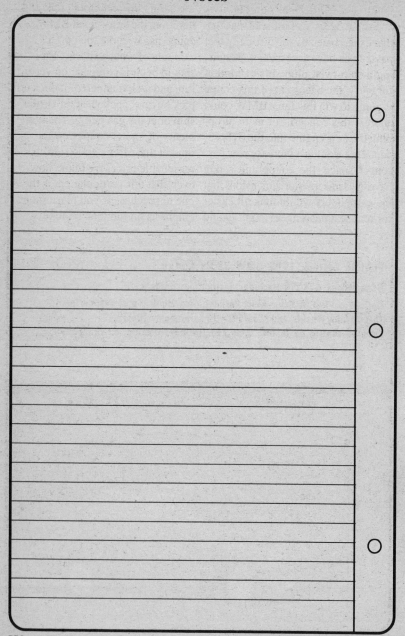